How to do just about Anything

READER'S DIGEST

How to do just about Anything

Published by the Reader's Digest Association Limited

LONDON · NEW YORK

HOW TO DO JUST ABOUT ANYTHING

Edited and designed by
The Reader's Digest Association Limited, London

First Edition Copyright © 1988

Second Edition 1994

The Reader's Digest Association Limited,
Berkeley Square House,
Berkeley Square, London W1X 6AB

Printed in Great Britain
ISBN 0 276 41993 6

Contributors

The publishers would like to thank the following people
for major contributions to this book

Writers

Dr Neville Carrington
Dr James Cox
John Crabbe
Brian Crichton
Mike Groushko

Ned Halley
Andrew Kerr-Jarrett
Peter Leek
Paulette Pratt
Sandra Shepherd
Judith D. Taylor

Rachel Warren
Michael Watts
Tony Wilkins
Dr David Williams
Tony Wilmott

Artists

Andrew Aloof
Art Beat
Dick Bonson
Leonora Box
Kuo Kang Chen
Andrew Clarke
Brian Delf
Colin Emberson

Guy Foster
Sarah Fox-Davies
Michael Gilbert
Terry Grose
Peter Harper
Mark Hart
Edward Williams Arts

Paul Hart
Inkwell Design & Art
Ivan Lapper
Malcolm McGregor
Jonothan Potter
Ann Savage
John See
Allan Thurston

Technical Adviser

Simon Gilham

Indexer

Michèle Clarke

About this book

HOW TO USE THE BOOK

Look up the subjects you require in alphabetical order, as you would in a dictionary. You will probably find them immediately – but if you cannot, turn to the complete index at the back of the book.

The index can also guide you to all entries in a given category. Under GARDENING, for example, are listed entries on lawn care, bedding plants, soil preparation, weed control and so on.

Many entries contain cross-references – printed in small capital letters – leading you to additional information. If, for example, the reference reads 'see GLUING', look up that entry – it will contain information needed for the job in hand. If the reference reads 'See also . . .' it will cover a related subject that may interest or be of use to you. The entry on OIL PAINTING, for example, contains both types – 'see STRETCHING A CANVAS' (which you may need to know) and 'See also WATERCOLOUR PAINTING' (which may interest you). As an additional aid, other entries occurring within the text are also printed in small capitals as instant cross-references.

WHAT SKILLS DO YOU NEED?

Most of the jobs in this book can be done by anyone who is reasonably handy. As you read the instructions – often amplified by clear illustrations – you may feel inspired to try your hand at jobs you have previously hesitated to tackle. Before starting, think how the procedures described apply in your particular home or special situation. Jobs in such areas as electric wiring, plumbing and car maintenance, for example, sometimes call for a degree of confidence and, perhaps, specialised skills. A mistake can prove both expensive and painful. So if you feel uncomfortable about a task, get help from someone more experienced.

Similarly, seek professional advice when necessary: consult a lawyer (the book tells you how!) about any important legal problem; see your doctor if a medical problem becomes worrying; have an architect or surveyor inspect a potential structural problem in your home; in an emergency, when a life is at stake, do whatever may be necessary to reduce the danger and summon medical help as quickly as possible.

OTHER SOURCES OF HELP

The entry on INFORMATION gives a list of specialist publications to consult on a wide range of subjects, should it become necessary. Many other entries include the address of the association, club or other body concerned with the subject which can help.

EGGS

Raw or under-cooked eggs (which are included in some mayonnaise and desserts) should not be given to the elderly and frail or to infants and pregnant women.

SELECTING TOOLS

Good tools make work easier, faster, more accurate – and safer. Buy tools of a reputable brand, but avoid very cheap tools, which will soon wear, or even break and cause injury.

The tools described here will handle most of your general repair jobs. Buy additional tools only when needed; consider renting expensive ones from a tool hire shop – especially if you will use them only occasionally.

Basic tools for home repairs A medium-sized screwdriver with a 6mm ($\frac{1}{4}$in) tip will drive most slotted screws; a stubby one for confined spaces is a help. A No 2 cross-slot screwdriver fits most cross-head screws in common use. A battery-powered, rechargeable, cordless screwdriver saves effort when a lot of work is involved.

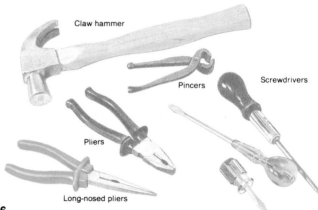

Claw hammer

Pincers

Screwdrivers

Pliers

Long-nosed pliers

Other good choices for a basic kit include: a 700g (1½lb) claw hammer; a 510mm (20in) panel saw, tenon saw, and junior hacksaw; a good craft knife and perhaps a 25mm (1in) wood chisel. Panel saws and tenon saws can be had with hardpoint teeth that never need sharpening, and cut wood more easily and efficiently. The general-purpose saw, which has specially treated teeth, can cut wood or metal.

To hold things in place while you cut or as glue sets, buy a pair of G-clamps – 100 or 150mm (4 or 6in) sizes are useful. For gripping and turning things, get general-purpose pliers, self-locking grips and a pipe wrench; pincers and long-nosed pliers are good additions.

A 2m (6ft) flexible steel-tape rule and combination square and spirit level should take care of marking, measuring and levelling tasks. Round off your hand tool set with a gimlet, bradawl and tacklifter.

The single most useful power tool you need is a drill: a 16mm (⅝in) chuck model with high and low (or variable) speeds, plus hammer action for masonry drilling, is versatile and powerful enough for most occasions. Get good-quality high-speed drill bits and masonry bits for use with it. Supplement the drill, if possible, with a small hand drill for working in spaces too confined for a power drill.

Tool safety Always use a tool designed for the task, especially if you have to exert force. Never use damaged, blunt or loose-handled tools. Wear safety goggles or spectacles when the work raises flying grit or other debris at eye level – wear a face mask, too, if necessary. Protect hands with thick gloves when handling rough materials, and with vinyl gloves when using strong or toxic liquids. For more safety tips, see the entry on POWER TOOL SAFETY.

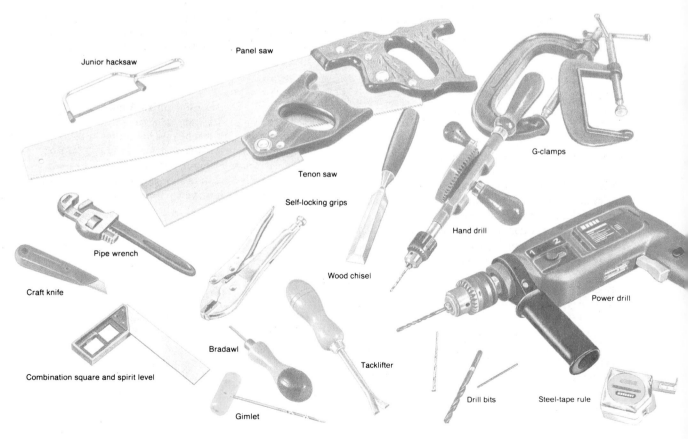

Junior hacksaw

Panel saw

G-clamps

Tenon saw

Self-locking grips

Hand drill

Pipe wrench

Wood chisel

Craft knife

Power drill

Bradawl

Tacklifter

Combination square and spirit level

Drill bits

Steel-tape rule

Gimlet

Abacus

How to use the oldest computer known to man

This simple calculating device was used by the Chinese thousands of years ago, and is still in use in some eastern countries. It is reliable – no batteries to wear out or digital display to fail – and makes a fascinating teaching aid for children.

A modern abacus is a wooden frame holding nine columns of beads on rods or wires. A crossbar divides the frame, with 2 beads on each wire above the bar and 5 on each wire below.

Numbers increase from right to left. In the lower part of the frame, the right-hand column represents ones, the next column tens, the third hundreds and so on. Each bead below the bar represents a single unit, each bead above represents 5 units, so that each full column has 15 units.

Making a calculation Calculations are made by moving the beads towards or away from the bar. When adding, the beads are moved to the bar, and when any column totals 10 or more – say 2 beads on the bar in the top section and 2 below – 10 units are moved away from the bar and a single bead in the next column is moved up to the bar. This is the equivalent of carrying one in arithmetic.

The final total is arrived at by noting the values of each number of beads against the bar, reading from left to right.

ABACUS

Counting with beads

3 8 0 2 5 8 5 0 1

Sum total Calculations of over 1500 million can be made on an abacus. Here the total is 380,258,501.

6 5 5

Adding To add 655 + 305, set up 655 by pushing to the bar five lower beads on wires one and two and a 5 and a lower bead on wire three, to display 655.

9 5 10

Add 305 Bring down one top bead (5) on wire one, move no beads on wire two and move three lower beads to the bar on wire three. From left to right the numbers now read 9, 5, 10.

9 6 0

The total Move away the top beads on wire one, and carry the 10 over by pushing up one lower bead on wire two. The total is shown by the values on each wire – 960.

Accident prevention

Avoiding accidental injuries at home, in the garden and at work

Falls account for most home injuries, ranging from bruises and sprains caused by slipping or tripping, to broken limbs and fatal injuries.

Have non-slip surfaces on floors, especially in the kitchen and bathroom, and use non-slip polishes on wooden floors. Fix rugs and mats to the floor and do not place them by the stairs or on landings. Repair or discard badly worn carpets, rugs and linoleum. Make sure stair carpets are sound and firmly fixed. Loose-fitting slippers and trailing hems on dressing gowns and long dresses can cause falls, particularly when worn by children, the infirm or the elderly. Repair all faulty footwear and clothing.

Wherever possible, keep shelves at a low height, and always use a strong stepladder to reach high shelves. Avoid overreaching and keep a hand free to steady yourself. Never stand on an upholstered chair, or one with a loose cushion.

Keep stairs, landings, entrance halls and outside steps and porches well-lit. Do not use long flexes on table lamps and other appliances – they can cause people to trip and fall.

Cuts come a close second to falls in home accidents, with the kitchen the main danger area. Use kitchen knives with care and keep them out of the reach of children. Do not use knives for purposes for which they were not intended, such as prising off jar or tin lids. Use a good tin-opener, preferably the 'butterfly' type, for opening sealed cans and never prise off the opened lid with your fingers.

The kitchen is also the place where SCALDS and BURNS are likely to occur, with the cooker playing the dual role of the family's best friend or worst enemy. Treat it with respect, cook on the back burners whenever possible and turn kettle spouts and steam vents away from the front of the cooker. Do not let saucepan and frying pan handles project over the edge of the cooker; if there are children in the house, fit a guard rail that will stop pots being pulled off. Avoid carrying utensils containing hot liquids from the cooker to another part of the room. Always use thick OVEN MITTS or an oven pad to pick up hot utensils.

Treat electricity in the home with extreme care, and always switch the power off at the fuse box before carrying out repairs, such as replacing a faulty switch (see ELECTRIC SOCKETS AND SWITCHES; FUSES AND FUSE BOXES) or replacing a blown bulb. Replace cracked or broken switches and sockets immediately. Unplug all electrical appliances when they are not in use, especially the TV set – which can cause a fire if it develops a fault – and electric blankets.

In the garden There are just as many hazards in the garden as in the house if proper precautions are not taken. Stepping on a garden rake may be good for a laugh in comedy films, but it is not funny in real life, so keep all garden tools in the tool shed when not in use. And take care when using them. Wear stout boots when digging.

Keep the garden path and any steps in good condition, checking regularly for loose or uneven paving stones on which people may trip – especially front garden paths and those leading to other entrances used by tradesmen, who can sue for injuries caused by negligence.

Lawn mowers should have a guard over the blades, and if you have an electric or motor mower never try to clear choked blades while the power is still on. Take care with an electric mower not to run over the lead. If this does happen, do not touch the wires: switch off the power at the mains or plug. A good safeguard is a circuit breaker fitted to the power socket – this will automatically switch off the power if the lead is cut – see CIRCUIT BREAKERS.

At work Safety at work is partly the responsibility of your employer, but he cannot be responsible for your careless-ness or negligence. Observe all safety rules and where applicable make use of protective clothing and equipment such as safety helmet, goggles, gloves and foot-wear. See also BATHROOM SAFETY; CHILD SAFETY; FIREWORK SAFETY; LADDERS; POWER TOOL SAFETY.

Acne

Treating yourself; when to see a doctor; some do's and don'ts

The most common of all skin complaints, acne is the scourge of teenagers, since it is they who suffer from it most. In its mildest form there may be only pimples and blackheads, though these can be dis-tressing at an age when personal appear-ance is important. In severe cases, pim-ples may turn into cysts.

The best home treatment is regular washing with medicated soap or deter-gent lotion and hot water. Keep a check on your diet to see if chocolate, nuts, sweets or fats make the spots worse. If the condition does not improve, or the spots turn to cysts, consult your DOCTOR. He may prescribe a lotion, antibiotics or a vitamin A or hormone preparation.

Do's and don'ts for acne sufferers

Do get as much sunlight as possible. Sun-bathing will often help acne to improve.
Do try proprietary antiseptic and kerato-lytic creams. A dispensing chemist will be able to advise you.
Do consult your doctor if there are cysts. Left untreated they may leave scars.
Do wash your hair regularly and keep it short. Hair falling on your face can increase the number of spots.
Don't use oily or greasy cosmetics. Ask your chemist to recommend a non-greasy cosmetic.
Don't squeeze or pick the spots – they will become worse and may leave scars.
Don't despair if spots do not respond to treatment immediately. It may take weeks or months, and acne is unlikely to go on getting worse indefinitely – sooner or later it will improve.

Acrylic

Using an unbreakable substitute for glass

Acrylic, a plastic material available in clear or coloured sheets, tubes and rods, can be cut with fine saws, shaped by filing, drilled and glued to make models, jewellery and boxes. Special adhesives, available at acrylic suppliers, are used to glue acrylic sheet. In resin form it can be moulded or used to encapsulate attractive and collectable objects such as flowers, shells and beads.

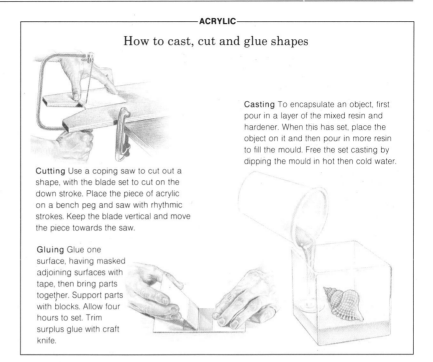

─ACRYLIC─

How to cast, cut and glue shapes

Casting To encapsulate an object, first pour in a layer of the mixed resin and hardener. When this has set, place the object on it and then pour in more resin to fill the mould. Free the set casting by dipping the mould in hot then cold water.

Cutting Use a coping saw to cut out a shape, with the blade set to cut on the down stroke. Place the piece of acrylic on a bench peg and saw with rhythmic strokes. Keep the blade vertical and move the piece towards the saw.

Gluing Glue one surface, having masked adjoining surfaces with tape, then bring parts together. Support parts with blocks. Allow four hours to set. Trim surplus glue with craft knife.

Kits for casting in acrylic are available from craft and modelling shops. The cast-ing material consists of a resin and a hardener, which when mixed sets in about 30 minutes. Any suitably shaped container can be used as a mould, so long as the inside is smooth.

To cut shapes, first make a bench peg – a piece of 10mm (⅜in) plywood with a V cut into it – and clamp it to a bench top. Mark out your design on the protective coating on the acrylic, which is left in place until the piece is cut out.

Aerobics

Enjoyable exercising for improving your stamina

The term 'aerobic' is from the Greek words meaning air and life. All forms of aerobic exercise increase the body's need for oxygen, which it obtains through an increase in the rate of blood flow through the heart. When this happens the heart pumps harder and, as it is largely muscu-lar, becomes stronger.

Any activity involving the rhythmic contraction of large muscles, such as those of the legs, requires stamina – the capacity to keep going without gasping for breath or going weak at the knees. Jogging, running, walking, swimming, cycling, skipping and even vigorous danc-ing are all good aerobic exercises. Full benefit comes from exercising at least three times a week.

Before taking up any form of exercise, first check your fitness level by taking your pulse for one minute (see PULSE TAKING). Before rising in the morning, the pulse rate/fitness levels are as follows:

RATE	FITNESS STATE
50	– very fit
50-70	– fit
70-80	– sedentary
80 plus	– take some exercise!

Whether you are fit or very unfit, work up to the exercises slowly, not more than 20 minutes at a time, and in any case observe the list of 'do's and don'ts' below.

Bearing them in mind, a simple fitness test is to step up and then down – use both feet – a 200mm (8in) high stair twice every five seconds for three minutes (*stop if you feel discomfort*). Rest exactly one minute then check your pulse: you are fit if it has returned to about normal rate.
Do consult your DOCTOR if you have a history of heart disease, high blood press-ure, dizzy spells, blackouts, diabetes, per-sistent back trouble, arthritis, are con-valescing or are worried about the effect of exercise on some other aspect of your health.
Do rest immediately if you feel pain or discomfort.
Don't make the mistake of thinking that if the exercises hurt they must be doing you some good.
Don't take exercise if you feel tired.
Don't exercise vigorously within two hours of taking a heavy meal.
Don't exercise if you have a heavy cold, feel ill or are at all feverish.

African violets

Growing a popular house plant

One of the most attractive house plants, the African violet (*Saintpaulia*) may flower all the year round with proper care.

Where they grow best Provide bright light throughout the year, but not direct sunlight. If you have fluorescent lighting, place the plant 300mm (12in) below the tube for about 12 hours a day. The plant will flourish in a temperature of 18-24°C (64-75°F), and high humidity is essential; stand pots on trays of moist pebbles; occasionally mist leaves with a fine spray of tepid water.

Watering Water moderately, enough to make the potting mixture moist at each watering. Place the spout below the foliage to keep water off the crown and leaves. Allow the top 13mm (½in) of the mixture to dry before watering again. Over-watering will cause the roots to rot.

Feeding At every watering, feed the plant with a dose of liquid fertiliser containing equal amounts of nitrogen, phosphate and potash and diluted to one-quarter strength – see FERTILISERS.

Potting and repotting Pot African violets in a mixture of equal parts of sphagnum peat moss, perlite and vermiculite, and add three or four tablespoons of dolomite lime to every four cups of the mixture – see POTTING HOUSEPLANTS. These ingredients are obtainable from gardening shops and centres. Choose a pot with a diameter of about one-third that of the plant.

Repotting is not necessary until about two months after the roots have filled the container – in fact, African violets thrive best when their roots are pot-bound, and the new pot should be only slightly larger than the old.

Three beauties Varieties of *Saintpaulia ionantha* available include 'Diana Red Double', in foreground; 'Diana Pink' and 'Diana Blue' behind.

Propagating Leaf cuttings can be propagated in potting compound or in water. Choose healthy leaves and cut the stems to about 25-50mm (1-2in). Cover the containers with plastic bags punched with small holes and secured by elastic bands. Leave for seven to ten weeks until the cuttings show signs of growth, then transplant to separate pots – see also PROPAGATING PLANTS.

Air beds

Repairing a punctured air bed

First find the puncture; if it is small, causing the air bed to deflate over a long period, half-inflate the bed and immerse it in a bath of water until air bubbles appear, then trace the bubbles back to their source.

Preparation Obtain a repair kit from a camping equipment shop. Kits for rubber-and-canvas beds have a rubber solution; those for plastic beds contain a liquid cement. Make sure you get the right one.

Clean the damaged area, using petrol or lighter fuel on rubber-and-canvas, but use only water on plastic as petrol will attack the material.

Allow the cleaned area to dry before making the repair.

Rubber-and-canvas bed Select a patch large enough to substantially overlap the puncture. Apply rubber solution to the punctured area, allow it to dry and apply a second coat. Treat the back of the patch in the same way, after first roughening it with glasspaper. When the solution is dry, press the patch firmly in position and leave to set for 12 hours.

Plastic Bed Spread only one coat of liquid cement on both the patch and bed. Apply the patch, pressing it firmly in position all round, and leave it to dry for five hours.

Air bricks

Replacing or inserting an air brick in a wall

Routine inspections to the outside of your house should include checking air bricks. They should never become clogged with earth or wet leaves, or covered up, so be sure to check them in autumn and again in winter – see CONDENSATION; VENTILATION.

Replace a damaged air brick as soon as possible – vermin and birds can get through the gap. Never block up an air brick, even for a short time.

In a cavity wall, the air brick goes through the whole thickness. In a solid wall, it fits on the outside, while the inner surface has a louvre. Before buying a new air brick, check the type you need.

To replace an air brick in a cavity wall, remove the old air brick by cutting

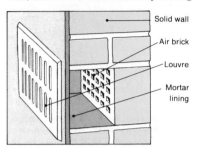

Solid wall air brick Fit the air brick on the outside. Line the hole with mortar. Attach the louvre with contact adhesive – see GLUING.

it out with a cold chisel and club hammer. Brush any dirt and loose MORTAR from the cavity. Next, spread a 13mm (½in) layer of mortar on the bottom of each hole in the inner and outer walls. Then spread a 13mm layer along the top and sides of the new air brick, before tucking it carefully into the hole. Before the mortar sets, scrape away the excess with a trowel. Repoint around the new air brick to match the surrounding wall – see POINTING. When the pointing has dried, clean up the wall with a stiff-bristled brush. See also BRICKLAYING.

Air filters

Renewing or cleaning your car's air filter

A dirty air filter will cause your car to use more petrol, because clogging of the filter will upset the ratio of air to petrol entering the carburettor. Check the filter every 6000 miles or every six months.

There are three main types of filter: a disposable paper element, a foam plastic element and, more rarely nowadays, a wire gauze element.

Paper element filters Undo the fastenings and lift off the lid. The paper filter consists of a pleated ring of perforated paper – the element – which will be dirtiest at the point where it faces the air intake. If the rest of the filter is clean, turn the element so that the dirty section is at the point farthest from the intake. If the element is dirty all round, discard it, clean out the filter housing with a rag dipped in paraffin or white spirit and fit a new paper element, available from car accessory shops.

Foam plastic filters Fitted mainly to specialist and high performance cars, these are replaced in the same way as paper element filters.

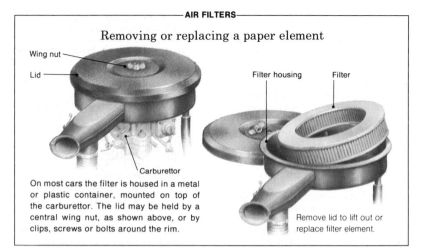

AIR FILTERS

Removing or replacing a paper element

Wing nut

Lid

Carburettor

Filter housing

Filter

On most cars the filter is housed in a metal or plastic container, mounted on top of the carburettor. The lid may be held by a central wing nut, as shown above, or by clips, screws or bolts around the rim.

Remove lid to lift out or replace filter element.

Gauze filters These consist of fine wire mesh which is oiled to catch dirt particles. To clean the filter, wash it thoroughly in a dish of petrol – do not use paraffin, which does not evaporate and if drawn into the engine will cause misfiring. Top up the oil level with clean engine oil, immerse the filter, and allow all surplus oil to drain off before refitting.

Allergies

Avoiding and treating common allergies: do's and don'ts

Allergies attack people in many forms, including HAY FEVER, asthma, ECZEMA and urticaria (also known as HIVES and nettle rash). An allergy erupts when your body reacts to a substance, or substances, it is sensitive to. These substances are called antigens, and they are mostly breathed into the lungs, or absorbed through eating or by physical contact.

The body defends itself against them by producing substances known as antibodies, and the 'battle' between antigens and antibodies triggers the release of certain chemicals, including histamine, from the surrounding cells. It is the histamine and other chemicals that cause allergic reactions – hence the term antihistamines for some of the medicines most commonly used to combat allergies.

Antigens which commonly cause reactions include pollen, animal hair and scurf, house dust mites, and a long list of foodstuffs: food colourings and additives, shellfish, eggs, chocolate, cheese and numerous others. The symptoms they produce include rashes, runny nose, watering eyes, sneezing, itching, blisters (isolated or in groups), restricted breathing, swollen eyes, lips or tongue, and weals on the skin.

Serious sufferers, who may not even know the source of their allergy, can often be treated successfully by a DOCTOR.

Medical tests are made to discover the cause. Drugs – even injections – may be prescribed.

The best treatment, however, is to avoid the cause. If it is found to be animal hair, try to avoid contact with dogs and cats. The doctor may trace it to dust mites which lurk in bed coverings, mattress hair, and the feathers of pillows and duvets. In this case, the remedy would be to change to polyester pillows and duvets, put a plastic cover on the mattress and vacuum the bedding daily.

'Damp dusting' the bedroom regularly, using a damp cloth, also helps to reduce the amount of dust present.

Antihistamine drugs often reduce hay fever and rashes: a single tablet can relieve itching from hives, for example, within an hour. However, some antihistamines can induce drowsiness as a side-effect, so should not be taken if you are driving or operating machinery. The majority of antihistamines – available as tablets, creams, nose drops, eye drops, syrups and elixirs – do not need a prescription.

Asthma and hay fever sufferers can use a preventative drug named sodium cromoglycate. It can forestall an attack, but does not work once the allergy has developed. The drug is available on prescription as eye drops, a nose spray or a powder inhalant.

Asthma sufferers get immediate relief from bronchodilators. Puffed or sprayed up the nose or in the mouth, they widen the bronchial tubes. Regular treatment with another inhaler, which contains steroids, helps to prevent respiratory allergies from developing and reduces swelling and inflammation in the airways. Most bronchodilators, and all steroid drugs, need prescriptions.

Do's and don'ts about allergies

Do make a note when you encounter something that triggers an allergy, and how you reacted. This will help your doctor when he makes his diagnosis. *Do* look for a pattern. Asthma only in spring suggests that the problem is grass pollen. A rash around the waist could be caused by elastic in a waistband. Nickel in a watch or bra strap may raise a rash. *Do* strive, having isolated the cause, to avoid it. If some foods bring distress, always check the ingredients of packaged foods.

Do remember that a baby may inherit asthma or eczema allergies. Breast feeding for six months, if possible, protects against antigens in cows' milk.

Don't expect instant results when you have removed sources of allergy. Animal hairs, for example, can lurk for months after the animal has gone.

Don't assume that a rash after taking penicillin means you are allergic to it. The virus or bacterium causing the illness could have brought on the spots. Check with your doctor.

Anagrams

How to play a fun word game; making your own anagram tiles

Any number from two to eight can play anagrams. You need a set of anagram tiles, each bearing a letter on one side.

If you do not have a set, use two sets of Scrabble tiles, or make your own from 2in × 4in index cards. Cut the cards into eight pieces 1in × 1in and print a letter on one side of each piece.

Prepare a number of tiles for each letter, roughly according to how often that letter is used in English. Here is one way of doing it:

A	18	F	4	K	2	P	4	U	8
B	4	G	6	L	8	Q	2	V	4
C	4	H	4	M	4	R	12	W	4
D	8	I	18	N	12	S	8	X	2
E	24	J	2	O	18	T	12	Y	6
								Z	2

Place the tiles face down on a table, leaving the centre of the table clear. Going around the table, each player turns over one tile and places it in the centre. Players have to spot one word of at least four letters from among the tiles that have been turned over.

Any player to spot a word calls it out (whether it is his turn or not), removes the tiles from the centre, and sets up the word in front of him.

You can capture a word from another player by adding one letter or more from the centre stockpile to the word, forming a new one. The first player who is able to assemble ten words wins. If all the tiles are used up before anyone has been able to make ten words, the player who has assembled the most words wins the game.

Ancient lights

Upholding your right to light from a window

A house that has enjoyed uninterrupted light to any of its windows for 20 years may be protected by law, so that no one can block or reduce that light. This is known as 'ancient lights' (not applicable in Scotland). Otherwise your right to daylight coming over a neighbour's land is not automatic. He can, given PLANNING PERMISSION, build an extension or some other building that will cut off the light, unless you have obtained a 'right to light'.

Check your title deeds: they may include such a right. On the other hand they may include a clause excluding you from obtaining that right. This is often done by landowners or developers who wish to build on adjoining land at some future date.

If you have no right to light, and are not prevented from acquiring it, you may be able to get a written agreement to it from your neighbour or the landowner. The law on 'right to light', however, is complicated and you should consult a solicitor – see LAWYERS.

Preventing a 'right to light' Though the law on obtaining a 'right to light' is vague, the law on stopping someone else getting it is less so. You can take steps to prevent your neighbour from acquiring the right if you want to erect a building that will obstruct his light, by lodging a light obstruction notice in your council's Local Land Charges Register. You must supply the dimensions of the proposed building, and you must also inform your neighbour of your action.

The notice is effective for one year, after that you must repeat the process at least once every 20 years – or your neighbour may acquire 'ancient lights'.

Animal smells

Getting rid of cat and dog smells

A number of simple precautions can control the smells of cats and dogs. First, keep the pet well groomed – see CATS; DOG CARE.

Provide a permanent sleeping place, and wash any bedding regularly. If it has slept on carpets, scatter baking soda, then vacuum thoroughly.

If your dog or cat still has a very strong body odour after brushing and cleaning, see a veterinary surgeon. The pet may have a skin disorder known as seborrhoea. This can be controlled by a medicated shampoo or, in mild cases, a human dandruff shampoo.

If its anal glands are impacted, the pet will bite or lick its backside more than usual, or rub it along the ground. Anal gland trouble, and other possible causes of smells, such as ear infection, need treatment by a vet.

If an animal makes a mess inside the house, scoop up the deposit and blot the area with paper towels. Apply lemon juice or ammonia to deal with the stain. Scrub the area with soap and water to remove the odour.

Keep some proprietary air fresheners handy, and place them as necessary.

Annuities

Boosting your retirement income

One way in which you can guarantee yourself a regular extra income when you retire is to buy an annuity.

What you get is interest on the capital and return of part of the capital, and the older you are when you buy the annuity the higher the income will be. A husband and wife can buy a joint survivorship annuity, which enables the surviving spouse to receive a reduced income.

If you are approaching retirement you can plan ahead by buying a deferred annuity, which you pay for by instalments. You can also use your home to obtain an annuity if you have paid off the mortgage – you take out a loan on the property to buy the annuity; your estate repays the loan when you die.

Where can I buy an annuity? From most life insurance companies, or through an insurance broker.

What is the minimum sum I have to pay? It varies – usually about £1000.

How often is the income paid? Usually monthly or half-yearly.

How long does the investment last? Until you die.

Is the income the same for women as for men? No, men get more than women, because women live longer than men and so get a lower income for a longer time.

How much annual income can I expect? For a purchase price of £10,000 at an interest rate of 11 per cent, your annual income would be:

Age	Man	Woman
65	£1457	£1311
70	£1642	£1437
75	£1915	£1629

Will I pay tax on the income? Only on that part which is made up of interest.

Is the income index-linked? Not usually – you receive the interest fixed at the time of purchase.

Can I get my capital back? No, once you have made an investment you cannot cash it in.

See also INVESTING; NATIONAL SAVINGS; PENSIONS; SAVING.

Antifreeze

Renewing the coolant in your car's radiator

The strength of the mixture of antifreeze and water in a car's cooling system should be checked at least every six months. Correct strength should be maintained all year round, because antifreeze also inhibits the build-up of sediments and rust in the system.

Further, the mixture has a high boiling point, which allows the engine to run at a higher temperature, improving efficiency and reducing the danger of overheating in hot weather.

The best antifreeze has an ethylene-glycol base. Mixed with anti-corrosive additives, it can stay undisturbed in the system for up to three years. Then the system must be flushed, and the coolant replaced with new antifreeze mixture – see RADIATOR FLUSHING. If you are not sure how long the coolant has been in, replace it.

The strength is tested with an antifreeze (not a battery) hydrometer, by drawing up some coolant from the radiator header tank or expansion tank. Hydrometers can be bought cheaply from car accessory shops – follow the maker's instructions.

If the coolant needs replacing, let the engine cool and place a container (a plastic bowl or bucket will do) under the radiator. If the drain tap has stuck, or the radiator does not have one, unclip and pull off the bottom hose. Remove the radiator filler cap to speed the flow.

Look closely at the coolant. If it contains bits of rust or sediment, the system should be flushed.

Check all hose clips and hoses. Replace any hose showing signs of cracking or internal weakness when squeezed.

Antifreeze damages paintwork. So before refilling, wrap rags around the filler neck to absorb splashes and spillages.

Close the drain tap or refit the bottom hose, if you have removed it, and tighten the hose clips. The fresh antifreeze solution is best pre-mixed in a 2 gallon watering can. If the car has an expansion tank, replace the coolant there with the correct mixture, making sure you fill the tank to the level marked on its side.

Run the engine, with the radiator cap off, until the coolant in the radiator is warm. Top up until the level remains constant, then replace the radiator cap. To check for leaks, spread newspaper on the ground beneath the engine and radiator, and find the source of any drips. Tighten clips or renew hoses as necessary.

Antifreeze is poisonous, so any kitchen container used for draining must never be used in the kitchen again. The old antifreeze must not be poured down a drain, but disposed of at a proper dump – consult your local authority.

Check the level of coolant at least once a week and always before a long trip. Top up only with the correct strength of antifreeze solution – plain water dilutes the mixture.

Antiques

Looking after antique furniture and bygones

Restoring antiques is a skilled craft, and if you have anything of great value that needs cleaning or repairing, take it to a professional restorer. If you are not sure of its value, get it valued by a reputable antiques dealer. Some of the large antiques auctioneers, such as Christie's and Sotheby's, have a valuation service.

There are, however, some jobs you can tackle yourself with reasonable safety provided you stick to a few simple guidelines and the pieces are not particularly valuable.

Cleaning and polishing Furniture that has accumulated a layer of grime over the years can be cleaned with a solution of one part each of linseed oil, vinegar and turpentine and a quarter part of methylated spirit. Shake the mixture well each time before using it, and apply with a soft cloth.

One of the beauties of antique furniture is the patina wood acquires with age, which is not the same as grime and should not be removed. Polish veneers and french-polished surfaces with furniture cream – on untreated wood use a proprietary wax polish, or you can make your own by melting an ounce of beeswax in three fluid ounces of turpentine.

Removing scratches and stains Scratches in a polished surface can be filled with a thin solution of shellac varnish and methylated spirit. Apply with an artist's brush until the filler stands above the surface. When it has hardened, sand it level with fine glasspaper. Polish with metal polish or a burnishing compound. See also SCRATCH MARKS.

Heat and water marks that have not penetrated through to the wood can be removed with metal polish applied with a soft cloth. A grey discoloration, called bloom, that sometimes appears on highly polished furniture can be treated with a solution of a tablespoon of vinegar to two pints of warm water. Wipe over with a soft cloth, wipe dry and polish.

Burn marks are treated in much the same way as scratches. First scrape away the burnt area down to the bare wood, sand with fine glasspaper and restain if necessary. Then fill and finish as for scratches.

Repairing damaged veneers Slight blistering of a VENEER can be repaired by pressing with a hot iron on top of several layers of blotting paper. If this does not work, slit the blister with a craft knife, insert a little PVA adhesive under the veneer and press with a warm iron. Use heavy books to weight down the repair for 24 hours to ensure good adhesion.

Repairing china Valuable porcelains, such as Meissen or Chelsea, should be entrusted to the care of an expert, but less valuable CHINA can be restored by anyone with a little care and patience.

There are a number of glues that can be used for mending china, the best being cyanoacrylate – the so-called 'super-glue' which bonds instantly. Before making the repair, clean both surfaces to be joined with methylated spirit and make sure that they fit together exactly. Apply the adhesive sparingly to one surface only – bring the two parts together and hold them firmly for about 30 seconds. Be very careful that you make an exact join first time – cyanoacrylate does not allow you a second chance.

Hairline cracks in china become more noticeable as dirt and grease build up inside them – soaking the piece for several hours in a strong solution of household bleach will clean out the cracks, making them almost invisible. Chips can be filled with a mixture of epoxy resin and finely powdered chalk, called whiting. If the piece to be repaired is a colour other than white, add powder paint to the mixture to obtain a matching shade.

Cleaning brass, copper, bronze, pewter and silver Clean heavily tarnished brass with a solution of 1 heaped tablespoon of salt and 2 tablespoons of vinegar to a pint of water. Remove a green deposit on copper, called VERDIGRIS, with paste made up of whiting and methylated spirit. Polish both metals with a mildly abrasive metal polish. Do not be tempted to lacquer polished copper and brass antiques – though it will save regular polishing it will also lower their value.

Bronze acquires a patina with age, in shades of brown or blue-green, which should *never* be removed. Do not polish bronze, simply wipe it occasionally with a soft cloth.

Polish pewter frequently, if neglected it takes on a dull grey finish which is difficult to remove. Use a proprietary pewter polish, not general-purpose metal polish which is too abrasive, and rub vigorously with a soft cloth.

SILVER and silver plate tarnish very quickly, but will retain their shine if cleaned regularly with a proprietary silver polish applied with a soft cloth or chamois leather. Always polish silver in straight strokes, not a crosswise or rotary motion. After polishing, clean in hot, soapy water.

Cleaning and repairing glass Soak badly stained cut-glass in a mixture of water and liquid detergent, to which a few drops of ammonia have been added. Broken glass can be mended in the same way as broken china, and special glass adhesives are available which give excellent results if the manufacturer's instructions are followed carefully.

Ants

Ridding your kitchen of a persistent pest

A cheap and effective way to drive ants from your kitchen and larder for good is to stop them from reaching their favourite snacks. These include jam, sugar, cakes and crumbs of all kinds, along with splashes and spillages of grease, gravy and syrupy juices.

Do not leave foods uncovered: keep jam, marmalade and honey jars firmly lidded; store cakes and biscuits in airtight containers; return food to the fridge. Sweep up or vacuum all crumbs and other small food scraps; scrub shelves and worktops thoroughly and regularly.

In addition, proprietary ant-bait jelly is available, or there are aerosol and puffer packs of suitable PESTICIDES and special insecticidal lacquer for spraying skirtings, shelves, pipeholes and door thresholds. In all cases, follow makers' instructions carefully and keep containers out of children's reach.

Increasingly, ants are living within the structure of centrally heated homes. Semi-tropical Pharaoh ants in blocks of flats need specialist treatment from a pest control company or your local council health department.

Ants may stage a wet-weather invasion of a house to escape from waterlogged nests outside. If they cannot reach the food they need they will leave of their own accord as the ground outdoors dries. There, however, they also spell trouble in the garden, swarming over fruit trees seeking the honeydew excreted by APHIDS, and attacking ripe fruit. They nest in the earth, where their tunnelling frequently damages plant roots.

To combat ants outdoors, dust the soil with HCH insecticide or destroy nests by pouring in a solution of HCH or trichorphon. The traditional method of pouring in boiling water seldom kills enough to eliminate them completely, as it will not reach the egg-laying queen.

Aphid attack If you see these tiny, transparent insects on a plant, such as this rosebud, take immediate steps to destroy them.

Aphids

Guarding plants against a tiny terror

Aphids are tiny, soft-bodied insects, also known as greenfly, blackfly or blight. Their numerous species – which include apple, black bean, cabbage and rose aphids – can severely damage many decorative plants, and most fruits and vegetables. They attack the tissues of stems, leaves and fruit to suck out the sap. They can also infect many garden plants indirectly by carrying sap they have sucked from a diseased plant to a healthy one.

Aphids multiply prodigiously in hot, humid weather. If they are not destroyed immediately, dense colonies will infest young shoots and the underside of leaves. In summer, spray or dust affected trees, shrubs, flowers and vegetables with a suitable insecticide containing HCH, carbaryl, permethrin, derris or malathion – see PESTICIDES. Or use a systemic insecticide – a chemical compound which enters the sap – based on menazon, oxydematon-methyl or dimethoate. This is sprayed or watered onto the foliage or soil. Inside the sap stream, the insecticide is toxic to aphids. Some gardening experts suggest that the insecticide should be varied from time to time, so that the aphids do not build up a resistance to a particular spray.

After using an insecticide on a food crop, you must delay before harvesting or picking. The package label will tell you how long to wait.

Indoor plants can be sprayed with resmethrin or permethrin, an allied product. Alternatively, discourage the aphids from reaching the foliage by wrapping the bases of plants with aluminium foil.

Appendicitis

What to do in an emergency case

Appendicitis can strike quite suddenly, causing pain in the abdomen. The victim often begins to feel this pain near the navel, from where it moves to the lower right side of the abdomen and intensifies into a constant ache.

The cause is inflammation of the appendix – a short tube, closed at one end, projecting from the junction of the small and large intestines.

Diagnosis is tricky because the symptoms vary, and may develop over four to 48 hours. But call a doctor if the pain gets worse, or becomes continuous and keeps the sufferer awake. Call anyway if the pain goes on after four hours. Watch also for these symptoms: NAUSEA, VOMITING, foul breath, loss of appetite for food or drink, pain when passing urine or walking, and a high temperature.

If you suspect appendicitis, seek urgent medical attention because hospital treatment – an operation to remove the appendix – will almost certainly be necessary. Without treatment, an abscess can develop; more commonly, you can develop peritonitis, a severe infection of the abdominal cavity.

While waiting for a doctor or ambulance, keep the patient still with a hot-water bottle wrapped in a towel on the abdomen.

Give no food, drink, laxatives, painkillers or drugs. Rinse the patient's mouth with sips of water.

In another form of appendicitis – called chronic – symptoms can come and go for months before an operation is recommended.

Appliqué

Stitching cut-out shapes to fabrics

To get the best results for appliqué work, choose natural lightweight or medium-weight fabrics, which are easy to handle. Be sure that all the fabrics are of the same type if they are to be laundered.

Ideas for appliqué designs abound, in magazines, design publications, collections of stencil shapes, and in colouring, art and needlework books.

To transfer designs, cut a cardboard pattern in the shape of each appliqué piece and trace the shape onto the appliqué surface. Add a 3mm ($\frac{1}{8}$in) seam allowance for hand sewing, 6mm ($\frac{1}{4}$in) for machine sewing. Layer the shapes so that you work from background to foreground. Shapes that do not stand by themselves should be positioned to overlap slightly.

Hand-sewing appliqués Fold and finger-press the seam allowance along the traced outline, to the reverse side, and

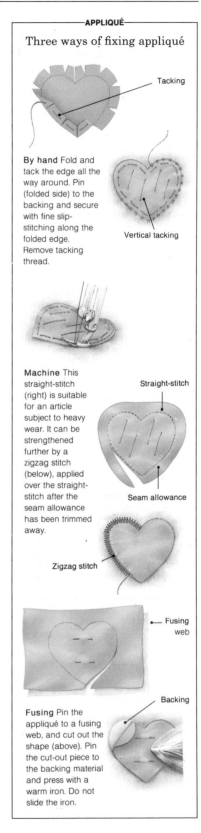

Three ways of fixing appliqué

Tacking

By hand Fold and tack the edge all the way around. Pin (folded side) to the backing and secure with fine slip-stitching along the folded edge. Remove tacking thread.

Vertical tacking

Machine This straight-stitch (right) is suitable for an article subject to heavy wear. It can be strengthened further by a zigzag stitch (below), applied over the straight-stitch after the seam allowance has been trimmed away.

Straight-stitch

Seam allowance

Zigzag stitch

Fusing web

Backing

Fusing Pin the appliqué to a fusing web, and cut out the shape (above). Pin the cut-out piece to the backing material and press with a warm iron. Do not slide the iron.

tack the folded edge as you go. Keep the tacking within the seam allowance width.

Pin the appliqué to the background and hold in place with vertical tacking stitches – see SEWING. Secure the appliqué with fine SLIP-STITCHING along the folded edges. Remove all tacking. Alternatively, you can use a running stitch or cross stitch, but you should remember that these are decorative stitches meant to be seen, and so will be part of the design.

Machine-sewing appliques Straight-stitch just outside the inner seamline on the appliqué. Trim the excess margin by cutting along the outer marked line. Fold the seam allowance to the reverse side and tack in place.

Position and pin the appliqué to the backing material; tacking with vertical stitches will keep the appliqué from shifting as you work.

To attach it by the straight-stitch method, set the sewing machine to medium stitch length, then carefully stitch along the folded edge of the appliqué. Pull thread ends through to the reverse side and knot them. Remove all tacking threads and pins.

To attach the appliqué by the zigzag method, position the appliqué and straight-stitch directly over the marked seamline. Trim away the seam allowance, as close to the stitching line as possible. Select a suitable width and length for the zigzag and sew over the raw edges and the straight-stitch.

Pull the thread ends to the reverse side and knot them. Remove tacking.

Securing appliqués by fusing A fusing web – a bonding agent that holds two fabrics together when melted between them – is used for this method.

Pin the fusing web to the reverse side of the appliqué material before marking and cutting out the shape, making sure the head of the pin is on the front of the shape. Pin the appliqué and web to the background material with two pins about 50mm (2in) apart. Press the tip of a warm iron between the pins to heat-fix the appliqué, then remove the pins, place a damp cloth over the appliqué and hold the iron on it until the area is dry.

Aquariums

Looking after fish in a tank

There are two types of aquarium fish – cold-water and tropical – and you will need two tanks if you intend to keep both types.

Start with a few fish and increase the number as you gain confidence. The goldfish, the most common cold-water fish, is ideal for the beginner. It grows to at least

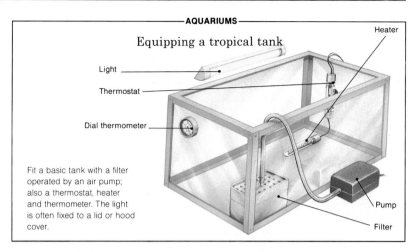

─ AQUARIUMS ─

Equipping a tropical tank

Light

Thermostat

Dial thermometer

Heater

Pump

Filter

Fit a basic tank with a filter operated by an air pump; also a thermostat, heater and thermometer. The light is often fixed to a lid or hood cover.

150mm (6in) in length, has a long lifespan and is easy to keep. Other popular cold-water varieties include shubunkin, koi, oranda, black moor and Japanese rice fish. These fish can be kept at living-room temperature – between 10 and 23°C (50-73°F).

A tropical tank can include many colourful species, such as guppies, the iridescent neon, swordtails, platties and Siamese fighting fish. But never put two Siamese males together – they will fight to the death! Tropical fish need a heater to keep the water between 22 and 26°C (72-79°F).

Choosing a tank The size usually depends upon how many fish will be in it, but as a general rule buy the biggest you can afford. A good size is 610mm × 300mm × 380mm (24in × 12in × 15in) – but the most popular sizes range from 460mm (18in) to 1m (39in) long. But make sure you have room for the size you buy. Place it on a firm, level surface or a sturdy stand and put a layer of polystyrene ceiling tiles under its base. Cover the top with glass or clear plastic to stop dirt getting in and the fish from leaping out. A cover will also reduce evaporation and help maintain an even water temperature.

Lighting can be daylight or fluorescent tubes in a hood that fits over the top of the tank. A north-facing window is ideal, but avoid too much direct sunlight; and cut down the amount of light if the water turns green or if there is an excessive growth of green algae. Install an air pump with a filter to keep the water clean and to maintain a high oxygen content. Some filters incorporate an electrically driven pump and do not need an air supply.

Setting up the tank Wash the tank with clean water and cover the bottom with 38-75mm (1½-3in) of well-rinsed aquarium gravel, sloping it towards the front. Add some well-washed rocks, pebbles or

driftwood as decoration. Plants can be plastic, or live ones such as Amazon sword, Cabomba and Vallisneria. Switch on the unit for a few days to ensure it is functioning properly.

Examine the dealer's stock carefully before buying your fish. Choose fish that are lively, well fed and free from blemishes. Do not overcrowd the tank – cold-water fish need a minimum of 4.5 litres per 25mm of fish (1 gallon per inch). Tropicals need 750mm² (12sq in) surface area for every 25mm (1in) of fish. When transporting fish in a plastic bag ensure that a constant temperature is maintained to avoid the danger of shock. Float the fish in the tank in their bag for ten minutes before releasing them.

Feeding Give your fish good-quality, staple food twice a day, but be careful not to overfeed them. They should be given no more than they can consume in five minutes. Supplement the diet with freeze-dried items, such as Tubifex worms. As a special treat, live brine shrimp (Artemia) can be given. If you go away for a day or two, the fish need not be fed.

Keeping fish healthy Check the temperature of a tropical fish tank daily and keep the glass clean. Algae can be removed from the sides with an algae magnet – two magnets facing each other, one on the inside, the other outside. Remove sediment and uneaten food with a siphon tube. Both appliances are available from pet shops. Change a quarter of the water every two or three weeks. Watch for any signs of disease – the two most likely to occur are fungus, which looks like patches of cotton wool on the body, and ich, which shows as white spots the size of a pinhead. Your dealer will advise on treatment.

If fish are gasping at the surface, the cause is most likely to be lack of oxygen, or too much heat. Avoid introducing parasites by disinfecting new plants and quarantining new fish in a separate tank for two or three weeks. Move fish that look unwell to a separate tank for observation. A fish with trailing faeces may be constipated and should be fed on a diet with a high fibre content – but ask the dealer to advise you.

Arbitration

Settling disputes without using courts

Civil court disputes about agreements and CONTRACTS may be lengthy and expensive. Arbitration, a less formal process that need not involve LAWYERS, may be a quicker and often cheaper alternative – for example, if your holiday fails to live up to expectations, or your car is not properly repaired.

There are some drawbacks, however. LEGAL AID is not available, and the arbitrator's decision is final. It can be appealed against only on a point of law, and only then if a court gives permission.

Fresh evidence that comes to light after arbitration is not grounds for reopening the case.

When arbitration applies The two parties to an agreement or contract – which need not be in writing to be legally valid – can jointly decide to seek arbitration voluntarily to settle a dispute; but sometimes arbitration is compulsory. It is frequently specified, for example, in service WARRANTIES, property leases, INSURANCE policies and the booking terms and conditions of holiday travel companies.

In those circumstances, if you have accepted the general terms of the agreement, you have accepted the arbitration clause, too, and are bound by it, so always read the small print carefully before you sign.

You may be able to have the arbitration clause struck out, reserving your right to go to court later if you wish. The snag is that the other party must agree, and it is unlikely that, for example, insurance companies would do so.

County court disputes involving amounts of less than £1000 are automatically referred to arbitration – see also SMALL CLAIMS. It is possible to object to that procedure, and to apply to the court registrar for a trial instead. However, that will be granted only if the registrar is satisfied that the issues involved are too complicated to be settled easily by arbitration, and if there is no prior agreement on arbitration.

The loser in a county court arbitration case involving less than £1000 does not have to pay the winner's costs – only set court fees. But both sides have to pay their *own* legal costs, if any. So this is a useful way to press a small claim over,

for example, a faulty washing machine or minor car damage.

In county court claims involving more than £1000, arbitration may be used only if both parties agree. In addition, the court may order costs to be paid.

Before county court arbitration begins, the normal pre-trial procedures must be followed. You must prepare a detailed summary of your case, and your opponent must file a reply. Then the registrar will normally hold an informal, private meeting at the court, to settle the arrangements for the hearing.

Arbitration hearings take a broader view than courts on what evidence is, or is not, permissible. They may, for example, take into account secondhand, or hearsay, evidence – what a witness was told by someone else – and documents not admissible in a formal trial.

Choosing an arbitrator In county court arbitration cases, the arbitrator is usually the court registrar, whose services are free; though a court fee must be paid to start proceedings. Agreements or contracts may specify other arbitration procedures, leaving the parties to decide jointly on a suitable person. He does not need any legal qualifications, although he must be qualified in a field relevant to the dispute – for example, as an official of the appropriate trade or professional association. Chambers of commerce or trade may be able to recommend a suitable candidate.

Written agreements and contracts containing an arbitration clause frequently specify that, if the parties cannot agree on an arbitrator, one will be appointed by the head of a named professional or trade body. Alternatively, the Institute of Arbitrators in London may be asked to suggest an arbitrator; it can also advise on procedures and likely costs.

There are no general rules for arbitration, though many trade associations have their own. With the agreement of the parties, the issue may be decided purely from written statements, without the need for a hearing. The parties may represent themselves at any hearing, or nominate someone, not necessarily a lawyer, to put their case. In independent arbitration cases, costs are decided by prior agreement, or by the arbitrator according to previously agreed rules.

Architect

Planning a new home, or extending the existing one

If you are planning to build a new home other than an 'off the shelf' design offered by a builder, you will need an architect to design it for you. Similarly an extension of any great size on an existing home will need his services – and not only in

the design. There will be other aspects on which you will need expert advice.

An architect can save you a great deal of time and money. He will draw up designs that will meet PLANNING PERMISSION and building regulations approval – see BUILDING PERMITS. He will also know how to get approval quickly, and how to get competitive estimates from builders once the work has begun – see CONTRACTORS. Finally, he will make sure it is up to standard.

How to find an architect Personal recommendation is the best guide; alternatively, contact the Clients Advisory Service at the Royal Institute of British Architects, 66 Portland Place, London W1N 4AD. Tell them what you have in mind – the style of house or type of extension – and they will supply the names of qualified members in your area.

How much will he charge? Architects' fees are governed by a scale of charges laid down by the RIBA. The fee is usually calculated as a percentage of the total cost of the building, and is payable as each part of the architect's work is completed. Generally, the higher the total cost the lower the percentage, and percentages for extension work are higher than for a new building. The scales of fees are published by the RIBA and obtainable from the architect's office.

Agree the costs with the architect from the outset; it is advisable to tell him how much you want to spend, so that he can then submit to you designs and plans that will suit your pocket. Make sure there are no hidden extras and ask him for a programme of work, stating at what dates the fees will be due and what work will be carried out at each stage.

Arthritis

Methods of relieving a painful ailment

Arthritis is not a single disease. More than 100 conditions, each featuring inflammation of one or more joints, are considered forms of arthritis. Many forms may occur once; others recur. Medical treatment can control arthritis, and may cure certain forms.

See a DOCTOR if any of the following symptoms persist for more than two weeks: recurring pain, or tenderness in the joints; morning stiffness; inability to move a joint normally; red, shiny skin over a joint that feels unusually warm; unexplained weight loss, fever or weakness combined with joint pain.

When people speak of arthritis, they usually mean osteoarthritis, the most common form, which stems from wear and tear on the joints and mostly afflicts people in late middle age. It strikes most often at joints in the fingers (which become lumpy), the spine, the hips and knees. In bad cases, muscles around the affected joints waste away.

Treatment for osteoarthritis usually includes painkillers to relieve the pain and inflammation; exercises to keep the affected joints flexible and to build muscle strength; diet for the overweight patient whose bulk may be causing stress to the joints. A doctor may recommend regular rest and some form of heat therapy, such as hot baths or showers. Other helpful measures include sitting in a straight chair, avoiding stairs, and keeping a leg up if the knee is affected. A physiotherapist may be able to help, using short-wave or ultrasound therapy. Although less common, rheumatoid arthritis (the condition often called 'rheumatism') still afflicts millions. It is a painful and destructive swelling of the joints, affecting women more often than men. It may first attack fingers and toes, then spread to include wrists, knees, shoulders, ankles, and elbows. Stiffness of the joints in the mornings is a characteristic feature. Anyone suspecting that they have rheumatoid arthritis, should contact a doctor. Mild cases are treated with aspirin, exercises, heat and rest. Other painkillers or stronger drugs, such as penicillamine or gold may also help. The doctor may arrange blood tests and X-rays, which could also disclose any other disorders.

In serious cases of both forms, surgeons can operate to replace joints with artificial joints made of special metal alloys or plastics.

Artichokes

Preparing and cooking globe artichokes

Use a large knife to cut off the artichoke stalk flush with the base, and slice 13mm (½in) or so off the top leaves. Trim away any sharp tips of the remaining leaves with scissors, and rub all the cuts with lemon to prevent discolouring.

Put the artichokes into a large enamel or stainless-steel saucepan or casserole of boiling water. Do not use an aluminium pan, which will discolour the artichokes. Salt the water with about 2 teaspoons for each 570ml (1 pint). Boil uncovered for 20-30 minutes according to size. Alternatively, steam in a steamer for 45-50 minutes over boiling water containing a little lemon juice or vinegar.

To test if they are done, gently tug a leaf from the base. If it comes away easily and its fleshy base is tender, the artichoke can be removed, using tongs. Spread apart the green outer leaves to expose the soft, purplish inner leaves, then remove the inner leaves to reveal the hairy choke. Use a spoon to scrape

away the hairs and expose the heart, or fond. Drain the artichokes upside down for 2-3 minutes. The choke can also be removed before cooking, but this is difficult as the leaves are quite hard. However, it cuts the boiling or steaming times roughly by half.

Artichokes are usually served one per person, with melted butter and perhaps lemon juice. Pull off a leaf, dip the fleshy stalk end into the butter and draw it through your teeth. Finish off with the fond, using knife and fork.

Artificial respiration

What to do if a casualty stops breathing

A person who has stopped breathing will die within minutes unless they have air in their lungs. As little as three minutes without oxygen can cause irreversible brain damage.

If you suspect that breathing has stopped when someone collapses or is injured, first open the airway by tilting the head and lifting the chin, then check

---

ARTIFICIAL RESPIRATION

Clearing the air passage; giving the 'kiss of life'

Clearing the air passage Before giving the kiss of life, clear the air passage. Place one hand on the forehead and tilt back the head – this opens the windpipe. Use your other hand to lift the chin and clear the tongue from the windpipe.

If there is obstruction, turn head, clear mouth with fingers. Make sure there is a pulse.

Mouth-to-mouth respiration
1 Tilt the head back to keep the air passage open. Pinch the nose with your thumb and forefinger, seal your lips around the open mouth and breathe into it, making the chest rise.

2 Remove your mouth and watch the chest fall; continue at a rate of one every six seconds (10 inflations per minute), until the victim starts breathing again.

Child respiration The kiss of life can be given to a baby or small child by sealing your mouth around both mouth and nose. Aim at about 20 gentle inflations a minute with a small child, or gentle puffs only for a baby.

by listening with your ear close to his mouth and nose, and watching carefully for chest movement. Look also for a blue-grey tinge on lips, cheeks and ear lobes.

If breathing has stopped, the cause may be simply a blocked air passage: food, vomit or blood may be obstructing it. Take immediate steps to ensure that the air passage is open, as illustrated.

If clearing the air passage causes breathing to restart normally, place the casualty in the RECOVERY POSITION and call for an ambulance.

If the casualty does not start to breathe after the air passage has been cleared, begin mouth-to-mouth respiration or, if the mouth is injured, mouth-to-nose respiration – applied in the same way as mouth-to-mouth except that the mouth is held shut while you seal your lips around the nose. It is best to have training in this technique. See also EXTERNAL CHEST COMPRESSION.

Asparagus

Growing and cooking a popular delicacy

Dedicated asparagus eaters can save considerable sums of money by growing this rather expensive delicacy for themselves in a permanent bed in the garden.

Nurserymen and good garden centres can supply the year-old asparagus crowns you need, which must grow for two more years before cropping. Mature plants produce crops in late April to mid-June.

Asparagus needs good drainage and strict weeding. How many you plant depends upon appetite, available space, and how many shoots, or spears, you expect to get from each plant. Plants need to be 450mm (18in) apart, with a further 300mm from the ends of each row. In the autumn before April planting, dig into the bed a bucket of manure or COM-POST per square metre (square yard).

In February, order plants (for delivery in early April), fork the bed into a good, crumbly tilth and rake in some FERTI-LISER. When the crowns arrive do not let their roots dry out – plant them immediately if the soil is in good condition; delay for perhaps two weeks if the weather is wet and cold, protecting them under damp sacks meanwhile.

To plant, dig trenches 200mm (8in) deep and 300mm (12in) wide spaced about 1m (3ft) apart. If the soil is of the clay type, mix gritty sand into the excavated earth to ensure good aeration and drainage. In the bottom of the trench, make a rounded ridge 75mm (3in) high, with its top still 125mm (5in) below ground level. Stand the crowns on this ridge with their roots fanned out in a circle, then cover them immediately with 50mm (2in) of sifted soil.

ASPARAGUS

Cooked fresh from the garden

Harvesting asparagus Clear away the soil from the stem and cut it below ground with a serrated knife when 100-150mm (4-6in) tall. If stems grow taller, they get woodier.

Cooking Boil in salted water for 10-15 minutes until soft. Immerse the harder lower parts but let the heads cook in the steam.

Thereafter, apply a general fertiliser at 70-100g per square metre (2-3 oz per square yard) annually in spring, and a mulch of well decayed manure or compost the following autumn after the dead stems have been cut back.

Hand weed the bed and support the growing stems with stakes and string along both sides if necessary – but do not cut them at all in their first season, and very little in their second. Cut mature plants when the spears are at least 100-150mm (4-6in) above ground, using a serrated-edged asparagus knife or a bread knife. Cut the stems at an oblique angle a little below ground. Crop two or three times a week until mid-June – do not let the spears grow too tall before cutting. After mid-June the spears must be left to develop into fern.

Enemies The plant has two serious enemies: the asparagus beetle and violet root rot. The beetles and their larvae feed on young shoots and leaves from early June, leaving the plants blackened and sticky. At the first signs, spray or dust with derris, malathion or gamma HCH – see PESTICIDES. The root rot fungus covers roots with purple-violet strands, and the top growth yellows and dies. No chemical cure is available: plants must be pulled up and destroyed, and no others planted in the same soil for several years.

Cooking asparagus Cut any woody bits from the bottoms of the stems and scrape the white parts downwards. Bundle and tie the stems, heads uppermost; place in salted water with the heads clear of the water and boil in a covered pan for 10-15 minutes, until the heads are soft to touch. Serve hot with melted butter and eat with your fingers.

Asphalt driveways

Laying a new drive or path with cold asphalt; repairing an old one

To lay an asphalt path or driveway, cold asphalt is spread over a layer of cold bitumen emulsion, then compressed with a garden roller. Both asphalt and bitumen are readily obtainable from builders' merchants and do-it-yourself centres.

First mark out the drive or path with string lines and small pegs. If it has a

ASPHALT DRIVEWAYS

Steps in laying down a new drive

First lay hardcore or cinder ash to make a firm bed for the drive. Over this goes a layer of bitumen, then the asphalt and, if desired, stone chippings. Use boards to give straight edges and a template board to give a smooth camber.

Stone chippings

Template board

Asphalt layer

Bitumen layer

Hardcore or cinder ash base

curve, mark it out with rope or a hose-pipe laid on the ground.

For a drive (which must bear considerable weights) excavate to at least 180mm (7in); for a path 75-100mm (3-4in). Fit any drain inspection chamber in a driveway with a heavy-duty cover; the drive must be laid flush with the cover. Protect any drains with a layer of concrete 610mm (2ft) wide and 100mm (4in) thick, set 300mm (12in) above the drain – see CONCRETE.

Line the sides of the excavated area with boards braced on the outside by pegs. For a path, lay a bed of cinder ash or hardcore 75-100mm deep; for a driveway it should be at least 180mm thick. Compact and level this bed with a garden roller. Choose a dry but not hot day for laying the bitumen over the hardcore. Use an old watering can to pour the bitumen over an area of about 2.5m² (30sq ft) at a time. Spread it to an even thickness with a stiff broom.

About 20 minutes later, when the bitumen has turned from brown to black, tip the asphalt onto it and rake it to an overall thickness of about 19mm (¾in). Roll it immediately, wetting the roller to stop the asphalt sticking to it. Add extra asphalt to any depressions formed.

If the path or drive is on level ground it should be cambered to let rainwater run off. To do this obtain a plank or board about 610mm (2ft) longer than the width of the drive, and trim one edge from the middle to the ends so that it forms a very shallow, concave template. Build up the centre of the drive with asphalt, then run the 'template' board across the surface from end to end.

At this stage, decorative stone chippings can be scattered thinly over the surface with a shovel, if desired. Finally roll the asphalt thoroughly in several directions to compact the surface. Allow two days for it to harden before driving a vehicle over it or removing the edging boards and pegs.

Repairing holes Use a cold chisel to chip away a square or rectangular section around the hole; dig out the old asphalt to a depth of at least 38mm (1½in) and sweep the hole clean. Fill with ready-mix tarmac, obtainable from builders' merchants, so that the tarmac stands a little above the surrounding surface. Firm the path by tamping it down with a punner – you can make one by nailing a piece of 25mm (1in) thick blockboard 150mm (6in) square to a length of 50×50mm (2×2in) timber; for a large patch use a roller. Leave to harden for 24 hours.

Repairing a broken edge Lay a length of timber along the edge and brace it with pegs on the outside, then repair as for a hole. Remove the edging board and pegs when the tarmac has hardened.

Aspic
Moulding food in a delicious jelly

Aspic is a clear jelly used to set food in a mould, to coat it and to hold a garnish in position.

To make aspic, skim the fat from four cups of cold meat, fish, poultry, or vegetable broth. Pour half a cup of the broth into a 3.4 litre (6 pint) saucepan, and sprinkle it with 2 tablespoons of unflavoured gelatine. Let it stand for 5 minutes until the gelatine is soft. Add the remaining broth and three egg whites beaten until they are frothy – see EGG SEPARATING.

Bring the mixture to the boil, whisking constantly. When a dense foam appears on top, remove the saucepan from the heat. Line a sieve with a teacloth that has been soaked and wrung out. Pour the liquid aspic through the lined sieve into a bowl. Let it stand until it sets as clear aspic.

Setting in aspic Pour a small quantity of liquid aspic into a dish or mould, then chill for about 30 minutes until set. Place pieces of meat, fish, poultry, or vegetables, and any garnish on the set aspic. Carefully pour in more liquid aspic until it comes two-thirds of the way up the food. Chill until this second layer is set, then cover the food completely with the remaining liquid aspic, and refrigerate again. To remove it from the mould, run a knife around inside the top edge, dip the mould into hot water for a few seconds, cover it with a plate then invert the mould.

Coating with aspic Allow the jelly to set to the consistency of unbeaten egg white, then place the food to be coated on a wire rack above a plate or tray. Spoon on the aspic until an even layer adheres. Leave until set, then repeat if necessary.

Decorate by dipping pieces of garnish – tarragon, carrot, olives, for example – in a little cool but liquid aspic before setting it in position with the point of a skewer. When set, glaze with more aspic. See also JELLIES.

Aspidistra
Looking after a Victorian houseplant

The aspidistra, also known as the parlour palm and cast-iron plant, has been popular from Victorian times. It has large, dark green and somewhat oblong leaves, and occasionally small purple flowers.

Its popularity endures because it is very easy to grow, and tolerates poor light, gas fumes, and extremes of temperatures.

Aspidistras thrive best when kept out of direct sunshine. In summer, water freely and wash the leaves occasionally. In winter, keep the plant fairly warm and avoid over-watering. A common sign of too frequent watering is the appearance of brown marks on the surface of the leaves.

Potting and feeding Use a soil-based potting mixture – 1 part fibrous soil to 1 part peat moss or leaf mould – and apply a standard liquid fertiliser every two weeks during the growth period. Repot only at three or four-year intervals, moving the plant into a pot one size larger when new growth begins in spring.

See also FERTILISERS; HOUSEPLANTS; POTTING HOUSEPLANTS.

Athlete's foot
Treating and avoiding an irritating infection

Athlete's foot, a form of ringworm, is a fungus infection most marked between the toes and on the soles of the feet. Damp and sweaty feet are particularly prone to infection. The condition is common among adolescents and sportsmen using communal changing rooms, where someone with bare feet suffering from the infection can easily spread it to others.

First signs are an itching, sometimes intense, between the toes and on the soles and sides of the feet. The skin, especially between the fourth and little toes, becomes soggy. It flakes and peels, and cracks appear between the skin creases. As it develops, small blisters and rashes may occur around the toes and soles, with the underlying inflamed skin showing bright red.

At the first signs of infection, wash the feet frequently, and dry carefully between the toes, keeping a special towel for the purpose. Change socks and footwear daily, or more often – especially if the feet tend to sweat. Treat the feet daily with a proprietary antifungal foot powder or cream from a chemist.

Diagnosis of athlete's foot is not infallible – the condition can be confused with types of ECZEMA and psoriasis. If in doubt, consult your DOCTOR. Also seek medical advice if the condition does not improve after using proprietary remedies, or if there is pain and swelling, with inflammation spreading towards the ankle. These symptoms could call for special treatment.

Some people guard against athlete's foot by wearing rubber or wooden sandals at gymnasiums, swimming pools, or in changing rooms. You can also avoid it by keeping your feet cool – wearing sandals, for example – changing sweaty socks and footwear after physical activity, long periods of standing, and on coming home from work.

Even when treatment is successful, reinfection is common through footwear and floor coverings, and because the fungus is difficult to dislodge from toenails. Guard against it by continuing to use a foot powder and to wash sweaty feet frequently, drying between the toes.

Auctions

How to bid, how to sell, and some pitfalls to avoid

Auction sales are a happy hunting ground for bargains – provided you bid prudently. It is easy to get carried away and pay more than you planned.

Before an auction sale starts there is a viewing period, when you can examine the goods on sale. Some particularly valuable items may have a reserve price, the lowest price the seller is willing to accept. The auctioneer will withdraw them if the reserve is not reached in the bidding. If you suspect there may be a reserve on something you are interested in, ask before the auction.

Making a bid When bidding starts, the auctioneer will ask for an opening bid at around the price that he hopes to get for the article. Do not bid immediately. Wait to see if he calls for lower bids, and when you are ready to make a bid raise your hand and be sure to catch his eye. It sometimes pays to delay your bid until the hammer is about to fall – this new competition may unsettle a rival bidder and cause him to drop out.

An item or group of items being auctioned is called 'a lot'. When a lot is knocked down to you the auctioneer or his assistant will ask your name. You must then pay for your purchase before you leave the saleroom. You are also responsible for removing anything you buy, so arrange transport if you intend to buy bulky items such as furniture.

If you find later that there is a fault in the item you have bought, you have no claim against the auctioneer or the seller. You can, however, claim your money back if the article is not as described – if, for example, a dish described as silver turns out to be silver plate.

All auctions are governed by the Conditions of Sale printed in the catalogue or displayed in the saleroom.

Selling by auction If you have goods to sell by auction, try to choose an auctioneer who specialises in the sort of articles you are selling. You can ask advice on setting a reserve – large companies have special valuing departments.

The auctioneer will get the best price he can, for his fee is a 10 to 20 per cent commission on the sale. He may withdraw a lot that fails to reach a reasonable bid, even without a reserve.

Avocado plants

Grow your own houseplant from an avocado stone

One of the more attractive HOUSEPLANTS can be quickly and easily grown from an avocado stone – though it will not bear fruit.

After removing the stone, wash it clean of any loose skin, pierce it three times around the middle with a skewer, and insert matchsticks in the holes. Suspend the stone, blunt end down, over the mouth of a jar or glass. Fill the jar with water until it reaches about 13mm (½in) up the stone.

Stand the jar in a warm, dimly lit place and check the water level daily, topping up as necessary.

After five or six weeks, when the stone

Growing Use matchsticks stuck into the stone to suspend it partly in water while it sprouts roots.

has sprouted bushy roots, plant about 75mm (3in) deep in a largish pot of JOHN INNES COMPOST No 1. When a stem with tiny leaves appears, put the plant in a warm, sunny, draught-free place. To stop it growing spindly and tall, cut the growing shoot at a height of about 150-180mm (6-7in). Water whenever the potting mixture gets dry, and spray the foliage occasionally.

According to how large you let it grow, the plant may need frequent repotting – see POTTING HOUSEPLANTS.

Axes and hatchets

Sharpening the blade and fitting a new handle

Whether your axe or hatchet is old or new, sharpen the blade with an oilstone before you use it. The handiest oilstone is a combination type, which has a medium grit surface on one side and fine grit on the other.

Lay the axe on a bench with its edge overhanging, and hold it steady by gripping the handle close to the head. Using first the medium grit, then the fine, work the oilstone across one side of the blade, inclining it towards the edge. Then turn the blade over and repeat the process on the other side.

Check the edge by sighting along its length: bright spots indicate blunt sections. Continue sharpening until the whole edge looks grey and becomes almost invisible.

You can also sharpen with a carborundum file. Clamp the axe or hatchet

head edge up in a vice. Hold the file flat against the blade and draw it upwards towards the edge, lifting off at the end of each stroke.

After sharpening with either oilstone or file, the blade can be honed to a really keen edge with an oiled handstone. Hold the circular stone in your palm, fingers gripping the groove cut around its side to protect them from the blade. Hone with a series of circular strokes along each side of the blade in turn, again keeping the angle constant.

If the edge becomes badly nicked, or dulled after frequent sharpening, have it reground at a hardware store or tool shop.

Replacing a handle A loose, split or broken handle is dangerous and must be replaced. To remove it, clamp the axe or hatchet head in a vice and saw off the handle close to the head. Drill holes in the wood inside the head, then use a chisel or an old screwdriver to force out the remaining wood.

Most new handles have a slot cut in the top by the manufacturers. If you buy one without a slot, make a saw cut lengthways across the top of the handle. Cut a thin hardwood wedge to fit. Using a wooden mallet, or nylon-faced hammer, drive the handle into the head until it is a tight fit. Now drive in the wedge until it is firmly stuck.

Saw off any surplus wedge still sticking out, then sandpaper the top of the handle flush with the head.

To make the handle even more secure you can drive in a single metal wedge – available from hardware shops – across the wooden one. Finally, smooth the handle with fine sandpaper and apply linseed oil with a soft cloth.

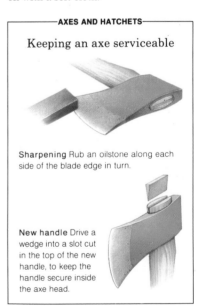

AXES AND HATCHETS

Keeping an axe serviceable

Sharpening Rub an oilstone along each side of the blade edge in turn.

New handle Drive a wedge into a slot cut in the top of the new handle, to keep the handle secure inside the axe head.

Baby alarms

Installing an early-warning system

A power-operated baby alarm has only two parts – the transmitter and the receiver. There is no connecting cable between the two and each unit runs from any electrical socket.

Place the transmitter near the baby's cot, not more than 1m (3ft) away. The transmitter is triggered by sound and works only when there is a noise of some sort close by. You can adjust its sensitivity.

The receiver can be placed anywhere where there is a convenient socket. If the two units are placed too close together – for example, on opposite sides of a wall – the receiver may emit a whistling noise known as 'feedback'. Simply move the units farther apart.

Baby bathing

Doing it safely; avoiding tears

It is not necessary to bathe a baby daily – two or three times a week is sufficient provided the head and nappy areas are kept clean – 'topped and tailed'. Evening is best for bathing – though not just after feeding – in a warm, draught-free room. Have all you need to hand before starting: clean cotton wool; baby soap; a large towel to put on your knees and another to wrap the baby in; a clean nappy and safety pins.

Pour about 75mm (3in) of warm water into the bath at about 35°C (95°F). Test it with a thermometer, or with an elbow or the inside of your wrist.

Soaping and rinsing Before putting the baby in the bath, soap him all over. Start with his head, applying soap with moistened cotton wool and making sure it does not get into his eyes. Clean his face with moist cotton wool, then rinse his head with water from the bath and dry by patting gently with a towel. Now lower the baby into the bath, holding one arm with your hand, so that his head is cradled against your forearm.

Continue to support him in this way and gently rinse his front with your other hand, then change hands and let him lean on your wrist while you rinse his back. Lift the baby out as soon as he is properly rinsed, using the same hold as you did when putting him in. Wrap him in a dry towel and pat dry.

Baby food

Solid foods for your baby, and how to make your own

Once your baby has teeth he can start taking solid foods in addition to breast or bottle feeds. Do not start too early, as it is unnecessary and he may become overweight – see also WEANING. The best time is between four and six months, beginning with cereals such as rice or oatmeal, cooked to a pulp in milk. Introduce one solid food at a time, so that you will know if any particular food disagrees with the baby.

Proprietary baby foods offer good nutrition, but you can easily prepare foods such as mashed ripe bananas, mashed hard-boiled egg and vegetable and meat purées. Do not add salt or sugar.

To make a meat purée, cut well-cooked chicken, beef or lamb into small cubes and grind them with milk to make a sauce-like consistency (or use a FOOD PROCESSOR). Do the same for a vegetable purée, using freshly cooked vegetables instead of meat.

Once baby can lift things to his mouth, let him practise biting on a rusk. Do not give him a biscuit, as a large piece could break off and cause choking.

BABY BATHING

Making it a pleasure for mother and child

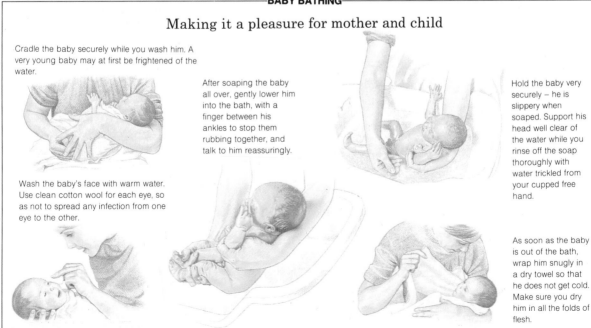

Cradle the baby securely while you wash him. A very young baby may at first be frightened of the water.

Wash the baby's face with warm water. Use clean cotton wool for each eye, so as not to spread any infection from one eye to the other.

After soaping the baby all over, gently lower him into the bath, with a finger between his ankles to stop them rubbing together, and talk to him reassuringly.

Hold the baby very securely – he is slippery when soaped. Support his head well clear of the water while you rinse off the soap thoroughly with water trickled from your cupped free hand.

As soon as the baby is out of the bath, wrap him snugly in a dry towel so that he does not get cold. Make sure you dry him in all the folds of flesh.

Baby winding

Bringing up the burps

Whether breast or bottle-fed, all babies swallow a certain amount of air, which floats on top of the milk in the stomach and makes the baby feel full. When the baby refuses to take more milk before the end of his feed this may mean that he needs winding. There are three ways of winding a baby:

● Hold the baby against your shoulder and gently rub or pat his back.
● Sit him upright on your lap and rub or pat his back while gently rocking him back and forth.
● Lay him face down across your knees, then pat his back as you rock him gently up and down.

Generally you need to wind him once during a feed and once afterwards. If you interrupt a feed too often he will cry and swallow even more air. If you wind him and nothing comes up, do not carry on more than a minute or two.

Backache

Caring for your back; how to prevent and ease lower back pains

The best way to avoid backache is to maintain a good, natural posture at all times – at work, at play, when relaxing and when sleeping. When backache does occur, a half-hour soak in a warm bath or lying on your back on a firm bed may help, or you can try the programme of exercises shown below. But if acute backache persists for more than two or three days, consult your doctor.

Lifting heavy objects Never try to lift anything that is beyond your physical capability – get help if possible, or follow the guidelines in LIFTING AND CARRYING.

Working in the garden Weeding is a backaching job if tackled in the wrong way. Do not bend from the waist to pull out weeds; go down on one knee, or both, as close to the weeds as possible to avoid stretching. This also applies to picking up any small object.

Sitting and sleeping Nowhere is good posture more essential than when sitting in a chair, or in the driving seat of a car. Do not slouch or slump when seated, or hunch your shoulders, and make sure the small of your back is well supported. Sleep on a firm mattress, preferably what is called an 'orthopaedic' bed, designed to support the spine where it most needs support. If you have a soft bed, put a stiff board under the mattress.

BACKACHE

These exercises can be performed whenever you have a few minutes to spare. The muscular stretches (below left) are designed to relieve stiffness in the neck and middle back. Joint stretching (centre and bottom right) increases the suppleness and general mobility of joints in the lower back.

Neck and middle back stretches
1 Sitting upright, with head down, place fingers on tips of shoulders, elbows in front. Hold for 2-3 seconds.

The pelvic tilt To stretch the muscles of the lower back. Lie on a firm mattress or the floor with knees up and feet flat. Gently tightening stomach muscles and lifting pelvis, try to flatten lower back against floor. Hold for 2-3 seconds; relax for 1-2 seconds; repeat.

2 Slowly rotate elbows upwards and outwards, raising head to look straight ahead. Hold for 2-3 seconds.

Joint stretching
1 Starting from pelvic tilt position, slowly raise knees towards chest, as far as is comfortable, to count of four.

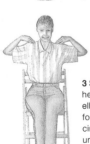

3 Slowly lowering head, bring elbows down and forward again in circular motion until back in original position. Hold and repeat.

2 Without straining, clasp hands around knees. Pull knees gently towards your chest. Relax tension, and repeat three more times. Let feet drop slowly back to ground to count of four. Repeat for 2-3 minutes.

Back-combing

Adding fullness to your hair-do

Back-combing makes a hairstyle look more substantial, and gives fine, limp hair greater body. Take a 25 × 75mm (1 × 3in) section of hair, comb it out, and hold it away from the scalp at 90 degrees. Using a fine-toothed comb, gently comb the section from the ends towards the roots.

A slight tangle will form at the base and the hair will stand away from the head. The more times you back-comb, the more fullness your hair will have.

You can tease your hair all over for a very shaped style, or do just one area that needs lift. When you have finished back-combing, brush or comb the surface of the hair lightly to smooth it.

Before washing it, gently comb out any knots. To avoid pulling out tangled hair, start combing near the ends, then from higher up until all the knots have gone.

WARNING Avoid back-combing too often; it can split and damage your hair.

Backgammon

Basic moves in a subtle board game

Backgammon is played on a board by two players, one using 15 white counters and the other 15 black or red ones. The board is divided into two identical sides, one for each player, consisting of 12 elongated triangles, called *points*, divided by a centre strip   the *bar*.

The two sets of six points divided by the bar are called the *inner table* and *outer table*. The points of the inner table are numbered 1-6, and those of the outer table 7-12, but the numbers are not marked on the board and must be memorised.

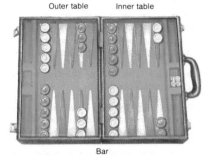

Outer table   Inner table

Bar

Setting the board Put two of your counters on your opponent's one-point, five on his 12-point, three on your own eight-point and five on your six-point. Your opponent does the same.

Your counters must move from your opponent's inner table, through his outer table, through your own outer table to your inner table, and then off the board. The first player to get all his counters off the board wins.

The first move is decided by the throw of a dice, the highest throw winning first move. Then two dice are thrown to determine the count for the opening move, and subsequently for alternate moves, each player using his own pair of dice. Two counters can be moved at a time, in which case one counter moves the number of points on one dice, and the second counter moves the number of points on the other dice. Or you can move one counter the total number of points on both dice.

A counter may be moved forwards onto a point not occupied by two or more of your opponent's counters; if it is occupied, the move is blocked and you must then try to move another counter or counters – but you must move the full number of points thrown by the dice. If you cannot, you forfeit your turn.

A single counter on a point is known as a *blot*, and if you land on your opponent's blot, called a *hit*, his counter is taken off the board and *barred* – placed on the bar. Your opponent must then return that counter into play before moving any other counters. To do this he must obtain a throw from the dice, one or both, that corresponds with a point from one to six on your inner table, and that point must not be blocked – occupied by your counters. If, however, he moves onto a blot, then your blot is placed on the bar.

Removing the counters from the board

is called *bearing off*, and you cannot start to bear off until all 15 of your counters are in your inner table. You may then bear off counters from points corresponding to the number thrown on the dice, or you can move counters within the table.

You must, if possible, use the full number. For example, if you have a counter on the six-point and you throw six, you can bear off the counter, but if the six-point is not occupied you must take a counter from the next highest point. You cannot, however, bear off a counter if a point indicated by the dice is vacant and there are counters on a higher point.

If, while bearing off, one of your counters is hit, and therefore barred, you must re-enter it as described. You cannot continue to bear off until your barred counter is back in your inner table.

Playing for stakes Backgammon is also a gambling game, played for a stake. A losing player who has managed to bear off at least one counter forfeits the stake, but if he has not managed to bear off any of his counters, he forfeits double the original stake – this is called a *gammon*. If the loser also has one or more counters still on the winner's inner table, he forfeits treble the stake – a *backgammon*.

Once the basics are assimilated, backgammon can become an absorbing and complex game. Those whose appetite is whetted can obtain further information from: The British Isles Backgammon Association, 2 Redbourne Drive, Lincoln LN2 2HG.

Backpacking

The last word in independent holidays

Backpacking is a handy term for a whole range of WALKING activities, from gentle weekend rambles with overnight stays at inns and YOUTH HOSTELLING to away-from-it-all cross-country hikes on which the walker carries everything needed for subsistence.

The pack With modern lightweight equipment and clothing there is no reason to carry a pack weighing more than 11kg (25lb). The items suggested would allow a solo walker to enjoy a 14 day holiday, provided he replenished his water daily and topped up his food supply along the way. There are few places, at least in Europe, where this is not possible.

Strapped outside the pack, for easy access in bad weather, go your water-proof and tent, together with the sleeping mat, which is waterproof. The mat can be rolled around food bought day by day, such as bread, cheese and fruit.

Since no rucksack is completely water-proof, anything you need to keep dry

should go inside a plastic bag or bags. This includes sleeping bags, spare clothing and food.

If two or more people walk together, the individual load is reduced by 1.5-2kg (about 3-4lb) – by sharing the tent, food and cooking equipment. Using inns or hostels, you can leave out most of the food, carry less water, and have no need for tent, sleeping bag, sleeping mat and cooking equipment, reducing the weight to no more than 4.5kg (10lb).

Another 0.5kg (1lb) or so of essential equipment goes in your pockets or about your person – knife, whistle, compass and maps.

For a warm-weather start, you should set off in a lightweight long-sleeved shirt, lightweight trousers and wearing or carrying a lightweight jacket. Lightweight clothing has two advantages: not only is it cooler and lighter to carry, but it dries quickly if you get wet or need to wash it. Long sleeves offer protection against SUNBURN and INSECT BITES AND STINGS, and can be rolled up to keep you cool, and down for warmth under a jacket.

By using the principle of layering, the clothing you are wearing, plus the spares in the pack, should keep you dry and warm or cool, as appropriate. To stay cool, stick with a light shirt and lightweight trousers or shorts. By adding successive layers – jacket, plus jumper plus thermal underwear – you can build up to a level which will allow you to keep warm on cold days.

Lightweight, waterproof boots with leather uppers and a rubber or composition sole, ridged for good grip, are the best general purpose footwear for backpacking – suitable for every sort of terrain, except snow and ice. Wear them with two pairs of socks – a thin inner pair and a thick outer pair. Try not to start a long trip with new boots; buy them well in advance and break them in on a few day trips first.

Boots, and all other equipment, should be bought from a specialist camping shop, most of which are run and staffed by enthusiasts, who are well worth consulting about every purchase. In particular, get their help in choosing boots and a rucksack, and in trying them on. Just as you need boots that fit your feet, so you need a pack that fits your back comfortably.

Equipped like this you should be able in summer to walk anywhere in Britain and on the Continent – except high mountains – see CLIMBING SAFELY. The same outfit would also serve for spring and autumn in lowland areas.

Planning the trip All backpacking needs some advance planning and the first thing to tackle is the route. For that, you will need maps – see MAP READING. In Britain, the Ordnance Survey 1:50,000

(1¼in to the mile) Landranger series and 1:25,000 (2½in to the mile) Pathfinder series are the most useful. Most countries produce equivalents to the OS maps, and many can be bought in this country from specialist map shops.

Footpath guides are also helpful. You may be able to borrow them from a library, or buy them from the regional tourist information office in the area to which you are going. If you are taking a tent (see TENTS) the Camping and Caravanning Club publishes a directory of members' sites – see CAMPING. If not, a list of hostels is available from the Youth Hostels Association, and there are many commercial guides published that give lists of farmhouse bed-and-breakfast accommodation.

In working out your itinerary, do not aim to walk more than 12-16km (7½-10 miles) a day at first, unless you are experienced and fit, and only then if you are using roads and footpaths through relatively flat and easy terrain. Two miles an hour is a good pace to begin with. This allows time to stop and look at things along the way and a ten-minute breather every hour. These breaks, plus an hour or two for lunch, should ensure that you get to your overnight destination while there is still daylight left – important if you are pitching a tent, or if the place where you are staying has rules about late arrivals.

With practice, you may be able to extend your daily walking range. But 24km (15 miles) a day is about the upper limit for all except the most dedicated. Steep hills, long grass and scrub, sodden ground, sand and scree (loose rock debris) will all reduce your rate of progress considerably, and so will wet, windy or very hot weather. Build a reasonable margin into your timetable to allow for them.

Do's and don'ts for backpacking

Do learn to read a COMPASS.

Do check your position regularly against the map to avoid getting lost.

Do tell someone where you are going, especially in wild country, and report to them when you arrive.

Don't press on if caught by fog or mist – wait for it to clear.

Don't walk alone, especially in wild country: two is a minimum party, three is better – in case of accident, one can stay with the casualty while the other goes for help.

Equipment in pack	
	Approx weight
Rucksack	0.70kg (1½lb)
Tent	1.60kg (3½lb)
Sleeping bag	1.10kg (2½lb)
Sleeping mat	0.23kg (½lb)
Waterproof	0.34kg (¾lb)

	Approx weight
Spare clothes	
Light shoes	
2 pairs thin socks	
Pair trousers/shorts	
Long-sleeved, lightweight shirt	
Pullover	
1 set of thermal underwear	
Woolly hat	
Gloves or mittens	
Needle and thread	
Total	1.60kg (3½lb)
Toiletries (including towel)	0.34kg (¾lb)
Clothespegs (4)	0.11kg (¼lb)
Torch	0.11kg (¼lb)
First aid kit	
Antiseptic cream	
50mm (2in) sticking plaster	
50mm (2in) crepe bandage	
Lint	
Moleskin (for blisters)	
Triangular bandage	
Aspirin/paracetamol	
Sterilising agent for water	
Total	0.23kg (½lb)
Food	
Muesli	0.45kg (1lb)
Dried milk	0.11kg (¼lb)
Pasta	0.45kg (1lb)
Salami	0.23kg (½lb)
Soup cubes	0.11kg (¼lb)
Tea/coffee	0.11kg (¼lb)
Herbs/onion	0.11kg (¼lb)
Dried fruit	0.45kg (1lb)
Water (1 litre plastic bottle)	1.00kg (2¼lb)
Total	3.00kg (6¾lb)
Knife, fork, spoon, tea towel	0.23kg (½lb)
Plate, mug	0.11kg (¼lb)
Cooker (gas), matches	0.45kg (1lb)
Pan	0.23kg (½lb)
Overall total	10.40kg (23lb)

Bad breath

Avoiding embarrassment; long-term remedies

The most common cause of bad breath – known medically as halitosis – is not taking proper care of TEETH and gums. Using breath fresheners or chewing mints may reassure an embarrassed sufferer, but these are camouflage agents, not cures.

Antiseptic mouth washes will kill some of the bacteria that can cause bad breath, but a more effective method is to clean the teeth and gums frequently – at least three times a day, preferably after meals. Use dental floss or dental sticks to get between the teeth, and brush the tongue with a soft toothbrush.

However, there are other causes of halitosis, including chest troubles such as chronic bronchitis, and infections of the throat and nose which generate mucus at the back of the throat. In such cases the problem should vanish as the ailment is treated. The widespread theory that constipation causes bad breath is unfounded.

As a general rule, those prone to bad breath should avoid tobacco (see SMOKING), onions, alcoholic DRINKS, GARLIC and spicy foods.

Badminton

Playing a strenuous racket game

Badminton is a form of ball-and-racket game in which the 'ball' is a feathered cork called a shuttlecock. Fast and furious when played well, the game was played by army officers in India in the 1860s, and takes its name from the Duke of Beaufort's Cotswold mansion, Badminton, where it was first played in England in the 1870s.

Stamina and swift reflexes are assets in deploying the wide variety of strokes used, from the full-blooded overhead smash into the far corner of the opponent's court to the delicate drop shot, barely clearing the high net.

The court may be indoors or out – usually indoors, so that wind or draughts do not affect the light shuttlecock. The court measures 13.4 × 6.1m (44 × 20ft) and has a level floor, usually of wood or composition material. It is marked out with 38mm (1½in) white lines whose width counts as part of the court.

A 762mm (2ft 6in) deep net is stretched tightly across the centre at a height of 1.55m (5ft 1in) at the posts, 1.52m (5ft) in the middle. The tightly strung racket weighs only 90-150g (3¼-5½oz) and the shuttlecock – the 'shuttle' or 'bird' – is made of leather-covered cork and goose feathers, or of synthetic materials.

Two players are matched in singles games, two pairs in doubles. They toss for service and choice of ends, the server starting from his right-hand service court then alternating between left and right. In singles, the server always starts in his right-hand court when his score is an even number; from the left court when his score is an odd number.

The server must keep both feet still and touching the ground inside his service court, and serve underhand, hitting beneath the shuttle. The serve is diagonal, and the bird must cross over the net, beyond the receiver's short service line, but inside his back and side lines.

The serve is good even if the bird clips the top of the net on its way; but if it is faulty, service passes to the opponent. If the service is good, the shuttle must be hit back over the net into the server's court before it touches ground. A rally continues until a player fails to hit the shuttle, hits the shuttle out of court or into the net, or commits a fault by:

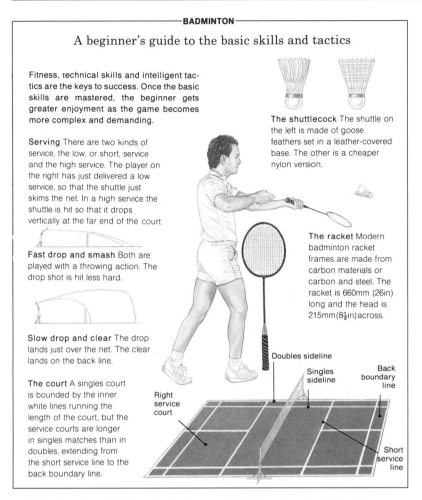

─ BADMINTON ─

A beginner's guide to the basic skills and tactics

Fitness, technical skills and intelligent tactics are the keys to success. Once the basic skills are mastered, the beginner gets greater enjoyment as the game becomes more complex and demanding.

Serving There are two kinds of service, the low, or short, service and the high service. The player on the right has just delivered a low service, so that the shuttle just skims the net. In a high service the shuttle is hit so that it drops vertically at the far end of the court.

Fast drop and smash Both are played with a throwing action. The drop shot is hit less hard.

Slow drop and clear The drop lands just over the net. The clear lands on the back line.

The court A singles court is bounded by the inner white lines running the length of the court, but the service courts are longer in singles matches than in doubles, extending from the short service line to the back boundary line.

The shuttlecock The shuttle on the left is made of goose feathers set in a leather-covered base. The other is a cheaper nylon version.

The racket Modern badminton racket frames are made from carbon materials or carbon and steel. The racket is 660mm (26in) long and the head is 215mm (8½in) across.

Doubles sideline

Singles sideline

Back boundary line

Right service court

Short service line

- Hitting the shuttle before it crosses the net.
- Hitting it twice during a stroke.
- Contacting the shuttle other than with the racket.
- Touching the net during a rally.
- Obstructing an opponent.

If the server loses, service passes to his opponent; if the receiver loses, the server gets a point and serves again. Only the server can gain points; if the receiver wins a rally he gains the service. A game runs to 15 points or, in women's singles, 11. A match is decided over three games.

In doubles, the full width of court is used. One partner of the serving pair serves first, service passing to their opponents when the ·first rally is lost. But thereafter each pair gets two serves: when a serving pair lose a rally, service passes from one partner to another; only when their second rally is lost do their opponents gain the service.

The principal strokes are the overhead and underarm clear (the lob), the smash, the drop and the drive – all played either forehand or backhand. When smashing, connect with the shuttle as high as possible, hitting it so that it flies downwards over the net. Drives, which skim the net, are despatched either straight or across court. A drop shot can travel slowly to land near the net, or quickly to skim the net and land near the service line.

Bail

Applying for release; providing securities

Bail means a security, usually a sum of money, exchanged for the release of someone arrested, as a guarantee that he will appear for the trial. A person arrested and charged with an offence may be granted bail by police or magistrates, allowing him freedom, usually on condition that he reports to a court or police station at a specified time or times until the case is heard.

Police cannot, however, grant bail to someone arrested on a warrant issued by a magistrate, unless it specifically allows them to do so. Bail is unlikely to be granted for someone charged with a serious offence, or who has broken bail conditions previously.

Any decision to grant bail at a police station must come from the senior officer there. If bail is refused, the accused person can ask for it when he first appears before magistrates (usually within 48 hours of arrest) if his case is not to be heard immediately.

If the offence is not punishable by jail, magistrates should grant bail – unless the accused has broken bail before and is thought likely to do so again, or is considered liable to commit another offence or interfere with witnesses. They may also grant bail but impose further conditions, such as surrender of passport, and a deposit of cash and other assets as security.

If magistrates refuse bail A person who is refused bail can be held for eight days in a remand centre or prison before reappearing in court. During that time he can ask to consult a solicitor about reapplying for bail – he cannot reapply himself. If he decides to do so, the solicitor can tell him whether LEGAL AID is available to pay the costs.

Alternatively, if his solicitor thinks he has a good case, he can advise him to appeal to a High Court judge against the magistrates' decision without waiting eight days. In this case the solicitor makes the appeal to whichever judge is on duty, in his private rooms ('in chambers'). Often the judge will hand down his decision the same day. No legal aid is available for such an appeal, but the accused can ask the Official Solicitor, who is a High Court official, to present his case instead. This procedure can take a long time.

Should the appeal succeed, the accused must meet all bail conditions or face up to three months' imprisonment and a fine in a magistrate's court, or 12 months' imprisonment and an unlimited fine in a Crown Court.

Providing securities Before magistrates will allow bail, they often ask the accused person to provide one or more people to guarantee securities other than those represented by his own assets. These are provided by sureties – people who will undertake to pay a certain sum if he absconds, and have the resources to do so – see SURETY.

Anyone intending to ask for bail should try to have one or more sureties present in court – police can advise magistrates as to their suitability. If the sureties are acceptable, magistrates may be prepared to grant the accused bail there and then.

Bail for young people A child under 14 must be granted bail unless suspected of murder or manslaughter. So must a young person aged 14-17, unless police or magistrates think it in his interest to remain in custody or a serious crime is involved.

Bail if convicted Someone convicted by magistrates can seek bail if sentence is delayed – say for a medical report or committal to a Crown Court. He can also apply if appealing against his sentence.

Ball cocks

Stopping an overflow from a lavatory cistern or cold water storage tank

A ball cock is a simple device for cutting off the supply when the water in a tank or cistern reaches a level just below the overflow pipe. The ball, or float, is hollow and may be made of copper, brass or plastic. It floats on top of the water. An arm attached to the ball is connected at its other end to a valve which operates on the water supply pipe.

As the tank fills and the ball rises, it operates the valve to cut off the supply. If a tank or cistern persistently overflows, either the ball is damaged and is not rising sufficiently to close the valve, or it is closing too late and the float needs adjustment. Alternatively, the valve itself may be faulty – either jammed with dirt or corrosion or in need of a washer.

Checking the ball You can alter the level of the ball by a screw adjuster or by slightly bending a metal arm. Grip the arm firmly with one hand close to the valve, and bend it downwards.

If the ball is submerged in the water for more than one-third of its diameter it is probably leaking. Unscrew the ball from the arm, shake it and listen for water inside. If it is faulty replace it with a new one, obtainable from a hardware shop or plumbers' supplier. Make sure that the arm is adjusted so that the water level remains below the overflow pipe.

Checking the valve The type of valve most commonly used in cisterns and tanks is known as a Portsmouth pattern valve. It consists of a piston fitted with a rubber washer which is pushed against the valve seat by the ball-cock arm. New washers are available from hardware stores. To replace a washer, first turn off the water supply – usually there is a tap or stopcock on the main supply pipe in the kitchen sink area.

The arm is attached to the valve by a split pin. Withdraw the pin with pliers and pull out the piston or lever it out with a small screwdriver. Clean the outside of a brass piston with wire wool. Unscrew the two parts of the piston and replace the worn valve washer in the cap with a new one. Turn on the water briefly to flush out the casing. Reassemble the piston and lightly grease it with petroleum jelly before reinserting it in the valve body.

Ball repairing

Mending a leaking vinyl ball

A puncture in a child's inflatable vinyl ball can be repaired with a heated screwdriver. To find the leak, inflate the ball with a bicycle pump and place it in a bowl of water, moving the ball around until air bubbles indicate the source. Dry the ball, marking the leak with chalk.

Heat the screwdriver over a gas ring or with a blowtorch, then rub the hot blade gently over the puncture to melt the edges, which will close together, forming a new seal as the vinyl cools.

Allow five minutes for the vinyl to harden, then reinflate the ball.

Ballroom dancing

Some basic steps to get you on the floor

Mastering the many steps and figures of ballroom dancing can prove both pleasurable and socially advantageous. Here are the basic steps of two popular dances – the waltz and the quickstep.

The waltz The waltz is danced to music played in 3/4 time, or three beats to the bar, with emphasis on the first beat. See the illustration opposite for the footwork of the waltz *step* and *turn*.

The man leads the *step*, moving forward with his right foot on the first beat (1), then taking one step forward and to the side with his left foot (2) on the second beat. On the third (3) beat he brings his right foot to the side of his left foot. The woman follows his steps, moving backwards. At the end of the first and second steps, both rise onto the balls of the feet, and up on the toes on the third step. The movements to the next bar are similar, but the man leads with the left foot.

For the man to *turn*, move the right foot forward and commence turning to the right (1). Move the left foot well forward and to the side, still turning (2), then close the right foot to the left foot (3). You should now have your back facing in the direction of the line of dance. To complete the turn, move the left foot back, continuing to turn right (4). Move the right foot to the side (5) and close the left foot to the right foot (6). The woman follows these movements backwards, left foot first.

The quickstep This is a brisk dance in 4/4 time – four beats to the bar. The man leads, taking a gliding step forward with the right foot skimming lightly over the floor, then follows with his left foot. This is known as the 'walk forward' and is followed by the 'chassé' – three steps with the feet closed on the second step. This can be danced side-close-side or forward-close-forward or back-close-back. It starts by a forward step on the man's right foot followed by the chassé taken side-close-side. The woman starts with her left foot, moving backwards.

This rhythmic little movement is the basis of the quickstep, which is danced slow, quick-quick, slow; slow, quick-quick, slow: a 'quick' equals one beat

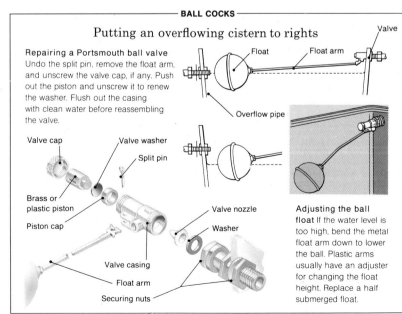

BALL COCKS

Putting an overflowing cistern to rights

Repairing a Portsmouth ball valve
Undo the split pin, remove the float arm, and unscrew the valve cap, if any. Push out the piston and unscrew it to renew the washer. Flush out the casing with clean water before reassembling the valve.

Valve cap

Valve washer

Split pin

Brass or plastic piston

Piston cap

Valve nozzle

Washer

Valve casing

Float arm

Securing nuts

Valve

Float

Float arm

Overflow pipe

Adjusting the ball float If the water level is too high, bend the metal float arm down to lower the ball. Plastic arms usually have an adjuster for changing the float height. Replace a half submerged float.

Learning the steps and turns for the waltz

The waltz is danced anti-clockwise, so you need to turn left at corners. But to do so you actually make a looping right turn through 180 degrees to follow the dance line.

- Right foot
- Left foot
- Right foot turning
- Left foot turning

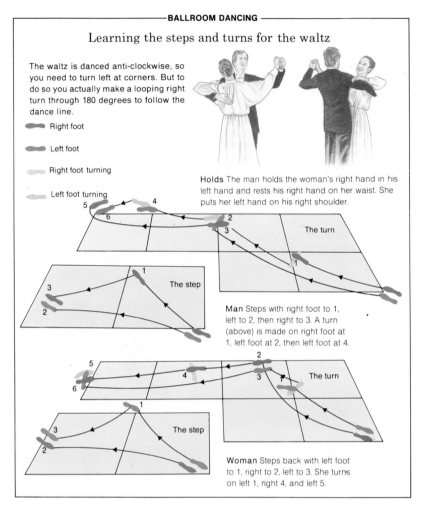

Holds The man holds the woman's right hand in his left hand and rests his right hand on her waist. She puts her left hand on his right shoulder.

The turn

The step

Man Steps with right foot to 1, left to 2, then right to 3. A turn (above) is made on right foot at 1, left foot at 2, then left foot at 4.

The turn

The step

Woman Steps back with left foot to 1, right to 2, left to 3. She turns on left 1, right 4, and left 5.

and 'slow' two, so the movement is completed in eight beats.

For the man to turn at corners, move the right foot forward, turning to the right. Move the left foot forward and to the side, pivoting on the ball of the foot, and close the right foot to the left foot, as in the chassé. Move the left foot back, still turning to the right. Bring the right foot back to the left foot, still turning, then move the left foot forward to continue the dance. The timing for this turning movement is slow-quick-quick, slow-slow-slow.

Balusters

How to tighten, repair or replace loose or damaged stair rails

Balusters, the vertical rails between stair treads and the handrail, are fixed in several ways. They may be butt-jointed and nailed at an angle (skew nailing) at both ends, butt-jointed at the top and fitted into a socket at the bottom, or socketed at both ends – see NAILING; WOOD-WORKING JOINTS. Some modern balusters are fitted into a groove at top and bottom and separated by fillets of wood.

Before attempting to fix a loose baluster or replace a broken one, find out how it is fixed.

Tightening a loose baluster To tighten a baluster butt-jointed at both ends, remove it by tapping it out with a mallet, driving it backwards at the top end and forwards at the bottom. Clean both faces of the join, apply PVA glue and renail the baluster in position.

Balusters socketed at one or both ends can be tightened by driving thin wedges, coated in PVA glue, into the gaps at the baluster ends. Trim off the ends of the wedges and make good the repair with wood filler and paint. On fillet-and-groove types, cut a new fillet to replace a lost one. Nail a top fillet in place.

Repairing a damaged baluster If a baluster is split along the grain, or has a clean break and is not badly splintered, glue the parts together with PVA and bind the joint with waxed string. Allow 24 hours for the glue to set before removing the binding.

Replacing a broken baluster Remove a baluster butt-jointed at both ends as described for tightening a baluster. Trim the new baluster – available from DIY shops – to length, either using the old one as a pattern or measuring between the handrail and stair tread. Glue and nail the baluster in position.

A baluster socketed at the bottom end can be withdrawn after the butt-jointed top has been tapped free. On some staircases the outer tread ends have mouldings which, when removed, allow the baluster to be pulled out of its socket sideways. Cut the new baluster to length, glue it into its socket using PVA glue; glue and nail the top butt joint.

To remove a baluster socketed top and bottom, cut it through flush with the underside of the handrail and withdraw it from the bottom socket. Clean out both sockets with a small chisel. Cut the new baluster to length, allowing about 10mm ($\frac{3}{8}$in) space above the baluster when fitted into the handrail socket. Glue both ends, push the baluster into the handrail as far as it will go, then drop it into

Simple repairs to stair rails

Nailing a butt joint On a slim baluster, drill a pilot hole for the nail to avoid splitting the wood. Tap the nail in on the skew (at an angle).

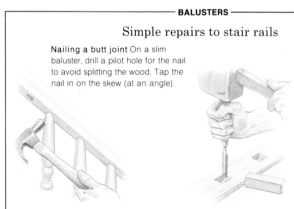

Fitting a new rail into sockets Cut the new baluster to length, making it 10mm ($\frac{3}{8}$in) short of full measure to give lifting space in the top socket. Chisel sockets clean (left). Glue the baluster at both ends and insert it top end first.

the bottom socket. The fillets used to separate balusters can be levered from grooves with an old chisel, if you need to remove a damaged baluster and fit a new one. No glue is needed. Cut new fillets if necessary when refitting.

Bandaging

Some ways of binding wounds and injuries

A well-stocked FIRST AID KIT should contain bandages suitable for all types of wounds and injuries.

Bandaging a minor cut A cut that is not bleeding profusely can be covered with a plaster. Clean and dry the cut and select a plaster with a gauze pad large enough to cover the wound. Replace it with a fresh one as necessary.

Bandaging a deep cut If a deep cut is bleeding heavily, apply a prepared sterile dressing – an absorbent pad with a bandage attached. Otherwise improvise a pad using perhaps a clean handkerchief, and tie it firmly in place with a bandage.

Try to use bandage of a width appropriate to the position of the wound: 25mm (1in) for fingers or toes; 50mm (2in) for hands; 75mm (3in) for arms or legs and 150mm (6in) for the trunk.

Start bandaging two or three turns below the wound, keeping even pressure, and finish two or three turns above it. Secure the bandage with a safety pin. If you do not have a safety pin, leave about 230mm (9in) of bandage free and cut it in half lengthways. Tie the two cut ends together at the base with a single knot, take the ends around the dressing above the wound and tie securely.

If there is a foreign body in the cut, do not remove it, as it may be plugging the wound. Cover the wound with a clean piece of cloth, then make a built-up dressing consisting of two or more small curved pads. To make a pad, put cotton wool or other material in a clean piece of cloth, and roll it. The pads should be made big enough to surround the foreign body and keep pressure off it. Hold the pads in place with diagonal strips of bandage, being careful not to bandage over the foreign body.

If possible, send someone to phone for an ambulance while you treat a severe wound or, when you have dressed the wound, take the patient to the nearest hospital casualty department.

Making an emergency bandage Use a square of clean cloth folded diagonally. Fold it as illustrated; fold it again for a narrow bandage.

Applying a tubular bandage Cut a piece of tubular bandage two-and-a-half times the length of the injured finger. Put the applicator tongs over the finger and slide on the bandage. Slip the applicator off the finger together with one end of the bandage, and turn the tongs so that the bandage is slightly twisted. Push the tongs back onto the finger and slide the bandage off them so that the finger is covered with two layers.

Bandaging a sprain Support the joint with a crepe bandage, which is applied in a figure of eight around both sides of the joint. If the pain is severe, however, seek medical attention.

Bank accounts

Opening an account, writing cheques and using bank services

A bank account keeps your money safe and enables you to pay bills by cheque or by direct debit and standing order – see also BUILDING SOCIETIES. Banks also offer interest on money not in current use, loans, financial advice and other services such as MORTGAGES.

How to open a bank account First choose your bank. Most offer similar services and make similar charges for services, so your choice may be governed largely by convenience – perhaps one with a branch close to your home or workplace. Several also offer home banking facilities through your computer or a television data service.

There are two types of bank account – current and deposit. To open an account, ask to see the branch manager and seek his advice about which type you need. Inform him also if your salary is to be paid directly into the bank.

Current account This is for everyday use. You can pay in or draw out cash at will, and write cheques which can be drawn against your account.

You can also have a cheque card, which guarantees that the bank will honour a cheque up to a fixed value even if your account is overdrawn.

Regular bills such as mortgage repayments and insurance premiums can be paid by standing orders – the bank pays from your account the amount specified on set dates, and will do so until you cancel the arrangement.

BANDAGING

Making and applying bandages for cuts and sprains

In first aid, bandages are used to keep a dressing in place; prevent germs entering a wound; maintain pressure on a wound to control bleeding; and to support an injured limb. Bandages can be improvised for certain types of cut or injury, out of sheets, pillowcases, stockings, scarves, or any other suitable material. If no bandage is available, a dressing can be secured with strips of adhesive plaster.

Avoid bandaging too tightly. After applying a bandage to an arm or leg, and again after ten minutes, check fingers and toes for cold, tingling, lack of feeling, or blue nails, and an injured arm for a weak pulse. If any of these danger signs occur, remove the bandage and re-apply it more loosely.

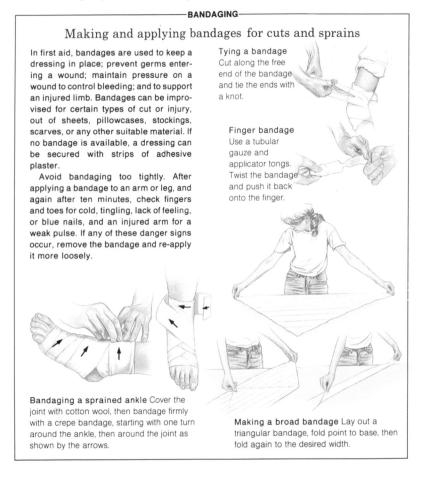

Tying a bandage Cut along the free end of the bandage and tie the ends with a knot.

Finger bandage Use a tubular gauze and applicator tongs. Twist the bandage and push it back onto the finger.

Bandaging a sprained ankle Cover the joint with cotton wool, then bandage firmly with a crepe bandage, starting with one turn around the ankle, then around the joint as shown by the arrows.

Making a broad bandage Lay out a triangular bandage, fold point to base, then fold again to the desired width.

You can also settle regular bills of varying amounts – such as electricity and gas – in a similar way, by what is called budget payment – see BUDGETING.

Another useful service offered by several banks is a 24 hour automatic 'cash till'. By using a special cash card you can draw money from a machine inside or outside the bank at any time.

Deposit account If you have surplus funds in your current account you can transfer them to a deposit account, on which interest will be paid. The amount of interest, as a percentage, is displayed in all branch offices.

Other sums for which you have no immediate use, or may wish to save (see SAVING) can also go in a deposit account. However, it is worth comparing rates of interest offered by building societies, NATIONAL SAVINGS and other savings/investment schemes – see INVESTING.

Writing a cheque A cheque written on anything is perfectly legal so long as it is legible, but it is much safer to use a cheque book provided by your bank. There are two types of cheque – 'crossed' and 'open'. A crossed cheque has two parallel lines and the words 'A/c Payee' or '& Co' across the face, denoting that it should be paid into the recipient's account. Such a cheque cannot be exchanged for cash and so is safer if it gets into the wrong hands. Write the name of the recipient clearly on the cheque, adding 'only' after it.

Cheques must be written correctly, or there could be problems for both writer and recipient. The date should be the current date; this is not essential, but a cheque cannot be cashed before the date marked on it. You can post-date a cheque to delay payment, but this is done only if the recipient – payee – agrees.

The amount must be written in words, except for the odd pence – for example: Seventy five pounds 60p. Draw lines across the remaining spaces so that the cheque cannot be altered, or write 'Only' after the amount. Write the figures in the box provided, leaving no space at the start and finish, so that extra figures cannot be added. Sign with your usual signature, and if you need to alter a cheque after writing it, initial the correction, too.

Keeping a check on your money Always fill in the cheque stub or the table near the end of the cheque book with the date, the amount drawn and the name of the payee. Some cheque books are now made without stubs, but the bank will usually supply a stubbed one if you ask.

Your bank will also send quarterly statements detailing all deposits and withdrawals, but you may be able to get statements more frequently if you wish –

for example, monthly – on request.

You can also ask for a statement, showing the balance in your account at the end of the previous day's trading, at any time during banking hours. Your current balance will also be displayed at certain automatic cash tills if you insert your card and press the correct buttons. On some it can also be displayed while cash is being dispensed.

Bankruptcy

What to do if you cannot pay debts, or if someone owes you money

If you know that you cannot pay your debts – even by selling all your assets – you can petition the court to declare you bankrupt. Apply on Form 6.27 obtainable from your County Court offices or, in London, the High Court (both listed in the phone book). Court officials will help you to fill in the form if you wish. When you return the form to the court, you must also send a statement of your financial affairs on Form 6.28.

An alternative is to apply to the court for an interim order, naming an insolvency practitioner who will help you draw up a proposal offering part or full payment of debts over a period of time. If creditors holding 75 per cent of the debt value agree, the proposal becomes binding. It avoids the expenses and restrictions of bankruptcy.

Creditor applying for bankruptcy If a debtor owes you, or you and others together, more than £750, you can petition the court to declare the debtor bankrupt. You must first serve a signed and dated statutory demand for repayment on the debtor. If the debtor has not paid three weeks after the date on the demand, you can present a petition to the court.

The mere fact of your petition may make the debtor pay. If not, you may expect eventually to receive payment, or part payment, from the sale of the debtor's assets.

The hearing of the petition The hearing is held at the County Court or the High Court in London. Debtor and creditor may be represented by their lawyers.

The court will reject a creditor's petition unless at least £750 is still owing. Instead of granting a bankruptcy order, the court may refer the matter to an insolvency practitioner to try to agree an arrangement for payment and avoid bankruptcy – provided that the debts exceed £2000 but not £20,000 and that the debtor has not been bankrupt in the previous five years. Even if the court makes a bankruptcy order, it may opt for a summary administration, which speeds up dealing with the matter.

If a bankruptcy order is made, bankruptcy starts at the date of the order.

Consequences of being declared bankrupt If you are declared bankrupt, control of most of your assets passes to the official receiver (a public official) or an insolvency practitioner appointed as trustee by the creditors. Further legal proceedings cannot be taken against your estate without the court's permission.

The trustee will give notice to all creditors if any payments are to be made and inform them of the date by which they must make claims. The costs of hearing and administering the bankruptcy are paid first. Then amounts owed in tax, VAT, National Insurance contributions and to former employees have preference. Personal creditors come last.

The bankrupt can keep necessary clothing, bedding, domestic appliances, tools and vehicles for business use – but the trustee may sell them and replace them with cheaper substitutes, retaining the balance for the estate.

Transactions made before the bankruptcy order may be set aside if they were designed to cheat creditors. The normal cut-off period for transactions is six months before the petition is filed, but it can be extended to five years.

The bankrupt's family may be entitled to live in the family home, especially in the first year. After that, all assets must be sold, including the home, except in exceptional circumstances.

The creditor's trustee can apply to the court for an income payments order under which a portion of the bankrupt's future income will be diverted to the estate – but the bankrupt must be left with sufficient income to meet his personal and family needs.

The bankrupt must meet the official receiver and trustee to give details of his property and affairs, and provide a statement of assets and debts within 21 days of the bankruptcy order. Concealment of property or relevant information is punishable by prison and/or a fine.

A bankrupt wishing to obtain credit in excess of £250 must disclose that he or she is an undischarged bankrupt; it is a criminal offence not to. A bankrupt needs the court's permission to act as a company director, and leave from the official receiver to have a bank account.

Discharge from bankruptcy In normal cases, the bankrupt is automatically discharged three years after the date of the bankruptcy order and is informed by the official receiver's department. A bankrupt who has been declared bankrupt within the previous 15 years must wait for five years and then apply to the court for discharge.

With some exceptions, discharge releases a bankrupt from all debts owed when the bankruptcy order was made.

Cooking light meals on a patio

Barbecuing is an ideal way of preparing a meal of meat cubes and vegetables spitted on long skewers. Sausages, pork cutlets, steaks and hamburgers will cook equally well. Turn meats once only during grilling.

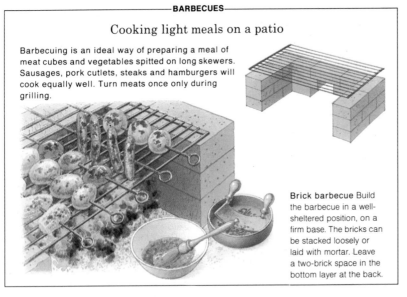

Brick barbecue Build the barbecue in a well-sheltered position, on a firm base. The bricks can be stacked loosely or laid with mortar. Leave a two-brick space in the bottom layer at the back.

Barbecues

Making a success of your barbecue parties

Before planning a barbecue party, master the art of lighting and controlling the fire and learn the approximate times for cooking various foods.

Prepare the food in advance, especially meats and poultry, which should be, if possible, marinated before grilling – see MARINATING.

Lighting the fire Charcoal is the best and most popular fuel for barbecues, available in lumps or briquettes. It can be lit by piling a small heap on top of crumpled paper and dry kindling in the centre of the barbecue. Or lay charcoal about 25mm (1in) deep on a bed of crumpled paper, pour over it an eggcup of methylated spirit and set alight. Non-toxic barbecue lighters are also available – liquid for squirting on, solid for inserting in the charcoal: follow maker's instructions. Never use petrol or lighter fuel – they are dangerous, smelly and taint the food.

After about 20 minutes, when the charcoal is burning properly, rake the pile into an even layer over the basket, cover with more charcoal and let it burn for a further 20-35 minutes. It should then look ash-grey in daylight or glowing red in the dark, and is ready for cooking. Keep a poker and fire tongs handy to move hot embers as necessary, and a bottle of water to sprinkle over flare-ups.

Barbecue cooking Meat properly grilled on a barbecue should be cooked uniformly without charring on the outside – unless you like it charred! Control the heat by raising or lowering the grille, or by dispersing embers with a poker or fire tongs. On some barbecues you can control it by adjusting air vents.

Cuts of lean meat, HAMBURGERS, sausages and pork cutlets grill well on a barbecue. Brush meat with cooking oil and turn only once during grilling. Allow 10-12 minutes each side for well-done steaks and hamburgers, halve that time if you like them rare. Sausages take about 5 minutes each side, lamb chops 5-10 minutes, pork chops 15-20 minutes (pork should always be well done).

KEBABS make tasty eating – any combination of small cubes of meat and vegetables threaded onto long skewers. Prepare them beforehand and allow two per person. Grill kebabs for 15-20 minutes, turning them once only.

Jacket potatoes can also be cooked on a barbecue. Scrub large potatoes clean, prick them, rub them with salt and wrap in foil. Cook at the edge of the grille for 50 minutes, or for 20 minutes among the charcoal.

Barbecue sauce Give your barbecue meal added zing with an appetising sauce. For a simple but effective one take 150ml ($\frac{1}{4}$ pint) of beef stock (or water at a pinch) and mix in 3 tablespoons of tomato ketchup and 2 each of Worcestershire sauce and wine vinegar. Add 2 tablespoons of brown sugar and a teaspoon each of celery salt and chili powder. Blend thoroughly, add tabasco sauce for extra bite according to taste, and spoon it over the food on your plate.

Building a homemade barbecue This is easily done using bricks and an oven grille. Pile the bricks to make a low, three-sided enclosure leaving a couple out of the bottom layer to provide a draught for the fire, and lay an oven grille on top of the bricks. Build the barbecue on a firm base, such as a patio, in a sheltered position. The bricks need not be bonded with MORTAR (unless you want the barbecue to be a permanent fixture) and can be dismantled after use.

Barometers

Your guide to the weather and how to read it

A barometer registers atmospheric pressure – the pressure exerted by the air above it. In general, a fall in atmospheric pressure heralds bad weather and a rise is associated with fine weather. So as pressure changes it is possible to predict weather several hours ahead. There are two types of barometer – mercury and aneroid.

The mercury barometer This works on the principle that a column of mercury in a tube will rise and fall with changes in atmospheric pressure. One end of the tube stands in an open dish of mercury, the other end is closed and contains a vacuum. When pressure at the open end rises it pushes the column up the tube; when pressure falls the weight of mercury causes the column to fall.

These changes in height are calibrated to show the changes of atmospheric pressure, the international units of which are the millibar and millimetres or inches of mercury. Normal pressure at sea level is 1013 millibars, equal to 760mm or 30in of mercury. A reading of 790mm (31in) indicates dry weather; one of 740mm (29in) forecasts rain.

The household mercury barometer often has a banjo-shaped case with a dial

The mercury and aneroid types

The instrument on the right is a mercury barometer; the one below is an aneroid. A moving pointer records pressure changes against a fixed one which can be preset.

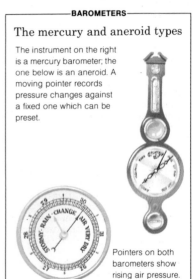

Pointers on both barometers show rising air pressure.

and pointer. In addition to its calibrated scale, the dial is also marked 'Stormy, Rain, Change, Fair, Very Dry'.

The aneroid barometer In this instrument, a pointer is attached to vacuum-filled metal bellows. The bellows expand or contract under atmospheric pressure, causing the pointer to move around a calibrated scale similar to that on a mercury barometer.

Changes in pressure can be noted on both types of barometer by setting a pointer on the barometer glass in line with the pressure-indicating pointer. As the pressure changes the indicating pointer will move to the left or right of the set pointer. See also WEATHER FORECASTING.

Basket repairs

Renewing a handle and mending the weave

A cane basket should be washed and scrubbed regularly in warm water. This will keep the cane supple and less likely to break. If any part of the basket does break off, it can be repaired with new cane obtained from a large store or handicraft shop.

Replacing a broken handle A basket handle consists of a bow of stout cane, bound with a cane strip.

Strip off the old binding and pull out the bow. Soak the new bow in warm water for at least an hour, then sharpen one end with a craft knife or trimming knife. Push the sharpened end into the basket to a depth of 50mm (2in).

Bend the bow to the correct height and shape and trim the other end to a point, allowing 50mm to push into the weave. Push the free end into the basket.

Working from the outside of the basket, insert the binding into the weave to the left of the bow. Push the other end in below the third row of cane, to the right of the bow. Take the binding over the top of the basket and across, inserting it below the third row of cane.

Pull the binding tight and wind it around the bow with its edges touching but not overlapping. To finish off, cross the binding to the left and right of the bow, weave the free end into the basket and trim it.

Repairing a hole in the weave Cut back all the damaged cane to the nearest staves, with the undamaged ends resting on the centres of the staves.

Soak the new cane for an hour or so, then insert one end between the strands and the stave at one side of the hole, leaving a 50mm (2in) tail.

Weave the cane across the hole, gently bend the cane around the last stave and weave in the other direction. Continue

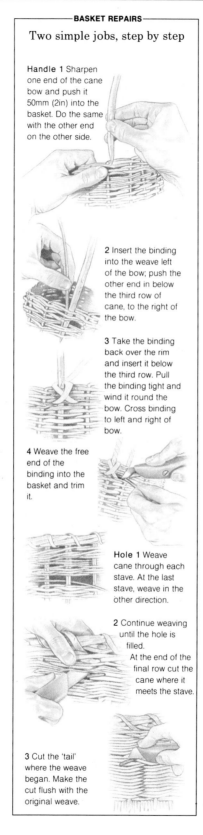

── BASKET REPAIRS ──

Two simple jobs, step by step

Handle 1 Sharpen one end of the cane bow and push it 50mm (2in) into the basket. Do the same with the other end on the other side.

2 Insert the binding into the weave left of the bow; push the other end in below the third row of cane, to the right of the bow.

3 Take the binding back over the rim and insert it below the third row. Pull the binding tight and wind it round the bow. Cross binding to left and right of bow.

4 Weave the free end of the binding into the basket and trim it.

Hole 1 Weave cane through each stave. At the last stave, weave in the other direction.

2 Continue weaving until the hole is filled.
At the end of the final row cut the cane where it meets the stave.

3 Cut the 'tail' where the weave began. Make the cut flush with the original weave.

weaving until the hole is filled, with each row alternate, passing on opposite sides of each stave. At the end of the last row, cut the cane where it meets the stave. Cut off the tail where the weave was started.

Bathroom safety

Neutralising danger spots; some do's and don'ts

The bathroom is full of hazards for the unwary, especially for children and the elderly or infirm – and the bath is one of the more serious potential danger spots.

Getting out of a bath is more difficult than getting into it. A rubber mat which grips the bottom of the bath with suction cups will prevent you slipping; a grab handle on the wall will help to steady you. When refurbishing a bathroom, consider buying a bath which has built-in handles and a non-slip area.

When bathing children, always run the cold water into the bath before the hot, in case a child falls in accidentally. An automatic thermostatic control can be fitted to a shower unit, so that it sprays water at a constant temperature, to guard against accidental SCALDS.

Do's and don'ts of bathroom safety

Do fit pull-cord ceiling switches to lights and wall-mounted heaters – wall switches are now illegal because of the danger from damp getting into them.

Do mop up water spilt on the floor – someone may slip on it. See that your bath mat has a non-slip backing.

Do store medicines and cleaning fluids in a locked cabinet well out of a child's reach.

Don't use electrical appliances in the bathroom – they can become 'live' if water vapour builds up inside the casing. An electric razor is the only exception, as long as it has a special socket which has an isolating transformer.

Don't fit a bolt or lock inside a bathroom door. If you have an accident, nobody will be able to get in to help – safety is more important than privacy.

Don't mix bleach with other cleaners. The mixture can give off a poisonous gas.

Don't leave young children alone in the bath – even an empty bath.

Bathtub sealing

Filling the gaps between the bath and the wall

Small gaps that appear around a bath or washbasin can be sealed with a silicone-rubber sealant – see SEALANTS. First clean out the gap thoroughly with a small, stiff brush, such as a dry scrubbing brush. Wash the surfaces with hot water and detergent to remove any traces of soap or grease.

Cut the spout of the sealant tube at an angle of 45 degrees and far enough back to ensure that a ribbon of sealant wide enough to fill the crack emerges. Squeeze the tube with an even pressure as you work along the gap. Run a wet finger along the sealant to get a smooth, even finish. Remove smudges with a wet cloth; or leave until the sealant has set, then remove surplus with a trimming knife.

Sealing large gaps Cover large gaps between a bath and tiled surround with quadrant tiles – see CERAMIC TILES. Apply waterproof tile adhesive to the two flat surfaces on the backs of the tiles; for corners use mitred tiles, applying adhesive to the mitred faces as well as the backs. Lay the tiles so that a cut tile will be in the centre of a row. Fit a round-end tile at each outer corner of the bath, in line with the edge.

Alternatively, use a flexible plastic strip, with silicone rubber sealant as the adhesive. Remove surplus adhesive while still wet. Set adhesive can be cut away with a razor blade. Use a silicone remover to get rid of any left.

Bathtub stains

Removing 'rust' marks and hardened deposits

Rust stains in an enamelled bath are caused by dripping TAPS, so first cure the cause – fit new tap washers.

Light rust stains can often be removed by rubbing them with half a lemon. For heavier stains use a 5 per cent solution of oxalic acid or a 10 per cent solution of hydrochloric acid, obtainable from a chemist. Wearing rubber gloves, apply the acid with a soft cloth and rinse the bath thoroughly afterwards.

Green copper stains can be removed with ammonia or oxalic acid.

For deposits caused by hard water, use a proprietary cleaner, following the manufacturer's instructions.

Batik

Making fabric designs using wax and dye

For more than 1400 years, the peoples of South-east Asia have been creating attractive, and sometimes flamboyant, designs on fabric by using batik – a technique in which those parts of the fabric to be left unchanged are covered in wax before the whole piece of material is dipped in dye. When the wax is removed, the areas beneath it reappear in their original colour.

Plain, light-coloured cotton is the best

BATIK

Tools and materials – and how to use them

Draw the design on the material using a soft pencil, after the material is stretched and tacked. Use the brush to cover large areas with wax and the tjanting pen for fine line-work.

Gently heat the wax to 77°C (170°F) so that it spreads easily. Check by using a thermometer.

Tjanting
Pencil
Hog's hair or sable brush
Thermometer

Stretch and tack the fabric to a frame. Put in tack 1, then stretch the fabric at the opposite side and press in tack 2; carry on as shown.

When the fabric is tacked tightly, draw the design using the soft pencil.

First colour

Brush the wax on areas you do not want dyed. Untack the fabric and soak it in the dye for 20 minutes. Rinse in cold water and let dry.

Second colour

For a second colour, re-tack and apply wax to areas not to be dyed. Untack and soak in the next dye. Rinse and dry.

fabric for batik work. Synthetic fabrics do not dye particularly well, and the colour may run straight through very thin silk. Thick wool is also unsuitable, as dyes can scarcely penetrate it.

If the fabric is new, wash it in hot, soapy water and rinse it to remove any dressing – an additive often used to stiffen the material; you may need to repeat the process. Once the fabric feels soft and free of dressing, dry it and iron it smooth. Then tack it, stretching it tight, to a wooden frame, and draw your design on it in soft pencil.

Preparing the wax The wax should be warm enough to spread evenly, but not so hot that it runs straight through the fabric. To make it, add 5 tablespoons of beeswax to 450g (1lb) of paraffin wax in a bowl, and gently heat the mixture in its bowl in a saucepan to around 77°C (170°F). Keep it at that temperature until you are ready to apply it. Special thermostatically controlled wax pans are available from craft shops if desired.

For colouring, use only cold-water

dyes that will not soften the wax further when they come into contact. If more than one colour is wanted, start with the lightest. Mix the dye according to the maker's instructions.

Apply the warmed wax with a small hog's hair or sable brush to those areas of the fabric that you do not dyed at this stage. Very fine lines can be drawn with a tjanting – a special pen which is filled by dipping it in the wax. Then untack the fabric from its frame and soak it in the dye for 20 minutes. Rinse it thoroughly in cold water and let it dry.

Removing the wax If you want to re-use the wax you have applied, boil the dyed fabric in water and let it cool. The wax will set on the surface of the water, and can be removed, to be melted again as necessary. However, boiling may cause some dyes to fade or run, and is not recommended unless wax is scarce.

To reduce this risk, you can remove the wax by ironing, although it cannot then be used again. Cover the ironing board with newspaper, with a layer of paper towelling on top of it. Lay the fabric on the paper towelling, then cover it with another layer of paper towelling on top. With a dry iron at one setting below *cotton*, press the fabric on both sides, changing the towelling as the wax accumulates on it – see IRONING.

Second colours If you are using more than one colour, tack the dyed fabric back on the frame, apply the wax to the areas you do not want to take up the next dye, untack the fabric and steep it in the new dye solution, as before. Rinse and dry before removing all the wax.

Finished batik fabrics should be dry-cleaned to remove any wax residue, unless you are using the material for curtains, in which case the residue helps to provide body. Frequent washing will cause the batik to fade.

Bats

Dealing with a protected animal

Because bats have become an endangered species, if a colony enters your home, your right to take action against them is very restricted. But first consider whether any action is needed – bats are quite harmless creatures.

Bats are not disease carriers, nor is their presence harmful to a building. Their droppings are dry and powdery, composed mainly of insect fragments. They are not a danger to health and will not damage timber or paintwork. Bats eat insects, including wood-boring pests, but they will not gnaw at your roof timbers. They do not build nests but simply cling or hang. It is extremely unlikely that a bat will become entangled in your hair, they have good eyesight and a unique 'radar' system.

Bats and the law All bats in Britain are protected by law. It is an offence to kill or injure a bat, or interfere with its roosting place or obstruct entrance to it. But you may destroy a badly injured bat that has no hope of recovery, or tend a disabled one until it can fly.

Occasionally a bat may enter a room through an open window near its roost entrance. If it is flying inside a room, open the windows and doors to allow it to escape. Pick up a crawling bat carefully, wearing gloves in case of bites. Take it outside and release it.

If you are squeamish about handling a bat, place a cloth over it and gather it up loosely with the bat inside.

During the breeding season, in late June, July and August, young bats may crawl through gaps around pipes or through floorboards. Take them outside at dusk and hang them on the wall near the roost entrance. They will be collected later by the mother.

If you need to disturb bats in your loft, or want to get rid of them, you must inform English Nature at Northminster House, Northminster, Peterborough, Cambs PE1 1UA. They will advise on how to comply with the law.

Battens

Using timber strips when lining walls

Battens are strips of TIMBER which have many uses, from making frameworks to providing fixings for roof tiles, PLASTERBOARD, decorative laminates and other wall coverings – see also PLASTIC WALL CLADDING; ROOF REPAIRS; WALL CLADDING. Frequently used sizes are 38×16mm ($1\frac{1}{2} \times \frac{5}{8}$in) and 50×25mm (2×1in).

For wall coverings, fix battens with hammer-in fixings, countersunk 50mm No 8 screws driven into wall plugs, or 50mm masonry nails.

The shape of the frame depends on the type of cladding to be used. For plasterboard, always use 50×25mm battens. Fix a single batten horizontally to the wall 25mm up from the floor and another 25mm from the ceiling. Check both battens with a spirit level to see that they are level, then hold a long batten vertically against the two battens and with a spirit level check at intervals to see that they are aligned. If they are not, pack them out with thin wedges of wood.

Now fix vertical battens, measuring and marking the fixing spots so that the battens will be spaced to half the width of the plasterboard, and the boards will butt at the centre of a batten. Check each batten with a spirit level and align with packing pieces where necessary.

It is more economical to use 1200mm (3ft 11in) wide plasterboard: if you use 900mm (2ft 1in) plasterboard, more battens are needed. For 13mm thick plasterboard 1200mm wide, fix battens at 600mm centres. Nail the plasterboard to the battens with 38mm ($1\frac{1}{2}$in) plasterboard nails.

Decorative laminate needs a sturdy framework of both vertical and horizontal battens. Fix horizontal battens flush with the floor and ceiling, and vertical battens at each end of the wall. Check and adjust the alignment as necessary. Space vertical battens at half board-width centres with equally spaced horizontal battens between them. Attach the laminate sheets to the frame with panel pins or adhesive.

BATTENS

Using them to support plasterboard and decorative laminates

The battens are fixed to form a rigid frame attached to the wall. For plasterboard, position the battens vertically apart at board width and half board width. For heavy laminates fix vertical and horizontal battens to support each board.

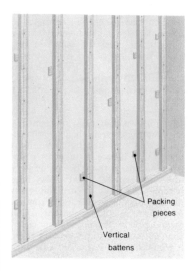

Use a spirit level to check that batten surfaces are level; align them with thin wedges of wood where necessary. Nail the plasterboard to the frame with plasterboard nails.

Packing pieces

Vertical battens

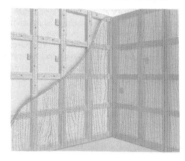

Laminates Fix both horizontal battens and vertical battens to support boards at centres and edges.

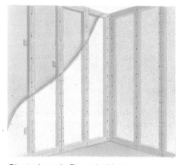

Plasterboards Fix vertical battens to support each board at its centre and butted edges.

Charging a car battery and maintaining its fluid level

A battery charger with an ammeter will show the rate of charge – the charge rate will fall as the charge level rises – and a hydrometer will check the final state of the charge.

Cell cover Sometimes there is a single cover on a filling trough. Put distilled water into the trough, and plastic level finders will feed the correct amount to each cell.

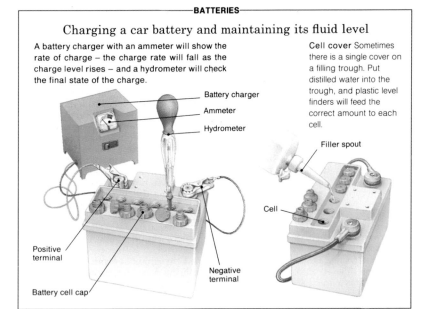

Battery charger

Ammeter

Hydrometer

Filler spout

Cell

Positive terminal

Negative terminal

Battery cell cap

Batteries

Maintaining and charging your car battery

To get the best from your car battery, check the fluid level and battery connections regularly – at least once a month. If the fluid level drops too low or the connections become loose or corroded the battery will not charge fully, and eventually will not hold enough power to turn the starter.

Checking the fluid level Battery fluid – or electrolyte – is a mixture of sulphuric acid and purified water, and its correct level is just above the battery plates, visible through the filler holes in the top. Some batteries are sealed for life and never need topping up, but in many the level drops over a period of time as water in the fluid evaporates.

To check and top up the battery, remove the caps or cover from the filler holes above each cell and fill to the correct level by adding distilled water – available from chemists. Some batteries have a see-through casing with a fluid-level mark on the outside. Do not allow electrolyte to splash on you or the car bodywork – it is corrosive. If it does, wash or hose immediately, using plenty of water. Before refitting the battery caps or cover check that the ventilation holes in them are clear. If they are blocked, clear them with a piece of thin wire.

In hot weather inspect your battery more frequently as the rate of evaporation may increase. If the level in one cell drops more than that in the others, it is possibly defective and the whole battery may have to be replaced – the cells are interconnected and a dud one means that the battery will not charge. If more than usual topping up suddenly becomes necessary, the battery may be overcharging. Have the charging circuit tested by an auto-electrician.

Checking the connections There are several types of battery connector, and the same rules apply to all – the mating surfaces of both connector and battery terminal must be free from dirt and corrosion, and in tight contact.

Use vinegar to remove the powdery deposit that forms on terminals, then clean the terminal with emery cloth or a wire brush until the metal is bright. Clean the faces of the connectors with emery cloth or a small, fine file. Smear the terminals with petroleum jelly (do not use grease) and refit the connectors tightly.

Charging a battery Frequent short trips at night or in bad weather may cause your car's headlights, windscreen wipers and heater to take more power from the battery than the engine's generator can replace. Again, the battery becomes too weak to turn the starter – an early sign of weakening becomes evident when the starter can only spin the engine slowly. If checks show that the connections are sound, remove the battery and have it recharged at a garage, or recharge it yourself.

A wide range of chargers is available from car accessory shops. Buy one that has high and low charging rates and an ammeter to show the rate of charge while it is operating. Before starting, remove the battery cell caps or cover so that gas generated in the electrolyte during charging can escape; do not charge in a confined or unventilated space – the gas can be ignited by a spark.

Most batteries have a capacity of 48amp hours – meaning they can deliver 48amps for an hour, 4amps for 12 hours and so on. Therefore a 2amp charge rate takes 24 hours to recharge a totally flat battery. In an emergency a high 10amp for 30-60 minutes is enough for the battery to start the car. However, frequent high-rate charges can damage the battery – better to charge at a lower rate for several hours, perhaps overnight.

Following the manufacturer's instructions, set the charger to high or low rate, as required. Disconnect the wires at the battery and, if possible, remove the battery from the car. Connect the crocodile clip on the charger's black lead to the negative (−) battery terminal, and the red lead to the positive (+) terminal. Plug the charger into a 13amp socket and switch on. Some chargers switch off automatically when the battery is fully charged – an advantage. Otherwise judge by the hours elapsed and by checking the electrolyte with a battery hydrometer. Either way, always unplug the charger before removing the clips and reconnecting the battery wires.

Checking with a hydrometer A hydrometer is a glass tube with a rubber bulb at one end, a rubber tube at the other and a float inside – cheap to buy from car accessory shops. It checks the battery's state of charge by measuring the specific gravity of the electrolyte. Squeeze the bulb and dip the tube into one battery cell. Release the bulb to draw up enough fluid to raise the float. Read off the graduation mark on the float stem against the fluid level in the tube. If it reads 1.27 or higher the battery is fully charged; below 1.13 the battery is flat.

Squeeze the bulb again to return the electrolyte to its cell, and test the other cells in turn. They should read within about 0.04 of each other; any large variation means a dud cell.

When refitting the battery in the car, always connect the supply terminal first. Most modern cars have a negative earth system, so the positive terminal is first; some older models have a positive earth system, where the negative terminal is connected first.

Battleships

A game for kids of all ages

Battleships is played on two identical boards marked out in squares. The squares are divided into 100 smaller squares, 10 across and 10 down, and numbered 1-10 one way and A-J the other.

Each player then deploys his fleet by

BATTLESHIPS

Winning a war at sea – without getting seasick

In the example shown here, one player has deployed a fleet of one battleship, one cruiser, two destroyers and two submarines. The crosses mark the shots fired.

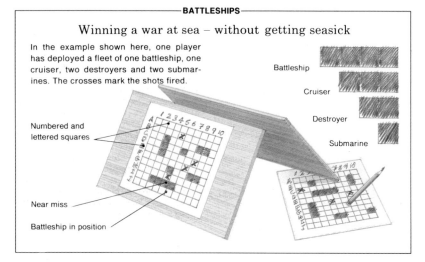

Numbered and lettered squares

Near miss

Battleship in position

Battleship

Cruiser

Destroyer

Submarine

filling in some of the squares – a battleship occupies 4 squares horizontally, vertically or diagonally; a cruiser occupies 3 squares and a destroyer 2 squares. You could also have an aircraft carrier (5 squares) and submarines with 1 square each. Both players must have identical fleets, which they deploy without letting their opponent know where they are.

The game begins when one player fires his first shot, by calling out the letter and number of a square. His opponent must then say if the shot has scored a direct hit, and on what type of vessel. All other shots are 'misses', though in some versions of the game a shot in a square immediately next to a ship is called a 'near miss', giving the firer clues as to the enemy's dispositions.

Each player takes it in turn to fire, with an extra go if he scores a hit, and marks his own board in the appropriate square so that he knows where his shots have fallen. A ship is sunk when all the squares it occupies have been hit, and the game ends when one player's entire fleet has been sunk.

In another version of Battleships, called Salvo, each vessel is allocated a number of guns – battleships and cruisers have two each and destroyers one. Players fire salvos from all their guns, instead of single shots. For example, if a player has a battleship, one cruiser and two destroyers he calls out 6 squares.

Beadwork

*Stringing beads and stitching
beads to fabric*

You can string beads using an ordinary sewing or darning needle, the size of the bead hole determining the size of needle and of the thread. Nylon pearl threading twist, obtainable from craft shops and haberdashery departments, is best for beads with a hole of 1.6mm ($^1/_{16}$in) or smaller. For larger beads any strong thread will do, such as polyester button thread or sewing thread – but any thread you use must be fine enough to pass through each bead twice.

Threading a necklace First decide how long you want the finished necklace to be, and allow two and a half times the length of the doubled thread for knotting between the beads. Arrange the beads in sequence on a piece of corrugated cardboard.

Begin threading by making an over-hand knot (see KNOTS) or fitting a clasp at the end of the thread. Feed the thread through the first bead and make another overhand knot. To pull the knot tight against the bead, insert a needle into the loop and pull the thread so that the knot tightens around the needle. Remove the needle. Hold the knot with a small pair of pliers or tweezers and pull the thread to tighten the knot against the bead. Continue threading, knotting between each bead.

There are several types of clasp you can use. One of the simplest and most secure is the screw clasp. Before threading the beads, make a thick knot in the end of the thread and pass the needle through one half of the clasp. Thread the beads and then feed the thread into the other half of the clasp and finish off with another thick knot.

Sewing beads to fabric Sew beads to clothing with dressmaker's cotton or polyester-covered cotton thread. On heavy fabrics use nylon thread.

Keep the material taut by stretching it on a frame or embroidery hoop. Anchor the thread with a knot or two tiny stitches sewn one over the other on the reverse side of the material, draw the needle through to the face side and thread on a bead. Make a backstitch, taking the needle through the fabric a bead-length behind and then ahead of the first stitch. Continue adding beads, keeping each tight against the next.

BEADWORK

Easy ways of threading, fastening and sewing beads

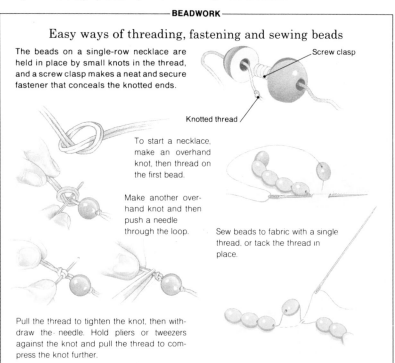

The beads on a single-row necklace are held in place by small knots in the thread, and a screw clasp makes a neat and secure fastener that conceals the knotted ends.

Screw clasp

Knotted thread

To start a necklace, make an overhand knot, then thread on the first bead.

Make another overhand knot and then push a needle through the loop.

Sew beads to fabric with a single thread, or tack the thread in place.

Pull the thread to tighten the knot, then withdraw the needle. Hold pliers or tweezers against the knot and pull the thread to compress the knot further.

Beards and moustaches

Giving a man a new image

Fashions in beards and moustaches come and go, and often seem curious or comical when their day has passed. One of the latest and oddest is 'designer stubble' – a permanent four-day growth – as worn by George Michael and other celebrities of pop music.

A full, neatly trimmed beard and moustache can disguise a narrow face and a pointed or weak chin, or it can offset a receding hairline. A full moustache without beard directs attention away from a large nose, broad face, protruding chin, or low hairline.

The early stages of growing either a beard or a moustache make you look unkempt – and feel uncomfortable. Persevere, however, washing your face frequently with soap and water to reduce itchiness; make sure you rinse the soap away thoroughly. If itching persists, try an anti-dandruff shampoo, but take care not to get any in your eyes.

In about three weeks there should be enough growth to begin clipping and shaping. Many men assume that beard care is less exacting and time consuming than shaving. In fact, whiskers, once grown, demand special care because they trap food, dirt and bacteria. They need a twice-weekly shampoo, and perhaps a conditioner to make the hair soft.

Trim a beard and moustache yourself at least once a week, and have them trimmed and shaped whenever you have a haircut. Trim when they are dry – wet whiskers lie differently, and snipping a damp beard can ruin the shape.

Designer stubble – despite its casual, even neglected, look – is even more demanding, if it is not to become a real beard or regress to a mere two-day shadow. Maintaining the authentic length can be done by shaving the opposite way to normal, holding the razor lightly. It may take a little while to get the hang of it, but if the first attempts result in a patchwork appearance, just shave off the lot and start again.

For foolproof, even stubble, you can buy an electric razor which has several interchangeable shaving heads for cutting stubble to different lengths that equal from two up to five days' growth.

Beauty creams

Making your own skin care preparations

You can easily make your own skin creams and lotions for FACIAL CARE and MANICURES. You only need water and a few inexpensive ingredients that are readily available from most chemists and health shops. These ingredients include:

glycerine, an oily liquid with good skin softening properties; beeswax, a mixer and emulsifier; cocoa butter, which combines with water to hold moisture near the skin; liquid paraffin, a lubricator and softener; and petroleum jelly, a softener. You can use ordinary tap water, but scented waters, such as rose or geranium water, give a light, pleasant fragrance to the creams.

Skin-softening cream Gently heat 1 cup of white petroleum jelly and 2½ teaspoons of cocoa butter in a heatproof mixing bowl on top of a pan of simmering water. Small globules of cocoa butter will form on top of the melted jelly. In a separate pan, warm 2 cups of water and 1 teaspoon of glycerine. Stir this mixture into the petroleum jelly and cocoa butter mixture. Let the cream cool until it starts to solidify, then add a few drops of perfume or essence that does not have an oil base. When it is completely cool, drain away the excess water. You will have about 1⅓ cups of skin-softening cream which you can keep in a screw-top jar.

Light moisturiser All skins need moisturisers of some kind in small amounts to counteract the drying effect of wind and sun. Dry skins need more moisturiser than oily skins. Moisturisers work by preserving moisture already in the skin. Mix equal parts of glycerine and rose water, or any herbal water.

Cleansing cream Use a kitchen knife or grater to shave half a cup of slivers from a beeswax block into a heatproof mixing bowl; you can buy beeswax from health stores or hardware shops. Add 2 cups of liquid paraffin and sit the bowl on top of a pan of simmering water until the beeswax melts. Let it cool to 49°C (120°F). In a separate pan, heat 1 cup of water to 49°C (120°F). Slowly pour the water into the oil and wax mixture, stirring as you pour. Cool the mixture – you will have about 3 cups – until it starts to solidify, then pour it into storage jars.

Bedding plants

Garden colour from spring to autumn

Bedding plants may be annuals (alyssum, lobelia, nemesia) or biennials (wallflowers, sweet williams); short-lived or tender perennials (DAHLIAS, BEGONIAS); or even shrubs (FUCHSIAS) – but they are alike in their use. They are put in garden beds only for their peak flowering time. They have been raised elsewhere in greenhouses, COLD FRAMES, or nursery beds, and after flowering they are lifted to make way for later-flowering plants. The annuals and biennials then go on the compost heap while the perennials or shrubs

may be overwintered in pots in GREENHOUSES or sheds until the time comes to plant them out again. By planting out a succession of bedding plants whose flowering times follow one another, you can keep the garden bright from spring until the autumn frosts.

You can raise your own bedding plants from seed. If you have space in the bed you can sow hardy summer-flowering annuals, including cornflowers, larkspur, poppies and some stocks, directly into their flowering positions from March until May. Less hardy flowers such as antirrhinums, lobelias and salvias may be sown in a greenhouse or cold frame in March and planted outdoors in most parts of Britain from late May. They flower from July to October.

For convenience, many people prefer to buy bedding plants ready-grown from nurseries. This may appear more expensive than raising from seed, but is not always so, when the cost of compost, and perhaps of heating a greenhouse, is taken into account. You can buy nursery-grown bedding plants in strips (usually between three and eight plants), or in boxes containing up to 48.

Continuous colour A succession of bedding plants – put in the bed for their flowering season and then replaced – gives a display of blooms from spring until autumn.

The monthly pageant Autumn-planted primroses and polyanthuses may flower in many parts of Britain during March. In April, they are joined by aubrieta, wallflowers, pansies and violas, with forget-me-nots beginning to display their distinctive blue. May and June bring love-in-a-mist, candytuft and honesty.

During May and June, spring-flowering bedding plants can be replaced or supplemented by those that flourish through high summer. Stocks, godetias, larkspur, cornflowers and alyssum bloom from June. Petunias, zinnias, dahlias, calendulas, mesembryanthemums and fuchsias will flower from July into a warm October. Some varieties of potted chrysanthemum can survive mild frosts that kill other bedding plants, and add a further touch of autumn colour.

Buying and planting When buying nursery-grown bedding plants, work out your exact needs beforehand, so that you do not over-buy. Look for plants that are stocky and bushy, rather than tall and leggy. Reject any with yellowing foliage.

Set the plants out as soon as possible; if you have to wait before planting, keep them well watered in a sheltered, well-lit spot outdoors. Plant them on a dull day or in the evening, so that they will not droop in the midday sun. Separate the plants by carefully pulling them apart with your fingers, and set them in the soil so that it is level with, or slightly higher than, the base of the main stem. Water them well immediately after planting, and in the evenings of dry days.

Bedwetting

Treat children with patience and care

Some children are four to six years old before their bladders are large enough to hold their water overnight, and they may wet the bed without even waking. The problem is not unusual after that age, and can persist long afterwards – one person in every 100 is still incontinent at the age of 18.

Even though the bladder is growing normally, the nervous system controlling it may be slow in developing. Or the child may be a very heavy sleeper, beyond awakening by nature's call.

A spell of bedwetting may be caused by a bad cough or by an irritation or infection in the urinary tract.

Anxiety can also be a major cause of bedwetting: a child may be worried subconsciously about such things as starting or changing school, moving house, parental rows or a new baby in the family. Parents may also induce anxiety by starting pot training too soon, or being too fussy and insistent about it.

Doctors advise against trying to train a child until he or she shows signs of being ready. Consult the family doctor if you suspect any form of anxiety as a cause of bedwetting, or if you suspect the cause may be medical – such as a urinary infection, or if the child dribbles urine by day or never has a dry night.

Treatment Unless the cause is an infection, the best treatment may be no treatment at all. Certainly refrain from scolding, punishing or shaming a bedwetting child – it will only make the problem worse. Instead, give praise when the bed is dry.

Until the trouble is overcome, fit the bed with a waterproof undersheet or mattress. Try to make sure that the child has nothing to drink a couple of hours before bedtime, and uses the lavatory just before getting into bed.

Essential parts of a multi-storey honey factory

The stacking-box hive lets beekeepers remove honeycombs with little disturbance to the bees – and add extra storeys.

Smoker and hive tool Smoke calms the bees while the tool is being used to remove frames when harvesting honey.

Roof This needs air holes and a waterproof covering. An inner cover allows the roof to be removed without exposing frames.

Supers Average of three needed to hold the bees and the honey.

Excluder Keeps the queen in the chamber below.

Brood chamber This is the young bees' nursery.

Floor Side rails support brood chamber to leave a gap for entry.

Beekeeping

The first steps in starting a rewarding hobby

Bees produce honey to store as food to see the colony through the winter. A beekeeper aims to coax his bees into producing more than they need, then takes the surplus for his own use. To this end he provides them with a good home, tends them carefully and ensures that they have enough food in winter. He may have to feed them as great a weight of sugar as the yield of honey from the hive, but comparing the prices of sugar and honey you may regard this as a very fair exchange. Taking an average over several years, an amateur beekeeper can expect to get 13.5kg (30lb) of honey a year from a single hive.

How to start beekeeping Join your local branch of the Beekeepers' Association. You can get the address from the British Beekeepers' Association, National Agricultural Centre, Stoneleigh, Warwickshire. Get to know other members who will let you help them. This way you will discover if you like bees. If you do not, the chances are that they will not like you, and you should perhaps find a different hobby. If the signs are that you and bees are mutually compatible, learn as much as you can about where to site hives, managing the colony, handling a swarm and collecting honey.

The necessary equipment – including the bees – can cost about £200. Though you may be able to save by getting good secondhand equipment from a local beekeeper.

Buying the bees Start with a nucleus – a small number of bees headed by a young queen – bought from a commercial producer, or perhaps your Beekeepers' Association. Buy early in the season – preferably May.

The hive A hive consists of a stack of wooden boxes, open at the top and bottom, standing on top of each other. The boxes contain frames in which the bees build their combs. Those in the upper boxes are used as honey stores; the lower ones form the brood chamber where the queen lays her eggs and young bees are reared. Start with a single hive, then the following year you may need a second, so that you can rehouse your bees if they establish a new colony. There are several designs of hive – the National is probably best for a beginner.

Protective clothing Most important is a bee-veil, made of net or plastic and attached to a broad-brimmed hat to keep it clear of the face and neck. The veil must reach your shoulders so that there is no gap for the bees to get in.

Protect your body with a zip-up jacket that has close-fitting cuffs; tuck your trousers into heavy socks.

Gloves will protect your hands, but they make it difficult to perform delicate tasks. It is better to work with bare hands: if you handle bees gently you are unlikely to get stung, or at least, not too often (see next page).

Bee smoker This is a container in which dry wood, rags or hessian can be burned, with a funnel and a bellows to pump out smoke. Use a large one that will smoke a long time. A tilted funnel works best.

Hive tool This steel instrument has a scraper at one end and a flat blade at the other. It is for prising apart the box sections that form the hive and for scraping beeswax from the frames.

Feeder To survive the winter, bees are fed with sugar syrup. There are several types of feeder, or you can make your own by perforating a lidded tin with small holes so the syrup can ooze out.

Dealing with stings Keep an antihistamine cream in the house because sooner or later you will get stung. Some people are extra allergic to bee stings, become dizzy and may even go into a coma. If you are one of those who react abnormally, get to a doctor or hospital for treatment as quickly as possible.

However, the usual reaction is pain at the area followed by a swelling, and most beekeepers soon become immune.

Remove the sting by pushing it out of the skin with a fingernail. Do not grasp the sting to pull it out, as this will pump more venom into the wound. The immediate pain can be eased by applying antihistamine cream, or a solution of 1 teaspoon of bicarbonate of soda in a tumbler of water. See also INSECT BITES AND STINGS.

Beer

Home brewing successfully – and your right to do it

The end product of home brewing is a refreshing drink that costs a fraction of the price of commercially produced beers. Kits are available from home brewing shops, supermarkets, department stores and chain store chemists, and the range covers many types of beer, from lager to stout.

There are two ingredients in a basic beer-making kit – hopped concentrated wort (malt and hops) and yeast. You will also need white sugar; in general the less sugar needed, the better the quality of the kit.

However, there is no sure guide to the quality of a home brew kit, other than personal recommendation or trial and error. The quality of the brew will also depend on using the right equipment, which should be kept scrupulously clean.

The equipment You will need: a food grade polythene fermenting bin to hold at least 23 litres (5 gallons); about 2m (6ft 6in) of 10mm diameter plastic tubing; about 40 one pint beer bottles; a corking machine and crown corks; a hydrometer and a thermometer; a long-handled plastic spoon, a 4.5 litre (8 pint) pan and a sterilising agent – made by dissolving four crushed Campden tablets and a teaspoon of citric acid in 570ml (1 pint) of cold water.

The brewing method Clean the plastic bin with sterilising fluid, rinse it with cold water, then stand it where you are going to ferment the beer. This should be somewhere with an even temperature of 18-24°C (64-75°F). If the temperature is too low, the yeast will stop fermenting; if it is too high, the yeast will mutate and produce odd flavours.

Instructions for mixing the ingredients vary according to which kit is used. Study the manufacturer's instructions carefully and have all the equipment you will need to hand before starting.

Fermentation will take about five to ten days, appearing first as a ring of bubbles, then a creamy, frothy head which will eventually collapse to form a mid-brown pancake across the surface of the beer. At this stage, skim off the froth and take a hydrometer reading. When the gravity is between 1000 and 1006, and remains so for 24 hours, it is time to siphon off the beer – see SIPHONING.

Use the plastic tubing to siphon off the brew, leaving as much heavy sediment as possible in the bin. Rinse the bin out immediately.

Sterilise the bottles and rinse in hot water. Siphon the beer into the bottles leaving a gap of at least 25mm (1in) at the top and add half a teaspoon of sugar to each bottle before corking. Keep the bottles in a warm place for four or five days for the sugar to ferment. Then move to a cool place for two weeks, after which the beer should be ready for drinking.

Once you have mastered the technique of brewing beer from a kit, you can, if you wish, move on to other brews such as lager and barley wine. Or you can try 'mashing' – making beer from ingredients bought loose from a home brewing shop. The shopkeeper can supply you with instructions, as well as ingredients.

Is it legal? There are no regulations covering the home brewing of beer or home WINE MAKING. You can make as much as you like – but you must not attempt to sell it. Selling it would make you liable for Customs duty. You would also have to apply for a licence under the Alcoholic Liquor Duties Act, which has strict regulations controlling such things as alcoholic strength and specific gravity.

Begonias

Growing and caring for a decorative plant indoors and out

Some begonias are valued mainly for their flowers, some for their decorative leaves and some for both leaves and flowers. Most are easy to grow, either indoors or outside in summer.

Begonias are divided into three groups: those with tubers, those with fibrous roots, and those with rhizomes – horizontal surface stems that send up leaves and flowers – see BULBS, CORMS AND TUBERS.

Growing begonias Nearly all begonias grow readily from stem cuttings (see PROPAGATING PLANTS); those with rhizomes grow from divisions of rhizomes. Some, such as rex begonias, prized for their many-coloured leaves, can be grown from leaf cuttings. *Begonia semperflorens* (one of the BEDDING PLANTS), which has white, pink or red flowers, can be started from seed.

BEER

Equipment for home brewing using a beginner's kit

All the ingredients for making 40 pints of beer are included in a beginner's kit, and it is possible to buy a kit that also includes the basic equipment. Buy beer bottles with the kit. Mineral water and soft drink bottles are not strong enough to withstand the fermentation pressures.

Fermenting bin

Beer bottles

Brewing kit

Plastic spoon

Siphon tube

Funnels

Winter-flowering begonia The hybrid 'Elatior begonia will brighten a windowsill in winter.

Start cuttings and tubers in early spring by planting in shallow trays of moistened peat moss, setting the tubers concave side upward, half in and half out of the peat moss. Stand each tray in bright, filtered light for about three or four weeks. When shoots have grown to around 25-50mm (1-2in), the plants can be transferred into 75-100mm (3-4in) individual pots.

Normal room temperatures are suitable for growing plants. Keep them in a strong light, but not direct sunlight except in winter. Provide humidity by placing the pot on gravel in a saucer or tray, with water not quite covering the gravel. Water moderately, and only when the top of the potting mixture is dry. Apply standard liquid fertiliser every two weeks.

The seeds of *Begonia semperflorens,* bushy plants with waxy leaves, should be sown in January or February, for bedding out in late spring. Their flowers will last from June to September. Scatter the seeds on top of fine-sifted potting soil and press them down gently. When the seedlings are large enough to handle, pot them individually in 75mm (3in) pots of JOHN INNES COMPOST No 1. *Begonia semperflorens* can also be sown in autumn for indoor blooms.

In the garden, lift tuberous begonias in November, store them in a dry place until the foliage has died, then clean and store them in a frost-proof place until spring.

Berries

Finding out which are safe to eat

Some of our most attractive-looking wild berries are poisonous – even deadly. Illustrated on the right are eight of the more tempting – and dangerous – of them, along with six of the best for eating or WINE MAKING.

Deadly nightshade, one to avoid completely, grows among ruins and in neglected gardens; its black berries are green

The delights and dangers of picking them

Wild berries abound in the countryside, in attractive clusters of red, black and purple – but few are safe to eat. Some can cause mild stomach upsets, but others can be fatal. Never pick berries for eating unless you are sure they are non-poisonous – if in doubt, leave them alone.

EDIBLE BERRIES

Blackberry The best known fruit of the hedgerows, but best picked before late September, when they become mushy and are attacked by the flesh-fly.

Sloes The fruit of the blackthorn ripens in September and although edible has an acid taste. It is used to make wine and to flavour gin.

Raspberry Though less common than the blackberry, the wild raspberry is of the same family. It is smaller than the cultivated raspberry.

Bilberry The blue-black berries, covered by a grape-like bloom, appear on the low, spreading shrubs in July.

Elderberry In autumn the bunches of small, black berries are easily recognisable. They are rich in vitamin C and are excellent for wine or jam making.

Strawberry Small and sweet, these berries grow wild on shady banks and in woods from June to October. They can be used for jam making, but are seldom found in large enough quantity.

POISONOUS BERRIES

Deadly nightshade The killer of the hedgerows. Every part of the plant is dangerous, and anyone suspected of eating a berry should be taken to hospital.

Bryony The poisonous berries grow in clusters, and change from green to yellow and then red in autumn.

Cuckoo pint The bright red berries cluster on a stalk in shady hedgerows and woods.

Spindle tree The pinkish-red fruits of this small tree can cause vomiting if eaten.

Guelder rose The leaves, bark and bright red berries of this shrub are all poisonous.

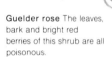

Holly The holly tree's berries provide winter food for birds, but contain seeds that are poisonous to humans.

Yew Though the scarlet berries are harmless, the seeds are poisonous.

Privet These purple-black berries appearing in autumn can easily be mistaken for elderberry in the wild, but are poisonous.

in early summer – and no less poisonous.

In country lanes and woods grow the wild *privet* and *guelder rose*, whose berries are also toxic.

The twiggy *spindle tree* appears in woods and hedges, and the *yew* in churchyards – the berries of both are poisonous.

Berry-pickers guide to the law On common land you can pick as many berries as you wish, but on a right of way across private land you must get the owner's permission.

Bicycle care

Lubricating your bike and adjusting the brakes and gears

To keep your bike in good condition and safe to ride (see BICYCLE RIDING), see that it is well-oiled and check brakes and gears regularly.

Inspect the bike while oiling it, so that you can make any necessary adjustments and renewals – to the brakes or chain, for example. Make sure all nuts, bolts and screws are secure and that no parts

are badly worn or damaged. Check the frame for RUST, and make sure the lights are working efficiently.

Fitting new brake blocks This is the same for both rod and cable brakes. Remove the brake-block shoe, hold it in a vice and prise out the old block with a screwdriver. Hold the shoe upright on the vice and tap in the new block until it butts against the closed end of the shoe. Refit the shoe, making sure that the closed end faces forward.

BICYCLE CARE

Keeping it running smoothly and stopping reliably

Lubricate all bearings and the chain every fortnight with proprietary cycle oil at the points shown. Some modern bikes have the hub, pedals and pedal crank bearings packed with grease during manufacture.

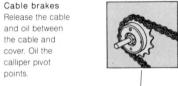

Cable brakes Release the cable and oil between the cable and cover. Oil the calliper pivot points.

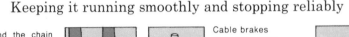

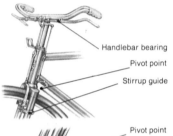

Head bearing Turn the bike upside down and run oil into the ball-races.

Front hub Turn the spring clip on the hub to expose the oiling hole. Inject with the hole facing upwards.

Chain Turn the chain slowly and trickle oil onto the links. Wipe off surplus oil.

Handlebar bearing

Pivot point

Stirrup guide

Pivot point

Stirrup guide

Rod brakes Oil the handlebar lever bearings and all the front and rear pivot points and stirrup guides.

Adjusting brakes The blocks on both cable and rod brakes should be set at about 3mm ($\frac{1}{8}$in) from the rim. If you cannot adjust enough to get this clearance, or if the blocks are more than half worn, fit new blocks.

Rear hub Inject a few drops of oil into the oil holes in the face plate of the gear wheel. Sealed hubs need no oil holes.

Pedals Inject oil through the holes in the end caps. Sealed pedals need no oiling.

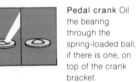

Pedal crank Oil the bearing through the spring-loaded ball, if there is one, on top of the crank bracket.

Front rod-brake adjustment Loosen the front clevis nut, hold the brake lever down and lift the stirrup to bring the blocks 3mm ($\frac{1}{8}$in) from the rim. Tighten the clevis nut.

Rear rod-brake adjustment Loosen the locknut on the rear stirrup adjuster. Move the stirrup until the brake blocks are 3mm from the rim. Tighten the locknut.

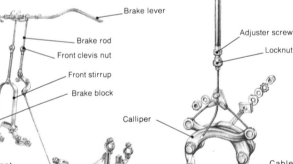

Brake lever

Brake rod

Front clevis nut

Front stirrup

Brake block

Calliper

Brake block

Stirrup adjuster

Adjuster screw

Locknut

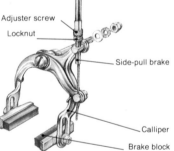

Adjuster screw

Locknut

Side-pull brake

Calliper

Brake block

Cable-brake adjustment Slacken the locknut and turn the adjuster screw anticlockwise to bring the blocks closer to the rim. Tighten the locknut.

Adjusting gears Gears help a cyclist to keep a steady pace without extra effort on varying gradients. Make sure they are properly adjusted. The derailleur-type gear assembly, used mostly on sports and racing bikes, has a cluster of different-sized sprockets on the rear wheel. The gear is adjusted at the carrier mechanism that moves the chain from one sprocket to another.

Hub gears are adjusted at the toggle-chain on the control cable where it enters the rear hub.

Keeping gears effective

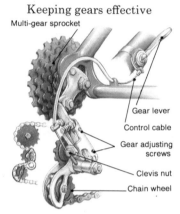

Multi-gear sprocket

Gear lever

Control cable

Gear adjusting screws

Clevis nut

Chain wheel

Derailleur adjustment Select first gear and screw in the upper adjuster until the chain runs centrally on the largest sprocket. Ensure a clearance of at least 3mm (⅛in) between the chain-wheel carrier and wheel spokes. Select top gear and screw in the lower adjuster until the chain runs centrally on the smallest sprocket.

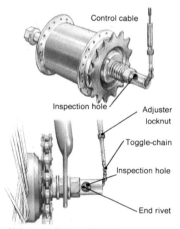

Control cable

Inspection hole

Adjuster locknut

Toggle-chain

Inspection hole

End rivet

Hub gear adjustment Select second gear and loosen the locknut on the cable adjuster. Turn the adjuster sleeve to pull the chain through the hub until you can see the end rivet in the centre of the inspection hole. Select third gear and give the sleeve another half turn. Tighten the locknut.

Mending an inner tube and refitting the tyre

Carry a puncture repair outfit when cycling, and spare valves or valve cores. You will also need three tyre levers to take off the tyre.

Removing the tyre Insert levers between tyre and rim on each side of the valve stem. Hook them on spokes. As a section of tyre edge comes free, move the centre lever on.

Removing the tube Press the valve stem up through the rim and gently pull the tube from under the free edge of the tyre. Ease it past the brake blocks.

Finding and patching the hole Pass the partly inflated tube through a bowl of water (above). Bubbles will pinpoint the hole. Deflate the tube, mark the puncture with an indelible pencil and clean the area with fine abrasive paper. Spread rubber solution thinly around the hole and allow it to become tacky. Apply the patch and hold for 30 seconds. Dust the edges of the patch with French chalk (left).

Bicycle punctures

Dealing with a flat tyre

If a tyre goes flat very slowly, check the valve first. Turn the wheel so that the valve is at the top, remove the cap and immerse the valve in a glass of water. If bubbles appear, replace the valve with a spare from your repair kit.

If it happens on the road, spit on your fingertip and put a film of saliva across the top of the valve to detect a leak.

If the valve is not faulty, check the tyre for anything that may have caused the puncture, such as a nail or a piece of glass, and note its position.

Removing the tyre and tube Upturn the bicycle so that it stands on its saddle and handlebars. Unscrew the knurled nut holding the valve assembly and push the valve up inside the wheel rim.

Insert tyre levers between rim and tyre and lever off the tyre. When a quarter of the tyre is free, run two fingers under the tyre edge to remove the rest.

Draw out the inner tube, partly inflate it, and find the puncture. Wipe the tube dry and mark the puncture with the indelible pencil provided in your repair kit. Cover the damaged area with a patch from the kit. Sprinkle French chalk over the repair to stop the inner tube sticking to the inside of the tyre.

Refitting the tube and tyre First, run your fingers round the inside of the tyre to check for projections or loose grit. If the tyre has been badly gashed, fit a new one as soon as you can. To replace the valve and inner tube, hold back the free edge of the tyre above the valve hole and push the valve stem through the rim. Fit the valve locknut finger tight and replace the valve core.

Partly inflate the tube and roll it over the rim and under the tyre edge. Then press the tyre back on the rim. If you find the last part difficult, move each thumb about 150mm (6in) back along the wheel and press the fitted tyre firmly towards the rim centre. Work inwards until the remainder slips into place. Loosen the valve locknut, push the valve into the rim and pull it out again. Tighten the valve locknut and inflate the tyre fully.

Bicycle riding

Choosing a bike and learning to ride it safely

When you buy a bike, make sure you can adjust the height of the saddle so that you can touch the ground with the soles of your feet when sitting on the saddle. When riding, your knee should be slightly bent when the ball of your foot is on a pedal at its lowest point.

Have the handlebars adjusted to give a comfortable reach without twisting your body when you turn them. Make sure you can easily use brake and gear levers.

Safe riding The Highway Code rules of the road apply to cyclists. Obey them at all times. Cyclists are especially vulnerable to some road hazards – memorising a few do's and don'ts will help you to avoid them.

Do wear light-coloured clothing or a reflective belt, armband or jacket when riding, so that you are easy to see.

Do watch out for car doors opening without warning, cars moving into or away from the kerb without signalling, buses pulling up at bus stops, pedestrians stepping onto crossings.

Do concentrate on the road ahead and avoid or slow down for potholes or bumps that may make you wobble or lose control.

Do keep to the left and ride in a straight line. When turning right, signal clearly in good time. Check before moving out.

Do make sure your lights work properly before riding at night.

Do ride slower than usual in wet or icy weather – brakes do not work as well as on dry roads, and skids are more likely.

Don't overtake vehicles on the right in the face of oncoming traffic. Do not ride on the nearside of a vehicle where you cannot see its signal lights – it may turn left across your path.

Don't ride on the footpath; it is against the law and a danger to pedestrians.

Bicycle touring

Equipping yourself for the open road

The best type of bicycle for touring, short or long distances and over flat or hilly terrain, is a lightweight model with a 10-speed derailleur gear – see BICYCLE CARE. If you intend to travel on poor roads, and will be carrying a heavy load such as CAMPING equipment, fit the bike with 32mm (1¼in) heavyweight tyres. Narrow, high pressure tyres will give you more speed, but are more liable to puncture.

Make sure the bike has good lighting. Generator lights, working from a small dynamo driven by the hub or tyre, give a good light, but they dim at slow speeds and go out when the bike stops. Battery lights, though less powerful, are adequate for short distances at night, and the front lamp can be used for map-reading or roadside repairs.

Tools and equipment Basic tools to carry are: puncture repair kit; three tyre levers; spare tyre valve; screwdriver; all-purpose or 100mm (4in) adjustable spanner; spare brake links and a rivet extractor; pair of long-nosed pliers. Also carry spare lamp batteries and bulbs and a small first aid kit (see FIRST AID KITS).

Clothing Special cycling shoes are available from sports shops, but you will need a different pair for walking. A good compromise is a pair of dual-purpose

cycling/walking shoes. Make sure they are comfortable for both.

Lightweight clothing is essential for warm days. Cotton-lined shorts, worn with a cotton T-shirt or open-neck shirt, are good choices. For colder days take a cycling jersey or jacket. For rainwear the best choice is clothing made from a PTFE membrane that keeps water out but allows perspiration to escape.

Carry reflective equipment to wear at night. This can be a crossbelt, armbands or a reflective jacket.

Baggage If you are travelling light, a large saddlebag attached to the saddle and saddlepost should suffice. For camping gear you need two panniers, one on either side of the rear wheel, with the load evenly distributed. Pack heavy items at the bottom.

Touring clubs Whether you tour alone or with friends, it is worth joining a touring club. The largest is the Cyclists' Touring Club – headquarters Cotterell House, 69 Meadrow, Godalming, Surrey GU7 3HS. The club has 60 District Associations, and helps members to plan tours at home and abroad.

Billiards

A tabletop game calling for skill and concentration

Billiards is played with three balls, two white and one red. The whites are the 'cue balls' – one for each player (one is marked with a black spot). The game opens with the first player striking the spot ball with his cue from any position

within the marked semicircle on the baulk line, called the 'D', to make it hit the red set on the 'billiard spot' at the far end of the table.

The object of the game is to score points with 'pots', 'cannons' and 'in-offs':

A pot This shot is made when a player hits another ball with his cue ball and sends it into a pocket. A potted red scores 3 points and the red is returned to its spot. Potting an opponent's white scores 2 points, but the ball remains in the pocket until the player's turn ends. The opponent must then restart from the D. Many players regard potting an opponent's ball as unsporting. It can also be counter-productive, because after potting it you cannot score a cannon.

A cannon All three balls must be on the table for a cannon, made when the cue ball hits both the red and the other white in the same stroke. It scores 2 points.

An in-off When the cue ball strikes one other and goes into a pocket, the player gets 2 points if it goes in off the white, 3 if off the red. The cue ball is returned to the D for the next shot.

Breaks and penalties A player's turn ends when he fails to score with a stroke, and the total score he makes during his turn at the table is called a 'break'. Points can be conceded to an opponent by incurring penalties. If a shot misses both other balls, or if the cue ball enters a pocket without hitting another ball the penalty is 2 points.

The game ends when a set target – such as 100 points – has been reached by either player, or at the end of a time

---

Potting the ball and playing a cannon

Billiard table The standard size is 3.7m × 1.8m (12ft × 6ft). The balls rebound from the rubber-lined inner edges of the table.

Baize-covered surface

Pocket

Red ball on spot

D semicircle

Cue ball

Baulk line

Cue

The cue ball is used to drive the red into a pocket, or hit both other balls in turn.

limit. Theoretically, endless breaks are possible – in 1907 a player named Tom Reece stayed at the table 85 hours 49 minutes, scoring 499,135. Play became so boring that the rules were changed, limiting the numbers of certain repetitive shots that could be played. See also POOL; SNOOKER.

Bird box

Building a nesting place to attract wild birds

An easily made nestbox may attract a family of birds to your garden. Put it up before mid-March, and face it away from the midday sun.

Materials All the sections of the box can be cut from one piece of softwood, preferably cedar, 150mm (6in) wide, 19mm (¾in) thick and 1450mm (4ft 9in) long. For assembly you will need two dozen 40mm (1½in) galvanised nails (see NAILING) and a dozen tacks. The roof should be hinged with a 150mm (6in) length of rubber, leather or waterproof canvas. Secure the roof with a pair of catches and screws.

Cutting the sections Mark off each piece – two sides, roof, base, back and front – on the board with a pencil, ruler and try square, and use a tenon saw (see SAWS AND SAWING) to cut them out. Make each side piece 200mm (8in) long at the front and 250mm (10in) at the back, to give a slope to the roof. Make the front 200mm (8in) long and the roof 215mm (8½in), and cut between the front and the roof at an angle of about 22 degrees (mark it with a protractor) to slope the back edge of the roof to fit against the back piece. Make the base 115mm (4½in) to fit within the sides; the back will be 460mm (18in) long.

For an entrance hole in the front, draw the circle with compasses and cut it out with a brace and centre-bit (see DRILLING) or coping saw. Make it 32mm (1¼in) for tits, tree sparrows and nuthatches, or 38mm (1½in) for house sparrows and redstarts. For an open entrance cut away half the front.

Assembly Nail one side to the back leaving 100mm (4in) at top and bottom. Nail the base to the back and side, then nail the other side to the back and base. Nail the front in place with the angled side uppermost, sloped forwards.

Tack the hinge to the roof at its angled end, then tack the hinge to the back. Make two wire hooks and staple them to the sides of the roof. Fit screws for the hooks to lodge on so that the roof will not be blown open.

Coat plain timber with a non-toxic wood preservative.

For fixing to a tree or wall

Make the roof slope, to throw off the rain, and hinged to allow annual cleaning. Dimensions for each piece are given below.

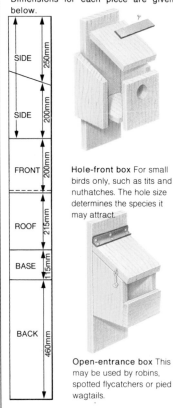

SIDE 250mm
SIDE 200mm
FRONT 200mm
ROOF 215mm
BASE 115mm
BACK 460mm

Hole-front box For small birds only, such as tits and nuthatches. The hole size determines the species it may attract.

Open-entrance box This may be used by robins, spotted flycatchers or pied wagtails.

Bird care

Looking after cage birds

Budgerigars, canaries and finches are the commonest cage birds. Most popular is the budgerigar, an affectionate little bird that is easy to tame. It can usually be taught to talk and is bred in various shades of blue, green, yellow and white.

When buying, look for birds that are alert, bright-eyed and sleek. Budgies may live up to 12 years, canaries usually about nine years, and finches only two and a half years. Top among the songsters is the roller canary, and the commonest finch is the zebra finch, named for its black-and-white striped tail and cheek markings.

The right cage Choose a cage large enough for the bird to fly around in, and equip it with at least two perches and with dishes for food and water. Make sure the floor has a removable tray, which is easy to keep clean; line it with sand-impregnated paper – available from pet shops. For finches and budgies, add a mirror, ladder or bell to amuse them.

Place the cage out of direct sunlight in a draught-free room. Clean it out and wash the dishes daily.

Feeding Budgies, finches and canaries are all seed-eaters. Seed mixtures are sold in pet shops. Provide ample food and water – birds left without will die in 24 to 48 hours. Dispensers are available for a few days' supply.

Also provide a small portion of leafy greens, such as lettuce or dandelion leaves, twice a week. Scatter mineral grit (needed for digestion) on the cage floor. Attach a cuttlefish bone to the side bars for the bird to rub its beak against.

Training A budgerigar can be let out of its cage once it is used to being handled. Begin by putting your hand into the cage and scratching the bird's head. When it gets used to this, press your forefinger gently against its breast to entice it to hop on your finger. Eventually it will come to your hand naturally when it is out of the cage.

Make sure you close all doors and windows before you let it out. Leave the cage door open so that the bird can return of its own accord. If it will not go back, darken the room to calm it and pick it up gently from behind with its neck between your first and second fingers. Never let canaries or finches out of their cage; they panic and could harm themselves by flying at the window.

Health and grooming A bird is not well if it has ruffled feathers, partly closed eyes and no appetite. Cover the cage on three sides to keep it warm and get it to a vet as soon as you can.

A budgerigar's claws and beak may grow too long. Hold it as described above and clip them carefully with scissors or nail clippers. A scaly beak, caused by mites, must be treated by a vet.

Bird table

Making a safe place for birds to feed

You can increase the number and variety of birds in your garden by putting out food for them. To keep them safe from cats, put the food on a bird table. Set it at least 3m (10ft) from bushes and trees where cats may lurk.

Materials Exterior quality 13mm (½in) plywood: one piece 460 × 305mm (18 × 12in). Softwood: 1.8m (6ft) of 25 × 25mm (1 × 1in); 1.6m (5ft 6in) of 50 × 50mm (2 × 2in). Angle brackets: four 100mm (4in) galvanised or enamelled. Galvanised nails, rustless 13mm (½in) woodscrews, hooks as required.

Method The plywood forms the table top. Cut the 25 × 25mm softwood into lengths that fit the table edges and nail them in place, leaving a small gap at one corner for drainage. The 50 × 50mm length of softwood forms the post. Fix the table top to it using the angle brackets, secured by the 13mm woodscrews.

Treat all the wood with non-toxic preservative and sink the post 460mm (18in) in the ground. Alternatively, put preservative on the bottom 510mm (20in) of the post and finish the rest of the post and the table with either exterior grade varnish or microporous wood stain – see STAINING WOOD.

Fix some hooks into the edges of the table for hanging strings of nuts and other titbits. As an extra precaution against cats, nail a ring of wire netting, about 230mm (9in) wide, near the top of the post. Spread the bottom edge to form a cone of netting.

Birdwatching

The first steps in a rewarding and fascinating hobby

You can begin birdwatching in your own garden. Position a BIRD TABLE in view of a window and, aided by a good illustrated guide, you will quickly learn how to identify birds by their plumage and other characteristics.

Of the 250 or so species to be seen regularly in Britain, however, only a small proportion, perhaps 25, are likely to descend upon your garden. For the rest you must travel farther afield.

To get the most from a day's birdwatching, visit one of the 2000 or so nature reserves run by such organisations as the Royal Society for the Protection of Birds, the county nature conservation trusts, the National Trust, the Wildfowl Trust and many local authorities. Before setting out, consult your guidebook to find out what species you are likely to see, and familiarise yourself with them. You may also find it worthwhile joining your local birdwatching society. Most societies organise visits to nature reserves and sanctuaries. Your local library can give you details.

To identify birds by their plumage at long range or to study them close to, you need binoculars with an eight or ten times magnification – but they are not essential for beginners. Even without them you can learn how to recognise birds by their silhouettes and flight behaviour.

However, learning to identify birds from their songs and call-notes alone is one of the most satisfying aspects of birdwatching. It is not easy, as many birds have similar songs, some mimic others and at times they all seem to sing at once – especially at dawn.

You will have little difficulty in recognising some of the more distinctive calls – the plaintive 'pee-wit' of a lapwing, the gentle 'coo-coo' of a wood pigeon, or the mournful 'coor-li' of a curlew as it wings its way across a moor.

Birth certificate

Registering the birth of a child; how to replace a lost certificate

Every child must be registered by the father or mother within 42 days of birth in England and Wales (21 days in Scotland) with the registrar of births and deaths for the sub-district in which the child was born. All the details about the child must be given in person. You can be fined if you fail to register the birth of your child.

There are two types of birth certificate – the short and the standard. The short certificate records only the name of the child, date of birth, sex and the district where the birth took place. The standard certificate records these details and also the name, address and birthplace of both father and mother. The short certificate is issued free of charge; for a standard certificate there is a fee.

You may need to produce your birth certificate whenever you are required to prove your age or identity. If you have lost it you can get a replacement, for a fee, from the Superintendent Registrar of the district where you were born.

Biscuits

How to make some teatime favourites

Keeping the biscuit tin topped up is easy if you make drop biscuits – so called because the dough is simply dropped in small mounds onto a baking tray. They need only about 30 minutes cooking and a number of recipes are available – here are two favourites – the first for ginger drops, the second for coconut wafers:

Ingredients (for 18 biscuits)
115g (4oz) plain flour
½ level teaspoon bicarbonate of soda
1 level teaspoon ground ginger
25g (1oz) golden syrup
25g (1oz) stem ginger, chopped
50g (2oz) butter or margarine
50g (2oz) demerara sugar
2 tablespoons milk

Grease two baking trays, then sift together the flour, bicarbonate of soda and ground ginger. Gently melt the syrup in a pan. Cream the butter and sugar until light and fluffy – then add the syrup and stem ginger, half of the sifted flour and 1 tablespoon of milk.

Stir gently, then add the remaining flour and milk and mix to a soft dough. Drop the mixture in teaspoons onto the baking trays.

Bake in the centre of an oven preheated to 180°C (350°F) – gas mark 4 – for 15-20 minutes.

Ingredients (for 18 biscuits)
50g (2oz) butter or margarine
50g (2oz) caster sugar
2 level teaspoons golden syrup
2 teaspoons lemon juice
50g (2oz) plain flour
25g (1oz) desiccated coconut

Grease two baking trays. Cream the butter and sugar until light and fluffy, then beat in the syrup. Add the lemon juice, sifted flour and coconut. Drop the dough in teaspoons onto the baking trays, allowing the wafers to spread.

Bake in the centre of an oven preheated to 180°C (350°F) – gas mark 4 – for 12 minutes, or until the edges of the wafers are golden-brown.

Bivouac tent

How to make a rough-and-ready shelter for sleeping outdoors

The tent consists of just a sheet of oiled cotton, 2.5 × 2.5m (8 × 8ft), available from camping equipment shops – or you can use a large sheet of horticultural-grade polythene. You also need a waterproof groundsheet, four meat skewers and a ball of strong string.

BIVOUAC TENT

A quick and easy-to-erect shelter

Oiled cotton or polythene sheet

Tie the string to a tree, then back over a forked branch stuck in the ground.

Putting up a bivouac Lay the oiled cotton or polythene sheet on the ground in the position you want the tent, with a length of string underneath at the centre.

Tie one end of the string to a convenient object, such as a tree, fence or large boulder, about 1m (3ft) from the ground. Wind the other string around anything that is also 1m high – perhaps a pile of stones or a tree branch driven into the ground. Now pull the string tight and tie it around a heavy rock on the ground. Move the rock back until the bivouac sheet is taut along its centre.

Use the four meat skewers to pin the corners of the sheet to the ground, forming the shape of the tent. Then replace each one with a heavy stone tied to the sheet. Tie more stones along the edges, then lay the groundsheet inside.

Blackjack

Playing a fast and exciting card game

Blackjack can be played by 2 to 10 players, each of whom tries to achieve a hand with a higher total than the dealer's hand without exceeding 21 points. The value of each card is: ace 1 or 11 (by choice of the player holding it); king, queen and jack 10 points each and all other cards their numerical value.

The dealer deals round the table twice, giving each player 2 cards, the first one face down, the second face up. In some versions of the game, each player bets on his first card; in another version bets are placed after the second card is dealt – rules must be agreed before play begins. A player who is dealt a pair can turn both cards face up and play them as separate hands, betting on each. When a player places a bet, he puts the appropriate number of tokens in front of him. The dealer does not bet, he pays out or wins the amount of each player's bet.

If a player scores 21 with only 2 cards, say an ace and a king, he turns his cards up and announces 'Blackjack'. He is paid double by the dealer and also takes over the deal, or he can sell the deal to the highest bidder.

After the dealer has dealt everyone 2 cards, the player on his left can ask for more cards to add to his total. Each card is dealt face up, singly, until he decides to *stand* (not to take any more cards) or exceeds 21, in which case his hand is *busted* and he pays the dealer his bet.

Play continues until it is the dealer's turn. He turns up his cards and decides whether to stand or draw more cards. If, for example, he stands at 18 he pays all those with more than 18 and collects from those with less. If he goes over 21 he pays out to all players with points totals of 21 or less. A dealer's Blackjack

beats all others, and he collects double from each player, or in some versions takes all bets from the table.

Most players stand or go bust when 4 cards have been dealt. If, however, a player draws 5 cards without busting, he wins double the amount of his bet.

Bleaching wood

Removing deep stains; lightening dark wood

Domestic bleach will remove most stains that have penetrated the grain of wood, such as ink stains. Strip the old finish from the stained area or the entire surface. When bleaching a dark spot, treat the whole surface so as not to leave a light area surrounded by dark.

Apply undiluted bleach to the raw wood with a clean sponge – wear rubber gloves. Leave for 20 minutes, then neutralise it with a 50/50 solution of vinegar and water. If after four hours the stain remains, repeat the process. To lighten naturally dark wood, use a wood bleach, following the maker's instructions.

Bleeding

Swift action to staunch wounds

If the wound is severe act quickly. Lay the casualty down. If a limb is involved and no fracture is suspected, elevate it. Press down firmly on the wound with any absorbent material or your bare hands, unless there is something embedded in the wound – in which case apply pressure alongside it. Maintain the pressure for ten minutes, after which the blood should be clotting.

If severe bleeding from an arm or leg wound continues, try to stop it by press-

ing on the appropriate artery – see illustration. For the leg use the femoral point. Lay the victim down, bend the injured leg at the knee and press down firmly in the centre of the fold of the groin with both thumbs, one on top of the other, against the rim of the pelvis.

For the arm, use the brachial point as illustrated. Do not press for more than ten minutes.

Blenders

Looking after your liquidiser

A blender, sometimes called a liquidiser, consists of a glass jar or jug containing a steel blade assembly at its base driven by a small electric motor. The rotating blade will liquidise fruits or blend ingredients for purées, sauces and drinks. Some blenders are available complete, others are an attachment to a food mixer.

If your blender fails to work, or suddenly stops working, check the plug connections and fuse – see FUSES AND FUSE BOXES; PLUGS. If it works intermittently, get it checked by a qualified repairer.

Sluggish operation of the blender may be caused by a build up of sediment around the blade and its shaft. Unplug the blender, empty it and turn the blade by hand; if it is stiff to turn, half-fill the jar with hot water and detergent, operate the blender for about ten seconds and then leave overnight. Thoroughly rinse with clean water. If this does not clear the fault, or if the blender now leaks through the blade shaft, replace the blade assembly or, if it is not detachable, buy a new jar assembly. Avoid trouble by cleaning the blender after use.

On some blenders, the jar can be unscrewed for cleaning. If it leaks at the base, check the rubber sealing ring. If it is damaged, fit a new one.

BLEEDING

Stopping blood flow at a pressure point

Use a pressure point only to arrest severe bleeding while a dressing for the wound is being prepared.

Femoral point The femoral artery can be pressed against the rim of the pelvis to reduce bleeding in an injured leg. Maintain the pressure for no more than 10 minutes at a time.

Brachial point The brachial artery runs along the inner side of the muscles of the upper arm. Press the artery against a bone to control bleeding from the lower arm, wrist or hand.

Blinds

Repairing Venetian and roller blinds

Regular maintenance should keep VENE-TIAN BLINDS trouble-free. Pay particular attention to the lifting and tilting mechanisms; they do not need lubrication, but should be kept clean to avoid jamming. Change frayed cords immediately, before they break – a broken cord is difficult to replace. Keep the slats clean by frequent dusting. If they become stained or greasy, sponge them with warm water and detergent. Replace broken or distorted slats.

Replacing slats Remove an end-cap from the bottom rail and slide out the bottom slat.

Unknot the lifting cord and draw both ends up through the slats until you reach the damaged slat. Remove it, slide in the replacement and re-thread the cords through the slats, weaving them in and out of the rungs. Knot the cord ends and replace the bottom slat and cap.

Replacing a frayed lifting cord You can fit a cord without removing the blind from the window. In the looped cord hanging at the side of the blind there is an equaliser, similar to a belt buckle. Slide this off the cord. Cut through both pieces of cord, about 150mm (6in) from the loop. Secure the new cord to the old with adhesive tape.

Remove an end-cap from the bottom rail and withdraw the slat so you can pull on the lifting cord ends to draw the new cord through. After replacing the slat and end-cap, hold the looped cord so the slats are level, and thread it through the equaliser.

Replacing a broken lifting cord You need access to the space inside the top rail for feeding the new cord along. The cords pass over pulleys above the lock slot and along the top rail. You thread one down the holes near one end of the slats and the other down the other set of holes, weaving them on alternate sides of the rungs that support the slats. Replace the bottom slat and cap after knotting the cord ends.

Roller blinds

Retensioning When a roller blind will not wind up onto the roller, it needs retensioning. Pull the blind down halfway, remove it from its brackets and roll the blind fully onto the roller. Replace it and pull it down. If there is still not enough tension to wind up the blind fully, repeat the procedure until the correct tension is obtained. You may have to twist the fitting rod a turn or two when inserting it into the bracket.

Fitting new material Blind material is available from large department stores and specialist fabric shops. Before buying a new length, measure the width of the roller and obtain material that is 25mm (1in) narrower, or buy a wider

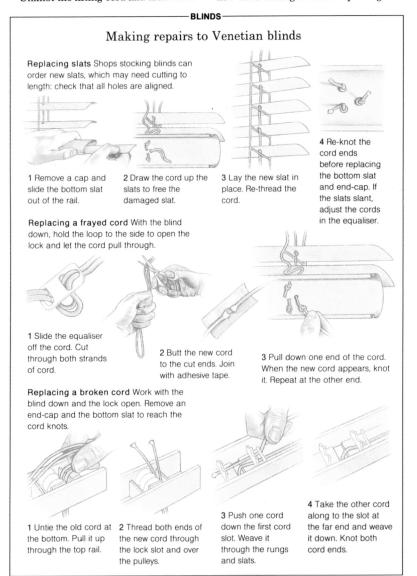

BLINDS

Making repairs to Venetian blinds

Replacing slats Shops stocking blinds can order new slats, which may need cutting to length: check that all holes are aligned.

1 Remove a cap and slide the bottom slat out of the rail.

2 Draw the cord up the slats to free the damaged slat.

3 Lay the new slat in place. Re-thread the cord.

4 Re-knot the cord ends before replacing the bottom slat and end-cap. If the slats slant, adjust the cords in the equaliser.

Replacing a frayed cord With the blind down, hold the loop to the side to open the lock and let the cord pull through.

1 Slide the equaliser off the cord. Cut through both strands of cord.

2 Butt the new cord to the cut ends. Join with adhesive tape.

3 Pull down one end of the cord. When the new cord appears, knot it. Repeat at the other end.

Replacing a broken cord Work with the blind down and the lock open. Remove an end-cap and the bottom slat to reach the cord knots.

1 Untie the old cord at the bottom. Pull it up through the top rail.

2 Thread both ends of the new cord through the lock slot and over the pulleys.

3 Push one cord down the first cord slot. Weave it through the rungs and slats.

4 Take the other cord along to the slot at the far end and weave it down. Knot both cord ends.

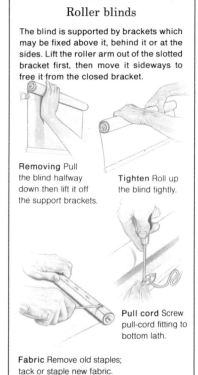

BLINDS

Roller blinds

The blind is supported by brackets which may be fixed above it, behind it or at the sides. Lift the roller arm out of the slotted bracket first, then move it sideways to free it from the closed bracket.

Removing Pull the blind halfway down then lift it off the support brackets.

Tighten Roll up the blind tightly.

Pull cord Screw pull-cord fitting to bottom lath.

Fabric Remove old staples; tack or staple new fabric.

piece and cut it to that measurement. Make sure there is enough material to cover the full length of the window plus 300mm (12in) to cover the roller and bottom lath.

On a wooden roller, the end of the blind is held to it by staples, tacks or adhesive tape. Remove them and either fit the new blind with more staples, or use small tacks. Follow the guideline marked for the old blind to ensure that the new one hangs straight.

A blind on a tubular metal roller is usually gripped in the seam of the tube. Cut the old material close to the roller with a trimming knife, then attach the new blind to the metal tube with contact adhesive, following the seam to make sure it hangs straight. Allow a contact area of at least 25mm (1in).

Unscrew the pull-cord fixture from the bottom of the old blind and pull out the lath. Turn up the bottom of the blind to form a sleeve for the lath. Fit the lath and pull-cord to the new blind.

Blisters

How you get them, and how to treat them

Blisters on hands and feet are mostly caused by friction. Feet suffer when ill-fitting shoes rub heels and toes; fingers and palms can be blistered by prolonged use of hand tools by do-it-yourselfers. Burns, skin irritants and insect bites can also cause blisters.

Treat by avoiding further friction, washing the blistered area gently with warm water and soap, and applying a dry sterile dressing. Healing should take about a week, perhaps longer if the skin beneath the blister is broken or infected.

Do not burst a blister deliberately, unless it is causing acute discomfort – you will increase the risk of infection. The fluid will be reabsorbed naturally and the blister will subside.

However, if a blister is broken accidentally, expose it to the air as much as possible, but cover it with a dry bandage if there is any risk of dirt getting in.

Should you decide to burst a painful blister, first wash both your hands and the blistered area thoroughly. Then heat a fine needle in a flame, let it cool briefly and, without removing the soot or touching the point, hold it flat on the skin and press firmly into one side of the blister, then the other. After removing the needle, press gently on the blister with cotton wool, wipe the area clean and apply an adhesive dressing.

Consult a doctor if a blister becomes infected, or where one occurs without any obvious cause. Multiple blisters occurring spontaneously may be symptoms of an infection such as chickenpox or IMPETIGO.

Bloaters

Serving salted-and-smoked herrings

Silver-skinned, subtly flavoured bloaters were a famed local delicacy in Great Yarmouth and along the East Anglian coast from before Victorian times. Now, with the decline of the herring fleets, they are a rather rare treat for any light meal.

Unlike kippers, bloaters are prepared for sale without splitting or gutting: the whole herring is lightly salted, left for 12 hours, and then smoked for 12 hours – traditionally over oak chippings. The result is a slightly gamey, though delicate, taste.

Local tradition has it that bloaters were invented accidentally by a Yarmouth fish-curer named Bishop in 1835. Other authorities hold that bloaters have been around for three centuries and more.

Because bloaters are only lightly cured, they do not keep for long, and should be eaten within 24 hours of being bought. Split along the underside with a sharp knife, scrape out the guts and brush with melted butter or oil. Cook under a hot grill for 3 minutes each side. Serve on their own, or with scrambled eggs.

Bloaters are also tasty 'raw'. Toss the gutted fish in olive oil and serve with potato salad. In an Irish dish, gutted and filleted bloaters are covered with Irish whiskey, which is then set alight. When the flames die down, the bloaters are ready.

Blood donors

A gift that could make the difference between life and death

Anyone over the age of 18 and under 65 and in reasonably good health may give blood to the National Blood Transfusion Service, for medical emergencies and treatment of disorders such as haemophilia and tetanus. Details of donor sessions – held regularly in most towns – are advertised in health centres and public libraries. Donors are not paid.

Regular donors generally give up to 0.5 litres (just under 1 pint) of blood twice a year. Each donation amounts to about 10 per cent of the total in the circulatory system of an average adult; its loss is made up naturally by the body in two to six weeks.

If you decide to become a donor, you will be asked some general questions about your health and required to sign a medical form. You also have to declare on another form that you are not at risk from AIDS or hepatitis. You should not give blood if you have taken medicines (including aspirin and paracetamol). A blood sample will be taken to test for anaemia. If the sample is satisfactory you will lie on a couch, and a nurse will inflate a cuff round your upper arm to make the blood vessels stand out. A local anaesthetic may be applied if you want it while a needle is inserted in your arm to draw off the blood. It is a painless process that takes 10-15 minutes. Once the needle has been removed, a plaster is put over the entry spot. You can have a drink of tea, a soft drink – and, at some centres, stout or ale – in the waiting room if you wish.

All the materials used for collecting blood are sterile and are thrown away after one use, so there is no risk of infection. If you have doubts about whether you are a suitable donor, get confidential advice from your doctor, a physician on duty at the donor session or the director of your local Blood Transfusion Centre.

Blowtorches

Gas-burning tools with many uses

Gas blowtorches burn butane gas contained in a pressurised canister. They vary in size from small units where the gas canister forms the handle, to larger sizes with a separate canister and a flexible tube connected to the nozzle.

Accessories include a flame spreader for PAINT STRIPPING and a copper bit for soldering (see SOLDERING AND BRAZING) – the two most frequent jobs for which it is used. A blowtorch is also handy for lighting a bonfire and for starting BARBECUES.

Paint stripping Before starting to strip the paint, make sure there are no newspapers or other flammable materials on the floor that could be ignited by droppings of burning paint. Use hardboard or a metal tray to protect the floor if necessary. Keep a bucket of water handy in which to drop any paint which smoulders or catches fire. Wear goggles and gloves for protection.

Fit the flame spreader, which pushes onto the blowtorch nozzle. Open the valve at the rear of the burner head and light the torch. Adjust the flame to about 38mm (1½in) long.

Hold the blowtorch nozzle about 75mm (3in) away from the paintwork and keep it moving slowly from left to right. In areas where you need to move the flame vertically, avoid a downward movement as you may burn your other hand. As the paint softens, strip it with a broad-bladed scraper. Do not use a blowtorch around windows as the glass may crack – use a chemical stripper instead.

Outside the house, check for birds' nests under the eaves and for rotten wood that could ignite. Have a garden water sprayer handy to damp down if wood starts to smoulder. Keep the torch away from plastic guttering, which melts easily – it is better to use chemical stripper here, or remove the guttering and replace it later, after repainting.

See also hot air strippers, page 326.

Soft soldering Soft solders, alloys of tin and lead, melt at temperatures below 500°C (1060°F) and are used for small joints and electrical connections. A flux is applied to help the molten solder flow – reels of solder with a flux core are obtainable from hardware stores.

Small joints can be soldered either with the torch flame set at about 13mm (½in) long, or with the copper soldering bit attached. To use the flame, thoroughly clean the parts to be joined and apply flux liberally, unless cored solder is to be used. Heat the general area of the joint with the outer part of the flame, then play the tip of the inner blue flame on the joint itself. Remove the flame and apply solder to the joint.

Body odour

What causes it and how to avoid it

Perspiration is the main cause of body odour, secreted through sweat glands. Bacteria can multiply in places where perspiration cannot evaporate quickly – armpits, feet and groin. The best remedy is bathing or showering daily – or more frequently if necessary.

Wash or dry-clean outer garments regularly. Keep underclothes fresh, changing them at least daily; choose those made of natural fibres – air circulates better through natural fibres than artificial ones, keeping down bacterial growth.

If these measures are not enough, use a deodorant, which contains agents to kill bacteria, or an antiperspirant to deal with sweating. The active ingredient of antiperspirants is an aluminium compound. Of the two most frequently used, aluminium chloride is more effective than aluminium chlorohydrate, but can damage clothing and irritate certain types of skin.

Start with a mild deodorant and apply before going to bed and first thing in the morning. Stop using any product that causes irritation.

Bolts

Assembling with bolts; loosening tight or rusted bolts

Use bolts and nuts when you want an assembly to have strength, and when constructing something you may need to dismantle again later – say a metal-framed greenhouse (see GREENHOUSES) or a wooden tool shed.

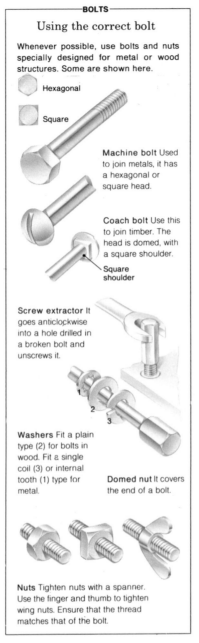

BOLTS

Using the correct bolt

Whenever possible, use bolts and nuts specially designed for metal or wood structures. Some are shown here.

Hexagonal

Square

Machine bolt Used to join metals, it has a hexagonal or square head.

Coach bolt Use this to join timber. The head is domed, with a square shoulder.

Square shoulder

Screw extractor It goes anticlockwise into a hole drilled in a broken bolt and unscrews it.

Washers Fit a plain type (2) for bolts in wood. Fit a single coil (3) or internal tooth (1) type for metal.

Domed nut It covers the end of a bolt.

Nuts Tighten nuts with a spanner. Use the finger and thumb to tighten wing nuts. Ensure that the thread matches that of the bolt.

When assembling metal parts use machine bolts, which may have square or hexagonal heads, or a domed head with a screwdriver slot. For joining timber use coach bolts, which have domed heads and square shoulders – as the bolt and nut are tightened, the square shoulder bites into the wood and so prevents the bolt from turning. Use a plain washer under the nut when using a coach bolt; plain washers under the head and under the nut on a machine bolt.

If you are joining metal, use a spring or toothed washer (or thread-locking sol-

ution) to stop the nut loosening. Always use correct-sized spanners so you do not damage the bolt head or nut, which will make dismantling difficult. For preference use spanners that completely encircle the bolt and nut, such as ring spanners or socket spanners. Never use pliers, pipe grips or a Stilson wrench. Hold the bolt head with one spanner, or with a screwdriver if the head is slotted, screw on the nut until it is finger-tight then tighten with a spanner.

Removing troublesome bolts If the corners of a nut or bolt head are so badly worn that a spanner will not grip, try using self-locking grips applied as tight as possible. If that fails, file two sides of the nut flat and use an adjustable spanner.

Rusted nuts and bolts can often be freed by applying penetrating oil or a chemical rust remover. Apply the oil or solution so that it can run down into the thread, leave it for at least ten minutes – the longer the better if the rust is thick.

As a last resort an obstinate nut can be driven off with a hammer and cold chisel. Place the chisel at an angle near a corner of the nut and drive it anticlockwise until the nut is loose enough to be removed by hand or with a spanner or self-locking grips.

If a bolt fitted into a threaded hole breaks off at the head, use a screw extractor – available from car accessory and tool shops – to remove the broken stub. The extractor is a tool rather like a large screw – but with a left-hand thread and a squared head. Using a twist drill about three-quarters the diameter of the broken bolt, drill a hole down into the bolt as deep as possible – see DRILLING. Insert the screw end of the extractor into the hole, then, using a spanner on the head of the extractor, turn it anticlockwise. As it turns, the extractor's threads bite into the bolt and it, too, turns anticlockwise and is unscrewed.

Bonnet catches

*Adjusting and lubricating;
releasing a jammed catch*

If the bonnet-release handle inside the car will not open the bonnet, the fault may be that the catch adjustment is too tight or that the mechanism has jammed through lack of lubrication. Either of these faults may have led to a third – a broken or overstretched cable caused by the additional strain.

Since bonnet catches are designed to foil car thieves they are not easy to open from outside the car, so preventing jamming is easier than unjamming.

How the catch works In most cars the catch has a spring-loaded spigot attached to the front of the bonnet, and a spring-loaded striker plate above the grille that clips into a groove in the spigot when the bonnet is pushed down.

The release cable runs from the release handle to a lever on the striker plate, and when pulled unclips the striker plate from the spigot. Correctly adjusted, the spigot should lock into the striker plate without undue pressure on the bonnet, which it should hold firmly down.

To adjust the spigot, first slacken the locknut. Screw the spigot up if the bonnet is too loose or down if it is too tight. Retighten the locknut. If the spigot does not enter the striker plate freely, loosen the screws on the plate, lower the bonnet carefully until the spigot itself aligns the plate, without actually locking it. Lift the bonnet and retighten the screw.

Keep striker plate and spigot lubricated with an occasional few drops of thin oil.

Releasing a jammed catch On some cars you can get at the underside of the catch by removing the grille. Once it is removed, use a strong screwdriver to lever the strike plate open; or you may be able to simply pull the release cable, if it has not broken at the catch. Otherwise you may have to get under the front of the car and reach up to free the catch or pull the cable end with pliers.

Once you have freed the catch, find the cause of jamming and rectify by adjustment, lubrication or having a new cable fitted.

Bonsai

The art of growing miniature trees

The beauty of the oriental art of bonsai is becoming increasingly appreciated in Britain and other western countries. Garden centres now sell trees ready-trained in traditional shapes – most of them destined never to grow more than knee-high. Kits are also available to cultivate specimens from seed.

The bonsai garden Most trees and many shrubs, apart from the fastest-growing species, can be transformed into bonsai. The evergreen Japanese white pine and Sargent juniper are popular for planting in individual containers, and are easily cultivated.

When groups, called 'groves', of bonsai trees are planted together in one container, they are usually left to grow straight. Maples, birches and oaks are suitable.

The container or tray (bonsai means 'tray planting') is an integral part of the design. Bonsai trays, with holes in the bottom and usually shallow, can be bought in various shapes – round, oval, rectangular and hexagonal, for example.

Natural stone and terracotta are among the most visually pleasing materials.

Training a tree It takes a year or more to train a bonsai tree from a seedling. Choose specimens in spring or summer, from plants whose main stem is approaching 10mm ($\frac{3}{8}$in) in diameter. If they are already growing in your garden, leave them there. Otherwise, pot them in JOHN INNES COMPOST No 1, and put them outdoors in shelter.

Begin training into a twisted shape immediately. Twist soft, thin wire round the tip of each seedling and bend it down to ground level. Keep the tip in place by securing it to twine tied below the rim of the pot.

Cutting back The main stem should be severed about 150mm (6in) from the base, when 13mm ($\frac{1}{2}$in) thick. Trim roots back.

By the winter, the main stem should be a full 10mm in diameter, and it is ready for the next stage in training. Sever the main stem about 150mm (6in) from the base. Carefully remove the tree from the soil or pot, and trim its roots back by about one-third, to fit a bonsai tray.

Put the tree in the tray, using soft, thin wire to anchor its roots to the holes in the tray's base. Twist more wire up around the trunk and branches to bend them to the required shape. Wind the wire evenly upwards at an angle of 45 degrees around the trunk and branches. Do not put too much tension on the wire and do not crisscross it. Fill the tray with John Innes No 1 compost, with a top layer of moss to give the appearance of grass. Put in a sheltered spot outdoors.

Care of your bonsai After a year, the bonsai's main root should be pruned a second time, and the tree rewired annually to allow for growth. Further shaping can be carried out by pinching off growth buds with your fingers. The leaf size of deciduous or broad-leaf evergreens may be reduced by snipping off the leaves (but not their stems) in early or mid-summer.

Most bonsai trees should be left outdoors apart from brief periods of showing indoors. In winter, they need a cool, frost-free place with good light.

Water bonsai often enough to keep the compost moderately moist, and mist them regularly. In spring and autumn, treat them once a month with a complete houseplant food, diluted to one-quarter strength.

Bookcase building

Making an attractive bookcase with only a few tools

You can make a simple bookcase using lengths of softwood (see TIMBER) 225 × 25mm (9 × 1in), 25 × 25mm (1 × 1in) BATTENS, a sheet of 3mm ($\frac{1}{8}$in) PLYWOOD or hardboard for the back, a few screws and a woodworking adhesive such as PVA. For finishing you need medium and fine grades of glasspaper, wood-filler and polyurethane varnish – see VARNISHING.

Remember when ordering timber that planed lengths come in nominal sizes – the 225 × 25mm will actually measure 221 × 21mm, because planing has removed the difference.

Measure the space where the bookcase is to fit, and decide how many shelves you will need and the height between each. Allow 150-200mm (6-8in) for paperback books, 200-300mm (8-12in) for hardbacks and 330mm (13in) for records.

List the main parts and their dimensions: two pieces for the top and bottom, with shelves of the same length, and two pieces for the sides.

Use a try square to mark the sides for shelf positions. Cut battens and drill

---

BOOKCASE BUILDING

Fitting it together

Side supports are sufficient for shelves up to about 1m (3ft) long. Give longer shelves extra support with back battens fixed by screws driven from behind the back panel.

Screws to fix top and base to sides

Side battens for shelves

Thin back panel

three 2.5mm ($^3/_{32}$in) countersunk holes – see DRILLING. Make one hole at the centre and one 25mm from each end. Screw the battens to the sides with No 8, 38mm (1½in) countersunk SCREWS.

At each end of the side pieces mark, drill and countersink three 2.5mm diameter holes, 13mm (½in) from the ends and spaced at 25mm from the front and back, and one at the centre.

Rest the front edges of the side, top and bottom pieces on a level surface. Apply woodworking glue (see GLUING) to the surfaces to be joined and join them together with No 8, 38mm (1½in) countersunk screws. Wipe off all surplus glue. Glue and panel pin the plywood or hardboard backing sheet in place.

Fill all the screwhead holes with wood filler (see STOPPERS AND FILLERS) and when it has set rub down flush with medium glasspaper. If the shelves are to be fixed, rest them on the battens and nail them firmly using lost-head nails.

Sand the unit with medium glasspaper followed by fine, then wipe clean with a rag dipped in white spirit. Apply two or three coats of polyurethane varnish, lightly sanding between coats.

Book-keeping

Understanding the double-entry system

When starting a business (see COMPANIES), you need to record day-to-day transactions in goods, money and services and to summarise them to show the overall position of the business.

Day-to-day transactions go into several account books – for example, sales, purchases, stock, expenses, cash – varying to suit the particular business. These are often called *books of original entry*. The information from them is then *posted* – entered – in the *ledger*. The ledger is the central book of the system, but no transactions go directly into it – all must reach it via a book of original entry.

Double-entry system In this method every transaction is recorded twice, because it has two effects on your business – for example, when you buy in goods, one effect is to increase stock; the other is that cash in hand is reduced.

So that both aspects are recorded, all the account books are drawn up with a matching set of columns: a *debit* side on the left and a *credit* side on the right.

The debit side is the receiving side, recording the value of everything that flows *into* the account. The credit side is the giving side, recording the value of everything that flows *out* of the account. What is termed debit and credit in book-keeping means virtually the reverse of their normal interpretation.

For every debit entry in one account, there must be a corresponding credit entry in the other. The difference between total credits and total debits in one account at the end of a book-keeping period – usually a month – is called the *balance*.

There is a credit balance when the credit total is greater; a debit balance when the debit total is greater. The closing balance of one book-keeping period becomes the opening balance of the next period. The difference between the two totals is added to the lower total to make the debit and credit totals equal before the period is ruled off.

Total debits and total credits in the ledger must always be equal; if not, the records contain an error that must be found and corrected.

Posting in the ledger The ledger records all day-to-day transactions. It can contain many accounts – individual ones for customers who have bought on credit, and for firms that have supplied goods on credit; plus general ones for wages, purchases, sales, cash, rent and the like.

Each account is again recorded as a debit or a credit – but from the point of view of the name on the account. From the *sales account book*, for example, the value of goods supplied to customers is entered on the debit side of each individual customer's account (an inflow to the account). The total value of goods sold is entered on the credit side of the sales account (value given out by the account).

But when transactions are posted from the *cash account book* to the ledger, they change sides (see illustrations) because they are now being recorded from a different point of view. When John Smith paid £100 in cash for goods, his payment was an inflow to the cash account book and recorded as a debit. In the ledger, John Smith's account shows the £100 on the credit side because it has moved out of his individual account.

On the other hand, the £300 paid to XYZ Ltd, shown as a credit in the cash account book (because the money went out of the account), is recorded in the

---

How a Mr John Smith balances his books

John Smith's ledger and cash account book show how the double-entry method works. They show how inflows to the cash account book change from being debits to credits.

Cash account Some payments are made in cash, others by cheque. The folio column gives a cross-reference to the account number in the ledger. The values entered here on the debit side would be entered on the credit side of the stock account. The rent and wages would be debited to the expenses account. The value of stock bought from XYZ and Bees would be debited in the stock account.

The ledger Each account would have its own page(s) or card(s). The initials refer to the book of original entry the transaction appeared in; the balance from that book is not posted in the ledger.

		CASH ACCOUNT BOOK							
DR	RECEIPTS				PAYMENTS				CR
Date	Particulars	Folio	Cash	Cheque	Date	Particulars	Folio	Cash	Cheque
			£	£				£	£
May 1	Balance		85	360	May 4	Rent	L4		150
6	Cash sales	L1	230		8	Wages	L4	180	
11	John Smith	L2	100		21	XYZ Ltd	L5		300
20	B. Green	L3		650	21	Bees Ltd	L6		220
22	Cash sales	L1	90			Balance carried down		325	340
			505	1,010				505	1,010
June 1	Balance brought down		325	340					

DR		LEDGER			CR
	1	SALES ACCOUNT			£
			May 6	Cash CB	230
			22	Cash CB	90
					320
	2	JOHN SMITH			
			May 11	Cash CB	100
	3	B. GREEN			
			May 20	Cash CB	650
	4	EXPENSES ACCOUNT			
May 4	Cash CB	150			£
8	Cash CB	180			
		330			
	5	XYZ LTD			
May 21	Cash CB	300			
	6	BEES LTD			
May 21	Cash CB	220			

ledger as a debit in the XYZ Ltd account, because it is value flowing into that account.

The company's overall position at the end of a period such as a financial year is summarised in the final accounts prepared from the ledger. The ledger is also the basis of assessment for tax.

Book repairs

Restoring damaged volumes

A number of simple repairs can be carried out on a damaged book to give it a new lease of life, provided it is a hardback covered with cloth or some other inexpensive material. Take leatherbound books to a professional repairer.

A detached back strip The back strip covers the back of the book and bears the book's title. If it has broken away, brush PVA glue (see GLUING) along the joints, align the back cover with the glued edge and press it into place.

Rub a flat implement, such as a table knife, along the joints to force out excess glue, then wipe them clean. Cover the back with waxed paper and wrap bandaging around the book to hold the back cover in place while the glue dries.

A loose cover If the book cover has become loose at the joints, open the book wide and use a knitting needle inserted between the spine and the back cover to apply PVA glue to the joints. Close the book, lay it flat and put a weight on it for 24 hours to hold it while the glue sets.

Cracked endpapers Endpapers, pasted inside the cover at the front and back of the book, sometimes crack at the hinge. Apply a thin bead of PVA glue along the crack and press the edges firmly together. Cut a thin strip of paper and press it into the glued crack. Close the book and weight it until the glue dries.

Torn pages Place a sheet of waxed paper under the tear. Carefully align the torn edges and brush them with PVA glue. Cover the tear with another sheet of waxed paper, rub gently along the line of the tear, then apply a weight for 24 hours. Afterwards, remove the waxed paper.

Loose pages When single pages of a book become loose, they can be glued back into place, as shown. Another method is to cut a narrow strip of paper the length of the book and no wider than the print margins of the pages. Fold it lengthways and glue the back with PVA adhesive. Glue one edge to the loose page and the other to the adjoining page. Place a strip of waxed paper in the fold, close the book and allow the glue to dry.

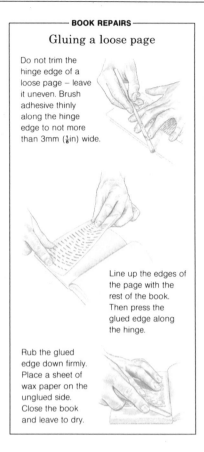

Gluing a loose page

Do not trim the hinge edge of a loose page – leave it uneven. Brush adhesive thinly along the hinge edge to not more than 3mm ($\frac{1}{8}$in) wide.

Line up the edges of the page with the rest of the book. Then press the glued edge along the hinge.

Rub the glued edge down firmly. Place a sheet of wax paper on the unglued side. Close the book and leave to dry.

Border plants

Choosing suitable plants to border a lawn or path

The most suitable plants for borders are hardy perennials, or to give them their full description, hardy herbaceous perennials. These plants, which bloom year after year, formed the basis of the herbaceous border which was an essential feature of early 20th-century gardens.

In recent years, however, the mixed border has gained popularity, particularly with owners of small gardens. It has the advantage that by mixing perennials with other plants such as annuals, roses, biennials and shrubs, it provides a varied display all the year round.

Obviously the shape and size of a border is governed by the feature it is bordering – usually a lawn or path – but it should be large enough to contain a selection of perennials within a framework of flowering shrubs and decorative evergreens. The shape can be rectangular, though an irregular shape, following the contours of a winding path for example, will add interest and allow the plants to be seen from several angles.

Planning a border There are hundreds

Year-long interest Showy annual blooms, reliable perennials, flowering shrubs, bulbs and bright autumn or evergreen leaves keep a mixed border alive all round the calendar.

of perennials to choose from. Their flowering seasons vary, so you can select them to give continuity of colour from spring to autumn, and when they die down, evergreens will prevent the border becoming bare and uninteresting.

The height to which plants grow is also important in planning a border, so tall-growing perennials such as lupins, delphiniums and phloxes should not be placed where they will obscure small plants like violas or polygonums.

Selecting border plants The range is so great that a good gardening book or a comprehensive grower's catalogue is an essential aid to selection. As a basic guide, however, some of the most popular plants are listed below.

Delphinium Tall-growing, about 1.5m (5ft), with a wealth of flowers in June and July. A good choice is a Pacific Hybrid such as 'Blue Bird', which has a clear blue flower with a white eye. Plant in autumn or early spring.

Lupin (*Lupinus*) The Russell strain of this plant thrusts up spires of colourful blooms in May to July to a height of about 1m (3ft). For a good mixture of colours, try the pink and white 'The Chatelaine', the blue and white 'The Governor', and the gold and yellow 'Chandelier'. Plant in autumn or spring.

Phlox An August-flowering plant with flowers of violet, wine-red and salmon-pink, and many other shades. Its dense flowers cluster on 1m (3ft) high stems. A good combination is violet-purple 'Border Gem' or the crimson 'Starfire' alongside the pale mauve 'Fairy's Petticoat'. Plant in autumn or spring.

Pinks (*Dianthus*) For the front of your border, old-fashioned pinks will give a bright and richly scented display. Their colours range from white through pink to deep red. Particularly attractive are 'Whiteladies' and 'Mrs Sinkins', both have double white blooms in June. Plant in autumn or spring.

Burning bush (*Dictamnus albus*) This plant gets its name from a spectacular and, for a plant, unusual characteristic. On hot summer evenings it gives off a volatile oil which can be lit, and a brief flash of fire surrounds it. Apart from its fiery nature it makes an attractive addition to a border with its 1m (3ft) high stems carrying fragrant white flowers in June and July. Plant autumn to spring.

Violas There is a wide selection of low-growing, free-flowering violas to light up a border from May to September, including 'Chantryland Orange', 'Hunters-combe Purple' and 'Boughton Blue'.

Polygonum For a low-level blaze of colour at a border edge, *Polygonum affine* is hard to beat. Growing no more than 300mm (12in) high, it spreads a wide clump of creeping stems with pink or red spikes of flowers in late summer and autumn.

Primrose (*Primula vulgaris*) Though past their best by April or May, prim-roses are a glorious prelude to the feast of colour a well-planned border provides.

Bottle gardens

Creating a miniature garden

Large, globular bottles, or carboys, with cork stoppers can be bought at garden centres, large florists and many department stores. You can buy them already arranged with a display of plants, but creating your own is more satisfying.

To negotiate the narrow neck opening you will need some special tools, all of which you can make yourself. Bamboo canes make ideal handles – wire a spoon to one to use as a spade, a wooden cotton reel to another for tamping down the soil, a sharp blade such as an old pen-knife blade for pruning and use two canes as tongs for inserting the plants. Attach a small sponge to a stiff wire for cleaning the inside of the glass.

Choose small, slow-growing plants, such as earth star (*Cryptanthus acaulis*), selaginella, friendship plant (*Pilea*) and fittonia, and decide upon their arrangement before placing the plants in the bottle. Ensure that small plants are not hidden behind larger ones, and that shapes and colours complement one another.

To prepare the bottle for planting, cover the base with a 25-50mm (1-2in) layer of charcoal chips and small pebbles. Add a 50-100mm (2-4in) layer of damp potting mixture, poured through a paper funnel. A combination of 2 parts of soil-based potting mixture, 2 parts coarse sand and 1 part of leaf mould or peat moss should suit most plants.

Use the spoon to smooth out the surface of the mixture and then make a hole for the first plant.

Remove the plants from their pots and shake off as much soil as possible from the roots. Holding the first plant gently between the two canes, lower it into its hole. Repeat the process with the remaining plants, then tamp down the potting mixture with the wooden reel. Finally moisten the sponge and clean the sides of the bottle.

Spray the plants with a fine mist, put the stopper in the bottle and place it in good, but not strong, light.

Except for occasional ventilation and pruning, the display should need no further attention for many months.

Boules

Playing bowls the French way

Visitors to France have often been intrigued by the sight of a group of men tossing metal balls in a village square. The game they play is boules, also called pétanque, and its popularity has spread to Britain.

In certain ways the game resembles English BOWLS, the object being to deliver the balls as close as possible to a small target ball – the jack or, in the French game, the cachonnet. In boules, however, the balls are metal and measure between 70 and 80mm (2¾-3⅛in) in diameter and are not biased. They can be delivered by throwing or rolling. Scoring is at a rate of 1 point for every ball of the same player that lies nearer to the cachonnet than those of his opponents. The game is played as singles, when each player has three or four balls, as doubles with three balls to each player, and trebles with two each.

The game can be played on any kind of level surface, preferably sand or gravel. The players toss for the right to choose the delivery circle, toss the cachonnet and deliver the first ball. The winner of the toss marks out a delivery circle about 330-480mm (13-19in) in diameter, which must be at least 1m (3ft) from any obstacle. Standing in the circle he then throws the cachonnet to a point that must be between 6 and 10m (20-33ft) from the edge of the delivery circle. If he fails to deliver correctly in three attempts the option passes to his opponent – but not the right to bowl first.

The first player delivers his ball, either by throwing or rolling, and must not cross or touch the circle line until his ball has landed or stopped rolling. A player of the other team then tries to throw his ball nearer to the cachonnet, or knock away the leading ball. The ball nearest the cachonnet leads, and it is then up to a player of the team not leading to throw until his team gets a leading ball. As the game progresses you can try to dislodge an opponent's ball from its place near the cachonnet.

The game ends when all the balls have been delivered, and the points are then added up. In the next game the cachonnet is thrown from within a circle drawn around the spot where it landed in the previous game.

Bowls

A game of skill and judgment

The ancient game of 'bowles' has evolved into two versions – flat green bowls, and crown green bowls.

Flat green bowls The game is played on a flat green, or lawn, usually 36.6-

---

BOTTLE GARDENS

The tools and techniques used for arranging plants

Inserting the plants requires dexterity and steady hands. It is best to start with the plants close to the side of the bottle, then work towards the centre.

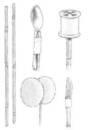

Canes, spade, sponge, tamper and pruning knife make up the tool kit.

Trickle potting mixture through a funnel, or a cone made with stiff paper, into the neck of the bottle.

Level the mixture with the spoon and make a hole near the edge, deep enough to take the roots of the first plant.

Use the canes to guide the first plant into its hole. Add more specimens, then tamp down the mixture and clean the glass.

40.3m (40-44yds) square and divided into six playing areas called rinks. The green is surrounded by a shallow ditch.

The object of the game is for each player to deliver a bowl closer to the jack, a small white ball, than his opponent. The jack is bowled by a player on the side starting first. It is bowled from the mat and must travel at least 22.8m (25yds).

In singles and pairs each player delivers four bowls, in fours, they roll two bowls each. In singles the first player to score 21 is the winner; in pairs and fours the side leading after 21 games, called 'ends', are the winners.

In each end, the player or team with the bowl nearest to the jack scores a point for each bowl closer to the jack than the opponent's most successful bowl. The winner of the end bowls the jack to aim at in the next end.

The bowls range from 120mm ($4\frac{3}{4}$in) to 130mm ($5\frac{1}{8}$in) in diameter, and though often made with lignum vitae and called 'woods', they may also be made of a composition material or hardened rubber. They are flattened slightly on one side of the running surface to make them biased, so that a wood rolls in a curved path, rather than a straight one.

Great skill is called for in judging the line along which to roll the wood and the force with which to deliver it, taking account of its bias and the characteristics of the green. The degree of curve imparted by the bias depends on the speed at which the wood is delivered: the slower the forward movement of the wood, the greater is the effect of the bias.

A player delivers a wood with at least one foot on or over a rubber mat, and the bowl must travel at least 13.7m (15yds) to remain in play. If not it is declared 'dead' and is placed on the bank. If a bowl touches the jack it is marked with chalk and is called a 'toucher'. It remains in play even if it rolls on into the ditch. All bowls except touchers that go into the ditch are declared dead, even if they rebound back onto the green.

Crown green bowls Perhaps even more demanding of the bowler's skills, this form of bowls is played on a green that rises 200mm (8in) to 460mm (18in) at its centre. Its surface is also irregular, adding to the hazard caused by the crown. The object of the game is the same as in lawn bowls, with variations in the rules, and it is played more in the north of England than the south.

Bow ties

Putting on the Ritz with a hand-tied bow tie

Bow ties, essential for dinner jacket or evening dress wear, can be bought ready tied in clip-on or neckband form. Apart from the conventional black or white, such ties are also available in many designs and colours for casual wear or, if your sense of humour runs to it, will light up, rotate or squirt water.

Ready-made ties, however, are for the impatient and careless dresser – the meticulous man ties his bow tie by hand, and the technique is really quite simple. Nor is tying a bow confined to gentlemen – a neat bow makes a smart finish to the neckline of a lady's blouse.

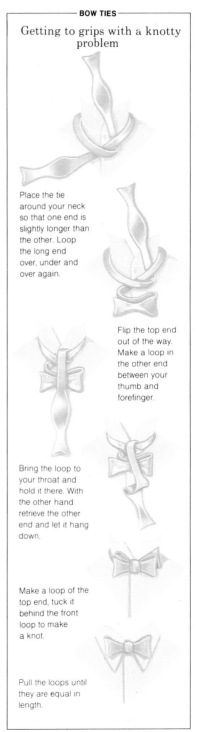

Getting to grips with a knotty problem

Place the tie around your neck so that one end is slightly longer than the other. Loop the long end over, under and over again.

Flip the top end out of the way. Make a loop in the other end between your thumb and forefinger.

Bring the loop to your throat and hold it there. With the other hand retrieve the other end and let it hang down.

Make a loop of the top end, tuck it behind the front loop to make a knot.

Pull the loops until they are equal in length.

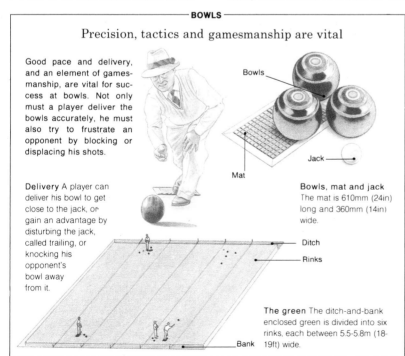

Precision, tactics and gamesmanship are vital

Good pace and delivery, and an element of gamesmanship, are vital for success at bowls. Not only must a player deliver the bowls accurately, he must also try to frustrate an opponent by blocking or displacing his shots.

Delivery A player can deliver his bowl to get close to the jack, or gain an advantage by disturbing the jack, called trailing, or knocking his opponent's bowl away from it.

Bowls

Jack

Mat

Ditch

Rinks

Bank

Bowls, mat and jack The mat is 610mm (24in) long and 360mm (14in) wide.

The green The ditch-and-bank enclosed green is divided into six rinks, each between 5.5-5.8m (18-19ft) wide.

---BRACKETS---

Fitting bracket to wall, and shelf to bracket

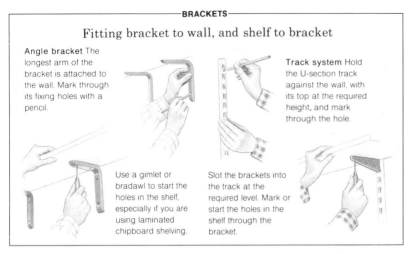

Angle bracket The longest arm of the bracket is attached to the wall. Mark through its fixing holes with a pencil.

Track system Hold the U-section track against the wall, with its top at the required height, and mark through the hole.

Use a gimlet or bradawl to start the holes in the shelf, especially if you are using laminated chipboard shelving.

Slot the brackets into the track at the required level. Mark or start the holes in the shelf through the bracket.

Brackets

Fixing shelf supports

There are two main types of brackets used for putting up SHELVES: right-angle brackets fixed directly to a wall; and track systems, which have arms that slot into a vertical channel and are adjustable for height.

The simplest type of right-angle bracket is made of pressed steel and is available in a range of sizes from 75mm (3in) to 300mm (12in). Some angle brackets have one arm longer than the other, the long arm being the one that is attached to the wall.

Decorative wrought-iron brackets, with a scrollwork design between the two arms, are still made by some blacksmiths; imitation wrought-iron brackets are available from most DIY and hardware shops.

Lightweight track systems, made of aluminium with a silver or gold anodised finish, are useful where shelf heights need to be altered from time to time, or where a combination of shelves of differing heights is required. The support arms hook into slots in the upright channels and can be adjusted at approximately 25mm (1in) intervals. Some systems have arms that slide in the channel, and are therefore infinitely adjustable. The arms are locked in position by the downward pressure of the shelf.

Fixing right-angle brackets Mark the wall with a pencil at the required height of the shelf. Hold a bracket against the wall with its top arm level with the mark and use a spirit level to check that it is vertical. Mark the wall through the screw holes with a pencil.

Drill the wall through the marked points using a masonry bit and insert wall plugs – see MASONRY DRILLING. Attach the bracket with SCREWS about 40mm (1½in) long, so that they go through the plaster and at least 25mm (1in) into the brickwork beneath. The screw gauge will depend on the size of the bracket holes – usually No 8 gauge for small brackets or No 10 for the larger sizes. Always use the largest gauge screw the screw holes will take. With a spirit level check that the top arm is horizontal. If it is not, pack behind the vertical arm with thin pieces of hardboard.

Fix the remaining bracket(s) in the same way, taking care that they are all at the same level. Lay the shelf across the brackets. Place a spirit level on it to check that it is horizontal. Mark its underside through the screw holes in the supporting arm with a bradawl or gimlet. Screw the shelf to the brackets with screws that will penetrate about half the thickness of the shelf.

Fixing track systems It is essential that the tops of each track are at exactly the same height, otherwise the shelves will not be level.

Make a pencil mark on the wall at the required height of the first track. Hold the track against the wall and mark the position of the top screw hole with a pencil. Drill and plug the wall and use a 50mm (2in) long screw to attach the track to the wall. Do not tighten the screw, let the track hang from it so that it swings like a pendulum. When it stops swinging it is vertical: hold it against the wall and mark the remaining screw holes. Drill and plug the holes and attach the track with No 8 or No 10 gauge screws.

Place a batten with a perfectly straight edge on top of the attached track, level it with a spirit level and mark the position for the top of the next track. Fix the second track as for the first. Continue fitting further tracks in the same way.

On a wall with an irregular surface, use packing pieces of thin hardboard behind one or more screw holes to keep the track from distorting.

Braising

Cooking meats and vegetables by moist heat

Braising is a combined roasting and stewing technique, which tenderises tough cuts of meat and brings out the flavours of vegetables, or blends them with other ingredients.

To braise meat or poultry, first brown in oil, butter or fat over medium heat, using a heavy pan – cast iron if you have one. Remove from the heat and add seasoning and water, stock or wine to half the depth of the food. For extra flavour, place the meat on a bed of chopped vegetables before adding the liquid.

Cover the pan with a close-fitting lid to prevent moisture from escaping. Simmer at low heat on a hob or in the oven at 160-170°C (325°F) or at gas mark 3, for two or three hours, until the meat can be pierced easily with a fork.

To braise vegetables, do not brown them, just dot them with butter and add enough liquid to cover the bottom of the pan to a depth of about 6-13mm (¼-½in).

Brake failure

Slowing and stopping in an emergency

If your brakes fail under normal driving conditions – for example, when you try to slow down for traffic signals – you should still be able to stop safely if you act quickly.

Apply the handbrake smoothly and at the same time pump the footbrake pedal in the hope that some hydraulic pressure will be restored to the main braking system. Keep a firm grip on the steering wheel with your other hand, because applying the handbrake may lock the rear wheels and cause the back of the car to slide sideways. If the rear wheels lock, ease off the handbrake.

As the handbrake slows the car, change down progressively through the gears, using the engine to help in the slowing process as you engage the lower gears. If the car has an automatic gearbox, move the selector level to L (low) or 2 (second gear).

If the handbrake and low gears are not slowing you enough to avoid an accident, try to steer the car up a slope or bank, or along a hedge or fence. This should help to slow it further and perhaps avoid a collision – even at the expense of damage to your vehicle.

Handbrake failure If the handbrake fails when you stop on your way up a steep hill, moving off again without first rolling backwards will be difficult. It can be done, however, by using the 'heel and toe' technique.

Keep the footbrake depressed by your

toe and swivel your foot so that the heel can be used to depress the accelerator. At the same time, select first gear and use your other foot to let in the clutch. As the car moves forward, remove your toe from the brake and accelerate normally.

Checking the brakes Regular weekly checks on the car's braking system should eliminate the chance of total brake failure while driving.

A leak in the hydraulic system, causing a loss of brake fluid, is the commonest cause. Check the fluid level in the master cylinder reservoir – usually mounted on or near the bulkhead of the engine compartment. Check it also before setting out on a long journey.

If at any time the level has dropped appreciably, there is a leak in the system which must be remedied by a garage as soon as possible.

Brass rubbing

Using a creative hobby to record history

More than 7000 medieval brasses survive in Britain's churches. Usually they are full-length portraits of the person commemorated, and so give a unique record of the costumes and heraldic symbols of the times.

And they can be copied faithfully on paper by brass rubbing.

Materials For a beginner, lining paper, as sold by home decorating shops, is adequate for most brasses. You will also need masking tape to hold the paper in place, two dusters, a soft brush and a cake or stick of hard, black wax, called heel ball, obtainable from an artists' suppliers or cobblers.

Finding brasses Any medieval church is likely to have monumental brasses, but before rubbing you must get permission

Rubbing Rub across the engraved lines with even pressure. Use the thumb as a barrier at the edge to stop the outline from blurring.

from the vicar or rector, or the dean in the case of a cathedral. It is best to ask in advance, either by letter or telephone, for several reasons: permission may be refused; others may be rubbing on the same day; or the church may be locked and the vicar away if you arrive unannounced. A small fee or a contribution in the church box may be requested. Many churches will not allow brass rubbing at weekends.

How to rub Clean the brass thoroughly with a duster and soft brush – even a small speck of grit can ruin the rubbing.

Cut a sheet of paper large enough to cover the brass and secure it to the floor or wall with short strips of masking tape. Make sure the paper is stretched absolutely flat, and firmly fixed.

Begin by rubbing the heel ball at the centre of the brass, applying a quite firm and even pressure. Rub across, not along, engraved lines. When you reach the edges of the detail, use the thumb of your other hand as a barrier to stop the heel ball going over the edge, otherwise the finished outline is blurred.

When the rubbing is complete, polish it with a soft cloth, remove the masking tape and carefully lift the paper. Dust off any loose flakes of heel ball and sweep up any flakes from the church floor. The rubbing can be framed – see PICTURE FRAMING, or simply pinned up to make an attractive wall decoration.

Bread-making

Baking fresh and crusty loaves

Successful home bread-making depends not only on using the correct ingredients in their correct quantities, but on very careful preparation and good kneading.

Most types of plain flour can be used, but the best is 'strong' flour, obtainable from grocers and supermarkets. This contains more gluten and is specially ground for bread-making so that it will give bread of light and open texture.

White bread The ingredients for making four loaves are: 1.4kg (3lb) of plain strong flour; 3-4 level teaspoons of salt; 25g (1oz) of lard; 15g ($\frac{1}{2}$oz) of dried yeast; 850ml ($1\frac{1}{2}$ pints) of warm water less 3 tablespoons.

Sift the flour and salt together into a large bowl. If you are using easy-blend dried yeast, mix it with the flour. Measure the salt carefully – too much will give the bread a heavy or uneven texture. Rub the lard into the mixture with the fingertips.

For dried yeast granules, dissolve 1 teaspoon of sugar in 285ml ($\frac{1}{2}$ pint) of warm water, then sprinkle in the granules. Stir and then leave for about 15 minutes to become frothy. Make a well

in the centre of the flour and pour in the yeasty water and the remaining plain water. Stir to combine the ingredients.

Work the dough with one hand until it leaves the sides of the bowl clean. Lift the dough onto a lightly floured surface and knead it for at least 10 minutes.

Kneading develops the gluten which makes the dough rise. Gather the dough into a ball with the fingertips and fold it downwards. Press down and away from your body with the palm of one hand. Give the dough a quarter-turn and continue kneading until it is no longer sticky and feels firm and springy. If you are in doubt about whether you have kneaded long enough, remember it is better to knead too much than too little.

After kneading, shape the dough into a round, put it in a lightly oiled polythene bag and set it aside to rise until it has doubled in size. It is best to let it rise slowly, at a low temperature over a long period – about 2 hours at normal room temperature, 6 hours in a cool room or larder and 24 hours in a refrigerator.

Divide the risen dough into four equal portions and knead it again for 2-3 minutes. Place each portion in a greased loaf tin, score the dough lightly along

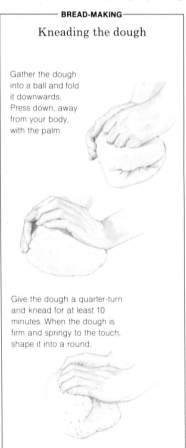

BREAD-MAKING

Kneading the dough

Gather the dough into a ball and fold it downwards. Press down, away from your body, with the palm.

Give the dough a quarter-turn and knead for at least 10 minutes. When the dough is firm and springy to the touch, shape it into a round.

the top with a knife, and brush lightly with salted water. Place the tins in lightly oiled polythene bags and leave in a warm place until the dough rises – called proving – to the top of the tins.

Remove the bags, brush the dough again with salted water and set the tins on baking trays.

Bake in the centre of the oven, pre-heated to 230°C (450°F – gas mark 8) for about 30 minutes, or until the crust is deep golden-brown. For really crusty bread, remove the loaves from their tins and bake for a further 5-10 minutes. Leave the bread to cool on a wire rack.

Baking wholemeal bread The procedure is basically the same as for white bread, but use wholemeal flour instead of strong flour, and add a level tablespoon of caster sugar to the flour and salt.

Breast examination

Checking for lumps and other irregularities

All women should examine their breasts once a month, and a doctor should be consulted about any abnormalities as soon as possible. Most lumps in the breast are *not* malignant, but early detection and medical treatment are advisable.

The best time for the examination is immediately after a period or, if you have had the menopause, on the first day of each month. Allow yourself plenty of time to carry out a thorough and unhurried examination.

Before carrying out a full examination, undress to the waist, stand before a mirror with your arms at your sides, and look for any visible lump, depression or difference in skin texture.

Note the size and shape of each breast, and if there are any irregularities report these to your doctor. In future examinations look for any unusual changes or differences – such as swelling or discoloration of either breast. Next, carry out the examination steps shown in the illustration (right).

Finally, if you buy a new bra of your usual make and size, and it feels uncomfortable, have a check-up – it could indicate a swelling.

Breast feeding

The natural way for mother and baby

There is evidence that breast-fed babies get more nourishment and emotional security than bottle-fed ones, and that they are less prone to gastroenteritis and cot death. Most women – 95 per cent – are able to breast feed successfully.

The most natural time for a feed is whenever the baby demands it. This may be up to a dozen times a day during the first couple of weeks, but should then settle down to a feed once every three or four hours.

When feeding, make sure that both you and your baby are comfortable. Wear clothes that open easily at the front and choose a low chair which allows your feet to be flat on the floor and supports your back. Sit upright and cradle the baby so that his mouth is level with a nipple, supporting the head with your elbow or forearm.

Gently stroke the baby's cheek that is nearest to the nipple. The baby's mouth

will turn towards it and begin to suck. Make sure the whole nipple is in the baby's mouth – sucking just the end of it closes the nipple openings and stops milk flowing.

If the baby seems to have trouble making contact with your breast, hold the breast between forefinger and second finger at the edge of the areola – the darker area surrounding the nipple – then gently press and guide the nipple into the mouth.

Use both breasts at each feed, transferring the baby from one to the other after 10-20 minutes. The baby will stop feeding when full, so do not worry if some feeds do not last as long as others. If only

---

BREAST EXAMINATION

Looking and feeling for possible warning signs

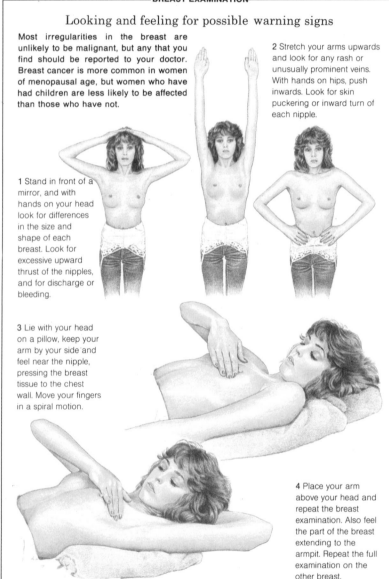

Most irregularities in the breast are unlikely to be malignant, but any that you find should be reported to your doctor. Breast cancer is more common in women of menopausal age, but women who have had children are less likely to be affected than those who have not.

1 Stand in front of a mirror, and with hands on your head look for differences in the size and shape of each breast. Look for excessive upward thrust of the nipples, and for discharge or bleeding.

2 Stretch your arms upwards and look for any rash or unusually prominent veins. With hands on hips, push inwards. Look for skin puckering or inward turn of each nipple.

3 Lie with your head on a pillow, keep your arm by your side and feel near the nipple, pressing the breast tissue to the chest wall. Move your fingers in a spiral motion.

4 Place your arm above your head and repeat the breast examination. Also feel the part of the breast extending to the armpit. Repeat the full examination on the other breast.

a little milk is taken at one feed, the difference will be made up at the next.

To remove the baby from your breast, slip your finger between the areola and the baby's lips, or gently pull down the baby's chin.

Bricklaying

*Learning basic techniques for
small building jobs*

Bricklaying is a skilled trade, and a major project such as building a house extension would be beyond most amateurs. But there are lesser jobs – building a garden wall or bricking-in a fireplace, for example – that can be undertaken with confidence by the average handyman. Before starting, however, you need to know the types and sizes of bricks available, the tools needed and the methods of laying used for differing jobs.

Types and sizes The cheapest bricks are *commons*, suitable only for using where they will not be damaged by frost, unless covered by rendering or plaster. *Facing bricks* are the most widely used for external work, or *engineering bricks* for a durable finish impervious to water.

The standard brick size is 215mm (8⅝in) long, 65mm (2⅝in) high and 103mm (4⅛in) wide. The end face of a brick is called the *header* and the long side the *stretcher*. When bricks are cut across their width they are called *bats*, further categorised by the size, for example a half-bat or three-quarter bat.

Types of bond All brickwork must be bonded, which simply means that the bricks are laid so as to give all parts of the structure equal strength and durability. Each row of bricks is called a course, and the vertical joints are staggered in alternate courses, so as to transmit the load evenly.

The simplest bond, in a wall of single-brick thickness known as a half-brick wall, is called *stretcher bond*, because the bricks are laid end to end with their stretcher faces showing. Double-brick thickness walls, called full brick, are built either with a *Flemish bond* of alternating stretchers and headers in one course, or an *English bond* of three courses of stretchers alternated with one row of headers.

An attractive garden wall can be built using *open bond*, sometimes called honeycomb, which is basically a stretcher bond with spaces between the bricks.

Tools A trowel for laying MORTAR and a board, called a *spot board*, to hold the mortar. You can make a single spot board using a piece of 300mm (12in) square plywood nailed to 25mm (1in) battens so that it is easier to lift. If the courses are to be laid to a height of 610mm (2ft) or more, you need a spirit level with separate bubbles for checking both vertical and horizontal alignment. Stretch a length of string between two stakes set either end of the wall, as a guide – see also LEVELLING.

At some point you will have to cut bricks, for which you need a bolster chisel with a 100mm (4in) wide blade, and a club hammer.

Types of bond used for brick walls

For walls half a brick thick – 100mm (4in) – *stretcher bond* is commonly used. *English bond* and *Flemish bond* are used for 215mm (8⅝in) thick walls, though Flemish bond is stronger and dearer. *Open bond* is a decorative stretcher bond.

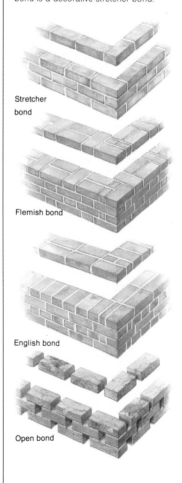

Stretcher bond

Flemish bond

English bond

Open bond

Building a garden wall, and the tools you will need

Have all the necessary tools to hand before starting: a spot board for the mortar; spirit level and string line for levelling; a mortar trowel and, for cutting bricks, a club hammer and cold chisel.

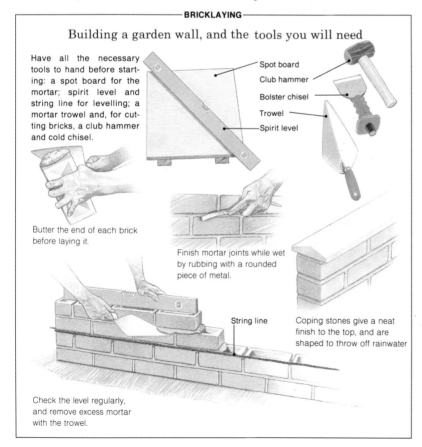

Spot board
Club hammer
Bolster chisel
Trowel
Spirit level

Butter the end of each brick before laying it.

Finish mortar joints while wet by rubbing with a rounded piece of metal.

Coping stones give a neat finish to the top, and are shaped to throw off rainwater

String line

Check the level regularly, and remove excess mortar with the trowel.

Laying If you are building a garden wall in stretcher bond and up to 1.2m (4ft) high, it will need a foundation three times the width of the wall and laid at least 460mm (18in) deep. Fill the foundation with CONCRETE consisting of 1 part cement and 4 parts mixed aggregate.

When the concrete has hardened, lay a bed of mortar and flatten it with the trowel to about 19mm ($\frac{3}{4}$in) thick, so the brick weight will press it down to 10mm ($\frac{3}{8}$in). Butter one end of a brick with mortar and lay it flat side down. Butter the end of the next brick to the same thickness, and lay it against the first brick. Tap it into position with the trowel handle. Continue along the course, checking frequently for level and tapping down any bricks standing above the level.

Start the next course with half a brick. Place a brick with its flat face uppermost and mark off the halfway line with a pencil and rule. Score the line with the bolster, then rest the blade on the line with the handle slightly tilted and give it a sharp blow with the club hammer. The brick should break cleanly in half.

Lay the course in the same way as the first, trowelling mortar into the indented top – called the *frog* – of each brick. As each course is laid, clean off all surplus mortar at the joints with the edge of the trowel. Before the mortar sets, smooth the joints with a piece of piping or an old metal bucket handle to make a neat finish – see POINTING. For the final course, lay the bricks frog side down or lay a course of precast concrete coping slabs for weather protection.

A half-brick garden wall up to 1.2m (4ft) high must be supported by piers at each end and every 1.8m (6ft). This can be done by setting two headers side by side to project from one side of the wall, then laying stretchers across them on alternate courses. Use three-quarter and half bat stretchers to alternate joints.

Bricking-in a fireplace The bricks can be laid directly on the hearth, and should be recessed by about 3mm ($\frac{1}{8}$in) to allow for a final finish of plaster. Lay an AIR BRICK in the second course for ventilation. Fill any gap at the top of the brickwork with mortar.

Bring-and-buy sales

Organising profitable fund-raising events

Bring-and-buy sales, like jumble sales and bazaars, are a popular way of raising funds. Provided any proceeds go to a recognised good cause – say the local church or a charity – and are not purely for someone's personal profit, there are few legal formalities.

Traditionally, those who attend donate home-produced items for sale – for example, sweets, cakes, flowers, vegetables, plants and handicrafts, which tend to dominate the stalls.

Advance planning Start planning at least four months ahead. Choose a sale organiser and several assistants, but not so many that arguments and confusion develop.

Decide on the site (often, a church or school hall), the date and the opening time. Try not to clash with other local events and remember that broadcasts of major events such as the Cup Final or the Grand National are likely to keep people at home.

Appoint people to organise publicity and accounts. There must be a record of all costs, such as hire of premises, printing bills and petty cash 'floats' for the stallholders.

Booking a hall If the sale is to be on private property, including church or school halls, book it well in advance from the owners or administrators. Let them know if you wish to hold a lottery – some halls do not allow it – and check that there are adequate kitchen facilities if you intend having a refreshment stall.

Most halls charge a fee unless the event is directly connected with them. Charge for admission – anything from 10p to about £1 – to recoup the fee and extras such as tea and biscuits for stall attendants. Any surplus can boost the profits.

You do not normally need police permission, but it is both useful and courteous to tell them well in advance. If necessary, they can help with car-parking arrangements.

Advertising and publicity Effective advertising need cost little. Many local newspapers do not charge for notices of fund-raising events – but they may not appear until a day or so before the sale.

Handmade posters, put up a week or two in advance, will arouse interest. Organise a children's competition for the best poster; award a small prize and you will have as many as you need.

Persuade friends and shopkeepers to put the posters in their windows, but remember that billposting on private property without the owner's permission is an offence. Ask to use school, church and public library notice boards.

Setting up stalls Church and school halls usually have trestle or folding tables that you can decorate as stalls. Otherwise, hire what you need – look under 'Furniture Hire and Rental' in *Yellow Pages*.

Draw a plan showing the position of the stalls. Allow space in front of and between them, and see that they do not block exits or lavatory doors.

Tickets, money and prices Tickets to be sold in advance need to be printed or duplicated; they should show the time and place of the sale. It is often simpler and cheaper to sell tickets at the door. In that case, a book or two of numbered tickets, available from most stationers, is adequate.

Pricing the goods on sale will depend partly on the neighbourhood, but also on the number of customers expected, and on whether any costs are not covered by ticket sales. A rough rule-of-thumb is that no item should be priced at more than half of what its equivalent would cost in a shop. But set arbitrary prices for handicrafts such as paintings or embroidery.

Keep the prices simple – say £1.50 for large sponge cakes, £1 for smaller ones, and 75p for half-a-dozen of the smallest. Show prices clearly on tickets and mark prices down towards the end of the sale, to try to sell every item.

Special attractions No official permission is needed for 'small lotteries' and attractions such as tombola or similar RAFFLES, run in conjunction with fund-raising events. 'Small' means that no more than £50 can be set aside to buy prizes, but they can be worth more if they are donated.

Lottery tickets may be sold only at the events, and any draw must take place during it. If you are in doubt about the legality of a lottery, get advice from your local council.

Live or recorded performances of music still in copyright need permission from the Performing Right Society, and may involve paying a royalty. The owner of the hall may already have a licence from the society.

A fee is also payable to tape or record manufacturers, but is waived (though permission must still be obtained) if the proceeds go to charity. See also GARAGE SALES.

Broken bones

Emergency treatment for fractures

Evidence of a broken bone may be as obvious as a fragment of the bone showing through the skin or a limb being obviously deformed. But it may be less evident – for example, prolonged pain at the point of an injury caused by a fall or a blow.

Even if you only suspect a fracture, send for an ambulance immediately. Do not move the injured person unless absolutely necessary – especially if you suspect a spinal injury, as this could cause further, and possibly fatal, damage.

While awaiting an ambulance, give emergency first aid, for severe BLEEDING or SHOCK. Do not give the casualty anything to drink. If you have to move the injured person – either because the ambulance is delayed or because you are advised to take the person to hospital yourself – secure the fracture so that the bone cannot move.

Securing a broken limb Tie a fractured leg to the sound leg with scarves, neckties or any other available materials, using padding material between ankles, knees and thigh. If a knee is broken, do not try to move it. Support it with a cushion or folded jacket. To immobilise a fractured arm, support in a sling and strap it to the body – see SLINGS.

Do not bend a broken arm by force. If it will not bend naturally, lay the casualty down in a comfortable position, put padding between the injured arm and the body and – avoiding the fractured spot – strap the arm to the body with three pieces of wide material.

Treating a fractured rib A simple rib fracture will cause sharp CHEST PAINS when the casualty breathes deeply or coughs. It can be eased by putting the arm on the injured side in an arm sling.

Difficulty in breathing and frothy blood at the mouth, however, indicate a more serious injury. Get an ambulance quickly. If possible, the injured person should lean towards the injured side of the body to help blood to drain away from the sound lung.

Budgeting

How to manage your money

A budget is a plan to organise your money to meet current expenses, to build up savings and to plan ahead. You can draw up the plan on a home COMPUTER, but all you really need is a ruled school exercise book, some scrap paper and perhaps a pocket calculator.

The task is simply to list your expected income and expenditure for a year ahead. Some people like to start their 'financial year' on January 1; others to start with the year on April 6. Keep a month-by-month check on how your actual income and expenditure is comparing with the forecast – and adjust your spending if necessary.

Keep your forecast figures separate from the actual income and spending figures, by using the front or back of the book or different coloured pens.

Forecasting income Using spare paper, list and add up your anticipated income from all sources for the year ahead – salary, pension and so on – counting the amount after income tax (see INCOME TAX RETURNS), NATIONAL INSURANCE and other deductions. If you are self-employed, work part-time or take seasonal jobs, base your estimated income on that of the previous year – if you earn more, the extra will be a bonus.

Add on any other amounts you regu-larly receive, such as interest on BUILD-ING SOCIETY savings, or share dividends.

You can divide the income into equal monthly parts – but beware of doing this if you receive it at irregular intervals.

Estimating expenditure Use last year's accounts, or paid bills and receipts, to help forecast expenses. Think if there may be any new items of expense looming. The expenses you should budget for are fixed costs, variable costs and savings.

Fixed costs These include rent or MORT-GAGE repayments, COUNCIL TAX, interest charges, HIRE PURCHASE instalments and, perhaps, life or medical INSURANCE. They also include the standing charges in gas, electricity and telephone bills.

Fixed costs are usually payable at regular intervals – monthly, quarterly, half-yearly or annually – so it is easy to decide which months to allocate them to in your budget. Make allowance for increases – in rents, service charges and insurance premiums, which tend to rise.

Variable costs These include daily living costs – heat, light and phone bills; food and household supplies; newspapers and magazines; fares and transport (including car insurance and repairs); clothes; house repairs and improvements; entertainment and holidays.

Most householders keep lighting and heating bills, so it is easy to enter the amounts in the appropriate month in your forecast. If you do not have details of previous spending on other items, such as food and clothing, keep track of it for a few months, and work out a monthly average to include in the budget. Allow for inflation at the current rate as a rough guide to estimate probable price increases.

Savings Try to build regular SAVINGS into your expenditure estimate. The money may be for a specific purpose – holidays, clothing, new household equipment – or it may simply be a nest-egg for emergencies, or perhaps INVESTING.

Adjusting spending Add up all the forecast spending for the period and subtract that total from the total income. Any money left over can be added to the savings allocation.

If expenses exceed income, see where you can make cuts. You cannot reduce fixed costs without changing your lifestyle, but look again at the variable costs and be prepared to reduce the savings provision.

You should now have a balanced budget, and you can transfer these final figures, broken down by month, to your notebook or ledger. Present them so that you can easily compare the forecast and actual figures.

BROKEN BONES

Body splinting a fractured arm or leg

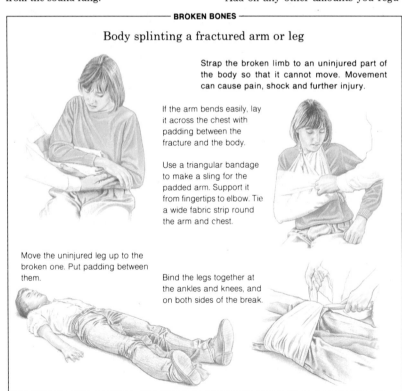

Strap the broken limb to an uninjured part of the body so that it cannot move. Movement can cause pain, shock and further injury.

If the arm bends easily, lay it across the chest with padding between the fracture and the body.

Use a triangular bandage to make a sling for the padded arm. Support it from fingertips to elbow. Tie a wide fabric strip round the arm and chest.

Move the uninjured leg up to the broken one. Put padding between them.

Bind the legs together at the ankles and knees, and on both sides of the break.

People with income from many sources, such as from a part-time business, may find it easier to use a double page for each month, entering income on one page, with spending on the facing page. See also BOOKKEEPING.

Building blocks

Using a convenient alternative to bricks

Standard building blocks are six times as big as bricks, so you can lay them almost six times as quick – but the same care must be taken as with BRICKLAYING.

Use them to build a wall or partition, either by themselves or combined with brickwork. They are made of precast concrete aggregates in various weights, densities, shapes and sizes.

Common blocks These are often called breeze blocks, and are the best choice for general use. Made of a lightweight aggregate of clinker from industrial furnaces, they accept nails and screws and are easily cut. Use this type of block for internal structures such as partition walls and the inner side of cavity walls.

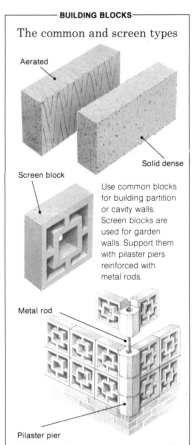

— BUILDING BLOCKS —

The common and screen types

Aerated

Solid dense

Screen block

Use common blocks for building partition or cavity walls. Screen blocks are used for garden walls. Support them with pilaster piers reinforced with metal rods.

Metal rod

Pilaster pier

The nominal size is 450 × 225mm (18 × 9in) – actual size, 440 × 215mm ($17\frac{5}{8}$ × $8\frac{5}{8}$in) – and thicknesses range from 50 to 220mm (2 to $8\frac{3}{4}$in).

Decorative walling blocks Concrete blocks made with an aggregate of crushed stone to simulate natural stone can be used for exterior walls in the same way as bricks. They are made in a range of sizes, but are usually larger than bricks.

Screen blocks Among the most popular precast concrete block is the pierced or openwork type – use it for jobs such as building a screen wall. The most common size is 300 × 100mm (12 × 4in), and there is an attractive range of decorative patterns. Some blocks each have a single design, some form a pattern when laid with others, and some have shaped outlines.

Screen blocks are not bonded, as bricks are – lay them in line to give a recurring pattern. Otherwise the method of laying is much the same as for bricklaying, but use stronger MORTAR. A wall built using screen blocks needs pilaster piers to support it at each end and every 3m (10ft).

Building permits

Obtaining approval for major alterations

If you want to put up a new building, or extend or structurally alter an existing one, anywhere other than inner London, you need approval from the Building Regulations Department of your local district council (regional or island council in some parts of Scotland). The approval covers safety, materials, habitability and construction standards.

If you go ahead without permission, you could be prosecuted or face an order to pull the structure down. The work may also need PLANNING PERMISSION. Separate applications for both planning permission and Building Regulations approval have to be made to the council on special forms obtainable from its offices.

You will need building permission for projects such as building an extension or converting a loft, for example, and perhaps for building a garage.

Building permission is not needed for general repairs, for some small buildings, for example a shed covering less than 30m² (323sq ft) made of non-combustible materials and sited more than 1m (3ft 3in) from the boundary, and for boundary walls and fences (although those may need planning permission). However, if you are in any doubt seek the council's advice – particularly if the work affects heating and sanitary systems and internal or external drainage.

Submitting an application The simplest method is to submit a Building Notice on a special form available from the council, at least two days before work is to be started. This is often sufficient for a small project, and detailed plans are not needed. If you are not sure, check your drawings and ideas with the local Building Control Officer well before submitting the notice.

For a more involved project, you may need to submit an application accompanied by a full set of working drawings plans, and elevations, so prepare them well in advance. Make it at least five weeks before you intend to start the work – preferably earlier.

When you apply for building permission, you will be charged a fee, related to the cost of the work and covering the costs of the local authority inspector who comes to examine the work during the course of construction.

If your scheme is turned down – either because it does not comply with rules or has not been properly prepared – you have little chance of winning an appeal. You will have to start again.

However, a local authority may agree to relax rules if, for example, it is persuaded that the materials you plan to use are reasonable, though not recognised in the regulations. If the council does not agree, you can appeal to the Department of the Environment (in Scotland, the Secretary of State for Scotland). The council will explain how to do that, but you will also need the advice of an ARCHITECT or building expert.

Inspecting the work During the work, and after completion, you must notify the building inspector at various stages, so that he can check that you are not contravening the Building Regulations. For example, you must give at least 24 hours' notice before laying concrete or other material over a site.

The building inspector can order work to be opened up for checking if required notice has not been given.

In London Inner London, the area once covered by the London County Council, has its own building laws, dating from the 1930s, and bylaws, though planning rules are the same as in the rest of the country. The applicant is required to prove his ability to meet certain minimum requirements regarding the safety and strength of the proposed building. The district surveyor for the area supervises the scheme as it is being carried out, charging a fee related to the cost of the project.

The plans must be submitted to the surveyor at least 48 hours before work begins. But, in practice, discussions start much earlier, to ensure that the scheme is at least broadly acceptable. Some details of the rules are also different.

Building societies

What they can offer; choosing and using them

Building societies offer profitable savings schemes, using the funds raised to finance MORTGAGES to those who wish to buy their own homes. Most societies offer a range of savings accounts, but in general the more you invest and the longer you can afford to leave it invested, the higher the interest rate you get. Their range of mortgage schemes enables borrowers to choose the arrangement they find most suitable.

Building societies can now offer a wide range of financial help besides loans on property, with some offering full banking services such as cheque books, credit and cash cards, standing orders, personal loans and OVERDRAFTS. Others are offering INSURANCE and a chance to deal in stocks and shares (see INVESTING). Some societies have even moved into estate agency services.

Certain societies have branch offices equipped with automatic tills which allow instant cash withdrawals from your account. In these, and other areas, building societies are now competing with banks – see BANK ACCOUNTS.

Building societies in general are more inclined to favour mortgage applicants who already have savings accounts with them, particularly at times when the society's funds are low.

Choosing a savings account Most building societies offer several different methods of saving. The interest paid on each is displayed in their branch offices. See also SAVING.

Ordinary share account Sometimes called 'paid up shares', an ordinary account can be opened with a minimum investment of £1. Withdrawals can be made at any branch at any time, though a few days' notice may be required for a large cash sum.

Subscription shares You are asked to invest a fixed monthly amount, usually a minimum of £1 and a maximum of £50. Withdrawals can be made at any time, and the interest rate is slightly higher than for an ordinary share account.

Tiered account Each building society has its own name for this type of account, but all work on the same principle, which is simply that the more you invest the higher the interest paid.

An initial investment of £500 is normally required, and higher interest bands start at £2000, £5000 and £10,000. If the account falls to below £500, interest is paid at the same rate as an ordinary share account.

Some societies allow any amount to be withdrawn at any time; others require notice, and limit the amount that can be withdrawn at any one time.

Term shares A lump sum is invested – usually a minimum of £500 or £1000 – for an agreed period of two, three or four years. Interest is paid to the investor.

Some societies arrange monthly interest payments, but the invested amount cannot be withdrawn until the agreed period has been completed – except in the event of the investor's death.

Individual building societies also offer other saving methods as well as those described above. For example, a 90 day account pays a good rate of interest but requires three months' notice for withdrawals.

Interest This is paid after the society has deducted income tax at the basic rate, though taxpayers on a higher rate must pay the difference to the Inland Revenue.

Non-taxpayers – many pensioners and children, for example – cannot reclaim the amount deducted for tax. Some other forms of saving would probably pay them better – see INVESTING and NATIONAL SAVINGS.

Interest is calculated at per cent/ annum, but may be credited to the investor's account twice yearly or, in some cases, monthly. If the interest is not withdrawn it is compounded – that is, interest is paid on the interest.

Opening and using an account Formalities are few – just take your initial deposit, cash or a cheque, to a building society branch and complete a simple form. You will be given or sent a passbook, in which deposits, withdrawals and interest are recorded. You must produce the book every time you make a deposit or withdrawal.

Deposits made by cheque cannot be withdrawn until the cheque has been cleared – normally in ten days. If you make a deposit using your own cheque book, the cheque must be made out to the building society, not to yourself. You can make a withdrawal by cheque made out to anyone you name – for example, to pay a bill – without charge.

Bulb forcing

Brightening winter with indoor blooms

You can bring a splash of springtime colour to midwinter rooms by forcing bulbs of narcissi, hyacinths and tulips, and crocus corms – see also BULBS, CORMS AND TUBERS. Forcing can make them bloom at Christmas – well before they would flower outdoors.

Nurseries and garden centres sell bulbs specially prepared for forcing. Buy the largest of each variety and make sure that the bulbs are clean and free from blemishes. The bulbs should feel hard, and tulip bulbs should have their brown tunic intact. Untreated bulbs can also be forced, although they bloom several weeks later than the treated kinds. A mixture of both types gives an extended indoor display until the garden awakens.

Set bulbs for forcing in September or October. Plant them directly into special decorative containers or use ordinary flower pots – but pots will need to stand in saucers or trays when they are brought inside, to stop furniture being damaged by water seeping from the drainage holes.

Containers without drainage holes should be filled with bulb fibre – a mixture of peat, broken oyster shells and charcoal. If you use flower pots, cover the drainage holes with crocks (bits of broken pot) and put a thin layer of coarse peat, moss or garden soil above them. Fill the rest of each pot with JOHN INNES COMPOST (No 1 potting).

Small bulbs, such as crocuses, should be set so that their tips are 25mm (1in) below the rim of the pot or bowl. Cover the tips completely with fibre or potting compost, but leave a gap of 13mm ($\frac{1}{2}$in) between the surface of the filling and the rim of the container.

Set large bulbs, such as hyacinths, so that their tips protrude slightly above the rim of the container or pot. Again, the filling should be 13mm below the rim. Use a deep container to allow for root development.

Place tulip and narcissi bulbs almost touching each other, and barely covered in compost. Space smaller bulbs and corms about 25mm (1in) apart and cover to a depth of 13-19mm ($\frac{1}{2}$-$\frac{3}{4}$in).

Fill the gap between surface and rim with water; that is enough to ensure that the fibre or compost becomes thoroughly moist. Wrap each container with a sheet or two of newspaper, covering all of it, including the top.

Then put the containers in a dark place. It should be cool – 4-7°C (39-45°F) – but not liable to frost. A shed, cellar or garage is often ideal. Otherwise bury them about 150mm (6in) deep in the garden and cover the replaced soil with a mulch of straw or grass cuttings – see MULCHING.

This creates an artificial winter for the plants. It should last about 8-12 weeks for untreated hyacinths, crocuses and daffodils, and other forms of narcissi; about 16 weeks for tulips – two or three weeks less for treated bulbs. If possible, inspect the plants occasionally. Make sure that fibre or compost is moist, but do not over-water.

Into the light When shoots of 25-50mm (1-2in) appear, or when the specified time has elapsed for buried plants, bring the pots or containers into a cool room indoors – about 10°C (50°F) – and place them out of direct light, removing their newspaper wrappings.

Keep them there until the shoots are 100-150mm (4-6in) long – normally in about two weeks. Then move them to a warmer, sunnier spot until coloured flower buds appear. Keep the fibre or compost slightly moist.

Once the flower buds take on colour, the bulbs are ready to display. Prolong flowering by placing them out of direct light and in a cool room at night.

Bulbs, corms and tubers

How they differ . . . and how to raise them

Bulbs – such as daffodils, tulips and lilies – are underground buds of tightly overlapping fleshy leaves or leaf bases, protected by dry, scaly outer layers.

Corms – such as crocuses, anemones and gladioli – are shaped like thick discs, formed from the swollen bases of plant stems. Unlike scaly bulbs, they are a solid mass of starchy material. Old corms shrivel as the food in them is used up by the developing plant.

Tubers, such as POTATOES, BEGONIAS and DAHLIAS, are swollen underground roots or stems. They produce shoots which in turn yield new plants.

Choosing for planting Bulbs and corms can bring year-round colour to the garden. Some members of the *Galanthus* (snowdrop) family produce blooms from October to March.

Crocuses, narcissi and tulips brighten spring, gladioli and lilies high summer. In autumn, outdoor cyclamens, colchicums and hardy nerines bloom. Most popular bulbs and corms should be planted in September/October, including any you intend to bring indoors for winter flowering – see BULB FORCING.

Whether you are selecting bulbs, corms or tubers, choose the biggest you can afford – they are more likely to produce large and plentiful flowers – and make sure they are healthy. Reject any with cuts, soft spots, signs of rot or dry, dusty-looking patches.

Site and soil preparation Many bulbs and corms look their best in small clumps or in massed drifts, with one colour to an area. Plant them also in borders – particularly in front of evergreens – or set them in the grass of your lawn.

Large-flowered, stately plants need more room to display themselves to advantage – lilies, for example. Put them in sites where the soil is well drained, to prevent rot. Prepare new beds by turning the soil spade-deep and adding peat moss

or well-rotted COMPOST, and organic FERTILISER. Add sharp sand, too, if the ground is clayey.

Lay out bulbs and corms on top of the ground in the pattern you prefer. Dig a hole for each with a trowel or dibber; for tall plants such as lilies and gladioli insert a stake or cane to give support eventually. Sprinkle in a little bone meal. If you are planting clumps, make each hole wide enough to take four to six bulbs, each a few inches apart. Put in the bulbs and replace the soil mixed with a little fertiliser. Keep the area weed-free while they are growing.

Corms of gladioli must be lifted around mid-October, before the first hard frosts, for winter storage in a frostproof shed or greenhouse. Lift gladioli corms carefully with a fork and remove any soil sticking to them. Trim off the roots with secateurs, and reduce the main stem to about 25mm (1in). Put them in a dry, warm, airy place for about ten days. When completely dry, break off the old, shrivelled corms and store new corms in trays in a frostproof place.

BULBS, CORMS AND TUBERS

Mixing them for the best effect

Bring colour to the garden all year round by carefully selecting bulbs, corms or tubers that flower at different seasons.

Bulbs Choose the biggest you can afford. Reject any with cuts, rot or soft spots.

Daffodil (left) and lily are ideal for garden borders.

Anemones make fine border plants and look their best planted in clumps.

Corms Put them in sites where soil is well drained to prevent rot.

Tubers These are underground roots that produce shoots to form new plants.

Bunions

Treating and avoiding a common foot problem

Ill-fitting shoes are the most common cause of bunions – painful but harmless enlargement and displacement of the joint of the big toe. Some people are more likely to get them than others, suggesting that heredity may also play a part.

Bunions often afflict women entering middle age; high-heeled shoes with pointed toes make the condition worse. But, for both men and women, the seeds of trouble are frequently sown in childhood or the teenage and early adult years, if shoes worn then are not chosen carefully for fit. Young bones are relatively soft and can be easily deformed without noticeable pain. It is only later, when the bones harden completely, that the real discomfort starts.

In severe cases, bunions can be treated by a simple surgical operation. Usually, however, that is not necessary. Felt pads, obtainable from chemists, to wear over the bunion, and loose-fitting, low-heeled shoes will reduce the pain and often eliminate it entirely.

At the first sign of incipient bunions, use this treatment to prevent them from developing. If they become worse, consult your doctor, who may refer you to a chiropodist.

Burglar alarms

Protecting your home against intruders

There is a wide choice of burglar alarm systems; some are suitable for DIY installation and others need to be fitted professionally. There are two basic types: one sounds an alarm if someone tries to break into your home; the other detects an intruder inside the house.

When buying, make sure that the alarm is loud enough to be heard over a good distance. Anything with a sound level below 95 decibels will not be effective. Tell your neighbours about it and choose an alarm with a bell that will stop after about 20 minutes, to avoid any false alarm causing a nuisance.

Break-in alarms There are three basic elements in this type of system – the sensors, control unit and the alarm itself, which can be a bell, siren or buzzer. The alarm should be fitted prominently on an outside wall, where just seeing it can deter an intruder. Some alarms are set off if the cover is removed, or the wiring circuit is cut.

The sensors can be magnetic switches attached to doors and windows. Movement of the magnet operates a switch which sends an electrical signal to the control unit, which in turn actuates the

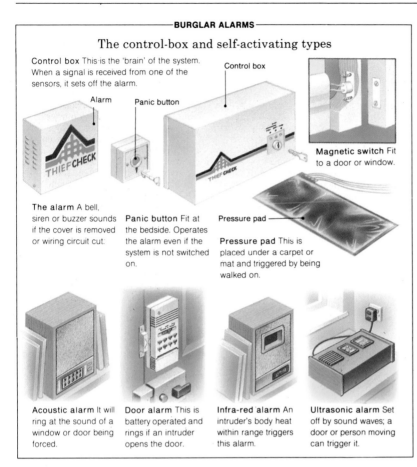

The control-box and self-activating types

Control box This is the 'brain' of the system. When a signal is received from one of the sensors, it sets off the alarm.

Alarm

Panic button

Control box

Magnetic switch Fit to a door or window.

The alarm A bell, siren or buzzer sounds if the cover is removed or wiring circuit cut.

Panic button Fit at the bedside. Operates the alarm even if the system is not switched on.

Pressure pad

Pressure pad This is placed under a carpet or mat and triggered by being walked on.

Acoustic alarm It will ring at the sound of a window or door being forced.

Door alarm This is battery operated and rings if an intruder opens the door.

Infra-red alarm An intruder's body heat within range triggers this alarm.

Ultrasonic alarm Set off by sound waves; a door or person moving can trigger it.

---

alarm. The power supply may be either mains or batteries, and some mains-operated systems have a battery back-up supply, so that if the power is cut off a battery will take over. The system is set with a key or by a code number, operated by a push-button panel.

There are small, single-box devices that will set off an alarm by movement of a door or the sound of a break-in. These are useful for a small flat or in a room which contains valuable possessions. This door alarm, battery operated, has a delay switch which allows several seconds for the householder to enter or leave without triggering it.

Internal alarms The simplest form of sensor is a pressure pad placed under a mat or carpet. These have the disadvantage that they wear with age and become unreliable. Also professional burglars will avoid walking where they are likely to be placed.

Far more sophisticated are ultrasonic and infra-red alarms. An ultrasonic alarm sends out sound waves which bounce back to it, and if anything interrupts the signal, such as a door being opened or a person moving, the alarm is triggered.

An intruder's body heat will set off an infra-red alarm, yet it is unaffected by a slowly warming radiator in the room. The unit can be installed in one room, or it can be extended throughout the house with extra infra-red detectors.

Avoiding false alarms Modern alarms are so sensitive that the risk of false alarms is inevitable. If you have an alarm fitted by a security firm, have it checked regularly.

Check a system you have installed yourself by rattling doors and windows to see that they are not loose – any slight movement may set off magnetic switches – and check pressure pads if fitted and replace them when necessary.

Burglar-proofing

Making your home 'as safe as houses'

Most burglars will enter a house only if it is easy to break into without making too much noise. If you make it difficult for a housebreaker he will go elsewhere. Fit good locks, bolts and latches on all doors and windows, and be security

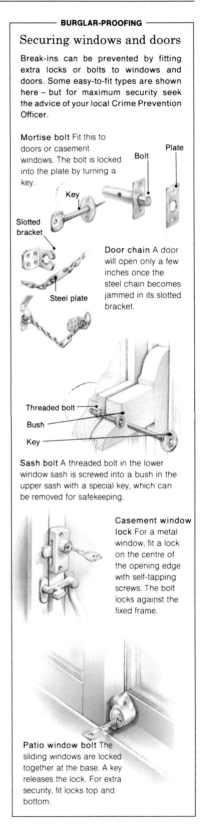

Securing windows and doors

Break-ins can be prevented by fitting extra locks or bolts to windows and doors. Some easy-to-fit types are shown here – but for maximum security seek the advice of your local Crime Prevention Officer.

Mortise bolt Fit this to doors or casement windows. The bolt is locked into the plate by turning a key.

Plate

Bolt

Key

Slotted bracket

Door chain A door will open only a few inches once the steel chain becomes jammed in its slotted bracket.

Steel plate

Threaded bolt

Bush

Key

Sash bolt A threaded bolt in the lower window sash is screwed into a bush in the upper sash with a special key, which can be removed for safekeeping.

Casement window lock For a metal window, fit a lock on the centre of the opening edge with self-tapping screws. The bolt locks against the fixed frame.

Patio window bolt The sliding windows are locked together at the base. A key releases the lock. For extra security, fit locks top and bottom.

conscious. Make sure every door and window is secured before going to bed or going out.

Types of locks and bolts Exterior doors have locks recessed into the door (mortise locks), or fitted to the inside face of the door (rim locks). The lock most commonly used for the front or main door is the cylinder nightlatch, which may be rim or mortise – see DOOR LOCKS.

Strong sliding bolts at the top and bottom of a door will resist a forced entry. They are best used in conjunction with a dead latch, or on a windowless door.

A chain bolt allows the door to open just enough to see who is calling, and the door must be shut again before the chain can be released.

Locking windows Burglars avoid breaking glass and will do so only to get at a window catch. But some windows, particularly older casement types, are easily opened with a strong blade or a screwdriver. A wide range of fittings is available to make windows more secure, including sash bolts, casement bolts and window stay locks.

Patio door lock This is mounted on the inner door and has a bolt that engages in a hole in the outer door. For maximum security, fit locks top and bottom – especially on aluminium-framed doors.

On wooden-framed French windows, mortise bolts engaging in the top frame and bottom still give reasonable security. Hinge bolts are a good precaution, especially on outward-opening doors – the bolts prevent the doors being lifted off their hinges.

Burns

Treating injuries from heat, chemicals and electricity

The emergency treatment for burns, caused by dry heat, and SCALDS, from boiling liquids or steam, is the same – cool them! In both cases, all but the most minor injuries need medical attention.

Remove the victim from the source of heat, taking care not to injure yourself in the process. If he has stopped breathing, give ARTIFICIAL RESPIRATION. If he is breathing but unconscious, clear his mouth with your fingers. Lie him in the RECOVERY POSITION.

Minor burns Treat minor burns by cooling the affected area in cold water for at least ten minutes, or until the pain has eased. This reduces the 'cooking' action. Cover the burn with a dry, sterile gauze pad or a piece of clean linen – see BANDAGING. Do not break any blisters that have formed, and do not apply butter, fats, creams or lotions.

Emergency action for minor and more serious burns

Deal promptly with burns to relieve pain and prevent infection. After first aid, take a young child, a sick or an old person to a doctor, however minor the burn. In serious cases, call an ambulance immediately.

Chemical eye burns With one hand hold the burnt eye open. For at least ten minutes flood the eye with gently running cold water or splash water on it from a basin or cup. Then get medical help.

Small burns Ease the pain of a superficial burn by cooling it under running water for at least ten minutes. Then cover the area of the burn with a sterile gauze dressing or a dry, non-fluffy material such as a clean handkerchief.

Deep burns Cool the burn, then cover lightly with a clean dressing – such as a pillowcase. Wrap a towel or similar material around the dressing to hold it in place.

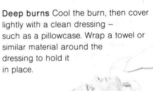

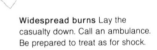

Widespread burns Lay the casualty down. Call an ambulance. Be prepared to treat as for shock.

Severe burns The severity of a burn is assessed according to the surface area of the skin affected, or the depth to which the burn has reached, or a combination of both. Deep burns are often less painful than those on the skin surface, because the nerve endings have been destroyed; the damaged area often looks charred, rather than scorched.

Cool severe burns with cold water, as above. Cover them lightly with sterile, non-fluffy dressings or a recently laundered cotton sheet while awaiting medical attention. Do not try to remove any charred clothing that is sticking to the skin. Remove any jewellery and loosen shoelaces, belt or waistband and collar. Raise burnt arms or legs above the level of the heart to reduce the blood flow to them. Put sterile gauze between burnt fingers or toes.

Any severe burn or scald needs urgent hospital treatment. As a rule this includes any deep burn or scald covering more than 9 per cent of the body. Treat for SHOCK. As a rough guide, each arm or the head represents 9 per cent of the skin area. The front or back of the torso, or each leg, represents 18 per cent.

If the victim is conscious, you may moisten his lips with cold water. Never try to give someone who is unconscious anything to drink.

Clothing on fire If someone's clothing catches fire, douse it with water or any other non-flammable liquid to put out the flames. If there is no suitable liquid to hand, use an article made of thick, non-synthetic fabric – a blanket or overcoat, for example – to wrap and smother the flames.

Electrical burns Remove the source of the electricity before touching the victim, or you may electrocute yourself. Switch off the power at the mains or plug, or pull the plug out of its socket by the insulated flex.

If you cannot switch the electricity off, use a dry wooden pole either to ease the live wire or appliance away from the casualty or to remove him from contact with the source – a live railway line, for example. Be ready to give artificial respiration if the victim stops breathing. Watch for signs of shock.

Chemical burns Treat burns from liquid chemicals by flushing with clean water for at least ten minutes before pausing to call for help. As you rinse the burn, remove any of the victim's clothing on which the chemical has spilt, taking care not to touch the area with your bare hands. Make sure that he is not lying, or sitting, in any of the chemical.

If the burn is from a dry chemical, brush as much of it away from the wound as you can, using a handkerchief, duster or soft brush and protecting your own hands. Remove contaminated clothing and check that the casualty is not lying, or sitting, in any of the chemical.

Chemicals in the eye should be flushed with water from a running tap, or splashed from a basin or other suitable container. Flush for at least ten minutes or until the pain eases. Lean the victim's head right back, preferably over a sink or bath, so that the sound eye is uppermost. Spread his eyelids wide open with the fingers of one hand while you pour with the other. Seek medical attention as soon as possible afterwards.

Business letters

Clear, effective and correct communication

Everyone has to write business letters from time to time – job applications, hotel bookings or complaints about faulty goods or services, for example. Keep them clear, simple and direct. Do not use words you are unfamiliar with. Try to strike a tone that is courteous and business-like without being pompous. Avoid slang, and check in a dictionary any spellings of which you are unsure.

If possible, type the letter or get it typed. Your local paper will carry advertisements for typing services, and the cost will be small. Leave wide, balanced margins, with a line of space between each paragraph. Do not try to cram everything on one sheet of paper.

Essentials to include Unless you have headed writing paper, set out your address and, if you wish, telephone number at the top right-hand side of your letter, with the date underneath. On the left, and slightly lower than your address, put the formal name – as it appears, for instance, on notepaper or a business visiting card – of the person to whom you are writing, his position or job-title, and the name and address of his organisation (the same information should also be written on the envelope). Underneath, add any reference number from previous correspondence.

If you know the person's surname, but not the first name or initials, put the company name and address first, with *For the personal attention of Mr Jones* underneath. Use the same formula if you want to write to the holder of a particular position but do not know his name – for example, the head of a company against which you have a complaint: *For the personal attention of the managing director.*

Make sure that your name, in the style by which you prefer to be addressed formally, appears legibly somewhere in the letter. Type it or write it in block capitals above your address or under your signature if it is not on a printed letterhead.

Beginnings and endings When writing to someone whose name you know, it is usual to include the name in the greeting at the beginning of the letter: *Dear Mr Brown*, or *Dear Mrs Smith*. All business letters that have a name in the greeting should close *Yours sincerely*, on a line by itself in the right-hand half of the page, above the signature.

In more formal letters, or where you do not know the person's name, use an appropriate impersonal greeting: for example, *Dear Sir*, or *Dear Madam*. Letters with any impersonal greeting should end with the phrase *Yours faithfully*, before the signature.

The impersonal approach is an easy, and perfectly polite, way around various problems of etiquette – for instance, if the person has a title or a professional qualification, and you are not sure of the way it should be used in a letter. Check with a reliable source, such as the person's business letterhead or visiting card, or by telephoning his secretary – the way in which the name and title is formally written. The Lord Rector; The Viscount Stanmore, PC, QC; The Right Hon Joan Black MP are examples. Use that style in addressing the envelope and at the head of the letter. Then open *Dear Sir*, or, to a woman, *Dear Madam.*

If you are writing to a company or other organisation, but not to a particular individual within it, begin your letter *Dear Sirs*, unless it is obviously an all-female group such as the Women's Institute; in that case, start *Dear Ladies* or with the rather old-fashioned *Mesdames*. When writing to the holder of a particular position, such as the managing director of a company, whose name and sex you do not know, begin *Dear Sir or Madam.*

Problem cases If you are not sure whether a woman should be greeted as Mrs or Miss, the style *Dear Ms White* has become accepted by many people; some women prefer it. Alternatively, use the impersonal *Dear Madam*, which is perfectly correct for women of any age.

Where the name does not give any clue to the sex of the owners – Chris Green, for example, or A.S. Robinson – and you know nothing about the person, use the name without any prefix for the address and at the top of the letter. A greeting repeating the name in full – *Dear Chris Green* – is by far the safest, to avoid giving offence.

When writing to a man, put *Mr* before his full name in the address or *Esq* after, but not both; use *Mr* in the greeting. As a courtesy, you should include your name in the way you prefer to be addressed formally, but it is considered incorrect for a man to style himself *Esq*, or for people to put *Mr*, *Mrs*, *Miss* or *Ms* before their own names. Show which is appropriate after your surname, in brackets.

Busy lizzie

Cultivating a favourite plant

Fast-growing busy lizzie (*Impatiens sultanii*) is an indoor and greenhouse favourite – see also HOUSEPLANTS; GREENHOUSE GARDENING. Given plenty of light and frequent watering in summer, it will produce a succession of white, pink, orange

Cheerful flowerer Eye-catchingly bright yet easy to grow, busy lizzie is ideal for introducing children to the pleasures of gardening.

or red flowers for months on end and spread spectacularly, eventually outgrowing even wide windowsills.

Relatives such as the red-flowered, brown-purple leaved dusky lizzie (*Impatiens petersiana*), also grown indoors, can be moved in their pots to open terraces or patios in summer. They make instant fillers for bare spots in sunny flowerbeds, too.

If you buy a ready-rooted busy lizzie, put it in a south-facing window for best results. Water sparingly in winter, but from spring onwards ensure that its soil is kept moist, watering it twice daily if necessary. Feed it twice weekly with houseplant food during the flowering season, and pinch out the growing tips occasionally to keep it bushy.

Taking cuttings Much of the fun children can get from busy lizzie and its relatives lies in PROPAGATING PLANTS from an established parent plant. This is easy to do, using cuttings taken at any time from April to September.

Choose healthy, strong, growing tips and cut them about 50-100mm (2-4in) long. Strip the leaves from the lower halves of the stems, and stand the cuttings in water in a light place, but out of direct sun. Within a few weeks, the cuttings will start to develop roots. Once these roots are sturdy, the plants can be transferred to individual pots containing JOHN INNES COMPOST No 2 (potting) or ordinary garden soil, and moved to a sunlit windowsill.

Butterflies

Attracting the queen of insects to your garden

Butterflies abhor wind. Many species adore sunlit meadowland, while others favour the dappled shade of open woodland. So a sheltered garden with sunny lawns and cooler clumps of tall plants, shrubs or trees reproduces their natural habitat best.

The choice of plants, as a source of nectar for adult butterflies and of protection and food for the caterpillars, is most important. Get the mixture right and you will have butterfly visitors from March or April until the last sunny days of September.

Unfortunately, neat weed-free borders filled with roses and gladioli, hydrangeas and lilies – all low in nectar – have little appeal for butterflies. The simpler flowers and tangled charm of old-fashioned cottage gardens, where stands of such gardener's foes as stinging nettles and thistles often flourish undisturbed in odd corners, are much more alluring.

Flowers for nectar Many traditional garden favourites are nectar-rich and will draw butterflies from neighbouring areas. The insects seem particularly attracted to yellow and purple blossoms. Primroses and polyanthuses are a food source for the earliest-appearing butterflies – small tortoiseshells, peacocks, brimstones, green-veined whites and orange-tips – from March onwards. So

Heady scent The nectar-rich blooms of *Buddleia davidii*, the butterfly bush, draw butterflies to them but can reduce the feeding insects to drowsy immobility.

are arabis, wallflowers, honesty, purple aubrieta and perennial yellow alyssum.

As spring turns to summer, and butterflies become more abundant, so does the range of flowers on which they feed. Lilacs and fragrant sweet rocket, which blooms in May, are particular butterfly favourites; valerian, which blossoms in June-August, attracts red admirals and painted ladies; while catmint and its relatives lure the green-veined white, as well as many bees.

For summer borders, plant thrift, sweet william, golden rod, and ox-eye daisies. Scarlet geraniums may draw brimstones. In autumn, late-flowering varieties of ice plant (such as *Sedum spectabile* 'Autumn Joy') and michaelmas daisies are a source of nectar when other blooms have faded.

Wild plants to leave undisturbed – or grow deliberately – include dandelions, bluebells, clover, red campion, daisies, knapweed and vetch.

Protection for caterpillars Butterflies lay their eggs on the plants on which their caterpillars feed – and virtually none of these plants, apart from grass and brassicas, grows in a well-cultivated garden. To encourage butterflies to breed, therefore, you must let part of your garden go almost wild. Clumps of nettles will encourage peacock and small tortoiseshells to lay their eggs.

Butter-making

Do-it-yourself dairy delights

Small, manually operated or powered churns are available for making butter at home, but no special equipment is necessary if you wish to try your hand at it.

An ample supply of milk or cream and a refrigerator are all that is required, together with a little patience.

There are bonuses, too. Buttermilk, the residue left as the butter itself begins to form, is rich in vitamins and some people find it a delicious drink, although its sharp taste does not appeal to all.

Starting with cream Butter is made only from the cream of milk. Buy single or double cream – as a rough guide, 570ml (1 pint) of double cream yields about 200g (7oz) of butter. Or obtain your own by allowing creamy milk (homogenised milk is no good) to stand in its bottles in the refrigerator for a day or two and then pouring the cream off.

For full-flavoured butter, let the cream ripen for two or three days outside the refrigerator in a warmish place, until it develops a buttery smell. A temperature of 20°C (68°F) is suitable. Cream that has

---

BUTTER-MAKING

The taste of success

Once you have churned cream into golden pellets, the art of butter-making consists of extracting the pellets from the buttermilk, then salting and shaping the pats.

Pour the churned mixture through a sieve. Rinse the pellets in cold water, changing the water several times until it remains clear.

Drain off the water and tip the butter onto a wooden breadboard. Squash and fold the butter to squeeze out all the remaining water and milk.

Salt the butter to taste, shape (and, if you like, mould) the pats and wrap them in greaseproof paper. They will keep for a week or two in a refrigerator, and for several months in a freezer.

not been ripened makes a blander butter, but it stays fresh longer. Experiment with various ripening times to find the taste you like best; if you save a drop or two of ripened cream from one batch it will speed up the ripening of the next.

Churning Once the cream is prepared to your satisfaction, you can churn it. But see first that the churn and other equipment are scrupulously clean, using water as near boiling as possible. Churning is best done with the cream at a temperature of about 16°C (61°F), so warm it lightly if it is a cool day. Butter will form at higher temperatures, but it remains soft and keeps poorly.

If you are using an electric mixer, attach a cake-mixing head and run it at slow speed, pouring the cream into the bowl a cup at a time. If you are using a wooden spoon, pour the cream into a bowl and beat it fast at first, slowing down as the cream begins to get heavy. Alternatively, put the cream into a clean, sealed glass jar and shake it vigorously.

With all these methods, the first sign of success is a change in the colour of the cream, from pale yellow to a rich gold. Keep stirring or shaking until the butter forms, first as small globules and then as large pellets.

Shaping the pats Strain and rinse the pellets, and tip the butter onto a wooden breadboard. With a spatula or large flat knife, squash, fold and refold the butter (in old-fashioned dairies, workers used handled wooden boards called scotch hands for this part of the process; you can still buy them). Tilt the board occasionally to let the surplus water run off.

Once most of the water has gone, salt the butter to taste by standing it for 10 minutes in a solution of salt and water. A mixture of about 90g (3½oz) of salt to 1.1 litres (2 pints) of water gives a moderately salted flavour, but you can weaken it if it proves too strong by remixing the butter with water and folding that out.

Buttonholes

Stitching by hand or machine

Work out the size of each buttonhole by measuring the width and maximum thickness of each button and adding the two together. Allow a further 3mm (⅛in) for the surrounding stitching – 1.5mm (¹⁄₁₆in) at each end.

For example, if the button is 25mm (1in) in diameter and 3mm (⅛in) thick, the hole itself will occupy 28mm (1⅛in). When the stitching is taken into account, the buttonhole will be 31mm (1³⁄₁₆in) long. Mark the centre line of the garment and the position of the buttons. The button placement line

must be marked on each half of the garment so that the centre lines will match when the garment is closed.

Mark the buttonhole ends. If the holes are to be horizontal, place them so that the ends nearest the edges of the garment are 3mm from the button positions. If the holes are to be vertical, the button position should be 3mm from the top of the buttonhole.

If you are working by hand, cut the holes before stitching. If you are using a machine, cut the holes after you have done the stitching.

For horizontal buttonholes, fan the stitches at the outer edge of the cut, where the button will rest. Form a rectangular bar at the other end. Vertical buttonholes are usually finished at both ends with the same stitch – either both fanned, or both bar-tacked.

Buttons

Sewing them on to stay

On all but very lightweight materials, buttons need a neck, called a shank, to help them stay fast when sewn on. Ordinary, flat, two-hole or four-hole buttons do not come with a shank, so you must make one from the thread as you sew them on.

To make a shank, lay a matchstick, toothpick or similar object across the top of the button, and sew the button on round it. That will produce enough slack in the thread to create the shank.

BUTTONS

With and without a shank

To sew a button on flat, anchor the thread with small stitches at the button position, then sew through the holes.

For a shank, loop the stitches over a toothpick, then pull it out so that the thread is left slack.

Pulling the button taut, wrap thread around the stitches beneath. Make a stitch through the shank.

Make six to ten stitches through the two holes in the button (or through each pair if there are four holes). Take out the toothpick or matchstick or whatever object you have placed across the button and pull the button away from the fabric, tautening the slack thread.

Bring the needle back between the fabric and the button, and wind the remaining thread tightly round the slack thread three or four times to finish the shank. Secure the shank by looping the thread through itself and cut off any left trailing.

See also BUTTONHOLES.

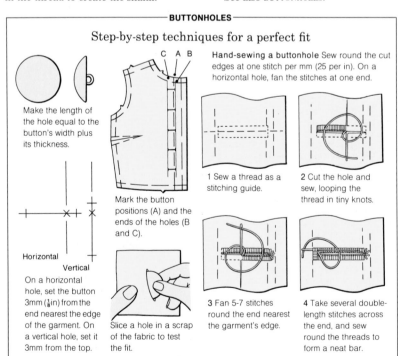

BUTTONHOLES

Step-by-step techniques for a perfect fit

Make the length of the hole equal to the button's width plus its thickness.

Mark the button positions (A) and the ends of the holes (B and C).

Horizontal / **Vertical**

On a horizontal hole, set the button 3mm (⅛in) from the end nearest the edge of the garment. On a vertical hole, set it 3mm from the top.

Slice a hole in a scrap of the fabric to test the fit.

Hand-sewing a buttonhole Sew round the cut edges at one stitch per mm (25 per in). On a horizontal hole, fan the stitches at one end.

1 Sew a thread as a stitching guide.

2 Cut the hole and sew, looping the thread in tiny knots.

3 Fan 5-7 stitches round the end nearest the garment's edge.

4 Take several double-length stitches across the end, and sew round the threads to form a neat bar.

C

Cabinet

A simple way to make a storage unit

An easy method of constructing a cabinet is to use veneered CHIPBOARD, finished either in white plastic or natural wood VENEER. The white needs no decoration, but the veneer must be sealed or varnished - see VARNISHING.

When buying the chipboard, get a roll of matching iron-on VENEER TAPE, to finish any visible cut edges.

Choose a cabinet width which exactly equals a standard width of board. This will ensure that the door will be the correct width without trimming down – though it will have to be cut to length.

Plan your cabinet so that as many cut edges as possible are hidden. In the design illustrated, only the top edges of the side pieces need edging strip. Use a fine-tooth handsaw to make cuts (see SAWS AND SAWING), and ensure that they are cut at true right angles, as all joints will be visible.

In the design shown, the side pieces are cut to the chosen cabinet height. But the top and bottom pieces are cut the chosen width, less twice the board thickness, so that they fit between the uprights. Any shelf pieces are cut 3mm ($\frac{1}{8}$in) shorter still, so that they are a loose fit on the shelf supports.

The cabinet components may be held together several ways. The simplest is to use plastic joints which come in two pieces. One piece is connected to each component, then a special screw pulls both pieces together. This system is ideal if units are to be dismantled at any time.

An alternative is to use DOWELS and PVA glue (see GLUING). Dowel joints are strong and, unlike plastic joints, do not obstruct the corners. Alternatively, insert plastic wall plugs or nylon chipboard fasteners, then use wood SCREWS (wood screws on their own do not hold in chipboard).

Special plastic caps are available to hide the screw heads.

Plastic shelf supports are available which fit into short holes drilled in the cabinet sides. Vertical rows of holes can be drilled so that SHELVES can be adjusted for height, as required. The shelves simply rest on the supports.

No backing is necessary if the cabinet is to hang on a decorated wall. But if a backing is required, use thin sheet PLYWOOD or hardboard, panel-pinned and glued to the back of the cabinet – see NAILING.

The simplest, and perhaps neatest, way to fit the door is to cover the whole front with it, using simple flush HINGES. Special cranked and adjustable cabinet hinges are also available, which are hidden inside the cabinet when the door is closed. Follow the maker's fitting instructions.

Use either a small plastic spring catch or a magnetic catch to hold the door in the closed position. A decorative knob or a metal edging strip may be fitted for opening the cabinet.

To hold the unit to a wall, use mirror plates screwed firmly to the back edges of the shelf side pieces then screwed into wall plugs - see MASONRY DRILLING; WALL FASTENERS.

Cacti

Raising succulent plants

Most cacti come from dry desert areas, but some are jungle-dwellers. The two kinds need slightly different care.

Desert cacti Plants such as the prickly pear (*Opuntia microdasys*) and Peruvian apple (*Cereus peruvianus*) grow wild in poor but fast-draining soil. A mixture of 1 part grit to 3 parts of JOHN INNES COMPOST (No 1 potting) is a suitable substitute. They need as much light as possible – a sunny windowsill is a good place to raise them indoors. The site should not get too hot in winter: 5°C (41°F) is warm enough.

From May to September, water desert cacti well, but allow the top 13mm ($\frac{1}{2}$in) of potting mixture to dry out before watering again. They benefit from being outdoors in a sunny, sheltered spot. But

---

CABINETS

Planning and assembling one, using chipboard

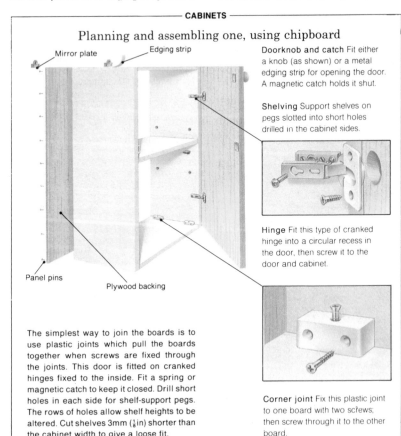

Mirror plate

Edging strip

Panel pins

Plywood backing

Doorknob and catch Fit either a knob (as shown) or a metal edging strip for opening the door. A magnetic catch holds it shut.

Shelving Support shelves on pegs slotted into short holes drilled in the cabinet sides.

Hinge Fit this type of cranked hinge into a circular recess in the door, then screw it to the door and cabinet.

Corner joint Fix this plastic joint to one board with two screws; then screw through it to the other board.

The simplest way to join the boards is to use plastic joints which pull the boards together when screws are fixed through the joints. This door is fitted on cranked hinges fixed to the inside. Fit a spring or magnetic catch to keep it closed. Drill short holes in each side for shelf-support pegs. The rows of holes allow shelf heights to be altered. Cut shelves 3mm ($\frac{1}{8}$in) shorter than the cabinet width to give a loose fit.

---

whether indoors or out, turn their pots partly round from time to time – so that the same side of the plant is not always facing the strongest light. Turning encourages them to grow straight.

After September, water desert cacti less frequently, and do not water them at all during December and January. Gradually start watering again from March. Over-watering causes desert cacti to rot.

Opuntia microdasys   Schlumbergera × buckleyi

Give the prickly pear (left) lots of light; keep the magenta-flowered Christmas cactus in a shady spot – warm and a little humid.

Jungle cacti These include the scarlet-flowered Easter cactus (*Rhipsalidopsis gaertneri*) and the magenta Christmas cactus (*Schlumbergera × buckleyi*) they must be kept out of direct sunlight at all times and need a year-round temperature of at least 7-19°C (45-66°F), and a slightly humid atmosphere. A centrally heated bathroom is a suitable place for them in winter. In summer they can go outdoors, in a shady, sheltered place. Use the same compost mix as for desert cacti, but add ⅓ part leaf mould or a peat substitute.

Keep the soil slightly moist during winter and early spring, when they should flower. After they have flowered, allow the soil to go nearly dry. Water them lightly in May and June, and give them another dry spell in July and August. Resume watering when buds appear in autumn.

All cacti Repot when the roots fill the pot. Wrap a newspaper around spiky varieties to protect your hands as you remove the plants.

Offshoots and seeds Many cacti put out offshoots, or side stems, that can be detached easily with your fingers from the parent plant. Remove offshoots in spring or summer. Set them in the grit and potting compost mixture, and treat them as adult plants. They will quickly take root. If the stems cannot be removed from the parent by plucking, cut them away and let them dry for a few days before potting, to deter rot.

To grow desert cacti from seed, prepare a mixture of 1 part sharp sand to 3 parts of sterilised John Innes seed compost. Put that over a layer of crocks (broken pieces of pot) in a pot or trough. Scatter the seeds on the surface, but do not cover

them with soil. Water them thoroughly.

Cover the pot or trough with glass or plastic, and put it in a temperature of 21-27°C (70-81°F). The plants need light when germination begins, but should be shaded from direct sun until they are established and ready for potting on.

Cake-baking

From basic sponges to Christmas cake

Success in cake-baking lies in following the recipe with care. Mix the ingredients in exactly the right proportions, for example, and follow precisely instructions on temperature settings and baking times.

Mixtures Flour, sugar and flavouring are the basic ingredients of most cakes. Eggs, fat and liquid, such as milk or water, are used in some recipes.

Self-raising flour cuts out the need for baking powder to make the cake rise. But use plain flour for light, whisked sponges, which have enough air in the mixture to rise on their own. Use a blend of both flours for rich cakes that would rise too much if they contained self-raising flour alone.

Choose the best-quality flavourings you can afford – fresh spices or rich, dark chocolate, for example. Dried fruits may harden if kept for a long time; essences such as vanilla can lose some flavour with keeping.

Have all ingredients at room temperature when you begin to prepare the mixture, so that they blend easily and do not curdle. Measure quantities precisely; dry ingredients measured in 'level teaspoons' should be levelled with the back of a knife blade.

The mixture for many simple, plain cakes is prepared by rubbing flour and fat together with the fingertips, to achieve a crumb-like texture. Raise your hands high when letting the mixture drop back into the mixing bowl – it helps to keep the mixture cool. Shake the bowl occasionally to bring larger lumps to the surface.

Creamed cakes, such as Victoria sandwiches, are made by blending fat with sugar. Cut the butter or margarine into small cubes and put it in a large bowl. If you are using a wooden spoon, beat the fat against the side of the bowl until it is soft. Add the sugar, and continue beating for about 10 minutes, until the mixture becomes fluffy and pale yellow, and drops easily from the spoon. Eggs should be added gradually, whether whole or beaten. Fold in the flour. Using an electric mixer (see FOOD PROCESSORS), the same process takes about 4 minutes.

Whisk eggs and sugar for whisked sponge mixtures in a deep bowl over hot (not boiling) water, unless you are using

an electric mixer. The mixture is ready when thick enough to leave a trail behind the raised whisk. Sift the flour two or three times and fold it carefully into the mixture with a metal spoon.

Tins and ovens Heat the oven to the required temperature while preparing the cake mixture. Prepare the cake tins, unless they are non-stick, as follows:

For sponges that do not contain fat, grease the tin evenly with fat. Now dust it with a mixture of flour and sugar in equal parts, shaking out any surplus.

For other cakes, grease the tin. Add a lining of greaseproof or non-stick baking paper and lightly grease that, too.

Cakes are generally baked in the centre of the oven. If you are baking two together place them side by side – but not touching.

Sponge cakes are cooked when the centre of the cake feels springy when pressed gently with the fingertips, and the cake has shrunk a little from the sides. Here is a basic sponge recipe – preparation time, 20 minutes; cooking time, 15 minutes.

Ingredients
75g (3oz) plain flour
Pinch of salt
3 eggs
75g (3oz) caster sugar
Filling and topping

Grease and dust with flour and sugar mixture two 180mm (7in) straight-sided sandwich tins. Sift the flour with the salt twice, into a bowl or onto a sheet of greaseproof paper. Break the eggs into a separate bowl and gradually whisk in the sugar. Keep whisking until the mixture is thick and light.

When the mixture is ready, carefully fold in the flour and salt. Divide the mixture evenly between the two sandwich tins, and bake just above the centre of an oven preheated to 190°C (375°F) or gas mark 5. Cook for 15 minutes, or until the sponge is pale or golden-brown and springy to the touch.

Allow to cool for 2 minutes, then use a palette knife to ease the baked sponges from the tins onto a wire rack, to finish cooling. Once cool, add filling to one sponge layer; put the other layer over it and add the topping. Suitable fillings are jam or jam and whipped cream. Glacé icing (see ICING CAKES) is a usual topping.

Christmas cake recipe Prepare this rich fruit cake at least a month ahead for Christmas eating. The recipe makes a round 230mm (9in) cake, or a 200mm (8in) square cake.

Ingredients
225g (8oz) seedless raisins
50g (2oz) large, stoned raisins
225g (8oz) sultanas

225g (8oz) currants
4 tablespoons cream sherry
225g (8oz) butter
225g (8oz) dark muscovado sugar
2 tablespoons black treacle
4 eggs
275g (10oz) plain flour
½ teaspoon salt
1 level teaspoon ground mixed spice
¼ teaspoon bicarbonate of soda
50g (2oz) blanched almonds, slivered
115g (4oz) glacé cherries, quartered
115g (4oz) candied peel, chopped

Put the raisins, sultanas and currants in a bowl and pour in the sherry. Stir, then leave in a warm place for several hours.

Grease the cake tin with butter and line it with a double layer of greaseproof paper, also greased with butter. Tie a double layer of brown paper around the outside of the tin, leaving an edge standing well above the rim, to prevent the cake from burning at the edges.

Prepare the cake mix in a large mixing bowl. First cream the butter and sugar together until light and fluffy, then beat in the treacle and add the eggs one at a time, beating well between each addition. Add a little flour to the mixture to prevent it from curdling.

Sieve the remaining flour with the salt, mixed spice and bicarbonate of soda and fold into the mixture along with the sherry-soaked fruit, almonds, cherries and candied peel. Stir well with a wooden spoon, but avoid overmixing which will make the mixture too soft. Pour the mixture into the cake tin and level the top.

Bake the cake in an oven preheated at 150°C (300°F, gas mark 2) for 1½ hours, then lower the heat to 140°C (275°F, gas mark 1) and bake for a further 1½-2 hours, or until a skewer inserted into the centre comes out clean.

After removing the cake from the oven, let it cool and then turn it out of the tin and peel off the lining paper. When it is completely cold, seal the cake in foil.

See also CAKE DECORATING; ICING A CAKE.

Cake decorating

The finishing touches in home baking

Add shaped decorations to your cake when the icing is nearly, but not quite, set – see ICING CAKES. For piped decorations wait until the icing is hard.

Edible decorations can be quickly made from fresh fruit, nuts or dried and preserved ingredients such as glacé cherries, angelica, mimosa balls, crystallised violets and rose petals. Sprinkles of chopped COCONUT, peanuts, or hundreds and thousands, pressed on with a spatula or by hand, enhance the flavour of a cake, and disguise any flaws in the icing.

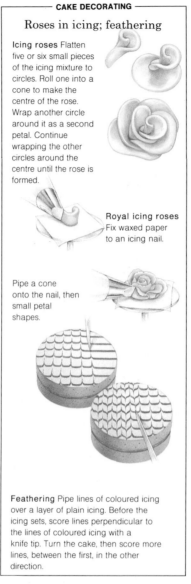

— CAKE DECORATING —

Roses in icing; feathering

Icing roses Flatten five or six small pieces of the icing mixture to circles. Roll one into a cone to make the centre of the rose. Wrap another circle around it as a second petal. Continue wrapping the other circles around the centre until the rose is formed.

Royal icing roses Fix waxed paper to an icing nail.

Pipe a cone onto the nail, then small petal shapes.

Feathering Pipe lines of coloured icing over a layer of plain icing. Before the icing sets, score lines perpendicular to the lines of coloured icing with a knife tip. Turn the cake, then score more lines, between the first, in the other direction.

Icing flowers A speedy way to make icing flowers is to blend 50g (2oz) of cream cheese with 225g (8oz) of icing sugar. Divide the mixture into several portions and add different food colourings to each – red, pink, yellow and blue for flowers, green for leaves. Shape the flower petals with your fingers. To make the leaves, flatten portions of the green mixture. Trim them to shape with a knife and score the tops to represent leaf veins.

Create more delicate roses from royal icing, using the plain or star-shaped small nozzle of an icing bag. Use a blob of icing to fix a small square of waxed paper to an icing nail (sometimes called a flower spinner). Pipe a centre cone onto the paper, and then pipe on small petal shapes. Work from left to right and over-

---

lap each petal slightly, until the rose is the size you want. Remove paper and rose from the icing nail, and let the rose set before gently placing it in position on the cake.

Feathering and piping Use the plain writing tube on your icing bag for feathering and writing messages. It can only be done with glacé icing.

Calligraphy

Turn your writing into an art form

Practise with a special calligraphy pen – either the fountain type which holds a supply of ink, or a plain pen-holder and nib, dipped in an inkwell.

Use high-quality waterproof, non-fading ink. Working on white bond or typing paper, copy or trace the letter strokes from the specimen alphabet shown, until you can make them accurately from memory and space the letters properly by eye. Hold the pen at a 45 degree angle, pulling it across the paper top to bottom or left to right.

Large stationers sell calligraphy pen sets, some of which have several interchangeable nibs. Sets are available for both left and right-handed people. They come also in different weights: a light pen gives more feel for the nib on the paper; a heavier one creates less friction as you write, making for a smoother action.

During long writing sessions, clean the nib occasionally – rinse it in water and wipe it, first with tissue and then with a lint-free cloth. When you have finished writing, clean the used nibs with a special cleaner, also available from art shops.

Once you are proficient, experiment with different coloured inks, and paper of different colours and textures. Real parchment, made from sheepskin, is expensive, and mistakes can be corrected only by an expert. But parchment-type paper is more widely available. Try making your own ink from acrylic paint, thinned with water and two or three drops of gum arabic per egg cup of colour. It dries quickly, so clean the nib often in warm water.

Quill penmanship An inexpensive and deeply satisfying method of working is to use a quill pen, cutting it yourself as ancient scribes did 1800 years ago. The flight feathers of various large birds are used, but the goose quill is preferred. To make the feather hard and springy, temper it by soaking in water, then dipping in hot sand. Use a sharp knife to strip the feathering from the bottom half of the shaft.

Cut a small scallop from one side of the end, so that the tip is hollow and

Practising an ancient craft

Hold the calligraphy pen at 45 degrees to the line of your arm. For vertical strokes, pull the pen from top to bottom towards you. For horizontal strokes, draw it from left to right. Keep your hand relaxed while writing. To vary the width of the strokes, turn your hand slightly so that the angle of the nib point on the paper is changed.

Pen holder

Reservoir

Nib

Fountain pen A reservoir above the nib holds the ink.

a b c d e f g h i j k l m n o p q r s t u v w x y z

A B C D E F G H I J K L M N O P Q R S T U V W X Y Z

Congratulations on your retirement

Calories in some foods	
Food cal – per 100g (3½oz)	Calories
Almonds	570
Apples	45
Bacon (fried streaky)	500
Baked beans	60
Bananas	80
Beef (fried rump steak)	250
Beef (stewed mince)	230
Beer (normal strength)	30
Bread (white)	230
Bread (wholemeal)	213
Butter	740
Cabbage (boiled)	10
Carrots (boiled)	20
Cauliflower	10
Cheese (Cheddar)	300
Cheese (cottage)	100
Cheese (processed)	310
Cheese (Stilton)	350
Chicken (roast)	150
Chocolate biscuits	520
Coffee (black)	5
Corned beef	220
Cornflakes (with milk)	205
Cream (single)	210
Dairy ice cream	170
Eggs	150
Fatty fish (herring)	243
Fish (white, fried in batter)	200
Fish (white, steamed)	80
Fruit cake	350
Ham	120
Lamb (grilled cutlets)	370
Liver (calf's, fried)	250
Margarine	730
Milk	65
Oranges	35
Peanuts (roasted)	570
Peas (boiled)	50
Pork (grilled chop)	330
Potatoes (boiled)	80
Potatoes (chipped)	250
Potatoes (roast)	160
Rice (white, boiled)	120
Sardines (in oil)	220
Sausages (pork, fried)	320
Soup (cream of tomato)	55
Spaghetti (without sauce)	120
Spirits	220
Sugar (teaspoon)	24
Tea (black)	2
Tomatoes	15
Veal (fried cutlet)	215
Wine	70
Yoghurt (flavoured)	80

curved underneath, like a steel nib. Push a knitting needle up into the shaft until you hear a slight click as the shaft cracks, to form the vertical split that allows the ink to flow smoothly.

Use a quill with the smoothly flowing ink made with an ink stick. Ink sticks are made in China and Japan of compressed soot, and are available from good art supply shops. Rub one end of a stick in a little water in a dish – make only small quantities at a time.

Calorie counting

Eating away your weight

The number of calories you consume controls your weight – see also DIETING. A calorie is a unit of energy in the form of heat – 1 calorie (1k cal) is the amount of heat required to raise the temperature of 1kg of water by 1°C.

Most of the calories in the food we eat are converted into energy by our bodies, and used up. But any that are not used are stored in the body as fat; it takes 3500 of these surplus calories to make 450g (1lb) of body fat.

Estimating your needs To keep your body weight at a reasonably constant level, you need to match the number of calories you take in through food and drink to those you burn up as energy in daily activities.

The number of calories burned each day varies widely from person to person, depending upon their sex, physical build, age, metabolism, health and physical activity.

For a rough idea of how many calories you burn up daily, multiply your present weight (in pounds) by 13.6 if you are not physically very active. If you are moderately active, multiply your weight by 16-18, or by 20 if you are very active.

You can get a more accurate figure by keeping track of the total number of calories you consume each day (*see table*) and by weighing yourself regularly. If you gain weight, you are taking in more calories than your body expends as energy, and vice versa.

When you have worked out the number of calories you need to keep your weight stable, use that figure as a guide, increasing your calorie intake when you are more active, and reducing it when you are not so active. Always maintain a balanced diet – see MENU PLANNING.

Remember that physical exercise is *not* an effective way to lose weight. You need to walk about 80km (50 miles) to use up just 450g (1lb) of body fat. Eating fewer calories is far more effective.

Keeping a check The table lists the calories in 100g (about 3½oz) portions of some common foods – an average helping.

Read labels on tinned, packaged and frozen foods. More and more manufacturers are now including calorie counts on them, expressed also as calories in 100g portions (k cal per 100g). Do not forget to include in your daily total anything added to your food, such as sauces, cooking fat or dressings.

Campfires

How to light one, even with damp wood

Choose the site for your fire carefully. It should be on level ground, well away from tree roots and overhanging branches. Clear a circle at least 2.4m (8ft) in diameter around the spot where the fire will go, scraping or digging away fallen leaves, turf, plants and decayed matter until you reach bare earth that will not burn. Pile the cleared material well away from the fire, to be used later to cover up the area again. See also CAMPING.

Gather wood from dead and fallen branches or trees (or use driftwood on a beach). Use a hand axe and cut into lengths of about 1m (3ft). Do *not* cut live trees or branches; not only is this destructive, but the wood smokes excessively and does not burn well.

The easiest campfires to build are:

The pyramid This is the best heat source, starting slowly, then burning for a long time without scattering sparks. Begin by laying a pile of tinder: dry twigs, pine cones, dead bark or pieces of paper. Lay two lengths of firewood, one on either side of the tinder and just touching it. Put another two lengths across the first two, near the ends.

Build up five or six layers of wood, alternately lengthways and across, to make a miniature 'log cabin'. Then make a 'roof' with five or six lengths across the top layer, and two more laid across these. Light the tinder.

The cone This is a good campfire for cooking: it lights quickly, even when the wood is wet, and provides a small, concentrated flame. Lay your tinder and arrange the firewood in a wigwam shape, upright and slanted inwards, in a rough circle around the tinder.

Fuzz stick Flaking damp wood makes it easier to ignite. Working from one end of a stick or branch, make a series of cuts around and along it to create feathery flakes still attached to it at the bottom. This exposes dry wood underneath, which will soon catch fire.

If the wood is damp, use a sharp knife to cut some pieces into 'fuzz sticks' as illustrated. Put the fuzz sticks upright around the inside of the cone, near the tinder. Once the tinder is lit, the fuzz sticks soon catch fire too.

Never leave a campfire unattended. To douse the fire, drown it thoroughly with water, or cover it with earth or sand. Bury any remaining charred wood. Scrape the site of the fire flat and cover it with the turf, leaves and other material that you cleared earlier, so that the ground seems little disturbed.

WARNING In many country and open areas, campfires are forbidden, so check before lighting one. Never light fires in forests, or on private land.

Camping

Equipping yourself for an outdoor holiday

Begin with a firm idea of what type of camping holiday you want, and tailor your plans to the transport you are using. Motoring will allow you to be a little indulgent in what you take – a luxury tent, collapsible beds and tables, and sporting equipment, for example. If you are BACKPACKING or BICYCLE TOURING, however, select only items that you can comfortably carry over long distances.

Some campers prefer to book sites in advance: local libraries often have campsite directories. National tourist offices have lists of sites abroad. If you choose not to book, remember that many coastal and mountain sites fill up quickly in summer.

Equipment TENTS can be anything from an improvised BIVOUAC TENT to a trailer model for towing behind a car. But it must be waterproof, well-ventilated, easy to put up and secure in strong winds. A built-in groundsheet is a great advantage. Whether the tent is new or old, check it before leaving – if possible put it up in your garden, to ensure that all ropes, poles and pegs are present, and that there are no tears. If its waterproofing property has deteriorated, it can be restored with an aerosol spray available from a camping equipment shop.

Take only lightweight SLEEPING BAGS if you are walking, with a sheet of foam rubber to go underneath for insulation against cold. If you are driving, you may have room for lightweight camp beds or inflatable AIR BEDS.

For outdoor catering, bottle-gas cookers are light and odourless. Paraffin pressure-stoves are cheaper to run, and work better than gas in the cold and wet. But they smell somewhat and can be dangerous if accidentally knocked over. Petrol stoves are available for motorised campers. If you plan to cook inside your tent, take a camp cooking table, with draught and splash shields.

A medium-sized frying pan and a 1.7 litre (3 pint) saucepan should suffice for basic cooking. Take a knife, fork, spoon and plastic soup bowl and mug for each camper. Do not forget to include a can-and-bottle opener and a torch and extra batteries. Carry water in plastic containers, or take a collapsible water-holder that fits into a backpack.

Away from official sites, you may need an implement, such as a light spade, for ground-clearing and digging. Specialist shops sell camping tools that incorporate a spade and a saw.

Clothing This should include rainwear, and a hat for protection against both rain and sun. Take stout shoes or boots for outdoor wear and walking, and light

shoes which can be kept dry to wear in and around the tent.

At the campsite Plan to arrive at least an hour before dark, so that you can see to pitch the tent. If it is not an official site, ask permission of the farmer or landowner before pitching your tent.

Choose a sheltered spot, but not one directly under trees. Make sure that the ground is not liable to become boggy, or even flood if it rains. A flat, well-drained area is best. Long grass is a sign of damp and coldness; thick undergrowth or stagnant water attract insects. Avoid fields showing recent signs that farm animals have been in them. Pitch the tent so that the entrance does not face the wind.

If you need a latrine, dig it well away from your tent, and downwind, preferably screened by bushes. Make it at least 1m (3ft) deep; leave the earth you have removed handy to sprinkle back after use. When you move on, refill the hole and replace turf. Dig a small hole near the latrine for greasy water; line the bottom with stones to promote drainage. Fill it in on leaving.

For cooking outside the tent, clear a hearth of bare earth, and keep the material you remove to fill it in again afterwards. Site it downwind from the tent but away from the latrine, and a safe distance from the tent – see also CAMPFIRES. Boil all water, or use purifying tablets, available from chemists.

Make a rule not to bring wet or muddy clothes and shoes into the tent.

Children and camping Many children love camping – even babies and toddlers – but you should plan activities to cater for their needs. Do not, for example, attempt long or difficult hikes. Children will require extra clothes, as they get far dirtier than adults, and possibly books, toys or games to keep them amused.

Older children will enjoy having their own tent. It gives them a sense of self-reliance, and it also gives you some degree of privacy.

Canapés

Savoury snacks to serve with drinks

Original French *canapés* were slices of bread fried in butter, perhaps with an anchovy or two on top. Now the term means any savoury appetiser with a base and a topping, served in one or two-bite portions, usually to accompany cocktails or pre-meal drinks.

Canapés can be cold or hot, and as straightforward or as ingenious as you like. Depending on their size, the ingredients and whether they are to be eaten as a prelude to a meal, allow two to six per person.

Bases These can be made with PASTRY, fresh bread of any type, fried bread, toast, plain biscuits (usually unsweetened or savoury), rye or crispbread. The bases should be thin and fresh – do not prepare canapés more than an hour or two in advance, or they may become soggy and impossible to pick up, or dry.

Shape bread or pastry bases, cutting them into squares, triangles or circles; some people remove bread crusts. Mould pastry into shallow 'boats' or tartlets.

Spread butter or margarine lightly on top of each base, or use a thin layer of cream or cottage cheese. Or try a herb butter, made by mixing 115g (4oz) of lightly salted butter with 2 tablespoons each of chopped parsley and chives.

Toppings For meat-lovers, top canapés with thin slices of chicken or turkey (on their own, mixed with MAYONNAISE and seasonings or, for turkey, dabbed with cranberry sauce). Cold roast beef goes well with stuffed olive, gherkin, mustard or horseradish. Garnish ham with glacé cherry, pineapple or apricot. Add a small slice of cucumber, tomato or stuffed or pickled olive to meat or game PATÉ.

Flaked fish, crab, lobster, prawns and shrimps can be used, either by themselves, or mixed with mayonnaise and herbs. For a special treat, try smoked salmon with lemon juice, black pepper and a sprig of dill, or smoked trout with horseradish. For an easy spread, mix tinned tuna fish with a dash of cream, lemon juice, tomato purée and Worcestershire sauce.

Hard cheeses, such as Cheddar, are a good standby. Garnish them with a chunk of fresh apple or pear, or with pickle. Cream and cottage cheeses go well with pineapple, peach or apricot, or with gherkins or olives. Add a sprinkling of black pepper.

For vegetarians and dieters, serve lightly salted, wafer-thin slices of cucumber that have been dipped in vinegar, with a sprig of dill. Sprinkle coarsely grated carrot with lemon juice and chopped parsley.

Serving Arrange the canapés on doily-covered serving plates, so that the colours of the toppings complement or contrast with each other. Keep them lightly covered, in a cool place, until you are ready to offer them round.

Canasta

A card game for two to six players

Canasta can be played by just two or three people playing solo, but usually the number is four or six, playing in pairs as partners. The object of the game is to score points by making *melds* – combinations of three or more cards of the

---

Combining cards for a meld

In this situation, the face-up discard pile is topped by a queen; the stock pile (left) always lies face down.

The pair of queens in this hand takes the queen on the discard pile. The discard queen could also be taken with one queen and wild two.

Three queens and a wild two (left) makes 50 points – enough for an initial meld, provided the player has not yet scored more than 1500 points in the game. On the right is a natural canasta, a set of seven cards with none wild. It is worth 500 points as a canasta, plus 5 points for each 7. A player could go out by forming his hand into this canasta and the meld of queens.

---

same rank. A seven-card meld is called a *canasta*. The first player or pair to score 5000 points wins.

The game is played with two standard packs of 52 cards, each with two jokers added, combined to form a pack of 108 cards. After shuffling, the pack is cut to determine who deals – the highest card winning. If a joker appears, the cut is repeated.

If two or three pairs of partners are to play, cards are drawn, and the two who draw the highest cards play together. Partners take alternate seats so that they do not follow each other in play.

The dealer places the cards singly, face down, starting on his left and dealing to himself last. Each player receives 11 cards if there are four or more players; 13 are dealt to three players or 15 to two players.

If a player gets a red 3, he places it face up on the table and gets a replacement card. The remainder of the pack is placed face down on the table to form a *stock pile*, and the top card is turned face up beside it to start a *discard pile*. If the top card happens to be another red 3, the next card from the stock pile is placed face up on top of the 3.

Play then begins with the person to the left of the dealer taking either the

card on top of the stock pile, or the face-up card if his hand contains a pair of the same denomination as that card or one of the denominations and a wild card. If red 3 is drawn, it must be placed on the table but no replacement card is drawn. To complete his turn a player must put a card face up on the discard pile.

Jokers and deuces (twos) are *wild*, which means that they can have any value you wish to make them. However, you cannot include more than three wild cards in making up any one meld. Players can lay their melds face up on the table and can add to them later – as can partners.

An initial meld must total at least 50 points (see below). This total can be reached by putting out two melds at once, for example, three jacks (10 points each) and three eights (10 points each). Once a player scores 1500 or more points, his initial meld must be at least 90 points. After 3000 points, his initial meld must be at least 120 points.

If a player can use the card on the discard pile in a meld, he can pick up the entire pile – provided it is not *frozen*. The pile becomes frozen if a wild card or a black 3 appears on top; the pile remains frozen until one of the players has a natural pair of the same denomination as the top card, or one card of that denomination and a wild card. The person who unfreezes the discard pile takes the entire pile.

A hand ends when a player can *go out* by putting down all his cards as melds, including a canasta. This may be either a *natural canasta* – a meld of seven cards with no wild ones added, or a *mixed canasta* – a meld of seven cards including wild cards.

All players total their bonus points – that is for *canastas, red threes, going out, going out with a concealed hand*. A red 3 (or threes) only counts as a bonus if the initial meld is made. Going out with a concealed hand means that neither a player nor his partner has laid any melds on the table.

Players can then count up the points values of the individual cards in their melds, but they must subtract the points still held in their hands from their melds and bonus points.

Points are allocated as follows:

HAND	
Mixed canasta	**300**
Natural canasta	**500**
Going out	**100**
Going out with a concealed hand	**200**
Joker	**50**
Two	**20**
Ace	**20**
King, Queen, Jack, 10,9,8	**10**;
7,6,5,4, or black 3	**5**
Red three	**100**
All red threes	**800**

Candle-making

A fun hobby, both decorative and useful

Many craft shops sell candle moulds and the basic ingredients for candle-making. The main ingredient is paraffin wax, available as blocks or granules. A material called stearin is usually added to the melted wax to make the candle hard, long burning and opaque. The usual proportion is 3 tablespoons of stearin to 450g (1lb) of wax.

If using dyes, dissolve them first in stearin and add the mixture to the melted wax. Small amounts of beeswax can also be added to paraffin wax to make it longer burning.

Heat the wax in a double saucepan, so that the wax in the top section will be melted gently by water heated in the lower section. Heat the wax to 98°C (208°F) if you are using metal or glass moulds, 83°C (181°F) if you are using plastic moulds. Measure the temperature with a sugar thermometer clipped to the rim of the inner pan.

Any suitably shaped carton, jar or tin, will do for moulding, but more decorative candles can be made in plastic moulds bought from a craft shop. If you use metal or glass moulds heat them to 43°C (109°F) and spray them lightly with silicone before you fill them.

Select a wick which is appropriate for the diameter of the candle: if it is too thin, the flame will be dowsed by the melting wax; if it is too thick the candle will smoke. The wick can be inserted either by making a hole in the soft candle with a knitting needle, by making a hole in harder wax with a hot skewer, or by securing the wick inside the mould before the wax is poured.

To secure a wick, knot its end, thread it up through a hole in the bottom of the mould, then seal the hole inside with a blob of melted wax and outside with Plasticine.

Place a piece of stiff wire across the top of the mould and tie the wick to it to hold it taut.

Hold the mould with an oven glove as you pour in the hot wax. Pour slowly to avoid bubbles, and if the mould is textured, turn it while pouring so that every crevice is filled.

Cool the mould in a bucket of water up to the level of the wax for about 30 minutes, then fill any hollow at the mouth of the mould where the wax has contracted. There may even be a bubble here which should be pierced, then filled with wax.

Allow the mould to cool overnight, then gently pull the candle from a rigid mould, or pull a flexible mould away from the wax. Trim the candle with a craft knife to remove any signs of mould seams.

Some craft shops sell rub-on colours which can be used to highlight a raised pattern on a candle, or give it an 'antique' finish.

Dipping One of the oldest and simplest ways of making candles is by dipping a wick into a melted wax mixture. However, it calls for patience, as the candle is built up only gradually, layer by layer.

Cut a wick considerably longer than the desired candle length, then find a container capable of taking the full wick length. Stand the container in a pan of water; fill it with wax and heat the water to melt it. Dip the wick in the melted wax, withdraw it, then pull it taut and hold it until the wax has set. This ensures a straight candle. Now dip again; withdraw and allow the wax to harden. Continue dipping until you have the required diameter. Dip the lower half more than the top half to give a tapered shape. Using containers of different colours you can make a candle with bands of colour.

Give a final glaze by dipping the candle first in wax which has been heated to about 92°C (198°F), then in cold water – but do not wet the wick.

Warning Do not heat wax above 100°C (212°F), because above this temperature it smokes, turns brown and becomes highly flammable. Do not let children heat wax unless they are supervised.

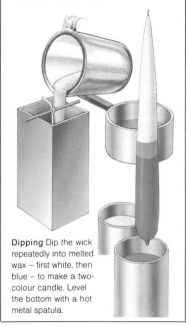

CANDLE-MAKING

Two ways to make them

Moulding Tie a wick in place on a stick across the top of a plastic (or warmed metal) mould. Melt the wax in a double saucepan and pour it in.

Dipping Dip the wick repeatedly into melted wax – first white, then blue – to make a two-colour candle. Level the bottom with a hot metal spatula.

Cane and bamboo

Re-seating chairs, and care of cane furniture

To replace the cane seat of a chair, first use tin shears or household snips to cut away any remaining canework. An old screwdriver will prise up and remove beading cane from the edges of the seat. Clean out all the cane holes with a brad-awl, and if the chair needs stripping and re-varnishing – see PAINT STRIPPING; VARNISHING – now is the time to do it. But make sure you do not block any holes, and let the varnish dry thoroughly before you start re-caning.

Materials You can buy the cane at craft shops. You need seating cane in three grades: No 2 split cane for the front-to-back and side-to-side canework; No 3 for the diagonal work and No 6 beading cane for the final surround. You also need a short length of thicker basket cane for plugging holes. Measure your chair seat before ordering cane, and the supplier will advise how much of each cane is required.

You also need about 20 golf tees for use as temporary pegs, to hold the cane in place while you pull it taut from hole to hole. On straight edges secure every second hole with a tee. On curves, secure every hole.

Method Soak all the cane in cold water for at least five minutes to make it supple, then store it in sealed plastic bags to prevent it from drying out.

As you thread the cane, make sure that you keep the smooth side up so that there is no roughness on the seat. When you start a new length of cane, secure the end under the chair in the nearest loop, twisting it through twice. Pull it up through the correct hole and peg it.

Cleaning cane and bamboo Where canework or bamboo is grubby, a mild household abrasive cream on a lint-free rag will remove the grime. Wipe off with a damp rag and allow to dry thoroughly before re-varnishing.

Apply at least three coats of varnish, and if the furniture is used outdoors, use an exterior grade varnish. A matt varnish looks more natural on bamboo. When the varnish is dry, apply wax polish.

Cannelloni

Making a filling pasta dish

Cannelloni is one of the larger varieties of tube-shaped PASTA – the name *cannelloni* literally meaning 'big pipes'. The tubes are about 75mm (3in) long and 25mm (1in) in diameter and can be bought dried and packaged or fresh from

---

CANE AND BAMBOO

Fitting new cane in a chair seat

Cut through the canework all round the seat, just inside the frame. Prise up the beading cane on top of the frame with a screwdriver. Push a bradawl into the top and bottom of each hole to clear it. Mark the centre holes at back and front with pegs. Count along the holes to the last in the back row (not the corner one) and then count the same number at the front. Mark these holes with pegs.

Starting Push a prepared cane down through the marked front hole so that about 75mm (3in) hangs below the seat. Put a peg in the hole to secure the cane. Pass the cane down through the marked back hole, pull taut and secure with a peg. Thread the cane through the next hole and move the peg to that hole.

First layer Continue threading between the front and back. When you reach the end of the back row, use side holes until you finish the row of front holes. Keep the four corner holes clear.

Second layer Thread cane from side to side in the same way, passing the canes over the first set. Start new canes as needed; secure all cane ends with pegs.

Third layer Fit a second set of front-to-back canes, passing them over the others.

Fourth layer Weave a second set across, passing under the first front-to-back layer and over the second.

First diagonals From the back corner weave under the cross canes and over the front-to-back canes. Take the cane down the front corner hole and up the next hole in the front row. Continue to the corner, then work the other half.

Second diagonals Start from the other back corner and weave over the sets of cross canes, under the sets of front-to-back canes.

Loose ends Drive plugs of thick cane into holes where canes start or end. Trim off hanging pieces under the frame.

Beading Bind a beading cane along each side with a length threaded up and down all the unplugged holes. Plug below to secure the bead and cane ends.

---

a delicatessen. Fresh cannelloni should be used in two or three days; dried, it lasts up to two years.

Dried pasta swells with cooking, so 50g (2oz) of cannelloni will yield 175g (6oz) when cooked. Cooking time is 15-20 minutes.

Cannelloni has little flavour of its own, but is a natural for stuffing with a savoury mix of meat, fish or vegetables, and serving with a sauce.

Here is a simple but delicious recipe sufficient for four servings:

Ingredients
8 tubes of cannelloni
450g (1lb) fresh spinach
225g (8oz) cooked chicken
25g (1oz) unsalted butter
25g (1oz) plain flour
200ml ($\frac{1}{3}$ pint) milk
Large tin chopped tomatoes
75g (3oz) grated Parmesan cheese
Salt and black pepper

Preparation Wash the spinach, put it in a large saucepan with no extra water, cover and cook over a low heat for 10 minutes. Drain through a colander, squeeze with a wooden spoon to remove all moisture, then chop coarsely. Dice or mince the chicken flesh.

Cooking Melt the butter in a saucepan, stir in the flour and cook gently for 1 minute, then slowly blend in the milk to form a smooth sauce. Bring to the boil and season with salt and freshly ground pepper. Simmer for 2-3 minutes, or until the sauce thickens. Remove the pan from the heat. Stir in the spinach and chicken.

Place the cannelloni in a pan of boiling salted water and boil for 15 minutes, or until just tender, then drain and cool for a few minutes. Preheat the oven to 180°C (350°F, gas mark 4). Fill a large piping bag fitted with a plain nozzle with the spinach and chicken, and stuff the cannelloni tubes. Arrange the tubes in a buttered, ovenproof dish and cover with the chopped tomatoes. Sprinkle with half the grated cheese.

Place the dish in the top half of the oven. Cook for 20-30 minutes. Serve with the remainder of the cheese.

Canoes and kayaks

Boarding and paddling – basic strokes and turns

The open canoes of today are very similar to those of the North American Indian. Kayaks, now used almost universally for recreation and sport, are descendants of a double-ended, decked Eskimo craft.

Canoes are propelled by a single-bladed paddle. Kayak paddles have a blade at each end, with the blades set at 90 degrees to each other.

Boarding Pull the canoe or kayak close to the bank with its bow facing upstream. With large-cockpit kayaks and racing canoes, kneel near the edge of the bank and place the paddle with one end on the bank and the other across the canoe in front of the cockpit, to form a bridge between bank and canoe.

For small-cockpit kayaks, the paddle is placed across the back of the cockpit with its greater length resting on the bank.

Grasp the back of the cockpit and the paddle shaft with your outside hand and push down on the shaft that rests on the bank with your inside hand, to support you while you get into the seat. Place the outside leg in the craft just past the centre line. Bring the other leg in straight under the deck (in a kayak), sitting down as you do so.

Paddling kayaks First hold the paddle shaft on your head so that your elbows form right angles. Mark the positions of your hands with a piece of tape, making sure that they are equidistant from each end of the paddle. Hold the paddle at these positions.

Reach forward without bending at the waist, twisting your upper body. Dip one blade well forward in the water so that only the blade is covered. Then pull the blade back in the water by first untwisting your body and allowing the opposite arm to move forward.

When the dipped blade is level with your hips, lift it out of the water, twisting your wrist as you do so to turn the opposite blade. Reach forward with the opposite blade and repeat as before.

Flat-bladed paddles can be used either way round. Curved or spooned paddles must suit the hand that controls the twisting action – if it is the right hand, say, the right spoon faces downwards while the left blade is in the water.

Paddling canoes Hold the paddle with one hand on the handle and the other about 150mm (6in) above the blade. Reach forward and dip the blade into the water, pulling back until the blade is level with your hips. Take it out, swing it forward and across the canoe and dip it in on the other side.

Steering and stopping To turn your canoe to the right, for example, either apply more power to the left-hand stroke or sweep the paddle in a wide semicircle from bow to stern.

To stop a kayak, use short, firm, backward strokes on both sides.

Safety Always wear a buoyancy aid or a lifejacket. Buoyancy aids are best for river canoeing, whereas lifejackets are necessary for sea or large expanses of open water.

Practise in a swimming pool before venturing onto a river. In particular, try capsizing your craft to make sure you can get out easily. Have someone at hand when trying this for the first time.

Tuition The British Canoe Union can tell you which is your nearest club. Their address is: John Dutteridge House, Ardbolton Lane, West Bridgford, Nottingham NG2 5AS.

Car accidents

What to do if your vehicle is involved

If you are not incapacitated by the accident, the first essential is to warn other traffic, so that more vehicles do not become involved. Call the police if anyone is injured. Anyone badly injured should not be moved without expert supervision. Keep any walking injured and those helping before the services arrive well away from moving traffic.

Once the injured are receiving attention, take particulars and find witnesses. Then record evidence on the spot. Try always to keep pencil and paper in your car for such an emergency.

The accident Even if your vehicle is undamaged, stop immediately if:
- Any person, apart from yourself, has been injured.
- Any vehicle, other than yours, has been damaged.
- A domestic animal other than a cat has been injured outside the vehicle.
- Damage has been caused to property.

Failing to stop is an offence involving a fine, endorsement on your driving licence and possible disqualification.

You may not have been directly involved in the accident, but if your vehicle contributed to it – for example, another driver swerved to avoid you and hit an obstruction – you must stop.

You must also remain long enough to exchange names and addresses with others involved, establish ownership of vehicles involved and take registration numbers.

If it is not feasible to stay – for example, if you hit an empty parked vehicle – you must report it in person to the police within 24 hours.

Apportioning blame It is prudent not to say too much at the scene of the accident. Do not admit blame – you could be confused and accepting more responsibility than the situation warrants.

You do not have to provide a written or verbal statement to the police. If, however, you wish to make a statement, write it yourself or make sure an officer writes it in your words, then initial it.

Recording evidence If a court action or claim is likely (see also CAR INSURANCE), take a note of:

1 Names and addresses of those involved drivers; a passenger supervising an L driver is also responsible. Passengers and witnesses need only tell the police, but may be willing to collaborate.
2 The names of other drivers' insurance companies, and their certificate numbers.
3 The amount of traffic at the time of the accident.
4 Time and weather conditions – and at night, the position of street lights at the time of the accident.
5 The exact position of other vehicles. Make a sketch. If you have a camera, take a photograph. Try to leave vehicles in place until the police arrive to measure distances. If one has to be moved, mark its original position with chalk.
6 Features such as broken glass or obstructions in the road; skid marks; road signs or crossings.

Under your sketch write a clear report of the sequence of events and the outcome. Note the names and addresses and telephone numbers of any witnesses willing to corroborate. Try to make copies of your evidence before parting with the original, in case it gets mislaid.

Accidents abroad The procedure will be similar, but regulations will probably differ. Continental handbooks issued by motoring organisations offer information country by country. Study the relevant ones before setting off.

Car aerials

Fitting them for good reception; and foiling vandals

Careful siting of your car aerial is as important as the quality of the aerial itself. Choose one which retracts and locks, or buy a flexible, rubber-covered one, which is virtually indestructible.

All types are readily available from car accessory and car radio shops.

Fitting an aerial Fix the aerial as far from the engine or as far from the ignition system as possible. Otherwise it will almost certainly attract electrical interference. For the same reason, keep the lead short and well away from wiring and electrical accessories.

You will probably need to drill a hole in the bodywork, usually 19-22mm ($\frac{3}{4}$-$\frac{7}{8}$in) in diameter – consult the fitting instructions – see also DRILLING. Take great care to avoid a slip damaging paintwork, or wiring or components underneath. Many car handbooks show a recommended aerial mounting point.

Stick a cross made with masking tape on the chosen site and mark on the tape the exact centre of the hole. Use a pointed centre punch and hammer to make a slight indent on the metal at that point, to prevent the drill tip from wandering.

Start with a small drill bit – no more than 3mm ($\frac{1}{8}$in) – then use progressively

Drilling the hole
Drill through a cross made with masking tape, to prevent the drill tip slipping.

larger ones until you have the correct size hole. Alternatively, use a hole saw of the correct diameter, or open a small hole with a round file. Mask the tip of the file with tape to avoid damaging the paintwork.

Use emery paper to rub the panel around the underside of the hole down to bare metal, to ensure good contact between aerial and bodywork. Poor contact or corrosion is often the cause of poor radio reception. Insert the aerial from beneath the hole and screw up the securing nuts tightly. Protect bare metal with undersealing compound.

Run the aerial lead back to the set and plug it into the appropriate socket – see CAR CASSETTES AND RADIOS.

Caravans and trailers

Choosing, hitching, towing and parking

Before buying or hiring a caravan, you need to know what your car can safely pull. Consult your car handbook, or ask your car dealer. Also, the Caravan Club has a useful free leaflet detailing car and caravan weight ratios: write to Caravan

Club, East Grinstead House, East Grinstead, West Sussex RH19 1UA enclosing a stamped, addressed envelope for a reply.

Equipping your car A suitable ball-and-hitch fitting to which a caravan can be attached is needed, plus the electrical fittings necessary to link the caravan with the car's rear lights, indicators, stop and fog lights.

Choosing a caravan Points to consider include: sleeping accommodation and how it intrudes on living space; cooking and fridge facilities; washing and lavatory arrangements; lighting and heating fittings; storage space and awning extensions.

Hitching up Make sure everything inside the caravan is stowed securely and all windows are shut. Check that the caravan brake is on, then wind up the corner steadying legs. Wind the jockey wheel so that the hitch coupling is just above the level of the ball on the car.

Back the car so that the ball is positioned just under the caravan coupling.

Remove the cover from the ball, lift the locking handle on top of the coupling, then lower the coupling onto the ball by winding the jockey wheel. When the jockey wheel is wound to its full extent, loosen the securing bolt and lift the jockey wheel assembly to its highest point, then secure it.

Secure the safety chain over the ball hitch; plug in the electrics and check that everything is working correctly.

If possible, have a helper to guide you and, if necessary, to help manhandle the caravan.

Towing and driving Remember that the car and caravan may measure more than

double the length of vehicle you are used to, and that in turning through narrow entrances the caravan will tend to cut corners.

Keep a sharp lookout for obstructions which would not touch your car, but could well hit the caravan – road signs, projecting rock faces, tree branches, narrow arches and so on.

When overtaking, allow more time and make longer warning signals than you would with just a car; and allow for the van length when pulling back into the left.

Parking Try to find a level piece of ground. The caravan should be equipped with a spirit level, so you may be able to move the van around a little until you are satisfied. Once settled, put on the caravan brake and, if there is the slightest slope, chock the wheels.

Remove the safety chain and disconnect the electrics. Disengage the coupling and place the cover over the ball hitch. Adjust the jockey wheel until the van is level, then lower the steadying legs. At this point it is best to take the van brake off – otherwise the brake shoes tend to stick to the brake drums.

Trailers As with a caravan, check that your car can safely tow the weight of the trailer and the sort of load it will carry. Consult your local dealer or a trailer centre. Similar towing equipment is usually required, but direction indicators may not be necessary.

Never overload a trailer, but load it with more of the weight to the front and distributed evenly on either side. Cover and secure the load, and never carry passengers. As with a caravan, allow plenty of room when overtaking and pulling back in.

CARAVANS AND TRAILERS

Reversing a trailer around a sharp corner

It is advisable to practise this manoeuvre in a quiet road or an empty car park. And if possible get some instruction from an experienced caravanner. Always remember that the trailer tends to swing in the opposite direction to that in which the car is being turned. The technique shown here – backing a boat and trailer down a ramp – applies also to caravans.

As car and trailer fall into line on the ramp, straighten the car's front wheels and begin to ease the trailer backwards.

Then, again with one hand, turn the wheel to the left. This swing of the front wheels turns the car in the same arc as the trailer.

Although you aim to back left, put one hand at the bottom of the steering wheel and turn it to the *right*. This jackknifes the car and trailer until the trailer's rear points towards the head of the ramp.

Carbon monoxide poisoning

Where it may lurk and what action to take

Carbon monoxide gas has no colour, taste or smell to warn of its presence, and when encountered in a confined space can be a killer. Swift action is necessary if someone inhales it. The gas is a by-product of combustion, and may be encountered in the following areas:

Bathroom Older GAS WATER HEATERS may have an inefficient flue, or the flue may have become blocked. If you experience headaches, dizziness or difficulty in breathing, turn off the gas supply, open the windows and inspect the flue.

If the heater is blocked, or has not been serviced recently, get it looked at immediately.

Kitchen The same dangers can apply to an old gas water heater in the kitchen, and also to a solid fuel or gas central heating boiler. Sometimes an EXTRACTOR FAN pulls air down the flue, bringing dangerous fumes with it. A boiler should have its own air supply in the form of a ventilator.

Garage Carbon monoxide is present in car exhaust fumes and you could be at risk in a confined space. Do not run the engine in the garage – particularly with the doors shut.

The car Inspect the exhaust system regularly, bearing in mind that the average life of the ordinary mild steel exhaust is about 18 months. Block holes and cracks between the engine and passenger compartment with a flexible sealant, to reduce the risk of fumes seeping in.

Caravans and boats The risks here are similar to those in a kitchen or bathroom, but are heightened by the confined space. Never use an unflued heater or cooker in a caravan or boat, and always make sure that the flues are kept clean.

Traffic jams Switch off the engine and the ventilation booster fan during long hold-ups, to avoid sucking fumes from other cars into yours.

HELPING A CASUALTY If you find someone affected by fumes, take a deep breath before entering the area. Pull the casualty well clear as quickly as possible into fresh air, or open all doors and windows.

If the casualty is conscious, recovery will be quite rapid. If unconscious, place in the RECOVERY POSITION and summon expert help. If the casualty is not breathing, the kiss of life (see ARTIFICIAL RESPIRATION) should be administered. Or an expert first-aider can apply EXTERNAL CHEST COMPRESSION if necessary.

CAR CASSETTES AND RADIOS

Fitting a set and speakers

1 **Replacing a radio cassette** Remove cassette and carrier. Insert new carrier; bend tabs with screwdriver until locked into dashboard. Fit rear mounting bracket if supplied. Connect all leads, as specified in handbook. Insert new cassette.

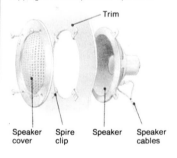

2 **Surface speakers** Remove the speakers from the pods. Position the pods and mark the screw holes. Drill the holes and an extra hole for wires. Attach the pods with self-tapping screws. Replace the speakers.

3 **Flush speakers** Remove the handles and trim panels on each door. Mark the speaker and screw holes. Cut out the speaker hole. Drill the screw holes and fit spire clips. Attach the speaker and cover.

Car cassettes and radios

Installing and maintaining them

Before buying a radio-cassette player, compare the various models available to see which one offers the most features within your price range.

The cheapest have only two wavebands, normally FM and AM, a manually tuned, analogue display, and a cassette player with fast forward and stop.

Medium-priced cassette radios have digitally tuned radios with either LED (light emitting diode display) or LCD (liquid crystal display) and a memory that stores your preferred stations.

The most expensive models are often fitted with RDS (radio data system), which automatically re-tunes your radio as you move around the country, and EON (extended other networks), which automatically interrupts the radio or cassette with the latest traffic news. The cassette player will probably feature track search, repeat and Dolby noise reduction.

Installing a set Most cars have space for the radio in the dashboard. Remove an existing radio and disconnect the aerial (see CAR AERIALS), speakers, earth and power leads.

Connect the replacement set according to the manufacturer's instructions. You will probably need to locate a live, positive feed that remains so even when the ignition is switched off. This is needed to maintain power to the rechargeable batteries that power the memory in the set. The positive wire should have an 'in-line' fuse incorporated in it to protect the set.

You may also need to locate a separate feed from the car light switch which illuminates the set's own internal light once the car lights are operated.

A negative feed is also required. If your car wiring does not appear to have one, locate a good earth on any metal part of the car, and attach to this a thick wire which in turn should be connected to the earth connection on the set.

Fitting speakers There are two types – surface-mounted and flush-mounted. Your choice may be largely governed by where they can be fitted.

For example, surface-mounted speakers go best in pods on the rear parcel shelf, but this is not practicable in estate or hatchback cars.

Flush-mounted speakers, however, can often be fitted into the door trims. Whichever type you buy, make sure they match the power output of the radio.

Attach the speaker pods to the rear parcel shelf. Place them well apart to get the best stereo effect. Run the wire from the set to the speakers under the carpet or under the trim on the inside of the door sills.

To fit flush speakers in the doors, first remove the inner door handles and window winders as described in the car's handbook or service manual. Prise off the trim with a screwdriver.

Choose a position for the speaker where it will not interfere with the window when it is wound down, and mark the outline of the speaker hole, slightly less than the overall size of the speaker, on the face of the trim.

Hold the speaker against the trim and mark the positions of the fixing screws. Cut out the speaker hole with a craft knife or trimming knife. Drill the screw holes and fit spire clips over them. The clips, obtainable from a car accessory shop, push onto the trim and are designed to take self-tapping screws. Attach the speaker, and if there is a separate grille, clip it onto the speaker.

To run the wires to the speaker, drill a hole in the door pillar and another in the door edge. Offset the holes by 25mm (1in) so that the wires will not kink when the door is opened or shut. Fit rubber grommets to the holes to protect the wiring. Connect the wires to the speaker and refit the door trim by banging the edge with the side of your fist to engage the spring clips.

When wiring speakers, make sure to connect the positive and negative wires to the appropriate terminals. The polarity may be determined by red (positive) and black (negative) wires which connect to terminals marked + (positive) and − (negative), or by terminals of different sizes so that they can only be fitted one way.

Cleaning and demagnetising After a while the pick-up heads of the cassette player become dirty, and may also become magnetised, caused by the friction of the tape. Most car cassette dealers sell cassette-care kits, which include a cleaning and demagnetising cassette. Follow the manufacturer's instructions.

Car horns

Repairing a faulty horn; stopping a continuously blowing horn

If your car horn fails, repair it as soon as possible – it is illegal to drive a vehicle without an audible warning device. The most likely fault is a blown fuse.

A blown fuse The fuses (see FUSES AND FUSE BOXES) are mounted in a box or on a panel usually on the bulkhead under the bonnet, or under the dashboard.

If the fuses are numbered, consult the car handbook to find which one protects the horn circuit. Alternatively, you may be able to see which one has blown.

Replace the fuse with a spare marked with the same amp rating – there is usually a spare in the fuse box. If the new fuse blows, there is a short circuit in the wiring which must be rectified by an auto-electrician.

If the horn works, check with your handbook to see if other circuits are protected by the fuse. Operate each in turn – one may be causing the fuse to blow.

If the fuse has not blown It is possible that the wiring connections to the horn

are corroded and must be cleaned up.

Pull the wires off their connectors, remove the horn and clean the terminals and connectors with fine emery cloth. If there is rust on the horn bracket at its mounting point, clean it and the mating area of the car body with a file and emery cloth until the metal of both is bright.

While the horn is removed, test it by connecting its terminals to the battery terminals using two lengths of insulated wire. If it works, bolt it back in position, connect it up and try sounding it again.

Finally, if the horn still fails to work, suspect the push-button switch. Often this forms part of a multi-function stalk switch on the steering column, and the complete switch unit must be replaced. Where the horn is operated by a button at the centre of the steering wheel, remove the button; clean and adjust the spring contacts beneath.

When a horn stays on If a horn will not stop blowing, tap the horn button – the switch may be stuck. If that fails, open the bonnet and disconnect the wiring to the horn. If the horn is difficult to get at, disconnect the battery to stop the horn blowing while you immobilise it – see BATTERIES.

Car insurance claims

Insuring your car; making a claim; dealing with a claim against you

Every car owner is required by law to be covered by insurance. This ensures that if an accident is caused by a driver's negligence, compensation is paid to anyone injured, or to the relatives of anyone killed.

Insurance policies There are four types of policy:
A *Road Traffic Act* policy is the cheapest and covers the minimum legal requirements. It compensates for injury or death anyone who has a legal claim against the driver.

It does not, however, cover claims for damage to another vehicle, which is covered by a *Third Party Only* policy. A *Third Party, Fire and Theft* policy also provides compensation if the car is damaged or destroyed by fire, or is stolen – it covers, too, damage caused by a thief.

A *Comprehensive* policy – the most expensive – gives all the benefits of Third Party, Fire and Theft insurance, plus cover for a wide range of other risks. These usually include: accidental damage, regardless of who is to blame; personal accident benefit; passengers' medical expenses; and loss or damage of items in the car.

It is best to shop around for insurance, or let an insurance broker or your motoring organisation do it for you (consult

Yellow Pages). They should get you the best value for money. A broker's services are free – they get commission from the insurance company. You can also buy insurance direct from some companies.

No-claims discounts Once insured you will start earning a no-claims discount: the insurance company will deduct a discount from your premiums if you have not made a claim or have not had a claim made against you. Most insurance companies give a 30 per cent discount after one claim-free year; this can rise to 60 or 65 per cent over four or five years.

Insurance claims If you are involved in an accident, and you consider that you were not to blame, you can claim against the other driver – see CAR ACCIDENTS.

Get a garage's written estimate for repairs to your car, then write either to the other driver or his insurance company stating that you hold him responsible for the damage and that he should pay for repairs. Inform your own insurance company of your actions.

If you have comprehensive insurance your insurance company will meet the repair bill, then claim the money from the other driver's insurance company if they agree that he was to blame.

With other policies, repairs cannot be put in hand until the other driver or his insurance company accept liability.

Claiming for fire or theft With Third Party, Fire and Theft cover, your insurance company will compensate you either for fire damage or the loss of your car if it is destroyed or stolen. If the estimate for repairs is high the company may send an engineer to inspect it. Should the cost be higher than the car's market value, they will write it off – and pay you the market value, or the value at which you insured the car if it is less.

In the case of a stolen car the insurance company will usually wait 28 days before settling your claim, in case the car is recovered.

Dealing with a claim against you If the claim is small – less than your no-claims discount – you may settle the claim personally. Tell your insurance company and make it clear to the claimant that the payment is in 'full and final settlement', without any admission of liability.

You can contest a claim that seems excessively high, but this could involve getting a qualified engineer's independent assessment. It is better to let your insurance company deal with it.

If you were undeniably in the wrong, your insurance company will settle the claim and you will lose part, but not necessarily all, of your no-claims discount for a period of time. In some cases where both drivers are claiming damages, each company will agree to pay for the repairs to the car it insures. This is known as a 'knock for knock' agreement and both drivers lose their no-claims discount.

Insurance abroad If you take your car abroad you may need a Green Card, which extends your normal insurance policy to cover you for driving overseas. Some insurance companies issue Green Cards free to their policyholders; the cost otherwise varies from company to company. In the European Community you have Third Party cover automatically, but not any fuller insurance.

The Automobile Association also issues Green Cards; they cost more than those issued by insurance companies, but give full comprehensive cover, even if normal insurance is only Third Party, Fire and Theft.

Car keys locked in car

How to avoid, or resolve, an embarrassing problem

You have parked your car, set the door locking button and slammed the door behind you – and your keys are still dangling in the ignition switch. You have a problem that could have been avoided had you taken a few simple precautions.

Not all cars have self-locking doors, but if yours has them, try to develop the habit of *always* locking them from the outside, using the key. As an extra precaution, carry a spare key with you, or conceal one somewhere on the exterior of the car.

You can buy a magnetic key case that fits under a wing or door sill, or you can tape a key behind a bumper or number plate.

If you do lock yourself out, however, the best thing to do is call the police. They will open the car for you within minutes. Alternatively, you may be able to open it yourself if the locking button is the type that looks like a golf tee, protruding from the door windowsill.

You will need a length of stiff wire, perhaps an opened-out wire coathanger. Bend the wire to make a hook about 10mm ($\frac{3}{8}$in) wide at one end, then work the hooked end of the wire between the door and door pillar. Pull on the door handle to make the gap as wide as possible, which will make manipulating the wire easier. Work the wire so that the hook catches on the button, then lift it up.

A loop of plastic baling tape will sometimes slip through a gap too narrow for coathanger wire. Slide the loop over the button, pull it taut, then raise it to lift the button.

Car locks frozen

Opening an iced-up car door

A quick and easy way to free a frozen car lock is to heat the key with matches or a cigarette lighter. Insert the hot key into the lock and leave it there for a few seconds for the heat to dissipate. Repeat if necessary until the key will turn normally – do not use force, as the key may snap.

You can also buy, from a car accessory shop, a lock de-icer, a small aerosol that squirts de-icing fluid into the lock. These usually take longer to work than a heated key.

When washing the car in winter, cover the keyholes with masking tape to keep out water. Keeping the locks well oiled will also help to avoid trouble, because oil will not freeze. Inject a few drops of thin oil into the keyhole, or run some oil onto the key and then insert it into the lock.

If the door latch freezes, operating the door handle lever or button a few times should free it. If this does not work, use an aerosol de-icer to inject fluid between the door and door pillar at a point just above the latch.

Carpet beetles

Getting rid of a damaging pest

These 3mm ($\frac{1}{8}$in) long beetles appear in spring. They are black, mottled cream and brown, or black with a white spot, and it is their larvae which do the damage.

They thrive in old birds' nests or among fluff in floor cracks and skirting boards, and in neglected cupboards, and feed on almost any natural fabric.

To avoid infestation, vacuum carpets regularly. Seal cracks in floorboards and skirting boards; if possible, change the position of large pieces of furniture and check the loft and airing cupboard for beetles or the moulted skin of larvae. Scatter mothballs among stored clothes and blankets or protect them by spraying with a mothproofing aerosol.

If you see signs of carpet beetles in a carpet, vacuum thoroughly and throw away or burn the contents of the vacuum bag immediately. Spray the carpet or other affected fabrics with a mothproofing aerosol.

Carpet cleaning

Save money by doing it yourself

It is possible to clean a carpet yourself with a carpet shampoo and shampooer, but antique or valuable carpets should always be cleaned professionally.

A carpet shampooer has foam rollers or brushes, sometimes both, that work the shampoo into the carpet as it is pushed back and forth. The shampoo is contained in a tank attached to the handle, and is fed to the rollers via a flow-control button or lever. An electrically operated carpet cleaner can be hired from a tool hire shop, dry cleaners or carpet shop. Operating instructions are supplied with it. Hot shampoo solution is placed into a tank in the machine, and this is fed through a flexible tube to a spray head fixed just in front of the machine's vacuum head. Dirt, old shampoo and most of the water applied to the carpet is sucked into the vacuum head, and into a collecting tank in the machine.

The best shampoo for home cleaning is dry foam, which is mixed with water to form the cleaning solution. If possible, use the brand recommended by the carpet manufacturer.

Before cleaning a carpet, vacuum it thoroughly. Treat any heavily stained spots with shampoo according to the manufacturer's instructions, and apply with a cloth, sponge or stiff brush, using a circular movement.

When the shampoo dries it forms crystals which can then be removed with a vacuum cleaner. Make sure the carpet is thoroughly dry before vacuuming – if heavy furniture has to be moved back before the carpet is dry, place aluminium foil under the feet to protect the carpet.

Carpet laying

Measuring and fitting for rooms

There are two commonly used methods of laying a fitted carpet: it can be tacked to the floor all round the edges of the room, or fixed to special strips of wood, nailed around the perimeter of the floor.

The strips are fitted with small spikes which hold the carpet in place, and they are used by most professional carpet fitters. A little more work is needed to nail down the strips, but they allow the carpet to be quickly and easily taken up at any time, simply by detaching it from its anchoring spikes.

First remove all furniture and any doors which swing into the room. Roughly position the carpet so that the pile sweeps away from the window, to avoid uneven shading in daylight.

Cut the carpet with either heavy scissors or a sharp trimming knife, allowing a margin of at least 38mm (1$\frac{1}{2}$in) on all sides up the skirting. Roll the carpet back halfway across the floor.

Nail the wooden strip to the floor, parallel to the skirting boards, but leaving a narrow gap of about 10mm ($\frac{3}{8}$in) between the strip and the wall. Repeat this process for the other half of the floor, excluding doorways.

Fitting a wall-to-wall carpet

Carpet

Gripper

Underlay

Fit the gripper strips with the teeth facing the skirting board. Take the underlay up to the edge of the strips, then lay the carpet. Using a knee-kicker (below), stretch it over the teeth and across the gap between strip and skirting.

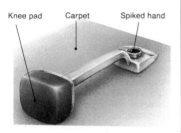

Knee pad   Carpet   Spiked hand

Push the spiked 'hand' at one end of the knee-kicker into the carpet and 'kick' the other, padded end with your knee. This stretches the carpet towards the skirting board. Repeat a couple of times, moving forward each time, until the knee-kicker touches the skirting board.

Unless the carpet to be laid has a foam rubber backing, it will need a separate underlay. This is made of felt or foam rubber and makes the carpet feel softer and thicker, as well as adding INSULATION and extending the carpet's life.

With the carpet rolled back, lay, cut and fit the underlay within the boundaries set by the wooden strips, dealing with half the room at a time. Staple or tack the underlay to the floorboards. If the underlay is laid on concrete, it should be held in place with an adhesive recommended by the manufacturer.

Unroll the carpet, anchor it temporarily along one side of the room with a few tacks about 150mm (6in) in from the wall. Then, starting from the centre of the opposite wall, stretch the carpet over the spikes of the wooden strip with the aid of a knee-kicker, which can be rented from tool hire shops.

When one side is fixed, remove the tacks holding the carpet along the opposite side. Again using the knee-kicker, re-stretch the carpet over the wooden strip, working from the middle of the wall outwards.

Trim the carpet to leave just a 10mm ($\frac{3}{8}$in) overlap along the two walls. Tamp the overlap firmly into the gap between the wooden strip and the wall skirting, by tapping a broad thin wedge into it

with a mallet. Repeat this process along the remaining walls.

The exposed edge of the carpet at a doorway should be protected with a strip of metal edging called a binder bar. A metal lip on the bar is slipped over the carpet edge, and the bar is nailed or screwed to the floor in the doorway. The metal lip is then hammered down to grip the carpet edge firmly.

Both the spiked wood strip (known as tackless fittings) and the binder can be obtained from DIY stores. Often, suppliers of new fitted carpets will fit it as part of the deal.

Carpet repairs

Mending small wear patches and burn holes

Small wear patches and burns are easily repaired – especially if you have any spare pieces of carpet, kept after it was laid.

Burn holes Remove any scorched fibres remaining with a sharp trimming knife or safety razor blade, to expose the backing beneath. Cut enough matching tufts to fill the hole from a place where it will not show, or a spare piece of carpet.

Dab the bottom of the hole and the ends of the tufts with a suitable latex adhesive, then insert the tufts into the hole. Leave to dry, then trim if necessary and brush to blend with the pile.

Worn patches If the pile is woven into the carpet backing, turn the carpet back and mark a square on the backing, over the damaged area.

Coat the area, plus about 25mm (1in) extra on all sides, with latex adhesive and rub it in with a rag or finger. This will prevent the carpet from fraying when you cut it. Now place a piece of wood under the damaged area on the pile side and, using a sharp trimming knife, cut out the marked square.

Cover the square hole in the backing with strips of hessian tape, overlapping the edges by about 50mm (2in).

Use the damaged square as a pattern to cut a new square from a piece of spare carpet, or from under heavy furniture where the gap will not show. Make sure that the pile in both runs in the correct direction and that any pattern matches.

Coat the back and edges of the new square with adhesive, taking care not to get it on the tufts. Press it firmly onto the hessian strips. Tap the edges lightly with a hammer to make them flush.

If the carpet is foam-backed, cut the damaged area from the tufted side. From a spare piece of carpet, cut a square slightly bigger than the damaged area and tack it temporarily into place to cover the hole.

Cut precisely round the new patch *and* through the carpet underneath. Remove the tacks, new patch and damaged patch. Turn back the carpet and stick strips of adhesive tape over the foam-back side of the hole. Roll the carpet face up again and press the new patch in place on the adhesive tape. Lightly hammer the edges down flush.

Car radio interference

Getting rid of buzzes and crackles

The ignition system, charging circuit and electrical accessories are the main sources of interference in a car radio. It may be transmitted through the aerial or conducted to the set along its wiring.

Before seeking the source of interference, check first to see that the radio has a good earth connection (see CAR CASSETTES AND RADIOS) and that there is a good earth contact beneath the aerial mounting and car body – see CAR AERIALS.

At this point, also check the aerial trimmer, a small screw on the side or front of the radio. With the radio tuned to a weak station, around the 250 metre (1200kHz) waveband, turn the screw with a small-bladed screwdriver until you get the maximum signal strength.

Most forms of radio interference are easily identified: a crackling or ticking noise that intensifies with engine speed

Suppressing electrical components

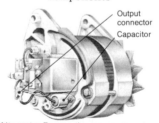

Output connector

Capacitor

Alternator Remove the rear cover and connect a 3mfd capacitor to the output connector. Mount the capacitor itself on the body of the alternator.

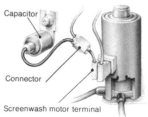

Capacitor

Connector

Screenwash motor terminal

Screenwash motor This is suppressed with a 1mfd or 2mfd capacitor fitted between the motor terminal and earth.

comes from the ignition; a whining sound that rises in pitch with engine speed is caused by the generator. Other noises are from electrical components, such as windscreen wipers or heater fan, and occur only when the component is switched on.

Ignition interference This takes the form of violent crackling generated by the high tension (HT) circuit. If the spark-plug leads and the lead from coil to distributor are carbon-cored – identifiable by the resistance value marked on the outer sheath – they have built-in suppression which may break down if the leads are stretched or damaged. Replace any suspect leads.

Copper-cored leads, used on many older cars, need a suppressor in the coil-to-distributor HT lead and suppressors on each spark-plug. There are two types of HT suppressor: one screws into the top of the coil, the other fits into the HT lead – cut the lead and screw the ends into the suppressor. Spark-plug suppressors are built into the spark-plug caps.

Low tension (LT) interference – the ticking generated by the contact breaker – can be cured by fitting a 1 Micro Farad (mfd) suppressor to the positive (+) connection on the coil. If you have an FM radio, fit a suppressor with two leads, attaching one lead to earth. Fit the suppressor under the coil mounting bolt.

Generator interference The generator, whether an alternator or dynamo, can be suppressed by fitting a capacitor – 1-3mfd for a dynamo, or 3mfd for an alternator – to the output terminal. Mount the capacitor under one of the generator fixing bolts, or as shown on page 81.

Interference from accessories All electric motors in the car generate a small magnetic field, but this is usually screened by the bodywork, when the bonnet is down. Interference may be conducted through the power supply cable to the set. Try re-routing the cable, or fit a choke in the cable. Alternatively, connect 1mfd or 2mfd suppressors between the supply to the accessory and earth.

Car roof racks

Gaining extra luggage space

Most roof racks, obtainable from car accessory shops, are adjustable to fit most car models. The fixing feet are held in the car's roof guttering and are held by clamps tightened either by bolts or by wing nuts. There are also models with clamping mechanisms designed for gutterless cars. Some cars have built-in fixing points for specially designed roof racks. Choose a rack that will fit

centrally over the roof area, with no overhang on any side.

The way you load a roof rack will determine its wind resistance, affecting both speed and petrol consumption. Lay the largest suitcases flat, with smaller items packed at the front. Lay smaller cases on top at the back, so that the load is higher there than at the front.

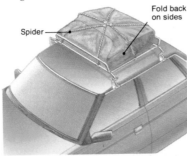

Spider

Fold back on sides

Economy drive Load higher at the rear end to minimise wind resistance – this cuts the amount by which fuel consumption is increased and maximum speed decreased.

For weather protection, cover the luggage with a tarpaulin or PVC sheet. Place the cover on the rack with the surplus ends hanging over the sides. Load the luggage and fold the sides of the cover over the top. Then take the front of the cover over to the back to make a neat 'parcel' with no folded edges facing the front. Secure the cover to the rack with rope or a bungee 'spider' – a stretch fastener which has elastic arms radiating from a central steel ring.

Never exceed the maker's recommended weight for roof loading, given in the owner's handbook, and inflate the tyres to the pressure for maximum load stated in the handbook.

Remove the rack when it is not in use. An unloaded rack can increase the car's petrol consumption by 5 to 10 per cent.

Car security

Protecting your vehicle against theft

Only the most sophisticated car security systems will deter a professional car thief, but there are fairly simple ones that will put off casual thieves and joy-riders. All can be fitted by the car owner.

One basic deterrent is to etch the windows with the car registration number. This will put off a thief because all the windows, as well as the number plates, would have to be replaced. Most car accessory shops sell etching kits.

The better electrical security systems will either set off an alarm if anyone tries to open the doors, or immobilise the ignition system if anyone but the owner tries to start the car.

One system has a pendulum unit which sets off the car horn if its balance is disturbed, for example by a door being forced. It is easy to fit and is in two parts, the pendulum unit and a key switch for setting the alarm, plus a few wires.

Another system has sensitive switches – similar to those that operate the car interior light – on all doors, the boot and the bonnet. If any of these are opened the car horn sounds and the headlights flash.

One of the more sophisticated devices has a set of push-buttons. A code number has to be 'dialled' before the car will start. Any attempt to bypass the unit sets off the horn.

Electronic technology is also used in a system that has ultrasonic sensors. Sound waves are transmitted inside the car, and if these are broken, perhaps by a window breaking, the alarm is activated.

Voltage sensors are used in another system. Any change in battery voltage – even the slight drop when a door is opened and the interior light operates – is detected and triggers the alarm.

A simpler device, such as a combination lock on the handbrake, will deter casual thieves. The handbrake release button cannot be depressed until the correct numbers are aligned on the lock.

There is also a telescopic bar with a hook at each end and a lock that holds the bar in a set position. One end hooks around a steering-wheel spoke and the other end hooks around the brake or clutch pedal. A similar device immobilises the gear lever.

Fit your security device in accordance with the manufacturer's instructions and display the warning sticker, if supplied. This is often a deterrent in itself.

Carving meat and poultry

Cutting up a joint or bird correctly

Make sure that your carving knife is sharp (see CUTLERY) and always use a two-pronged fork with a guard to protect your thumb should the knife slip. A smaller sharp knife will also be useful if bones have to be removed. In recent years, electric carving knives have gained popularity, as they take much of the effort out of the job.

Most meats should be left in a warm place for 10 to 15 minutes after they have been taken out of the oven. This makes it less likely that the flesh will crumble when you come to carve it.

Boned and rolled meats present no carving problems, but remember that all meat is best cut across the grain, as this makes it more tender. Where there are bones, a knowledge of exactly where they lie in the joint makes carving easier.

Cut beef in thin slices, pork and veal slightly thicker, and lamb thickest of all.

The basic techniques for slicing meat safely and without waste

Leg of lamb Position the leg meatiest side up and slice down to the bone. Take out two slices, each about 6mm (¼in) thick. Continue slicing from both sides of the cut, keeping the slices fairly thick. Turn the joint over, remove unwanted fat and carve horizontal slices along the leg.

Loin of lamb Use a small knife to remove the chine bone. Find the natural divisions between the bones and cut the meat into thick slices.

Saddle of lamb Make your first cut across the joint, then another at right angles to the first, down the centre so that you can remove the meat from the bone. Carve each piece in thick slices. Turn the joint over and carve the fillet lengthways.

Shoulder of lamb Position the joint with the fat side uppermost. Cut a long slice about 13mm (½in) thick from the centre of the joint right down to the bone. Carve slices from both ends of the first cut. Carve horizontal slices from the bone until all the meat has been removed.

Rib of beef Remove the chine bone at the thick end of the meat; loosen the meat by sliding the knife point between the meat and the rib bones. Carve down through the meat, keeping the slices thin.

Sirloin of beef Use a small knife to loosen the meat from the bone. Position the meat so that you can carve down to the bone, keeping the slices thin. Turn the meat over, remove the bone and continue carving downwards.

Best end of lamb Ask your butcher to remove the chine bone and also the thin outer layer of skin. Carve with the fat side uppermost and find the fleshy meat between the ribs with a small knife. Divide into cutlets.

Blade of pork Remove the crackling, then carve downwards around the hump-shaped bone, cutting two or three slices down to the bone, but leaving them attached. Then cut across the base of the slices to release them.

Hand of pork Remove the crackling, then detach the rib bones from the underside. Carve slices down from each side of the bone, then turn the joint over and carve the remaining meat horizontally.

Pork loin Use a small knife to remove the chine bone. It should come away quite easily. You can now cut right through the meat. Angle the knife slightly to increase the size of the slices, and cut back crackling.

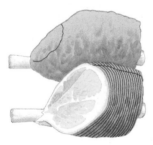

Duck Cut off the thighs and wings close to the body, then cut downwards through the centre of the breast. Carve slices parallel with the centre cut.

Whole gammon Remove a small triangular section at the knuckle end, then carve in an inverted V-shape along the bone, taking a thin slice first from one side, then the other, until all the meat is removed.

Chicken Insert a knife into the thigh joint, turn the bird and cut around the thigh, then remove the leg. Repeat with the other leg. Divide the legs into thighs and drumsticks. Cut off each wing, including a portion of breast. Lay the bird on its back and cut off the breast meat in thin slices from either side of the breastbone. Carve **turkey** and **capon** in the same way.

Duckling Use poultry shears or a knife to split the bird along the centre of the breastbone, from the neck to the back opening. Cut through the backbone to halve the bird.

Car washing and polishing

*Maintaining a car's finish inside
and out*

Clean your car and its interior every few weeks – more frequently in winter – and polish it once every six months. Choose a dry, warm day, but do not wash the car in direct sunlight as it will dry too quickly, leaving unsightly smears.

Interior Clean this first and, if practicable, unbolt and remove the front seats, and take out carpets and underfelt. Vacuum the floor pan and any carpet trim that cannot be removed.

Vacuum the carpets and if necessary clean them with a proprietary carpet cleaner. If there are worn patches, fit rubber mats, which can be loose-laid or stuck down with a latex adhesive. Car accessory shops stock them.

Vacuum the upholstery and clean with an upholstery cleaner. Use a special cleaner for vinyl. Lightly wash the roof headlining with a diluted cleaner.

Add a few drops of methylated spirit to warm water to clean inside the windows and windscreen. Try not to damage the electrical elements on a heated rear window – use a sponge and wipe along the line of the elements, not across.

Exterior Use plenty of clean water to wash down the bodywork, applied either with a hose or bucket. Start from the top, and if you use a hose, direct it under the wheel arches and sills to dislodge any build-up of mud. Do not hose the wheels, as water may get into the brake drums; use a stiff brush dipped in water.

If dirt still adheres to the bodywork, wash the car with warm water and a few drops of proprietary car-wash fluid. Do *not* use household detergents, which can streak the paintwork. Use a clean sponge or soft brush, and immediately after washing rinse thoroughly with cold, clean water and dry with a CHAMOIS LEATHER.

Remove obstinate tar spots, bird droppings, tree sap or insects with a soft cloth dipped in white spirit.

Pull the windscreen wiper arms away from the screen and wipe the blades with a sponge and undiluted windscreen washer fluid. Wash the windscreen and windows with clean water.

Polishing There are many brands of car polish available, some in paste form and some liquid; many contain wax that will give the car a deep shine and protect its finish.

After washing the car, apply the polish according to the manufacturer's instructions. Polish with a soft cloth, or with a buffing mop fitted to an electric drill (taking care not to damage any decorative trim). After polishing, clean tarnished chrome with a proprietary chrome cleaner.

When paintwork is dull and will not polish, try a cutting compound – a slightly abrasive polish which will cut through the grime and expose the bright paintwork beneath. But take care – used too often it will remove layers of paint. Do not use cutting compound on metallic-finish paintwork.

Casino

A card game for two or four people

The game is played by two opponents or two pairs of partners. A standard 52 card deck is used, and the object of the game is for a player, or team, to score 21 points before the other player – or team – can do so.

In ranking an ace counts as one, the other cards according to their numbers – two, three, four . . . up to ten, with the picture cards having no ranking. The deck is shuffled and cut for deal. Low card wins, and the dealer distributes cards clockwise starting on his left, placing the cards face down.

The dealer gives two cards at a time until each player has four; then he deals four cards face up onto the centre of the table, and sets aside the remaining cards face down as a *stock pile*.

When a hand is finished, the dealer again deals four cards per player from the stock pile – but does *not* deal four cards to the centre of the table. When the stock pile is exhausted, the deal passes left for the next round.

Play begins with the player on the dealer's left. If he has a card of the same denomination as one face up on the table, he may play this card – taking both the played card and the card from the table. If two or more cards of the same denomination are on the table, he may take them also. The exception is picture cards, where only one may be taken at a time.

He may also capture combinations from the board. For example, if he has a ten in his hand and there is a three and a seven on the table, he may take both of these cards by playing his ten. If two such denominations appear on the table, both adding up to ten, he may take both on the same play. And if a ten is also exposed at the same time, it may be collected along with the denomination. Play that takes every card from the table is called a *sweep*. And a sweep means a bonus point in the scoring (see below).

If a player is unable to play a card, he puts a card from his hand face up on the table with the others. When all players are out of cards, the deal is repeated, using the stock pile. Cards are not, however, dealt onto the centre of the table, even if it is bare.

The person making the last successful play on the final hand of the round claims all cards left on the table. At the finish of each round, players count and sort through the packs gathered from the table and points are awarded as follows: sweeps, point each; aces, point each; little casino (2 of spades), one point; big casino (10 of diamonds), two points; most cards captured, three points; most spades collected, one point.

Further rounds are played until a player, or team, at the close of a round, has scored 21 or more points, and so wins the game.

There are various strategies open to players. For example, *building combinations* on the table. A player holding a ten may see a five and a four on the table. If, in addition to the ten he holds an ace, he can pair the five and four on the table; and placing his ace on the pile he announces that he is *'building tens'*. On his next turn he can play his ten and gather the combination.

He can only build in this way if he can actually make the play on his next turn. But, before his turn comes round again, another player may steal his combination, provided that player holds a ten.

Also, another player may *raise the bid*. If one player announces he is building sixes, the next player may raise the bid to an eight by placing a two from his hand on the combination.

A strict rule is that a player cannot raise his own builds. For example, if he says he is building eights, he may not change it by adding yet another card on his next turn. He must play the eight and gather the cards. Also a card that raises a build must come from a player's hand – never by using cards from the table.

To prevent other players from raising a build, a player may resort to a tactic known as the *call*. For example, if a five and a three lie on the table, and a player holds a pair of eights, he can make a pile of the five and three and add one of his eights, announcing *'eights call'*.

Similarly, if there is an eight and a five on the table, and a player holds an eight and a three, he may play his three onto the five with the same effect – calling *'eights'*. Now no other player can raise the build. But even this tactic is not foolproof, since someone else holding an eight may take in the cards.

Casserole

*Covered-dish cooking in an oven
or on a hob*

For this you need a cooking pot complete with lid, and they are available in various materials. China, earthenware and porcelain pots are generally for oven use only, unless marked *flameproof* – see COOKWARE.

Pots made of cast iron, or steel coated with vitreous enamel, can be used either on the hob or in the oven – and the same applies to flameproof glass. If the casserole is cooked on top of the cooker, the heat must be kept low.

Meat, fish and vegetables can all be cooked deliciously in a casserole. To get a good consistency, combine 3 parts solids with 1 part sauce to prevent the dish becoming either too watery or too stodgy.

Cut meat into small pieces, dip in seasoned flour then brown in a FRYING pan with a little fat or oil. Drain the meat then place it in the casserole. Next, brown prepared vegetables in the frying pan, and put in the casserole with the meat. Finally, prepare the sauce.

This may be made simply by sprinkling flour onto dripping in the frying pan, heating it for a few minutes, then adding stock or water and seasoning. Bring to the boil, then pour this sauce over the ingredients in the casserole.

Put the lid on and place the casserole in the oven set at 150-180°C (300-350°F), gas mark 2-4, or on the hob. Cooking time should be slow. Two to two and a half hours is normal for good quality stewing steak and lamb. Allow longer for the tougher cuts of meat, less for tender lamb and chicken. Check the seasoning and thickness of the gravy before serving; gravy can be thickened with a little flour if necessary.

Cassettes and recorders

Testing, cleaning, demagnetising; unjamming tapes

Electrical and mechanical faults and breakages are best left to the supplier or a repair shop. Poor performance and sound reproduction are due often to lack of cleaning and maintenance.

There are some simple tests you can make if the machine stops working completely. Remove the cassette, switch on and look to see if the capstan that turns the cassette is working. If it is turning,

the tape has jammed or broken (see below). If not, try these further tests:

Battery-operated machine Remove batteries and clean their connections with fine emery paper to improve contact. Replace batteries and try again. If this fails, fit new batteries. If this also fails, seek expert advice.

Mains-operated machine Check the connections to the machine and the wiring to the power plug, also the fuse in the plug – see FUSES AND FUSE BOXES; PLUGS. Tighten or reconnect loose or broken wires. Replace a blown fuse. If the machine does not work and/or the fuse blows again, seek expert advice.

Tape problems Always keep cassettes in their boxes – left loose they attract dust, which affects performance.

If the machine runs smoothly until a cassette is inserted, check that the spools and tape run freely, and the tape is not twisted or jammed in the cassette.

Where a tape has snagged badly in the recorder, cut the tape and pull an end through: you can rejoin it by using a splicing kit available from dealers.

If the tape has snagged inside the cassette, ease out the tangled portion, then lay the creased section on a clean, smooth surface and press the wrinkles out with your fingers. Rewind the tape. Where tape is damaged, cut off the damaged piece with a razor blade and rejoin, using the splicing kit.

Cleaning Keep the recorder dust-free, and clean it once a week or after every ten hours of play. Dealers and electronics shops sell service kits containing a cleaning brush, tape head cleaning fluid and a tape head cleaning cassette.

Sometimes, the tape head develops a magnetic charge which can also distort recording. Special demagnetising cassettes are available to deal with this.

See also CAR CASSETTES AND RADIOS.

Easy-to-fit types and patterns

Ball and wheel castors are made with plate or peg-and-socket attachment. The plate type should be used where the castor is to be fitted to cross-grain wood, such as under the frame of a bed, which would split if drilled to take the socket for a peg-and-socket castor.

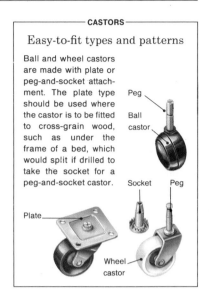

Peg

Ball castor

Socket *Peg*

Plate

Wheel castor

Castors

Making furniture mobile

There are two main types of castors – small swivelled wheels for fitting to furniture – wheel and ball. Both are available from hardware and DIY stores.

Wheel castors These come in differing patterns and sizes, ranging from simple fixed wheels of metal or plastic to rubber-tyred models.

There are also twin-wheel castors which can carry heavier loads, and are more manoeuvrable than single wheels.

Ball castors These, too, come in a number of sizes but are handed *left* and *right*. So a set normally consists of two right-hand and two left-hand castors. For best results, put left diagonally opposite left, and right diagonally opposite right.

Two ways of fixing castors are:

Peg and socket This is used for fixing into end-grain wood. Drill a hole to the size given with the instructions and tap the metal socket supplied into the hole.

Push the peg of the castor into the socket – it is usually locked in place by a firm tap with a mallet or rubber hammer.

Plate A plate may be fixed to a castor, or supplied as a separate unit into which a peg attached to the castor will fit. The plate should be screwed into cross-grain wood, and should sit well within the thickness of the timber, so that the screws are not too near the edges. Always drill start holes into the wood to prevent the screws from splitting it.

Any legs to which castors are being attached must be set vertically, not splayed.

Cleaning tape heads; unjamming cassette tape

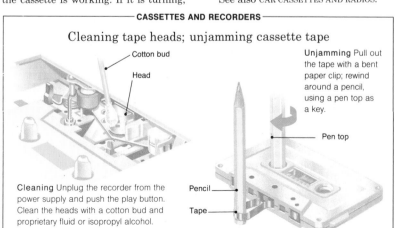

Cotton bud

Head

Unjamming Pull out the tape with a bent paper clip; rewind around a pencil, using a pen top as a key.

Pen top

Pencil

Tape

Cleaning Unplug the recorder from the power supply and push the play button. Clean the heads with a cotton bud and proprietary fluid or isopropyl alcohol.

Caterpillars

*How to stop them destroying
your plants*

Caterpillars can do untold harm to growing plants – flowers, fruit and vegetables – in a very short space of time. But the only harmful butterfly caterpillar is that of the cabbage white, which has a voracious appetite for brassicas. Most other caterpillars are the larvae of moths. All of them hatch out from eggs laid in the spring, and begin feeding immediately.

Here is how to spot some of the worst offenders:

Buff-tip moth Hairy caterpillar with orange stripes and a black head. Likes the leaves of fruit trees, mostly in midsummer.

Cabbage white butterfly Caterpillars green, black and yellow, to be found stripping the leaves from any brassicas. Their black droppings also foul the vegetables.

Codling moth Small and pale pink, these caterpillars start as eggs laid on the young fruits of apple or pear. On hatching they immediately tunnel, usually through the eye, into the core where they feed from July to September.

Pea moth The caterpillar is pale yellow-green, and tunnels into pea pods to feed on the peas.

Tortrix moth There are several species, of different colours, and they feed on the foliage of roses and other ornamental shrubs and trees. They can be identified by their habit of wriggling backwards when disturbed.

See also CUTWORMS.

Dealing with caterpillars They can be controlled by insecticides (see PESTICIDES), most of which kill by contact or are stomach poisons – applied either by a direct spray or through systemic formulations which are absorbed by the plant.

Treat infested plants as early as possible, especially the kind where caterpillars will eventually burrow into fruit and so gain protection from the insecticide. Insecticidal dusts are available for treating soil or leaves which may be harbouring caterpillars.

Before choosing an insecticide, check that it is safe to use on the plants you wish to treat. This is most important with flowering fruits and vegetables which are to be harvested. Derris and trichlorphon are the best insecticides for edible crops – the produce can be harvested within two or three days of the last application.

In addition to chemical attack, regular handpicking of plants to remove egg clusters or visible caterpillars will help.

Recognising aristocrats of the feline world

The majority of domestic cats in Britain – some 5 million of them – are of unknown ancestry. Those whose ancestry can be traced back for several generations, through breeding records, can be registered for showing – there are more than 30 varieties or breeds. Here are four of the more popular ones:

Snowy-white Chinchilla

Siamese

Persian

Short-haired tortoiseshell

Cats

*Choosing them, training them and
keeping them healthy*

Cats are independent creatures, but they still need care and attention to keep them healthy and happy. Neglect soon leads to scavenging, an unkempt appearance and possibly disease. Alternatively, overfeeding and pampering can soon make a cat overweight, and its general health will suffer from lack of exercise.

Choosing Look for a sleek coat with no thin or bare patches. A cat or kitten should be clean on the hind legs and under the tail. Check how it responds to handling and play: lack of response and a general lethargy may indicate poor health or neglect. If in doubt, consult a vet. If you live in the country, where the cat will roam free, keeping down rats and mice, a short-haired tabby of country origin will like the life.

A town cat will prefer the fireside, and dislike unpleasant outdoor conditions. Your choice here may be the black, white and coloured strains which have inbred with the tabbies, or the more highly prized strains which you will see being preened at the shows.

Should you prefer a thoroughbred, first visit a large cat show. There you will see the shorthaired cats – the Siamese, Burmese and Abyssinian – and the spectacular long-haired varieties – Persians, Colour-points and Chinchillas. Their breeders will be able to give you expert advice.

Feeding A wide variety of canned, moist and dry proprietary foods can give your cat a well-balanced diet. Do not feed dry foods alone.

Some adult cats like to eat twice a day; others prefer one main meal. Milk can be given occasionally, but not all cats like it. Fresh water should always be available. Restrict liver and fish to not more than twice weekly. Too much of either causes dietary problems. Avoid fatty scraps, poultry skins, and all bones from meat, fish or poultry.

Grooming Daily grooming is advisable, so you will need a brush, or a comb with rounded tips, to stimulate the skin and remove loose fur. Long-haired breeds need grooming twice a day in spring, when their hair moults. Check regularly for FLEAS, which can cause worms and disease. If you find any, treat the cat with a proprietary spray or powder.

If a cat seems off-colour and uninterested in food, there are additives containing extra vitamins available from pet shops as a pick-me-up. But if the cat does not respond, and there are signs of deterioration or perhaps loss of hair, seek advice from a vet.

Training Where a cat is new to your home, allow it to explore the place freely, but keep it indoors for at least ten days. Provide a litter box, partially filled with an even layer of commercial cat litter, and remove soiled litter daily. The container should be totally emptied and cleaned with a safe disinfectant at least twice a week.

Apart from keeping an eye on the cat's general health, it is wise to have a vet immunise any new cat or kitten against feline enteritis and cat flu. Annual booster injections are needed. Holiday kennels will rarely accept cats that have not been immunised.

The vet will also advise on checking for worms and having a cat neutered if it is not to be used for breeding.

CAT'S CRADLE

How to make one, and turn it into a 'soldier's bed'

1 Loop the string around the palm of each hand. Hook your right middle finger under the loop on the right palm, then repeat using the left middle finger.

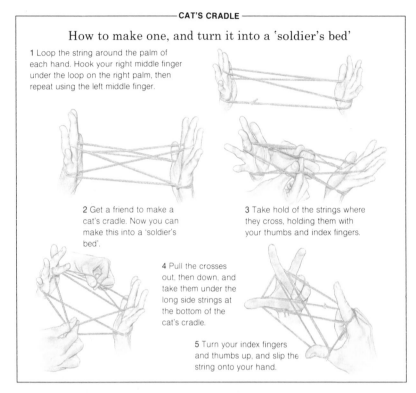

2 Get a friend to make a cat's cradle. Now you can make this into a 'soldier's bed'.

3 Take hold of the strings where they cross, holding them with your thumbs and index fingers.

4 Pull the crosses out, then down, and take them under the long side strings at the bottom of the cat's cradle.

5 Turn your index fingers and thumbs up, and slip the string onto your hand.

Cat's cradle

Having fun with a loop of string

This is a string manipulation game based on a loop of string. By getting a partner to pick up the strings at various points where they cross, and transferring them over to their own hands, a variety of patterns can be formed.

Ceiling rose

Renewing a light fitting

Before buying a new ceiling rose, examine the old one to see what kind you need. Switch off the power at the main fuse box (see FUSES AND FUSE BOXES) and remove the fuse that controls the lighting circuit.

Unscrew the rose cover and let it slide down the pendant flex.

Note how many terminals are in use in the rose. If only three are holding wires, the rose is fed from a JUNCTION BOX; buy a rose with similar terminals – or use one with more terminals and leave some unconnected.

If the old rose has four terminals in use, the wiring is of the loop-in system, where no junction box is employed. All wires pass through this rose, so you need to obtain one with the same number of terminals, or more.

Fitting Undo the terminal screws holding the pendant flex in the old rose with a small screwdriver and remove flex, rose cover and lampholder.

Loosen the remaining terminal screws holding the wires coming down through the ceiling, noting where each of the wires is connected.

In a loop-in rose, make sure the black wire from the switch cable (connected beside the brown flex wire) has a red tag on it.

Straighten all the wires then undo the screws holding the rose to the ceiling. In older homes, the rose may be in two pieces, the first piece attached to the ceiling, and the second piece screwed to the first.

Remove the old rose and brush away any dust and plaster debris. The new rose should fit into the same screw holes as the old.

Feed the wires in the ceiling through the hole in the centre of the new rose and secure the rose in place with the two fixing screws. If it is not situated directly under a joist, nail a wooden strut between JOISTS and screw into that.

Connect all the wires as illustrated, screwing each of them tightly into the correct terminal.

Prepare the new piece of flex and connect it to the lampholder as illustrated. For plastic fittings, two-core flex is needed, but metal fittings need three-core flex, connecting the earth wire to the rose and the metal fitting.

Cut the new flex to length, thread it through the rose cover.

Bare just enough of the insulated wires for them to pass over the anchor points in the ceiling rose and connect to the outer terminals.

Only the outer sleeve of the flex should show when the cover has been threaded on the flex and screwed into place.

CEILING ROSE

How the two different types are wired

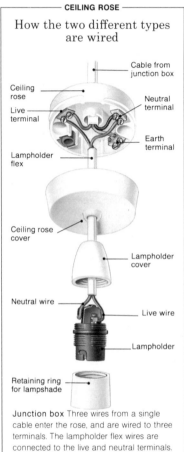

Cable from junction box

Ceiling rose

Neutral terminal

Live terminal

Earth terminal

Lampholder flex

Ceiling rose cover

Lampholder cover

Neutral wire

Live wire

Lampholder

Retaining ring for lampshade

Junction box Three wires from a single cable enter the rose, and are wired to three terminals. The lampholder flex wires are connected to the live and neutral terminals.

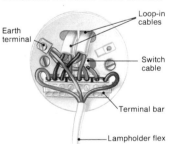

Loop-in cables

Earth terminal

Switch cable

Terminal bar

Lampholder flex

Loop-in Three cables enter the rose. Screw all the green/yellow-sleeved wires to the earth terminal, the three reds to the centre threesome, the two loop-in blacks and the blue to the outer threesome, the red-tagged black from the switch cable and the brown to the outer twosome.

Central heating

The systems available, and how to maintain them

Gas, oil, solid fuel and electricity are all used to. heat central heating systems. Except for two of the electrical systems they all use the 'wet' principle: water is heated by a central boiler, then pumped to radiators placed throughout the house. A thermostat maintains an even warmth by switching the pump on or off when the temperature rises or falls around a preset level.

Some wet systems also heat domestic tap water, by feeding hot water from the central heating pipes through tubes in a separate water storage cylinder. The central heating water and tap water supply are always kept separate. In the central heating system the same water is circulated continuously, topped up occasionally by water from a feed and expansion cistern usually situated in the roof space.

The two electrical systems use off-peak power, which is cheaper during certain hours of the night. In one, air is drawn over a heated storage block, then blown through ducts to the various rooms.

The storage block is rather like a larger version of the storage heaters used in the other electrical system, though this heating system is not strictly 'central', as each storage unit is a heat source in itself.

The heaters can be controlled in several ways – some release their heat at a greater rate at the end of the day, by either manual or automatic controls; others are fan-assisted and some have a thermostat-controlled fan.

Choosing a system There is little difference in the running costs of the four systems, though oil prices tend to fluctuate more than gas, solid fuel and electricity. Gas and electricity, however, gain an advantage in that fuel to operate them does not have to be stored on the premises.

Looking after your central heating Electrical heating systems need little or no maintenance, but to get the best from a wet central heating system, have it serviced once a year, during the summer months while it is not in use.

Get the servicing done by a member of the Heating and Ventilating Contractors' Association (head office: 32-34 Palace Court, London W2 4JG). If gas work is involved he should also be a member of the Confederation for the Registration of Gas Installers (CORGI).

There are, however, a number of things you can do yourself to ensure trouble-free heating:
● During the summer, switch on the pump once or twice to keep it free; open and close the pipe and radiator valves

---

Replacing a leaking radiator; replacing a pump

If a radiator leaks from a hole or welded seam, close the control valve. If there is also a lockshield valve, remove the cover and close it with a spanner – if there is not, drain the system. Disconnect the radiator joints at both ends. Catch any water spillage in a bowl. Lift the radiator off its brackets. Fit a replacement and wrap thread-sealing tape round the threads. Reconnect the joints. Open the lockshield to refill, and bleed the system.

Lockshield valve Count the turns needed to close it. Reset open with the same number.

Air lock Release the air by turning the bleed screw with a specially designed key.

On/off control

Control valve Turn it off and on by hand to shut off or restore the water supply.

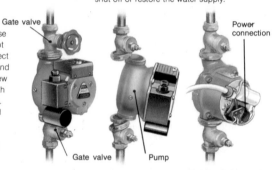

Changing the pump Close the gate valves if any, if not drain the system. Disconnect the pump from the pipes and electrical contacts. Fit a new pump of the same type with connections the same size. Restore the water flow and check that unions are watertight. Reconnect the electrical wiring and bleed the air from the system.

Gate valve · Power connection · Gate valve · Pump

---

occasionally to prevent them sticking.
● Go into the roof space at least once yearly and check that the ball valve in the feed and expansion cistern pivots freely. A smear of petroleum jelly on the pivot will help keep it free and prevent corrosion.
● Clean the fuel filter of an oil-fired system regularly. Turn off the oil supply at the tank and switch off the electrical ignition system. Remove the screws holding the filter unit and withdraw the filter. Wash it in petrol and let it air-dry before refitting.
● Clean a solid-fuel or oil-fired boiler every six months (but leave any adjustments of the control mechanisms to a qualified engineer). Cover the burner of an oil-fired boiler with a clean rag, then wire brush the furnace walls and remove the carbon dust with the extension hose of a vacuum cleaner.
● In a solid-fuel boiler, replace damaged or worn fire bars and patch damaged fireclay linings with a repair kit obtainable from a builders' merchant. To ensure maximum efficiency, always use the correct fuel for the burner. Your solid-fuel merchant will advise you if you tell him the make and model. Empty cold

ash from the ashpan whenever it becomes full. Have the flue cleaned at least once a year.

Problems and cures
Most faults that arise during the running of central heating are easily rectified.

Air locks A radiator that is warm at the bottom and cold at the top has air in it which must be bled out. Switch off the circulation pump and slacken the bleed screw at one end of the top rail of the radiator. A special key for this, obtainable from a hardware shop, fits over the squared end of the screw. Place a jar or hold a cloth under the bleed screw. At first air will escape with a hiss, and if you place one hand on the radiator you will feel the heat rising. When it reaches the top, be ready to close the screw when water flows from it.

If radiators do not heat up fully, this may be due to poor water circulation caused by air locks in the pipes. To clear them, open the vent plug on top of the circulation pump and close it when water begins to flow. Use a small spanner to slacken the nipple in the flow pipe from the pump. Close it when water escapes.

Water leaks Leaking pipe joints and radiator connections can usually be repaired only by remaking or replacing the joint (see PLUMBING), though a leak from a compression joint may be cured by tightening the joint. Take care not to overtighten or you may make the leak worse. To repair a joint you will need to drain or partly drain the system.

If a radiator leaks from a small pinhole or from a welded seam it must be replaced. Close the control valve at one end of the radiator, and if there is a valve at the other end, remove the cover and close the valve with a spanner, counting the number of turns. This valve, called a lockshield, is preset to control the flow of water; it must be reset to the same position when it is reopened.

Closing both valves isolates the radiator so that there is no need to drain the system. But if the radiator has only one valve, drain the system.

Use a spanner to disconnect the joints at both ends of the radiator. Place a bowl under the joints to catch any remaining water.

Lift the radiator off its fixing brackets and replace it with one of the same type and size.

Wrap PTFE thread-sealing tape around the threads before reconnecting the joints of the replacement radiator. Open the lockshield valve by the same number of turns taken to close it.

Refill the system if it has been drained. Open the control valve and the bleed screw until all air has been expelled.

Changing a pump The circulation pump is more prone to failure than any other component. If you suspect the pump is faulty, switch it on and put your hand on it – you should feel a slight vibration. Or listen to check that it is running by placing a long screwdriver against the casing and holding the other end against your ear.

To replace the pump, close the gate valves in the pipes on either side, or drain the system. Make a note of how the electrical connections to the pump are made and remove them with a screwdriver. Unscrew the union nuts connecting the pipes to the pump.

Be sure to replace the pump with one of the same type, or with the same size connections. If possible, take the old pump with you when you buy the new one from a central heating appliances supplier.

Fit the new pump and open the gate valves, or refill the system; check that the unions are watertight. Reconnect the electrical wiring. Bleed air from the system.

Cool radiators If the top floor radiators are cold, check that the feed and expansion cistern has water in it and that the ball valve is operating. Depress the valve

arm; if no water comes through, repair or replace the valve – see BALL COCKS.

Cool radiators farthest from the boiler indicate that the system is out of balance. The lockshield valves on the radiators are set so that those farthest from the boiler receive more water than those nearest to it, the valve on the last one being fully open. Only attempt to rebalance the system yourself if the problem is minor, otherwise get expert help.

Cold patches in a radiator are caused by blockages – usually of sludge – which can be cleared by flushing.

Flushing First remove the radiator (see above). Completely remove the bleed screw and push a cork or wooden bung into the pipe connection at the bottom rail. Take the radiator outside and lay it flat on the ground. Put a garden hose into the open end of the bottom rail and flush until clean water flows freely from the bleed hole. Remove the hose and refit the radiator.

Draining the system The system must be drained if you remove radiators that cannot be isolated – for example if there is only one valve on a radiator, or if the whole system is blocked. First turn off the water at the feed and expansion tank stop valve, or tie up the ball valve arm. Fit a garden hose to the drain cock on the boiler return pipe, at the bottom of the boiler, and secure it with a hose clip.

Run the hose out to a convenient drain and open the drain cock with a spanner. Open all the radiator bleed screws, and the bleeds on the pump and its return pipe. Allow the system to empty.

Close the drain cock and all the bleed screws. Slowly refill the system at the feed and expansion tank. Filling slowly lessens the risk of air locks – any that do occur should be bled out of the system.

Ceramic tiles

Tiling a wall or floor; replacing a broken tile

There is a wide range of colours, patterns and finishes in ceramic tiles for both wall and floor covering, but there are important differences between the two types.

Floor tiles These are fired at a higher temperature than wall tiles. They are also slightly thicker and more difficult to cut. They are available in sizes 100 × 100mm (4 × 4in), 150 × 150mm (6 × 6in) and 200 × 100mm (8 × 4in).

Wall tiles The commonly used sizes of ceramic wall tiles are: 108 × 108mm ($4\frac{1}{4}$ × $4\frac{1}{4}$in) and 150 × 150mm.

For covering the main area of a wall or floor, field tiles are used. These have

square, unglazed edges and some have spacer lugs to ensure uniform spacing when butted together. Border tiles have one rounded and glazed edge and are known as RE (round-edge). Tiles for corners have two adjacent round edges and are termed REX. Universal tiles are glazed on all edges and can be used as both field and borders.

The top edge of a row of field tiles can be finished with *quadrant tiles*, which are like a narrow strip of a round-edge tile.

Tiling a wall The wall surface must be clean, dry and perfectly flat. Remove any wallpaper or loose flakes of paint and fill holes in the plaster – see PAINT STRIPPING; PLASTER PATCHING; STOPPERS AND FILLERS; WALLPAPER REMOVAL.

Make sure that your starting point is level. If you are tiling a complete wall, fix a temporary horizontal batten (see BATTENS) with its upper edge a tile width from the floor or skirting, and level it with a spirit level.

Mark off a number of tile widths on another batten and use this as a measuring staff to mark the tile positions on the wall batten. Start marking from the centre of the wall, or from the centre line under a window. Aim to have any cut tiles at each end and of the same width.

Decide at which end of the wall you wish to begin fixing the tiles, and nail a vertical batten to the wall at this point, aligning it with a plumb line or spirit level. Check the intersection of the two battens by placing some loose tiles in the angle – they must fit perfectly square.

Use an adhesive recommended by the tile manufacturer and spread it evenly over the wall, covering an area of about four rows of six tiles. Ridge the surface with a notched spreader. Press each tile firmly onto the adhesive and work in horizontal rows. If the tiles do not have spacer lugs, use matchsticks as spacers, or plastic, cross-shaped spacers available at DIY shops. Make frequent checks with a spirit level – every third or fourth row – and wipe off any surplus adhesive.

To tile into a recess, tile the wall surrounding the recess first, then lay a row of glazed-edge tiles inside the recess so that their edges overlap the straight edges of the surrounding wall tiles. Fix cut tiles at the rear of the recess.

Cutting wall tiles In general, modern tiles are too hard to cut with a wheel cutter or tile spike. A platform tile cutter, obtainable from DIY shops, will probably be necessary. It will cut tiles up to 11mm ($\frac{3}{8}$in) thick. If in doubt, buy one or two tiles and test for the best cutting method, rather than investing in a lot of tiles you find hard to cut and trim.

Cutting floor tiles Many floor tiles can be cut with a platform cutter, but some may need a special cutter from a hire shop.

---- CERAMIC TILES ----

Marking exact guidelines and laying tiles

Tiling a wall Do not assume that a floor or skirting board is level. Fix a horizontal batten a tile width up, and level it with a spirit level. Fix a vertical batten and check it with a plumb line. Then mark off the tile widths on the battens. Put the first tile in the right angle where the battens meet to make sure it is a perfect fit. Remove battens after 24 hours when the adhesive has set, to finish tiling.

Tile types From left to right: field, border (round-edge), corner (REX) and quadrant.

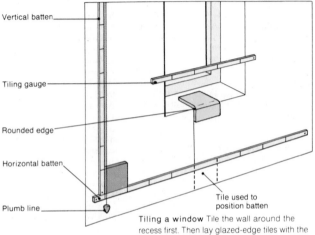

Vertical batten

Tiling gauge

Rounded edge

Horizontal batten

Plumb line

Tile used to position batten

Tiling a window Tile the wall around the recess first. Then lay glazed-edge tiles with the glazed edges facing into the room. Fix cut tiles to the rear of the recess.

Tiling a floor Draw a line on the floor from the centre of the doorway to the far wall. Make sure the line is 90 degrees to the door. With a measuring staff, mark off the drawn line in tile widths. Then nail a batten at the far wall where the last tile ends. Use masonry nails lightly tapped in. Nail another batten along a wall at right angles to the first to form a corner. The marked line and the second batten must be parallel. Spread the adhesive over about a square metre of the corner with a notched trowel. Starting at the joint made by the battens, press each tile into place. Leave a gap for grouting between tiles with no spacer lugs. Scrape off surplus adhesive before moving on.

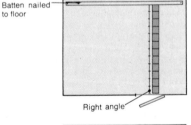

Batten nailed to floor

Right angle

Right angle

Marked line

Second batten

Door

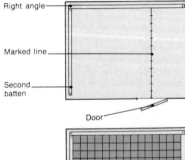

Whole floor tiled except for borders

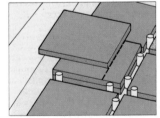

Grouting gap Instead of using the usual 3mm ($\frac{1}{8}$in) plastic spacers, you can make wider grouting a decorative feature by using lengths of 6mm ($\frac{1}{4}$in) dowel rod.

Grouting After the tile adhesive has set – usually in about 24 hours – fill the spaces between the tiles with grout, available in powder form to be mixed with water, or as a ready-mixed paste. Mix the powder to a stiff consistency.

Spread grout liberally with a sponge, pushing it well into the joints. Use a clean, flat sponge to wipe away the excess grout before it sets. As the grout begins to harden, run a stick with a rounded tip along the joints to give a neat finish. When the grout has set, polish the tiles with a soft cloth. Ready-mixed grout in a range of colour shades is also available. See also TILE REGROUTING.

Laying floor tiles Concrete floors provide the best base for ceramic tiles, though they can be laid on a wooden floor lined with sheets of 13mm ($\frac{1}{2}$in) plywood or chipboard.

An adhesive recommended by the tile manufacturer can be used on both wooden or concrete floors. However, if a concrete floor is not perfectly level, it is better to level it, using a self-levelling floor compound – see UNEVEN FLOORS.

Cutting floor tiles Floor tiles need a special cutter which can be hired from a hire shop. Or you can have them cut by the tile stockist.

To mark where a tile is to be cut, put it face down on top of the last full laid tile, then place a second tile on top, fitted against the wall. Use a felt-tip pen to mark where the second tile overlaps the first, then cut the first tile along the line. The uncovered part will fill the gap. If you are having the tiles cut, number each space and corresponding tile.

Grouting floor tiles Allow 24 hours for the adhesive to set and fill the spaces with grout as for wall tiles, but leave the grout flush, rather than finishing with a rounded stick.

Replacing a damaged tile First dig out the grouting surrounding the damaged tile with a sharp tool, such as a pointed scraper. Then chip away the tile with a hammer and cold chisel, working from the centre. Scrape out the old adhesive, apply fresh adhesive to the back of the new tile and press it into position. Regrout the spaces around the tile.

Chafing dish cooking

Adding an Edwardian touch to your table

The elegant chafing dish, fashionable in Edwardian times, remains not only decorative, but delightfully useful. It is ideal for slow, even cooking or rapid FLAMBÉ COOKING – even for keeping food warm on the sideboard. Best of all, delicacies

Cooking at the table A chafing dish set on a trivet over a small spirit burner enables you to cook a dish such as crêpes suzette at the table and serve it hot on the spot.

can be served straight out of the dish and onto your plate, the moment they are cooked.

A traditional chafing dish – often silver or silver plate – comprises a shallow pan with a domed cover, set on an ornate trivet (stand) containing a small spirit burner. Genuine Edwardian ones may be found in antiques shops or acquired at auctions; new ones are available from some large department stores or high-quality kitchen equipment shops – many restaurants use them.

For breakfast, EGGS can be scrambled to fluffy perfection; kidneys and mushrooms lightly sautéed in butter; bacon crisped just enough in its own fat . . . perhaps best of all you can delight luncheon or dinner guests with such treats as CRÊPES SUZETTE or *Poires flambées*, a French recipe for pears in brandy:

Ingredients (for 4)
4 ripe, firm dessert pears
4 pieces of stem ginger
25g (1oz) unsalted butter
2 tablespoons brandy
1-2 tablespoons ginger syrup
2 tablespoons double cream

Preparation Peel the pears, cut them in half and scoop out the cores with a teaspoon. Quarter each piece of stem ginger and set aside.

Fill the chafing-dish burner with methylated spirit, light it and adjust the flame to give a moderate heat.

Cooking Put the butter in the dish and set it over the heat. When it has melted fry the pears, cut side down, until they are golden-brown. Turn them and fry the other sides.

Fill a warmed tablespoon with brandy, set it alight and pour over the pears; repeat with the remaining brandy. Arrange the pears on plates, two halves on each, with two pieces of ginger in each cavity.

Add the ginger syrup and cream to the juices in the pan and stir over a gentle heat to make a sauce. When the sauce is well blended and thoroughly heated, spoon a little over each portion and serve immediately.

Chain saw

Sawing safely, and servicing

This is a powerful and useful tool, but handling it calls for strength, care and a degree of skill. An average handyman will find it fast and efficient for dividing long branches into shorter logs, or for rough-cutting heavy timber. But felling and trimming a tree is best left to a skilled operator.

WARNING Never use a chain saw when you are up a tree or ladder. The saw requires both hands and a tight grip: should you or the saw slip, it could cause you serious injuries.

The saw can be driven by a petrol engine or electric motor. For home use the electrical type is the handiest. If you need a more powerful, petrol-driven model, rent it from a tool hire centre.

All chain saws come with clear instructions on safety and use. Study these carefully before sawing. Wear close-fitting clothing which will not snag on obstructions. Put on ear defenders, heavy gardening gloves, safey goggles, and if possible a safety helmet. Wear heavy shoes or, better still, safety boots with steel toecaps.

Preparing the saw The chain must be very thoroughly oiled – it is not possible to over-oil. Soak a new chain in a chain oil recommended by the makers for at least an hour before it is used.

The saw also has an oil reservoir, and this must be kept topped up to the recommended level: some have an oiling button which, when pressed, feeds oil onto the chain. Press the button before every cut, and regularly while cutting.

If the saw is used a lot, remove the chain and guide bar every few hours and clean thoroughly. At the same time, check for wear or for burrs on the metal. Consult the maker's instructions on how to deal with these.

The chain must also be sharpened at recommended intervals. Buy a sharpening kit designed for your particular model, and use it according to the instructions.

An electric saw must be plugged into a 13amp socket – never a lighting socket – and the plug fuse should also be 13amp – see PLUGS; FUSES AND FUSE BOXES. For extra safety, plug into a socket which incorporates a CIRCUIT BREAKER. With an extension lead, use a shrouded socket

at the end meeting the chain-saw cable. Most chain saws come with the male part of the shrouded connector already fitted. A socket can also be supplied.

Using the saw Make sure the wood you are cutting is firmly held on trestles. It is unwise to cut wood resting on the ground in case the saw touches the ground and is damaged, or kicks back (see below). Make sure the chain is not touching anything when you switch on.

Grip the saw firmly with both hands, thumbs and fingers encircling the handles. Keep all parts of your clothing and body well away from the moving chain, and watch carefully as you cut. Do not force the saw, or the chain will stretch.

Be prepared for kick-back: the saw can suddenly jerk upwards or backwards as it hits an obstruction such as a nail buried in the wood, or a solid object close to it. A firm grip at all times ensures that the saw is always under control.

Now try a cut. With the wood supported at both ends, first cut *down* about one-third of the way through. Then cut up from below to meet the first cut. If the support is at one end only, cut one-third of the way *up*, then cut down, to prevent the wood pinching the saw. On a saw horse always cut outside the supports.

While cutting, keep helpers and children well out of the way in case of accidents. As soon as you stop cutting, unplug the saw from the power supply.

Chair repairs

Remaking joints and mending breaks

The main problem encountered with older furniture is loose joints, caused by the failure or shrinkage of the animal glue used to hold the chair together. Do not waste time trying to squirt fresh glue into the joints: use a mallet or rubber hammer to knock them apart completely. Scrape off all the old glue, back to bare wood. Apply PVA-based glue (see GLU-ING) to the tenon part of each piece (see WOODWORKING JOINTS), then tap them back in place.

Where a component such as a leg is very loose, saw two notches in the end of the tenon, and insert small wooden wedges. Apply glue to the tenon, then tap the leg back: this will force the wedges into the slot, expanding the tenon inside the housing. Wipe away surplus adhesive before it sets.

QUICK TIP Another approach to an ill-fitting joint is to use a special glue which expands as it dries, also acting as a filler. Buy it at a DIY shop.

Where a square-section or turned rail has broken, tap the chair apart so you can remove the broken pieces. Check

Fixing loose joints

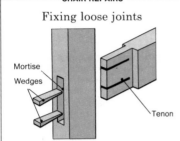

Mortise

Wedges

Tenon

When fixing a very loose joint, saw two notches in the end of the tenon and insert a thin wooden wedge in each. Glue the tenon and tap it into the mortise. Wipe off any surplus adhesive before it sets, using a clean rag.

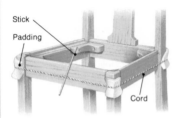

Stick

Padding

Cord

To keep the seat frame and legs of a chair rigid when gluing, use a length of cord as a tourniquet. Turn the stick to tighten it. Use soft padding at the four corners to prevent the cord from marking the chair legs.

that the broken pieces will fit together tightly before gluing. Apply PVA-based wood glue; tap the pieces together with a mallet or rubber hammer, if necessary, and clamp them while the glue sets. Put scrap wood between the clamp and the repaired piece, so that the clamp jaws do not mark it.

If the break is across the grain of a large rail, insert DOWELS to strengthen the repair.

Where shape makes it awkward to hold pieces together, wind a length of cord tightly around the break.

Where broken rails are of dowel rod, take a broken piece to a local DIY supplier and get some new dowel of similar diameter, and roughly matching in colour (use a wood dye if necessary – see WOOD STAINING). Cut and shape as required to make a new rail using a rasp and/or sandpaper.

If seat joints are loose, check the reinforcing blocks at the four corners. They may be screwed in place; if so, undo the screws and remove the blocks. Clean off all old glue down to the bare wood. Apply new PVA-based wood glue and screw the blocks back in place, using slightly larger gauge screws.

For a sagging seat – see REUPHOLSTERING.

Chamois leather

Keeping it supple and long lasting

Often referred to as a wash leather, the chamois leather is made from the hide of the chamois goat or from the underlayer of a sheep's skin. A good skin is highly absorbent and ideal for window cleaning and for drying car bodywork after washing. But it will wear and tear quickly if it is not properly looked after.

If a chamois becomes heavily soiled, rinse it in warm water, then knead it in soapy water, working soap into the skin. When clean, wring it out gently – never twist a chamois tightly – as it tears easily when wet, then immerse in fresh soapy water. Use pure soap flakes, not detergent. Squeeze it lightly, then hang it up to dry without rinsing. Rub and stretch the leather gently while it is drying to prevent it going hard.

Cheese sauces

Making a savoury topping and cauliflower cheese

A cheese sauce (see SAUCES) makes an excellent savoury covering for EGGS, fish (see FISH CLEANING) and broccoli, as well as the more usual cauliflower. Ideally, the cheese used should be a tangy one – such as mature Cheddar – to add a sharp taste. Here are two ways of making a cheese sauce – the roux method and the blending method. Use the same ingredients for each:

Ingredients
(enough for two people)
285ml (½ pint) milk
25g (1oz) butter
25g (1oz) plain flour
½ teaspoon mustard powder
50g (2oz) Cheddar cheese
Pinch of cayenne pepper or ground nutmeg

The roux method (roux being an equal volume of butter and flour cooked together) and the blending method. In the roux method the flour is cooked first, giving less of a raw flour flavour than in the blending method. Heat the milk gently in a saucepan. Remove when warm and cover with a pan lid. Melt the butter over a gentle heat in another pan and mix in the flour with a wooden spoon. Cook gently for 2 minutes, stirring all the time. Then add the mustard powder.

Remove from the heat and add the warm milk, stirring all the while. Return the pan to the heat and bring the sauce to the boil, still stirring. Then simmer for about 5 minutes, giving the mix an occasional stir.

When the sauce is smooth and creamy,

slowly add the grated cheese, stirring it in as it melts. If it feels too thick, add a little extra milk to thin it. Season to taste.

The blending method Mix the flour with a few tablespoons of your measured milk, and blend to a smooth paste in a bowl. Bring the remaining milk to the boil and pour it over the paste, then return it to the pan. Bring it to the boil over a low heat, stirring all the time with a wooden spoon. Simmer the sauce for 2-3 minutes until thick, then add the butter and the mustard powder and cayenne pepper or nutmeg. Cook for 5 minutes. The cheese is then added as with the roux method.

Here is a quickly made dish in which the sauce is used:

Cauliflower cheese Strip off any outer leaves from a cauliflower, rinse it thoroughly, then cook in a little fast-boiling salted water until tender. Do not overcook. Drain off the water and place the cauliflower in an ovenproof dish. Pour the hot cheese sauce over the hot cauliflower; sprinkle with a little extra grated cheese, and brown under a hot grill.

Chemical toilets

How they work, and how to care for them

Chemical toilets are a necessity for caravanners and campers staying at less established sites. Types available include:

Single container This is the most basic design, comprising a container with a seat, anti-spill lid and a top flap to cover the seat. A chemical added to the container sterilises, neutralises and disinfects the contents, which can be poured into the site tank.

Twin tank This type can be flushed. A moulded upper tank which holds flushing water is wrapped around a seat and bowl. From this waste can pass via a sealed trap to a holding tank below. A chemical is used in the lower tank to sterilise and deodorise the contents. This tank must not be filled with drinking water.

Flushing may be by hand bellows, or, in more sophisticated models, by means of an electric pump operated off the car battery.

There is also a choice between units which recycle the flushing water and those which rely on a supply of fresh water. The recycling type is useful where water supplies are limited, but those which use fresh water tend to be generally cleaner in operation.

Holding tanks vary in capacity from

10 litres (2 gallons) to 24 litres (5 gallons), but the larger sizes can be heavy. Some tanks are fitted with an indicator, so you know when to empty the toilet.

Plumbed-in This system is suitable only where there is a plumbed-in supply of water, plus an adjacent sewer to take away effluent.

It can be fitted with a battery-operated macerator pump, which grinds the waste so that it can pass through a 13mm ($\frac{1}{2}$in) hosepipe, making disposal simpler. Alternatively, a hand-operated bilge pump with a 32mm ($1\frac{1}{4}$in) pipe can be fitted.

Chemicals Each toilet manufacturer offers a range of chemical products, in liquid or powder form, both for neutralising waste and to keep the toilet bowl clean and germ-free. There is also a special toilet paper designed to dissolve easily when in contact with the chemicals. Read makers' leaflets for details.

Maintenance Clean portable toilets with a mild, non-abrasive cleaner suitable for plastics – see CLEANING SOLVENTS AND POWDERS. Before storing, rinse out the lower tank with a solution of 1 cup of household bleach to 4.5 litres (1 gallon) of water. Or use a cleaner recommended by the manufacturer. Do not use resin-based sanitary fluid as it will cause the sealing gaskets to swell.

Check all rubber sealing gaskets periodically, and smear them with petroleum jelly.

The most used part of the toilet is the pump. Most models should last the lifetime of the toilet, but should you experience problems, parts are available from dealers or the manufacturers. Each part has a reference number which should be quoted when spare parts are required.

Chess rules

Starting to play the king of board games

This ancient game for two people is played on a chequered board of 64 squares, with pieces that are generally white for one player and black for his opponent. Each player has 16 pieces – one king, one queen, two rooks (or castles), two bishops, two knights and eight pawns – arranged, as shown, in two ranks to start. The object is to break through your opponent's defence and capture his king (*checkmate*).

Each type of piece can be moved only in a particular pattern. Except for the knights, no piece can normally jump over or pass through another piece on the board. But any piece can capture any opponent's piece by moving to the same square. A captured piece is removed.

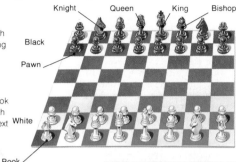

CHESS

Positioning and moving the pieces

The board Position the board so that there is a white square in each player's right-hand corner. The king and queen occupy the two centre squares on the back row, black queen on its black square, white queen on its white square, facing each other. On the back row, a rook (or castle) goes in each corner with a knight next to it and a bishop next to that. The eight pawns each occupy a square on the front row.

Knight · Queen · King · Bishop
Black
Pawn
White
Rook

King moves The king can move in any direction, but not to a square that puts it in check. It moves one square except when castling.

Knight moves The knight moves one or two squares forwards, backwards or sideways and then two or one squares in a direction at right angles to the first – three squares in all.

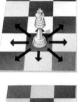

Castling The king moves two squares towards a rook, and the rook moves over the king to the vacant square the king has just crossed. The move can be made only in these circumstances: the king must not be in check, the king and rook must not have been moved previously and the squares between them must be vacant. Also the king cannot move across a square that is under attack.

Pawn moves A pawn can only move forwards, except when capturing. But for its first move only it can go forwards one or two squares. Afterwards it may go only one square at a time. It cannot capture an enemy piece on a square ahead of it, and its progress is blocked until the enemy piece is moved or taken. An advancing pawn that reaches the opponent's back row is promoted to any piece of higher value, other than a king.

En passant A passing pawn can be taken.

Capturing Pawn moves diagonally when taking.

First moves Pawns move one or two squares.

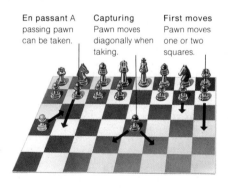

The *king* can move in any direction, only one square at a time, except when castling. It cannot be moved to a square that would put it *in check* – that is, where it would be captured by the opponent's next move. Nor can any piece of the same colour as the king be moved if that would leave the king in check.

The *queen* can also move in any direction, in a straight line over as many unoccupied squares as seems advantageous. That freedom makes her the most powerful piece on the board.

A *rook* can move forwards, backwards or sideways over any number of unoccupied squares. It cannot move diagonally. If you want to bring your two rooks closer to each other for an attack, or to move your king to a better-protected area of the board, you may *castle*. This stratagem counts as one move. Always move the king first when castling, to make it clear to your opponent what you are doing. Castling is the only case in which a king moves more than one square, or in which a piece other than a knight jumps over another piece.

A *bishop* can move diagonally forwards or backwards over any number of unoccupied squares. Each bishop is thus confined to squares of the same colour throughout the game.

A *knight* always moves to a square of a different colour from the square it is standing on. It may jump over any pieces in its path.

A *pawn* can move only forwards, up the board. From its starting position, it can advance either one or two squares; after that, it can advance only one square at a time. But it can capture a piece that is diagonally in front of it, one square to the left or right.

If you have advanced a pawn to the fifth rank, and would capture one of your opponent's pawns if he advanced it from the starting rank by one square, he cannot elude you by using the two square advance. If he tries, you may capture his pawn (now on the square to the left or right of yours) *en passant*. His pawn is removed from the board, and yours moves diagonally forwards one square – to the empty square his pawn has just passed over.

If you manoeuvre one of your pawns into your opponent's back rank, you can declare the pawn to be any piece of higher value, other than a king. A queen is usually chosen, because of its power; it is possible, by *queening* a pawn, to have two queens of the same colour.

Moves alternate, with white always playing first; it is customary to change colours with your opponent after each game. Only one piece can be moved at each turn, except when castling. You should warn your opponent when you put his king in danger by saying *check* (though the warning is not obligatory). He must then move his king out of check, or capture the piece that is threatening it, or block the attack by moving one of his other pieces into the attacker's path.

If your opponent cannot do any of these things, it is checkmate, and the game is over.

A game is a *draw* if neither player can possibly win. A *stalemate* occurs when the player whose turn it is cannot make any legal move, but his king is not in check; it counts as a draw.

Chest pains

Recognising dangerous symptoms and taking emergency action

Pains in the chest may mean serious, even life-threatening, illness – or they may have a relatively harmless cause, such as indigestion. Unless you are certain that the cause is minor, get medical attention immediately – particularly if severe pain is accompanied by pallor, sweating or difficulty in breathing, or the victim has a history of heart or breathing disorders.

Heart attacks Symptoms of a HEART ATTACK include an intense, crushing pain in the centre of the chest, radiating to the shoulders, arms, neck or jaws, accompanied by shortness of breath and a rapid and weakening pulse. Sometimes the symptoms are less severe.

If you suspect someone has had a heart attack, be ready to give ARTIFICIAL RESPIRATION and CHEST COMPRESSION if necessary. Put the victim in a comfortable, half-sitting position with knees up and head and shoulders supported. If he is conscious, give one aspirin and tell him to chew it slowly. Loosen his clothing at the neck, chest and waist.

Encourage him to breathe normally and to stay calm. Reassure him that a doctor or ambulance is on the way.

Angina Exertion, a cold wind, an emotional upset or even a heavy meal can temporarily reduce the oxygen supply to the heart, producing pain across the upper part of the chest, and lasting for minutes. This is called angina.

Angina attacks usually pass off in 10-15 minutes if the victim sits and rests. Give painkillers in doses prescribed by the victim's doctor.

Other causes Other possibly serious causes of chest pains include respiratory diseases such as pneumonia, pleurisy and lung cancer. They are accompanied by breathing difficulties and, often, by fever.

A hot sensation behind the breastbone after a meal (heartburn) may indicate a duodenal ulcer, but is more often simply indigestion that can be cleared up with antacid tablets or medicine. Shingles, a virus infection, can produce a sharp chest pain, usually on one side only, several days before blisters appear.

See also CHOKING, COUGHING.

Chewing gum removal

Solving a sticky problem

To make the gum easier to remove, harden it by rubbing it with an ice cube wrapped in plastic film, or put the gummed-up article in a plastic bag in a freezer compartment. Carefully pick the hardened gum off using a blunt instrument or fingernails. Take care on woollens and loose fabrics.

If traces remain on fabrics after removing, use a little lightly beaten egg white on washable fabrics or a solvent dry-cleaning fluid, spray or paste – see CLEANING SOLVENTS. Follow the maker's instructions and test beforehand on an area that does not show.

Do not use ordinary dry-cleaner on suede, leather, rubber, plastic or water-proofed fabrics. Try clean, cold water on rubber and plastics.

QUICK TIP When using dry-cleaners on fabrics, put the stained area face down on a clean paper towel, so that it absorbs the stain; move the stained area so that it is always on a clean patch.

Chilblains

Treating and preventing painful swellings

Itchy, painful chilblains are brought on by exposure to cold and made worse by damp. The reddish-blue inflammations, which can be up to 50mm (2in) across, most commonly affect fingers, toes and the backs of the legs.

Treat chilblains by protecting them at all times from further cold. Keep affected areas warm and dry with protective clothing. Never warm chilblains in front of a fire or other heat source, and do not scratch them. They should clear up in a few weeks. If they persist, consult your pharmacist, who may recommend a cream to counteract itching.

To prevent chilblains, wear warm and waterproof clothing and footwear out of doors in winter. Keep your bedroom warm and wear bed socks.

QUICK TIP A traditional cure for chilblains is a concoction of 250g (9oz) of celery stalks boiled in 1 litre (1¾ pints) of water. Allow the mixture to cool, then dip your hands or feet into it for five minutes.

Childbirth

Coping with an emergency delivery

Make every effort to contact a doctor or midwife – dial 999 if necessary. It is technically illegal in Britain for anyone without formal qualifications to supervise a birth, but exceptions are recognised in genuine emergencies, such as when medical help is delayed through bad weather.

Keep calm. Reassure the mother and anyone else present. Most births take place without difficulty.

The first signs Labour begins with pains that develop in the small of the back, moving to the lower abdomen as contractions start. The interval between contractions is usually about 30 minutes at first; gradually they become more frequent and painful.

This stage usually lasts for several hours. Allow the mother to move about, make herself comfortable, and to visit the lavatory as often as she needs. Tell her to relax, and not to bear down. Give her occasional sips of water, but nothing to eat.

Getting ready Wash your hands and scrub your nails in running water, but do not dry them. Keep washing frequently throughout the birth. Tell anyone with an open cut or an infection to stay well away from the mother, and later from the newborn child.

Find the cleanest materials you can to use as bedding, towels, cloths and swabs. Try to have replacements for when they become soiled. Line the bottom of a cot, basket, box or drawer with a folded blanket, towel or shawl. If possible, have another shawl ready to cover the baby. Do not put a pillow in the cot.

Prepare a bed for the mother, or improvise one on a clean surface. Cover it first with a plastic sheet or, failing that, with newspapers. Spread a clean towel or sheet over the plastic or newspapers. Fold a blanket in three from top to bottom and wrap it in a clean sheet, to cover the mother's upper body during delivery. Collect plenty of pillows or cushions for the mother to lean on, and a blanket or warm garment in case she feels cold.

Get a nappy for the baby, and for the mother a sanitary towel, a large bowl for her to sit on to deliver the placenta, and a smaller one in case she vomits. Put all these items, with the towels and cloths, within easy reach of the bed.

When contractions quicken As the contractions become more frequent, watery fluid may run from the vagina (the 'breaking of the waters') and there may be some seepage of blood. Put the mother on the bed on her back or side. Breathing in and out with the contractions, without holding the breath, can reduce pain.

As the contractions become stronger and more frequent, the mother's need to bear down becomes irresistible. Encourage her to hold her breath while bearing down with each contraction.

As the birth approaches, the contractions occur every two or three minutes. Get the mother to bend her knees, and to grasp her thighs behind them, so she can pull on her legs at the same time as she is bearing down.

When the head emerges Support the baby's head as it appears, gently holding it so that it does not pop out. Tell the mother not to bear down, but to pant in quick breaths. Support the baby's body carefully with one hand as it emerges. Do not pull the baby at any stage during birth.

Once the baby is fully born, wipe away any blood or mucus from its mouth. If it does not breathe immediately, hold it carefully with the head lower than the body. If breathing does not start then, blow hard on the baby's chest; do *not* slap its back.

Aftercare As soon as the baby is breathing normally, lay it gently on its back, being careful not to pull on the umbilical cord. Do not cut the cord: the doctor or midwife will do this.

Do not wash the baby. Wrap it warmly in a clean towel or blanket, ensuring that the top of its head is covered but so

Delivering a baby in an emergency

In an emergency an unqualified person may have to deliver a baby – although normally it is illegal.

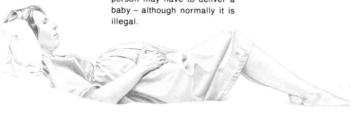

First stages When contractions become strong and frequent, make the mother lie in a comfortable position – on her back or side – with her knees bent. Put pillows under her shoulders. As the baby's head begins to appear, tell the mother to pant quickly. Put a clean towel under her buttocks and another on the bed between her legs.

When the head is out Support the head as it emerges. If the head is covered with a caul, or membrane, remove it quickly – but very gently.

When the shoulders emerge Carefully support the shoulders as they emerge, but do not pull them. After one shoulder has appeared, the other will follow if you raise the head gently. Support the rest of the body with one hand as it emerges. At no stage pull the baby.

Clearing mucus and blood When the baby is fully born, use a clean cloth to wipe mucus and blood from the mouth. If it does not breathe immediately, hold it carefully with the head lower than the body to drain any mucus.

Cord around the neck If the baby's head emerges with the cord around its neck, hook a finger under the cord and ease it over the head.

Breech birth If the bottom appears first, simply support the body as it emerges. When the shoulders are out, gently ease the body up so that the mouth is clear to breathe.

that it can breathe easily through the mouth and nose. Give it to the mother to hold, or put it next to her on the bed, on its side with its head low.

Wrap the mother in blankets while you are waiting for the placenta (afterbirth) to be expelled. This usually happens 5-15 minutes after the birth. Place a bowl between her legs to catch the placenta. The process of expulsion can take up to 20 minutes. Keep the placenta to show the doctor or midwife. If the placenta is only partly expelled, or does not emerge at all, get medical attention as soon as possible.

Wash the mother and put a sanitary pad in place. Make her comfortable and tidy, and put the baby to her breast if she wants it. Once the afterbirth is delivered and any bleeding has stopped, she may eat and drink if she wishes. When the mother has fed the baby, or if she is too tired, put it in the cot on its side with its head low.

Children's tantrums

Handling displays of temper and unruly behaviour

Between the ages of two and four almost all children indulge in tantrums, fits of uncontrolled rage during which they are incapable of responding to reason. They may hurl toys and other objects and fling themselves around.

Such outbursts are worrying – even frightening – to parents, but they are a natural part of growing up. Dealt with calmly they subside quickly, and the child does not suffer lasting harm. By the age of about five most children are growing out of these outbursts.

Tantrums, and the uncooperative behaviour that accompanies them, are a sign that, for the first time, the child is recognising that he is a separate person, able to express his own likes and dislikes. However, he has not yet learnt to compromise; every time his will is thwarted, there is potential conflict.

How to cope Accept that tantrums are neither naughtiness nor spite, but part of a child's process of adjusting to the world. There is no point in trying to reason with the child, in arguing or in punishing him.

Keep as calm as you can, if necessary leaving the room so that he can work out his temper on his own. Do not be drawn into a head-on battle of wills as your anger will only feed his. Use your adult understanding to avoid clashes – for example, by distracting the child, by making him laugh or by gentle deception to get him to do what you wish.

Outbursts over food are common. Do not force the child to eat; he will not starve as long as food is available. Do not worry about tantrums in public. The opinion of strangers does not matter.

In all tantrums, the child will become relaxed and reasonable once he is satisfied he has made his point. Until that stage is reached, just be patient.

Get advice from your doctor if you find yourself reacting violently to tantrums, or if they irritate you so much that you no longer enjoy the child's company.

Child safety

Preventing childhood accidents

As soon as your baby learns to crawl, reorganise furniture and the contents of cupboards and shelves so that only safe, sturdy objects are near the floor and that breakable or dangerous items are high up where they cannot be reached.

Ensure that handles, knobs and bolts on inside doors are well above the child's reach; remove keys from interior locks. Padlock, or put a high bolt on, sheds, greenhouses, workshops and cellars; keep tools and implements inside when not in use.

Fit childproof catches or bars to windows. Put gates, designed for the purpose, at the top and bottom of staircases. Install childproof locks and a safety seat in the car.

Poisons Household cleaners, hair dyes and shoe polish are among the poisons found in most homes; sheds, garages or cupboards under the stairs may contain paint strippers, weedkillers or insecticides. Store them, in their proper containers, on high shelves, and put them back there immediately after use. Do not allow young children to play in a garden recently treated with weedkillers (see WEED CONTROL) or PESTICIDES.

Keep all medicines, including vitamins, in a locked cabinet high on a wall and contained in childproof containers. Do not leave aspirins or other medicines in handbags. Lock alcoholic drinks away. If your child swallows poison, do not deliberately make him sick; get medical attention immediately and if possible keeping any remains of the poison and its container to show the doctor – see POISONING.

Burns and shocks Keep matches and cigarette lighters out of reach. Put secure guards in front of fires and radiant heaters, and never use freestanding heaters in a room where a child may go. Buy flame-retardant clothing for the child, particularly for nightwear.

In the kitchen, turn saucepan handles to the back of the stove while cooking, or use the back burners. Keep knives and scissors in a high drawer. Put all electrical equipment, such as mixers, safely away immediately after use. Do not allow tablecloths to dangle near the floor, where a child can pull them down.

Avoid hot-water scalds by turning the thermostat down to 54°C (130°F). Never leave a hot-water bottle in a cot with a child, nor put a cot against a radiator.

Prevent electric burns and ELECTRIC SHOCKS by plugging electric points with special plastic covers. Do not leave flexes within the child's reach and use extension flexes only as a temporary measure.

Avoiding suffocation Keep all objects small enough to be swallowed away from young children; do not give them toys with parts that might come loose, or foods on which it is easy to choke, such as pieces of apple or carrot, nuts or hard sweets. Take care, too, with ribbons, strings and cords.

Store plastic bags out of reach, or knot them up small before throwing away – a child putting one over its head could suffocate. Never use a plastic bag to cover a child's mattress. Be careful of large items, such as an unused refrigerator or trunk, which could trap a child; lock them or remove the catches.

Never leave a child unattended near a bath containing even a little water. Cover GARDEN POOLS with wire-netting so a child cannot slip in.

Buy a sturdy playpen where the child can play safely, while you do chores.

As soon as a child is old enough to understand, teach it road drill and warn against taking sweets from strangers.

See also ACCIDENT PREVENTION.

Chimney fires

Action to prevent a serious blaze

Chimneys become a fire risk if soot is left to accumulate inside them. Coal and wood fires produce most soot, and where these fuels are used chimneys should be thoroughly cleaned annually. Even oil and gas CENTRAL HEATING systems produce some soot.

Smouldering soot can suddenly erupt into flames, threatening the chimney and, if unchecked, the entire house.

If a chimney catches fire
● Call the fire brigade.
● Move carpets and furniture away from the fireplace.
● Seal off the draught to an open fire by shutting doors and windows.
● Smother the fire in the grate with earth; or douse it with soapy water – detergent helps water to cling to the coals, and the steam produced also helps to put out the fire up the chimney.
● Put a fireguard in front of the grate to stop hot soot falling into the room.
● Check other rooms through which the chimney passes. If their chimney walls are hot, move furniture away.

China

Care and repair of dishes and ornaments

Fine china, especially if handpainted, should always be washed separately from other dishes and cutlery, preferably in a plastic bowl, using hot but not boiling water and a mild detergent. Avoid using any cleanser which contains an abrasive. Use a soft brush to clean any crevices. Rinse in clear, warm water. If a dishwasher is used, avoid adding too much detergent.

China should be rinsed as soon as possible after use, especially if it has contained vinegar, salt, lemon juice or wine. Tea or coffee stains can be removed by wiping with a damp cloth dipped in bicarbonate of soda or borax, before rinsing. Hardware shops and china stores sell special products for removing stubborn stains.

To protect china
● Put only ovenproof dishes in a hot oven.
● Do not put hot food on cold plates.
● Cool dishes to room temperature before stacking them.
● To prevent chipping, put paper towels between plates when stacking them.
● Lay cups on their sides in groups of four, with the handle of each cup inside the bowl of another, and place the group on stacked saucers.

Repairing china Mend breaks with one of the slow-setting epoxy glues (see GLUING), which allow time to reposition the pieces if necessary, and are waterproof when cured. First, clean broken edges with methylated spirit, applied with a brush. Mix the glue according to the maker's instructions, then apply a thin coat to both edges to be joined and press together. Repairs to handles are unlikely to be strong enough to withstand normal use.

To achieve a good join, an even and constant pressure must be applied for at least 12 hours, until the glue has set. This can sometimes be achieved simply by applying a weight or by binding the pieces together with adhesive tape or gummed paper.

To repair plates which have broken in two, hold the two halves together with clothespegs until the glue dries. Another approach, useful when a plate has broken into more than two pieces, is to prepare a mould by taking an impression in modelling clay, obtainable from a crafts shop, from a matching plate. Glue the broken pieces and fit them together in the mould, then leave to set.

Use the frayed end of a matchstick dipped in methylated spirit to remove any surplus adhesive before it dries. Remove partially hardened adhesive with a razor blade or sharp knife.

Fill chips in china with a mixture of epoxy resin and whiting – finely powdered chalk obtainable from hardware shops.

Before it is completely set, cut off any surplus with a sharp knife. When set, carefully rub the filled surface with a piece of dampened 600 or 700 grade wet-or-dry paper until it is smooth.

Positioning and gluing awkward shapes

Place an awkwardly shaped ornament in a box of sand, with its broken surface protruding. Glue the edges of both pieces and carefully position the broken piece.

Mend a broken cup handle by holding the glued parts together with 38mm (1½in) gummed paper. The paper will shrink as it dries out, putting pressure on the join.

Chinese checkers

Playing star wars with marbles

This is a game for two to six players, using coloured marbles – or sometimes pegs – which fit into holes on a six-pointed, star-shaped board. The object of the game is for each player to try to get his marbles across the board from one point of the star to the other point directly opposite it before any of his opponents can do the same.

Each player has marbles of a single colour. If there are only two players they each have 15 marbles. If there are three or more players, they have 10 marbles each.

Moves are taken in turn. The player

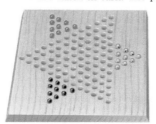

Three-way stretch For a three-handed game of Chinese checkers the players set out their marbles in alternate points of the star.

---

can only move one marble at a time, and that only to an empty hole immediately adjacent – unless a jump is possible. If another piece – either an opponent's or his own – is occupying the adjacent hole, he can jump over it, provided the hole on the other side of the intervening piece is free.

Multiple jumps are possible in any direction, where several pieces are separated by single empty holes. The jumped pieces are not removed, as they are in DRAUGHTS.

Chipboard

Working with versatile boards

This boon to do-it-yourselfers is made from wood chips bonded together under high pressure. It can be cut and drilled, though the glues used for bonding the wood chips tend to blunt tools. Because of its granular composition it will not take woodscrews – special chipboard SCREWS are available. Or you can drill and plug it with DOWELS to take ordinary woodscrews. Chipboard is cheaper than timber and available in a larger range of sizes.

Chipboard is made in thicknesses of 12mm, 18mm, 22mm and 25mm (½in, ¾in, ⅞in and 1in), in sheets ranging from 1.2 × 2.4m (4 × 8ft), the standard size, to 1.8m × 600mm (6 × 2ft). There are several grades of hardness. Standard chipboard is suitable for interior use only, since it easily absorbs damp, even when painted. There are special grades available for exterior use.

Unfaced chipboard is ideal for re-covering a floor, for laying a floor in a roof space, or for making a flat roof over an extension or garage, when it should be covered with bituminous felt. There is also a wide range of chipboards available faced with VENEER or with laminates of various kinds. For shelving, worktops and furniture building – see CABINETS. Facings range from white melamine to simulated wood grains: the natural wood veneers that are available include mahogany, teak and oak. Iron-on edging strips are available to veneer sawn edges – see VENEER TAPE.

Working with chipboard As well as dowels, there are special plastic inserts, obtainable from DIY shops, for plugging chipboard to make fastenings with wood or self-tapping screws.

When using a combination of chipboard and timber, always screw or nail through the chipboard into the timber. Chipboard can also be glued with any woodworking adhesive, the strongest being PVA or urea – see GLUING.

It can be cut with panel, tenon, circular or jig saws (see SAWS AND SAWING) and edges finished with plane and glasspaper.

Chip pan fire

Tackling a blazing chip pan or frying pan

Fire starts in a pan containing cooking oil when the oil gets too hot and becomes volatile. When you see smoke coming off oil, it is getting close to the point where it will ignite. Turn off the heat immediately and do not move the pan until it has cooled down.

If a pan ignites, leave it where it is, turn off the heat and smother the flames with a fire blanket if you have one – see

How to douse the flames Leave the pan where it is. Turn off the heat. Smother the flames with a fire blanket, wet cloth or large saucepan lid, held in front of your face as a shield.

FIRE EXTINGUISHERS. Alternatively, cover it with any wet cloth, such as a large towel or tablecloth, or a saucepan lid that is larger than the top of the pan. Keep some such item handy when using a chip pan.

Do not try to put out the fire with water – it will spread the flames. Do not be tempted to pick up the pan and rush out of the house with it; the flames are likely to flare up fiercely and may blow back on you.

Once the fire is out, keep the pan covered until the oil is cool – for at least 30 minutes.

If you are unable to put out the fire, or if it spreads, close all the doors and windows, get out of the room and call the fire brigade.

Chiselling

Using a versatile woodworking tool

A set of bevel-edge chisels and a mortise chisel will do most chiselling jobs required by a handyman. A general-purpose set of chisels would comprise four bevel-edge chisels with 6, 13, 19 and 25mm ($\frac{1}{4}$, $\frac{1}{2}$, $\frac{3}{4}$ and 1in) wide blades, and a mortise chisel with a 6mm ($\frac{1}{4}$in) blade.

Using a bevel-edge chisel To cut the slot for a halving or housing joint (see

WOODWORKING JOINTS), clamp the timber firmly, then make two saw cuts the width and depth of the slot.

Pare away the waste a little at a time, working from both sides of the slot. Cut upwards at first, making two slopes to a peak in the centre, then chisel away the central waste. Lightly shave the bottom until it is smooth and check for flatness.

To cut a recess for a door hinge, mark out the length, width and depth of the hinge on the door edge. Holding the chisel vertically, tap the handle with a wooden mallet to cut along the length and width of the recess and down to the depth line. Clean out the waste with the chisel, working from the front edge.

Using a mortise chisel A mortise chisel has a thick, straight-sided blade and a stout handle designed to withstand the blows of a mallet required to chop out a deep recess, or mortise.

Whether cutting a mortise-and-tenon joint or perhaps making recesses for DOOR-LOCKS, it is best to first remove most of the central waste with a series of drilled holes. Clean out the sides with a chisel.

Shaping wood by paring To make a rounded end on a piece of wood, clamp the wood securely on a bench or in a vice. Hold the chisel vertically, with the thumb of one hand on top of the handle. Keep your head over the work.

Pushing down with the thumb, pare off the corners as illustrated until you have an almost perfect curve. Smooth the curve with a rasp and sandpaper.

Taking care of your chisels A chisel is usually protected by a plastic guard over the cutting edge – keep it on whenever the tool is not being used.

Chisel blades have two angles forming the edge: a broad one at 25 degrees and narrower one at 30 degrees – the actual cutting edge. The 30-degree angle is honed and must be renewed from time to time (some chisels have to be honed when new – check when buying).

To keep chisels sharp, use an oilstone – see illustration (below right). Provided the chisels do not get very blunt or chipped, a combination oilstone with fine and medium sides will do. Lightly coat the surface with thin oil or white spirit before using.

To sharpen the blade rub both sides on the medium stone until the burr falls off, leaving a razor-sharp edge. Lightly rub the blade on the fine stone for a final edge.

WARNING Chisels are sharp and can be dangerous if not used properly. Always cut away from your body, and make sure the piece of wood you are working on is securely held in a vice or clamp. Keep both hands behind the blade as you work.

CHISELLING

Basic chisel techniques

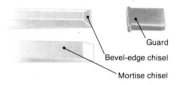

Guard
Bevel-edge chisel
Mortise chisel

Bevel-edge chisels are used for making housing and halving joints or cutting shallow recesses – for hinges, for example. A mortise chisel is used for making mortise-and-tenon joints and cutting deep recesses.

Cutting a housing joint Clamp the timber firmly in a vice. Saw two cuts the width and depth of the intended slot and chisel out the wood between the cuts.

Cutting a mortise Drill holes down the centre of the intended slot, using a bit with a diameter slightly less than the slot's width. Chisel away the remaining waste.

Making a rounded end Hold the chisel vertically. Cut the corners of the wood at 45 degrees, then those left by the cuts.

Sharpening a chisel Hold the chisel blade to a lightly oiled stone at an angle of 30 degrees. Rub it to and fro until a burr forms. Rub the blade's other flat side until the burr turns back. Go on rubbing each side until the burr falls off.

Chocolate truffles

Making special, melt-in-the-mouth treats

Chocolate truffles are simple to make in an interesting range of flavours. The following recipe makes 12 chocolates:

Melt 75g (3oz) of plain chocolate in a small bowl over a pan of hot water. Add one egg yolk, 15g (½oz) butter, a teaspoon of top of the milk or single cream, and one teaspoon of rum, brandy or any liqueur of your choice. Beat the mixture until thick, then chill in the refrigerator until firm enough to handle.

Spoon the mixture out into 12 equal portions and roll into balls. Dip in chocolate vermicelli or drinking chocolate powder to give the truffles a professional finish, and put each one in a little paper cup. Store in an airtight container in a fridge, or use within a week of making.

Choking

Clearing a blocked breathing passage

Knowing what to do when someone chokes allows you to act quickly and calmly, avoiding panic.

The first sign of choking is often a violent coughing fit. If the victim cannot speak, the breathing passage is probably blocked. In the desperate struggle to breathe in, the obstruction often becomes even more firmly lodged.

Treating someone who is conscious
Remove food and/or false teeth from the mouth and get the victim to cough as vigorously as he can. This alone might be enough to dislodge the obstruction from his breathing passage.

If that fails, bend the victim over and slap him firmly between the shoulder blades. As soon as breathing starts again, get him to sit quietly and take sips of water until fully recovered.

With a child, lay him over your knees with his head down. Support the chest with one hand, then give up to five firm slaps between the shoulder blades with the heel of the other hand. Each slap should be strong enough to dislodge the obstruction.

Hold a baby with one hand as illustrated. With the fingers of the other hand, slap him firmly between the shoulder blades up to five times. Use much less force than for an adult or older child. Avoid putting your finger in a baby's mouth unless you can see the object to be removed.

Abdominal thrusts This is a more violent remedy which may prove necessary if blows to the back fail to restore breathing. It can, however, be a dangerous technique, causing damage to the liver and

How to treat a choking person

Always treat a choking as a life-or-death emergency. The first sign is often a coughing fit. The victim's face may turn blue and the veins in the head and neck become swollen. If he cannot speak, the breathing passage is probably blocked

Backslaps for an adult If the victim is still conscious, bend him over so that his head is lower than his chest. Slap him firmly between the shoulder blades up to five times with the heel of your hand. Deliver the slaps with enough force to induce an involuntary cough.

Abdominal thrusts Only try this technique as a last resort. Stand or kneel behind the victim. Clench your fist and put it, thumb inwards, over the stomach between waist and rib cage. Grasp the fist with the other hand. Pull both hands towards you with a quick inward, upward thrust. Repeat up to five times. If this fails, alternate five backslaps and five thrusts.

Backslaps for a baby Hold the baby so that jaw and chest are supported and the head pointed downwards. Slap him with your fingers between the shoulder blades.

Self help If there is no one to help you, clench a fist and place it thumb side against the stomach just above the navel. With the other hand jerk the fist firmly inwards and upwards several times.

Unconscious victim Put the heel of one hand between the navel and bottom of the breastbone. Cover with the other hand. Give a quick upward thrust with your arms straight.

other internal organs and should be used only as a last resort.

Stand or kneel behind *an adult* victim and administer the thrusts as illustrated (see previous page). They should drive out any air that is still remaining at the bottom of the lungs and with it the obstruction. Repeat up to five times, checking the victim's mouth to see if the obstruction has come up.

Only use abdominal thrusts on a child if you have been trained to do so. Use only one hand, and less force than for an adult. Otherwise, start immediate artificial respiration. Do not use abdominal thrusts on a baby.

Treating someone who is unconscious Once the victim has become unconscious, the throat muscles may relax sufficiently to allow air to get past the obstruction.

Start mouth-to-mouth respiration to force air into the lungs (see ARTIFICIAL RESPIRATION). If there is someone else present, get them to telephone for an ambulance.

If the lungs do not inflate after the first breath roll the victim onto his side, with his chest against your thigh and his head well back. Give five hard blows on the back. See if the obstruction has been dislodged. If it has, hook it out of the mouth with a finger.

If not, turn the victim onto his back and tilt the head well back. Straddle his thighs. Administer up to four quick upward thrusts as illustrated (see previous page).

Check the mouth to see if the obstruction has been dislodged, and remove it if it has. If not, resume mouth-to-mouth respiration. If the lungs again do not expand, repeat the sequence of backslaps, thrusts and mouth-to-mouth respiration.

Treating yourself If you are choking and there is no one available to help you, treat yourself as illustrated (see previous page).

Cholesterol

Cutting down on foods that spell danger

Cholesterol, a white, soapy-textured fat-like substance, is produced naturally by the body and is essential for life.

Abnormally, it can be deposited on the walls of the arteries of many people with heart disease. These deposits restrict the amount of blood passing along the arteries, leading eventually in some cases to a HEART ATTACK.

Some foods, such as eggs and meat, contain cholesterol, and it was once thought that extra cholesterol taken in with our food was responsible for raising cholesterol levels in the blood. Research has shown that this is not so: the body tends to produce less cholesterol to balance the amount taken in.

It is now known that dietary fat is the culprit – particularly the saturated fats contained in cream, cheese and some margarines. Diets which include a lot of saturated (animal) fats seem to stimulate the body to produce more cholesterol. And in diets where more vegetable oils are eaten, less cholesterol is produced in the blood – see also CALORIE COUNTING; DIETING.

Keeping down your cholesterol This can be achieved by simply cutting down on the amount of animal fat included in your diet.
● For cooking use vegetable oils, such as sunflower, corn, soya bean, rapeseed and olive.
● Avoid fried foods.
● Use skimmed or semi-skimmed milk.
● Change the balance of your diet by avoiding meat and eating more vegetables and pulses (beans, lentils, split-peas and so on).
● Trim the visible fat from meat before cooking; remove the skin of poultry.
● Choose margarines that are high in unsaturated (vegetable) fats.
● Eat fewer cakes and biscuits: they contain high proportions of fat.

Chopsticks

How to eat the oriental way

The next time you dine at a Chinese or Japanese restaurant, ask the waiter for chopsticks, or use chopsticks the next time you have a Chinese meal at home.

If possible, hold them in your right hand – the Chinese consider it impolite to use the left one, even if you are left-handed.

Do not be shy about lifting the bowl up near your mouth to avoid messy eating. It is not considered bad manners, and both the Chinese and Japanese do it as a matter of course.

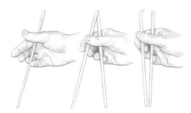

Rest one stick (the lower) on your third finger, with the thicker end in the crook between your thumb and forefinger. Hold the other (upper) stick between your thumb and forefinger and rest it on your middle finger. Keeping the lower stick rigid, move the upper stick up or down to pick up food. Pick up small portions at a time and work rice or noodles into a mass to make lifting easier.

Christmas decorations

How children can have fun making their own

In the Christmas holidays, children can make simple decorations from everyday oddments.

Snowman's head Cover a blown-up balloon with strips of newspaper, stuck on with wallpaper paste. Build up three or four layers of newspaper, then finish off with a layer of white tissues. When dry, draw on eyes, nose and mouth.

Decorative wall plaques Loops of wire threaded through foil dishes or paper plates covered in baking foil can be used to hold holly, paper flowers, ribbon bows or gold-painted fir cones. Hang the plaques on picture hooks.

Wall displays Cut shapes from stiff cardboard, and cover with brightly coloured wrapping paper. Then cut out pictures and motifs from old Christmas cards and glue them onto the shapes. Hang with coloured cords – see also CHRISTMAS TREES.

CHRISTMAS DECORATIONS

Making them with oddments

Silver ball Take eight shallow foil dishes. Fold in the edges of each so that the base forms a triangle. Staple one side of each dish to one side of another, until all eight are joined in a ball. Then thread a cord through a hole in the top.

Drinking straw star Press the centres of eight coloured straws onto a drawing pin and spread out the arms evenly. Weave gold or silver wrapping string under and over the arms to make a central disc.

Wall plaque Pierce four holes in a foil dish or paper plate and thread through two wire loops to hold the decoration.

Christmas trees

*Selecting and planting one that
will last for years*

Trees are supplied by the Forestry Commission to retail centres or are raised and sold by private growers.

Trees with roots can be planted out after Christmas, then dug up and taken into the house again the following winter. Norway spruce, however, is fastgrowing and eventually will be too tall to take indoors.

It can then become a permanent feature of the garden, but as it can eventually grow to 40m (130ft), careful siting is important. The tree does well in slightly acid soil, but should thrive almost anywhere provided it is kept well watered while in the house.

Some tree dealers are said to scald the roots to prevent planting out, but this is not Forestry Commission practice. It would, says the Commission, not be worth the time and bother, as few people plant them out, and even then many die for a variety of other reasons.

When selecting a rooted tree, check that the roots are not damaged. If it is not to be potted immediately, stand it in a bucket of water in a cool place. Once potted, water the tree daily and keep it away from any heat source. This will help keep the tree healthy and minimise needle shedding. A tree less than 1m (about 3ft) tall will stand the best chance of surviving when planted out.

If you intend to plant out the tree, try to keep it in the house for no more than ten days, which will improve its chances of growing. Unfortunately, early January is not the best time to plant any tree, so to give your Christmas tree the best chance of survival break up any frozen soil thoroughly with a fork and work plenty of peat, garden compost or leaf mould into the soil. Dig a hole deep enough to cover the roots, and after planting spread more peat and compost around the base of the tree.

Cigarette scorch marks

*Dealing with them on fabrics and
furniture*

Holes burnt by a fallen cigarette on clothing or a piece of furniture require fairly drastic treatment – see also ANTIQUES; CARPET REPAIRS; TABLE REPAIRS. But scorch marks can sometimes be removed, if there is no other damage.

Fabrics Light scorch marks in linen may disappear if rubbed with a slice of lemon and left in the sun. Or try dabbing the mark repeatedly with hydrogen peroxide solution – 1 part 20 vol. peroxide to 6 parts cold water. But test the material first for colourfastness, in an area where any bleaching will not show. After treatment, rinse with clean water. On delicate fabrics, apply a borax solution – 1 tablespoon borax to 500ml (about 1 pint) warm water. Soak and rinse; launder according to laundering instructions.

Heavy scorch marks in woollens are almost impossible to remove.

Furniture Very light burns may polish out with a good proprietary furniture polish or a metal polish applied on a soft cloth, working with the grain.

Carpets On a wool carpet, rub the burn immediately with a slice of potato. This usually removes the singe from the surface. The brown tips on the ends of threads sometimes wash out, or they can be carefully trimmed with scissors, brushed and then rubbed with coarse glasspaper.

Cigarette smells

Getting rid of tobacco fumes

There are several ways to clear a room of stale cigarette fumes: open windows and use an electric fan if possible; use a proprietary air freshener; or put out a dish of ammonia or vinegar. Burning a candle in the room for a short while will also help.

Where the problem is constant, an air purifier is a good investment. A small, inexpensive one that circulates air through carbon filters can be moved around to stand wherever it is most effective.

If you have a warm-air heating system (see CENTRAL HEATING) you can have an air purifying unit attached to it.

Circuit breaker

*Fitting an automatic safeguard
against electric shocks*

This is a valuable safety device which switches off current instantly if a breakage or fault occurs in an electrical appliance, or if the flex or cable carrying power to it is damaged – see ELECTRIC WIRING.

An RCD (Residual Current Device), as it is called, works by checking constantly on the current flow to earth. The moment this current exceeds a preset level, the RCD switches off, and will not allow power to be restored until the fault is remedied.

Available in several forms, an RCD may be incorporated into a new mains fuse box (see FUSES AND FUSE BOXES), to protect all circuits. Or you can buy one incorporated into a power socket, to replace an ordinary socket – see ELECTRIC SOCKETS AND SWITCHES. This protects anything plugged into that socket. Or there is a plug-in RCD that fits into a socket and has one socket outlet on it to receive the plug of an appliance.

Finally, special plugs which also contain an RCD are available – but great care must be taken when using one not to knock the rather delicate mechanism inside. Only the appliance to which the plug is fitted is protected. If an extension lead is used, remember the circuit-breaker plug must go into the house socket, not the extension lead socket. Otherwise the actual extension lead would not be protected.

Circuit breakers are available in several current ratings and degrees of sensitivity: consult an electrical supply shop when buying.

Circuit testing

Two simple faultfinding devices

When an electrical appliance fails, always disconnect the appliance from the mains before trying to find the fault.

A couple of simple aids will suffice for faultfinding. Make a basic circuit tester as shown, and buy a special circuit-testing screwdriver. This should have a metal contact, which may double as a pocket clip.

If, for example, a table lamp will not light:

1 Try another bulb; if that fails, remove it and, with the lamp switched on, touch the circuit-testing screwdriver tip to each bulb-holder pin in turn. If the neon lamp in the screwdriver glows in contact with either pin, current is reaching the pin but not the bulb. The pin is not making contact with the bulb terminal.

2 If the neon does not glow, unplug the lamp and test the fuse in the plug (see PLUGS) with the circuit tester. If the circuit tester's bulb fails to light, replace the fuse.

3 If the fuse is sound, try another appliance in the socket. If that works, the fault is in the flex.

Remove the flex from plug and lamp, then use each wire of the flex to complete a circuit through the test circuit. One will probably light the bulb; the other not. If practicable, replace the damaged section with a new length of flex, joining it to the rest with a purpose-made flex connector. Do not try to join lengths of flex with insulating tape. It is often as cheap to replace the entire flex.

4 If the second appliance does not work, check the fuse in the circuit supplying the socket. If this is sound the lamp switch may be faulty.

If possible, remove the switch and apply the test circuit to it as shown (see next page).

If a fuse blows again when replaced, get an electrician.

Locating some common faults

Circuit tester Screw a torch bulb-holder to a piece of wood. Then use a strong elastic band to strap on a 4½ volt battery. Use bell wire to connect one crocodile clip to the bulb-holder and the bulb-holder to a battery terminal. Attach the other crocodile clip to the other battery terminal with bell wire.

Attach clips to the ends of the fuse. The bulb will light if the fuse is sound.

The table lamp may fail to light because of a fault in the on/off mechanism in the switch. With the lamp unplugged, remove the switch cover and attach a clip to the live terminal on each side of the switch. The circuit bulb should go on and off when the switch is operated. If not, the switch must be replaced.

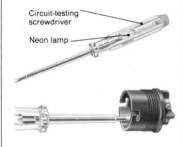

Circuit-testing screwdriver

Neon lamp

With the table lamp plugged in and switched on, touch each pin in the bulb-holder in turn with the tip of the circuit-testing screwdriver. The neon lamp will glow if the current is reaching the pins.

Citizen's arrest

Detaining a wrongdoer: your rights within the law

Every citizen has the right, under certain circumstances, to make a citizen's arrest when someone commits a crime. But your powers of arrest are limited.

You can arrest someone for what is termed an *arrestable offence* – usually one carrying a maximum penalty of five or more years of imprisonment – or for a breach of the peace. But you must be sure that the crime has been committed, otherwise you can be sued.

You cannot arrest someone on suspicion of a crime about to be committed. For example, if you see someone loitering suspiciously near a neighbour's house, you have no right to arrest him, because no crime has been committed.

If you do arrest a person, you must tell him why. If he resists, you are entitled to use reasonable force – but you must get him to a police station immediately or as soon as possible. If you detain the person longer, he could charge you for false imprisonment or assault. Where possible, you should call on passers-by for help, and obtain their names and addresses in case they are needed as witnesses.

You have no right to question or search the person you arrest to seize evidence. The suspect must be handed over to the police, while you remain available for questioning.

In practice it is inadvisable to make a citizen's arrest unless the offender surrenders meekly. If he attacks you or runs away, there is little you can do. If you see something suspicious, call the police immediately, or get someone else to do so. Keep the suspect under surveillance until the police arrive.

Citrus houseplants

Growing them from pips and cuttings

Attractive pot plants can be grown using the pips of oranges (see also ORANGE TREES), tangerines, lemons or grapefruit. Or, if you have access to existing plants, cuttings can be taken and used for propagating new plants – see PROPAGATING PLANTS.

To grow from pips, fill a 75mm (3in) pot with a good rooting mixture and plant a number of pips, spacing them well apart. Water well, then cover the pot with polythene to retain the moisture, and place in a warm spot – such as in an airing cupboard or on a shelf above a radiator.

Germination of the pips takes from four to six weeks; when the shoots are through, gradually expose them to light. Place them 250-300mm (10-12in) below

fluorescent lights for 15-16 hours a day, or near a brightly lit window, but not directly in the sun's rays.

When the shoots have several sets of leaves on them, carefully transfer them to individual pots filled with potting compost. Keep them warm and they will grow steadily – 100-150mm (4-6in) in a few months. But it may be several years before they flower indoors.

To grow from existing plants, take stem cuttings 75-150mm (3-6in) long. Dip one end of each cutting in a hormone rooting powder, then plant it in an individual small pot containing a mix of equal parts of peat moss and coarse sand or perlite. Moisten it well, then enclose the whole pot in a polythene bag and place it in medium light, at a temperature of 18-24°C (64-75°F).

Rooting should take about six to eight weeks, after which take off the bag and keep the rooting mixture damp until you see new growth at the tip. The new plant is now ready to receive monthly feeds of half-strength liquid fertiliser.

When you find roots emerging from the drainage hole in the pot, transfer the plant into a larger pot filled with a soil-based mixture and treat it as the mature plant from which it was taken.

Care of mature plants Keep the plants in a sunny situation. Do not feed in winter if the light is bad. Water moderately and keep plants above a temperature of 10°C (50°F).

Clarifying butter

Removing all but the pure fat for cooking

Butter adds its own distinctive flavour to cooking – but it can pose problems, because it easily burns. The answer is to cook with clarified butter. This retains the flavour of the original, but does not burn over a high heat.

Clarified butter is particularly useful in sautéing such dishes as mushrooms, fish, shellfish, veal and chicken breasts, where delicacy of flavour .is important. It is, however, relatively expensive, 225g (8oz) of butter produces only 150g (5oz) of clarified butter.

To clarify butter, melt a sufficient quantity (allowing for loss while clarifying) in a small, heavy-based pan over a gentle heat. Cook the butter, without stirring it or allowing it to brown, until the foaming stops. Take the pan off the heat and let it stand until the milky deposits have sunk to the bottom. Pour the clear yellow liquid (preferably through a piece of muslin) into a bowl.

Stored in a refrigerator, the clarified butter will quickly solidify and keep for at least three weeks. Throw away the milky deposits.

Cleaning and polishing materials

Making use of household resources

Many items commonly found in the kitchen, bathroom and garage can be used for cleaning and polishing jobs – see also CLEANING SOLVENTS; DUSTING AND CLEANING. Here are just a few.

Ammonia Add 1 part ammonia to 3 parts warm water to clean grubby paintwork, laminates and bathroom surfaces. After cleaning, wipe the surfaces with clean water to remove all traces of ammonia. Do not let fumes or splashes reach your eyes. Wear protective gloves and ensure good ventilation while using.

Baking powder This is a good grease loosener and deodoriser, and is less abrasive than scouring powder. Make a paste with clean water; rinse thoroughly after use with clean water and polish with a soft, dry cloth.

Bleach Household bleach can be used for removing stains from white cotton and linen only. Dilute 15ml (1 tablespoon) in 1.1 litres (2 pints) cold water. It can also be used to whiten bare wood. Wear protective gloves and safety spectacles.

Borax Laundry borax is safe on most materials. Use 15ml (1 tablespoon) in 570ml (1 pint) warm water for sponging and soaking. For stains, such as red wine, on white cottons, sprinkle on the powder and pour hot water through the material.

Brick Rub a piece of matching brick, dampened with clean water, on brick fireplaces to remove marks. Never add detergents or soap.

Dough The soft inner part of a loaf – preferably white bread – compressed into a ball makes a gentle rubber for removing marks from wallpaper.

Glycerine This is useful for lubricating and softening stains. Use 1 part glycerine to 2 parts water. Apply to an old, dried stain. Leave for ten minutes. Rinse thoroughly before carrying out any treatment to remove stains.

Hydrogen peroxide Dilute 1 part in 4 parts water for removing stains from clothing. Test on an unseen area first.

Jeweller's rouge A fine abrasive powder, useful for cleaning silverware other than silver plate.

Lemon juice Will remove marks from marble. Do not leave it on too long because it will eat into the marble and cause staining.

Metal polish In either liquid or wadding form, it can be used for removing scratches from acrylic plastics – such as baths.

Methylated spirit Apply with a soft cloth to remove marks from polished surfaces – except french polish. It will also soak up some ball-point pen marks and grass stains. Never use on acetate or triacetate fabrics.

Paraffin Mixed with equal parts of methylated spirit it makes a cleaner for dirty glass.

Salt Soak bloodstained items in salted cold water. To treat iron mould stains, cover the stained area with salt; pour lemon juice over the salt and leave for an hour. Rinse and repeat the treatment if necessary.

Steel wool For marks on vinyl tiles or parquet, rub with fine steel wool dipped in white spirit. On wood, work only in the direction of the wood grain to avoid scratching.

Talc Sprinkle onto a damp stain; leave until talc discolours, then rinse out. Repeat as necessary.

Vinegar White vinegar can be used for removing marks from marble. See also lemon juice.

Wood ash Applied with a damp rag, this mild abrasive will remove marks on polished furniture.

WARNING Many household chemicals can be harmful. Keep them out of reach of children, and if mixtures are made, label them carefully. *Never* store chemicals in old squash or lemonade bottles.

QUICK TIP Mop up spilt red wine with a white napkin – then, with a clean napkin underneath, pour enough white wine over the stain to saturate it. Leave to soak, then rinse out the stain with lukewarm water.

Cleaning solvents

How to use spot and stain removers

Cleaning solvents are mainly used for removing grease marks and stains from materials which cannot be washed. It is best to use them while the mark is still fresh.

The cleaners come either as a liquid, often in a bottle with dabbing pad, or in an aerosol can.

Before use on the stain, test on a portion of the material which will not be visible – such as a hem.

Spray an aerosol from the distance recommended on the can. Leave it to dry then brush off the powdery deposit with a soft brush. Repeat the treatment if necessary.

To use a liquid solvent, lay the stained area face down on a clean, absorbent, white or colourfast cloth, then either use the pad on the bottle, or dampen another cloth with solvent and lightly dab the fabric. Work from outside the area to the centre of the mark to prevent the stain from being spread. If the cloth underneath becomes discoloured by the stain, move to a clean part of the cloth.

Use as little solvent as possible. Sponge the area with clean water to avoid ring marks as soon as the stain has gone, then wash the item or have it dry cleaned as recommended on the care label.

WARNING Some cleaners are flammable and poisonous. So keep them away from children and naked flames, and ensure ample ventilation.

Climbing plants

Give them sun or shade – and a little support

Climbing plants can be used indoors (see also HOUSEPLANTS) to divide areas of a room, as a feature on a wall, and around a door or window. You can train them up canes, miniature trellises or ladders. Outdoors they can conceal unsightly walls – see also PLANTING and PROPAGATING PLANTS.

Indoors Few common indoor climbers – apart from black-eyed susan (*Thunbergia alata*) – like direct sun, or close proximity to radiators and other sources of dry heat. Ivies (*Hedera*), however, need plenty of light. Feed them and keep the soil moist during the growing season; allow the soil almost to dry out between waterings in the winter.

Grape ivy (*Rhoicissus rhomboidea*) spreads well in cool, shady rooms that do not become too cold in winter. Monsteras (Swiss cheese plants) and the creeping fig (*Ficus pumila*) have aerial roots; train the upper ones on a moss stick. Keep both monsteras and creeping figs in shade or semi-shade, and see that their soil is always slightly moist – see also PHILODENDRONS.

Ivies usually attach themselves to their supports. Other plants may need tying loosely with raffia or garden twine. Thinner shoots can be attached to a wall with a loop of transparent sticky tape: cut one strip of the size you want, and another 25mm (1in) longer. Stick the shorter strip to the inside of the longer one, so that the adhesive does not touch the shoot itself.

Wall flowers Tie wisteria to wires fixed firmly on a sunny wall. In February cut back the sideshoots to three or four buds.

Outdoors Ivies and parthenocissus (Virginia creepers and their relatives) grow in any soil, in sun or partial shade, and need no extra support; they will flourish even on north-facing walls. Wisterias need supporting wires on walls, but will find support of their own from pergolas; they need sun and rich, loamy soil.

Popular clematises also need support on walls; they prefer a limy soil, with plenty of leaf mould to hold moisture, and sun or partial shade.

QUICK TIP Fast-growing Russian vine (*Polygonum baldschuanicum*) rapidly screens sunny outside walls. It flourishes in moist soils, and produces sprays of white flowers from July. Support young vines with wires.

Climbing safely

Knowing the risks, seeking advice

Climbing and mountaineering are activities with an element of danger, so it is important to get proper advice and to know how to use the right equipment.

Boots Correct footwear is vital. Look for waterproof boots with good ankle protection and a stiff sole with deep tread.

Clothing Weatherproof clothing is essential for any journey into the mountains. It must be windproof and waterproof, and have a good hood. The layering principle is used, in which different layers of clothing carry moisture away from the skin but retain warm air. Breathable fabrics help ensure comfort, and avoid over-heating through perspiration. Good socks help to avoid blisters, and gloves, hat and scarf can provide important extra warmth.

Winter Anyone venturing onto a mountain in winter will need to have crampons and carry an ice axe. The ice axe can be used to help stop an accidental slip becoming a fatal fall. Crampons are necessary on hard snow and ice. They must fit boots correctly.

Helmets Because head injuries are likely to be especially serious, you should wear a helmet to protect you from falling objects or from striking your head if you fall.

Technical equipment Chocks, karabiners, slings and ropes are all used by climbers to protect them from falling. It is important to know how to use this equipment correctly, particularly belaying devices.

Instruction There are many good books which describe climbing techniques and training methods. It is also possible to get instruction from experienced climbers, qualified instructors and guides, and at outdoor centres and climbing walls. For details about centres and instructors contact the Mountain Leader Training Board, Capel Curig, Gwynedd LL24 0ET (Tel: 016904 272). Information on climbing walls and other publications are available from the British Mountaineering Council, Crawford House, Precinct Centre, Booth St East, Manchester M13 9GH (Tel: 0161 273 5835).

Clubs There are over 350 climbing and mountaineering clubs in Britain. Details about different clubs are available from the BMC.

Do's and don'ts of climbing

Do plan your route carefully, taking account of the experience and skill of the members of your party, and the hazards of the particular ascent.
Do make sure you have the right equipment and the knowledge of how to use it.
Do check the weather forecast.
Don't park inconsiderately or cause access problems because of inappropriate behaviour.

Clock cleaning

Keeping an old timepiece in trim

Dirt and dust are the main household enemies of mechanical clocks and watches. Ideally, they should be professionally cleaned from time to time – once a year for small wristwatches, less frequently for larger clocks.

You can clean a clock movement yourself. Remove it from its case and soak in liquid lighter fuel for at least 15 minutes. Wipe with a lint-free cloth, and dry the moving parts with a hair dryer. Lubricate the movement with a light oil, applying it with a matchstick to the spindle bearings in the movement plates.

To reduce the risk of dirt getting into the mechanism, keep clock and watch cases closed. If a mechanical clock stops without reason, put a rag soaked in lighter fuel in a container inside the case, and close it. The fumes are often enough to dislodge dirt, though the process can take several weeks. Wind clocks and watches carefully, to avoid breaking the spring; always move the hands clockwise when setting the time.

If an electrical mains-operated clock keeps stopping, that is usually a sign of a loose wire in the FUSED CONNECTION UNIT or plug and socket to which the clock is attached – see PLUGS; ELECTRIC SOCKETS AND SWITCHES. Switch the electricity off at the mains before checking. These clocks should be oiled every two years, or in accordance with the maker's instructions.

Batteries in quartz and other electric clocks generally last one to five years – ask when you buy. Erratic movements of the hands or digital numbers show the battery is running down.

Clothes storage

Protecting and keeping clothing smart

Store clothes in wardrobes in which air circulates freely; if there is a lack of air, clothes quickly become musty and decay – see also MOTHPROOFING. Do not pack too much in or clothes will be crushed.

Unless a garment is to be washed or dry-cleaned, hang it up or fold it neatly as soon as you take it off. Fasten buttons and zips, and adjust collars, sleeves and legs to their proper positions.

Use a soft clothes brush to brush jackets, trousers, skirts and coats before putting them away.

Thick wooden hangers are best for heavier clothes, such as suits, and padded hangers for other garments. Use well-shaped hangers to preserve shoulder-lines. Sweaters and cardigans should be folded and stored flat, or hung over towel-rails fixed inside a wardrobe.

QUICK TIP To keep trousers and slacks from slipping off hangers, glue a strip of felt to the bar; this will also reduce the mid-knee crease.

Organise drawer space with dividers and boxes, and do not cram in too many clothes. Minimise creases in folded garments stored for any length of time by

CLOTHING ALTERATIONS

CLOTHES STORAGE

Making the best use of space in a wardrobe

Open shelves, rails, drawers and wire baskets have a role to fill in a well-planned wardrobe.

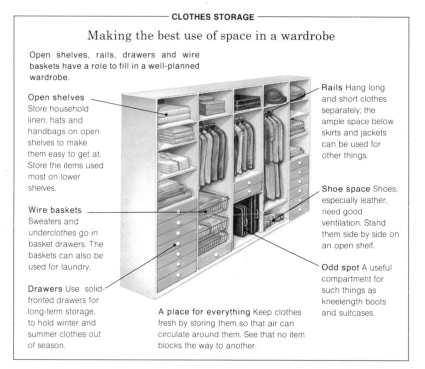

Open shelves Store household linen, hats and handbags on open shelves to make them easy to get at. Store the items used most on lower shelves.

Wire baskets Sweaters and underclothes go in basket drawers. The baskets can also be used for laundry.

Drawers Use solid-fronted drawers for long-term storage, to hold winter and summer clothes out of season.

Rails Hang long and short clothes separately; the ample space below skirts and jackets can be used for other things.

Shoe space Shoes, especially leather, need good ventilation. Stand them side by side on an open shelf.

Odd spot A useful compartment for such things as kneelength boots and suitcases.

A place for everything Keep clothes fresh by storing them so that air can circulate around them. See that no item blocks the way to another.

Tailoring garments to your shape and size

When clothes are a poor fit, because the wearer is not standard size or has lost or put on weight, a few simple alterations will ensure a perfect fit.

Taking in Take in a skirt waist by adjusting the seams and darts. If the skirt is too wide at the hips, unpick the hem and take in the excess from waist to hem.

Letting out On a skirt with a side zip, fit a triangular elastic insert centrally at the back.

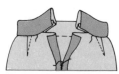

Trouser alteration Take in trousers at the back by cutting the waistband and taking in the fabric at the seam.

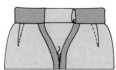

Letting out trousers If there is not enough fabric at the seam to increase the waist, fit a wedge-shaped insert of similar fabric into the waistband and seam.

Bodice adjustment Ease tightness round the bust by unpicking the side seams and darts, then widen the darts, lifting fabric into each dart on the lower stitch line.

---

laying tissue paper on their backs before folding.

When storing winter or summer clothes, wash or dry-clean them before you put them away for the season. Do not starch washable items going into storage. Label bags, chests or boxes with lists of their contents, so that you can easily find items you need.

Do not store wool, cotton or silk in plastic for more than a few months, because these fabrics need to breathe; protect them with old sheets or tissue paper. Avoid all plastic containers in places where damp is a problem. See also PACKING.

Accessories Clean, dry and air boots and shoes before storing them. Use shoe or boot trees to preserve their shape. Preserve the shape of hats by filling their crowns with loosely crumpled tissue paper. Arrange belts, ties and scarves on a tie-rack or a swinging towel bar. Put a LAVENDER BAG or POTPOURRI in lingerie drawers.

Clothing alterations

Improving fit: adjusting for weight loss or gain

Before altering any garment, examine the seams and darts carefully to see how they have been sewn and how much room they leave for alteration. To ensure a neat finish, always press out the creases after you have unpicked a seam or dart,

and press them again after restitching.

Adjusting waistlines To take in the waist of a skirt; unpick and remove the waistband and zip and open the seams and any darts. Turn the skirt inside out. Distribute the excess material evenly between the seams and darts, and pin and restitch them. Replace the zip and waistband, allowing for any extra overlap needed on the waistband. See also SEWING and SEWING MACHINES.

To let out skirt waists a little, unpick the waistband and open seams and darts. Reduce the seam allowance and darts, distributing the reduction evenly, pin and restitch.

If more room is needed at the waist on skirts with a zip at the side, cut through the waistband at the centre back and unpick the back seam to a depth about three times the width of the waistband. Turn in the raw edges and stitch in a triangular elastic insert. On skirts with a back zip, put two smaller elastic inserts into the side seams.

To adjust the waist of trousers or slacks, turn the garment inside out, cut the waistband at the centre back and unpick part of the back seam. If the trousers are too loose, take in the excess material at the centre back and taper it from the waist down. Restitch the seam and waistband, trim off the excess seam, and sew the waistband back to the trousers.

If the trousers are too tight, cut a wedge-shaped insert from the same or similar material. The top of the wedge

should be slightly wider than the amount by which the waist will be let out, to allow for seams, and long enough to fold back over the waistband, also with a little extra for a seam. Taper the bottom of the wedge to a point. Stitch the insert into the waistband and seam, turning the top edge of the insert over and down and stitching it, with raw edges folded in.

Hipline adjustments To reduce the width of skirts at the hips, unpick the waist seam at the sides. Stitch new side seams, parallel to the existing ones and tapering to the waist. Divide the excess material equally between the two new side seams. Unpick the original side seams, trim the seam allowance and restitch the waist seam.

If a skirt is too tight at the hips, undo all the vertical seams and let each out by the same amount. With some skirts and dresses that have waistline seams, you can widen the hips by raising the skirt at the waistline, so long as the garment is not too straight and narrow, and is long or has a generous hem.

Put the garment on, and raise the skirt until the hipline feels comfortable. Tie string round the new waistline, and mark it with tailor's chalk. Take the garment off, and remove the waistband or open the waist seam.

Trim the top of the skirt 16mm ($\frac{5}{8}$in) above the chalk mark. Take in any darts, lengthening them as needed, and the side seams at the waistline, to fit the waistband or waist seam. Unstitch and lower hem if necessary – see HEMS.

Realigning darts For a proper fit, darts should slope towards the fullest part of the body area they are accommodating. To realign them at shoulder, bust, waist or elbow, unpick them and pin them in their new positions on the right side of the garment. On the wrong side, mark new stitching lines with tailor's chalk.

Tack on the right side and try on the garment before final stitching. When they are stitched, press the darts towards the centre of the garment. Looseness or tightness at the bust can be corrected by adjusting bust darts and side seams.

Large abdomen To adjust for a protruding abdomen, unpick the front waist seam and the side seams. Let out the side seams by up to 10mm ($\frac{3}{8}$in), and the front of the waistline seam by up to the same amount, tapering a new waist seam to the original stitching at the sides.

Hollow back To adjust a garment to fit a hollow back, open the back waist seam. Raise the back waistline by making a deeper seam at the centre. Taper the new stitching to the old.

Cockroaches

Ridding your kitchen of unwholesome pests

To deter cockroaches, keep your kitchen as free as possible from moisture and damp. Do not leave any food uncovered or in paper bags (use metal, china, glass or plastic containers). Wrap all waste before disposal and block cracks where the insects may hide. Keep working surfaces, shelves and floors immaculate.

Repair leaky PLUMBING; wring out and dry dishcloths, sponges and tea towels after use. Seal openings around pipes and cabinets with silicone rubber sealant. Clean frequently under and behind low furniture and appliances.

If your kitchen does become infested, remove food, cooking and eating utensils, and all shelf linings. Dust or spray wall openings, under low equipment and other suspected hiding places with a commercial insecticide formulated for crawling insects, such as diazinon, fenitrothion or bendiocarb. Follow the maker's instructions carefully. Reline the shelves (if you use a spray, allow about four hours for it to dry before putting fresh paper on shelves). Repeat the dusting or spraying, and reline the shelves again, about three to six weeks later, in case a new generation of cockroaches hatch from any hidden egg capsules unaffected by the first treatment.

Cold frames

Growing vegetables in a frame

A cold frame, so called because it is not artificially heated, can be a substitute for a greenhouse, or a 'halfway house' where greenhouse plants can be acclimatised before they go outdoors. See also GREENHOUSES; GREENHOUSE GARDENING.

Properly used, a frame should rarely be empty. In winter, protect cauliflower plants in it, ready for setting out in early spring. You can sow onion and lettuce seeds there in January, two months earlier than in open ground.

In April plant out the onions and lettuces and in their place in the cold frame put french and runner beans. Follow these in late May with cucumbers or melons which will grow in the frame during summer. In September start the cycle again by sowing cauliflower seeds.

There are several types of cold frame available in wood, aluminium, plastic or galvanised steel, with glass or ACRYLIC sheet covers.

Filling the frame Several weeks before planting, dig well-rotted manure or compost into the soil at the rate of a bucketful to the square metre or square yard. Just before planting rake 75g (3oz) of general fertiliser into the topsoil, together with about half a bucket of moist peat. This will ensure that the ground is moist for overwintering crops. After planting, scatter slug pellets in the frame. Ventilate the frame by sliding the top to one side or propping it open. If you make two frames you can give the right conditions to plants that need different temperatures. During frosts, cover the frame at night with sacking or an old blanket, and remove the covering during the day.

Colds

Coping with the symptoms of a common affliction

There is no cure for the common cold, nor is immunisation against it possible, but some of the symptoms can be relieved, making the condition more bearable until the cold clears up on its own. This normally happens after a week to ten days.

If you have a slight temperature, take plenty of fluids, especially cool drinks, to replace the fluids being lost by perspiration.

Do not wrap up in extra clothes or blankets, and do not heat up the room or sit in front of a hot fire. Rather, allow the body to lose some of the excess heat being generated.

A headache or other aches and pains can be relieved with painkillers taken in recommended doses.

Steam inhalation may help to relieve nose congestion. Half fill a bowl with boiling water, place a towel over your head so as to trap the steam, and inhale for a few minutes at a time.

As soon as you feel able, take a walk in the fresh air.

Cold truths and untruths

● *Colds get better on their own.* True – but if symptoms persist after ten days, consult your doctor.

● *There are no medicines that will cure or shorten the duration of a cold.* True.

● *Colds are caused by getting wet or physically cold.* Untrue – but infection is more likely if you are generally run down.

● *Vitamin C is effective in treating a cold.* Untrue – there is no medical evidence to support the theory.

Cold sores

What to do about painful blisters around the mouth

A common virus, herpes simplex, causes cold sores in and around the mouth. They usually clear up in ten days to three weeks, but may recur, brought on by illness (usually a cold), stress, exposure to extreme cold, sunburn, or menstruation.

Severe outbreaks of cold sores, those in babies or infants, or those where blisters are near the eye, should be treated by a doctor, as there may be secondary infection. Frequently recurring attacks can be a sign of another, underlying, medical disorder.

Do not touch the blisters and then other parts of your body – particularly your eyes. The virus is found in the blisters, and is easily spread.

The symptoms of cold sores may be alleviated. Ease the pain of those in the mouth by frequent rinses with diluted proprietary mouth washes and sips of iced water. A soothing cream or salve can soften cracked lips. Spirit of camphor may dry up external blisters.

Sometimes, particularly in the first attack, doctors may prescribe antiviral tablets or ointment or an antibiotic cream.

If you are prone to cold sores, use a sun-screening lip salve when you are out of doors.

Colic

Soothing a baby's mysterious tummy ache

Many babies between the ages of about two weeks and three months suffer from colic – attacks of acute abdominal pain, usually during the evenings. By itself, colic is not serious, but get a doctor's advice immediately if it is accompanied by other symptoms such as vomiting, diarrhoea or blood in the motions, or if the attacks are so severe and persistent that they are exhausting the child or the mother.

Colic occurs in breast-fed, as well as bottle-fed, babies – often immediately after feeding. If you are bottle feeding, check that the hole in the teat is the correct size, and that you are holding the bottle tilted so that the teat is always full of milk. See also BREAST FEEDING.

If you have just started giving the baby solids (see BABY FOOD; WEANING), stop in case the child is reacting to one or other of them. Do not add solids or change the milk (although a small proportion of babies are allergic to cow's milk and may do better on soya-bean milk).

Try gently rocking the baby in your arms, rubbing its back, or placing a warm pad on its abdomen. If that does not work, take the baby for a walk in its pram, or even for a drive. Colicky babies usually thrive and gain weight normally, despite the discomfort that colic causes them.

Collections

Money for good causes

Collections in the street, or from house to house, are used by a wide range of charities and other organisations to raise money from the public.

If you want to organise a house to house collection, for instance for the local branch of a charity, check at the local police station to see if they will authorise it, or whether you need permission from the local council. For a street collection, council permission is essential. A check will be made on your identity, and on how much money is going to the charity. The authority will also make sure that no other collection

takes place on the same day.

All collectors must wear identifying badges and carry a certificate authorising them to collect. This also applies to people selling goods door to door on behalf of a charity. If you suspect that someone is not genuine, or you want to complain to the charity about them, ask to see their authority, and note the name and address of the organiser on the certificate.

Colour blindness

Give your eyes the coloured dot test

Difficulty in distinguishing between colours, especially red and green, is an inherited defect. It rarely causes problems, but it could prevent a person from taking up an occupation demanding perfect colour vision – such as an airline pilot or communications operator.

Opticians and doctors test for colour blindness with colour plates on which patterns may be visible only to people suffering from the disorder, or only to people who do not have it. Often, they use test cards covered with irregular spots – some are shown above.

View the plates in a room lit by natural daylight (electric light or direct sunlight can distort the results), from a distance of 760mm (30in), with your line of vision at right angles to each plate. You are allowed three seconds to decide what you see on each plate.

Companies

Setting yourself up in business

There are three ways in which you can carry on a business: on your own as a sole trader; with co-owners in a partner-

ship; or as a limited company. In a limited company you can be one of at least two owners (through a shareholding) and, at the same time, an employee.

Setting up a limited company is the most complicated and expensive of the three. But there is one big advantage – if the business should get into deep financial difficulties, the personal property of the people running it or owning its shares cannot be seized and sold to meet the debts. Sole traders and members of a partnership do not have the same protection. However, banks and creditors often demand security for loans to companies, either over the property of the company or from the directors. This may include asking for a mortgage over the directors' homes. You ought to seek professional advice before agreeing to this.

Getting the expert's advice If you are thinking of starting up in business, first find a good accountant, one who is recommended or one with good qualifications, and ask him or her about the best way for your business to trade. For a sole trader or a member of a partnership, there are few special legal formalities involved, other than keeping proper accounts. Provided that the Inland Revenue and the Department of Social Security agree, you will be classed as a self-employed person for tax (see INCOME TAX RETURNS) and NATIONAL INSURANCE purposes. You can do most of the things a limited company can do – for example, employ staff and buy or lease property and equipment for use in the business. Many of your business expenses can be offset against your earnings for income tax purposes.

Financial risk This depends much on the kind of business. If expenses are low and you are unlikely to incur substantial

Testing for colour-vision deficiencies

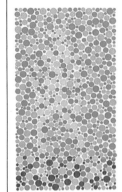

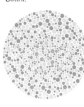

People with normal vision see a girl in a bikini and hat. Those with colour deficiencies do not see the bikini.

These test plates should be viewed in a room lit by natural daylight, not under artificial light or in direct sunlight. If you do not see the correct image on any of the plates, ask your doctor or ophthalmic optician to give you a comprehensive test.

People with normal vision see a teapot. Those with colour-vision deficiencies see a mug.

People with normal colour vision see an umbrella. Those with colour deficiencies see a walking stick.

refunds to customers, you may not need to become a limited company. If overheads such as rent, wages and the cost of materials, equipment and stock are heavy, you could benefit from forming a company.

You should also consider setting up as a limited company if you are in a business – such as a booking agency – which takes advance payments for future services which you may be unable to deliver.

Most business disasters occur when suppliers' bills cannot be paid; some are precipitated when dissatisfied customers demand refunds or sue.

Forming a company If you decide on this course, engage a solicitor who specialises in company law; the basic cost is more than £100.

You must submit various documents to the Registrar of Companies, including the *memorandum and articles of association*. The memorandum must state: the name of the company; whether its registered office will be in England, Scotland or Wales; the business purpose for which the company is formed; and the maximum amount of capital which may be put into the company (the authorised share capital). This authorised share capital is divided into shares – each of which has a nominal value.

The articles of association lay down the rules governing the day-to-day running of the company – such as the way in which directors are appointed, and the powers they have. Once the company is registered, you must comply with the rules requiring notification of changes of shareholders, directors, and other details such as the address. You must also file annual accounts audited by a qualified accountant, though it was announced in 1994 that this requirement may be relaxed.

Companies normally have at least two shareholders, and either two directors or a director and a company secretary; but a company can be established with only one shareholder or owner. It is often convenient to involve a wife, husband, partner or other family members aged over 18. All directors can be paid fees for their work, but income tax and NATIONAL INSURANCE must be paid through the PAYE scheme.

Private limited companies These companies (denoted by Limited at the end of the name) cannot sell shares to the public; the rules for share disposal are decided, with legal advice, when the company articles are drawn up.

Public limited companies These companies (which must have Public Limited Company or plc at the end of the name) can sell shares publicly. The authorised share capital must be at least £50,000.

Shares issued (sold) must be at least £50,000 before they start trading.

All limited companies must pay corporation tax on their net profits. Full-time directors, as employees, are liable to PAYE tax on their salaries. Fees and share dividends are also taxed. Limited companies can provide fringe benefits such as pensions as a business cost. However, tangible benefits – for example, a company car – that remain as assets on the company books can be seized to meet any debts.

Compass

How to find your way across country

You can navigate over totally unfamiliar country with a good degree of accuracy using an Ordnance Survey map and a compass (see also MAP READING). A walker's compass is best – the compass itself is set in a clear plastic straightedge, which has calibrated markings for checking map references, sometimes a magnifier for map reading and an engraved 'direction of travel' arrow.

Checking your position To find out exactly where you are, open the map out so that the arrows on it which identify north are visible. On large-scale maps, 1:50,000 or larger, there are two arrows on the top edge or side which define true north and magnetic north.

Lay the compass down on the map and swivel the map round until the arrow for magnetic north and the compass needle are aligned.

Now look around you for a landmark that can be easily identified on the map – for example a church, a small lake or hilltop. Find the landmark on the map and lay the straightedge so that it touches the symbol on the map. If you do not have a walker's compass, use any object that has a straight edge, such as a cigarette packet, book or ruler. Look along the straightedge, and turn it until it points towards the landmark but still touches the symbol on the map. Do not turn the map.

Draw a line along the straightedge, back to the position of your eye. Now find other landmarks and repeat the procedure – your position is approximately where the lines cross.

Plotting a route Decide in which direction you wish to travel and lay the straightedge on the map along that line, without moving the map – use the 'direction of travel' arrow on a walker's com-

Finding your approximate position

When lining up landmarks and map symbols, any straight-edged object can be used as a sighting instrument if your compass does not have one. Hold it and the map up to eye level, without turning the map.

Open out the map until you can see the two arrows on the top edge, which point to true north and magnetic north. With the compass on the map, turn the map until the compass needle is exactly in line with magnetic north.

Look for a landmark and lay the straightedge on the symbol for it on the map. Turn the edge to point to the landmark. Pencil along it. Repeat with other landmarks. You are near where the lines meet.

pass. Sight along the line and pick out a distinctive feature to use as an objective. When you reach it, plot your next line of travel.

QUICK TIP If you get lost without either map or compass, you may be able to find a compass course with the aid of a watch. Point the hour hand at the sun – on an overcast day look for the brightest part of the sky – and an imaginary line dividing the angle between the hour hand and 12 on the watch will point due south. In summer time, first turn the watch back one hour, to GMT (Greenwich Mean Time). See also NORTH STAR.

Complaints

Seeking satisfaction for faulty goods and services

A substantial body of legislation now exists to protect customers buying goods and services. Most manufacturers and shopkeepers are also aware that dealing quickly and fairly with complaints is good for business. In many cases all you need to do is complain to the immediate supplier of the goods or service for the fault to be righted or some reparation made. But if you fail to gain satisfaction there are several courses of action you can take.

Much of the legislation – including the Weights and Measures, Trade Descriptions and Consumer Safety Acts – is administered by local authorities through trading standards officers. These officers can not only give you free advice, but may be able to pursue the matter if it involves a criminal breach of these or other consumer protection laws. For example, an article purchased from a shop may be dangerous as well as defective. Alerting the trading standards officer may ultimately lead to the product being removed generally from sale. Your local Trading Standards Department can be found in the telephone book, listed under local council departments.

Some aspects of consumer protection – notably the Fair Trading and Consumer Credit Acts – are the responsibility of the Government-appointed Director General of Fair Trading. But initially, your local trading standards officer is the best person to go to for advice. A Citizens Advice Bureau can also help; the publicly financed National Consumer Council and the self-supporting Consumers Association take an active interest in customer complaints, though the latter will deal only with complaints made by subscribers to the association.

Making a complaint A customer has a right to expect that any goods or services he buys match their description and are adequate for the purpose for which they

were intended. If not, he can complain and, if necessary, take legal action to obtain compensation or to get his money back.

Defective goods A complaint about goods bought from a shop should be made to the shop, which is legally responsible for the goods it sells. Shops cannot evade responsibility by referring the buyer to the manufacturer. In agreeing to sell the goods to you, the shopkeeper in effect guarantees that they are satisfactory.

Recent legislation makes the manufacturer also liable for defective goods, whether or not he was negligent, but only where there has been injury, or where property worth more than £375 has been damaged or lost.

Unsatisfactory services A complaint about services – for example, building work on your house – should be made to the supplier of the service, in this case the builder. It is implicit in your contract with him – which need not be a written contract – that he will do the job with reasonable care and skill – see CONTRACTORS. If he fails to do this you can sue him for breach of contract or negligence – see LAWYERS; SUING.

If your initial, informal approach fails to bring satisfaction, complain fully in writing, fixing a time limit for a reply – say 14 days. Send the letter by recorded delivery so that the shop, firm or individual cannot deny receiving it. Keep a copy of your letter for future reference.

Complaints about officials If you feel yourself the victim of unfair or unjust treatment by government officials, complain to your local councillor or, if the complaint concerns a department of central government, to your local MP. If they fail to get satisfaction, your case can be investigated by an ombudsman – see OMBUDSMEN.

Going to law There are now so many sources of free or inexpensive advice about consumer rights that it is not usually necessary to consult a solicitor, unless and until you have decided to take your case to court.

Sometimes a formal solicitor's letter, costing a few pounds, can underline the seriousness with which you view your complaint and help you to obtain satisfaction. But it could also spark off a lengthy legal correspondence with your opponent's solicitor, which might prove costly. There are now many insurance schemes which cover legal expenses for consumer and other problems.

Unless the matter is serious, the cost of litigation may not be worth while. If the amount involved in the claim is £1000 or less (see SMALL CLAIMS) you will almost certainly have to pay your own legal costs, win or lose. If the sum involved is

more than £1000, and you lose, you may be ordered to pay all or part of your opponent's legal costs in addition to your own.

The lesson is clear: do not start court proceedings unless you are certain that your case can be proved. A solicitor is the best person to advise you on that.

Compost

Making fertiliser from garden and kitchen waste

Good compost can be made in the garden at little cost other than some patience: it is simply the product of several months of bacterial action, during which rotting vegetable matter is converted into a sweet-smelling, brown, crumbly humus.

A wide range of raw materials can be used: vegetable trimmings, the dead tops of plants, non-seeding weeds, grass clippings, old leaves, egg shells – even shredded newspaper, if it does not form more than 10 per cent of the mixture.

It is best to make compost directly on ground that has been well forked over, so that any excess water can drain away. Then add a layer of waste about 150mm (6in) deep. If the material is dry, saturate it with water before sprinkling on a compost activator to aid decay.

Sprinkle with sulphate of ammonia or one of the proprietary rotting compounds obtainable from gardening shops. Build up the heap with more layers in the same way. Soil or bonfire ash may be added 25mm (1in) thick between layers. Decomposition may be speeded by turning the heap after two months and forking the less-decomposed material to the centre of the heap and the rotted compost to the outside. Cover with a final layer of soil and plastic sacks. When the heap reaches a height of 1.2m (4ft), start a new heap.

Several types of compost bin are now available, at varying prices. A simple homemade compost pen can be made by forming a cylinder from a length of chicken-wire about 1m (3ft) wide. Bend the cut wire ends at one edge of the cylinder round the mesh along the other edge to secure. Line with plastic sacks to retain warmth.

See also JOHN INNES COMPOST.

Computers

Choosing and using a home computer

With a personal computer, normally referred to as a PC, you can entertain and educate yourself and your family, compose and record music, balance your household budget and bills, analyse your investments, prepare letters, reports and documents, and draw graphics and pictures. With the advent of the compact disc, computers can now offer a full encyclopedia on disk along with many thousands of other reference 'CD-books' and games. PCs can, with the addition of a 'plug-in' board, accept both still photographs and video/TV pictures, and can be used to edit videos.

With a *modem* (a device that permits your computer to talk to another via a normal telephone line) you may access your bank account and pay bills, order goods from mail-order services, access information lines, and send and receive facsimile documents.

The PC consists of the *processing unit,* the *keyboard*, and the *VDU* (visual display unit) or screen.

The processing unit is the box that contains the CPU (central processing unit), its memory and storage devices – *hard disk(s), floppy disk(s),* and, if fitted, a CD player and tape back-up unit. The keyboard, which resembles that of a standard typewriter, allows the user to 'communicate' with the computer. The VDU displays what is typed or drawn by the user. Most computers today also come with a *mouse,* which allows the user to move the computer *cursor,* or pointer, around the screen and select various options. Some computers have *pens* that act in a similar fashion to a mouse but offer the user a more familiar object.

A hard disk is normally not removable, and is located inside your computer's processing unit. This disk holds the computer's operating system as well as your programs and files. A floppy disk is removable, and is so named because, originally, both the disk and its cover were flexible or 'floppy'.

The CD player that is now available with PCs is being used to access the many millions of characters, in addition to graphics, photographs and even music and video excerpts, that are stored on a CD.

Tape back-up or data cartridge back-up units are designed to back-up, or copy, your hard disk quickly, and often only require just one tape cartridge, as each cartridge can hold large quantities of data.

Today the most popular PCs operate under the *MS-DOS* system (*M*icro *S*oft *D*isk *O*perating *S*ystem), but *Windows* has been added to make the PC more user-friendly and remove the need for the user to know much about the system. Windows offers the user a *graphical user interface,* which instead of using text-based 'menus', as does MS-DOS, employs graphics, pictures and *icons* (symbols) to represent various applications, services and options.

Buying a computer Computers vary in price from around £500 to £5000, according to specification, memory size, speed and disk capacity. If you buy a well-known, modern, MS-DOS based computer, you can always upgrade it later by adding more memory or disk capacity, or indeed by upgrading the processor.

The first thing to consider is how much you want to spend. The second most important consideration is, what do you want the computer for? If it is solely for home use, for you and your children, a cheaper, less powerful, model with a hard disk of around 100mb (megabytes) capacity will probably be ideal. If you want your computer to run Windows, you should select a computer with at least 4mb main memory. If speed and facilities such as facsimile are required, a more powerful model with a larger hard disk will be required.

If you plan to use your computer for graphics and picture manipulation, the computer you need will be a much more powerful model with a 500mb hard disk and 8-16mb main memory.

You may decide that you need a portable or lap-top computer. Again, these vary in price according to their specification. Before buying your computer, read some of the many computer magazines that are available, talk to friends who already use one, and visit a computer superstore where you can see many models being displayed.

When buying a printer, consider how much you want to spend and what you want it for. If it is solely for home use, for you and your children, a *dot matrix* or *ink-jet/bubble-jet* printer will be ideal. If quality of output is important, a *laser* printer is the one to buy.

You can spend anything from around £150 to £5000 on a printer, depending on specification, Expect to pay around £150-£200 for a monochrome ink-jet/ bubble-jet printer, around £500-£1000 for a colour ink-jet/bubble-jet printer, £500-£2000 for a monochrome laser printer and up to £5000 for a colour laser printer.

A *package* is the name used to describe a program or suite of programs that allows you to carry out various tasks on your computer. If you want to maintain your share portfolio or prepare and manage budgets, you will need a *spread sheet* package. If you need to keep records, you will need a *database* package; if you wish to prepare graphics and pictures, you will need a *graphics* package; and if you want to create letters, reports and documents, you will need a *word processing* package. Prices vary, but £200 is probably the average for a simple package. If you buy a 'bundled' package – several at once – you will get a much better deal and will probably find all the items listed above for around £300.

When you have decided on your package budget and requirements, shop around before buying. It is likely that you will be able to negotiate a deal whereby a shop will give you a special price if you buy everything from there.

Guarantees and service Read the guarantee carefully. Exactly what does it promise? If something goes wrong, will your dealer make repairs, or will you have to send the computer to a distant factory? Test the system thoroughly before sending off the guarantee card.

If you buy a relatively expensive computer, ask about a service contract to keep down the cost of repairs when the guarantee runs out. Check your house contents insurance, too.

Computer care Heat, dust, damp, cigarette smoke, static electricity and the electromagnetic fields generated by all electrical devices are enemies of your computer system. Set it up somewhere out of direct sunlight and away from radiators or fires.

Leave room for air to circulate freely around the machine's intakes and vents. Keep the computer clean and cover it when you are not using it.

Disks should be stored away from loudspeakers, televisions, electric fans, laser printers, the screen itself, and other electrical equipment. They should always be kept in a dry, dust-free location without extremes of temperature. Store your disks in a suitable dustproof disk box. Never leave your disks where there is a risk of damage or contamination, especially from liquids. Never try to clean your disks.

Disks, if used and stored properly, are generally reliable. However, if the information stored on them is of great importance, you should keep another copy of the information on a separate disk, because with use the magnetic coating can deteriorate, leading to disk errors and potential loss of data.

If you receive any 'static' shocks where you work, protect your computer by either spraying the carpet beneath with an anti-static spray from a computer store, or, when working on your computer, keeping your feet on a rubber mat.

Surges in the electricity supply can cause data errors or lead to computer failure. If possible plug your computer into a supply that does not serve large applicances, and fit an anti-surge plug that will minimise any sudden power increases.

Concrete

Mixing and using; laying driveways and patching

Concrete is made by mixing cement, sand and stones (aggregate) together in measured proportions, then adding water. Ordinary Portland cement is grey, but a range of other colours is available, including white. The cement used must always be dry, fresh and free from lumps, and is best bought fresh for each job.

Sharp sand is used for concrete mixes, not the soft builders' sand used for MOR-TAR. Aggregate may be either gravel or crushed stone, and varies in particle size according to the type of work in hand. There are various ways of getting your concrete, again depending on the job.

Bagged mixes These are available in paper sacks, requiring only the addition of water: ideal for small jobs, but relatively expensive.

Separate ingredients Buy them from a builders' merchant, either loose or bagged. Hand mixing is hard work, so consider renting a mixer from a local tool hire centre – see HIRING.

Bulk delivery *Yellow Pages* lists companies who will deliver bulk concrete of the required mix to your door, but it is not always possible to order small quantities.

Site-mixing In this system, concrete is mixed as required from the back of a special lorry. Only the amount you actually require will be mixed.

Mixes

Most concrete work in the garden can be tackled with one of three basic mixes.

Mix A A general-purpose mix for jobs such as garage floors and drives: 1 part cement, 2½ parts sand, 5 parts coarse aggregate by volume.

Mix B Use this where strength and wear resistance is needed – for paths, pools and steps, for example: 1 part cement, 2 parts sand, 4 parts coarse aggregate by volume.

Mix C This is a mix for bedding mortar for paving slabs: 1 part cement, 3 parts sand by volume.

Always use a minimum of water for mixing: it makes stronger concrete, and is much less messy.

Calculating quantities

To find out how much concrete you need, use Table 1. Working in metric, read across the area scale on the left of the table to the line for the required thickness of concrete, then down to the total quantity scale. This will give you the amount in cubic metres. For imperial, read from the right, but the final figure will still be in metric (ready-mixed concrete is sold by the cubic metre).

When you have calculated the volume required, use Table 2 to see how much of each ingredient you need for a particular mix. It is wise to err a little on the generous side when ordering.

Laying paths and driveways

Make the same basic preparations for both jobs, but for a driveway, which bears much heavier traffic, it is important that the foundations be that much stronger.

First mark out the route, clearing off all grass and topsoil. Use string stretched between wooden pegs to mark straight runs. For curves, lay a garden hose along the ground.

Paths Remove surface material down to a depth of at least 75mm (3in) below the proposed path level. Fill any soft areas with hardcore or broken stone and stamp it well down so that you form a really firm base.

Driveways Excavate to a depth of at least 180mm (7in), then cover with at least 75mm (3in) of hardcore, well rammed down.

To contain the concrete, make up a *formwork* of boards held by pegs driven into the ground outside the formwork. Adjust the boards so there is a slight fall or slope across the width of the path. To allow for drainage, slope it away from a house wall.

Divide the formwork into bays every 3m (10ft) by placing a hardboard strip across the path or drive. This allows for expansion of the concrete.

If the soil or foundation material is very dry, damp it before the first concrete is laid. Fill one bay from one end, piling the concrete higher than the formwork, then levelling it with a board laid across the formwork and moved back and forth, in a zigzag fashion. It is best to create a slight ripple on the surface so that the concrete will not become slippery in wet or icy conditions.

The concrete must not dry out too

Making a solid surface for a path or drive

Ram down a hardcore bed and set up timber formwork to the surface height required. Make a crossfall for drainage and insert joints to allow for expansion. Lay the concrete within two hours of mixing, and level and compact (tamp) it with a board edge.

Tamped concrete surface with rippled effect

Tamping beam

Formwork

Hardcore bed

Crossfall set with spirit level and wooden shim

Expansion joint

Formwork support peg

Calculation tables

The amount of concrete needed (Table 1) depends on the area and thickness to be filled. The quantities of ingredients (Table 2) vary according to the amount of concrete and the mix to be used.

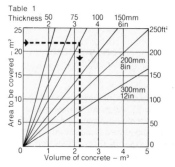

Table 1

Table 2

Quantities for 1m³ of concrete	Mix A		Mix B		Mix C
Cement (50kg bags)	6		7		11
Sand (m³)	0.50		0.50		1
Coarse aggregate (m³)	0.85	1.10*	0.75	1.00*	0

*All-in aggregate

Example: Area to be concreted 2 × 11 = 22m²

From Table 1, 100mm thick requires 2.3m³
From Table 2 the quantities required for Mix A

Cement 2.3 × 6 = 14 bags
Sand 2.3 × 0.50 = 1.25m³
Coarse aggregate 2.3 × 0.85 = 2m²

quickly, as this would weaken it. On hot days, cover the concrete with damp sacking or sheet polythene. Keep the concrete moist in this way for at least three days. If frost is likely, cover the sheet with a layer of earth or sand, or a 75mm (3in) deep layer of straw (but it is best to avoid laying concrete in frosty weather).

Continue filling bays, removing the expansion pieces as the concrete begins to harden. The complete formwork can be removed after a day or two, taking care not to damage the edges of the path or drive.

Fencing A special bagged, fast-setting concrete is available for setting fence posts. The mix is added to the hole dry, then water is added. Setting takes about 5 minutes.

Repair work and patching
Clean out all loose material from pot-holes and cracks, slightly undercutting the surface where possible. To fill holes or cracks, make up Mix C adding a proportion of PVA adhesive (see GLUING) to equal parts of the mixing water. This will greatly improve adhesion to the old material.

When resurfacing, just before covering with Mix C, coat the area to be repaired with PVA adhesive mixed 1 part to 3 of water. Add the Mix C concrete, then smooth and level it.

Condensation

Dealing with damp caused by poor ventilation

Condensation occurs when moisture suspended in warm air comes into contact with a cold surface. It is mostly seen on single-glazed windows and mirrors in bathrooms, but it can appear on any cold surface, including walls, floors and, in extreme cases, furnishings and even clothes in wardrobes.

Apart from the damage it does to decoration, the deposited moisture encourages mould growth – see MILDEW AND MOULD.

Condensation occurs on cold, mainly dry days. If you encounter damp patches on walls on wet, muggy days, suspect structural DAMP – not condensation. Steam-producing processes in the home – washing, bathing, cooking, clothes drying – cause condensation, and blocking in chimney flues and efficient DRAUGHT-PROOFING aggravate the problem.

The best way to deal with condensation is to extract the damp air with EXTRACTOR FANS in the kitchen and bathroom – see also VENTILATION. Make sure that the doors to these rooms are kept closed when steam is being produced; if moist air is allowed to escape into the rest of the house it will condense in the coldest spots.

Condolence letters

Writing the right words to the bereaved

When there is a death in the family, or affecting close friends or business associates, it is usual to write a letter of condolence. Try to let the person know that you are thinking of them at this time, that you sympathise with their loss, that you held the person in esteem and will miss them too. Say also that you will make yourself available should any form of help be needed.

Keep your letter brief and to the point. Do not bring in any other news – save it for a later letter. Do not be afraid to express your own personal feelings at the news. If it was the result of a long illness, the feeling may be one of relief that the person is no longer suffering.

Sample – to a close friend
Dear ......, I was so sad to hear of the death of your mother – but in a way relieved that the suffering you mentioned is over for her. She was a lovely lady, and we were always warmed by her cheery greeting and interest in our family. I am sure she will be greatly missed by your family. You will be much in our thoughts over the next few weeks – and if there is anything at all we can do to help, please give me a call. Just a reminder, our phone number is ....
Yours affectionately,

Sample – for a business associate
Dear Mrs ...., As a colleague of your husband for eight years, I was shocked to hear of his sudden death. And I am writing to offer you and your family my sincere condolences. Fred was very much liked by his colleagues, and those he dealt with on behalf of our company, and we will always remember him for his willingness to help.

Should you need any assistance regarding his business affairs here, please do not hesitate to get in touch with me on this number .... Our personnel department will be in touch concerning pension and so on.

Please notify us of the date of the funeral. A number of us wish to attend. And please let us know where flowers should be sent.

Yours sincerely,

Conjunctivitis

Dealing with a painful eye problem

The white of the eye and inside of the eyelid are covered with a thin, transparent membrane called the conjunctiva. Inflammation associated with these membranes is called conjunctivitis. See also EYES; STYES.

Symptoms Trouble can develop quite slowly, the eyes looking red and congested, and feeling gritty and irritated. The eyes become sticky, and you may find a crusty deposit around them after a night's sleep.

Causes The most common cause is a virus or bacterial infection which responds to treatment, but irritants such as tobacco smoke, cosmetics and even some proprietary eye preparations may lead to conjunctivitis. In small children it can be caused by blocked tear ducts.

Occasionally conjunctivitis may be an outward sign of an allergy; on rare occasions it may indicate a serious eye disease.

Treatment Bathe a sticky eye in boiled water left to cool. Do not cover the eye with an eye patch. It can aggravate the infection. With a small child, massaging the lower eyelid near the nose may help to clear a blocked duct.

If the problem persists after two or three days, consult your doctor, earlier if there are severe pains.

If you have recently visited a tropical country, consult your doctor as soon as symptoms develop, as you may have picked up a virus which could eventually affect your vision.

Prevention Avoid irritants like tobacco smoke. Do not use proprietary ointments, eye drops or washes if you feel these may be a source of irritation.

Wash your hands well after treating someone with conjunctivitis – it can be passed on by direct contact. And see that the infected person has his own face flannel and towel, which no one else should use.

Constipation

Ways to avoid worrying bowel problems

It is quite common and normal for a baby to go for a week without emptying the bowels, but with adults, when waste material (faeces) stays in the rectum for several days, it becomes difficult to pass – and this is constipation.

Lack of exercise, poor diet or nervous tension can all cause constipation. WALKING, JOGGING or SWIMMING are good exercises for stimulating the bowel muscles. Eat plenty of roughage, such as bran, wholemeal bread, leafy vegetables and fresh or dried fruits.

Take plenty of fluids, preferably water, fruit juice and milk.

Laxatives that stimulate the bowel can be taken, though they should be discontinued as soon as normal habits are restored. Suitable short-term laxatives include castor oil, cascara, figs, senna and Epsom salts. For chronic or persistent constipation there are bulk-forming laxatives which can be taken to supplement a high-roughage diet. There are a number of proprietary brands, available from chemists without prescriptions.

If you think the cause is nervous tension, or if constipation persists for more than two weeks, seek medical advice.

Contact lenses

Finding out which type is best suited to you

Contact lenses of many different types are now available to meet different needs. Comfort and convenience are important considerations in deciding which to choose. It is important also to seek expert advice before reaching a decision. See also EYES; EYE TESTING; COLOUR BLINDNESS.

Consult an optician who is a qualified contact lens specialist – with a Diploma in Contact Lens Practice (DCLP). These are the main types of lens he can prescribe:

Hard lenses The cheapest, oldest and most durable type available, these are more resistant to scratches than gas permeables and are long lasting, easy to clean and maintain. But they are prone to pop out or slip off-centre.

The hard acrylic lens also lacks lubrication and stops oxygen reaching the cornea, which can cause irritation. It usually takes a month or more of gradually increasing usage for the wearer to adjust to them.

Soft lenses More expensive but flexible and more comfortable, they are usually made of water-absorbing plastics, and allow some oxygen to reach the eye. Because they are bigger than hard lenses they are more stable, covering a substantial portion of the eye, extending under the lid.

However, they provide marginally less clarity of vision than hard lenses, and are more fragile and easily damaged: usually they last for only a year or two. They also require frequent cleaning in special solutions, which can cost the wearer £200 a year more.

Extended-wear lenses This type of soft lens allows more oxygen to reach the eye, enabling the wearer to keep them in longer – possibly up to 30 days. However, most specialists recommend that you take them out every few days to clean them.

These are particularly useful for those who have difficulty handling contact lenses – people with arthritic fingers, for example.

Gas permeable lenses These combine some of the best features of hard and soft lenses. They are almost as hard as conventional hard lenses and give excellent vision. They can also allow more oxygen to reach the eye than even the best of the soft lenses, though only a few do so. While more durable than soft lenses, they are nevertheless fairly brittle. They are less resistant to scratches than hard lenses and need more cleaning. Here are some tips for prospective contact lens wearers:

Lens care Always use the disinfecting and storage solutions recommended for your lenses. Keeping them in water could lead to an eye infection.

Repositioning a slipped lens Roll your eye towards the lens. Gently press the lid to push the lens back into place.

Finding a lost lens To find a hard lens, shine a torch about the spot where the lens was lost; the lens will reflect the beam. A lens can flip out a considerable distance, so expand your search over several square yards if you fail to find it where expected. If necessary pull a stocking or tights over the head of a vacuum cleaner, and vacuum the area: the lens will be trapped in the fine mesh.

Contractors

Finding and dealing with a builder

A contractor is someone you engage to do work for you – and if the work is on your home, that probably means a builder. But as work on a home may involve many skills, some of it may have to be sub-contracted. You need to establish at an early stage whether to give your contractor permission to find sub-contractors, or engage them under direct contract to you – see CONTRACTS.

The second course could reduce costs – particularly if you can arrange to buy materials, fittings and appliances through discount stores.

Whichever way you choose, make it clear to the builder where the demarcation lies. This will influence his estimate for the job. Only if he chooses the sub-contractors will he be responsible for the quality of their work.

Finding a builder If you are employing an ARCHITECT he can help you to find a reliable builder through his own contacts. If you have to find one yourself, recommendation is the safest way. Talk to someone who has had a good job done, or if you see local work you like, ask who carried it out.

Otherwise check adverts in your local press and *Yellow Pages*. Choose a firm belonging to some relevant body – the Federation of Master Builders, British Decorators' Association, National Register of Warranted Builders, or Guild of Master Craftsmen. Always plan to meet a representative personally.

Estimates Establish exactly what you want doing and check that the builders can meet your requirements in full – either with their own workmen or helped by sub-contractors. Make it clear at this stage if you plan to do any of the work yourself.

Get a written estimate from each firm, then choose which you feel best meets your requirements. Accept the chosen estimate and embody this in a formal agreement with a full specification which can be signed by the builder.

Payment Most builders expect monthly payment in arrears – at the end of a month's work. Small jobs may require weekly payments. Never pay in advance other than for the purchase of specific fittings – even here it is best to pay the supplier direct.

Arrange to withhold a proportion of the money until you are entirely satisfied with the work done – 5 per cent is a reasonable amount. Otherwise, if there is a dispute, you have no lever to encourage an unreliable builder to put matters right. See also BUILDING PERMITS; PLANNING PERMISSION.

Contracts

How to make binding agreements

A contract is simply an agreement between two 'parties' – people or organisations – usually involving an exchange of goods or services by one for some form of payment by the other.

In most cases they can be concluded by a spoken agreement, or even without speaking at all. For example, someone who picks an item from a supermarket shelf and pays at the cash desk without saying a word has created a contract for that purchase with the shop. See also COMPLAINTS; CONTRACTORS.

Some contracts, however, must be in writing and signed. These include contracts for the sale of houses or flats, leases for more than three years, agreements in which one person guarantees another's debts, and hire purchase and other consumer credit agreements. Employment contracts need not be in writing, but most employees are entitled to at least a written summary of their terms of employment after being in a job for 13 weeks.

Minors under 18 can enter many types of contract, although the law discourages people from granting them loans or credit. In general, a contract disadvantageous to a minor cannot be enforced.

Getting it in writing Important contracts should always be in writing – it saves trouble if there is a dispute later. A solicitor can draw up the document for you, or you can do it yourself. There is no specific form of words that you need use – though there is certain information that must be stipulated in employment particulars. But all the important details should be included and clearly set out – the full names and addresses of the parties, and what has been agreed, such as a price, rate of pay, delivery date, quantities or materials to be used. Make two copies. Sign and date both yourself, and get the other person to do the same. Keep one copy, and give your co-signatory the other.

If you are asked to accept a contract, read all associated documents carefully first, particularly any small print; estimates, quotes and receipts may all contain terms that form part of the contract. The courts will not help you if you overlooked and therefore accepted a particular condition, provided that condition is lawful.

If you have any doubts, get advice from a solicitor or other expert. Should you object to a particular condition, strike it out of the contract before signing, or tell the other party in writing (keeping a copy) that you do not accept it; it is then up to him whether or not to go ahead with the amended contract.

The terms of contracts cannot be significantly altered once they have been reached, unless both parties agree. If you agree or suggest changes to a contract that is in force, set the changes out in writing, too.

When a contract is broken A contract is broken if one party backs out of it entirely, or substantially changes the terms without permission from the other. The injured party can then claim compensation or damages for any loss he has suffered as a result.

Sometimes a dispute can be settled without going to court, through a third party; standard contracts used by builders and other suppliers often specify a body to undertake this task – see ARBITRATION.

Disputes over employment contracts can be pursued through industrial tribunals or the courts – but not both at the same time. Other cases of breach of contract are dealt with by the civil courts; but the process can be lengthy and expensive, so get legal advice before starting an action.

Getting out of a contract You may get out of a contract if you can show that the other party broke it first, or that you were lured into it by a false statement. You may also escape if you can show that there is a fundamental flaw in the contract, or that the circumstances

under which you entered it were unlawful; in both cases, it will be invalid.

A contract condition that takes away someone's legal rights – for example, to compensation for injury through negligence – can be challenged in the civil courts. The Unfair Contract Terms Act makes some unfair conditions automatically void – among them attempts by a dealer to reduce his obligation to ensure that the goods he sells are of suitable quality and fitness for ordinary use.

If you are sued for breach of contract, and found to be liable, damages awarded against you will be linked to the loss suffered by the other party. For example, if you order a television set but then refuse to pay on delivery, you might be required to give the dealer the profit he has lost – but the court would not order you to accept the set.

Cookers

Using and maintaining gas, electric and solid fuel cookers

Whatever type of cooker you have, using it properly gives the best results and cuts fuel bills, while keeping it in good order will ensure years of reliable service.

Gas cooker All gas hobs give direct heat that can be instantly controlled. There are usually four burners, including one small and one large.

Do not allow the flames to extend up the sides of a pan – the contents will not heat any quicker and the flames will leave stains (see CLEANING AND POLISHING MIXTURES; COOKWARE), as well as creating a fire hazard when frying.

Clean the burner holes regularly with a stiff bristle brush. Wipe any spillages from the burner head or frets immediately, or they will bake on hard.

Unless your oven is self-cleaning, clean it regularly, before it becomes too big a job – see OVEN CLEANING. If there is a glass door on the oven, or a door with a glass panel, clean it with a damp cloth dipped in bicarbonate of soda or a strong solution of detergent and hot water.

Do not try to make adjustments to the gas supply or any faulty operation on a gas cooker. Have it checked by a British Gas official or by a gas fitter approved by the Confederation for the Registration of Gas Installers (CORGI). You must also employ an approved fitter to install a gas cooker – it is illegal to fit it yourself.

Electric cooker A standard cooker has an oven, a grill and a hob with boiling rings or plates, or heating areas under a ceramic hob.

The pans for electric hobs should have perfectly flat bases so that there is full contact between the hob and the pan. The heated areas may take 30 minutes to

cool down after being switched off.

The door and shelves of an electric cooker need to be cleaned regularly, following the maker's instructions. Never allow dirt and grease to build up anywhere, as it will reduce the efficiency and life of the elements. Never use aluminium foil to line the shelves, sides or floor, as it can damage the elements.

On some older cookers the hob elements consist of a spiral ring in a metal sheath that can sometimes be replaced when worn out. Some cookers have solid metal plates which are simply unplugged, but others need access to the terminals under the cooker top plate.

First check that you can get access to the terminals. Switch off the cooker at the mains, then remove the elements and check at an electrical supply shop whether you can obtain replacements of exactly the same type and size.

Oven elements are usually behind panels in the sides, or at the back in a fan-assisted oven. They can be replaced only by a qualified service engineer.

Solid fuel cooker Heat is stored in a solid fuel cooker, which is designed to stay alight continuously. Some models provide hot water for CENTRAL HEATING and the domestic supply.

Check the heat gauge each morning to make sure the cooker temperature is correct. It will be too low if the lids of the hotplates are left open or if the flues or chimney are blocked. Clean the flues once a month: the manufacturer's instruction booklet will tell you how. Have the chimney swept yearly.

The temperature will be too high if the ashpit door is not tightly closed. Clean its machined edge regularly with a wire brush. Follow the instruction book on fuel, riddling and refuelling.

Wipe the outside of the cooker daily with a damp cloth. The oven doors lift off for cleaning; do not put them in water or the insulation will be damaged. Inside, the ovens need to be brushed out occasionally. Use a wire brush to clean the hotplates.

Cooking with a candle

Boiling water and cooking a meal

A single candle can give enough heat to boil a kettle and cook a basic meal such as egg and bacon. It can be used outdoors or indoors in an emergency.

Making a candle cooker Cut a 125mm (5in) household candle so that the bottom piece is slightly longer than the top. Expose its wick, and the two pieces will be the same length.

Wrap each piece twice round in brown paper, trimmed to the length from the tip of the wick to the base. Secure the paper with sticky tape or string. Stand the two

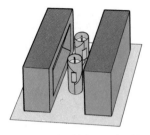
Emergency cooker Make sure the side supports rise clear of the candles.

half candles between two bricks laid with their hollows facing inwards – or you can use concrete slabs, or tiles stacked high enough to clear the candles.

Cooking Light the candles *and* the brown paper around them. Set the kettle or pan on the bricks over the heat. A pint of water will boil in 10-15 minutes. An egg will fry in about five minutes.

Make sure the candles are properly extinguished after use.

Cookware

Choosing and caring for your pots and pans

Saucepans and other cooking utensils are made in five main materials: aluminium; copper; stainless steel; cast iron; and heat-resistant glass. There is also plastic ware for MICROWAVE COOKING. Price, durability, efficiency and ease of cleaning are the main points to look for.

Aluminium The cheapest material, aluminium is lightweight and durable, will not rust, is easy to keep clean and conducts heat well. Thick, heat-retaining pan bases are needed for electric hotplates and solid fuel cookers.

Clean them with hot, soapy water and a scouring pad. Boil a weak solution of vinegar or lemon juice and water in the pan to shift stains. Never use soda.

Copper The material is an excellent heat conductor and extremely durable, but it is expensive and discolours badly. Copper utensils are usually lined with tin or silver, which wears thin in about three years. Clean the inside with soapy water only, and the outside with a proprietary copper polish or with half a lemon dipped in vinegar and salt.

Stainless steel It cleans easily just with hot soapy water, but is a poor heat conductor. To overcome this, the best saucepans have a base of copper, or aluminium, or mild steel sandwiched between stainless steel.

Cast iron Not only is this an excellent heat conductor, it also retains heat and

so makes pots and pans economical to use. Once the pan is heated, the heat source can be turned low.

However, cast-iron utensils are heavy, which makes them awkward and dangerous to lift when full. Wash in hot, soapy water, rinse and dry, then rub with cooking oil or unsalted fat to prevent rust.

Heat-resistant glass Most glass cookware is for oven use only, but some is flameproof, which means that it can be used on direct heat. Consult the maker's instructions.

Enamelled and non-stick cookware Enamel can be fused onto cast iron, steel or aluminium, and is found on almost every type of kitchen utensil from frying pans to roasting tins. They last for years if properly cared for. Enamel chips and scratches easily, so use only wooden or plastic spoons or spatulas. Clean only with hot, soapy water. To remove stains, soak pans in warm, soapy water.

Non-stick pans allow you to cook with little or no fat. They clean easily with a sponge and warm soapy water. Never use abrasive cleaners or metal utensils, which scratch the surface.

Microwave ovenware The ultra high-frequency waves generated in a microwave oven will pass through almost any material except metal, which reflects the waves and may damage the oven. Containers made of specially formulated plastics are available: buy a set designed to make the best use of oven space.

Corks and corkscrews

Correct ways to open the wine

The corks sealing bottles of good WINE seal in enough air to enable the wine to mature to perfection. If the cork dries out and shrinks, too much air gets in and the wine becomes vinegary or musty. So keep corks moist if you are storing wine for more than a few days, by placing the bottles on their sides – see WINE STORAGE.

Prepare for opening by cutting off the cover, down to the bulge on the bottle neck. Wipe the area clean if necessary, particularly if there is a white, powdery deposit around the neck.

On a traditional corkscrew look for a thin, widely spaced thread on a spiral at least 60mm (2½in) long, with a sharp tip. The edge of the thread should not be too sharp, or it can fragment the cork.

Make sure the handle is long enough to give good leverage, with a plain finish that allows a firm grip; and that handle and spiral are connected securely.

Screw a corkscrew down through the cork and, when the spiral end protrudes through the cork, pull, holding the bottle between your knees. If the cork is really

tight, stand the bottle on the floor and press down on it with one hand while pulling the cork.

Lever corkscrews remove much of the effort. Three useful types are illustrated.

Opening sparkling wine Tear off the foil. Tilt the bottle away from you, and untwist the ring of the wire muzzle, keeping hold of the cork with the other hand. Remove the muzzle and, still holding the cork, twist the bottle until you feel the cork begin to rise. Ease the cork out gently, and pour the wine immediately.

QUICK TIP If pieces of cork fall into a bottle during opening, quickly strain the wine through a clean piece of linen.

CORKSCREWS

Three ways to pop your cork

A corkscrew should have an open spiral (1) not a central core (2) to reduce its bite nor a sharp edge (3) to cut up the cork.

1 2 3

Boxwood The upper crossbar is used to drive the spiral into the cork. The lower crossbar is then turned in the same direction, driving the spiral upwards and thus withdrawing the cork.

Butterfly The side levers swing upwards as the spiral is driven into the cork by turning the top handle, which also serves as a bottle opener. The toothed levers are then pushed down together, and a ratchet action forces the spiral upwards to pull the cork.

Waiter's friend With the handle extended, the spiral is screwed into the cork. The hinged section is then folded down to engage with the bottle rim, turning the handle into a lever for pulling the cork.

Making a three-straw braid

Even this simple dolly can be plaited in different ways. In the method shown, the north and south pointing straws lie side by side throughout and are not angled to cross over each other.

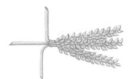

Starting Tie three straws together with thread just below the ears of grain. Spread the straws to point north, west and south.

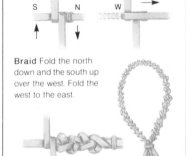

Braid Fold the north down and the south up over the west. Fold the west to the east.

Finishing Continue folding until the braid is as long as you want. Loop it, tie it with thread, trim the ends and tie on a ribbon.

Corn dollies

Making an ancient harvest decoration

Corn dollies are thought to be a survival of the ancient pagan custom of using the last stalks of the harvest to make an image or idol for the corn spirit to live in during the winter. Dollies range from the very simple to the extremely elaborate, and are not always in the shape of a doll.

The best material for making corn dolly decorations is a traditional variety of winter wheat which, unlike more modern varieties, has a long, hollow stem and a small head. Traditional wheats are now grown by some farmers specially to meet the needs of corn dolly makers. But rye, oats and, though less satisfactorily, barley can be used.

If possible the corn stalks should be cut by hand to prevent them from being crushed, and ideally a week or two before the corn is fully ripe to avoid the grain

dropping when the stalks are handled. Unless the stalks are being used immediately, dry them in the sun or in an airing cupboard to prevent mildew.

Grade the stalks into fine, medium and thick for different kinds of work. Remove the outer sheath. Leave the ears on some of the stalks. Only the length between the ear and the first joint is used. Store in a dry place.

Before starting to make a dolly, soak the straw in water for up to three hours to restore its natural pliability. Leave any straw not being used immediately in a dampened towel, so that it does not dry out. To join straws, slide the thinner top end of one into the hollow bottom end of another. Use buff-coloured thread for tying several straws together. Blue is the traditional colour of ribbon for many dollies, but other colours are used.

Cornices and covings

Restoring old cornices and fitting covings

In many old houses the decorative cornices – between wall and ceiling – become clogged with paint. With patience they can be restored.

Inevitably a certain amount of mess will be made by the work, so it is best tackled first as part of a redecorating project. In most cases the paint is likely to be distemper or emulsion, which can be removed or softened with water. If it is an oil-based paint you will have to apply a paint remover – see PAINT STRIPPING; DISTEMPER REMOVAL.

To clean with water, use a small sprayer filled with warm water and soak a small area at a time. Leave it for about 30 minutes, then carefully scrape out the paint with an old screwdriver, pointed stick or similar tool. Brush away the loosened paint frequently.

Apply paint remover with an old paintbrush, and follow the manufacturer's instructions about soaking time and removal.

You may be able to repair damaged moulding with plaster of Paris. Mix only a small amount, stirring the plaster into the water to make a smooth, stiff paste. Dampen the cornice with clean water, then build up the repair in layers, using an artist's palette knife or a clay modelling tool – see MODELLING IN CLAY. Work quickly, as plaster of Paris sets in about three minutes. There are also proprietary products for this type of repair – follow manufacturer's instructions.

Fitting covings Curved covings can be used to hide cracks between a wall and ceiling, or to add character to a room. There are several types; one, made of gypsum plaster, is sold by builders' merchants who will also supply the special

Cutting coving to fit

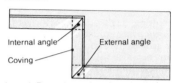

Polystyrene   Plaster

Cut expanded polystyrene to the exact length with a sharp, wetted knife; you cannot sand it. Preformed corners are sold; fix them first. Cut plaster coving with a fine-toothed saw; it needs mitring at corners.

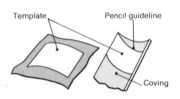

Internal angle   External angle

Coving

Length For an internal angle, measure the coving to fit from corner to corner. For external angles measure from corner to corner and add on the width of the coving for each angle. Then mitre the ends.

Template   Pencil guideline

Coving

Mitres Cut out the templates supplied with the coving. Test them on your corner and adjust as needed. Hold the template on the coving and pencil a guideline for sawing.

adhesive needed (see GLUING); others, sold in DIY shops, include polystyrene, polyurethane and fibrous plasters.

For a neat finish, cut the coving from the front – polystyrene or polyurethane with a knife, plaster with a fine-toothed saw. You can sand the cut plaster with fine glasspaper, but the other types cannot be smoothed. The method of fitting, except for the different adhesives used, is much the same for all types and the wall and ceiling must be bare and clean.

Remove wallpaper, ceiling paper or paint down to the plaster. Apply adhesive to the back of the coving. When using plaster coving, use an old paintbrush to wet the appropriate area of wall and ceiling with clean water.

Press the coving into position. With plaster coving leave a 3mm ($\frac{1}{8}$in) gap between each length, remove excess adhesive from the coving edges with a scraper and use it to fill the gap. Butt the ends of polystyrene or polyurethane coving. Wipe off excess adhesive with a clean rag.

At corners, press the mitred ends of

plaster coving firmly together and fill the joint with adhesive, using a flexible knife. When the adhesive has hardened, smooth the joints with fine glasspaper. Special preformed corner pieces are available to overcome the problem of cutting neat mitres in plaster or polystyrene coving.

Plaster coving can be painted after priming with a plaster primer. Polystyrene coving can be left unpainted. If you do paint it use emulsion, gloss paint would create a fire hazard.

Corns

Relieving a painful foot condition

The best cure for corns is to remove their cause, which almost always is ill-fitting shoes. Painful corns can be treated at home or by a chiropodist, but will recur as long as pressure and friction on the skin continue.

A corn consists of a central core surrounded by thick layers of skin. After soaking in warm water for about 15 minutes the hard skin can be carefully pared with a sharp, sterile blade, though this treatment is better carried out by a chiropodist. Alternatively, the skin can be rubbed down with a pumice stone or emery board.

Corn plasters will keep the shoe pressure off corns. There are also proprietary corn-removing preparations available from chemists, which encourage the skin to peel.

Eventually, the hard core itself will come out.

Consult your doctor if corns become ulcerous, or if the foot bones are so deformed that no shoes are comfortable to wear.

Cosmetics

Using make-up to highlight your favourable features

Make-up can give your face a smooth finish, protect the skin, conceal flaws and blemishes and add expression and colour. Choose the best make-up for *you*, never borrow someone else's cosmetics. If you have dry skin, use an oil or cream base foundation. For an oily skin choose a water-based or oil-free foundation.

Before buying a foundation cream, test the shade by dabbing a little on your face and neck, in natural daylight if possible, or on the inside of your wrist. The right shade will almost disappear as it blends with your skin. If you use a concealer to hide blemishes, choose one that is slightly lighter than the foundation.

Cheek colour, or blusher, need not match your lipstick exactly, but should be in the same colour range. An orange-pink cheek colour, for example, should not be used with a bluish-pink lipstick. A powder blusher is best for oily skin; cream rouge for a dry skin.

Preparing your skin Before applying cosmetics, wash your hands, pin back your hair and clean your face and neck with cleansing cream or a cleansing lotion. Then tone, using a proprietary toner or rosewater diluted with distilled water – 1 part to 3 parts. Dab small spots or pimples with cotton-wool balls dipped in witch hazel or another astringent lotion. Blot the skin dry using a soft tissue.

Next apply a moisturiser. Use a concealer stick or cream to cover blemishes and blend it with the surrounding skin. Use the concealer also to minimise any dark circles there may be under your eyes; pat it in gently with fingertips on the delicate skin under the eyes.

Applying foundation and powder To give your face an even colour, smooth on a little foundation cream with your fingers or use a slightly damp sponge. Apply it with upward and outward strokes to avoid dragging the skin down. Blend the foundation up to your hairline and down to just under your jaw.

Powder-type blusher and eye shadow work best if you powder your face first. If you use cream-based rouge and eye shadow, apply them first and powder afterwards. Apply loose, translucent powder with a powder brush; use a powder puff or cotton wool for pressed powder, brushing off any excess with a large, soft powder brush.

Contouring with highlighter and contour powder Choose a contour powder that is slightly darker than the foundation, and a highlighter without sparkle for day wear. Use contour powder to make certain areas of the face less prominent, and highlighters to make them more prominent. For a receding chin, apply highlighting powder with a medium size brush in a crescent about 25mm (1in) below the bottom lip line, blending carefully. Disguise a protruding chin in the same way, but using contour powder.

Contouring with blusher and rouge Apply a blusher or rouge to your cheeks, temples and forehead. To position it, locate the 'apples' of your cheeks (the parts that are most prominent when you smile) and the hollows (the areas just below the intersection of cheekbone and jaw). Then shape your face into a more perfect oval.

To make a long, narrow face appear wider, stroke the colour from the outermost hollows of your cheeks towards your ears. To slim a round face, put colour on the apples in tiny crescents below the eye area.

Soften a square face by stroking the blusher or rouge along the undersides of both apples back towards your ears and along the jawbone. Keep cheek colour two fingers width from your nose, and above the level of the nostrils.

Follow with eye shadow and mascara (see EYEBROWS; EYE MAKE-UP), and finish off with lipstick. Outline your lips with a lip pencil and apply the lipstick with a lip brush.

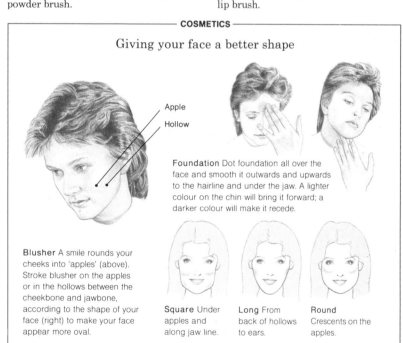

— COSMETICS —

Giving your face a better shape

Apple

Hollow

Blusher A smile rounds your cheeks into 'apples' (above). Stroke blusher on the apples or in the hollows between the cheekbone and jawbone, according to the shape of your face (right) to make your face appear more oval.

Foundation Dot foundation all over the face and smooth it outwards and upwards to the hairline and under the jaw. A lighter colour on the chin will bring it forward; a darker colour will make it recede.

Square Under apples and along jaw line.

Long From back of hollows to ears.

Round Crescents on the apples.

Couch grass

Getting rid of an ugly invader

Couch grass spreads by long, sharply pointed wiry rhizomes – underground stems – and produces green spiky flowers. It is common on waste land, and all too common in gardens, where it can spoil the appearance of a lawn and choke vegetable and flower beds. It cannot be eliminated from a lawn by lawn weed-killers (see WEED CONTROL; PESTICIDES), which are formulated to kill broad-leaved weeds without harming any kind of grass.

When preparing ground for a lawn, remove all roots and shoots of couch grass before seeding. If, however, couch grass does reappear it will succumb to regular mowing over two or three years.

If couch grass is well established in a lawn, you will have to dig out every clump completely or use a poison which will clear the ground of all growth; afterwards reseed or returf the bare ground.

In beds, frequent and thorough hard-weeding or total clearance with a chemical are the solutions. Do not use a hoe on couch grass; it will simply multiply from fragments of rhizome left in the soil.

Coughs

Coping with minor coughs and recognising serious ones

Coughing is an automatic reflex that helps to keep unwanted matter out of the lungs. It can be triggered by inhaling, for example a small bit of food (see CHOKING) or noxious chemical fumes. Most commonly, though, it is a result of the common cold (see COLDS) when excessive amounts of mucus tend to collect in the upper respiratory tracts.

Getting relief Coughs due to colds usually disappear without treatment within a few weeks. But you may need relief in the meantime in order to sleep or work – drink warm or cold liquids or suck boiled sweets or lozenges.

Cough medicines There are two main types of effective cough medicine: expectorants, which loosen the mucus so that it can be coughed out, and suppressants, drugs which suppress the cough reflex. Expectorants can be bought over the counter. Do not take them before driving or operating machinery, as some can cause drowsiness.

As coughing is an important protective reflex it can be dangerous to suppress a cough, and doctors are not always willing to prescribe suppressants.

When coughs are more serious If the cough is severe, produces thick, yellowish mucus, or is accompanied by a high fever, or if it persists for more than three weeks, you should see a doctor. Persistent coughing may be caused by smoking, an allergy or bronchitis. Consult a doctor if there is blood in the mucus.

Council tax

Reductions and benefits

Council tax must generally be paid by all local residents to their councils in respect of every house, or part of a building used as a home.

Buildings exempt include empty homes, and houses being rebuilt or left unfurnished for short periods. Check with your local council for full details.

Where only one person lives in a house, you can usually claim a 25 per cent discount. Some groups of people are not counted as residents: they include students, school leavers, some trainees, hospital patients, and care workers. So, for example, if a student and a trainee are living at home with a single parent, the parent can claim the discount. Discounts are also available for some disabled people.

People on low incomes may claim Council Tax Benefit, which will give them cash to pay all or some of the tax. If you are on social security benefits or have a low income, check the details with your local council.

Covenants

Increasing the value of a cash gift

A deed of covenant is a written and sealed deed under which you can make a series of payments to another person or a charity, and, in the case of a charity, increase the value of those payments by obtaining tax relief (see also INCOME TAX RETURNS) if done properly.

If, for example, you agree to pay a *gross* annual sum of £1000 to a charity, you can, under a covenant, deduct tax from the gross amount at the basic rate and pay the remainder to the charity. You keep the deducted amount, provided you are liable for at least that much tax on your income, and the charity claims the sum from the Inland Revenue.

So, if the basic rate of tax is 25p in the pound, you pay the charity £750 (£1000 minus £250) and the charity claims the £250 from the taxman. But for the covenant to work like this, you must be liable for at least £250 income tax.

Certain conditions must be met when making a covenant to charities. The agreement must run for more than three years, except where it ends earlier because of something uncertain, for example, your death; you may not benefit from making the payments – you may not receive goods or services in return, for example; the covenant must be in writing and signed, sealed and dated before a witness and it cannot be backdated.

Covenant payments that you make to a charity earn tax relief at the highest tax rate you pay.

Crab

How to prepare a popular shellfish

Crabs can generally be bought ready-cooked. Choose one that feels heavy for its size and has stiff claws, all attached. Shake the crab and listen for water inside the shell – if there is water, do not buy the crab.

Extracting the meat Most parts of the crab contain meat, from the richly flavoured brown meat in the upper shell to the flaky white meat in the legs and claws. The stomach sac and gills (or 'dead men's fingers') are inedible.

Dressing a cooked crab

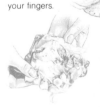

After removing the legs and claws, hold the shell upside down and pull off and discard the tail.

Push the body from the shell by pressing outwards with both thumbs, while holding the shell upright with your fingers.

Pull off the white bulbous gills and the feathery wisps attached to them. Make sure to remove them all, and discard them.

Thoroughly clean out the shell and place the brown meat in the centre and the white meat on each side.

Before extracting the meat twist off and set aside the claws and legs. Then lift off and discard the tail, a circular or pointed flap in the crab's belly. Hold the crab upright in both hands with the tail end uppermost and the upper shell towards you and push the body free from the upper shell with your thumbs. Pull the whitish, bulbous gills from the body and discard them. Some gills may also have fallen into the shell – be sure to discard these, too.

With a spoon, scrape the brown meat out of the upper shell. Be careful to avoid the spongy stomach sac which should be discarded. Take the body and, with a skewer, poke the white meat out of the leg and claw sockets. Keep the white meat separate from the brown. If necessary, cut the body in half to extract all the meat. Crack open the claws and legs with nutcrackers or a wooden mallet, remove any shell fragments and pick out the meat with a skewer.

Dressing a crab Scrub the upper shell thoroughly, both inside and out. Break the edge of the shell back to the dark line near the outer edge. Arrange the crabmeat in the shell, putting the brown meat down the middle and the white meat on either side of it.

Cradle cap

Treating a baby's scalp rash

An oily, scaly, yellowish crust sometimes forms on a baby's scalp. It is caused by excessive secretion by the skin's oil glands and is quite harmless and easily treated.

Apply baby oil or petroleum jelly to the baby's head and leave it on overnight. Then gently brush or comb the softened crust with a baby brush or a fine-toothed comb. Wash the scalp with a mild shampoo.

Repeat the treatment until the cradle cap disappears or is reduced. If it persists after three or four weeks, consult your doctor, who may prescribe special lotions and shampoos.

Cramps

Coping with spasmodic abdominal pain

The spasmodic stomach cramp pains are caused by involuntary tightening of the muscles and are usually a symptom of acute gastroenteritis. See also STOMACH ACHES.

There are a number of causes of the complaint, among them FOOD POISONING, food allergy (see ALLERGIES), FLU, CONSTIPATION and overindulgence in alcohol.

The sufferer should rest and take no solid foods until the cramps have subsided and any other symptoms, such as NAUSEA, VOMITING and DIARRHOEA, have passed. Frequent but small amounts of clear liquids such as water and lemon tea should be taken.

With this treatment, gastroenteritis should clear up in 24 to 48 hours, but if the cramp persists for more than three or four hours, or is accompanied by high fever, a rigid abdomen, continuous vomiting or a pain radiating to the left or right shoulder, a doctor should be consulted. See also PERIOD PAINS.

Crazy eights

Eights are wild in a quick card game

Two or four people can play this game, for which you need a standard 52 card pack.

Dealing If two people are playing, deal seven cards to each player; if three or four people are playing, deal them five cards each. Place the rest of the pack face down on the table to form a *stockpile*. The dealer then turns the top card face upwards beside it to start a *discard pile*.

The play Each player, in turn, discards a card from his or her hand that matches either the suit or the rank of the top card on the discard pile. For example, if the top card is the seven of spades, you can discard any spade or any seven and place it on top of the pile.

Alternatively, you can discard an eight – a wild card in this game. You decide which suit you wish the eight to represent and it is given the rank of the card on which it is laid – if the card beneath is a three, for example, then the eight is treated as a three. Once you have discarded, you can, if you wish, take one card from the top of the stockpile.

If you are unable to discard, you must draw from the stockpile until you come to a card that you can discard. If the stockpile has been used up, you forfeit your turn to the next player.

Scoring The first player to discard his or her last card gets points for all the cards remaining in the other players' hands. Each eight is worth 50 points; each court card is worth 10; and each ace, 1. Other cards score at their face value.

If the game comes to a standstill because the stockpile is used up and no one is able to discard, each player adds up the points for the cards left in his or her hand and the player with the lowest score wins that round.

The winner is the first person to reach a score – 100, for example – agreed on at the beginning of the game.

A path to set off your garden

Lay crazy paving on a suitable base and a bed of mortar. Not all pieces will be of the same thickness, so apply more mortar under the thinner slabs.

Crazy paving
Mortar
Concrete
Sand
Hardcore

Crazy paving

Laying an attractive garden path or driveway

Broken paving slabs are the best material for a crazy paving path; they are obtainable from your local authority's highways department, or buy them from a builders' merchant.

Prepare the path foundation by removing topsoil to a depth 100mm (4in) deeper than the thickness of the slabs – 230mm (9in) for a driveway. Lay 100mm of hardcore. Spread 13-25mm ($\frac{1}{2}$-1in) of sand over the surface and roll it in.

For a driveway make a crossfall, a slope from side to side for drainage – see CONCRETE. Spread a 100mm layer of concrete over the sand and hardcore and leave to harden for two or three days. A layer of concrete is not needed for a path.

Lay a 25mm bed of MORTAR (1 part cement/4 parts sharp sand).

Select slabs with straight edges for the borders, laying these first, filling in with smaller pieces and leaving joints 13-25mm wide. Tap the stones in place with the shaft of a club hammer and check regularly with a spirit level. Fill the joints with mortar and level it flush with the slabs.

Credit and credit cards

Obtaining credit and using a credit card

Credit lets you have the use of major purchases during the period when you would otherwise be saving for them. You can buy better quality or at a better price when the chance arises.

However, you generally pay more than if you buy outright for cash, and you have to bear in mind that rises in interest rates may put up repayments or that your income may fall.

How to obtain credit If you want a relatively small sum (a few hundred pounds, for example) one of the easiest ways of getting the money on credit is with a bank overdraft (see BANK ACCOUNTS). You can borrow as much – or as little – as you like up to a limit agreed with your bank manager; you pay interest only on the amount that you are overdrawn, not on the overall limit. You normally have to repay within a year.

For larger sums (up to about £10,000), you can get a 'personal loan' from your bank. This is for a fixed sum, usually for a specific purpose such as buying a car or carrying out home improvements. It is repaid, plus the interest, in monthly instalments over a period of up to five years.

Alternatively, you can open an 'ordinary loan account' with your bank. This is similar to a personal loan, but can work out cheaper because the interest rate is not fixed. Personal loans can also be arranged with finance companies, but the interest rates can be higher.

A common way of buying goods, such as television sets, cars or refrigerators, on credit is by HIRE PURCHASE (HP), or by credit sale. This is arranged with the shop selling the goods. With hire purchase agreements you are technically hiring the goods until you have finished paying for them. You generally pay in monthly instalments for up to three years. Credit sales are effectively the same as hire purchase agreements except that you own the goods from the beginning. Hire purchase is often convenient, but almost always more expensive than a bank loan.

To raise money for major home improvements or repairs, you can increase your mortgage (see MORTGAGES). This may involve a number of extra costs – revaluing the property, for example – but the repayments are usually spread over a longer period, and so you pay less per month.

Annual percentage rate of charge When comparing the cost of different forms of credit, make sure you are quoted the annual percentage rate of charge (APR). This shows in a comparable form the annual costs of different forms of credit, taking into account not only interest rates and the size of repayments but other costs such as service charges. The higher the APR, the more costly the credit.

Security For smaller loans you are unlikely to be required to provide security. For large ones, though, you may have

to, and in some cases offering security could lead to lower interest rates. Your home, investments or an insurance policy that can be cashed in for a large sum are usually acceptable as security.

Credit cards With a credit card you can get short-term, interest-free credit on goods up to a limit set by the credit card company. You can use the card wherever a sign indicates that the shop or business accepts the card. The credit card company will send you a monthly statement showing how much you owe and the minimum amount you have to repay.

If you repay the debt in full before the date indicated on the statement, you will not be charged interest. If you let the debt run on, however, you will probably be charged higher interest rates than for a bank loan.

You can also obtain cash from a bank with your credit card – up to the limit set by the credit card company – but interest is charged from the moment you take the cash.

A number of large department stores have 'account cards' which are used in the same way as credit cards for buying goods in their shops.

If you lose a credit card, report the loss immediately to the credit card company. If a thief uses it after you have reported the loss, you will not have to pay anything. Even if the thief uses it before you report the loss, you will only have to pay the first £50 of any bills incurred.

Crêpes suzette

Delicious pancakes cooked at the table

Crêpes is the French word for thin pancakes, and *crêpes suzette* is a popular recipe in which the pancakes are cooked in an orange juice and flamed (see FLAMBÉ COOKING) in liqueur. For a small dinner party they make a delightful sweet, especially if cooked at the table in a CHAFING DISH.

Ingredients (for 12 pancakes)
25g (1oz) unsalted butter
50g (2oz) caster sugar
Juice of 2 oranges
Juice of half a lemon
2-4 tablespoons orange liqueur

Cook the pancakes and keep them hot between two plates over a saucepan of gently boiling water.

Melt the butter in the chafing dish, stir in the sugar and cook gently until it is a golden-brown caramel. Add the orange and lemon juice and stir to make a thick sauce.

Drop a flat pancake into the dish, fold it twice and push it to the side of the dish. Repeat with the next pancake.

When all the pancakes are in the sauce, add the orange liqueur and set it alight when hot. Shake the chafing dish gently to blend the flamed liqueur evenly with the sauce.

Place the pancakes on a hot serving dish, pour over the sauce and serve at once.

If you do not have a chafing dish, crêpes suzette can be made in the kitchen using a large frying pan.

Cribbage

Playing an absorbing card game for two

A standard 52 card deck is used, and the object of the game is for each player to score 61 or 121 before his opponent.

The deal is decided by cutting the cards, and the *lowest* card wins. The dealer then deals six cards each, dealing one at a time, and each player then places two cards face down to form the *crib*. The remaining deck is then cut by the non-dealer and restacked to form the *stock*, and the dealer's opponent turns up the top card – the *starter*.

The dealer's opponent leads by laying down a card face up and announcing its value – kings, queens and jacks count 10, aces 1 and all other cards at face value. The dealer then plays a card and announces the total value of the two cards played. Players keep the cards they play in front of them.

Play continues until a player cannot lay a card without the total going over 31. That player then announces 'go', and his opponent plays all the additional cards possible without pushing the total over 31. Play then reverts to the player who called 'go', who starts a new play, starting from scratch, using his remaining cards.

Scoring The chance to start scoring occurs when the starter is turned up – if it is a jack, called *His Heels*, the dealer gets 2 points. During play a card that brings the total to exactly 15 or 31 scores 2; if 31 is not reached the card bringing the total nearest to 31 scores 1. Playing the last card scores 1.

A *pair*, two consecutive cards of the same value, scores 2; a *triplet*, 6; a *four*, 12. The cards of a *sequence*, three or more cards in a numerical run, each score 1 point. The scores go to the player whose card completes or adds to a combination or sequence.

The scores are kept on a cribbage board, which has four rows of 30 holes, two rows for each player, and two or four extra holes to hold the pegs at the start of the game. Each player has two pegs, which he uses to keep track of his score as the game progresses. He starts by advancing one peg along the holes of the outer row to mark his first score, then uses the second peg for the next score. He returns down the inner row until 61 is scored, or goes round again in a game where 121 has been agreed as the target score.

When all the cards in the players' hands have been played, a second round of scoring commences, with the dealer's opponent counting up the combinations in his hand in conjunction with the starter. Then the dealer counts up his combinations, also using the starter, and then he tallies the points he finds in the crib, also including the starter. The crib always goes to the dealer; the loser of any game deals for the next game.

In the second score count, pairs, sequences and other combinations earn the same scores as when playing, but this time including the starter.

A single card can be used in more than one combination. For example, a four-card hand of 9-9-8-7 scores as follows: three for each run of three (7,8,9 twice), two for the pair (two 9s), and two for two cards totalling 15 (7 and 8) – total score 10. A five-card hand such as 9-9-8-7-6 scores 16, counted as follows: fifteen for 2 (9 and 6), fifteen for 4 (9 and 6 again), fifteen for 6 (8 and 7), 2 for a pair (9s)

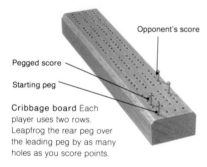

Opponent's score

Pegged score

Starting peg

Cribbage board Each player uses two rows. Leapfrog the rear peg over the leading peg by as many holes as you score points.

makes 8, and 4 for a run (6,7,8,9) twice makes 16.

A player with the jack of the same suit as the starter, *His Nobs*, adds 1 point.

A four card flush – four cards of the same suit – scores 4 if it is in the hand but not in the crib. A five-card flush, or four cards of the same suit as the starter, scores 5, whether in a hand or the crib. If a player overlooks points in his hand, his opponent can call 'muggins' and score the points for himself.

Crime compensation
How a victim can seek recompense

Compensation can be obtained not only for personal injury inflicted by a criminal, but for other kinds of loss – for example, if you are a victim of fraud, or the relative of a victim who has been killed.

If you are the victim of a crime you can sue the person convicted of it for damages in the civil courts. But this involves legal costs, which may be high, and you cannot be certain how much will be awarded as damages or whether the criminal will be able to pay.

Two other sources of action are, however, open to you and will not involve you in paying legal costs: a criminal court (a crown court or magistrates' court); and the Criminal Injuries Compensation Board.

Compensation through a criminal court cannot be considered until someone has been found guilty of a crime. The courts are powerless to help where, for example, the crime is unsolved. In such cases, it is worth applying to the Criminal Injuries Compensation Board.

Crown or magistrates' courts At the trial you can apply for a compensation order. If it is granted, the criminal has to make a compensatory payment either immediately in full, or over a period by instalments.

There is no limit to the amount a crown court may award in damages, but a magistrates' court may award compensation up to £2000 only. Neither court can grant awards to victims of road traffic offences or to the dependants of somebody killed as the result of a crime.

In assessing the compensation to be awarded, the criminal court will take into account physical and psychological suffering caused by the injuries, and factors such as loss of earnings, or extra expenses incurred. The sum awarded will take into account the amount the criminal could reasonably be expected to pay over a two-year period.

After an award in a criminal court, the victim can usually still make a claim through the civil courts.

Criminal Injuries Compensation Board You can apply to the board for an award to be paid out of state funds.

The board can award compensation for personal injury resulting directly from a crime of violence that has been reported without delay to the police. It will also consider compensation claims from anyone injured while arresting a suspect, or helping a police officer to discharge his duties; from dependants of people killed as the result of a crime; from anyone who may have paid a victim's funeral expenses. It will not, however, consider claims arising from road traffic offences – the civil court or the Motor Insurer's Bureau deal with these.

The board will only consider claims that it believes deserve compensation of at least £1000. The size of an award depends on the particular circumstances of the case – the victim's age, for example. A typical award for a broken arm might be £4000, for the loss of an eye £20,000, and for the loss of a limb £30,000. The amounts awarded are the same as a court would grant.

A fixed bereavement award of £3500 is payable to the victim's husband or wife, or – where the victim was unmarried and under 18 – to the parents.

Claim forms can be obtained from the Criminal Injuries Compensation Board, Morley House, Holborn Viaduct, London EC1A 2BP.

Crochet
Getting started with the basic stitches

Like knitting, crochet is a way of making a piece of fabric from one long piece of yarn. Unlike knitting, though, you form the interlocking loops of yarn that make up the fabric with a single crochet hook – a special needle with a small hook at the end.

The yarns range from delicate, lustrous cottons to thick wools and even strands of leather. The range of crochet hooks is just as varied, from fine steel for crocheting cotton, linen or silk, to thick plastic for making rugs. The hooks are numbered in the same way as knitting needles: the larger the number, the smaller the size.

The first – or foundation – row of any piece of crochet is made using the chain stitch (see illustration overleaf), and it is used as the base for the first row of working stitches from which the rest of the fabric develops. The basic working stitch is the double crochet (see illustration overleaf). It is the simplest of the working stitches and produces a flat, close-knit fabric.

Holding the yarn It takes a little practice to hold the yarn in such a way that you can quickly and easily take up the working length on the hook and at the same time keep the loop on the hook firmly tensioned.

A common method of taking up the yarn is to hold a working length from the ball in your left hand, looped over your index finger, under your second and third fingers, and wrapped round your little finger to anchor it. Leave a length of up to 50mm (2in) between your index finger and the hook, and use your index finger to control the tension.

Use the thumb and second finger of your left hand to hold the base of the loop on the hook to keep it taut while drawing the yarn through it. If you are left-handed, hold the yarn in the same way, but in your right hand.

Crocheting fabric Make the number of chain stitches required, keeping the stitches the same size so that the crochet is neat. When following a pattern, remember that the first loop on the hook does not count as part of the foundation row.

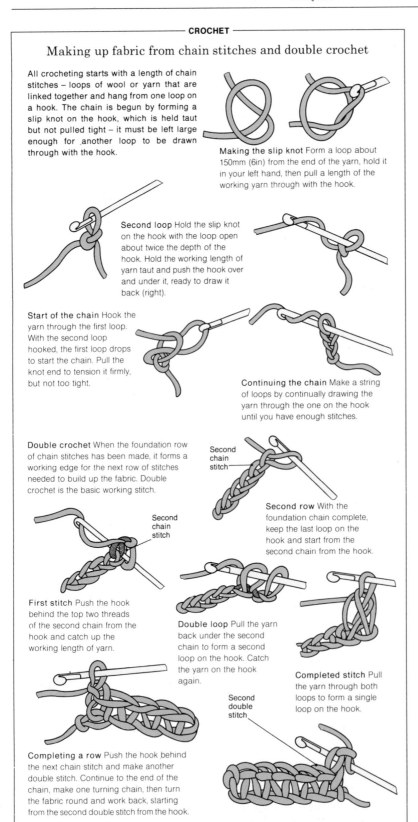

CROCHET

Making up fabric from chain stitches and double crochet

All crocheting starts with a length of chain stitches – loops of wool or yarn that are linked together and hang from one loop on a hook. The chain is begun by forming a slip knot on the hook, which is held taut but not pulled tight – it must be left large enough for another loop to be drawn through with the hook.

Making the slip knot Form a loop about 150mm (6in) from the end of the yarn, hold it in your left hand, then pull a length of the working yarn through with the hook.

Second loop Hold the slip knot on the hook with the loop open about twice the depth of the hook. Hold the working length of yarn taut and push the hook over and under it, ready to draw it back (right).

Start of the chain Hook the yarn through the first loop. With the second loop hooked, the first loop drops to start the chain. Pull the knot end to tension it firmly, but not too tight.

Continuing the chain Make a string of loops by continually drawing the yarn through the one on the hook until you have enough stitches.

Double crochet When the foundation row of chain stitches has been made, it forms a working edge for the next row of stitches needed to build up the fabric. Double crochet is the basic working stitch.

Second chain stitch

Second row With the foundation chain complete, keep the last loop on the hook and start from the second chain from the hook.

First stitch Push the hook behind the top two threads of the second chain from the hook and catch up the working length of yarn.

Double loop Pull the yarn back under the second chain to form a second loop on the hook. Catch the yarn on the hook again.

Second double stitch

Completed stitch Pull the yarn through both loops to form a single loop on the hook.

Completing a row Push the hook behind the next chain stitch and make another double stitch. Continue to the end of the chain, make one turning chain, then turn the fabric round and work back, starting from the second double stitch from the hook.

Build up the fabric with successive rows of double crochet.

American patterns Before using a new pattern, check whether it is British or American. American patterns use different terms – the British double crochet, for example, is the American single crochet.

Casting off To finish a piece of crochet, cut the yarn a few inches from the hook. Catch the loose yarn with the hook and pull it back through the loop on the hook. Pull it tight. Thread the loose yarn through a sewing needle and sew it neatly into the crochet.

Croquet

A lawn game of skill and concentration

Croquet is played on a lawn, or court, on which six hoops and a central peg are set out as illustrated. The object is to knock balls through the hoops with a mallet, going round the court twice, and finishing by striking a ball to hit the central peg.

The first player or team to do this wins the game, irrespective of the number of strokes taken. Four balls are used, coloured red, yellow, blue and black. In a singles game, each player uses two balls, the red and the yellow always being paired against the blue and black. A team consists of two players, and each plays his own ball throughout the game.

The inside width of the hoops is 95mm (3¾in), and the diameter of the balls is 92mm (3⅝in). So, with only 3mm (⅛in) to spare, a player cannot expect to *run a hoop* in the same way that a golfer makes a long putt. Instead he must manoeuvre the ball towards the hoop with a series of shots until it is close enough to be safely knocked through.

Play begins from behind a baulk line, and the player who plays first is called the *striker*; his opponent is the *outplayer*. A player is allowed only one shot at a time, until he runs a hoop, when he is allowed an extra shot. But he can gain bonus shots by making his ball strike any of the other balls on the court.

This is called a *roquet* and earns the player two extra shots. He then places his ball so that it is touching the roqueted ball, and strikes his ball so that both balls move. This is known as a *croquet* shot, and the opponent's ball may be *croqueted* to any part of the court.

When the striker's ball has come to rest, he takes his second bonus shot – called the *continuation* stroke – with which he can either try to run a hoop or roquet the same ball twice in a turn. If he fails either to roquet or run a hoop his turn ends.

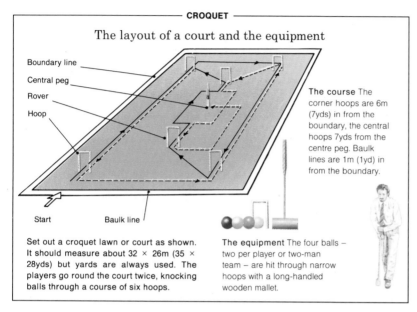

CROQUET

The layout of a court and the equipment

Boundary line
Central peg
Rover
Hoop

The course The corner hoops are 6m (7yds) in from the boundary, the central hoops 7yds from the centre peg. Baulk lines are 1m (1yd) in from the boundary.

Start   Baulk line

Set out a croquet lawn or court as shown. It should measure about 32 × 26m (35 × 28yds) but yards are always used. The players go round the court twice, knocking balls through a course of six hoops.

The equipment The four balls – two per player or two-man team – are hit through narrow hoops with a long-handled wooden mallet.

The skill of croquet is the use of roquet and croquet shots to position the ball to make a run of the hoop possible, and also to place an opponent at a disadvantage. A turn in which more than one hoop is scored is called a *break*. The last hoop to be negotiated is called the *rover*, and the ball then has to be played to strike the central peg, which is 38mm (1½in) in diameter and stands 460mm (18in) out of the ground. When the ball strikes the peg it is said to be *pegged out*.

Croquet originated in France in the 13th century, but did not become popular in England until the middle of the 19th century.

The game is played by people of all ages and both sexes – men and women compete on equal terms. Its governing body is the Croquet Association, whose headquarters are at the Hurlingham Club, London SW6. They can advise you of a club in your area.

Croquettes

Making tasty deep-fried fritters

Croquettes comprise a crunchy outer coat and savoury filling, and are very simple to make. A wide variety of grated or finely chopped cooked vegetables, as well as cheese, seafood, poultry and other meats, can be used for the filling.

Where necessary, the ingredients can be bound together with creamed potato or a thick white sauce (see SAUCES), then moulded by hand into various shapes. Traditionally they are cork-shaped, about 25mm (1in) wide and 38mm (1½in) long and are rolled in breadcrumbs, dipped in beaten egg, then deep-fried in cooking oil until they are a deep golden-

brown – see FRYING.

Here is a recipe for potato croquettes:

Ingredients
900g (2lb) potatoes
50g (2oz) butter
Milk
2 eggs
Breadcrumbs
Vegetable cooking oil
Seasoning

Boil and mash the potatoes. Transfer to a clean pan and add the butter, a little milk and seasoning, and put the pan over a gentle heat. Beat the mixture until light and fluffy, adding a beaten egg.

Roll the mixture into wine-cork shapes, then roll each croquette in fresh white breadcrumbs. Beat the second egg and roll the croquettes in it, then in more breadcrumbs.

Fill a deep, heavy-based saucepan fitted with a wire basket one-third full with oil and heat over a moderate heat to 190°C (375°F). Test the temperature by dropping a cube of white bread into the oil. If it browns in 40-50 seconds, then it is hot enough for the croquettes.

Fry the croquettes for 2-3 minutes and drain thoroughly. Fry again for a further 2-3 minutes and serve.

Crutches

Using walking aids when injured

Crutches must be the right height for the patient. Modern elbow crutches should have the handgrips set at wrist height with the user standing.

To stand up, grasp both crutches with one hand and hold them upright on your

injured side. Push against the chair with your free hand until you are standing on the uninjured leg. Now move one crutch to the unaffected side and grip it comfortably.

When standing, hold the crutches at a slight angle outwards from the body – about 100mm (4in) away from the feet.

There are two ways to walk with crutches – either by taking your weight partly on the injured leg and partly on the crutches in alternation with your sound leg, or by using the crutches and your sound leg to take all the weight, with none on the injured leg. When using a single crutch, hold it in the opposite hand to the injured leg.

CRUTCHES

Walking with an injured leg

Preparing to stand Grasp both crutches by the handgrips using the hand on your injured side, and hold them upright.

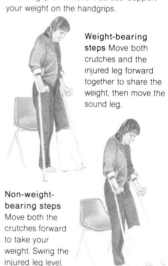

Getting up Use your free hand to push yourself up to stand on the uninjured leg. Take the crutch for the uninjured side by its handgrip and move it across. Support your weight on the handgrips.

Weight-bearing steps Move both crutches and the injured leg forward together to share the weight, then move the sound leg.

Non-weight-bearing steps Move both the crutches forward to take your weight. Swing the injured leg level. Step forward with the other leg.

Cultivator

Using and maintaining one

A garden cultivator is a powerful aid for breaking in a new or neglected garden, especially a large garden, but takes a little time to master. You may find it bucks and moves from side to side, but you will soon control this with practice. When you get your cultivator – whether it is new, secondhand or hired – try to have a test run with it before you take it home, and be sure to get the right booklet with operating instructions. Apart from helping you to use the machine, the booklet will help you to trace faults and, if you need spare parts, to find the name and number of every piece. Most cultivators are petrol-driven, but some models run on mains electricity. The more expensive models can have other equipment attached to them, such as grass cutters, lawn rakes and sprays.

The right cultivator to use There are two basic types of cultivator. The most common type has the engine set above the blades. It is heavier to work than the other type, which has the engine set behind the blades, but digs deeper and is the best for neglected ground and heavy clay soils.

When the engine is set behind the blades the cultivator is easier to control and is best used for digging light soils and for cultivating between plants.

Using the machine Before you use the cultivator, make sure you know how to stop it instantly. Do not use it on frozen or waterlogged ground.

Try to relax your arms and let the machine do the work. Walk forward slowly, giving the cultivator time to do the work.

On rough or hard ground, set the cultivator at reduced throttle speed. If the machine starts to run away on hard ground, release the clutch and go over the ground again.

Adjustment and maintenance Before you do any work on the machine, remove the spark plug lead – and leave it off until you have finished the work. Only work with the spark plug lead in place when you are adjusting the engine's running.

Handle Set the handle in the most comfortable position for you. Release the clamp, then remove the pivot bolt to release the handle. Set the handle in the position you need, replace the pivot bolt in the most convenient hole and tighten the clamp.

Wheels On wheeled models, clean and grease the wheel bearings regularly to make the machine easy to move about.

Oil Check that the engine and transmission oil levels are correct. Check them each week while the machine is being used regularly.

With a new machine you may be advised to change the engine oil after the first five hours of use. Otherwise change it after every 25 to 30 hours of use or once a year, whichever is the sooner.

Filter A clean air filter on the carburettor will help to prevent dirt from getting through to the engine. Clean the filter regularly, especially if you use the cultivator in dry, dusty conditions. Remove the filter housing and take out the thick gauze, foam pad and thinner gauze. Wash them in clean petrol or in detergent and water. Let them dry and replace them in

the right order. If the foam pad is still very dirty after washing, replace it with a new one.

Starting A cultivator is not always in regular use and may be difficult to start after a long lay-off. Keep a new spark plug ready to aid starting.

Idling speed Adjust the idling speed after running the engine to warm it. Turn the throttle stop screw clockwise to increase the idling speed, anticlockwise to reduce it. The setting is correct when the engine just ticks over gently at minimum throttle setting.

Fuel intake If the engine splutters or misses when you accelerate, the fuel mixture needs adjusting. Run the engine until it is warm, then set the throttle control lever to slow speed. Adjust the idling jet screw so that the engine idles fastest, then give the screw a quarter turn anticlockwise.

You may have to reset the idling speed after altering the fuel intake.

Clutch Check in the operating manual how far the lever should move before the clutch engages. To adjust it, loosen the nut locking the jockey arm that controls the tension on the belt. Then position the arm to take up some of the slack in the belt. Check that when the clutch is disengaged, the belt is completely slack and not binding on the engine pulley. Retighten the nut to lock the arm in position.

Cut out The engine should cut out when the throttle control lever is returned to stop. If it does not, adjust the throttle cable adjuster until the engine cuts out.

Cleaning Wipe or brush off as much dirt as you can after each outing.

Winter storing Have the cultivator serviced at the end of the season then rub over the blades and all other metal surfaces with an oily cloth before you put the cultivator in a dry shed for the winter.

CULTIVATORS

Driving a machine that takes the hard work out of digging

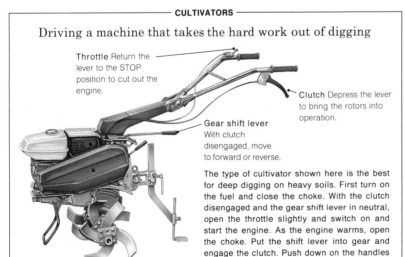

Throttle Return the lever to the STOP position to cut out the engine.

Clutch Depress the lever to bring the rotors into operation.

Gear shift lever With clutch disengaged, move to forward or reverse.

The type of cultivator shown here is the best for deep digging on heavy soils. First turn on the fuel and close the choke. With the clutch disengaged and the gear shift lever in neutral, open the throttle slightly and switch on and start the engine. As the engine warms, open the choke. Put the shift lever into gear and engage the clutch. Push down on the handles as the machine moves forwards.

Cupboards and wardrobes

Ideas for making the most of space

In kitchens and bedrooms, shelved cupboards that once gave adequate storage soon become cluttered as new items such as crockery and clothes are added. You can increase cupboard space by making new cupboards (see also CABINETS; CLOTHES STORAGE) and fitting them with space-saving ideas, or adapting those ideas in old cupboards.

Wire or plastic trays, which can be bought at hardware or DIY shops, can

Fitting out a cupboard with simple space-savers

Clips

Hooks

Towel rail

Wire baskets

Wire trays

A tall broom cupboard can be made to hold much more than brooms, by fitting hooks, clips, rails and wire baskets.

be stacked in a cupboard to increase the amount of usable space and provide easy access to their contents. They may be of different depths – a deep tray at the bottom and shallow ones above, for example – and fitted so that they can either be fully or partly withdrawn, like a drawer.

Attach runners for each tray to the sides of the cupboards. The runners can be strips of wood, plastic or angle metal. Allow about 50mm (2in) clearance between the top of each tray and the bottom of the one above. If the trays are not to be fully withdrawable, fasten a light chain between the back of the cupboard and the back of each tray. Adjust the chain length so that the trays cannot be withdrawn more than halfway.

The back of a cupboard door can also provide storage space. A wide range of inexpensive and easy-to-fit wire or plastic baskets is available from DIY shops for screwing to a cupboard door. The baskets can be deep or shallow, narrow or wide and will swing into the unused spaces above shelves when the door is closed.

Lengths of curtain wire or a towel rail fitted inside a wardrobe door will hold such things as ties, scarves or belts. In the same way, leads for electrical appliances can be stored in a kitchen cupboard. Strong spring clips screwed behind a tall kitchen cupboard door will hold brooms and mops.

In wardrobes, clothes often hang on a wooden rail which may in time sag under

their weight. Remove the rail and fit a curtain track (see CURTAIN RAILS) with wheeled or nylon glides for the curtain hooks, to the top of the wardrobe or under a top shelf. The clothes hang on coathangers hooked into the glides.

This also allows a little extra space at the bottom of the wardrobe, which can be fitted with SHELVES for shoes.

The inside of a wardrobe door is a good place for a full-length mirror, but mirror glass is heavy and may weaken hinges not designed to take the weight. Mirror tiles are the answer, attached by placing a self-adhesive foam pad at each corner and in the centre.

Mark a line at the height you want the top of the mirror to be, using a straightedge and spirit level to ensure that it is level. Fit the top row of tiles against the line; position them carefully, as the adhesive pads grip immediately, leaving no chance of adjustment. Fit the remaining tiles below, leaving a paper-thin gap between their edges. A pack of 36, 150mm (6in) square tiles will make a 0.6m × 1.3m (2ft × 4ft 6in) mirror.

Curry powder

Making your own blend of a spicy flavouring

Different SPICES such as black pepper, chilli pepper, cayenne, coriander, cumin, turmeric, ginger, mace, cinnamon and cloves are blended to make curry powder. It can be bought already ground and blended, but you can make your own curry powder using whole or ready ground spices.

Roast whole spices in an oven at 150°C (300°F, gas mark 2) for 20 minutes. Let them cool, then grind them individually in a blender or with a mortar and pestle.

Using the ground spices, blend: 2 teaspoons each of cinnamon and turmeric; 1 teaspoon each of cumin and ginger; $\frac{1}{2}$ teaspoon each of cloves, black pepper and chilli pepper.

Use the blended curry for making curry sauces, to serve with meats, fish, or egg dishes such as curried eggs:

Ingredients (serves 4-6)
8 eggs
50g (2oz) butter
1 large, finely chopped onion
1½ tablespoons curry powder
285ml (½ pint) chicken stock
Salt and freshly ground pepper
1 teaspoon arrowroot
150ml (¼ pint) single cream
3 tablespoons desiccated or grated fresh coconut
Juice of half a lemon

Boil the eggs for 10-12 minutes, then cool them under running water. Shell the eggs and put them to one side.

Melt the butter in a pan over low heat and add the chopped onion and curry powder. Fry the onion gently, stirring until tender, then add the stock. Season with salt and pepper and simmer for 10 minutes. Mix the arrowroot with the cream and stir into the sauce. Simmer for 5 minutes.

Add 75ml (2½fl oz) of boiling water to the coconut. Allow it to cool then pour through a fine sieve into the curry sauce. Add the lemon juice and check the seasoning.

Halve the eggs and place in an oven-proof dish. Pour in the sauce, cover with foil and place in an oven preheated to 160°C (325°F, gas mark 3) for 15 minutes. Serve with boiled, long-grain rice.

Curtain rails

Choosing and fitting tracks and poles

Curtains are hooked into gliders or rings which slide along a track or pole as the CURTAINS are opened and closed.

Some tracks have obtrusive brackets and channels which need to be concealed by pelmets or VALANCES. Others have a neat front with all the fittings concealed so that no PELMET or valance is needed. Poles are meant to be seen and never have pelmets or valances.

Most tracks are held to the wall or ceiling by brackets spaced about 300mm (12in) apart. Some tracks have fronts that imitate poles and have false rings, but they are fitted like tracks. A few tracks have no brackets but screw direct to the wall or ceiling. Poles are held by just one bracket at each end – with an extra one in the middle if the pole is 2.4m (8ft) or longer.

Tracks are plastic or metal and can usually be curved to fit a bay window. Poles are wooden, plastic or metal. They are designed only for straight runs, but some shops will order a curved pole for you if you ask them to.

To avoid a gap where the pair of curtains meets, the track should have an overlap. Tracks concealed by pelmets or valances are fitted in two halves with an overlap bracket holding one half in front of the other at the centre of the window. On other tracks and poles, the overlap is made by a special glider arm that carries the leading edge of one curtain over the leading edge of the other curtain.

Cording sets are built into many tracks or can be added. Cords threaded along the track and hanging down at one end are pulled to open and close the curtains without the fabric being handled.

Unless the curtains are to go in the window recess, buy a track to extend at least 150mm (6in) beyond the window at each side so that the curtains can draw well back to let in as much light as

---

Different ways to hang curtains

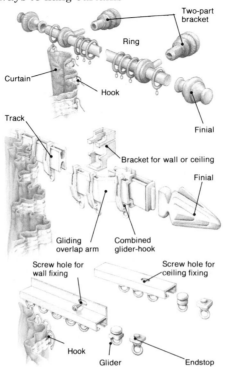

Poles One bracket near each end is enough to support poles up to 2.4m (8ft) long if lightweight curtains are being used. For heavy curtains, an additional, central bracket, may also be needed. Do not fix the brackets over the glazed area because the curtains cannot be drawn beyond the brackets, so you will lose light. A curtain ring outside the bracket keeps the outer curtain edge in place.

Track on brackets You can screw most brackets either horizontally into a wall or upwards into a ceiling. The track clips, slots or slides onto the brackets. Gliders to receive the curtain hooks (or combined gliders and hooks) slide or clip onto the track. A central glider arm makes the curtains overlap. Finials or endstops keep the gliders on the track.

Tracks without brackets You can buy different tracks, depending on whether you need to screw them to wall or ceiling. Endstops prevent the gliders from sliding out of their channel – they have screw eyes you can drive against the channel top; the eyes hold the hook at the outer edge of each curtain.

Labels in illustration: Two-part bracket; Ring; Curtain; Hook; Finial; Track; Bracket for wall or ceiling; Finial; Gliding overlap arm; Combined glider-hook; Screw hole for wall fixing; Screw hole for ceiling fixing; Hook; Glider; Endstop

---

possible. Tracks and poles come in several standard lengths together with brackets, gliders or rings, endstops or decorative finials, and fixing screws. The screws, however, are not always long enough to penetrate the necessary 38mm (1½in) into the masonry or timber behind the plaster or plasterboard – see DRILLING; MASONRY DRILLING. If no standard pack is the right length, buy the next size up and cut the track or pole to length with a hacksaw or general-purpose saw. Smooth the cut with abrasive paper if a wood pole is being fixed.

Positioning the track or pole For wall fixing, draw a pencil guideline at least 50mm (2in) above the top of the window. Measure up from the window or down from the ceiling and align the track or pole with whichever is nearer or it will always look askew. Mark drilling spots on the line, one 50mm from each end and any others spaced evenly about 300mm (12in) apart. For a track without brackets, hold the track on the line and make marks through the fixing holes. Some brackets for poles have their fixing holes above centre on the back of the bracket; allow for this when you mark the drilling spots.

Drill at the marked spots, using a masonry bit; you may need a drill with a hammer action if the lintel is concrete.

For ceiling fixing, draw the guideline on the ceiling about 38mm (1½in) out from the wall top. Use a metal detector to locate the lines of pins holding the plasterboard to the joists. Or, from above, drill through the plasterboard on either side of a joist. From below, the holes will show the position of the joist. Make sure the drilling spots are under joists or the fixing will not be strong enough to support the weight of the curtains.

For fixing in a window recess, mark the spots for the brackets on the top frame if it is wooden. If it is metal or PVC, mark, drill and plug holes in the top of the recess.

Fitting Screw the brackets in place. With some ceiling fixings, you have to put the brackets on the track first. Fit the track or pole onto the brackets. Many tracks have two-part brackets; one part screws to the wall, the other part is positioned on the track and slots down into the first part. Others have screws that tighten the brackets' grip on the track. Screw a bracketless track direct into the prepared holes. Slide or clip the gliders onto the track.

On a pole with real rings, slide on all but two of the rings before you put the pole on the brackets. Tighten any screws in the bottom of the brackets until they bite into the pole.

Curtains

Choosing, measuring, cutting and sewing them

First decide on the length and style of heading you want for the curtains and fix the track or pole – see CURTAIN RAILS. French windows, patio doors and tall sash windows need floor-length curtains. Windows with sills well above floor level can have floor or sill-length curtains.

Floor-length curtains give a room an elegant, formal look; sill-length ones, which should hang to 100mm (4in) below the sill, are suited to informal rooms.

Do not hang floor-length curtains over a radiator – all its heat will be lost behind them. Instead fit sill-length curtains, or hang them to 50mm (2in) above the radiator. See also CENTRAL HEATING.

On a narrow landing or in a very small room, you can hang the curtains inside the window recess. But make sure they do not touch the glass and that they end 10mm (⅜in) above the sill. If not, they will pick up dirt and moisture.

Headings The gathering or pleating at the top of the curtain is formed by drawing up cords running along the tape sewn across the curtain top. Gathered, pencil-pleated, cartridge-pleated, pinch-pleated, smocked, trellised and ruffed headings can all be made by different heading tapes. The width of curtain needed varies according to the chosen tape.

Fabric Always choose curtain fabric – dressmaking fabric does not wear well and upholstery fabric is too stiff to gather and hang well.

If you choose a large pattern, there will be more wastage – and so greater cost – than with a small pattern, when you match panels to make up the right width. Buy from one roll, if possible – colours may vary on different rolls.

Most fabrics are faded by sun, so make curtain linings to protect them. Lining also improves the way the curtains drape and improves INSULATION. Match the sewing-thread colour to the main fabric, not the lining. Use synthetic thread (made in one thickness) on man-made fabrics, cotton thread on natural fabrics. Number 40 cotton is the thickness for medium-weight fabrics, 60 for thin fabrics.

Measuring The curtain 'drop' is measured from the bottom of the curtain track glider or ring to the required length – 25mm (1in) above the carpet or other floor covering, 100mm (4in) below the sill or 50mm (2in) above a radiator. Add on 75mm (3in) for the top turning and 150mm (6in) for the hem at the bottom.

If the heading is to stand up above the glider, to hide the track, add on the depth of the heading tape; it can vary from under 50mm to about 150mm. Also add

---

Basic steps in making lined curtains

Lined curtains last longer, keep out more light and keep in more warmth than unlined ones. Pin, tack, then sew together panels of fabric for the curtain and for the lining to make the width you need – allowing for the fullness your chosen heading tape needs. With a patterned fabric, make sure the patterns match accurately before you tack and sew the panels. With a plain fabric, make sure all the panels will be the same way up. Press seams and trim lining to make it 50mm (2in) narrower than the curtain before sewing them together.

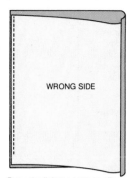

WRONG SIDE

Lay the lining on the curtain, putting right sides together. Pin the right-hand edges together.

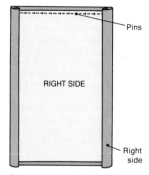

WRONG SIDE

Draw the lining across to align with the curtain at the left. Pin the left-hand edges together.

RIGHT SIDE

Pins

Right side

Sew along the two pinned lines. Turn the curtain right side out. Pin the lining across the top.

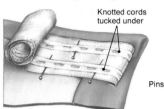

Knotted cords tucked under

Heading tape Pin and tack on the tape with the raw ends tucked under. Knot the cords that will be at the centre. Make sure the other ends hang free. Machine the tape top and bottom in the same direction to avoid puckers.

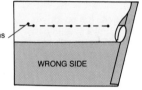

Pins

WRONG SIDE

Fold up, pin and tack a double hem onto the wrong side of the lining. Sew it by machine or hemstitch it by hand.

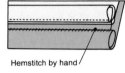

Hemstitch by hand

Fold back the lining and make a double hem on the curtain. Pin and tack it in place, then sew it by hand with hemstitch.

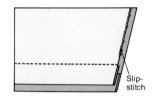

Slipstitch

Finish sewing the bottom end of the lining to the curtain turning at each side. Sew by hand using slipstitch.

---

on the length of one pattern repeat.

Multiply the width of track or pole by the width required for the heading style – $1\frac{1}{2}$-2 for gathers, $2\frac{1}{4}$-$2\frac{1}{2}$ for pencil pleats and 2 for cartridge and pinch pleats and for smocked, ruffed and trellised headings. Add on 300mm (12in) for side turnings and an overlap where the curtains meet.

Divide the total by the roll width of fabric (often 1.2m or 48in, but different in some fabrics and linings). The answer tells you the number of panels required for the pair of curtains; always take the next whole number above the answer.

Multiply the number of panels by the curtain drop to find the total length.

Cutting out Cut the fabric into panels of the required length, making sure each panel starts at the same point of any pattern. Use a set square to make sure you cut at a right angle across the fabric.

Trim off the selvedges – the tightly woven strips at the sides. If you have an odd number of panels, cut one in half lengthways and put the half-widths at the outer edges of the curtains.

Joining panels Pin together the edges of the panels for one curtain, right sides together, about 20mm ($\frac{3}{4}$in) from the edge. Check that the patterns match accurately and adjust the pins as necessary.

Tack the panels together along the pinned line (see SEWING) then machine along the tacking with a plain seam.

Take out the tacking and press the seams open.

Join the panels for the linings in the same way, then trim off 50mm (2in) down one side.

Putting in linings Spread out one of the main curtains, right side up, and spread the lining over it right side down. The lining's top edge should be 20mm ($\frac{3}{4}$in) below the curtain top. Join the lining and curtain together at the sides so that a tube is formed. When you turn the tube right side out and centre the lining, there will be 25mm (1in) of curtain fabric turned over the lining down each edge.

Pin across the top of the lining to hold it in place 20mm below the curtain top. Press the side seams.

Trim the bottom edge of the lining to make it 25mm shorter than the main curtain. Make separate double hems on the lining and curtain. At the sides, sew the lining to the curtain by hand.

Putting on heading tape Fold the top 50mm (2in) of the curtain over the lining and pin it in place. Cut heading tape the width of the curtain plus 65mm (2½in). Fit it across the curtain top over the raw edge. If you planned the heading to stand

up above the track, position the tape farther from the curtain top. If the tape is a deep one, sew the end as well as the top and bottom. Take out the tacking.

Pull on the cords while you slide the curtain along them, until it is the right width. Knot the cords separately and wind the surplus round a cord tidy. Do not cut it off; it allows you to open the curtains out flat for washing or cleaning. Distribute the gathering evenly.

Slip curtain hooks into the tape pockets – one at each end and others about 75mm (3in) apart. Use split hooks for cartridge pleats and pinch pleats, standard plastic or metal hooks for other headings.

Slip the hooks into the gliders or curtain rings on the track or pole. Open the curtains and run a finger and thumb down the folds from top to bottom.

Cushions

Making them with foam or loose fillings

To make a square or rectangular foam-filled cushion, buy a block of high-density polyether foam, 100mm (4in) thick and to the dimensions required for the cushion. To soften and protect the foam surface, cover with thin polyester wadding secured with upholstery net. Choose a hard-wearing fabric with a firm close weave for the cover. Cut two pieces the size of the foam, and round one piece stitch PIPING 13mm ($\frac{1}{2}$in) from its edge.

Lay the two pieces together, right sides facing and the piped piece on top, and stitch together 13mm ($\frac{1}{2}$in) from the edge along three sides. Turn the cover right side out and insert the foam filling. Close the opening with SLIPSTITCHING.

Using loose fillings Down, feathers, kapok or foam chips can also be used to fill cushions, but they must be contained in an inner cover made from a closely woven fabric such as cambric.

Make the inner cover 'inside out' and leave one side open. Turn the cover right side out, pack with filling and slipstitch the opening. Make the outer cover in the same way as for a foam-filled cushion, to the dimensions of the filled inner cover.

Cutlery

Caring for kitchen and eating implements

All cutlery needs careful looking after, whether workaday kitchen knives or the best silver, if it is to retain its usefulness and appearance.

Care Kitchen knives should be kept so that their blades never touch, and sharp edges cannot come into contact with fingers. House them in a wooden knife block, or store them in racks or on a magnetic knife holder fixed to the wall. Store good-quality tableware in a lined cutlery box, with divisions for each piece.

Sharpening Kitchen knives that are in regular use should be sharpened once a week. Most are hollow-ground by the manufacturers at an angle of 15-20 degrees, so hold them at this angle when sharpening.

There are several ways of sharpening: by drawing a blade across a stone; using a hand-held steel; using a sharpener with discs which the knife is pulled through; or using an electric knife sharpener.

Table knives can also be sharpened using one of these methods.

Sharpen a scallop-edged blade only on the smooth side, and use a sharpening stone (see SHARPENING HAND TOOLS), never a knife sharpener. If it is really blunt, have it professionally sharpened. Saw-edge blades cannot be sharpened at home – have them done professionally.

Remember, a blunt knife is more dangerous than a sharp one – it is the blunt one that slips.

Always dry table cutlery after washing it in warm water. This prolongs its life, especially in hard-water areas where the water can cause pitting in stainless steel.

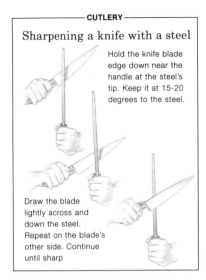

— CUTLERY —

Sharpening a knife with a steel

Hold the knife blade edge down near the handle at the steel's tip. Keep it at 15-20 degrees to the steel.

Draw the blade lightly across and down the steel. Repeat on the blade's other side. Continue until sharp

Never use water that is too hot on knives with bone or ivory handles, as it can loosen the adhesive holding on the handles. Wash silverware items separately to avoid scratching: remove stains with silver polish before washing.

Repairs If a handle comes loose, pull it off and clean out all the old adhesive, both from the tang and from inside the handle. Insert an epoxy resin adhesive into the hole and push back the tang – see GLUING. Wipe away surplus adhesive and leave the repaired item to set for the recommended time.

Place a bent blade on a flat metal surface and tap it straight with a hide or rubber hammer. The soft face of the hammer will not mark the blade. If necessary, smooth after hammering with a fine grade slipstone or fine emery paper.

To remove heat stains, rub the blade with fine grade wet-or-dry abrasive paper used wet. Or use fine grade emery paper. Small nicks in edges can be honed away from unplated or stainless-steel blades with a fine grade slipstone. For a deeper nick, use a fine hand file, then finish off with fine emery paper.

If fork tines are bent towards each other, force an old wooden ruler between them to push them apart. If they are out of line, sandwich them between two pieces of card, then place in vice jaws and tighten. Any further adjustment can be done with pliers, separated from the metal by card to avoid damage.

Bent fork and spoon handles can be levered straight between slightly opened vice jaws. Line the jaws with card to protect the cutlery from scratches. For a severe bend or kink, lay the handle on a flat metal surface and tap the handle with a hide or rubber hammer.

Valuable silverware is best not repaired at home: take it to a reputable silversmith or jeweller.

Cutworms

Getting rid of a garden pest

These fat greenish-brown or grey-brown caterpillars remain in topsoil during daytime, emerging at night to feed on the stems and leaves of a variety of garden plants and vegetables. Often they will cut stems off at ground level, which gives them their name.

Thorough and frequent digging and weeding are the best ways to protect your soil from cutworms. Treating the soil with gamma-HCH, bromophos, or diazinon or chlorpyrifos granules will also help – see PESTICIDES.

CV (Curriculum vitae)

Selling yourself to a prospective employer

Literally translated from the Latin, *curriculum vitae* means 'the course of one's life'. When a prospective employer requires you to supply your CV, however, he is interested not only in your past working life and its relevance to your application for a job but also in your interests and hobbies.

Take great care in preparing it. Present it in a clear, concise manner, tabulating all the facts of your previous positions, in reverse chronological order; your educational qualifications and career-related training; the standard of your education – for example, school, college, university; any honours, awards or outstanding achievements.

If relevant, list any foreign languages spoken, or any skills you have which are not reflected in your work record, but may be applicable to the job for which you are applying.

Do not state why you left your last job, or previous jobs; or, if you are still employed, why you are dissatisfied with your present job. Do not grovel – 'I would deem it a great favour if you could see your way to granting me an interview' – rather try in your letter to make your prospective employer wonder how he has managed without you in the past.

Use plain, simple English. Do not try to impress by using big words or vogue words or phrases; avoid such terms as *in-depth* study, *in the field of*, *meaningful* and *hopefully*.

Write your CV on good-quality paper, and if you have a good, clear hand write in longhand.

Alternatively, have it typed professionally. Typing services can usually be found advertised in a local paper. Check thoroughly for spelling, punctuation or typing errors.

Put your full name, address, age and home and business telephone numbers at the top of the page, and send in your CV with a covering letter.

Dahlias

Growing the Aztecs' flowers

Dahlias – flowers of Aztec origin – fall into two main groups: those grown annually from seed and those grown from tubers or cuttings of tubers – see BULBS, CORMS AND TUBERS. Seeds (see SEED SEWING) are usually sold to be grown as BEDDING PLANTS, in mixtures of different colours; to produce specific blooms, you need tubers or pot-grown plants.

The plants may grow to anything from 300mm (12in) to 1.8m (6ft) tall with single or double blooms 50-250mm (2-10in) in diameter, depending on type. They flower from late July until the autumn frosts.

Preparing the ground Dahlias need plenty of light and, preferably, a bed of their own. Good, medium, loamy soil is ideal, but they should thrive in any reasonable soil. Prepare by manuring well in autumn before planting the following May or June – see SOIL PREPARATION.

Choosing Buy the biggest tubers you can afford, as they are more likely to produce large and plentiful flowers. Make sure they are healthy – reject any which have cuts, soft spots, signs of rot or dry, dusty or shrivelled-looking patches. Buy young, potted dahlias in late spring.

Planting All but dwarf dahlias need staking. Dig a 150mm (6in) hole for each plant and drive in a stout 1.5m (5ft) cane to a depth of about 300mm (12in).

Insert the tuber gently, taking care not to damage it, and keeping the remnant of the stem uppermost. Mix the displaced soil with bone meal and a handful of moist peat – use it to refill the hole, then water the plant.

Dig holes and stake out potted plants as you would tubers, keeping the ball of soil around the roots intact. Water after planting, and again within two days in dry weather.

Damp

Keeping it out of your home

Unless checked, damp in the home will quickly cause wood rot, rust or ruined decorations. So make regular checks of the areas most at risk – at least once a year, before winter.

Roof Do not venture on your roof without a roof ladder, which hooks over the ridge. Even then – take care. First check the ridge tiles: frost can attack the holding mortar, making them loose. Refix them with MORTAR.

Next, examine the main roof tiles or slates for damaged or missing ones and replace them – see ROOF REPAIRS. Loose slates can often be secured with a blob of epoxy-resin-based filler – see STOPPERS AND FILLERS. Tiles may only need hooking back over battens by their nibs.

See that chimney pots are secure. Pots over flues no longer in use should be capped with a half-round tile or a special capping pot to allow ventilation but keep out rain. Work on a chimney stack should usually be left to a builder with the necessary scaffolding. It is seldom a job for the amateur.

Check that gutters are secure without sags. Clean out all the debris, and make sure downpipes are not blocked. Rainwater spilling onto a wall can cause internal damp problems – see GUTTERS AND DOWNPIPES.

Flat roof areas are prone to leaks. Fine cracks can be sealed with a rubber-bitumen waterproofing compound. Where break-up is serious, the roof should be re-covered. Examine all FLASHINGS and repair or renew as necessary.

Walls Look for missing mortar between bricks and repair as necessary – see POINTING. Porous brickwork can be coated with a silicone water repellent, available from builders' merchants. This stops rain getting in, but still allows the wall to breathe.

On rendered surfaces, fill any cracks with mortar mix before redecorating. Add a little PVA glue to the water when mixing the mortar to improve adhesion. A good masonry paint will seal hairline cracks, as most of these paints contain a gap-filling additive – such as sand, nylon fibre or mica flakes.

See that any damp-proof course (dpc) is not bridged by something leaning against the wall above it. If it is damaged, you can rent equipment from a tool hire centre to inject a damp-resisting fluid into the wall, forming a new dpc.

Make sure that all AIR BRICKS around the house are kept free of obstructions: underfloor VENTILATION is vital to prevent DRY ROT.

Doors and windows Seal gaps and cracks around frames with an exterior grade mastic – see SEALANTS. Do not use putty or mortar, both of which harden and crack with age.

Replace all cracked or missing glazing putty – preferably with a glazing mastic. Take new paint 3mm ($\frac{1}{8}$in) onto the glass to seal any gap between putty and glass. Cracked glass can be temporarily sealed with waterproof adhesive clear tape.

Indoors Inspect all joints in water pipes, particularly near CENTRAL HEATING radiators. Tighten loose compression joints.

Examine tanks and cisterns for leaks. Older tanks may rust; they are best replaced with new flexible plastic tanks. See that overflows are not blocked. If water is dripping from an overflow, check the BALL COCK – it may need repair.

Dandelions

Clearing them from a lawn

Unchecked, dandelions can play havoc with a lawn. Their roots deplete the soil of essential nutrients; their broad leaves deprive the grass of light; and they are said to exude a growth-inhibiting gas.

Dandelion control One method of controlling dandelions is to pull out individual plants as they appear. But make sure to pull out all their long taproots, or they will simply grow back again. Pull them when the soil is wet, using a hoe to free the roots.

If you have a bad invasion of dandelions, apply a proprietary broadleaf hormone weedkiller directly to young plants – see WEED CONTROL. You should not have to repeat the treatment more than twice.

Dandruff

How to keep it under control

Dandruff – scales of dead skin flaking from the scalp – may occur at any age, but is especially common among young adults. Although it is often associated with the condition known as seborrhoea (excessively greasy skin), it can affect any scalp – dry or oily. In general, the oilier the skin, the worse the dandruff. At its worst – greasy scales which stick to the hair and skin – it can cause severe irritation.

Dandruff cannot be cured as such,

only controlled. In mild cases, twice-weekly use of a detergent shampoo may be sufficient – see HAIR CARE. Treat severe dandruff with a proprietary application containing salicylic acid, tar or selenium. Follow the maker's instructions for frequency of use. (Pregnant women and nursing mothers should avoid selenium.)

If the condition persists after several weeks, consult a doctor, who can determine if the cause is ECZEMA or dermatitis and recommend other treatments.

Darning

Mending holes and frayed areas

Darning is really a process of re-weaving, and should follow closely the style of the original fabric. At its neatest, it should be almost undetectable. Work in good light, using a darning needle of suitable size and threads from the garment hem if you can, or wool or thread as similar as possible to the original. Use long needles to span larger holes. Use sizes 14-18 darning needles with yarn.

A hole is easier to mend if spread (but not overstretched) over a curved surface such as a darning mushroom.

The darn needs to be bigger than the hole, so that end stitches go into good, strong fabric. Avoid making a square darn, which puts all the strain on only a few threads.

DARNING

Weaving the thread

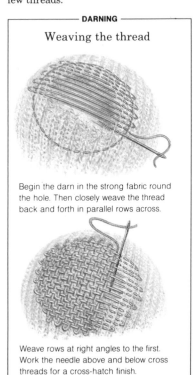

Begin the darn in the strong fabric round the hole. Then closely weave the thread back and forth in parallel rows across.

Weave rows at right angles to the first. Work the needle above and below cross threads for a cross-hatch finish.

Start by making a frame of running stitches around the hole, about 25mm (1in) from its edges, to strengthen and hold the area of worn fabric. Now work the wool or thread from side to side in parallel rows kept close together. Leave a small loop at the end of each row to allow for the thread shrinking. Then work rows at right angles, passing the needle above and below threads, and alternating this on each row.

For a large hole, tack a patch of net underneath the fabric and darn through this to reinforce the repair.

QUICK TIPS For good results it is best to shrink darning wool before using it. Leave it in a steamer for ten minutes or hold it in steam from a kettle. Do not knot the thread when starting, and cut it close when finishing.

Darts

A game for teams or individuals

The game is played by throwing darts at a circular board marked in concentric rings and with 20 numbered wedges. It can be played by two or three players singly, or by teams of two or more. In a singles game, each starts with a score of 301; teams start with 501 per team. The points scored by each dart thrown are subtracted from the starting score. The first player, or team, to reach zero wins.

Single darts are thrown to decide who starts, the player nearest the bull (centre) leading off. Each player throws three darts in his turn at the board. But the player (or team) can usually only open their scoring with a double – a dart landing in the narrow outermost ring of the board, where it scores double the number marked on the wedge. A player (or team) who fails to score a double with his three darts, must try again on his next turn, and so on until he succeeds. Scoring must also be completed with a double or a bullseye. There are usually three games, or legs, to a match.

The bullseye at the centre of the board is worth 50 points, and the small ring surrounding it 25. Between the 'double' ring and the bullseye is another narrow ring: a dart landing in it scores treble the number marked on the wedge. The highest number of points a single dart can score is 60 (treble 20).

For tournament games the' score required is always 501, and the board is mounted so that the bullseye is 1.7m (5ft 8in) from the floor. The player throws from the oche – a line marked on the floor 2.37m (7ft 9¼in) from the board.

Outside tournaments, a number of variations can be played on the traditional game, using the same clock-face board – going around the board in a sequence of doubles, for example.

Death watch beetle

Recognising and destroying it

This beetle thrives on old or decaying hardwoods, and can cause considerable damage – but these days is found only in older properties. It is evident when woodwork is pitted with pin-sized holes, which are, however, larger than those of the furniture beetle – see WOODWORM.

The adult beetle has mottled brown wing cases with a flattened front segment. It is about 6mm (¼in) long, and lays its eggs in cracks on a rough wood surface. The eggs produce curved, fleshy white larvae, which can sometimes be seen before they start to eat their way into the wood. They tunnel for about four years – some taking as long as ten years – after which they emerge as adult beetles, ready to repeat the cycle.

Timber weakened by the beetle must be cut out and burned, and new wood treated with a preservative inserted. Wood which is not badly damaged should be treated with a special insecticidal woodworm fluid either brushed or sprayed on the timber. You can rent the necessary equipment from a tool hire centre – it includes spray, fluid and face mask. In addition, get an injector with a nozzle for injecting the fluid into some of the holes – the deeper the fluid penetrates, the more effective the treatment.

If in doubt about an attack, call in a specialist woodworm company offering a free survey and guaranteed treatment.

Debt collectors

What they may and may not do

Anyone who is owed money is entitled to try to recover it himself, or to hand the matter over to a debt collector or collection agency to act on his behalf. The collector or agency must have a licence from the Director General of Fair Trading, and strict rules apply to them.

It is a criminal offence to harass a debtor or his family by, for example, threatening violence or court proceedings. It is also illegal to publicise the debt – for example, by parking outside a debtor's home in a vehicle marked 'Debt Recovery Service' – or by mentioning the debt to local traders. Shops must not display 'shame lists' of debtors, but trade organisations may exchange lists of them privately.

A collector's powers are limited to asking politely for the money owed. If the request is declined, he can apply to the court for a judgment against the debtor. That merely confirms that the money is owed; if the debtor still refuses to pay, the collector may ask the court for an enforcement order.

This entails seizure by bailiffs of goods to the value of the debt, or the interception of payments made to the debtor – his salary, for example. In most cases, bailiffs may not force entry into a debtor's premises, though they can enter through an unlocked door or open window, but anyone refusing them admission may be threatening a breach of the peace or be in contempt of court.

Bailiffs are not entitled to seize essentials such as clothing belonging to the debtor and his family, their beds or the debtor's tools of trade. Unless the debt is for rent, they also cannot take goods belonging to people other than the debtor, including those of his family or goods on hire.

Goods still subject to a hire purchase agreement belong, in law, to the hire purchase finance company; they cannot be seized to help pay off general debts other than rent. However, if the debt is to the finance company, and the court order is for recovery of those particular goods, the bailiff can use any force necessary to enter the premises and carry them off – see HIRE PURCHASE.

If you believe you are being wrongly pursued for a debt, seek advice from a solicitor. If a collector threatens violence or otherwise harasses a debtor or his family, the police should be informed. Goods seized in error by a bailiff may be reclaimed through the court that ordered the seizure. If the sale of seized goods raises more money than is owed, the balance is returned to the debtor, less about 15 per cent of the total seized for court fees.

Deckchairs

Repairing and re-canvassing them

At the end of summer, give woodwork a light rub over with glasspaper, then apply clear preservative. Allow the canvas to air dry before storing.

At the start of a season, dust the framework with a damp rag, and lightly oil all pivot points.

Where wood has split, apply PVA-based waterproof wood glue (see GLUING) liberally to the pieces to be joined, then bind or clamp the repair until the glue has set. If a joint is loose, pull it apart; clean off old adhesive and coat with waterproof glue. Reassemble, and clamp together until the glue has set.

Where a rivet has worked loose, place a block of metal against the rivet head, then tap the other end where the washer is, working around the edges of the rivet. Apply a little oil if it is a pivot point.

If canvas is perished or damaged, lever out the tacks with a tack lifter. Buy replacement canvas from a department store or hardware shop and cut to length, using the old canvas as a guide. Fix with new large-headed tacks into new holes. See also GARDEN CHAIRS.

Découpage

Decorating with cut-out pictures

The art of *découpage* was developed in 17th-century Europe in imitation of expensive Chinese and Japanese lacquer ware. Pictures or shapes cut from paper are glued to smooth-surfaced objects of wood, metal, glass or porcelain, such as boxes, trays, vases, plates and lamp bases. Pictures can be cut from magazines, catalogues or greetings cards, or bought from craft shops.

Tools needed Small, sharp, fine-pointed scissors; several small pieces of synthetic sponge; a rubber hand roller; a craft knife; fine quality soft-bristled paintbrushes; either a burnisher (sold by craft shops) or a small spoon; a felt-covered sanding block.

Materials needed White (PVA) glue (or acrylic adhesive for glass or porcelain); clear sealer fixative, available in sprays; very fine wet-or-dry abrasive paper; perhaps wood stain and sealer; fine steel wool; the clearest varnish available; pum-

---

DÉCOUPAGE

Preparing the cut-outs

Before cutting out the paper designs, seal the paper on both sides by applying two coats of sealer fixative. Allow the first coat to dry before applying the second.

Cut round the outline using nail scissors. Hold them at an angle to bevel the under edge.

After gluing the cut-out, place a clean, damp cloth over it and press it smooth with the hand roller.

---

ice powder and linseed oil for a very fine finish on wood; Plasticine to hold the cut-outs in place.

Preparation Seal the paper, then cut out designs with scissors angled inwards to bevel the under edges.

Strip old wood of its finish (see PAINT STRIPPING). Wrap the wet-or-dry round the block and sand old and new wood several times until smooth, wiping it clean after each sanding with a lint-free cloth. Next, apply wood stain if you are using it, followed by a coat of sealer. If the object is also to be painted, apply sealer before painting. Remove RUST from metal objects, then seal.

Making the design Work in a dust-free room. Using tiny pieces of Plasticine, arrange the pictures in several ways on the object until you have a pleasing design; mark their positions lightly with a pencil. Glue the backs of the cut-outs before finally positioning them – the largest first, then the smaller ones. With clean fingers, squeeze out excess glue and air bubbles. Finally, wipe off remaining glue with a damp sponge.

Lay a clean, damp cloth on the design and press smooth with the roller. Work from centre to edges. Through the cloth, press down the edges of the cut-outs with the burnisher or the back of a spoon. Allow two or three hours to dry.

Varnishing Do not varnish on humid days, as the finish may be affected. Apply ten coats of varnish; leave each to dry for 24 hours. Lightly dry-sand and wipe with a cloth between coats.

When the tenth coat is dry, wet-sand the surface to a smooth, cloudy finish with wet-or-dry paper wrapped round a sponge and dipped in soapy water. Apply six to ten more coats of varnish, wet-sanding after each third coat, including the last, and dry-sanding after others. Lightly smooth with fine steel wool.

Finish wooden objects by polishing with a mixture of 1 part pumice to 2 parts linseed oil, rubbed in hard. Wipe clean with a cloth, and polish with white wax.

QUICK TIP To check whether wood is smooth after sanding, rub the surface with an old pair of tights. If the material catches, more sanding is needed.

Dehydration

Recognising the symptoms, and what to do

Adults usually take in about 2.4 litres (4.3 pints) of water each day in their food and drink. If the body loses more water than it absorbs – as a result of illness (particularly diarrhoea and vomiting), over-exertion, extreme heat or the action of certain drugs – dehydration sets in, leading to SHOCK and, eventually, death. Babies and old people are most at risk.

In all cases of dehydration, get medical advice immediately. The symptoms are a dry mouth, coated tongue, thick saliva and pallor. The face looks pinched, with sunken eyeballs, and the victim may become irritable and lethargic. Urine production is low.

If the victim is conscious and able to keep fluids down, give small sips of water, fruit juice, tea or other liquids – but not alcohol, which is itself dehydrating – until medical help arrives. If the cause is extreme heat, move the sufferer to a cool place. Over-exertion or high temperatures that produce profuse sweating cause the body to lose salt as well as water, and that needs to be replaced, too – see HEAT EXHAUSTION.

Severe vomiting, diarrhoea or both can lead to dehydration in an infant or adult, if the condition lasts for more than 24 hours; in babies under six months, it can set in after bouts of sickness or diarrhoea spread over six hours. In both cases, a DOCTOR should be contacted. If the victim keeps vomiting liquids, the lost fluid may have to be replaced intravenously in hospital.

See also DIARRHOEA; VOMITING.

Dents in cars

Knocking or pulling out, filling and respraying

First knock out the dent. If you can get your hand behind the dent, push it out firmly by hand. Alternatively, beat it out gently with a ball-pein hammer (see HAMMERS), holding a flat piece of wood against the outside to stop you beating it out too far.

If you cannot get your hand behind the dent, drill a small hole in the deepest part of the dent, then screw in a long self-tapping screw until only about 13mm ($\frac{1}{2}$in) of the screw sticks out. If the dent is small, grip the head of the screw with self-locking grips or a claw hammer and pull the dent out.

To pull out a larger dent, use a claw hammer levered on a long piece of wood. Do not pull the dent out higher than the surrounding surface.

Filling Remove all the paint from the dent and for about 25mm (1in) around it, using an electric drill with a wire brush or sanding disc. Score the metal with any pointed tool, such as a bradawl.

Buy body filler and cellulose stopper from a car accessory shop. Mix the filler according to the maker's instructions. Apply it quickly to the dent, using a plastic spatula or flexible wallpaper scraper. Spread the filler evenly and firmly, so that it is slightly higher than the

surrounding surface. Leave it to harden for the recommended time.

Once the filler has hardened, shape roughly with a rasp or special bodywork shaping tool. For final finishing, rub it with wet-and-dry abrasive paper wrapped around a sanding block and dipped in water. Start with coarse, 80-100 grit paper and move on to progressively finer papers, finishing with 400 grit.

Brush off any dust and let the surface dry, then check it for imperfections with your fingertips. Fill any pits or imperfections with the cellulose stopper. Let the stopper harden and rub it down with fine grit paper. Clean the area with a cloth and leave to dry completely.

Respraying For respraying, you will need an aerosol can of primer and one

of top-coat paint, obtainable from car accessory shops. Make sure it is the same colour as your car – the shop will have the paint manufacturer's list of car makers' colours and code numbers. You can find your car's paint code number on the serial number plate in the engine compartment. Do not spray in damp conditions, or on a windy day if you are working in the open air.

First, remove any wax or grease from the surrounding paintwork and rub the paintwork lightly with wet-and-dry paper. Rinse and wipe dry. Carefully mask any lights, windows, door handles, bumpers, badges or trim.

Shake the can of primer thoroughly. Spray a thin coat on the repaired area. Leave it for a few minutes, then spray on more. Continue until the repaired area is

Pulling out with a claw hammer; filling

A dent cannot be beaten out so that the surface is completely smooth again – because the metal stretches. Beat or pull out the metal to just below its original level, then fill in what is left of the dent with plastic body filler and cellulose stopper.

Sanding down Use an electric drill with a sanding disc or wire brush to remove paint.

Final touches Rub the filler smooth with progressively finer wet-and-dry paper.

Pulling out Fit a screw in the dent. Lever a hammer on scrap wood to pull the dent out.

Shaping Shape the hardened filler, leaving it slightly higher than the bodywork around.

Before spraying Remove wax or grease from the paintwork with a cloth dipped in white spirit. Rub with 600 grit wet-and-dry paper dipped in water. Mask lights, windows and bumpers with brown paper.

Top coat Spray on in even, horizontal bands, keeping the nozzle 300mm (12in) from the surface and letting each band overlap slightly.

evenly coated with paint that blends in reasonably well with the surrounding paintwork. Let it harden for as long as practicable – say overnight. Then rub lightly with 600 grit wet-and-dry paper dipped in water.

Shake the can of top coat thoroughly, then carefully spray a very thin layer onto the repaired area. Leave to dry for a few minutes, then spray on another thin coat. Repeat until the paint blends with the surrounding paintwork. If the paint runs, let it dry completely, then rub it smooth with 400 grit wet-and-dry paper, used wet, and repaint.

When the last coat is touch dry, carefully pull off the masking. After a day or two prime a damp cloth with mild paint cutting compound and rub the edges of the newly painted area to blend it in completely with the old paintwork, except on metallic-based paint on which you spray two coats of clear lacquer over the base colour coat. Do not wax polish the new paintwork until it has weathered for about six weeks.

Dentures

Daily care to avoid problems

After each meal, remove dentures and brush them thoroughly, using a medium-texture toothbrush and a proprietary denture paste. Rinse the paste away with lukewarm water and keep brushing until the dentures are completely clean.

While the dentures are out, brush the gums gently with a soft, wetted toothbrush, then massage them with your finger. If possible, rinse your mouth and dentures with water after meals.

Each night, take the dentures out before going to sleep, and put them in clean, cold water to keep them fresh. Change the water nightly. About once a fortnight add a cleanser, or half a cup of white vinegar, to the water to prevent calcium from building up on the dentures.

Gum problems When natural teeth are removed, the gum shrinks quite quickly for six months and more slowly after that. Anyone with newly fitted dentures may find that they become loose, and may need to visit the dentist to have them adjusted.

Dentures should be checked by the dentist if they become uncomfortable, or if the wearer develops mouth ulcers or inflammation, swelling or bleeding of the gums. In any case, they should be examined regularly.

QUICK TIP In an emergency, reattach a broken tooth to the plate, or repair the plate itself, with fast-acting extra-strength glue. But go to the dentist as soon as possible for a permanent repair.

Descaling

Keeping kettles and pipes from furring up

Descaling compounds, usually based on formic acid, are supplied by hardware shops in liquid form or as a powder. Both should be handled with care: guard your eyes; wear rubber gloves; and keep the chemical off fabrics.

Kettles Buy a sachet of descaling powder, fill the kettle about two-thirds full of tepid water, and pour in about one-third of the powder. It will bubble for a time; wait until bubbling ceases, then check to see if all the scale has been dissolved. If not, add more powder, and continue the process until the inside surfaces are clear.

In extreme cases, it may be necessary to empty out the kettle, refill with clean water, then boil until the scale starts to crack up and fall off in chunks. Remove the broken material, empty the kettle, and refill two-thirds with tepid water and use more descaler.

Before using the kettle, fill it with clean water, boil for 10-15 minutes, empty out, then rinse in running water.

Plumbing Modern CENTRAL HEATING systems are not affected by furring, as the water passing through the radiators is sealed in and not replaced in any quantity.

In older systems where domestic water and heating water are combined, scale can build up in the pipes. It can also fur up the boiler – usually recognised by a knocking noise inside when water is being heated.

Special descaling chemicals are available through plumbers' merchants which, when circulated through the system, will dissolve the scale. Flush the system afterwards to remove the chemicals.

Special crystals are also available, packed in a net container to be suspended in the cold water tank. Replace every six to eight months. See also WATER SOFTENERS.

Diarrhoea

Common causes and remedies

Bouts of diarrhoea lasting more than half a day are potentially serious in babies under a year old and in frail, elderly people, because loss of body fluids can lead to DEHYDRATION; get medical advice. In others the attack often clears up in a day or two if the sufferer rests, avoids food, and drinks plenty of liquids.

In the case of an otherwise healthy child or adult, consult the DOCTOR if the diarrhoea lasts for more than three days, or if it is unusually severe and is

accompanied by frequent VOMITING, abdominal pain, a high temperature or blood in the motions. Get advice, too, if several people are simultaneously affected, or if the sufferer has recently returned from abroad.

Occasional attacks of diarrhoea may be brought on by unwise eating or drinking, stress, or a viral or bacterial infection. Recurring attacks may indicate a food allergy or a disorder called irritable bowel – see a doctor.

No change is necessary in the diet of breast-fed babies suffering from diarrhoea. But the mother should avoid spiced foods, such as curry.

For babies not being breast-fed, stop milk and solids and, as often as possible, give boiled water or diluted orange or apple juice (not squash). Ideally, give a glucose and electrolyte mixture, such as Dioralyte, available from chemists.

Toddlers can be given clear liquids until bowel motions become less frequent, and then go straight to solids that do not contain milk.

Older children and adults should have a day or so of clear liquids only, and then another day or two of bland, non-fatty foods. Over-the-counter medicines containing kaolin, morphine, methylcellulose or codeine phosphate may help. Make sure to use the correct dosage, usually half the adult dose for children, as specified on the label.

Holiday tummy If you are going abroad, particularly to hot countries, ask your doctor or pharmacist for advice on medicines to take to reduce the risk of stomach upsets.

High-risk foods to be avoided abroad include uncooked fruit and vegetables, raw seafood, shellfish, raw or underdone meat, egg products, cream and mayonnaise. Treat ice cream with caution.

Dieting

Healthy ways to lose weight

There is no miraculous crash diet that will make you lose a large amount of weight in a few days. Diets claiming to accomplish that are at best ineffective – weight loss is rapidly regained once normal eating is resumed – and at worst dangerous to health. So are drugs that either reduce appetite or increase the rate at which the body uses up energy. Most doctors will not prescribe them because they can have dangerous side effects. However, your DOCTOR can advise you about dieting and monitor your progress.

The best way to lose weight and become healthier is to eat a balanced diet. You must provide your body with sufficient amounts of carbohydrate, protein, fat and vitamins to stay healthy, but if you eat fewer calories than your body uses for energy you will lose weight – see CALORIE COUNTING.

Avoid snacks in between meals, but eat regularly. If you miss meals you may become so hungry that you overcompensate and eat too much when you do have a meal. Have only moderate portions – most things are fattening if you eat or drink too much of them.

Eat lots of high-fibre foods. It will help you to diet (and make you less likely to develop bowel problems). A bran cereal for breakfast fills you up so that you won't be ravenous by mid-day. Eat wholemeal bread and foods made of wholemeal rather than white flour. Bran, boiled or baked potatoes, rice and vegetables are filling and are not fattening. Eat just enough to satisfy your appetite.

Reduce the amount of fat that you eat to an absolute minimum. You can supply your body with an adequate amount of essential fat-soluble vitamins by eating only a small amount of fat each day. Butter, cream, lard, pastries, cakes, pies and meat fat are all fattening. See also CHOLESTEROL.

Use skimmed milk rather than whole milk, because it has less cream. Try not to eat butter with your baked potato or bread. The fat in chipped or roast potatoes or the butter on slices of bread can treble their calorie content. Similarly, salads are only slimming without mayonnaise or an oily dressing.

Reduce the sugar in your diet as much as you possibly can: it is fattening, causes tooth decay and is unnecessary in your diet. You can get all the carbohydrate you need by eating potatoes, rice, wholemeal bread and a moderate amount of fresh fruit.

Drink low-calorie drinks which do not contain sugar as a sweetener. Alcohol is fattening. It is also an appetite stimulant and will reduce your willpower to stick to your diet.

Regular EXERCISES, in conjunction with a carefully chosen diet, will improve muscle tone and so reduce flabbiness as well as helping you to lose weight.

Do not expect quick results. Although you may lose weight rapidly at first, it evens out. Dieting requires willpower and is not easy.

Dimmer switch

Fitting one in place of a rocker switch

A dimmer switch allows you to vary the amount of light given out by a bulb from its full brightness down to a glimmer. In most cases a dimmer switch can be fitted in place of a standard rocker-switch (see ELECTRIC SOCKETS AND SWITCHES) without alteration to the existing wiring. Dimmer controls vary from rotary to sliding swit-

ches and touch plates, and may be combined with the on-off control. Some have a push-pull knob for on and off, so that you can have the light come on at a desired setting. When buying a dimmer, make sure it is what you want. Some are not suitable for spotlights, some supply current up to a certain wattage rating only. Special switches are needed for FLUORESCENT LIGHTS, and should be fitted only by a qualified electrician.

Before working on a switch, turn off the power at the mains and remove the fuse for the relevant circuit from the fuse box – see FUSES AND FUSE BOXES. To make doubly sure, turn the light switch on and off before starting work.

Fitting Remove the screws in the old switch cover, and keep them – if the ones supplied with the dimmer switch have a metric thread they may strip if you try to fit them to your mounting box. Pull the old switch from the mounting box, note which way the wires are connected, then disconnect them. If the earth wire is connected to a terminal on the mounting box, do not disconnect it unless it is bare, in which case cover it in green-and-yellow PVC sleeving and reconnect it.

Reconnect the wires to the correct terminals of the dimmer switch. If it is a one-way switch, there will be three wires – a red, a black with a red sleeve, and the earth. If it is a two-way switch, it will have either one cable with red, blue and yellow wires, or two cables – one with red and black wires, one with red, blue and yellow wires. The red, blue and yellow cable connects the two switches, the other is connected to the lighting circuit. A two-way switch usually has terminals marked COM (common), L1 and L2 (sometimes A, A1 A2). Either the red or yellow wire may have been connected to COM, the other to L1 – you must reconnect them as they were before. The blue goes to L2. Screw the dimmer switch to the mounting box. Tighten the screws evenly to avoid cracking the switch cover. Replace the fuse, restore the power, and test the new dimmer switch.

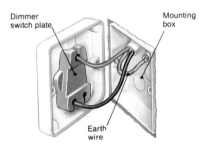

Dimmer switch wiring A simple, one-way dimmer switch has the same type of connections as a rocker switch. The red or red/black wires can go to either terminal, as both are 'live'.

Dishwashing by hand

Avoiding damage and removing stains

To prevent chipping, it is best to wash CHINA and glass dishes in a plastic bowl, and to put protective rubber collars on taps. Given time, wash one piece at a time, to avoid chipping or breakages. Wash the least greasy items – usually glasses – first; then wash cutlery, dishes and pots and pans in that order. After washing the glasses and dishes, rinse them in another bowl of hot water.

Drying SILVER should be dried by hand to get a bright shine. Use lint-free towels (linen is best) to dry and polish each piece while it is still hot from rinsing. Dishes, glass, stainless-steel cutlery and pans are better stacked to dry by themselves in the air – preferably on a rack. Polish glass with a lint-free cloth.

Removing stains and dried food Try not to let dishes or pans get stained or encrusted with dried food in the first place. Rinse the dishes soon after use, even if you cannot wash them. Rinse egg or milk off with cold water, also bowls in which pastry and other flour-based foods have been mixed; rinse off other foods with hot water. Be particularly careful to rinse or soak tea and coffee pots and cups, both stain badly.

To bleach a stained dish, rinse it in a solution of one part 30 per cent hydrogen peroxide to three parts water. Or try rubbing with baking soda, but take care not to damage the pattern.

If food dries on plates, do not scrape with abrasives or sharp objects; simply soak them.

See also DISHWASHER; PANS BURNT.

Dislocated joints

Emergency action and treatment

A joint becomes dislocated when bone ends are knocked or wrenched out of position. The most common dislocations are of the shoulder or jaw, but any joint can be affected – toes, fingers, ankles, wrists, elbows, hips or between the vertebrae in the back and neck. The injury is usually accompanied by torn ligaments (a sprain) and sometimes by a fracture.

The symptoms may include severe pain, swelling, bruising, and difficulty in moving the joint. Often, the affected limb or digit is carried at an awkward-looking angle.

Never try to push a dislocated joint back into position: treat it as a fracture – see BROKEN BONES. Remove or cut away tight clothing or rings near the affected joint, immobilise it as appropriate, support an injury to the arm or shoulder with a SLING, and call for medical attention immediately.

You can apply cold compresses or ice packs to try to relieve swelling and pain. Do not give the victim anything to eat or drink, in case a general anaesthetic is required as part of medical treatment.

Once a dislocated joint has been returned to its proper position – perhaps in a simple manipulation performed by the doctor, or sometimes of its own accord – it is tempting to regard the injury as healed. It is not; damaged ligaments and tissues take weeks to recover. If the victim returns too soon to normal use of the joint, pain and swelling may recur, and there is a risk of long-term damage.

Young children sometimes suffer partial dislocations, particularly of the elbow or shoulder, that do not show on X-rays. The only symptoms may be pain and tenderness. A doctor or nurse can reposition the joint by manipulation.

Distemper

Safeguarding your dog; symptoms to watch for

Prevention is the only really effective way to combat distemper, a highly contagious and potentially fatal virus disease that can affect dogs of any age, but which is most prevalent among younger animals. In general, the older a dog is, the less likely it is to die from the disease, although it may be left with muscle spasms, epilepsy or temporary or permanent partial paralysis. Puppies should be vaccinated against distemper at the age of about 10-12 weeks; annual booster injections are recommended – see DOG CARE.

An unvaccinated dog can catch distemper from direct contact with (or airborne infection from) an infected dog, ferret or mink. Distemper may be carried on the nose, or on the pads of the paws. Humans and cats cannot catch canine distemper, but humans may carry the virus on the hands or clothes. If your dog becomes infected, avoid contact with other dogs or have a complete change of clothing when going outdoors.

The illness takes three forms. Digestive distemper is accompanied by high fever, vomiting, diarrhoea, loss of appetite and severe dehydration. Respiratory distemper has the same symptoms, but there is coughing, too. Nervous distemper, which is sometimes the final stage of the other two forms of the illness, is accompanied by nervous spasms, muscle contractions and, possibly, paralysis.

At the first symptoms of possible distemper, even in vaccinated dogs, take the animal to a vet; a delay of a day or two could be fatal. The vet may inject the dog with a serum, though the results are not always successful.

Distemper removal

Stripping it from ceilings and preparing for redecoration

Distemper is a water-based paint – no longer produced, but often found in old buildings. Any non-washable distemper – with soluble glue in it – should be stripped off before redecorating. It is generally found painted onto ceiling paper.

Non-washable distemper Use a sponge to soak the surface a number of times with water, then scrape off both the paint and paper with a broad stripping knife. Be careful not to damage the plaster with the stripping knife. If the paint and paper do not come off easily, soak them with wallpaper stripper overnight. Once the distemper has been stripped, wash the surface thoroughly with clean water.

Washable distemper This does not contain glue, and does not need to be removed before redecorating. Simply clean the surface by sponging down with warm water and detergent and rinse with clean water. Rub down any areas of loose or flaky paint with fine glasspaper.

However, since new paint or ceiling paper may not stick too well to residues of distemper, it could pay to cover surfaces with a coat of oil-based primer sealer before redecorating.

Distress signals

Attracting attention in emergencies

Repeated sound signals made by any means available – such as blasts on a whistle or horn – are the most effective means of attracting attention in many emergencies.

The SOS in MORSE CODE (three dots, three dashes, three dots) is universally recognised; so is the mountain distress signal of six whistle blasts a minute, followed by a minute's silence.

In daytime, distress signals can be flashed with a mirror or other shiny object to reflect the sun. At night, use a lamp or torch to make the Morse SOS.

In the wild People on foot in open country are difficult to spot from a distance or from the air, and sound signals may be hard to trace – though you should still make them if possible. Light one or more fires if you can, using damp wood or grass to produce smoke once the fire has taken. Wear your brightest coloured clothes outermost, and wave a large flag of bright clothing.

To assist in rescue from the air, spell out the words HELP or SOS on the ground in letters at least 6m (20ft) long improvised from branches, stones or clothing, or stamped out in snow.

Signal to the aircraft with a mirror (in daytime) or torch (at night). If you are being rescued by a helicopter, light a small smoky fire, near the pick-up point to show the wind direction to the pilot. Indicate firm ground with an H.

At sea Continuous sounding of a foghorn or the firing of a gun or other explosive device at one-minute intervals are recognised signals that a vessel is in difficulties.

A radio transmitter should be tuned to the international distress frequency, Channel 16 VHF (156.8 mHz) or 2182kHz MF. If danger is grave and imminent, repeat the word 'Mayday' three times, give the name of the craft three times and repeat 'Mayday' once more.

Repeat the name of the vessel, and give its position, a brief description of the emergency and help needed. Say 'over' at the end of the message, and listen for an acknowledgment before putting out the call again.

If you need urgent help but are not in immediate danger – for example, because of engine failure or if someone is missing overboard – use the signal 'Pan Pan' instead of 'Mayday'.

On larger, well-equipped boats, light a fire of oily rags in an oil drum on the deck, or set off red flares or an orange smoke canister. If you have International Code flags, fly the letters NC, with the flag N above the C. Otherwise, fly any square flag above or below anything resembling a ball. A piece of orange canvas with a black square and circle is an additional sign for attracting aircraft.

On the smallest boats, a national flag flown upside down is recognised as a sign of distress. Or stand where you are clearly visible to passing vessels or the shore and slowly raise and lower your outstretched arms.

Diving

Taking the plunge headfirst

The standing forward dive is best learned by building up to it gradually. Start by sitting on the edge of a swimming pool with your legs dangling in the water. Stretch your arms straight above your head so that your hands meet. Lower your head and tuck your chin into your chest. Now bring your arms and body down, keeping them in a straight line, and simply fall downwards and forwards into the water. To resurface, turn your hands and head upwards.

Kneeling dive Next, dive from a partly kneeling position. Kneel on one knee only at the edge of the pool. Stretch your arms overhead and tuck your chin into your chest. Fall downwards and forwards, pushing your hips upwards as

Learning to take a header

To build up confidence for a standing dive, start from a sitting position on the edge of a pool. Practise until you feel ready to tackle the next stage.

Sit with arms outstretched then roll forwards, giving a push with your heels.

For a standing dive, launch yourself upwards and arch over, keeping arms and legs together.

Straighten the legs as you arch over. Enter the water with arms and legs in a straight line and together.

your knee leaves the ground and propelling yourself into the water with your feet. Straighten your legs and bring them together as you enter the water.

Standing dive Now try a standing position. Curl your toes over the edge of the pool with your arms overhead and your chin tucked into your chest. Bend forwards at the waist, keeping body and arms straight, and roll downwards and forwards, entering the water hands first two to four feet from the edge.

WARNING When diving in the sea, a lake or river, never dive into water of an unknown depth. At least 2m (7ft) is needed for a standing dive. Check for underwater hazards, such as rocks or logs. People with chronic ear infections or sinus problems should consult a doctor before diving.

Doctor

Registering with or changing an NHS practitioner

If you move to a new district, find and register with a local doctor immediately. Do not wait until you fall ill, as it may take some time to find a doctor who can take you on his list, and medical records may take weeks to transfer.

If you are receiving continuous medical treatment, ask your previous doctor for a letter explaining the circumstances, which you can pass to the new doctor.

Lists of doctors are kept at the office of the local NHS Family Health Services Authority – Health Board in Scotland – (address in telephone directory), public libraries, main post offices and Citizens Advice Bureaus.

For extra guidance, ask your new neighbours about their doctor, how easy it is to see him and what arrangements are made when the doctor is away.

Having chosen a doctor, visit his surgery to ask whether you can register. Take your National Health Service medical card, and those of any other members of your family who want to register, too.

A doctor can refuse to register you without giving his reasons. This usually means that his list is full. However, every citizen has the right to be registered: if you have difficulties, again contact the Family Health Services Authority or Health Board who will allocate you to a doctor. If you need immediate treatment you can go to any general practitioner for a period of 14 days.

Expect to be invited for a 'health check' at your new surgery, where your height, weight, blood pressure and so on will be measured, and you will be asked about smoking, alcohol intake and other matters.

Temporary stays If you are away from home and need emergency treatment, contact any local GP. If you are staying for more than 24 hours he may ask you to register temporarily by filling in a form (FP19).

Changing GPs You can change your doctor without giving any explanation. But first, find a new one who will accept you, and sign on. Your medical records will be transferred automatically from your old doctor to your new one.

Dog barking

Curbing a noisy pet

A dog will naturally bark the occasional warning – at a strange sound perhaps, or an unaccustomed step – and should not be discouraged from doing so, but random barking is a nuisance. Try to start curing it early – bad habits are easier to curb in a young dog, before they become entrenched, than in an older one.

When the dog starts barking for no apparent reason while you are present, simply tell it to stop. It does not matter what word you use – 'no' is as good as any – but be commanding and consistent and always use the same word. If a firm 'no' does not work, repeat the word and at the same time give a quick jerk on the dog's collar. As soon as it stops barking, praise it quietly.

If a dog barks incessantly while you are out, you will soon hear about it from your neighbours. To avoid further embarrassment, and possible complaints to the police, you must take positive steps to stop its solitary barking.

Pretend to leave the house, wait for it to start barking, then return quietly and catch it in the act. Reprimand it as before, again praising it quietly when it stops.

To stop a dog becoming a solitary barker, get it used to being alone gradually: go out for just brief periods at a time. It may help to leave a radio switched on. Soon you should be able to leave it alone for longer spells, comfortably settled in its basket, surrounded by a few familiar 'toys' such as a ball or a bone.

See also DISTEMPER; DOG BITES; DOG CARE; OBEDIENCE TRAINING.

Dog bites

Emergency treatment; coping with an attacking dog

A dog bite can introduce germs from its mouth into the bloodstream, possibly causing infection. If the skin has been broken and the victim has not been immunised against tetanus during the previous five years, the victim should see a DOCTOR as soon as possible for an antitetanus injection. Serious wounds should be treated by a doctor at a hospital casualty department.

As an immediate treatment, wash the wound and surrounding area thoroughly with soap and warm water or a mild antiseptic. Dry the skin gently, wiping away from the wound, and cover it with a clean dressing held in place by a bandage – see BANDAGING.

If a dog attacks you, offer it a forearm covered with a sweater or jacket if possible. Push your forearm down hard into its throat to weaken its grip, and keep pushing until it lets go. Do not pull your arm away until the grip is released, as this will cause a lacerated wound instead of a clean one. If the dog returns to the attack, try to grasp it by the back of the neck and push it through a door or gate that can be firmly closed.

Any unprovoked attack by a dog should be reported to the police: failure to control a dog is an offence.

Dog care

Choosing one and looking after it

Buying a dog is a commitment which may continue for 15 years or more, so it should be planned rather than done on impulse.

When deciding what to buy – small or large, mongrel or pedigree – take account of such factors as availability of space, cost of upkeep and where you live (having regard to such things as toilet needs and exercise). For example, a large, boisterous dog that needs exercise is not an ideal choice for someone in a small, town flat.

Mongrel or cross-bred dogs often make excellent pets. The advantage of a pedigree dog is that you can be sure of its eventual looks and size, and have some guarantee of its breeding and health. Also, you can choose a dog for the purpose for which the breed has been developed, or for its characteristics.

For example, if you want a family dog, a good all-rounder, one of the gun dog breeds – perhaps a Labrador, or Spaniel – would probably suit better than a Terrier or Collie. If you live in an area calling for a good watchdog that is large enough to offer you protection, a German Shepherd or Boxer is a better bet than a Chihuahua.

Buying If you buy an adult dog, you avoid the bother of puppy rearing – but you may know almost nothing about the animal. It could have a poor health record or bad habits which are not immediately obvious. In this case you would probably be safer taking one from someone you know rather than a stranger. Another precaution is to consult the vet who has records of its vaccination (see below) or other treatment.

When buying a puppy, find someone specialising in the breed you want, either from adverts in dog magazines or by consulting the breed society (address available through the Kennel Club, 1 Clarges Street, London W1Y 8AB).

When you are shown a litter of puppies, choose one which is obviously fit: plump and lively, with clear eyes, a shiny coat, white teeth, firm, pink gums and fresh breath. Avoid any puppy which seem listless or unwell.

The breeder will usually recommend taking delivery of the puppy after it has turned eight weeks old. You will be given its pedigree and other documentation, including details of any treatment received (such as worming or injections), and probably a diet sheet.

Feeding For an adult dog, try to continue its usual diet and feeding times. With a puppy, the breeder will advise you – probably to cut feeds from four to three daily as the puppy grows. After six months, a young dog needs only two feeds a day, reducing to one meal of an adult dog food daily by the end of the first year.

Never feed a dog titbits between meals, and always leave a dish of fresh water within reach.

Grooming The average dog will need brushing once or twice a week, and you can use these sessions to check for any skin problems or hidden injury. Start brushing a puppy gently and soothingly so that it gets used to a routine. Equally, you can soon accustom a pup to being bathed occasionally. Adult dogs tend to keep themselves quite clean, but the odd bath may be necessary. Towel the dog thoroughly afterwards (or if it has been swimming) and keep it warm until the coat is completely dry. Professional grooming and/or clipping may be desirable for certain breeds, such as Old English Sheepdogs and Poodles.

Exercise Dogs need regular exercise – to run free for at least an hour a day as they mature. Shorter bursts suffice for small puppies, who tire quickly and need

---

DOG CARE

Buying a dog for a purpose

The advantage of buying a purebred dog is that you will know what its characteristics are likely to be when fully grown.

Family dogs Get a sturdy Labrador or Cocker Spaniel if you want an affectionate pet.

Guard dog For a good pal and sturdy defender, buy a German Shepherd dog.

---

to sleep between meals. Adult dogs should be exercised before meals; not afterwards, when their stomachs are full and they are inclined to rest.

During these exercise periods you can start training your dog – see OBEDIENCE TRAINING. A quick, responsive puppy should know all the basic commands well before it is six months old.

Health Signs which call for veterinary attention include persistent loss of appetite, dullness of the eyes, a dull coat, listlessness, vomiting, diarrhoea and excessive thirst or urinating.

Dog fights

Preventing them and parting the dogs

The best way to deal with dog fights is to avoid them – and often you can. Call your dog to heel (see OBEDIENCE TRAINING) if you spot another dog when yours is running free. If your dog is on the lead, walk swiftly past or away from any dog which looks like giving trouble. The worst thing you can do, in a tense situation between dogs, is to stand by and let them engage in a confrontation.

Most dog fights end quite quickly, so often there is no point in intervening. If you have to break up a serious fight, take care *you* do not get bitten: dogs move faster than most human beings can react.

If you are alone, do not put out your hands – this is the quickest way of getting bitten. Instead, try distracting the dogs by creating a loud noise – shout, whistle or even bang a dustbin lid.

If someone else is on hand, you may be able to simultaneously grab one dog each by the collar or scruff of the neck. Timing is important: it is useless to haul one dog off if the other is still unrestrained. Do not drag fighting dogs apart if one has its teeth sunk into the other, as this will only result in even worse wounds. Try slapping its side or flank to make it let go.

If your dog is bitten in a fight, clip away the fur around the wound and clean it with warm water and a little disinfectant. Cover and bandage the wound if it looks serious and take the dog to a vet. See also DOG BITES; PET INJURIES; PET MEDICATION.

Doll repairs

Putting back arms and legs

Most modern dolls are made of plastic, with head and legs held in place by flanges. Sometimes a flange splits or tears, causing the limb to fall off. It can be repaired quickly and simply by heating the blade of an old knife or screwdriver

Re-stringing the head, body and limbs

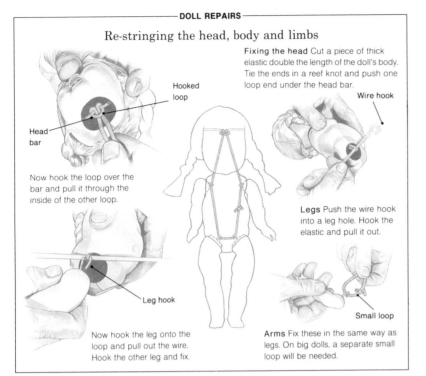

Hooked loop

Head bar

Now hook the loop over the bar and pull it through the inside of the other loop.

Leg hook

Now hook the leg onto the loop and pull out the wire. Hook the other leg and fix.

Fixing the head Cut a piece of thick elastic double the length of the doll's body. Tie the ends in a reef knot and push one loop end under the head bar.

Wire hook

Legs Push the wire hook into a leg hole. Hook the elastic and pull it out.

Small loop

Arms Fix these in the same way as legs. On big dolls, a separate small loop will be needed.

and touching it to the torn edges.

As the plastic begins to melt, remove the knife and squeeze the split edges together. If it is a long tear, work on 13mm (½in) at a time. When the repair is complete, finish off by reinforcing the inside of the flange with a strip of adhesive tape. Press the flange home into the body of the doll.

Re-stringing The traditional method of holding the limbs of dolls together is by round elastic, which in time can break. The doll can be easily reassembled, using new elastic and some strong wire, as illustrated. Use round elastic, about 6mm (¼ in) thick.

See also TEDDY BEAR REPAIRS.

Dominoes

Playing a popular pub game

Any number of people from two to nine can play. There are 28 dominoes in a set, and each is divided in half by a line. Within each half the surface is either blank or marked by dots, ranging in number from one to six. Seven of the dominoes are *doubles*, with the same values on either side of the line, ranging from double blank to double six. The rest have different combinations of values – for example, 6-5; 4-1; 3-0.

There are several variations on the game, but all share the same central objective: to get rid of all your own hand

of dominoes before your opponents can lose theirs.

Starting play Lay all the dominoes face down on the table and swirl them round until they are thoroughly mixed – the dominoes equivalent of shuffling cards. Each player then draws a domino to decide who leads off – the one drawing the highest value goes first.

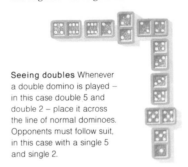

Seeing doubles Whenever a double domino is played – in this case double 5 and double 2 – place it across the line of normal dominoes. Opponents must follow suit, in this case with a single 5 and single 2.

Block dominoes This is a game for two players. Each draws seven dominoes to form his hand, concealing them either by holding them in his hands, or by standing them on end directly in front of him, so that only he can see the dots. The remaining dominoes, still face down, are then moved to the side of the table to form the stock or reserve.

The leading player places any domino from his hand face up in the centre of the table. The other player then has to follow suit, butting the half of a match-

ing domino against the appropriate half of the lead player's domino, and so on. The dominoes are laid end to end, except for doubles, as shown.

If a player cannot follow suit he calls out 'Go!' or raps the table and allows his opponent to take another turn – until he can follow suit. Play ends when one player has used all his dominoes.

The loser counts the dots on the dominoes he still holds, and the total number is passed to the winner as his score for that hand.

Where both players cannot follow suit, each counts the dots in their hands, the winner being the one with fewest. He scores the points difference between the two hands.

A points total of 50 is generally set as the grand game-winning total. After each hand all the dominoes are shuffled again and the players draw another seven dominoes from the stock. The previous loser is given the opportunity of opening play in the next game.

Door bells and chimes

Fitting and faultfinding

Battery-operated door bell or chime kits can be bought in most hardware and electrical shops. Only a low voltage is needed. Long-life batteries should last for up to two years.

Fitting a battery-powered unit Site the bell or chime above the door or where it can best be heard – preferably within 9m (30ft) of the bell-push. For a greater distance, you may need thicker wire or stronger batteries – check the maker's recommendations. Otherwise, the sound may soon fade out. Fix the unit to the wall following maker's instructions.

Site the bell-push on the door jamb and drill a hole through the jamb just wide enough for two-core bell wire – see DRILLING. Connect the bell wire to the two bell-push terminals, thread it through the hole and screw the bell-push on.

Run the wire to the bell by a convenient route and fix it to woodwork with plastic cable clips at 300mm (12in) intervals. Then connect it to the two bell terminals. It does not matter which inner wire is connected to which terminal.

Locating faults If the door bell does not work, try new batteries. If it still does not work, check the connections in the bell and bell-push – see CIRCUIT TESTING. Reconnect any loose wires.

If the bell-push appears faulty, put the blade of an insulated screwdriver across its two terminals. If it rings, the bell-push is corroded or defective. Disconnect its wires and clean the contact points with fine sandpaper. If it still does not work, fit a new bell-push.

Doorknobs

Tightening loose knobs on interior and exterior doors

There are three basic kinds of doorknobs: screw-on and door-mounted knobs for inside doors, and pull-knobs for front doors. Each needs to be tightened in a different way, if it becomes loose.

Screw-on knob Older doorknobs have a small grub screw at the base, which secures the knob to the end of a spindle running through the door. If the grub screw is loose, the knob may eventually come off the spindle. Tighten it as shown.

Door-mounted knob Later doorknobs have a plate at the base, which is screwed to the door. The knob fits onto a smooth spindle running through the door. If the plate becomes loose, remove the screws and fill the holes with plastic wood. Then remount the fitting. If the knob is still not steady, remove the screws and turn the plate slightly on the door. Mark the new screw holes, drill them and refit the plate and doorknob.

Pull-knob Many front doors are closed by a decorative pull-knob, which does not turn. If it becomes loose, remove the screws and fill the holes with plastic wood. Then replace the fitting, ensuring that the screws are strong enough to keep the knob firm. Or drill out and plug the old holes, and screw into the plugs. Some pull-knobs, fitted to one side of a door only, have a spindle that passes through the door and has a nut and washer on the end. If this type of knob becomes loose, tighten the nut.

DOORKNOBS

Tightening when loose

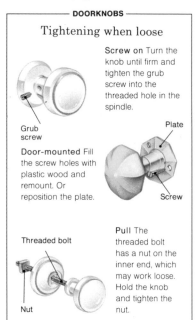

Screw on Turn the knob until firm and tighten the grub screw into the threaded hole in the spindle.

Grub screw

Door-mounted Fill the screw holes with plastic wood and remount. Or reposition the plate.

Plate

Screw

Pull The threaded bolt has a nut on the inner end, which may work loose. Hold the knob and tighten the nut.

Threaded bolt

Nut

How to fit a night latch

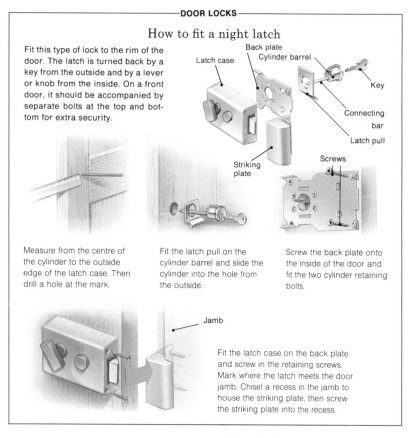

Fit this type of lock to the rim of the door. The latch is turned back by a key from the outside and by a lever or knob from the inside. On a front door, it should be accompanied by separate bolts at the top and bottom for extra security.

Latch case
Back plate
Cylinder barrel
Key
Connecting bar
Latch pull
Striking plate
Screws

Jamb

Measure from the centre of the cylinder to the outside edge of the latch case. Then drill a hole at the mark.

Fit the latch pull on the cylinder barrel and slide the cylinder into the hole from the outside.

Screw the back plate onto the inside of the door and fit the two cylinder retaining bolts.

Fit the latch case on the back plate and screw in the retaining screws. Mark where the latch meets the door jamb. Chisel a recess in the jamb to house the striking plate, then screw the striking plate into the recess.

Door locks

Fitting new ones

Locks for external timber doors come in two basic types: rim night latches and mortise locks. See also BURGLAR-PROOFING.

Rim night latch This has two main components: a cylinder with a key-operated pin tumbler on the outside of the door, and a knob mechanism inside.

Measure from the centre of the cylinder to the outer edge of the latch case and mark the distance from the door edge. Then drill a hole the diameter of the cylinder body at the mark, using a power drill or handbrace and drill bit – see DRILLING.

Fit the latch pull onto the cylinder and slide the cylinder into the hole from the outside. Screw the back plate onto the inside of the door, and fit the two cylinder screws.

Fit the latch case onto the back plate, ensuring that the connecting bar protrudes through the plate and engages in the lock. Cut the bar to length with a hacksaw, according to the thickness of the door, and following the maker's instructions.

Shut the door and mark the position of the latch on the door jamb. Then chisel a recess (see CHISELLING) for the striking plate and screw it to the jamb. Make sure the door closes properly and that the lock works. If not, set the door keep a little deeper into the jamb.

Mortise lock This has a deadlock – a steel bolt housed in the door which engages into a striking plate set flush in the jamb.

Hold the lock against the inside of the door and mark the length and width of the lock casing on the door stile. Using the marks as a guide, transfer the width marks to the edge of the door. Measure the thickness of the lock and mark the outline centrally between the width marks. Drill and chisel out a mortise to accept the lock body.

Push the lock casing firmly in the recess, mark around the face plate and then remove the casing again. Chisel a recess the thickness of the face plate along the marked outline.

Then, holding the lock against the side of the door and aligned with the mortise, push a bradawl through the key and spindle holes to mark where the key and handle spindle will go. Remove the lock and drill holes of the same diameter as the key and spindle holes. Keep the drill

How to fit a mortise lock

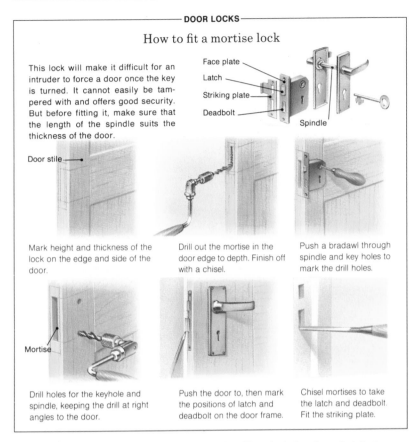

This lock will make it difficult for an intruder to force a door once the key is turned. It cannot easily be tampered with and offers good security. But before fitting it, make sure that the length of the spindle suits the thickness of the door.

Face plate
Latch
Striking plate
Deadbolt
Spindle

Door stile

Mark height and thickness of the lock on the edge and side of the door.

Drill out the mortise in the door edge to depth. Finish off with a chisel.

Push a bradawl through spindle and key holes to mark the drill holes.

Mortise

Drill holes for the keyhole and spindle, keeping the drill at right angles to the door.

Push the door to, then mark the positions of latch and deadbolt on the door frame.

Chisel mortises to take the latch and deadbolt. Fit the striking plate.

at right angles to the door as you work.

Enlarge the bottom of the keyhole with a padsaw (see SAWS) to make it the correct shape. Push the lock case into the mortise with the bolt protruding, and screw the face plate to the door edge.

Fit the handle spindle and key, then screw the handle plates to each side of the door – ensuring that the handle fits over the spindle. Push the door to and mark the positions of latch and deadbolt on the frame. Hold the striking plate against the marks and pencil in the areas where the latch and deadbolt will fit.

Chisel out mortises for the latch and bolt and a recess for the striking plate. Make sure the door closes properly and screw in the striking plate.

Doors

Curing a door that squeaks, jams or sags

A few drops of oil on each hinge will usually quieten a squeaking door. Work the oil in by pulling the door backwards and forwards several times.

There are three main causes of a door jamming: swelling of the timber, sagging at the hinges and sticking at the bottom edge of the door.

Swelling A timber door shrinks in summer and swells in winter. To stop it jamming, plane down the swollen edges (see PLANING) removing the door from its hinges if necessary. Fit flexible draught strip to the door frame (see DRAUGHT-PROOFING) to seal the gap in summer.

Sticking If a door sticks at the bottom on new carpeting, remove it and plane as much wood from the bottom as is necessary.

Sagging Tighten the hinge screws as necessary. If the screws will not tighten, drill out the screw holes, insert wall plugs and use new screws driven into the wall plugs. If the door still sags, unscrew the top hinge from the frame, then deepen the hinge-flap recess by CHISELLING. Replace the hinge, screwing it as tight as possible. This will lift the door.

Double glazing

Simple ways to insulate your windows

Flexible plastic sheeting such as polythene, PVC or plastic film (but not ordinary cling film) can provide simple, temporary double glazing when stretched across the inside of a window frame. Make sure the frame is clean and dry, then line it with double-sided adhesive tape and cut a sheet of plastic to overlap the frame by about 50mm (2in).

Remove the protective paper from the tape and press the sheet onto it, starting from the top and stretching across to the sides and down to the bottom. Run your thumb along the edges to ensure a perfect seal. Trim off the excess. When using plastic film, apply warm air from a hairdryer to the attached sheet. This will shrink the film and remove any creases.

For a more permanent installation,

Fitting secondary panels with a DIY pack

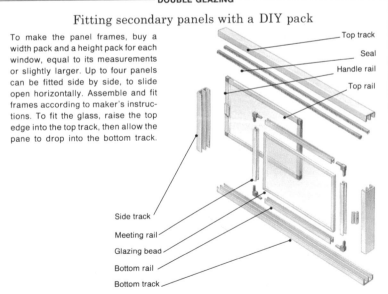

To make the panel frames, buy a width pack and a height pack for each window, equal to its measurements or slightly larger. Up to four panels can be fitted side by side, to slide open horizontally. Assemble and fit frames according to maker's instructions. To fit the glass, raise the top edge into the top track, then allow the pane to drop into the bottom track.

Top track
Seal
Handle rail
Top rail

Side track
Meeting rail
Glazing bead
Bottom rail
Bottom track

build a timber frame, which can be removed during summer and replaced the following winter. Use lengths of 13mm × 25mm ($\frac{1}{2}$in × 1in) BATTENS. When the frame is attached to the window, the 13mm thickness plus the thickness of the window frame will give a good IN-SULATION gap of about 19mm ($\frac{3}{4}$in). Make the frame about 13mm smaller all round than the window frame, to allow room for fixing clips.

Cut four battens to length, mitre the corners (see MITRE JOINTS) and join with corrugated metal fasteners. Stretch polythene or PVC sheet across the frame and fasten it with tacks or staples and trim off the surplus. For a neater appearance, tack 6mm ($\frac{1}{4}$in) strips of batten along the edges of the sheet. Fasten foam self-adhesive draught excluder to the inside of the frame to give an airtight seal.

Use equally spaced plastic L-shaped clips to hold the frame. Fix them to the window frame with countersunk screws.

Glazing with glass or acrylic Simple secondary glazing kits are available from DIY shops. They consist of channelling and track made of plastic or aluminium to fit in the window recess or to the existing window frame, and are sold in a range of sizes (see illustration). Glass is not supplied – get it from a glazier after you have assembled the frames. Alternatively, use clear ACRYLIC, which you can cut to size yourself with a fine-toothed hacksaw. Allow at least one hinged or sliding panel per window so that it can be opened for ventilation or for escaping from fire.

Dowels

Using them to make joints in wood

Dowels, or short hardwood pins, are used to join together pieces of wood when making or repairing furniture such as tabletops or chair frames – see also WOOD-WORKING JOINTS. Dowel joints are made by drilling corresponding holes in two pieces of wood, inserting glue and dowels, then clamping the pieces together until the glue sets.

Ready-made dowels are available in various sizes from DIY stores; they have grooves running along them to let excess glue escape. Or you can make your own by using a hand saw to cut pieces of dowel rod into short lengths, then use the same saw to cut grooves in them.

Choose a dowel with a diameter one-third the thickness of the wood into which it will be inserted. It should be about 3mm ($\frac{1}{8}$in) shorter than the total depth of the two dowel holes. The depth of each hole should be at least two-thirds the thickness of the wood being drilled.

A simple way to align dowel holes is to mark them with panel pins. Tap the

pins into their required positions on one of the pieces to be joined, leaving about 6mm ($\frac{1}{4}$in) protruding. Now snip off the pinheads with pincers. Place the two pieces of wood together and tap the first piece with a mallet, so that the pins leave marks in the second piece. Finally, remove the pins with pliers.

Drill holes to the required depth (see DRILLING) where marked, ideally using a woodboring or dowel bit, which has a centring point for accuracy and drills a flat-bottomed hole. Clear out the wood shavings. Glue the dowels to halfway and insert them into one piece of the wood. Glue round the rims of the holes. Then glue the projecting parts of the dowels and push the joint together. Wipe off any excess glue and leave to set, clamping as necessary.

Dowelling kits are also available from DIY stores. They include a drill bit with a depth stop, and a metal jig which clamps to the workpiece to ensure accurate drilling. Some kits also include metal centre points for aligning the holes. These can be used instead of marking with panel pins.

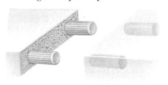

Dowelled joint Glue chamfered wooden pins into matching holes to make a strong butt or mitre joint in wood or chipboard.

QUICK TIPS To cut grooves along homemade dowels, clamp the saw upside down in a vice, and rub the dowel along the teeth of the saw, wearing gloves to avoid possible injury.

Dowels fit more easily if their ends are slightly chamfered. Ready-made ones usually have this done; you can chamfer homemade ones quickly with a pencil sharpener.

Down pillows

Keeping them fluffy and in good shape

The best pillows have all down filling, others may have down and feathers. A down pillow should last at least ten years: choose one with good, close-woven ticking to prevent the down coming through. It should also be 'washable'.

Down pillows should be washed only when necessary. Knead gently in warm soapy water, then rinse several times in warm water. Hang to dry by the corners of the ticking.

To re-cover a pillow, wash and dry it, then open the ticking at one end by about

300mm (12in). Leave a gap of the same size in one end of the new ticking and sew the two together so that the holes match exactly. Shake the down through the hole into the new ticking, then tack across the new cover to seal it before unpicking the join. Oversew the new ticking to finish it neatly.

Drains

Dealing with smells, blockages and overflows

There are two main types of domestic drain: open gullies and closed drains.

Gullies are underground immediately outside the house and receive waste water from sinks, baths, basins and washing machines, and also rainwater from downpipes. Water passes through the gully into a closed drain. A gully has a grid at ground level which you can lift off to reach the U-shaped trap below.

Closed drains receive waste from gullies and lavatory outlet pipes and carry it to the main sewer. They run underground but pass through inspection chambers which you can reach by taking off the manhole cover.

Gullies Smells or overflow will occur if the grid, or the trap below, becomes clogged – with grease or tea leaves, for example, from the kitchen sink or with leaves from nearby trees.

To clear the grid, put on long rubber gloves, scoop out any debris with an old garden trowel, then lift out the grid and plunge it up and down in a bucket of hot water and detergent to clean it thoroughly.

Clean the grid three or four times a year to rid it of grease, and pour a little domestic bleach over it every week or two.

If an overflow does not clear when you have cleared and lifted the grid, the U-shaped trap below is blocked. Again wearing long rubber gloves, scoop out any rubbish in the trap with an old trowel bent to a right angle or an empty tin can. If necessary, break down the obstruction with a trowel or old brush handle. When the trap is cleared, hose it down with the water on full pressure or pour down several buckets of water. Alternatively, fill the bath with water and then pull the plug.

Drains Occasionally a gully overflows because the drain it leads to is blocked. If the obstruction is farther away from the house, waste seeps out round the manhole cover of one of the inspection chambers. If the drain is only partly blocked, you will notice that baths, sinks and the lavatory pan are slow to empty.

To locate the blockage look in the inspection chambers. Remove the man-

─── **DRAINS** ───

Understanding a drainage system

Waste water and sewage from the house, and also rainwater from the gutters, are fed into a closed drain which has inspection chambers, and leads to the main sewer.

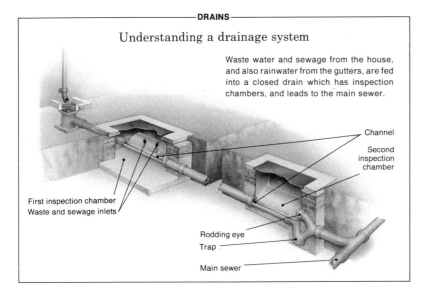

Channel

Second inspection chamber

First inspection chamber
Waste and sewage inlets

Rodding eye

Trap

Main sewer

hole covers in turn, starting with the one nearest to the house.

If the first chamber is clear, and you have cleared the gully, the blockage is between the chamber and the gully.

But if the first chamber is full, look in the next one, and so on. When you come to a chamber that is empty, the blockage is between it and the previous chamber.

To clear the blockage hire a set of drain rods, complete with rubber plunger and a corkscrew head (see HIRING). Fit the plunger to the screw end of the rod. Then screw on a further length or lengths of rod at the other end. Push the rods up the drain towards the blockage, turning them clockwise so that they do not unscrew, and pushing hard against the blockage.

If the blockage does not shift, withdraw the rods, still turning them clockwise. Replace the plunger with the corkscrew and twist it clockwise into the blockage until it breaks up and the waste runs away down the slight slope of the drain.

Cleanse the drain thoroughly by releasing a bathful of water, flushing the lavatory and running the cold taps in the bathroom. Hose down the sides of the inspection chambers, their rims and covers, or clear them with buckets of water. Clean the rods with watering cans of water with disinfectant added. Throw away the gloves.

To stop any smells escaping from the manhole, you can smear the lips of the covers with car grease before replacing them.

If all the inspection chambers on your property are full, the blockage is in the trap built into the chamber nearest the sewer. You can clear this through the rodding eye – a plugged pipe end projecting above the trap. You will have to locate this among the waste, remove the

plug, and insert the rods through it. Or you can pay the local council's environmental health department to deal with it. They will also test drains that are not blocked but still let off offensive smells – probably due to a leak.

Draughtproofing

Sealing windows, doors and floors

Draughtproofing is the cheapest and most effective form of INSULATION for your house.

Windows and interior doors Seal these with foam or rubber self-adhesive strip stuck on the frames. The strip is normally about 6mm ($\frac{1}{4}$in) thick and 10mm ($\frac{3}{8}$in) wide and lasts for one to five years.

Clean the frames with warm water and washing-up liquid. Let them dry and then cut the strip to length with scissors or a trimming knife. Gradually peel the protective backing from the length as it is stuck in place. Fit the ends of the strip snugly into the frame corners.

Sprung nylon or metal strip – available from DIY stores – can also be used, particularly on window and door frames with uneven gaps, and on sash windows. It lasts longer than foam or rubber. The strip is usually pre-holed, and fixing pins are supplied. Cut it to length with tinsnips or dual-purpose scissors. Apply it with the raised edge facing away from the window or door.

Gaps in or round the frames of casement windows and doors can be sealed with silicone rubber sealant, available from DIY and hardware stores.

Interior and exterior doors Several draught and threshold excluders are available, including foam strip, nylon

brush and sprung nylon or metal strip.

Cut to length the self-adhesive foam strip. Stick strips along the sides and top of the door frame. Nylon brush strip is either self-adhesive or is fixed in place with panel pins. Sprung nylon or metal strip is also pinned.

For extra protection, a nylon brush excluder can be fitted to the base of a door – to the outside of interior doors and the inside of exterior doors.

Excluders for outside doors are usually in two parts: one is screwed to the base of the door; the other to the threshold under the door. Some excluders also deflect rain.

Floors The best way to draughtproof a timber floor is to cover it with sheet hardboard (see also UNEVEN FLOORS) and then carpet or vinyl – see also CARPET LAYING; VINYL FLOOR COVERINGS. Alternatively fill gaps between floorboards.

Gaps of more than 6mm ($\frac{1}{4}$in) should be filled with thin strips of wedge-shaped softwood. Apply woodworking glue to both sides of a strip and tap it into the gap with a mallet. Leave a small amount of strip above the floor. When the glue has set, plane off the excess wood – see PLANING. Sandpaper any roughness.

Smaller gaps can be filled with a flexible coloured sealant applied with a sealant gun, but it is expensive for large rooms and cannot be stained. Fill small gaps on stained floors with PAPIER-MÂCHÉ. When set, it can be sanded smooth and stained.

Never block external AIR BRICKS.

─── **DRAUGHTPROOFING** ───

Stopping door draughts

Threshold Fit a threshold excluder to the bottom of a door to stop draughts.

Frame Stick foam strip to the frame of interior doors. The foam is compressed as the door shuts, sealing any gaps.

Draughts

A board game for two people

The game is played on a square board which is divided into 64 smaller squares, coloured alternately light and dark. Each player has 12 'men' – round discs – which are also in contrasting colours, usually black and white or red and white.

The two players sit on opposite sides of the board, with the dark corner squares to each player's left. Each player places his men on the dark squares of the three rows nearest him. The two centre rows are left empty. The object is for each player to try to capture all or most of his opponent's men.

Black, or red, moves first, and moves can be made only on the dark squares, forwards and diagonally at the same time. When a man occupies a square adjacent to one occupied by an opponent's man, and there is a vacant square beyond it, the player may capture his opponent's piece by jumping over it. The captured man is then removed from the board. A series of jumps can be made in one move if there is a sequence of alternate men and vacant squares.

If a player fails to make a possible jump, either by an oversight or because doing so would place his man in a capturable position, he can be 'huffed' – his opponent captures the man that should have made the jump and removes it from the board. Should a player have the choice of two different jumps at one turn, he can only make one, and loses the other man by being huffed.

When a man is successfully moved to occupy a square in the opponent's rear row, it becomes a 'king', and is crowned by having a man of the same colour placed on top of it.

Unlike the ordinary men, a king can move both forwards and backwards, and is not forced to jump when the opportunity arises.

The game ends when all one player's men have been captured, or he has so few men left he has no hope of winning. If neither player can win – for example if each has only one man left – the game is drawn.

Drawer construction

Making and fitting drawers

A drawer can fit flush with the front of a cabinet (see CABINETS) or it can be made with a false front – a board that overlaps part of the cabinet front, concealing the gap between the cabinet and the sides of the drawer. A flush drawer has to be more precisely made, because the gap remains visible.

Flush drawer Before making a drawer, plan it carefully on graph paper. Use 25mm (1in) planed TIMBER for the front. The sides and back can be made with 19mm ($\frac{3}{4}$in) wood and the bottom with 3mm ($\frac{1}{8}$in) PLYWOOD.

First, cut out and prepare the wood. To make the front, which will be attached to the sides with a rebated joint (see WOODWORKING JOINTS), use a piece of wood slightly longer than you want the front to be; this allows for final trimming. Using a tenon saw, power saw or routing tool (see ROUTERS) cut a rebate (a right-angled groove) at each end of the front.

Use a saw, power saw or routing tool to cut a horizontal groove just above the inside bottom edge of each side piece and the front piece. The drawer bottom will slide into these grooves. Cut another horizontal groove – wider this time – a little over halfway up the outer side of each side piece. These grooves will engage

Making a flush drawer with rebated joints

Cut all the pieces to size before making the joints. Note that the back is shallower than the front, to allow the bottom to be slid into grooves.

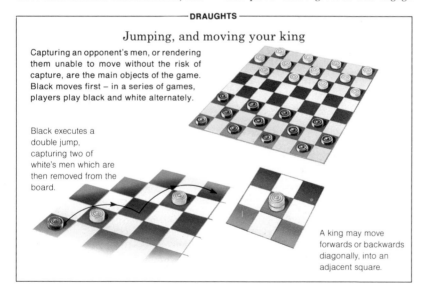

If the drawer is to fit on side runners, make sure the grooves are perfectly true, and rub in candlewax to make the drawer run smoothly.

Rebated joint

Side

Glue the front to the sides, and secure the joint with pins.

Front

with the side runners in the cabinet. Finally, cut vertical slots on the inner sides, near the back of each side piece, into which the back of the drawer will fit (see illustration).

Assemble by fitting together the back and sides. Using a suitable adhesive such as PVA (see GLUING), attach the front to the sides. Knock in pins to strengthen the rebated joint and check that the drawer is square, while allowing the glue to set for the recommended time.

Check that the drawer is still square, then slide in the bottom. Fix the bottom to the underside of the back, with panel pins. Carefully trim the front with a plane to make it fit neatly into the cabinet – see PLANING.

Making a false-fronted drawer This is made in the same way as a flush drawer, but it has two fronts. The first is fitted flush between the side pieces; then the second, or false, front is fixed to the first. The first is glued and pinned in place. The false front should be 10mm ($\frac{3}{8}$in) larger on each side than the drawer opening. Attach it with screws driven in from the rear. Kits for making drawers of various types and sizes are available from DIY stores.

Jumping, and moving your king

Capturing an opponent's men, or rendering them unable to move without the risk of capture, are the main objects of the game. Black moves first – in a series of games, players play black and white alternately.

Black executes a double jump, capturing two of white's men which are then removed from the board.

A king may move forwards or backwards diagonally, into an adjacent square.

Drawer repairs

Fixing loose, sticking or broken drawers and runners

Wooden drawers on wooden runners sometimes work loose and jam when the runners or grooves (rebates) in the drawer sides become worn. See also DRAWER CONSTRUCTION.

Remove the drawer and measure the depth and width of the rebates. Obtain a length of hardwood strip that is slightly larger than these dimensions. Cut two pieces to the length of the runners and plane them so that they slide easily in the rebates – see PLANING.

Run a pencil along the top of each of the old runners to mark their position. Now carefully remove the old runners – they may be screwed or pinned and glued – and fit the new ones, using PVA adhesive and countersunk screws.

If the old runners were screwed, drill fresh holes in the new runners, so that the new screws will not enter the same holes as the old ones. Wipe off any surplus adhesive immediately. Allow 24 hours for the adhesive to set before re-fitting the drawer.

A sticking drawer Damp or high humidity may cause wooden drawers to swell and stick. If a drawer is completely jammed, switch on a fan heater about 1.2m (4ft) away and leave it for a few hours. If sticking persists after the drawer has dried out, lightly sandpaper the runners, then rub them with a candle stub or soap, to 'lubricate' them.

Replacing a split drawer bottom Remove the drawer and carefully knock the back out of its joints – use a wooden mallet or a hammer with a piece of wood to protect the surface. If the joints stick, moisten them with steam from a kettle.

Slide out the damaged bottom and fit a new piece of plywood or hardboard cut to the same dimensions. With a small chisel, clean out old glue from the corner joints on the back and sides. Refit the back with PVA glue and allow to set.

QUICK TIP As a temporary repair to a split drawer bottom, glue a 50mm (2in) wide strip of stiff canvas along the underside of the split, using PVA or contact adhesive.

Drawstrings

A quick way to replace a broken drawstring

A shoelace makes a quick replacement drawstring in a child's garment. Use a lace which is longer than the part of the garment into which it is going to fit, to allow for the ends to be tied. Thread the metal tip of the lace into one end of the opening and work it round to the other side. Tie a knot in the lace at each end of the opening big enough to prevent it slipping out.

For bigger garments, use a length of cord or ribbon, which can be bought by the metre from haberdashery stores. Tie a safety pin to one end of the cord and thread it through the drawstring channel in the cloth. Remove the safety pin and knot the cord at each end.

Drilling

Making accurate holes in wood and metal

To achieve complete accuracy in almost all drilling operations, use an electric drill mounted on a drill stand. This will ensure that the hole is drilled at right angles to the work surface. Also, because the drill is controlled by a lever attached to the stand, pressure can be exerted more evenly and controlled more finely and the depth of drilling can be preset.

Drilling wood Holes in wood can be drilled with an electric drill, a swing brace or a wheel brace. A swing brace is operated by pushing the middle of the brace round in a circular sweep. It bores holes accurately and can be used with special bits which are far larger than standard twist drills.

A disadvantage with the swing brace

Vertical drilling If you do not have a drill stand, place a try square with the blade upright near the drilling point. Keep the drill bit parallel with the square as you drill.

is that it cannot be used in confined spaces, unlike the wheel brace. This is a much more compact hand drill, operated by turning a small drive wheel at the side. Although much slower than the electric drill, it is more easily controlled.

The best type of electric drill to use is a variable or two-speed drill. This enables you to choose a slow speed in starting the hole, and increase it when satisfied that the hole is exactly where you want it, and is at the correct angle.

Before drilling, mark the hole position with a cross. Drill at the intersecting point, starting slowly until the drill bit is established, then more quickly.

To avoid splitting the wood at the underside of the hole, drill only until the tip of the bit appears underneath; then turn the work over and start drilling from the other side. Alternatively, put a piece of scrap wood under the piece you are drilling.

If you are drilling to a fixed depth, adjust the drill stand to drill the correct depth, or fit a depth stop to the drill bit. This can either be a special stop, available from tool or DIY stores, or simply a piece of insulation tape wrapped around the bit to mark the depth you want to drill to.

For jobs where absolute accuracy is vital – to house DOWELS, for example – it is best to use one of the many types of metal jigs available.

Drilling metal Mark the work to be drilled with a cross and indent the intersecting point with a hammer and centre punch. Hit the punch hard, so that it makes a deep indentation, which will prevent the drill wandering. Clamp the metal firmly so that it does not move when drilling begins. If necessary, stick a cross of masking tape over the drilling point to prevent the drill bit slipping and scratching the surface.

If the hole is to be fairly large, first drill a pilot hole, using a small drill bit, before using one of the correct size. For a large hole you may have to use several drills, starting with a small one and increasing until the correct size hole is reached. A high-speed twist drill is essential for drilling hard steel, and it is advisable to use one for all thick metals. Ordinary twist drills are cheaper, but tend to lose hardness.

Use the high-speed drill at the slow setting on your drill. When drilling deeply, pause occasionally to lubricate the hole with a drop of light machine oil.

Large holes Holes up to 100mm (4in) in sheet materials, such as wood, plastics and soft metal, can be made with a circle cutter, which has a twist drill at the centre and a cutting blade at the end of an adjustable arm. Alternatively, holes up to 75mm (3in) can be cut in thin metal, wood and plastic using a hole saw, which has a saw blade in a circular shape with the drill bit in the centre.

See also MASONRY DRILLING.

Drinks

Mixing cocktails and a popular punch

Cocktails, with their exotic names and elaborate mixture of alcoholic drinks, fruit juices and other ingredients, were popular in the Twenties and Thirties; the Eighties have seen them rediscovered.

Chill the bottles in the fridge for several hours before mixing cocktails, and keep a selection of short and tall glasses in the fridge, if possible. Alternatively, fill each glass with ice while the drinks are being prepared. Empty them before pouring the drinks.

Have plenty of ice available for chilling the drinks.

The measures given here are for the standard versions of four popular cocktails; they can be expanded, strengthened or diluted as required.

Dry Martini

Dry vermouth
Gin
Strip of lemon rind
Small green olives

Mix 1 part of vermouth to 2 parts of gin in a jug containing plenty of ice. Stir until chilled, and strain into small, wide-rimmed cocktail glasses. Add more gin for a drier martini; more vermouth for a less potent one. Serve with an olive on a cocktail stick in the glass. Twist a strip of lemon rind over the glass to release the oils, and then drape it over the edge.

Tom Collins

Gin
Lemons
Sugar
Soda water

Squeeze the lemons and allow the juice of one lemon and a teaspoon of sugar per tall glass. Pour a measure of gin into each glass, add crushed ice and top up with soda water. Stir well to keep the drink effervescing.

Tequila Sunrise

Tequila
Grenadine
Orange juice

For each glass, allow one measure of tequila to half a measure of Grenadine and top up with ice and orange juice.

Planter's Punch is a universally popular drink, which can be served cold or hot.

Planter's Punch

Rum
Sugar
Unsweetened lime or lemon juice
Angostura bitters or Grenadine
Soda water
One orange

The basic rule of thumb for making this drink is to mix 1 part of lime juice to 2 parts of sugar and 3 parts of rum. Add a dash of Angostura bitters or Grenadine to taste.

When serving cold, top up with ice and 4 parts of soda water. Garnish the glasses with orange slices. To serve hot, omit the ice and soda and top up with hot water. See also SOFT DRINKS; TODDIES.

Driving in bad weather

How to avoid trouble in fog, snow and on wet or icy roads

The first rule when you have to drive in bad weather is to slow down.

In fog Drive on foglights or dipped headlights, night or day. It is compulsory to switch on sidelights and either dipped headlights or a pair of foglights whenever visibility is bad. Switch on windscreen wipers and demisters. If your car has high-intensity rear lights, switch them on. Open the driver's window so that you can hear what is going on.

Do not try to overtake a car ahead – stay well back, so that if it stops suddenly you have time to pull up safely. Remember that at only 20mph your stopping distance is about 12m (40ft) on a dry road.

Do not rely on the car in front to lead you – follow your own course using the kerb and road markings as a guide. In town, watch for parked cars. If you have to stop, try to park off the road; switch on your four flashing hazard lights if you are forced to stop on a dual carriageway or motorway hard shoulder. See also MOTORWAY DRIVING.

In snow In heavy snow, observe the same rules as for fog, but stay in as high a gear as possible, to counter wheel spin.

Try to keep moving; if you have to stop, decelerate gently, brake gently and change gear slowly and smoothly. A sudden change in speed through heavy braking or harsh gear changing may cause the wheels to lock and skid – see SKIDS.

Avoid accelerating when the front wheels are not pointing straight ahead, which could provoke a rear-wheel slide. Do not try to steer while braking, which will cause a front-wheel skid.

Moving off in snow, use second gear and pull away slowly, smoothly and gently. If the wheels start to spin, ease off the accelerator and let the car roll forward a little, or backward on a slope, before accelerating again.

Stuck in snow If wheelspin prevents you starting off in snow, pack something behind the driving wheels – gravel or sacking, for example. In winter, carry a shovel and sacking in the boot.

Make sure the front wheels are as straight as possible, select second gear and drive forward gently. Do not use reverse gear unless you have to – this very low gear may provoke wheelspin. Once the car is on the move, do not stop until you are on firm ground.

In the wet Stopping distances on a wet road are twice those on a dry one. Take special care when the roads are wet after a long, dry spell – oil and rubber dust can combine with water to make the surface treacherous.

Make sure your TYRES are in good condition and correctly inflated. At high speeds tyres with a deep tread will stop a car in half the distance taken by tyres with tread depths at the 1mm legal limit.

In heavy rain, speeds above 35mph can cause aquaplaning, when tyre treads cannot disperse the water quickly enough, so the car rides on a cushion of water, losing all adhesion to the road. If this occurs, take your foot off the accelerator and hold the steering as straight as possible. *Do not touch the brakes.* When the tyres grip, continue at reduced speed.

On ice Extra vigilance is needed during freezing conditions because ice can form in patches and is not always easily spotted. So-called 'black ice' is particularly dangerous. It forms when rain freezes as it hits the ground, but there is no apparent change in the appearance of the road.

Drug overdose

Treating in an emergency

An overdose of drugs of any kind requires medical attention. Depending on the drug involved and the amount taken, symptoms may range from dizziness (sometimes with slurred speech) to outright collapse.

If breathing has stopped and there is no pulse, you must start resuscitation at once: make sure that the victim's airway is clear, use ARTIFICIAL RESPIRATION and, if you are trained in first aid, EXTERNAL CHEST COMPRESSION. If the casualty is unconscious but still breathing, turn him or her into the RECOVERY POSITION.

In either case, get someone to telephone 999 and ask for an ambulance as soon as possible. Save any pills, medicine bottles or containers, together with any vomited matter, to help the doctor identify the drug.

Even if the casualty is conscious and seems to be recovering, you should still seek medical aid, otherwise his condition may worsen later on. Ask him about the drug so that you can tell the doctor if the victim loses consciousness.

WARNING Do not try to induce vomiting in someone with a drug overdose. It may be harmful.

See also DRUG RECOGNITION.

Drug recognition

Telltale signs of drug abuse

Symptoms of drug abuse are difficult to recognise at an early stage, because they are barely perceptible. But there are tangible clues to look for if you suspect that someone you live or work alongside is using drugs. They include packets of unlabelled tablets, capsules, powders, seeds, greenish-brown 'tobacco' (which may be cannabis), odd-smelling cigarette stubs, needles and syringes. Smoking herbal cannabis leaves a lingering smell in a room and on furnishings and clothes.

The appearance of a confirmed addict will yield unmistakable clues. Use of stimulants, such as amphetamines and cocaine, brings a pronounced emotional 'high', during which the eye pupils are enlarged. This is followed by a 'hangover' effect, possibly accompanied by a dry cough, peeling lips and excessive thirst.

Many solvents contained in such household products as glues, cleaning fluids, nail-varnish remover and paint thinners have a sedative effect when sniffed, but can also cause hallucinations and sores round the mouth. They are also toxic, and can lead to death.

Sedative drugs, including heroin, morphine and barbiturates, induce symptoms rather like drunkenness – unsteadiness, trembling, confusion and sometimes loss of consciousness. Heroin and morphine make the pupils of the eyes contract.

Cannabis smokers tend to become relaxed and sleepy; sometimes the appetite increases and the eyes become reddened. People taking LSD become hallucinated, causing them to become disorientated and giggle inappropriately, or show signs of terror if they are experiencing nightmarish visions. Ecstasy users may appear calm and serene, but can become agitated if challenged. They may appear clumsy and unco-ordinated.

A pronounced change in behaviour is often the most indicative sign of increasing drug use. The addict may change his style of dressing, and begin to mix with quite different friends. Moodiness is common, also deteriorating performance at school or work, unpunctuality and slack personal hygiene.

If you suspect that your teenage child might be taking drugs, take a soft line and try to establish why. It may only be a passing phase, in which case a quiet talk on the risks he or she is taking may work. But if drug-taking has become a regular habit, get medical advice.

Dry-mounting photographs

Preparing pictures for display

Photographs can be displayed on mounting boards – available from art supply shops – with or without a border. To make a clean edge on both print and mount, place them on a hard, flat surface and cut them to size with a craft knife guided by a steel straightedge.

Although rubber contact adhesive (see GLUING) is the easiest to use, it will, in time, discolour the print. Instead, use dry-mounting tissue available from photographic equipment shops, a thin,

resin-based waxy sheet, which adheres when it is heated, and does not deteriorate even in damp conditions.

Place the photo face down and lay the tissue on top. Set an electric iron at the 'wool' setting and tack the tissue to the back of the photo by touching the centre with the tip of the iron. Experiment first with a disposable photo, so as to find the right temperature.

Trim the tissue to the same size as the photograph. Place the print, face up, on the mounting board then cover it with brown paper. Using the iron set at the correct heat, press down firmly so that the tissue bonds the photograph to the mount.

Ironing does not give such a good result with enlargements bigger than 200 × 250mm (8 × 10in). It would be better to have these mounted professionally.

Dry rot

Avoiding, recognising and repairing it

Dry rot is a fungus that, in time, reduces wood to a flaky mass which crumbles when touched. It is less common than WET ROT, but more serious. It can spread through doors, windows, floorboards, skirtings, joists – in fact, the whole structure. It can travel through brick walls and attack adjoining buildings – and has even been known to attack furniture that has been stored or moved very infrequently, affecting chair and table legs, for example.

The first sign of dry rot may be a musty, mushroom-like smell. Despite its name, dry rot thrives in damp, warm, still conditions. A tiny leak in the PLUMBING system, or a faulty damp-proof course can be the initial cause, providing the moisture on which the fungus thrives. Strands spread from the initial spores and eventually fruiting bodies form, looking like giant pancakes. These release

Spotting dry rot Fine fronds spread through timber and masonry, and grow into discs like dirty cotton wool. The wood they feed on splits along and across the grain.

microscopic spores, like red dust, which can be blown to new areas.

The best protection is to ensure that you have a dry, damp-free, well-ventilated house – see AIR BRICKS; CONDENSATION; DAMP; VENTILATION. But if dry rot is detected it is vital that all traces are immediately eliminated. The British Wood Preserving Association at 150 Southampton Row, London WC1B 5AL, will supply a list of specialist companies, many of whom offer a 20 year guarantee on their work — a good plus point if you decide to sell your house or flat.

If you decide to do the work yourself, remove and burn all affected timber at least 610mm (2ft) and preferably 1m (3ft) beyond the furthest extent of the decay. Treat all timber and masonry within 910mm of the cut-away with a dry-rot fluid, available from most DIY stores. Remove any plaster from the walls near the affected area and brush down with a wire brush. Collect and burn all debris.

Drill masonry in the affected area at regular intervals with downward-sloping holes 13mm ($\frac{1}{2}$in) deep. Funnel in dry rot fluid and allow it to seep through the brickwork. Before fitting new timber, treat it with dry-rot fluid. Finally, paint all surfaces within 1.5m (5ft) of the affected area with fungicidal fluid.

Dusting and cleaning

Labour-saving ways with household chores

The amount of cleaning a house needs can be reduced significantly by a careful choice of furnishings. When furnishing a room, consider how much dusting, cleaning or polishing it will need.

Furniture such as tables, sideboards and wall units offers fewer corners in which dust can collect – if it is simple in shape. For armchairs and settees, choose loose covers in soft, washable furnishing fabrics which can be easily removed and laundered at home. Study the manufacturer's instructions on cleaning before buying; check with the manufacturer or supplier if no instructions are supplied. When adding ornaments to a room, remember that cleaning them, if there are too many, can become a major task. Do as much dusting as possible with vacuum-cleaner attachments. Bed-making is often easier if you use a DUVET.

Hard floors Seal wood and cork floors with a polyurethane sealer, which can then be cleaned using a damp mop.

Carpets Clean with a vacuum cleaner as necessary – heavy traffic areas need daily vacuuming; keep them free of grit because it can cut the pile. Avoid dragging heavy furniture over carpets as this will damage the pile.

Walls Brush high mouldings and picture frames with a cornice brush. Use a vacuum cleaner with a brush attachment, or a cloth-covered brush or broom, to remove cobwebs and dust, working from the bottom up. Wash painted walls, or washable wallpaper, with a sponge wrung out in a mild detergent solution. Clean a small area at a time – about 610mm (2ft) square – and work from the bottom up to avoid streaking; runs of dirty water are much easier to remove from a clean, damp surface than a dry, dirty one. Rinse with cold water, working from the top down. If necessary, scrub gloss paint with a soft brush.

Remove grease stains on wallpaper by rubbing gently with a chunk of dry white bread.

Tiles Wipe aluminium or ceramic tiles with a sponge wrung out in a mild detergent solution. Rinse and dry with a CHAMOIS LEATHER. Clean grouting with an old toothbrush dipped in bleach solution. Make sure that you protect yourself with gloves and avoid splashing bleach onto the surrounding area. Clean mirror tiles with a chamois leather wrung out in vinegar water – use a tablespoon of vinegar to 570ml (1 pint) of lukewarm water.

Clean vinyl and quarry floor tiles with a brush attachment on a vacuum cleaner and wash as necessary – vinyl need only be wiped with a sponge mop wrung in warm, soapy water, then in plain water.

Furniture The wood in much modern furniture is coated with hard-wearing lacquers which only need an occasional wipe with a damp cloth. Greasy marks on antique furniture (see also ANTIQUES) should be removed with a chamois leather wrung out in vinegar water (see **Tiles** above). Repolish the surface with your usual wax polish – never mix polishes.

Pieces which are french polished can be treated in the same way. Use a wax polish occasionally on oak, pine, walnut, beech and elm and waxed mahogany. On teak and afrormosia, use a teak oil or cream twice a year only. Dust or buff otherwise. Clean cane furniture with a vacuum brush attachment. Wash as necessary with warm salt water, but do not over wet. Dry naturally, away from direct heat, or it will warp.

Use a cloth lightly dipped in warm turpentine to clean gilt frames.

Fabrics Most modern upholstery fabrics carry labels recommending cleaning methods. A special padded-head vacuum-cleaner attachment is useful for removing animal hairs. Although many fabrics are stain resistant, a spillage should be mopped up immediately to prevent staining. See also CLEANING AND POLISHING MATERIALS; CLEANING SOLVENTS.

Venetian blinds Drop the blind to its full length and turn the blades until they are as upright as possible, then vacuum clean with a brush attachment. Turn the blades the other way and vacuum the other side. Wash if necessary.

Duvets

Cleaning the quilt and making a cover

Duvets should have removable covers that can be washed regularly. The duvet quilt itself needs occasional cleaning.

Duvets with synthetic fillings such as polyester can be washed according to care label instructions. However, if you are washing the duvet yourself a single duvet is probably just as much as you can cope with.

Have a double duvet washed at a launderette. They should not be cleaned because the filling retains poisonous fumes. Those with natural fillings of down or feathers – or a mixture of the two – should be professionally cleaned.

When washing a duvet in the bath, knead it gently in warm, soapy water, rinse and then squeeze out any liquid. Try not to drag a wet duvet out of the bath without supporting its weight evenly. Spread it out to dry, or hang it over parallel clothes lines or a rotary clothes line. Do not use a tumble dryer or the filling will not stay evenly spread.

Making covers New duvet covers can be made from bed sheets, or lengths of cotton or polyester-cotton sheeting. You need two rectangular pieces of material each 2.11 × 2.13m (6ft 11in × 7ft) to make a cover for a duvet 1.98 × 2.03m (6ft 6in × 6ft 8in) to fit a standard-sized double bed. The cover is made slightly bigger than the duvet for easy fitting.

Place the two pieces of fabric together, right sides facing and edges matching. Pin them together, leaving a central gap of about 1m (3ft) at the bottom end to push in the quilt. Machine-stitch around the cover about 13mm ($\frac{1}{2}$in) from the edge, leaving the opening unstitched.

Turn over the seam allowances round the opening and press flat, then turn the cover right side out and press. Pull apart an appropriate length of Velcro fastening and pin one strip along the inside of each side of the opening. Machine-stitch round each strip close to the edge.

For a firm finish, machine-stitch all round the cover again, except for the opening, in line with the stitches on the inside edge of the Velcro tape.

Instead of using Velcro, you can turn under and stitch the seam allowance at the opening, and sew on four pairs of tapes for tying the gap together or attach PRESS-STUDS.

See also DOWN PILLOWS; EIDERDOWNS.

Dyeing

How to dye; which dye to use for different fabrics

Most articles that can be washed can be dyed at home. You can do the dyeing in a washbasin, sink, bath or washing machine. There are three basic kinds of home dyes: cold-water, multipurpose hot water and wash 'n' dye.

Cold-water dyes Colourfast powder dyes, these are best for natural fibres, and can also be used on viscose rayon and polyester-cotton mixtures. They are particularly suited to BATIK and TIE-DYEING.

Multipurpose hot-water dyes Mix and use these powder dyes strictly according to makers' instructions. They suit most man-made materials – including nylon, acetate and some rayons – as well as natural fibres. Any liquid mixture left over can be stored in an airtight container for about two weeks.

Wash 'n' dye A mixture of dye and detergent, for use in washing machines, these dyes are particularly suited to large articles such as curtains, bedspreads and loose covers. Some dye will remain in the machine's pump, so always rinse the machine on a hot wash setting, with a tablespoon of detergent and a cup of bleach added.

Using dyes Always wear rubber gloves, old clothes and a plastic apron when dyeing, and test a piece of the fabric to see if the dye takes well and produces the colour you want. Note that dyeing will not cover another colour, it will mix with it. For example, a yellow dye used on a blue garment will turn the garment green. You can buy a dye stripper, which will remove the original dye.

Remove stains before dyeing, or they will show through – see CLEANING AND POLISHING MATERIALS; CLEANING SOLVENTS. Scorch marks cannot be covered up by a dye.

Dyes work best on cotton, linen and nylon. On polyester, pale shades are produced and fabrics containing polyester and nylon mixtures emerge with a two-tone effect. Wool can be dyed by following closely the dye manufacturer's instructions, but never dye wool in a washing machine, as the material will probably shrink.

Fabrics that cannot be dyed at home include acrylic, angora, camel, cashmere, glass fibre and mohair. And fabrics with a special finish – such as drip-dry cottons and showerproof raincoats – should not be dyed as the finish will be spoilt.

WARNING Do not wash home-dyed articles in biological washing powder – the colour will come out.

E

Earache

*What to do about them at home;
when to see a doctor*

Severe earache is usually a sign of ear infection, particularly in children. Infections of the middle ear (behind the eardrum) are very common among children under ten, especially during winter, and may be associated with a cold, cough or fever. With adults the condition is rarer. The pain is caused by inflammation of the eardrum and a vacuum in the middle ear. A baby may keep crying and rubbing its ear lobe.

Let the sufferer rest, and to ease pain, give painkillers in the recommended dosage. Cool drinks will help reduce temperature, and replace body fluids lost through fever. Do not probe the ear, and do not use eardrops unless they are prescribed by a doctor.

When to get medical help Consult a doctor if earache persists despite the use of painkillers, such as paracetamol, or if a child is feverish and crying inconsolably.

Earhole infections An infection of the outer-ear canal may result in pain and discharge, either from a scratch or burst boil or from a more general infection. The condition is sometimes known as 'swimmer's ear' because ear infections are often contracted while swimming.

Get the infection treated by a doctor within 48 hours. Meanwhile, proprietary painkillers should give relief. Do not allow the infected ear to get wet and do not probe it.

QUICK TIP To help prevent infection, place two or three drops of olive oil in the ears before swimming. See also RINGING IN THE EARS.

Ears

*Care, protection and the removal
of foreign bodies*

Keeping your ears clean should not extend to removing the moist wax produced by small glands in the outer-ear canal – it protects delicate ear tissue from infection. If impacted wax causes deafness or a congested feeling in the ear, get the ear syringed by your doctor.

To clear impacted wax, it may help to place two or three drops of a softening agent (from chemists) or olive oil in the ear at night, keeping it in with a plug of cotton wool. Put olive oil in the ears for at least three consecutive days before having them syringed.

Protecting your hearing Some loss of hearing may accompany ageing in a natural way, and cannot be prevented. What can be avoided is deafness caused by exposure to loud noise. A noisy workplace, over-amplified rock music and the noise of gunfire when shooting can all injure the ears. Wear ear protectors – muffs (resembling earphones) are better than earplugs – when there is any risk to your hearing. Have a hearing test at least once a year if you work in noisy surroundings.

Removing a foreign body This is a job for a doctor. Never probe inside the ear to extract anything stuck in the ear canal – you are likely to do further damage. If you have anything lodged in your ear, or suspect that a child may have, get medical help at once.

WARNING Do not try to clean wax or anything else from the ear canal with cotton-wool buds. You risk pushing the wax – and possibly shreds of cotton wool – deeper into the ear. Cotton buds are intended for gently cleaning the outer ear.

Earthenware

*Repairing broken pots, vases or
ornaments*

Broken garden pots or ornamental earthenware can be mended with an epoxy adhesive – the type made up of a hardener and a resin for mixing just before application – to give a water-resistant repair – see GLUING.

Preparation Thoroughly scrub all the exposed edges with an abrasive powder, rinse clean and allow to dry. Damp earthenware should be given two days in a warm room to dry out completely – the adhesive will not work on a wet or soiled surface.

Before gluing, reassemble the article as best you can, placing all the pieces together in the most workable sequence. If there are several pieces, number them with chalk to show the right order for assembly.

Gluing Mix adhesive as directed and spread on both edges. Force the glue into the porous surfaces using an applicator or a sharpened stick such as an ice-lolly stick. Make the join and keep the pieces together with masking tape. Where there are several joins to make, glue each piece and allow it to set before adding the next one – a prolonged process as epoxies may take several hours to harden.

Earthenware cooking pots and crockery are unhygienic after repair, because chipped glaze will admit food particles to the porous material beneath, risking a build-up of germs. They can, however, be used as vases or plant pots.

Earthquakes

*What to do during an earth tremor
and in the aftermath*

Areas where there are most likely to be earthquakes include southern Europe, central and South-east Asia, Japan and the Pacific coasts of both North and South America. But nowhere can be guaranteed safe. Two earthquakes in Britain shook large areas of central Wales and the Midlands in April and May 1984.

Indoors When a quake begins, move away from windows, ceiling lights, mirrors and tall furniture. In built-up areas you are safer indoors than out, ideally under a sturdy desk, bed or table, or in a doorway – the frame gives extra protection. Stay away from the exits and lifts in a tall building.

Outdoors Move away from anything tall that might fall, such as buildings, pylons and trees. If you cannot find an open area, shelter in a doorway – but not in a basement or other underground structure which might collapse or be sealed off by rubble.

In a car Stop, and lie on the floor of the car, keeping as low as possible. An earthquake may involve a number of tremors at irregular intervals. Stay where you are until you hear an all-clear from the rescue services, or a radio broadcast.

Aftermath Following a serious quake, listen to the radio or TV for instructions; use the telephone only for emergencies – leave lines clear for rescue services. If you smell gas, turn it off at the meter or cylinder, open windows and leave. If the water is cut off, you may have a limited supply in the cold tank and hot-water cylinder if they are undamaged, but boil before drinking. Do not flush toilets until you know sewage pipes are intact. Stand to one side as you open cupboards, in case the contents fall out. Check your own home for structural damage. Stay clear of any structures that might be weakened and could suddenly collapse.

If you are on holiday, contact the nearest British Consul for advice on how to leave the area. Drink only boiled or bottled water.

Earwigs

Combating a garden pest

Earwigs feed at night, making ragged holes in the leaves and flower heads of chrysanthemums, clematis and DAHLIAS. They also attack vegetables such as cucumbers and TOMATOES. They are especially active in greenhouses and occasionally enter houses.

You can trap the earwigs with straw-filled, inverted flower pots left overnight on the ground near infested plants. Shake the pots out each morning over a bowl of hot water to kill the earwigs.

Protect plants by dusting or spraying with trichlorphon – see PESTICIDES. Clear away garden rubbish regularly, as earwigs use it for shelter.

Eczema

Coping with – and avoiding – a common skin problem

There are several types of this common skin complaint, also called dermatitis. All are characterised by ITCHING, reddening and swelling leading to blisters that weep, sometimes becoming infected, and leaving the skin with a crusty, scaly appearance. See also ALLERGIES.

Some 90 per cent of eczema cases first appear during babyhood, and half have cleared up by the age of two. Only a small number of cases afflict people into adulthood.

Causes and treatment Doctors are not certain what triggers many cases. But one type, contact eczema, may be caused by contact with chemicals, detergents, dyes, jewellery containing nickel and even garden plants. Cosmetics and deodorants can cause eczema on the face and body. Contact eczema clears up if the irritant is identified and avoided. Where the cause is elusive, a doctor may arrange skin tests to establish the culprit.

Another type of eczema is atopic eczema, commonest in children, which often runs in families with a history of hay fever or asthma. Chronic atopic eczema may be prevented by avoiding, if possible, things that exacerbate it – such as cold, windy weather and emotional stress. Do not wear wool next to the skin. Keep your bedroom as dust free as you can and do not use feather pillows or duvets.

Early stages may be relieved by moisturising cream. Doctors usually treat later stages with steroids. Sufferers find it difficult not to scratch the affected areas, but this aggravates the symptoms, and causes infection and bleeding.

The National Eczema Society, 4 Tavistock Place, London WC1H 9RA, can give more information.

Efflorescence

Dealing with white stains on exterior and interior walls

White, salt-like, powdery crystals, known as efflorescence, can stain new brickwork, stonework or plaster. The salts rise to the surface as the material dries out. Efflorescence may occur on old masonry if it is damp.

Removing Do not decorate over efflorescence, as it will mar paintwork or wallcoverings, and do not try to wash it off – this will make it worse. Brush it off regularly with a dry, stiff-bristled brush – not a wire brush. Alternatively, use a chemical masonry cleaner, available from most builders' merchants.

Preventing Efflorescence disappears once the wall is dry. If it does not do so, treat the wall for DAMP. If the wall is to be decorated, apply an alkali-resisting primer before using oil-based paint – see PAINTS.

To discourage efflorescence on brick or stonework, coat the wall with a silicone water repellent, which will keep out damp.

Egg decorating

Dyeing and painting eggs

You can decorate eggs before you eat them – to add colour to Easter festivities, for example. Or you can make a pinhole at each end, blow the contents into a bowl, and decorate the shells to keep as ornaments (see illustration).

For colourful soft-boiled eggs, use white-shelled eggs and add food colouring – blue, green, red and yellow are available – to the cooking water. Also add two tablespoons of vinegar – it makes the colour adhere better.

If you boil an egg in plain water with an onion skin added, the shell will be coloured a rich yellow. Or put some petals, a small flat flowerhead or a ferny leaf against the shell, tie onion skin round it and parcel the lot in white cloth. The imprint of the flower or leaf will be pale against a golden shell.

Designer eggs Use hard-boiled eggs (cooled immediately under cold running water to avoid yolk discoloration,) to make more elaborate, multicoloured patterns by a method similar to BATIK.

You need a range of vegetable dyes, a fine paintbrush or a needle, and either melted beeswax or candle wax – or use a white wax crayon. Dip the brush or needle into the melted wax, or use the crayon, and mark on the shell the part of your design that is to be white.

Always immerse the egg first into the palest dye you intend to use – such as yellow. Turn it to give an even coating and allow it five minutes or more to take on the depth of colour you want. Leave this coating to dry.

Next, wax over the areas you want to keep in the first pale colour, then immerse in the second dye, and so on, using the dyes in sequence lightest to darkest.

Finally, place the egg in a warm oven, with the door open, until the wax starts to look shiny. Take the egg out and carefully wipe away the wax with a paper towel.

EGG DECORATING

How to make eggs into ornaments

Preparing First dye the eggs with a background colour by dipping them in a cold-water dye, with two tablespoons of vinegar added. Leave to dry, then blow.

Colouring Paint a design on the shell with acrylic paint or inks. When it is dry, finish the surface with clear varnish.

Eggs

Storing fresh, cooking them just right – and washing up afterwards

An egg box is stamped with the packing date – the week number of the year. Eggs stored in a cool larder should stay fresh for a fortnight. In a refrigerator they can keep for up to eight weeks. Take eggs out of the refrigerator at least 45 minutes before cooking.

Keep separated eggs in a refrigerator in covered containers. Yolks, protected by a covering of water or milk, will keep up to four days; whites up to a week.

Freshness test A fresh egg put in cold water will sink and settle on its side; a less fresh one will sink but stay upright. An egg that floats is past its best – and may be rotten.

Boiled eggs Pierce the larger end of each egg with a pin or an egg piercer. The pocket of air in the large end swells during cooking, but escapes through the pinhole instead of bursting the shell. If eggs do crack, add a little vinegar to the water; if egg white appears, add a teaspoon of salt.

Fill a saucepan with enough cold water to cover the eggs, bring to the boil, then lower the heat to a simmer – or the eggs will be tough. Simmering times are:

Size 5 (Medium)	Sizes 3-4 (Standard)	Size 2 (Large)
Soft-boiled (runny yolk)		
2¼ min	2½ min	3 min
Medium-boiled (soft yolk)		
3½ min	4 min	4½ min
Hard-boiled (solid yolk)		
6 min	7 min	8 min

Immediately you have taken an egg out, crack an end with the back of a spoon to stop it continuing to cook in its own heat. A hard-boiled egg should be plunged into cold water to cool it quickly. To peel a hard-boiled egg, tap round its centre to crack the shell then pull off the half shells.

Fried eggs Heat about a tablespoon of fat for each egg in a frying pan over medium heat; use butter, oil, bacon fat, lard, or a mixture. Break the eggs one at a time into a cup and slide each into the hot fat. Cook until the white sets, basting with a spoon.

Poached eggs Half fill a shallow pan with water and add a teaspoon of vinegar or a pinch of salt. Bring to a simmer. Break each egg into a cup. Stir the water to create a whirlpool and gently slip the egg into it. Cook until the white sets. Lift out with a perforated spoon.

An 'egg poacher' steams rather than poaches eggs, in individual containers which are suspended over simmering water that should half fill the pan base. Butter the containers, break an egg into each container, put on the lid and cook the eggs for about two minutes, or until the whites have set.

Scrambled eggs Allow two eggs per person. Adding a tablespoon of milk per egg, mix in a bowl and season to taste. Melt about 15g (½oz) butter per egg in a heavy saucepan over a medium heat and add the beaten eggs. Stir continuously until the eggs are thick and creamy. Serve immediately or the eggs will continue to cook and solidify. See also OMELETTES.

Washing up Use tepid water to clean off congealed egg. Hot water will harden it and make it difficult to remove.

Egg separating

Dividing the white from the yolk

Work over a bowl. Break the egg across its centre by tapping it sharply either with a knife or on the rim of the bowl. Hold the egg upright and lift off the top half of the shell. Most of the white will run into the bowl and the yolk will stay in the lower half of the shell. Slide the yolk from one half of the shell to the other until all the white has run into the bowl. Now you can slip the yolk into a separate bowl.

Alternatively, break the egg into an egg separator set on a cup. The yolk will be held by the central bowl; the white passes through slits round it.

Do not let the shell edge pierce the yolk as it slides from one half to the other. Use the edge to free clinging egg white.

Eiderdowns

Cleaning and storing

An eiderdown is a very thick quilt intended for use over a sheet and blankets, with a bedspread over or under it. Eiderdowns are not to be confused with DUVETS.

Cleaning The covering may be of natural fabric such as cotton, or it may be synthetic. Fillings are either of natural feather-down mixtures or polyester. An eiderdown with natural filling must be dry-cleaned. Before putting it back on the bed, air thoroughly for several days to get rid of the cleaning-solvent fumes. Eiderdowns with synthetic filling are mostly washable – follow the label instructions. The eiderdown can be tumble-dried, hung over parallel lines or spread on clean sheeting to dry flat. Do not spin-dry or wring out by hand as you will weaken the QUILTING stitches.

Storing Roll the eiderdown up in a clean sheet and store it in a dry place. Do not wrap it in plastic because this prevents air circulation and can lead to mildew. Air the eiderdown thoroughly before use by draping it over a washing line in fresh windy weather.

Repairs If a number of quilting stitches need renewing, use a quilting loop if possible. This stretches tight the part of the eiderdown you want to repair and gives easy access between the stitches.

Electric blankets

Choosing, using safely and faultfinding

The electric blankets in use in Britain are of three main types:

Electric underblankets These are usually for preheating the bed, and must be switched off before you get in. All these types are laid over the mattress and tied securely to it, to prevent them from creasing.

Electric overblankets These resemble conventional blankets in appearance and weight, but the central part contains heating elements; the areas round the perimeter, which tuck under the mattress, are not wired. The blankets have graduated heat settings and thermostatic controls, and can be left on through the night. There are similarly equipped electric DUVETS.

Electric pads These are small electric blankets, inside a washable cover. They can be folded or bent around a limb to give heat relief from pain, or placed in the lap and used in a similar way as a hot water bottle in bed or in a chair.

Be careful to place the flex where no one will trip over it.

Safety: Do's and don'ts
Do store the blanket in a dry place, laid flat or rolled to stop it from creasing.
Do follow the manufacturer's instructions in every detail.

Do check regularly for signs of wear, scorching or uneven spacing between heating wires. You can do this by examining the blanket with a bright light behind it.

Don't pin a blanket or anything else to the mattress.

Don't use when creased or folded.

Don't use with an adaptor for plugging in more than one appliance – it could be switched on accidentally.

Don't buy a secondhand blanket.

Don't dry-clean. Washable blankets should be laundered according to the manufacturer's instructions.

Don't switch on the blanket while it is wet. Dry by spreading over a drying rail. A spin dryer may be used, but not a tumble dryer as this may damage or displace the wires.

Faultfinding If the blanket fails to heat, check the socket outlet by plugging a working appliance into it – see ELECTRIC SOCKETS AND SWITCHES. If the socket is working, check that the plug connections are firm – see PLUGS. If they are, replace the fuse in the plug – see FUSES AND FUSE BOXES. If this does not remedy the fault, return the blanket to the manufacturer.

Never try to repair an electric blanket yourself.

Electric shock

Rescuing and treating a shocked victim

An electric shock can kill or cause a large number of injuries, including severe BURNS and asphyxiation – see CHOKING; LIGHTNING.

Never touch an electric shock victim directly until the power has been turned off. If you do, the current may pass through you as well.

If someone receives an electric shock at home or at work, turn off the main switch at the consumer unit (see FUSES AND FUSE BOXES) if you know where it is and can get at it. Otherwise, switch off at the socket and pull out the plug if it is accessible. Do not use the switch on the appliance, as a faulty switch could be the cause of the trouble.

If you cannot turn off the power at once, push or pull the victim away from the current with a non-conducting material such as a long, thick piece of dry wood – a broom handle, for example. Stand on a dry rubber mat or a pile of newspapers as you do so. Do not touch the victim with your hands. Never use anything damp, wet or made of metal. If you are in the garden, do not stand on the ground but on a dry board or other safe surface.

Once the contact with the electricity is broken, dial 999 for an ambulance if the casualty is or has been unconscious or is burnt or feels unwell. If the breathing or heartbeat has stopped, give ARTIFICIAL RESPIRATION; if you are trained to do so apply EXTERNAL CHEST COMPRESSION as necessary. Then move the casualty into the RECOVERY POSITION.

After treating them, cover any burns with a clean dry cotton sheet or handkerchief until medical help arrives.

If the accident involves high-voltage supply cables or a railway line, call the emergency number displayed on the

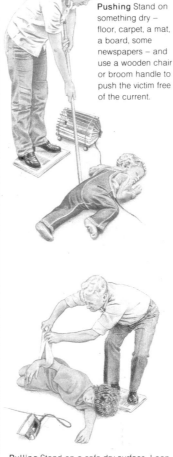

ELECTRIC SHOCK

Action to take to save a victim

Act swiftly to save a victim of electric shock. Switch off the power or push or pull the victim free without touching him.

Pushing Stand on something dry – floor, carpet, a mat, a board, some newspapers – and use a wooden chair or broom handle to push the victim free of the current.

Pulling Stand on a safe dry surface. Loop or wind a dry rope, towel, scarf, or pair of tights round the victim's arm or foot without making direct contact. Pull the casualty free of the electric current.

pylon or substation or in the railway station; or dial 999 for the police. Call for an ambulance while you wait for the power to be turned off. The casualty will need quick medical treatment.

Keep at least 18m (20yds)) away from fallen high-voltage cables. They could be damaged and electricity from them may be conducted over a wide area by wet ground or moist air.

Electric slow cookers

Using and caring for them

The plug-in cooker is in effect a ceramic CASSEROLE with a built-in heating element. It cooks food at comparatively low temperatures, without loss of liquid, flavour or nutrients. The pot needs a 13amp plug fitted with a 3amp fuse. Its electricity consumption is low – 80-170 watts an hour. Most foods take 8-12 hours to cook; they never reach boiling point but the temperature is high enough to make them safe by killing bacteria. The pot has either a simple on/off control or a high/low setting. Some models automatically switch to the low setting after a certain time.

You can leave the pot cooking unattended while you are at work, to provide a hot evening meal. It is suitable for stews, pot roasts, SOUPS AND STOCKS as well as patés (see PATÉ) and terrines. The slow process also works well for custards, SAUCES, poached fruit and steamed puddings.

Techniques A recipe book is provided with the cooker because slow-cooking methods can differ from conventional techniques. For example, vegetables need more time than meats. Most recipes include liquid to conduct the heat to the ingredients, but the amount may be smaller than in oven cooking because there is no evaporation. The long cooking intensifies natural flavours, so seasoning should be only light. A slow cooker will not brown meat or vegetables but this can be done first in a FRYING pan.

Care and cleaning Do not leave food to cool in a slow cooker. Transfer it to another container and when it is cold, put it in the refrigerator.

WARNING Never immerse the cooker in water. Wipe the casing with a damp cloth. Fill the pot with hot water, rub it with a nylon scrubber then empty it and wipe it dry. The pot in some models can be removed from the casing for serving from or when washing up.

On the whole, slow cookers are easy to clean because the low temperature cooking means that food does not bake onto the inner surface of the pot.

Checking connections

Do not examine a socket (or a light switch) until you have turned off the mains and removed the circuit fuse. Use insulated screwdrivers with blade tips to suit the screw size.

Releasing Remove the mounting screws and ease the socket away from its mounting box until you can see the terminals on the back of the socket.

Checking Pull gently on each of the wires. If any can move, tighten the terminal screw. If a single wire comes loose, release all the wires at that terminal. Re-insert them all together and tighten the screw firmly.

Positioning Put sockets 150mm (6in) or more above a floor or work surface to be safe from knocks and avoid bending a plug-flex sharply.

Electric sockets and switches

Inspecting, removing and fitting new

If a socket feels warm or if an appliance plugged into it does not work, but works in another socket, check that the faulty socket is properly connected.

If a socket is cracked or broken, replace it as soon as possible and do not use it in the meantime. Electric shock or a fire could be caused by something making contact with the wiring inside.

If the damaged socket is a single one, you may decide to replace it with a double one. No extra wiring is needed but you will have to fit a double mounting box. There are kits designed to fit over a single box and convert it to a double socket, but these protrude from the wall. Check with a spirit level that the new box is horizontal before you fix it.

If the box is in the skirting board, use a mallet and chisel to enlarge it – see CHISELLING. You will probably also have to cut into plaster and masonry behind it. Do this as for a box in a wall.

If the box is to be recessed in the plasterboard of a stud partition wall (see PARTITIONS), you need a mounting box with lugs to grip the plasterboard.

Fitting a new socket or switch

Turn off the main switch at the consumer unit or fuse box and remove the fuse for the circuit you want to work on. Unscrew the socket or switch from its mounting box and release the conductors from the terminals on its back.

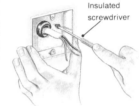

Insulated screwdriver

Old mounting box To fit a double socket in place of a single you will have to fit a larger box. Take out the screws holding the back of the box to the wall. Ease out the box.

Drill holes

Wall cavity Pencil around the new box. Drill holes along the lines – see MASONRY DRILLING. Use a club hammer and chisel to cut out plaster and masonry to the required depth.

Plasterboard

Sprung lug

Box in plasterboard Enlarge the hole with a hacksaw. Use a plastic box with sprung lugs. Feed in the cables (no grommets are needed) and fit the box with lugs held inwards. Release them to grip the plasterboard between box rim and lugs.

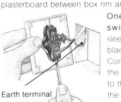

Earth terminal in box

One-way light switch Put red sleeving on the black conductor. Connect this and the original red wire to the terminals on the back of the switch.

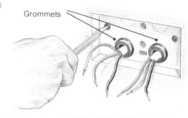

Grommets

Box in masonry Mark, drill and plug holes for screwing the box to the back of the cavity. Fit grommets in the most convenient entry holes in the box, feed in the cables and screw the box firmly into the cavity.

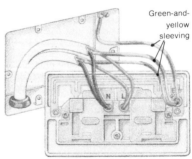

Green-and-yellow sleeving

Connecting the socket Match the wires – red with red, black with black, and green-and-yellow with green-and-yellow. Insert the red wire tips together into the terminal marked L and screw them down firmly. Connect black to N and green-and-yellow to E or ⏚. Screw the socket to the mounting box until the two just meet.

For a surface-fitted mounting box, drill and plug the wall to receive the fixing screws – see MASONRY DRILLING. Use toggled wall plugs in plasterboard – see WALL FASTENINGS. Knock out the most convenient entry hole. Feed in the cables and screw the box firmly in place.

Connecting the socket If the tips of the conductor wires are blackened or broken, cut them off and prepare the cable again, stripping off about 16mm (⅝in) of the insulation. Use a sharp knife to cut off some of the outer sheathing if necessary to allow the conductor wires to reach the terminals comfortably – but take care not to nick the insulation. If any earth conductor wires are bare, cover them with green-and-yellow plastic sleeving, leaving 16mm bare at the tip.

There will be one, two or three cables entering the box. Match together the tips of the conductor wires but do not twist them together before connecting them to the correct terminals, as shown. When you screw the socket in place, do not dislodge or pinch the wiring; and do not overtighten screws – the socket may crack.

Replace the circuit fuse and turn the main switch back on. If you need an extra socket at another position, you can add one on a spur – see SPUR CONNECTIONS.

Light switches Replace a cracked switch at once to prevent anyone from touching the wires, and to prevent damp from getting in and perhaps making normally safe parts live. You might want to replace a sound switch with one of a different style – for example, a rocker switch, a brass switch to match other fittings, or a DIMMER SWITCH. Do not fit a metal switch unless the lighting cable has an earth conductor wire. When replacing a switch on a two-way system, be sure the new switch is also two-way.

Before unscrewing the switch plate, you must turn off at the mains and remove the circuit fuse – see FUSES AND FUSE BOXES. Unscrew the switch plate, ease it away from the wall and note which terminal each wire goes to.

There is no need to release the earth conductor from its terminal in the mounting box. Connect the new switch in the same way as the old one. Screw the switch plate in place, replace the circuit fuse, and turn the main switch back on.

Electric wiring

*Recognising, connecting and
replacing cables and flexes*

Cable is used for the permanently fixed wiring in a house. It carries power from the consumer unit (see FUSES AND FUSE BOXES) to ceiling lights; ELECTRIC SOCKETS AND SWITCHES and FUSED CONNECTION UNITS. Cable can be routed in the wall

plaster, run between the PLASTERBOARD faces of PARTITIONS, hidden under floorboards or above the ceiling. Cable can be fixed along the surface of a wall or ceiling and concealed by plastic trunking. When fitting cable, route it above a ceiling or below floor level, then take it in conduit vertically to a switch or socket.

Never route cable across a wall midway up, or take it diagonally across; there is a danger of piercing it if you hang a picture or drill the wall to screw a fixture to it. Before fixing anything to a wall, check it thoroughly with a metal and wiring detector.

Cable should be held in place about every 250mm (10in) along the route. You can secure it with cable clips. Use cable clips also where the cable runs alongside JOISTS; fix the cable 50mm (2in) below the top of the joist. Where cable runs at right angles to joists, feed it through holes drilled through them 50mm below the top. Within stud partition walls, cut notches in the timber framework to receive the cable and secure it in them with clips. Where cables are run in walls, always use plastic conduit.

Cables of different sizes are used for the various household circuits, depen-

---

ELECTRIC WIRING

Where the cables and flexes go

Mark the fuse carriers in the consumer unit to show which circuit each fuse protects. Separate circuits run from the unit to supply upstairs and downstairs lights and sockets. Many homes have additional circuits – for example for an electric cooker or a shower heater unit.

● **Lighting circuit** It links a chain of ceiling roses (and perhaps junction boxes) and ends at the last one. Cables branch off it to switches.

● **Single appliance circuit** An appliance that is a large user of electricity has its own circuit. It could overload a shared circuit.

● **Ring circuit** Sockets are on a circuit that starts from and returns to the consumer unit.

Two-core flex You can use flex without an earth conductor only for double-insulated appliances and non-metal light fittings.

Three-core flex For most appliances fit flex with an earth conductor, choosing the right conductor size and type of sheath.

Fitting new flex Uncover the terminals. Feed in the flex, prepare its end and connect blue to N, brown to L, green-and-yellow to E or ⏚

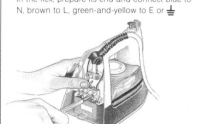

Two-core-and-earth cable Most cable has three wires in an oval sheath. Use the correct cable size for each circuit.

Two-way switch cable For a light to turn on and off at two places use three-core-and-earth cable; its colours are distinctive.

Extending a flex Use a purpose-made connector to suit the flex size. Connect the earths at the centre, both browns on one side and both blues on the other.

ding on how much current they have to carry; the size is given in square millimetres.

A lighting circuit is wired with 1mm² twin core and earth cable and protected by a 5amp fuse. The circuit can supply a maximum of 1200 watts at one time.

A ring circuit (or ring main) is wired with 2.5mm² twin-core-and-earth cable. It can be connected to any number of sockets or fused connection units, but the cable length should not exceed 80m (90yds); generally a floor area up to 100m (120yds) can be served safely by one ring circuit.

The circuit is protected by a 30amp fuse and can supply a maximum of 7200 watts at one time. SPUR CONNECTIONS can be added on cable branching off the ring.

In older homes, sockets are supplied by radial circuits – separate cables run from fuse boxes to individual sockets. They are safe provided the cable is sound, but you cannot add spur sockets.

Appliances using large amounts of electricity frequently should have their own individual circuits. A cooker up to 13kW needs 6mm² cable and a 30amp fuse; above 13kW it needs 10mm² cable and a 45amp fuse. A shower circuit up to 13m (14yds) long needs 6mm² cable and a 30amp fuse; a longer cable run needs 10mm² cable. An immersion heater needs 2.5mm² cable and a 20amp fuse. All these cables must contain an earth wire.

When to replace cable Round-pin sockets supplied by cable made of rubber-insulated conductor wires sheathed in rubber or lead, or run in metal tubing (conduit), indicate that your wiring is 40 years or more old. The rubber will probably be brittle by now, and may crumble, exposing the wires. Even if the sockets are 13amp square-pin ones, check that they have not simply been connected to old cables. These cables should be replaced as soon as possible.

Round bakelite or brass light switches mounted on wooden blocks are also signs of 40-year-old wiring that should be replaced as soon as possible.

Radial socket circuits need replacing only if the cables are of the old type. Modern twin-core-and-earth PVC-sheathed cable installed as a radial system is quite safe.

To find out if your wiring is radial, turn off the main switch and look inside an old socket in a living room. If only one cable enters the socket, the wiring may be radial. Examine the two sockets nearest the first, one on either side of it. If each of these also has only one cable entering, the wiring system is radial.

Flex This connects an appliance or light to a circuit. The connection may be made with a plug and socket, a fused connection unit, or – for fixed lights – a CEILING ROSE. Most appliances – irons, toasters,

washing machines, for example – are sold with flex already wired into them; others – such as kettles, tape recorders, sewing machines – have a flex with a push-in connector to insert into the appliance. However, the flex for a pendant light has to be connected to the lampholder – see LIGHT FIXTURES.

The conductor wires in flex consist of many fine strands to give the required flexibility. The greater the current carried, the thicker the wire must be and the more strands it contains. Sheathing depends on how hot the wires become – some can take up to 60°C (140°F), others up to 85°C (185°F). The sheathing may be PVC or rubber with a fabric outer cover. The rubber type is for appliances which themselves become hot and could damage PVC – irons and kettles, for example. Electrical supplies shops have charts showing exactly what a given appliance requires.

Preparing flex for connection Use a sharp knife to slit the outer sheathing lengthwise. Take care not to nick the insulation on the wires inside. Peel back the sheathing and trim off enough to let them reach the terminals easily. Now use a wire stripper to remove the insulation from about 16mm (⅝in) at the end of each wire. Gently twist the tip of each bared wire. Wind insulating tape around a cut in fabric sheathing, to prevent fraying.

Extending a flex Never lengthen flex by simply twisting wires together and wrapping insulating tape around the join. Use a purpose-made connector, either fixed or detachable. Buy one of the right amperage for the flex. In a detachable connector, fit the half with pins to the appliance flex, and the half with the holes to the flex from the power source.

Embroidery

Learning some basic techniques

Embroidery is done with a variety of stitches and may be used as decoration, to outline designs, or fill in solid areas. For example, backstitch is a small, straight stitch used for outlines, or as a base line for decorative stitches; blanket stitch, which is a linked L-shaped stitch, is used for finishing edges; chain stitch, which is formed by linked loops, is suitable for outlining or filling; cross stitch, an X-shaped stitch, is used for borders, outlining or filling in; and stem stitch is used for forming stems in floral designs and for outlines along curves.

When sewing, secure the fabric in a hoop or frame to keep it taut, but make sure the weave is not pulled askew. Do not work with more than 510mm (20in) of thread, to avoid fraying and knotting.

Making five basic stitches

The following are commonly used stitches; sew each in the sequence illustrated and following the numbered order of needle insertion. Use an embroidery hoop gripping the fabric between the rings.

Backstitch Bring the needle out at 1, insert it at 2 and pull it out at 3.

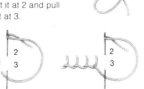

Blanket stitch Bring the needle out at 1, insert it at 2 and pull it out at 3, looping the thread under the needle.

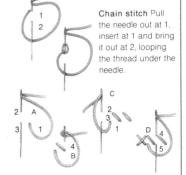

Chain stitch Pull the needle out at 1, insert at 1 and bring it out at 2, looping the thread under the needle.

Cross stitch Bring the needle out at 1, insert it at 2, pull through at 3 and insert at 4 (as for A and B). Alternatively, bring the needle out at 1, insert at 2, pull out at 3 and continue. On the return row insert at 4 and pull out at 5 (as for C and D).

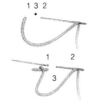

Stem stitch Bring the needle out at 1, insert at 2 and pull it out at 3, half a stitch's length between 1 and 2. Repeat.

To secure each thread at the start, hold the end along the reverse side of the fabric and stitch over it for a length of 50mm (2in). To finish off the thread, slide the needle under 50mm of stitching on the reverse side; never make a knot.

Enamelling

Basic principles of an ancient art

Enamel is powdered glass coloured by metallic oxides, laid over a metal backing and heated. It melts and fuses to the metal, forming a hard, glossy and decorative surface on jewellery and other ornaments.

Materials Enamels (called vitreous enamels) are sold in three forms: transparent, opalescent, and opaque. Transparent enamel includes the basic, colourless enamel known as flux.

All types may be sold either in lumps – for grinding down at home with a jeweller's pestle and mortar – or in coarse, powdered form. There is a wide range of colours, but the colour of the finished product may differ greatly from that of the powder. Test-fire on a sample of the metal backing you intend to use to check the finished colour. You need a liquid binder to bind the enamel to the metal before firing – use a proprietary type or gum tragacanth.

Metals suitable for the backing are 90 per cent pure copper and gilding metal; silver and gold are also used by skilled enamellers. You can buy jewellery blanks and bowls ready for enamelling.

Equipment For most jobs you need a kiln – in effect a small electric oven capable of reaching very high temperatures. A soldering torch can be used, but gives a less satisfactory finish. The kiln should open at the front and have a temperature control and indicator. You will also need racks for supporting the enamelwork during firing, and tools for handling heated items and a heat-proof glove.

A range of fine-meshed sifters is necessary for separating the basic coarse-ground form (usually 60-mesh grade) into the finer grades needed for detailed designs. The finest grade is 600-mesh.

You will need an enamelling shovel – or simply a small spoon – for handling powdered enamels. If you intend to use wet enamels, buy a palette, spatula and fine paintbrushes.

For smoothing the surface of the enamel after final firing you need three carborundum stones – fine, medium and coarse. To restore the glossy finish by hand, use a damp felt buff. There are machines for polishing with a felt buffing wheel. In both cases, the felt should be coated with cerium oxide. All items are sold by craft shops or jewellery suppliers.

ENAMELLING

Fusing decorative powdered glass onto metal

Enamelling involves preparing the metal, applying enamel in ground and decorative layers, each fired at high temperature, and stoning it smooth. Special tools are needed.

Carborundum stones

Wide spatula

Firing kiln

Enamelling shovel

Sifter with handle

Screen firing rack

Firing fork

Tongs for handling hot work

Protective glove

Cutting the backing metal Scribe the shape required. Cut it out with a jeweller's saw, which has a thin blade.

Applying binder Use a wet paintbrush to coat binder on the cleaned metal before enamelling either ground or decorative layers.

Applying enamel Put the enamel powder in a sifter and shake it gently over the binder to form a thick coat. Then fire it.

Finished work

Preparation Cut the backing metal to shape using a jeweller's saw. Clean the metal with emery paper and afterwards 'pickle' it in a nitric acid. Solder on pins or other fixings with enamelling solder, which will withstand the heat of the kiln – see SOLDERING AND BRAZING.

Use the sifting meshes to grade the enamel powders starting with the finest mesh. Shake the powder onto a clean sheet of paper. Pour the powder into a clean bottle for storing and mark the grade on the bottle immediately. Sift the remaining powder through the next-finest mesh, and so on. Tap the sifter against the workbench to clean it between colours.

When heated, the enamel and metal expand at different rates and the metal can warp. To avoid this, fire a coat of enamel on the back of the metal (this is known as counter-enamelling). First paint anti-fire scale on the front to prevent damage; when it is dry coat the edges and back of the metal with binder and sift on 60-mesh grade enamel. Wait for the binder to dry, then fire it until the enamel is glossy.

Peel off the anti-fire scale and apply a ground-coat of 60-mesh grade to the front of the metal in the same way, and fire it.

Decorating Build up the enamel in thin layers, each individually fired, cooled and cleaned before the next is applied. To clean, wash with soap and water, rinse, dip into ammonia and rinse with running water.

Designs can be applied by STENCILLING. Another method is wet inlay – mixing the powder with binder and applying it with a paintbrush.

Firing Allow an item a minute and a half in the kiln before inspecting, then recheck every half minute or so.

Firing times vary according to the type of enamel and the thickness of the metal. Firing is complete when the enamel is smooth and shiny and has a slight glow.

Finish off the piece when it has cooled by smoothing it first with a rough carborundum stone, then with a smooth one, and buffing it to an even sheen.

Endowment policies

*Choosing the right policy
to meet your needs*

An endowment policy combines life assurance with a savings scheme – see also INSURANCE. The policy is drawn up for a specified term – for example, 10, 15 or 20 years.

When the policy matures at the end of the term, the policyholder receives a lump sum. If the policyholder dies at any time during the term, the amount insured is paid out to the beneficiary named in the policy.

With or without profits? There are two basic kinds of endowment policy, the non-profit type and the with-profit type.
Non-profit This is for a stated amount that applies both to the life insurance sum and to the payout that will be made when the policy matures.
With profit The policy, which costs more in premiums than the non-profit type, increases in value through the addition of bonuses.

Paid annually, these bonuses come from money the company earns by investing your premiums; the size of each bonus varies according to how successful the company's investments are. There is no guarantee that a bonus will be paid at all in any given year, but once a bonus has been added to the value of the policy, it cannot be taken away by the company.

In addition to annual bonuses, the insurance company may pay a 'terminal bonus' when the policy matures. Again, this is at the company's discretion, and the amount will depend on how well investments have performed during the policy's term.

A further type of policy is the *unit-linked* one, in which income the company has earned by investing your premiums in a unit trust is reinvested on behalf of the policyholder to build up the lump sum. Most unit-linked policies include a relatively modest level of life assurance cover.

Choosing the right company Independent insurance brokers will advise on different types of policy and the merits of different companies. For an indication,

you can investigate insurance companies' past investment performances for yourself. Comparative tables, showing what sort of profits the leading companies have earned for their policyholders in recent years, regularly appear in specialist publications such as *Money Management* and *Planned Savings* – both available from larger newsagents.

Always keep firmly in mind that past performance is no certain guarantee of how well a company will perform in the future.

Endowment policies are often taken out to cover the amount of a loan. See also MORTGAGES.

Epileptic fit

*What you can do to help if
somebody has one*

In epilepsy, uncontrolled electrical impulses from the brain's nerve cells cause the sufferer to have recurrent seizures. These can come on without warning, but usually pass in a few minutes with little or no ill-effect.

Recognising the symptoms A major epileptic fit or *grand mal* is most commonly characterised by loss of consciousness, collapsing to the ground and involuntary jerkings of the whole body. During the fit, the victim may also bite his tongue, foam at the mouth and lose bladder or bowel control.

The fit will usually last for only one or two minutes, but the sufferer may remain unconscious for a short time before waking up, and even then will probably be feeling confused and groggy.

How you can help
● Do not interfere. Only try to move a victim who may be in danger, such as in a busy road. Do not attempt to restrain him.
● Give the victim space. Move any objects he may collide with.
● Try to catch a victim about to fall. Ease him to the ground. Find something soft to cushion his head. Loosen clothing at his neck if you can.
● Look for a card or bracelet – carried by many epileptics – which may give emergency information.
● Do *not* try to force anything into a victim's mouth – this will not help to prevent him choking on or biting his tongue, and may cause injury. Offer the sufferer a drink only when he is fully conscious and in control.
● When convulsions are over, put the victim into the RECOVERY POSITION. Do not leave him alone until he has recovered completely.
● Summon medical help if there is any injury, if it is the victim's first fit, or if he

has repeated fits. The time and duration of the fits should be noted, for passing on to the doctor.
● Call for medical help if the victim fails to regain consciousness within 10 minutes.

Escargots

*Edible snails: a home-grown recipe
for a famous French delicacy*

Canned, precooked snails are sold in delicatessens, along with bags of ready-to-use shells. Prepare them according to the directions on the labels, and add your own snail butter according to taste.

Snail butter With 115g (4oz) of butter, blend 1 tablespoon finely chopped shallot, 1 teaspoon finely chopped parsley, and 1 peeled and crushed garlic clove; now season with salt and freshly ground black pepper. Push a little of the butter into each shell, followed by a snail, then seal the shell with more butter. At this stage you can, if you wish, deep freeze the snails – see FREEZING FOOD.

Cooking Arrange the snails on a dish with their open ends upwards and place in a hot oven for 10-15 minutes or until sizzling. Serve immediately with small pieces of fresh bread.

Special equipment Give each person a slender two-pronged fork to draw out the snails. As well as the forks, you can buy special tongs for holding the shells. You can also buy escargot plates with six or 12 recesses; if you cook the snails on these, the butter stays in small pools round each snail.

Eviction notice

*What you can do about a notice
to quit your rented home*

A letter from your landlord giving you notice to quit is the first step in what may be a lengthy procedure – and which will not necessarily end in you being evicted.

Read the letter carefully. It should be quite clear on four points:
● It should state the address of the premises and the landlord's intention to take full possession, either personally or via an agent.
● It must give at least four weeks' notice, or longer if the terms of your tenancy agreement require it.
● The letter should state that, if you have not vacated by the date when the notice expires, the landlord will then have to apply to a court for a possession order to allow eviction.
● The notice must refer to your rights

under the Rent Acts, pointing out that if you are uncertain of them, you should seek legal advice (see LAWYERS), assisted by LEGAL AID if necessary. The notice should tell you, too, that information is available from, among others, Citizens Advice Bureaus and rent tribunal officers.

Provided the letter includes all these points, you should seek advice at once. If it does not include all these points, it has no force in law.

Are you a protected tenant? Under the Rent Acts and Housing Acts, many tenancies – furnished and unfurnished – have security of tenure; that is, the landlord cannot evict you without good reason.

A tenant is normally protected in the following circumstances: if the rent is above £250 (£1000 in London) and below £25,000 a year, or, if the letting began before April 1, 1990, the rateable value was below £1500 in London or £750 elsewhere; if the landlord does not live on the premises; and if it is an unfurnished letting (or furnished, but the letting began before August 13, 1974).

You are not likely to be a protected tenant if you are a council, Crown or housing association tenant; if the accommodation goes with your job; if the landlord lives on the premises and has made it clear from the outset that the premises must be vacated at the end of the letting period. Students are not protected; nor are tenants in short tenancies, holiday lets or 'serviced' flats or houses.

If you are protected, and do not want to leave, the landlord has to obtain a possession order from a court and can do so only on one or more well-defined grounds. Among these are:
● The offer of an equivalent home in the same locality, where you will have the same legal protection as at present.
● A sound claim that you have breached the tenancy agreement by falling behind with the rent or upsetting the neighbours, damaging the property or some other cause.
● The landlord or the landlord's family need the property for themselves. (Unless, that is, you have been an unfurnished tenant from before March 23, 1965, or a furnished tenant from before May 24, 1974, and the landlord has bought the property since then. In such a case you can stay.)

A judge may still refuse a possession order or make a suspended one – if, for example, you can satisfy the court that you have paid up the rent and will not get into arrears in the future.

If the court does decide to grant a possession order, you will be given four weeks to leave. If you do not get out within that time, the court can appoint a bailiff to evict you – by force if necessary.

If you are not protected, and your tenancy agreement dates from before November 28, 1980, you may be entitled to a hearing by a rent tribunal. You must apply within 28 days of the date your notice to quit comes into effect. Ask at your town hall or Citizens Advice Bureau how to apply.

If your tenancy dates from later than November 28, 1980, your landlord must still get a court order to evict you, and you will still be given reasonable time to move.

Exercises
Building up suppleness and strength

Exercise should be taken slowly, at a pace that is comfortable for you. Repeat the routine at least three times a week for a period of 20 to 30 minutes each time. See also RELAXATION EXERCISES.

The stretch-and-flex exercises given below will improve suppleness. To get full benefit, stretch until you feel mild tension, then hold briefly at that

— EXERCISES —

Stretching and flexing in sequence

Before attempting any of the exercises illustrated – or any other form of vigorous exercise – see AEROBICS and take careful note of the do's and don'ts.

Trunk twists

Arm crossovers

Arm circles

Alternate leg raises

Sit-ups Level 1

Press-up Level 1

Press-up Level 2

Sit-ups Level 3

Reach and climb

Hold the halfway position

Side bends to left and right

Sitting stretches

Cat back, arching and dipping back

position. They are followed by press-ups, sit-ups and leg raises, which are for building-up muscle strength.

Head rolls Turn head to left, back to centre, then to right, centre. With chin on chest, slowly turn head left, back to centre, then right, centre.

Shoulder shrugs Stand with arms at sides, roll shoulders towards ears, drop shoulders. Repeat three times.

Arm circles Stand comfortably, with feet slightly apart, looking straight ahead. Slowly raise your outstretched arms, with palms together and follow them with your gaze. Raise them as high as you can above your head. Lower and separate your arms, push them as wide and far back as you can, slightly arching your back.

Ankle rotation Sit on the floor with straight legs together. Slightly raise one foot, flex and point four times, then circle foot twice in each direction.

Side bends Stand with your arms straight down by your sides, feet about 300mm (12in) apart. Lean your head to the right, bend your upper body sideways to the right, and push the palm of your hand as far down the side of your leg as you can in comfort. Repeat to the left side. Bend each side for 30 seconds.

Trunk twists Stand with feet apart and arms stretched out to the front, palms downwards. Swing one arm to the side, and farther back by twisting your trunk and turning your head. The arm should go through 180 degrees. Return arm to the front and repeat with the other.

Reach and climb Stand with legs apart. Reach one arm up as far above your head as possible, then lower it slightly and reach with the other arm. Continue reaching with each arm alternately, trying to stretch a little higher each time.

Arm crossovers Stand with knees relaxed, hug and cross arms in front of your body, then fling them out to the sides.

Sitting stretches Sit on the floor with your back straight and with legs apart and stretched out, toes pointing up, knees relaxed. Reach forward over one leg to a point a few inches above your toes. Hold at least 15 seconds; repeat over the other leg. Put the soles of your feet together and hold your ankles. Bending from the hips and keeping your head up, gently pull yourself forward until you feel a stretching in the groin area.

Alternate leg raises Lie on your side, both legs extended. Move upper leg up and down, toes pointing up. Repeat on the other side. Repeat on both sides, this time with toes pointing down.

Cat back Get down on hands and knees. Pull your stomach in, put your chin on your chest, and arch your back upwards like a cat. Then relax. Reverse the motion by bringing your head up and dipping your spine to form a shallow U.

Press-ups and sit-ups There are various levels of these exercises, according to how fit you are. Start with the *Level 1* exercise and do it at the rate of ten a minute. Then gradually speed up until you can do 16 to 20 a minute with ease. When you have achieved *Level 1* comfortably, move on to *Level 2*. Do this exercise at the same rate as for *Level 1* until you feel able to move on to *Level 3*.

Press-up levels In each level, take up the press-up position by crouching down, legs together and putting your palms about 300mm (12in) apart on the floor. Move your feet back until you are flat out. *Level 1* Lift head and shoulders only; hold for a few seconds. *2* Push up till your arms are straight, but keep your knees on the floor and move back to a kneeling-squatting position. Reverse motion, returning to floor. *3* Keeping your body straight, push up until your arms are straight. Bend your arms until your chest is 75-150mm (3-6in) from the floor.

Sit-up levels Start by lying on your back, fully stretched out, legs together, arms down by your sides. *Level 1* Raise arms and shoulders only. *2* Tuck your feet under a heavy item such as a sofa. Lie flat with your hands clasped behind your neck. Sit up slowly, pausing halfway, until your torso is at right angles to your legs. Maintain the position briefly, then return slowly to starting position. *3* Place arms atop your thighs and raise your body, sliding your hands towards your ankles.

Extension leads

Using them safely; repairs

An extension lead is intended only for temporary use – with a power tool, for example, and not for the permanent connection of any appliance or fitting. Remember that trailing wires are hazardous, so always connect an extension lead to a power socket as near as possible to the point where you intend to work. Plug the appliance into the extension-lead socket before you connect the extension lead to the mains socket outlet.

You can buy an extension lead already made up with a plug and socket, and in a range of lengths. The easiest and safest to use are contained on a spool which has the socket mounted in its side. Always withdraw the lead fully from the spool – if left wound while in use, it could overheat and be damaged.

Choose an extension lead rated at the highest wattage you are likely to require. It is safest to buy one with 1.5mm^2 twin core and earth flex and a 13amp plug; it will not be overloaded if used with an appliance such as an electric fire. When using an appliance with a rating of less than 700 watts, fit a 3amp fuse in the 13amp plug – see PLUGS.

You can make an extension lead by using a length of twin core and earth 1.5mm^2 flex and a 13amp plug and trailing socket. Choose brightly coloured flex easy to see outside, and a rubber-clad plug and socket.

An extension lead with a two-part flex connector, instead of a trailing socket, must be fitted with the socket half of the connector attached to the end of the flex that has the mains plug fitted to it. The pin half must be fitted to the appliance flex, so that the pins can never be live while the connector is separated.

As a safety measure, you should use an RCD (see CIRCUIT BREAKER) which cuts off the power instantly if a fault develops.

Lead repairs Replace a plug or socket that is cracked or broken. If the lead insulation becomes damaged, cut off the damaged section if it is near one end and refit the connector. Failing that, the whole lead must be replaced.

WARNING Never try to repair damaged insulation by wrapping adhesive tape round it, and do not join lengths of flex by twisting the wires together and binding with tape.

External chest compression

A first-aid technique that can save life in an emergency

WARNING Chest compression is only used when the heart has stopped beating. It must be learned from a qualified first-aid instructor and should be applied only by a person who has had the necessary training. If applied wrongly or unnecessarily it could be lethal.

Compressing the chest of a casualty whose heart has stopped can, in conjunction with ARTIFICIAL RESPIRATION, save the victim's life. The technique squeezes the heart between the breastbone and spine, which makes it manually pump blood around the body. The restored blood supply to the brain can restart the natural pumping of the heart.

Has the heart stopped? Feel for the pulse in the neck, as shown on page 159.

Emergency action when the heart stops beating

Checking the pulse To check the pulse, feel the carotid artery in the hollow of the neck between the Adam's apple and the long muscle at the side.

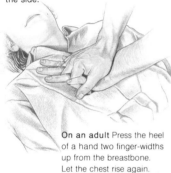

On an adult Press the heel of a hand two finger-widths up from the breastbone. Let the chest rise again.

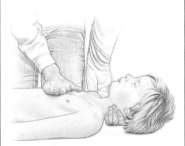

On a young child Use one hand only to compress the lower breastbone by 25-38mm (1-1½in). Give 100 presses a minute with one lung inflation after every 5.

On a baby Support the baby along one arm with its head cradled by your hand and tilting slightly down. With two fingers only, press down 13-25mm (½-1in) on the middle of the breastbone.

If *no* pulse is detected, proceed with chest compression.

The technique Position the heel of one hand on a point two finger-widths up from the bottom of the breastbone. Place your other hand over it and, keeping your fingers and thumbs raised off the chest, press down 38-50mm (1½-2in).

The compressions should be repeated at normal pulse rate – 80 per minute. After 15, inflate the lungs twice by artificial respiration; repeat the sequence. Check for a neck pulse after every 10 breaths.

If the pulse returns When you detect a pulse, stop compression but continue artificial respiration until breathing restarts. Check the neck pulse often, and resume compression if it stops.

Children and babies Where the victim is a child under ten use one hand only.

Hold an infant as illustrated. This position also permits mouth-to-mouth or mouth-to-nose respiration. Use two fingers only to give 100 presses a minute, with one lung inflation after every five.

Extractor fan
Installing a powered ventilator in a window

Electric-powered extractor fans draw air from a room to the outside. They are needed mainly in kitchens, toilets and bathrooms to get rid of smells and moisture-laden air. Most fans can be reversed to draw in cool air.

There are two basic types of fan – centrifugal and axial flow. Axial flow types are suitable for window mounting.

Choose a fan with ample capacity to ventilate the room. Its capacity is given in cubic metres per hour. Calculate the volume of the room in cubic metres (length × width × height) and multiply this by the number of air changes needed an hour (4-6 in a living room; 10-15 in a kitchen or toilet; 15-20 in a bathroom). Thus a kitchen 3 metres long, 2 metres wide and 2.4 metres high has a volume of 14.4 cubic metres. Multiply this by 10-15 air changes (144-216) and you know you need a fan with a capacity of 144-216 cubic metres an hour.

Install the fan in a non-opening pane of glass and across the room from the

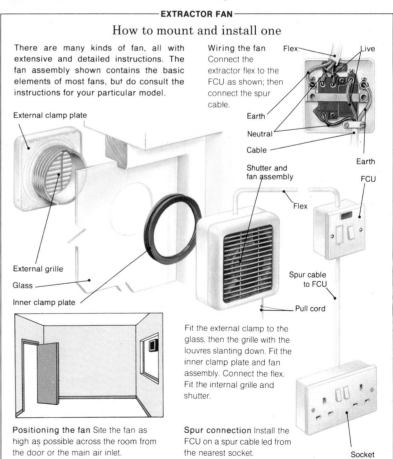

EXTRACTOR FAN

How to mount and install one

There are many kinds of fan, all with extensive and detailed instructions. The fan assembly shown contains the basic elements of most fans, but do consult the instructions for your particular model.

Wiring the fan Connect the extractor flex to the FCU as shown; then connect the spur cable.

Flex — Live — Earth — Neutral — Cable — Earth — FCU

External clamp plate

Shutter and fan assembly

Flex

External grille
Glass
Inner clamp plate

Spur cable to FCU

Pull cord

Fit the external clamp to the glass, then the grille with the louvres slanting down. Fit the inner clamp plate and fan assembly. Connect the flex. Fit the internal grille and shutter.

Positioning the fan Site the fan as high as possible across the room from the door or the main air inlet.

Spur connection Install the FCU on a spur cable led from the nearest socket.

Socket

main entry point for air. This ensures air is drawn right across the room. Do not put the fan near a boiler or gas heater unless these have their own flues – or fumes could be drawn into the room.

The fan can be controlled by the switch of a wall-mounted FUSED CONNECTION UNIT or by a built-in pull-cord switch. Choose one with a pull-cord for a bathroom unless the fused connection unit can be well out of reach of a person using the bath or shower. Make sure the fan has a shutter which closes when you switch it off.

Installing the fan Make the hole in the window (see GLASS CUTTING), unless the window has sealed DOUBLE GLAZING. For this, do not attempt to cut the hole yourself – ask the window supplier to install a pane with the hole made and its edges sealed.

Fit the external clamp plate, making sure any rubber seal is positioned correctly. Fit the external grille, then the inner clamp plate and fan assembly.

Connect the flex to the connector block in the fan assembly, brown to L, blue to N and green-and-yellow to E or ⏚. Use the size of flex recommended in the maker's instructions. If the fan is double insulated (marked ▣) there will be no earth terminal: use a two-core flex without an earth conductor wire.

Fit the internal grille and shutter – again following the maker's instructions.

Connecting to the power supply Turn off the main switch at the fuse box (see FUSES AND FUSE BOXES) and withdraw the fuse for the circuit on which you will be working.

Install a fused connection unit (FCU) on a spur led from the nearest socket – see SPUR CONNECTIONS. In a bathroom, make sure the FCU is well out of reach of anyone using the bath or shower. If this is not possible, install the FCU just outside the bathroom and lay cable from it to a flex outlet plate near the fan. The plate fits over a standard socket mounting box.

When the FCU is installed, replace the circuit fuse and turn the main switch back on.

Eyebrows

Shaping and colouring them

Plucking can improve eyebrow shape, as long as you retain the natural line. Use tweezers to pluck out stray hairs between your brows and below them, and any that extend too far beyond the outer corner of the eye. Do not pluck the top of the brow, as this will destroy the natural line.

Just before plucking, press a warm, wet facecloth over your brow. Heat will

Plucking, trimming and applying colour

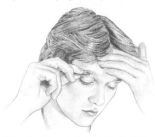

Brush eyebrows daily with an eyebrow brush or a soft toothbrush. Apply a touch of petroleum jelly to keep them in shape.

Trimming the eyebrows Pluck each hair with a swift, sharp movement, pulling in the direction the hair grows and holding the skin over the eyebrow taut.

Eyebrow span Hold pencil against outer edge of nostril. The brow's inner boundary is where pencil crosses it. To mark the outer edge, swing pencil to outer corner of eye.

Eyebrow pencil Thicken or darken the brows with an eyebrow pencil in short, feathery strokes. Choose a colour slightly darker than the natural colour of the eyebrows.

make the hair roots a little easier to extract. Pluck hairs out one at a time. Refresh the area afterwards with a cotton-wool pad soaked in a skin-toning lotion.

WARNING Never apply a hair-colouring product to your eyebrows; the strong solution could seriously damage your eyes.

Eye injuries

Dealing with foreign bodies in the eye; treating a black eye

Avoid rubbing or touching an injured eye, as this may cause a foreign body to cut into the surface or a liquid irritant to spread further. Attempt to remove an

How to give emergency treatment

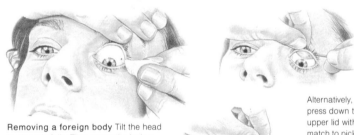

Removing a foreign body Tilt the head backwards fully. Then grasp the lashes of the upper lid gently and pull the lid back. Try to remove the object with a piece of gauze folded into a point.

Alternatively, press down the upper lid with a match to pick up the object on the inner lid. Pull up the eyelid against the match and remove the object.

Impaled object On no account must you try to remove the object. Cut a hole in a piece of gauze and put it over the eye. Put a paper cup or pad over the gauze to keep it firmly in place. Secure it with a bandage tied round the head.

Dressing an eye If a foreign body cannot be dislodged, tape a clean gauze pad over the eye. Seek medical help immediately. Use the same technique to protect a healing eye.

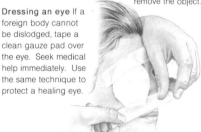

object such as a speck of grit or an eyelash only if it is floating on the white or under an eyelid. First, try flushing it out. Tilt your head to the injured side and trickle cold or tepid water over the eye from a shower spray or jug. You can also try blinking your eyes underwater in a washbasin or sink.

If flushing fails to do the trick, try lifting the object off the eye with the twisted corner of a tissue or clean handkerchief. Sit in front of a well-lit mirror and gently pull up the upper eyelid (or draw down the lower one).

To remove an object from high up under an eyelid, you need a helper to roll the lid back over a matchstick. Pull the lid by the lashes gently back over the match to expose the underside. The speck can then be removed with the corner of a tissue or clean handkerchief.

Immovable foreign body Do not try to remove anything that is firmly stuck to the eye or on the pupil or iris. Close the eye and cover it with a pad of cotton gauze or cotton wool. Tape the pad lightly in place to keep eye movement to a minimum, and see a doctor as soon as possible. Follow the same procedure if an eye continues to give trouble after a foreign body has been removed.

Impaled object Do not attempt to remove any splinter, of glass or metal for example, or any other object impaled in the eye. Call an ambulance at once. If you are tending a casualty, protect the injured eye: cut a hole in a piece of clean cloth and place it over the eye, being careful not to touch it. Over the cloth place a paper or plastic cup and hold this in place with a bandage. If necessary, cover the uninjured eye to stop natural eye movement.

Chemicals Any chemical that gets into the eye can cause serious damage. Flush the eye immediately with water, holding the eyelids open if necessary. Continue washing out the eye for 10-15 minutes, then cover the eye with a clean dressing and get to a hospital. See also BURNS.

Black eye A blow violent enough to cause a black eye may injure the eye itself, so see a doctor without delay. An ice-pack or cold compress will help reduce swelling and pain.

Eyelets and grommets

Reinforcing holes in leather and fabrics

Metal eyelets are used to reinforce small holes in fabrics or leather to take thongs and laces, such as in a leather drawstring purse, or to take buckle holes. Grommets are larger than eyelets, and are used on

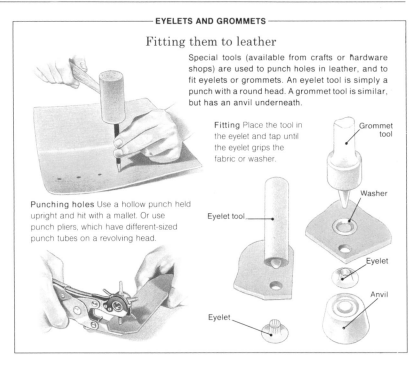

EYELETS AND GROMMETS

Fitting them to leather

Special tools (available from crafts or hardware shops) are used to punch holes in leather, and to fit eyelets or grommets. An eyelet tool is simply a punch with a round head. A grommet tool is similar, but has an anvil underneath.

Fitting Place the tool in the eyelet and tap until the eyelet grips the fabric or washer.

Punching holes Use a hollow punch held upright and hit with a mallet. Or use punch pliers, which have different-sized punch tubes on a revolving head.

Grommet tool

Washer

Eyelet tool

Eyelet

Anvil

Eyelet

heavy fabric and plastic sheets such as tarpaulins, tents and groundsheets. The method of fitting both is similar, and the materials and tools are obtainable from craft shops or hardware stores.

Fitting eyelets To pierce holes in leather, use a hollow punch and mallet, or punch pliers. When using a punch, place the work on a firm surface, protected by a sheet of hardboard or fibre board. Hold the punch vertically and strike it sharply with a hammer or mallet to cut a clean hole.

Punch pliers have punch tubes of several diameters on a revolving head; select the desired diameter tube, hold it over the work and squeeze the handles to cut the hole.

Place an eyelet in the hole with its head on the facing side – the side that will be visible – and hold the work on a firm surface. Place the eyelet tool, a punch with a round head, over the top rim of the eyelet and tap it sharply until the eyelet grips the material.

Fitting grommets To make the hole in fabric or plastic, use a sharp knife or small pair of scissors. The grommet tool comprises a punch and an anvil; grommets are in two parts – the eyelet and a washer. Place the eyelet in the hollow side of the anvil. Insert the top of the eyelet through the hole in the facing side of the material. Place the washer around the eyelet, convex side up. Place the grommet tool over the rim of the eyelet and tap the tool sharply until the eyelet rim grips the washer.

Eye make-up

Enhancing your eyes

Choose eye-shadow colours that contrast with or enhance the colour of your eyes, rather than those that match it exactly. Violet eye shadow, for example, accentuates the green in hazel eyes; topaz makes brown eyes look deeper. Mauve, coral and grey are flattering to blue eyes.

Eye shadow should also complement your skin tone and the colour of your clothes. Muted shades look best in daytime; use iridescent or bright colours at night, if at all. Mature women should choose eye-shadow cream.

If your eyes are the classic oval, brush a medium shade on the eyelid down to the lashes, a slightly darker shade along the underside of the bone between lid and brow. Blend the colours up and out.

Prominent eyes will recede if you use a dark shade over the entire lid almost to the bone of the brow.

To make close-set eyes seem farther apart, use a pale shade on the third of the lids near the nose, a darker shade near the temple. You can reverse the process to make wide-set eyes seem closer together.

Eyeliner Use a liquid or pencil eyeliner to emphasise shape, in either black, brown or a toning shade to complement the choice of eye shadow. Make a thin line as near the eyelashes as possible, taking care not to stretch the delicate skin around the eye.

EYE MAKE-UP

Applying eye shadow, mascara and eyeliner

Eye shadow can help to redefine eyes that are not a perfect oval shape. A light colour tends to bring an eye area forward and a dark colour subdues it.

Classic oval eyes Use a medium shade on the eyelid, down to the eyelashes.

Small or deep-set eyes Apply pale shading from under the eyebrows down to the eyelashes, to make the eyes look larger.

Extending with a V-shape Apply a small V of a darker shade beyond the outer eye corners to make eyes appear larger.

Close-set eyes Apply a pale shade to the lid near the nose and a darker shade near the temple to make the eyes seem wider apart.

Mascara Hold the mascara brush vertically when coating the tips of the lashes. Then sweep it horizontally over the lashes from base to tips.

Eyeliner Make a thin line with the pencil as close to the lashes as possible. Smudge the line with the little finger for a natural effect.

Mascara For a wide-awake look, use an eyelash curler before applying mascara. Hold the curler near the base of the lashes and squeeze. Do the same towards the tips of the lashes.

Apply mascara with your eyes open. Should any lashes clump, separate them with a clean mascara brush or a fine comb. Use a cotton bud for cleaning-up afterwards.

Removing make-up Remove eye make-up each night by gently wiping with cotton wool soaked in eye make-up remover.

See also EYEBROWS.

Eyes

Eye disorders and what can be done about them

Never neglect eye problems. Many disorders can be treated or prevented if you heed certain danger signals and see an optician about them quickly.

Symptoms you should report to the optician

● Sudden partial or total blindness in one or both eyes – go to the optician immediately.
● Severe pain in the eyeball.
● Seeing a double image.

● Vision obscured by grey or blurred area in one or both eyes.
● Noticeable difference in size of the two pupils (this may be caused by the use of eye drops).
● Redness in the eye.
● Any pain or other symptom lasting more than three to five days.
● Persistent inflammation of the rims of the eyelids.

Anyone who is having difficulty seeing clearly should make an appointment with an eye specialist for EYESIGHT TESTING. Anyone over 40 with eyesight problems should also be tested for *glaucoma*, a disease of the eye which, if not detected and treated early, can cause blindness. Have an eye examination every two years – particularly if there is a history of glaucoma in your family.

A common age-related eye disorder is *cataract*, a misting of the lens affecting most people aged over about 65. Your doctor can advise you when surgery – replacement of the lens – will help.

A condition most common among people over 55 is *macular degeneration*, in which damage to the focusing point at the centre of the retina causes blurring and distortion of vision. In some cases the condition can be treated by destroying the abnormal blood vessels which cause it, using a laser. Where treatment is not possible, the doctor will recommend using magnifying glas-

ses to improve your vision.

A minor disorder is floaters – black dots or threads that seem to float in front of the eyes. They are caused by minute leaks of blood into the eyeball. Do not worry about them; they need no treatment and often disappear in a few weeks.

Children A baby or child who squints or appears 'cross-eyed' should be seen by a doctor as soon as you notice the condition. The child will not grow out of a squint, and left untreated it could lead to impaired vision in one eye.

See also CONJUNCTIVITIS; CONTACT LENSES; EYE INJURY; STYES.

Eyesight testing

Checking the quality of your vision

If you find it difficult to focus clearly, or have blurred vision or aching eyes, you may be suffering from one of the so-called refractive errors. There are four main ones: myopia (short-sightedness); hypermetropia (long-sightedness); presbyopia (a type of long-sightedness starting in middle age); and astigmatism (distortion of vision).

For any of these conditions, the best course is to see an optician for an eyesight test.

Optician An optician is trained and equipped to test vision. It is best to go to an ophthalmic optician, who will also check that your eyes are healthy. The optician tests the vision of each eye separately, using a chart from which you read letters of diminishing size from a set distance. He may make further tests – including asking you to look at a chart through a pinhole aperture, or to look at diagonal lines and/or a circle with lines radiating from the centre.

If there is a refractive error, the optician will do more detailed tests, and will probably prescribe spectacles, or you may be able to have CONTACT LENSES instead.

Regular tests Try to have regular eye checks, because refractive errors cause increasing discomfort if not corrected. Also, tests will detect any early signs of diseases such as glaucoma (see EYES) which can have serious consequences if not treated.

Children Undetected sight problems can hamper learning, so a child's eyesight should be tested from school age – or even before if you notice a squint (see EYES). Eye testing should continue at yearly intervals until the person is around 20 years of age.

See also COLOUR BLINDNESS.

F

Facial care

Cleansing, toning and moisturising

Safeguard your complexion by developing a daily programme of facial care that includes a thorough morning wash, either repeated in the evening or substituted by a nightly cleansing, toning and moisturising routine.

For washing, use the simplest high-quality soap you can buy, without added disinfectants or perfume; medicated soaps may help combat septic skin conditions such as boils, but are otherwise not necessary.

If you use a face flannel, ensure it is always clean and fresh. After soaping your face, rinse it well with plain water, and pat it dry with a clean, soft towel.

Cleansing Always remove make-up at night. Take off mascara with a cotton bud dipped in eye-cleansing lotion, and eye shadow with a pad of clean cotton wool moistened with the lotion. Dab face-cleansing cream generously over the nose, chin, forehead and cheeks.

Massage it into the skin, starting under the throat with a gentle, upward motion. Massage up to the forehead, then across under the eyes to the nose, and finally back over the chin. Remove the cream with soft tissue pads or damp cotton wool held in each hand, again starting from the throat and working up.

Toning Use a toner to remove any traces of dirt, make-up or cleanser immediately after cleansing. Choose one that just tingles; if it stings, it is too strong.

Soak a clean cotton-wool pad lightly in the toner, and use it to wipe the face gently; apply it first to the forehead and cheeks, then to the crevices around the nose and finally to the chin. Avoid the delicate areas around eyes.

Moisturising Weather and washing both remove natural moisture from the skin, drying and tautening it. A thin layer of moisturiser after toning helps to keep your face smooth and supple.

Dot moisturising cream lightly over the face. Start from the centre of the forehead and work the cream outwards, using the fingers of both hands. Pat the cream gently around the eyes and cheeks, then work it around the jawline, chin and mouth, finally massaging it with upward strokes over the throat.

Facials and masks An occasional facial treatment will remove deep-seated impurities and stimulate circulation. To give yourself a home facial, buy some camomile tea bags and a facial, or 'beautifying', mask from a chemist: a clay-based mask may benefit oily skins; creamy masks contain additional moisturising agents for drier skins.

Remove all make-up and cover your hair with a shower-cap. Pour boiling water over two of the camomile tea bags in a basin. Drape a towel over your head to trap the steam, and hold your face about 300mm (12in) above the water for up to ten minutes.

Blot dry with a towel or tissues, then apply the mask according to the maker's instructions, taking care not to get it too close to your eyes, mouth or hairline. Leave it on as directed, generally up to ten minutes, then remove it with toner and cotton wool, rinse your face in cool water, blot dry and apply moisturiser.

See also BEAUTY CREAMS; COSMETICS.

FACIAL CARE

A plan of action for removing make-up

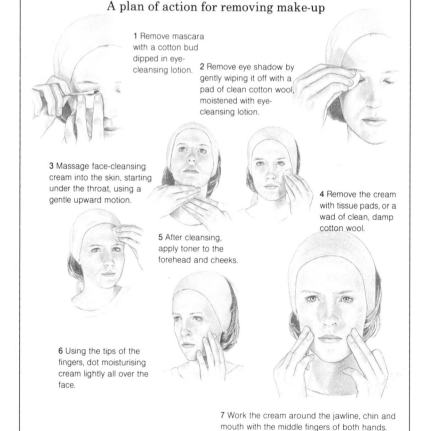

1 Remove mascara with a cotton bud dipped in eye-cleansing lotion.

2 Remove eye shadow by gently wiping it off with a pad of clean cotton wool, moistened with eye-cleansing lotion.

3 Massage face-cleansing cream into the skin, starting under the throat, using a gentle upward motion.

4 Remove the cream with tissue pads, or a wad of clean, damp cotton wool.

5 After cleansing, apply toner to the forehead and cheeks.

6 Using the tips of the fingers, dot moisturising cream lightly all over the face.

7 Work the cream around the jawline, chin and mouth with the middle fingers of both hands.

Fainting

What to do if someone feels faint – or faints

Faintness – a weak, light-headed and unsteady feeling – is caused by a temporary reduction in the supply of blood, and the oxygen it carries, to the brain.

Often it is brought on by being in a hot, stuffy room, but there are other possible causes, such as a sudden fright, pain, stress, or a drop in blood sugar level through missed meals or excessive

DIETING. Sometimes, faintness can occur after standing still for a long time, or on rising suddenly after bending.

Warning signs are pallor or a greenish tinge to the face, frequent yawning, a cold and clammy skin and beads of sweat on the face, neck and hands. The victim should sit or lie down by an open window or, outdoors, in the shade. Loosen a tight

Treating a casualty Lay someone who has fainted on their back and raise their legs.

collar or belt and put his head between his knees until the feeling passes.

If you see someone faint, try to break his fall, and check if he is breathing. If his breathing is normal, loosen any tight clothing and raise his legs above the level of his head, either holding them or propping them on something suitable. Indoors, open windows; outdoors, protect the victim from the sun. After the victim recovers – usually in a few minutes – keep him lying down a little longer.

If the victim is not breathing, check that his airway is clear and, if necessary, give ARTIFICIAL RESPIRATION. You should also seek medical advice if the fainting fit lasts for more than a few minutes, or if you suspect that the cause of the fit may be injury or illness – see UNCONSCIOUSNESS.

Family trees

How to trace your ancestry

Start by trying to trace your direct line of descent through your parents, grandparents and so on, backwards in time. Later, if you are successful, you can try adding the collateral lines forward from a distant forebear through brothers, sisters, aunts, uncles and cousins.

Using a loose-leaved notebook, with one entry to a page, write down the dates and places of birth, marriage and death of your immediate ancestors, and the names of spouses, with any other rel-

evant information, such as jobs or details of a military career.

You will almost certainly be able to find all you need about your immediate family – parents and grandparents. But after that, the trail may become harder.

Look for clues in family documents – a Family Bible may contain lists of births, marriages and deaths of several generations – and photograph albums; question relatives. Anything that provides a name or date will help. A baptismal certificate, for example, may lead to a church in a particular locality. Church and parish registers and gravestones are often sources of information.

Local newspapers keep files of back-issues in which you may be able to trace missing details of births, marriages or deaths if you know the approximate dates. They also sometimes carry summaries of wills – occasionally invaluable for identifying 'missing' forebears.

All wills entered for probate since 1858 have been recorded with the Principal Registry of the Family Division of the High Court, Somerset House, Strand, London WC2R 1LP, either directly or through a local probate office. Copies can be consulted for a small fee.

Reference books may assist you to track down an ancestor who was a clergyman, doctor, lawyer, civil servant or member of the armed forces. Ask at your local library. Detailed lists are also published of university graduates, and pupils of some schools.

County Records Offices – address available from the county council – preserve rate books listing names and addresses of property owners, electoral rolls, quarter session and other court records (dealing not only with offences, but such things as taxes). They also keep, or know the whereabouts of, old parish registers and manorial rolls.

Major sources Once you have exhausted all the sources in your ancestors' locality, you may need to consult some major national sources. The Public Record Office, Chancery Lane, London WC2A 1LR, keeps information on census returns, Chancery Court proceedings, agreements (such as land transfers) made in front of justices, hearth taxes between 1660 and 1674, manorial rolls and subsidy rolls of people levied for taxes. For admission, you must obtain a reader's ticket from the enquiry desk when you arrive.

The General Register Office, St Catherine's House, 10 Kingsway, London WC2B 6JB, has records of births, marriages and deaths in England and Wales since 1837 – before that date, baptisms, marriages and burials were recorded in parish registers (see above).

Researchers at the GRO are not allowed to work with the registers themselves, but only with the indexes, from which a copy of the register entry can

then be ordered for a fee. The information in the indexes is compiled in alphabetical order by surname (remember spellings can sometimes change over the generations); the register entries are compiled according to registration date.

In Scotland, the General Register Office, New Register House, Edinburgh EH1 3YT, contains records of births, marriages and deaths since 1855, census records from 1841 to 1891 and parish registers before 1855. For Ireland, births, marriages and deaths since 1864 are listed in the Registrar-General's Office, General Register Office, Joyce House, 8 Lombard Street, Dublin 2. Similar information for Northern Ireland is kept by the Registrar-General's Office, Oxford House, Chichester Street, Belfast.

The British Library in London, the national libraries of Wales and Scotland and the university libraries of Oxford, Cambridge and Trinity College, Dublin,

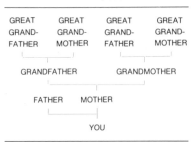

The family tree

GREAT GRAND-FATHER	GREAT GRAND-MOTHER	GREAT GRAND-FATHER	GREAT GRAND-MOTHER
GRANDFATHER		GRANDMOTHER	
FATHER	MOTHER		
YOU			

Intimate relations The chart shows how you are related to the rest of your family, following a direct line from your great-grandparents.

all have large collections of documents and records that you may need to consult.

Consulting experts If the task of tracing your family tree proves too daunting to accomplish alone, you could join the Society of Genealogists, 14 Charterhouse Buildings, Goswell Road, London EC1M 7BA. The society has its own vast collection of records, mainly for England, but also covering other parts of Britain and old colonies overseas.

They include a vast index of baptisms and an attempt to detail the marriages of England from 1530 to 1838, listing 7 million names. Work on this is being continued by the Church of Latter Day Saints of Salt Lake City, USA. The Scottish Genealogy Society, 21 Howard Place, Edinburgh EH3 5JY, assists members with research in Scotland.

The Federation of Family History Societies, 5 Mornington Close, Copthorne, Shrewsbury, Shropshire SY3 8XN, has a list of local societies who will also help. If you want to engage a professional researcher, contact the Association of Genealogists and Record Agents, 1 Woodside Close, Caterham, Surrey CR3 6AU.

Fences

Repairing damaged posts and rails; maintaining a chain-link wire fence

A rotting fence post should be repaired or replaced as soon as possible – before the whole section of fence it supports collapses. New posts, concrete spurs and any other fittings needed, such as metal extension brackets, are available from timber merchants, garden centres and DIY stores.

Replacing a rotten post If the fence is more than 1.2m (4ft) high the post must be sunk 610mm (2ft) into the ground. You would therefore need a post at least 1.8m (6ft) long. For a 1.8m high fence the post should be 2.7m (9ft) long. It is best to buy one that has been vacuum-pressure impregnated by the manufacturer, but apply more preservative yourself – see WOOD PRESERVATIVES.

To keep the fence upright while the rotten post is removed, prop it up with two long wooden BATTENS nailed to or wedged under the panel top or upper horizontal (arris) rail, one batten on either side of the post about 610mm from it. Remove a fence board on either side of the post and saw through the arris rails flush with the post. Dig out the post. If it is set in concrete, use a metal bar to lever it up out of the concrete, then remove the concrete, first breaking

it up with a bolster chisel or pickaxe.

Fit the new post, so that at least 460mm (18in) of it is below ground (760mm [30in] for a 1.8m high fence). Ram hardcore (broken bricks, stones and other hard debris) about 150mm (6in) deep into the hole around the post. Fill the rest of the hole with alternate layers of hardcore and CONCRETE, rammed well down. Check with a PLUMB LINE that the post is straight before the concrete sets hard.

When the concrete is hard, attach the arris rails to the new post with metal extension brackets, using galvanised SCREWS. Paint the brackets to stop them rusting. Refix the fence boards on either side of the post.

Supporting a partly rotten post A post rotted only at ground level can be saved by sawing off the rotten section and supporting the sound section with a concrete spur. Most posts are usually 75mm (3in) or 100mm (4in) square. Make sure to buy a spur that fits your post.

To fit a concrete spur, support the fence on each side and remove the rotten end of the post from the ground, breaking up any concrete with a bolster chisel or pickaxe, then removing it. Dig a hole for the spur, about 300mm (12in) square and 610mm (2ft) deep so that it will be able to fit against the side of the sound section post that faces away from the fence. Set the spur in the hole with its longer face against the post. Use a spirit level or

plumb line to check that it is upright. Drill holes in the post to match those in the spur, then join them together with galvanised coach BOLTS.

Fill the hole with hardcore and concrete (see above).

Repairing a broken arris rail If the rail has broken at the post, remove the fence board by the post and saw the rail free. Attach it to the post once more with a galvanised metal extension bracket, using galvanised screws.

If the rail has broken in the middle, repair it with a galvanised metal bridging bracket. Get a helper to hold the broken halves tightly together. Position the bracket over the break and attach it to the rail with galvanised screws.

Tightening a chain-link fence Make sure the posts are secure – the end posts should be braced with struts and set in concrete. Use pliers to tighten the wire at the eyebolt at the end post. If the wire is still loose, tighten the straining bolt at the end post.

If the mesh of a chain-link fence starts to rust, it should be completely removed, and replaced with new mesh, preferably plastic-coated.

Ferns

Growing them indoors and out

Some of the more exotic ferns, such as lace fern and the maidenhair ferns, come from warm climates, and in Britain must be grown indoors – see also HOUSE-PLANTS. Ferns from temperate climates, such as royal fern and most of the *Dryopteris* ferns, can be grown outside.

Indoors Keep indoor ferns out of direct sunlight; they do best in bright, filtered light at room temperature. During the growing season, water plentifully with tepid water, so that the roots are kept moist, but not sodden, as long as the temperature remains at 15°C (60°F). Feed once a month with nitrogen-rich FERTI-LISERS, diluted to half the recommended strength. When temperatures are over 21°C (70°F), mist spray the fronds daily with tepid water; hold the sprayer 610mm (2ft) away from the plant.

Reduce watering during winter, letting the top of the soil in the pot dry out between waterings. Do not feed in winter. Ferns are susceptible to attack by several pests, including APHIDS, scale insects and MEALY BUGS.

Always check the label of an insecticide (see PESTICIDES) before using it on a fern. Some insecticides could kill the fern as well as the insects.

Potting Repot a fern only when its roots fill the pot – tip the fern out temporarily

---

FENCES

Repairing posts and rails on a garden fence

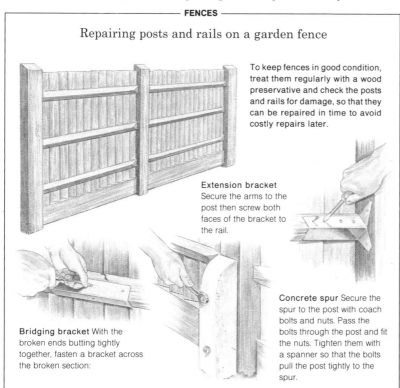

To keep fences in good condition, treat them regularly with a wood preservative and check the posts and rails for damage, so that they can be repaired in time to avoid costly repairs later.

Extension bracket Secure the arms to the post then screw both faces of the bracket to the rail.

Bridging bracket With the broken ends butting tightly together, fasten a bracket across the broken section.

Concrete spur Secure the spur to the post with coach bolts and nuts. Pass the bolts through the post and fit the nuts. Tighten them with a spanner so that the bolts pull the post tightly to the spur.

Foliage plants for home or garden Grow lace fern indoors. Plant robust royal ferns outdoors. They grow to a height and spread of 1.5m (5ft)

Lace fern

Royal fern

to check. Repot it in a pot one size up, in a mixture of two parts sterilised potting compost, two parts peat moss or leaf mould, one part coarse sand or perlite, and some charcoal granules.

A number of ferns, such as maidenhair ferns, can also be grown in hanging baskets, with a drip tray filled with water or moist pebbles about 150mm (6in) below, to provide humidity.

Outdoors Plant outdoor ferns in autumn or spring. Choose a spot shaded from the midday sun and high winds. Before planting, fork sterilised bone meal and plenty of leaf mould or garden COMPOST into the soil. Cover the surface of the soil with more leaf mould or compost after planting. Add more leaf mould or compost each autumn and spring. Do not water ferns unless the soil dries out completely in a very hot spell.

Fertilisers

What to use in a garden and for houseplants

All plants need three major nutrients: nitrogen for healthy leaves and stems; phosphorus (in the form of soluble phosphates) for healthy roots, fruit and seeds; and potassium (in the form of potash) for the production of flowers and for maintaining growth and all-round health. Plants also need minute quantities of trace elements such as iron, manganese and zinc. Most general fertilisers provide these nutrients.

Types available Compound fertilisers provide all the major nutrients in various proportions; single fertilisers contain only one or two. Organic fertilisers, such as bone meal, provide the nutrients in

natural rather than artificial chemical form. They are slower acting than chemical fertilisers but last longer. They should be applied earlier than chemical fertilisers.

How much of these nutrients a fertiliser contains is indicated by the NPK number. A fertiliser labelled 10:6:4, for example, has 10 per cent nitrogen (N), 6 per cent phosphorus (P) and 4 per cent potassium (K); the rest is mostly inert filler. The percentages are always listed in the same order.

Fertilisers can be granular or, for quick absorption, liquid. There are also foliar feeds – special liquid fertilisers which are sprayed onto leaves for rapid absorption when plants need a quick boost.

In the garden The most important fertiliser here is a balanced general compound, which has 7 per cent of each of the three major nutrients, or alternatively the organic fertilisers, blood, fish and bone meal. Apply them, as directed by the manufacturers, to prepare soil for spring planting and sowing.

Apply more about halfway between planting or sowing and the start of the harvest.

Straight nitrogen fertilisers, such as sulphate of ammonia, should also be used in spring. Apply them, as directed, to the soil around vegetables such as spring cabbages which have come through the winter, to help to stimulate spring growth.

Mix phosphatic fertilisers, such as bone meal, into the topsoil before planting herbaceous perennials, shrubs, roses, bulbs, climbers and trees. Tomato fertilisers, which are high in potash, can be applied throughout the growing season to assist all flowering and fruiting plants.

When using fertilisers, keep strictly to the recommended amounts. If in doubt, remember that too little is safer than too much.

If you use mainly chemical fertilisers, you should also feed the soil with organic matter which will form humus. Humus is the gummy substance which binds the soil particles together into groups so that air and water can circulate. Provide this organic matter by digging in manure or garden COMPOST.

Indoors Feed HOUSEPLANTS only during the growing season and never when the roots are very dry. Most of them flourish on a balanced general fertiliser, but flowering plants benefit from a little potash-rich fertiliser as well.

To keep foliage plants lush, a nitrogen fertiliser such as ammonium nitrate can be used occasionally as a liquid feed. For a quick tonic to an undernourished plant, spray the leaves with a general foliar feed diluted to a quarter of its normal strength.

Be careful not to give houseplants too much fertiliser at one time, or their roots may be damaged. It is generally safer to dilute a fertiliser to half the recommended strength and apply it more frequently.

Fever

Treating a high temperature

A raised temperature, shivering, chills and a feverish feeling may be symptoms of a common illness, such as a cold or influenza – or it may be the first sign of something more serious.

For most people normal temperature is 37°C (98.6°F), though for some it may be up to 0.5°C (1°F) above or below this. Children's temperatures can often go as high as 40°C (104°F) at the beginning of a relatively minor illness. An adult's temperature does not usually rise so high – though the illness may be more serious.

What to do The patient should rest in a warm, but not hot, room, drink plenty of fluid, such as broth, fruit juice, noncarbonated soft drinks and water, and take paracetamol or a similar safe painkiller, following carefully the instructions for dosage on the packet. If the temperature rises above 39°C (102°F), sponge the patient all over with tepid water.

Consult a DOCTOR about a baby who is in pain, who is unusually floppy or drowsy, who has a hoarse cough with noisy breathing or has continual vomiting or diarrhoea. Fever is usual in any infection and is not, in itself, important.

With adults, you only need to consult a doctor if the patient shows any other symptoms of a potentially serious illness, such as the breathlessness and cough of pneumonia.

Child's fever fits In a child of five years or less, a swift rise in temperature may cause a seizure or fever fit. During the fit, the child first goes still for a few seconds, then starts to twitch arms and legs rhythmically. The fit may last for up to 15 minutes – rarely more. Such fits can be very frightening for parents, but scarcely ever have any serious side effects. Do not let the child see you are concerned – your apprehension may communicate itself to the child and frighten it in turn.

Lay the child on his side, making sure there is nothing to block his airway. Cool the room. Remove his clothes and sponge him down with tepid water.

If this is the first time he has had such a fit, or he is less than 18 months old, call a doctor or ambulance immediately. If he has had a similar fit before, contact your doctor during the next surgery hours to ask for further advice.

FIGURE DRAWING

Getting the proportions right

Draw an egg-shape for the head and use it as the basic measure. A standing figure is eight heads tall, the legs about four heads tall. Depict the parts of the body first as simple boxes, cylinders, triangles. Join them with curving lines for the figure's outline.

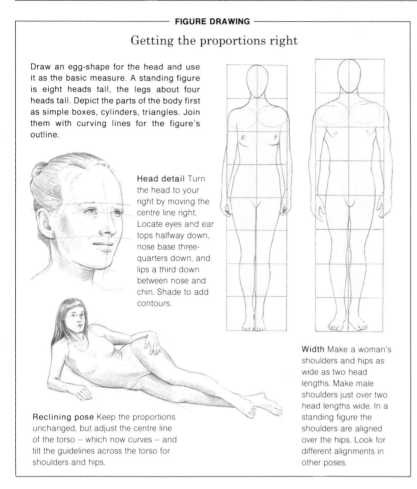

Head detail Turn the head to your right by moving the centre line right. Locate eyes and ear tops halfway down, nose base three-quarters down, and lips a third down between nose and chin. Shade to add contours.

Reclining pose Keep the proportions unchanged, but adjust the centre line of the torso – which now curves – and tilt the guidelines across the torso for shoulders and hips.

Width Make a woman's shoulders and hips as wide as two head lengths. Make male shoulders just over two head lengths wide. In a standing figure the shoulders are aligned over the hips. Look for different alignments in other poses.

Figure drawing

Learning to draw people

Drawing a full length human figure requires much practice. Use an HB pencil, a good, all-purpose drawing tool, which has a point midway between hard and soft. Pencils and a sketching pad or white drawing paper can be bought at an art supply shop.

It is essential to understand the body's proportions. Most artists use the head as the unit of measurement: a standing figure is roughly eight times the length of the head. The torso is about three heads tall, and the upper and lower legs are each two heads tall. The elbows are about three head-lengths down from the top of the head.

Each part of the body can be represented by geometrical shapes: an egg-shape for the head; an oblong box for the torso; cylinders for the upper and lower arms and legs; squares for the hands and triangles or wedges for the feet.

Within these shapes draw vertical and horizontal guidelines to locate features, such as eyes, nose and mouth on the face; shoulders, nipples and navel.

Now begin rounding off the shapes with curves to outline the true shape, and sharpen the contours by shading.

When you have finished drawing each part of the body to your satisfaction, try linking them together in a full-length figure. Begin with a standing front view, then try other poses such as kneeling, sitting and crouching, and back, side and three-quarter views.

Look for alignments between the various parts – in a front view shoulders align with hips, elbow with waist, chin with torso centre line. As the pose changes, so will the points that align.

Filing

Keeping your affairs in order

A well-organised filing system arranged chronologically, by subject, or alphabetically can save considerable amounts of both time and energy. Use a system or combination of systems that suits your needs; for example keeping a check on household affairs or running a club or society.

You can, of course, file your papers on shelves or in shoe boxes. But they will be safer from damage in a metal filing cabinet. Clearly identify each file's subject on its folder tab.

Chronological files Label five or six folders with your working days of the week. Arrange them in a drawer of the filing cabinet, then add an extra folder labelled 'Next week'. Drop into the appropriate folders reminders of engagements, calls to be made and errands to be completed as well as, for example, bills to be paid.

Keep items in their folders until they have been dealt with, then discard them or move them into another filing system. You can transfer records of all paid bills, for example, to a financial file subdivided into months. Keep bank and credit-card statements in this file, too.

Subject files Arrange the subjects alphabetically. Subdivide where appropriate as in the financial file. Subject files are very flexible; you can retitle or subdivide as you go, or you can consolidate a number of files into one.

Alphabetical files If you have a lot of correspondence, this system will help you to find letters quickly. File alphabetically by surname and put the most recent letters to the front of each folder.

A box of index cards is an alphabetical file of many uses. It can help you keep your address list up to date or catalogue your books, record collection or recipes.

Fingernails

Dealing with problems and injuries

Fingernails grow continually, and if they are not cut, they split and break. Generally they give little trouble, but problems can occur.

Black nails Injuries which crush a nail – such as jamming a finger in a door – cause bleeding beneath the nail, which usually blackens. In time the discoloration usually recedes as the nail grows. If the bleeding is extensive, the nail may come off or you may need to have a doctor remove it.

Brittle nails Poor health or an inadequate diet (see DIETING) may cause nails to crack or break easily. If you suspect this is the cause, try eating more lean meat, fish, fresh fruit and vegetables. Extreme dryness of the nails can also cause brittleness. In this case, apply a nail cream – available from chemists – night and morning, keeping the nails cut short until the condition improves.

Loose nails Prolonged use of nail hardeners containing formaldehyde may loosen nails. The flesh beneath becomes infected and discoloured. The condition is slow to heal, although keeping nails cut short can help. Loose nails may also be associated with skin diseases such as eczema: seek medical advice.

Nail furrows Furrows or grooves along a nail are often the result of a minor injury or a cyst near the cuticle. The furrows may split open, causing pain and possibly infection. If there is a cyst, or if the finger becomes inflamed, see a doctor. Otherwise, keep the nail clean and trim off any loose fragments.

Less prominent ridges can be smoothed with a nail-buffer.

Pitted nails An occasional dimple or pit in the nails is not abnormal, but their appearance can be improved by nightly treatment with an anti-irritant consisting of glycerine and boracic (boric) acid. Buy them from a chemist and mix according to his directions. Do not use nail varnish and remover until the pitting clears up.

White spots Tiny white flecks appear spontaneously in some people's nails, or they may occur as a result of slight injury to the cuticles. They are harmless and will eventually grow out.

Yellow nails Yellow staining on the nails is sometimes caused by nail varnishes, especially when they are used without a base coat. The stains are edged out by a new growth.

Flaking nails Constantly putting your hands in detergent or soapy water causes the outermost nail layers to flake off. Wear rubber gloves when washing dishes or clothes, and work nail cream into the nail base every day.

See also NAIL BITING.

Finger painting

Pictures without paintbrushes

Finger paints are available from art supplies shops, along with finger-painting paper – although you can make do with any glossy paper, or a sheet of foil, oilcloth, or a glass or enamel tray.

You also need: wooden spatulas (or ice-lolly sticks) to ladle out the paints; two dishes of clear water; sponge or rags; masking tape; and a wad of newspaper or blotting paper.

Tape a sheet of painting paper onto the work surface and set out the paint jars, each with its own spatula. Pour a little water onto the paper and spread it round evenly with your palm or a sponge. Use a spatula to spoon out a blob of paint

from one of the jars. Spread this, too, on the paper with your palm, then use a finger to draw in it.

Beginners – especially young children – should start with a single colour, experimenting with different shapes and designs. Further colours can be added later – each one dropped onto the paper next to the others before being worked into the picture. Keep a dish to wash your hands in between colours to avoid spoiling them.

The beauty of finger painting is that you can change your pictures as you fancy while painting them. Or you can wipe them out and start again.

Later you can explore the possibilities of using ordinary household items such as combs, rags or pieces of wood to draw through the wet paint, adding to your range of shapes and effects.

Leave the finished painting to dry on several layers of newspaper or on a few sheets of blotting paper. If it dries buckled (cockled), iron it flat between these absorbent layers.

See also OIL PAINTING; WATERCOLOUR PAINTING.

Finger weaving

Multi-strand plaiting for making belts and bands

Finger weaving is the technique of interweaving yarn threads with your fingers to make long strips of loosely woven material which are ideal for use as belts, scarves or headbands. The only equipment you need is a flat or round stick, about 300mm (12in) in length, and nine

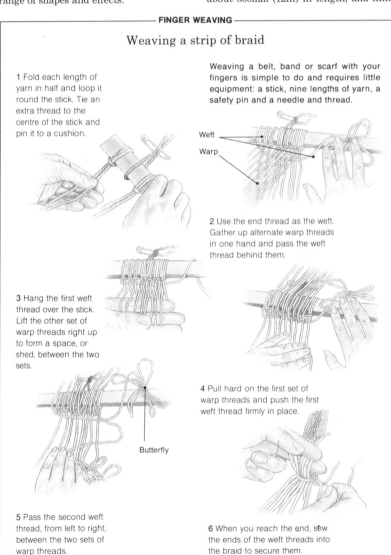

FINGER WEAVING

Weaving a strip of braid

1 Fold each length of yarn in half and loop it round the stick. Tie an extra thread to the centre of the stick and pin it to a cushion.

Weaving a belt, band or scarf with your fingers is simple to do and requires little equipment: a stick, nine lengths of yarn, a safety pin and a needle and thread.

Weft

Warp

2 Use the end thread as the weft. Gather up alternate warp threads in one hand and pass the weft thread behind them.

3 Hang the first weft thread over the stick. Lift the other set of warp threads right up to form a space, or shed, between the two sets.

Butterfly

4 Pull hard on the first set of warp threads and push the first weft thread firmly in place.

5 Pass the second weft thread, from left to right, between the two sets of warp threads.

6 When you reach the end, sew the ends of the weft threads into the braid to secure them.

lengths of yarn, which are looped onto the stick to be used alternately as *warp* and *weft* threads.

A simple basic design is the diagonal stripe. For this, cut nine 4.6m (5yd) lengths of yarn – three light-coloured, three medium and three dark. Double the lengths of yarn and attach each one at its centre to the stick with a loop, so that you begin with 18 lengths hanging from the stick. Now loop a piece of thread round the middle of the stick and secure the whole assembly to a cushion with a safety pin.

To prevent the yarns becoming tangled, you need to wind each one up into a *butterfly*. Take each thread individually and loop it round your thumb; then pass it across the palm and loop it behind the little finger, bringing it back again to the thumb over and over again in a figure-of-eight formation. When you have completed six or eight loops, wind the thread around the centre of the butterfly and tie it there. The hanging strands are called the warp threads and those that you weave through the warp threads are the weft threads.

To begin weaving, make what is known as a *shed* – a space formed by holding alternate warp threads apart to allow the weft to be passed through. Pass the first weft thread through this shed. Lift the other set of alternate warp threads (the odd numbers) to make a shed for the second weft thread. Pull the first warp threads down and push the first weft into place, laying the end of this thread over the stick.

Carry on as illustrated until the desired length of braid has been woven. Finish by sewing in the final weft thread.

Fire

What to do in an emergency

Think out beforehand alternative escape routes from each part of the house. If you were trapped upstairs, for example, which room and window would it be easiest to get out of? Which has the clearest drop and the softest ground underneath? Are there any balconies, garage roofs, or any other features which might ease your way to the ground? Do all the windows open easily? If they have locks, are the keys close to hand?

If fire breaks out, take precautions when following your escape route:

● If a door feels hot, or if smoke is seeping around the edges, do not open it – try another route. There are probably flames beyond the door, and they would become fiercer in the draught created by opening it. Even if the door is cool, crouch down, and open it only enough to look beyond it before proceeding. If it opens towards you, keep your foot against it to prevent the pressure of hot gases beyond the door

from forcing it wide open.

● Try to close all doors and windows behind you, to minimise draughts and so slow the spread of the fire.

● Keep as near as possible to the floor, since smoke fills the top of a room first.

● Do not jump out of an upstairs window unless it is unavoidable. Make a rope by knotting together sheets, trousers or any other stout material. Secure one end round a bed leg or wardrobe and put the other end through the window. Climb down as far as you can before jumping, to reduce the risk of injury.

● If there is no safe way down, shut the door, open the window and shout for help. A solid wooden door can take about 30 minutes to burn through. If there is any water available, douse the door and walls with it.

● Stuff pieces of cloth – wet, if possible – into the cracks round the door to keep out smoke and fumes.

● If you are in a high-rise block or hotel and the stairway is blocked by fire, go to a higher floor – or even the roof.

● If your clothing catches fire, wrap yourself tightly in a rug, blanket or heavy curtain to smother the flames, and lie down to stop flames rising to your head. Roll over slowly, if necessary, to smother flames, but not too fast or they could burn you more extensively. If there is nothing to wrap yourself in, cross your arms over your chest with hands touching shoulders, and roll on the floor.

See also CHIMNEY FIRES; CHIP PAN FIRE; FIRE EXTINGUISHERS.

Fire extinguishers

What to use and where to keep it

The simplest and most useful fire extinguisher is a fire blanket or large, damp towel. A bucket of water is safe to use on some fires but should not be used for others – chip pan and electrical fires, for example – and in any case makes a mess. See also FIRE.

If you are considering buying a purpose-built fire extinguisher for the home, make sure it is big enough to be useful – a capacity of 1.4kg (3lb) is a minimum, and even this would be sufficient for only a small fire. Aerosol extinguishers are too small for all but the smallest fires.

There are five types of general-purpose extinguisher, which come in colour-coded containers:

Blue *Dry powder* Use on flammable liquids or electrical equipment. This is the most suitable for keeping in the home and the least dangerous to use.

Red *Water* Use on burning wood, paper or cloth. Do not use on electrical equipment which is still switched on, or on flammable liquids such as petrol, spirits,

oil or cooking fat. Do not use on a TV set even if it has been switched off.

Black *Carbon dioxide* Use on most types of fire, but do not use for oil-burning stoves or small fires.

Cream or White *Foam* Use on flammable liquids.

Green *Vaporising liquid* Use on all large fires, including electrical fires. Do not use in confined spaces because it gives off poisonous fumes.

Using an extinguisher

● Make sure it is suitable for the fire concerned.

● Switch off the current if electrical equipment is involved.

● Crouch to keep clear of the smoke, and sweep the extinguisher from side to side.

● Aim it at the base of the flames and work steadily in from the edge.

● Learn how to use the extinguisher in advance, so no time will be lost.

● Have the extinguisher serviced by the manufacturer every year.

Fitting a fire extinguisher in your car Fit a 1.4kg (3lb) extinguisher containing either dry powder or a vaporising liquid known as BCF. Both are safe for electrical equipment. BCF, which is being phased out, emits fumes that are toxic in a confined space, so air the car afterwards.

Keep the extinguisher where you can reach it instantly – secured under the dashboard, or in the driver's footwell – not in the boot. Get it checked yearly.

WARNING If a fire breaks out in your home, get everyone out of the house before attempting to tackle it, and get someone to call the fire brigade. Do not attempt to tackle a fire if it is fierce or spreading, or looks like becoming so.

Firelighting

Laying and lighting fires

Set aside any large cinders from the dead fire and brush the soot from the back and sides of the fireplace. Sprinkle a little water on the ash to keep the dust down, then remove it.

Lighting with matches Use plenty of dry paper, squeezed loosely into balls or twists. With a little more time, you can make paper crackers, which burn more slowly and give the wood time to get well alight. Roll a sheet of newspaper diagonally and press the roll flat. Double it to a V shape and fold the arms of the V backwards over each other again and again to form a short, concertina-like cracker.

Lay crisscrossed layers of short, dry sticks on the paper. Or use two or three firelighters in place of paper and wood. Finally, put the coal or other solid fuel and the cinders round the wood and on top of it. Use small or medium-sized pieces and set coal with the grain running upwards. Open any draught-control adjuster, then light the paper.

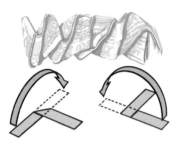

Paper cracker Roll up a sheet of newspaper, flatten it, fold into a V, and fold back each half repeatedly to form a concertina shape. Use as many crackers as necessary.

Gas pokers If you have a convenient gas supply point, use a gas poker. Set it in the base of a pyramid of cinders and solid fuel and ignite the gas – use a taper if you cannot reach it with a match. Leave the poker in position until the fuel is well alight. Calor-gas pokers are available if you have no mains gas.

Fireplaces

Repairing and sealing them off

The principal weak point of a fireplace is usually the fireback. Check it periodically for cracks. These let smoke and heat get behind the fireplace and can weaken the chimney brickwork.

Dealing with a cracked fireback If you have a badly cracked fireback have it replaced completely. Small cracks can be filled with fire cement available from builders' merchants or DIY shops.

Remove soot and loose dirt from the fireback with a stiff bristle or wire brush. Clean out the cracks with a sharp-pointed tool such as a trowel. Use a paintbrush to soak the cracks with water.

While the cracks are still wet, fill them with the fire cement, applied with a putty knife. Now work the clay in as firmly as possible with a trowel. Remove any excess cement and smooth the filled surface using a wetted finger. Leave it to dry for several days before lighting a fire.

Loose or damaged tiles Refix loose tiles with special heat-resistant tile adhesive, available from DIY shops or builders' merchants. See also CERAMIC TILES.

To replace a damaged or broken tile, first break it up with a hammer and cold

steel chisel, starting in the centre and working outwards. Wear thick gloves and safety goggles as protection against flying pieces of tile. Make sure the wall and the edges of the surrounding tiles are clean, by scraping off any old mortar.

Spread fresh adhesive both on the back of the new tile and on the base – use an old paintbrush or applicator supplied with the adhesive. Press the new tile carefully into place, then wipe off any surplus adhesive with a damp cloth. Regrout the joint after 24 hours.

Blocking a disused fireplace A fireplace can be blocked either temporarily or permanently. Before doing so, make sure you have the chimney swept, and have the chimney pot capped with a half-round ridge tile or a cowl.

To block the fireplace permanently, brick up the opening (see BRICKLAYING), laying an air brick at the centre near the bottom – see AIR BRICKS. Plaster the brickwork (see PLASTER PATCHING), to match the surrounding wall, leaving the air brick clear. When the plaster has set, drill and plug the surface to take a louvred ventilation grille over the air brick – see MASONRY DRILLING. The grille, available from DIY shops, and air brick will prevent CONDENSATION forming in the flue and possibly staining the walls.

To block a fireplace temporarily, drill and plug the wall and screw four 50 × 25mm (2 × 1in) BATTENS inside the opening, to make a frame for the cover. Recess the frame so that the cover, when fitted, will be flush with the surrounding chimney breast. Cut a piece of hardboard or PLYWOOD to cover the opening. Using a padsaw, cut a hole at the centre near

the bottom and fit a louvred grille – see SAWS AND SAWING. Screw or nail the cover to the battens and decorate.

If the fireplace is linked to a common flue serving a fireplace still in use, do not fit a grille, through which hot soot may fall. When blocking this fireplace temporarily, use a fire-retardant board.

Firework safety

Avoiding injuries on bonfire night

Guy Fawkes night can end in tragedy when fireworks are not properly handled. Safety measures recommended by the Firework Makers' Guild are:

● Keep fireworks in a closed box; take them out one at a time and put the top back immediately.
● Follow the instructions on each firework carefully – read them by torchlight, never by a naked flame.
● Light the end of a firework fuse at arm's length – preferably with a safety lighter or fuse wick.
● Stand well back; never return to a lit firework – it may go off in your face.
● Never throw fireworks; never put unlit fireworks in your pocket; keep pets indoors.
● Let off your fireworks on a clear site, away from buildings and trees, and stage your display before lighting the bonfire.
● Never light and hold a firework that does not clearly indicate that it is safe to do so; hand-held fireworks should have wooden or plastic handles, and should have a colourful rather than a vigorous spray, shower or explosive effect. Most

---

FIREPLACES

Filling cracks: Blocking off a flue

Cracks in a fireback can lead to heat damage in the chimney brickwork. Always fill small cracks and replace a severely cracked fireback. Alternatively, block the fireplace altogether.

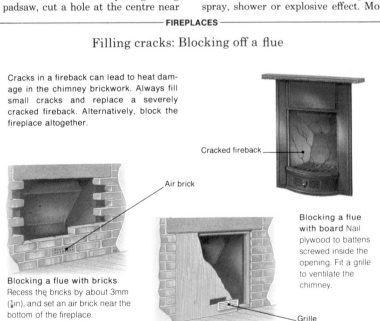

Cracked fireback

Air brick

Blocking a flue with bricks Recess the bricks by about 3mm (⅛in), and set an air brick near the bottom of the fireplace.

Blocking a flue with board Nail plywood to battens screwed inside the opening. Fit a grille to ventilate the chimney.

Grille

others are clearly marked 'Not to be held in the hand'.

● Inspect the site after a display and damp down any remains.

If there is an accident, administer first aid treatment for BURNS and, according to the severity of the injury, seek emergency help. Retailers are forbidden by law to sell fireworks to children under 16 and should not display fireworks until three weeks before November 5.

The Firework Makers' Guild publishes its safety recommendations in *The Firework Code*, which is distributed by the Firework Information Office, PO Box 29, Hove, East Sussex BN3 5RP. The code and posters are also available from firework retailers.

First aid kits

What you need in the home and outdoors

A first aid kit should enable you to treat minor injuries and cope with more serious ones until the casualty gets proper medical help. You can buy ready-made kits from a chemist, or you can assemble your own – perhaps two, one for the home and a smaller one for the car.

Keep a first aid kit in a well-sealed plastic container. Tape to the inside of the lid a card giving the address and telephone number of your doctor and the address of the Accident and Emergency Department of your local hospital. Give also medical details of you and your family such as blood groups, allergies and conditions such as diabetes or asthma.

Mark the container clearly 'First Aid Kit' with, perhaps, a white cross on a green background for quick recognition. Keep your home kit on a shelf out of the reach of children, but where it can be found easily in an emergency. All the family should know where it is kept.

A kit for the home A home kit should have the following items:

● Antiseptic wipes and lotions, for cleaning cuts and wounds.

● Cotton wool, for applying antiseptic and lotions.

● Calamine lotion, for skin inflammations.

● Adhesive dressings, or plasters, of different sizes, for covering small wounds.

● Sterile dressings of different sizes, for covering larger wounds.

● Sterile eye dressing, for eye injuries.

● Tubular gauze, for finger injuries, and tongs to apply it with.

● A roll of 25mm (1in) plaster.

● Triangular bandages, for making a bandage or a sling.

● Crepe or conforming bandages, for sprains and wounds in joints.

● Painkillers, such as paracetamol.

● Antihistamine cream, for insect stings and bites.

● Safety pins, for pinning bandages.

● Tweezers, for removing splinters.

● Blunt-ended scissors, for cutting plaster and bandages.

Outdoors When you are going on holiday or week-ending outdoors, take the first aid kit with you and add to it a foil – or 'space' – blanket. This folds into a tiny packet, but unfolded can be wrapped around a casualty to keep him or her warm in freezing conditions.

In the car A more compact car kit could consist of:

● Adhesive dressings.

● Sterile dressings.

● Triangular bandages.

● Crepe bandages.

● Antiseptic cream, for grazes.

● Scissors.

● Assorted safety pins.

● Antihistamine cream, for stings.

● Calamine lotion, for sunburn.

Fish cleaning

Preparing fresh fish for cooking

Fresh fish are often sold ready prepared, but if you catch or buy fresh fish you must clean, skin, fillet and bone them yourself for cooking.

Cleaning For round fish, such as herring, first cut off the fins with scissors, then remove the scales by holding the fish by the tail and scraping the blunt side of a knife blade along the body from tail to head. Rinse loose scales away under the tap.

To gut the fish, slit it along the belly from just below the head to just above the tail, with a sharp knife. Scrape the entrails away and rinse inside the fish with cold water, rubbing it with salt to remove any black skin. Trim away the gills and cut off the tail, using a sharp knife or kitchen scissors. The head can be left on or cut off just beneath the gills.

Smaller round fish such as sprats and sardines need very little preparation: simply cut off the head and gently squeeze out the entrails. Rinse the fish and dab it dry with a cloth or a paper towel.

For flat fish, such as plaice, cut off the fins and gills. Lay the fish dark side down and make a semicircular split just below the head, to remove the entrails. The head and tail can be cut off, too, with a sharp knife or kitchen scissors. Wash the whole fish in cold water and dry with paper towels.

Skinning Round fish can be skinned, but are usually cooked with the skin on. To skin small, whole round fish, use a

sharp knife to cut straight down the back and to loosen the skin on one side of the head. Then dip your fingers in salt and, gripping the cut end of the skin firmly, draw it down to the tail. Do the same on the other side of the body.

Flat fish often have the dark skin removed before cooking, but the white skin is left in place. Lay the fish on the work surface with the white skin downwards and make a cut across the point where the tail joins the body. Run a thumbnail between the cut skin and the flesh to free the skin along both edges. Then, again dipping the fingers in salt, hold the fish down by the tail with one hand and use the other to strip the skin back towards the head.

Remove the dark skin from fillets of flat or round fish by putting the fillet, dark side down, on the work surface and inserting a knife blade between skin and flesh, starting at the tail end. Hold the skin tightly at the end and 'saw' the flesh away from the skin.

Filleting After cleaning, fillet a large round fish, such as a haddock, by cutting off the head and slicing deeply along the back and down to the backbone with a sharp flexible knife. Hold the blade at an angle to the bone and cut the first fillet away from it, working from head to tail. Then insert the knife point beneath the backbone in order to lever it away from the flesh. Now pull the backbone from the remaining fillet and cut off the tail.

Flat fish are filleted into four pieces by slitting down the backbone on the dark side and making a semicircular cut just below the head through half the thickness of the fish. The first fillet, from the side nearest you, can now be separated from the bone with short sharp strokes of the knife. Cut it free along the outer edge and at the tail. Remove the second fillet in the same way before turning the fish over to fillet the light side.

Boning After cleaning a large round fish, such as salmon or salmon trout, cut off the fins and gills, and cut a small V shape around the tail to stop the skin shrinking. Rinse the fish and then poach it – see POACHING. Cut the skin of the cooked fish just below the head and above the tail, and gently peel it off. Then cut the backbone below the head and above the tail leaving head and tail intact. Slice the fish down the backbone and ease the bone out through this cut, taking care not to break the fish.

Before boning smaller round fish, such as herring and mackerel, remove the entrails, head and tail. Slit the fish along the underside and spread it open, with the exposed flesh downwards, on the work surface. Press down with your fingers along the length of the backbone to loosen it. Then turn the fish over and, starting from the head, run your thumb

Methods of cleaning, skinning, filleting and boning fish

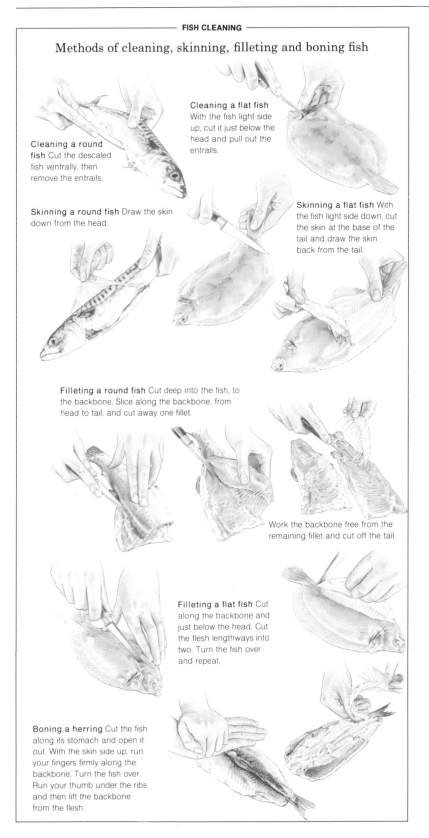

Cleaning a round fish Cut the descaled fish ventrally, then remove the entrails.

Cleaning a flat fish With the fish light side up, cut it just below the head and pull out the entrails.

Skinning a round fish Draw the skin down from the head.

Skinning a flat fish With the fish light side down, cut the skin at the base of the tail and draw the skin back from the tail.

Filleting a round fish Cut deep into the fish, to the backbone. Slice along the backbone, from head to tail, and cut away one fillet.

Work the backbone free from the remaining fillet and cut off the tail.

Filleting a flat fish Cut along the backbone and just below the head. Cut the flesh lengthways into two. Turn the fish over and repeat.

Boning a herring Cut the fish along its stomach and open it out. With the skin side up, run your fingers firmly along the backbone. Turn the fish over. Run your thumb under the ribs and then lift the backbone from the flesh.

between the ribs and flesh on one side, loosening the bones. Repeat on the other side. Lift up the backbone and pull it clear. The fish can be folded back into shape for cooking or cut into two. See also GRILLING.

Fish hook removal

What to do if you become the catch

If the fish hook is well embedded in your flesh – say, in a finger – do not try to pull it back out of the wound, as the barb will tear the flesh. If possible, get to the casualty department of a hospital to have it removed. In an emergency, however, push the rest of the barb through the skin, working it forwards and up, until it is clear of the wound. Clip off the barb with the wire-cutting section of a pair of pliers and pull out the shaft.

Clean and use antiseptic on the wound as soon as possible, cover it (see BANDAGING) and see a doctor if necessary. You may need a tetanus injection if you have not had a booster in the last five years.

Fishing

River, lake and sea fishing techniques

Freshwater fishing is classified as either fly or game fishing for salmon or trout, or coarse fishing, for any other fish. Fly fishermen attract fish to the hook with lures made to resemble flies or small water creatures – see FLY TYING. In coarse fishing the hook is baited with food (for example, maggots, worms or bread) and is either held on the bottom with a weight or suspended just below the surface by a float. Sea angling generally uses the same techniques as coarse fishing, though with stronger equipment.

Ledgering A weight, known as a ledger weight, on the coarse fisherman's line holds the bait down where it will attract fish feeding near the bottom, such as bream, tench and barbel. The line runs freely through the ledger weight so that the fish feels no resistance when it takes the bait. The hook can also be attached to the line on a short link, known as a paternoster. Ledgering is good for fishing in both still and running water.

Assemble the FISHING TACKLE and bait the hook. Stand where your shadow will not fall on the water and frighten away any fish. Attract fish to the stretch of water by throwing in groundbait or hook bait; throw it just upstream if you are fishing running water.

Buy groundbait in a fishing-tackle shop or make your own by drying out stale bread in an oven and crumbling it

How to cast a bait or lure

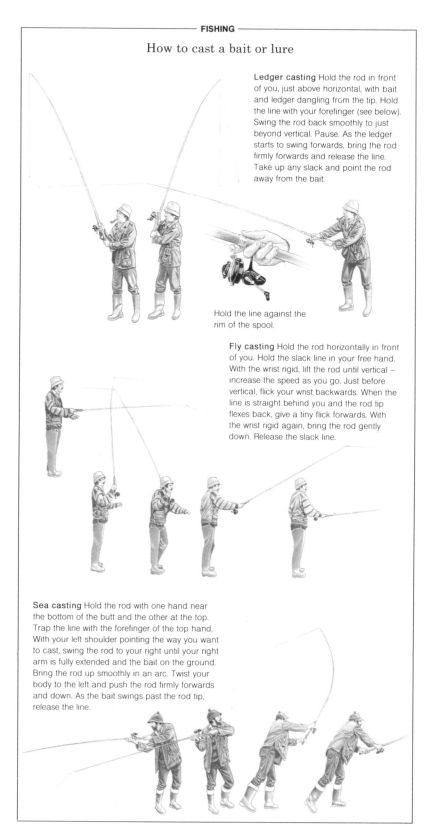

Ledger casting Hold the rod in front of you, just above horizontal, with bait and ledger dangling from the tip. Hold the line with your forefinger (see below). Swing the rod back smoothly to just beyond vertical. Pause. As the ledger starts to swing forwards, bring the rod firmly forwards and release the line. Take up any slack and point the rod away from the bait.

Hold the line against the rim of the spool.

Fly casting Hold the rod horizontally in front of you. Hold the slack line in your free hand. With the wrist rigid, lift the rod until vertical – increase the speed as you go. Just before vertical, flick your wrist backwards. When the line is straight behind you and the rod tip flexes back, give a tiny flick forwards. With the wrist rigid again, bring the rod gently down. Release the slack line.

Sea casting Hold the rod with one hand near the bottom of the butt and the other at the top. Trap the line with the forefinger of the top hand. With your left shoulder pointing the way you want to cast, swing the rod to your right until your right arm is fully extended and the bait on the ground. Bring the rod up smoothly in an arc. Twist your body to the left and push the rod firmly forwards and down. As the bait swings past the rod tip, release the line.

finely. At the water's edge soak a small handful of groundbait and press it into the size of a table-tennis ball or an orange, depending on the number of fish you hope to catch. Throw in just a few balls or the fish will fill themselves and not be interested in the hook bait.

Cast the baited hook using a fixed-spool reel, as illustrated. After casting, take up any slack line, point the rod away from the bait, and lay it in rests with its tip near the water.

Fix a quivertip or swingtip to the rod end. A quivertip is a small device made of glass or carbon which quivers at the slightest touch on the hook. A swingtip is a rubber device which hangs from the rod tip and swings upwards when a fish bites. If either moves, trap the line against the rod butt with a forefinger, then raise the tip firmly but gently, to make sure the fish is securely hooked. Pull in the fish, keeping the rod tip up and the line taut, until you can reach it with a submerged landing net and bring it to land.

Float fishing A float and a small weight holds the bait at the depth you want. Try adjusting the distance between the weight and the float, you can suspend the bait at any depth where fish are likely to be feeding. Float fishing is suitable in both running and still water.

Assemble the tackle and attach a plummet weight to the hook. Lower the plummet and float into the water where you want to fish. If the float submerges, draw it up the line closer to you; if it flops over, push it down closer to the plummet. Adjust it until it floats upright. You now know the depth of the water and can adjust the float to hold bait at the depth where fish are feeding.

Attract fish to the water you are fishing with groundbait and bait the hook. Cast the bait and float as in ledgering. If you are fishing still water, simply cast into the water you want to fish and lay the rod in rests. If you are fishing running water, use the technique known as trotting, with the float attached by its top and bottom. Cast the bait slightly upstream of the stretch you want to fish. Hold the rod steady for a moment so that the bait moves ahead of the float. Then lower the rod and let the float, preceded by the bait, move downstream. Keep the line between rod and float taut.

When a fish bites, the float may not plunge dramatically. In running water, in particular, it may merely hesitate or flicker slightly.

Casting a fly Before you attempt fly fishing, master the art of casting. You can practise on a lawn with a small piece of paper at the end of the line instead of a fly.

Put together the tackle and cast as illustrated. At the end of the cast, the line should run out smoothly and the paper land lightly.

Fly fishing for trout There are two principal forms of fly fishing for trout: wet fly fishing and dry fly fishing. Wet flies are fished underwater and are meant to look like tiny water creatures, minnows or drowning insects. Dry flies are fished on the surface of the water and are meant to look like insects alighting momentarily. See also FLY TYING.

When wet fly fishing, you can use as many as three flies at a time. In running water, cast directly across the stream and let the flies drift around with the current before you cast again. In still water, gradually pull in the line to draw the flies towards you. Keep your eye on the line where it enters the water. If it makes an unusual movement, strike.

Dry fly fishing is done only in running water. Cast just upstream of where you think a fish is, then let the fly drift down over the fish's nose, pulling gently so the line does not go slack. When you see a fish bite, pause for a moment to let it take the fly before striking.

Fishing for salmon The techniques for salmon fishing are essentially the same as those for wet fly fishing for trout. But the equipment used is stronger and the flies are larger and brighter.

Another effective technique for catching salmon – as well as most coarse fish – is spinning. In spinning, a bright artificial lure, usually made of metal, is cast out, then pulled rapidly through the water. Its erratic movements make it look like a small sick or injured fish.

Sea angling from a beach or pier Fish that can be caught from the shore include mackerel, bass, flounder and cod. You can use an artificial lure on the hook, or bait it, for example, with lugworms, small crabs or baby squid.

When fishing with bait, attach a weight near the tip of the line to help carry the bait out to sea. When fishing from a beach, always fish an incoming tide, otherwise your bait will be in increasingly shallow water. Cast the bait out as illustrated. You can hold the rod or set it on rests until a fish bites.

See also FISHING RIGHTS.

Fishing rights

Getting permission and a licence to go fishing

You may not fish in a freshwater river, stream, lake, pond or canal without permission from the owners of the fishing rights. The rights in a river belong to the owners of the land adjoining it, and cover

the half of the river bed on their side.

Fishing rights on lakes and ponds belong to the owner of the surrounding land. Information on canals can be obtained from the Fisheries Officer of the British Waterways region concerned.

The simplest way to obtain permission to fish in fresh water is to join a local angling club which rents fishing rights from the owner of the water.

Fishing licences In all waters in England and Wales you must also have a licence to fish in fresh water. You can get one from the fisheries officer of the local water authority, or from a fishing-tackle shop or angling club. In Scotland you do not need a licence for coarse fishing, but must have one for salmon and trout fishing.

Close seasons It is illegal to catch certain fish at certain times of the year. In England and Wales the close season for coarse fishing is March 15 to June 15; for salmon, November 1 to January 31; and for trout, October 1 to the last day of February, although local bylaws can vary the dates. The close season for rainbow trout is laid down by local bylaws. In Scotland the close season for trout is October 7 to March 14, the close season for salmon varies from river to river.

Sea fishing No licence is needed for fishing in the sea and tidal waters, and there is no close season. You do not need permission to fish from the shore as long as no local bylaws forbid it, but you must obtain permission from the owner, usually the council, for pier fishing.

Fishing tackle

Choosing and caring for rods and equipment

Most fishing rods are made from carbon fibre or hollow glass fibre. Carbon fibre makes lighter, stronger rods than glass fibre, with what some anglers regard as a better casting action.

Other equipment There are three principal kinds of reel for holding and winding lines – centrepin, fixed-spool and multiplier.

The simplest is the centrepin, a rotating drum on a central spindle. On a fixed-spool reel, the drum stays still but a rotating pick-up arm pulls the line in. The multiplier is a centrepin reel geared to wind in the line at great speed.

Coarse and sea-fishing lines are generally made from nylon monofilament. Modern fly-fishing lines are made from plastic-coated synthetic materials which float or sink. Make sure to buy a line that suits your rod – a tackle-shop assistant will guide you, if necessary.

Rods, reels, floats and lures

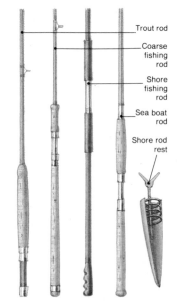

Trout rod

Coarse fishing rod

Shore fishing rod

Sea boat rod

Shore rod rest

Rods and rests Different kinds of rod have been developed for particular kinds of fishing – even particular fish. Make sure to get the correct type. For coarse fishing and sea angling, you can also use a rod rest.

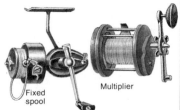

Fixed spool

Multiplier

Reels Use a fixed-spool reel for most coarse fishing. For fly fishing, use a centrepin reel. A multiplier is good for spinning or bait fishing with heavy tackle.

Centrepin

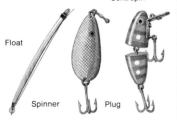

Float

Spinner

Plug

Floats and lures A float suspends bait in the water and indicates if a fish has taken the bait. Spinners and plugs are lures – or artificial baits. When buying them get the advice of a local fishing shop, where they will know what is best for local waters.

For fly fishing you also need a selection of leaders – lengths of nylon monofilament about 1m (3ft) long which are tied to the outer end of the line – the flies themselves, and a landing net.

For ledgering you need a net, rod rests and ledger weights. For float fishing, you need a net, rests, floats and weights.

Looking after fishing tackle Always clean a rod after use. Rub it with a clean damp cloth, followed by a dry one. After sea angling, first remove all traces of salt by washing in fresh water. If you are not going to use your rod again for several weeks, smear the exposed metal parts with petroleum jelly. Wipe it off before using the rod again.

On a rod used regularly, check the rings every three months. If the line has cut grooves in any of them or they are cracked, replace them. Clean inside the ferrules (which hold the rod sections together), with a meths-soaked cloth wrapped around a stick. Retouch any damaged VARNISHING – especially on split-cane rods – to keep out water.

Clean a reel after use. Take off the line and rub the reel with a clean damp cloth, then a dry one. With a fixed-spool reel, rub the outside and all moving parts with thin oil on a rag. With a centrepin reel, pull the two halves apart and rub with thin oil on a rag. If you have been sea angling, wash the reel in fresh water, wipe it dry, then cover it with a thin layer of petroleum jelly to prevent corrosion. Every six months, pull a reel apart, clean and lubricate with thin oil.

Store fishing tackle in a dry place out of sunlight. Keep rods in cloth covers loosely tied in the middle.

Flagstones

Making and re-laying paths; curing unevenness

Precast concrete flagstones are commonly 50mm (2in) thick and 460mm (18in) or 610mm (2ft) in length or width.

Making a path Clear the area to be paved of all topsoil, and mark the width of the path, using string and wooden pegs. Try to work in multiples of flagstone widths to reduce the need for cutting them to size. Allow 10mm ($\frac{3}{8}$in) jointing gaps between slabs (use wooden spacers while laying).

Consolidate any soft ground by ramming hardcore or rubble into it. If the path is close to the house, give it a slight crossways slope away from the house, so that rainwater can drain away.

There are three different ways of laying flagstones:

Sand bed Prepare a bed of sand 38-50mm ($1\frac{1}{2}$-2in) thick, and lay the slabs on it. Use a spirit level to ensure the surfaces lie flush, tapping them down as necessary with a cushioning block of wood and a club hammer. There is, however, a risk of movement or settlement with this method.

Mortar blobs Make bedding MORTAR of one part cement to four of sharp or concrete sand and the minimum of water. Mix it so that it just binds together but does not slump (collapse). For each slab, lay five generous blobs – one for each corner and one in the middle – and lay the slab on these, tapping it level as for a sand bed.

Bed of mortar Lay down a thin layer of sand to fill in any gaps in the hardcore. Make up the mortar mix as for blobs, but put down a complete layer 25mm (1in) thick. Lay the slabs on this, again tapping them level.

Re-laying If a flagstone rocks or is uneven, use the edge of a spade to prise it up. Clean the underside and stack it vertically. Level off or build up the sand bed, then re-lay, tapping level.

If mortar blobs were used, chip away the old mortar – either from the flagstone or the bed – with a cold chisel. Mix new mortar and re-lay the slab.

If the slab was on a mortar bed, it should remain trouble-free unless undue weight has been put on it. In this case, lift the slab, break up the old mortar with a club hammer, and clear it out. Lay a new mortar bed and replace the slab.

Jointing With new and repaired paths, it is best to fill joints with mortar – wait for at least two days after laying. Sand can be used, but it encourages the growth of weeds. Mix the mortar using one part cement, two of sand and the minimum of water so the mix feels dry and crumbly. Use an old paintbrush to damp the joints with clean water, then fill each joint with mortar, using a small bricklayer's trowel.

When the gaps are filled, draw a piece of bent tubing or dowel (see DOWELS) along each joint to give a slight hollow.

Flambé cooking

A culinary spectacle

In this method of cooking, brandy, or another spirit or liqueur, is poured over food cooked in a wide shallow pan and set alight just before the dish is served. The result is not just spectacular: the flaming alcohol leaves its flavour to enrich that of the food.

Kebabs, shellfish, steaks, veal escalopes and other dishes which do not require long cooking are suitable for flambéing. A number of desserts also respond well to the flame treatment: the best known is probably CRÊPES SUZETTE.

For the diners to enjoy the spectacle, prepare the dish at the table, using a CHAFING DISH or a small spirit burner. Cook the food in the shallow pan until it is ready, then pour on the spirit with the pan still over the heat. When the spirit is hot, put a lighted match to the edge of the pan and the rising vapour will burst into flames. Shake the pan gently to incorporate the liquor evenly in the sauce and serve straight from the pan as soon as the flames die.

WARNING Do not wear lacy cuffs, and tie back long hair. Never flambé near furnishings which might catch fire.

FLAGSTONES

Laying a flagged path for heavy wear

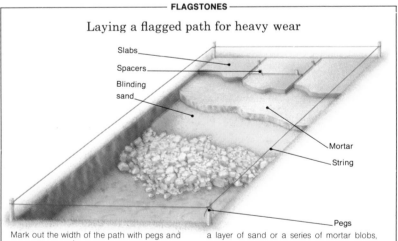

Slabs
Spacers
Blinding sand
Mortar
String
Pegs

Mark out the width of the path with pegs and string. Clear away the topsoil. Ram hardcore or rubble into any soft ground. To make a hard-wearing path to bear a heavily laden wheelbarrow, for example, lay down a thin layer of what is called 'blinding sand' with mortar on top. For an ordinary path, put down a layer of sand or a series of mortar blobs, one at each corner and one in the middle. Lay the slabs on top using wooden spacers to leave 10mm ($\frac{3}{8}$in) gaps between them. With a spirit level, make sure the slabs are flush with each other. Tap uneven slabs down with a wooden block and club hammer.

Pointing and bending flashings

Flashing

Mortar

Wedge

Re-pointing Secure flashing with wedges during pointing. Fill wedge holes later.

Wedge

Zinc or lead

Bending metal flashing Set a sliding bevel at the angle needed for a snug fit (above). Bend the metal carefully over the edge of a board (right) until it matches the angle set on the bevel.

Sliding bevel

Flashings

Repairing and renewing; fixing leaks

A flashing is a waterproof semi-flexible strip used to seal a gap between two surfaces – such as brickwork and a roof. Lead flashings were once common, but are now expensive. For matching patched-in repairs, you can use cheaper materials such as zinc or bituminous felt. Both are sandwiched into the MORTAR joints. For completely renewing flashing, it is easier to use self-adhesive metal-backed flashing tape.

Repairing If a flashing has pulled out from a mortar joint, rake out all the crumbling pieces with an old chisel. Brush out the gap, then damp it all thoroughly.

Re-point with mortar mix – see POINT-ING. Add only a limited quantity of water, to produce a dryish mix, that will not spill on the brickwork and stain it. If the flashing needs to be held in place while the mortar is applied, push wooden wedges, or tiny rolls of lead or bitumen felt into the gaps. When the mortar has dried, remove the wedges and fill the holes with mortar.

Patching To replace badly damaged flashing, chip away any mortar still holding it in place, using a cold chisel and club hammer, and lever out the old material. Clean out the joint to a depth of at least 25mm (1in), then dust the gap with an old paintbrush.

Buy a roll or sheet of lead, zinc or bituminous-fibre flashing and cut it to the required width (down a roof slope, it will have to be stepped to fit into mortar joints). With metal, work with 1.5m (5ft) lengths; each has to be bent to shape, so use a sliding bevel – a sort of adjustable try square – to set the angle between wall and roof.

Lay a zinc or lead strip on a board, and use a wooden mallet to lap over 19mm ($\frac{3}{4}$in) of material for the edge which will go in the wall. Then place the centre of the strip over the board edge, and shape the strip to match the angle set on the sliding bevel. Shape bituminous-fibre material by hand when it is in position, using a blowtorch or hot-air gun to soften it as you work. It will hold the required shape when it hardens again.

Make sure the roof and wall where the flashing will go is clean, then damp the gap in the brickwork with clean water. Insert the edge of the strip into the gap, and wedge it there with wood, rolls of flashing or scrap lead strip. Apply a wide band of bituminous waterproofing compound to the roof where the flashing will lie. Gently tap down zinc or lead flashing with the wooden mallet until it is in close contact with the compound.

Fill the gap in the brickwork with fresh mortar, pushing it well in. When it is dry, remove the wedges and fill the holes with mortar.

Where cracks in the flashing are letting water in, seal them with a bituminous sealant or mastic compound, applied with a small trowel. If necessary, use strips of glass-fibre tape or hessian sandwiched between layers of sealant to reinforce it. Materials are available from DIY stores and builders' merchants.

If the flashing shows signs of deterioration but is still bonded to the wall, apply a coat of flashing primer, then cover it with a strip of self-adhesive flashing tape, pressed well down to give a weatherproof seal. The primer is supplied by the tape manufacturers, and some packs have a can of primer.

Renewing Remove the flashing completely, scraping out all debris, as before. Then clean off the area with a stiff brush. Fill in the joints with mortar and let it harden before fitting self-adhesive flashing tape (this is not tucked into the joint).

First coat the surface with the primer to ensure thorough adhesion.

Normally, the flashing can be bonded firmly in place, but where considerable structural movement is likely – such as where a garage joins a house wall – do not press the tape fully home, to allow for any small gap opening and closing.

At internal corners, cut the lower edge of the tape and overlap it. At external corners, patch in a square with the upper edges cut and splayed round the angle, then lay the main tape with the lower edges cut and splayed over the patch.

Flat feet

Helping children to avoid them; relieving them

Children are born with flat feet. It may take many years before a child has developed muscles that are strong enough to support the normal arched shape of the feet, and until then the feet will look flat when weight bears on them.

Children with knock-knees put more pressure on the inner edges of the feet and so are more likely to be flat footed. In the vast majority of cases flat feet are painless and no treatment is required. Children with painless flat feet are best left untreated but, whenever possible, allowed to run around without shoes and socks so that the feet can develop normally. Shoe wedges sometimes help reduce wear on shoes, but will not speed the development of the foot arches.

Some people's joints are supported by particularly elastic ligaments which means that their joints remain very flexible into adult life. Other people's feet tend to point outwards so that their body weight presses down on the foot arches rather than on the centre of the feet. Their foot arches tend to flatten out when they stand so that they continue to have flat feet into adult life.

Although the condition is usually painless and no treatment is required, there are exceptions. If the deformity is present at birth and the feet are so rigid that they cannot be gently manipulated into a normal position the baby may require splints or surgical correction. Occasionally flat-footed adults develop 'foot strain' in which case the feet are painful, particularly after standing or walking. They may also develop other foot deformities such as bunions or curly toes which require treatment. Flat-footed children and adults should be sure to wear well-fitting shoes and, if necessary, lose weight. Regular exercise will strengthen the muscles, and arch supports in the shoes may be comforting. If foot strain is very painful a period of rest and strapping of the foot followed by gradually increasing exercise will usually provide relief. If it does not, consult your DOCTOR.

Fleas

Ridding your furniture and carpets of them

It is usually cats and dogs that bring fleas into a home – and more often in summer when fleas thrive; they tend to die off in cold weather. Fleas live by sucking blood from the host animal. They do not live on the host all the time but usually in carpeting, bedding or furniture with easy access to the host. If their preferred host is not available, they will make do with the blood from a human or another animal for a short time. Their bites cause pink spots that itch for three or four days and then disappear. Calamine lotion will ease the itching.

Fleas may get onto humans when they cuddle their pets; or may reach them from a chair or bed that a pet has been allowed on; or, more commonly, they may bite children because children play on carpets that are harbouring fleas.

Regular treatment is best to keep fleas down. There are veterinary insecticidal shampoos for ridding dogs of fleas, but with cats especially, it is easier to dust on a veterinary flea powder. Sprinkle the powder on carpets also and suck it up later with a vacuum cleaner. Wash the pet's bedding regularly and spray it, and upholstery that may be affected, with an aerosol insecticide based on permethrin or methoprene.

Once fleas have moved in, carry out a thorough treatment to kill adult fleas. Repeat it ten days later to kill fleas that have matured during the ten days, but have not yet laid any eggs.

Flooding

Taking precautions and surviving

In an area prone to flooding, ask the local water board if there is a system of warnings, and be alert for them. If your home is liable to flooding, keep a supply of sandbags ready and always have emergency supplies in the house. Check your insurance policies and find out from the insurance company whether any special provisions affect you. When flooding threatens, block gaps under all outer doors with sandbags placed outside them. If you do not have real ones, improvise by filling plastic bags or pillowcases with sand or garden soil. Or pack the gaps with carpets or blankets. If rising water seems likely to reach window level, sandbag windowsills in the same way.

Indoors, turn off gas and electricity at the mains to minimise the risk of fire and electric shock. If there is time, try to minimise damage by taking valuables, appliances, furniture and even carpets upstairs. If your home is a bungalow, put what you can in the roof space and raise the rest as high as possible – onto shelves, tables and on top of built-in furniture, for example.

If the flood water continues to rise, take all food upstairs and as many drinks and filled drinking vessels as you can, and fill baths and basins with drinking water. Take up warm clothing, matches and candles and a portable stove, if you have one, on which to cook. Take up a battery-powered radio so that you can hear about aid and rescue, and about weather prospects.

In an isolated area, try to keep handy some sort of signalling device – a torch, whistle, or oily rags for burning, for example – to summon help – see DISTRESS SIGNALS.

A serious and prolonged flood may force you out onto the roof. Take rope or sheets to tie yourself to a chimney-stack, so that you will not be swept away. Before going outside, put on warmest clothing and footwear. Eat and drink as much as you can to build up energy reserves, and take your signalling equipment with you.

Do not leave your home unless your life is in danger there. If, as a last resort, you have to go for help, try to improvise a raft from any buoyant material, such as an airbed, a cabinet or wardrobe or planks of wood (floorboards, for example) lashed together with sheets. Make sure it floats before boarding and take something to paddle with – perhaps a tray or broom – and also a signalling device.

If you are on foot in flood water, remember that even a small stream, swollen by fast-flowing water, may be powerful enough to sweep you away. Look for a walking staff of some kind to use as a third leg for stability and also to probe for depth. Watch out for debris which can knock you over.

Floor refinishing

Restoring and repolishing floorboards

Floorboards which have been sealed instead of covered, to let the natural beauty of the wood show, become scuffed and scratched in time – especially if not protected by slip mats or rugs.

Restoring Strip away the old finish with an industrial floor sander and an edging sander – see SANDING. You can rent them from one of the hire shops – see HIRING. Clear the room of furnishings and seal over the doors with plastic sheeting, or fine dust will spread everywhere. The sander has a wide abrasive belt and a dust bag to pick up most of the dust produced. However, you should wear a face mask and ear-muffs – sold in DIY shops – to avoid breathing in the dust and to protect your ears from being damaged by the row from this extremely noisy machine.

Before you use the sander, check the floor for protruding nails or tacks, which could damage the abrasive belt. Use a hammer and nail punch to knock nails down below the surface; pull out tacks with a claw hammer or pincers.

A fine abrasive belt will remove an old decorative finish, but if the floorboards have uneven areas that need levelling, use a coarse belt first and then a fine one. Use the edging sander in corners or other spots which the sander will not reach. Vacuum thoroughly to remove all traces of dust. Wear thick socks or rope-soled or white-soled footwear when you are sanding and refinishing to avoid making marks on the floorboards.

Refinishing DIY shops sell a range of wood stains or dyes, from light oak through to ebony – see STAINING WOOD. Buy a small amount first to try on a hidden patch; stains often look different after application. The sealing compound enriches the colour of the wood so you should try this on a small patch of floor before deciding whether you need a stain or dye. Sand off your trial patches before starting the whole job.

If you are going to put on a stain or dye, apply it with a paintbrush or pad (see PAINTBRUSHES, PADS AND ROLLERS) or a pad of lint-free cloth. Apply evenly, so the finish will not look patchy.

When the stain is dry, lightly sand over the floor with a sanding block, using fine abrasive paper and working with the grain of the wood, to avoid scratches. This will remove any roughness where the stain has raised the wood grain.

Dust off thoroughly, then apply a first coat of flooring-grade wood seal or varnish – see VARNISHING. A good way to do this is with a 'rubber' – soak a cotton-wool wad with the sealer, then wrap it in a piece of lint-free cloth, such as an old handkerchief. Use it to rub the seal or varnish well in. Allow it to dry thoroughly for the time recommended by the maker.

Now brush on two or three more coats, allowing each to dry before the next is applied. The layers will provide a tough finish, but it is still wise to protect the areas that are walked on most with mats or rugs.

Floor repairs

Dealing with damage; curing squeaks in wooden floors

Undue weight on one section of flooring can crack or split a board. You should lift and replace the damaged section.

If the boards are butt-joined, slip a wide-bladed chisel – called a bolster – in at the end of the board to lever it up. If

FLOOR REPAIRS

Lifting and filling

Lifting butt-joined boards Cut the board just before a joist. Prise up the end with a bolster until the nails rise enough for you to draw them out with a claw hammer.

Filling small gaps Press in papier mâché with a filling knife and clean off the excess. Leave the filling to set hard, then smooth it with medium-grade sandpaper.

you are lifting a long section, raise the end, then lever up alternate sides, slipping a scrap piece of wood into the gaps to keep them open.

Once the board is up, remove all nails from it and saw off the damaged section, cutting back to the centre of the nearest joist. Buy a replacement length of the same thickness.

Nail short BATTENS to the sides of the JOISTS beneath the old board to support the replacement length, then nail the new board in place.

If the boards are tongued and grooved, use a general-purpose saw (see SAWS AND SAWING) to cut between the boards for the full length of the piece to be removed. Start the cut with the end of the saw. Take great care not to cut into electric cables or pipes beneath. Alternatively, use a power circular saw, with its depth of cut set to about 13mm ($\frac{1}{2}$in), which will be just enough to cut through the tongue without cutting into any pipes or cables.

This cut will remove the whole tongue from one board. Now insert the bolster and lever along the cut side to lift the board along one edge. This will loosen the floor nails. Now use a claw hammer to remove the nails.

When fitting the new length of board, you may be able to work its tongue into the groove of the neighbouring board – if too much damage was not done easing the old board out. Then carry on as for butted boards.

Rotten boards If you find cracks across the wood grain and a musty smell, suspect DRY ROT. If the wood is dotted with small holes, suspect WOODWORM.

Worn boards In older homes, the wood may have worn away due to constant use. You may be able to turn the board over. Follow the steps outlined for cracks and splits, then turn the board over and refit it. You may need to fit small wood packing pieces between the board and the joists if the board does not lie flat. Glue them in place with PVA wood adhesive before nailing down the reversed board. Replace a badly worn board with a new one.

Shrunken boards Recently installed CENTRAL HEATING may cause this problem. Fill small gaps with PAPIER MÂCHÉ. Do not use proprietary fillers: they will break up and drop out. Fill large gaps with slips of wood cut to a slight wedge shape, glued, then tapped into place with a mallet or rubber hammer. When the glue has dried, plane off any protruding wood flush with the surface.

Squeaks These are caused by one board edge rubbing against another. Puff talcum powder between the boards, or screw through boards where they pass over a joist (often the board groans as the screw is tightened down).

Loose boards These often occur where the flooring has been lifted to install piping or cable, then carelessly replaced. Screw the loose board firmly onto the joists – a screw will hold it tighter than a nail and is easily removed if access is needed again.

Flower arranging

Basic design principles; keeping the flowers fresh

The materials you need include containers of various shapes and sizes, 50mm (2in) wire mesh, pinholders, Plasticine or floral clay and blocks of special porous material, obtainable from florists.

The mesh is cut to size and crumpled into the base of the container to hold flower stems at different angles. Or stems can be pressed onto a pinholder, which is secured to the container bottom by a wedge of Plasticine or floral clay.

A porous block – especially useful for holding flowers in shallow containers – should be soaked before use and kept moist. It should also be stored in a plastic bag when not in use to keep it moist, as it does not easily absorb water a second time. It is held in position by a special adhesive tape, stocked by florists, or it can simply be impaled on a pinholder. Oasis is not suitable for very soft stems.

FLOWER ARRANGING

Making different shapes

Massed Cut all the flowers slightly longer than the container, using enough to fill it. The rim will give sufficient support.

Use a deep container.

Arrange the side stems at right angles to the centre stem.

All-round Place the long centre stem first, then use the same length for the lowest stems. Fill in evenly with shorter stems.

Place the flowers in the same way as an all-round design.

Long and low Cut the centre stem short but the side stems long to extend out over the rim of the container and dip to the table.

Use flowers with long stems to make a semicircular outline.

Front facing Raise the mesh or holder higher at the back and put the focal stem three-quarters of the way back.

Before starting an arrangement, consider the decor of the room and the position of the display, the basic shape and scale you want to achieve and the flowers available. If you are using large blooms like roses or chrysanthemums, you may choose a solid shape, such as an oval or a triangle. With tall, slender flowers such as gladioli, you may want to work in curves.

Colour can be used sparingly for gentle harmony, like putting together two shades which are close to each other in the spectrum, such as violet and blue. Or you can make dramatic contrasts with different colours. Dark, strong colours catch the eye more quickly than restrained, delicate ones. So, bolder colours should feature low in the visual centre of your arrangement.

To begin, partly fill the container with fresh water before inserting any flowers. The water level can be topped up when the arrangement is complete. Strip away leaves from the parts of the flower stems which will be submerged.

Massed arrangement This is the simplest type of arrangement – a bunch of marigolds or cornflowers, for example, massed tightly together. The emphasis is on colour rather than design. The success of the arrangement depends on using a suitable container – high enough to give support and not too wide at the neck – and on using enough flowers. A sparse bunch will simply flop.

All-round design In this kind of display, use a wide-necked container to give room for the stems to radiate out in all directions. To give additional support to the central stems, raise wire mesh in the centre to form a mound above the rim.

The main focus of all-round design is the tall central stem, which must be vertical. Arrange the side stems at right angles to it. Place stems of intermediate length between the focal and side stems, all leaning away from the centre.

Do not concentrate exclusively on one side; the arrangement will be seen from all sides. Fill any gaps with shorter stems or foliage, remembering that stems should radiate from a central point, not cross one another.

Long, low arrangements This kind of display is suitable for a dining table. Use a shallow container so that diners can see each other across the table. Make the arrangement round or oval to suit the shape of the table.

Front-facing arrangements These are suitable for standing close to a wall. Make the focal point nearer the back and the outline semicircular. Place the front-facing flowers down from the top centre to below the level of the rim and use extra flowers at the sides.

Keeping flowers fresh Cut garden flowers early in the morning, before the sun gets to them. Do not buy flowers that have been standing in the sun. Never place an arrangement in full sun, beside a fire or radiator, on top of a television set or near strong lamps, because heat causes cut flowers to wilt. Keep them out of draughts, too, as these cause water loss. If a little mild disinfectant is added, the water need not be changed daily, but fresh water must be added to keep up the level.

Glass vessels are not ideal for flowers, since they let in sunlight which causes bacterial decay (and foul water shortens the lives of flowers). However, you can buy preservatives from florists or garden centres to add to the water; alternatively, add to each pint of water, a teaspoon of sugar and half a teaspoon of bleach.

QUICK TIP Revive wilted blooms by cutting the stems underwater, by standing the stem ends in boiling water, or by letting the flowers float in water for a while.

Flower drying

Preserving blooms for dried-flower arranging

The simplest way to preserve flowers is to hang them up for several weeks to dry naturally. A faster way is to use chemicals, which can sometimes complete the drying in a matter of days. You can preserve a great range of flowers – helichrysum and xeranthemum from the rock garden, delphiniums, foxgloves, larkspur and poppies from the summer border, iris pods from beside the pond and hydrangeas from the early autumn shrubbery. An even greater range of grasses dries successfully.

Picking and preparing Gather the plants on a dry day, picking flowers before they are fully open and grasses before they start to shed their seeds. Prepare them immediately. Pull the leaves off flower stems. Wire helichrysums, xeranthemums and other flowers with large heads and thin stems, or the dried stem will be unable to support the flower. Before wiring, cut off the stem 25mm (1in) below the flower. Use florists' wire and remember to make a hook on the piece for each flower to prevent it from slipping right through.

Natural drying Tie small bunches of stems together with string. Use slip knots which can be tightened as the stems shrink. Hang the bunches upside down in a warm, dry, well-ventilated place until crisp and dry. The place should ideally be dark, or at least well away from direct sunlight, which bleaches colours.

— FLOWER DRYING —

Using chemical dryers

Wiring Bend over the tip of the wire. Push the wire down through the flower centre until the hook grips the flower.

Drying Coil the wire and sit the flowers face up on the drying agent. Spoon drying agent into and round them to cover them up.

Drying with chemicals Use alum or borax powder, silica-gel crystals or even well-washed and dried sand. Cut off the stems and wire the flowers. Use an airtight tin or plastic box with a 13mm ($\frac{1}{2}$in) layer of the drying agent covering the base evenly. Do not try to put too many flowers in one box, they must not touch each other. Trickle the drying agent on them so that the petals are not displaced. Seal the lid with sticky tape.

Check on flowers in silica gel after two days. Uncover the edge of one to see if it is crisp; if it is not, leave for another day – but no longer, or the flowers will be too brittle. If sand is used, allow three or four days for drying. Flowers in borax take three or four weeks to dry. Take out the flowers very carefully – the petals are easily damaged.

All three drying agents can be reused indefinitely, provided that the moisture they have absorbed from each batch of plants is first dried out in a moderately warm oven (not more than 120°C or 250°F – gas mark $\frac{1}{2}$).

Flower pressing

Keeping memories of summer

Gather flowers when there is no rain or dew on them, and press them straight away. Flat or single flowers press successfully – as do ferns and brackens. Heavy flower heads and succulent plants are less suitable for pressing.

Put fleshy flowers, such as daisies, between sheets of blotting paper and thinner flowers, such as buttercups, between paper towels or sheets of newspaper. Lay the flowers out carefully between sheets of paper and place them in the middle of an old telephone directory or in a purpose-made flower press. Leave them for four to six weeks.

Arrange ferns and thick green leaves between paper towels and lay them under a carpet or rug, where they will be regularly walked over for a few months. The longer the pressing time, the better the colour will last.

When the plants are ready, arrange them on a piece of card with tweezers to make a pleasing picture or greetings card. Dab latex glue behind each plant with a matchstick and press it down lightly to secure it. Cover a picture with glass and fit it into a picture frame, or seal the edges of the glass and card together with adhesive tape. Store spare pressed flowers and leaf sprays singly in transparent paper bags.

Flu

Recognising and dealing with symptoms; avoiding

Flu symptoms include: headache; aching muscles and back; fever (although you will feel cold); sweating; general weakness; nasal catarrh and sneezing; coughing, sometimes with sputum; and pain behind the breastbone, which is made worse by coughing.

When a flu epidemic is at its height, a DOCTOR can see patients in high-risk categories only: those who are known to have heart conditions or chronic lung disease, young children and people over the age of 65.

Anyone else with flu should not attempt to go to work. Go to bed and take plenty of fluids to replace the loss caused by FEVER; meals should be light and easily digested. Painkillers may be taken in recommended doses, and proprietary cough medicines or hot lemon and honey drinks may ease COUGHS.

The worst effects of flu are over within two or three days, although the aches and pains and the fever may last for a week and the weakness (perhaps with mild depression) may persist for several weeks. Most flu sufferers should make a complete recovery.

However, pneumonia can be a complication of flu, especially in the elderly or chronically sick. This is why high-risk patients should seek to prevent flu by immunisation. Each year vaccines are produced for the specific flu viruses which are likely to be prevalent the following year. Immunisation in September or October should give protection for the winter.

Flummery

A sweet pudding recipe from Scotland

Flummery has become a nationally popular dish, but its traditional Scottish name is Sowans. The original basic ingredient was oatmeal but, instead, you can substitute cracked wheat. Properly made, flummery has a smooth, jellied texture, is white in colour and has a delicious and distinctive flavour.

Ingredients (for six to eight)
3 heaped tablespoons of fine oatmeal, or 4 heaped tablespoons of cracked wheat
Juice of two oranges
2 tablespoons caster sugar
150ml ($\frac{1}{4}$ pint) cream
Finely grated rind of two oranges
4 tablespoons of honey, brandy or whisky
150ml ($\frac{1}{4}$ pint) of whipped cream

Soak the oatmeal or cracked wheat for 24 hours in enough cold water to keep it covered. Pour off the water and cover the grain again with about 1.1 litres (2 pints) of fresh, cold water. Leave to stand for another 24 hours.

Stir well and strain the liquid into a pan. Add the strained orange juice and sugar then boil, stirring frequently, for about 10 minutes, or until thick. Allow to cool a little, then stir in the cream.

Pour into a large dish, or into individual small dishes, sprinkle with the grated orange rind and leave to set.

To serve, top each dish with 2 teaspoons of honey, brandy or whisky, and 1 heaped teaspoon of whipped cream.

Fluorescent lights

Installing and replacing; tracing faults

The fluorescent tube is a very efficient and economical form of lighting. It should last 5000-7000 light hours – up to seven times longer than a tungsten filament bulb. And a 40 watt tube gives about as strong a light as a 200 watt bulb does.

A 1.2m (4ft) 40W tube is suitable for a kitchen or bathroom. Pelmet lighting, where the tube is hidden, needs a 1.5m (5ft) 65W or 80W tube. In the garage, use one or more 1.2m 80W.

A warm white-coloured tube gives maximum output, and is suitable for the kitchen. A de-luxe warm white gives the best results in living or dining areas.

Slim fluorescent tubes twisted into compact shapes are beginning to replace conventional bulbs. They are more expensive, but a low-energy lamp will use only one unit of electricity every 60-100 hours, compared with one every 10 hours for an ordinary 100-watt bulb.

Installing A conventional fluorescent tube light fitting needs to be supplied by a twin-core-and-earth lighting cable (see ELECTRIC WIRING) because the metal baseplate of the fitting must be earthed. If you are fitting it in place of a pendant light, turn off the power at the main switch on the consumer unit or fuse box (see FUSES AND FUSE BOXES) and examine the light's CEILING ROSE. If the rose is wired by the loop-in method you will have to transfer the connections to a JUNCTION BOX above the ceiling and feed the new length of cable for the light fitting (see LIGHT FIXTURES) through the hole in the ceiling. If the ceiling rose of the light you are replacing has only one cable entering it, there is already a junction box above the ceiling; in this case you only need to disconnect the conductor wires from the terminals and take down the base of the ceiling rose.

FLUORESCENT LIGHTS

Connecting the fitting to the lighting circuit

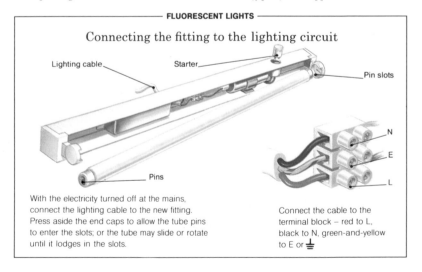

Lighting cable

Starter

Pin slots

Pins

N
E
L

With the electricity turned off at the mains, connect the lighting cable to the new fitting. Press aside the end caps to allow the tube pins to enter the slots; or the tube may slide or rotate until it lodges in the slots.

Connect the cable to the terminal block – red to L, black to N, green-and-yellow to E or ⏚

Connecting to the fluorescent fitting
Feed the cable into the light fitting through the grommeted hole located close to the terminal block. Then offer the unit up to the ceiling. Ideally, screw the fitting to a suitable ceiling joist – see JOISTS. You can locate one by knocking on the ceiling or probing it with a fine needle. If there is no convenient joist, fit wooden struts between joists with skew nails (see NAILING) and screw the fitting to the struts. If the fitting is only lightweight, you may be able to use cavity fixings to give a secure anchorage to plasterboard.

With the unit in place, connect the prepared wires of the cable to the terminal block – black at N and opposite the blue wire, red at L and opposite the brown wire, earth (covered with green-and-yellow sleeving) at E or ⏚ and opposite the green-and-yellow wire. Now screw on the cover which hides the wiring.

The tube has two small pins at each end, and these must be located in holes in the end caps – usually by springing the caps apart. In other models, the pins slide into place, then the end cap is turned to anchor the tube in place. This may complete the installation – or there may be a decorative diffuser which needs to be clipped in place.

Replace the circuit fuse and turn the electricity back on at the main switch.

Faultfinding Before examining any of the fittings, turn off the electricity at the main switch. If a tube is not lighting, check that good contact is being made with the pins, and that they are housed correctly in their recesses. If there is a small cylindrical starter (the device that sparks the gas in the tube) remove it and try a new one. If this fails, replace the tube with a new one.

A tube that looks dim and flickers slightly is probably just getting old – tubes become less efficient as they age. If a tube flickers when switched on, but fails to light up, suspect the starter: change it for a new one.

Fly tying

The basics of the art

Thousands of patterns exist for FISHING flies. Some are realistic imitations of insects and water creatures that a fish eats; others (salmon flies, for example) are fanciful creations designed to awaken the hunting instinct in a fish. The materials used range from cock feathers to animal fur, from silver tinsel to raffia.

For trout fishing, the two main groups of flies are dry flies, which float on the water, and wet flies, which are made of more absorbent materials and go under

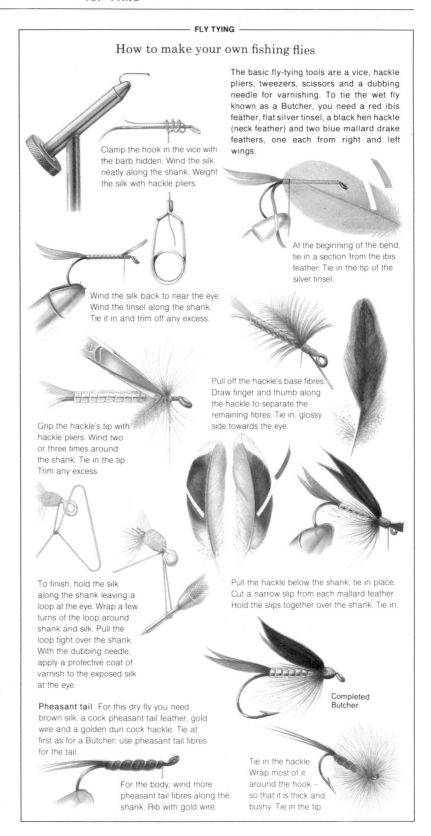

How to make your own fishing flies

The basic fly-tying tools are a vice, hackle pliers, tweezers, scissors and a dubbing needle for varnishing. To tie the wet fly known as a Butcher, you need a red ibis feather, flat silver tinsel, a black hen hackle (neck feather) and two blue mallard drake feathers, one each from right and left wings.

Clamp the hook in the vice with the barb hidden. Wind the silk neatly along the shank. Weight the silk with hackle pliers.

At the beginning of the bend, tie in a section from the ibis feather. Tie in the tip of the silver tinsel.

Wind the silk back to near the eye. Wind the tinsel along the shank. Tie it in and trim off any excess.

Pull off the hackle's base fibres. Draw finger and thumb along the hackle to separate the remaining fibres. Tie in, glossy side towards the eye.

Grip the hackle's tip with hackle pliers. Wind two or three times around the shank. Tie in the tip. Trim any excess.

To finish, hold the silk along the shank leaving a loop at the eye. Wrap a few turns of the loop around shank and silk. Pull the loop tight over the shank. With the dubbing needle, apply a protective coat of varnish to the exposed silk at the eye.

Pull the hackle below the shank; tie in place. Cut a narrow slip from each mallard feather. Hold the slips together over the shank. Tie in.

Completed Butcher

Pheasant tail For this dry fly you need brown silk, a cock pheasant tail feather, gold wire and a golden dun cock hackle. Tie at first as for a Butcher: use pheasant tail fibres for the tail.

For the body, wind more pheasant tail fibres along the shank. Rib with gold wire.

Tie in the hackle. Wrap most of it around the hook – so that it is thick and bushy. Tie in the tip.

water. Salmon flies are similar to trout wet flies, but are considerably larger and more elaborate.

The principal parts of the fishing fly are the body, the hackle (representing the legs), the tail and usually wings.

Equipment Start fly tying by buying a beginner's kit, with a basic selection of fly-tying materials and all essential tools. The materials may include hooks, coloured silks, gold wire, fluorescent nylon floss, gold and silver lurex and oval tinsel, raffine, chenille, a selection of feathers (including hackles), fur and animal hair, beeswax and varnish. The tools are a vice; two hackle pliers; tweezers; fine-pointed scissors; and a dubbing needle for applying varnish and teasing out materials. Other useful tools are tiny brushes, a bobbin holder and a hook for making whip finishes.

Tying a wet fly A simple wet fly is the Butcher. First, clamp a hook in the vice with the jaws of the vice hiding the barb. Use a reasonably large (size 8 or 6) hook with a down-turned eye. Thoroughly wax a length of black silk by running it through the beeswax.

Hold the end of the silk along the shank of the hook with the end towards the bend. Wind a few turns of silk along the shank towards the bend, then snip off the excess end of silk. Continue winding the silk to make a neat layer from the eye to the beginning of the bend. Clip hackle pliers onto the silk to prevent it unwinding off the hook. Snip a 6mm (¼in) wide slip (section) out of the ibis feather and tie it in at the bend with two or three turns of silk. Tie in also a length of flat silver tinsel. Wind another layer of silk back to near the eye – but leave plenty of room to tie in the hackle and wings there later. Wind the tinsel back along the length of the hook to near the eye and tie it in with two or three turns of the silk. Trim off any excess tinsel.

Pull the fluffy fibres off the base of the hackle. Hold the tip of the hackle and draw finger and thumb along it from tip to base to separate the fibres. Tie in the base of the hackle. Grip the tip of the hackle in the hackle pliers, then wind three or four turns of hackle round the shank. Carefully wind the silk through the hackle, then tie down the hackle's tip with a turn or two of silk. Trim away any excess hackle. Between forefinger and thumb pull the hackle fibres to hang below the shank. Tie the hackle in this position with three or four turns of silk.

Cut a 6mm wide slip from each mallard feather. Grip the slips firmly between finger and thumb, with the convex sides outwards, and hold them along the top of the hook so that their tips stick slightly beyond the bend. Wind two or three turns of silk loosely over the slips, then carefully pull the silk tight to hold the slips

securely. Conceal any ends of feather with a few turns of silk before tying off.

To tie the silk with a whip finish, hold the silk with your left hand along the shank, leaving a loop at the eye end. Keep the loop taut to prevent the silk on the hook unwinding. Wind four or five turns of the loop over the silk and the hook shaft. Keeping the loop taut with the dubbing needle, pull the silk in your left hand until the loop closes over the hook and the whip finish is complete. Alternatively, use a purpose-made tool.

Cut off the silk, then use the dubbing needle to apply a coat of varnish to the whip finish and silk at the eye.

Tying a dry fly Use a cock hackle for a dry fly – it is stiff and helps to keep the fly afloat. For this simple dry fly, a Pheasant Tail, use a size 10-14 hook with an upturned eye.

Follow the same method as for the Butcher. Clamp the hook in the vice. Wax the silk and wind a layer of it along the hook shank. For a tail, tie in a few fibres from the pheasant tail. Then tie in a few more fibres from the pheasant tail and a length of gold wire for the body. Wind the silk back to near the eye, leaving plenty of room to tie in the hackle. Wind the pheasant tail fibres along the shank and tie them in near the eye. Wind the gold wire over the fibres in neat spirals and tie it in with two or three turns of silk.

Choose a suitable hackle; its fibres should be about one and a half times the distance between the barb and the shank of the hook. Prepare the hackle and tie it in as for a wet fly. With hackle pliers, wind most of the hackle round the hook back towards the bend. Tie it in. The hackle should be much bushier and thicker than the hackle of a wet fly.

Snip away any excess bits of hackle feather, holding the hackle back out of the way with your hand. Conceal any ends of feather with a few turns of silk, then make a whip finish and varnish as for a wet fly.

Foam mattress

Choosing and caring for them

Foam mattresses are made from latex (rubber) or polyurethane or from layers of both. Latex is softer and more bouncy, but polyurethane is cheaper and generally lasts longer. When choosing, try out several until you find the most comfortable one for your needs. It should be 100-125mm (4-5in) thick and give slightly to cradle the body, yet be firm enough to give support. Make sure that the cover will allow air through and that you have a suitable base for the mattress such as a slatted or spring base. Make sure, too, that a polyurethane mattress is filled with fire-retardant, combustion-modified

polyurethane foam, and has a cover that will not catch fire from a lighted match.

Looking after a foam mattress There is no need to turn it – just clean it occasionally with a stiff brush or the upholstery attachment of a vacuum cleaner. It does not give off the fibres that mattresses with wadding do; this means it needs cleaning less often – and makes it suitable for people allergic to fibres. Pull back the bedclothes each day to air it well and dry out any moisture.

Blot up any liquid immediately. You can remove most stains by sponging with cold water or with a sponge dipped in a cool detergent solution and squeezed almost dry. Use a hairdryer to dry off the mattress, or if a large area is damp, prop it up in front of, but well away from, a fan heater. You can use a dry foam cleaner on the mattress, but never use solvent-based cleaners, carbon tetrachloride or strong chlorine solutions or the foam will break up; it will also retain harmful fumes.

Fondue

Cook-as-you-eat at the table

Fondue is a Swiss dish of melted cheese flavoured with Kirsch, cooked in a special fondue pot. Traditionally, Gruyère cheese is used, but Emmenthal or Gouda can be used. Cheddar is not suitable.

To cook a fondue you put the pot over a spirit burner in the centre of the table, and each person dips chunks of bread on long-handled forks or skewers into the melted cheese. Twist the forks or skewers after lifting them out of the fondue each time – or you will end up with sticky strings of cheese all over the place.

Fondue pots are fireproof earthenware dishes, but you can use a flameproof dish or heavy-based saucepan. The spirit burner keeps the fondue cooking gently while you eat it. Turn the heat down when the fondue gets low and starts to form a crust on the bottom of the dish.

Here is a fondue for four to six people:

Ingredients
2 cloves garlic
150ml (¼ pint) milk
350g (12oz) grated Gruyère, Emmenthal, or Gouda cheese
450ml (¾ pint) dry white wine
1 tablespoon Kirsch
Pinch of grated nutmeg, salt and freshly ground white pepper
1 French loaf

Preparation Crush the garlic and rub it round the sides and base of the cooking dish. Add the milk and cheese and cook over a very low heat, stirring continuously with a wooden spoon, until the cheese melts and the mixture becomes smooth and creamy. Gradually blend in the wine and Kirsch. Season with the nutmeg, salt and pepper, then heat the fondue through without boiling.

Heat the loaf in the oven until crisp. Cut into 25mm (1in) cubes. Light the spirit burner on the dining table and put the fondue on it. Leave until it is bubbling gently.

Food mills

Processing and puréeing the simple way

A food mill or mouli purées (see PURÉE-ING) and sieves food at the same time and is hand-operated. A perforated metal disc like a grater sits in the bottom of a metal bowl, and the food is pressed through the disc by a close-fitting blade turned by a handle.

The food mill has several advantages over a liquidiser or FOOD PROCESSORS. You can decide the texture of foods like paté by choosing a fine, medium or coarse disc; and soups and sauces (see SOUPS AND STOCKS; SAUCES) are less watery because the ingredients are not pulped. A food mill is also ideal for preparing baby food because it removes skin, pith and pips.

Always dismantle and wash the various parts thoroughly in detergent and warm water after use, to avoid leaving food particles trapped in its crevices and perforations.

Food poisoning

Treatment and prevention

Food poisoning is caused by viruses, bacteria, or their poisons, in infected food. Others, such as rotaviruses, campylobacteria and staphylococcal bacteria multiply in under-cooked or reheated foods and cause severe vomiting from two to eight hours after eating.

Salmonella bacteria are usually passed on by way of infected food-handlers, flies, dirty cooking utensils, or from certain food sources such as chicken or milk, and cause severe diarrhoea within 12 to 36 hours.

Other symptoms of food poisoning include: abdominal cramp, colicky pain, sweating, weakness and dehydration; there may also be traces of blood in the vomit or motions.

Anyone with suspected food poisoning (known to doctors as gastroenteritis) should take nothing by mouth except sips of water. Only when the stomach seems settled is it wise to try a little light nourishment such as dry biscuits, jelly, blancmange or clear soup. Avoid irritants such as tea, coffee or acid soft drinks, which may revive the symptoms. Proprietary medicines may help control the diarrhoea – a chemist can recommend one.

Most cases of food poisoning clear up within a day or two, but see a DOCTOR:
● If the symptoms are severe and last for more than three days – more than six hours in the case of a baby or small child.
● If there is blood in the motions.
● If you experience any untoward symptoms such as double vision.

To minimise the risk of food poisoning, wash your hands scrupulously after using a lavatory and before handling food. Discard any food which you suspect may be contaminated, such as processed meat or fish and dairy products such as milk, custard, cream or mayonnaise, which have been standing for a long time at room temperature.

Thaw frozen foods completely so that they cook through to the centre, and never refreeze food once it has thawed – see FREEZING FOOD.

Do not eat any food which you suspect may have been prepared in unhygienic conditions (particularly when you are abroad).

Avoid cans of food which are damaged – dented or bulging at the ends – or split, because they are likely to be contaminated.

Never attempt to can food at home. A rare but serious form of food poisoning known as botulism, which can prove fatal within 24 hours, is nearly always traced to products which have been improperly canned. It is caused by the bacterium *Clostridium botulinum*, which grows without oxygen at low temperatures and is resistant to boiling and heat.

Early symptoms include double vision, difficulty in swallowing and pronounced weakness. There may also be VOMITING and DIARRHOEA. If botulism is suspected, seek medical help at once.

Food processors

Using and caring for a useful appliance

The food processor is the most versatile time-saving implement in the kitchen, fitted with accessories for specialised tasks such as chopping, shredding, slicing, mixing dough and liquidising.

It is important to remember that the food processor works very fast. Use only short bursts of power to chop or purée – as fruit and vegetables can easily become watery. Meat should be chilled thoroughly before processing to prevent it from being liquidised.

You can process all the ingredients of a complicated recipe by starting with the more solid ones and then adding in the softer ones. For example, PASTRY can be made by processing the chilled butter, margarine or other fat with the dry ingredients, then pouring liquid through the food tube and processing only until a ball of dough is formed.

For soups and purée (see SOUPS AND STOCKS; PURÉEING) add 150ml (¼ pint) liquid to soft or cooked ingredients in the bowl and process 15-20 seconds at a time.

Clean and dry all parts of the processor thoroughly after use, following the maker's instructions. The metal blades are as sharp as good knives and should be kept in the storage containers supplied.

WARNING Keep hands well away from the blades when using a processor. Push pieces of food through the food tube with the plastic pusher and wait for the motor to stop before opening the bowl. When pouring out the blade, hold the blade in place with a wooden spoon or remove it just before tilting the bowl.

See also FOOD MILLS.

Food storage

Keeping it fresh and wholesome

The flavour and nutritional value of foods can be impaired if they are not properly stored. Without exception, foods stored at lower temperatures remain fresh longer than those left near a source of heat – a radiator, cooker or hot-water tank – or in full sunlight.

Fruit and vegetables Soft fruits and green vegetables, including salads, should be bought fresh every two or three days and stored in a ventilated cupboard or larder, or they can be kept for two or three days in a refrigerator. Vegetables such as onions and potatoes and hard fruits in good condition will keep well for up to several months if stored in a cool, dark dry place such as a garage or a cellar.

Fish Wet fish should always be kept chilled. Really fresh fish will keep overnight in a sealed plastic bag, in the coldest part of a refrigerator.

Poultry This may breed harmful bacteria and must also be kept, loosely wrapped, for one or two days in a cool larder or two to four days in the refrigerator. See also GAME BIRDS.

Meat Fresh meat can be kept in a cool larder for one day, or in a refrigerator for two or three days. Raw and cooked meats must be kept in separate, closed containers in the refrigerator to prevent evaporation and smells. Cooked meats should be eaten within one day after refrigerating.

Dairy products Butter, fats and cheese can be bought weekly and stored in a cool larder or refrigerator – see also EGGS. Keep in their wrappers, or in a covered container. Keep hard cheese in foil.

Other foodstuffs Vegetable oils deteriorate unless kept cool; keep just a small bottle of oil near the cooker and refill as necessary from your store.

Dry ingredients such as flour and sugar should be stored in dry, airtight containers. Plain flour will keep for six months, self-raising two or three months and wholemeal flour two months. Spices keep well in airtight containers in a cupboard, but dried herbs – which should never be exposed to light – lose their flavour after six months. See also FREEZERS; FREEZING FOOD; HERB PRESERVING.

Foot care

*Dealing with problems and
avoiding foot ache*

Badly fitting shoes, too much walking or standing, and being overweight are the usual causes of aching feet. The ligaments become strained, leading to pain in the middle of the foot; discomfort may also spread along the inside of the foot and into the calf.

Foot strain of this kind usually disappears with rest. If the pain continues, you should consult a doctor.

More serious foot problems can also be caused by wearing the wrong shoes. Shoes which are too tight cause BUNIONS, CORNS and calluses and if worn constantly will deform the feet. Shoes that are too loose slip up and down as you walk and this can lead to BLISTERS. Constant wearing of high heels – heels higher than 50mm (2in) – also compresses the toes and may cause bunions, curly or overlapping toes and backache.

Shoes should be chosen for comfort rather than certain fashions, especially in the case of children and elderly people. They should grip at the heels, support the arches and cushion the soles of the feet. Shoes should not pinch your feet at any point, and should have room for you to wiggle your toes. If you plan to go hiking, buy strong walking shoes (or boots) which are roomy enough for two pairs of socks – see BACKPACKING; WALKING. Harden your feet with surgical spirit, applied daily for about two weeks before you go hiking.

The best way to strengthen the feet is to go barefoot as much as possible. This improves the mobility of the toes, reduces tension in the feet and helps you to relax generally. It also makes the feet less prone to the formation of calluses – ridges of troublesome hard skin which form on the sole of the foot. They can be smoothed away by gentle rubbing with a hard-skin remover, available from a chemist, which has an abrasive surface.

Use it once a week, but if the skin is too tough to remove, have it pared away by a chiropodist.

See also ATHLETE'S FOOT; CHILBLAINS; INGROWING TOENAILS.

Forms of address

*How to address public officials
and clergymen*

Conventions associated with letter writing range from the simple use of Esq as a courtesy when addressing an envelope to a man, to more complex forms when writing to people of title or rank. Some of these forms of address are as follows.

The Queen or Queen Mother Letter begins: Madam, With my humble duty. In the body of the letter, substitute 'Your Majesty' for 'you' and 'Your Majesty's' for 'your'. Letter ends: I have the honour to remain, Madam, Your Majesty's most humble and obedient servant. Addressed on envelope as: Her Majesty The Queen, or Her Majesty Queen Elizabeth The Queen Mother.

Other members of the royal family Letter begins: Sir or Madam. In the body of the letter, 'you' becomes 'Your Royal Highness' and 'your' becomes 'Your Royal Highness's'. Letter ends: I have the honour to be, Sir (or Madam), Your Royal Highness's most humble and obedient servant. Envelope: His (Her) Royal Highness The Duke (Duchess) of .... Other forms include: His Royal Highness The Prince of Wales, Her Royal Highness The Princess of Wales, Her Royal Highness The Princess Anne, The Princess Royal, and His Royal Highness The Prince Edward.

Archbishops of Canterbury and York Letter begins: Dear Archbishop. Letter ends: Yours sincerely. Envelope: The Most Reverend and Right Hon the Lord Archbishop of Canterbury/York.

Bishop Letter begins: Dear Bishop. Letter ends: Yours sincerely. Envelope: The Right Reverend the Lord Bishop of ....

A parish priest of the Anglican Church Letter begins: Dear Mr Smith (or Dear Father Smith, if preferred) or Dear Vicar (or Rector). Envelope: The Reverend John Smith.

The Pope Letter begins: Your Holiness or Most Holy Father. Letter ends: I have the honour to be Your Holiness's most obedient servant (or, in the case of Roman Catholics, most humble child). Envelope: His Holiness the Pope.

A cardinal Letter begins: Your Eminence or My Lord Cardinal, or (socially)

Dear Cardinal Jones. Letter ends: I have the honour to remain Your Eminence's obedient servant (or, for Roman Catholics, devoted and obedient child) or (socially) Yours sincerely. Envelope: His Eminence Cardinal Murphy or, if also an archbishop, His Eminence the Cardinal Archbishop of ....

Members of HM Government May be addressed formally as Dear Sir or Madam, or (socially) as: Dear Prime Minister, Dear Foreign Secretary. Envelope: The Secretary of State for Foreign Affairs.

Members of Parliament No special convention, other than to address envelope as: John Smith, MP.

The Lord Chief Justice Letter begins: My Lord, or (socially) Dear Lord Chief Justice. Envelope: The Rt Hon the Lord Chief Justice of England.

A Judge of the High Court Letter begins: Dear Sir, or (socially) Dear Judge. Envelope: The Hon Mr Justice Jeffreys.

A Judge of the County Court Letter begins: Dear Sir. Envelope: His Honour Judge Jeffreys.

A Queen's Counsel When a barrister becomes a Queen's Counsel the letters QC are shown after his or her name. This includes county court judges but not higher legal appointments.

A lord mayor The lord mayors of London, York, Cardiff and Belfast are styled 'The Right Honourable'. Lord mayors of other cities are styled 'The Right Worshipful'. Letter begins: My Lord Mayor, or Dear Lord Mayor. Envelope: The Right Honourable the Lord Mayor of London.

The mayor of a city or borough Letter begins: Mr Mayor, or Dear Mr Mayor. Envelope: The Right Worshipful the Mayor of Canterbury (in the case of a city) or The Worshipful the Mayor of Lambeth (for a borough).

There are many other forms of address, which you should be able to find in the reference section of any public library.

Freezers

*Choosing, maintaining and
faultfinding*

There are two kinds of freezer: upright freezers and chest types. Upright freezers, which look like ordinary refrigerators, take up less floor space than chest types but need space for the door to swing open. They have sliding basket drawers for easy loading and unloading.

Chest freezers are generally cheaper than upright ones and the storage space in them is more adaptable. Also they tend to lose less cold air than upright ones when opened. On the other hand, they take up more floor space and can be awkward to load and unload.

Freezers vary in size according to their cubic capacity. For each cubic foot of net volume (not including shelf and basket space) you can store roughly 9kg (20lb) of frozen food. The smaller ones are about the size of a refrigerator or washing machine. Larger ones, such as a double-door upright freezer, are about twice that size. A combined fridge-freezer is a small upright freezer with a refrigerator on top or underneath – see REFRIGERATORS.

Looking after a freezer A freezer should be defrosted and cleaned at least once a year – preferably when its stocks are low.

Disconnect the freezer, then take out any food and wrap it in several layers of newspaper. Store the food temporarily in a cool place – defrosting usually takes a few hours. Line the bottom of the freezer – and the floor around it if it is an upright – with newspaper. Put bowls of warm water inside to speed up the defrosting. Use a plastic spatula or freezer scraper to scrape excess frost from the inner sides – do not use anything sharp because it could damage the lining.

Leave the door or lid open, and when the frost has melted, mop the water up with a sponge and cloth. Alternatively, if the freezer has a defrost drain hole or spout, simply let the water drain into a container.

Remove any food stains on the lining with warm water with a little bicarbonate of soda dissolved in it. Do not use detergent, as its odour might be transferred to the food. Also, do not use abrasive cleaners – they might damage the lining.

Reconnect the freezer when it has dried out. Leave it on the lowest setting with the door or lid closed for an hour before returning the food.

Repairs If the door or lid seal is damaged, buy a new one and screw it in. If the seal is clipped into a recess rather than screwed, get a dealer to replace it.

If no power, or only intermittent power, is reaching the freezer, first try replacing the fuse and checking the connections in the plug – see CIRCUIT TESTING; PLUGS. If this makes no difference, there might be an excessive build-up of ice. Switch off and allow the freezer to defrost.

If power is reaching the freezer but it is not cooling properly, feel the condenser or evaporator system at the back. It should be warm. If it is not, get a qualified repair contractor to check it, and replace it if necessary.

What to do in a power cut Do not open the freezer, or you will let warm air in. Keep the room where the freezer is as cool as possible. It takes 12-24 hours for food to thaw in an unopened freezer, and it should stay in good condition for about eight hours. Leave the freezer unopened for at least two hours after the power has been restored. Should the power failure be prolonged, remove the food as you would for defrosting.

See also FREEZING FOOD.

Freezing food

What you can freeze and how long it will keep

Food you can keep in the freezer ranges from simple packets of peas or beans to elaborate precooked dishes that need only to be reheated. You can buy food ready-frozen from supermarkets or freezer centres or you can freeze, for example, garden vegetables, cuts of meat or dishes you have cooked.

Preparing food for freezing Unless it is carefully packaged, food will lose much of its flavour and texture when frozen. Only use packaging material that is greaseproof, moisture- and vapour-proof and durable; special freezer packaging is best. Useful packaging material includes heavy-duty polythene bags, foil containers with lids, plastic boxes and wax cartons.

Package food in small parcels so that it freezes and defrosts as quickly as possible. Exclude as much air as possible – though with liquids a little space, about 25mm (1in), should be left at the top to allow for expansion. Allow food to cool before placing in the freezer.

Make sure you label and date the packages. The most suitable implements are a wax crayon or freezer-proof pen.

With the exception of bread and undecorated cakes, food should never be refrozen once it has defrosted.

What not to freeze Eggs in their shells burst when frozen. Cream (though not whipping or double cream), yoghurt and mayonnaise separate when thawed – so do foods made with gelatine. Dishes that include egg yolks or unwhipped cream should be frozen without the cream or egg yolks.

Other foods that do not freeze well include vegetables with a high moisture content, such as lettuces, raw tomatoes, cucumbers, radishes and celery; soft cheeses; and bananas.

Freezing breads and cakes All breads, scones and buns freeze well. Bread can be kept in the freezer for up to a month; scones and buns can be kept for longer, up to six months.

Cakes are best frozen without icing. Un-iced sponges will keep frozen for up to six months, rich fruit cakes for up to a year. If you do freeze an iced cake, first freeze it unwrapped until the icing has set hard; then wrap it, protecting the icing with an inner layer of waxed paper, and return to the freezer. Do not keep it for more than two months.

Freezing pastries, pies and pre-cooked dishes Uncooked pastry will keep for up to five months in the freezer. Pre-baked pies also keep well frozen, fruit pies for six months and meat ones for four months. Other precooked dishes that freeze well for up to two months are stews, casseroles, pizzas and the sauces for pasta dishes. Add more salt and spices if necessary when reheating.

Freezing fish, meat and poultry Freeze fish only if it is absolutely fresh. Scale and gut smaller round fish (see FISH CLEANING), then freeze them whole. Simply remove the heads and tails of larger round fish before freezing. Flat fish should be cut into fillets and packaged with sheets of waxed paper between the fillets. Fish can be kept frozen for up to six months.

Freeze only good-quality meat. Remove as much fat and bone as possible. Wrap the meat with plenty of layers of packaging to avoid freezer burn. Separate cutlets, chops, steaks and hamburgers with wax paper. Freeze meat quickly; slow freezing reduces its quality. Pork will keep frozen for up to nine months, beef and lamb for up to a year.

Before freezing poultry or game, remove the giblets and freeze separately. Wash the bird and dry it. Do not stuff it before freezing; the stuffing will make it slower to freeze and defrost. Poultry and game will keep frozen for up to nine months; giblets for six months.

Vegetables and fruits Vegetables should be blanched before freezing to destroy enzymes that cause loss of colour and flavour. Dip them in boiling water for two to five minutes, depending on the thickness of the vegetable. Cool by placing them under running cold water. Vegetables can be kept frozen for up to a year.

Fruit usually keeps its flavour well when frozen, but tends to become softer in texture. Freeze fruit that is ripe but still firm. Overripe fruit is best frozen as a purée.

There are three ways of freezing fruit: dry freezing, sugar freezing and syrup freezing. When fruit is dry frozen, it is first frozen loose and unwrapped on a paper-lined tray. Then it is packed in a container or bag and returned to the freezer. This method is suitable for whole soft fruits such as blackberries, strawberries, raspberries and gooseberries.

Sugar freezing is suitable for juicy fruit such as strawberries, raspberries and cherries. Thoroughly mix the fruit with 115g (4oz) of caster sugar for every 450g (1lb) of fruit, and pack in a container or bag. Fruit such as cherries should be stoned before freezing.

Alternatively, firm-textured fruit such as peaches and apricots can be frozen in syrup. Dissolve 450g (1lb) of sugar in 570ml (1 pint) of water, then chill the syrup in the refrigerator. Peel, halve and stone the fruit, then pour over 285ml ($\frac{1}{2}$ pint) of syrup for every 450g of fruit. Put some crumpled wax paper under the container lid to hold the fruit under the syrup.

Sugar or syrup freezing fruit tends to discolour it, so add some lemon juice.

French polishing

How to apply it, and repair it

French polish is a traditional furniture finish that has been largely superseded by the tougher polyurethane finishes which are less affected by heat and water. But it still offers an excellent means of finishing furniture.

The simplest way of applying French polish is to buy a proprietary DIY material, but it may still be bought in a number of forms in specialist paint shops under the name of garnet polish, button polish, white polish or transparent polish. All are based on shellac, varying only in colour. And all are applied in a similar manner.

Applying French polish Careful preparation is vital. Timber must be clean, dry and well smoothed with fine glasspaper, then the dust removed, ideally with a tacky rag – a special duster

impregnated with a resin which is tacky enough to pick up fine wood dust, but not sticky.

Choose the shade of polish you require, keeping in mind that the darker polishes darken the wood considerably. Experiment with both the technique and the colour first on a scrap piece of wood. If a more drastic colour change is required, stain and smooth the wood before polishing – see STAINING WOOD.

The secret of successful French polishing is to apply it on a polishing rubber, which you can make using a lint-free cloth, such as an old, clean white handkerchief and a wad of clean cotton wool. Make sure the cloth has no wrinkles. Polish should ooze slightly through the cloth, but avoid over-soaking.

Work the polishing rubber evenly over the whole surface to be polished in a continuous figure-of-eight movement. Continue until the surface has an even layer of polish, then after a few minutes, repeat the process several times to build up a series of thin layers. Make sure that edges and corners get their share of the polish.

The next stage is called spiriting off. Leave the surface for at least eight hours then make a new rubber with a double layer of cloth, and soak the cotton wool in methylated spirit. Squeeze the pad until almost dry: too much spirit would merely dissolve the polish.

The aim of spiriting off is to remove any marks left by the rubber and to give a sparkling finish. Use a figure-of-eight motion applying increasing pressure as the rubber dries out. Use fresh cloth from time to time, then finally work in the direction of the wood grain, continuing until the surface is perfect. Although the polish dries fairly quickly, it takes several days to harden completely.

Repairs to French polish You can establish whether a surface has been French polished by applying a lint-free cloth dipped in methylated spirit to the surface. A light rub will immediately soften a French-polished surface and there will be a deposit on the cloth. Other finishes, such as polyurethane, will be unaffected by the methylated spirit.

Scuff marks Prepare a solution of 5 parts methylated spirit, 2 parts raw linseed oil and 1 part pure turpentine. Make up a soft cloth pad and use a figure-of-eight motion to work the mixture over the damaged area. If there are deeper scratches, use neat methylated spirit to soften the existing polish so that it can be blended together over the scratch marks.

Bad damage Strip off the existing finish with neat ammonia, acetone or varnish remover. Then proceed as for new French polishing.

Heat marks Rub the affected area with a mixture of 1 part pure turpentine and 1 part raw linseed oil or camphorated oil.

Spilt alcohol This acts as a solvent to French polish. Wipe off spills as soon as possible and leave the surface to dry. If polish has been removed by the alcohol, treat the area with French polish substitute, obtainable from many hardware stores. Apply it with a small brush until the surface has been built up. Leave to dry hard, smooth with flour-grade abrasive paper, then use the rubber, as for scuff marks.

Scratches Special scratch repair sticks are available from many DIY shops, supplied in a number of wood colours. Rub the appropriate colour stick into the scratch, then blend it in by rubbing over lightly with a soft cloth.

Cigarette burn Gently remove the damaged polish with a razor blade tip. If the damage is shallow, use a scratch repair stick. If deep, drip in some melted coloured beeswax, available from paint stores. You may need vegetable dye to colour the beeswax to match the existing finish. See also CIGARETTE SCORCH MARKS.

Water stains White marks can often be polished out by rubbing the area with metal polish wadding. Rub vigorously to generate heat. Black marks may not respond, in which case the existing polish will have to be removed and new polish applied.

WARNING If you have valuable ANTIQUES in need of restoration, do not try to polish them yourself. Get them treated by a reputable furniture restorer. This way you will be assured of retaining the full value of the piece.

FRENCH POLISHING

Making a polishing rubber; how to apply it

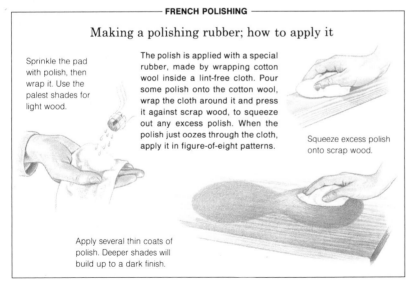

Sprinkle the pad with polish, then wrap it. Use the palest shades for light wood.

The polish is applied with a special rubber, made by wrapping cotton wool inside a lint-free cloth. Pour some polish onto the cotton wool, wrap the cloth around it and press it against scrap wood, to squeeze out any excess polish. When the polish just oozes through the cloth, apply it in figure-of-eight patterns.

Squeeze excess polish onto scrap wood.

Apply several thin coats of polish. Deeper shades will build up to a dark finish.

FRISBEES

How to hold it; how to throw it

Holding Place your thumb on top, index finger along the rim, and the little finger inside the rim.

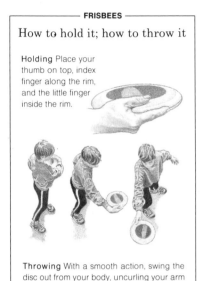

Throwing With a smooth action, swing the disc out from your body, uncurling your arm and hand. At the last moment, release the disc, flicking your wrist.

Frisbees

Throwing a flying toy

A windless day and a good quality flying disc are all you need to learn this modern version of the ancient sport of disc throwing. Flying discs are available from toy shops and some sports shops.

Making it fly Hold the disc against your chest as illustrated, then swing it away from your body, releasing it at the last moment. Having mastered the basic throw, add a short run of up to 9m (30ft) before the release. Raise both arms to catch the returning disc at the last moment and grab the edge with both hands.

Refinements To make the disc curve in flight, tilt it at the moment of release and flick the wrist less.

To make the disc hover, then float gently earthwards, swing the disc upwards almost vertically and give it a much stronger flick of the wrist.

To bounce the disc off the ground, hold it underarm rather than against your body and aim at a point 3m (10ft) away.

Frostbite

Avoiding it; emergency treatment

Frostbite is always a possibility in freezing weather, but is most likely in temperatures below −7°C (19°F) especially in high winds. It develops as the skin cools and blood vessels become constricted, cutting off the blood supply. Any part of the body may be affected, including well-clad hands and feet, but most vulnerable are exposed parts such as the nose, ears, cheeks and chin.

The affected part feels increasingly cold and stiff, accompanied by a tingling sensation which becomes acutely painful. The skin hardens and turns blue or white. Eventually the area goes numb and there is no further feeling of cold or pain.

It is essential to combat frostbite at once, otherwise gangrene may set in. First, seek shelter and remove any clothing or jewellery, such as rings and watches, which may be in contact with the affected part. Next, warm the area slowly, preferably with your hands or against some other part of the body. Do not apply intense heat of any kind or attempt to rub the affected part.

As circulation returns, the flesh may turn blue and develop blood-filled blisters – do *not* break or treat them with any medication. If possible, wrap the affected part in cloth and cover this with some heavier protection such as a coat or blanket.

The intense pain caused by frostbitten flesh thawing out may be eased by raising the affected part above the level of the chest.

Do not attempt any further treatment beyond hot, sweet drinks if these are available. Instead, get the victim to hospital as fast as possible.

Frost protection

How to stop pipes and tanks from freezing

With the recent improvements in standards of loft INSULATION it is even more vital that all plumbing in the loft itself is well protected. An insulated loft remains very cold because heat is not allowed to rise through the ceilings.

Tanks Lag any cistern or tank in the loft, either with a tank lagging set, or with glass-fibre blanket wrapped around and tied or taped in place – both types of insulation are available from DIY stores. Try not to compress the insulation too much. Cover each tank with a lid, but make a hole and fit a plastic funnel immediately below the expansion pipe. Then, if it overflows, water will be directed into the tank. Cover the lid with insulation.

Do *not* insulate the loft floor under the cold water tank: this will allow a little warmth to rise from below to keep the chill off it.

Pipes Lag all pipes with flexible foam plastic sleeves, available from DIY and hardware stores. These may be taped in place or, in some types, snap closed.

Make sure all bends and joints are well protected, and include overflow pipes.

Cold air can sometimes blow up overflow pipes, so make sure the pipe end is fitted with a simple flap, or an open-ended polythene tube.

Other areas Try to ensure that no pipes anywhere in the house are in direct contact with exterior walls. Put some form of insulation, such as lengths of expanded polystyrene, between pipe and wall.

A CENTRAL-HEATING system can freeze if switched off during severe weather – with drastic results. When a home is left for short periods, leave the heating on if possible, with thermostats set low so that the chill is kept off the house. For long periods of absence, drain the whole heating system, using the drain cock on the boiler.

Tie up the ball valve in the expansion tank – or turn off the water supply to it, otherwise it will refill as you empty. An alternative is to put a special antifreeze solution into the system by way of the expansion tank. Ask a plumbers' merchant or central-heating supplier for details.

Make sure there are no dripping taps, which may cause the waste pipe to ice up.

Frozen pipes

Thawing them out; emergency repair

Try to deal with a frozen pipe before it can thaw and leak water. As soon as you realise that a pipe has frozen – if there is no water at a tap for example – examine it for signs of damage. A telltale glint of ice in a crack, or a joint with ice formed round it, will reveal a burst.

Tracing a pipe Pipes are most likely to be frozen in the loft or against an outside wall. If the kitchen cold tap is not working, the blockage is in the rising main just inside the house; if it does work but the tank is not filling, the rising main is blocked on its way to the tank.

Sealing and thawing the pipe As soon as you spot a burst, make an immediate repair with a proprietary burst pipe kit, or an epoxy repair paste reinforced with glass-fibre bandage.

When the pipe has been sealed, wrap it with hot-water bottles or heated rags, or play a hair dryer on it.

Dealing with a burst If a pipe thaws before you can repair it, turn off the mains water immediately. Put buckets under the burst to catch the water, and run all other taps and flush toilets to empty the loft cold-water tank quickly.

Repair the pipe as before, or call a plumber. See also PLUMBING.

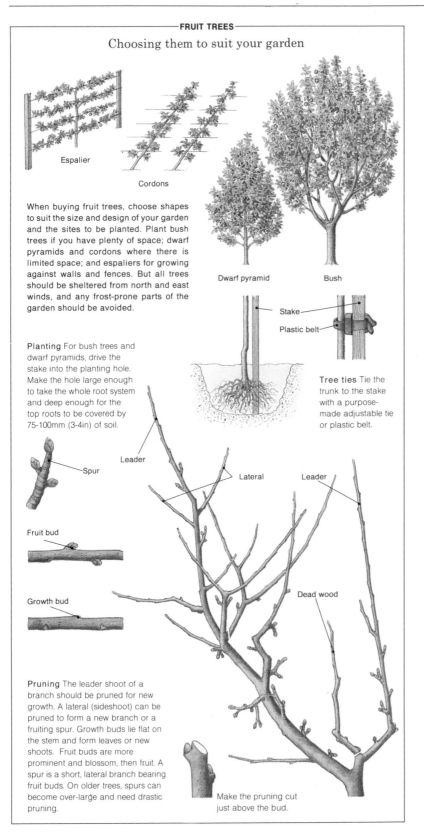

FRUIT TREES

Choosing them to suit your garden

Espalier

Cordons

When buying fruit trees, choose shapes to suit the size and design of your garden and the sites to be planted. Plant bush trees if you have plenty of space; dwarf pyramids and cordons where there is limited space; and espaliers for growing against walls and fences. But all trees should be sheltered from north and east winds, and any frost-prone parts of the garden should be avoided.

Dwarf pyramid

Bush

Stake

Plastic belt

Planting For bush trees and dwarf pyramids, drive the stake into the planting hole. Make the hole large enough to take the whole root system and deep enough for the top roots to be covered by 75-100mm (3-4in) of soil.

Tree ties Tie the trunk to the stake with a purpose-made adjustable tie or plastic belt.

Leader

Spur

Lateral

Leader

Fruit bud

Dead wood

Growth bud

Pruning The leader shoot of a branch should be pruned for new growth. A lateral (sideshoot) can be pruned to form a new branch or a fruiting spur. Growth buds lie flat on the stem and form leaves or new shoots. Fruit buds are more prominent and blossom, then fruit. A spur is a short, lateral branch bearing fruit buds. On older trees, spurs can become over-large and need drastic pruning.

Make the pruning cut just above the bud.

Fruit trees

Buying, planting, pruning and harvesting the fruits

Most gardens can now accommodate fruit trees because of the range of dwarfing rootstocks they are raised on.

Apples and pears can also be grown flat against a wall or fence in two shapes – the cordon, which consists of a slanting main stem with short, fruiting spurs; and the espalier, which carries fruit on horizontal branches spreading to each side. Plums always tend to sprawl; bushes and fans are the shapes that take least space.

Although fruit trees will grow in most soils, they must be sheltered from north and east winds and sited where spring frost will not destroy the blossoms. Late-flowering varieties are best suited to cold areas; plum trees, which all flower early, are not often successful in the north.

A wide choice of varieties is available: the nurseryman can advise you on different ones. Although some are technically self-fertile, most crop better if other varieties are in flower at the same time in your (or a neighbouring) garden.

Some popular varieties of apple, pear and plum trees are:

Apples
Cox's Orange Pippin A crisp, juicy, well-flavoured dessert apple. Flowers mid-season; use November to January.

Discovery White-fleshed, rosy-red, sweet dessert apple. Flowers mid-season; use in August.

Bramley's Seedling Considered the best cooking apple, fluffy and well-flavoured, but suitable for the garden only in dwarf form. Flowers mid-season; use October to March.

Pears
Conference Long, slender and dark green with yellowish, juicy, sweet flesh; a regular cropper. Flowers mid-season; pick in October to eat a month or two later.

Doyenné du Comice One of the most delicious of all pears – large, rounded, yellow-green when ripe with succulent white flesh; crops irregularly. Flowers late; pick in October to use one to three months later.

Winter Nelis Bears well-flavoured, small, dark russet fruit; a good cropper. Flowers late; pick in October to use in December.

Plums
Victoria A light red, yellow-flushed plum suitable for cooking and dessert. Flowers mid-season; reliable heavy crop in late August.

Marjorie's Seedling Large, blue-black fruit best used for cooking and bottling; regular heavy cropper. Flowers late; pick in late September.

Coe's Golden Drop Sweet, yellow high-flavoured dessert fruit, but not a heavy cropper. Flowers early; crops in late September.

Planting Fruit trees can be planted from October to March, though early autumn is best as the ground is still warm and encourages root formation.

Dig a hole wide enough to take the outspread roots, and deep enough for the top ones to be covered with 75-100mm (3-4in) of soil. Fork the soil at the bottom of the hole to improve drainage, and add some well-rotted COMPOST to poor soil.

For bush trees and dwarf pyramids, drive a stake into the planting hole – see STAKING PLANTS. For cordons or espaliers to be grown against a wall or fence, fix horizontal support wires at 610mm (2ft) intervals, with the lowest wire 760mm (2½ft) above the ground.

Stand the tree in the hole about 100mm (4in) from the stake, or 230mm (9in) from a wall, spread out the roots and sift in fine soil, making sure that it settles between the roots. Firm the soil thoroughly with your feet. Make sure that the grafted joint is at least 100mm above ground, or it may form its own roots. Water regularly and liberally during the first season.

Pruning During the first four years, prune during winter to make the tree produce a strong framework of branches in the required shape. Always remove crossing branches and those keeping light and air from penetrating the tree. And take out any dead wood. Once the tree begins to bear fruit, prune also in the summer to promote fruit buds.

Pruning cuts are made just above a fruit bud in summer and just above a growth bud in winter. Fruit buds are large and round, growth buds are smaller and lie flatter on the stem. Use sharp secateurs, to make each cut slant in the same direction as the bud. Do not leave a stump above the bud; it will die.

During summer pruning (in late July and early August), cut back leading shoots by one-third to half their length. Prune sideshoots to leave three or four buds on each.

Picking the fruit To test whether an apple is ready for picking, place the palm of your hand beneath it and give a simultaneous lift and gentle twist. The apple should part easily from its spur. Store apples in a cool, slightly moist atmosphere.

Most varieties of pears ripen *after* picking. Harvest early varieties by cutting the stem with a sharp knife when the fruit is mature but still hard. Pick later varieties when the stalk parts easily from the spur after a gentle twist. Store pears in a cool, dry place.

Pick plums so that the stalk comes away with the fruit. For bottling, cooking or freezing, pick them before they are quite ripe.

See also CITRUS HOUSEPLANTS; ORANGE TREES; PESTICIDES.

Frying

*Browning food in deep fat;
cooking crisp potato chips*

For deep-frying, use a deep pan fitted with a wire basket or, better still, an electric deep-fryer with a built-in thermostat to control the temperature. A temperature of 190°C (375°F) is suitable for most deep-frying; if you do not have a thermostatically controlled fryer, test the temperature by dropping a cube of bread into the oil – at the correct temperature it will brown in 60 seconds.

Fill the pan to no more than one-third with good quality cooking oil, such as sunflower or corn oil, and heat it over a moderate heat. Frying times vary according to the size and type of food. For foods containing previously cooked ingredients, such as CROQUETTES, allow 2-3 minutes. Fritters need 3 to 5 minutes and potato chips 4 to 6 minutes.

Fish or chicken pieces can first be coated in batter or egg or breadcrumbs. Fry fish for 5 to 10 minutes, chicken for about 15 minutes.

Ingredients (for batter)
115g (4oz) plain or self-raising flour
Pinch of salt
1 egg
150ml (¼ pint) milk

Sift the flour and salt into a bowl. Using a wooden spoon make a hollow in the centre of the flour and drop in the lightly beaten egg. Slowly pour half the milk into the flour, gradually working the flour into the milk. Beat the mixture until it becomes smooth and free of lumps. Allow it to stand for a few minutes, then add the remaining milk, stirring continuously until the batter is bubbly.

Dip the prepared fish or chicken in seasoned flour and then into the batter.

Potato chips For golden, crispy chips, deep-fry them twice. First dry them on kitchen paper to prevent the oil from bubbling and sputtering. Place the chips in the wire basket, lower them into the heated oil and cook for 4 to 6 minutes – remove the basket from the pan and stand on absorbent paper. Re-heat the oil and fry the chips again for 1 or 2 minutes. See also CHIP PAN FIRE.

Fuchsias

Growing and caring for them

Garden fuchsias will grow in almost any well-drained soil, with the addition of humus, such as peat or leaf mould, and a little bone meal. Plant young shrubs in May or June, when frosts are over. They need full sun or light shade, and frequent watering during dry spells.

Cut the plants down to the base at the end of November, MULCHING deeply with bracken, ashes or peat.

Tender fuchsias for greenhouse cultivation (see GREENHOUSE GARDENING) or for summer BEDDING PLANTS should be grown in 150-230mm (6-9in) pots of JOHN INNES COMPOST No 3.

Indoors Stand the pots on a tray of damp pebbles in a sunny spot. Mist-spray them several times a day and keep well watered.

In March, trim the plants lightly, water and start them into growth at a temperature of 10°C (50°F).

In GREENHOUSES, provide a humid but airy atmosphere during the growing season and lightly shade the glass. In winter, fuchsias should be kept only barely moist, and at 4-7°C (39-45°F).

Fuchsias indoors Garden fuchsias do not transfer well into the home. It is best to start with small plants, about 100-125mm (4-5in) high, in spring. Pot them in a soil-based potting mixture in 125mm (5in) pots as soon as they have produced good top growth and the roots have begun to fill their pots. See also HOUSE-PLANTS; POTTING HOUSEPLANTS.

Keep in a cool temperature, about 16°C (61°F), and water plentifully during the growth period, keeping the potting mixture thoroughly moist. Feed weekly with liquid FERTILISERS.

Propagation Take tip cuttings, 75-100mm (3-4in) long, from shoots without flowering buds in March. Set them singly in 50mm (2in) pots of equal parts of peat and sand at a temperature of 16°C (61°F) and cover them with a polythene bag. The cuttings will take root in three to four weeks, and can then be transferred to 75mm (3in) pots of John Innes potting compost No 3. See also PROPAGATING PLANTS.

Fuel economy

*Getting good fuel consumption
from your car*

Driving economy is achieved by the skilful and unhurried use of the accelerator, gears and brakes. Think ahead all the time, making allowances for the movements of other traffic and anticipating when you may need to slow down or stop.

Never switch on the starter in short bursts because this may damage the flywheel. Switch on for 10 seconds, and if within that time the engine does not start, switch off and wait for 20 seconds before trying again. If you switch on for too long it will eventually run the battery down – see BATTERIES.

In cold weather, in a manual gearbox car without an automatic choke, pull the choke out all the way before starting the engine. Once the engine fires, drive off immediately, and push back the choke gradually as the engine warms up. You use less petrol if you can warm up the engine while driving rather than letting it idle. Do not rev the engine when it first starts.

Always accelerate gently and smoothly, and change into a higher gear at the right time – that is, when the speed you have reached in the lower gear can be maintained in the higher gear without accelerating.

If your car has a rev counter, try to change gear at between 2000 and 3000 revolutions per minute (rpm), the engine speed at which most cars run efficiently.

If your car handbook or service manual gives the maximum speeds the car is capable of in each gear, halve these figures to find the right road speed for changing gear. For example, if the maximum speed in third gear is given as 50mph, change up or down at 25mph.

Fast driving and fuel economy are not compatible. A car travelling at 80mph may use twice the amount of petrol it consumes at 30mph. For most cars a cruising speed of 50mph will give the best fuel consumption – the saying 'Fifty is thrifty' is worth remembering.

When approaching a corner or sharp bend, start to brake gently well ahead, then change gear directly from top to second just before the bend. Harsh braking and unnecessary gear changing wastes petrol. Stay in second gear as you negotiate the bend – never brake or change gear while cornering – and accelerate smoothly away from it.

When climbing a hill, do not try to stay in a high gear too long. If possible, try to build up enough speed beforehand to climb the hill in a low gear at a constant speed. Never try to save petrol by coasting down a hill in neutral or with the ignition switched off – it is illegal, the saving will be negligible and the car could become uncontrollable.

If your car has an automatic gearbox, always drive with the lever in the 'Drive' position – automatic gearboxes sense for themselves when to change gear economically. If you need to override the gearbox manually, select the 'Low' or 'Intermediate' position rather than use the 'kickdown', which increases petrol consumption.

See also CAR ROOF RACKS.

Funeral arrangements

Coping with a death in the house

Arrangements are normally handled by the dead person's next-of-kin or, if there is a will, by named executors who have agreed to take responsibility for settling his or her affairs.

First call in a doctor – usually the person's GP – to certify death. The doctor will complete a medical certificate showing the cause of death, and give you either this or a tear-off strip from it, entitled 'Notice to Informant'. Keep this for registering the death.

Where there is doubt as to the cause of death, the doctor must report the death to the coroner (in Scotland to the Procurator Fiscal) – a fairly common situation, occurring with one in every five deaths. It can happen, for example, if a doctor has not seen the person recently, and the cause of death is not obvious. A post-mortem examination may be needed.

In such a case, the death cannot be registered or the funeral go ahead until the coroner or fiscal gives permission. When the cause of death is established, the coroner's or fiscal's office may register the death directly, or ask the next-of-kin to do so. Otherwise, the doctor who completes the medical certificate will give you the address of the local registrar of births, deaths and marriages.

Visit the registrar in person within five days of the death. If you are unable to attend, write informing him of the death, then visit him within 14 days.

The registrar will require the Notice to Informant, the deceased's full name, place and date of birth, occupation, place and date of death, usual address, National Health Service Medical Card and, if he or she was married, the age of the surviving partner. He will also ask whether the dead person was receiving a pension or allowance from public funds.

He will give you a death certificate; also a disposal certificate, which the undertaker must have before the funeral.

Extra copies of the death certificate (available from the Registrar for a small fee) are needed to obtain any life assurance, the death grant, widow's benefit or other entitlements. The DSS booklet *What to do after a Death* (D49) details benefits available.

The certifying doctor may also be able to suggest an undertaker if you do not know of one in the area. The undertaker will take away the body and discuss funeral arrangements and costs.

The funeral can be an earth burial, cremation or burial at sea. For cremation, there are additional forms to be filled in: the undertaker can advise you.

You are not obliged to follow a dead person's preferences for the funeral, even if these are set out in the will. But if the deceased had contracted to donate his or her body (or organs) for medical purposes, you must contact the relevant hospital or medical institution at once.

Relatives and friends should be notified of a death at the earliest opportunity. You may also wish to put a notice in the local newspaper.

Fuses and fuse boxes

*Why fuses blow, and how to
replace them*

A fuse is a planned weak link in an electrical circuit, and if something goes wrong, the fuse disintegrates ('blows') cutting off the electricity supply. The main reasons for a fuse blowing are:

Old age In time, a fuse wire may corrode and fail for no apparent reason. Replacing the fuse wire (see below) will restore power.

Overloading a circuit If too many appliances are connected to a particular circuit – perhaps through using too many adaptors – the wiring will overheat and the fuse melt. In a fuse-wire carrier this is seen as globules of melted fuse wire. Replace the fuse wire and reduce the load on the circuit.

Damaged wiring or a faulty appliance This may cause the fuse to blow with a bang, blackening the fuse carrier and vaporising the wire. The fault must be traced (see CIRCUIT TESTING) or the faulty appliance unplugged before the fuse is repaired.

Replacing a fuse In older homes, fuses are in fuse boxes, each fuse protecting a particular circuit – either power or lighting – see ELECTRIC WIRING.

Before touching the fuses, switch off the current at the mains switch. Now pull out the fuses one at a time to see which has blown. Replace each one before removing the next.

Always re-wire using fuse wire of the same amperage. Never increase the amperage – substituting, say, a 15amp wire for a 5amp one – unless a mistake had been made previously. Replace the fuse and switch on at the mains. If it blows again, there is still a fault in the circuit, which must be found.

Replacing and repairing a blown fuse

First turn off the main switch and take off the fuse cover. If you have rewirable fuses, check for damaged wires. Remove any melted fuse wires and insert new ones. If you have a consumer unit with cartridge fuses, replace the blown cartridge fuse with a new fuse of the same rating. If your consumer unit contains miniature circuit breakers (MCBs) the button or lever on the MCB will be switched off. Check the relevant circuit before resetting the MCB.

Main switch

Rewiring
Unscrew the melted wire and replace with wire of the same thickness and rating.

Fuse cover

Fuse wire

Changing a cartridge Remove the fuse holder, take the two halves apart and prise out the fuse. Replace with one of the same amperage.

MCB Reset the button or lever

In more modern homes, there is a compact main switch and fuse box combined, known as a 'consumer unit'. A typical unit may contain six fuses – perhaps a 30 or 45amp for a cooker; 30amp fuses for socket outlet ring circuits; a 20amp fuse for a shower; a 15amp fuse for an immersion heater, and 5amp fuses for lighting circuits. Instead of cartridge fuses, the unit may contain miniature CIRCUIT BREAKERS.

You cannot see whether a cartridge fuse has blown. You can test it quickly and easily with a metal-cased torch. Remove the fuse from its carrier and take the end off the torch. Hold the cartridge so that one end of it touches the battery and the other end touches the metal case. Switch on the torch. It will light if the cartridge is sound.

QUICK TIP Keep a torch, insulated screwdriver and a selection of cartridges or fuse wires near the fuse box or consumer unit in case of emergency.

Fused connection unit

Fitting a power point for a fixed electrical appliance

You can fit a fused connection unit (FCU) instead of a plug and socket to connect an electrical appliance to the power circuit – see PLUGS; ELECTRIC SOCKETS AND SWITCHES. A plug allows you to move an appliance from one spot to another, plugging it in as needed. But appliances such as wall-mounted heat-

ers, extractor fans and freezers are never moved and so do not need plugs.

If they are wired into FCUs, there is no danger of damaging or accidentally removing a plug. An FCU is the only power point, apart from a shaver socket, which you are allowed to install in a bathroom.

You can fit the FCU to replace a socket on a ring circuit (see ELECTRIC WIRING) or you can lead an extra spur of cable from an existing socket to supply the FCU – see SPUR CONNECTIONS. The FCU fits a standard single mounting box of the kind installed for a socket.

Choose an FCU with a switch. It can also have a red neon indicator, to remind you that it is switched on.

Connecting the flex Connect the appliance flex to the FCU first, while you have room to work; then switch off power at the mains (see FUSES AND FUSE BOXES) before you connect the FCU to the circuit.

The flex fitted to a freezer or washing machine should be long enough to let you pull it forward for occasional cleaning or maintenance.

Use a sharp knife to strip off about 75mm (3in) of the outer sheath – just enough for the insulated conductor wires to reach the FCU terminals comfortably. Use wire strippers to take off 16mm ($\frac{5}{8}$in) of the brown, blue and green-and-yellow insulation.

Feed the flex through the side or front entry of the FCU, securing it with the flex grip if there is one. Make sure that the outer sheath goes through the entry.

Connect the conductor wires to the terminals marked Load or Out.

Connecting the FCU to the circuit Turn off the main switch at the consumer unit (main fuse box) and withdraw the fuse for the circuit you are working on.

If you are replacing an existing socket, take out the screws holding it and release the insulated conductor wires from the terminals behind the socket.

If you are fitting the FCU at a new power point, prepare the cable end by stripping the outer sheath and insulation on the conductor wires in the same way as on the flex. The earth wire in cable is bare; slip a short piece of green-and-yellow plastic sleeving over it.

If the FCU is on a ring circuit there are two cables to connect; match the tips together – red with red, black with black and green-and-yellow with green-and-yellow. If the FCU is on a spur branching off the ring circuit, there will be only one cable to connect (see illustration). Use the terminals marked either Mains, Feed, Supply or In.

Prise the fuse holder from the front of the FCU and fit the correct cartridge fuse in it – 3amp for appliances of up to 720 watts, 13amp for higher-wattage appliances. The wattage is shown on a small metal plate fixed on the appliance.

Press the FCU gently over the mounting box without disturbing the connections. Screw it in place until the FCU just meets the box; do not screw it too tight or the FCU may crack.

At the consumer unit, replace the circuit fuse and turn on the main switch.

Connecting an FCU to a spur

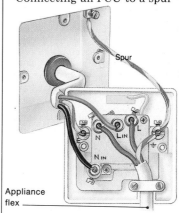

Spur

Appliance flex

Connect the appliance flex to the Load (or Out) terminals: brown to L; blue to N; green-and-yellow to E. or ⏚. Then connect the spur to the Mains terminals: red to L; black to N; green-and-yellow-sleeved earth to E, or ⏚. Connect a sleeved earth wire from the earth lug on a metal box to the earth connection on the FCU.

G

Game birds

Preparing and cooking grouse, pheasant and other birds

Grouse, pheasant and all other game birds need to be hung before plucking and drawing, to let the flavour develop and the flesh become tender. Each bird should be suspended by the neck from a hook in a cool, dry place well-protected from flies and rats.

The period of hanging depends on the age of the bird, the weather and individual taste (the longer a bird is hung, the stronger its flavour). An average is five to ten days (two or three days for wild duck). The bird is ready when the breast feathers, or those just above the tail, can be plucked easily.

Complete the plucking (see PLUCKING BIRDS), drawing and trussing as you would for POULTRY, or pay a poulterer to do it for you. Leave the feet on and set aside the giblets for GRAVY.

WARNING If the flesh has a green or bluish tinge, the bird has been hung too long and should not be eaten.

Young game birds are excellent for roasting, while BRAISING is better for older, tougher specimens. A young bird has smooth, supple feet and legs, a breastbone that gives slightly at the tip when pressed with the fingers, downy feathers on the breast and under the wings, and pointed (rather than rounded) tips to the long wing feathers.

Allow one grouse per person, or one between two people if the bird is plump.

A pheasant serves four people; pheasants are often sold in a brace of a cock and a smaller hen bird, but may also be bought singly.

Before roasting a game bird, sprinkle salt and pepper inside it, put in a knob of butter and cover the breast with bacon strips to keep the meat moist.

Set the bird on a slice of toast in the roasting tin; baste it often during roasting. The toast soaks up the juices and is eaten with the bird.

For the last 10-15 minutes of cooking, remove the bacon strips, and sprinkle the breast lightly with flour. Continue cooking until brown.

Serve grouse whole, or halved lengthways, on the toast, with game chips (potato crisps) or matchstick potatoes, and fried breadcrumbs. Offer a strong, giblet gravy, a green salad, sprouts or braised celery and redcurrant jelly or cranberry sauce – see SAUCES. The same accompaniments are suitable for pheasant, with bread sauce in place of the jelly or cranberry sauce.

Carving roast pheasant Cut the drumsticks from either side of the body. Hold the knuckle end of the drumstick in one hand, and slice the meat downwards all round it. Carve thin slices from the thigh bones. Cut off both wings. Carve the lighter breast meat in long, thin downward slices, from either side of the breastbone, as you would for chicken – see CARVING MEAT AND POULTRY.

Serve each guest a mixture of slices of breast and either leg meat or uncarved wing.

Roasting time for game birds

Bird	Season (approximate)	Temperature	Time
Capercaillie	Oct 1-Jan 31	200°C (400°F) mark 6	30-45 min
Grouse	Aug 12-Dec 10	200°C (400°F) mark 6	30-45 min
Partridge	Sept 1-Feb 1	200°C (400°F) mark 6	30-45 min
Pheasant	Oct 1-Feb 1	220°C (425°F) mark 7	20 min per 450g (1lb)
Pigeon	All year	220°C (425°F) mark 7	20 min per 450g (1lb)
Ptarmigan	Aug 12-Dec 10	200°C (400°F) mark 6	30-45 min
Quail	All year	220°C (425°F) mark 7	20 min
Snipe	Aug 12-Jan 31	220°C (425°F) mark 7	20 min
Woodcock	Oct 1-Jan 31	220°C (425°F) mark 7	20 min

Wild duck are in season from September to mid-February. Roast teal for 15-25 minutes according to taste, mallard or wigeon for 30 minutes, at 220°C (425°F) mark 7.

GARAGE DOORS

Rotting door bottom

Hinge

Brace

Backing rail

Area for repair

Drill a starting hole above the backing rail. Saw and prise out the rotten wood. Cut tongued-and-grooved lengths of timber to size and fit the pieces together. Glue all the joints, then glue and screw the wood to the backing rail. Countersink the screws and fill before painting

Garage doors

Repairing hinged doors; maintaining up-and-over

Hinged timber doors If the door is sagging, but otherwise sound, it may be possible to simply unscrew and reset the top hinge (see HINGES) about 6mm ($\frac{1}{4}$in) farther into the door frame. This lifts the bottom edge of the door.

If the door frame is loose at the joints, unscrew it from the hinges. Carefully knock apart the loose sections with a mallet or rubber hammer, to avoid damaging the wood. Clean off all old glue; re-glue using a waterproof adhesive (see GLUING), checking with a try square that the door is square before the glue sets. The most important component of the door is the brace, running from the bottom hinge to the corner diagonally opposite. Make doubly sure that this is firm.

If the door bottom has rotted, replace with new TIMBER, as illustrated. Cut well back into the sound wood, to make sure the rotted area has been eliminated. Do not try to patch rotted areas with wood filler – it will soon fall out, and the rot will spread.

Where a door panel has rotted, use a chisel and mallet (see CHISELLING) to cut away one side of the beading all around the panel until it can be removed. Measure the old panel, then use a panel saw to cut a new one – ideally from exterior-grade plywood – and secure it in place using waterproof glue. Replace the cut-away beading with new beading, available from timber merchants. Mitre the corners (see MITRE JOINTS) and glue and pin in place.

Check the paintwork regularly and repaint as necessary, to avoid damp penetrating the timber.

Up-and-over doors Panel rot is common where a wooden door projects beyond the door frame when open – rainwater can collect on it, and eventually causes rot. Replace a rotted panel as for a hinged door.

Metal doors are prone to RUST – especially if knocked or scratched. Clean off all loose rust with a wire brush, or an abrasive disc in a power drill, then paint the area with a rust inhibitor, which you can buy from car accessory or hardware shops.

Aluminium doors can accumulate a whitish deposit which, in fact, can form a protective surface. Or you can paint them with a zinc chromate primer, followed by good quality enamel.

Give opening mechanisms an occasional oiling at all pivot points, and check that any running channels for wheels are clean. Do not oil springs.

Garage sales

Planning them and pricing the goods

Americans on short-term tours of duty in Europe popularised garage sales here, to dispose of household goods and personal effects they did not wish to ship home. Now the term has come to mean any sale of secondhand household items held in a garage or other area of a private home.

There are no laws specifically applying to garage sales, but they may be technically forbidden under tenancy agreements. However, take care not to give neighbours or a landlord grounds for complaint – for example over noise, or obstruction caused by parked cars. You are also bound by the SALE OF GOODS Act, which means that anything you sell must correspond exactly with its description.

Plan your sale six weeks or so in advance. Most garage sales are held at weekends. Assemble, clean and repair the items you are selling. Get a few friends to help in your preparations, and on the day of the sale. They may have items of their own to include; if so, use different-coloured price tags to make clear what has been bought from whom.

Advertise the sale about a week beforehand in your local newspaper, giving the date, time, place and a summary of the goods for sale. Put a poster in your front garden or window, but remember you need permission from the owner to display posters on private property not belonging to you.

Price goods clearly with removable sticky labels. As a general rule, you should charge from 10 to 30 per cent of what the item would have cost new, depending on age and condition. Be cautious about including antiques or other collectable items; they may be better sold through a dealer or auction house.

Display the goods with similar items grouped together. Put clothes on an improvised rack, books on shelves or in boxes, tools on trestle tables. If you are selling electrical goods, put them near a power point where they can be demonstrated.

Have a good supply of small change – say, £20 – in your cash box. Be open to offers on prices, and mark them down towards the end of the sale if you want to, so that everything goes.

See also ANTIQUES; AUCTIONS; BRING-AND-BUY SALES.

Garden chairs and seats

Keeping them in good repair

Tubular metal frames get knocked about while in use – and while being stored for winter. Do not ignore chips and scratches; they quickly rust. Rub damaged or rusted areas with fine abrasive paper, then treat them as for RUST.

Keep all moving joints oiled. Wipe away surplus oil to avoid staining cushions or clothing.

Check all cushions for tears or open seams before you store them. Sew up any

damage with strong matching thread. Store the cushions in a dry place. Somewhere indoors is much better than a garage or shed. Replacements can often be ordered through the original supplier.

The strain on the cover of many garden chairs and loungers is taken by support cords under the metal frame. If a cord breaks it is not usually possible to make a satisfactory repair with any other kind of cord, but repair kits of extra-strong rubber bands and hooks are sold by garden centres and hardware stores.

Timber seats Wooden garden furniture that stands outside all year should be checked for loose joints every spring and autumn. Tap apart any loose joints with a rubber hammer – or an ordinary hammer over a piece of scrap wood – to avoid bruising the furniture. Chisel off all old adhesive, then apply new waterproof wood glue (see GLUING) to the joints and tap them back together. If the tongue of a joint has shrunk and glue cannot bridge the gap, use an epoxy-based wood repair paste instead.

Varnished wood that is in good condition, apart from signs of weathering, needs rubbing down with fine abrasive paper. Working with the grain, clean off the dust and re-coat with exterior-grade varnish – see VARNISHING.

If varnish is flaking, strip it off with a chemical stripper (see PAINT STRIPPING), rub the bare wood smooth, then apply one of the exterior-grade WOOD PRESERVATIVES rather than varnish – they will not flake or crack. Use an oil type stain to change the colour of the wood.

See also DECKCHAIRS.

Gardenias

Exotic blooms indoors

The shrub *Gardenia jasminoides*, sometimes called Cape jasmine, is not difficult to grow, but getting it to flower needs care. In a greenhouse or as HOUSEPLANTS gardenias reach about 460mm (18in) high. They like fairly high humidity and bright light, though not strong direct sun. A room temperature of 16-24°C (61-75°F) is suitable for most of the year. However, in late spring and summer, when the flower buds are forming, a constant temperature of 17°C (63°F) is needed; a sudden change will make the buds fall.

Water throughout the year. In summer, give enough room-temperature water to moisten all the potting mixture and allow the top 13mm (½in) of mixture to dry out before watering again. Mist the plants occasionally, also using water at room temperature; take care not to dampen buds or flowers, as that may discolour or damage them. Between March and September, feed the plants

---

GARDEN CHAIRS AND SEATS

Replacing support cords

Eye   Hook

Remove all the cord. Put hooks in the eyes of one flap and lodge a rubber band on each. Working from the centre, pull the bands to hook in the eyes opposite.

Extra-strength rubber band

every two or three weeks with 'acid' pot plant FERTILISERS. Gardenias hate lime so do not use tap water in hard-water areas. In winter, allow the top 25-50mm (1-2in) of potting mixture to dry out between waterings.

When roots appear on the surface of the soil or through the drainage hole in the pot, repot the shrub in a mixture of leaf mould and peat moss in equal parts. Soil-based lime-free potting mixtures are also suitable. You can encourage gardenias to flower in winter by pinching out the summer buds.

Garden ponds

Building with plastic or glass-fibre lining

Check the slope of the ground with a spirit level on a length of wood – see LEVELLING. If the edge of the pond is not level the water level will spoil the appearance of the pond. Choose a spot for the pool well away from trees and open to plenty of daylight.

Before you decide finally on the size and shape of the pond, select the liner – either a flexible liner sheet or a rigid plastic or glass-fibre shell.

Flexible liner The best and most durable liners consist of a double layer of PVC with nylon netting sandwiched between it, or black butyl rubber sheeting.

Dig the hole with its walls sloping in from the top. This reduces the risk of collapse and frost damage. Remove all sharp stones, roots or other obstructions that could damage the liner.

Line the hole with damp sand, about 25mm (1in) thick, to cushion the liner. Dampening the sand makes it stick to the sides.

Stretch the liner over the hole and anchor its edge securely with bricks, stones or slabs. Run water onto the liner from a garden hose. The water will stretch the liner until it touches the sides and bottom of the pond, though it will be necessary to move the weights from time to time.

When the pond is full, remove the anchoring bricks or slabs and cut off surplus liner with scissors, leaving a flap about 150mm (6in) wide lying on the ground around the pond. Cover the flap with paving, mortaring the slabs or broken pieces in place so that they overhang the water by at least 25mm – see MORTAR. Take care not to drop any mortar into the pond, as it will poison plants and fish. If any does drop in, empty the pond, clean it out and refill.

Rigid shell There are two main types – vacuum-formed plastic or the more durable and expensive moulded glass fibre. Both are installed in the same way.

GARDEN PONDS

Digging a pond; fitting a flexible liner

Design your preferred shape of pond, keeping it simple to make fitting the liner easy. Lay out the shape and mark it. Then dig the hole for the pond, about 460mm (18in) deep. Line the pond with damp sand at least 25mm (1in) thick, and then fit the liner.

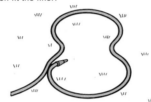

Marking out the shape Lay out a garden hose on the ground to form your desired shape, then mark the shape using wooden pegs.

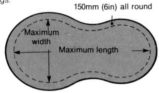

150mm (6in) all round

Maximum width

Maximum length

Sizing the liner Add twice the depth of the pond to both its maximum length and its maximum width. Add 150mm (6in) for the rim.

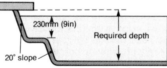

230mm (9in)

Required depth

20° slope

Shaping the walls You can make a ledge for plants about 230mm (9in) below water level. Slope the walls at an angle of 20 degrees.

Dig the hole as closely as you can to the shape of the shell but make it larger so there is a definite gap all round when you put the shell in place. As a rough guide, place the shell in position right side up and sprinkle sand around the outline. When the hole is the right size, line the base of the hole with at least 25mm (1in) of sand. Put in the shell and fill the gap round the outside with sieved soil up to the level of any shelf. Check with a spirit level that the rim of the shell is level in both directions. Then fill the pond with water up to the shelf level. Continue filling the gap with damped sand or sieved soil rammed down while water pours into the pond. This ensures firm support for the shelves. Edge the pond with paving, mortaring it in place to overhang the water by at least 25mm.

SAFETY NOTE Wherever small children are likely to be near the pond, fit

tough plastic garden mesh about 6mm (¼in) below the water line, anchored by pegs or metal hooks under the paving.

This will also prevent birds or cats from removing fish from the pond.

Garden walls

Repairing and maintaining the brickwork

Damaged pointing Dig out all loose and crumbling MORTAR to a depth of at least 13mm (½in), using the tip of a trowel, or a narrow steel chisel and club hammer. Use an old paintbrush to remove dust, then damp the joints well with water, using the same brush. Fill the joints with mortar mix – 1 part cement, ¼ part of hydrated lime to 3 parts soft builder's sand – then smooth off with a piece of bent copper tube, to make a weathered joint – see POINTING. Otherwise match existing joints. If you have to buy materials just for this job, buy a dry mortar mix available in small quantities, to which only water is added.

Loose bricks Chip away the mortar around the bricks until they can be removed. Chip off old mortar from the bricks, then 'butter' the edges with mortar and lay a bed of mortar in the hole to be filled – see BRICKLAYING. Ease the bricks in; tap home with the handle of the club hammer, then finish pointing.

Flaking bricks Hack out all the flaking brick with a chisel and fill with mortar coloured to match the brick. If flaking is excessive cut out the damaged brick and replace it with a new one. To prevent further flaking (spalling) treat the wall with silicone water repellent to prevent damp from entering the wall.

Mould or moss Treat the wall with a proprietary fungicide, diluted as instructed on the pack. More than one treatment may be necessary. When the mould has gone brown or black, brush it away. See also EFFLORESCENCE.

Garlic

Adding a unique flavour to food

For the true garlic taste, buy whole garlic bulbs; garlic salt, garlic granules, or garlic paste, sold by most grocers and supermarkets, are adequate substitutes, but lack the same intensity of flavour.

Choose bulbs that are plump and firm, with no discoloration. Buy only enough for a week or two at a time – the flavour weakens after two or three weeks. Store bulbs in a dark, dry place or in an aerated jar at room temperature.

The bulb encloses small, curved segments called cloves; most recipes need only one or two cloves, but Chinese dishes, for example, may require more. Pull the clove from the bulb and peel it. The skin will come away easily if you put the clove on a chopping board, concave side down, and press it with your thumb.

Garlic can have different degrees of strength, depending on how it is prepared. Uncooked garlic imparts more flavour than cooked – the longer the cooking time, the milder it becomes. Cut-up or pressed garlic is stronger than a whole clove.

For the most delicate flavour, rub a peeled clove against the bowl in which the food will be prepared, or sauté a whole clove in oil, and remove it before adding the food to be cooked. Cook until the garlic cloves are just golden – they burn easily in hot oil and develop an unpleasant, bitter taste.

Most hardware and kitchenware shops sell special garlic crushers for pressing garlic; catch the juice released by crushing and add it to salt to make your own garlic salt.

Garnishing

Decorating dishes attractively

If possible, garnish with at least one ingredient from the recipe. Herbs, for example, can be treated in several ways to add colour to a dish, and also complement the flavour of some foods.

Tomatoes, mushrooms, onions, celery and radishes are among the ingredients that can be used – see illustrations.

Herbs The leaves or flower heads of parsley, sage, chives or tarragon make a natural garnish for many dishes. Use small sprigs or single leaves on individual plates or, on larger serving dishes, make up small bouquets of mixed herbs. Sprinkle chopped fresh herbs over dishes which have little natural colour of their own. See also HERBS IN COOKING.

Vandyke tomatoes Cut a zigzag pattern around the centre of a small tomato, using a small, sharp knife and cutting right through to the core. Separate the two halves. You can then, if you wish, scoop out the halves and fill them with diced peppers and cucumber.

Fluted mushrooms Use very white button mushrooms of a uniform size. Score the mushroom cap from the centre to the edge at regular intervals with a small, pointed paring knife, removing a narrow strip of flesh each time. Remove the stem. To prevent the mushrooms from discolouring, boil them in water with a few drops of lemon juice for about three minutes.

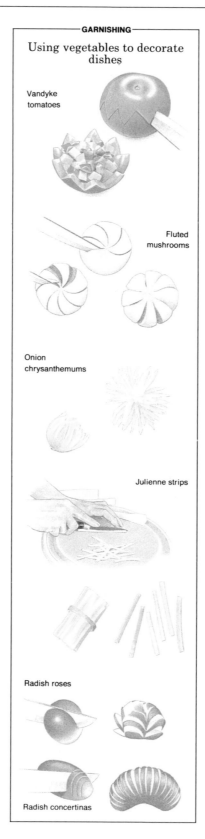

— GARNISHING —

Using vegetables to decorate dishes

Vandyke tomatoes

Fluted mushrooms

Onion chrysanthemums

Julienne strips

Radish roses

Radish concertinas

Onion chrysanthemums Peel a small onion and, using a very sharp knife, cut into quarters lengthways, stopping just short of the base. Make several more cuts and gently press the onion open to form petals. Soak in iced water for one hour – the petals will then open up.

Radish roses Remove the stalk and cut a slice off the base so that the radish will stand upright. Starting near the base, cut a row of scallop shapes round the radish, keeping them joined at the base. Continue to cut rows of scallops to the top of the radish. Place in iced water for one hour; it will open like a rose.

Radish concertinas Make cuts close together along the length but not right through. Gently open out.

Soup garnishes Cut thin strips (julienne strips) of carrot, celery or turnip, boil lightly and add to a consommé just before serving. For a consommé royale, beat a tablespoon of stock into one egg, steam the mixture until firm, cut out shapes with pastry cutters and add to the soup before serving.

Gas escape

What to do if you smell gas

If you smell gas, or suspect a leak, put out cigarettes and any naked flames such as pilot lights or candles immediately. Turn off any electric fires or motors (such as a vacuum cleaner) in the room, but do not turn any other electric switches either on or off, or even allow an electric doorbell to be used (tape over the push button). A spark from operating any electric switch could cause the gas to explode. Open all doors and windows to let the gas escape, and leave them open.

Check that no gas taps have been left on accidentally, and that no gas jets or PILOT LIGHTS have gone out. If a tap has been left on or blown out, turn it off and leave the room for the gas to clear.

If no gas appliances are on, there is probably a hidden leak. Turn the supply off at the meter immediately and leave the house. Telephone the British Gas emergency service (listed in the telephone directory under 'Gas'), or dial 999 and ask for the police. Tell your neighbours what is happening.

Stay out of the house until the leak has been traced and repaired, and the smell of gas has cleared. Make sure all gas taps are off once the gasmen have finished; relight pilot lights.

Never try to repair gas appliances or pipes yourself. By law, such maintenance must be carried out by a trained engineer such as those authorised by British Gas or the Council for Registered Gas Installers (CORGI). Use qualified gas fitters to install all appliances, whether they are new or secondhand, and have them serviced regularly – see GAS ROOM HEATERS; GAS WATER HEATERS.

Bottled gases Liquefied petroleum gas – usually propane or butane – sold in cylinders or metal bottles to use, for example, in mobile gas fires and on boats and in

Turning off Use the handle on the meter valve to turn the pivot, so the line on the pivot is at right angles to the gas pipe.

caravans, can be as explosive as household gas, and is also poisonous. If you suspect a leak, extinguish cigarettes and naked flames, close the valve on the cylinder tightly and open doors and windows. Check that all connections are as tight as possible (using a spanner, not your fingers) and inspect rubber hoses for wear or damage, replacing any leaky sections. Do not light appliances or turn on electrical switches until the smell of gas has dispersed. Ventilate lower levels – such as the bilges of a boat – after a leak has occurred.

QUICK TIP Rub soapy water along rubber hoses with the gas supply on. Bubbles will mark any leak.

Gas room heaters

Maintaining and using them safely

Simple care can help to maintain the efficiency of gas heaters and to keep them working safely. But never attempt to install, move or overhaul them yourself. By law, those are jobs for an officially approved installation company belonging to the Council for Registered Gas Installers (CORGI), or for your British Gas office.

If a heater develops a major fault, turn off the gas supply to it and call the gas board immediately. Try to have gas heaters and CENTRAL HEATING boilers professionally serviced once a year. See also GAS ESCAPE.

Between services, vacuum gas heaters regularly with a brush attachment to keep them free of fluff and dirt, particularly around the air inlet grille (usually on the bottom of the heater) and the outlet grille (usually at the top front). A blocked inlet can damage some types of gas fire by causing them to overheat, though certain models have a thermal cut-out device to prevent this from happening; never hang clothes to dry over the outlet. Check the external casing of a gas fire for signs of discoloration, which

will indicate that products of combustion are escaping instead of going up the chimney.

Periodically check the flue to ensure that it is not blocked. On convector heaters – the sort without clay bars, called radiants, that glow when alight – remove the front panel occasionally and clean inside the casing. On radiant and radiant/convector heaters, occasionally vacuum the area behind the radiants. On all models, check the holes in the gas jet from time to time; if any seem blocked by dirt or accumulated carbon, clear them with a fine needle.

If a clay radiant becomes damaged, buy a matching replacement from your local gas showrooms. Most modern radiants are box radiants. They are protected by a metal grille slotted into the sides of the fire, which is taken out to replace the broken radiant. On a fire with horizontal bar radiants, remove the radiants carefully. Make sure that no broken bits fall into the burners. Refer to the user's instructions supplied by the heater manufacturer.

Both convector and radiant heaters may have an automatic lighting device, powered by a battery that has to be replaced when it is exhausted. On convector heaters, the battery may be under or at the side of the casing. To replace it on underside fittings, slip off the locating clip and remove the battery; on side-mounted models, pull off the covering panel. On radiant fires, the batteries are under the panel at the front of the heater. Later models have a press-button spark ignition, with no batteries needed. Some log/coal-effect fires ignite when the control tap is turned on.

Some radiant fires have an electrically operated fire-effect panel, lit by a bulb. To replace a worn-out bulb, remove the electrical plug from the socket and lift out the fire-effect panel. Remove the metal spinners (they give the flickering appearance when the fire is working) to get to the bulb. Take it out, fit a new bulb and reassemble. See also GAS WATER HEATERS; PILOT LIGHTS.

Gas water heaters

Maintaining and using them safely

Have gas water heaters checked and serviced annually by a qualified gas engineer. Most modern types have a removable front panel that enables you to clean them inside and inspect their PILOT LIGHTS if necessary, between services; that is not possible on some older models, which must be disconnected by an engineer for cleaning and adjustment.

Modern water heaters usually have a built-in (or balanced) flue to take in fresh air and to expel the waste products; ensure that the flue does not become

obstructed. If you have an old-type water heater with an ordinary overhead flue in your bathroom, make sure you have permanent ventilation. Better still, have a balanced flue heater installed.

If you have a small sink heater without a flue, guard against a possible build-up of poisonous carbon monoxide by never running the heater for more than five minutes at a time, and by having adequate permanent ventilation.

Gates

Maintaining and mending timber and metal ones

Timber gates may sag because their joints or hinges are loose, because they have no brace or are wrongly hung, or because their posts are leaning.

Remove the gate from its hinges and check the joints. Tap apart any loose ones with a mallet or rubber hammer or with an ordinary hammer over a piece of scrap wood. Chisel off any old adhesive, and apply waterproof wood adhesive – see GLUING. Reassemble the joints, checking with a try square that the corners are perfect right angles.

Make sure there is a brace and that it is soundly fitted. If it is loose, take it off and refit it with waterproof glue and galvanised screws. If there is still some movement in the gate, screw on metal braces. Straight pieces, T-shapes and L-shapes are available from DIY stores.

If the hinges are loose, remove them and refit them with SCREWS of a larger gauge and perhaps a little longer if the thickness of wood allows. If necessary, plug the holes with wooden DOWELS or fibre wall plugs and screw into them. Replace damaged hinges.

Dig out a leaning gate post. If it has rotted, replace it with one of similar size, made of pressure-impregnated timber.

Make the post hole deep enough for the post top to be level with the one on the other side when standing on a brick placed at the bottom of the hole. Get a helper to hold the post upright in position while you check with a spirit level that it is vertical, and also level with the other post, (see LEVELLING) and that the opening allows clearance for the gate catch and hinges. Anchor the post by ramming hardcore round it, leaving 100mm (4in) at the top for a CONCRETE collar. Slope the top of the concrete. To stop posts sagging inwards on soft ground, lay a 200mm (8in) concrete strip between them.

If you fit a new gate, coat it liberally with one of the WOOD PRESERVATIVES before VARNISHING or painting it – see PAINTING EXTERIORS.

Metal gates These rarely fail under strain. It is usually a hinge which gives

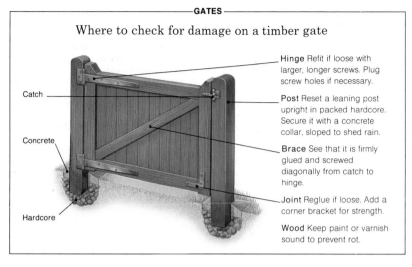

GATES

Where to check for damage on a timber gate

Catch

Concrete

Hardcore

Hinge Refit if loose with larger, longer screws. Plug screw holes if necessary.

Post Reset a leaning post upright in packed hardcore. Secure it with a concrete collar, sloped to shed rain.

Brace See that it is firmly glued and screwed diagonally from catch to hinge.

Joint Reglue if loose. Add a corner bracket for strength.

Wood Keep paint or varnish sound to prevent rot.

way. This is often a pin or an eye mortared into a brick pillar, and may pull out eventually.

Lift off the gate, remove the hinges from the pillar and tap out the MORTAR with a hammer and cold chisel. Enlarge the holes for the hinges, using the hammer and chisel. Brush PVA adhesive inside the holes then refit the hinges. Hold the gate in place on the hinges to check their position before sealing them in with brick mortar. Support the hinges with timber props while the mortar sets.

If paintwork is damaged, RUST may attack the metal. Remove all loose rust with a wire brush and coarse abrasive paper, then treat the bare metal for rust before repainting.

Take care to paint all the intricate curves of the metal. You may find an aerosol or spray gun easier to use than a brush – see SPRAY PAINTING. Apply several thin coats rather than one thick coat to avoid paint runs.

Hinges and latches Lubricate gate hinges with grease – not with oil because it evaporates too quickly. Use oil on latches but wipe away any surplus or it will get on people's hands.

On a wrought-iron gate, drill a hole through the top of the hinge pin (see DRILLING) and fit a split pin through it once the eye is hooked over – this makes the gate more difficult to steal.

Geraniums

Growing them and keeping them through the winter

True geraniums are hardy plants that grow in sun or partial shade in most types of soil; and most kinds survive winters outdoors. However, their name has been popularly borrowed for pelargoniums, which are more delicate and

are killed by winter frosts. They, too, flourish in sun or partial shade (needing at least four hours a day of direct sunlight) in most types of soil. Their showy blossoms range from the familiar bright red to pink or white, and some varieties have scented leaves.

Plant out pot-grown geraniums in beds or window-boxes after the last frost has passed, spacing them 200-380mm (8-15in) apart. Feed them monthly with FERTILISERS low in nitrogen, and pinch back new growth to keep the plants bushy. Remove dead flowers to encourage new ones, and water in dry spells, allowing the soil to become slightly dry between waterings.

To keep plants over winter, transfer them to pots indoors (see POTTING HOUSEPLANTS) well before the first frosts are due. Cut stems back about halfway and use the smallest pots that will accommodate the roots. Put the plants on a sunny windowsill or in a cool greenhouse. They prefer cool rooms with a minimum temperature of 7°C (45°F) and are sensitive to gas, so windowsills in kitchens with gas boilers or cookers are not suitable. Keep the soil just moist. Cut the plants back again when new shoots are about 100mm (4in) long. Feed weekly with potplant fertiliser in spring, in preparation for the transfer outside.

Grow new pelargoniums from 100mm cuttings taken from the tips of established, healthy plants in August or September – see PROPAGATING PLANTS. Strip all but three leaves from each cutting, and put the cuttings around the edges of a large pot in an equal mixture of damp sand and peat.

Place the completed pot inside a polythene bag in which you have pierced a few air holes. Do not let the bag touch the leaves. Stand the pot in a cool greenhouse or conservatory or on a sunny windowsill.

Once the cuttings have rooted (three to

four weeks), transfer them to individual pots of John Innes potting compost No 1. Take care to keep the soil moist. Repot the cuttings in January or February, using medium-sized pots containing JOHN INNES COMPOST No 2.

German measles

Precautions, symptoms and treatment

This common infectious disease, also called rubella, is not normally serious and an attack usually confers immunity for life. However, if a woman gets it during the first 16 weeks of a pregnancy, it may severely affect the unborn child – causing stillbirth, blindness, deafness or heart disease. Anyone with German measles should keep away from newly pregnant women. If you contract the disease and come inadvertently into contact with a mother-to-be, be sure to let her know, so that she can get advice from her DOCTOR if she has not been immunised.

Because other viruses can mimic German measles, doctors routinely offer immunisation against German measles, measles and mumps to all children in their second year, even if they have already had one of these illnesses. The injection may produce a mild rash and joint pains, clearing up after a few days.

Women who are unsure whether they have had it should ask their doctor for a blood test – similar tests are made automatically early in pregnancy – to establish whether or not they are immune. If an injection is needed they should avoid pregnancy for at least three months afterwards, as immunisation can also affect an unborn child.

Rashes and pains German measles takes 14 to 21 days to develop after exposure to the infection. First symptoms may be a general feeling of illness, followed within a few days by a rash of small, pink spots starting behind the ears or on the face, and spreading over the rest of the body.

Glands, particularly behind the ears, may swell, and there may be pains in the joints, sometimes severe, especially in young women. The rash lasts for up to five days and the sufferer is infectious to others from five days before until four days after the rash appears. The joint pains may persist for two weeks.

Most cases are treated at home. Keep the victim indoors for four days after the rash appears, and give painkillers as necessary. Consult the doctor if the joint pains are severe, or if the patient develops a high temperature, severe or persistent headache, or becomes unnaturally drowsy. Get medical advice if you suspect that any woman in early pregnancy has been exposed to infection, and is not known to be immune.

Coping with different shapes

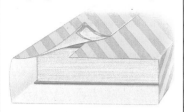

Rectangular box Centre the package, top down, on the paper and bring the paper up round it. Turn under the overlap by 25mm (1in), stick double-sided sticky tape along the fold and press down.

Neat ends Press the top of the paper over one end of the box, tucking it right into the angles at the sides so that the paper slants down there. Press the slanted sides into sharp creases then fold them inwards. Press them in firmly at the base of the box so the bottom of the paper slants in at the sides. Fold the raw edge over and tape the fold to the top edge of the paper.

Jar or bottle Use two squares of soft paper, laying one on the other with their corners alternate. Centre the jar, draw up the paper all round and tie it with ribbon.

Tube Bring the paper up round the tube and stick it as for a box (top). At each end of the tube tie a ribbon to gather the paper. Spread the gathers evenly.

Gift wrapping

Covering boxes, bottles and tubular shapes

Use double-sided sticky tape to seal the wrapping in place. It is put on the underside of the paper so that no tape shows on the finished parcel.

To gift wrap a square or oblong package such as a box or a book, use a piece of wrapping paper long enough to wrap right round it with a 50mm (2in) overlap. The paper should be as wide as the package plus the depth of the package plus 25mm (1in).

When you bring up the paper round the package, it must fit snugly, not be loose, or the parcel will be untidy. It helps to tape one edge of the paper to the package inside so you can pull the other edge tightly round; you cannot do this, however, if tape might damage the contents – say a book jacket. Instead, press the two edges of the paper together with the flat of both hands before you stick down the overlap.

If your package is too large for a single sheet of wrapping paper, lay two or more sheets on the table wrong side up. Make a 13mm ($\frac{1}{2}$in) fold on each adjoining edge, turning one edge up and the other edge under. Slip one fold inside the other and tape under the top fold to hold the seam in place.

To wrap an awkward shape such as a jar or a bottle, use pliable paper such as tissue, foil or coloured Cellophane. Cut out two squares, each with sides as long as twice the height of the jar plus three times its width. When you have gathered the paper round at the top, fan out the corners over the securing ribbon to resemble petals.

Lay a soft, flat gift such as a scarf on a piece of cardboard before wrapping. Or buy or make a cardboard tube and push the gift inside. You can then make the wrapping look like a Christmas cracker. Allow 75mm (3in) of paper to extend beyond the tube at each end for the cracker look.

WARNING Gift wrapping paper is not robust enough to use as an outer covering for mailing. Cover the wrapped gift with strong brown paper before posting – see PARCEL TYING.

Gilding

Using gold leaf the craftsman's way

If a picture frame is sound (see PICTURE FRAME REPAIRS), you can gild or decorate it with gold leaf.

The simplest method is oil gilding, for which you will need: gesso; small paint brushes; fine abrasive paper; dark reddish-brown paint; shellac; a small hog's-hair brush; oil-based gold size; gold leaf; a gilder's cushion; a drinking straw; a gilder's knife; a 100mm (4in) wide camel-hair brush called a gilder's tip; a squirrel-hair brush. All these materials are sold in specialist art shops.

First prepare the frame. Apply several coats of gesso, letting each coat dry thoroughly. Then rub smooth with abrasive paper and paint with the reddish paint. Finally seal with two coats of shellac.

For the next stage, apply the gold size, making sure you work it well into all parts of the moulding. It will take about two hours to dry. Wait longer if it still feels tacky.

Put the gilder's cushion near the frame so that you don't have to move the leaf very far. Open the book over the cushion and lift out some leaves for cutting.

Transfer cut pieces to the frame piece by piece, overlapping them a little, then tap them into place.

Fill in any small areas left bare with tiny fragments cut from a leaf, and transferred to the frame on the end of a soft brush. If any spots have dried apply more size before the leaf.

A cheaper way A good effect can be obtained, but more cheaply, using gold or silver foil.

Cut the foil into 38mm (1$\frac{1}{2}$in) squares and crumple up each square, to give a crinkled texture, before spreading it flat for use. Mix PVA adhesive (see GLUING) with water and apply it to the frame with a toothbrush.

Press squares of foil onto the frame and work them into its contours. Brush more glue over the surface and allow it to dry before applying antiquing glaze.

Repairing a gilt frame For touching in damaged areas of gilt, use wax gilt. Choose a shade to match your frame and rub the wax on the bare patches.

Gingerbread men

Making a children's party treat

To make gingerbread men, combine 115g (4oz) soft brown sugar, 115g treacle, 75g (3oz) butter, 1 teaspoon each of ground cinnamon and ground ginger, and half a teaspoon of ground cloves in a heavy-based saucepan.

Cook over a low heat and stir, gradually bringing the mixture to the boil. Remove the saucepan from the heat and allow the syrup to cool to room temperature. Stir in 1$\frac{1}{2}$ teaspoons of baking powder.

Mix together 450g (1lb) plain flour, sifted, and a pinch of salt in a bowl. Make a well in the centre of this and pour in the cooked mixture, adding one lightly beaten egg. Incorporate the flour and

Gold leaf on a picture frame

Sizing Use a hog's-hair brush to paint a thin coat of gold size evenly over the prepared frame. Leave it to dry – the dry size squeaks as you draw a finger over it.

Getting the leaves Move a few gold leaves from the book to the cushion, either by sucking each up onto the end of a drinking straw or by blowing them out of the book.

Preparing a leaf Use the gilder's knife to lift one leaf to the centre of the cushion. Cut a piece from it to fit a portion of the frame.

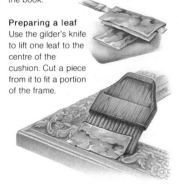

Lifting into place Rub the bristles of the gilder's tip on your face or palm to pick up a little grease, then press it onto the leaf, which will cling to it. Lift it onto the frame and apply it.

Fixing When you have applied several pieces to the frame, use the squirrel-hair brush to tap them gently onto the wood. Twirl the brush as you tap, especially into mouldings, to make the leaf stick.

syrup by stirring from the centre. Turn out the mixture onto a floured board and knead it lightly. Then form it into a ball and wrap it in greaseproof paper. Chill for about 30 minutes.

Preheat the oven to 160°C (325°F), gas mark 3. Roll out the dough to 3mm ($\frac{1}{8}$in) thick. Use a cutter to stamp out the gingerbread men, or cut the shapes with a pointed knife. Place the figures 50mm (2in) apart on greased baking sheets and bake for 8-10 minutes, until lightly browned. Remove with a palette knife and cool on wire racks. Use piped glacé icing to make faces on your gingerbread men and to outline the figures.

Gin rummy

A variation on rummy

For this card game for two players you need one full pack of 52 cards, and a pencil and paper to keep the score. The aim of each player is to make sets of three or four cards of the same denomination – for example, three kings, four eights, three sixes or sequences (runs) of three or more consecutive cards of the same suit – such as the two, three, four and five of spades. Points are awarded according to the outcome of each hand, and the first player to reach 100 is the winner.

In scoring, aces equal 1 point each, and each picture card counts as 10; the other cards are counted at their face value. Each set or sequence must consist of at least three cards, and you cannot use the same card twice in making them up; for example, the king of spades cannot appear as part both of a set of kings and in a sequence of spades. As the points values imply, aces are played low – queen, king, ace is not a sequence, and neither is king, ace, two. However, ace, two, three is a sequence.

The rules of play and scoring vary slightly in different card schools, so check before you start. Here is one widely accepted version of the game:

The deal and play The players cut the pack to decide the dealer; the player drawing the lower card deals to the non-dealer and then to himself alternately, until both players have ten cards each. (Throughout the rest of the game, the dealer is the player who won the previous hand.) The rest of the pack is placed face down and the top card is turned face up beside it.

The non-dealer may, if he wishes, pick up the exposed card to help him make a set or sequence, discarding a card from his hand, face up, in its place. If the non-dealer cannot make use of the exposed card, the choice passes to the dealer. He may pick up the exposed card, discarding one of his own. If neither player wants the first exposed card, the non-dealer

must pick up the top card from the unexposed stock, afterwards discarding one onto the exposed pile. Play continues alternately, with each player picking up either the top card from the exposed pile or from the stock, and discarding one card onto the exposed pile. Only the top card on the exposed pile is available if wanted.

Once either player has made enough sets or sequences in his hand so that the total value of any unplaced cards is 10 points or less, he may end the hand by 'knocking' – that is, rapping on the table, and laying out his hand in sets, sequences and unplaced cards. You may 'knock' only immediately after you have picked up a card and discarded one. You are not obliged to knock once your unplaced cards total 10 points or less, but can continue until a final discard leaves you with the whole hand in sets and sequences – a 'gin'.

The skill in gin rummy lies in timing the decision to knock. Your opponent's discards can give you a clue about his progress towards ending the hand.

Scoring Once one player has 'knocked' or declared gin, the other must lay out his hand. He may add any of his unplaced cards to the declarer's exposed sets or sequences. For example, he could add a spare jack to the declarer's set of three jacks. Then the scores are added up.

A gin using all ten cards carries a bonus of 20 points, whether or not the opposing player managed to dispose of all his unmatched cards. The points values of any remaining unmatched cards are totalled for each hand; if those for the declarer are lower than those for his opponent, the declarer collects points equivalent to the difference. If the non-declarer is left with a total equal to or below that of the declarer, the non-declarer collects the difference in value plus a bonus of 10 points (the 'undercut').

The dealing of hands continues until one player has reached 100 points. Then, if the game is played for stakes, there is a second calculation to determine how much the winner collects. First, he receives 100 points for reaching 100 first, or 200 points if his opponent has not won a single hand. Then each player receives a bonus of 20 points for each hand he has won; the winning bonus is adjusted by the difference between the two hand bonus totals.

Finally, the points collected by each player during the game are totalled. The winning bonus is adjusted by the difference between these points totals, to produce the net points score.

In a variation of the game, to begin the discard pile the top card of the stock pile is turned up. If this card is a spade, the score for the hand is doubled. The value of the turned-up card sets the limit for knocking.

Glass cutting

Straight lines, curves and circles

Using the right tool is the key to cutting glass without breaking it. Choose a cutter with a small, hardened steel alloy wheel, preferably one to which replacement wheels can be fitted. Do not choose the professional tool with a diamond chip tip – it takes more practice than an amateur can afford.

Try always to use new glass. Old glass changes in nature, becomes increasingly hard to cut and tends not to break along the scored line.

You will also need: a steel tape for measuring; an accurate straightedge to guide the glass cutter; some white spirit to lubricate the cutting wheel, and a chinagraph pencil or felt-tipped pen to mark the cutting line.

Straight cuts Lay the glass on a completely level surface clear of any debris. An open newspaper is a useful aid to cutting, as the rules between columns are very accurate, and are at true right angles to horizontal rules. Glass laid over the newspaper can be positioned using the rules as guides.

Measure the glass accurately. It is very hard to remove an extra sliver later. Mark the glass with the pen or pencil, then position the straightedge on the line. Lubricate the cutter wheel with white spirit and set it on the line at the point farthest from you. Hold the cutter so that your forefinger applies pressure to the wheel and then draw the cutter towards you, pressing hard enough for you to hear the wheel whispering over the glass. Draw it along the line in one clear run. Do not stop halfway.

Lift the glass and tap lightly along the underside of the score mark with the handle of the glass cutter. Now place the glass on top of the straightedge, aligning the score mark exactly along the edge. Press the glass down firmly; it will snap cleanly along the score.

If only a thin strip has to be removed, place the glass so the strip overhangs a table. Grasp the strip between thumb and forefinger to snap it off.

To snap off a very thin sliver, use pincers or the edge of the glass cutter. For this operation wear protective gloves and safety spectacles.

Cutting a circle Use a special cutting tool that has the cutting head fitted to an arm on a suction pad. You can lock the head at any position you wish on the arm.

Mark two diagonal lines across the pane of glass from the corners with pen or pencil. Measure and mark the required radius of the circle along one of them. From the point where the diagonals cross, set the cutter to match the radius exactly, then fix the suction pad

Using two cutting tools

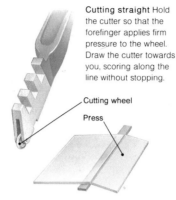

Cutting straight Hold the cutter so that the forefinger applies firm pressure to the wheel. Draw the cutter towards you, scoring along the line without stopping.

Cutting wheel

Press

Tap the underside of the score mark with the cutter handle. Place the glass on top of the straightedge and press down.

Suction pad

Arm

First circle

Cutter

Cutting a circle Slide the cutter to the required radius and score a circle. Move the cutter inwards about 19mm (¾in) and score another circle.

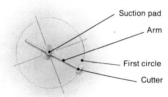

Second circle

Diagonal cuts

Score lines from the centre to the inner circle to form wedge shapes. Gently tap them out. Score lines around the outer circle and gently tap out the segments.

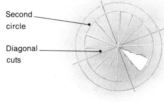

on the glass where the diagonals cross. Check that the wheel is on the radius mark; apply even pressure and score the circle on the glass without stopping.

Move the cutter in about 19mm (¾in) and score another circle. Score lines along a straightedge from the inner circle to the centre – rather like the spokes of a wheel. Now tap out the wedge-shaped pieces from the inner circle, first

tapping under the scored lines and then pressing out the pieces.

Score lines from the remaining circle to meet the hole, all round the remaining 19mm (¾in) of waste glass, then tap out the remaining pieces with an ordinary wheel cutter. Nibble off any remaining pieces with pincers.

Cutting a curve Mark out the required curve accurately on paper and lay it under the glass. Score the curve freehand, following the pattern and making it in one continuous stroke until you run off the edge of the glass. Make score lines radiating out from the curve on the waste side of the glass and tap the waste away, section by section.

Glasses

Matching the glass to the drink

There are eight main types of drinking glasses, each designed to complement the taste and bouquet of the wine or spirit it is intended to hold. The best quality glasses are full-lead or lead crystal; full-lead crystal contains 30 per cent lead oxide, lead crystal contains 25 per cent lead oxide, and it is this addition that gives glassware its brightness, clarity, weight and strength. The thinner and finer the glass the better the wine or spirit tastes.

Crystal glassware, however, is expensive, so if you want to collect a full set of glasses for all occasions you may need to do so over a period of time, starting with three basic types.

Sherry glass Sometimes called a copita, this pear-shaped glass is also suitable for port, Madeira and liqueurs.

Wine glass There are three different shapes of wine glass – the Paris goblet, tulip glass and hock glass. Of these, either the Paris goblet or tulip glass can be used for drinking both red and white wines, though the tulip glass can also be used for sparkling wines such as champagne and spumante. Sizes of wine glasses are: 5oz; 6¼oz; 8oz; 10oz and 12oz.

Whisky tumbler A squat, straight-sided glass with a heavy base (Scotsmen do not like to have their drink knocked over), the whisky tumbler will hold about 225ml (8fl oz) and so can also be used for long drinks such as beer or lager.

These three types can later be added to with more distinctive and sophisticated glasses, designed for the full appreciation of good wines and spirits.

Champagne glass Champagne or spumante, the Italian sparkling wine, should be drunk from a tall, conical glass called a flute, which allows the bubbles to rise

| Port or sherry | White wine | Champagne flute | Hock | Paris goblet | Brandy | Whisky tumbler | Lager | Beer jug |

Brandy glasses are shaped to trap fumes in the funnel. Port glasses allow fumes to disperse in the funnel. The champagne flute is designed to prevent the bubbles from dissipating too rapidly. Beer glasses are either jug-shaped or straight-sided: beer quality is not affected. But some beer drinkers claim that silver or pewter tankards will keep the beer cooler. A hock glass often has a coloured stem that reflects attractively into the wine.

evenly and rapidly. The dish-shaped version is not really suitable for sparkling wine as it allows the bubbles to dissipate too quickly.

Port glass The ideal shape for this glass is a bulbous base narrowing to a funnel top. Port has a pungent aroma, which would be almost overpowering if allowed to escape through a wide-topped glass. A port glass should be filled to between a half and two-thirds of its capacity, so that the fumes can disperse in the funnel formed at the top.

Hock glass Perhaps the most elegant and sophisticated of all wine glasses, there are designs for each region of these German wines. The Rhine-wine hock glass has a brown stem to reflect colour into the wine, whereas Alsace wine is drunk in a glass with a green stem. The glass for Moselle wines is engraved to catch the light and bring out the green-gold colouring of the wine.

Brandy glass A thistle-shaped glass which, like the port glass, traps the fumes in its funnel top. Some brandy drinkers prefer the 'balloon' glass, designed to be cupped in the hand so that body heat warms the brandy to evaporate the fumes more quickly.

Beer: glass, jug or tankard? Some beer drinkers prefer their beer in a straight-sided glass, others opt for a handled jug. Neither type affects the quality of the beer, but since a pint of beer weighs just over 450g (1lb) a firm grip on a handle lessens the chance of a full pint slipping through your fingers.
Pewter or silver tankards also have a handle, and often a glass bottom.

QUICK TIP Cut glass gives an attractive sparkle to drinking glasses, but is often imitated by moulded glass. To tell the difference, run a thumb along the pattern – the edges of cut glass are sharp, whereas moulded glass has rounded edges.

Glassware

Cleaning and looking after it

To retain the lustre and brilliance of crystal glassware (see also GLASSES), wash each piece separately in warm water with a little liquid detergent added; rinse in clean water, dry and then drain on kitchen paper or a tea towel. Store glasses in a closed cupboard, standing right way up. Storing them rim down may chip the edges.
Leave badly stained cut glass overnight in a mixture of water, detergent and a few drops of ammonia. To remove lime deposits, fill the glass with distilled water, leave it for a week, then gently remove the crust with a toothbrush.
If glassware – such as a decanter – becomes stained inside, put in a tablespoon of silver sand, obtainable from a gardening shop, and a weak solution of warm water and liquid detergent. Swill the contents round, but check frequently that the glass is not being scratched.
To remove a stopper that is stuck in a decanter, apply a mixture of two parts white spirit, one part glycerine and one part salt between neck and stopper. After 24 hours, wrap a hot cloth round the neck and ease out the stopper.

QUICK TIP To free ordinary table glasses that are stuck together, fill the top one with cold water and dip the bottom one in warm water.

Gluing

Choosing the right adhesive

For most general household jobs you need a selection of adhesives. There is, however, no adhesive for polythene – it has to be welded; and nylon, too, cannot be glued.
For all repairs involving adhesives, keep the pieces clean and dry. Even the grease from your fingertips can weaken a bond. Do a dummy run first if a number of pieces are involved, to make sure where and how they fit. Numbering the pieces helps. Take time over complicated repairs, allowing one part to set before bonding on the next.
Store all adhesives out of reach of children, especially cyanoacrylates, PVC, polystyrene cement and epoxy resin, all of which give off toxic fumes. When children are using a suitable glue, such as PVA, supervise them closely. Protect surfaces and keep the room well ventilated.
The adhesives most used are:

Cellulose and starch-based Used for wallcoverings. They are supplied ready-mixed or as powders for mixing with water. Some are applied to the back of the wallcovering, some to the wall.

PVA A non-flammable adhesive available in a wide range from plastic bottles for school use to tubs for building work. The adhesive is white, creamy in consistency, and can be diluted with water. Once set it is water-resistant and almost clear. It is effective on wood, bonds MOR-TAR to tiles, bricks and pavings, bonds one layer of concrete to another, and can seal a concrete floor to prevent dust coming off the surface. As a general household adhesive, PVA is applied to only one of the surfaces to be bonded together, and the surfaces need clamping together while the glue sets.

Clear resin A general-purpose household adhesive for sticking card, flexible materials like leather, and for model-making. It is not a very strong adhesive, and should not be used for jobs such as fixing a broken pottery handle. Apply it straight from the tube – usually to both surfaces. Apply the resin, wait until it is only slightly tacky, then press the surfaces. Apply the resin, wait until it is only slightly tacky, then press the surfaces together.

Epoxy resin This is supplied in a pack containing two tubes, one of adhesive and the other of hardener. Mix equal amounts from the two tubes. Once mixed, the adhesive starts to harden and the hardening cannot be slowed down or stopped. Of the two versions available – standard and quick-setting – standard makes a stronger bond. Apply to one surface only and clamp or tape the surfaces until the resin sets. Use the resin for mending or bonding metals, china and glass, and some rigid plastics. It is not suitable for flexible materials.

Expanding foam Although designed as a gap filler, foam is highly adhesive, and can anchor loose slates and tiles.

Formaldehyde This is the ideal glue for woodworking – especially outdoor work – as it is waterproof, heat-resistant, and produces a strong joint. Apply it to one surface, then clamp together the surfaces to be bonded while the adhesive sets.

Rubber-based A white latex type is used for bonding textiles, fabrics and leather, and a rubber-resin type, called contact adhesive, for sticking down large areas of laminate or similar board. They are not suitable for wood because they retain some flexibility. Black rubber adhesive is highly water-resistant, making it ideal for repairs to rubber seals, waterproof boots, boat and caravan exteriors, and canvas and tarpaulin sheets.

Apply the adhesive to both surfaces, wait for it to become touch-dry, then bring together the two surfaces.

When using contact adhesive on large areas, such as for PVC or cork floor tiles, take care to choose adhesives where the solvent is water. Many types contain solvents that give off dangerous fumes. When working on large areas, make sure the room is well ventilated.

Cyanoacrylate Often called superglue. The clear, thin liquid gives a bond in seconds. Apply it straight from the small tube to one surface. Bring together the surfaces for bonding quickly and accurately, pressing them to make good contact with each other. Use on metals, glass and china but not on domestic crockery because it softens in warm water. If you accidentally bond fingers together, soak them in warm soapy water for a few minutes and they will separate.

U/V activated A clear, liquid adhesive for glass. It leaves no glue line and, once set, is detergent and waterproof. The adhesive will not set until exposed to natural daylight or sunlight, but then it sets quickly. It is not suitable for china or stoneware, because the light cannot penetrate the material.

Panel adhesive Supplied in a cartridge for use in a mastic gun, this can be used for fixing plasterboard or timber panelling to a wall, attaching skirting boards and architraves, and in general replacing nails for many jobs.

PVC This adhesive softens the surface of PVC material, ensuring a good bond. Apply it from the tube to both surfaces for bonding and press them together until bonded. PVC glue is ideal for repairing flexible plastic items such as macs, beach balls and the covering of kitchen stools or garden chairs.

Polystyrene cement Like PVC adhesive, this softens the plastic to which it is applied. Use it on both surfaces to ensure a good bond. It is used mostly by modellers who make up kits. If you use it on decorative polystyrene, keep it off the surface to avoid disfigurement.

Golf

Beginner's guide to playing an ancient game

Golf is a game played on a large outdoor obstacle course having a series of holes spaced far apart. Each hole is located in an area of smoothly mown grass, known as the green, and is approached by a roughly mown strip of grass, called the fairway. At the opposite end of the fairway from the green is the tee, the point from which the approach to the hole starts. Full-size golf courses consist of 18 holes, each one with a fairway from 90-550m (100-600yds) or more long. The object is to hit a golf ball from the tee (a plastic peg set in the ground by the golfer), along the fairway to the green and finally into the hole, in as few strokes as

---

GOLF

How to hold and swing the club; which irons to use

Backswing arc

Downswing arc

Follow-through

The swing Hold the club in your left hand, with the back of your hand facing the target and the club face aligned with the ball. Now wrap your right hand round the handle. The Vs formed by your thumbs and index fingers should point upwards.

Swing the club back, turning your shoulders and bending your left knee. Bring the club down just inside the backswing arc and follow through. Your left hip should shift towards the target. During the backswing and downswing keep your head still, the angle of your spine constant, and look at the ball.

The grip

Aligning the club   Backswing   Downswing   Follow-through

Irons Each iron has a different weight and a typical performance (the average distance that you hit a ball in normal conditions). Use a No 9 for a distance of about 110m (120yds), a No 7 for 123m (135yds), a No 4 for 155m (170yds), and a No 2 for 183m (200yds).

No 9   No 7   No 4   No 2

possible. A target number of strokes is set for each hole, according to its distance from the tee. This is called the par for the hole; only expert golfers can achieve par figures for a whole round. The task is made more difficult by hazards such as trees, streams, rough grass and cunningly sited sand-filled bunkers.

Rules and scoring The rules are laid down by the Royal and Ancient Golf Club of St Andrews but individual clubs have their own supplementary rules.

There are two main forms of play and scoring:

Stroke play The player counts the total number of strokes taken to complete a round of 18 holes. The player or side with the lower score wins.

Match play The game is played hole by hole by individuals or sides, and a hole is won by the side completing it in the fewest strokes. The winner is the individual or side that has won more holes than there are holes left to play rather than the side completing the round in the fewest strokes. Someone who has won the first ten holes, for example, cannot lose, and is said to have won '10 and 8' – that is, ten holes up with eight left to play.

In both types of play, if the game is tied at the end of the agreed number of holes and the winner must be decided, the players normally restart from the first hole, until someone wins a hole – known as a 'sudden death play-off'.

Stroke and match play rounds can be between two players (singles) or, in competitions, between many more; the competitors tackle their round in pairs. In *foursomes*, the two partners take alternate strokes at the same ball. In *four-balls*, each partner plays his own ball, but only the better score for each hole is counted. In *greensomes*, each partner drives from the tee and they then choose which ball they will play second discarding the other and continuing with alternate strokes.

Choosing clubs There are four categories of golf clubs, each with its specific use in playing each hole. 'Woods' can be used on the fairway for long approach shots to greens. The driver is used for hitting the ball from the tee on long holes; 'irons' for short holes or long shots after the drive; 'wedges' for short lofted shots over an obstruction or out of a bunker; and a 'putter', for rolling the ball on the green.

A beginner can learn basic golf with a small selection of clubs, either borrowed or bought secondhand.

The usual choice for a full set of clubs is three woods, eight irons, a wedge, a sand-wedge (for bunkers) and a putter. If you join a golf club, you can seek advice

from the club professional, who often runs a shop selling clubs and kit. He will know more about your game than an assistant in a sports goods store.

Standard-length clubs are suitable for most players, there is a standard length for men, one for women and one for boys. Clubs with shorter or longer shafts can be made specially to order. Short players will need clubs with a flatter lie than a tall golfer requires – the lie is the angle of the shaft to the ground when the club rests flat on its sole.

Club heads and shafts come in a variety of materials. The heads of woods may be persimmon, wood laminate, graphite or steel. Steel is the best choice for shaft material. The overall weight of the club should be proportionate to your strength and ability; average players do best with light clubs. Choose rubber grips, which are easy to clean and work when wet, rather than leather.

The choice of putter is very personal but it should sit squarely in your hands, align easily, feel well balanced and not wobble when you play your stroke. Experiment with different styles of putter – the blade, flange and mallet types are the most popular.

Common faults Two of the most common faults when playing golf shots are the hook, in which the ball curves from right to left (for a right-handed player), and the slice, in which the ball curves wide to the right. A focus for correcting either is *The Line*, an imaginary line from the ball at rest to the hole or another designated target.

Gourds

Growing ornamental fruits for winter decoration

Some members of the cucumber and melon family bear bulbous fruits which develop hard outer skins in shades of green, yellow and orange. Harvested in early autumn and allowed to dry for several weeks, the fruits can be polished and varnished to make attractive indoor ornaments.

Cultivation Gourds are natives of tropical America, but with care can be grown outside in Britain. Sow seeds in early May in pots of seed compost, placed in a COLD FRAME. Plant out at the end of May in any well-drained soil and in full sunlight.

Set the plants at intervals of 1m (3ft) and train them up trelliswork or a fence. There are a number of varieties of gourd plants, including apple-shaped, egg-shaped, pear-shaped, small-waisted and club-shaped.

Harvesting When the fruits are hard

and the stems brittle, cut them with a sharp knife, wipe them clean and leave to dry.

Making ornaments Polish the gourds with a soft cloth, then coat with clear varnish. Depending on their shape and size, hang the gourds singly or in groups. Small ones can be used as Christmas tree ornaments. See also CHRISTMAS DECORATIONS; CHRISTMAS TREES.

Gout

Relieving and treating a painful ailment

Contrary to popular belief, gout is not caused by over-indulgence of food and alcohol. It is a disorder in which excesses of uric-acid salts collect in various parts of the body, and the causes are uncertain. Nor is it an ailment confined to the feet – the ears, tendons, knees, elbows, hands and kidneys can also be affected.

The symptoms of severe pain, swelling, redness and tenderness usually develop suddenly and mainly affect joints, often the joint of the big toe. In chronic cases hard lumps form on the ears, hands and feet. Once the condition has started, the sufferer is liable to attacks for the rest of his life. However, women are rarely affected and acute attacks may be frequent or few and far between.

Treatment Only treatment by drugs prescribed by a doctor will relieve the condition, and a doctor should be consulted as soon as the condition is suspected. Being overweight can also aggravate the condition.

Prevention If blood tests show a level of uric acid in the blood which is higher than normal, attacks can be avoided by taking long-term drugs, such as allopurinol, to keep levels of uric acid down.

Grants

Obtaining cash aid to improve your property

Local councils can help some home owners and tenants to repair or improve their properties. Since 1990, these grants have been restricted by the Local Government and Housing Act 1989 to those with particular needs or with low incomes or savings.

Your council can tell you if you are entitled to a grant, what work they will consider assisting, and how much the grant might be. Even if you are entitled to some help, the council may not be able to afford it.

Disabled facilities grant An owner or

tenant of a house or flat can apply for this grant to convert it for use by a disabled person. The work must be necessary and appropriate for the disabled person, and it must be reasonable and practicable to carry the improvements out. Work to improve the disabled person's access and movement, and help with cooking and heating, normally get a grant. The person applying must also meet the income and savings tests that apply to all grants.

For all other grants, the house must have been built or converted at least ten years before the application was made. No application can be made for work that has already been started, and it can only be made by an owner or tenant (or two or more of them together).

Renovation grants These assist the repair or improvement of a home, or the creation of a home by conversion, by the owner or tenant. Grants must be made in many cases if the work is necessary to make a home fit for human habitation, for example because of excessive damp or lack of proper drainage.

Common parts grants These grants are aimed at helping owners or tenants to repair the common parts of a building consisting of two or more homes. At least three-quarters of the flats must be the main homes of their tenants or owners, and the tenancies must be protected or have at least five years to run.

HMO grants These grants pay for improvement of a house in multiple occupation (HMO). This means that the house is lived in by two or more people who are not part of the same household.

How much will you get? The size of the grant depends partly on how much of the work the council consider is necessary for the repairs or improvements, and how much you are entitled to after your income and savings are taken into account.

The council check the cost of the work by asking most applicants to provide at least two quotations from local builders to do the work. They will also have their own views on the costs of some improvements, and on an upper limit on the total you can claim. You cannot usually avoid this limit by making a series of applications. The earlier ones will be taken into account each time.

The council will also require full details of all your sources of income and savings, including income from savings and the amount of your savings. If your income or savings are above set limits, you lose grant in proportion to the amount of the excess. Those with higher incomes or savings may receive no grant.

Conditions The council will impose conditions on any awards of grants that they make. These include requiring the person receiving the grant to repay it if the property is sold soon after obtaining the grant.

Grants are also made towards the cost of repairs to a building of architectural or historic interest. You cannot get a grant for installing central heating unless it is part of a general improvement scheme. For all grants, do not start work until the grant has been approved.

Gravel paths

Laying and maintaining one

Prepare a hardcore sub-base 100mm (4in) deep (see ASPHALT DRIVEWAYS), allowing a depth of about 25mm (1in) for the gravel surface. Cover the hardcore with a 25mm layer of sharp sand, making sure that any gaps are properly filled.

To prevent the gravel spreading from the path, line each side with a suitable edging, such as kerbstones or timber formwork which has been well soaked in one of the WOOD PRESERVATIVES.

Use 10mm or 20mm pea gravel, obtainable from a builders' supplier. Spread it with a rake to a depth of about 13mm ($\frac{1}{2}$in), then roll and compact it with a garden roller. Spread a second layer of the same depth, and roll it again.

Rake and roll the surface regularly as it becomes disturbed, and treat it with weedkiller once a year.

Gravy

Making sauce from the juices of meat and poultry

There are two types of gravy – thick and thin. To make thick gravy, pour off most of the fat from the roasting tin, leaving about 2 tablespoons of sediment. Stir in a tablespoon of plain flour and blend it thoroughly with the sediment, over a low heat.

Continue to stir while cooking, until the mixture thickens and turns brown. Gradually blend in about 285ml ($\frac{1}{2}$ pint) of hot brown stock (you can, if necessary, make that from a stock cube) or vegetable liquid.

For special occasions, use a little wine or dry cider with the liquid in which vegetables have been cooked or instead of it. Bring the gravy to boiling point for a minute or two. Taste and season as required, adding gravy browning if necessary. Strain into a warmed gravy boat or jug to serve.

To make thin gravy, pour all the fat from the roasting tin, leaving only the residues from the meat. Add 285ml ($\frac{1}{2}$ pint) of hot vegetable liquid or brown stock, stir well and boil for up to 3 minutes.

For an instant gravy, melt 25g (1oz) of lard or butter in a small saucepan and fry half an onion in it, finely chopped, over a hot ring, until the pieces of onion turn dark brown. Stir in 25g of plain flour, and gradually mix in 450ml ($\frac{3}{4}$ pint) of stock. Simmer for 5 minutes, season and add gravy browning to taste.

For giblet gravy, add finely chopped cooked poultry giblets and giblet stock to the thick gravy after it has been prepared.

For a cream gravy, use equal parts of turkey or chicken broth and milk as the liquid in the thick gravy recipe, and cook until smooth.

QUICK TIP To thicken a gravy to which you have added too much liquid, boil briskly for an extra minute or two to reduce it.

Greenhouse gardening

Heated and unheated greenhouses; caring for plants, a greenhouse calendar

An unheated greenhouse (see GREEN-HOUSES) lengthens the growing season, allowing plants to be started into growth in early spring for planting out in the garden later. Plants kept in the greenhouse will grow on well into the autumn.

A heated greenhouse greatly increases the range of plants that can be grown – and also the cost of growing them. A greenhouse kept at a minimum temperature of 13°C (55°F), known as a 'warm house', will use almost twice as many heating units as a 'cool house' of the same size, with a minimum temperature of 4°C (40°F). Heating costs can be reduced by lining the greenhouse with polythene sheeting or, better still, bubble polythene, and by minimising draughts.

For many gardeners a cool house is the most satisfactory. It can be heated in several ways including a solid-fuel boiler, electrical heating and oil-fired heating. Three heaters that are easy to install and efficient are: a fan heater, which distributes heat evenly throughout the greenhouse; an electric convector heater; or a paraffin heater.

An advantage of electric heating is that it can be thermostatically controlled; a disadvantage with paraffin heaters is the CONDENSATION created, which calls for the greenhouse to be ventilated at all times. Roof ventilators help to control temperature and are essential – automatic types are available – and roller BLINDS are useful for shading in strong sunlight.

Caring for greenhouse plants Use potting and seeding mixtures, not garden soil, for your plants – see also JOHN INNES COMPOST. Check the soil daily for moisture, and water as necessary. On hot summer days, spray the plants – except those with velvety, silvery or hairy leaves – with water. Feed plants every two or three weeks with a liquid fertiliser.

Buy your plants from a reputable nursery or garden centre, and check carefully for pests and signs of disease. Recheck regularly and remove dead flowers and decaying leaves. Apply PESTICIDES as needed.

Keep the greenhouse and surrounding area clean, and do not use it to store garden tools, which can harbour pests.

A greenhouse calendar

January Plan the number and types of plants to be grown in the coming year. In an unheated greenhouse, sow broad beans for planting out in March; in a cool greenhouse take cuttings of late-flowering chrysanthemums, sow cauliflowers and maintain 10°C (50°F).

February In a warm greenhouse sow TOMATOES towards the end of the month, for planting in the greenhouse in April. Pot rooted chrysanthemum cuttings.

March Prick out tomato seedlings and prepare a bed in a cool greenhouse for planting them in April. In an unheated greenhouse sow french beans late in the month, and sow tomatoes for planting out in May.

April Sow sweet corn and runner beans in an unheated greenhouse, for planting out in May. Plant tomatoes in a cool greenhouse in a prepared bed. Pot tuberous BEGONIAS. Increase ventilation as the weather gets warmer.

May Early in the month, sow marrows and courgettes in an unheated greenhouse, and plant out at the end of the month. Remove any sideshoots from the tomatoes.

June Ventilate the greenhouse freely during hot spells. Turn off artificial heat, water and spray freely.

July/August Pick tomatoes, remove sideshoots and feed every week. Sow cyclamen seeds and cinerarias. Artificial heating is not necessary.

September Restart heating at the end of the month. Sow annuals for a spring display, potting in 75mm (3in) pots. Pot spring-flowering bulbs – see BULBS, CORMS AND TUBERS.

October Reduce watering and cease feeding. Take off the lateral buds of late-flowering chrysanthemums.

November Complete potting of autumn-sown annuals. For a cool greenhouse, lift and pot hardy perennials for late winter flowering, but leave outside.

December Bring in hardy perennials lifted in November. Clean out the greenhouse, and wash the glass to make the most of weak winter light.

Greenhouses

Maintaining, repairing and fitting them out

Like all structures that are exposed to the weather, greenhouses need regular maintenance, with a thorough check before the winter season.

Timber frames Check for rot damage to timber – particularly at joints where the rain may have got in. Small areas of damage can be repaired with an epoxy-based wood repair material. Cut out all soft wood when it is dry with a chisel and mallet, then use a wood-hardening liquid to toughen up the remaining wood before applying the repair material with a filling knife. Fill the repair to just above the surface, then when it has hardened, rub it down until the whole surface is smooth.

Fill any remaining cracks and gaps with exterior-grade wood stopping (see STOPPERS AND FILLERS), then treat the timber with one of the WOOD PRESERVATIVES, or with an oil stain preservative or a microporous paint – see PAINTS. Ordinary gloss paint is not ideal on greenhouses, as it is prone to peeling.

If the greenhouse is made of Western red cedar, treat the timber with a red cedar preservative. This restores the rich, warm colour of fresh cedar which, if left untreated, becomes a silvery grey after weathering.

Replacing glass Most glass is bedded in linseed oil or acrylic putty (see PUTTYING) and fixed with glazing sprigs. Replace glass in dry weather, as putty will not stick to wet wood. To remove a broken pane, pull out the sprigs with pincers, then, wearing a tough gardening glove, knock in the broken pieces. Spread plenty of newspaper inside the greenhouse to catch the broken fragments. Chip away the old bedding putty with chisel and mallet.

Treat the rebates you have cleaned with wood primer, to seal the surface of the wood, before applying a new bed of putty. Measure for the new pane of glass, reducing the size by 3mm ($\frac{1}{8}$in) on each dimension so the glass will not be a tight fit in a frame. Order horticultural grade glass, which is cheaper than ordinary window glass.

Use either new putty or a glazing sealant (see SEALANTS) as a bed for the new pane. Press the glass in place, pressing only around the edges, then knock in glazing sprigs to hold the glass firm. The heads of the sprigs should protrude about 5mm ($\frac{3}{16}$in). Slide the hammer across the glass so there is no risk of cracking

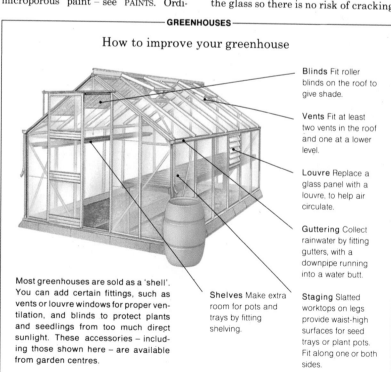

GREENHOUSES

How to improve your greenhouse

Most greenhouses are sold as a 'shell'. You can add certain fittings, such as vents or louvre windows for proper ventilation, and blinds to protect plants and seedlings from too much direct sunlight. These accessories – including those shown here – are available from garden centres.

Blinds Fit roller blinds on the roof to give shade.

Vents Fit at least two vents in the roof and one at a lower level.

Louvre Replace a glass panel with a louvre, to help air circulate.

Guttering Collect rainwater by fitting gutters, with a downpipe running into a water butt.

Shelves Make extra room for pots and trays by fitting shelving.

Staging Slatted worktops on legs provide waist-high surfaces for seed trays or plant pots. Fit along one or both sides.

it. Trim off surplus putty with a putty knife.

Metal frames If the greenhouse is of aluminium or galvanised steel, there should be little problem with corrosion, but if it is steel-framed it may rust. Clean off all loose rust with a wire brush. Protect your eyes against flying bits with safety goggles. Then treat the rusted areas with rust-inhibiting liquid or galvanising paint. When dry, apply either a primer and top coat of gloss paint, or use a rust-inhibiting enamel.

The whitish film that may form on aluminium frames is a white oxide deposit, and acts as a protective layer. There is no need to paint over it.

Replacing glass The method of holding glass in metal frames is different from that used for wood. Some form of spring clip is used to hold the glass in place, and you need to check to see which kind you have, and how they are removed. Try not to damage them as they may be difficult to replace. Use horticultural glass for replacement work, and have it cut 3mm ($\frac{1}{8}$in) smaller all round than the frame so the glass is not a tight fit.

In older metal greenhouses, the glass may be bedded in putty, but the more modern and simple method is to use neoprene or foam rubber strips under the glass to cushion it. These need not be stuck in place. The pressure of the clips holds them firm.

Dirty glass Glass often gets coated in algae, which cuts down the light. Use a fine garden spray to apply correctly diluted fungicide to the glass. This will kill the mould.

Fitting out a greenhouse A number of accessories can be fitted in a greenhouse. These include: louvre ventilators, which may be installed at the sides and back to improve air flow; and automatic vent openers, which work to a preset temperature, as illustrated.

Grilling

Simple cooking with intense heat

This method of cooking by direct heat is suitable for steaks, chops and other relatively small and tender cuts of meat and poultry, sausages and fish cakes, many fish and some vegetables. Because little or no fat needs to be added in the process, many people use grilling as an alternative to FRYING, for dietary reasons. Grilling done at a high setting sears the food rapidly, sealing in the natural juices; on grills with an adjustable setting, low heat can be used for gently cooking through.

As a general rule, grills inside a gas oven should be used with the oven door closed, those in an electric oven with the door ajar; but read the maker's instructions.

For best results, the top surface of the food to be grilled should be 75mm (3in) from the heat source, unless the portions are more than 50mm (2in) thick. Then, the food will be better cooked if it can be moved slightly farther away from the heat or the heat can be turned down.

Have the food at room temperature. Preheat the grill and brush the grill rack lightly with cooking oil, to prevent sticking. Trim most of the fat from meat to be grilled, and snip the fat that is left on to prevent curling during grilling. Tough meat benefits from MARINATING in a blend of oil, wine or vinegar, herbs and spices for 1-3 hours before grilling. Halfway

Guide to cooking times (total for both sides)	
Beef steaks 25mm (1in) thick	7 min (rare)
	10 min (medium)
	15 min (well done)
Lamb chops	12-15 min (well done)
Lamb cutlets	7-10 min
Pork chops	15-20 min
Pork sausages	10-15 min
Bacon rashers	5-10 min
Bacon chops	10-15 min
Gammon steaks	10-15 min
Veal chops	12-15 min
Veal escalopes	4 min
Fish fillets	4-5 min
Fish (whole, and thick steaks and cutlets)	10-15 min
Small chicken halves	30-40 min
Chicken joints	20-30 min

through the cooking time, turn the food over; use tongs or a spatula for turning, rather than a fork, which may break the heat-sealed surface of the food.

White fish, such as plaice or sole, should be lightly brushed with melted butter or oil and sprinkled with lemon juice beforehand, and basted during grilling. Oily fish needs no brushing or basting. The fish is cooked when the flesh flakes on testing with a knife. Score whole fish with three or four diagonal cuts on each side. This allows the heat to penetrate evenly and stops fish from splitting. Thin fish fillets and fish steaks need cooking on one side only.

To grill a small chicken, split it lengthways and arrange the halves skin side down on the grill rack, which if possible should be 125mm (5in) from the heat; at that distance, allow 15-20 minutes for each side. Brush with melted butter or oil, baste during grilling to keep the chicken moist and juicy, and turn it frequently. It is ready if the juice runs clear when you pierce a thigh with a fork.

Vegetables such as tomato halves, mushroom caps and slices of courgette can be grilled with meat or fish. Brush them with cooking oil and add them towards the end of the cooking time.

QUICK TIP When grilling fish, line the grill pan with aluminium foil. This will prevent fishy smells lingering in the pan, and will also aid grilling by reflecting the heat.

Ground cover

Using low-growing plants to cut weeding and hoeing

Carefully chosen ground-cover plants can eliminate weeding in hard-to-reach places such as round the base of SHRUBS or HEDGES. They can also refresh fallow vegetable plots, or provide a substitute for grass lawns in areas where a lawn

Plant low-growing plants to provide ground cover and reduce the need for weeding. *Polygonum amplexicaule*, in the background, is a hardy perennial, and rue (*Ruta graveolens*), in the foreground, is an evergreen subshrub; both grow in dense bushy clumps.

might not receive enough light or rain.

Almost any low-growing plant or shrub can be used as ground cover provided that the soil and conditions of sun or shade are suitable. Favourites include blue-flowering evergreen periwinkles (good in shade), sun-loving dwarf hypericums, ivies and prostrate varieties of conifer such as *Juniperus sabina* 'Tamariscifolia' or a rose such as 'Max Graf'. Low-growing perennials include polygonums, *Sedum acre* (stonecrop) and aubrietas. *Saxifraga × urbium* (London pride) and *Stachys lanata* (Lamb's tongue) do very well even in poor soil.

Slow-spreading lily of the valley is good for small corners where the soil is damp and partly shaded. Alyssum is a useful filler between larger plants in summer, and reseeds itself year after year. The evergreen *Lamium galeobdolon* 'Florentinum' (best in shade beneath trees) and *Hypericum calycinum* benefit from once-a-year mowing on a high setting, to keep them dense and leafy. Chamomile, planted in sun on sandy soil and mown to maintain it at a height of 38-50mm (1½-2 in), is an attractive alternative to grass for a small lawn, and gives a pleasant smell whenever it is walked on. It may need mowing once or twice a year, and it is best to use a rotary mower with the blade set 50mm (2in) high. Red clover, mown or left unmown, enriches the soil with nitrogen, and is suitable for fallow vegetable plots or for sowing round the base of fruit trees.

When PLANTING, leave 1m (3ft) between woody shrubs such as prostrate juniper, 300mm (12in) between such trailing plants as periwinkle and ivy. Slow-growing small plants should be placed 100mm (4in) apart.

Apply a thick mulch of peat or straw (see MULCHING) between the young plants. Keep the soil moist, except for sedums, which prefer it dry.

Guarantee

Obtaining your rights when goods have a warranty

If you buy goods that turn out to be faulty or unfit for their purpose your right to redress is from the retailer who sold them, not from the manufacturer – see SALE OF GOODS. The manufacturer, in law, is liable only if the defective goods cause foreseeable injury or damage, when he may have to pay compensation to anyone who suffers as a result – see COMPLAINTS.

However, many manufacturers voluntarily offer to repair or replace faulty merchandise during a specified period of time after it has been bought, under a guarantee or warranty – see WARRANTIES. According to the Unfair Contract Terms Act of 1977, a guarantee or warranty may not diminish a customer's statutory rights to have defective goods put right, or to claim compensation from the maker if the defect causes an injury or damage.

On the other hand, because the guarantee is a voluntary agreement, the manufacturer is within his rights to limit his responsibility to repair or replace the goods. The most obvious limit is the time for which the guarantee is valid, but others may exclude labour costs, or require the customer to pay for return of the goods to the factory.

Such clauses, however, mean only that the manufacturer is not liable; you can still reclaim, say, the labour and postage costs from the shop where you bought the faulty goods.

Most manufacturers' guarantees require you to complete and return a postcard to the maker within 10 or 14 days of buying the goods. In practice, few check on whether the card has been sent back, provided it is clear that the goods are still under guarantee.

However, it is advisable to return the card; similarly, to observe the guarantee conditions on installation, use and repairs, otherwise the guarantee may be invalidated.

Guitar repairs

Mending a cracked body; fitting strings and fret wires; replacing a machine head

A crack in the belly of a guitar can be repaired with glue under pressure, but great care must be taken – too much pressure may cause further damage.

Prepare by making a wooden frame 25mm (1in) wider than the width of the part of the belly to be repaired, and 13mm (½in) deeper. Make it by cutting four lengths of 25 × 25mm (1 x 1in) wood to the required size, then GLUING and nailing them together. Now cut three softwood wedges, 75mm (3in) long and tapered from a thickness of 25mm. Wrap the wedges in a soft cloth.

Remove the strings from the guitar. Clean out the crack with a fine artist's brush. Melt a little animal glue, sometimes called Scotch glue, and brush it into the crack.

Position the frame round the guitar and gently tap in a wedge at each side to clamp the instrument so that the crack just closes. Check that the edges of the crack do not overlap. Remove any surplus glue.

Tap in the third wedge above the crack to keep the edges flush. Allow 12 hours for the glue to dry.

Fitting a new string Remove the ends of the broken string from the bridge and machine head. Thread the new string through its hole in the bridge.

Cross the short end of the string over the bridge, under the string and under the loop you have made. If the string does not have a ball-end, push the end through the loop several times and pull the string tight.

Feed the free end of the string through the hole in the machine head and turn the head clockwise. Wind the string four or five turns on its roller, making sure that it does not overlap.

Fitting a new fret If one of the wires across the fingerboard – called frets – becomes worn down or works loose, fit a new one cut from a length of fret wire. This can be obtained from a musical instrument shop.

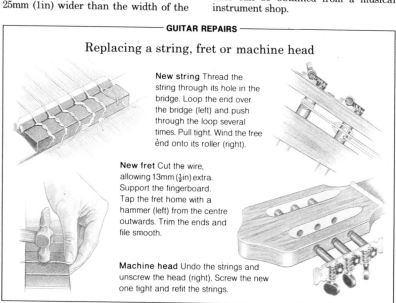

── GUITAR REPAIRS ──

Replacing a string, fret or machine head

New string Thread the string through its hole in the bridge. Loop the end over the bridge (left) and push through the loop several times. Pull tight. Wind the free end onto its roller (right).

New fret Cut the wire, allowing 13mm (½in) extra. Support the fingerboard. Tap the fret home with a hammer (left) from the centre outwards. Trim the ends and file smooth.

Machine head Undo the strings and unscrew the head (right). Screw the new one tight and refit the strings.

Remove the strings and lift or gently prise out the fret. Measure a new wire, allowing 13mm (½in) extra, and cut it with side cutters. You should make sure you do not disturb the natural curve of the wire.

Place a block of wood under the fingerboard, position the fret wire and lightly tap it home with a small hammer, working from the centre outwards. Trim the wire flush with side cutters and smooth the ends with a fine file.

Replacing a machine head There are six machine heads on a guitar – the metal plates that hold the tuning roller and cog mechanisms. Sometimes they are mounted three a side on two plates, sometimes there are six individual plates. If a cog wears or breaks, free all the strings and unscrew the head from the guitar. Obtain an identical head and fit it, screwing it up tightly and evenly. Refit the strings on their rollers. If an identical head is not available, buy a new pair and fit both.

Guitar tuning

Keeping the strings of your instrument on pitch

To tune a guitar you first correctly pitch the high E string, using a pitch pipe, E-tuned pitch fork or a tuned piano. The remaining five strings are then tuned to match one another.

High E is the first and thinnest string on the guitar – that is, the lowest one on the fingerboard for a right-handed player. The remaining strings are: 2nd, B; 3rd, G; 4th, D; 5th, A; 6th, E.

If you are tuning to a piano, tune to the E above middle C. A pitch pipe is tuned for all the guitar strings; find the highest of the two E pipes and blow gently and evenly to give the note.

A tuning fork gives the most accurate note; hold the handle between your thumb and first finger and strike the prongs against your knee, then hold the end of the handle on the guitar bridge and the vibrating prongs will produce the note.

Tuning the 1st string While the tuning note is sounding, pluck the 1st string and compare the two notes. To raise the pitch of the string, turn the tuning peg clockwise, or anticlockwise to lower the pitch. Turn the peg a little at a time, and continue tuning until the notes match exactly.

Tuning the 2nd string Press the 2nd string just behind the 5th fret – 5th from the guitar head – with the tip of the second finger of your left hand. Play the 1st string twice, then play the 2nd string and tune it to match the 1st.

The remaining strings are tuned in the same way, tuning each to the one previously tuned, as follows: 3rd string, press behind the 4th fret and tune to the 2nd string; 4th string, press behind the 5th fret and tune to the 3rd string; 5th string, press behind the 5th fret and tune to the 4th string.

Guns

Licensing and choosing sporting guns; care and maintenance

There are two kinds of certificate covering the ownership of guns: a shotgun certificate, covering all smooth-bore weapons with a barrel length of 610mm (2ft) or more; and a firearm certificate covering all other guns, such as rifles and pistols. You must have a certificate before you can buy a gun. For a handgun or practical rifle (military type weapon) you need to be a member of an approved club, which must have the facilities to use the particular weapon you have. You do not need to be a member of a club to own a rifle for hunting. However, in all cases each application is thoroughly investigated by the police. Certificates will not be granted for automatic or semi-automatic rifles or pistols.

No certificate is required for a low-powered airgun.

A shotgun certificate authorises you to own any type of shotgun. A firearms certificate specifies the type of arms and ammunition you can buy and use. Nobody under the age of 14 can obtain a certificate, and the police may refuse an application by anyone they consider unfit to have a gun.

There are, however, circumstances when people do not need a certificate. They are: when shooting at an artificial target at a time and place approved by the police – such as a small-bore rifle and pistol club; when you borrow a gun from a certificate holder, provided you fire the gun in the holder's presence and on land owned or rented by him; when someone carries guns for a certificate holder, such as a gun-bearer at a game shoot – though he is not, however, allowed to fire the gun.

Application forms for shotgun and firearms certificates are available at most police stations. Shotgun certificates cost £17 and firearms certificates £48; they are valid for three years.

Choosing a gun Shotguns are made in several bore sizes, and in three barrel configurations – side by side, one above the other (called an over and under) and single-barrel 'automatic' shotguns. For game or clay-pigeon shooting, choose one that comes to the shoulder easily and is comfortable to handle.

If possible, attend a shoot or go to a local clay-pigeon club and try out a few guns, to find which suits you best. Failing that, a gunsmith will let you handle several models, without firing them.

Similarly, for small-bore or pistol shooting, go to a club and take advice from members. If you have difficulty finding a club, write to the National Small-bore Rifle Association, Lord Roberts House, Bisley Camp, Brookwood, Woking, Surrey GU24 0NP, or the Clay Pigeon Shooting Association, 107 Epping New Road, Buckhurst Hill, Essex IG9 5TQ.

Gun care Keep your gun locked in a cupboard or cabinet, and *never* leave it loaded. Lock ammunition in a separate drawer. *Never* point a gun at anyone, even if you are sure it is not loaded. When carrying a shotgun it should be empty and open at all times. Load it only when you are ready to use it. 'Break' the action, that is open the breech, and keep the safety catch on until you are ready to fire. Pump action guns should be carried with bolts back and with chambers and magazines empty. You should carry the gun in the crook of your arm.

Clean the gun after each use, keeping it free of dirt and moisture. Use a commercial solvent and phosphor-bronze brush cleaning rod to clean the bore followed by cloth patches to remove the excess oil. Also clean between the barrel and the rib. Fold an oiled cloth and push it between the rib vents, or use an old toothbrush. Lubricate all working parts with a thin coat of gun oil.

If you have an automatic shotgun, strip it down and wash the trigger plate in paraffin, or spray it with a specially formulated aerosol solvent. Keep the extractor claws scrupulously clean, and replace them if they become worn.

WARNING Always wear ear protectors when shooting.

Gutters and downpipes

Clearing and repairing, and fitting new ones

Gutters can become clogged with debris in autumn, and damaged by ice in winter. So it pays to check them before and after winter to see that they allow a free flow of water.

Put up a ladder (see LADDERS) at a point farthest from a downpipe, with at least three rungs above gutter level so you have a good handhold. Anchor the ladder so that it cannot slide by screwing a ring bolt into the fascia board (the board to which the gutter is screwed) and rope the ladder to the ring bolt.

Pour a bucket of water in the gutter as fast as possible to create a surge of water. Then watch to see what happens. If the water flows smoothly away, there should be few problems. If it gathers in a pool at one point, the gutter is sagging. If necessary re-position the ladder and check the brackets holding that section of gutter. The SCREWS may be loose or have rusted away. In which case replace them with rustless screws of a slightly larger gauge – No 10 screws instead of No 8 – if they will pass through the bracket holes. If not, plug the holes in the fascia board with exterior-grade wood stopping (see STOPPERS AND FILLERS); wait until it sets, then replace the screws. If you find that the fascia board has rotted, remove the gutter and replace that section of board.

If you find water drips from gutter joints, scrape away all debris from the joint. With metal guttering, the holding bolt may have rusted away. Remove it, reseal the guttering with bituminous gutter sealant (see SEALANTS) and replace the bolt. Tighten it up with a spanner until sealant is squeezed out.

If the gutter is plastic, check that the spring clip holding the sections together is in place and is not damaged. If it seems loose when in place, suspect the gasket seal. Separate the sections and remove the neoprene gasket. It should be sponge-like and soft. If it is compressed and hard, replace it with a new gasket, bought from any hardware or DIY shop which stocks plastic guttering.

If you find a metal gutter is cracked, and the damage is slight, seal the crack with a gutter sealant.

Where water fails to flow away, suspect a blocked downpipe. This may be caused by leaves, or an old bird's nest which has becomed lodged in the pipe. Never push the blockage down. Try to hook it out from above with a length of bent wire. Or, as a last resort, where the blockage is out of reach, hire a Sani-snake tool which worms its way through an obstruction so you can pull it up.

To clean any remaining debris, use a garden hose to spray down inside the pipe. When clear, fit a plastic or metal cage over the mouth of the downpipe, so that nothing else can get in.

If you find a rust hole in metal guttering, remove all loose rust, then repair the hole with an epoxy-based repair paste. Smooth it before it sets. The paste acts as a rust-inhibitor as well as making a permanent repair. If a length of gutter is badly damaged by rust, it should be replaced rather than patched up.

Cracks in downpipes are often caused by a blockage in the pipe which, when it freezes, expands with enough force to crack the pipe. If not badly damaged, repair with epoxy resin repair paste reinforced with glass fibre bandage. Coat the pipe with paste, covering the damaged area; wrap glass fibre bandage over it, pressing it into the paste, then coat over the top with paste.

Making repairs, fitting new sections

Bitumen sealant

Rustless bolt

Leaky joint In metal guttering, remove the old bolt and separate the guttering. Spread bituminous sealant onto the end of the lower section and set the upper section into it. Put in a rustless bolt.

Cracked pipe
Cover a crack in a metal pipe with layers of epoxy resin repair paste under, then over glass fibre bandage.

New gutter Screw a bracket to one end of the fascia board and tie a weighted builder's line to it. Hold the last gutter bracket at the other end, run the line over it and make sure it is horizontal. Calculate the fall, mark bracket positions and fit them.

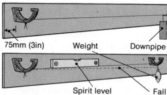

75mm (3in)   Weight   Downpipe

Spirit level   Fall

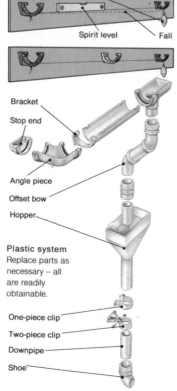

Bracket
Stop end
Angle piece
Offset bow
Hopper

Plastic system
Replace parts as necessary – all are readily obtainable.

One-piece clip
Two-piece clip
Downpipe
Shoe

Replacing guttering Where a metal gutter is in bad condition, remove it and replace it with plastic guttering. Removing cast-iron guttering is a two-man job as the sections can be very heavy. Try to find a way to rope a section at a time and lower it to a helper. Do not try to handle a full length on your own. It can easily topple you off the ladder.

To release a gutter length, try to undo the nuts which pass through the gutter sections. If totally rusted up, try penetrating oil or rust solvent. If this fails, cut through the bolt with a small hacksaw.

Once the gutter is down, unscrew the brackets from the fascia board. This too may be hard work if the screws have rusted.

If the fascia-board paint is in good condition, fill all screw holes with plastic wood, and spot paint when hard. If the board needs redecorating, this is the ideal time to do it.

Every gutter must slope down from the closed end towards the downpipe, so that water flows away. This is called the fall, and should be at least 25mm (1in) in every 3m (10ft). So the first job is to calculate the correct fall.

Position a bracket as high on the fascia board as is practical, 75mm (3in) from the end of the board. This will be the closed end of the gutter. The downpipe will be at the opposite end of the board. Hold the downpipe gutter section in place, then measure 75mm in to mark the position of the last gutter bracket. Calculate the correct fall of the gutter and re-position the bracket. In extreme cases it may not be possible to get the correct fall because of the long run. In this case you will have to position the downpipe centrally, or near the centre if there is a window, and run the gutters down to it from either side.

Use the string to mark the locations of intermediate brackets on the fascia board – at least one every 610mm (2ft). Study the instruction leaflet supplied with the gutter as to how much is needed to overlap into the joint sections. And be sure to cut the gutter dead square so that it fits neatly into its housing. A fine hacksaw is the best cutting tool. Work from the base of the gutter to the edges. Smooth the cut edges with a file or with fine glasspaper.

The downpipe sections need careful measuring to allow for the necessary overlap where one pipe sockets into the next. With plastic guttering these are bonded to each other with a special solvent, and once the joints have been sealed, they are impossible to undo.

Cast-iron downpipe is usually held by brackets which are fixed to the wall with heavy pipe nails. But plastic brackets are best fixed by drilling and plugging the wall, and then screwing the brackets in place – see MASONRY DRILLING; WALL FASTENERS.

Haemorrhoids

Treating and avoiding them

Haemorrhoids, or piles, are small, rounded, purplish-blue lumps occurring either inside or outside the anus. They are swollen or enlarged veins and are sometimes caused by pressure, such as prolonged constipation or pronounced straining to empty the bowels. They may itch or be painful or bleed.

External piles usually heal within a week or two, often leaving loose tags of skin. Internal piles may give trouble from time to time and sometimes they protrude through to the outside. They can be pushed back with a hot sponge.

In either case, hot baths or hot compresses relieve the discomfort and there are soothing ointments available from a chemist. Strict hygiene is essential. If the pain or bleeding is severe or persistent, see your doctor, who may recommend surgical removal.

To prevent piles, avoid straining or chronic constipation. Make sure there is plenty of roughage in your diet, including whole-grain bread, cereals, fresh fruit and vegetables, and take plenty of fluids.

Hair care

*Brushing, shampooing,
conditioning and drying*

The outer layer of each hair is called the cuticle, and consists of overlapping, scaly cells. If the hair is properly cared for, the cells of the cuticle lie flat, and the hair looks smooth and shiny. If the cuticle becomes dry or damaged, the hair is dull, lifeless and unmanageable.

The cuticle tends to be broken down by the sun, a very dry atmosphere, a too-frequent use of HAIR DRYERS, heated rollers and electric curling tongs or brush, BACK-COMBING, colouring, straightening and permanent waving. Split ends, which make hair frizzy and unmanageable, can result from constant perming, strong bleach, or sharp combs or brushes. Ask a hairdresser to cut them off.

A balanced diet containing adequate protein and vitamin C, and gentle treatment to preserve the natural balance of moisture, oils and acidity will help to keep hair healthy. See also DANDRUFF; HAIR COLOURING; HAIR LOSS; HOME PERMS.

Brushing Thorough brushing removes tangles and distributes natural scalp oils

evenly, to make the hair look shiny; however, if you overdo it, you may split or thin the hair. Brush once or twice a day, and before shampooing, using a brush that is kept scrupulously clean.

The coarser and thicker your hair, the stiffer the brush bristles should be. Natural bristles are considered best, but many brushes have plastic or nylon bristles. Styling brushes for wet hair generally have plastic bristles. They should all have rounded ends and smooth shafts to avoid damaging the hair or scalp.

To brush correctly, bend at the waist and pull the brush gently and slowly through your hair from the nape of your neck forwards; this protects the more fragile hair at the top of your head and round your face. Finish, depending on your hairstyle, with a few backwards and sideways strokes.

Shampooing For most people, a weekly shampoo is sufficient, although if you work in a dirty environment or your scalp is extremely greasy, you may need to shampoo more frequently. Proprietary shampoos clean with a mixture of detergent, soap, water and oils; extra ingredients such as herbs, beer, tar extracts, egg or cucumber may give the hair a pleasant smell, but other claimed effects – for example, making the hair shinier or more manageable – are only temporary. Expensive shampoos are not necessarily better than cheaper ones.

Before shampooing, brush or comb thoroughly, but not too vigorously, to loosen dirt and dead cells. Use either a clean brush or a clean comb with widely spaced, smooth teeth. Then wet the hair thoroughly with warm water from a spray or a jug over a basin. Make sure that the underlying layers of hair are thoroughly soaked.

Pour about a teaspoon of shampoo into the palm of the hand. Massage it evenly into the hair with the fingertips (not the nails), building up a thick, creamy lather all over the scalp. Rinse thoroughly with lukewarm water until every trace of shampoo is removed. If you shampoo daily, one lather is normally enough. If you wash your hair less frequently, gently massage another teaspoon of shampoo into the scalp, and rinse the hair again until the water coming from it is absolutely clear.

Conditioning Conditioners – which usually contain oil, emulsifier and waxes – coat the cuticle of each hair

with a fine oily film. That makes the hair easier to comb after washing, and gives an appearance of smoothness and body. However, most of the effect is washed away by the next shampoo.

Read conditioner labels and experiment to find the one you like best. Apply a conditioner after each shampoo, following the instructions on the label. If your hair tends to oiliness, condition only the ends. If it is fine and also oily, try conditioning immediately before applying the shampoo; a light residue of the conditioner may remain afterwards.

Drying Remove water from your hair by blotting, not rubbing, it with a warm dry towel. Get rid of tangles with your fingers or with a wide-toothed comb, working from the ends back to the scalp; do not use a brush, which can cause damage. If possible, let the hair dry naturally once most of the water and tangles are removed; do not dry it by the heat of a fire. Use a hairdryer, rollers or electric curling tongs or brush for the final touches.

When using a hairdryer, hold it at least 150mm (6in) from your head, to avoid dehydration and singeing of the hair.

QUICK TIP When blow-drying your hair, brush it, in the final stages, *against* the direction in which it will finally lie, to give it more body and bounce.

Hair colouring

Dyeing it at home

Hair dyes can be used to enrich or liven the natural tones of your hair, to disguise oncoming greyness – or to change the colour completely. There are four main types of dye:

Permanent dyes These penetrate the inner core of each hair, remove the original colouring and replace it permanently with another. They will lighten dark hair, but for a drastic change, say dark brown to blonde, it would be necessary to pre-bleach the hair to pale yellow first, then apply a toning colour. Bleaches remove some of the hair's colouring without replacing it with another.

Use permanent dyes if you want to change the colour radically, say from brown to blonde, or to disguise large amounts of grey or white hairs. Bleach can be used to streak or highlight sections of hair, or just lighten the ends.

Semi-permanent dyes Only the outer layer of each hair is affected by these dyes, which wash out after about a month. They will not change the colour radically, but are good for enhancing or enriching – for example, the red tones in brown hair or disguising a few grey hairs.

Temporary dyes These dyes or rinses simply leave a layer of colouring around each hair which will wash out with the next shampoo. Use them to freshen up colour – for example, hair that has already been dyed with a more permanent dye, but has faded in the sun.

Natural vegetable dyes The best known of these widely used dyes is henna, which adds rich red tones to brown or dark hair. They can last for several months, but do not alter the structure of the hair and leave it full of body and shine. They should not, however, be used on hair that is more than 10 per cent grey, as reds tend to become orange.

Using dyes at home Kits for home dyeing are readily available from chemists and hairdressers. Most are applied like shampoo – though some permanent dyes are applied with a special brush to dry hair. Make sure to buy a kit made by a reputable manufacturer, and follow carefully the instructions given with it. Carelessly used, dyes can damage your hair or give it an unflattering colour.

If you want to streak, highlight or tip your hair, get someone to help you. If you want to dye it a completely different colour it is safer to go to a trained hairdresser. It is also a good idea to consult a hairdresser if you want to perm or straighten your hair at the same time as dyeing it.

Never colour your hair on the spur of the moment. If using a permanent or semi-permanent dye, first make sure that you are not allergic to it. Mix a small amount and apply some to an area of skin about 25mm (1in) square on the inside of the elbow. Leave it for over 24 hours, making sure that it does not get rubbed off. If redness or itching develops, do not use the dye.

With any dye, remember that your own hair is unlikely to end up exactly the same colour as the one shown on the packet. Much depends on the original colour of your hair. To test in advance how your hair will react to the dye, snip off about 30 strands from different parts of your head. Following the instructions, colour these strands in a little dye, then look at them closely in full daylight to make sure they are the colour you want your hair to be. See also HAIR CARE; HAIR LOSS; HAIR PIECES; HAIR SETTING.

Haircutting

Basic styles for cutting it yourself

There are two basic ways of cutting hair. The simpler is to cut all the hair straight across at the back, sides and front to the same length. This is known as a club cut. Club cutting is used most often to give a pageboy or bobbed hairstyle. The other method is to cut the hair at the back, sides and front in layers, with the layers of hair underneath longer than those above, to produce a tapered effect. This is known as a layered or graduated cut. Shapes are achieved by the angle at which the hair is held.

Both types of cut can be made at home. As a rule, cut hair when it is wet, bearing in mind that it will look shorter when dry. Do not attempt to cut hair into a completely new style at home. The illustrations below show how to make a club cut.

Layered cut Divide the hair into five sections, as for a club cut. Cut the hair on the nape to the length you want it to be (at chin level is usual), with the sides slightly shorter than the centre to form a shallow V-shape. Clip away any hair growing below the line you have established, as for a club cut.

Take down the bottom 25mm (1in) layer of hair from the side sections at the back. Let the hair hang down, then take a small vertical bunch, including some of the nape hair, between your first and second fingers pointing downwards. Hold the bunch out from the scalp and cut upwards. Cut to the same length as the nape hair. Continue cutting in similar bunches across both sections.

HAIRCUTTING

Making a simple club cut

Cut your hair while it is wet, and use sharp haircutting scissors, available from chemists. You should be able to trim the front yourself, but you may need help when cutting the back and sides.

Divide the hair in the front into two sections, from forehead to crown, along the line of the normal parting. Clip the two halves in place, using hair clips. Part the hair in half at the back along a vertical line down the centre of the scalp. Clip-up these two halves to leave a thick fringe along the nape.

Cut the hair on the nape to the length you want, making the sides slightly shorter than the centre to form a V-shape. Cut any hair growing below the V-line with the scissors held flat against the neck.

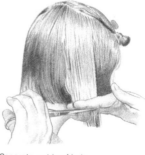

Separate a strip of hair about 25mm (1in) wide from each of the back sections. Grip between the first and second fingers held horizontally. Cut the strip to the same length as the hair on the nape.

Separate the bottom 25mm (1in) from each of the front sections and cut to length. Continue to bring down strips and cut them to match the original line until all the hair is cut.

Take down the next 25mm layer of back hair. First cut it horizontally, holding it between horizontal first and second fingers, so that it is slightly shorter than the layer below. Then take bunches between downpointing first and second fingers and trim to the same length. Repeat until all the back hair is cut in layers.

Take down 25mm of hair from one of the front sections, hold it between horizontal first and second fingers, and cut it to the length you want it to be. Continue cutting 25mm layers of hair in the front sections in the same way as the back hair, first horizontally so that it is slightly shorter than the first layer, then vertically. Cut the top hair, in 25mm layers, pulling it down and holding it between horizontal first and second fingers. Establish the length of the first layer at the eyebrow or slightly higher.

Trimming a fringe For a feathery, uneven fringe, pull the front hair straight out from the forehead, then twist it tightly and cut straight across the end.

For an even, straightedged fringe, comb forward the bottom 6mm ($\frac{1}{4}$in) layer of hair above the hairline on the forehead. Wet it and press it against the forehead. Cut straight across. Bring down the next 6mm layer of hair and cut it very slightly longer than the first, so that it forms a slight curve over the forehead. Repeat, cutting each layer very slightly longer than the previous one.

Hairdryers

How to find faults and make repairs

Most modern hairdryers are pistol-shaped. The circular casing at the back contains the motor and fan, and the heating element – a spiral wire – is contained in the barrel. The switches are in the handle. The fan draws air in through a grille, then drives it over the heating element and down the barrel onto the hair. When using a hairdryer, hold it about 150mm (6in) from the head.

Finding and mending a fault If a hairdryer does not work, first press the reset button. If this has no effect, replace the fuse in the plug – see FUSES AND FUSE BOXES; PLUGS. If it still does not work, or only intermittently, check and renew if necessary the connections in the plug.

If this makes no difference, unplug the dryer and check inside. Remove the screws that hold it together (they are sometimes hidden under a label) and gently prise the two halves apart with a screwdriver. Check and renew if necessary the connections in the dryer.

Using a soft brush, clean out any hairs that may be clogging the grille, fan or motor. If you have a circuit tester, check the flex and fit a new one if necessary – see CIRCUIT TESTING.

If the dryer still does not work, the motor probably needs replacing. Return it to the dealer or manufacturer.

If the motor works but there is no heat, replace the heating element. Fit a new unit of the same kind yourself or get the dealer or manufacturer to do it for you.

Hair loss

What happens and what you can do about it

An average healthy scalp sheds about 100 hairs a day as part of the natural process by which hairs grow, fall out, and are replaced. A faster rate of loss can lead to thinning or to partial or total baldness.

The loss may be temporary, in which case a doctor, dermatologist (skin specialist) or trichologist (hair and scalp specialist) may be able to advise you on ways to help the hair to return.

Temporary hair loss has many possible causes. Lack of protein resulting from too-strict dieting or from iron-deficiency anaemia is quite common; sometimes a change in diet to increase the amount of meat, eggs, cereals and fresh peas and beans, and the intake of vitamin C, may work (see MENU PLANNING); although if you suspect you could be anaemic you should consult a DOCTOR.

Illnesses whose symptoms include a high fever are another frequent cause. So are scalp diseases, radiation and some forms of drug therapy, hormonal imbalances (for example, those following childbirth), and chemical hair treatments such as HAIR DYEING and permanent waving – see HOME PERM.

Frequent use of tight rollers, too-vigorous brushing or scalp massage and the wearing of 'tight' hairstyles – for example, ponytails – can accelerate hair loss, too; generally, the hair will return to normal on its own once these causes have been abandoned – see HAIR CARE.

Permanent, partial or complete baldness, or hair thinning, is hereditary, and mainly affects men. However, women going through the menopause often find their hair thins – and stays that way. Toupees or wigs can be used to disguise permanent baldness – see HAIRPIECES.

Hair-weaving, in which false hair on a thin net is set against the scalp, and then woven tightly in with the remaining natural hair, can lead to scalp irritations; the weaving must be redone every few months. Transplants of healthy hair-growing skin from elsewhere on the body to the bald area have had some success, but transplants are expensive, may produce surgical complications and do not look entirely natural.

Hairpieces

Styling aids; how to conceal baldness

A hairpiece may be a full wig or a toupee (a partial wig) worn to conceal baldness; or it may be a postiche (usually a switch of long hair) to dress in coils, curls, braids, or some other elaborate way to enhance a natural head of hair.

The most natural-looking hairpieces are made from fine human hair, but they are expensive and difficult to look after. Hairpieces of coarse human hair are cheaper. Synthetic hairpieces are cheapest of all, and easiest to maintain.

The backing of a wig or toupee may be hard plastic – perforated for ventilation – with hair inserted in it. A synthetic fibre mesh is another type of base which loses its shape faster than a hard one but is lighter and not as hard to wear. The ideal base, lightweight but expensive, is loosely woven real hair. A poorly ventilated hairpiece will cause perspiration, the build-up of oils secreted by the scalp and even bacterial infections. It is best to wear a hairpiece for as short a time as possible. If you can leave a day between wearings without embarrassment, so much the better. Wash and condition your scalp and remaining natural hair daily; keep the hairpiece scrupulously clean, following the wigmaker's instructions.

A full wig should fit closely but not be tight. Hold the front on the forehead and ease the base down at the sides and back. A toupee may be held by an adhesive, or secured to natural hair with surgical thread, or be held by pulling natural hair through the backing.

A postiche has to be pinned tightly to the natural hair and this can damage the hair, accelerate hair loss and even lead to baldness with constant use. Wear a pin-on hairpiece for special occasions only, and attach it carefully.

Hairpin crochet lace

Making and joining strips of lace

This type of lace takes its name from the two-pronged frame or fork on which it is made, which often resembles a large hairpin. Any type of yarn is suitable for this lace, from thin cotton to thick knitting wool.

Yarn is wound round the prongs of a hairpin and worked into a series of loops in the centre, or spine, with a crochet hook – see CROCHET. The width of the strips can vary, depending on the distance between the prongs. In addition to a variety of widths, hairpins are also available in different lengths, from 10mm ($\frac{3}{8}$in) to 100mm (4in).

The finished strips can be woven together and used to make clothes.

HAIRPIN CROCHET LACE

Hairpin crocheting a strip of lace; joining the strips together

1 Using a slipknot, tie the end of the yarn to the middle of the left prong and take it across the right prong.

2 Wind the yarn behind the right prong and hold it taut. Slip the crochet hook under and through the knot.

Join loops of yarn together on the hairpin with a chain stitch and work them up into strips. Join the strips by placing them side by side and weaving, chain or slipstitching the loops on the side of one strip into those of another strip.

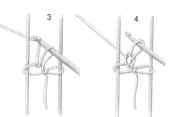

3 & 4 Pick up the yarn and draw it down through the loop so that you have a loop round each prong and one on the hook. Hook up the yarn again and draw it through the hook loop to form a second loop.

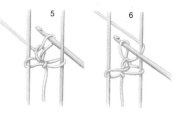

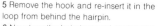

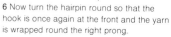

5 Remove the hook and re-insert it in the loop from behind the hairpin.
6 Now turn the hairpin round so that the hook is once again at the front and the yarn is wrapped round the right prong.

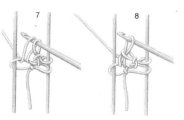

7 & 8 Draw the yarn under the top strand of the left loop on the hairpin so that you have two loops on the hook. Hook up the yarn once more and draw it through both loops on the hook so that only one is left.

9 Repeat steps 3-8 until the hairpin is filled or until the strip is the length you want.

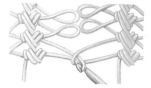

Joining the strips
1 Hook up a loop first from one strip, then one from the other.

2 Draw the second loop through the first, then repeat.

5 The strips can also be joined with a slipstitch. Hook up a loop from the sides of two strips, catch up a loop of extra yarn and draw it through.

3 Work up the strip from bottom to top in this way.

4 Stitch the final loop into the work.

Hair plaiting

Making a neat and simple pigtail

One of the tidiest ways of dressing long hair is to arrange it in a traditional plait or pigtail.

Draw all the hair back and divide it into three equal strands at the nape. Grasp the left strand and take it across the centre strand, so that it now becomes the centre strand. Take the right strand, pass it across the centre strand, so that it in turn becomes the centre strand. Continue in this way until the strands

---

HAIR PLAITING

Plaiting a pigtail

1 Divide your hair into three strands. Take the left strand over the centre strand and hold it in your right hand. Pull what is now the left strand aside and release the first strand, which is now the centre strand.

2 Take the right strand over the new centre strand and hold it in your left hand. Pull the new right strand aside and release the new centre strand. Take the left strand over the centre strand again, clasp it in your right hand and pull the new left strand aside with your left hand.

3 Continue plaiting in this way until you reach the end of the strands; now secure the plait with an elastic band.

are too short to plait, then wind a covered elastic band round the end of the plait to hold it in place – leaving a short tail dangling below it. With practice it should not take more than a minute or two to make a plait.

Hair setting

Creating waves with rollers, and curls with pin curls

Whether your hair is long, medium or short, you can set it at home with rollers to give waves or body and bounce. The smaller the diameter of the rollers, the tighter the hair will be rolled.

When you take out the rollers and brush the hair, tight rolls will make a wavy style. If the hair has been loosely rolled, removing the rollers will reveal a sleek, smooth style but with plenty of fullness and a curve at the ends. Use large hairpins or plastic roller pins to secure the rollers.

HAIR SETTING

Using rollers

Use medium rollers for body and bounce. Working upwards from the neckline, roll the hair at the sides and back downwards. Roll the front section of the fringe forwards.

Hold the tip of a section of hair on the top of the roller with the thumbs. Turn the roller downwards to wind on the hair.

Push a hairpin through the roller at 45 degrees to the scalp. If the hair is rolled under, point the pin towards the crown; if rolled upwards, point the pin down.

Pin curl Wind the strands like a snail. Clip across the curl diagonally and flat against the head.

Apply some setting lotion, gel or mousse to make the set last longer; comb it evenly through the hair. Divide the hair into three main sections, one on top of the head from forehead to crown, one running round the head from the top of one ear to the top of the other ear, and the third from ear level to nape.

As you deal with each main section, divide it into sections as wide as the rollers you are using and as deep as the diameter of the roller. Comb one of these sections out from the scalp, hold the tip of the section on top of the roller with your thumbs, then turn the roller down towards the scalp until all the hair is wound round it. Push a hairpin or roller pin diagonally through the roller, not in the direction you have rolled it but the opposite way until the tip is braced against the scalp.

When you are using narrow rollers, set the nape section first with the rollers arranged horizontally. Then set the middle section, arranging the rollers vertically. Last of all set the top section, using slightly larger rollers, working from forehead to crown and rolling the hair back towards the crown.

When you are using large rollers, set the top section first, then the middle section – arranging the rollers horizontally – and then the nape section.

For hair that is too short to go on rollers – round the ears and at the neckline, for example – make pin curls. Use the fingers of one hand to wind a small lock of hair round the index finger of the other hand. Wind from base to tip. Slide the lock off, press it flat against the scalp and secure it with hairgrips or clips.

Let your hair dry completely before you take out the rollers and hairgrips. Brush out the hair into the style you want. You can spray on lacquer to hold it in place.

For a quicker set, you can use rollers that are electrically heated; or you can use electrically heated curling tongs or a heated curling brush instead of rollers. Your hair must be dry or almost dry when you use electric curling aids. You can use a little setting mousse for a better result on fine hair. Deal with the hair in sections as with heated rollers.

See also HOME PERMS.

Hallmarks

How to identify gold, silver and platinum

Gold and silver objects have been hallmarked in England since 1363, as a guarantee of purity. Anyone trading in precious metals – including antiques dealers – must display an official notice issued by the British Hallmarking Council, explaining the system.

The hallmark not only assures a cus-

HALLMARKS

What the symbols mean

To identify the towns where items were assayed, study the symbols. The letters in a shield are London marks, showing the styles for successive periods.

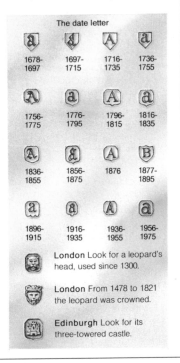

---

tomer that he is buying genuine gold and silver (and now, platinum), but enables him to identify the sponsor or manufacturer of an article, and the place and date of testing the precious metal content.

Silver hallmarks There are usually four symbols in a hallmark: the sponsor's or maker's mark, the standard mark, the assay mark, and the date letter. A fifth mark, the sovereign's head, is found on most silver assayed between 1784 and 1890.

Sponsor's mark Before the 18th century, sponsors or makers used emblems or symbols as their mark, but in 1739 it became law for initials to be used. For example, the initials PL under a crown mean that the article was made by the famous London silversmith Paul de Lamerie, under royal patronage.

Standard mark This confirms that the metal is sterling (92.5 per cent) silver. The English mark is a lion *passant* (on four feet), the Scottish a lion *rampant* (on hind feet) – before 1975 it was a thistle. Imported silver has figures denoting the minimum weight content in parts per thousand.

Until 1822 the English mark was a lion *passant gardant* (with its head turned, looking over one shoulder), although between 1697 and 1720 this was replaced by the seated figure of Brittania. During that time the standard of fine silver was raised from 92.5 per cent to 95.84 per cent. The Brittania mark is still used on silver of this purity – known as Brittania silver.

Assay mark This signifies the office responsible for testing and marking the article. Today there are only four such offices in the UK: London, Birmingham, Sheffield and Edinburgh. The marks are: London, a leopard's head; Birmingham, an anchor; Sheffield, a Tudor rose (before 1975 a crown); Edinburgh, a castle. Dublin (Republic of Ireland) also has an assay office, signified by the figure of Hibernia (before 1923 it was a crowned harp).

In the past there have been many other assay offices, and some the collector may come across are: Chester, a sword and three wheatsheaves; York, five lions on a cross; Newcastle, three castles; and Exeter, a three towered castle.

Date letter It is almost impossible to identify date letters without reference to a guide. The best guide is *Bradbury's Book of Hallmarks*, obtainable from most large bookshops. The letters of the alphabet are shown in a shield and denote the year in which an article was assayed. Different forms of letters, italic or Old English, are used and the shape of the shield also differs for certain years.

Commemorative marks Three special events are commemorated by an additional mark: the Silver Jubilee of George V and Queen Mary in 1935, showing their crowned heads facing left; the Coronation of Elizabeth II in 1953, her crowned head facing right; the Queen's Silver Jubilee in 1977, her uncrowned head facing left.

Gold hallmarks The sponsor's mark, assay mark, date letter, and commemorative marks on gold are the same as for silver, except that the Sheffield (assay) mark has always been a rose, and the Birmingham anchor is on its side.

Standard mark Since 1975 the mark has been a crown followed by figures giving the minimum weight content in parts per thousand. Before 1975 the content was given in carats and only 18 and 22 carat was marked with a crown (in England) or a thistle (in Scotland). On imported gold, both numbers appeared.

A carat is the number of parts of gold in 24 parts of the final alloy. The commonest carats are 22 (now expressed in parts per thousand as 916), 18 (now 750), 14 (now 585) and 9 (now 375).

Foreign gold and silver Since 1842 all imported gold and silver articles have been stamped with a special assay office mark. The current marks are: London, the sign of the Constellation Leo; Birmingham, an equilateral triangle; Sheffield, the sign of the Constellation Libra; Edinburgh, St Andrew's Cross.

Certain foreign hallmarks, known as Convention hallmarks, are also recognised in the UK under an International Convention. They consist of a sponsor's mark, a common control mark, a fineness mark showing the parts per thousand and an assay mark.

Platinum hallmarks Platinum has been hallmarked only since 1975. The platinum standard mark is an orb inside a pentagon, and the figures giving the weight content in parts per thousand. Assay marks are the same as for silver.

Halloween games

Duck-apple, broomstick races and dressing up

Ducking or bobbing for apples heads the list of favourite Halloween games. Float plenty of apples in a large tub or bowl of water, first laying down some plastic sheeting to protect the floor. Get the duckers to kneel down beside the tub. With their hands behind their backs, the players must each bite into an apple and lift it out of the water.

You can either make a group of children all compete at the same time, in which case the first one to lift out an apple wins; or you can make them do it one by one and time them. In this case the winner is the child who takes the least time to lift out an apple.

For a drier variant, suspend apples by their stems from strings in a doorway. The children clasp their hands behind their backs and try to bite into the freely spinning fruit.

Murder in the dark This is a fun game if you are entertaining older children. Give out slips of paper, one marked 'detective', another marked 'murderer' and the rest left blank. The detective must leave the room, but the others must not tell each other what is on their slips. Turn out the lights. In the dark, the murderer prowls and grasps the neck of the victim, who gives a blood-curdling scream and falls to the floor. The lights are then turned on and the detective returns to ask questions until the murderer is exposed.

The murderer may lie, but everyone else must answer truthfully. The detective must deduce which person is the murderer from the answers given concerning positions and actions at the time of the event.

Halloween relay races Give relay races a seasonal flavour – try a witches' relay, for example. Divide the children into teams. Every child must in turn run to the end of the room or garden and back while straddling a broomstick, then pass the broomstick to the next member of his team. The first team to complete wins.

Dressing up Another essential ingredient of Halloween is dressing up in costumes and masks. Use bits of old towels, curtains, tablecloths, sheets or old clothes from, for example, charity shops to make frightening or amusing costumes. Or you can buy unbleached muslin, felt, nylon netting or fabric lining, then dye it the colour you want – see DYEING. Use lightweight cardboard wrapped with aluminium foil to simulate armour, and decorate it with poster or acrylic paints.

To make a mask, first design it on a piece of newspaper. Cut out the outline to make a pattern, then use it to cut out the mask in cardboard. Decorate the mask with poster paints, glitter, sequins or crepe paper. Tie on a length of elastic to keep it on.

Make-up adds a final touch. Use women's make-up, or theatrical make-up (greasepaint). If you use greasepaint apply it over a base of cold cream rubbed into the skin. Use an eyebrow pencil to draw on beard stubble, moustaches or side whiskers. To grey your hair, dust it with cornflour or talcum powder.

You can make yourself look bald by wearing a swimming cap painted flesh colour. Cut out holes for your ears. Add a few strands of hair, if you like, by stringing lengths of thread knotted at the ends through holes cut into the cap. See also JACK O'LANTERNS.

Hamburgers

Mixing and cooking them

Though beef is the traditional ingredient for hamburgers, a mixture of pork and beef mince also makes burgers with a good flavour and texture. They should be 13-19mm ($\frac{1}{2}$-$\frac{3}{4}$in) thick – any more and they will not cook through evenly.

Ingredients (serves 6)
450g (1lb) minced lean pork
450g (1lb) finely mince lean beef
1 egg, beaten
Salt and freshly ground black pepper
Pinch of ground nutmeg or coriander
40g (1$\frac{1}{2}$ oz) fresh white breadcrumbs

Mix the pork and beef together. Put the beaten egg into a bowl and season with salt, pepper and a little nutmeg or coriander. Then stir in the breadcrumbs. Add to the mince and mix together thoroughly.

Divide the mixture into six round

shapes and chill in the refrigerator until ready to cook.

For BARBECUES, allow 5-8 minutes each side, turning carefully so that the burgers do not break up. On a cooker, grill the burgers under a moderate heat for about 10 minutes on each side – see GRILLING.

Hammers

Which type to use; replacing handles

The most commonly used has a steel head with a hickory or ash wood handle. Also available are hammers with steel heads and glass fibre handles, and with steel heads and handles – mostly used for claw hammers. These usually have a perforated rubber grip to stop your hand slipping on the shaft, and to absorb much of the shock of impact. A hickory shaft can be broken under strain, but glass fibre and steel shafts are virtually indestructible.

Apart from the way these are made, hammers also come in a variety of patterns, each with its own purposes:

Claw hammer This head has a split end, or claw, for pulling out nails. Use the handle as a lever once the nail is gripped.

Pin hammer This is a light hammer for driving panel pins, fine nails and tacks. The head is flat at the back for starting small nails.

Cross pein A larger version of the pin hammer, it comes in a number of patterns, of which the commonest is the Warrington.

Ball pein The ball-shaped pein at the back of the head is used for beating metal or for setting RIVETS.

Club hammer This has a heavy steel head, up to 1.8kg (4lb). Use it to hit a steel chisel (see CHISELLING) or bolster, or a hand-held masonry boring tool – see MASONRY DRILLING. Wear protective gloves and safety goggles.

Soft-faced hammer The head usually has a different material – such as copper, rubber or nylon – on each face. One of the most useful is a hammer with one soft and one hard rubber face.

Many have also removable faces that can be changed for different uses, or replaced when badly worn. The hammer is used for hitting a surface you do not wish to damage.

Mallet (joiner's or carpenter's) The head is flat faced and usually made of beech. Its main job is to hit chisels with wooden handles.

Choosing the type for the job

Make sure you have the right hammer before starting on a job; use claw, pin and cross-pein hammers for light carpentry; ball peins for engineering work; mallets and soft-faced hammers for easily damaged surfaces; and heavy hammers, such as club and sledgehammers, for breaking up masonry, driving in posts and similar tasks.

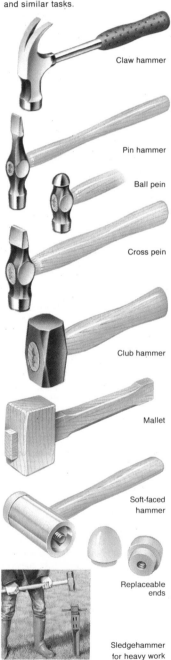

Claw hammer

Pin hammer

Ball pein

Cross pein

Club hammer

Mallet

Soft-faced hammer

Replaceable ends

Sledgehammer for heavy work

Sledgehammer This has a heavy head up to 9kg (20lb) with a long handle for heavy driving. Flat-faced, ball-pein or straight-pein types are available. Light blows can be made by holding the hammer just below the head and dropping the head onto the object to be driven. For heavier blows, hold it near the end of the shaft and swing it like an axe.

Repairing a hammer

Loose head On older hammers the shaft may shrink, or steel or hardwood wedges may have worked loose. If wooden wedges are loose, remove them, apply waterproof wood glue and tap back in place. With steel wedges, push slivers of hardwood into the holes, then hammer back the wedges.

Damaged shaft If the handle is cracked or badly damaged, clamp the hammer head in a vice and drill holes in the handle to weaken the grip of the wedges holding it in place. When possible, wiggle out the remaining wood. If it will not move, chisel it out with a thin wood chisel and mallet.

Take the hammer head to your tool shop and get a new shaft of suitable size. It may need some sandpapering down to make it a tight fit. If the handle is not cut to take wedges, grip it in a vice and make saw cuts in the top end, slightly deeper than the depth of the wedges. Put the head on the shaft, then tap the other end of the shaft firmly against a hard surface to drive the head onto the handle. Saw off any excess wood above the head, then drive in the wedges until they are flush with the end of the handle.

Hamsters, guinea pigs and gerbils

Caring for some popular pets

Children love pets that are tame and friendly, parents love pets that are easy to feed and care for – hamsters, guinea pigs and gerbils fill both bills.

Hamsters These small creatures are clean and almost odourless, and so are ideal for keeping indoors. They are, however, aggressive until they become used to their owner, and are always aggressive with their own kind and so should be

Gerbil

Hamster

Guinea pig

housed separately. It is best to buy either an adult that is tame or a youngster ready to be tamed.

Rough treatment of a nervous young hamster will always result in a sharp nip, and the best time to get him used to being handled is when he is being fed. Hamsters store some of their food in cheek pouches, then eat it later, and it is while he is busy pouching that you can run a finger down his back. Increase the caresses each time until he will allow you to pick him up when he has finished eating.

The cage for a hamster should be at least 610mm (2ft) by 300mm (1ft), and should be made of hardwood, heavy plastic or metal – otherwise the hamster will quickly gnaw its way out. Cover the front or top with small-mesh wire-netting and line the floor with plain paper (not newspaper) or a thick layer of sawdust. Hamsters tend to use the same place in their cage for droppings, so put down a small metal tray covered with sawdust, and clean it every day. Remove old stored food twice a week, and change the paper or sawdust once a week.

Food should consist of a mixture of rolled oats, wheat, sunflower seeds or one of the packaged foods available from pet shops. In addition, lettuce or cabbage should be given, and root vegetables such as carrot, turnip or swede, or pieces of apple can be given occasionally. Make sure there is always a supply of drinking water. Provide a piece of sweet wood, such as apple, hazel or willow, to give the hamster something to gnaw on.

Hamsters are nocturnal, and are also vulnerable to extremes of hot and cold. They should be kept in a room at a constant temperature of 18°C (64°F), and out of draughts. The cage must be out of reach of cats or dogs, and not near windows or radiators. Make sure you have soft, natural fibre bedding. Hay is not suitable as it can wound cheek pouches.

A well-treated hamster should live for more than two years.

Guinea pigs Sometimes called cavies, these creatures can be kept indoors or outdoors, though the choice is often determined by space: a hutch for a pair should be 1050mm (3ft 6in) by 610mm (2ft), and 610mm high. The wire-netting front should be 25mm (1in) or 13mm ($\frac{1}{2}$in) mesh and, if outdoors, roofed with roofing felt.

The hutch should contain a box about 250mm (10in) square and 150mm (6in) high for sleeping quarters, which should be lined with soft hay. Cover the floor of the hutch with sawdust or peat. Change the hay and floor covering at least once a week.

Feed guinea pigs with mixed cereals, plus green food. It is essential to supply vitamin C every day. A piece of sweet wood, such as apple, hazel or willow, will give them something to gnaw on and keep their teeth in trim, and there should always be fresh water for drinking.

Gerbils These desert creatures, a little smaller than a rat in size, are easy to handle, as they do not bite in fear as, for example, hamsters do. They can be fed on the same foods as hamsters, but not too much sunflower seed. Add small quantities of lettuce, sprouts, carrot or firm fruit such as apple. Gerbils drink very little, but water should always be available.

Gerbils are tunnellers, and the best way to keep them is in a large aquarium filled three-quarters full with loamy soil or soft peat. Replace the soil about three times a year. Some of their tunnels will run close to the glass, so that their activities underground, as well as above, can be seen.

Gerbils are susceptible to heat exhaustion, so do not leave a cage in full sun. They have intense curiosity, and can be let out of their cage under supervision.

Gerbils breed rapidly. Ask your pet shop to sex them carefully if you do not wish for a breeding pair.

Handbag repairs

Cleaning and mending handbags;
replacing handles

You will need a few LEATHERWORK tools and materials: an awl, craft knife, clear resin adhesive (see GLUING), needles (including a curved one) and waxed thread as well as long-nosed or needle-nosed pliers, a nail punch and hammer, and possibly rivet pins (see below). You may also need special leather stains, available from shoe repair shops.

Cleaning Wash a leather bag with a leather soap, and when clean and dry, rub in a leather softener. A PVC bag can be cleaned with a soft cloth and soapy water or a mild detergent solution. Rinse and leave to dry.

Treat stains on suede with a suede stain remover or a grease solvent; when dry, steam the bag over a kettle spout to raise the pile. If areas have become smooth, rub with a fine glasspaper; treat with suede cleaner and finish by brushing with a copper-wire brush.

Cuts and tears Find a spare piece of material similar to that of the bag, and cut a patch large enough to cover and overlap the cut or torn area. Apply a thin layer of clear resin adhesive to the *inside* of the damaged area. Similarly apply a thin layer to the patch. Allow both surfaces to become touch-dry. Carefully bring the damaged edges together in their correct position, then apply the patch to the inside, pressing it firmly in place. The bond will be immediate. Now lay the bag down, and press the edges of the damaged area well onto the patch from the outside. If done carefully, the damage should be almost invisible.

Restitching a seam Pull out the damaged or perished thread with a stiff needle or scissors point. For resewing, choose a needle which will pass through the existing holes, and thread it with waxed thread, knotting the end. Put the knot on the inside of the bag, then copy the existing stitching. With a single running stitch (see SEWING), continually go forward two holes and back one. Extend the new stitches a few holes past the repaired area (use the awl to make holes) before cutting the thread.

Damaged handle Take the bag to a leatherware shop or shoe repair shop and try to get a handle that is a match, or near match. If it is ready-riveted, use a craft knife to cut the damaged handle from the bag, then long-nosed or needle-nosed pliers to open the D rings enough to remove them from the bag.

Insert the D rings through each end of the handle. Now put the rings back on the bag, squeezing them gently with pliers to close them again.

If you cannot get a handle, buy a strip of calf leather at least twice the width of the damaged handle and about 75mm (3in) longer. Turn the two edges back so that they meet, and glue them in place with clear resin adhesive. Buy a leather stain which matches the colour of the bag, and stain the new handle.

Buy two rivet pins from a local craft shop. These come in two pieces, which can be pressed together to hold the new handle in place, one at each end.

Trim the corners off the handle, then turn each end back about 32mm (1$\frac{1}{4}$in). Use a nail punch and hammer to make a neat hole through both thicknesses of handle. Now pass one end of the handle through one D ring; push a rivet through the holes.

Position the cap on the end of the pin, and, holding the rivet over a solid surface, tap the cap home with a hammer. Repeat the process with the other end. If any bare ends of leather show a different colour from the handle, use a spot of stain to match them in.

Loose clips If the clasp of a snap-shut handbag works loose, it is usually possible to tighten it by using a pair of long-nosed pliers to adjust one or both sections of the clasp.

The fault may also lie partly with loose hinges. Tighten each hinge by placing the pin of the hinge on a hard surface and lightly tapping the other end of the pin with a hammer until the whole hinge tightens up. Do this gently.

Changing colour Leather stains may be used to change the colour or darken a handbag – but take care, some leather stains can also stain clothing. For PVC materials there are special paints in a limited range of colours which will permanently recolour the fabric.

Hanging plants

A decorative, space-saving way to display plants

In rooms or hallways where floor space is limited, hang plants at or above eye level in windows and sunny corners. Or to relieve the expanse of a large window area hang a variety of containers at different levels, in a group. Use a terracotta bowl or plastic or ceramic planter, or a wire basket. All of these containers are available at plant shops or garden centres.

Suspend a planter from a secure ceiling hook or wall bracket, using chains, wire or rope. A particularly attractive display can be made by using a MACRAMÉ hanger, with two or three plant holders hung one above the other. Make sure the planter can be easily reached for watering, and is not in a draught or heavy shade. Some hanging containers have pulleys which allow them to be raised or lowered, making it easier to water the plants inside.

Check the soil every few days (it soon dries out) and water and feed as required – see HOUSEPLANTS. Turn hanging plants round every two or three weeks so that all sides get the same amount of light.

─── HANGING PLANTS ───

Planting in a wire basket

Line with sphagnum moss and plastic sheet. Pierce plastic for drainage and trim off. Fill with compost.

Arrange trailing plants around the edge of the basket and set upright plants in the centre. All should need the same amount of watering.

Suitable plants for hanging In bright areas hang alyssums, lobelias, petunias, oxalis, chlorophytum (spider plant), dwarf nasturtiums, asparagus fern or ivy-leaved geraniums. In shady spots grow maidenhair fern (see FERNS), *Maranta leuconeura kerchoviana* (rabbit tracks), BEGONIAS, FUCHSIAS, ivy, WANDERING JEW or zebrina.

When planting a hanging basket make sure that the overall effect is not too weighty. Mix plants which have feathery foliage, such as asparagus fern or spidery dizygotheca, with plants which have dense, broad foliage, such as cissus. Counterbalance plants which have trailing stems with plants that climb upwards.

Try to vary the foliage, offsetting sober-leaved plants such as ficus, against flamboyant plants such as codiaeum.

Hang nails

Removing and preventing them

A hang nail is an outgrowth of skin along the side of a fingernail. It is often caused by frequent immersion in water, when the outer skin layer splits away from the cuticle, or by picking or biting the fingernail.

Remove a hang nail as soon as you notice it, before it becomes painful and possibly infected. Use clean, sharp nail scissors and clip it close to its base. Wash your hands and apply some antiseptic cream and a plaster. If the finger becomes very painful, or pus forms, consult a doctor.

To prevent hang nails, wear rubber gloves when washing dishes, and use hand cream frequently. Avoid biting or picking your nails and try to stop if it has become a habit – see NAIL BITING.

Hangover

Coping with the morning after

The aftereffects of heavy drinking are caused not only by alcohol but also by preservatives and chemical by-products from fermentation, called congeners, in the drinks. There are usually more congeners in dark-coloured drinks than light-coloured. Alcohol is a diuretic causing dehydration through increased urination; congeners taken in large quantities poison brain cells.

Brandy, blended whisky and red wines have high alcohol and congener contents and so tend to produce the worst hangovers. Gin, vodka, white wine and malt whisky contain fewer congeners and are less likely to cause a bad hangover.

These are only general rules, however, as the amount of congeners can vary from brand to brand, and the effect they can have varies from person to person.

One way of avoiding a hangover is to discover which drinks and brands of drinks affect you most, and keep off them. This applies also to beers and lagers – some brews and brands of drink may affect you more than others. Another way is to alternate alcoholic drinks and SOFT DRINKS such as mineral water. Whichever way you choose, never drink on an empty stomach.

Most spirits and liqueurs, often with a high alcohol content, can be diluted with water, soda or other soft-drink 'mixers' to reduce the dehydration and stomach irritation they cause. Aim at reducing the rate at which alcohol enters your bloodstream by drinking slowly.

After a drinking spree, drink as much water as you can to compensate for the loss of body fluid.

If you have a headache, take paracetamol rather than aspirin, which will irritate an already irritated stomach.

Traditional cures There is no stimulant (such as coffee) or drug that will speed the rate at which alcohol is removed from the bloodstream. Nor will an alcoholic drink on the 'morning after', or a 'hair of the dog that bit you', help. Water will be just as effective in reversing the dehydrating effect of alcohol, and reliance on an early morning drink can lead to alcoholism.

Hay fever

Avoiding and relieving seasonal allergies

The term hay fever covers allergic reactions (see ALLERGIES) to a host of substances – including plant pollen, animal hairs, dust, perfumes or cosmetics, tobacco fumes, food additives and alcohol.

Symptoms – which often appear in childhood – include sneezing, coughing, wheezing, blocked or runny nose, headache, swollen, streaming eyes and loss of a sense of smell.

Hay fever is usually most widespread in spring or summer, but can occur all year round if sufferers are constantly exposed to substances to which they are allergic. The commonest of these are house dust and mattress dust, which affects the sufferer at night.

The best way to avoid hay fever is to identify the substance to which you are allergic (it may be obvious) and avoid it as much as possible. For example, stay out of woods, fields and gardens during the pollen season; steer clear of domestic animals and smokers; vacuum bedrooms, furniture and mattresses frequently.

See your DOCTOR, who may prescribe antihistamines, sprays or eye drops. Some of these actually prevent hay fever, whereas others merely alleviate the symptoms.

Sometimes the symptoms are so severe that they affect your work or interfere with school examinations, in which case your doctor may prescribe a short course of steroid tablets or steroid injections to alleviate the symptoms.

Even without treatment, the symptoms usually become less troublesome as you grow older – and sufferers often find that the problem disappears altogether after middle age.

Headaches

Easing minor ones; recognising serious ones

Many headaches are caused by prolonged tightening of the face, scalp and neck muscles. Aching is felt generally at the back of the head, though sometimes at the front, and the muscles at the back of the neck feel tense.

Such tension headaches generally come towards the end of the day, after periods of anxiety or intense concentration – when driving long distances, for example. They rarely last for more than a few hours, though some sufferers may continue to feel tense for a time afterwards.

To ease the pain, relax the tense muscles; if possible, have a short rest or nap. Or relax over a cup of tea with a friend. A MASSAGE or a hot compress applied to the forehead and base of the skull may also help. If none of these measures are possible or do not work, take mild painkillers in doses recommended by the manufacturer.

If the headaches recur Everybody has headaches from time to time – some more often than others. If, however, you seem to be having an unusual number of headaches, try to identify the cause and find a way to deal with it.

Common causes include anxiety and overwork. Try to reduce your workload and to alter your lifestyle to reduce tension. Make sure you get enough fresh air and exercise.

When to see the doctor Consult a DOCTOR immediately if a headache is accompanied by drowsiness or follows a head injury, or if a very severe headache starts suddenly.

Consult a doctor quickly if:
● A headache shows no signs of easing after two or three days.
● If it is made worse by moving the head or coughing and continues for more than three days.
● If it is accompanied by other symptoms, such as stiffness in the neck or back, or by blurred vision or vomiting.

See also MIGRAINE; RELAXATION EXERCISES.

Head and face injuries

When to give first aid in an emergency

If someone has suffered a head injury, possibly through a fall or a road accident, get them to a DOCTOR or to the Accident and Emergency Department of the nearest hospital as soon as possible – particularly with elderly people and anyone who has, however briefly, suffered UNCONSCIOUSNESS. In such cases there is a danger of internal BLEEDING or brain damage.

While waiting for help, ensure that the casualty is breathing through a clear airway. If unconscious, place him in the RECOVERY POSITION. If he is not breathing, give ARTIFICIAL RESPIRATION.

Scalp wounds Due to the large amount of blood, these often seem more serious than they really are. Stop the bleeding by applying direct pressure to the wound with a clean handkerchief or towel, or a dressing and bandage – see below.

Broken jaw Someone with a broken or dislocated jaw often has a wound inside the mouth – sometimes caused by teeth which have been broken in the accident. He may have difficulty in speaking and there may be a profuse flow of saliva – frequently blood-stained. The jaw should be supported until the casualty reaches hospital, as illustrated.

Clear the mouth of any blood or broken teeth with your finger, but keep teeth in case they can be replaced.

HEAD AND FACE INJURIES

How to apply dressing and bandage

The flow of blood from a scalp or face wound should be checked with a pad dressing, and fixed in position with a bandage or plaster. A suspected broken jaw should be supported with a bandage. Get the casualty to a doctor or hospital as quickly as possible.

1 Gently place a pad dressing on the wound to stop the bleeding.

2 Secure the dressing with a triangular bandage or cloth. Cross the two ends at the neck.

3 Take the two ends round to the forehead and tie them firmly. Draw the point of the bandage downwards at the back.

4 Hold the bandage gently and bring the point up over the crown. Fix it in place with a safety pin or adhesive tape.

Bleeding face Press a clean, folded handkerchief or a pad of paper tissues over the cut. When the bleeding slows, put a fresh pad over the first and fix it in place with sticking plaster.

Broken jaw Get the casualty to hold a pad under the chin. Bandage the pad in place and tie the ends on the top of the head. Loosen slightly if the teeth are clenched tight.

Face injuries Severe bleeding can make facial injuries appear far worse than they really are. Deep wounds need to be stitched by a doctor or at a hospital, but most cuts need little more than cleaning and bandaging.

Hearing aids

Relieving deafness with a tiny microphone

In most cases of deafness, whatever its cause, a hearing aid will partly restore hearing.

The symptoms of partial deafness are not always quickly recognised, but include difficulty in picking up high or low-pitched sounds, and in understanding what is being said to you by someone speaking at a normal voice level, particularly where there is background noise.

First consult your DOCTOR, who will arrange for you to visit the audiology department of a hospital. There a specialist will remove any wax in your EARS and conduct tests to find the level and range of your deafness. Using an instrument called an audiometer, he will transmit tones to you through headphones, and as you signify those you can hear and those you cannot, he will draw a chart showing the range of your hearing loss. He will also determine the extent to which each ear is affected and will prescribe one or two hearing aids as necessary.

The commonest type of hearing aid is worn behind the ear. It contains a tiny microphone and amplifier which transmits sounds through a plastic tube to an earpiece. At the hospital a mould of your ear will be painlessly taken, to provide you with a personal earpiece. At a later visit you will be given the earpiece and a hearing aid tuned to compensate for your personal hearing loss.

Living with a hearing aid Remember that a hearing aid is no more than that – it cannot fully carry out the functions of the human ear. For example, in a crowded room the human ear can ignore background noises and concentrate on one only, such as a personal conversation, but a hearing aid will pick up all the noises at the same volume level. Similarly, with a hearing aid it is difficult to hear someone clearly if their head is turned away from you.

Do not be afraid to tell other people about your problem, and ask them to co-operate by speaking clearly and without shouting. You may also learn in time how to lip-read, putting the lip movements and sounds together.

Your hearing aid will have three switch positions, marked M, T and O. M is the 'on' position and O the 'off', the T position is used when using a public telephone – it will cut out background noise and enable you to carry on a normal conversation.

Some theatres and cinemas also have a 'loop system' for hearing-aid users. With it you can switch to T and hear only what is being transmitted through the theatre's speaker system, and not the annoying crackle of crisp bags or sweet wrappers from the person in the seat behind you. The presence of a loop system is usually proclaimed in the foyer; if not, ask the manager or an attendant if there is one.

Looking after your hearing aid The tiny, button-size batteries will last several weeks and are easy to replace. Keep the earpiece clean and rinse it occasionally in a weak antiseptic solution. Replace the plastic tube from time to time – the hospital will show you how – as it will go brittle with age and crack. A crack or hole in the tube will cause the hearing aid to whistle. If the tube or earpiece becomes blocked with wax, hold it under a running hot water tap to clear the blockage, then blow through it to expel water droplets.

Heart attack

What to do in an emergency situation

A heart attack is caused by a reduction of the blood supply to the heart. It may result from a narrowing of the arteries, caused by a build-up of fatty deposits, or blockage by a blood clot.

The symptoms include: severe pains in the chest, sometimes spreading down one or both arms and into the neck and jaw; dizziness; shortness of breath and a weak or irregular pulse. The victim may also lose consciousness. In the weeks leading up to the attack the victim may feel unusually tired and breathless, and may suffer from severe indigestion.

Emergency treatment If the patient is conscious, place in a half-sitting position with knees bent. Support head and shoulders with pillows or cushions, and place another cushion under knees. Give an aspirin to chew slowly.

Call the patient's DOCTOR, or dial 999 and ask for an ambulance. Inform the ambulance service that you suspect a heart attack.

Loosen clothing round the patient's neck, chest and waist to help circulation and breathing. *Do not give anything to eat or drink.*

Check the patient's breathing and pulse. If he loses consciousness but is breathing normally, place him in the RECOVERY POSITION. If he stops breathing, give ARTIFICIAL RESPIRATION, and if the heart stops beating, give EXTERNAL CHEST COMPRESSION if you are trained in it.

Heartburn

Relieving and avoiding a burning pain in the chest

A hot sensation behind the breastbone, commonly called heartburn, is caused by stomach acids flowing back into the oesophagus, the food pipe. It usually occurs after meals.

Weakness of the valve at the lower end of the oesophagus, where it joins the stomach, allow the acids to flow back. Obesity, over-indulgence in food or drink, wearing tight corsets and belts, or bending down or lying flat after a meal, can all trigger an attack. Heartburn may also affect pregnant women, whose muscles are more relaxed than usual.

Antacids that neutralise the hydrochloric acid produced by the stomach will help to relieve heartburn. They are obtainable from chemists without prescription, and may be taken in tablet or liquid form.

Avoid substances that will aggravate the condition, such as alcohol, tobacco smoke, aspirin, garlic, onions, chocolate and coffee. Eat smaller meals and sit upright while eating. Do not wear tight clothes, and avoid stooping.

If the symptoms persist, and are accompanied by other symptoms such as bleeding or difficulty in swallowing, consult your DOCTOR.

Heat exhaustion

First aid for a person overcome by heat

Overexposure to high temperatures or overactivity in hot weather causes loss of salt and water from the body through excessive sweating, and can bring about heat exhaustion.

The symptoms include muscle cramp in the legs and arms, dizziness, headache and nausea. The breathing is fast and shallow and the pulse fast but weak. The victim will look pale, have cold, clammy skin, and feel tired and weak. He or she may collapse if the condition is not treated quickly.

Put the casualty in a cool, shaded place and remove any heavy clothing. Check the body TEMPERATURE. If it is higher than normal – above 37°C (98.6°F) – the casualty may be suffering from HEAT STROKE.

To replace the lost fluids and relieve cramp, make up a drink of lightly salted cold water – a quarter teaspoon of salt to each pint – with fruit juice added to improve the taste. Give the casualty small amounts of this liquid every ten minutes.

If the casualty is unconscious, place him or her in the RECOVERY POSITION and get medical help.

Green screen A tall evergreen hedge, such as yew, gives shelter and privacy to a garden.

Heat stroke

What to do for bodily overheating

Exposure to high heat and high humidity can produce heat stroke, which must be treated quickly, as an attack can prove fatal. Babies and old people are particularly at risk.

Heat stroke may occur suddenly, with the body TEMPERATURE rising to 40°C (104°F) – see THERMOMETERS. The skin is hot, dry and flushed, and the breathing may be noisy and the pulse jumping. The person may complain of headache, dizziness and nausea.

Put the patient in a cool room, in a half-sitting position. Remove clothing and wrap sheets or towels soaked in cold water around the whole body.

Call a DOCTOR or ambulance as soon as possible, or get someone else to do it while you are treating the patient.

Fan him until the body temperature drops to 38°C (100°F) – check the temperature every five minutes. Continue fanning, and if the temperature rises again, restart the cooling treatment.

Heat stroke can bring on UNCONSCIOUSNESS. Place the person in the RECOVERY POSITION and continue the cooling treatment while awaiting medical help.

Hedges

Planting and caring for a living fence

A high hedge can shield a garden from the wind or from the eyes of neighbours. It can also make an effective noise barrier. Low hedges are an attractive way of dividing up a garden.

For a tall hedge it is best to plant evergreen SHRUBS – such as holly – or deciduous shrubs that keep their dead leaves for all or most of the winter, such

as beech and hornbeam. For low, dividing hedges, try barberry, box, cotoneaster or privet.

Planting If possible, plant the shrubs either in autumn or early spring, and start with plants less than about 600mm (2ft) high. Shrubs grown in containers can be planted at any time.

Dig over the soil about two weeks before planting, removing perennial weeds, and work in FERTILISERS.

Stretch a string line between two pegs to mark the position of the hedge, then stick in canes at intervals of 300-460mm (12-18in) along the line to show where each shrub goes. Make either a single row, or for a denser hedge, a staggered double row. Dig a hole for each shrub, or a trench for several. Make each hole deep enough for the base of the stem (or the soil mark on the stem) to be at soil level, and wide enough for the roots. Break up the subsoil at the base of the hole.

Mix the soil from the hole with COMPOST or well-rotted manure, about 1 part to 2 parts soil.

Water a container-grown shrub before removing it from the container. Hold each shrub by the base of its stem to position it in the hole. Fill in the soil mixture round it and tread well down. Then water each shrub thoroughly. Tie the shrub to its cane until well established.

Pruning and trimming With the exception of conifers and slow-growing evergreens such as yew and holly, prune hedge shrubs immediately after planting – see PRUNING SHRUBS. Prune quick-growing shrubs by half. Prune others by one-third on top and harder at the sides. The following winter prune by the same amount. Trim sides, but not tops, of conifers and slow-growing evergreens.

Once the hedge is established, prune it as necessary – check the recommended time for the particular shrub. Trim hedges so that the bottom is slightly thicker than the top.

Hedge trimmers

Maintaining, sharpening and using them safely

Most domestic hedge trimmers are powered by their own electric motors or connected to a mains electricity supply. Regularly maintained, they give years of trouble-free service. Always unplug a trimmer before servicing.

Overhaul After a period of hard use, or at an interval recommended by the makers, check the whole appliance. Undo the nuts holding the gearbox cover in place and remove the cover. Store loose pieces in a plastic bag. Remove the

---

HEDGE TRIMMERS

Keeping your trimmer in good order

Lubricate a trimmer regularly, as directed by the manufacturer. Use light machine oil and grease. Clean the blades after use, making sure you remove all gummy deposits.

Gearbox cover

Fixed blade

Blade-drive block

Blade bolts

Gear wheels

Driven blade

On most trimmers, one blade is fixed while the other moves. The moving blade has a peg drive.

Felt pad

Blade bar

blade bolts, noting the position of any concave washers under the blade bar. Carefully remove the fixed blade, then lift the driven blade from its peg on the driven gear wheel.

Use a fine wire brush to remove debris and gummy deposits from the surfaces and teeth of both blades. Then use a file to sharpen the blade teeth, but do not alter the angle of the teeth edges. Grip each blade in a vice while you work, moving the blade so you can work as close to the vice jaws as possible. Finish by rubbing each blade flat on an oiled oilstone using a circular motion, to remove any burrs.

Check gearwheels and the blade drive-block for wear or damage, and replace with new parts if necessary. Soak the felt dust-excluder pad with oil, working it in with your fingers, then pack the gear-wheels with grease. Reassemble in reverse order.

Check the full length of the cable for damage. Bind any slight scrapes with plastic tape, but if the outer sheath is damaged, cut out the damaged section and re-join the cable with a waterproof connector (never with insulating tape). Put the female part of the connector – not the protruding pins – on the length of cable connected to the power plug.

When fitting a new plug (see PLUGS) choose a rubber one.

Safety If your power socket is not protected by a built-in RCD (see CIRCUIT BREAKER), plug an adaptor-type RCD into the socket, *then* plug in the hedge trimmer. Should you accidentally cut the cable, the RCD will immediately cut off the power. See also POWER TOOL SAFETY.

Read the instruction book carefully concerning the limitations of the tool. Other safety tips:
● Work with the cable looped over a shoulder so that it trails well away from the cutting blades.
● Always hold the trimmer with both hands.
● Watch out for fencing wire or other metal obstructions which would damage the blades and cause an accident.
● Unplug the trimmer whenever it is left unattended, for however short a time.
● Do not work in wet weather, or leave the tool out in rain.

Hems

How to mark and stitch them

To finish the hem of a garment you have made, or to alter the hem of a ready-made article (first unpicked and pressed), put on the garment, and the shoes you usually wear with it. A helper can measure up from the floor and put pins horizontally at the desired hemline on the right side of the fabric. If you have no

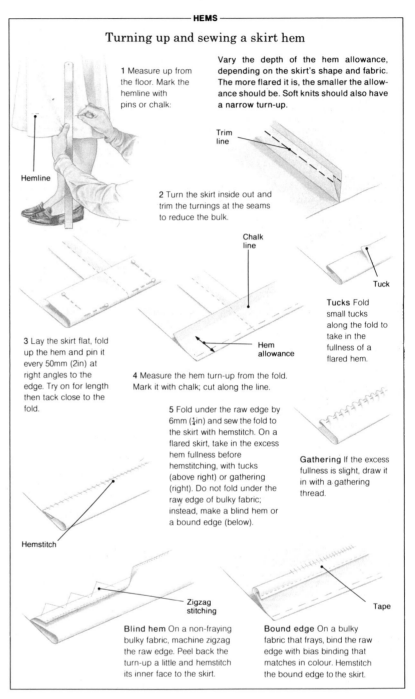

Turning up and sewing a skirt hem

1 Measure up from the floor. Mark the hemline with pins or chalk:

Vary the depth of the hem allowance, depending on the skirt's shape and fabric. The more flared it is, the smaller the allowance should be. Soft knits should also have a narrow turn-up.

Hemline

Trim line

2 Turn the skirt inside out and trim the turnings at the seams to reduce the bulk.

Chalk line

Tuck

Tucks Fold small tucks along the fold to take in the fullness of a flared hem.

3 Lay the skirt flat, fold up the hem and pin it every 50mm (2in) at right angles to the edge. Try on for length then tack close to the fold.

Hem allowance

4 Measure the hem turn-up from the fold. Mark it with chalk; cut along the line.

5 Fold under the raw edge by 6mm ($\frac{1}{4}$in) and sew the fold to the skirt with hemstitch. On a flared skirt, take in the excess hem fullness before hemstitching, with tucks (above right) or gathering (right). Do not fold under the raw edge of bulky fabric; instead, make a blind hem or a bound edge (below).

Gathering If the excess fullness is slight, draw it in with a gathering thread.

Hemstitch

Zigzag stitching

Tape

Blind hem On a non-fraying bulky fabric, machine zigzag the raw edge. Peel back the turn-up a little and hemstitch its inner face to the skirt.

Bound edge On a bulky fabric that frays, bind the raw edge with bias binding that matches in colour. Hemstitch the bound edge to the skirt.

helper, you can use a chalk marker which puffs a line of chalk onto the fabric at the desired level; make sure that the fabric will not be permanently marked by the chalk.

If the hem is on a jacket, not a skirt, you can lay the garment flat, pin the hem yourself, and adjust the pins if necessary when you try the jacket on.

Instead of SEWING a hem, you can use

iron-on bonding web to secure it. Prepare the hem as for sewing, then slip a 25mm (1in) wide strip of bonding web under the turning so that the web is just covered. Press all along the turning with a hot dry iron over a damp cloth until the cloth is dry – see IRONING; PRESSING. The web is not suitable for flared skirts but is a quick aid for straight and gathered skirts, also trouser hems.

Herb gardening

*Growing herbs for fragrance,
beauty and usefulness*

HERBS are grown principally for the kitchen (see HERBS IN COOKING), but many also make attractive plants – for example, borage, thyme and rosemary with their bright flowers; sage with purple, gold-edged or grey-green leaves; fennel, dark and feathery; and parsley brilliantly green and profusely curled. Some herbs should be grown where you will brush against them – mint and fennel, for example – and others, such as creeping thyme, where you will tread on them, so that you can enjoy the fragrance they release.

Planning It is most convenient to grow herbs in a plot near the kitchen door, but since most herbs are Mediterranean plants, it should be south-facing and in full sun. A plot sloping to the south is ideal, especially if the soil is light, even poor, and alkaline. Dig the plot to a spade's depth in winter; if the soil is heavy, work in one bucket of peat substitute or COMPOST to each square metre. Rake the soil fine in spring.

Plan to have the taller plants at the back – the evergreen rosemary and bay, the perennial fennel, and biennial angelica. Put the small plants at the front where they will not be overshadowed – the evergreen thyme, perennial chives, hardy biennial parsley, marjoram which should be treated as a half-hardy annual, and the hardy annual summer savory. In between you can grow borage and dill (hardy annuals), the evergreen sage; balm, GARLIC, mint and tarragon (hardy perennials); the hardy biennial chervil; and the half-hardy annual basil.

Propagation Sow hardy annuals and biennials from spring onwards, and half-hardy annuals later when the risk of frosts is over. Sow in drills about 13mm (½in) deep and 250mm (10in) apart. Thin the plants as they grow to prevent crowding. Parsley seeds are slow to germinate and may take a month or six weeks; soaking the seeds in water for 12 hours before sowing may speed germination. Alternatively, you can let some of your plants run to seed and transplant the seedlings to the required spots in spring.

You can buy small plants of perennials for planting out in spring or autumn. You can also raise perennials from seeds sown in spring in a nursery bed for transplanting to the permanent spot in autumn. If you are already growing the perennials, you can increase them by dividing and replanting them in spring or autumn.

Shrubby plants – rosemary, thyme, bay, sage – can be grown from 100-200mm (4-8in) hardwood cuttings taken from July to September and inserted in a nursery bed or frame to root for planting out the following spring. See also PROPAGATING PLANTS; SEED SOWING.

Care Keep the plot weed-free. Trim back shrubby plants each year to keep them compact. Confine rampant perennials such as mint and balm by surrounding them with tiles or metal lawn-edging strip driven to 150mm (6in) deep. Alternatively, plant them in an old bottomless bucket inserted into the ground. Parsley and angelica need more moisture than most other herbs so water them regularly and often in dry weather. Apply a little general fertiliser during the growing season – see FERTILISERS.

Smaller-growing annual herbs can be raised from seed in late summer and transplanted to pots for wintering indoors on a sunny windowsill. Small perennials also can be potted to winter indoors so that you can continue to use your herbs fresh throughout the winter. Evergreens can be grown in pots or tubs to have within reach on a balcony or patio during winter. Feed herbs in pots or tubs every fortnight and water them when the soil feels dry.

Herb preserving

Drying and freezing

Most herbs can be picked when they are in bud and just ready to flower (usually in May or June), for drying and use in the winter. This is the time when their flavours are at their best – see HERB GARDENING; HERBS IN COOKING.

Pick on a warm, dry morning, after the dew has dried off them but before the sun gets too hot. These are the conditions when the oil content is highest. Pick carefully, one variety at a time, discarding any dead or withered leaves.

Drying Oven-drying is quick and convenient. You can make use of the residual heat after the oven has been used for baking. Stretch some muslin or other fine cotton fabric over a cake rack. Dip small bunches of the herbs in boiling water for a few seconds to clean them and to help to preserve the colour. Shake off the moisture and put the herbs on kitchen paper until the water has drained off them. You can take the leaves of mint, sage and other large-leaved herbs off the stems.

Lay the herbs on the rack and place them in the oven (switched to its lowest setting), leaving the door slightly ajar. Turn the herbs over after 30 minutes, to ensure even drying. Leave in until they are crisp – usually after about an hour.

Air-drying herbs takes up to ten days, depending on the temperature and ventilation. Tie the herbs in bunches and dip them in boiling water for a few seconds.

Shake out each bunch and leave it to dry on kitchen paper. Then wrap a piece of muslin or other fine cotton fabric round each bunch to keep out dust and hang the bunches downwards in a warm, dry, airy place, such as an airing cupboard. The herbs are dried when the leaves and stems feel brittle.

To store dried herbs, crush them with a rolling pin, remove any bits of stalk and pack them in small airtight containers, labelled with the contents and date. Try to avoid glass containers as the colour will fade from the herbs.

Freezing Non-evergreen herbs – basil, chives, fennel, mint, parsley – freeze well. Wash and dry the herbs and put them into polythene bags, labelled and sealed, for the freezer. Chopped herbs can be frozen with a little water in a refrigerator ice-cube tray. When the cubes are solid, put them into sealed polythene bags for storage in the freezer for up to six months. To use, put a cube or two in a fine strainer and run cold water through to melt the ice and leave the herbs ready as a garnish or to add to a dish.

WARNING Do not shake dried herbs into a cooking vessel straight from a container. Steam may get into the container, and cause mould.

See also FOOD STORAGE; FREEZING FOOD.

Herbs in cooking

*Using them to add or enhance
flavour*

The leaves, flowers and even the seeds of herbs are used in cooking to enhance flavour. They are best when used fresh but they can be frozen or dried for winter use (you need only half as much dried herb as fresh or frozen). If you grow herbs (see HERB GARDENING), it is easy to dry your own – see HERB PRESERVING. If you buy dried herbs, get them from a shop with a rapid turnover where they have been kept away from the light in airtight containers, otherwise they fade and go stale. Choice of herbs is entirely subjective, but certain herbs go especially well with particular foods.

Balm The leaves have a strong lemon scent when crumpled. Use in OMELETTES, STUFFINGS, SAUCES and fruit drinks.

Basil Strong, clove-like flavour. Use with oily fish, roast lamb, chicken, duck and goose; also used in omelettes, tomato dishes, soups (see SOUPS AND STOCKS), SAUSAGE MAKING and SALADS.

Bay Use with oily fish, pork, veal and goose; also in stews, sauces, PÂTÉS, terrines, milk puddings and custards.

Bouquet garni A small bunch of parsley, thyme, marjoram and bay tied with string, to put in soups and stews during cooking.

Chives Member of onion family. Use finely chopped to garnish egg and cheese dishes, baked potatoes, salads.

Dill Mild aniseed flavour. Use with fish, salads (especially cucumber), MAYONNAISE, and sauces. Dill seed is also added to pickles – see PICKLING.

Garlic Traditional Mediterranean ingredient with a strong onion flavour. Used in stews, dressings and herb butters. Use with soups, salads, tomato and shellfish dishes, PASTA and PIZZAS. See also GARLIC.

Marjoram A spicy, sweet flavouring to use with oily fish, roast lamb, pork, veal, chicken, duck and partridge; also in soups, stews, omelettes, tomato and mushroom dishes.

Mint Used in sauces and JELLIES, traditionally with roast lamb. Use to flavour peas, new potatoes and carrots and as a garnish.

Oregano A relative of marjoram. Use with chicken, spaghetti sauces, pizza and salads.

Parsley A peppery-flavoured garnish, traditionally used with fish, sauces, cooked vegetables, salads and eggs.

Rosemary Sharp, astringent flavour. Use sparingly with oily fish (when grilled), roast lamb, pork, duck and poultry.

Sage Strong, slightly bitter flavour. Used in stuffings (for roast pork, chicken and duck), sausages and MEAT LOAF.

Tarragon Use in chicken and veal dishes, omelettes or with oily fish; also used in hollandaise and tartare sauces, SALAD DRESSINGS and mayonnaise.

Thyme Strong, sweet-flavoured, versatile herb used with oily fish, roast pork, veal and poultry; also used in STUFFINGS, and with some cooked vegetables.

See also GAME BIRDS; GRILLING; POACHING; POULTRY; ROASTING MEATS.

Hiccups

What you can do to stop them

Hiccups occur when the diaphragm dividing the chest from the abdomen goes into spasm and interrupts the normal breathing pattern. This may be caused by a large meal, too-hearty laughter, or a hastily swallowed hot drink.

The simple cure for hiccups is to breathe in carbon dioxide – the gas you breathe out with each breath. You can do this by cupping your hands over your nose and mouth and breathing in and out several times; you can use a paper bag instead of your hands – but not a plastic bag or you may suffocate.

Most attacks of hiccups are over within 20 minutes. If an attack persists for more than a day, you should see a DOCTOR.

Hinges

Using the right hinges for the job; hanging doors

Hanging a door Two hinges are sufficient for most interior DOORS, but a solid exterior door will need three. You will need six or eight countersunk SCREWS for each hinge.

The stiles (upright timbers) are extended at the top and bottom of a new door, to protect the corners from damage until the door is to be hung. Saw them off (see SAWS AND SAWING) before wedging the door in place 6mm ($\frac{1}{4}$in) above floor level, to measure for trimming.

Once you have marked where the door meets the door frame, make another line inside this to allow the door to clear the frame and swing inside it to meet the doorstop. The clearance should be 2mm ($^1/_{16}$in) on a flush door, 3mm ($\frac{1}{8}$in) on a panelled door because it is more liable to expansion. Plane to the inner marked line – see PLANING.

If the frame has already had recesses cut in it for a previous door, position the recesses in the new door to match them. Otherwise, chisel recesses in the door (see CHISELLING) and make recesses in the frame to match them.

Hanging a cupboard door Most cupboards now are plywood or fibreboard, and the door edges will not hold screws.

HINGES

Fitting them to doors, cupboards and gates

Interior door Use 75mm (3in) or 100mm (4in) steel butt hinges, placed so knuckles clear the door. Cut round as deep as the hinge thickness.

**Cut across the area every 6mm ($\frac{1}{4}$in). Pare out in sections with the chisel flat side down.

**Screw the hinges on the door. Position it open, clearing the floor. Fix each hinge to the frame with one screw. Test the fit. Put in the other screws.

Cupboards For a lightweight inset door made of plywood or fibreboard, use face fixing hinges (right). Fix them with raised-head screws, letting the knuckle determine the spacing between door and frame. For a lay-on plywood or fibreboard door, use concealed hinges (below).

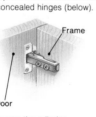

Frame

Door

Recess the cylinder inside the door and screw in the plate to secure it. Screw the arm inside the frame.

Plate

Cylinder

Arm

Gates Position the hinges on the gate's cross rails, drill start holes through the screw holes and screw on the hinges. Position the gate, raised 50mm (2in) above the ground. Drill start holes on the post for the hinge flap and drive in the screws.

They need hinges fitted on the face or back of the door and frame. Allow a clearance of 2mm ($^1/_{16}$in) for an inset door to swing easily into the carcass and allow a lay-on door to overlap 16mm ($^5/_8$in) onto the carcass. Make sure the screw length is less than the thickness of the door. The concealed hinges for a lay-on door are adjustable after the door has been hung.

Hanging a gate The simplest hinge for fixing a small wooden gate to a timber post is the T-hinge. Allow sufficient clearance for the hinge movement and catch at the sides. Special hinges are needed for heavy pairs of GATES on posts, and for gates on brick piers.

Hire purchase

Your rights and responsibilities when buying on credit

Under a hire purchase agreement the buyer does not own the goods until he has paid the last instalment. The shop or trader sells the goods to a finance company, which becomes legal owner and lends the goods to the customer.

The hirer pays a deposit and then pays the balance, with interest, by fixed amounts over an agreed period. The Government may lay down rules about the size of deposit and period of hire.

Most advertisers of hire purchase facilities must quote the Annual Percentage Rate of Charge (APR). The lower the APR the less you pay in the long run. Your bank will tell you what the APR would be on a personal loan or an overdraft; often it is cheaper to borrow the full purchase price from the bank – see BANK ACCOUNTS.

If you fail to keep up the payments, the seller may repossess the goods – but will need a court order if you have paid more than one-third of the total price. Normally a court will make an order allowing you to keep the goods and pay reduced instalments.

You cannot return the goods, unless they are defective, until you have paid half the total price and all instalments due so far. If you want to end the agreement early by paying all the outstanding amount you may still have to pay the full amount of interest.

Signing an agreement Every hire purchase agreement must contain a 'signature box', warning you that you are legally bound by the agreement and you must not sell the goods before they become legally yours. Do not sign a form without the warning.

The agreement must state the cash price and the price including hire purchase charges. You must also receive a copy of it when you sign.

If when you sign you are not at the seller's trade premises, the law allows five days (14 days if you are buying from a mail-order catalogue) for you to change your mind and write to the seller cancelling the agreement, without paying anything.

When you sign you declare that you know the true price of the goods and that they are satisfactory – so before signing, examine them. But you may still have a right to sue if they prove unsatisfactory.

Hiring

Renting cars, tools and other goods

An increasingly wide range of goods can be hired – cars, CONCRETE mixers, TELEVISION SETS and VIDEO RECORDERS, marquees, men's morning dress, ladies' ball gowns, for example.

To find out where to hire them, consult *Yellow Pages* – under Hire Services or the name of the particular item you want to hire.

Rental agreements Always read a rental agreement carefully before signing it – to make sure that it does not impose conditions that are unacceptable to you.

It is wise always to insure hired goods for their full value – see INSURANCE. Some hire shops offer an insurance scheme for damage to equipment. If hired goods prove unsatisfactory, you are entitled to a replacement.

Car hire You must have a valid driving licence, and many companies will require the driver to be over 21. To hire luxury cars, you normally have to be over 25.

Within Britain you can usually pick up a hire car in one place and drop it off at another depot of the company elsewhere. Some companies will arrange for you to pick up or leave a car at a major railway station, airport or other location in Britain or abroad.

Most car-hire companies base charges for shorter-term hirings on time and mileage; for hirings longer than a few days, time is usually the only basis.

Basic third-party insurance (see also CAR INSURANCE CLAIMS) is usually included in the charge, but you generally have to pay extra for personal accident cover.

Television and video hire Check on what notice you must give to end the agreement. The rate charged may reduce as the hiring period lengthens.

Tool hire Hire shops or centres offer a wide range of equipment – from power drills to lawn mowers, welding equipment to ladders. Apart from the hire charge, you will usually have to pay a deposit – and will pay for 'consumable parts' such as sanding belts and discs.

Hire shops will usually advise you on how to use equipment. You are responsible for insuring against injury, damage or loss.

Skip hire To leave a hired skip in the street, you must get local authority permission – and can be fined without it.

The owner is responsible for lighting the skip at night and showing his name and address clearly. If you hire for a month or more, you will be regarded as the owner.

Hives

Relieving their itching

Hives (urticaria) are swollen, ITCHING areas of pale skin surrounded by angry red weals. They can occur anywhere on the body and vary in size from pimples to saucer-size eruptions. They may disappear within hours, move to different sites, or last for several days or weeks.

Mostly they are an allergic reaction to certain foods – for example, strawberries, shellfish, chocolate, eggs or cheese. Drugs such as codeine and aspirin can also cause flare-ups – as can dust, pollen and an individual's sensitivity to sun, cold or light.

There is no effective home cure, but the itching may be relieved by applying calamine lotion or cold compresses, or by taking antihistamines.

If the itching becomes unbearable, or if there are complications – such as swelling of the mouth, tongue or throat – see your doctor without delay.

Homelessness

How to obtain shelter in an emergency

If you are homeless, or at immediate risk of being made homeless, you are entitled to free advice and assistance from the local housing authority. In certain recognised emergencies, you are entitled to be given temporary or permanent accommodation, too – if, for example, homelessness is the result of fire or flood, or if the people affected include a pregnant woman, dependent children, an elderly person or someone who is mentally or physically handicapped or ill.

In these and other cases, contact the local council's housing department – get the address from the telephone directory, a public library or any council office. Most councils have a homeless persons officer. The Citizens Advice Bureau can also give assistance and so, in some cities, can Shelter Housing Aid Centres and other housing charities.

Who can claim help In law, people are homeless if they have no accommodation they are entitled to occupy. In addition to disaster victims, they include evicted tenants (see EVICTION NOTICE), people turned out by their relatives, and legal immigrants who have nowhere to live.

Others legally considered homeless, although they have accommodation, include those who cannot gain entry to their homes, women at risk of assault by a husband or cohabitee, and caravan or houseboat dwellers with no site or mooring for it.

Someone who is likely to become homeless within 28 days is entitled to the same help as those already without accommodation. Local authorities consider people as still homeless if they are living in temporary short-term accommodation – for example, a relative's house, a charity night shelter or a women's refuge.

What the council will do If your case is officially classed as an emergency, the local authority may send you to stay temporarily in one of its reception centres or hostels, or give you a short lease on an empty property. In the last resort, it may put you in a guest house or hotel.

Whenever it is possible, families will be allowed to remain together. If you have any property – for example, articles saved from a fire – the council is obliged to store or protect it until it can be reclaimed; whether or not a charge is made for this service depends on your income.

What happens after temporary accommodation has been arranged varies according to circumstances. If the council considers that you became homeless 'intentionally' through your own actions – such as deliberately giving up a satisfactory home, or refusing to pay rent – it is obliged to keep you in accommodation only long enough to give you a reasonable chance to find your own.

The council is not obliged to provide a permanent home, though it must give advice and assistance. Anyone evicted for genuinely being unable to meet the rent or mortgage payments, however, is unlikely to be classed as intentionally homeless; the council may grant Housing Benefit to help with rent.

If the council decides that you are not legally responsible for your plight, it must eventually provide, or help you find, adequate permanent accommodation, such as a council house or flat or, if you can afford it, private accommodation. In some cases, it may assist you to move to another area where you have a better chance of obtaining accommodation.

Non-emergency cases If your case is not recognised as an emergency you can claim council advice and assistance, but not the right to accommodation. In prac-tice, most single people, (other than unmarried mothers or mothers-to-be) and childless couples are not classed as emergency cases.

When more than one council is involved If a council decides that you have closer connections with another area, it passes responsibility to that housing authority. If two authorities disagree about responsibility in an emergency, one must provide temporary accommodation until the matter is sorted out. When someone has no local connections – because he has just arrived from abroad, for example – the first local authority to which he applies for help is held to be legally responsible.

Income support Homeless people are entitled to income support. In London and Glasgow there are special Social Security offices which deal with homelessness. Families in temporary accommodation receive income support to cover the board and lodging charge, and any meals not included, and an allowance for personal expenses. See also NATIONAL INSURANCE.

How to complain If you feel you are not getting the help to which you are entitled, complain to a local councillor, the local MP or the ombudsman – see OMBUDSMEN. If a council fails to consider your case on its merits or handles it unfairly, you can ask the courts to over-rule its decision or to extend a period of temporary accommodation pending the outcome of the full court hearing. You may be able to claim damages if the council has broken a statutory obligation to provide accommodation. The Citizens Advice Bureau or Shelter Housing Aid Centre may be able to help you in formulating and presenting the complaint.

Home perm

How to do your own permanent waving

Before giving yourself a home perm, trim your hair (see HAIRCUTTING). If you have any split ends (see HAIR CARE), make sure you cut them off. Do not use a home perm on hair that has recently been coloured (see HAIR COLOURING), or that is dull or very dry. The hair is probably out of condition. Consult a hairdresser if you are in any doubt – otherwise your hair could be damaged by chemicals used in the perm preparation.

Do not use a home perm if your scalp is inflamed or has developed a sore. Wait for it to heal.

The perm should last up to six months, but the time it lasts and the amount of curl it produces will vary according to the length and texture of your hair. Short hair will be curled more than long hair. There are perm kits for normal hair, and kits for hair that has been coloured some time ago.

All kits normally contain an alkaline waving solution to soften the hair before it is wound on the rollers; a neutralising solution which sets the hair into its new waves; a plastic cap; and endpapers which help keep the hair in the rollers.

You also need towels, a plastic comb and plastic rollers. Read and follow the maker's instructions.

The success of a perm depends on how long you leave the waving solution on your hair. Different kinds of hair absorb the solution at different rates. If chemicals are left on for too long, they can severely damage the hair.

To find the right timing for you, do a test on one small lock of hair 24 hours before the perm, carefully following the kit instructions. You should also do a patch test on your scalp, to make sure you are not allergic (see ALLERGIES) to the solutions; do not use the perm if the test patch becomes sore.

It takes two or three hours to complete a home perm – and there should be no distractions. Take the telephone off the hook and ask a friend to help you put in the rollers. Keep the solutions away from your eyes and throw away leftovers; they cannot be kept for later use.

See also HAIR SETTING.

Home worker

Dealing with tax and rate problems

If you regularly work from home, either self-employed or as an employee, you may be able to recoup some of the costs involved, in the form of allowances on your taxable income. To qualify for the allowances, you must convince your tax inspector, by letter, telephone or a visit, that a significant part of your working time is spent at home.

You will also need to keep a careful record of your business expenses. Keep a file of all bills and receipts, to support your claim, and submit it with your INCOME TAX RETURNS each year.

The inspector decides what allowances you are entitled to receive; if you disagree, you can appeal to the tax commissioners. When submitting your claim, list all your expenses that could conceivably relate to your business. The inspector may disallow some of them, but probably will not offer to include any you have forgotten to mention.

What you can claim You can claim tax relief in any or all of three categories:
● Raw materials, such as fabrics for dressmaking.
● Business equipment, for example, a

typewriter, computer or filing cabinet.
● Operating expenses – these can include electricity bills, telephone charges, stationery and postage costs, rates, accountant's fees and insurance premiums for business equipment. Travel costs arising from business are also a deductible expense.

When the list of items for relief has been agreed, the tax inspector will decide what proportion of the cost of each can be offset against tax. If you buy stationery that is used solely for business, the full cost will probably be allowed.

If you use a car for both business and private needs, the inspector will want to know how much motoring time you devote to each. If you are claiming some household running costs, the inspector takes into account the amount of time spent working from home and the facilities set aside at home for business use.

For example, if you live in a six-room house, work entirely from home, and have set aside one room mainly for business, the inspector starts his calculations by assuming that one-sixth of your household running costs qualify as business expenses. However, he may reduce that proportion by arguing, for example, that you would have had to heat and light the room for part of the time regardless of your business activities.

Getting permission You cannot change the use of your home to a shop or workshop without PLANNING PERMISSION from your local authority. Obtaining planning permission means that you must apply to the local council, and that your neighbours will have a chance to object. If you change the use of your property without getting permission, the authority can stop you doing so.

If major alterations are needed to the property you will need BUILDING PERMITS. Further, your property may cease to be a home, and so you become liable to pay business rates to the local council on the property, not just the COUNCIL TAX. In practice, if you only use part of your home for a business, and it does not interfere with the neighbours or involve changing the building in any way, the local authority may not be unduly concerned.

Check leases and covenants If you live in rented accommodation, your tenancy agreement may forbid you to work at home. Freehold or leasehold agreements may include covenants forbidding or restricting commercial use of private housing. Check the wording of your lease or title deeds. See also TENANTS.

Capital gains tax If you use part of your home solely for business, you may have to pay capital gains tax when you sell the premises. Moreover, you are still liable for the tax even if there was some

domestic use, too – for example, if your children did homework there, or you kept a spare bed in it for guests.

To avoid possible future complications, always make clear on your claim for income tax relief on household running costs that your work room is sometimes used privately.

Insuring your assets Household contents INSURANCE policies cover inexpensive business items such as pocket calculators and manual typewriters. But you may need to make special arrangements to protect more expensive business necessities – for example, computers, stocks of goods for resale or large quantities of cash.

If you are regularly visited by numbers of clients or customers, you may be charged more for your contents policy. Check your policy and if in doubt ask the insurance company. However, if you have to pay an extra premium, that will be tax-deductible as a business expense.

Employment rights If you work from home, you are liable for the same NATIONAL INSURANCE charges, and qualify for the same benefits, as others who are employed or self-employed. If you are self-employed, you are responsible for buying your own national insurance stamps. See also SELF-EMPLOYMENT.

Full-time employees who work from home are covered by the same employment protection laws as those who work on the employer's premises. They are not covered by most of the rules on health and safety at work, but can sue an employer for negligence if injured by a faulty machine that the employer has provided.

Hooks and eyes

Sewing them to garment openings

Hooks and eyes are small but strong fasteners. They may be used alone on an opening or to supplement another fastening. See also PRESS-STUDS; VELCRO FASTENERS.

On overlapping edges, use a straight eye. Sew the hook on the underside of the overlap, with the tip at least 3mm ($\frac{1}{8}$in) from the edge to prevent it from showing if there is a pull on the opening, but not so far away that the end of the overlap will droop.

Attach with whipstitch (see SEWING) round each fixing hole, then pass the needle and thread through the fabric and whipstitch the hook near the end to hold it flat.

Mark on the underlap where the end of the hook falls. Place a straight eye on the mark and whipstitch one hole. Pass the needle and thread through the fabric and whipstitch the other hole.

Where to sew them on

Lapped edges Sew the hook on the inside of the overlap about 3mm ($\frac{1}{8}$in) from the edge. Position the straight eye on the underlap where the end of the hook falls.

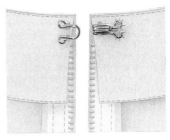

Edges that meet Sew the hook and eye on the inside. Position the hook 2mm ($\frac{1}{16}$in) from the edge and the round eye to extend slightly beyond the edge.

On waistbands Use this special hook and eye set, designed to prevent the hook from slipping out of the eye. Position as for lapped edges.

Covering hooks and eyes A fine finishing touch is to cover both with closely spaced blanket stitches, using a single strand of matching silk twist.

Hopscotch

A playground game that keeps you on the hop

Using a stick, scratch a numbered hopscotch pattern (as illustrated) on a 3-4.6m (10-15ft) length of bare ground – or chalk it on a pavement.

Stand in front of space 1 and toss a small stone into it. Hop on one foot into the space, then pick up the stone – still on one foot – and hop back to the starting point.

Now toss the stone into space 2. Hop into space 1, then 2. Retrieve the stone and hop back to the starting point, one space at a time. Continue like this until you reach space 10 and hop back to the starting point.

You lose your turn to an opponent if you fail to toss the stone into the right space; if your foot or stone lands on a line; or if you lose your balance and put both feet on the ground. After your opponents have had their turns, start again where you left off. The first player to complete the course wins.

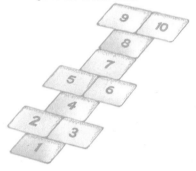

Hopping course Chalk or scratch a hopscotch course of 10 compartments. Number the compartments.

The rules of hopscotch vary from place to place. Sometimes the first person to complete the course marks a section with his or her initials and the game continues with that person allowed to rest on both feet in the initialled section, while other players have to hop over it.

Sometimes the stone is tossed into a space and the player hops to the space as normal – but then instead of picking the stone up and hopping back to the starting point, the player kicks the stone from space to space back to the start.

In some versions certain spaces are rest areas, in which you may put both feet down – or two spaces side by side are occupied simultaneously, with a foot in each space.

Courses may also be marked differently. Sometimes the course is simply a long rectangle divided in half lengthways, each half then divided into four or five sections – to give eight or ten equal sections in all.

Mastering the basic skills

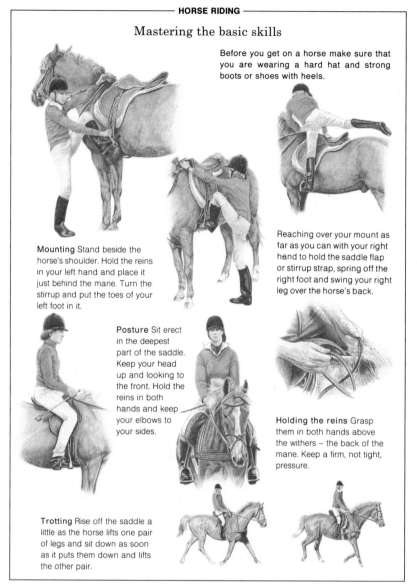

Before you get on a horse make sure that you are wearing a hard hat and strong boots or shoes with heels.

Mounting Stand beside the horse's shoulder. Hold the reins in your left hand and place it just behind the mane. Turn the stirrup and put the toes of your left foot in it.

Reaching over your mount as far as you can with your right hand to hold the saddle flap or stirrup strap, spring off the right foot and swing your right leg over the horse's back.

Posture Sit erect in the deepest part of the saddle. Keep your head up and looking to the front. Hold the reins in both hands and keep your elbows to your sides.

Holding the reins Grasp them in both hands above the withers – the back of the mane. Keep a firm, not tight, pressure.

Trotting Rise off the saddle a little as the horse lifts one pair of legs and sit down as soon as it puts them down and lifts the other pair.

Horse riding

Beginner's guide to mounting and controlling a horse or pony

A reputable riding school is the best place to learn how to ride, but a knowledge of the basic techniques will help.

Mount a horse as illustrated, lowering yourself gently into the saddle at the end and slipping your right foot into the right-hand stirrup. Reverse the procedure to dismount.

Riding position Hold yourself in the saddle with your shoulders squared and the back slightly hollowed. Hold the reins in both hands – only hold them in one while you are signalling on a road.

To test the stirrup length, take your feet out of the stirrups and let your legs hang straight – the length is about right if the bottom of the stirrup iron touches your ankle. Put the ball of each foot on the stirrup tread, with your heels down and toes pointing out slightly. Keep your thighs, knees and upper calves lightly gripped against the saddle. Hold your lower legs back, so that your ears, shoulders and heels are aligned.

Controlling the horse Signal lightly on the reins and use your voice, legs and weight to guide the horse.

To go forward at a walk, tighten the reins briefly, then slacken them and lean forward slightly. Squeeze the horse's sides with your legs. Release the pressure when the desired pace is reached.

To turn right, pull steadily back on the right rein and slacken the left. Apply pressure with the inside of your left leg. Reverse the procedure to turn left. To stop or slow the pace, pull back slightly on both reins and shift your weight back and down in the saddle.

Trotting When a horse trots it lifts its fore and hind legs in diagonal pairs, which results in a bouncing movement. To counteract this, rise out of the saddle when one pair of legs is lifted and return to the saddle when the other pair is lifted. Lean forward and push down on the stirrups, straightening your knees just enough for your seat to clear the saddle. Come down immediately, then rise again.

Horseshoes

A pitching game for two or four

The object of this game is to pitch horseshoes with an underhand throw to encircle a 360mm (14in) high stake. It is set in the ground at a slight angle so that the top is 75mm (3in) nearer to the pitcher than the bottom. Substitute horseshoes (available from some sports shops) are generally used.

The game is usually played on a flat, bare clay surface by two players singly or four in two pairs. Two stakes within chalked boxes are set up as illustrated. Each player in turn pitches two shoes from the box at one end towards the stake at the other. The score is calculated and the players change ends. In doubles each partner is at the opposite end.

Games are played to either 21 or 50

points. A shoe encircling the stake (called a ringer) scores 3 points, but a player's ringer becomes void if his opponent subsequently achieves one as well. A shoe leaning against the stake counts 2 points and the shoe on the ground nearest to the stake is worth 1 point, provided it is within 150mm (6in). If there are no ringers or leaners, having two shoes nearer the stake than an opponent's shoe counts 2 points.

The tactics of the game are to knock an opponent's shoes away from the stake.

Hoses

Repairing a dripping and damaged hose

Most hoses are made of plastic which makes them far less prone to deterioration than rubber ones. Some have polyester fibre reinforcement which gives added strength and makes the hose more pliable – especially in cold weather.

Most garden centres and hardware departments stock a range of hose connectors, nozzles and sprinkler attachments.

Nozzle or joint dripping Unscrew the plastic nozzle or connector and look for damage. Throw away and replace any cracked fittings. If the fitting is sound, clean out any grit. Check that any rubber expansion ring is not damaged. You can try to get a replacement for a split or perished ring, but in many cases you will have to buy a completely new fitting.

Badly deformed hose This may be caused by bad storage in cold weather. Connect a deformed hose to the hot-

water tap and run water through until the hose softens enough for recoiling. A hose is best stored on a hose reel – it keeps its shape and is easier to unwind and wind up again after use.

Damaged hose If there is a small cut in the hose, you can bind it with pipe repair tape. This will withstand the pressure of the mains water. If the damage is substantial, cut out the damaged section with a sharp knife, trimming the ends square. Then rejoin the two pieces, using a union connector.

Alternatively, if you have a short spare piece of piping of the right diameter, push the hose onto it from either side until the hoses meet; clamp both hose ends on tightly using two worm-drive hose clips.

Houseplants

Providing the proper environment for healthy plants

There are two main groups of houseplants – foliage plants (grown for the appearance of their leaves) and flowering plants. Although all need light, air, water, warmth, and occasional feeding and pruning, the conditions in which they thrive best vary. Check on the care label before buying, or consult a book giving the specific needs of different types of plants.

Light Most flowering plants can be grown in direct sunlight, but most foliage plants need light shade or full shade. Generally, plants with variegated or coloured leaves need more light than plants with dark green foliage. Make sure their light needs are being met. Too much sun will scorch leaves, but too little light results in thin stems, feeble growth and pale leaves.

South and west-facing rooms normally have the best light, but plants near south-facing windows may need to be moved during the hottest part of the day, or they will wilt. Desert CACTI and GERANIUMS are among the few plants that thrive in a full summer sun.

Plants grow towards the light, so turn them round periodically so that they grow evenly. Do not, however, turn a flowering plant that is in bud. If a bud is exposed to a drastic change of light, it may drop off.

Air Plants must have air circulating freely about them, but avoid draughts, particularly cold ones. Dust leaves regularly so that the pores are kept clear and the plants can breathe properly. For hairy-leaved plants, such as African violets, use a fine paintbrush. Wipe large-leaved plants on both sides with a damp pad of cotton wool.

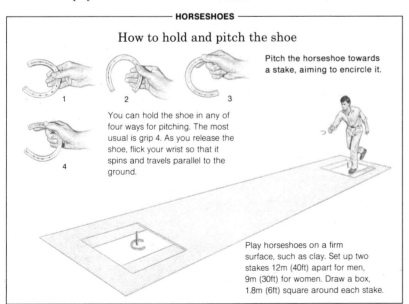

HORSESHOES

How to hold and pitch the shoe

1 2 3

Pitch the horseshoe towards a stake, aiming to encircle it.

4

You can hold the shoe in any of four ways for pitching. The most usual is grip 4. As you release the shoe, flick your wrist so that it spins and travels parallel to the ground.

Play horseshoes on a firm surface, such as clay. Set up two stakes 12m (40ft) apart for men, 9m (30ft) for women. Draw a box, 1.8m (6ft) square around each stake.

Except for desert cacti and SUCCULENTS few plants thrive in dry air. If you have central heating – which dries the air – provide humidity by using a humidifier or standing one or two pans of water in the room. Occasionally spray your plants with a mister. Make sure the water is at room temperature. Do not spray plants standing in direct sunlight as the leaves will scorch.

Alternatively, place the pot in a larger container lined with moist peat – or put the plant for an hour or two in a steamy bathroom or kitchen.

Warmth Most plants prefer constant temperatures, ideally 10-18°C (50-64°F) and not more than 24°C (75°F). Do not place plants near fans or radiators, and on cold winter nights move them away from windows.

Food Feed plants liquid plant food once a fortnight during the growing and flowering seasons. Mix the feed in water according to the maker's instructions. It is better to give too little food than too much. Do not feed plants when the soil is dry or if they are sick.

Water The amount of water needed by different plants varies considerably, but most need more during the growing season – late spring and summer. Generally, it is better to give too little water than too much, and a good soaking regularly is better than frequent small amounts. Clay pots dry out faster than plastic ones. Water plants such as African violets and cyclamens from the bottom, so that the water is drawn up into the pot.

Growing tip

Pinch off the growing tip of a plant in the spring or early summer to make it bushier.

Pruning Prune plants with a vigorous growth – such as FUCHSIAS and GERANIUMS – by cutting back just as growth begins.

Many houseplants need little pruning other than cutting away dead leaves. If a plant does become straggly, or pale, cut off the shoots just above a leaf joint with scissors, secateurs or a sharp knife.

See also PLANT CARE DURING HOLIDAYS; POTTING HOUSEPLANTS; PROPAGATING PLANTS; WANDERING JEW.

Houses and flats

Buying and selling property in England and Wales

Because buying a house or flat is probably the most expensive purchase you will ever make, take your time about choosing it.

When you start house-hunting you may find that your dream home will cost more than you can afford, so aim for a good compromise. Make a list of requirements and decide on the priorities, then whittle the list down until you can get a home at the right price and as close as possible to your ideal.

Shopping for a home You can buy a house or flat from a private seller, through an estate agent or, in the case of new property, from a builder or property developer. Look at advertisements in your local paper, or in one of the national house-selling magazines if you intend to move to a new locality. If you cannot find what you want, visit several estate agents to see what they have to offer, and ask them to send you details of houses coming on the market within your price range. Pitch your top price a little above your maximum – most house-sellers are prepared to come down on their original asking price. Estate agents will send you literature, arrange viewing appointments, and transport you there if necessary, without any charge to you.

Getting a mortgage Before starting on the house-hunting trail, make sure that you can get a mortgage – see MORTGAGES. If you are buying through an estate agent he will ask if you have arranged a mortgage, and if not will probably offer to get you one. Most mortgage terms offered are standard, but interest rates can vary, so compare the rates offered with those of several BUILDING SOCIETIES and banks. You may also be able to get a mortgage from your local council. If you are saving with a bank or building society, you are more likely to get priority at a time when credit facilities are under Government restraint.

House-hunting Do not try to visit too many houses in a day, two or three is enough. Take a notebook to jot down any points you may want to remember, otherwise you will find it difficult later to recall which was the house with the nice kitchen and which was the one with a hole in the roof. When you find somewhere you like, arrange to make a second visit for a more thorough inspection. Look at every room and note the general condition and state of decoration – you may see things that you will want a surveyor to examine more closely, such as damp patches on walls or cracked ceilings. Try to visualise how your furniture will fit into each room, and take a

tape measure with you if you have any particularly large items.

Ask the owner to show you some recent gas and electricity bills, especially if the house has central heating, and what general and water rates are paid.

If you see any faults in the house, ask the owner if he will have them put right before the sale, or reduce his price.

Check whether the property is freehold or leasehold. When you buy freehold property you own the house and the land it is built on. With leasehold property – most flats or maisonettes are leasehold – you pay ground rent to a landlord until the lease runs out. Ask the length of lease still unexpired – you may not be able to get a mortgage if it is only 60 years or less. Most flatholders are also required to pay into a maintenance and building insurance scheme.

If you decide you would like to buy, get a solicitor (see LAWYERS) or licensed conveyancer to advise you about an offer and to handle conveyancing – transfer of property from the seller to you – if the purchase goes ahead.

Put in an offer directly to the owner if it is a private sale, or through the estate agent. Make your offer a little less than the asking price, but be prepared to pay the full price if the seller refuses to bargain. Also arrange a surveyor's inspection.

Engaging a surveyor Although the mortgagees (the bank or building society holding your mortgage) will send you a copy of the valuation survey, you should have an independent structural survey – especially on old property. Engage a surveyor as soon as you have made an offer – he may find things that will put you off buying the property and you can then withdraw the offer before the solicitor's costs start to build up. Your solicitor may be able to recommend a surveyor, but you can save money by asking the mortgagees for the name of their surveyor, and getting him to do a structural survey at the same time as he carries out the valuation survey.

If you have already suspected woodwork diseases or rising damp you can arrange a free inspection without obligation by most of the large specialist firms. In some areas you can also get the electric wiring inspected. Ask at your local electricity showrooms if it is free, or how much it costs.

Tell your surveyor if you have had any such inspections, so that he will not duplicate the work.

If you are buying new property, it will be covered by the ten-year guarantee of the National House-Building Council. Read the guarantee carefully, however, to see what it covers and how to make a claim. But it is still advisable to engage a surveyor, to check that the building work is being properly carried out.

Buying a property If you can arrange for the same solicitor to act for both you and the mortgagees, there will be only one fee to pay. Get in touch with a solicitor as soon as possible, giving all the details of the proposed transaction. He will carry out all the necessary searches into the transaction – dealing with land registration, paying STAMP DUTY if applicable, checking the title deeds and leasehold, if any, and making sure that there are no restrictive covenants or likely local development schemes that could trouble you later. Your solicitor will also draw up a contract (as will the seller's solicitor) and when he is satisfied that all is in order, will ask you to sign the contract. He will then arrange with the seller's solicitor to exchange contracts and fix a completion date agreeable to both you and the seller. When this is done, both you and the seller are committed to going through with the transaction, and you must put down your deposit on the property. On completion the mortgagees will provide the rest of the money in exchange for the title deeds and the empty property. You will then be given the keys.

A licensed conveyancer can also deal with the purchase or sale.

Selling a house or flat You can sell privately or through one or more estate agents. If you do it privately you will have to make your own assessment of the value, or get it done for a fee by an estate agent. If you put the sale in the hands of an estate agent he will charge a commission – which may be anything from $\frac{1}{2}$ to 3 per cent of the amount he sells the house for. You can put the property in the hands of several estate agents, but the commission may be less if you let one agent handle the sale exclusively.

When you accept an offer, tell your solicitor the name and address of the buyer and his solicitor, and the agreed price. As with buying, the exchange of contracts and completion will follow in due course. A straightforward sale will be completed in from six to eight weeks.

On completion day your solicitor will send you a cheque for net proceeds (the sale price less the mortgage payments due, the estate agent's fees and any other fees). He will also send his bill, which he may deduct from the sale price.

Houses and flats in Scotland

*Buying and selling north
of the Border*

In Scotland, most properties are bought through a solicitor rather than an estate agent, at a Solicitors' Property Centre. Here details of property are advertised as in an estate agent's office in England. The seller usually fixes an 'upset price' – offers being invited in excess of this price. If several people show interest, a time limit is set for offers. He instructs his solicitor to accept the highest bid made in that time.

You arrange a survey and based on the surveyor's report your solicitor will guide you on how much more than the upset price to offer. However, you are not allowed to know what other bids have been made.

When you make an offer in writing it is binding, provided the seller also accepts it in writing. The seller has to decide which offer to accept, and his written acceptance creates a contract known as 'missives of sale'.

The Scottish system has advantages and disadvantages: it is possible to buy a house in one week, from the first viewing to acceptance of the offer; but before making an offer you must engage a solicitor and a surveyor, with no guarantee that your bid will be accepted, and so could incur heavy costs to no avail if you make several unsuccessful offers.

When selling property in Scotland your solicitor acts as your agent, preparing particulars of the house, advising you on what price to ask, advertising the property, dealing with offers and negotiating the sale. He then deals with the conveyancing in much the same way as an English solicitor.

A new system of land registration in Scotland, called the Registration of Title, was set up in 1981 and is being gradually extended to replace the old Register of Sasines, which is kept in Edinburgh.

House-training pets

Toilet training for cats and dogs

When a cat is new to your home, allow it to explore the place freely, but keep it indoors for at least ten days. Provide a litter box, partly filled with an even layer of commercial cat litter, and remove soiled litter daily. Empty the container and clean it with disinfectant at least twice a week.

A kitten should not be allowed outside or where it could come into contact with other CATS until it has been injected against feline enteritis and flu. This is a two-stage course of injections given when the kitten is nine and thirteen weeks old.

A puppy should not be allowed outside your own house or garden until it has had a course of injections against DISTEMPER and other serious infectious diseases. By this time it is usually about three months old.

Train the puppy to relieve itself on a sheet of newspaper always placed in the same part of the floor. Praise it when it goes where you want it to. In a few days the puppy will automatically head for the spot where you have trained it to go.

Once the puppy can go outside, get it into a routine of being taken outdoors immediately after a meal (and every two hours or so in between). Take the puppy straight to the place where you want it to relieve itself, and praise it immediately it does so.

As the puppy grows, it will be able to contain itself long enough for you to get it outside. But be alert to its needs – if the door to the garden (or the room with the newspaper) is closed and the puppy goes and sits anxiously beside it, that is your cue to rush it outdoors.

If there are any accidents, do not scold the puppy: its inclination is to be clean, so have patience and it will soon learn how to be so.

See also DOG CARE; OBEDIENCE TRAINING.

Hypothermia

Treating victims of creeping cold

Hypothermia, a dangerous lowering of body temperature to 35°C (95°F) or below, can occur indoors or outside. Its onset is gradual and the symptoms are often misleading. They include apathy, shivering, cramps, slurred speech, stumbling gait and erratic, rather confused behaviour. But the overriding symptom of hypothermia is that the skin feels deathly cold – even parts of the body which are normally always warm, such as the armpits and the stomach. If the condition is not recognised and dealt with quickly enough, the shivering will stop and the victim may lapse into unconsciousness and die.

Those most susceptible to hypothermia are babies (especially those which are premature, of low birth-weight or sick) and old people. With very small babies, the cause is most often a cold bedroom at night, but the condition is difficult to recognise because the skin tends to turn bright red. With old people the cause is generally insufficient heating, food and warm clothing in cold weather.

What to do If you suspect hypothermia, call an ambulance immediately.

Move the victim to a warm room if possible, lay him or her down (in the RECOVERY POSITION if unconscious) and wrap the body in a blanket.

Do not attempt any vigorous treatment such as exercise or rubbing the limbs. This draws blood away from the deep core of the body (and, therefore, from the vital organs) where it is needed to sustain life.

If the victim is conscious, give him or her a warm, sweet drink, but not alcohol, which lowers the core temperature.

Remove any wet clothing as soon as you can, since water draws warmth away from the body faster than air.

Ice cream

Making it yourself

Ice cream is easy to make at home, and no special equipment is needed. Here is a simple recipe for vanilla ice cream, enough for six servings. About an hour before you are ready to freeze the ice cream, set the freezer at its coldest setting. Return the setting to normal after the ice cream has been frozen.

Ingredients

285ml (½ pint) milk
1 vanilla pod
1 whole egg
2 egg yolks
75g (3oz) caster sugar
285ml (½ pint) double cream

Put the milk in a saucepan, add the vanilla pod and bring almost to the boil. Remove from the heat and leave to infuse for 15 minutes. Remove the pod.

Beat the egg and egg yolks until pale and creamy, then add the sugar and beat for a further 2 or 3 minutes. Stir in the milk. Pour the mixture into a clean pan. Heat gently, stirring all the time, until it thickens enough to coat the back of a wooden spoon – up to about 10 minutes. Pour into a bowl and leave to cool, stirring from time to time to prevent a skin forming. When cool, lightly whip the cream. Fold it into the custard.

Pour the custard into a 600-900ml (about 1-2 pint) freezer container. Freeze, uncovered, until it is slushy and ice granules are forming at the edges – about an hour. Turn into a chilled bowl and beat until smooth. Return to the freezer container, uncovered, and freeze for several hours until firm. Cover and refreeze.

Homemade ice cream can be stored in the freezer for up to three months. About an hour before serving, transfer it from the freezer to the refrigerator to soften.

Ice removal

Making steps, paths and drives safe in winter

Prevention is better than cure, so if possible remove snow from steps and paths immediately after a snowfall, before it can get compacted to form ice. Use a simple snow pusher made by inserting a square of hardboard between the tines of a garden fork. Then sweep away the residue with a stiff broom.

If ice does form, you can chip it away with a spade, or sprinkle it lightly with salt to melt it. Do not use large amounts of salt, as this will damage CONCRETE.

With the path clear, sprinkle sand, gravel or ash on the surface to give a grip should a frost occur overnight and the path freeze over.

Where steps are very smooth and prone to icing, coat them with exterior grade emulsion paint or tile paint with a quantity of silver sand added. The gritty surface will afford better grip – though it will not last more than a couple of seasons.

Ice skating

Getting started; basic figure skating

Dress comfortably for ice skating – and warmly for outdoor skating.

Skates can usually be rented at ice rinks; use figure skates. The blades of figure skates have two knife-sharp edges, one running the length of each side of the blade, enabling the skater to glide on an inside or outside edge.

The boots should fit snugly and hug the heel, but at the top you should be able to insert two fingers on one side.

Before getting onto the ice, accustom yourself to the skates by walking around on them. Keep on the slip-on covers – or guards – which protect the edges. Skate guards are not provided with rental skates, but can be purchased when buying your own skating equipment. At first you will have trouble balancing, but this will soon pass.

Getting onto the ice Choose a time when the ice is uncrowded. Remove the guards from the skates and step carefully onto the ice, holding onto the barrier. Keeping hold of the barrier, pull yourself away from the entrance, sliding your skates along the ice as you go. Do not attempt to walk normally on them.

Let go of the barrier and accustom yourself to standing unsupported on the skates. Balance yourself, and twist your ankles slightly to feel the blade edges of your skates grip the ice.

Pushing off and forward Keep your body straight, head up, knees slightly bent and feet a few inches apart. Relax your arms, holding them at waist level. Position your feet so that they form a T-

Learning how to move and stop

Pushing off With right instep against left heel and knees slightly bent, straighten the right leg and glide on the left skate.

Snow-ploughing to a stop The easiest way to stop is to force both heels outwards and bring the knees together.

Making a T-stop Bring the instep of your free foot against the heel of your skating foot. Lower it to the ice gradually.

Getting up Kneel, hands flat on the ice. Bring one foot forward, then the other foot forward. Rise slowly.

shape with the left heel touching the right instep. Bend both knees and transfer your weight to your left foot. Dig into the ice slightly with the inside edge of your right skate.

Push yourself off by straightening your right leg, and glide forward on your left skate keeping your knee bent. Raise your right leg behind you with the toe pointing outwards and downwards an inch or two above the ice. You should find yourself gliding in a slight curve to the left.

Bring the right foot forward and lower it onto the ice beside the left foot. Glide forward on both skates. Practise pushing off in this way, first with one foot then with the other.

Now try sustaining the forward movement. Push off on your right skate. When you start to run out of forward movement, lower the left foot onto the ice at a 45 degree angle to the right foot with the left heel against the right instep. Transfer your weight onto the left foot and push off on your left skate. Raise your right leg behind with toe pointing out and down. Continue in this way.

Cornering and stopping When negotiating corners or bends, cross your feet one in front of the other. Most ice rinks operate in an anticlockwise direction, so, with your left foot forward, leaning on the outside edge, bring your right foot from behind to brush the inside of your left foot and continue through, crossing wide in front of your left foot. When your right foot touches the ice, transfer your weight onto it and lift the left foot off the ice. Your right shoulder should be pointing forwards and your left shoulder behind you. Repeat until you complete the bend.

You can stop by using the snow-plough method or, when you are more confident, the T-stop. Bring your free foot against the heel of the skating foot to form a T-shape. Gradually lower the free foot until the outside edge of the skate is touching the ice. Slowly transfer your weight onto this skate until you stop.

Making a figure of eight Take up a T-position, with your right heel against your left instep and your right shoulder and arm pointing in the same direction as your right foot.

Push off on your right skate, keeping your right knee bent. Raise your left foot off the ice with the knee slightly bent and the toe pointing downwards and outwards. Skate in a circle to the right, leaning into the circle so that you are skating on the outside edge of the right skate. Keep your body and skating leg rigid, with your right shoulder and arm pointing round the line of the circle. Do not bend your ankle.

When you have gone halfway round the circle, start to turn your shoulders

so that the left shoulder comes forward. At the same time start to bring the free, left leg forward. Straighten your right skating leg momentarily as the left leg passes it. When these movements are finished, you should be where you started.

Bring your left skate down at 45 degrees to the right. Push off on your left skate and make a circle to your left, following the same procedure as for the right, only in reverse.

Falling Do not be afraid of falling when skating – but learn to do it correctly. Keep your hands up as you start to slip. Bend your knees and sit down.

WARNING If skating on a frozen pond or lake, make sure it has at least 100mm (4in) of clear ice or 200mm (8in) of cloudy ice. Check for cracks, weak spots or broken areas. Do not skate alone.

Icing cakes

Two ways of decorating small or large cakes

To add a finishing touch to small cakes, sponges and layer cakes, ice them with soft glacé icing. Decorate large fruit cakes with royal icing, which is harder and is the traditional finish for Christmas and birthday cakes, but first coat the cake with MARZIPAN to prevent the cake staining the white icing.

Glacé icing The following recipe makes enough icing to coat the top of a cake 150-200mm (6-8in) in diameter, or 12-18 small cakes or buns.

Ingredients
115g (4oz) icing sugar
1-2 tablespoons warm water
Colouring or flavouring if desired

Sift the icing sugar into a deep bowl and gradually add the water, stirring with a wooden spoon until the mixture is thick enough to coat the back of the spoon. Add more water or sugar to get the right consistency, and add a few drops of colouring or flavouring if desired.

Put the cake, or cakes, on a wire tray over a plate. Pour the icing over the cake – just enough to cover the tops of small cakes or buns – or spread it over a large cake with a palette knife.

Royal icing This recipe makes enough icing to cover the top and sides of a cake which is 250mm (10in) in diameter and 50mm (2in) deep.

Ingredients
4 egg whites
800-900g (1¾-2lb) icing sugar
1 tablespoon lemon juice
2 teaspoons glycerine

Whisk the egg whites in a large bowl until frothy. Gradually stir in half the sifted icing sugar, then beat until the icing is smooth. When half the sugar has been added, beat in the lemon juice. Add more sugar a little at a time and beat until the icing forms soft peaks when pulled up with a wooden spoon. Stir in the glycerine, which will stop the icing from going hard.

To make royal icing in an electric mixer, set the control to medium speed and whisk the egg whites before adding the icing sugar. Do not overbeat the icing as it will become rough and will not spread smoothly.

Leave the icing, covered with a damp cloth or cling film to prevent a crust forming, for 24 hours before using it. Spread it evenly over the top and sides of the cake, with a palette knife which has been dipped in water, to a thickness of about 3mm (⅛in). On a Christmas cake you can lift the icing into small peaks to create a snow effect. Leave to set for 24 hours before decorating – see CAKE DECORATING.

Immersion heaters

*Adjusting the thermostat;
replacing the heater element*

An immersion heater can be mounted inside the hot water cylinder in a number of different ways – with a single heater element mounted vertically or horizontally; with two separate elements mounted horizontally and spaced well apart, or with a dual element mounted vertically. The advantage of two elements is that either a large or a small amount of water can be heated, according to need – by switching on one or both elements, or the larger element can be used on cheap night rate electricity. An immersion heater is sometimes used to supplement a boiler, which does not have the same degree of heat control. See also WATER HEATERS.

Adjusting the thermostat A temperature of 60°C (140°F) is recommended for domestic hot water. Any hotter than this and you increase the risk of hard water scale forming on the heating element – see also WATER SOFTENERS. To check or set this temperature, turn off the heater at the main switch and remove the relevant fuse (see FUSES AND FUSE BOXES), then undo the screw securing the heater cover. Inside is a thermostat: insert a screwdriver in the slot and turn the screw to the recommended setting. Replace the cover and circuit fuse, and switch on the power again.

Element descaling If the heater has run at too high a temperature for some time, you may find the water does not heat quickly, or there are rumbling noises in the cylinder. This happens when a coating of lime scale forms on the element, which can cause it to burn out.

Remove the element from the cylinder, then immerse it in a DESCALING fluid.

Removing an element Switch off the electricity supply at the main fuse box; if the cylinder is also heated by alternative means, allow it to cool. Turn off the water supply to the cylinder.

Either turn off the gate valve in the feed pipe from the cold water storage cistern, or drain the cistern by tying up the ball cock (see BALL COCKS) and running the bathroom cold taps until the water stops flowing. Drain water from the cylinder drain cock – the amount

you will need to drain will depend on the location of the heater element or elements, but the water must be drained to below the level of the heater fitting.

A special immersion heater spanner is needed to remove the element, which fits over the large nut holding it in place, as illustrated. If necessary, the spanner is usually available from a tool hire shop.

Use the special spanner to unscrew the heater element and lift it from the cylinder.

Replacing an element When putting in a new element, always use the new washer supplied with it, to ensure a watertight seal. If you are simply replacing an element after descaling it, get a replacement washer from a plumbers' merchant or hardware store which stocks immersion heaters.

Screw in the element, tighten it with the special spanner and replace the wiring. Use heat resistant three-core cable (at least 1.5mm^2 – see ELECTRIC WIRING); make sure that the terminals are tight and the wires tucked well in, so that the cover does not catch on them.

If you want to replace a single element heater with a dual model, consult an electrician: you probably need two flexes connected to a special changeover switch.

Installing an immersion heater for the first time is straightforward if the cylinder already has a fitting to accept it. Otherwise a hole must be cut, and this is best left to an expert.

Immunisation

Protecting your child against serious diseases

From their birth until the time they leave school, children should have a series of immunisations against various serious diseases.

Have the vaccinations done by your family DOCTOR if possible, because there are certain circumstances under which a child should not be vaccinated, and your doctor will know of them. For example, a child that has suffered brain damage, is prone to epileptic fits or has a close relative with epilepsy should not be immunised against whooping cough unless the doctor considers it safe. Similarly it may not be safe to give measles vaccine to a child suffering from leukaemia or Hodgkin's disease, or if the child has an allergy – for example, EGGS. You should also tell the doctor if the child is on any kind of drugs.

When a baby is two months old, vaccination is given against diphtheria, tetanus, whooping cough and HiB (haemophilus influenza). At the same time polio vaccine is given in the form of drops. Four weeks later the treatment is

---

IMMERSION HEATERS

Renewing an immersion heater; setting the thermostat

To renew an immersion heater, turn off the main switch and remove the relevant fuse from the fuse box. Drain the cylinder. Remove the heater cover, disconnect the wires, unscrew the heater with the appropriate spanner and extract it. Insert the new heater, screw it home and rewire as shown below. Screw on the retaining cap.

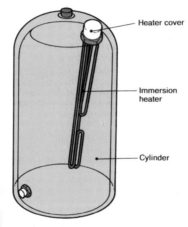

Heater cover

Immersion heater

Cylinder

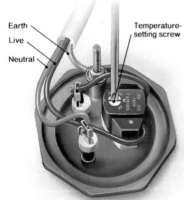

Earth
Live
Neutral
Temperature-setting screw

Resetting the thermostat Unscrew and remove the heater cover. Adjust the temperature-setting screw with a screwdriver, to 60°C.

Alternative spanners Use a flat immersion heater spanner to unscrew the old element and draw it out. For a deep-lagged cylinder, use a large box spanner, turned with a bar.

Taping up the element thread Bind PTFE thread-sealing tape about three times anticlockwise round the thread on the element plug. Screw into the cylinder.

repeated, and again after a further four weeks.

At 13 months immunisation against measles, mumps and German measles is given in one injection.

Diphtheria, tetanus and polio immunisations are given again at between four or five years, and at 10-13 years a vaccination against tuberculosis may be given if a skin test shows that the child does not have a natural immunity to the disease.

At 15 years, or on leaving school, children should have further tetanus and polio immunisation.

Impetigo

What it is and how to treat it

Impetigo is a skin infection which generally affects the exposed parts of the body, particularly the face, hands or knees. It is most common in children – though it occasionally occurs in adults too.

The first symptoms are red spots which become watery BLISTERS. These burst leaving yellow, crusty sores. Impetigo is highly infectious, and more spots and sores rapidly develop around the original area of infection. If not treated it can last for several weeks.

Treatment Consult the DOCTOR as soon as possible. He may prescribe an antibiotic ointment to be applied to the infected areas or, if the attack is severe, he may prescribe antibiotic tablets or mixture.

You should also wash the infected area frequently with antiseptic diluted in warm water to help to restrict the infection. If the sufferer is a child, make sure he does not touch or scratch the sores. Wash his towels, flannels and clothes separately from those of the rest of the family.

Properly treated, impetigo should clear up rapidly.

Income tax returns

What to declare, and claim

There are two important things to remember when filling in a tax return – it is illegal not to declare all your taxable income, and you should be sure to claim all the reliefs and allowances due to you, or you may pay more than necessary.

Taxable income Your pay from your job is taxed under Pay As You Earn (PAYE) and is deducted from your salary by your employer, unless you are self-employed – see HOME WORK; SELF EMPLOYMENT. On your tax return you must state your gross salary for the year, which is shown on the form P60 given to you by your employer at the end of each tax year.

You may also be taxed on expenses paid to you by your employer, as reimbursement for out-of-pocket expenses you have incurred while carrying out your duties. If you are, you should state on your tax return that these were expenses notified to the tax inspector by your employer on form P11D.

If you receive benefits in kind (or 'perks') instead of cash payments, you may pay less tax. How much less will depend on whether you earn more than £8500 from your employment in any one year, including perks. If you earn less, you will not pay tax on most benefits in kind, including the loan of a car, a uniform or other clothes, on free or cheap meals supplied in the staff canteen, or on most other benefits. The general rule is that if you cannot sell the benefit, you cannot be taxed on it.

If you earn over £8500, you pay tax on these perks, but at special rates. You will usually still be better off receiving the loan of a car rather than the cash to buy or hire one. Small interest-free loans will also be of benefit, but you will be charged tax if you are given a free season ticket. You will normally be charged tax on the amount it costs the employer to provide your benefit.

If you have a part-time job in addition to your main employment, carry out work at home for which you get paid, for example freelance writing, or run a small business such as a market stall or a mobile disco, you must declare your income from that source.

Payments made to you by your employer in lieu of notice or as redundancy pay are not taxed, up to a limit of £30,000. Neither is a lump sum paid for an injury that ended your job.

Most PENSIONS are taxable, some that are not include: industrial injuries disablement pensions, war widow's pensions and war disablement pensions. Some social security benefits are taxable or part taxable. Included among them are widow's pensions, industrial death benefits, invalid care allowance and unemployment benefits or income support arising from unemployment.

If you are receiving rent from letting property it is taxed as investment income, but for furnished property part or all of the income may be taxed as earnings. Income from holiday lettings is treated as earned income, and should be shown separately from other furnished property on the tax return.

Interest from most types of investment is taxed, those that are not include: ENDOWMENT POLICIES; NATIONAL SAVINGS certificates; Premium Bond prizes and BUILDING SOCIETIES Save-As-You-Earn schemes. Betting and lottery wins are also tax-free.

The interest on savings with Building Societies and BANK ACCOUNTS is taxed before you get it, and if you are a non-tax payer you cannot claim it back. Even though the tax is paid at source, you must enter the amount of interest, and the name of the Building Society or bank on the tax return form. Interest on National Savings Bank ordinary deposit accounts is exempt from tax on the first £70 that is earned, but the full amount must be entered.

Tax allowances Everyone is allowed to earn a certain amount before paying tax, and the amount depends on your marital status.

The incomes of married couples are no longer added together for income tax purposes. Instead, everyone is treated as a single person, given a personal allowance (the same amount for everyone) and subject to independent taxation.

If you are married and living with your husband or wife, you can claim a married couple's allowance. This is normally given to the husband, but if both request it, the allowance is transferred to the wife.

An unmarried couple living together do not get this allowance, nor does a single parent. However, if they, or one of them, claims child benefit for one or more children (see SOCIAL SECURITY) they can claim an additional personal allowance of the same amount as the married couple's allowance.

If you are divorced or separated from your wife (or husband) and paying maintenance, you can claim tax relief on the amount of the maintenance, up to the level of the married couple's allowance. More generous rules apply if the maintenance started before March 14, 1988.

If you are over 65 a higher allowance is paid, and it is further increased if you are over 75. A special allowance is paid if a taxpayer is blind, and registered as such with the local authority.

You can get tax relief on MORTGAGES, but this is limited to the interest paid (not the repayments) on the first £30,000 of a loan on a house. This is allowable if the house is bought as an only or main home, or it is let for over half the year. If two or more people buy the house jointly, the relief is shared between them. If they bought the house before August 1988, each can claim full relief.

Dealing with the taxman Whenever you are in doubt about any aspect of your tax return, write to, telephone or visit your Inspector of Taxes. Similarly, notify him if you think that your PAYE coding is wrong, if you do not agree with your tax bill, or you discover that for years you have not been claiming an allowance you were entitled to.

Indelible ink

Using it – and removing it

Certain so-called indelible inks can, if you know how, be removed. But ink used in clothes markers and laundry markers is intended to be just that – indelible.

When using ball-point markers, mark the fabric first with a soft pencil and then go over it with the pen. This avoids blurring and spreading.

As mistakes and accidents may occur, buy the kind of marker which requires ironing to fix the ink. Provided you catch any stain before ironing, the ink can be removed with methylated spirit as for a mark caused by a ball-point pen – see CLEANING AND POLISHING MATERIALS.

To remove 'indelible' ink marks, first try soap – by far the safest treatment for most fabrics – and rinse in lukewarm water. Or soak the mark in hot, sour milk which can work effectively, if slowly, but may further stain the fabric. Hair lacquer may take away the mark – but may also leave a mark of its own.

Methylated spirit works quickly to remove ball-point, felt pen and some other inks. But it may also remove any dye and should not be used on acetate, triacetate or nylon material. Whichever remover you use, test its effect on an inconspicuous piece of the same fabric first.

If all else fails, write to the ink manufacturers for cleaning advice and ask what kind of dye the ink contains or if they can recommend a solvent. If necessary, take the stained material to a dry cleaner, give the dye name and ask if anything can be done. Fabrics such as silk chiffon and brocade should always be dry-cleaned.

See also CLEANING SOLVENTS; STAIN REMOVAL.

Indigestion

What to do about discomfort after eating

Indigestion is usually caused by eating too much rich, fried or fatty foods, or by drinking too much alcohol. Symptoms include burping, HICCUPS, discomfort in the top of the abdomen, a hot sensation behind the breastbone (see HEARTBURN), flatulence and NAUSEA.

To relieve the symptoms take half a teaspoon of bicarbonate of soda in a glass of water, or antacid tablets which can be bought from a chemist without a doctor's prescription. Drink small amounts of non-alcoholic fluids, and rest in an easy chair.

For more lasting relief, smoke less and change your eating habits. Eat smaller amounts more often and more slowly. Cut down on alcohol, spicy foods, dairy products, beans, onions and seasonings

such as black pepper, vinegar and garlic.

Occasionally, indigestion can be caused by duodenal or gastric ULCERS or a hiatus hernia. If symptoms occur frequently, grow progressively worse, or are accompanied by VOMITING, abdominal pain, coughing, or loss of appetite or weight, see your DOCTOR.

Information

Finding sources

Sources of information can be surprisingly close to hand. A pocket diary, for example, often contains maps, metric conversion tables, sports fixtures and information of a specialised nature, depending on its particular theme.

Daily newspapers give weather forecasts, TV programmes and many other entertainment listings – not to mention currency exchange rates, share prices and sports results. Local information, entertainment and events appear in local newspapers; classified press advertisements cover a wide range of goods and services. Local radio stations may also offer consumer advice and information.

A telephone provides quick contact with a vast range of information sources; the directory lists emergency numbers and telephone services, and sometimes numbers for specific information such as weather, sporting results or even cookery. *Yellow Pages* directories list major local and national companies.

Impartial advice on goods and services is provided by the Consumers Association, 2 Marylebone Road, London NW1 4DX; they also publish the monthly *Which?* magazine, examining and assessing consumer products.

If your query concerns activities or services administered by the local council, consult your telephone directory and contact the relevant department.

Her Majesty's Stationery Office, PO Box 276, London SW8 5DT, will answer questions on published government documents and books, which can also be ordered or bought direct from its bookshop at 49 High Holborn, London WC1V 6HB. An invaluable HMSO annual is *Britain – An Official Handbook*.

To contact government departments direct, look up their address in *Vacher's Parliamentary Companion*, usually available at your local library, where other major reference books may include:
* *Black's Medical Dictionary*.
* *Burke's Peerage* (and *Landed Gentry*).
* *Citizens Advice Notes* – a digest of government legislation.
* *Councils, Committees and Boards*.
* *Crockford's Clerical Directory*.
* *Debrett's Correct Form* and *Etiquette and Modern Manners*.
* *Dictionary of National Biography*.
* *Directory of British Associations*.

* *Elderly People – Rights and Opportunities* by J. Manthorpe.
* *Encyclopaedia Britannica*.
* *Everyman's Dictionary of Dates*.
* *Gray's Anatomy*.
* *Guide to Social Services*.
* *Guinness Book of Records*.
* *Keesing's Record of World Events* (a daily record).
* *The Oxford Companion* arts series.
* *Reader's Digest – You and Your Rights*.
* *Research; a Handbook for Writers and Journalists* by Ann Hoffman, published by A. & C. Black, provides sources of information and contact addresses for national and international information.
* *The Statesman's Yearbook* (a world gazetteer).
* *The Times Atlas of the World*.
* *The Times Atlas of World History*.
* *Whitaker's Almanack* (a condensed year book and general reference encyclopaedia).
* *Who's Who* (also its international edition).
* *Willing's* or *Benn's* guides to newspapers and periodicals.

Ingrowing toenails

Relieving the pain and preventing a recurrence

The front corners of an ingrowing toenail – usually on the big toe – dig into the surrounding skin, causing pain and inflammation. The usual cause is wearing shoes that are too tight, or cutting off the corners of the nail.

To lessen the pain and prevent possible infection, soak pieces of gauze in surgical spirit and tuck them beneath the corners of the nail twice a day. Never cut away the sides of a nail.

If the area becomes infected, or if the pain persists, see your doctor – who may prescribe an antiseptic ointment or antibiotic. If the problem persists, a small operation can be performed, under local anaesthetic if necessary, stopping any further nail growth. To prevent the condition, wear comfortably fitting shoes, avoid tightly fitting socks, and use nail clippers to cut your nails so that they are square, not curved.

Insect bites and stings

Dealing with a painful and occasionally serious problem

In most cases, insect bites and stings are more painful than dangerous. But they can be serious, and in rare cases prove fatal if the sufferer has an allergic reaction (see ALLERGIES) or if he is bitten or stung in the throat or mouth. If necessary, take a sufferer to the Accident and Emergency Department of a hospital.

Bees, wasps and ants The pain caused by a bee or wasp sting is immediate and sometimes intense. The site becomes inflamed and swollen and starts to itch. If the sufferer is allergic to the sting, severe swelling may occur rapidly – followed by swelling on other parts of the body. He may collapse, become unconscious (see UNCONSCIOUSNESS), or stop breathing. Make sure that the airway is clear, start ARTIFICIAL RESPIRATION and then get expert medical help.

Honey bees are the only insects which leave the entire sting in the wound. Scrape out the sting with a fingernail. Apply antihistamine cream to the wound. Wasp and ant stings should also be treated with the cream.

Stings to the throat or mouth can make the throat swell rapidly, blocking the airway. To reduce the swelling, give the sufferer sips of cold water, or an ice cube to suck. If his breathing is difficult or noisy, get expert medical help as soon as possible.

Mosquitoes and midges Bites from mosquitoes and midges may not be noticed at first – the itching starts later. Wash the bites with soap and cold water and apply antihistamine cream. If there is an allergic reaction – such as severe swelling – get medical attention quickly.

See also BEEKEEPING; INSECT REPELLENTS; TICKS; WASPS.

Insect repellents

Keeping pests away

Insecticide sprays and powders are the most effective way of dealing with household insect pests. They are sold in most supermarkets and hardware and chemists' shops.

A cheap and easy-to-make (if rather smelly) insect repellent is a solution of equal quantities of paraffin, milk and water. Mix the paraffin and milk first and then add the water. Apply the solution to walls, windowframes, light fittings and so on. Hair lacquer makes a handy spray for gumming up the wings of flying insects. Flies are said to be repelled by mint, and hanging baskets of mint are a useful deterrent.

Mosquitoes and gnats are most troublesome if you live near a river or lake. To keep them off your skin – particularly at night – cover the whole body with a proprietary insect repellent, available as a gel, stick or spray. The most effective types contain diethyl toluamide. Also apply repellent to sheets and clothing – they last longer on cloth than on your skin. Failing these, use camomile lotion, oil of cloves – or plain vinegar.

Flexible fly screens which fit over window openings are available. See also INSECT BITES AND STINGS; MOTHPROOFING.

Insomnia

How to overcome persistant sleep problems

There are no firm rules about how much sleep is necessary, but on average most adults sleep about eight hours a night. Others need up to ten hours sleep, and some people need as few as four or five.

Losing a couple of hours sleep at night does you no physical harm, but it may make you irritable, nervy or listless.

Poor sleeping can have a number of causes, the most common of which is worry – about money, work or your personal life. Depression can also disrupt sleep, particularly through early waking.

Avoid taking stimulants – tea, coffee, cigarettes – shortly before going to bed; eating rich and indigestible meals late in the evening; taking naps during the day; becoming agitated by tackling work problems or watching an exciting film shortly before going to bed.

There are several effective ways of relieving insomnia. Take daily exercise such as JOGGING, BICYCLE RIDING or walking the dog. Have a warm bath at bedtime, or have a drink of malted milk or warm milk in bed. Make sure the amount of bedding is right for the room temperature, so that you are not too hot or too cold. Try reading in bed in order to relax, or simply count sheep. Take up RELAXATION EXERCISES or YOGA.

If insomnia persists, see your DOCTOR. Sleeping pills, which can help lessen STRESS or tension, are only a temporary solution to the problem, and do not deal with the root causes. Some people become dependent on the pills, and it is best to avoid them if possible.

Insulation

Keeping the cold out and the warmth in

Efficient insulation, combined with DRAUGHTPROOFING, can cut fuel bills by as much as 50 per cent. So money spent on insulation is a good investment. Before you begin, check with your local authority or Citizens Advice Bureau for the latest details of GRANTS towards loft insulation and tank lagging. It is important that should a grant be available, you apply for it before any work is done. You will also be told which materials are acceptable by the local authority, and what thicknesses should be used.

Effective insulation in areas like the loft space will put plumbing more at risk, so be sure to protect pipes and tanks – see FROST PROTECTION; PIPE LAGGING.

The roof space This is the first area to tackle, as up to 25 per cent of the warmth in your home can escape through the roof. Make sure you have safe access to

Spreading loose-fill insulation evenly

To get the loose-fill to an even depth, use a T-shaped gauge made from scrap wood. The gauge's arms should rest on the joists.

the loft – ideally by means of a loft ladder. If the loft is not boarded over, place stout planks across the floor JOISTS so you have something to walk or kneel on. Never put your weight on the lath-and-plaster or PLASTERBOARD between the joists – your feet will go through.

You have the choice of insulating the loft floor, or, if the loft is to be used for more than storage space, you can insulate the underside of the rafters. Insulating the floor gives the best heat saving. If you insulate the rafters, the whole loft space will become warm – and that can be a very large volume of heat.

The most common material used is glass fibre blanket supplied in rolls, usually 400mm (16in) wide. It is, however, very bulky – both to get home and to get up into the loft space. Choose 100mm (4in) thick blanket for the best results.

Before you start work, vacuum the whole area and, at the same time, take the opportunity to check for signs of WOODWORM. Wear a face mask to keep dust and fibres out of your lungs, and wear gloves tucked into an old long-sleeved shirt.

If the space between the joists is less than 400mm, use a panel saw to cut the blanket while it is still rolled and in its wrapper. Some insulation blanket is supplied with a foil or plastic backing, to prevent condensation in the roof space. Otherwise, buy foil-backed building paper or polythene and lay it between the joists before laying the blanket. Lay foil-backed paper foil-side down.

Roll out the blanket between joists. Continue laying rolls, butting the ends as rolls run out. Take the insulation close to the eaves, but leave a small air gap of about 50mm (2in) so that some air can circulate in the loft space to reduce the risk of condensation. Lag the hatch door as well. Cover it with blanket held in place with string wound round tacks hammered along the door edges.

Other materials available for loft insulation include vermiculite and pelleted mineral wool, which are tipped between joists to a depth of about 100mm. To get a regular thickness, make up a simple depth gauge from scrap wood. One part should rest on the two joists, while a centre piece spreads the loose-fill to the correct depth.

Do not take insulation under the cold water storage tank. This will allow some heat from below to reach it and keep the chill off.

If you wish to insulate the roof rather than the loft floor, the job is simple provided there is bitumen felting under the tiles. Lay insulating blanket between the rafters, holding it in place with string wound around tacks. Nail insulation board or sheet plasterboard to the rafters with plasterboard nails. Make sure adjoining sheets meet at the centre of a rafter.

If there is no felting and you can see daylight through cracks, fix waterproof building paper down between the rafters, pinning it to the sides of the rafters with brass drawing pins. Start at the top and work down, overlapping sheets by at least 100mm. Be sure to run the bottom edge of the paper out at the eaves so that no rainwater or melting snow can drip into the loft space. Once this has been done, you can insulate as you would for a felted roof.

Cavity walls There is no DIY system for filling the cavity. Get quotes from specialist companies, recommended by the National Cavity Insulation Association, PO Box 12, Haslemere, Surrey GU27 3AH. Companies offer either a dry pelleted system, or a foam system. Both are equally effective if installed correctly. The foam tends to be cheaper than the dry system. The job is normally completed within a day.

Solid walls Special insulating plasterboards are available with which to line internal walls, but it is a complex job, involving the removal of SKIRTING BOARDS, architraves, ELECTRIC SOCKETS AND SWITCHES. The alternative is to consider cladding the outside of the wall either with shiplap boarding or vertical hung tiling. This causes less disturbance, but can be a costly exercise – see WALL CLADDING; PLASTIC WALL CLADDING.

Floors Timber floors need no insulating, as timber is a natural insulator. However, older timber floors may allow draughts through between the boards, and a covering such as underlay and carpet (see CARPET LAYING) or foam-backed vinyl (see VINYL FLOOR COVERING) will help. CONCRETE floors are much colder and heat can be lost by absorption into the concrete. Again, covering concrete with cork tiles, vinyl or carpet will

insulate the cold surface. Even PARQUET or strip wood flooring gives protection.

Windows Heavy curtains will help insulate windows, but best results will be achieved by draughtproofing and DOUBLE GLAZING.

See also FROST PROTECTION.

Insurance

Insuring your life and your home

There are three basic types of life insurance: term, whole-life and endowment – see ENDOWMENT POLICIES. A term policy is taken out to cover an agreed period of time; if you die within that time your dependants receive the amount you have insured yourself for – but you get nothing back if you live beyond the term. A whole-life policy provides permanent protection for your family, who will receive benefits when you die.

The cost of life insurance varies from company to company, but the younger you are, the lower the premiums will be, and above a certain age, usually 50, you may be required to have a thorough medical check-up.

How to buy insurance You may be attracted to one particular insurance company by personal recommendation or by a newspaper advertisement, but you can also consult an insurance broker or other insurance intermediary. His services will usually cost you nothing, since he earns his living from the commission he gets from the insurance company (those selling motor or household insurances may charge a fee). So it is in his interest to sell you an expensive policy, but if you are sure of the type you want, how long it is to run and the premiums you can afford to pay, and are determined not to be persuaded otherwise, you should be able to get a policy that suits you – not the broker. A broker's advice can be particularly useful when buying a with-profits endowment policy – he will know which companies are the most prosperous, and therefore pay the best bonuses.

Insuring your possessions There are two types of insurance you can buy to protect your home and its contents. A buildings policy, sometimes called a 'bricks and mortar' policy, insures you against the cost of the loss of or damage to your home. If you have a mortgage the mortgagee will insist that you have such a policy and will arrange it for you.

The cover you get varies from company to company, but usually includes such things as fire, floods, accidental breakage of glass, storm damage and burst water pipes. It will not cover you for normal wear and tear or damage that

has been caused by your own neglect.

The amount that you should insure your home for should be the cost of rebuilding, not its sale value. Rebuilding costs will depend on the area in which you live, and one way to get an accurate estimate is to ask a local builder. You can, however, make a good estimate yourself by using the leaflet 'Buildings Insurance for Home Owners', published by the Association of British Insurers. To obtain the leaflet, send a stamped, addressed envelope to: The Association of British Insurers, 51 Gresham Street, London EC2V 7HQ.

As building costs are rising all the time it is best to have an index-linked policy – the cover is linked to an index of building costs and is adjusted monthly.

Contents insurance policies cover the loss or damage of household effects, personal effects, valuables and money. They will also cover you for certain legal liabilities. For example, compensation you may have to pay if your dog bites the postman, or if you or a member of your family cause injury to others or damage their property. (But not motoring accidents – see CAR INSURANCE.)

There are three types of contents insurance: indemnity, new-for-old, and a mixture of both. An indemnity policy only compensates you for the actual value of items lost. With a new-for-old policy, however, you get what it would cost to replace the items, whatever their age or condition. The sum insured under these policies must equal the cost of replacing the contents by new, otherwise you may not recover a loss in full.

With the mixed policy, some items such as furniture, electrical appliances and TV, radio and hi-fi equipment get new-for-old cover, the rest get indemnity.

To estimate the value of your home's contents, make a room-by-room INVENTORY. If you are insuring valuable things like jewellery and antiques, have them valued professionally.

International road signs

Recognising them and understanding their meaning

Many of the road signs used throughout Europe are already familiar to British drivers, and those that are not are usually easily identifiable by the symbol displayed. All international road signs fall into two main categories – those that must be obeyed, and those that warn.

Traffic signs that must be obeyed are usually circular with a red border, or blue with a white rim. The exception is the 'Give Way' sign – an inverted red triangle. Warning signs are usually rectangular or triangular (not inverted). Some blue rectangular signs inform, such as 'Tourist Office', and 'Camping site'.

Getting to know the more common signs

All European road signs have some features in common which may help you to understand them. Important ones you may encounter are shown here.

Danger warning signs

Road intersection – drivers on the 'thinner' road must give way.

Level crossing.

Level crossing with gates.

Road leads onto river bank or a quay.

Swing bridge.

Road intersects a tram line.

  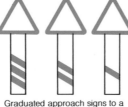

Cattle crossing.

Crosswind.

Graduated approach signs to a level crossing.

Informative signs

Advance warning of a diversion.

Direction of a priority road.

Tram stop.

Mountain road open or closed to traffic, and the name of the pass.

Standing and parking signs

Parking prohibited on the left on odd dates, and on the right on even dates.

Exit from a limited duration parking zone.

Prohibitory and regulatory signs

No vehicles loaded above fixed amount of flammables or explosives.

No vehicles loaded above fixed amount of water pollutants.

No entry for motorised or animal-drawn vehicles.

No entry for vehicles wider than 2m (6ft).

No entry for vehicles over 5 tons laden weight.

No entry for motorised vehicles pulling a trailer other than a semi-trailer or single-axle trailer.

Use of audible warning devices prohibited.

Do not pass Customs without stopping.

Local prohibitions on vehicles end.

End of a 'no overtaking' zone.

Signs regulating priority at intersections

Give way.

Priority road.

Priority ends.

Signs giving notice of facilities

Breakdown service.

Camping and caravan site.

Youth hostel.

Starting point for walks.

Introductions

Following the rules of etiquette

When introducing people, the essential rules to remember are that men are introduced to women, younger people to those who are older, and people of lesser rank or importance to those who are more important. Traditionally, too, an unmarried woman is introduced to a married woman. Occasionally, these rules conflict, in which case they have to be interpreted with flexibility and common sense. It may well be more appropriate, for example, to introduce a young woman to an elderly and distinguished man, than the other way round.

Making an introduction When making an introduction, speak clearly so that the people being introduced are able to catch each other's names straightaway. Whether you introduce them simply by their Christian and surnames ('Mary, this is Mike Patterson – Mary Downing') or more formally, using Mr, Mrs, Miss or their rank or title, depends largely on their ages and the formality of the gathering. If you are in any doubt, it is usually safer to err on the side of formality, especially with introductions to older people.

When introducing a child or teenager to an adult it is customary to give the child or teenager's Christian name but to introduce the adult more formally: 'May I introduce my son Simon. Simon, this is Dr Steel.' The adult can then if he wishes invite the younger person to call him by his Christian name.

It is also polite to tell the people being introduced something about each other. But do not feel you have to give their life stories, or even say what their jobs are. You are trying to launch them into an interesting conversation – and at the end of a busy day, for example, work may be the last thing they feel like talking about. 'Cathy and I were at college together' or 'Mike is a cricket fanatic' might be more suitable openings.

If you are the host or hostess of a reasonably small party or gathering, you should introduce each guest to all the others. At a larger party, introduce each guest to at least one other, preferably someone with whom he or she will have plenty in common. At very large gatherings or receptions, it is quite normal for the guests to introduce themselves to one another.

Being introduced When being introduced to someone, it is polite to stand up, if you were sitting, and to shake hands. At the same time you should say, 'How do you do?', 'Good morning', 'Good evening' – or in informal gatherings simply 'Hello'.

It is especially important to shake hands with foreigners. In most countries, the handshake is used much more than in Britain and to omit it can be regarded as unfriendly or rude. If someone is introduced to a group of people, make an effort to include him or her in the general conversation.

Inventory

Making a room-by-room valuation of your possessions

When you take out a home contents INSURANCE policy you must make sure that the sum insured is equal to the full value of all your possessions. If it is not, and you lose everything, say by FIRE, the insurance company will only pay you the amount for which you are insured, and you could be faced with heavy costs when you replace the lost items. And if some of your possessions are partly damaged, the insurance company will only pay a proportion of the value, based on the proportion of the sum insured to the total value.

You should also know the individual value of each item, so that you can claim on your insurance if any are damaged, stolen or destroyed.

Calculating your sum insured Go from room to room, not forgetting the garage and shed, carefully estimating what it would cost to replace every item at current prices. Have JEWELLERY, ANTIQUES and paintings valued professionally. For items covered by an indemnity policy, deduct an allowance for wear and tear and depreciation. As a price guide, check with advertisements and retailers' catalogues.

Make up a chart and enter the values in the end column, then add up the figures. If your policy is index-linked, the total is the sum insured you need. If not, add a suitable allowance for inflation in the year to come. Up-date your policy annually if it is not index-linked, and always keep two copies of the inventory in different places – for example in a bank safe-deposit box or with the insurance company.

Investing

Putting your money to work in stocks and shares

Governments and companies raise part of the money they need to operate by issuing securities, usually in the form of stocks or shares. People buying shares own a proportion of the company's assets, which entitles them to shares in its profits and, in the event of the liquidation of the company, to a share of the residual assets after all other creditors have been paid.

The securities themselves have a value, too. Many can be bought or sold at any time on a stock exchange, or, in the case of some small companies, the unlisted securities market.

Interest payments from stocks and shares are liable to income tax. If you sell a holding at a profit, you may have to pay capital gains tax. In addition, there are fees for buying and selling charged by banks, market makers or stockbrokers, or anyone else acting on your behalf, and STAMP DUTY has to be paid on purchases, except new share issues. Take all those deductions into account when deciding whether to invest.

Choosing an investment Stocks and shares are not suitable places to put emergency funds that you may need in a hurry; those are best left in BUILDING SOCIETIES or BANK ACCOUNTS to earn interest. On the other hand, if you have some spare capital, securities can give you a better chance to build it up, while increasing your income, too – though you can also lose if the share price falls.

Stocks, which pay a fixed rate of interest, are a safer investment than ordinary shares, which do not (though if a company does well its dividends to ordinary shareholders can be generous). The most popular kinds are issued by the government and local authorities; government stocks are sometimes called gilt-edged securities, or gilts, because the interest is guaranteed.

Many British government stocks can be bought through the NATIONAL SAVINGS Stock Register (details from post offices) – charges are lower than buying through a stockbroker, so small investments, say a few hundred pounds, can be made.

Before buying, look at the stock carefully. First, how long will your money be tied up, and can you get it if you need it? Local authority loans or bonds, for example, are generally issued for a fixed period of one to seven years, and cannot be sold during that time (except by the heirs of a holder who dies). Yearling bonds and local authority stocks are traded on the stock exchange at any time, though you may not get what you paid.

Second, what interest is offered? It will almost certainly be less than the rate available at the time of purchase from banks and building societies; on the other hand, as it is fixed in advance, you may do better in the long term than you would with another investment where the rate is adjusted according to economic circumstances.

Index-linked British government stocks, which can be sold at any time, pay an income adjusted according to the retail price index.

Companies issue two forms of stocks: **Debentures** secure a loan for periods of from 10 to 40 years, and pay guaranteed interest. Some types may be redeemed by the company for their issue price once the agreed period has expired. Debenture holders have first claim on the assets of a company that gets into difficulty.

Ordinary shares and unit trusts Holders of ordinary shares in a company are not guaranteed a dividend if it does badly. If it does well, the management proposes the amount to be paid and whether, for example, it should be given in the form of cash or perhaps further shares. However, the proposal must be approved by a shareholders' meeting in which ordinary shareholders usually form a majority – so they influence the final decision heavily.

Property bonds and managed bonds, like UNIT TRUSTS, spread the funds of small investors across many investments. Property bonds invest in property and real estate; managed bonds hold a mixture of investments in property, fixed-interest securities and ordinary shares.

Getting advice Study the financial pages of newspapers. Compare interest rates where those are guaranteed, and the conditions on which they are offered. Watch out for new shares issued when a company is floated on the stock exchange. They are not subject to Stamp Duty, VALUE ADDED TAX (VAT) or to a commission.

Look, too, at yield – the income derived from an investment expressed as a proportion of its current price. It is not the same as interest; government stock, for example, originally offered at £100 at 6 per cent interest always bears the same interest rate. If general interest rates rise to, say, 8 per cent, the sale price will fall, so that the yield keeps pace. To provide a yield of 8 per cent the price would fall to £75.

A company's price-earnings ratio is calculated from its earnings, after tax and other deductions, divided by the number of ordinary shares. That figure is then divided by the quoted share price to give the ratio, expressed as X/1. A large company with a good earnings record might have a P/E of 16/1 or more. Remember, however, that yields, P/E ratios and other statistics are historical information; they show what happened in the past – not what might happen.

Unit trust, local authority bonds and stocks and some other forms of stocks and shares can be bought directly through newspaper advertisements. Otherwise, a market maker or stockbroker can make the purchase for you; most of them charge commission of around 1.5 per cent with a minimum fee which could be equal to more than 1.5 per cent – if the amount you are investing is less than about £1000. High Street banks, and some investment consultants, will manage your investments if the sum is more than £10,000.

Invisible ink

Simple ways to write secret messages

You can write messages invisibly with bottled or freshly squeezed lemon juice, or the juice squeezed from a grated onion. If you choose onion juice, let it stand for a few moments beforehand. Dip a toothpick or wooden cocktail stick into the juice, and write on hard-surfaced paper.

Anyone who knows the trick can make the message appear by holding the paper near a warm light bulb or electric iron. Take care not to let the paper catch fire.

You can also write invisibly with milk. Once it has dried, rub pencil shavings or cigarette ash lightly over the paper.

Invitations

How to send and reply to formal and informal invitations

Most invitations today are made by telephone or by an informal, written note. But for more formal occasions – such as a 21st birthday party – engraved or printed vellum cards are normally sent out. They are obtainable from most good stationers, who will advise about wording.

Usually, the names of the host and hostess are printed in the centre of the card – and that of the prospective guest is written in the top left-hand corner or beneath. The host's address is printed at the bottom left-hand corner, and the function, date and time at the centre, below the name of the host. If dinner dress is to be worn, simply put 'Black Tie' at the bottom, alongside *RSVP*.

Invitations for WEDDINGS are sent out at least six weeks before the event, invitations for cocktail parties, dances and so on are usually sent out about three or four weeks before the event. Formal invitations should be replied to promptly in equally formal third-person terms. For example: 'Mr Arthur Brown thanks Mr and Mrs Peter Jones for their kind invitation to an At Home on Tuesday, September 10th at eight o'clock at 32 Acacia Avenue, Middletown, which he has great pleasure in accepting/which he regrets he is unable to accept.' Informal invitations are normally replied to by telephone, or by a warm, friendly note.

Irish coffee

How to float the cream on top

Irish coffee is most popular as a stylish after-dinner drink. To make it, heat a stemmed glass and pour in a measure of Irish whiskey, adding sugar to taste. Then fill the glass to within about 25mm (1in) of the brim with piping hot coffee.

Stir briskly and, before the coffee has settled, slowly add chilled double cream so that it floats on top.

The best way to do this is to pour the cream slowly over the back of a small spoon held over the glass. Let the drink stand for a few minutes. Then drink the coffee-and-whiskey mixture through the cold, frothy cream, savouring the contrast between the two.

For Highland coffee you should use Scotch whisky instead of Irish; and for Gaelic coffee use brandy.

Ironing

The best way to iron clothing

Always iron at the temperature given on the fabric label, or at the setting identified by a symbol, that is, 'cool' (one dot), 'warm' (two dots) or 'hot' (three dots) – see IRONS. Iron items that require the lower iron setting first. Iron dark or embroidered fabrics, acetates, acrylics, rayons, silks, triacetates and woollens on the reverse side to prevent surface shine (see SHINE REMOVING). Iron cotton (unless cotton piqúe) on the right side. Iron nylon, linen, polyester and polyester mixture on either side.

Ironing shirts and blouses Iron while damp, starting with the seams and double thicknesses on the inside. Then iron the collar, placing it flat on the ironing board, reverse side up, and press from the points towards the centre. Turn the collar over and repeat. Press the sleeves next, beginning with the insides, then the outsides of the cuffs. Place the sleeve flat on the board, and iron the sides, avoiding the top edge. Then centre the seam underneath and iron the top.

If a blouse sleeve has gathers at the shoulder, iron it on a sleeve board or over the end of the ironing board, using the tip of the iron for the gathers. Drape the shoulders over the end of the board in turn, and iron them. Then lay the back of the shirt flat and press it, including the seams on the outside. If the shirt has a pocket, press the inside of it first. Finally, iron both front panels and hang the shirt in a warm, open space to dry.

Ironing skirts First iron the waistband of a skirt over the end of the board. On a pleated skirt, tack the pleats into place first, iron a little below the waist; turn the skirt around and iron the rest of each pleat length. Iron a skirt with gathers or unpressed pleats from hem to waist.

Ironing trousers Iron the top of the trousers first by pulling them over the end of the ironing board with zip or buttons undone. Iron each section in turn, rotating the trousers until all the sections are pressed – see PRESSING.

Lay the trousers flat on the board, legs on top of each other, with the sides and seams aligned. Fold back the top leg and iron the inside of the bottom leg. Turn the trousers over and repeat on the other side. Then iron the outside of each leg; iron the creases with a damp cloth between the iron and the material.

Irons

Choosing, maintaining and repairing them

The three main types of electric iron are the dry iron, the steam/dry iron and a steam/dry iron with a spray. All have a heat selector, usually with temperature settings that show the types of materials that should be ironed at each setting. These are: Hot (210°C), cotton, linen, rayon; Warm (160°C), polyester mixtures, wool; Cool (120°C), acrylic, nylon, acetate, triacetate, polyester. Modern irons are also marked with dot symbols that correspond to the labelling systems on clothes – one dot for cool; two dots for warm, three dots for hot.

The steam/dry iron also has a setting for steam. In the body of a steam iron a small valve allows water to drip from a tank onto the top of the hot soleplate. Here it is converted to steam, which passes through holes or grooves in the base of the iron.

Steam irons are useful for ironing clothes which have become too dry for normal ironing. Some irons also incorporate a spray, which jets a fine mist of cold water ahead of the iron when a button on the handle is pressed – a useful refinement for stubborn creases or overdry clothes. Others deliver an extra burst of steam, instead of water.

Choosing a hand iron Decide which type is most suited to your needs, then look for one that feels comfortable and balanced in your hand. Sheer weight is not necessary; it is the correct heat for the fabric, combined with the right amount of dampness that gives good results.

Look also for the special features provided by different makes of iron. These include a warning light that glows when the iron is switched on and goes out when the selected temperature is reached; a water gauge that indicates how much water is in the tank; and a flex that can be adjusted to suit left- or right-handed users. Always choose an iron that carries the BEAB Mark of the British Electrotechnical Approvals Board, which signifies that the model has been tested and approved for safety to British Standards Institute requirements.

Use and care of your iron The three-core flex must be properly wired to a 13amp plug with a 13amp fuse – see ELECTRIC WIRING; PLUGS. Never connect an electric iron to a lighting circuit, which is not designed to handle the load of about 1kW at which most irons are rated. A flex-holder, clipped to the edge of the ironing board, will prevent undue wear on the flex, and will stop it trailing across the fabric being ironed.

Always use distilled water, obtainable from chemists, in a steam iron, unless the manufacturer states that tap water can be used. When filling or emptying, make sure the iron is unplugged from the electrical supply. Empty the tank immediately after use, and while the iron is still hot. Stand and store an iron on its heel rest, and do not wrap the flex around the iron while it is still hot.

Replacing a flex As soon as the sheathing on the flex begins to chafe or fray, replace the flex. Buy a length of three-core, fabric-covered flex with a rating of at least 6amps – if the iron is rated at more than 1440 watts, use 10amp flex.

Before you start, make sure the iron is unplugged.

Remove the cover at the back of the handle. Note carefully the connections of each coloured wire – blue (neutral), brown (live) and green/yellow (earth) – disconnect them and draw the flex through the rubber flex protector.

Feed the new flex through the flex protector and into the connection enclosure. Strip off about 65mm (2½in) of the outer sheath – or enough for the wires to reach the terminals easily. Bare the ends of the wires to about 13mm (½in). Connect them to the correct terminals, as noted earlier.

QUICK TIPS To remove marks from the soleplate, rub the iron over a damp piece of coarse cloth stretched across the ironing board. For obstinate deposits from synthetic fabrics, use a proprietary cleaning paste or stick. As a last resort, rub gently with very fine wire wool, but without roughening it – and never on a non-stick soleplate.

When cleaning a steam iron, hold it in the ironing position so that particles do not lodge in the steam vents.

Itching

Treatment and relief

Itchiness can be caused by several ALLERGIES and disorders. Calamine lotion and antihistamine medicines give some relief, but the cause must also be treated.

Allergies An allergy to certain drugs or foods, or contact with irritants, can cause skin disorders such as ECZEMA and HIVES.

Eczema is a red, weeping, itchy rash which tends to occur in skin creases, and is common in asthma and HAY FEVER sufferers. It is relieved by steroid and moisturising creams.

Itchy weals, usually a sign of hives, can be relieved by antihistamine tablets. See a DOCTOR immediately if the mouth or throat swell, or if breathing is difficult.

Infections Scabies is a highly contagious and very itchy infestation by a tiny mite which burrows into the skin. Your doctor or chemist will prescribe a suitable lotion, which should be used by all members of the household.

Fungi and yeasts, such as 'thrush', affect the groin and other warm, moist areas, causing itchy rashes. Consult a doctor for diagnosis and treatment.

Prickly heat Hot, humid weather may cause red pimples or blisters, which can be avoided by wearing loose clothing and keeping cool. Frequent baths and calamine lotion will ease the itching – see PRICKLY HEAT.

Stress This can cause anal itching (also caused by poor hygiene and HAEMORRHOIDS), or an uncontrollable urge to scratch exposed areas, called neurodermatitis – see STRESS.

Treat anal itching by washing the anus regularly, cleaning with moist tissues and changing underwear often. Avoid constipation and scratching. Consult a doctor if there is any bleeding.

Neurodermatitis can be treated with antihistamines and covering the itchy areas so that they cannot be reached.

Ivory

Care and cleaning

To retain its creamy colour, ivory must be exposed to the light. If you keep ivory-handled CUTLERY in a drawer, or the ivory keys of a PIANO constantly covered, they will eventually turn yellow. The pale colour will also last longer if you do not store the ivory where it will come into contact with smoke from cigarettes or a coal or wood fire.

To prevent ivory from drying out, do not keep it in a hot, dry atmosphere, and oil it frequently with almond oil.

To clean ivory, gently remove any marks with a cotton bud dipped in white spirit, wipe with a soft, clean cloth, and buff it dry. Put discoloured ivory handles or ornaments in the sun to fade.

Do not soak ivory in water, which can cause hairline cracks to increase as well as loosening the glue holding any metal parts in place.

Badly stained, yellowed or cracked ivory should be restored or repaired by a jeweller; piano keys should be 'scraped' professionally, or replaced.

Jacking a car

Doing it safely; using axle stands

The jack supplied in a car's tool kit is intended for jacking the car to change a wheel – do not use it on its own to support the vehicle while you are carrying out any other work, especially if you intend to work underneath it. Any force you exert may cause the car to fall off the jack, or the jack may simply collapse due to wear or damage – use axle stands instead (see below).

Changing a wheel can be hazardous if the proper procedure is not carried out. Though the car will not drop on you if it slips off the jack while a wheel is removed, the brake drum or disc may be damaged.

Avoid changing a wheel on a sloping, uneven or loose surface. In an emergency, such as a flat tyre, try to get the car onto a firm, level surface. It is a good idea to carry a block of wood, about 300mm (12in) square and 25mm (1in) thick, in the car to set under the jack if you have to use it on a loose surface.

Loosen the wheel nuts or bolts *before* jacking – if you loosen them while the car is jacked the force required may roll the car off the jack.

The type of jack and the location of the jacking points vary from car to car – make sure you know how your jack works, and where the jacking points are, before using it. The car handbook, if you have one, explains jacking procedures; otherwise, ask a garage dealing with the make or model of the car. *Never* try to jack the car under the body other than at the jacking point.

Find the jacking point for the wheel you wish to remove – some cars have only one jacking point on each side of the car and both wheels on one side are lifted simultaneously. Apply the handbrake and chock the wheel diagonally opposite the one you are going to remove. Jack up the car until the wheel is just off the ground. If you are changing a punctured wheel remember that the inflated spare will need more ground clearance than the flat tyre.

Remove the loosened nuts or bolts, lift the wheel off its studs and fit the spare wheel. Tighten the nuts/bolts finger-tight, working diagonally. Lower the jack until the weight of the car is on the wheel. Tighten the nuts/bolts with a wheelbrace or socket spanner, then lower and remove the jack – see SPANNERS AND WRENCHES.

JACKING A CAR

Raising it to change a wheel

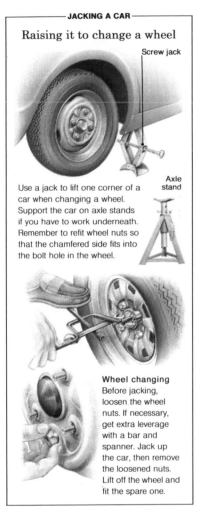

Screw jack

Axle stand

Use a jack to lift one corner of a car when changing a wheel. Support the car on axle stands if you have to work underneath. Remember to refit wheel nuts so that the chamfered side fits into the bolt hole in the wheel.

Wheel changing
Before jacking, loosen the wheel nuts. If necessary, get extra leverage with a bar and spanner. Jack up the car, then remove the loosened nuts. Lift off the wheel and fit the spare one.

Using axle stands Always use axle stands to support a car if you are going to work underneath it. Available in pairs from car accessory shops, they are tripod shaped with a central pillar which can be adjusted for height by pushing a steel peg through holes in the pillar. Though called axle stands, they can be used to support a vehicle under any structural member strong enough to support its weight, such as jacking points, or main suspension members if work requires the suspension raised. Never use them under unsupported sheet metal, steering arms or the engine sump.

To set an axle stand in place, jack up the car as before, push the stand into position as required, then gently lower the car onto it. To remove the axle stand when work is complete, jack up the car until you can pull the stand clear, then lower the car to the ground. Finally, remove the jack.

Jack o'lanterns

All lit up for Halloween

To make this children's lantern you need a flat-bottomed, large, round pumpkin or a swede, and an ordinary candle. Place the pumpkin on several layers of newspaper. With a dark crayon or soft pencil, draw a face on a well-rounded side. Position the mouth high enough so that the candle will not be seen.

Cut different faces – here are two ideas

With a paring knife, cut out a bevel-edged lid around the pumpkin stem. The opening should be large enough for your hand to pass through. Slice the stringy membrane from the lid. Dig out the seeds and membrane from the inside of the pumpkin with a long-handled spoon. Carve the face with a sharp knife, using sawing strokes rather than one continuous cut. Place a candle in a holder in the bottom of the pumpkin. When the candle is lit, close the lid and keep the lantern away from curtains or other flammable objects. Do not leave it unattended or in the care of children.

See also HALLOWEEN GAMES.

Jacks

A game for nimble fingers

Using small stones, this game has been played throughout the world since prehistoric times. Today it is played with a small rubber ball and ten plastic jacks, each with several prongs.

You start by dropping the jacks onto a flat surface all at once. Then, using only one hand, toss the ball in the air, pick up a jack and catch the ball after it has bounced once. Set the jack aside. Keep picking up one jack at a time until you have set aside all ten. This is called *ones*. Next, in *twos*, pick up two jacks each time, and in *threes*, three groups of three and one. In *fours*, pick up two groups of four and two, and in *fives*, two groups of five. In *sixes*, pick up six and four, in *sevens*, pick up seven and three, in *eights*, pick up eight and two, in *nines*, pick up nine and one. Finally pick up all ten jacks.

You lose your turn if you fail to pick up all the required jacks; if you fail to catch the ball after one bounce; or if you touch any jack other than the ones you have to pick up. When your turn comes again, start at the stage at which you last played. The first player to complete all ten stages is the winner.

The rules of jacks differ from country to country, and there are several variations of the game.

Jackstraws

Playing the pick-up-sticks game

Also known as spillikins, or fiddle sticks, this game is played with 50 thin wooden or plastic sticks – the jackstraws – and the aim is to pick up one straw at a time from a tangled pile, without moving any of the other straws.

A jackstraw's colour indicates its value. Green is worth 1 point; red 2 points; orange 5 points; yellow 10 points. The one blue straw is worth 20 points. Once you have it, you can use it to lift other straws. If you pick up a green, red and orange stick in that order, each stick counts as a double score – the total score for the three sticks being 16.

How to start the game
Hold the straws in a bunch and release them onto a flat surface. Pick them up one by one with your fingers, trying not to move the other straws.

If another straw does move, your turn ends, and the next player takes over, starting again from the beginning with all the sticks.

Each player keeps a record of his score at the end of his turn. Play continues until each player has had a turn or a number of rounds. The player with the most points wins.

Jam making

Preserving fruit with sugar

Jam originated as a means of preserving fruit. Essentially, it is fresh ripe fruit simmered on its own or with water until it starts to break down, then boiled rapidly with sugar until it reaches the point – known as setting point – where it begins to gel. The gel, or set, is a result of a reaction between the sugar and pectin, a substance found in varying degrees in ripe fruit. Acid must also be present to help to release the pectin.

Pectin and acid Some fruits are naturally high in pectin and acid and make excellent, firmly set jams. They include black and red currants, cooking apples, damsons, gooseberries and some plum varieties. Less high in pectin and acid are apricots, greengages, blackberries, loganberries and raspberries. Jams made from these do not set as firmly.

Fruits that are low in pectin and acid include cherries, strawberries and rhubarb. To make jam with these you may have to add extra pectin and acid in the form of lemon juice – 2 tablespoons of juice for each 900g (2lb) of fruit; or redcurrant or gooseberry juice – 90ml (3fl oz) for each 900g of fruit. Pectin can be bought from a chemist or grocer. Add it according to the maker's instructions at the same time as the sugar. Alternatively, add one grated cooking apple for each 450g (1lb) of fruit. Acid can be added in the form of citric or tartaric acid – $\frac{1}{2}$ level teaspoon for each 900g of fruit.

When choosing fruit for making any kind of jam, make sure it is fresh, firmly ripe and dry. Remove stalks and bruised portions. With cherries and damsons, you may leave the stones in, or remove them, as you wish. With other stoned fruit, halve and stone them.

Strawberry jam This recipe for strawberry jam makes about 2.3kg (5lb) of jam.

Cook in a large, heavy-based aluminium or stainless-steel pan. It should be no more than one-third full of fruit, otherwise the jam may boil over. Use granulated or preserving sugar; brown sugar affects the taste. It is a good idea to warm the sugar for 15-20 minutes beforehand in an oven set at 110°C (225°F) – gas mark $\frac{1}{4}$.

Other jams are made in essentially the same way. Tough-skinned fruit such as plums and blackcurrants, may need to be simmered for up to 45 minutes before the fruit begins to break down. The time taken to reach setting point varies from 3 minutes to 20 minutes.

Ingredients
1.8kg (4lb) strawberries
Juice of 4 large lemons
1.4kg (3lb) warmed sugar
Small knob of butter

Steps in making strawberry jam

Cook gently until the juices run. Stir in the sugar until it dissolves. Add the butter and boil hard for about 15 minutes.

To test for setting point, put a teaspoon of jam onto a chilled saucer. Refrigerate for a minute, then push the edge of the jam with a finger. The surface should wrinkle up and break.

Fill each jar to the very brim using a ladle; the jam will shrink as it cools. Wear oven mitts and beware of splashes.

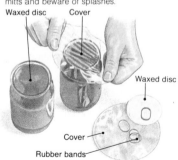

Put disc, wax side down, on jam. Dampen one side of cover and lay it, damp side up, on the jar. Secure it with a rubber band.

Preparation and cooking Prepare the strawberries, and simmer with the lemon juice until they are tender and the juices run. Add the sugar and butter, and boil until setting point is reached. Remove from the heat and skim off any scum with a slotted stainless-steel spoon.

Let the jam stand for 5-10 minutes until a skin forms on the surface, then stir so that the fruit is evenly distributed. Pot and seal as illustrated.

Testing for setting point Jam sets at about 105°C (220°F). The most reliable way of testing for setting point is the saucer, or wrinkle, test, also illustrated.

If it has not reached setting point, return the pan to the heat for a further 5 minutes, then repeat the test.

Potting and sealing Clean and dry the jars, then warm for a few minutes in the oven. If a bubble forms against the glass, tilt the jar (wearing oven mitts) to let it escape.

If using plastic-coated screw-top covers, put them on immediately. If covering with Cellophane or plastic, put a waxed paper disc, waxed side (that is, smooth side) down, on top of the jam in each jar. Dampen one side of the covers and stretch them gently as you lay them, damp side up, on the jars. Hold in place with rubber bands. Wipe any splashes off the jars with a damp cloth. Label the jars with the contents and date, once they have cooled.

Jellies

Making and potting fruit juice preserves

Many fresh fruits can be made into delicious jellies. For best results, work with modest quantities. In general, all you need do is to prepare the fruit as you would for JAM MAKING. Use fruits rich in pectin and acid, and with strong flavours. The yield for jellies will be less than for jam, as no pulp is used.

Wash the fruit thoroughly, crush BERRIES to extract the juice and cut other fruits into pieces. Do not remove the peel or cores, as these are rich in pectin.

Put the prepared fruit in a large aluminium or stainless-steel saucepan, cover it with water and simmer until it is tender – usually for 45 minutes or an hour. Then strain it through a scalded jelly bag, leaving the juice to drip through into a bowl for at least an hour. Do not squeeze the jelly bag, as this will result in cloudy jelly.

Measure the quantity of strained juice and add sugar in the specific amounts given below. Then return the juice to the pan and boil quickly, continuing to boil for about 10 minutes or until the setting point is reached. Take the saucepan off

the heat and remove any scum, using a heated stainless-steel spoon.

Fruit especially rich in pectin, such as blackcurrants, can be boiled a second time to give a further extract. If you intend doing this, allow the cooked fruit to drain the first time for only 15 minutes. Then return the pulp to the pan with half the quantity of water you used for the first extract.

For the second extract, simmer the fruit for 30 minutes, strain it and leave it to drip for an hour. Combine the two extracts, add sugar and finish cooking. Do not keep the extracted juice too long before boiling it with sugar, or it will lose pectin.

Here are some recipes for fruit jellies:

Blackberry
1.8kg (4lb) blackberries
570ml (1 pint) water
Juice of 2 lemons
Sugar

Simmer the fruit with water and lemon juice until it is tender. Strain once through a jelly bag and measure juice. Add 450g (1lb) of sugar to each pint of juice and continue according to general instructions.

Blackcurrant
1.8kg (4lb) blackcurrants
1.7 litres (3 pints) water
Sugar

Simmer fruit with 2 pints of water for first extract; return strained pulp with 1 pint of water for the second extract. If only one extract is required, use 3 pints of water. Allow 450-575g (1-1¼lb) of sugar to each pint of juice.

Crab apple
1.8kg (4lb) crab apples
1.7 litres (3 pints) water
Sugar

Simmer the washed and chopped fruit until it is cooked to a pulp (and the liquid reduced by one-third). Strain and allow 450g (1lb) of sugar to each pint of juice.

Damson
2.7kg (6lb) damsons
1.7 litres (3 pints) water
Sugar

Use all the water to simmer the fruit for a single extract. Add 450g (1lb) sugar for each pint of juice.

Gooseberry
1.8kg (4lb) gooseberries
1.7 litres (3 pints) water
Sugar

There is no need to top and tail gooseberries. Proceed in the same way as you would for blackcurrant jelly.

Redcurrant
2.7kg (6lb) redcurrants
1.7 litres (3 pints) water
Sugar

Take two extracts, following the general instructions and the recipe for blackcurrant jelly.

Pour fruit jellies into warm, sterilised jars, seal with wax discs (wax side down, as for jam) and Cellophane or plastic covers and allow them to cool. Do not forget to label the jars when you add the outer lids. Store the jars in a cool, dry, dark place.

Jet lag

Helping your 'body-clock' adjust to changing time zones as you travel

Rapid movement across the world's time zones in modern airliners disrupts the body's natural (circadian) rhythms, causing a condition known as jet lag.

It can take more than a week for the body to adjust to the time zone and night/daylight cycles at the ultimate destination. The air traveller's sleep patterns are upset; he or she becomes fatigued and disorientated; concentration suffers and short-term memory and some mental skills (such as the ability to do simple arithmetic) may be affected. If possible, you should wait at least 24 hours after completing such a journey before conducting business affairs.

To minimise the effects, try to book a flight arriving in the evening local time, so that you get a night's rest soon after landing.

During the flight, drink plenty of fluids – water or fruit juice preferably – but avoid carbonated drinks which may cause stomach discomfort and flatulence. Avoid alcohol, tea and coffee, which tend to add to the natural dehydration experienced at high altitudes. Avoid smoking, too, because tobacco inhibits the absorption of oxygen. Try to sleep as much as possible.

Jewellery

Cleaning it and making small repairs

The beauty and brilliance of jewellery can be maintained by cleaning, either in warm soapy water or with a proprietary jewellery care product, gently using a soft brush (such as a mascara brush) to loosen dirt.

Dry and polish pieces with a chamois leather. Opal, amber and turquoise are easily damaged and should be polished only with a chamois leather or a soft cloth.

For diamonds, use a solution made from 1 tablespoon of ammonia and a few soap flakes in 2 cups of warm water. Rinse afterwards in clear, warm water and dip them in surgical spirit to restore their lustre.

Wash pearls in warm, soapy water. However, the best way to keep them in good condition is to wear them next to your skin, as their surface benefits from contact with natural oils present in the skin.

Take care, however, as they can be damaged by make up, perfume and hair lacquer.

Immerse solid silver jewellery in a solution of 1 tablespoon of washing soda to 570ml (1 pint) of hot water until the tarnish has been removed, then rinse and dry thoroughly.

A piece featuring stones of any kind should be cleaned instead with silver polish. Gold and platinum can be washed in warm soapy water.

Leave repairs to valuable jewellery to a professional, but you can carry out simple repairs to fashion jewellery – made of non-precious or semi-precious metal or stones – at home.

Use small jeweller's pliers for these repairs, and always work in good light over a soft cloth which will trap any stones or other small parts which may come adrift and might otherwise roll away out of sight.

Securing loose stones Imitation stones are often set in claws. If a claw breaks, it will have to be replaced by a jeweller, but if it merely works loose you can tighten it with smooth-jawed pliers. Squeeze the pliers gently but firmly against the claw, easing it inwards until it clasps the stone tightly.

If a stone comes out of its setting, it is

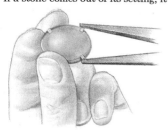

Loose stone Using small jeweller's pliers, squeeze the claws that hold the stone gently, bending them inwards until they clasp the stone firmly in its setting.

usually because the adhesive has lost its effectiveness. To make good, use an emery cloth wrapped round a needle file to rub away the old adhesive, both from the back of the stone and from the mounting. Apply a thin coating of epoxy resin adhesive (see GLUING) to the stone and the mount, reposition the stone and leave it to set.

Jigsaw shapes

Cutting up cardboard for a tricky game

To play jigsaw shapes, a game leader is elected. He or she takes some sheets of cardboard, each in a different colour, and cuts out identical sets of shapes – squares, triangles or rectangles. Each shape is then cut into five or six identical pieces – the smaller the pieces, the more difficult it will be to complete the puzzle. A set of pieces is then given to each player, and the object of the game is to reassemble them into their original shapes. The first person to complete a set wins the game.

You can also play jigsaw shapes with two teams, each taking it in turn to cut out the shapes and piece them back together.

Jogging

Equipping yourself; warming up; getting started

Jogging is an aerobic exercise (see AEROBICS; PULSE TAKING) which requires the proper clothing and a phased programme. Jogging shoes should have a good support around the heel; a well-cushioned midsole to reduce impact shock; good flexibility; a wide sole; an arch support and a thumb's width of space between the big toe and the shoe tip.

It is best to jog on a resilient surface such as dirt, grass or a cinder track. If you must jog on paving, asphalt is better than concrete.

First warm up with about ten minutes of EXERCISES. Start jogging at a slow, comfortable pace – how long you jog is more important than how far or how fast. Jog until your heart rate is at your training level for aerobic exercise, and keep it there for 20 to 30 minutes. When you finish, slow down to a walk and then cool down with more exercises, so that your heart rate drops to normal.

Do not take up jogging without consulting a doctor first if you are not in good health or are over the age of 35. See also JOGGING INJURIES.

Jogging injuries

Treating minor strains and sprains

Most JOGGING injuries are caused by overdoing the exercise, wearing unsuitable shoes or failing to carry out the warm-up exercises properly. The injuries can range from muscular soreness to major problems with an ankle, knee or hip joint, or with muscles. See also SHIN SPLINTS.

Do not ignore any pain or signs of fatigue, breathlessness or weakness. Continuing to jog when all is not well can result in a more complex or even permanent injury.

Do not jog if you feel physically tired – you are more likely to pull a muscle or sprain a joint. Treat minor SPRAINS AND STRAINS immediately, and continue the treatment until the pain ceases. If the injury does not respond to your own treatment, consult your DOCTOR. Do not resume jogging until an injury has completely healed.

John Innes compost

Making your own mixtures

There are many proprietary seed and potting composts available from garden shops, based on the mixture formulated by the John Innes Horticultural Institution. But if large quantities are needed, it is simple (and cheaper) to buy the ingredients and make your own, according to John Innes formulas.

To mix small batches you need a potting bench – a tray or box which has two sides, a back and a plastic or metal surface which can be kept clean and sterile. It is usual to work in bushels, one bushel being the amount that will fit into a box 560 × 250 × 250mm (22 × 10 × 10in) without compacting.

To make John Innes seed compost (working in parts by volume), mix 2 parts of sterilised medium loam with 1 part each of fibrous peat and coarse sand. To each bushel of this mixture add 40g (1½oz) of superphosphate of lime and 20g (¾oz) of ground chalk or limestone.

There are three grades of John Innes potting compost: No 1, for slow-growing plants; No 2, suitable for most purposes; and No 3, recommended for fast-growing and vigorous plants such as TOMATOES and chrysanthemums.

For No 1, mix 7 parts (by volume) sterilised medium loam with 3 parts peat and 2 parts coarse sand. To each bushel add 115g (4oz) of John Innes base fertiliser and 20g (¾oz) of ground chalk or limestone. John Innes base fertiliser is made up of 2 parts hoof and horn meal, 2 parts superphosphate of lime and 1 part sulphate of potash. The quantity of fertiliser and chalk is doubled for No 2 and trebled for No 3.

Mixing the compost Make small quantities of compost at a time. Measure out the exact amounts you will need of peat, fertiliser (if using it), sterilised loam, chalk and sand. Put some of the sand into a bucket and mix into it the fertilisers, lime and ground chalk. Then spread the different ingredients on the potting bench in layers; mix them together thoroughly. Use all the compost as soon as possible. See also COMPOST.

JOISTS

Replacing an old joist

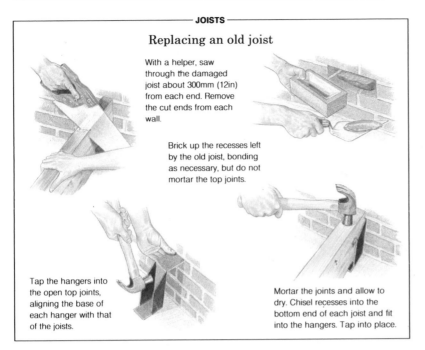

With a helper, saw through the damaged joist about 300mm (12in) from each end. Remove the cut ends from each wall.

Brick up the recesses left by the old joist, bonding as necessary, but do not mortar the top joints.

Tap the hangers into the open top joints, aligning the base of each hanger with that of the joists.

Mortar the joints and allow to dry. Chisel recesses into the bottom end of each joist and fit into the hangers. Tap into place.

Joists

Making under-floor repairs

Floor joists are usually built into the brickwork of a house during construction, but you can replace damaged joists, using galvanised steel hangers which can be fitted into the walls to support new joists. Builders' merchants supply hangers for most joist sizes. First remove the floorboards over the joist – see FLOOR REPAIRS.

Before replacing joists on an upper floor, try to minimise the damage to the ceiling underneath. If possible, slide a knife blade along the bottom of the joist to locate the nails holding the ceiling. Press down gently around the nails to loosen them, and have a helper in the room below to remove them.

You will probably have to replace the ceiling with PLASTERBOARD if a number of new joists have been fitted; otherwise you should be able to repair minor damage – see PLASTER PATCHING.

Get a helper to hold the damaged joist while you saw through it, as shown. Pull it clear, and remove the cut ends from each wall, disturbing the brickwork as little as possible. Brick up the recesses left by the old joist, bonding as necessary, but do not MORTAR the top joints, where the hangers go – see BRICKLAYING.

Tap the hangers into these open top joints, lining up the base of each hanger with that of the joists. With the hangers in position, fill the joints in the brickwork with mortar and allow to dry.

Chisel recesses in the bottom of each

end of the new joist to fit it over the base of the hangers – see CHISELLING. Fit the joist into the hangers, tapping it into place with a hammer. Check that its top edge aligns with the other joists.

If you need to run a cable through the new joist, drill a 25mm (1in) hole through it about 50mm (2in) below its upper edge.

Bowed joists An uneven floor may be caused by bowed or twisted joists. To correct this problem, take up the floorboards and nail timber struts at intervals between the joists to straighten them. See also UNEVEN FLOORS.

WARNING If there is an electricity cable passing through a damaged joist, switch off the power at the mains before removing the cable.

Judo

First steps in an ancient art of self-defence

The aim of judo is to 'disable' your opponent by means of a throw, stranglehold, arm lock or a 30 second hold-down. The sport, derived from the ancient art of ju-jitsu, is practised by the young and not so young, and by both sexes.

You wear loose-fitting jacket and trousers, called *judogi*, but remain barefooted. The jacket is fastened by a belt whose colour denotes the wearer's standard, ranging from white for novices to black for the highest of the grades of mastery (*dan*).

The best way to learn is to join a

judo club recognised by the British Judo Association, 7a Rutland Street, Leicester LE1 1RB. You need not be fighting fit, but if you are not so young, have a medical check-up: back or knee problems can be aggravated by judo.

Falling The main emphasis in judo is on throwing your opponent, and since every competitor must expect to be thrown frequently, the first thing a club will teach you is how to fall properly – the breakfall. This helps to overcome the fear of being thrown.

The simple rules for falling properly are: roll as much as possible; the moment before you hit the mat, beat the mat hard with your free arm to lessen the impact; and tuck in your chin so that your head will not jerk back and hit the floor on impact – see illustrations on next page.

Throwing Once the breakfall is mastered you can learn some basic throws. Position and timing are more important than physical strength. It is essential to get your opponent off-balance. The type of throw used depends much on opportunity: three useful ones for beginners to learn are the *Osoto-gari*, *Ippon-seoinage* and *Ko-uchi-gari*.

Osoto-gari When your opponent is moving his right leg towards you, move close to him and use your right hand to grip the lapel about level with his collarbone. Bring your left hand over his right arm, gripping the jacket at the sleeve.

Now bear down with your left arm and upwards with your right hand, to push your opponent off-balance, onto his right heel. At the same time take a short step forward with your left foot and move towards your opponent until your chests touch.

Swing your right leg beyond his right leg, then swing it back so that the back of your right thigh contacts the back of his, and sweeps his leg from the ground. Swing your upper body downwards as your right leg comes back and up.

Ippon-seoinage (one-arm shoulder throw) From a facing position, grip your opponent's right sleeve tightly near the elbow with your left hand and move your right foot forward diagonally. Bring your left foot round, so that you are turning away from your opponent and bend your legs; at the same time swing your right arm up under his right armpit. Your right bicep must be under the armpit, and pulling down with your left hand will ensure that his arm is tightly trapped – essential if the throw is to succeed.

Moving into position for the throw, bend your legs and thrust out your right hip. Pull forward and down with your arms, curl your body forward, straighten the legs and off-load your opponent from your back and right shoulder.

JUDO

Learning to fall, and three basic throws

Learning to fall without injury when thrown is essential: always land with a breakfall. Once proficient at the breakfall, you can learn some basic throws.

Breakfall Crouch (left), then roll back with your chin tucked in. Strike the mat hard with your free arm as soon as the upper part of your back touches the mat (right).

Osoto-gari 1 Pull down on your opponent's right sleeve. Push him back with your hand on his left shoulder.

2 Step onto your left foot and swing your right leg from behind his. Use your arms to push him over.

3 As his left leg lifts off the ground and your right leg sweeps up, swing your body down towards the mat.

Ko-uchi-gari 1 As your opponent moves his right foot forward, twist yourself to the left and throw your right foot between his legs.

2 Bring the sole of your foot against the heel of his right foot and sweep it forward, at the same time pushing him down to the left.

Ippon-seoinage
Facing your opponent, grip his right sleeve with your left hand. Move your right foot diagonally in front of your left and pivot on your right foot, turning your back to your opponent and bringing your right bicep under his right armpit. Bend your legs, then straighten them and pull him forward and down.

Kesa-gatame Lean across your opponent's upper body and wrap your right arm round his neck. Grab his left arm and tuck it under your left arm, trapping the wrist. Hold his sleeve tight at the elbow.

Ko-uchi-gari This is a very fast leg throw, used when an opponent has his legs wider apart than usual. Grip his right sleeve at the elbow with your left hand, and his jacket at the left collarbone with your right hand.

Move your feet so as to turn slightly left, then swing your right foot through his legs and bring the sole of your foot sharply back against the heel of his right foot, sweeping it forward. Push forward and down with both hands and follow through, using your body weight to push him to the mat. Do not fall on top of him.

Hold-down In competitive judo a hold-down can score a win – the opponent must be held down on his back for a count of 30 seconds. One basic hold-down is *Kesa-gatame.*

Sit by your opponent's right armpit. Secure his arm and head tightly – as illustrated. Spread your legs.

Arm locks and *strangleholds*, used to force an opponent to submit, require expert tuition. Strangleholds especially can be dangerous. Many instructors will not teach them to people under 16.

To indicate that you submit, tap either your opponent or the mat twice – and your opponent must release you.

Jugged hare

Preparing and cooking

Jugged hare is a rich hare stew. In spite of its name you do not need a stoneware jug to cook it – any deep, heavy-based pan will do. Get your butcher to joint the hare. Make sure he gives you the blood as well in a separate container.

Ingredients (for six people)
1 jointed hare
1 large onion
2 carrots
2 sticks celery
50g (2oz) streaky bacon
50g (2oz) butter
Salt and black pepper
Bouquet garni
Grated rind of $\frac{1}{2}$ lemon
850-1000ml ($1\frac{1}{2}$-2 pints) beef stock
25g (1oz) plain flour
4 tablespoons port
Blood of the hare

Preparation and cooking Peel and roughly chop the onion, carrots and celery. Remove the rind from the bacon and chop the bacon. Fry the bacon in a deep, heavy-based pan until the fat runs, then add the butter. Add the hare joints and fry until well browned. Add the chopped vegetables, salt and pepper, bouquet garni and lemon rind. Pour in enough stock to cover the meat and bring to the boil. Cover tightly and cook over very low heat for $2\frac{1}{2}$-3 hours or until tender.

Mix the flour with a little water to make a smooth paste and stir into the stew. Cook for a further 2-3 minutes. Mix the port and blood. Remove the pan from the heat and stir in the port and blood mixture. Serve at once. Do not reheat the stew – or the blood will curdle.

Juggling

How to amaze your friends with dexterous prestidigitation

You can use any conveniently sized balls for juggling – tennis balls are an ideal size and weight. The first rule to learn is never to look at your hands. To acquire this basic skill, start by tossing one ball from hand to hand so that it arcs directly before your eyes. Toss the ball by letting it roll from your fingertips and catch it in the palm of your cupped hand.

Practise this technique until you can toss and catch the ball about 200 times without looking at your hands. Now begin working on a simple circular pattern; toss the ball with your right hand, catch it with your left and quickly toss it back across your body at waist level. Do this about 200 times, then another 200 times in the reverse direction.

Now you are ready to tackle two balls. Start with one in each hand. Toss one in the air and pass the other quickly to the throwing hand. As the first ball starts to fall, toss the second. Catch the first ball, pass it back to the throwing hand and, as the second ball starts to fall, toss the first one again. When you can do this 100 times in each direction, try one-handed circles; toss each ball just as the other begins to fall. Then try a straight up and down pattern; toss each ball straight up as the other starts to fall.

By this time, though you may not be

How to connect and disconnect jump leads

Park the cars close together, so that the leads reach – but be sure that the cars do not touch each other. First connect the two positive (red lead) terminals. Then connect one end of the black (negative) lead to the negative terminal of the working battery and the other end to any unpainted metal part of the faulty car away from fuel or brake pipes. Start the working car, rev it and start the other car. When the engine is running normally, disconnect the leads in the reverse order.

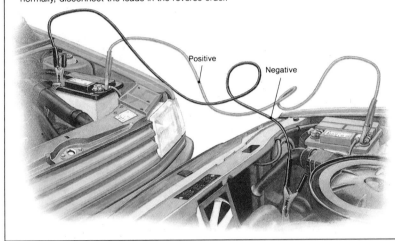
Positive
Negative

ready to apply for a job at a circus, you should be adept enough to try juggling with three balls. Start with two in your right hand and one in your left. Toss one ball from your right hand, and as it arcs toss the ball from your left hand to rise beneath the first and arc at the same height. Catch the first ball and toss the last ball as the second arcs, and so on, keeping all three balls circulating.

Jump-starting a car

Getting on the move when the battery is flat

If your car battery is very low, a boost from the battery of another car could be all you need to get started – and your own battery will then be charged by your car's charging system. The batteries of the two cars are connected by a pair of jump leads, which can be bought from a car accessory shop and are a useful item to carry in the boot in case of emergency.

Park the second car so that the two battery compartments can be easily connected by the jump leads. Make sure everything is switched off in both cars. Do not let the two cars touch – particularly if one of them has a positive (+) earth electrical system and the other a negative (−). No matter how the batteries are earthed, connect the positive terminal on one battery to the positive terminal on the other, and the negative to the negative. Always connect the positive lead first and disconnect it last.

A set of jump leads has one pair of connectors with black plastic handles, and the other with red. Connect the positive terminals with the red clips and the negative terminals with the black clips.

Start the second car, and once its engine is running smoothly try to start the faulty car. Rev up the engine of the second car slightly. When the faulty car starts, leave it running and disconnect the leads – first the negative and then the positive.

Some cars with fully electronic ignition, fuel injection systems or engine management computers can be damaged by the surge of current caused by connecting and disconnecting the leads. In this case, disconnect the leads of the battery and lift it out of your car. Then connect the leads as described above, and run the second car for about 20 minutes. This should recharge your battery. See also BATTERIES.

Junction box

Fitting one into a lighting circuit

For some types of LIGHT FIXTURES it is necessary to replace the CEILING ROSE with a junction, or joint, box. In most houses built since the mid-1960s, the lighting circuit is wired to the 'loop-in' system, in which three cables are connected to each ceiling rose except the last one on the circuit – see ELECTRIC WIRING. One cable runs from the main fuse box (see FUSES AND FUSE BOXES) or the previous

Practising the technique

Two-ball juggling Toss the green ball, then pass the red to the right hand ready for tossing as the green ball starts to fall.

Three-ball juggling As the green ball crests, toss the red. As the red crests, toss the blue and catch the green.

ceiling rose on the circuit. One goes to the light switch and the other goes to the next ceiling rose in the circuit.

Where FLUORESCENT LIGHTS, spotlights or tracklights are being fitted in place of pendant lights, the light fittings provide no connecting points for the lighting circuit cable coming in and then going on to the next lighting point. You must transfer the connections from the loop-in ceiling rose to a junction box above the ceiling and lead a cable from it to the new fitting.

Switch off the power at the main fuse box and remove the circuit fuse. Unscrew the ceiling rose cover and release all the conductor wires from the terminals. You will have to lift floorboards in the room above (or go into the roof space) and draw the cables above the ceiling. Screw the base of the junction box to a joist.

Lay lighting cable (see ELECTRIC WIRING) from the junction box to the lighting point. Prepare its ends for connection. Put green-and-yellow sleeves on all bare earth wires.

If the switch cable is not marked, you will have to identify it. Turn on the light switch, grip the tip of the red wire in what you think is the switch cable with the clip of a circuit tester (see CIRCUIT TESTING) and connect its other clip to the tip of the black wire. The tester will light up if it is the switch cable. Put a red tag on its black wire.

Make the connections in the junction box as illustrated. If you are adding an extra light – for OUTSIDE LIGHTING, for example – there will be two light cables and two switch cables to connect; use the same terminals for both.

Screw the new light fitting securely in place; the screws should be driven into a joist or into wooden struts nailed between JOISTS.

Feed the cable into the new light fitting. Screw the black wire tightly in

place at the terminal marked N and the red at the terminal marked L. Screw the earth wire into the terminal marked E or ⏚.

Replace the circuit fuse and turn the electricity back on at the main switch.

Jury service

What to do if you are summoned

Most people in Britain between the ages of 18 and 65 can be called to serve on a jury. Nearly always the summons is for serious criminal cases, although juries can be empanelled for certain civil cases. It is an offence, punishable by a fine, to ignore the summons or to fail to attend court when required. However, you may apply to the court to be excused jury service if you have a valid reason, such as illness, blindness or deafness, pregnancy or certain domestic or business difficulties. General inconvenience is not a valid reason.

If you wish to be excused, write giving your reasons to the Clerk of the Court immediately you receive the summons.

Jurors, chosen at random from the electoral register, are usually summoned about six weeks before they are due to serve. The summons specifies the date on which jury service is to begin, but not when it will end (since it is impossible to know how long a trial will last). The summons may have a minimum period of service – usually about two weeks.

Who can refuse jury service Members of some professions can refuse without having to give a reason. These include doctors, dentists, nurses, midwives, members of the armed forces, peers and MPs. You can also refuse if you have served on a jury – apart from a coroner's jury – within the previous two years.

Who may not do jury service There are three categories of people who may not sit on a jury. The first category is professional – magistrates, coroners, barristers, solicitors, legal executives, prison governors, prison officers, probation officers, police officers (including special constables), clergy, nuns, ministers of religion and anyone in a comparable job. They may not serve on a jury for ten years after leaving the occupation.

The second category is criminal – anyone who, in the last ten years, has served any custodial sentence or had passed on him any suspended sentence or community service order, or who has been placed on probation in the last five years. The third is non-residential – anyone who has not been resident in the United Kingdom, Channel Islands or Isle of Man for at least five years since the age of 13.

The trial On the appointed day, a panel of jurors will be on hand for a particular case and the final 12 are picked by ballot from these. As each name is read out, the juror sits in the jury box. A juror who is challenged by the defence and turned down returns to the jury pool and waits to be called for another case.

When all 12 jurors are seated, each one takes an oath that he or she will follow the proceedings and give a true verdict; if a juror casts an improper vote (due to bribery perhaps), he or she faces imprisonment for up to two years.

During the trial, which consists of opening and closing statements by the prosecution and defence, evidence and cross-examination of witnesses and the judge's summing up, jurors may take notes. They may even question a witness by way of a written note to the judge. If a member of the jury has to leave the courtroom during the hearing, he has to ask the court usher, and the judge orders a brief adjournment. Jurors must not discuss the case with anyone.

After the summing up, the usher leads the jury to the jury room and locks them in. Now they must elect a foreman (who will act as their spokesman) and consider their verdict. Jurors must stay together until a verdict is reached; sometimes they may have to be accommodated overnight in a hotel. The ideal is for all the jury to agree. If this is not possible, a majority verdict – supported by at least 10 of the 12 – is acceptable. If the jury fails to agree, the judge must discharge the members and order a new trial.

Jurors are not paid for their services, but they can claim subsistence and travel expenses. They may also claim an allowance for loss of earnings, as employers are not bound to pay wages to anyone absent on jury service. Anyone who is sacked because he or she has been away on jury service can claim UNFAIR DISMISSAL; the employer may also face an action for contempt of court.

JUNCTION BOX

Siting and wiring the box

Position a junction box so that the cables can reach it easily. Make sure you connect wires to the correct terminals in the box.

Junction box

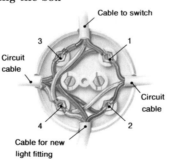

Cable to switch

Circuit cable

Circuit cable

Cable for new light fitting

Siting Screw the box to a joist so that cables are 50mm (2in) below floorboards, and secured by cable clips – especially where they enter the box.

Wiring Connect the red circuit and switch cable wires to No 1 terminal. Connect the black circuit and light wires to No 2 terminal. Connect the red light wire and red-tagged switch wire to No 3, and the earths to No 4.

Kebabs

Cooking on skewers

Kebabs are a Middle Eastern dish, excellent for cooking on BARBECUES. To make them, pieces of meat, vegetables, and sometimes fruit, are marinated (see MARINATING), put on skewers and cooked.

Traditionally, the meat used is lamb, as in the recipe given here, but beef steak and pork fillet also make good kebabs. Or you can try scallops, prawns, mussels, lamb kidneys or cocktail sausages – or combinations of these ingredients.

Vegetables and fruit that can be used include onions, green and red peppers, tomatoes, button mushrooms, slices of blanched courgettes, fresh or tinned pineapple cut into cubes, apple cut into cubes and apricots or peaches, stoned and halved. Apricots go well in lamb kebabs and pineapple in pork kebabs.

This recipe for lamb kebabs makes enough for four people. Use 200-250mm (8-10in) skewers. They should be flat rather than round – or the food will slide round the skewers when you turn them.

Ingredients
700g (1½lb) boned shoulder or leg of lamb
1 medium-sized onion
1 green or red pepper
4 small tomatoes
12 button mushrooms
For the marinade:
4 tablespoons olive oil
1 tablespoon lemon juice
¼ teaspoon ground coriander
1 crushed garlic clove
Salt and pepper to taste

Preparation Trim the fat from the lamb and cut into 25mm (1in) cubes. Peel the onion, then cut it into quarters and separate the layers. Cut the pepper into 13mm (½in) squares. Put the lamb, onion and pepper into a dish. Whisk together the marinade ingredients and pour them over the ingredients in the dish. Mix well, then cover and leave for at least an hour.

When ready to cook, cut the tomatoes in half. Pour off the marinade, reserving it. Divide the marinated ingredients, the tomato halves, and mushrooms between four skewers. Thread them on the skewers, alternating the ingredients and packing them closely together.

If you are using a barbecue, cook the kebabs on the rack for about 10 minutes, turning once, then brush with marinade and cook for 4-5 minutes more or until browned on the outside and pink in the centre. If using a grill, set the grill to a moderate heat. Turn the kebabs at least twice while cooking and brush with marinade.

Serve on a bed of rice with lemon wedges.

Kedgeree

A hearty breakfast from the Raj

Kedgeree (or *Khicharhi*) was originally an Indian dish. But in the 18th century it was introduced into Britain, where it became popular as a substantial breakfast dish. In its anglicised form, it consists of smoked haddock, eggs, rice and spices. It can equally well be served for lunch or supper.

This recipe makes enough for four people.

Ingredients
450g (1lb) smoked haddock
75g (3oz) butter
1 large chopped onion
½ teaspoon hot curry powder
175g (6oz) long-grain rice
2 hard-boiled eggs
1 tablespoon chopped parsley
1 tablespoon lemon juice

Preparation Place the haddock, skin side up, in a wide pan. Cover it with boiling water, then simmer very gently for 10 minutes. Remove the haddock from the water, reserving both.

Melt 50g (2oz) of the butter in a large pan. Add the onion and brown it gently. Stir in the CURRY POWDER and cook briefly, then stir in the rice. Cook for a minute or two, stirring all the time. Pour in 570ml (1 pint) of the haddock water. Cover and simmer very gently for 15-20 minutes until tender.

Discard the skin and bones from the haddock, and flake the flesh. Shell and chop the eggs. When the rice is cooked, fork in the haddock, eggs, parsley, lemon juice and remaining butter. Keep over a very gentle heat for about 5 minutes to let it heat through. Serve on a hot dish.

Kennel

Building a made-to-measure home for your dog

Building a two-room kennel will provide a warm, dry, outdoor shelter for your dog. Make it large enough for the dog to sleep or lie down in the inner room without being cramped, allowing an extra 150mm (6in) to the length and

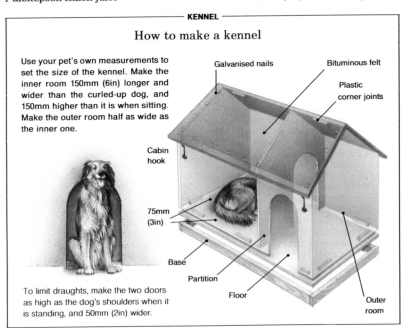

KENNEL

How to make a kennel

Use your pet's own measurements to set the size of the kennel. Make the inner room 150mm (6in) longer and wider than the curled-up dog, and 150mm higher than it is when sitting. Make the outer room half as wide as the inner one.

Galvanised nails
Bituminous felt
Plastic corner joints
Cabin hook
75mm (3in)
Base
Partition
Floor
Outer room

To limit draughts, make the two doors as high as the dog's shoulders when it is standing, and 50mm (2in) wider.

width measurements of the dog taken when it is lying curled up. Make the outer room half as wide as the inner one.

For the height, measure from the floor to the top of the dog's head when it is in a sitting position, and add 150mm. Make the doorways shoulder high and 50mm (2in) more than the shoulder width.

Add the length and width measurements of the two rooms together, and make a floor to this size using 18mm ($\frac{3}{4}$in) exterior grade PLYWOOD. For a base, build a frame the same size as the floor, using 50 × 100mm (2 × 4in) TIMBER softwood. Fit the floor to the base, using 32mm (1$\frac{1}{4}$in) No 8 woodscrews.

Make the walls and inner partition from 18mm exterior grade CHIPBOARD, with end walls cut at 45-degree angles for a sloping roof. Cut doorways in the partition and in one wall.

Use 18mm exterior grade plywood for the roof panels; join them at the apex with plastic corner joints. Allow 50mm extra on the length and width measurements of the roof panels to provide eaves. Cover the roof with bituminous felt, held with galvanised clout nails.

Assemble the walls, base and inner partition using plastic corner joints or screwing through short 25 × 25mm (1 × 1in) BATTENS, as illustrated. For cleaning, make the roof detachable, held by cabin hooks.

Paint the outside walls and base with one coat of primer, followed by undercoat and gloss (see PAINTING EXTERIORS) or one of the WOOD PRESERVATIVES.

Place the kennel where the dog can see family comings and goings. Disinfect regularly; cover the inner room with shredded newspaper, changed weekly.

Kettle repairs

Patching a hole; replacing an electric element

Aluminium kettles cannot easily be repaired by soldering, but a small hole can be plugged using cork and tin plate.

Cut out both ends of a tin can, using a tin opener. Hold a 10p coin in the centre of one disc and cut round it with a strong pair of scissors. Do the same with the other piece of tin.

Lay the coin on a 3mm ($\frac{1}{8}$in) thick piece of cork and cut round it. Sandwich the cork disc between the two tin discs on a scrap piece of wood and hammer a large nail through the centre. Remove the nail, and through the hole it has made pass a 3mm machine screw through one tin disc and through the hole in the kettle. Slip the cork disc over the screw inside the kettle, and then the other tin disc.

Screw a nut onto the screw until it is finger-tight. Hold the nut with the fingers and tighten the screw with a screwdriver. Do not overtighten; the cork should be

---

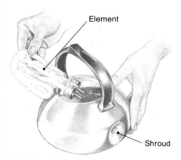

KETTLE REPAIRS

Replacing a heating element

Element

Shroud

1 Hold the element and unscrew the shroud on the outside of the kettle. Pull the element out through the top of the kettle and clean off any scale inside.

2 Slip the inner washer on to the new element, fit the tail of the element through the hole, slip on the outer washer, then screw the shroud back on.

---

firmly compressed but overtightening will cause it to crumble. Fill the kettle with water; if it still leaks, tighten the patch a little more.

Replacing a kettle element Remove the old element and fit a replacement as illustrated. Take off any scale around the connector hole with detergent, or scrape it off with a blunt knife, then refit the new element.

Keyholes

How to cut one in a door or drawer

The essential tool for cutting a keyhole is a padsaw, or keyhole saw – see SAWS AND SAWING. It has a wooden or metal handle into which interchangeable saw blades are clamped.

To start, drill a hole a bit larger than the diameter of the key barrel – see DRILLING. From the bottom edge of the hole, measure and mark off the depth of the tang of the key and drill a smaller hole.

Select a padsaw blade that will enter the top drilled hole and fit it into the handle. Make two straight cuts down to the lower hole. Use a small file to clean the sides of the slot.

Keys

What to do if a key breaks in a lock

A broken key in a lever-type lock may be easy to remove if the tip of the key protrudes at the back of the lock. Simply push the broken section back through the lock with a thin metal rod, such as a knitting needle, or a piece of stiff wire. If this cannot be done, remove the lock, turn it face down and gently tap the back to dislodge the broken piece.

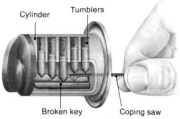

Cylinder

Tumblers

Broken key

Coping saw

To remove the shaft of a broken key, try to hook it out with the teeth of a thin padsaw, jigsaw or coping-saw blade.

A broken key in a cylinder lock (see DOORLOCKS) is more difficult: try inserting a very fine padsaw or coping-saw blade into the key slot, so that its teeth engage with the teeth on the key. Then carefully pull out the broken piece. You may be able to withdraw it far enough to grip it with a pair of pliers and pull it out.

If all else fails, partly dismantle the lock so that the cylinder can be withdrawn, then tap it gently on a hard surface to dislodge the broken key.

Kippers

Grilling, frying, jugging and slicing them cold

Kippers are herrings that have been gutted, then salted and smoked. The best-quality ones come from Loch Fyne in Scotland, Northumberland, East Anglia and the Isle of Man – but these are becoming sadly rare.

When buying kippers, choose ones that are oily and plump. Buy them whole on the bone rather than filleted in vacuum packs.

Kippers can be grilled, fried or jugged – left to cook in boiling hot water. The best-quality kippers can also be cut into thin slices and served cold – rather like smoked salmon. Serve cooked kippers with a knob of butter on top, a dash of lemon juice and plenty of brown bread and butter.

Grilling Put the kippers, skin side up, on a piece of kitchen foil in the grill pan. Grill for about 5 minutes until the skin starts to go crisp and come away from the flesh at the edges. Do not grill the other side.

Frying Grease a frying pan lightly with butter. Heat it, then put in the kippers. Fry each side over a medium heat for 2-3 minutes.

Jugging This is the simplest, and many people say the best, way of cooking kippers. Put them tail up in a heavy stoneware or heatproof jug, then pour in enough freshly boiling water to cover them. Leave for 5-10 minutes, depending on their size, then drain well and serve.

Slicing This only works with the very best-quality kippers. Lay the kippers out flat, then using a sharp knife cut them horizontally into wafer-thin slices. Serve with bread and butter and lemon quarters. See also PATÉ.

Kitchen cabinets

Fitting ready-made or self-assembly units; fitting worktops

Floor-standing and wall-mounted kitchen cabinets are mostly made to standard metric sizes. The standard base units are 600mm (2ft) or 1200mm (4ft) wide, 600mm deep and 900mm (3ft) high including worktop. Wall cabinets are only 300mm (12in) deep and are 600mm or 1200mm wide. Many manufacturers offer variations of widths of all units, and special units for corners or small spaces.

Kitchen cabinets can be bought ready-made or in kit form with full assembly instructions. Whichever you choose, first take detailed measurements of your kitchen and draw a scaled plan so that you can decide where the units will fit. Where possible range two or more base units along a wall, to avoid cutting a worktop and to provide a spacious work surface. Remove any SKIRTING BOARDS, so that the units will fit flush to the wall.

Fit wall cabinets centrally over the base units, and allow 400-460mm (16-18in) between the worktop and the bottom of the cabinets.

Fitting base cabinets When assembled, either in a factory or at home, base cabinets are perfectly squared, but your walls are almost certainly not – and the floor may not be level. If necessary you can level the floor (see UNEVEN FLOORS), but to align the cabinets with the walls you will need packing pieces. Place a cabinet in position and note the gap between its back fixing points and the wall. Make packing pieces to fill the gap, using PLYWOOD or thin BATTENS.

Mark the wall through the cabinet fixing holes, drill the wall (see MASONRY DRILLING) and fit wall plugs – see WALL FASTENERS. Drill a hole through each packing piece, slip them into the gap and screw the cabinet to the wall. Use a spirit level to check that the unit is standing

level. If it is not, fit thicker packing pieces as required.

Fitting worktops If a worktop has to be cut to length, use a jigsaw or handsaw – see SAWS AND SAWING. If the cut edge will be visible, cover it using VENEER TAPE of the same material as the work surface.

Lay the worktop on top of the cabinet, or cabinets, and push it hard to the wall to cover the gap at the rear. Fasten the worktop to the cabinets with chipboard SCREWS inserted up through plastic corner joints attached to the cabinet top rails. Make sure that the screws are the correct length and will not protrude through the worktop surface.

Fitting wall cabinets With the worktop in place, measure up from it and mark a line on the wall for the location of the cabinet. If you are going to tile the space between worktop and cabinets (see CERAMIC TILES) make the measurement multiples of the tile size, allowing for grouting. Build up temporary supports for the cabinet to stand on – wood blocks or bricks – and mark the fixing holes.

Align the wall cabinet centrally above the base cabinet, and use a spirit level to see that it is true vertically and horizontally. Mark through the cabinet fixing holes in the back panel and drill and plug the wall. Screw the cabinet to the wall and remove the supports.

Kites

An easy-to-make high-flier

A box kite will fly well in most winds. You can make one with a few cheap materials obtained from a DIY shop and craft or model shop.

Materials

Eight 300mm (12in) square expanded polystyrene ceiling tiles
Four 910mm (36in) sticks of 10mm (⅜in) square balsa
Adhesive tape
Balsa cement
PVA adhesive
Reel of nylon thread, string and one curtain ring

Lay four tiles in line, chamfered edge down, and tape them together with two parallel strips of adhesive tape placed about 150mm (6in) apart. Leave about 50mm (2in) of tape free at one end of each strip.

Turn the tiles over and apply PVA adhesive to the chamfered edges of the tiles. Fold the tiles to make an open-ended box, securing the end tiles with the tapes. Make a second box in the same way. Allow the glue to set.

Glue the balsa sticks into the inside corners of the two boxes with PVA adhesive, leaving 13mm (½in) projections at each end. Tie a length of nylon thread to one projection, loop it around the pro-

---

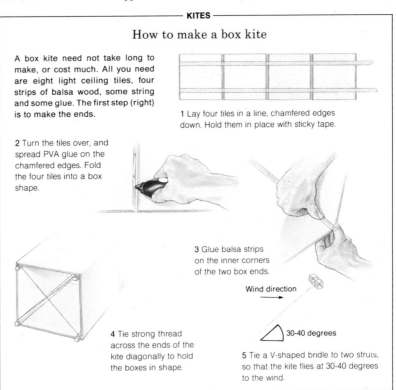

KITES

How to make a box kite

A box kite need not take long to make, or cost much. All you need are eight light ceiling tiles, four strips of balsa wood, some string and some glue. The first step (right) is to make the ends.

1 Lay four tiles in a line, chamfered edges down. Hold them in place with sticky tape.

2 Turn the tiles over, and spread PVA glue on the chamfered edges. Fold the four tiles into a box shape.

3 Glue balsa strips on the inner corners of the two box ends.

Wind direction

4 Tie strong thread across the ends of the kite diagonally to hold the boxes in shape.

30-40 degrees

5 Tie a V-shaped bridle to two struts, so that the kite flies at 30-40 degrees to the wind.

jection on the opposite corner, then around the next projection and across to the fourth, to cross-brace the box. Repeat at the other end. Dab balsa cement on the thread at the loops and where the threads cross.

For the kite to fly successfully it must be attached to its flying line by a bridle. This consists of a piece of string, about 1.2m (4ft) long, folded in half and looped through the curtain ring. Tie the two free ends of the string to two of the balsa sticks to form a V. Attach one end of the reel of nylon cord, the flying line, to the curtain ring, using a round turn and two half-hitches – see KNOTS.

Flying the kite Stand with your back to the wind, and jerk the line as the kite rises. To fly correctly the kite should face the wind at an angle of about 30 to 40 degrees. The lighter the wind, the greater the angle required. To adjust the angle, slide the ring along the bridle, so as to alter the relative lengths of the two arms. When you get the adjustment right, the kite should rise without any need for you to run.

Knitting

Basic stitches for beginners

The craft of knitting consists of two basic stitches – knit stitch and purl stitch – and two variations – slipstitch and twisted stitch. Before you can begin to knit, you must cast a row of stitches on one needle. There are two ways of doing this using only one needle: single casting on and double casting on.

Single casting on First, form a slip knot for the first stitch about 150mm (6in) from the yarn end. Pass the yarn from the ball over and around the left thumb. Insert the needle under the loop on the thumb. Slip the thumb out of the loop and pull the yarn down to close the loop around the needle. Continue in this way until the number of stitches that you require is cast on.

This method produces a delicate edge that is particularly good for a hem edge, but the first row is hard to knit.

Double casting on For this you need a double length of yarn. Make a slip knot a measured distance from the yarn end, allowing 25mm (1in) for each stitch. Wrap the short end of the yarn over the left thumb and the yarn from the ball over the left index finger. Slip the needle through the thumb loop, then scoop the yarn from the index finger and draw a loop onto the needle. Release the thumb loop; tighten the loop in the needle by drawing the short yarn forwards with the thumb.

This method produces a firm elastic

How to make the stitches

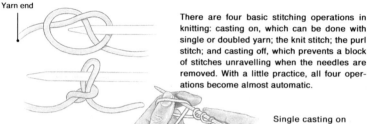

Yarn end

There are four basic stitching operations in knitting: casting on, which can be done with single or doubled yarn; the knit stitch; the purl stitch; and casting off, which prevents a block of stitches unravelling when the needles are removed. With a little practice, all four operations become almost automatic.

Slip knot Make it for single and double casting on. Form a loop then catch the yarn on the needle.

Single casting on Once the slip knot is on the needle, pass the yarn from the ball round your left thumb, and hook the loop with the needle.

Double casting on 1 Loop the measured yarn end on your thumb and the yarn from the ball over your left index finger.

2 Slip the needle up through the thumb loop and round the finger loop (see arrow).

3 Draw the finger loop through the thumb loop. Withdraw your thumb and pull the stitch tight.

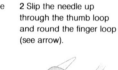

Knit one 1 Push the right-hand needle through the first stitch and behind the left needle. Hook the yarn round.

2 Draw the loop you have made on the right-hand needle back through the stitch on the left.

3 Allow the first stitch to slide off the left-hand needle and pull it tight, ready for the next stitch.

Purl one Push the right-hand needle through in front of the left needle. Hook the yarn round (left) and pull the loop through.

Twisted stitch Enter the back of the loop, hook yarn as for knit stitch. Purl normally on next row.

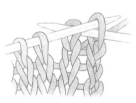

Casting off 1 Work two stitches. Catch the first in left needle.

2 Pull first stitch over second and off the right needle.

3 Work the next stitch in the row. Repeat 1 and 2.

edge which is suitable for any pattern that does not require a delicate edge. For a beginner, it is easier to control than single casting on.

Knit stitch For this stitch, hold the needle with the cast-on stitches in your left hand and the other needle in your right hand.

Insert the needle into the first stitch from the front. With the right index finger loop the yarn clockwise round the right-hand needle. Then draw this loop through the stitch on the left-hand needle with the point of the right-hand needle. Finally, slip off the first stitch on the left-hand needle, leaving a new stitch on the right-hand needle.

With practice, you should achieve even tension and speed.

Purl stitch Cast on and hold the needles as for the knit stitch. Start with the yarn at the front of the work. Insert the point of the right-hand needle into the front of the stitch from right to left – with the point over the left-hand needle. Then with your right index finger pass the yarn over and around the point of the right-hand needle in an anticlockwise direction. Finally, draw the loop through the stitch on the left-hand needle and onto the right-hand needle. Slip off a stitch on the left-hand needle.

Purl stitches tend to be looser than knitted stitches. With experience, you should develop even tension – especially if you keep your index finger close to the work.

Purling or knitting all rows is called *garter stitch*. Purling and knitting alternate rows is called *stocking stitch*, and purling and knitting alternate stitches on one row is called *rib stitch*. Where knitting pattern instructions refer to garter stitch, assume that all rows are knitted unless otherwise stated.

Slipstitch This stitch is slipped from the left to the right needle without being worked. The yarn is carried either in front of or behind the stitch. If carried in front, the yarn strands form the pattern. If carried behind, the slipstitch becomes the pattern.

To make a *slipstitch knitwise*, hold the yarn at the back of the work. To make a *slipstitch purlwise*, hold the yarn at the front of the work. To make a *slipstitch purlwise on a knit row*, hold the yarn at the back of the work.

Twisted stitch A chain-like pattern is produced by twisting stitches. Knit or purl into the back of the stitch instead of into the front – so that the loop of the stitch crosses right over left. When making a twisted stitch by knitting into the back, hold the yarn at the back. When purling into the back of a stitch, hold the yarn at the front.

Casting off The simplest and most often used method is *plain casting off*.

Unless the pattern instructions say otherwise, the stitches are worked from the right side and in the same sequence in which they were formed. That is, you knit the knit stitch and purl the purl stitch.

Work the two stitches at the beginning of the row. Hold the yarn behind the work and insert the left needle in the front of the first stitch. Then pull the first stitch over the second one and off the needle. Continue until the desired number of stitches is cast off. At the end of a row, break the yarn and loop the end through the last stitch. Pull tightly to secure the row.

Knots
Tying basic knots for using ashore and afloat

Although there are many kinds of knot, they basically fall into two types: hitch, knots and bend knots. Hitches are used to attach a line to a post or rail; bends are used to tie two pieces of rope, possibly of different thicknesses, together.

Whichever type of knot you tie, a rope has two parts in relation to the knot – the standing part, which you do not manipulate, and the working end. A loop between the two can be overhand (the working end over the standing part) or underhand (the working end under the standing part).

How to tie seven useful knots

The best way to learn an unfamiliar knot is to practise it using fairly thick rope or clothesline. In this way it is easier to become familiar with the knot's pattern than it is using thin string. This page shows in detail how to tie seven common knots, useful in a variety of situations.

Figure-of-eight To make a 'stopper' knot – one that will not roll down the rope under pressure – make an underhand loop, then an overhand one. Pull the working end through the first loop, so that it resembles the number 8.

Half hitch and slip knot The simplest hitch knot is the half hitch. Make a loop and pass the working end through it. If you double the end before you push it through, the result is a slip knot.

Clove hitch Used to tie a rope round a fixed object such as a bollard, this knot is formed from two overlapping loops. To stop it slipping, add a half hitch.

Round turn and two half hitches Another useful mooring knot. Loop the rope twice round the bollard, making the second loop overlap the first. Secure it with two half hitches.

Reef knot Use a reef knot (two overhand knots tied in opposite directions) to join two ropes of equal thickness, or for tying a first aid bandage. To undo it, pull one of the free ends towards the other. That will convert it into a sliding knot, like the two half hitches on the left.

Sheet bend To join two ropes of different thicknesses, use a sheet bend. Form an overhand loop in the thicker rope, then pass the end of the other rope through the loop. Pull the thinner rope round and behind the standing part, then back through the loop.

L

Lace cleaning

*How to wash and when
not to iron*

Lace must be cleaned with the greatest possible care. Rubbing or wringing lace can make holes in it, especially if it is old or has been exposed to sunlight.

Small lace articles such as gloves can be washed by putting them in a closed container partly filled with soapy water, and shaking gently. Then rinse them in clear, warm water and lay them flat on a towel to dry. They will not need ironing.

Larger articles such as veils should be gently agitated in a bowl of warm soapy water and then rinsed in clean warm water, making sure that the temperature of both lots of water is the same. Stretch the larger articles flat to dry; if necessary, hold them in shape with stainless-steel pins. Again, they should not need to be ironed.

If lace does have to be ironed – because of stubborn wrinkles – always iron on the 'wrong' (underneath) side. If the lace is old or fragile, place a piece of muslin or tissue paper between it and the iron. Use a cool iron – see IRONING.

To clean lace curtains and tablecloths at home (they can be dry-cleaned) first of all fold them into a neat square. Then leave them to soak overnight in warm, soapy water. Gently press the water out of them by hand, and spread them flat out to dry – either on a table or on clean grass out of the sun.

To give fresh body to lace, dip it in a solution of gum arabic. Pour 250ml (about $\frac{1}{2}$ pint) of boiling water on 25g (1oz) of gum arabic, stir well and let it cool. Allow the solution to dry and then lightly press the lace with a cool iron under tissue paper or muslin. See also CURTAINS.

Ladders

*Types of ladders, and how to use
them safely*

For general use around the home, two types of ladder will serve most purposes – platform steps and an extending ladder. Platform steps are suitable for decorating jobs; the platform that drops into place when the steps are opened out is useful for holding pots of paint or tools.

An extending ladder is for working at greater heights; for example, when maintaining roof guttering (see GUTTERS

Carrying, lifting and securing them

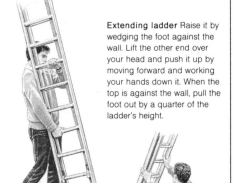

Carrying a ladder Always carry it vertically, to avoid accidentally hitting someone behind you. Bend the knees slightly and grip a rung just below waist level with one hand. With the other hand, grip a rung at eye level. Rest the ladder against a shoulder and straighten up. Steady the ladder with the upper hand as you walk.

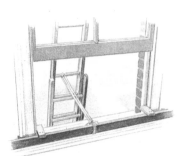

Extending ladder Raise it by wedging the foot against the wall. Lift the other end over your head and push it up by moving forward and working your hands down it. When the top is against the wall, pull the foot out by a quarter of the ladder's height.

Stepladder Before standing on the steps, make sure that the two sections are fully apart and locked into position by the locking stays or ropes. On some ladders a platform locks the two sections into place.

Securing the foot Tie it to well-fixed stakes. On uneven ground, keep the ladder level by setting a wide board with a batten nailed to it under the lower leg. On soft ground, set the board under both legs.

Securing to a window Secure a length of rope to one rung and tie it to a stout batten or plank fixed behind a window frame. Nail small pieces of wood to the ends of the batten to prevent it from sliding sideways.

AND DOWNPIPES) and painting upper windows – see PAINTING EXTERIORS. The most durable and easy to use are made of aluminium – light to carry and to handle and virtually maintenance-free.

Using ladders and stepladders safely
Always take all precautions against falling when using any kind of ladder at any height.

Never rest a ladder against glass, glazing bars or guttering. The ladder must extend at least three rungs above the work point so that you have something to hold on to. You can buy stand-off brackets to hold the ladder away from the wall when working on guttering. Lash the top of the ladder to a ring bolt screwed into the fascia board.

Always look straight ahead when climbing a ladder, not down or up. Hold onto both sides of the ladder and climb one rung at a time. Never stand on the top rungs; the minimum safety position is about four rungs down. When working on a ladder, never overstretch to one side – it may slip sideways. Always keep one hand free to hold the ladder while working.

Positioning an extending ladder For maximum safety and ease of climbing, the base of a ladder should stand away from the wall at a distance of a quarter of the ladder's height. At this distance, on firm, level ground, the ladder should be stable, but as an extra precaution place a bag of sand or cement against the foot.

Ladder care Store all ladders in a dry place – and under lock and key. Ladders left outside are an invitation to burglars. If you have nowhere to store a long ladder, padlock it to a house wall on purpose-made ladder brackets.

Protect wooden ladders with wood preservative and a coat of clear varnish – see WOOD PRESERVATIVES; VARNISHING. Never paint a wooden ladder, as this will hide dangerous defects. Check the rungs regularly to see that they are not loose or rotted. Do not attempt to repair or replace a faulty rung, have the work done by an experienced joiner.

Check tie rods, sliders and support brackets on an extending ladder, and tighten them if necessary.

Lampshades
Cleaning and re-covering

Clean a lampshade made from a washable material – linen, crepe, chiffon or plastic – with a mild solution of warm water and detergent. Rub gently with a soft cloth and then rinse well under running cold water. Pat dry with a towel and leave standing until it dries.

Covering a wire-frame shade

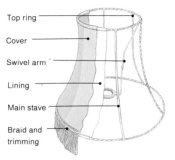

Top ring — Cover — Swivel arm — Lining — Main stave — Braid and trimming

You will need lining and covering fabric, 25mm (1in) wide cotton binding, 19mm ($\frac{3}{4}$in) wide insulating tape, 13mm ($\frac{1}{2}$in) wide braid, fringe and brown paper.

1 Bind the staves and the top and bottom rings. Fit the pattern paper round half of the frame and fold it round the rings and side staves.

2 Remove the paper, lay it flat, mark the fold lines with a pencil and cut along the lines. Lay the paper shape on the lining material, and cut out two pieces, allowing an extra 25mm (1in) all round the shape.

3 Stitch the lining pieces together and fit inside the frame. Pin round the bottom and top rings. Make up the cover and fit it over the frame, stitching it in place.

If the material sags after washing, tighten it by rotating the shade near gentle heat. Fibreglass shades need only to be wiped with a damp cloth.

Lampshade re-covering First strip off the old covering and lining, and clean the staves thoroughly with wire wool. Starting from the top, diagonally bind the two main staves of the frame – the ones to which the swivel arms are attached – with cotton binding. Finish off each binding with a loop knot, cut off the surplus and then bind the top and bottom rings.

Bind the other staves vertically with strips of insulating tape if they are not already plastic-coated.

Wrap a piece of brown paper round half of the frame, folding it around the top and bottom rings and around the two main staves. Remove the paper, lay it flat and pencil along the fold lines. Cut out the shape.

Hold the pattern on the lining material, and allowing 25mm (1in) all round, cut out two pieces.

Pin one piece to the frame, around both main staves, and pencil in the lines of the staves. Unpin the material, place the two pieces together and stitch 6mm ($\frac{1}{4}$in) outside each line – see SEWING.

Make two cover pieces in the same way, but stitch along each line, not outside. Trim the seams with scissors.

Place the lining inside the frame, with its seams in line with the main staves. Fold the lining around the bottom ring and pin it in position. Smooth out the lining gently to the top ring. Pin the lining around the top ring, snipping the seams to fit around the ends of the swivel arms. Stitch it to both rings and the main staves. Trim off the surplus material.

Turn the seams of the cover inside and fit them against the main staves on the outside of the frame. Carefully pin the material round the rings and main staves, tensioning it to make a smooth fit, then stitch to the rings and staves. Trim off the surplus.

To finish off, stitch fringed trimming round the bottom ring, and overstitch braid around the top and bottom rings. Alternatively, stitch bias binding round the rings.

Lapidary work
Polishing stones and pebbles in a tumbler

The simplest technique for polishing stones and pebbles is tumbling, whereby a rotating tumbler grinds them to a smooth, shiny finish. The basic equipment is a small barrel turned by an electric motor, abrasive grits and a polishing agent. All are available from crafts shops.

Choosing stones Many of the stones and pebbles found on the seashore or on river beds have a beautifully coloured core beneath their dull outer covering. They will tumble into fine polished stones suitable for all kinds of decorative work, such as making pendants or filling a glass vase or bottle.

Not all stones, however, are suitable for polishing. Some, such as sandstone, are too soft. Limestone is also soft, but can be tumbled, although only with other limestone pebbles.

Take a sharp penknife and a small file when hunting for suitable stones. If neither will mark a stone, it is suitable for tumbling. If the file but not the knife marks it, the stone can be tumbled with others of its kind.

Tumbling When tumbling, always load the barrel to its full capacity, otherwise the stones will chip instead of grinding smooth. The weight specified in the barrel capacity is the weight of the stones, grit and water combined.

Use a grit of 80 to 100 mesh for rough grinding and 400, 500 or 600 mesh for fine grinding.

Select the stones you wish to grind, choosing stones of different sizes, but do not use stones that are too large; for example, if the tumbler has a capacity of 1.5kg (3lb) do not use stones more than 25mm (1in) in diameter.

Place the stones in the barrel until it is almost three-quarters full. In a 1.5kg barrel add 1 heaped tablespoon of silicon-carbide grit and enough water to barely cover the stones. Use proportionately larger quantities of grit for larger barrels. Close the lid of the tumbler, place it on the rollers and start the motor.

Stop the tumbler every 24 hours and take out a few stones and wash them in clean water. Check them for smoothness and put them back in the tumbler if they are not chipped or blemished. Continue tumbling until the stones are ready for fine grinding. Very hard, rough stones can take weeks.

Remove the stones and pour the sludge in the barrel into a plastic bag, which can be disposed of with household rubbish. Wash the stones and the barrel well to get rid of all traces of grit. Examine the stones and put aside any that are not ready for fine polishing.

Place the stones you have selected back in the barrel, and make up the capacity to three-quarters full with other rough-ground or polished stones. Add 1 heaped tablespoon of fine grit, cover the stones with water and begin tumbling them again.

Check every 24 hours, until the stones are perfectly smooth and flawless – it will probably take at least a week. Remove the stones, wash them and the barrel and dispose of the sludge in a plastic bag as before.

Polishing In a 1.5kg (3lb) barrel, add 1 heaped tablespoon of cerium oxide (the polishing agent) to the stones, and cover with water as before. Add a little wallpaper paste to cushion them against damage. Polishing time may be from three days to a week.

When the stones have been polished, wash them and the barrel. Put the stones back, add $\frac{1}{2}$ teaspoon of detergent and cover them with water. Tumble them for four to eight hours to remove the film left by the polish.

Rinse the clean stones under a running tap and dry them in a soft cloth.

Laryngitis

Getting relief for a hoarse voice

Inflammation of the larynx (voice box), called laryngitis, produces hoarseness and sometimes loss of voice. Acute laryngitis is infectious, can strike suddenly, and generally lasts for less than a week; it is usually accompanied by a cough and sore throat and, often, by a raised temperature. Chronic laryngitis may last for days or weeks, and recur. There is, however, no pain in the throat. Chronic laryngitis can be brought on by emotional STRESS, excessive use of the voice, SMOKING, or irritants such as dust.

Treat both types of laryngitis by resting the voice as much as possible. Do not smoke. In cases of acute laryngitis, take extra liquids and painkillers in recommended doses. Cough syrups may ease the symptoms.

Contact the DOCTOR if the high temperature associated with acute laryngitis lasts for more than three or four days, if the victim coughs up blood, or if the voice remains hoarse for more than three weeks.

In cases of chronic laryngitis, contact the doctor if the hoarseness lasts for more than three weeks.

Latches and catches

Choosing the right catch for the job, and fitting it

Most DIY and hardware shops stock a range of easy-to-fit latches and catches. They can be fitted in addition to locks or bolts, or where locking is not required.

Door latch Most interior doors can be fitted with a mortise latch, which holds the door closed but cannot be locked. The easiest type to fit is the tubular latch, requiring only two holes drilled in the door and a recess in the frame for the striker plate.

Mark the position for the latch on the door edge. Using a brace and bit, drill a hole slightly larger than the diameter of the tubular latch, and slightly deeper than its length – see DRILLING. Insert the latch and mark the outline of the faceplate on the door edge.

Chisel out a recess (see CHISELLING) so that the faceplate will fit flush with the door. Withdraw the latch and measure the length from the faceplate to the handle hole. Transfer this measurement to the door, and drill a hole large enough to take the square handle bar. Refit the latch and secure the faceplate with countersunk screws.

Fit the handle bar assembly knob or lever handles – cut the bar to length if necessary, using a hacksaw. Fit the handle plate over the bar and screw it to the door. If you are fitting knobs, first screw the rose to the door around the bar, then put the knob on the bar and fix it with the grub screws that come with it. See also DOORKNOBS; DOOR LOCKS.

Hold the striker plate against the door frame, opposite the latch faceplate. Mark its outline, chisel a recess and screw the striker plate to the frame.

Gate latches A popular latch for a full-height gate (see GATES) is the Suffolk latch. It is particularly useful because it has a bar that can be raised from both sides, with a handle and thumb lever on both sides on the outside.

Cut a slot in the door by drilling a series of holes and then cutting the outline with a padsaw – see SAWS AND SAWING. Screw the backplate to the gate, with the lever at the bottom of the slot. Fit the bar so that it rests on the lever in its fully dropped position, and fit the catch on the gate frame.

A simple and effective gate fastener is the automatic latch, in which a striker arm triggers a catch when the gate closes. There are several types, and all consist of two parts – one for the gate and one for the gatepost. Screw each part in a convenient position, making sure that the striker arm swings freely into the catch.

Cupboard catches For doors on CUPBOARDS, magnetic catches are easy to fit. Some magnets can be quite powerful, so match the catch to the size of door. Attach the magnet to the inside of the door frame and its keeper plate to the door, so that the two make contact when the door is closed. Elongated holes in the magnet housing and the plate provide adjustment for the fixing screws.

Ball catches or roller catches can also be used on cupboard doors – there is a wide range of sizes, and the larger catches can be used on room doors. The ball or roller is spring loaded and is pushed back into its housing by the striker plate as the door is closed. When the door is fully closed, the spring pushes the ball or roller into the striker plate to hold the door firmly closed.

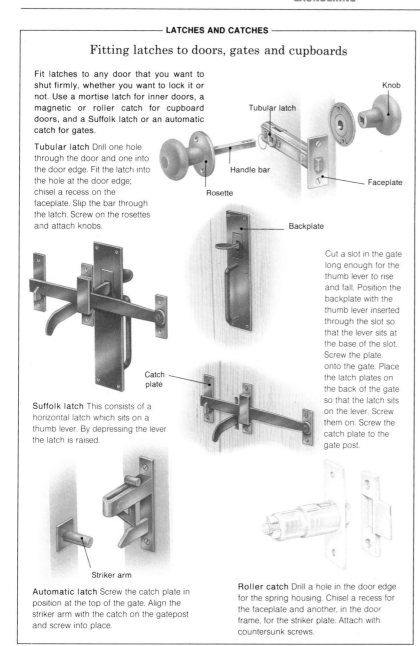

Fitting latches to doors, gates and cupboards

Fit latches to any door that you want to shut firmly, whether you want to lock it or not. Use a mortise latch for inner doors, a magnetic or roller catch for cupboard doors, and a Suffolk latch or an automatic catch for gates.

Tubular latch Drill one hole through the door and one into the door edge. Fit the latch into the hole at the door edge; chisel a recess on the faceplate. Slip the bar through the latch. Screw on the rosettes and attach knobs.

Knob

Tubular latch

Handle bar

Rosette

Faceplate

Backplate

Cut a slot in the gate long enough for the thumb lever to rise and fall. Position the backplate with the thumb lever inserted through the slot so that the lever sits at the base of the slot. Screw the plate onto the gate. Place the latch plates on the back of the gate so that the latch sits on the lever. Screw them on. Screw the catch plate to the gate post.

Catch plate

Suffolk latch This consists of a horizontal latch which sits on a thumb lever. By depressing the lever the latch is raised.

Striker arm

Automatic latch Screw the catch plate in position at the top of the gate. Align the striker arm with the catch on the gatepost and screw into place.

Roller catch Drill a hole in the door edge for the spring housing. Chisel a recess for the faceplate and another, in the door frame, for the striker plate. Attach with countersunk screws.

Laundering

Washing your things the right way

Sort your clothes and other laundry into groups, according to which treatment they need. Most clothes are now clearly labelled with internationally recognised symbols indicating how they should be washed and at what temperature (see the chart on the next page).

Generally, white cotton and linen articles should be washed in very hot water – 95°C (200°F) in a machine, 50°C (120°F)

by hand; most other white and colourfast articles in hot water 50-60°C (120-140°F) in a machine, 50°C (120°F) by hand; and woollens, silks and acrylics in warm water 40°C (105°F), in a machine and by hand.

If you are washing fabrics of different kinds at the same time, wash as for the most sensitive among them and use the lowest temperature recommended. Bear in mind, though, that if you mix articles in this way too often, some are likely to deteriorate – white articles, for example, will start to turn a dull grey if not washed in hot enough water. Wash whites to-

gether, rather than with coloureds. If an article is unlabelled, err on the side of washing it too gently.

Machine washing First make sure that all pockets are empty. Mend any rips and tears which could be made worse during washing – see MENDING; PATCHING; SEWING. Tie belts and strings and do up zips and hooks. Button cuffs to centre buttons. Treat any stains – see STAIN REMOVAL.

Load the clothes into the machine and select the programme – see WASHING MACHINES. Be careful not to overload the machine – or the clothes will come out creased and inadequately washed. Cottons should be loaded so that the drum is full but you can still put your hand in and turn it around. Towelling and man-made or drip-dry fabrics should be much more loosely packed. Mix large items, such as sheets, with smaller ones so that the load is even.

Launderettes In most launderettes, the machines have only two programmes – hot and warm. Wash white and colour-fast cotton, linen and rayon articles in the hot programme. Wash most man-made fabrics in the warm programme. Woollens and silks should be washed by hand at home.

Hand washing The label will usually indicate the temperature at which a garment should be hand washed: 50°C (120°F) is hand hot – as hot as the hand can bear; 40°C (105°F) is warm – the water should be pleasantly warm to the hand; 30°C (85°F) is cool and the water should feel cool to the hand.

Most articles should be given a short soak before being washed by hand. If they have bad protein stains – such as egg yolk, gravy or blood stains – soak them in a biological detergent if the fabric is suitable, following the detergent and garment manufacturers' instructions. Otherwise soak them for about two hours in warm water with ordinary soap powder dissolved in it, according to the instructions on the packet. Dissolve the soap powder or detergent in the water before adding the clothes. Do not soak white and coloured articles together, or the whites will take on some of the colour.

Articles that should not be soaked beforehand are those made from wool, silk, non-colourfast and drip-dry fabrics and fabrics with flame-resistant finishes. Simply wash them following instructions on the 'care' label.

Wash large articles such as blankets in a bath or large sink as they will be damaged in an automatic machine. Wash drip-dry articles on their own. When washing woollen or acrylic articles, move them gently under the surface of the water, trying not to squeeze or rub.

LAUNDERING

Understanding washcare codes

Symbol	Wording	Washing temperature	Suitable fabrics
95	'Wash in cotton cycle/programme' or 'wash as cotton'	Machine very hot 95°C Hand hand hot 50°C *normal action, rinse/spin*	White cotton and linen without special finishes
60	'Wash in cotton cycle/programme' or 'wash as cotton'	Machine hot 60°C Hand hand hot 50°C *normal action, rinse/spin*	Cotton, linen or viscose without special finishes where colours are fast at 60°C
50	'Wash in synthetics cycle/programme' or 'wash as synthetics'	hand hot 50°C *reduced action, cold rinse, reduced spin or drip-dry*	Nylon, polyester/cotton mixtures, polyester cotton and viscose with special finishes; cotton/acrylic mixtures
40	'Wash in cotton cycle/programme' or 'wash as cotton'	warm 40°C *normal action, rinse/spin*	Cotton, linen and viscose where colours are fast at 40°C but not at 60°C
40	'Wash in synthetics cycle/programme' or 'wash as synthetics'	warm 40°C *reduced action cold rinse, reduce spin*	Acrylics, acetate and triacetate including mixtures with wool; polyester/wool blends
40	'Wash in wool cycle/programme' or 'wash as wool'	warm 40°C *much reduced action, normal rinse/spin (do not hand wring)*	Wool, wool mixed with other fibres; silk
	Hand wash	see garment label	
	Do not wash		

Rinse clothes in warm or cold water after washing.

Washing powders Be sure to use the right kind of washing powder. With automatic washing machines, for example, you should only use low lather 'automatic' powders or liquid detergents. If you live in a hard water area, add water-softening powder to the washing powder. It will prevent hard water deposits building up in the machine pipes. Also, use the right amount of powder – follow the machine manufacturer's instructions.

Use biological detergents for soaking out stains (see above) or for the biological soak or pre-wash cycle of certain washing-machine programmes. Fabric conditioners, or softeners, can be added in the last rinse to keep fabrics soft and to cut down static electricity in man-made fabrics.

Never use chlorine bleach on silk, rayon, drip-dry and deep-coloured cotton materials.

Lavender bag

Making a fragrant cupboard freshener

Gather the lavender from your garden on a dry summer's day just before the flowers open. Tie it in small bunches and hang it to dry naturally in a warm, dark place for a few days – see FLOWER DRYING.

Make a sachet or bag about 75mm (3in) across, using a rectangular piece of attractive material. Fold the fabric in half, wrong side outwards, and seam the two opposite sides – see SEWING. Turn the bag inside out and fill it with the dried lavender flowers.

The open end can be hemmed (see HEMS) and secured with ribbon or machine-stitched together. A lace trimming adds an attractive finishing touch. Keep the bag in a cupboard or drawer where it will bring a refreshing fragrance to linen and clothes.

Fragrant bundles Bind lavender stalks just below the flower heads. Bend the stalks back over the heads, then tie up with ribbon.

Lavender sticks To make them, bind 12-18 freshly picked long-stemmed lavender flowers together just below the flower heads. Bend the stalks back over the flower heads and secure with a ribbon. Dry (as above) and use the sticks to perfume cupboards and rooms.

Lawn care

Keeping grass green and healthy

To keep your lawn green in dry spells, give it a thorough weekly soaking, preferably in the early morning before the sun is at its height. More frequent, light waterings only produce shallow roots and encourage weeds.

Do not cut the grass too short. The ideal height, in most cases, is about 25mm (1in); let it grow slightly longer in dry spells or if it receives hard wear.

Begin regular mowing of established lawns in early spring, when the grass is dry and has reached a height of about 50-75mm (2-3in). Before mowing, scatter worm casts and remove debris, using a besom or wire rake.

The first cut should remove the top one-third of the grass, but afterwards you can use a slightly lower mower setting – see LAWN MOWERS. Then mow once or twice a week until mid-autumn. If the grass becomes badly overgrown, mow it once on a high setting and again, on a lower one, three or four days later.

And what to do with the grass cuttings? At the beginning and end of the season, when the cuttings may be long and the soil damp, collect the cuttings in the grass-box and put them on the compost heap. At other times leave them on the lawn to rot down and feed the grass. The reason for collecting them at each end of the season is that they may encourage moss if they do not rot down quickly.

Fertilising the lawn An annual feed with fertiliser is sufficient for most lawns. The best time to give it is in late spring, when growth is most vigorous, but you can apply lawn fertiliser at any time during the summer. Compound FERTILISERS containing nitrogen, phosphate and potash are most suitable. There are many proprietary brands; those specifically designed for lawns tend to have a high proportion of nitrogen – which stimulates rapid growth and makes the grass green. The proportions are shown on the side of the container. One designated 10-6-4 is nitrogen-rich; one labelled 7-7-7 contains equal parts of the three nutrients.

Choose a day when the grass is dry, but the soil beneath is damp. If the fertiliser is in the form of granules, ensure that it is spread as evenly as possible; you can buy or hire wheeled fertiliser spreaders to make the task easier. Water the lawn afterwards.

Apply liquid fertiliser from a watering can, preferably with a bar attachment in place of the normal rose. Mark the lawn with strips of twine or tape to show the area already covered, to prevent overlapping.

Lawn problems In mid-autumn, vigorous use of a wire rake will remove dead leaves and other debris that could encourage fungal diseases such as fusarium and dollar spot.

Aeration is necessary once a year on heavy or compacted soils. It improves drainage and growth, and may discourage moss. Choose a day when the soil is moist. With an ordinary garden fork, make sets of holes 100mm (4in) deep at 100mm intervals across the lawn; do not lever the fork too hard, as that may damage the grass. For large lawns, you can buy or hire mechanical aerators that serve the same purpose.

Isolated weeds that mar an otherwise well-kept lawn can be removed by hand; a potato-peeler is useful for digging them out, with their roots, without leaving large bare patches. Or you can use a spot weedkiller – see WEED CONTROL.

Selective weedkillers, combined with a lawn fertiliser, can be applied according to the makers' instructions in spring or early summer, two or three days after one cut and the same period before the next. If you use separate fertilisers and weedkillers, apply the weedkiller three weeks after the spring treatment with fertiliser. For liquid weedkillers, use a watering can with a fine rose, but take care that it does not drift onto nearby beds. With both liquid and solid weedkillers, mark the areas treated with twine as you go along, to prevent overlapping.

Moss in a lawn is a symptom usually of waterlogging or excessive shade. Proprietary moss-killers or lawn sand (a mixture of fine sand, iron sulphate and sulphate of ammonia in the proportions 24:1:3 is one formula) may temporarily remove the moss. However, it will return unless the cause is dealt with – for example, by improving aeration and drainage of the soil, or by cutting down an overhanging tree.

Bare patches may also be the result of waterlogging or the presence of a tree. Again, in such cases, the cause must be removed.

Bare patches due to wear should be re-seeded in spring or late summer.

Fork over the area and rake it smooth. Sprinkle a handful of Growmore over each square metre or yard, and then sprinkle on the grass seed. Protect the seed from birds with netting and stakes, and water in dry spells. See also TURFING.

Popular lawn grasses Most lawn seed mixtures contain three or four species of grass which are blended for different purposes, such as a fine-quality lawn or a hardwearing one where children can play.

For top-quality lawns, for example, *Chewing's fescue* is mixed with *Browntop* in the proportion 70:30.

Rye grass Mixtures with rye grass are the cheapest and suitable for lawns that get heavy wear and tear. Traditional varieties are coarse, but some newer strains are finer and can give a good appearance.

Crested dog's-tail This is tough, slow-growing and suitable for most soils. It is used for a hardwearing lawn of fine quality.

Fescues These grasses grow anywhere. *Chewing's fescue* and *hard fescue* resist drought well. *Creeping red fescue* is fine and hardwearing, but should not be cut too short.

Rough-stalked meadow grass This flourishes in partial shade, unlike its relative, *Smooth-stalked meadow grass.*

Timothy This grass is suitable for heavy soils and exposed gardens. *Velvet bent* likes damp soil and shade. *Browntop* is hardwearing, with fine, dense leaves.

Lawn mowers

Care, servicing and simple repairs

A lawn mower will only perform efficiently if it is kept clean and well lubricated. So make a habit of removing caked soil and crushed grass clippings while they are still damp and store the mower under cover. Before doing any maintenance work on an electric mower, always unplug it; on a motor mower, disconnect the spark-plug.

The two most important areas are the cutting blades and the wheels or roller. Use an old kitchen knife to cut away any build-up of mud on the wheels or roller, as this affects the depth of cut. When clean, spray lightly with an aerosol protective oil.

Lubrication varies according to mower type, so read the instruction manual. Some mowers require grease, others oil, while others need neither, as the bearings are lubricated during manufacture, then sealed for the life of the mower.

As a general rule, oil or grease the machine after every eight hours of mowing. Then lubricate the whole machine and spray with aerosol oil before storing for winter.

During the mowing season, keep an eye on all nuts and bolts. They can work loose with the vibration of the machine. This applies particularly to adjustable wooden rollers. Make sure also that the adjusting nuts are easy to turn, that all oiling points are clear of debris and the protective caps are in the closed position.

Blade care Check the blades on a cylinder mower for damage caused by stones or other hard obstructions. Use a file to remove any burrs, and straighten any slight bends by firmly tapping the appropriate blade with a hammer. See that the cylinder is in the right position in relation to the fixed bottom blade. If the gap is too big, the machine will not cut; too close, and it will seize up.

To check for correct alignment, hold a sheet of paper between the cylinder blades and the fixed blade and rotate the cylinder. The blade should cut cleanly through the paper along its full length. Adjust the cutting action by turning the adjusting screws at each end of the cylinder.

If the cylinder blades are blunt, they can be sharpened by using grinding paste. Coat each blade with paste, then turn the rotating cylinder backwards by hand so the paste is trapped between cylinder and bottom blade. When sharpening is complete, wipe the paste from all blade surfaces.

If the bottom blade is rounded and beyond sharpening, remove it by undoing the holding screws. Take the blade to a local lawnmower stockist and get an identical replacement blade. If the new blade has a coating of protective paint, clean it off to bare metal before fitting.

Rotary mowers There are two types of rotary mower: hover mowers which float on a cushion of air, and the larger models mounted on wheels, allowing for adjustment of height of cut. With both types, cleaning the underside is important, as a build-up of debris can soon affect the efficiency of the mower. Clean off caked mud and grass after each session. The propeller-like cutting blade revolves at very high speed and is easily blunted by obstructions, so check the blade after every use. Always stop the machine and wait for the blade to become stationary before touching it. With electrical models, always unplug before servicing.

To remove burrs, remove the blade from the machine by removing the large

---

LAWN MOWERS

Adjusting for height of cut; adjusting and changing blades

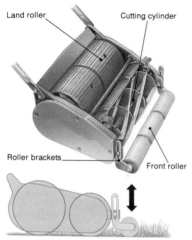

Land roller

Cutting cylinder

Roller brackets

Front roller

According to the length of the grass you are cutting, adjust a mower's height of cut. Keep the blades well aligned so that they cut cleanly.

Slacken the bolts holding the roller brackets to the mower. Raise or lower the roller, then tighten the bolts at the desired position.

On a different type of mower, slacken the knob on each bracket. Pivot the bracket on the support bar, then tighten the knob.

Height of cut Adjust the height to which the grass is cut by raising or lowering the mower's position on the front roller brackets.

Locknut

Blade adjusting Slacken the locknuts on the adjusting screws at each end of the cutting cylinder. Slightly undo the screws, then tighten again until some paper held between cylinder blades and fixed blade is cut cleanly along its length. Tighten the locknuts.

Rotary mowers Some rotary mowers can be fitted with plastic blades – for safer mowing. Use plastic blades only for grass cutting. For cutting denser growth, such as weeds, use metal blades. Use a strimmer (below) for trimming edges and, for example, around trees.

Plastic blades

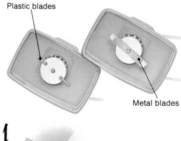

Metal blades

Changing blades
Push plastic blades in and up to remove. Bolt on metal blades.

holding screw or nut and remove the blade and spacer. Clamp the blade in a vice and use a file to remove burrs and sharpen the cutting edges. If the blade is too badly damaged, take the blade to a local stockist and get an identical replacement blade.

It is important that the blade remains well balanced, as an unbalanced blade will cause severe vibration and may damage the bearings. Trouble could be caused by filing off too much metal from

one end. You can check this by clamping an old knife with a narrow blade in a vice horizontally and balancing the mower blade on the knife by means of the central hole. If the mower blade drops on one side, file more off the heavier side until the blade balances well.

The fast rotating blade is a potential danger to any foot which slips under the rim of the mower, and to eliminate this risk many manufacturers offer a plastic blade or cord which cuts grass but

nothing else. Obviously the plastic materials are far less durable than steel, so you need spare plastic blades. Some machines are supplied with both types of blade. Check this point when buying.

Engines The petrol engine on a power mower needs regular maintenance. Remove and clean the spark-plug at least twice a year – see SPARK-PLUGS. Scrape off carbon deposits from the nose and electrodes of the plug with a plug file or a folded piece of fine emery paper. Check the gap between the electrodes with a feeler gauge of the thickness recommended in the service manual. Use a gapping tool to adjust it by bending the earth electrode towards or away from the central electrode.

Check the carburettor air filter, which must be kept clean. Remove a sponge type filter element, wash it in liquid detergent, rinse and allow to dry. Apply a few drops of engine oil, squeeze to distribute the oil evenly, then replace the element – see also AIR FILTERS. A clogged fuel-pipe filter will impede the petrol flow: pull the pipe off at the carburettor and check that fuel flows freely. If it is obstructed, renew the fuel pipe and/or filter (some are integral). When filling with fuel, use a funnel fitted with a fine gauze filter to keep out impurities. Keep the oil reservoir topped up to the right level at all times.

Cables With an electric mower, regularly check the cable for signs of damage, and replace damaged cable immediately or cut out a damaged section and re-join the cable with a waterproof cable connector. The socket half must be fitted on the cable connected to the plug.

Check the plug for loose connections and make sure the cable is correctly anchored by the securing strap. If you have to fit a new plug, fit a rubber one.

For complete safety, use an RCCB CIRCUIT BREAKER between the power supply and the mower.

If the mower is battery-operated, see that the battery is kept fully charged (see BATTERIES) and that it is topped up to the correct level with a proprietary topping-up fluid or distilled water.

Remove terminal leads occasionally and clean the posts with a wire brush. Wipe the case dry with an old rag, then coat the posts and terminal lead ends with petroleum jelly (not grease).

Lawyers

Seeking legal advice

Most types of legal work involving a court hearing can be dealt with only through a solicitor, unless one of the parties chooses to conduct his own case. Depending on the nature of the action, the solicitor may instruct a barrister (called an advocate in Scotland) to appear on his client's behalf.

Solicitors also deal with many other forms of legal transaction – property conveyancing or the administration of a dead person's estate, for example. They can give general advice on the law, too, although sometimes another expert may be a more suitable choice – for example, a chartered accountant in matters relating to tax.

All solicitors are subject to strict rules on qualifications and how they run their businesses. They can be fined or struck off in the same way as doctors for professional misconduct. They are entitled to charge for all work done for a client, including telephone calls and letters, based on the length of time it takes. You will find that a fee of £40-£60 an hour is quite normal.

However, although all solicitors are governed by the same rules, one firm may differ from another in two important ways. The first is in the fees they charge, including whether or not they participate in various schemes that reduce the cost of legal advice. The second is the area of law in which they specialise; one firm, for example, may concentrate on domestic and family issues, while another may do most of its work in the commercial or criminal fields. If you are choosing a solicitor, therefore, it pays to shop around.

Solicitors now advertise, and are listed in local classified telephone directories. Public libraries keep copies of *The Solicitors' and Barristers' Directory and Diary* which gives the area in which each firm specialises.

Choosing a solicitor Consult the register in your library and pick two or three firms specialising in the field of law with which you are concerned. Telephone each and give them details of your case. Ask whether they understand it and are prepared to take it, and for a rough estimate of the likely cost.

If asked in advance, some solicitors will quote a fee of up to £10 for a 30-minute first interview. That is usually time enough for the solicitor to determine whether the case is worth pursuing, and for you to decide whether he is the right person to pursue it. Subsequent interviews will be charged at the solicitor's normal, higher rates.

Ask the firm, too, if they participate in the 'green form' – 'pink form' in Scotland – advice schemes (see below). These schemes can, in many circumstances, reduce your bill for work done out of court. (Court costs may be partly defrayed if you qualify under the rules for LEGAL AID.)

If they do not participate, try other firms. If they do, tell them from the beginning that you intend to consult them under those schemes.

Green (or pink) form schemes Under them, solicitor's charges are offset for people of limited means.

Ask the solicitor to fill in on your behalf a form giving details of your disposable income (weekly earnings less deductions for specified expenses such as tax and allowances for dependants) and disposable assets (excluding home, furniture, clothing, car and tools of the trade). He will be able to advise you regarding your entitlement.

However, if you are involved in a civil claim for money and you win, the solicitor's full fee can be deducted from the amount you are awarded.

Disputes with solicitors If you disagree with your solicitor's bill, ask for a breakdown in detail. If you are still not satisfied, ask the solicitor for a certificate from his professional body stating that the amount is 'fair and reasonable'.

Complaints about solicitors should be referred to the Law Society, 113 Chancery Lane, London WC2A 1PL, or the Law Society of Scotland, 26 Drumsheugh Gardens, Edinburgh EH3 7YR.

Other sources of help

Citizens Advice Bureaus give advice on all sorts of legal problems at no cost; their staff include lawyers and trained volunteers.

Legal advice centres or Law Centres give help not involving court work; they are staffed by qualified lawyers.

Specialist organisations include consumer advice centres, dealing with shoppers' rights, and housing advice centres; both are operated by some local authorities, and do not charge for advice. Independent bodies such as Shelter can also help with housing problems; the National Council for Civil Liberties may assist with matters involving civil rights.

Addresses and telephone numbers of any local branches of these bodies can be found in the telephone directory or a public library.

Trade and professional organisations and societies often include free or low-cost legal advice as a service to members. Most trade unions, for example, retain lawyers to assist in legal problems; the AA or RAC may be able to help motorist members.

Leaded lights
Removing, replacing and repairing

A leaded-light window consists of small glass panes set individually into pieces of H-section lead – called cames. The glass is sealed with putty – see PUTTYING. Problems can arise with them – especially in older houses.

Leaks Mark the leaking areas during wet weather, using a wax crayon. When dry, ease open the cames on the outside face of the leaded light and scrape out the old putty. Squeeze a little clear silicone rubber bath sealant into the gaps. Then, with a helper applying counter-pressure from the other side, carefully press back the lead.

Broken pane Chisel through the soldered joints at both sides of the pane and turn back the lead with the chisel (see illustration). Now, wearing safety goggles and sturdy gardening gloves, remove the pieces of broken glass and clean out all old putty, brushing the cames clean.

Measure carefully for the replacement pane (see GLASS CUTTING), then bed the cames with clear silicone rubber bath sealant or metal casement putty. Ease the new pane into place, then press down the lead as before, ensuring it makes a good contact with the glass.

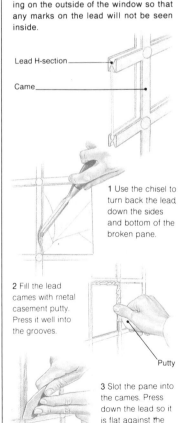

LEADED LIGHTS

Replacing a broken pane

First chisel through the soldered joints at both sides of the broken pane – working on the outside of the window so that any marks on the lead will not be seen inside.

Lead H-section

Came

1 Use the chisel to turn back the lead down the sides and bottom of the broken pane.

2 Fill the lead cames with metal casement putty. Press it well into the grooves.

Putty

3 Slot the pane into the cames. Press down the lead so it is flat against the glass.

Remove surplus putty with a putty knife while it is still soft, then burnish the cut joints with an abrasive pad or fine glasspaper.

Apply SOLDERING flux to the cleaned lead, then place a little solder on each cut joint using a moderately hot soldering iron. Rub the iron over the new joints to give an effect which matches the other panel joints.

Bulging lights High winds and, in the case of door lights, constant slamming, can cause bulging. Remove the whole panel from its frame. If it is held with putty, remove the putty with an old wood chisel and a hammer. Remove any metal glazing sprigs with pincers. If there is also an outer wood beading unscrew it, or prise it out gently if it is nailed.

Lay the panel on a flat surface. Open up all loose joints and remove any putty which has deteriorated. Fill the gaps with silicone rubber sealant, then press the lead into tight contact with the panes. Work on both sides of the window. Allow the sealant to set, then carefully replace the panel in its frame – see WINDOW PANES.

Colour problems Where new glass is put into a coloured pane, you can colour it with special stains available in kits. Full instructions are supplied for applying the stains.

Leather garments

Caring for and cleaning coats, jackets and gloves

Do not put leather or suede garments away immediately after wearing them – leave them out for a while to air. If they have got wet, put them on a hanger and let them dry naturally, not near heat. Suede clothes should be brushed regularly with a rubber brush or pad – never a wire brush. Do not brush suede when it is wet.

Blow into leather gloves directly after use to puff them up, and pull the fingers gently into shape.

Cleaning coats and jackets If possible, avoid cleaning or washing leather garments as this tends to spoil the attractive patina that leather develops over time. If a garment has become badly soiled, however, get it dry-cleaned at a shop with a specialist leather cleaner.

Some garments can be washed to remove minor stains. How you wash them depends on how the leather was tanned. Follow the instructions on the label. See also STAIN REMOVAL.

Washing gloves Most leather gloves are washable, but make sure by checking the label. To wash them, dissolve soap flakes or special glove soap in warm water. Wash the gloves on the hand – unless they are made from doeskin, which tears easily when wet. Squeeze water gently into the leather but avoid wringing the gloves.

After washing, remove the gloves carefully and rinse them several times in tepid water. Press them gently between towelling. Then blow into each glove to separate the inside surfaces, and hang them up to dry by lightly pegging at the corner of the cuff at the side seam. Keep them out of sunlight or direct heat. When they are almost dry, put them on your hands or stretch them gently.

Gloves that are not washable should only be cleaned professionally.

Leather work

Cutting and stitching; making a belt

A good craft shop should supply the small pieces of leather and specialist tools needed to make a start. Different thicknesses and types of leather are used for different projects, ranging from cowhide, or pigskin up to 4mm ($\frac{1}{6}$in) thick for belts, to chamois suede, doeskin or buckskin as thin as 1mm ($\frac{1}{32}$in).

Essential tools are: a craft knife with replaceable blades; leather shears; punches for making holes; rawhide mallet; steel rule and awl. Various other tools for bevelling, shaving and embossing can be added later.

─── **LEATHER WORK** ───

Special tools to work with; making a belt

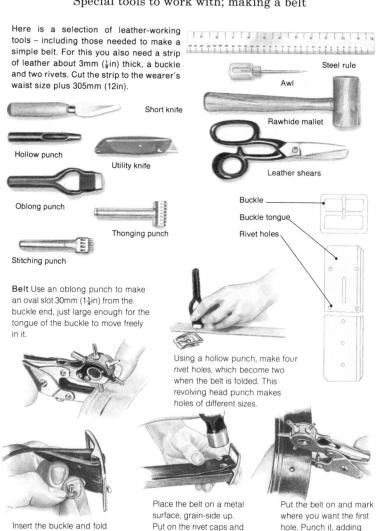

Here is a selection of leather-working tools – including those needed to make a simple belt. For this you also need a strip of leather about 3mm ($\frac{1}{8}$in) thick, a buckle and two rivets. Cut the strip to the wearer's waist size plus 305mm (12in).

Steel rule

Awl

Short knife

Rawhide mallet

Hollow punch

Utility knife

Leather shears

Oblong punch

Buckle

Buckle tongue

Thonging punch

Rivet holes

Stitching punch

Belt Use an oblong punch to make an oval slot 30mm (1$\frac{1}{4}$in) from the buckle end, just large enough for the tongue of the buckle to move freely in it.

Using a hollow punch, make four rivet holes, which become two when the belt is folded. This revolving head punch makes holes of different sizes.

Insert the buckle and fold back the strap. Fit the rivets from underneath.

Place the belt on a metal surface, grain-side up. Put on the rivet caps and tap them sharply with a hammer or mallet.

Put the belt on and mark where you want the first hole. Punch it, adding extra holes at 25mm (1in) intervals.

Cutting The hardest part is getting your knife to follow a marked line – the blade tends to wander. To help avoid this, make a card template then draw around it with a pencil onto the good side of the leather.

Now use the awl to trace your lines, applying enough pressure to make an indentation which the knife blade can follow. If the leather is thick, do not try to cut through in one pass. Go part way through, then repeat the cuts until the leather is penetrated.

Cut on something yielding, such as scrap flooring vinyl, hardboard or plywood – hard materials like laminate or metal will quickly blunt knife blades. Use the steel rule as a guide for straight cuts – and always cut away from the fingers holding the rule.

When cutting a curve, slowly rotate the leather with one hand while continuing to cut with the other.

Leather shears are useful for cutting curves, and irregular lines in lightweight leather.

You may need to thin the leather at a given point – either to join two pieces or where thick leather is to be folded. This operation can be done with a tool called a *safety beveller*, used like a potato peeler, or a shoe knife. Always work away from the fingers holding the leather.

Dyeing If you want to dye the leather yourself, buy oak-tanned leather which is a neutral shade, or oil-tanned which is light yellow. Leather dyes are available in a wide range of colours, but tend to be dark until diluted with dye solvent. Test the dye on scrap leather. Do not dye the actual job until all cutting, hole punching, edging and tooling have been done.

Gluing Use a clear resin adhesive, which dries clear and remains flexible when dry – see GLUING. Apply it to both surfaces, allow them to become touch-dry, then press them firmly together to make an immediate bond. Keep the adhesive off the face of the leather – it is difficult to remove.

Stitching Mark the stitch line with a pencil and a straightedge or steel rule, using compasses for curves. To make a series of evenly spaced holes, use a stitching punch or awl for sewing with thread, or a thonging punch for sewing with laces or thongs. Practise on waste material until you feel able to tackle the real thing.

Two kinds of needle are used: harness needles, which have a blunt point designed to go into prepared holes; and gloving needles, which have a very sharp point, designed to be used on thin leather – usually where no stitching holes have been made.

Both come in a range of sizes, and both needle and thread are matched to the size of hole being used or made. Use linen button thread for sewing, waxing it with a wax block so that it slips easily through the leather, and the stitches are long-lasting. Silk thread may be used for fine leather, and carpet thread or sailmaker's twine for thick leather.

Use narrow strips of leather in place of thread for thonging. There are two types of thongs, round and flat; both are supplied in several colours as well as natural. The needle used has prongs on which the thong is impaled, secured by a spring clip.

Fittings Many of the fittings available are attached to the leather, rather like PRESS STUDS, with a tool called a press stud or garment setter. These fittings include eyelets to take thongs or laces; press studs and rivets for fastening thick sections of leather permanently together; and decorative studs.

Making a belt As a first project, make a single-buckle belt – see illustration. A good choice of leather would be vegetable-tanned cowhide, which is both strong and supple. Make sure that the grain runs along the length of the belt, to reduce stretching.

The width is governed by the inside measurement of the buckle chosen, so buy the buckle first.

The width and thickness of the belt determine the size and position of rivets – choose them to suit.

Dye all cut edges with a felt brush, and push a little dye through the holes, using a pipe cleaner as a brush. Now dye the grain side of the belt by rubbing with a piece of lambswool dipped in the chosen dye. Use a cloth to apply neat's-foot oil to the outer side of the belt. Rub it in by hand, then finish by polishing with newspaper.

A plain belt can be decorated with grooves made by a stitch grooving tool; edges can be neatly bevelled with another tool called an edge-shaver.

Left-handedness

Teaching left-handers how to cope in a right-handed world

About 10 per cent of the population is left-handed. It first becomes apparent in children before the age of six. Until then a child will probably use one hand or the other when playing or drawing. But gradually he will transfer everything – pencils, knives, books – from his right hand to his left.

Parents should accept the fact that a child is left-handed, and not try to change it. The dominant hand is ruled by the brain area that also controls talking, writing and reading. Interfering with the process can lead to speech problems, as well as difficulty in reading and writing. In addition, the child may become puzzled, frustrated and anxious.

Instead of criticising or 'correcting' him, help him. Learning to write can be troublesome for left-handers, because the left hand, as it moves across the page, covers and sometimes smudges the words just written. Give the child a pen or pencil that will not smudge and get him to hold it far enough from the point to let him see what he has written.

When the child starts school, make sure the teachers know that he is left-handed, and not just being 'difficult'. At mealtimes, lay plates and cutlery the right way round for him. Some left-handers prefer to sit at a corner of a table and to the left of a right-hander, so that their elbows do not collide.

Left-handers often come into their own at sports. In racket games such as tennis and squash they have an advantage over opponents who are accustomed to the spin, angles of return and playing style of right-handers. And when a left-hander and a right-hander are batting together in cricket, the field placings have to be constantly changed. For left-handed golfers left-handed clubs are now widely available. See also GOLF.

Tools and household appliances probably cause left-handers the most problems, but more and more left-handed implements such as scissors, tin-openers, potato peelers and secateurs, are becoming widely available. Left-handed implements can be obtained from Anything Left Handed, 57 Brewer Street, London W1R 3FB.

Leftovers

Turning them into appetising meals

When cooking leftovers, always transform them into a new dish. Simply reheated in their original form, their texture and flavour will be faded and limp. But new dishes made with them can be excellent.

Do not combine lots of different leftovers in one dish. Use each one to make a separate dish. Mix the leftovers with plenty of fresh ingredients and sufficient sharply flavoured seasonings and spices to give the new dishes good flavour and texture.

The sooner you use up leftovers, the better: the flavour and texture will be retained and you avoid the risk of food poisoning. Meat should not be kept in REFRIGERATORS for more than three days, fish for more than two days and vegetables for more than five days. See also FOOD STORAGE.

Meat leftovers Small amounts of meat can be used to make a meat sauce to go with PASTA. Larger amounts can be used to make CASSEROLES, curries or pies – see CURRY POWDER; PIE MAKING. Meat can always be made to go further by adding a little canned meat.

A classic dish for using up leftover beef is *cottage pie*, or with lamb, *shepherd's pie*. Cook two chopped onions in butter or oil until soft. Add about 350g (12oz) of minced leftover meat and cook until brown. Add some stock or gravy, tomato ketchup and a little Worcestershire sauce. Mash 450g (1lb) of cooked potatoes adding a little butter and milk.

Put the meat in a greased ovenproof dish and spread the mashed potatoes on top. Bake in an oven preheated to 220°C (425°F, gas mark 7) for about 30 minutes until browned on top. There should be enough for four to six people.

Poultry and fish leftovers Many dishes, from paella to chicken à la king, can be made with chicken or turkey leftovers. For one of the simplest dishes chop up the meat and mix it with chopped hard-boiled eggs, cucumber, apple, green or red pepper, celery and radishes. Fold the mixture into MAYONNAISE spiced with curry powder or horseradish. Chicken can be made to go further by adding tinned tuna fish.

Mix fish leftovers with prawns or other shellfish and make into a pie. Alternatively, combine them with a creamy sauce (see SAUCES) to fill PANCAKES or spread over toast. Fish can be made to go further with tinned tuna or salmon.

Vegetable leftovers Cooked vegetables can be used the next day in SOUFFLÉS or OMELETTES, or mixed into a salad. They can also be added to meat dishes or puréed to make soup – see PURÉEING.

Alternatively, cut up crisp vegetables, heat some butter in a frying pan or wok, add the vegetables and toss over a moderate heat until they have absorbed all the butter.

It is also a good idea to keep the liquids in which vegetables have been cooked as well as any peelings or trimmings for use in soups – see SOUPS AND STOCKS; GRAVY.

Leftover egg yolk, and whites Leftover yolks can be beaten into creamy soups, white sauces or mashed potato, or they can be used to make mayonnaise, Hollandaise sauce or custard. Whites can be used to make a MERINGUE or for ICING CAKES. Or you can add them to scrambled eggs, mousses, fruit purées or soufflés.

Stale bread Use stale bread to make breadcrumbs. Remove the crust, then dry the bread in a cool oven at 120°C (250°F, gas mark ½) for a few hours. Crumble it with a rolling pin and store in an airtight container. Use for coating meat or fish before sautéeing or deep FRYING. You can also fry breadcrumbs in butter to add to casseroles or serve with game.

Slightly stale white bread can be used to make bread-and-butter pudding. Cut 8 slices of bread. Butter them, remove the crusts and cut into quarters. Butter a heatproof dish and place the bread in the dish in layers, butter-sides up. Sprinkle sultanas and grated lemon rind between each layer.

Beat 2 eggs with 2 level tablespoons of vanilla sugar or caster sugar. Bring 570ml (1 pint) of milk almost to the boil and pour over the beaten eggs. Strain the custard through a sieve onto the bread. Sprinkle another level tablespoon of sugar on top and leave to stand for 15 minutes. Bake in an oven preheated to 180°C (350°F, gas mark 4) for about 30 minutes until lightly browned on top.

Legal aid

Help in meeting court bills

Anyone who is a party in a court case, whether charged with a criminal offence or involved in a civil action, may be entitled to legal aid, to help meet the court costs. But to qualify he must submit to a rigorous scrutiny of his earnings and assets. If his financial means are above certain limits, legal aid will be refused.

A solicitor (see LAWYERS) will be able to give you a rough idea of whether or not you qualify for help. Then you must obtain and fill in a legal aid application form. Civil case forms are available from solicitors' offices or Citizens Advice Bureaus. In a criminal case, a defendant should ask the magistrates' clerk for one when he appears in court.

Legal aid cannot be obtained to pay for legal advice not connected with a court case. A separate kind of legal aid, known as the green form scheme (pink, in Scotland) is available for legal advice and assistance.

Cases involving libel or slander do not qualify for aid. Nor do such matters as claims for redundancy payments, social security appeals or UNFAIR DISMISSAL, heard before tribunals, rather than courts.

What the forms ask Applications for legal aid are intended to establish the applicant's disposable income and assets. Disposable income is the amount left over from earnings after specified expenses, such as tax bills, rent or mortgage payments, have been met. Disposable assets are savings and items such as jewellery that could be used to raise money; they do not include your house, furniture, clothes or the tools of your trade.

Property that is the subject of the dispute in a civil action, such as a piece of land, is excluded from the assets. A spouse's income is not included in defended divorce actions.

Submitting an application In criminal cases, the completed form must be returned to the magistrates' clerk. If aid is refused, the defendant can re-apply to the magistrates, or finally to the crown court, if he is sent there.

In civil cases, the completed form must be sent to the local office of the Legal Aid Board – address in telephone directory. If you have a solicitor, ask him to check the application before it is sent.

The Legal Aid Board will ask the Legal Aid Assessment Office of the Department of Social Security to verify the financial details, and you may be interviewed by an income support officer. If your application is rejected, you may be able to appeal to the society's appeals committee, but if that turns you down you cannot take the matter further.

Civil claim settlements In most civil cases, the loser pays his own and the winner's costs. If the loser is on legal aid, his contribution to his own costs is limited to the amount specified when the aid was granted; however, he may have to pay something towards the winner's costs. If the legally aided person wins, but costs are not paid by the loser, the amount of legal aid is deducted from the damages or property won.

Lettering a sign

Centring the words without using a ruler

To make a neat sign without complicated measuring, start with pencil sketches on scrap paper until you have a pleasing arrangement of letters. Then print the first line of letters on scrap paper the same width as your poster or signboard.

Blacken the back of the paper with a soft pencil and fold the paper in the centre of the line of words. Pencil a light line down the middle of the poster or board. Tape the paper lightly to the surface, matching the fold to the line. Then trace over the letters to transfer them.

Continue until you have transferred each line of your sign. Then go over the letters lightly in pencil, straightening their lines and evening their height and thickness. If you need to erase, use an ordinary rubber. Broaden the letters with a broad-tipped marker or a flat-ended lettering brush and poster paint.

Alternatively, you can buy a stencil alphabet and stencil your sign – see STENCILLING – or use Letraset transfer letters.

An outdoor sign should be made on wood and protected with two or three coats of clear varnish.

Plastic tube method; concrete and fencing

Use a length of transparent plastic tube filled with water to find true level between two distant points – when laying a path, for example – or around corners.

Hold both ends of the tube upright. Align the water level at one end with your starting level. Get a helper to use the other end of the tube to position the second point on a level with the first – the water level in the tube is on the same plane at both ends.

Levelling concrete Drive a peg into the ground so that its top is at the level you want the concrete surface to be. Drive in other pegs, using a batten and spirit level to make sure their tops are level with one another.

Fencing on a slope Divide a fence on a slope into equal horizontal sections stepped at different levels, with each step the length of a fence panel. Use a spirit level and true board to get the posts level. Use the spirit level to get the fence panels horizontal before nailing into place.

Levelling

Finding a true horizontal plane

Finding a true level is vital for many jobs around the house and garden. Here are a few examples:

Shelving Use a spirit level to ensure that SHELVES are horizontal. Fix one bracket; then ask a helper to hold the next bracket in place while the shelf is rested on both. Lay the spirit level on the shelf and move the loose bracket up and down as necessary until the bubble is central in the vial. Then mark the screw holes on the wall through the holes in the bracket.

For finding a vertical – see PLUMB LINE.

Foundations Any CONCRETE slab upon which a structure is to be erected must be truly level.

Use pegs, a straight wooden batten (see BATTENS) and a spirit level. Sharpen some short battens at one end and drive one into the ground at a corner of the area. Set it with its top at the right level for the surface of the concrete. Drive in a second peg no more than 1.5m (5ft) from the first. Lay the batten across the tops of the two pegs, then lay a spirit level on the batten. Adjust the second peg until the batten is horizontal. Continue with more pegs all over the area until the batten is horizontal when it is laid across any two pegs. The tops of the pegs are then all level with each other.

The same technique can be used to make foundations for a garden wall – see BRICKLAYING.

An alternative way to get the tops of the pegs level – especially useful in large areas with long distances between pegs – is to use a length of flexible transparent plastic tube. Fill the tube with water, making sure there are no air bubbles.

Tip out some water to leave air at each end. Holding both ends of the tube upright, align the water level in one end with the top of the first peg. Get a helper to hold the other end against another peg. Adjust the peg so that its top is level with the water in the tube – and so level with the top of the first peg.

This method is useful for finding true level between any two distant points, in different rooms of a house, for example, or around a corner.

Lice

Detecting and eliminating nits in the hair

The first sign of head lice is likely to be intense ITCHING of the scalp. Scratching can produce a secondary infection, with blisters, spots or yellowish, crusty sores. The lice themselves may be visible through a magnifying glass; their grey eggs, called nits, can often be seen near the roots of the hair.

Chemists sell remedies for head lice, which should be used according to the maker's instructions (they are not suitable for babies under the age of six months). If the hair is short enough, comb it afterwards with a fine-toothed nit comb to get rid of remaining eggs.

Frequent washing with hot, soapy water or a medicated shampoo may help to deter lice. However, they spread very quickly, particularly among young schoolchildren; they do not signify an unclean home or person. Anyone with whom an infested person has been in close contact can catch them, and should be told the problem exists.

Seek medical advice if home treatment fails to remove the lice, if a young baby is infested or sores are badly inflamed.

Lifesaving

Rescuing a panicking or exhausted swimmer

Do not go into the water yourself except as a final resort – and only then if you are a strong and experienced swimmer. Avoid direct physical contact with the person in difficulties if possible; someone in danger of drowning develops a desperate strength that can endanger the would-be rescuer.

If the victim can be reached from land – for example, a river bank – hold out a pole, shirt or jacket for him to grasp. Get someone to hold you, to prevent you from being dragged in, or hold onto a firm object with one hand while you use the other to help the victim. If he is too far from land for you to reach directly, throw him a buoyant object, such as a beach ball or a life buoy, to keep him afloat until he can be rescued. If you throw a rope, try to land it just beyond the victim, so you can then pull it close for him to grasp.

To perform a rescue from a small boat, reach for the victim over the stern, rather than the side, to lessen the risk of capsizing. Wedge your feet under a fixed seat, or get someone to hold them. Reach over the stern, grasp the victim's wrists, and get him to grasp yours.

In the water If you are confident of undertaking an in-water rescue, take a piece of clothing, a towel or other suitable object for the victim to hold. If he is conscious and the water calm, give him one end of the object, tell him to lie on his back, and tow him to safety.

When the victim is unconscious, turn him on his back, put your hand around his chin and straighten your arm, locking the elbow. Tow him using side stroke. In rough water, keep his head well up by putting your arm across his chest,

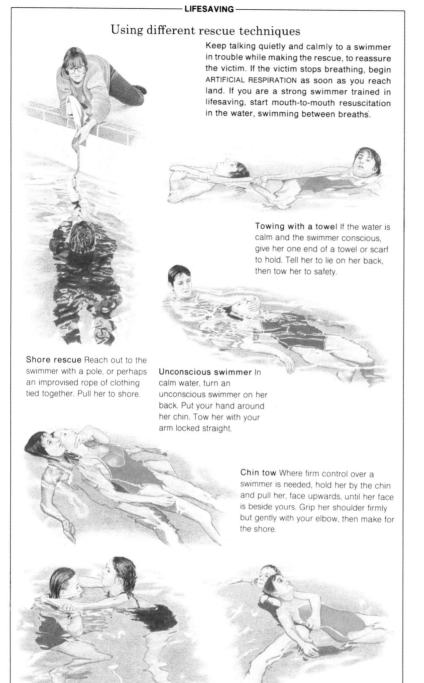

Using different rescue techniques

Keep talking quietly and calmly to a swimmer in trouble while making the rescue, to reassure the victim. If the victim stops breathing, begin ARTIFICIAL RESPIRATION as soon as you reach land. If you are a strong swimmer trained in lifesaving, start mouth-to-mouth resuscitation in the water, swimming between breaths.

Towing with a towel If the water is calm and the swimmer conscious, give her one end of a towel or scarf to hold. Tell her to lie on her back, then tow her to safety.

Shore rescue Reach out to the swimmer with a pole, or perhaps an improvised rope of clothing tied together. Pull her to shore.

Unconscious swimmer In calm water, turn an unconscious swimmer on her back. Put your hand around her chin. Tow her with your arm locked straight.

Chin tow Where firm control over a swimmer is needed, hold her by the chin and pull her, face upwards, until her face is beside yours. Grip her shoulder firmly but gently with your elbow, then make for the shore.

Grabbed by someone drowning If a drowning swimmer grabs you from in front, tuck your chin into your shoulder. Take hold of her arms, then push them up and over your head. If she grabs your leg, push her away firmly with your free foot.

Cross chest tow If the sea is rough, put your arm across the swimmer's chest, holding her around the lower ribs with your hip in the small of her back – this keeps her head above the water. Swim to the shore using side stroke.

holding him round the lower ribs, with your hip in the small of his back; use side stroke to swim to safety.

Where firm control over the casualty is required, take his chin from behind and pull him, face upwards, until his head is by yours. Grip his shoulder with your elbow and swim steadily towards the shore, as illustrated.

Getting free Turn quickly onto your back and swim out of reach if the victim tries to grab you. If necessary, use your foot to push him off. If he grabs you from the front, tuck your chin into your shoulder, take hold of his arms, and push them up and over your head.

See also DISTRESS SIGNALS.

Lifting and carrying

Correct methods to avoid back trouble

Lifting heavy or awkward objects in the wrong way is one of the commonest causes of back pain – see also BACKACHE. Reduce the risk of such injury by making your relatively strong leg muscles do most of the work.

──── **LIFTING AND CARRYING** ────

Keeping your back straight

Keep your back straight, whether squatting down to lift a heavy object from the floor, or bending your knees to lift something only waist high.

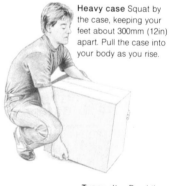

Heavy case Squat by the case, keeping your feet about 300mm (12in) apart. Pull the case into your body as you rise.

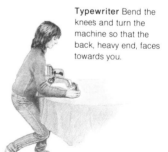

Typewriter Bend the knees and turn the machine so that the back, heavy end, faces towards you.

When lifting, do not stoop or bend your back. Bend at the knees instead, squatting right down if necessary; keep your back naturally straight and your feet comfortably apart. Draw the object close to you, grasp it and straighten your legs to bring you back to a standing position.

Adopt the same principles when putting something down. Try to avoid bending your spine when putting a load into a car boot.

If you have a bad back do not try to change a car wheel. It involves manipulating a heavy weight in a stooped position and at arm's length. For similar reasons do not try to lift a baby at arm's length over the raised side of a cot. Lower the side first so you can hold the baby close.

When carrying luggage or shopping, two even loads – one in each hand – are less likely to damage your back than one very heavy one, which weighs you down lopsidedly and puts strain on the spine. If you use suitcase wheels or a shopping trolley, try to make sure that the overall height allows you to push or pull without stooping as you walk.

Lifts

What to do if you are trapped in a lift

The greatest danger when a lift breaks down is that the people trapped inside it will panic. Modern lifts are very safe – so stay calm and reassure those with you that the lift will not plunge uncontrollably down the shaft. This is because automatic brakes, usually set under the lift floor, clamp onto the steel guide rails running down the sides of the shaft. The brakes work even if there is a power cut.

To summon help, press the alarm button or use the telephone. If there is no alarm system, bang on the doors with your hand or a heavy object, and shout. Once you contact someone outside, ask him to call the lift engineer.

If the engineer is not available, lift rescues can be handled by the fire brigade: tell your contact to dial 999.

Do not try to escape from a stalled lift without expert help from outside. Even if you force open the inner lift doors it is extremely unlikely that you will be able to reach and open the outer doors onto a landing. And in attempting to climb out you could easily slip on the grease and oil that build up on the outside of a lift.

Do not try to clamber through any hatch in the ceiling of the lift. When a hatch is opened, the lift is prevented from moving by an electrical contact. But if an open hatch accidentally falls shut, the lift could unexpectedly move, throwing you off balance. You could also trip over the lift cables in the darkness of the shaft, or slip on the grease and fall off.

Most calls for help are normally answered quickly. But at the start of a weekend, or late at night, there may be no one around to answer your call. In such cases keep calm and wait, even if help does not come for hours – or even days. Try to attract someone's attention as soon as the building reopens.

Meanwhile, do not smoke, as this will eat up your supply of air. If someone has difficulty in breathing, loosen the clothing around his neck and make him put his cupped hands over his mouth and breathe in and out that way. The main discomforts will be heat, hunger and thirst – but you *will* survive until help comes.

Light fixtures

Replacing old with new

The most common type of room lighting is the pendant light, in which a lampholder is attached to a flex suspended from a CEILING ROSE. There are, however, a number of fixtures which can replace pendants, to give better illumination or highlight certain features in the room. They include FLUORESCENT LIGHTS, spotlights and track lighting. If you fit a multi-spot or a track with three lights, make sure that you do not overstep the 1200 watts total load a lighting circuit can take.

Whichever you choose, the wiring to it should be a single cable containing a red (live) and black (neutral) wire and possibly an earth wire. If the light fitting is metal, the wiring must have an earth conductor wire.

Turn off the main switch at the consumer unit or fuse box, remove the circuit fuse (see FUSES AND FUSE BOXES) and unscrew the ceiling-rose cover. If there is only one cable connected to the rose, you can wire this cable direct to the new fixture.

If there are two or three cables, you will have to transfer the connections to a JUNCTION BOX fitted above the ceiling. You can then run a cable from the junction box to go direct into the new light fixture.

Fitting a spotlight The spotlight reflector is mounted on a baseplate by a bracket, which allows the lamp to be turned or swivelled in any direction.

Fitting track lighting or a spotlight

You can fit track lighting or a spotlight in place of a ceiling rose, after switching off power at the main switch and unscrewing the rose. These examples show how to wire fittings where the rose had a single cable.

Spotlight Screw the spotlight backplate to the ceiling in place of the rose base. Connect the terminal block wires as shown. Screw the spotlight base to the backplate.

Backplate

Terminal block

Spotlight base

Pencil line

Ceiling hole

Track light 1 Hold the track against the ceiling with the side edge of the terminal block covering the ceiling hole. Draw a pencil line along the side of the track.

Cable

Pencil line

2 Place each fixing clip so its centre is over the pencil line. Mark the screw holes through it. Use a gimlet to start the holes, then drive in the screws.

Fixing clip

Terminal cover

3 Push the cable wires through the hole in the top of the track and connect the red wire to L, black wire to N, and green and yellow to E or ⏚.

Release the conductors from the ceiling rose and unscrew the base of the rose from the ceiling. Remove the backplate on the spotlight base and screw it to the ceiling in place of the ceiling-rose base. Connect the red wire of the lighting cable to the terminal marked L and the black to that marked N. They will be opposite the brown and blue respectively of the wiring already in the new fixture.

Cover the bare earth conductor wire with green-and-yellow plastic sleeving and connect the wire tip to the earth terminal on the backplate. Screw the spotlight base to the backplate.

If any heat-proof sleeving is included in the spotlight pack it must be used. Follow the maker's instructions.

Fitting track lighting Switch off at the mains, remove the circuit fuse, then remove the existing light fitting. Release the conductor wires from the ceiling-rose terminals and unscrew the base of the rose from the ceiling.

Take the cover off the end of the track to expose the terminal block. Hold the track against the ceiling with the side edge of the terminal block covering the hole in the ceiling and draw a pencil line on the ceiling along the side of the track.

Position track fixing clips with their centre over the pencil line and mark through the screw holes. Where the clip is directly under a joist attach it to the ceiling with wood screws. If there is no joist, use cavity plugs. Space the clips at regular intervals. Partially insert the side screws in the clips.

Pass the lighting cable through the hole in the track, adjacent to the terminal block. Push the track into the clips and tighten the side screws. Connect the cable wires to the terminal block – red opposite brown at the terminal marked L and black opposite blue at N. Cover the bare earth conductor wire with green-and-yellow sleeving and connect it at E or ⏚. Ease any excess cable back through the hole in the ceiling and replace the terminal block cover.

To fit a spotlight, open the arm of its fitting and slot the grooved end into the track channel. Position the spotlight where required and close the arm to lock the light into the track. Insert additional lights in the same way.

Lightning

Treating someone struck by lightning; precautions in a thunderstorm

If someone has been struck by lightning there is a fair chance that he will suffer only SHOCK and minor BURNS. Lightning is most likely to kill if it strikes the head and passes through the body to earth. It may also cause severe burns, BROKEN BONES due to muscular spasms and cuts. In addition, clothing may catch fire and metal watchstraps or jewellery melt.

Treatment If the casualty's clothes catch alight, lay him on the ground immediately to keep the flames off his face. Otherwise, he could die from burns caused by breathing in the flames or from lack of air. Put out the flames by dousing them in water or wrapping the person in a thick coat or blanket or towel. If he is unconscious put him in the RECOVERY POSITION.

Treat burns by cooling them with cold water, then cover them with a dressing the inside of a folded handkerchief will do. Secure it with a strip of clean cloth. Dial 999 and ask for an ambulance without delay. Keep the casualty warm and reassure him that medical help is on the way.

Taking precautions Although you are unlikely to be struck by lightning during a thunderstorm, it is worthwhile taking basic precautions:
● Do not shelter under tall trees – especially isolated ones. Lightning tends to strike the highest points in the area.
● Keep off high ground and away from metal fences and structures. If you are caught in an open area, lie flat.
● If you are close to a tall object that might attract lightning, sit on something dry with your feet together and off the ground. Hug your knees to your chest with both arms – and do not touch the ground with your hands. Keep your head well down.
● Stay in your vehicle if you are driving – it is one of the safest places to be during a lightning storm because the tyres act as insulators. But do not ride a bicycle or a motorcycle in such conditions.
● Seek shelter only in substantial buildings – avoid isolated barns or shelters.

Lino cuts

Using lino to print designs on to paper

Lino cuts are specially suitable for printing large simple designs. Lino is easy to cut, but you will not be able to produce the delicate lines and textures achieved with a woodcut or etching plate.

Arts or crafts shops stock the materials you need:
● Blocks of lino – sold in various sizes.
● Tools – usually a set of nib-like gouges which fit into a uniform handle.
● Oil-based or water-based block printing ink (for children, water-based is easier to clean up afterwards).
● A rubber roller.

You will also need a sheet of carbon paper, a piece of clean, flat glass or Perspex and a rolling pin.

LINO CUTS

Cutting and inking them

Cutting Use a gouge to cut along the edges of the design. Gouge out 'trenches' around the areas to be removed and work inwards to prevent any accidental cuts.

Inking Run the roller over the glass or Perspex sheet, working lengthways and crossways.

Making the design Draw your design on a piece of white paper. Then lay the carbon paper face down on the lino and place your design on top. Trace the drawing with a sharp, hard pencil.

Paint the areas that will be background or in relief with a colour that contrasts with the lino. Use a small gouge to crisscross the background and a larger gouge to cut along the edges of the design.

If the lino becomes hard and difficult to cut, put it on a radiator or in a low oven for a few minutes to soften it.

When you have finished cutting, wash the block in warm, soapy water and dry.

Printing Using the rubber roller, carefully roll out a layer of ink on the glass or Perspex, working lengthways and crossways to avoid making lumps or air bubbles. Then run the inked roller with equal care over the lino block, covering only the raised areas. Gently lay your blank paper or card over the inked block, then use a rolling pin to press the paper firmly onto the design. Remove gently and leave to dry.

Lipstick stains

Ways of removing them

Act quickly to remove a lipstick stain; the longer it is left the more difficult it will become.

Scrape off any pieces with a blunt knife. Then moisten a clean cloth with dry-cleaning solvent and dab at the stain, working towards the centre so as not to spread it. Turn the cloth to a clean area as soon as it becomes dirty.

If the stain is on loose fabric, hold a clean white cloth behind it. Where possible, launder according to instructions – see LAUNDERING.

Leave it to dry naturally; artificial heat may damage the fibres.

Another method for fabrics (but not carpets) is to dab the stain with methylated spirit, leave for five minutes and then wash the area with warm water and rinse. However, methylated spirit may draw out dye, so check for colourfastness.

A third method for fabrics is to squirt washing-up liquid directly onto the stain, dampen the area, then rub it briskly, forming thick suds and rinse. Handkerchiefs can be boiled or bleached. See also STAIN REMOVAL.

Lobster

Preparing and eating

Cooked lobsters are available in all good fishmongers. To prepare one for serving, lay it back uppermost on a chopping board and slice it in half from head to tail with a large, sharp knife. Spread out the two halves and remove the gills, the stomach sac in the head and the dark intestinal vein running down the tail. Keep the greenish liver (also in the head) and the coral-red roe (in the tails of females), to use as a garnish. Serve with wedges of lemon, mayonnaise or sauce vinaigrette and a green salad.

Eating You need a knife and fork, a pair of nutcrackers and a two-tined cocktail fork or skewer (restaurants have thin, long-handled lobster forks).

Use the ordinary fork to remove all the meat you can from the head, body and tail. To get meat from the large claws, break them from the body and crack them in several places with the nutcrackers; use the cocktail fork or skewer to work the flesh out from either side of the thin membrane running down the middle of each claw, and to push out any meat remaining in the tail. Break off the side feelers with your fingers and suck the meat from them.

Dressed lobster This is done in the kitchen before serving. Break off the claws, crack them with a hammer and work the flesh away with a skewer. Use a smaller skewer to pick the meat from the feelers. After you have cut the lobster in half and taken out the gills, stomach and tail vein, scrape out all the meat from the head, body and tail.

Divide all the meat you have extracted. Wash the half-shells, put the meat back in them and serve. Garnish with the liver and the roe.

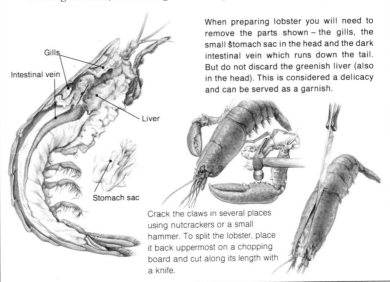

LOBSTER

Slicing in half, removing inedible parts and cracking claws

When preparing lobster you will need to remove the parts shown – the gills, the small stomach sac in the head and the dark intestinal vein which runs down the tail. But do not discard the greenish liver (also in the head). This is considered a delicacy and can be served as a garnish.

Gills

Intestinal vein

Liver

Stomach sac

Crack the claws in several places using nutcrackers or a small hammer. To split the lobster, place it back uppermost on a chopping board and cut along its length with a knife.

Lost dogs and cats

How to guard against losing them; how to go about recovering them

You are legally obliged to provide your dog with a collar and clear identification – such as a metal disc giving your name and address – in case it gets lost.

This does not apply to CATS, which have no legal status. Even so, it is a good idea to fit your cat with an elasticated collar and identity disc. For both cats and dogs, the collar should be a snug fit, but not too tight, so that it does not slip over the animal's head.

An owner who lets his dog out without a collar can be fined heavily. If the dog causes an accident, the owner can also be sued for damages. Similarly, if a dog is dangerous, the owner is legally responsible for keeping it under control.

Some local authorities have no-go areas for dogs; and dogs on highways or in public places must nearly always be kept on a lead. It may be an offence to let a dog foul certain roads and parks.

In rural areas, it is an offence to let your dog chase or molest farm animals. If it does so you can be heavily fined and the magistrate can order you to have the dog destroyed. A farmer is legally entitled to shoot a dog only as a last resort if the dog is actually attacking an animal and if the owner is not present.

If you do lose a pet Work outwards from the spot where the animal was last seen, searching in widening circles. A dog usually comes to your call, but a cat may crouch in hiding. Use a torch when searching dark areas – the light reflecting from an animal's eyes makes it easier to spot.

If you cannot find your pet, tell the local police station and nearest animal shelter – consult *Yellow Pages* under 'Animal Welfare Societies'. Tell neighbours and the postman; put notices in local shop windows. You can also advertise in a local newspaper, perhaps offering a reward for its return. Also check the paper's 'Lost Animals' section if there is one.

Anyone finding a stray dog is legally bound to return it to its owner or inform the nearest police station. If the dog is not claimed after seven days, it may be sold or painlessly destroyed. If you hit a dog while driving a vehicle, you must report the incident to the police. See also DOG CARE.

Louvre doors

Cleaning and painting them

Dust louvre doors with a duster or the brush attachment of a vacuum cleaner.

The simplest way of painting louvre doors is to use aerosol paint or a spray gun – see SPRAY PAINTING. Enamel is the easiest to use, as it requires no primer.

Make a simple spray booth out of scrap cardboard to collect any over-spray, and apply paint in very thin coats, building up coats until you are satisfied with the finish. Allow each coat to dry; avoid any heavy application, which will cause the paint to run. If this happens, let it dry for 24 hours, rub down with fine sandpaper and respray.

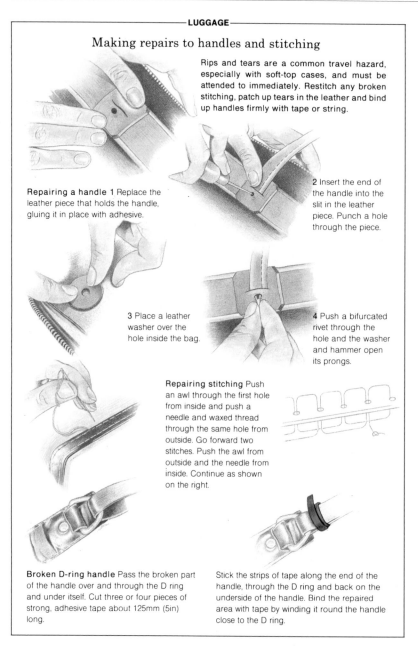

Making repairs to handles and stitching

Rips and tears are a common travel hazard, especially with soft-top cases, and must be attended to immediately. Restitch any broken stitching, patch up tears in the leather and bind up handles firmly with tape or string.

Repairing a handle 1 Replace the leather piece that holds the handle, gluing it in place with adhesive.

2 Insert the end of the handle into the slit in the leather piece. Punch a hole through the piece.

3 Place a leather washer over the hole inside the bag.

4 Push a bifurcated rivet through the hole and the washer and hammer open its prongs.

Repairing stitching Push an awl through the first hole from inside and push a needle and waxed thread through the same hole from outside. Go forward two stitches. Push the awl from outside and the needle from inside. Continue as shown on the right.

Broken D-ring handle Pass the broken part of the handle over the D ring and under itself. Cut three or four pieces of strong, adhesive tape about 125mm (5in) long.

Stick the strips of tape along the end of the handle, through the D ring and back on the underside of the handle. Bind the repaired area with tape by winding it round the handle close to the D ring.

Luggage

Mending tears in suitcases, protecting corners and repairing a broken handle

All forms of luggage benefit from a little regular care and attention.

Treat leather suitcases with a leather dressing, then polish with a soft shoe brush or duster. Plastic fabrics need an occasional wash with a mild solution of water and detergent.

Do not use oil on lock mechanisms. It attracts dust and grit. Instead, use a dry lubricant such as powdered graphite.

If the case tears, undo any interior lining near the tear and find a piece of similar fabric or leather large enough to cover the damage. Apply clear resin adhesive, or vinyl adhesive for a vinyl case (see GLUING), to the case interior and the patch, and leave until touch-dry. Then position the patch over the damage and press the surfaces together. Hammer lightly and check that the edges of the tear are in close contact. Replace any interior lining.

The corners of rigid cases can be streng-thened by fitting vulcanised fibre corners which are held in place by RIVETS. Note, however, that they cannot be fitted to rounded corners. The corners and rivets can be bought at a leatherware shop. Use bifurcated rivets and small washers.

When riveting is complete, make sure there are no rough edges inside the case.

Where stitching is frayed or broken, remove all damaged thread, and restitch. Rub beeswax along the stitching to prevent further fraying.

If a case handle breaks, use pliers to pull the D rings open far enough to release them from the case. Take the remains of the handle to a leatherware shop and find a new handle of similar size. Fit the handle on the rings, then reinsert the D rings and press them back together with the pliers.

Emergency repair Use self-adhesive fabric tape or adhesive strapping tape.

If tape is not available, use thick string and a piece of strong material about 19mm ($\frac{3}{4}$in) wide such as the end of a case strap in leather or webbing, or a sandal strap. Hold it to the top of the broken handle, pass it through the D ring, then hold it to the underside of the handle. Bind it firmly in place with the string, putting turns close together.

If the handle has broken completely, discard it and use an old necktie wound round the D rings as a makeshift handle, or use a section of webbing strap.

Lumbago

Dealing with a severe lower back pain

If you suffer a severe attack of lumbago – the general term for crippling lower back pain – stop all physical activity at once. Lumbago often occurs when lifting or stooping, and further exercise of any kind will probably make you feel worse. Back exercises are only appropriate when intense pain has subsided. See also BACKACHE; LIFTING AND CARRYING.

Aspirin, ibuprofen or paracetamol may bring some relief; bed rest – lying flat and keeping warm – is usually beneficial. A hot-water bottle or an electric pad may bring relief. If your mattress is soft, ask someone to lay a flat board beneath it; or alternatively lie, well-wrapped in bedclothes, on the floor.

Any movement is likely to increase the pain; turn slowly and try to avoid reaching out for bedside objects.

The condition may later require skilled help, but there is usually little a doctor can do in the first few hours. If the pain persists more than two or three days, or increases, ring your DOCTOR.

He may prescribe stronger painkillers, and refer you to a specialist after the initial attack has subsided.

Mackerel

Cooking a fish that must be fresh, or quick-frozen

Fresh from the water, mackerel make a delicious meal, but they go off rapidly after only a few hours, unless quickly frozen – see FREEZING FOOD.

To prepare mackerel for eating, scale and gut them. Remove heads and tails; fillet if required – see FISH CLEANING.

Mackerel can be grilled, baked or shallow-fried, poached, or steamed as fillets – see POACHING; STEAMING. Many people enjoy them served plain, with a wedge of lemon or sprinkling of lemon juice.

A traditional Somerset dish is mackerel baked in cider.

Ingredients (to feed four people)
4 freshly caught mackerel with heads removed, gutted and washed
Salt and black pepper
2 dessert apples
1 small onion
200g (7oz) Cheddar cheese
65g (2½oz) butter
50g (2oz) fresh white breadcrumbs
4 tablespoons dry cider

Peel and coarsely grate the apples, onion and half the cheese. Melt the butter in a small pan. Mix the grated apple, onion and cheese with the breadcrumbs in a bowl and add 1 tablespoon of melted butter. Season the prepared mackerel and stuff them with the mixture. Hold each fish together with two or three wooden skewers along its belly.

Grate the rest of the cheese finely. Put the mackerel side by side in an ovenproof dish. Sprinkle the cheese over them, pour on the rest of the melted butter and add enough cider to cover the base of the dish. Lay a piece of buttered kitchen foil loosely over the dish and bake for 25-35 minutes in the centre of an oven preheated to 180°C (350°F) or gas mark 4. Serve with lemon wedges, chopped parsley and baked potatoes in their jackets.

Macramé

First steps in decorative knotting

Macramé (the word comes from Arabic and means 'striped towel' or 'embroidered veil') is the craft of ornamental knotting – see also KNOTS. To do it, you need only cord, a pair of scissors, various sizes of pins, and a rigid work surface that

---

Making some of the basic knots

Start with cords seven or eight times the length of the finished piece, to allow for knots. Secure them to the mounting cord using lark's head knots.

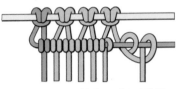

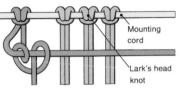

Mounting cord

Lark's head knot

Double half hitch 1 Take the left-hand (dark blue) cord across the other cords. Take the second end of the dark blue cord round the first, then over again. Pull the end through the loop and pull tight.

2 Tie a similar knot with the next cord (light blue) and continue across the row until all the cords are tied.

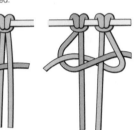

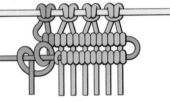

3 Turn the mounting cord in the opposite direction. Then, working from right to left, tie a reversed double half hitch with each cord.

Square knot
1 Take the first cord over the second and third and under the fourth.

2 Take the fourth cord back under the third and second cords and up through the loop.

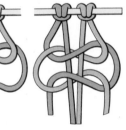

3 Bring the right cord over the two centre cords and under the left cord.

4 Take the left cord under the two centre cords and up through the loop formed by the right cord.

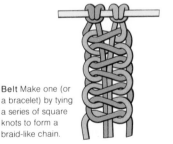

Belt Make one (or a bracelet) by tying a series of square knots to form a braid-like chain.

---

will hold pins – you can make one out of heavy cardboard or buy one.

Household string makes an ideal cord to practise with. As you become more adept, use cotton, linen, jute, or artificial fibres (which need dampening beforehand). Knitting wools are generally too stretchy, but WEAVING wools are suitable.

To practise the basic knots, cut four lengths of cord each 610mm (2ft) long

and one of 150mm (6in) to use as a mounting cord; knot each end of the mounting cord and pin it firmly to the top of the work surface. Fold the long cords in half and space them at equal distances along the mounting cord. Use lark's head knots, in which the folded end of each knotting cord is turned over the mounting cord and the two lengths of the knotting cord are passed through it.

As you become more skilful at macramé, you can work other features into your design. For example, a thin wooden rod, or a series of curtain rings, in place of the mounting cord, can become the top of a macramé curtain. You can attach plastic or wooden beads to the ends of the knotting cords to add a decorative touch to the bottom of the curtain.

Magic tricks

Creating simple but effective illusions

The art of magic is the art of misdirection – using 'patter' (an engaging line of talk), gestures, props or any other means at your disposal to draw the attention of onlookers away from the hands that are performing the trick.

Learn one magic trick at a time. Practise in front of a mirror until you can make your gestures look natural and they become automatic. Never look at your 'working' hand while you are doing a trick.

Here are some simple illusions for the home conjuror:

Disappearing coin Hold a 20p piece between your thumb and the index and middle fingers. Pretend to take the coin in your other hand, but instead, as that hand closes around the coin, push the 20p deep into your palm. Relax your muscles so that the loose flesh of the palm folds around the edges of the coin.

Later, you can retrieve it with the first two fingers of that hand, so that it 'appears' from anywhere you choose. The technique is called 'palming'.

Mystery handkerchief Put a coin in the centre of a handkerchief, and fold the handkerchief into three consecutively smaller triangles. Grasp the bottom corners, one in each hand, and hold the cloth taut, tilting it backwards and forwards. The coin will slip into your hand; palm it. Wave the handkerchief with your other hand while you pass the coin into your pocket, or onto your lap, unseen by the audience.

Loose change Select a volunteer from the audience. Say you can tell him his age and how much loose change he has in his pocket, provided it is less than £1. Get him in secret to write down the following:

His age – say 10
Double it – 20
Add 5 – 25
Multiply by 50 – 1250
Subtract 365 – 885
Add the amount of change (for example, 65p) – 950

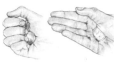

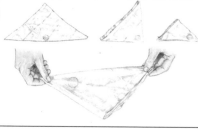
Ask for the last figure (950) and, in your head, add 115; that gives 1065 in the example given. The first two figures are always the age (10) and the second two (65) the amount of change. The formula always works so long as the change is less than £1.

Mystic ashes Ask members of the audience to name some famous people. Appear to write each on slips of paper you have ready; in fact, write the first name you are given on all the slips. Put the slips in a hat and ask an onlooker to draw one of them, folding it so you cannot see what is on it. Put the remaining slips in an ashtray and burn them, muttering 'magic' words and studying the ashes. Then announce the name on the unburnt slip.

Colour-changing cards Before your magic show, arrange a pack of cards so that black and red cards appear alternately. The edges of the red cards should stick out a fraction at the top of the pack, and the black cards should stick out by the same amount at the bottom.

Hold the cards firmly, and – with practice – you will be able to flick through the pack with your thumb so that only the red cards are visible to the audience. Then blow on the pack and surreptitiously turn it round. When you flick through again, only the black cards will show.

Push the cards together and flick through the pack a third time. Both black and red cards will now be visible.

Orange to apple Prepare an orange beforehand by peeling it carefully. Use four upward slices through the skin, leaving it joined at the top. Find a small apple and put the orange peel around it, so that it is completely hidden. Set the 'orange' on a table in front of your audience; if they are not too close, they will not spot the slices in the skin. Display a

large handkerchief to show that it does not conceal anything. Cover the 'orange' with it. As you remove the handkerchief, secretly take the orange peel with it; crumple the handkerchief and put it, with the concealed orange peel, in your pocket. Hey presto, the orange has turned into an apple.

Magnet

Making your own

If you lay two bar magnets end to end, the ends will either attract or repel each other. This is because a magnet's atomic components correspond to the earth's magnetic field, creating a north-seeking pole at one end of the bar and a south-seeking pole at the other. A basic principle of magnetism is that like poles repel each other and unlike poles attract each other. This principle is used when making a simple magnet.

You need two bar magnets and the steel bar you wish to magnetise. Lay the steel bar in a horizontal position and hold the magnets by their tips, one in each hand, with the two ends that attract, north and south, pointing downwards. Stroke the steel bar simultaneously with the two magnets, working outwards in opposite directions, from the centre of the bar.

The stroking will magnetise the bar by realigning its atoms to create its own north and south poles at either end.

You can magnetise a bar by stroking it along its length with a single magnet, but this tends to produce only one strong pole.

A magnet can be made more effectively by making a coil with about 500 turns of insulated copper wire. If you put a steel bar inside the coil and pass direct current from a battery through the wire, the bar becomes magnetised, retaining its magnetism when the coil is removed.

Manicures

Keeping hands and nails in trim

A weekly manicure at home can help to keep your hands and nails looking good – see FINGERNAILS. For it you need: cotton wool; emery boards; nail or cuticle cream; nail scissors; nail brush; hand cream; an orange stick or a hoof stick (which has a shaped end for cleaning and a rubber tip for easing back cuticles); a nail buffer; and perhaps an oily nail-varnish remover. Work in a good light so that you can see what you are doing clearly.

Start by removing any old nail varnish. Hold a piece of cotton wool soaked in varnish remover against the nail for a few seconds, and then wipe the nail from the base towards the tip.

Wash your hands thoroughly in warm, soapy water. Do not soak the hands too much; it will soften the nails. Dry your hands gently with a soft towel and massage the nails and cuticles with cuticle cream.

Use a hoof stick, or the blunt end of an orange stick soaked in cuticle cream, to ease the cuticles gently away from the nails; this facilitates nail growth. Be careful not to push the hoof stick too deeply into the cuticle or you will damage the nail.

Clean gently under the nails with the sharpened end of the hoof stick or orange stick wrapped in cotton wool. Wash the hands to remove excess cream and scrub the nails with the brush. Dry the hands again gently.

Using the nail buffer, buff the nails with single, one-way only strokes to smooth them. Shape the nails with an emery board working in one direction only towards the middle from each side. Filing back and forth causes nails to split.

Run the nails along a piece of fabric to check that they are smooth. If any snags are left, smooth them away with the finer side of the emery board. Do the same with any rough or snagged areas of cuticle.

Massage the hands with hand cream, and in addition to the weekly manicure, use the cream at least twice every day to prevent the hands becoming dry.

Applying varnish Wipe your nails with varnish remover and make sure that they are dry and free from soap. Spread one hand flat on a towel laid on a table. With the other, apply one thin coat of colourless varnish to the little finger.

Paint the centre of the nail from the cuticle to the tip, and then brush down either side. Remove any surplus varnish with the brush. Varnish the other nails on that hand in the same way, and then those on the other hand.

Let the varnish dry and, using the same technique, apply two thin coats of

Cuticle care and filing

Soften cuticles before pushing them back off your nails – so that they leave the nails cleanly and without splitting. File the nails into a smooth, elegant shape.

Softening cuticles Massage cuticle or nail cream all over the nails. Wait for three minutes for the cream to take effect.

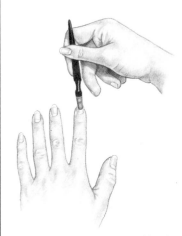

Pushing back cuticles Use the rubber tip of a hoof stick to ease each cuticle gently down and away from the nail. With circular movements remove any bits of cuticle left sticking to the nail's surface.

Buffing and shaping Smooth the nails with a buffer, then shape them with an emery board. When shaping, use only upward movements from the nails' sides to tips. Leave enough nail growth at each side to maintain strength.

coloured varnish. Let the first dry before putting on the second; wipe off smudges with a cotton bud or tissue dipped in varnish remover.

When the second coat is dry, apply a top coat of colourless varnish over the nails and under the tips. Let the varnish dry completely before you do anything with your hands.

Map reading

Understanding a map; finding where you are

All maps are drawn to a scale that relates the area of land covered proportionally to the area of the map. For example, a scale of 1:50,000 means that 1cm on the map represents 50,000cm (0.5km) on the ground – this is equivalent to 1¼in to the mile.

A map for use by a local planning authority, showing buildings and plots of land in detail, would be on a scale such as 1:1250 (roughly 50in to the mile), but a map of Europe in one sheet would be on a scale such as 1:4,000,000 (1in to 64 miles). A map covering the whole of Britain in one sheet needs a scale of 1:1,000,000 (1in to 16 miles). Every good map gives a scale in linear form for measuring distances (see ROUTE PLANNING), and has a key showing the various signs and symbols used to indicate features such as rivers, roads and churches. Once you have familiarised yourself with these symbols, the map will become an aerial picture of the land around you.

Maps are usually drawn with north at the top, and are gridded in squares related to the scale. On small-scale international maps, the grid lines are the lines of latitude and longitude. Larger-scale maps may have the grid lettered or numbered so that each square can be identified.

The National Grid Maps prepared by the Ordnance Survey have a grid reference system (see illustration overleaf) covering the whole of Britain. The 1:50,000 Land-ranger Series has references that can be used to identify any point down to 100m (about 100yds).

Contours, heights and gradients All points on a map of a particular height above sea level are joined by a line known as a contour. The map key will tell you how far apart each contour line is on the ground – usually a distance of 5 or 10m (about 16-30ft). Some lines are broken by a number, with the tops of the figures pointing uphill. These represent the altitude in metres of that particular line.

The closer together the contour lines, the steeper the slope. The gradient – the steepness of the slope – is calculated by

Using a grid reference; interpreting Ordnance Survey map symbols

Use a grid reference to find a point on a map. To understand the symbols used, consult the legend – or key. On the right are some symbols used on Ordnance Survey 1:50,000 Landranger maps.

Grid references With a national grid reference you can pinpoint anywhere in the country on an Ordnance Survey map. A grid reference gives two letters and some figures. Below, as an example, is how to find the summit station on Snowdon on a Landranger map using its reference – SH609543.

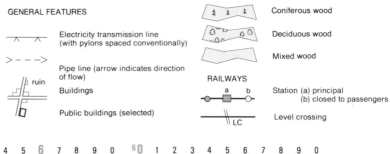

GENERAL FEATURES

Electricity transmission line (with pylons spaced conventionally)

Pipe line (arrow indicates direction of flow)

Buildings

Public buildings (selected)

Coniferous wood

Deciduous wood

Mixed wood

RAILWAYS

Station (a) principal
(b) closed to passengers

Level crossing

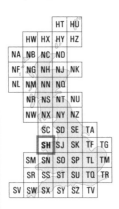

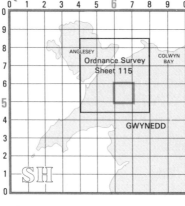

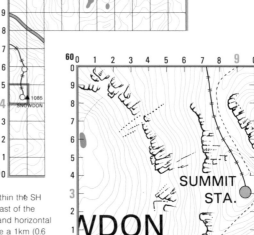

SH609543 The letters **SH** indicate the 100km (62 mile) square of the national grid (above) in which Snowdon lies. In a six-figure grid reference, as given, the first three figures are read along the map from left to right, the second three up the map; if the reference is four figures only, the first two read along, the second two up. The figures **6** and **5** – the first and fourth of the reference given – indicate a 10km (6 mile)

square (shown in red above) within the SH square, lying to the north and east of the crossing point of vertical line 6 and horizontal line 5. The figures **0** and **4** locate a 1km (0.6 mile) square (shown in blue above) within the 10km square. On a 1:50,000 map, look along to find line 60 and up to find line 54, then look in the square to the north and east of their crossing point.

SH609543 The station is finally pinpointed by figures **9** and **3**, whose grid lines are normally estimated by eye – 9 along and 3 up.

---

dividing the distance by the change of height. Steep slopes on roads are frequently marked by an arrow which points downhill.

A gradient of 1 in 10 means that the slope rises 1 metre in every 10, so the lower the second figure, the steeper the hill. On an Ordnance Survey map, the symbol ⇉ means 1 in 5 or steeper (20% +). The symbol ⇾ means 1 in 5 to 1 in 7 (20% to 14%).

Locating your position on a map If you get lost along minor roads while driving, you can spot your position with the help of a village name and one or two physical features you can see, or have just passed, such as a river or railway line. Find them on the map and hold the map flat so that each of them is in the same direction from you as the actual feature. This will show you roughly where you are and in which direction you must travel to get back to your planned route.

If walking across country, find three prominent landmarks, such as a church, a hill or a wood, and relate your position to them in the same way on a larger-scale map – as explained in COMPASS.

Marble

Maintaining and polishing a beautiful stone

Marble is a fairly delicate stone, so treat it gently whenever you are cleaning and polishing it.

Remove grease with pure soap only, or white spirit. Never use bleaches, abrasives or detergent, and never immerse it in water.

Then rinse off thoroughly with clean water. Dry quickly with a CHAMOIS LEATHER. To reduce the risk of staining, brush interior marble occasionally with a mixture of white shellac and methylated spirit – add enough methylated

spirit to make the shellac workable.

Marble in the garden can be protected in winter with a wooden cover. To save it from normal weathering use bleached beeswax, available from some hardware shops. Mix it with white spirit until it has the consistency of butter, and apply it sparingly. Do the job on a summer's day when the marble is warm and will absorb the wax. Wipe off any surplus beeswax mixture.

Most stains on marble should be removed by a professional, but you can remove smoke stains, from fireplace marble for example, yourself. Gently rub the marble with powdered pumice and water. If the stain persists, rub with the juice of a lemon – but do not leave it on as the acid in the lemon will attack the stone. White spirit will often remove greasy stains. Allow plenty of ventilation, do not smoke, and if the fire is a gas fire, turn out the pilot light.

Mending breaks in marble is best done with an epoxy resin adhesive – see

GLUING. Fill small holes and chips, or build up missing pieces with a mixture of marble dust and epoxy resin adhesive. Instead of the marble dust you can use kaolin powder and an appropriate colouring.

When the repair is complete, polish with colourless microcrystalline wax, then buff with a clean, soft cloth.

Marbles

How to play the classic games

The practice of making marbles from small pieces of marble in the 18th century gave the game its name. Today's marbles – small, translucent, coloured balls – are made of glass.

The standard marble is about 16mm (⅝in) in diameter, but the marble used to shoot with – called the *taw* or *shooter* – is slightly larger and more fancy. It is usually an *alley*, a large marble once made of coloured alabaster, but now of coloured glass.

To shoot the marble, get down on one knee and balance the taw on the first finger of one hand with the thumb. Rest your knuckles on the ground and then flick the marble off your finger with your thumb.

Among the most popular games of marbles are ringers, bossout, and long taw.

Ringers A circle about 3m (10ft) in diameter is drawn on the ground. Two markers are also drawn at the circle's edge and opposite each other. One is the 'pitch' line, the other the 'lag' line. Thirteen marbles are then placed as illustrated below in the form of a cross in the centre of the circle.

Two to six players take part, and before the game begins they decide the order of play by each kneeling in turn at the pitch line and shooting the taws towards the lag line. The player whose shooter comes to rest closest to the lag line takes the first shot, the player who is next closest is the second to play, and so on.

The purpose is to knock the marbles forming the cross out of the ring. The first player shoots from the pitch line and if he knocks one of the target marbles out he shoots again. But if he fails, the next player takes his turn. Players get a further turn if they knock an opponent's shooter lying inside the circle out of the circle.

After his first shot, a player makes subsequent shots from where his marble lies, if it is inside the circle. If it lands outside, the player may shoot from any point the same distance from the centre as where the marble came to rest.

The game continues until all the marbles forming the cross are shot outside the ring. The winner is the player who knocks out the most.

Bossout Two players take part, each with the same agreed number of marbles. The first shoots a marble as far as he likes. His opponent then shoots at it. If he hits the target marble, or gets close enough to span the distance with the thumb and little finger of one hand, he wins it. It is then his turn to shoot a target marble.

But if he misses the first target marble, or cannot span the distance, he leaves his marble where it is and it becomes the target marble for the first player, who takes aim from the spot where his original target marble was.

The game continues until one player has won all the marbles.

In this game, players do not use an alley because of the danger of losing it.

Long taw This is played in just the same way as bossout, except that there is no spanning. The target marble must be hit for the opponent to win it.

Marinating

Tenderising meat and adding flavour

Meat, fish and game can all be made more tender – and more tasty – by steeping them before cooling in a blended liquid, called a marinade.

Marinades usually consist of oil, seasoning and an acid ingredient which tenderises the flesh – usually wine or vinegar, but lemon juice or natural YOGHURT can be used. Afterwards, the marinade can be heated and served as a sauce, thickened or unthickened – see SAUCES.

Use a glass or ceramic bowl or dish for marinating, and a wooden spoon for stirring the mixture. Roughly, allow 115ml (4fl oz) of marinade for each 450g (1lb) of meat or fish.

Generally, the longer the flesh is marinated, the more tender it becomes. A soaking of at least 1 hour is recommended, and 2-4 hours will allow the full flavour to develop. A single large piece of tough or aged meat may benefit from 8-12 hours; marinating for 12 hours cuts the cooking time by a third.

If time is short, and the meat is fairly tender, score its surface lightly with a sharp knife to allow the liquid to penetrate and soak it for 30 minutes.

The ingredients of marinades are largely a matter of choice; however, too much salt or soy sauce in the mixture tends to make meat dry. Here is a quickly made, simple marinade suitable for 1.4kg (3lb) of cubed meat:

Mix 1 cup of olive oil with ½ cup red wine vinegar or dry red wine. Add 1 chopped onion or 2 crushed garlic cloves, thyme, tarragon or rosemary to taste and season.

Add the meat, and toss to coat it thoroughly. Cover and let it stand for 3 hours at room temperature or 6 hours in the refrigerator. Stir every hour or two.

Marmalade

Making it dark, chunky and delicious

Traditional homemade marmalade takes time to make but the taste well repays the effort. This recipe uses bitter Seville oranges, which are in the grocer's in abundance in January and February.

MARBLES

How to shoot with taws in a game of ringers

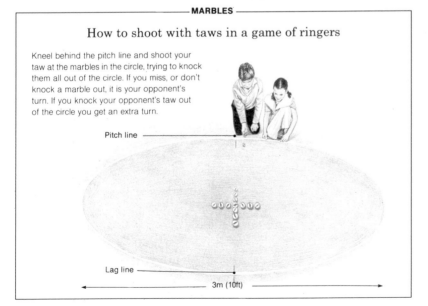

Kneel behind the pitch line and shoot your taw at the marbles in the circle, trying to knock them all out of the circle. If you miss, or don't knock a marble out, it is your opponent's turn. If you knock your opponent's taw out of the circle you get an extra turn.

Pitch line

Lag line

3m (10ft)

Ingredients – for 4.5kg (10lb)
1.4kg (3lb) Seville oranges
2.8 litres (5 pints) water
Juice of 2 lemons
1.4kg (3lb) brown sugar
1.4kg (3lb) white sugar

You will also need a piece of muslin, glass jars and a large preserving pan or heavy-based saucepan.

Scrub and dry the oranges and shave off the peel with a potato peeler, leaving as much pith as possible on the orange. Chop the peel into 6mm (¼in) strips.

Cut the oranges in half and squeeze out the pips and juice; separate and save both. Cut away the pith from the orange pulp, place pips and pith in the muslin and secure tightly. The pith and pips release pectin, which sets the marmalade.

Cut up the remaining orange pulp and place it in the pan, with the chopped peel, muslin bag, orange and lemon juice and water.

Boil the mixture over a low heat for about 2 hours, or until the peel is quite soft and the liquid has reduced by half. Press the muslin bag between two spoons, then remove it.

Add the sugar, stirring until it has completely dissolved. Turn up the heat and boil rapidly for 15-20 minutes until the mixture reaches setting point – see JAM MAKING.

Skim off the surface scum and let the marmalade cool for 10 minutes, stirring occasionally to distribute the peel.

Pour the marmalade into clean, dry, warm jars, cover with waxed paper discs and seal with metal tops or clear Cellophane secured with rubber bands or thin string.

Marquetry

Using wood veneers to make pictures

Marquetry is the craft of producing designs or pictures using thin wood VENEER in various colours and graining, or mother-of-pearl, metal, ivory, bone and tortoiseshell. To start with, stick to wood.

Very few tools are needed, but what is required is a steady hand and patience. The blades of your knives must be kept sharp, so you need a sharpening stone for honing blades – or the type of knife where blade sections can be snapped off to expose a new sharp section as the blade becomes blunt.

To start with, choose a very simple design which does not involve too much fine cutting. A craft shop stocking marquetry supplies can offer designs and patterns, along with a wide selection of wood veneers. If you do your own picture, simplify the detail – and try to

include some objects which would be made of wood. Use only four or five veneers, looking at the colours and the grain patterns.

Start by selecting a sheet of veneer the size you want your finished picture to be, and draw your pattern or picture onto this piece. If your design is the same size, use transfer paper, available from art supply shops, to transfer the pattern direct. But if the scale is different, divide your pattern and the veneer into squares, then transfer your design square by square to the new size – see PATTERN TRANSFER. Make sure your design is a perfect rectangle, or allow enough spare

veneer around the picture area for trimming.

The simplest way of producing your design is by the window method. This involves cutting the required shape into the base veneer, removing the cut piece, then filling the hole with your selected veneer cut to fit. You need to progress in an orderly manner, so plan to start at one corner and work outwards.

When you have cut out the pieces, apply PVA adhesive to the edges, using a sliver of veneer as a brush. Do not put glue on the underside of the pieces. Work on only one piece at a time. Trying to prepare a number of pieces together only

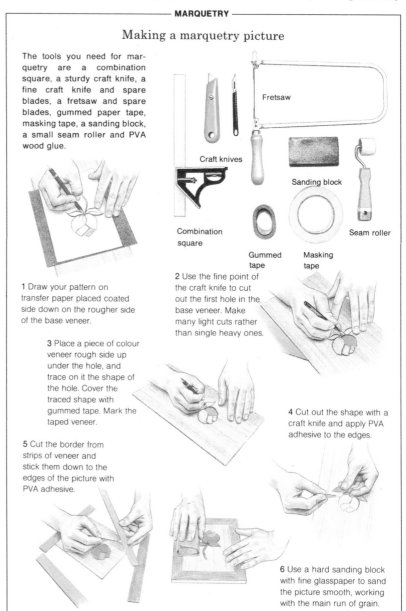

MARQUETRY

Making a marquetry picture

The tools you need for marquetry are a combination square, a sturdy craft knife, a fine craft knife and spare blades, a fretsaw and spare blades, gummed paper tape, masking tape, a sanding block, a small seam roller and PVA wood glue.

Fretsaw

Craft knives

Sanding block

Combination square

Gummed tape   Masking tape

Seam roller

1 Draw your pattern on transfer paper placed coated side down on the rougher side of the base veneer.

2 Use the fine point of the craft knife to cut out the first hole in the base veneer. Make many light cuts rather than single heavy ones.

3 Place a piece of colour veneer rough side up under the hole, and trace on it the shape of the hole. Cover the traced shape with gummed tape. Mark the taped veneer.

4 Cut out the shape with a craft knife and apply PVA adhesive to the edges.

5 Cut the border from strips of veneer and stick them down to the edges of the picture with PVA adhesive.

6 Use a hard sanding block with fine glasspaper to sand the picture smooth, working with the main run of grain.

aggravates any cutting errors, and makes fitting more difficult.

Hold each applied piece in place with masking tape applied to the underside of the base veneer, leaving it in place until the glue has dried. At this stage, remove the masking tape and also peel away the gummed paper tape taking care not to pull up the veneers. You may have to wet the gummed paper with a damp cloth to assist its removal. The rest can be sanded away later.

Do not worry if the surface of the design looks uneven; SANDING down will transform it.

With the design complete, prepare the baseboard upon which it will be mounted. This can be of PLYWOOD or medium-density fibreboard which will not warp, and it should be at least 13mm ($\frac{1}{2}$in) thick and large enough to contain the whole picture, plus a decorative border. Allow 25mm (1in) for the border. Cover the back and edges of the base with veneer, matching it to the background veneer of your picture.

Using the combination square to line up the corner points of the baseboard and picture, cut the four corners of the border to form mitred joints. As with the main picture, hold the border with masking tape until the PVA adhesive is dry.

Check your picture, then apply contact adhesive to the back of the picture and the face of the baseboard. Allow both to become touch-dry, then carefully position the picture and press it into place. Use the wallpaper seam roller, working from the centre out, to ensure that good contact is made, then lay a scrap piece of board over the picture and apply a heavy weight and leave for 24 hours.

Put the picture aside for a week to let the veneers contract and settle, then sand it smooth. Start with 50 grit paper, moving to 80 and 220, then finally 400 for fine finishing.

Plain wax polish may be used to seal and finish the veneer, but for a really fine finish use French polish see FRENCH POLISHING.

Marriage

Getting a licence for a church or register office wedding

A couple planning marriage in England or Wales can choose between a church wedding and a register office wedding. For marriages in Scotland, see below.

Church of England weddings The couple (or just one of them) must make an appointment with a clergyman in the parish where they live. Details of the marriage will be noted and their names will then be read out in the parish church.

This is called *publishing the banns*, and must be followed for three Sundays. It allows anyone who knows of a legal obstacle to the marriage such as an existing marriage to report it to a church officer. If there is no such obstacle, the couple can marry at any time in the following three months. The fee for the marriage is £90, and the marriage certificate costs £2.00.

Common licence If a couple do not wish banns to be published, they can apply for a *common licence*, obtainable from the Bishop's Surrogate of the diocese where either of them has lived in a parish of that diocese for at least the past 15 days. It costs £45 and allows the couple to marry in a church in that parish at any time in the following three months.

Special licence A couple who cannot meet the 15 day residence qualification, but want to marry urgently – for example, because of business commitments or travel plans – can apply to the Archbishop of Canterbury's Office in Westminster, London, for a special licence. They must have a letter of approval from the vicar of the church where they plan to marry.

The licence can only be issued by the Archbishop of Canterbury, who must approve of the reason or reasons given. The fee is £90. The licence will not be issued if either party is divorced.

Weddings in other churches To marry in any church other than the Church of England, the couple must first obtain a certificate from the superintendent registrar in the district where they are living, in the same way as for a register office marriage. They also need to make arrangements with their chosen church.

Register office marriage If a couple prefer a civil ceremony, they (or one of them) must make an appointment with the superintendant registrar of marriages in the district where they are living. One or both must have lived in the district for seven days, and a *registrar's certificate* is issued after notice of their intentions has been displayed at the register office for three weeks. The wedding can then take place at any time within three months from the day notice was given.

Where parties live in different districts, each must give notice in their own district. The notice and marriage fees come to £39 if both live in the same district; £57.50 if they do not.

By issuing a *combined certificate and licence* sometimes wrongly called a special licence a superintendent registrar can allow a couple to marry after waiting only one clear weekday. One of them must have lived in the district for the previous 15 days and the other must be physically present or usually resident in

England and Wales on the day notice is given. The fee is £66.50.

Marriage in Scotland A couple planning to marry in Scotland must each complete a *Marriage Notice* at the office of their local district registrar.

Their names and the date on which they intend to marry are then displayed in a prominent place in the registrar's office usually in the window. If, after 14 days, no one has shown a legal impediment to the marriage, the registrar issues a *Marriage Schedule* giving permission to wed and stating where and when.

There is a joint fee of £11.50, plus a £13 marriage fee for a civil ceremony in a register office. There is also a £3 fee for a marriage certificate.

Religious weddings in Scotland can be conducted by church officials of various denominations, including ministers of the Church of Scotland and Roman Catholic priests. The local district registrar has a list of the *celebrants* the people who are authorised to conduct marriages. Their fees vary.

See also WEDDINGS.

Marzipan

Making and using it to coat cakes for icing

Marzipan, also known as almond paste or almond icing, can be used to top rich fruit cakes or provide a smooth foundation when ICING CAKES. See also CAKE BAKING; CAKE DECORATING.

This recipe makes enough marzipan to cover the top and sides of a 230mm (9in) diameter cake, ready for icing:

Ingredients

175g (6oz) icing sugar
175g (6oz) caster sugar
350g (12oz) ground almonds
1 egg
2 teaspoons lemon juice
2 teaspoons brandy (optional)

Sieve the icing sugar into a bowl. Add the caster sugar, almonds, egg, lemon juice and brandy, if used. Mix to make a smooth dough and briefly knead the mixture in the bowl, then shape it into a ball.

Do not handle the marzipan more than necessary, otherwise it will become oily. Wrap it in greaseproof paper or a plastic bag and store in a cool place until needed. The marzipan will keep for up to 2 weeks in a refrigerator.

Applying marzipan If the top of the cake is domed, slice off most of the dome. Put the cake upside down on a cake board so that the bottom is now on top.

Brush the cake surface with lightly beaten egg white (see EGG SEPARATING) or apricot glaze to help the marzipan to stick. To make apricot glaze, mix 2 heaped tablespoons of apricot jam with 2 teaspoons of water or lemon juice.

Divide the marzipan in half, then divide one half into half again. Sprinkle a pastry board with sieved icing sugar and roll out each of the smaller portions to strips a little wider than the depth of the cake, and about half its circumference in length. Trim one long edge of each strip straight with a knife, using a clean ruler as a straightedge, and trim the ends so that each strip is a little less than half the circumference of the cake.

Press the strips of marzipan against the cake sides, butting the strips on one side and leaving a small gap on the other. With a straight-sided tumbler or jam jar, roll the marzipan onto the side of the cake, closing the gap. Trim the top edges with a sharp knife.

Roll out the remaining portion of marzipan and use a cake tin as a guide to cut out the piece for the top of the cake. Lay the marzipan in place and gently roll it until it fits the top exactly.

Warm a palette knife in hot water, then dry it and use it to seal the gap between the top and side layers of marzipan.

Cover the cake with a tea towel or greaseproof paper and leave for at least 24 hours before icing.

If the cake is going to be kept for a long time, leave it to dry for a week before icing.

Masonry drilling

Boring holes in brickwork and concrete

Special twist drills, or masonry bits, are available for drilling holes in brick walls, concrete floors and precast concrete pieces, such as lintels, gateposts and fence posts. The drills have a carbide tip and are made in sizes that correspond to wall plug sizes – see WALL FASTENERS.

For most brickwork, use a masonry bit in a power drill, set at a slow speed which will make drilling more accurate and will prolong the life of the bit.

For concrete or engineering bricks, however, you need either a power drill that has a hammer action, or a hammer action attachment which fits into the drill chuck. The hammer action drives the bit backwards and forwards at high speed while it is rotating. See also DRILLING.

If you do not have a power drill, or are working where there is no power supply, use a hand-boring tool and a club hammer. The tool has interchangeable fluted bits, which are available in sizes to suit wall plug sizes, and fit into a hardened steel handle.

Wear a thick glove on the hand hold-

Using a hand-boring tool Grip the handle of the tool firmly and keep it horizontal. Strike the head with firm, straight blows. Turn the fluted bit in the hole after every three or four blows to clear the debris out of the hole.

ing the tool, and protect your eyes with safety goggles. Be sure to keep the tool at right angles to the brickwork at all times, otherwise the hole will become tapered and the wall plug will not grip properly.

Massage

A relaxing routine for the whole body

A gentle massage helps the body to relax, and provides a pleasant sensation, but do not use it to treat any form of illness or injury. Leave the treatment to someone with medical qualifications. When giving a massage, make sure that you, too, are relaxed – see RELAXATION EXERCISES. Otherwise, the tension in your body will make it difficult for you to relieve your partner's tension.

Take off anything that might catch against your partner's flesh – such as rings, a wristwatch or bracelet – and make sure that your fingernails are cut short and smooth. Before starting, make sure that the room is warm and the lighting restrained.

Have your partner lie face up on a firm, padded surface such as a carpeted floor or a table covered with a blanket. Do not use a bed, as the 'give' in the mattress will absorb most of the pressure. Your partner should be nude or wearing underwear, and if you use baby oil or vegetable oil for the massage, warm it first in your hands. Avoid rigorously massaging the front of the neck. Never apply too much pressure to the lower back or stomach, and never apply direct pressure to the spine.

The upper body First stroke your partner's face gently with your fingertips, moving from the centre outwards and ending with a circular motion at the temples. Massage along the cheeks and jawbone. Use a firm press-release action along the eyebrows. With your fingertips,

massage the scalp hard enough to move the skin.

Then cradle your partner's head as you work the neck muscles with your fingers. Gently lay the head down and, with a hand on each shoulder, push downwards towards the feet. Knead the muscles along the tops of the shoulders. This is a good massage for someone who wants to relax after a hard day's work.

The torso Place your hands, palms down, with the heels resting just below your partner's collarbone, thumbs touching. Begin a gliding stroke downwards, applying medium pressure to the chest and less to the stomach.

Now place your hands, fingers down, on your partner's side and pull the flesh upwards, alternating hands and squeezing the flesh as you work along the entire side. Repeat on the other side. Finally, work the top of your partner's chest with your fingertips.

Arms, hands and legs Grasp your partner's wrist with both hands and apply a firm, gliding stroke towards the armpit; take your top hand up over the shoulder. With both hands, pull firmly back down the sides of the arm and over the fingers.

With your partner's elbow bent and resting on the surface, encircle the wrist with your hands and slide them firmly downwards to the elbow. Return, applying no pressure.

From the same elbow-bent position, massage the inside of the lower arm with your thumbs. Place your partner's hand on your shoulder and apply the same technique to the upper arm. Finally, grasp your partner's arm in both hands and wring your hands vigorously back and forth along the entire length. Repeat the process on the other side.

In turn, massage the palm of each hand with your knuckles. Work the back, then the front, of the hands with your thumbs. Gently twist each finger, bending it slightly backwards and forwards as you knead it from the base to the tip.

Use the same series of procedures for the legs as you did for the arms, first stroking up and pulling down the whole leg, then sliding up the upper leg, then sliding up the lower leg.

With your hands supporting the knee, trace the furrow around the kneecap with your thumbs. Drum lightly on the kneecap with your fingertips; then work circles on either side of the bone. Wring the legs, as you did the arms, and work the feet, as you did the hands, applying extra pressure to the heels.

The back Have your partner turn over onto the stomach, with the head to one side. Knead the buttocks; then twist the knuckles of your index fingers into the hollows on either side. Vibrate the entire area with the heel of your hand.

MASSAGE

Techniques for relieving tension and relaxing muscles

1 Massaging the face, head and neck can relieve headaches and eyestrain. Begin by stroking the face with your fingertips (right), then gently massage the temples with circular movements (far right).

2 Stroke the cheeks gently but firmly, then with your fingertips massage along the jawbone.

3 With the thumb and forefinger of each hand, pinch firmly along the lines of the eyebrows.

4 Place your hands well behind the neck and massage the neck muscles with firm upward strokes.

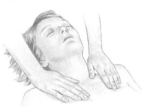

5 Place your hands below the collarbone and make gliding strokes over chest and stomach.

6 Pull the flesh upwards, with one hand after the other, squeezing as you work along each side in turn. Then with circular movements work around the chest and breastbone (right).

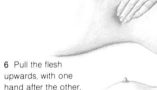

7 Take the wrist in both hands and stroke upwards, then pull firmly back down the sides and over the fingers.

8 Grip the wrist firmly with one hand, and with the other massage the inside of the lower arm.

9 Massage the palm of each hand, making small rotary thumb pressures in each palm.

10 Massage the legs in a similar way to the arms, using firm, gliding strokes and pulling down on the insides of the thighs.

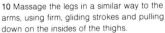

11 With your partner lying face down, massage the buttocks (left). Then work your thumbs along either side of the base of the spine and press into the furrows with first and middle fingers (right).

Use a long, gliding stroke down the back, then work your thumbs up the furrows on either side of the spine. On the return, dig the tips of your index and middle fingers deeply into the furrows. Knead the upper back muscles; then rub your hands briskly over the back.

Next, rake your partner's body with your fingertips. Then drum the muscles with the outer edges of your hands. Finish the massage by feathering the body with light fingertip strokes.

Maternity leave

Knowing when you are eligible; how to apply

A woman who has worked at least 16 hours a week for the same employer for more than two years, or at least eight hours a week for more than five years, is entitled to 18 weeks' maternity leave. Six weeks' leave will be at 90 per cent of the woman's average weekly earnings if she is earning a figure for which NATIONAL INSURANCE contributions are payable (£57 or more per week in April 1994). The remaining weeks are at a lower, set rate (£48.80 a week in April 1994). If the woman has not worked for the same employer for the required time, all her maternity pay will be at the lower rate.

Under the regulations, the leave period can start between six and 11 weeks before confinement; the balance is taken afterwards. To qualify for your full entitlement, you should not work for anyone during your leave period. Leave and pay may be jeopardised if you go abroad outside the EEC or are taken into legal custody during this time.

An employer cannot normally dismiss a woman because she is pregnant. However, if her condition 15 weeks or more before the birth makes it impossible to work properly (or if the law does not allow her to do that job while pregnant), and if she is not able to take time off for sickness (when she would get statutory sick pay), she may be 'fairly' dismissed if no other suitable job is open. She is still entitled to statutory maternity pay. See also UNFAIR DISMISSAL.

Self-employed women who have been paying flat rate National Insurance contributions can get maternity allowance.

Mayonnaise

Making a popular dressing for salads and cold dishes

The trick of making perfect mayonnaise lies in not using cold ingredients, and in adding the oil very slowly to prevent the mixture curdling.

Make sure that all the ingredients are at room temperature, and take the eggs out of the refrigerator at least an hour before starting.

Here is a recipe that will make about 285ml ($\frac{1}{2}$ pint) of mayonnaise – enough for four to six people.

Ingredients

2 egg yolks
1 tablespoon lemon juice or wine vinegar
285ml ($\frac{1}{2}$ pint) olive oil
$\frac{1}{2}$ teaspoon French mustard
$\frac{1}{4}$ teaspoon salt
$\frac{1}{4}$ teaspoon freshly ground black pepper
1-2 tablespoons hot water

Put the egg yolks (see EGG SEPARATING) into a mixing bowl with the lemon juice or wine vinegar as flavouring (do not use malt vinegar – it is far too strong). Beat with a balloon whisk, or an electric whisk, until well blended. Then beat in the mustard.

Start adding the olive oil drop by drop from a jug or a bottle with a lip, and whisk continuously. After about a quarter of the oil has been added, the mayonnaise takes on the consistency of thin cream. Now pour in the rest of the oil more rapidly, still whisking continuously.

When all the oil has been added, whisk in 1-2 tablespoons of boiling water. This will lighten the texture of the mayonnaise and help to stop it from curdling. Season the mixture to taste with salt and pepper, and add more lemon juice or vinegar as necessary.

If the mixture does curdle, break a fresh egg yolk into a clean bowl. Add the curdled mixture drop by drop, whisking as before.

Covered, mayonnaise will keep in the refrigerator for 2-3 days. Beat it again before serving.

This recipe may be varied with the addition of flavourings such as chives, parsley, garlic, capers and gherkins, all finely chopped. These can be added last to the beaten mixture.

Mealy bug

Getting rid of a greenhouse pest

Mealy bugs attack mostly plants kept in heated places such as greenhouses.

The bugs tend to form colonies, looking rather like blobs of cotton wool, where leaf shoots branch from a plant's stem. They also suck the plant sap, causing weak or stunted growth.

Controlling mealy bugs Spray larger plants thoroughly with malathion or with diazinon and repeat, if necessary, after a fortnight. To get rid of bugs on small or houseplants, use a watercolour paintbrush to paint the colonies with a solution of one of the same PESTICIDES. Repeat the treatment if necessary.

Measles

Treating a contagious infection in children

Measles is usually a disease of childhood, contracted by being in direct contact with another sufferer. A week to ten days later, the first signs will be a raised temperature, sore red eyes, a dry cough and, a day before the brownish-pink rash appears, you may see small white spots on the inside of the cheeks.

Treatment Call a DOCTOR as soon as you suspect measles, and put the child to bed. Rest and plenty of fluids are necessary to reduce the FEVER, even if the child refuses food. The child may be quite unwell for several days.

The doctor may prescribe antibiotics if he finds signs of ear or lung complications. Otherwise, no medicines are prescribed except, perhaps, paracetamol to reduce the temperature.

The illness may last five to seven days after the spots appear. Recovery is usually complete.

Prevention Immunisation – carried out shortly after the child's first birthday – is now considered the best protection, and is effective in most cases.

Meat loaf

A simple and economical main dish

For a tender meat loaf use lean stewing steak, and mince it finely yourself. The ready-minced beef normally on sale is too coarse for this dish. This recipe takes about 20 minutes to prepare, $1\frac{1}{2}$ hours to cook and feeds four to six people.

Ingredients

700g ($1\frac{1}{2}$lb) stewing steak, finely minced
1 onion, peeled and minced
50g (2oz) fine white breadcrumbs
$\frac{1}{2}$ teaspoon dried thyme
$\frac{1}{2}$ teaspoon dried oregano or marjoram
1 clove garlic, crushed, or $\frac{1}{4}$ teaspoon garlic salt
$\frac{1}{2}$ teaspoon salt
$\frac{1}{4}$ teaspoon freshly ground black pepper
2 eggs, beaten
450ml ($\frac{3}{4}$ pint) stock, reduced to 150ml ($\frac{1}{4}$ pint) by fast boiling
15g ($\frac{1}{2}$oz) butter

Preheat the oven to 150°C (300°F), gas mark 2.

Mix well all the ingredients, except the butter, and mould them into an oblong shape. Use the butter to grease an oblong 900g (2lb) loaf tin, about 200mm (8in) long, and press the mixture into it evenly.

Stand the loaf tin in a shallow roasting tin containing enough boiling water to come halfway up its sides – this stops the meat loaf from sticking to the bottom. Bake uncovered in the centre of the oven for $1\frac{1}{2}$ hours. If necessary, add more boiling water to maintain the level.

Turn the loaf onto a warmed serving plate, and serve with fresh TOMATO SAUCE, ketchup or barbecue sauce.

Meditation

Relaxing your mind to counter stress

Daily meditation can help to lower blood pressure, reduce stress, and promote feelings of physical and mental well-being. People who practise meditation claim that it releases the mind from the flood of outside stimuli, as well as from the continuous flow of its own thoughts; and that the meditator achieves a condition unlike either sleep or ordinary wakefulness.

Choose a quiet place where there are no external distractions, such as television, radio or background music. Sit in a comfortable, upright position.

Close your eyes and breathe evenly through your nose. Now relax your entire body, from your feet to the top of your head. See also RELAXATION EXERCISES; YOGA.

Now picture a peaceful scene – perhaps a blue sky or a green meadow – or concentrate on a word or phrase of your own choosing and repeat it to yourself silently or aloud. Should distracting thoughts, feelings or sensations intrude, simply concentrate on your chosen word or image. This may be difficult in times of stress, but with practice the unwanted thoughts and tensions should decrease and finally disappear.

Meditate once or twice a day for anything from 10 to 20 minutes. At the end of this time, open your eyes and sit quietly for a minute or two before resuming your daily tasks.

Memory improvement

Practical ways to overcome forgetfulness

Memory has two forms, short-term and long-term, and it is short-term memory that often lets you down. For example, you may rapidly forget the name of someone to whom you have just been introduced; yet you can remember the name of someone you have not seen or heard from for years. But, with practice, your all-round memory can improve.

Start by repeating the name of someone new until it is firmly lodged in your mind. In doing so, you prevent any new information from entering your mind – and driving out the previous item. If you see more of this new person, then his name – and possibly his address and telephone number – will be transferred to your long-term memory.

Tricks can also help. If you have trouble socially remembering names and faces, try connecting the name with some aspect of the person's appearance or personality. For instance, does Bob bob his head when he talks? Is Jean wearing jeans? Is Michael fair-haired like the actor Michael Caine? Does Rose have rosy cheeks?

Keep a special list of business associates and contacts and review it regularly, imagining the people's faces. In addition, once or twice a day, quickly review what you have recently learned.

If possible, speak the new information aloud, visualise it, and then write it down. All three actions will help to move the items into your long-term memory – and to keep them there.

Mending

Repairing tears in materials and seams

To mend a tear in, for example, a shirt or skirt, tack a piece of stiff paper to the underside of the material so that the edges of the tear are held together, or use a small piece of iron-on Vilene.

Choose some thread that matches the

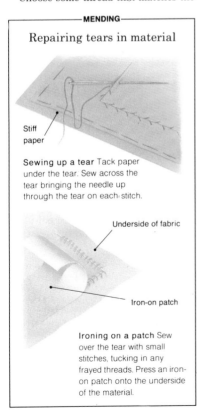

── MENDING ──

Repairing tears in material

Sewing up a tear Tack paper under the tear. Sew across the tear bringing the needle up through the tear on each stitch.

Stiff paper

Underside of fabric

Iron-on patch

Ironing on a patch Sew over the tear with small stitches, tucking in any frayed threads. Press an iron-on patch onto the underside of the material.

material, then sew the tear with small slanting stitches. Push the tip of the needle down through the tear and the paper and under the material, then bring it up through the paper and material just to one side of the tear. Turn the needle, then bring it back down through the tear, under the material on the other side and up again. Continue until the tear is sewn up. Then tear away the paper.

Iron-on repairs Another way of mending a tear is to use iron-on bonding web or an iron-on patch.

On a lightweight fabric you may be able to take matching material from a hem. Lay it behind the tear with a piece of bonding web between the two layers, and apply a hot iron over a damp cloth.

For heavier material, such as denim, buy iron-on patching material and iron it to the back of the tear, making sure that the edges of the tear are touching.

Mending a seam If the fabric is torn at the seam unpick the seam and sew the edges of the tear as described above.

Stitch the seam together again either with a machine or by hand. Use short stitches and go on beyond the section that has come undone at each end.

See also DARNING; PATCHING.

Menu planning

Achieving balance and variety

Menus fall into two main categories – those for entertaining, and those which provide nutritionally well-balanced meals for day-to-day living.

Menus for entertaining Bringing together the right combination of different dishes to form the perfect meal is an art which comes with experience. Here are a few basic rules:
● Consider your guests' likes and dislikes.
● Suit the occasion. Celebration meals require something special, can be formal with 4-6 courses, or can be a buffet with a wider selection of dishes. Informal gatherings need only 2-3 courses.
● Consider your ability, and the facilities and equipment available. Inexperienced cooks are wise to choose dishes with which they are confident. Confident cooks should exercise restraint; over-enthusiasm can result in meals that are too complex and overtax the diner's digestion.
● Respect the seasons. Food in season will always have the best flavour, and will be cheaper.
● Take into account the time of year. Steak and kidney pudding, which would be very welcome in winter, would not be so popular on a hot summer day.
● Avoid exclusively cold dishes, even in

summer. Introduce something hot – for example, hot buttered new potatoes with parsley make an excellent accompaniment to cold salmon or chicken.
● Select dishes which provide a combination of soft and crisp or crunchy textures.
● Avoid repetition of the same food, or style of cooking. For example, don't follow a tomato soup with a pasta dish laden with tomato sauce, or serve two or three courses of fried foods.
● Co-ordinate the colour scheme: a colourful meal is a more interesting one.
● Refresh and re-stimulate the palate by serving cheese after the main course, before the dessert.
● Choose wines to complement and enhance each course. As a general rule, serve white wine with fish and poultry, red wine with red meats, and sweet wines with the dessert.

Nutritionally well-balanced meals A healthy, well-balanced meal is one which provides the body with adequate amounts of protein, vitamins and minerals, energy-giving foods and dietary fibre, with a limited amount of fat, sugar and salt. At least one healthy meal should be eaten every day.

Each of our daily meals should consist of a combination of the following foods:
● To encourage growth: fish, poultry, meat, cheese, eggs, milk, bread or other cereal products, nuts, peas or beans.
● To provide vitamins and minerals not commonly found in other foods, and also fibre: plenty of fresh fruit and vegetables. These should be eaten raw for maximum benefit, as cooking destroys many of the valuable vitamins.
● To provide energy: fats, bread and cereals, enough to satisfy the appetite.

Mercury

How to handle quicksilver

Although a metal, mercury is liquid at normal temperatures – but not wet. It cannot be picked up, mopped up or brushed up without breaking into globules. In the home it is most likely to be found in THERMOMETERS, and if a thermometer is broken the spilt mercury – sometimes called quicksilver – can be difficult to remove.

If mercury spills on a carpet it may be swept up, but silvery traces are likely to remain. Do not vacuum it – under heat, mercury becomes a highly toxic vapour.

On a flat surface, try rounding up spilt particles by slipping a stiff, thin sheet of paper beneath them. Wrap them well and dispose of them in a dustbin.

Mercury is poisonous if inhaled, or if it gets into the bloodstream, or is absorbed through the skin. But, if swallowed, it usually does no harm as the gut cannot absorb it.

Meringues

*Making a feather-light topping, or
a delicious small cake*

Meringue is made from stiffly beaten egg whites mixed with sugar. It makes a superb topping for pies and puddings such as lemon pie or queen of puddings, or can be baked to make small cakes filled with whipped cream.

To make the meringue, whisk 2 egg whites (see EGG SEPARATING) in a bowl, using a balloon whisk or egg beater, until stiff. Add 50g (2oz) of caster sugar and continue whisking until the meringue will stand in soft peaks and keeps its shape. Then, using a metal spoon, fold in 50g (2oz) of caster sugar by slowly and gently turning the mixture.

For a topping, spread the meringue evenly, from the edge of the pie or pudding to the centre, and sprinkle caster sugar over it before placing in the oven.

To make the cakes, place rounded dessertspoons of the mixture onto a lined baking sheet and bake the meringues in an oven preheated to 110°C (225°F), gas mark ¼ for 2 hours. Turn off the oven and leave the meringues in the oven for 1 hour more.

Gently remove the meringues from the baking paper, and sandwich pairs with whipped cream.

Metal detecting

Choosing and using a detector

All metal detectors use the same basic principle – the machine sets up an electromagnetic field which is disturbed by any metal object that comes within its range. Transmit-Receive (TR) detectors give an audible signal.

By using headphones to pick out the sounds and cut out background noise – and also by adjusting the controls – you soon learn to distinguish true finds from unwanted signals such as minerals in the ground. More sensitive 'motion' models do much of the work for you, but have to be kept moving over the ground all the time to emit a response.

Detectors vary in size, price, gadgetry and sophistication. Some work best on farmland, others in parks or on beaches – even underwater.

Using the machine To avoid upsetting landowners and archaeologists:
● Ask permission before detecting on private land.
● Follow the Country Code.
● Disturb the ground as little as possible.
● Do not spread litter.
● Report any finds of historic, valuable or lethal objects to the landowner and the police – see TREASURE.
● Avoid archaeological sites, because it is illegal to use a detector on scheduled ancient monuments.

Metalworking

Shaping and joining sheet metal

An engineer's vice firmly attached to a sturdy bench is essential for metalwork – one with a jaw width of 150mm (6in) will be suitable for general work.

Materials Sheet mild steel and aluminium are the easiest to cut, drill and shape, though the choice will depend on the function of the finished piece. For example, aluminium is the best choice where lightness or resistance to corrosion is required.

The thickness of sheet steel and aluminium is given in gauge numbers – the lower the number the thicker the metal – 16 gauge (1.6mm thick) being suitable for most jobs.

Measuring and marking Lay the sheet on a flat surface and measure and mark out the shape you require. Use a rule as a straightedge to join up marked points with a scriber. Before marking, coat the steel with engineer's blue (similar to blue ink) or a wide marker pen so that the scribed lines stand out clearly.

Use the scriber to mark a straight line as illustrated. Scribe a circle or an arc with dividers, also illustrated.

METALWORKING

How to mark, cut and bend pieces of metal

Before starting work, gather the tools necessary. For marking and measuring, you need a metric and an imperial steel rule; a try square for marking right angles; a sliding bevel for marking other angles; a fine-pointed scriber for marking straight lines; a punch and spring dividers with hardened points for inscribing arcs and circles.

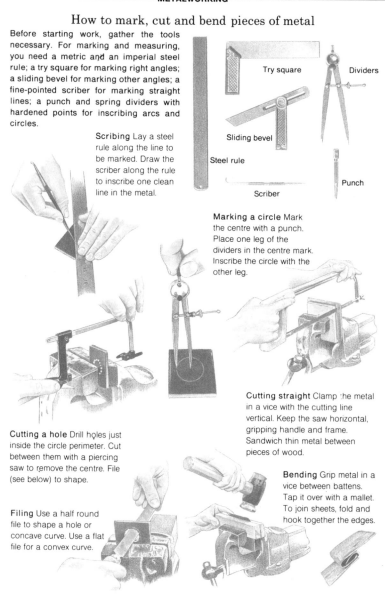

Scribing Lay a steel rule along the line to be marked. Draw the scriber along the rule to inscribe one clean line in the metal.

Marking a circle Mark the centre with a punch. Place one leg of the dividers in the centre mark. Inscribe the circle with the other leg.

Cutting straight Clamp the metal in a vice with the cutting line vertical. Keep the saw horizontal, gripping handle and frame. Sandwich thin metal between pieces of wood.

Cutting a hole Drill holes just inside the circle perimeter. Cut between them with a piercing saw to remove the centre. File (see below) to shape.

Filing Use a half round file to shape a hole or concave curve. Use a flat file for a convex curve.

Bending Grip metal in a vice between battens. Tap it over with a mallet. To join sheets, fold and hook together the edges.

Cutting Use a hacksaw (see SAWS AND SAWING) with a blade which allows at least three teeth to be in contact with the metal at the same time. The thinner the material the finer the blade, but for soft metals such as aluminium, use a coarse blade to avoid clogging. Fit the blade with teeth facing forward.

Clamp the metal firmly as illustrated. Cut with long, even strokes, pressing down on the forward stroke and releasing the pressure on the backward stroke. Use the full length of the blade. After cutting, clean burrs from the edge with a fine file.

Cut out a hole as illustrated using a piercing saw – a deep-framed saw with a very fine blade – or use a hole saw (see DRILLING) or an abrafile fitted into a hacksaw frame. Use a piercing saw to cut curved lines. Cut just outside the line and finish off by filing as illustrated.

Bending To make an angled bend, place the metal between two 25mm (1in) wooden BATTENS and clamp in the vice. Adjust the metal sheet so that the bend line is level with the top of the battens. Bend using a hide-faced or boxwood mallet with light blows along the length of the bend. To form a curve, shape a hardwood block to the required curve and bend the metal round it.

Joining To join two edges, fold each edge into a hook shape by hammering over a piece of scrap metal, then hook them together as shown. Hammer the seam flat with a steel hammer. See also RIVETING; SOLDERING; WELDING.

Meter reading

Calculating electricity and gas consumption

There are two types of domestic meter in use, for both electricity and gas. The older meters have a series of dials and pointers, and more modern meters have a digital display read from left to right. If you have an Economy 7 electricity meter, it has two digital indicators – one for the lower-priced night-rate electricity, the other for the day rate.

To check consumption, subtract the previous reading – recorded on your last account – from your new reading.

Reading an electricity meter The dial-type meter has six dials, each pointer revolving in the opposite direction to its neighbour. From left to right they record consumption in units – in ten thousands, thousands, hundreds, tens and singles. Ignore any dial registering tenths or hundredths of a unit – usually coloured red.

With a digital meter, write down the figures from left to right, ignoring the $\frac{1}{10}$ figure on the extreme right.

How to read dial and digital meters

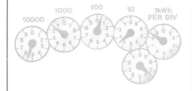

Electricity meters Read a dial meter from left to right – but ignore the dial (usually coloured red) recording tenths of units. If a pointer is between figures, write down the lower one. This meter reads 51038.

With digital meters read from left to right; ignore the figure on the far right.

Gas meters Read only the four dials – usually at the bottom – with black hands. Read from left to right. If a pointer is between figures, write down the lower figure. This meter reads 7429.

With digital gas meters, read the first four figures from left to right.

Reading a gas meter To read the dial-type meter, use only the four black-hand dials. With the digital meter, read the first four figures only, from left to right. The figures refer to hundreds of cubic feet.

Metric conversion

Working out imperial and metric measures

The modern metric system – strictly known as the Système International d'Unités (SI), or International System of Units – is a system of weights and measures based on the original metric system founded in France during the French Revolution in the 1790s. The

modern form was agreed at an international conference in 1960.

The basic units of SI are the metre for length, the kilogram for mass and the second for time. Other units such as the litre for liquid volume are derived accordingly – 1 millilitre is equivalent to 1 cubic centimetre.

Larger or smaller units are formed by multiplying or dividing the basic units by multiples of ten. The multiples are indicated by a series of prefixes – such as *kilo* for a thousand times, as in kilometre, which is 1000 metres; or *milli* for a thousandth part of, as in millilitre, which is one thousandth of a litre.

Conversion table To convert from imperial to metric, multiply the imperial amount by the figure in the third column. To convert 5lb into metric, for example, multiply by 0.45 to get 2.25kg.

To convert from metric to imperial divide the metric amount by the figure in the third column. To convert 20km into miles, for example, divide by 1.61 to get a little under $12\frac{1}{2}$ miles.

	Imperial	Metric	Conversion figure
Length	inches	millimetres	25.4
	inches	centimetres	2.54
	feet	metres	0.30
	yards	metres	0.91
	miles	kilometres	1.61
Area	square inches	square centimetres	6.45
	square feet	square metres	0.09
	square yards	square metres	0.84
	acres	hectares	0.41
	square miles	square kilometres	2.59
Volume	cubic inches	cubic centimetres	16.39
	cubic feet	cubic metres	0.03
	cubic yards	cubic metres	0.76
Liquid volume	fluid ounces	millilitres	28.41
	pints	litres	0.57
	gallons	litres	4.55
Weight	ounces	grams	28.35
	pounds	kilograms	0.45
	tons	tonnes	1.02

Mice as pests

Getting them out – and keeping them out

House mice live indoors all year long, whereas field mice intrude mainly in the autumn and winter.

Mice enter houses through heating and ventilation ducts, from under floorboards, along plumbing or through broken AIR BRICKS. They usually build their nests near a food source and forage at night, eating the first morsel they come across. Keep all foodstuffs safely out of their way – in containers, cupboards or a refrigerator. Plug all holes, however small, with cement or plaster reinforced with wire wool.

If the problem persists, put down spring traps or poison baits – obtainable from hardware shops. Chocolate and cereals, nuts or peanut butter make more effective baits for a trap than the traditional cheese. Place traps at right angles to the wall with the treadle towards the wall. To avoid catching your fingers, use a pencil to move the set traps into position.

Alphakil is a quick-acting, humane and safe mouse-killer; others include Rodine 'C' or Ratak. The Rentokil Mouse-killing System includes three bait boxes and a poison bait.

Try to place mousetraps and poison out of the way of family pets and warn children not to touch them.

Mice as pets

Feeding and looking after them

Mice make easy-to-care-for and affectionate pets. Once they get to know you, they may scamper up your arm and nestle in the nape of your neck.

Start by buying a pair at a good pet shop. A buck and doe can produce up to 20 litters a year, with from six to 12 young in each litter. So if you want to keep the number down to two, buy a pair of females. Two males will fight. The pet-store owner can identify the sex for you.

If you decide to buy a breeding pair you should remove the buck before the female has her litter and keep the pair separate until the young mice are fully weaned.

Mice are best kept in a wire and metal cage – they can chew their way out of a wooden one.

They eat about a teaspoon of food a day, mainly bits of bread, canary seed, oatmeal, green vegetables and fresh fruit. As a treat you could give them a little grated cheese. Stale bread should be offered in milk or water. Change the drinking water in the bottle twice a week.

Mice usually urinate and defecate in the same spot, so it is a good idea to place a disposable aluminium pie plate, filled with sand or cat litter, at that spot. Clean the plate every two days.

If you take good care of them, your mice – white, black, brown, or spotted – should live for about three years.

Microwave cooking

How to make almost instant meals

Microwave ovens cook with invisible radiation rather than heat. The microwaves are high-frequency electromagnetic waves bounced off the oven walls into the food. They are absorbed by the water molecules in the food and converted into heat.

Microwave ovens cook much more quickly than conventional ones; potatoes can be baked in their jackets, for example, in under ten minutes. Plates and dishes do not get hot in a microwave (except for some heat transferred from the food) because they have no water molecules.

Certain foods do not cook well in a microwave. They include PASTRY and YORKSHIRE PUDDING, which need hot air around them to rise, egg custard, MERINGUES and fruit cakes – see CAKE BAKING.

Meat cooked in a microwave will not be crisp and brown on the outside – though some microwaves have special browning dishes or conventional heating elements that can be used at the end of cooking time to brown the meat. Tougher cuts needing long, slow cooking should not be cooked in a microwave.

On the other hand, food that would normally be boiled or poached (vegetables, fruit and fish, for example) can be much better cooked in a microwave. They keep their texture better and lose fewer nutrients.

Using a microwave Cook food in the dishes in which it will be served – but do not use metal dishes or dishes with metallic decorations, or the metal may cause an electric arc that could damage the oven.

If you want food (vegetables, for example, or fish) to stay moist while being cooked in a microwave, cover the dish with clingfilm. If you want it slightly crisper, leave it uncovered. With irregularly shaped meat joints, shield thinner parts of the joint for part of the cooking time with kitchen foil held in place with cocktail sticks – otherwise these parts will cook more quickly than the rest. Prick the skins of vegetables such as potatoes or tomatoes to prevent them bursting through internal pressures.

For the length of time to cook a particular food, consult the manufacturer's booklet. Some microwaves have probes or sensors which are poked into the food before cooking and will stop the oven when the food reaches the right temperature. Make sure that the food is piping hot throughout before eating it.

MICE AS PETS

Providing them with healthy living quarters

Buy a wire cage for your mice, about 600mm (2ft) long and 300mm (12in) high and wide. It should contain a water bottle, food dispenser, litter dish, an 'upstairs' sleeping box complete with ladder and a bed of straw or chaff, and preferably an exercise wheel.

Metal cage

Sleeping box (with bedding)

Pie dish

Water bottle

Ladder

Food dispenser

Clean the cage with a safe disinfectant and change the bedding every day.
Clean out the litter dish every other day.

Many microwaves have turntables which rotate a dish during cooking to make sure it is evenly exposed to the microwaves. If yours does not, give the dish a quarter turn four times during cooking. Alternatively, stir dishes such as stews and casseroles thoroughly from time to time.

Thawing and reheating food A microwave is exceptionally useful for defrosting and reheating food. A 1.4kg (3lb) joint of meat, for example, can be defrosted in under half an hour – and a plate of food for a latecomer to a family meal can be reheated in a few minutes without becoming soggy or losing its flavour.

To defrost food, put it in the microwave for three or four minutes, then remove it. If the food can be stirred, break it up as much as possible with a fork – otherwise, let it stand for a few minutes so that the heat can soak in from the outside towards the centre. Return to the microwave for a further three or four minutes, then remove and either break it up some more or leave to stand. Continue in this way until the food is evenly defrosted. Alternatively, put the food into the microwave on the defrost (lowest power) setting and leave it until it has thawed completely, but it will take longer to thaw this way.

When reheating a plate of food, put foods such as potatoes, which take longer to reheat, around the edge of the plate where they will get the full force of the microwaves.

Migraine

Treating severe and recurrent headaches

About five people in a hundred suffer from migraine – one of the recurrent HEADACHES which occur in two forms: *common migraine*, in which the headache only is present; and *classic migraine*, in which the headache is accompanied by several alarming but not dangerous symptoms.

Classic migraine begins with a warning – often soon after waking – that an attack is about to take place. The warning often takes the form of bright spots or zigzag lines before the eyes. The sufferer may soon experience numbness or tingling in the face, a hand or a leg. There may be slight difficulty in speaking – and the symptoms may gradually spread throughout the body.

After a while, these symptoms disappear and are followed by a severe, throbbing headache. Sometimes, nausea and vomiting also occur. A migraine headache can last from a few hours to several days – and the attacks may come as often as two or three times a week.

They are sometimes brought on by overwork or emotional STRESS, by alcoholic drinks, or by eating certain foods – including chocolate, cheese and citrus fruits. The headache is caused by the blood arteries leading to one side of the person's head contracting and expanding.

Any severe, prolonged or recurrent headache should be reported to your DOCTOR. If migraine is diagnosed, he may prescribe special drugs – some of which prevent attacks if taken regularly, and others which are taken as soon as an attack starts.

During a migraine attack, the sufferer should lie down in a darkened room and rest. If an attack is prolonged, eat only light, bland foods, to reduce the risk of vomiting.

More women than men are migraine victims; the contraceptive pill can cause attacks. The attacks tend to become fewer and less severe as the sufferer gets older – sometimes disappearing altogether in later middle age, often, in women, at the time of the menopause.

Mildew and mould

How to avoid and remove them

The growth of both mildew and mould is encouraged by DAMP, CONDENSATION and lack of VENTILATION.

Mildew This is a very fine form of mould growth, most noticeable on white fabrics. If ignored, it can form a stain which is very hard to remove.

Exposing a stained article to sunlight will kill off the mildew, but if a stain is left, apply lemon juice to washable fabrics and leave to dry. A peroxide solution may also be used on washable fabrics.

With dry-clean fabrics, moisten the stain with lemon juice, sprinkle with salt and leave to dry in the sun, if possible. Sponge lightly with clean water and allow to dry. Alternatively, use a proprietary fungicide, following the instructions carefully. See also CLEANING SOLVENTS; STAIN REMOVAL.

Moulds Large mould growths may be encountered on paintwork and wallcoverings, including the grouting between tiles.

On paintwork, they may appear as blackish deposits – mainly on painted metalwork. Mould can be killed with a proprietary fungicide, though in severe attacks a number of applications may be necessary. Do not use household bleach, which although it seems to work, has only a temporary effect. The mould will recur in a matter of months.

Allow the fungicide to work, then wipe off any debris with a clean rag.

On wallcoverings, the mould may

appear as brown or purple spots which actually stain the surface. To kill the mould, the wallcovering must be stripped off and the wall treated with a fungicide. When repapering, use a paste containing a fungicide to discourage further mould growth – see WALLPAPERING; WALLPAPER REMOVAL.

In extreme cases, mould may affect clothing in cold wardrobes, carpets – and even bedclothes. The answer in each case is to make the rooms drier and warmer. The most serious form of mould growth is DRY ROT, which can cause very severe structural damage.

Mirrors

Hanging, cleaning and restoring them

In many old houses, mirrors can be hung from picture rails by chains and hooks that clip over the rail. In houses without picture rails, or for a neater look, there are several fixing methods available – see illustration on the next page.

For all mirrors that are stuck or screwed to the wall, make sure that the wall is flat. If necessary, line the wall first by fixing a piece of plywood or chipboard to it using countersunk screws to secure it in place.

Many plain unbacked mirrors are best held by mirror clips – some designed to be fixed, others slotted so they can be slid into place. Usually, six clips are required – two fixed ones to support the bottom edge of the mirror, and four sliding clips, two at the top and one each side.

Lightly mark the position of the mirror on the wall, then position the two bottom clips and mark the wall for screw holes. Drill and plug the wall (see MASONRY DRILLING), then screw the two clips in place, using countersunk nylon washers usually supplied with the clips. These cushion the mirror, and prevent the screws marking the mirror backing. Sometimes two washers are supplied – one to go between wall and clip, and the other between clip and mirror. This allows for any slight irregularity in the wall surface.

Rest the mirror on the two fixed clips and lightly mark the positions of the sliding clips. Remove the mirror and mark the required hole positions, making sure the clips will be able to slide out far enough to allow the mirror to be put in place. Drill and plug holes as before; position the mirror, and slide the clips in to hold the mirror firm.

Never overtighten any kind of mirror screw – it could crack the mirror.

Cleaning Use a proprietary window-cleaning fluid, applied with a clean cloth, then polished with a soft duster.

Fitting them to walls

Adhesive pads Fix mirror tiles to flat walls using adhesive foam pads. Make sure the paintwork is sound, but strip off wallpaper, so that all the pads make contact with the bare wall.

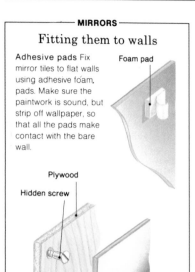

Foam pad

Plywood

Hidden screw

Hidden screws Fit plywood backing to the wall using countersunk screws, then fix the mirror to the backing, using clips screwed into the sides and bottom of the backing.

Mirror clips Fix plain unbacked mirrors to a wall using sliding clips – see text.

Mirror screws Drill and plug the wall, fixing the mirror with dome-head screws, which have decorative heads hiding their slots – see SCREWS. If the mirror is not ready-drilled, get a glazier to do it for you.

Restoring There is no DIY method of restoring discoloured or damaged silvering. Take the mirror to a glazier and get a quote for resilvering.

Remember when buying mirrors that those used in a bathroom should be suitably protected, otherwise the silvering will be affected by damp. So ask the shop assistant to advise you.

Mites on plants

Recognising and dealing with tiny plant pests

Mites are tiny, sometimes microscopic creatures related to spiders and ticks. Many cause serious damage to plants, either by feeding on the plant tissues or by passing virus diseases to the plants.

Red spider mites There are two kinds: the fruit tree red spider mite, which attacks fruit trees, particularly apples, plums and damsons; and the glasshouse red spider mite, which attacks greenhouse and HOUSEPLANTS as well as some shrubs and herbaceous plants – see GREENHOUSE GARDENING.

Although they are two distinct species they have a similar effect on plants they attack. The leaves become finely mottled and turn yellow or rusty brown – and in bad attacks they fall. Glasshouse mites leave a fine silk webbing on leaves.

To control fruit tree mites, spray in winter with DNOC/petroleum wash, and again, immediately after flowering, with derris, dimethoate, dinocap, benomyl or malathion. To control glasshouse mites, spray regularly with dimethoate, or use biological control (red spider predator *Phytoselulus* is easily obtained).

Gall mites As their name suggests, the symptoms of gall mites are galls or swellings on the leaves and buds of a plant. To control, spray the plant in spring with lime sulphur.

Blackcurrant gall mites – or big bud mites – are the most serious pest of blackcurrant bushes. The mites infest the buds, which then become greatly enlarged and fail to develop. To control them, remove and burn the swollen buds in early March, then spray with a solution of lime sulphur or benomyl when the flowers first open. Repeat three weeks later.

Blackcurrant gall mites also transmit a virus disease called reversion. Its symptoms are poor crops and plant growth and leaves that are smaller than usual with fewer lobes; the flower buds are hairless and bright magenta in colour. The only way to deal with the disease is to dig up the plants and burn them.

Bulb scale mites Twisted, malformed leaves and rust-coloured streaks on stems and foliage are symptoms of an infestation. These mites attack principally narcissi and hippeastrums. If plants are badly infested, destroy them. With less severe cases, in winter, when the bulbs are dormant, immerse them for two or three hours in water kept at 44°C (111°F).

Tarsonemid mites There is no really effective way of controlling tarsonemid mites. They make leaves of plants they attack curl at the edges – and in severe cases, distort completely. They also cause discoloration and scarring on the surface. DAHLIAS, BEGONIAS, pot cyclamens, FUCHSIAS and greenhouse plants such as FERNS are particularly susceptible. Spraying with lime sulphur will help to limit infestations.

Mitre joints

Making neat corner joints in wood

A mitre joint is formed by cutting two meeting pieces of wood at an angle of 45 degrees, so that when joined they make a perfect right angle.

This type of joint is commonly used in PICTURE FRAMING. If you plan to do a lot of framing it would pay to invest in a mitre block or box, or even in a special corner jig. These are all designed to guide a saw blade at the correct angle while the piece of wood is held in place.

Cutting and joining them

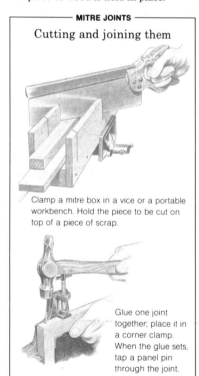

Clamp a mitre box in a vice or a portable workbench. Hold the piece to be cut on top of a piece of scrap.

Glue one joint together; place it in a corner clamp. When the glue sets, tap a panel pin through the joint.

Mitre clamps will hold the pieces in position while the glue is setting.

For the occasional mitre joint, you can use a combination square, or a sliding bevel set at the correct 45-degree angle. Usually it is the inside dimension of a frame which is important, so one end of the picture-frame moulding is mitred, then the internal length marked on the moulding and the second angle marked.

Keep the saw upright while the cut is made; this is vital if the two mitres are to fit properly. Use a tenon saw with fine teeth and clamp the moulding firmly in a vice or to the bench with a clamp while cutting – see SAWS AND SAWING.

Some pieces of wood, such as skirting boards, are too wide to fit into a mitre box. Draw a square on the edge, then draw a diagonal cutting line, continuing it down the face. Cut to these two lines.

The simplest way of joining the mitred pieces is to glue and pin them. Clamp the two pieces in a corner clamp, having applied adhesive to the meeting faces. Make sure they are in tight contact. When the adhesive has set, knock a panel pin through the corner and remove the corner carefully from the clamp. Repeat the process for the other three corners.

Large frames may need strengthening. One method is to cut into the corner with a tenon saw and insert a sliver of veneer coated in glue. Wipe off any surplus glue, and then let the glue set. Trim off the surplus veneer.

Alternatively, you could join the pieces with dowel joints – see DOWELS.

Mobiles

Making moving sculptures

A mobile is a delicately balanced assemblage of lightweight objects suspended by strings. The least breath of air will set a mobile in motion.

To make a simple mobile, tie or glue various shapes (circles, squares, animal forms, flowers) to a central string. Cut the shapes from art paper or medium-thick cardboard. To add texture and eye-appeal, incorporate coloured plastic beads, balsa wood, or natural objects such as shells and nuts.

More complex and interesting mobiles can be created by incorporating one or more horizontal arms into the structure. Slender wooden DOWELS or coathanger wire make good arms.

Use string or nylon fishing line to hang an object or shape from each end of an arm. Hold the arm between your thumb and forefinger to determine the point of balance, knot a string there, and lift the mobile by the string to make sure it hangs level.

Create other arms by the same procedure and add them to the structure. Work from the bottom up, checking the balance of the assemblage whenever a new arm is added. For extra appeal, vary the size of the shapes and the lengths of the threads. Mobiles made with shells or metal make an attractive, tinkling noise when they are disturbed by a draught.

Hanging a mobile Display it in an open area where it can move freely and be seen.

Another interesting method is to hang shapes within shapes – smaller circles within larger ones, for example. As they are disturbed, the shapes spin inside each other in different directions.

Modelling in clay

An easy way to create your own sculptures

Self-hardening clay, available from craft shops, is a useful medium for learning to sculpt – it is as pliable as firing or casting clays, hardens naturally without the addition of a hardener, and can be reconstituted and used again if your first efforts are unsatisfactory.

Modelling tools with variously shaped tips and wire loops are also available from craft shops.

Sculpting a head For a largish head, say one-third life-size, make an *armature* – a basic framework or matrix on which to fix the clay. Use a piece of $300 \times 25 \times 25$mm ($12 \times 1 \times 1$in) wood nailed to a flat base, as illustrated. A few nails partly driven into the top of the armature will help hold the clay during modelling.

Smooth the head with the hacksaw blade, then shape the eyes, nose and mouth, as shown, with the modelling tool. Cut out two eyelids from a flat piece of clay, press them into position and shape them with a wetted sable brush.

Make eyebrows and ears from rolled

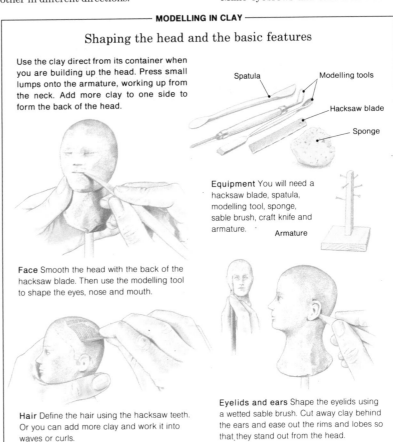

— MODELLING IN CLAY —

Shaping the head and the basic features

Use the clay direct from its container when you are building up the head. Press small lumps onto the armature, working up from the neck. Add more clay to one side to form the back of the head.

Spatula

Modelling tools

Hacksaw blade

Sponge

Equipment You will need a hacksaw blade, spatula, modelling tool, sponge, sable brush, craft knife and armature.

Armature

Face Smooth the head with the back of the hacksaw blade. Then use the modelling tool to shape the eyes, nose and mouth.

Hair Define the hair using the hacksaw teeth. Or you can add more clay and work it into waves or curls.

Eyelids and ears Shape the eyelids using a wetted sable brush. Cut away clay behind the ears and ease out the rims and lobes so that they stand out from the head.

strips of clay, press them into place, and shape with a small spatula. For the ears, lay another strip inside the outline to thicken the edges. Then use the modelling tool to detail the ears, finishing with a wetted sable brush.

Use a craft knife to cut away clay from behind the ears, then ease away the edges and the lobes so that they stand out from the head. The hacksaw teeth can be used to define the hair; or add extra clay and work it into waves or curls.

Go over the facial details with a sable brush dipped in water, bringing out cheek lines, nostrils and mouth. Finally, smooth over the head with a piece of natural sponge soaked in water. The model will harden in about two days. Then you can, if you wish, paint the head with poster or enamel paints.

If you are not satisfied with your first attempt, and wish to try again after the model has hardened, break it into lumps about the size of large pebbles, place them in a plastic bucket and add a little water. Cover the clay with polythene and leave for four or five days, when it will be malleable again.

Moles

Coping with a lawn destroyer

Moles are not easy to get rid of and you may have to use more than one of the following methods. Probably the most effective is to use a chemical based on aluminium ammonium sulphate, available in garden centres.

Put it down in the runs – and if that gets rid of the moles put down more along the boundaries of your garden to stop them coming back. The chemical will only deter moles and not kill them; it can be used to drive away CATS.

Other ways of discouraging moles are to push rags soaked in creosote down runs, or to bury bottles upright, as far as their necks, where moles are active. They dislike both the smell of creosote and the hum of the wind in the bottles.

Alternatively, you can remove their main food source, earthworms, with a proprietary wormkiller. If you feel more drastic action is necessary, use a mole trap or one of the proprietary smoke generator deterrents.

Mops and mopping

Day-to-day floor care

There are two ways of mopping floors – dry mopping, much like sweeping, and damp mopping, for wiping or washing.

Dry mopping Wool or synthetic mop heads are best for dry mopping, since their 'static cling' attracts dust. Some

are oil-treated or impregnated and not only pick up dust easily, but polish and help to preserve wood flooring. However, they tend to turn floor wax gummy, so should only be used on unpolished floors.

When using a dry mop, avoid lifting the mop head, which scatters dust. Work towards the centre of the floor, pulling the dust along as you go; then shake it out into a plastic bag or lined bin.

Wash a soiled mop head in a mild solution of detergent and water, then leave it to dry head up.

Damp mopping Vinyl or ceramic floors are most easily washed with a long-handled sponge mop, which has a replaceable head hinged for wringing, the water being squeezed out by pressing a lever.

First dry mop the floor, or sweep up dust and grit with a vacuum cleaner or soft household broom. Then dip the mop into a bucket of clean, hot water, squeeze out the excess and wipe a section of floor. Rinse and wring out the mop, wipe the floor and leave it to dry.

To wash a grimy floor, use a household cleaning powder or fluid. After wetting the floor with the household cleaner (diluted or undiluted, according to instructions), leave it for a short while, then mop to remove the dirt. Rinse and wring out the mop, wipe the floor and leave it to dry.

Abrasive and alkaline cleaning agents can damage vinyl tiles and other kinds of flooring – so when choosing a cleaning product, read the label carefully and make sure that it is recommended for your floor. Never flood vinyl-tiled or jointed sheet flooring (see VINYL FLOORING) – water can seep between the joints and destroy the adhesive.

After using a mop, rinse it and shake out the water outdoors. Wash the mop head in warm, soapy water, rinse, wring out and dry head up.

Morse code

A universal way to make signals

The American inventor Samuel Morse devised his code – in which letters are represented by combinations of short and long signals – in about 1838. He established which letters are most often used and gave them short signals ('e' is a single dot); those least used (such as 'q') were given the longer signals.

His code simplified the sending of telegraphic messages, and it can be written in dots and dashes or signalled with flash lamps or by radio bleeps. The international distress signal SOS – three dots, three dashes and three dots – was introduced in 1912, 40 years after Morse's death. The catchphrase 'Save Our Souls' came some time later. See also DISTRESS SIGNALS.

The language of dots and dashes	
A ·—	N —·
B —···	O ———
C —·—·	P ·——·
D —··	Q ——·—
E ·	R ·—·
F ··—·	S ···
G ——·	T —
H ····	U ··—
I ··	V ···—
J ·———	W ·——
K —·—	X —··—
L ·—··	Y —·——
M ——	Z ——··
1 ·————	6 —····
2 ··———	7 ——···
3 ···——	8 ———··
4 ····—	9 ————·
5 ·····	0 —————

Mortar

How to mix; proportions for different strengths

Cement, sand and hydrated lime or a liquid plasticiser mixed with water make up the mortar used for bonding bricks – see BRICKLAYING.

For small jobs, buy ready-mixed bags of mortar, to which only water is added. For jobs involving more than 150 bricks, it is cheaper to buy the ingredients from a builder's merchant and mix your own.

Mortar becomes unusable within two hours of mixing, so make small batches to avoid waste. Generally there are two mixes – a standard mix, and a strong mix. Mix ingredients by volume.

Standard mix 1 part Portland cement; 1 part hydrated lime or plasticiser; 6 parts soft sand for bricks, or 5 for BUILDING BLOCKS.

Strong mix 1 part Portland cement; 1 part hydrated lime or plasticiser; 3 parts soft sand.

Making the mix Measure out the sand on a flat, clean surface. Measure out the cement and add it to the sand. Mix them thoroughly with a clean shovel, and add the hydrated lime or plasticiser.

Make a crater in the top of the pile and pour in a little water. Shovel from the outside of the pile into the middle. Keep turning and adding water until the mix is stiff but pliable and falls off the shovel cleanly.

Mortgages

Ways of borrowing to buy a home

A mortgage is a loan obtained by using the property you wish to buy as security. There are, however, several kinds of mortgage and you should examine the alternatives carefully to decide which suits you.

Repayment mortgage This is the most straightforward: a building society, bank or other finance company advances you a loan, which you repay by monthly instalments over a number of years – see BANK ACCOUNTS; BUILDING SOCIETIES. The usual mortgage period is 20 or 25 years; with a shorter period, the monthly instalments are higher.

The monthly instalments are partly repayment and partly interest, and tax relief is given on the interest up to a maximum loan of £30,000 – see INCOME TAX RETURNS. Each payment pays back some of the capital you borrow, plus interest on the amount still owed. As the amount owed diminishes, a higher proportion of each payment goes towards paying off the capital.

Endowment mortgage With this, you take out a fixed-term endowment insurance policy to cover the loan – see ENDOWMENT POLICIES; INSURANCE. You have to pay insurance premiums and interest on the loan, but are entitled to tax relief on the interest. At the end of the term, the policy produces a lump sum which is used to pay off the loan.

If the policy is 'with profits', you may receive a cash payment too. If you die before the end of the term, the insurance company pays off the mortgage.

Having trouble in paying? If you are made redundant or suffer a serious accident or illness, you may find it hard to meet your monthly payments. That may happen, too, if the mortgage interest rate rises sharply. If you are in difficulties, tell your building society or bank manager about the problem straight away. They may be able to extend your mortgage period, or allow you to pay the interest only for a time, so as to reduce your outgoings.

Pension mortgage To take out a pension-linked mortgage you have to be self-employed or a member of an employer's pension scheme which will grant pension mortgages.

You make contributions to a pension fund, and at the end of the loan period part of the fund is used to pay off the mortgage.

The main advantage is that the repayments of capital are subject to tax relief as well as the interest payments.

Getting advice As well as building societies and banks, local authorities, mortgage finance companies, insurance companies and even your employer may be willing to offer you a mortgage. But they have different rules and interest rates.

Before committing yourself, obtain professional advice about the mortgage most suitable for you, how much you can afford to borrow, whether you need a mortgage protection policy and whether you are better off with a building society or other lender. Your solicitor, accountant or bank manager will all be able to help. Insurance brokers and mortgage brokers will also give you advice, but they will have a vested interest in the mortgage they recommend, as they receive their commission from the company that lends you the money.

Since the lender is entitled to seize your home if you fail to keep up payments, it is advisable with many types of mortgages to take out a *mortgage protection policy* from an insurance company. It will then pay the monthly instalments if you die before the end of the mortgage term.

This saves your dependants from the burden of monthly payments or repaying the balance.

You can also insure against payments incurred during a long illness.

How much to borrow? Single people can usually borrow up to two and a half or three times their gross yearly salary. Couples can borrow three times the gross yearly income of the higher earner, plus once the income of the other. If you are self-employed, the lender will ask to see your accounts and will base the loan on your previous year's income, or your average income over three years.

Interest Rates are linked to the prevailing bank base rate – but are higher, and can fluctuate considerably. If rates rise sharply, you may be able to get a repayment mortgage extended, but not an endowment mortgage.

Banks may charge an arrangement fee for a mortgage. Most lenders – including building societies – insist on a valuation of your property, for which you have to pay. Most buyers employ a solicitor to vet and handle a mortgage agreement as well as the purchase of the house – see LAWYERS.

Mosaics

Making pictures from glass and ceramics

Mosaics are patterns or pictures made from small pieces of coloured stone, glass, ceramics and other durable materials. They are available in two basic forms, one for decoration, as an alternative to the larger ceramic tile, and the other as a craft, producing pictures and patterns.

The largest selection of decorative mosaics can be found in the specialist tile centres and stores, and they are offered in two types. With the first, miniature tiles are mounted, evenly spaced, on a backing of tough netting, to form squares. To use them, apply tile adhesive to the wall with a notched spreader as for normal CERAMIC TILES, then bed the whole square into the adhesive. The net ensures the correct spacing between each small piece of mosaic.

The second type is also applied as a square, but this time the mosaic tiles are mounted face down on paper, where they are firmly held in place. Before fixing to the wall, lay the square face down, and fill gaps between the pieces with grout until it is flush with the surface. Then, apply tile adhesive to the wall as before and fix the square to it while the grout is still wet. Once the adhesive has set, soak off the paper face with water, exposing the decorative surface of the mosaic.

Then, with both systems, fill all remaining gaps between mosaic pieces with grout. When this has dried, polish the surface to remove surplus grout.

Where gaps have to be filled with less than a full square of mosaic, the netting or the paper is merely cut through with a knife at the appropriate point. Or, for smaller gaps, individual pieces can be detached and set into adhesive.

If you are interested in mosaics as a craft hobby, first find a local craft shop, or a mail order company, which can supply mosaics. The technical term for these small pieces is *tesserae*, and they are available in glass, glazed and unglazed ceramic, and *smalti* – which is the term for glass pieces with irregular surfaces which increase the reflective properties of the mosaic.

Apart from using the standard tesserae, you can be adventurous and include small shells, pebbles or chips of marble.

The only tools that you need to add to a standard tool kit are a pair of tile cutters and tweezers. The tile cutters resemble pincers with very sharp jaws, and with these you can cut pieces of mosaic to any size or shape. But, because the bits will fly, wear protective safety spectacles or goggles.

The traditional adhesive for mosaics is cement MORTAR, but this tends to make a mosaic heavy. Instead, use ceramic

---

MOSAICS

Two ways of creating patterns and pictures

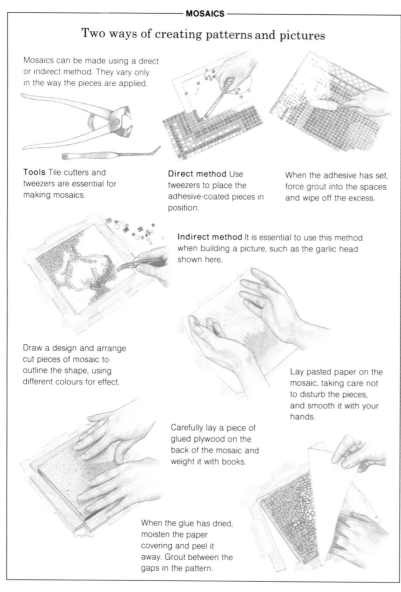

Mosaics can be made using a direct or indirect method. They vary only in the way the pieces are applied.

Tools Tile cutters and tweezers are essential for making mosaics.

Direct method Use tweezers to place the adhesive-coated pieces in position.

When the adhesive has set, force grout into the spaces and wipe off the excess.

Indirect method It is essential to use this method when building a picture, such as the garlic head shown here.

Draw a design and arrange cut pieces of mosaic to outline the shape, using different colours for effect.

Lay pasted paper on the mosaic, taking care not to disturb the pieces, and smooth it with your hands.

Carefully lay a piece of glued plywood on the back of the mosaic and weight it with books.

When the glue has dried, moisten the paper covering and peel it away. Grout between the gaps in the pattern.

---

tile adhesive or, for smaller mosaics, PVA adhesive – see GLUING. To apply the mosaic to a surface, coat the under face of each piece with adhesive and press them in place, leaving a small gap between pieces. Once the adhesive has set, fill all the gaps with grout, pressing it well in place. An artist's palette knife or sponge makes a good applicator.

Allow the grout to dry, then polish the surface with a soft duster.

Apart from this direct method of applying mosaic, there is also an indirect way. Lay the pattern out on a suitable flat surface, with the required gaps between each piece. Then pin strips of wood around the arrangement to contain the design and prevent the outer pieces from moving.

Coat tracing paper with a water-soluble paste, and paste the paper to the upper face of the tesserae. When the paste has dried, carefully lift the entire mosaic and place it in position on a bed of permanent adhesive on a piece of plywood. When this adhesive has dried, moisten the paper and remove it, then fill the gaps between tesserae with grout.

The advantage of this method is that you can play around with the design, moving pieces to get the most pleasing picture or pattern. Only when the design is complete is the paper stuck in place.

With a mosaic which has a rough surface, it may be necessary to use a stiff-bristled brush to clean and smooth the grouting prior to a final polish. The finished mosaic can be treated with wax floor polish.

Mothproofing

Protecting your clothes, carpets and furniture

Moth larvae cause the damage. Small, whitish maggots – about 6mm ($\frac{1}{4}$in) long – with brownish heads, they eat wool and hair, but do not like man-made fibres, cotton or linen. So the items most at risk are woollens, fur coats, carpets and rugs, blankets, upholstered furniture and some curtains.

Before storing (see also CLOTHES STORAGE), clean or wash the items, then seal them in large polythene bags with adhesive tape.

Before sealing up woollens, spray with a moth killer. The clothes will need a good airing before wearing again.

As a further precaution, sprinkle drawers with moth repellent crystals, available from chemists. Or make up small gauze sachets in which to put the crystals, then hang the sachets in storage spaces. A slow-release insecticidal vapour strip can be hung in wardrobes to kill adult moths.

If you suspect that an item of clothing may contain moth grubs or eggs, lay it on an ironing board, cover it with a damp towel, then apply a hot iron – see IRONING. The heat and steam will kill off any intruders.

Thoroughly vacuum infested carpets, then lightly spray them with moth killer. Or, if possible, lift the carpet and underlay and sprinkle powdered moth repellent crystals or powder on the floor and into any cracks between boards before re-laying the floorcovering.

To protect upholstered furniture, vacuum it regularly, paying particular attention to crevices and hidden areas. Then spray lightly with aerosol mothproofer.

Motorcycles

Riding safely; essential maintenance

A newcomer to motorcycle riding should seek training before venturing onto the road. Your nearest training centre can be found by contacting local road safety council departments or libraries.

Confidence in yourself and your machine is the key to riding safely. Build confidence by ensuring that your machine is in first-class order, and by learning to handle it on a training ground, or on private land, before gaining experience on the roads.

Clothing Always wear protective kit when riding. It is essential for comfort and protection. Helmets are required by law in Britain and most other countries – this applies to pillion passengers as well. Make sure the helmet is comfortable and a snug fit. You must wear eye protection, either goggles or a visor which conform to British Standard 4110-1979 (XA, YA or ZA). Helmets must conform to the standard laid down for each type.

Leather clothing, including gloves, is still the best for motorcycling: it cheats the wind, resists tearing and protects your skin if you fall. However, it is expensive and is not waterproof. For the beginner a good-quality two-piece oversuit in neoprene would be suitable. Never be tempted to ride bare-armed or wear shorts on a sunny day – a fall and consequent slide along the road surface can literally strip the flesh from your bones. Again, leather is favoured because it 'breathes' and absorbs sweat, giving comfort as well as protection.

In wet weather wear a waterproof oversuit. It will also conserve body heat. Do not wear clothing which is too tight – it inhibits circulation. If necessary stop and warm up by doing exercises to regenerate body heat. Periodically wiggle fingers and toes to aid circulation.

Difficult conditions Try not to ride in snow, unless you really have to. When riding in snow, use throttle and brakes gently. Ride on fresh snow if possible – it offers more grip than snow compacted by other vehicles. When riding on packed snow or ice, keep a light grip on the bars, grip the tank with your knees and keep your feet on the footrests. This will make the machine feel more stable.

Slow down by changing down through the gears rather than using the brakes. Watch out for wet leaves in autumn: they are extremely slippery. Be alert also for manhole and drain covers, especially when wet; they create a change in the surface level, and can be slippery. After a long dry spell a sudden shower makes roads treacherous, washing oil and rubber out of the road surface and making it extremely slippery.

Watch also for fuel spillage, especially on roundabouts where vehicles with full tanks often spill excess fuel.

Roadcraft Make sure you are conspicuous by wearing bright clothing (including a fluorescent sash), and by positioning yourself correctly on the road. In the daytime, if visibility is poor, use headlights.

Approaching right-hand corners, keep to the left. This lets you see farther round the corner than by riding in the middle of your half of the road, or in the crown of the road. Similarly, for left-hand corners move towards the crown of the road before entering the corner.

Essential maintenance Regular checks on your bike are essential for riding safety. For a start keep it clean: while using the sponge and rags you will notice if a silencer bracket has fractured

or a brake calliper bolt become loose, and so on. Spotted at an early stage, these problems can be prevented from becoming disasters.

The following checks should be made daily, if practicable, and certainly before long trips:
● Tyre pressures and tread depth.
● Lights and battery electrolyte level.
● Brake and clutch lever and pedal adjustments.
● Chain tension and lubrication.
● Oil levels.

For detailed guidance on maintenance consult your owner's manual, or local dealer: modern machines are so varied that specific guidance is needed.

Tyre and brake checks are the most important for safety. Never ride on old or split tyres, or with patched inner tubes. Most tyre manufacturers say tyre performance is impaired once tread depth is down to 2mm – 1mm more than the minimum of 1mm tread depth required by law over the whole of the tread area.

Most modern machines have brake-wear indicators for drum brakes, and inspection windows for pads used in disc brakes. Hydraulic disc brakes are self-adjusting, but check fluid reservoir level against the mark on the reservoir. Inspect the fluid pipes closely for leaks, and rectify any faults immediately.

Where a drum brake does not have a wear indicator it should be dismantled for inspection and cleaned, at the intervals recommended in the manual. If you do the job yourself, be careful not to inhale brake dust. Have brake shoes replaced if necessary. If in doubt, consult a garage.

Motorway driving

Learning the rules; avoiding trouble

Learner drivers, cyclists, moped riders and pedestrians are barred from motorways. So are tractors and other agricultural vehicles, and certain invalid carriages. Maximum speed is 70 mph.

When driving on a motorway, remember that traffic is travelling much faster than on an ordinary road. Concentrate at all times, and use your driving mirrors. See also MOTORWAY SIGNS.

Motorway do's and don'ts Special rules apply to motorway driving: breaking them can lead to a fine or disqualification.
● Do not reverse or make a U-turn. If you miss your exit, you must carry on to the next exit.
● Do not pick up or set down a passenger or hitchhiker on any part of a motorway, including slip roads to and from it.
● Do not use the hard shoulder or verge, except in an emergency such as a break-

down, accident or illness. Even then, do not stay on the hard shoulder any longer than is necessary.
● Do not drive too close to the vehicle in front, especially in wet or foggy conditions.

Lane drill In a two-lane carriageway, keep to the left-hand lane except when overtaking. In three-lane carriageways, you can stay in the middle lane if there are slower-moving vehicles ahead in the left-hand lane, but move back to the left-hand lane as soon as possible.

The right-hand lane in a three-lane carriageway is for overtaking only. It may not be used at all by vehicles over 3 tonnes (except coaches) and vehicles with trailers.

Do not overtake a vehicle on its left – unless traffic is moving slowly, and the traffic on the right is moving more slowly than yours.

If you feel sleepy, stop at a service area or turn off at an exit and take a short walk. Do not stop on the hard shoulder.

Breakdown If your vehicle breaks down, steer left towards the hard shoulder as soon as a glance behind shows it is safe to do so. Stop on the hard shoulder and switch on your hazard warning lights. Get out *on the nearside* and place a red warning triangle 140m (150yds) behind you, on the hard shoulder.

If necessary, get any passengers out of the vehicle (again on the nearside), off the hard shoulder and onto the motorway banking or verge. Otherwise, they should stay inside the vehicle – do *not* let them stand on the hard shoulder.

Do not attempt repairs. Posts to the left of the hard shoulder have arrows pointing to the nearest telephone. Walk to the nearest post and note the number and letter on it, so you can be located quickly. Then walk to the phone (do not cross the carriageway if you see one nearer) and lift the receiver.

A police operator will answer, asking for your location, car make and model, registration number, and cause of your breakdown. Even if you do not know, tell him the symptoms and what happened. If you belong to a motoring organisation, tell him you want their assistance. Do not hang up until he tells you – the telephone is one-way only, so he cannot call you back. Wait for assistance.

Motorway signs

Understanding what they mean

Motorways have special signs warning of hazards such as fog, ice, or an accident ahead.

Danger ahead The central panel of the signal will indicate either a temporary speed limit or that one or more lanes of the carriageway have been closed ahead. Slow down and do not resume normal speed until you come to a sign showing the end of restriction signal – a lighted diagonal bar without flashing lights.

Some motorways still have older signs consisting simply of a pole supporting amber lights. If these are flashing, slow down to a maximum speed of 30mph.

Some overhead signs and those at the entrance to motorways have red lights, as well as amber ones. If these are flash-ing, stop at the sign. Alternatively, the amber lights of overhead signs may have flashing arrows in the central panels. If the arrows are pointing diagonally down-wards, change to the lane indicated.

Direction and information signs
Motorway signs are always blue. Turn-off signs indicate the number of the exit in the bottom left-hand corner and how far ahead the exit is. Leading up to the exit itself are three 'count down' mark-ers, which have diagonal white bars.

MoT test
Ensuring that your car will pass

The purpose of an MoT (Ministry of Transport) test is to make sure that a car complies with the law's requirements for roadworthiness.

The test must be carried out by an authorised examiner at an approved testing station displaying the triple tri-angle sign.

Any car more than three years old has to be tested annually and must pass on all points. The test can be done from one month before the existing MoT certifi-cate, or tax disc, is due for renewal. The new certificate runs from the expiry date of the old one.

If the car does not pass, the owner will be given a V21 form (Refusal to Issue a Test Certificate Notice), stating clearly where the car has failed. It is illegal to use a car that has failed the test – except to drive it home or to a garage to have the defects put right. Nor can a tax disc be renewed without a valid test certificate.

You will greatly reduce the chances of failing the test if you give your car a series of checks beforehand.

Lighting equipment Both headlamps should be equally bright and work when dipped and on main beam. They should be aligned slightly to the left.

The front sidelights, red tail-lights and rear stop lights should give a steady light and be equally bright.

Make sure there is no crack in the red tail-light lenses. Check that the rear number-plate light works and that the two reflectors are undamaged and effec-tive. Test them with a torch in the dark.

Finally, test the indicators.

Brakes Check the brakes on a quiet stretch of road driving at about 20mph. Slip the gear into neutral and apply the brakes normally. The car should stop in a straight line without veering to the right or left and with no vibration.

Now repeat the process, but this time apply the brakes hard. The car should stop in a straight line again. Repeat the test with the handbrake. The car should come gradually to a halt and both rear wheels should lock. Check that the hand-brake can hold the car on a steep hill.

Tyres and wheels TYRES on the same axle should have the same size and con-struction. Check that the front wheels are not fitted with radial tyres if the back ones have cross-ply tyres; this combi-nation is illegal.

Check for cuts or bulges on the side walls. Check too that there are no cracks or dents in the wheel rims.

Other parts Make sure that the SEAT BELTS are in good condition. They should

---

— MOTORWAY SIGNS —

Reading the signals

In dangerous conditions, flashing amber lights warn of hazards ahead. Slow down immedi-ately. Blue motorway signs indicate junctions and other information.

Motorway warning signs are normally in the central reservation. They may indicate: temporary speed limit (left and centre); or lane ahead closed (right).

On busy motorways signals may be placed overhead, each panel applying to the lane below. This sign indicates 50mph limits on left and centre lanes, and 'change lane' on the right.

Temporary maximum speed.

Move to the next lane on the left.

Leave motorway at next exit.

End of temporary restriction.

Direction sign at junction leading straight onto motorway.

Exit from motorway 1 mile ahead.

Exit ½ mile ahead – usually the second sign.

The final indication of exit from motorway.

'Count down' markers at exit from motorway.

be securely anchored and the webbing of the belts should not have any broken strands – though some scuffing on the surface is permissible. Check that the WINDSCREEN WIPERS and WINDSCREEN WASHERS work effectively; the wiper blades should not be split, cracked or perished.

Check the body, especially the chassis, door sills, wheel arches and subframe, for RUST damage. If parts of the body that contribute to the overall strength of the car are excessively weakened by rust, the car will fail the test.

Unless you are experienced, it is best to let a garage check steering and suspension. But you can easily check the steering by turning the wheel while the car is stationary.

If the car has rack-and-pinion steering there should be no more than 13mm ($\frac{1}{2}$in) movement at the steering-wheel rim before the road wheels start to turn, or 50mm (2in) if the car has a steering-box system.

The SHOCK ABSORBERS should be working effectively and not leaking: inspect them and do the 'bounce test' detailed in the entry on shock absorbers. Suspension springs must be undamaged and securely anchored.

Check the exhaust system for leaks and to see that it is supported securely.

Moulding food

Turning out puddings in attractive shapes

To give a sharper and more attractive design to JELLIES, custards, mousses and puddings, use a tin or aluminium mould. Puddings are much more easily unmoulded from these than from china which tends to grip the pudding.

Before filling the mould, rinse it under the cold tap and shake off any surplus water. Stir a pudding mixture gently to

A stunning pudding can be created by setting a jelly in an elaborate ring mould and filling the centre with whipped cream, fruit or a mousse of a contrasting colour. Jelly should be eaten within 24 hours of making, because it toughens if you keep it for too long

make sure the ingredients are evenly distributed. Jellies, mousses and other moulds usually take 2-3 hours to set in a refrigerator. If left longer, they tend to lose some of their flavour.

To unmould any chilled pudding, loosen the edges with a knife, dip the mould up to the rim in hot water for 5-10 seconds. Rinse the serving plate under the cold tap for a moment or two and shake off any excess water. Then gently turn the mould out onto the slightly moist plate and slide it into position.

Mouldings

Using specially profiled strips of wood

Mouldings are lengths of wood which have been specially shaped, or profiled, and this shaping may be functional or purely decorative. The decorative ones can be used as they are, or, by combining two or more mouldings, you can build up more complex and intricate designs.

Lengths may be glued together, and clamped while the glue sets, then the moulding held in place by using panel pins for fine mouldings and oval nails for larger ones – see NAILING. Remember the long head-axis of an oval nail should go

---

— MoT TEST —

Points to check before submitting your car for the test

Check brakes, steering and suspension, lights, reflectors, tyres, seat belts, exhaust, chassis structure, horn and windscreen wipers.

Wipers Examine the wipers for damage and replace if there are any signs of wear. Both washer jets should work efficiently.

Horn Check that this operates as soon as the horn button is pressed, and that its sound is clear and loud.

Seat belts Make sure that they and their mountings are firmly anchored, and the webbing in good condition.

Suspension Check that the springs are not worn or rusted.

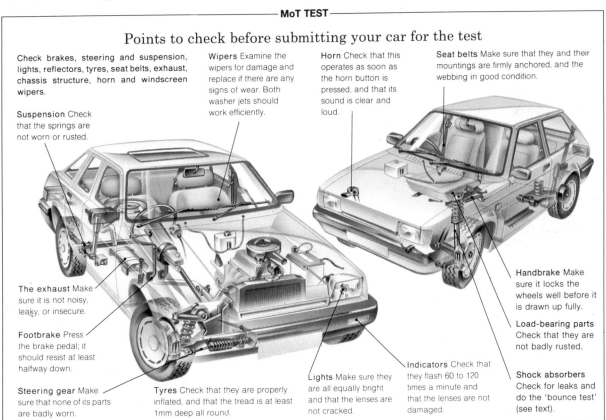

The exhaust Make sure it is not noisy, leaky, or insecure.

Footbrake Press the brake pedal; it should resist at least halfway down.

Steering gear Make sure that none of its parts are badly worn.

Tyres Check that they are properly inflated, and that the tread is at least 1mm deep all round.

Lights Make sure they are all equally bright and that the lenses are not cracked.

Indicators Check that they flash 60 to 120 times a minute and that the lenses are not damaged.

Handbrake Make sure it locks the wheels well before it is drawn up fully.

Load-bearing parts Check that they are not badly rusted.

Shock absorbers Check for leaks and do the 'bounce test' (see text).

along the grain of the wood to avoid splitting it.

Hockey stick, quadrant, architrave and decorative mouldings are illustrated. Common types of moulding are:

Dowel Used mainly for making DOWELS and strengthening WOODWORKING JOINTS.

Glazing bar Used as channelling for glass in GREENHOUSES and glass lean-to buildings. Available ready-primed in red or white for painting, or in red cedar for natural finishing.

Picture rail Usually fixed to a wall prior to final plastering, using cut nails. These are sunk just below the wood surface, then the holes filled with putty prior to painting.

Picture frame Available in a wide range of designs, many of which can be combined with other mouldings to form more complex mouldings. Accurate mitres are essential for making frames – see MITRE JOINTS; PICTURE FRAMING.

Channel Available in a number of sizes, and used for holding sliding doors. A shallow grooved channel is used at the bottom, in which sliding doors stand. Then a deeper channel is used at the top so that the doors can be lifted into it, then dropped into the lower channel.

Hockey stick Useful for edging or lipping tables and work tops. This moulding is also widely available in plastic, with a special moulding designed to hide and protect the edges of ceramic TILING – such as on window ledges.

Carved and embossed These are available in a wide range of patterns and sizes, and are designed to add an attractive finish to furniture. Again several types can be combined.

Moving house

Planning, packing and moving in

Start planning your move as soon as you have decided on the removal date. Begin by getting rid of all unwanted items: charity shops and jumble sales will take items in reasonable condition; the rest can go to the local rubbish tip – or the refuse collection department of your local authority may be able to advise you about 'special collection' facilities, sometimes available for a small fee.

If you do not have too many possessions, you can hire a van and do your own removal – driving, loading and unloading, perhaps aided by friends or family. Vans are available in various capacities for hire on a daily basis. With an ordinary driving licence you can hire a van up to 7.5 tonnes – see HIRING.

Estimate carefully the size you will need, and try to make the move in one journey, returning the van immediately afterwards.

Allow plenty of time for loading and unloading – it takes longer than you think – as well as for journey time.

If, however, you are moving the full contents of a home, employ an experienced removal company. The best are found by personal recommendation; alternatively, check in *Yellow Pages* under 'Removals' and choose a company that is a member of the British Association of Removers.

Getting an estimate The company will send an estimator to decide what size of van is required; make sure that he knows exactly what is to be moved. Forgotten items that involve an extra journey can bring heavy additional charges.

Go through the house with the estimator, pointing out any fittings – such as carpets and curtains – that you are leaving behind. He will tell the removal foreman, but as an extra precaution, label all items to remain, *Not to be removed*.

The estimator will also ask if you are doing your own packing, or want it done by the removers. This will cost extra, but may be worth while if you are short of time to do your own – for example, if you are self-employed.

If you are taking fitted carpets with you, ask the estimator if they can be lifted by the removal company in advance, or if you must do it yourself. The removal men will not take up fitted carpets on moving day; they will only roll them up and carry them out. They will not refit them – see CARPET LAYING.

Fix a date and time of removal with the estimator, and arrange INSURANCE cover for your possessions, from when they are loaded to when they are unloaded, including any storage period. Removal firms usually offer insurance at about 10 per cent of the removal charge, but it may be cheaper to obtain a temporary extension of your home contents insurance.

The removal company will send you a written quotation: check it carefully for date and time, then confirm your acceptance and ask the company to confirm in writing. Once agreed in writing, it becomes a contract (see CONTRACTS) and

---

── MOULDINGS ──

Using them for practical and decorative jobs

Hockey stick Use this type of lipped moulding for edging – the body of the moulding covers any exposed edge while the lip extends over the top surface, covering any gaps.

Architrave Disguise ugly joints between walls and the frames of doors and windows throughout the house.

Quadrant Fill any awkward right-angle gaps with a length of quadrant. To allow for movement, pin to one surface only.

Decorative Fix these carved and embossed mouldings with glue and small panel pins.

its terms cannot be altered, except by any special provisions in the quotation. Check that these are fair and reasonable before signing.

Packing The removal company will provide packing cases free: use them to pack china and glassware, double-wrapped in newspaper. Collect strong cardboard boxes for other items and use plastic dustbin liners for linen, bedding and curtains.

You must take down curtains, fixtures and fittings, and dismantle self-assembly furniture.

Pack clothes in suitcases and garment bags (see PACKING), but small items can be left in their drawers. To transport pot plants, make a metal foil tray and place it in the bottom of a cardboard box. Water the plants thoroughly and put them in the box on the day of the move.

Pets cannot be taken in the removal van – you must take them with you. CATS can be taken in cartons available from a pet shop; birds can be carried in their cages; goldfish in a plastic bag containing ten times as much air as water. Tropical fish can also be placed in plastic bags, but put the bags in cardboard boxes and fill the spaces with expanded polystyrene chips or granules to maintain the temperature. If the journey is long, the fish may have to be tranquillised by a vet, as stress can kill them.

Pack delicate equipment such as hi-fi, video-recorder and computer gear in their original boxes, if possible, or get boxes that are a close fit and pack them with newspaper.

Run down the contents of REFRIGERATORS and FREEZERS and defrost as near to removal day as is convenient. A freezer can be kept in use if you are moving only a short distance – the contents will keep without thawing for up to eight hours. Arrange to have it loaded last and taken off first, so that it can be quickly reconnected.

Gas appliances permanently connected to a supply, such as GAS HEATERS and COOKERS, must be disconnected by British Gas or an approved gas fitter. Arrange for him to call on the morning of the move, and for reconnections at your new home. You may also want an electrician to disconnect electrical appliances.

At the same time arrange for the gas and electricity meters to be read – you will then be charged only for units used up to that time. If you have a telephone, notify the sales office of the telephone company of your move, so that they can make up your final bill. If you are moving only a short distance, you may be able to retain the same number.

Other people you need to notify include the local authority and water company, your employer, bank, credit card companies, insurance companies,

Inland Revenue, Department of Social Security and any clubs or organisations of which you are a member. Send your car registration document to the Driver and Vehicle Licensing Centre, Swansea SA99 1BN. Send your driving licence to the same address, with your new address filled in on the reverse side of the licence.

The Post Office needs seven days' notice to redirect your mail. Fill in Form P944G, available from post offices, and your mail will be redirected for up to a year for a small charge. Remember also to cancel milk, newspapers and any other regular deliveries.

Moving out Before removal day make a room-by-room plan of your new home, numbering each room. Then number the articles to be moved, so that the removal men know where each piece goes. Give the plan to the removal foreman when the van arrives.

Before it leaves, make sure the driver knows the way; give him a rough map if he does not, and tell him of any access or parking problems there. If there are parking restrictions outside the house, tell the remover in advance, so that they can arrange police cooperation.

Give the foreman the house keys if you are not travelling ahead, though it is best to be there first if you can.

At your old home, have a final check to see that everything has been loaded before the van leaves, then shut all windows and turn off the water at the stop valve and the electricity at the consumer unit – see FUSES AND FUSEBOXES. Hand over the keys to the new owner or estate agent as soon as you know that your solicitor has been paid.

As soon as possible after the move, check the condition of your goods: any claims for damage or breakages must be made within seven days.

Muggers

Fighting back if you cannot escape

If you are attacked in the street, try to escape, but be prepared to defend yourself if you have to. Try to judge the situation: if an armed mugger wants your cash, it may be safer to hand it over than to risk injury. But faced with a potential killer and no way of escape, fighting back may be the only alternative.

There are several ways of disabling an assailant. They are all dangerous and one or two could be lethal. Never use them except in an emergency, and practise them beforehand with extreme caution.

If you are forced to defend yourself, do so without warning. Strike as hard, as fast and as often as you need to. If necessary, use more than one technique – and

Effective ways to combat an attacker

Shin scrape and stamp Scrape the heel of your shoe down the assailant's shin, then grind your heel into the top of his foot. High heels are particularly effective.

Eye jab Form your fingers into a V and ram them hard into your attacker's eyes – causing intense pain and temporary blindness.

Brolly or walking stick Use both hands to wield an umbrella or stick and thrust its end forcefully into the assailant's face, stomach or genitals.

shout and scream as loudly as possible. A handbag or attaché case also makes a powerful defence weapon if swung forcefully at an attacker's face or head. Here are some effective countermeasures:

Throat jab Hold the fingers of one hand straight and rigid and jab them into an attacker's throat. Use either the ends of the fingers or the edge of your hand.

Eye jab Make a V with your forefinger and middle finger and jab them hard into an attacker's eyes. This will cause him great pain and temporary blindness.

Stomach jab Use this if an attacker comes up behind you and clamps his arms around your neck. Twist your body slightly, clench your fist, raise your arm and jab backwards with your elbow as hard as you can. Catch him in the stomach, aiming to wind him. This should relax his grip, allowing you to break free.

Shin scrape and stamp If the stomach jab fails to break his grip, lift a foot and scrape the heel of your shoe down his shinbone, finally grinding your heel into the top of his foot. This is particularly effective if a woman victim is in high heels, or a man is wearing stout shoes or boots.

Knee in the groin Move in close to an attacker and bring your knee up hard into his groin. This will double him up in agony – provided he is not wearing a coat and has no time to twist away.

Twisting the little fingers If you are grabbed by the throat, grasp the attacker's little fingers and wrench them up and away from your neck. This will cause him great pain, and probably break his fingers.

Using an umbrella or walking stick These make formidable defence weapons. Hold the stick or brolly in both hands and jab its pointed end hard into an attacker's face, stomach or genitals.

Mulching
Keeping soil moist and weed-free

In hot, dry weather soil should be mulched – covered with a layer of decaying vegetable matter – to keep it moist. As well as slowing evaporation, a mulch will keep plant roots at an even temperature, supply them with nutrients as it decomposes, and smother weeds.

A mulch can consist of COMPOST, peat, manure, rotted straw or sawdust, leaves, or pulverised bark. Always water dry soil thoroughly before mulching it, and do not mulch cold or frozen soil.

In spring or early summer spread a layer of mulch 50-75mm (2-3in) thick over the roots of trees, SHRUBS and herbaceous plants. Avoid touching plant stems with mulch, and do not mulch annual seedlings until they are well established. Runner beans and peas can be mulched with damp peat, leaf mould or garden COMPOST no more than 13mm ($\frac{1}{2}$in) deep.

Strips of black polythene make a good mulch for crops such as bush TOMATOES and strawberries, as they stop the fruit from resting on the soil. Put down slug pellets first, and cover the corners of the strips with soil to keep them in place.

Peat should be soaked before use, and when straw is used as a mulch it should be sprinkled with a nitrogenous fertiliser (see FERTILISERS) at about 50-75g (2-3oz) per square yard. This will balance the loss of nitrogen caused by the decomposition of the straw. At the end of the growing season, turn the mulch into the soil.

Mulling ale and wine
Warming drinks for winter

Mulled ale is a traditional old English beverage. It has the consistency of thick soup and is a splendid drink for cold winter nights. Mulled wine – a more recent introduction from the Continent – turns an otherwise undistinguished red wine into a warming drink on a cold day, or a special treat for autumn and winter parties. Here are two recipes – the first for ale, the second for wine:

Ingredients (2 large glasses)
2 eggs
570ml (1 pint) light ale
3 teaspoons caster sugar
$\frac{1}{4}$ teaspoon grated nutmeg
25g (1oz) butter, cut in pieces

Beat the eggs with 2 tablespoons of ale in a bowl.

Heat the rest of the ale, gently, in a saucepan. When hot, but not boiling, stir the ale slowly into the egg mixture, beating all the time.

Pour it back into the pan and add the sugar and nutmeg. Reheat but do not boil. Add the butter and serve in heatproof glasses or tankards.

Ingredients (6-8 glasses)
285ml ($\frac{1}{2}$ pint) water
4-6 cloves
50mm (2in) piece of cinnamon stick
50mm (2in) piece of lemon rind
75g (3oz) caster sugar
1 bottle red table wine

Put the water, cloves and cinnamon in a saucepan together and simmer them for 5 minutes.

Add the lemon rind and sugar. Heat

gently and stir continuously until all the sugar has dissolved.

Pour in the wine and heat until the liquid steams; it should not boil.

Remove the lemon rind, cloves and cinnamon stick and pour the drink into heatproof glasses. See also TODDY.

Mumps
Treating a child's complaint that can be serious for adults

Mumps epidemics occur every three or four years and usually affect children over the age of two. But adults can also suffer from this highly infectious and common disease.

The main symptom is swelling of the saliva-producing gland in front of one ear and over the angle of the jaw. A day or two later the opposite gland may also become swollen. Pain and swelling may occur in other glands – such as the testicles in males after puberty, the ovaries in females, and the pancreas in both sexes. With women this is often accompanied by stomach pain.

Both sexes may also have earache or pain when eating. Because mumps is infectious before any of these symptoms appear, there is no way of stopping the disease from spreading.

Mumps usually clears up without treatment within a week. But if testicles are swollen, if there is severe headache, stiff neck, or if your eyes are bothered by the light, you should see your DOCTOR. He may prescribe painkillers or treat any suspected complications. Immunisation is included in a vaccine given to children at the age of 13 months.

Muscle aches
Easing stiffness and soreness

Any unaccustomed exertion – such as running for a bus – can make muscles stiff and sore. Relaxing in a hot bath, pressing hot towels to the affected area, or using heat-producing liniments and lotions can help. Gentle MASSAGE helps to get the muscles back to work. If necessary take ibuprofen or paracetamol according to the instructions of the packet.

A pulled muscle will be swollen as well as painful. Reduce the swelling with an ice pack – a bag or folded cloth filled with crushed ice. Bandage it to the muscle for 20-30 minutes. Then remove the ice pack and bandage the area firmly but not so tightly as to stop circulation – see BANDAGING; FIRST AID KITS. Rest the muscle until the pain passes and take paracetamol if required.

If the pain or swelling is intense, or if it lasts longer than 48 hours, see your DOCTOR. See also CRAMPS.

Mushrooms

*Growing them at home and
cooking them*

Mushrooms can be grown in boxes
indoors – for example, in a dimly lit cellar or shed – or outdoors in a shady
corner of your lawn. Making COMPOST
for indoor growing is difficult, so buy
ready-mixed compost from a nursery or a
commercial grower, or buy a mushroom-
growing kit which consists of mushroom
spawn and the correct compost in a plastic tub.

Spawn can also be bought separately.
If you intend to plant it in the lawn,
make sure that it is suitable for growing
in grass.

Growing outdoors Pick a warm, damp
day between late spring and early
autumn and, with a trowel, lift small
squares of turf about 50mm (2in) thick
and 300mm (12in) apart. Place a walnut-
size piece of spawn into each hole and
replace the turf. The mushrooms will
grow in 10-12 weeks.

Growing indoors Plant the spawn at
any time about 50mm (2in) deep in a tub
or box of compost, allowing 300mm (12in)
between each piece.

Water the compost lightly. Ten days
later, cover the compost with a layer of
sterilised loam, obtainable from a nursery. This will help to maintain an even
temperature and stop moisture from
escaping.

Kits have their own instructions,
which may differ from those given here.

Cooking Mushrooms taste best if they
are cooked and eaten soon after picking.
Before cooking them, trim the base of the
stalks, then wipe the mushrooms with a
damp cloth.

Harvest time Pick mushrooms grown indoors
between eight and ten weeks after planting. They
taste best when they are cooked and eaten
immediately after picking.

For *steamed mushrooms*, cover and
cook them in the top of a double saucepan, with a little butter and salt, for
about 20 minutes. For *fried mushrooms*,
slice them thinly and fry in butter for 3-
4 minutes; serve them with the pan juice.
For *grilled mushrooms*, brush them
whole with butter and place under a

moderate heat for 6-8 minutes, turning
them over once during the cooking.

Whichever way you cook them, they
are delicious served on toast, in OME-
LETTES, with bacon or with liver, or in
pies, CASSEROLES and stews.

Musical chairs

*Playing a traditional game
for children's parties*

A number of chairs, one less than the
number of players, are placed back-to-
back in two rows. To the accompaniment
of a piano, or music from a tape or record-
player, the players march round and
round the rows of chairs. When the music
stops, everyone tries to find a seat. The
player left standing drops out of the
game, a chair is removed and a new
round begins.

The game continues until only two
players and one chair remain. Then, one
chair is placed in the centre of an area
marked by two further chairs (approximately 1.2m (4ft from the centre chair).
The two players move anticlockwise
round the perimeter of the area. The
player who sits on the chair when the
music stops is the winner.

Mussels

*Finding, preparing and cooking a
delicious mollusc*

Mussels can be found on beaches, clinging to rocks or stones. They should only
be gathered during the colder months –
from October to April.

Do not take mussels from a beach
where refuse or sewage are pumped into
the sea, and only gather those that are
alive: if a mussel closes up after being
gently prised open a little, it is alive; if
it is open, or opens easily, discard it.

Preparing When buying mussels, make
sure they are alive and fresh – and avoid
any with broken shells. Scrub them with
a stiff brush in cold, salted water to
remove any grit. Then use a sharp knife
to scrape off the beard, or black weed,
from the outside of the shells.

Cooking Cook mussels in a large, heavy-
based pan containing about 13mm (½in)
of water or white wine, and some
chopped parsley and onions. Cook with
the lid on for about 5 minutes, until
the shells open. Discard any that remain
closed.

Take the pan off the heat, take out the
mussels with a slotted spoon, and remove
a half shell from each one. Keep the
mussels warm under a dry cloth and
strain the cooking liquid through muslin.
Serve the mussels with the liquid poured

over them. They go well with brown or
wholemeal bread. See BREAD-MAKING.

To make mussel brose (or broth), cook
2.3 litres (4 pints) of mussels in water
vigorously for 6 minutes. Then put the
juice in a small pan.

Toast 2½ tablespoons of oatmeal under
a medium grill until golden-brown.

Remove the mussels from the shells.

Heat 15g (½oz) of butter in a pan and
cook two finely chopped shallots in it
until transparent. Add the mussels and
a pint of milk, and heat without boiling.

Bring the mussel juice to the boil and
add the oatmeal. Mix well and add to the
soup, off the boil. Season, sprinkle on
parsley, and serve.

MUSSELS

Cleaning and preparing for cooking

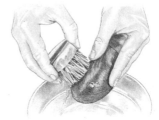

Put the mussels in a pail of cold salted
water and use a stiff brush to scrub off
any remaining grit.

With a sharp knife, scrape the shell clean
and prise away any barnacles. Rinse in
several changes of cold water to remove
any remaining grit.

Hold the shell on end and cut away the
beard of seaweed-like strands protruding
from the shell edges.

Nail-biting

Curbing a nervous habit of children and adults

Nail-biting is a common childhood habit that may extend into later life. Like all nervous habits, the only certain cure is by exercising willpower – which can be particularly difficult for a child to understand.

As nail-biting may be a physical response to emotions such as anxiety, insecurity or boredom, reprimands are unlikely to be effective.

An appeal to vanity will sometimes work; a girl can perhaps be offered a manicure set or clear nail varnish to encourage nail consciousness.

Adult nail-biters should try to keep their fingers busy with spare-time hobbies such as model-making, painting, needlework or carpentry. See also FINGERNAILS.

Nailing

Which nails to use and where to use them

There are dozens of different types and sizes of nail, and it is important to choose the right one for the job in hand. Here are the more common ones, and what they are used for:

Round wire nail This is ideal for work where appearance does not matter too much, as the nail heads remain visible on the surface of the wood. However, the sections of wood being nailed should be fairly large, otherwise the round body of the nail will cause splits. Available in sizes 20-150mm ($\frac{3}{4}$-6in).

Oval wire nail Used in joinery work, this is far less likely to split wood if the long head-axis follows the grain. The head can also be hit flush with the wood, or sunk and the hole filled using a nail punch and putty or wood filler – see STOPPERS AND FILLERS. Sizes 25-150mm (1-6in).

Lost head nail A much finer round nail, this has a head specially designed to be punched below the surface. Again, the hole is filled with putty or wood filler. Sizes 12-150mm ($\frac{1}{2}$-6in).

Panel pin This is a very thin round nail, for joinery and cabinet work and for

---

Basic techniques

Two pieces of wood can be joined very securely with nails, but problems can occur if you are not familiar with some basic techniques. Here are four of them:

Fixing thin to thick Always nail a thin piece to a thick piece. Otherwise the nails will not penetrate the thin piece far enough to grip.

Fixing to end-grain If you cannot avoid nailing into end-grain, drive the nails in at opposing angles for better grip (skew nailing). Also use wood glue.

Avoiding splits When nailing near an end, cut the wood over-length, nail it and cut off the excess. Put nails in different grain lines.

Nailing hardwood Hardwood splits easily, so first drill start holes with a twist bit thinner than the nail shank.

---

securing MOULDINGS. The small head is easily punched into wood then covered with putty or wood filler. Sizes 15-50mm ($\frac{5}{8}$-2in).

Tack The large head enables a tack to be used for fixing carpets, underlays and fabrics to wood. Sizes 6-30mm ($\frac{1}{4}$-1$\frac{1}{4}$in).

Clout nail Another round nail, but with a large head, the clout nail is used mainly for fixing roofing felt or wire fencing. All clout nails used outdoors should be galvanised or made of aluminium alloy. Sizes 20-100mm ($\frac{3}{4}$-4in).

Plasterboard nails The jagged shank is designed to improve the holding power of the nail in PLASTERBOARD. Sizes 30mm (1$\frac{1}{4}$in) and 40mm (1$\frac{1}{2}$in).

Hardboard pin Sometimes called a deep-drive pin, this is for securing hardboard sheet. The diamond-shape head sinks into the board, effectively hiding itself. Sizes 15-50mm ($\frac{5}{8}$-2in).

Cut floor brad This flat nail is cut from sheet metal and used to fix floorboards. It gives a good grip, and the blunt tip cuts through wood fibres – rather than pushing them aside – to avoid splitting the wood. Sizes 12-150mm ($\frac{1}{2}$-6in).

Cut clasp nail Again cut from sheet metal, the clasp nail is for securing heavy timbers to timber or masonry. It gives a good grip – for example, it is used to hold picture rail to a wall. Sizes 25-200mm (1-8in).

Annular nail This is often called a ring nail; it has teeth which grip very firmly into wood and is used in naturally soft timbers like Western red cedar, where ordinary nails do not grip well. It is also useful for fixing PLYWOOD and other large sheet materials. Sizes 20-100mm ($\frac{3}{4}$-4in).

Masonry nail A specially toughened nail which can be hammered direct into masonry, it must not penetrate too far or its wedge action may split a brick or block – 15mm ($\frac{5}{8}$in) into solid masonry is a good average. Protect your eyes when using masonry nails, as they can shatter. Sizes 15-100mm ($\frac{5}{8}$-4in).

Nailing tips

● When nailing, always use the correct type of hammer for the job – see HAMMERS.

● When nailing two pieces of wood of different thicknesses, always fix the thinner piece of wood to the thicker. Choose a nail about two and a half to three times longer than the thickness of the thinner piece.

● If there is the slightest risk of splitting the wood – and that applies to all hardwood – drill start holes – see DRILLING. Choose a drill bit which is smaller than the shank of the nail.

● When using oval nails in line, avoid nailing along the same grain line, otherwise the build-up of pressure exerted by the nails will split the wood along that grain.

● Reduce the risk of round wire nails splitting wood by blunting the point to a flat surface. This surface then cuts through the wood fibres, rather than pushing them aside.

- Increase the holding power of a nail by driving it in at an angle. This is called *skew nailing*.
- To get even more holding power, use nails long enough to go right through the wood, then turn them over – or *clench* them. On pieces of wood of similar thickness, drive in nails for clenching from either side.
- To sink nails into wood, use a nail punch (or nail set) and hammer. Where it is difficult to locate small pins and tacks, use a push-pin tool, which holds the pin magnetically while you position it. Then drive it home with a pin hammer.
- Avoid nailing into the end-grain of wood. If it is unavoidable, drive in nails at opposing angles for better grip, and use wood glue.

Removing nails Where a nail head is visible, lever it up slightly with a tack lifter, an old chisel or the claw on the handle of carpenter's pincers, until the claws of a claw hammer can be inserted under the nail head. Protect the wood with a small block of scrap wood under the lifting tools.

If a nail is bent over, straighten the bent section with an old chisel and with pliers, until the claw hammer can be used to draw it. If a nail has lost its head, pull it out with carpenter's pincers.

If a nail is hidden, chisel away the wood around it until it can be gripped with pincers. To avoid damage to decorative wood, such as picture rails, it may be possible to lever the wood away from the cut clasp nails, leaving the nails in the wall to be wiggled out with pincers. However, cut clasp nails are so hard to remove that you may have to twist off the head with the hammer claw and drive the shank below the surface.

Names

Choosing them and what they mean

There are no hard-and-fast rules about choosing forenames for your child. You can have as few or as many as you like – and you can even make them up. However, the registrar of births or the vicar performing a christening may object to dozens or to any considered unsuitable.

You are not legally obliged to give the forename when you register the birth, but most people do. Nor are you obliged to give a forename afterwards, but of course everyone has at least one.

If you change your mind about the name, you can alter it within a year of registration by applying to the registrar, unless the child has already been baptised. In that case, the name must, in law, stand until the child is 18, when he or she can seek to change it – a lengthy legal process.

Some families have a tradition of names that they use in succeeding or alternate generations – Winston among the Churchills, for example. Others prefer a free choice. Fashions in forenames, other than the most straightforward ones, tend to go in cycles of about 15 years. If you choose a name that is very fashionable at the time – particularly if it is unusual – you may be 'dating' your offspring; he or she may be one of many children with the same name in the same school class.

Consider the accepted abbreviations for your chosen name. You may love 'Charlotte', but you will not be able to stop your daughter's friends from calling her 'Charley' or 'Lottie'. Look at the initials; Charles Augustus Dobson, for example, sounds impressive, but CAD has obvious drawbacks.

Unisex names such as Evelyn or Jan can lead to teasing at school. So can names that have become ridiculous or unpleasant through association with fictional characters or slang.

Some people suggest that a short forename goes well with a long surname, and vice versa. According to their argument, John or Jane would sound better than Nathaniel or Wilhelmina in front of a surname such as Ollerearnshaw; conversely, Smith can carry with dignity such forenames as Alexandra or Jonathan. It is purely a matter of taste.

Names have entered English from many sources – Latin, Greek and Hebrew, French and German and even the Hollywood film studios. Gary, for example, was dreamed up for the actor Gary Cooper from a place name in Indiana (his agent's home town).

Here are some popular forenames, with their original meanings.

Boys
Adam, *Hebrew*, red earth
Alan, *Celtic*, harmony
Alexander, *Greek*, protector of men
Andrew, *Greek*, manly
Anthony, *Latin*, clan name
Benjamin, *Hebrew*, son of the right hand
Brian, *Celtic*, hill or strong
Charles, *German*, manly
Christopher, *Greek*, bearing Christ
Colin, *French*, variant of Nicholas
Daniel, *Hebrew*, God is my judge
David, *Hebrew*, dearly loved
Dennis, *French from the Greek*, of Dionysius, god of wine
Dominic, *Latin*, of the Lord
Edward, *Old English*, prosperous
Evan, *Welsh* form of John
Ewan, *Gaelic*, youth
Frank, *German*, free (also as Francis)
Gavin, *Celtic*, battle hawk
Geoffrey, *Old German*, peace
George, *Greek*, farmer
Graham, *Scottish family name*, from place name 'Granta's homestead'
Guy, *French from German*, wood

Harold, *Old English*, powerful army
Henry, *German*, home ruler
Hugh, *German*, mind
Ian, *Gaelic* for John
Ivan, *Russian* for John
Jacob, *Hebrew*, supplanter
James, *Greek/Latin from Hebrew*, Jacob
Jeremy, *Hebrew*, exalted
John, *Hebrew*, grace of God (Jonathan means gift of God)
Joseph, *Hebrew*, Jehovah added (a child)
Julian, *Latin*, name of Roman clan
Justin, *Latin*, just
Keith, *Scottish*, place name
Kenneth, *Gaelic*, handsome one
Kevin, *Irish*, handsome at birth
Lee, *Old English*, meadow or clearing
Leo, *Latin*, lion
Leslie, *Scottish* surname
Lewis (or Louis), *French/German*, famous warrior
Luke, *Greek*, from Lucania (a place in southern Italy)
Malcolm, *Gaelic*, disciple of Columba
Mark, *Latin*, warlike
Martin, *Latin*, of Mars
Matthew, *Hebrew*, a gift
Michael, *Hebrew*, who is like God?
Miles, *unknown*, may be *Latin* for soldier or from *Old German*, merciful
Neal (or Neil), *Irish*, champion
Neville, originally a Norman surname, from Neuville in Normandy
Nicholas, *Greek*, victorious people
Nigel, *Irish*, champion
Noel, *French*, nativity
Oliver, *French*, possibly from *Latin* for an olive, or from *Old German*, elf-host
Patrick, *Latin*, nobleman
Paul, *Latin*, small
Peter, *Greek*, a rock
Philip, *Greek*, lover of horses
Richard, *Old German*, hard ruler
Robert (also Robin), *German*, bright fame
Roger, *German*, fame or spear
Roy, *Gaelic*, red, or from *French*, king
Samuel, *Hebrew*, Shem is God
Sean, *Irish*, as John
Simon, *Hebrew*, obedient, or from *Greek*, snub-nosed
Stephen, *Greek*, crown
Stewart (or Stuart), *Old English*, keeper of the household
Terence, *Latin*, Roman family name
Thomas, *Aramaic*, twin
Timothy, *Greek*, honouring God
Victor, *Latin*, conqueror
Walter, *Old German*, ruling people
William, *German*, helmet of resolution
Zachary, *Hebrew*, God remembers

Girls
Alice, Alison, *German*, noble
Amanda, *Latin*, worthy of love
Amy, *Latin*, beloved
Angela, *Greek*, a messenger
Ann, Anne, Anna, *Hebrew*, gracious
Barbara, *Greek*, foreign
Belinda, *Italian/German*, possibly beautiful serpent
Bridget, *Irish*, lofty or august

Camilla, *possibly Etruscan*, the Queen of the Volsci
Caroline, *Latin*, feminine of Charles
Catherine, *Greek*, pure
Charlotte, *French*, noble
Chloe, *Greek*, a young green shoot
Christine, *Latin*, a Christian
Clara, Clare, Claire, *Latin*, bright
Cora, *Greek*, a girl
Deborah, *Hebrew*, a bee
Diana, *Latin*, from the goddess
Dorothy, *Greek*, God's gift
Elizabeth, *Hebrew*, consecrated to God
Emma, *German*, whole
Eva, Eve, *Hebrew*, causing life
Felicity, *Latin*, happiness
Fiona, *Gaelic*, white
Frances, *German*, free
Georgina, *Greek*, farmer
Grace, *Latin*, grace
Helen (also Ellen), *Greek*, bright
Hilda, *German*, female warrior
Irene, *Greek*, peaceful
Jane, Jean, Janet, Joan, Joanna, *various*, feminine forms of John
Jennifer, from *Welsh* Guenevere, King Arthur's wife
Judith, *Hebrew*, a jewess
Julia, *Latin*, name of a Roman clan
Katherine, *Greek*, pure
Laura, *Latin*, laurel
Linda, *German*, a serpent
Lindsay, *Scottish*, surname
Louise, *French*, feminine of Louis
Lucy, *Latin*, shining
Margaret, *Greek*, pearl
Mary, *Hebrew*, wished-for child
Mavis, *French*, song thrush
Melissa, *Greek*, honey bee
Miranda, *Latin*, admirable
Natasha, diminutive of Natalia, *Latin*, Christmas Day
Nicola, *Greek*, victorious
Olive, Olivia, *Latin*, olive
Patricia, *Latin*, noblewoman
Prudence, *Latin*, discreet
Rachel, *Hebrew*, ewe
Rebecca, *Hebrew*, a heifer
Rosalind, *German*, compound of horse and serpent
Roxana, *Persian*, daybreak
Ruth, *Hebrew*, the meaning is unknown
Sally, diminutive of Sarah
Samantha, the origin is unknown, became popular following American TV series *Bewitched*, 1970.
Sarah, *Hebrew*, princess
Selina, *Latin*, heaven
Sophie, *Greek*, wisdom
Stella, *Latin*, star
Susan, *Hebrew*, lily
Sylvia, *Latin*, wood
Teresa, *Latin*, the meaning is unknown
Tracy, *French*, from place names, also diminutive of Teresa
Ursula, *Latin*, she bear
Valerie, *Latin*, strong
Vera, *Russian*, faith
Veronica, *Latin*, true image
Virginia, *Latin*, chaste
Zoe, *Greek*, life

NAPKIN FOLDING

Two quick and easy designs

Cone fold Fold the napkin into three, with the top and bottom thirds overlapping. Fold the right-hand edge of the napkin inwards by one-third.

Hold the top right-hand corner between thumb and forefinger, with the palm up.

Turn the hand so the napkin wraps around it, with a point at the back of the hand. Take the bottom left-hand corner across to meet the point. Finally, hold the two corners together and turn them up like a cuff. Stand the cone up, with the free corner standing out.

Fan fold Fold the napkin in half. Fold up one end by about 25mm (1in), then make concertina pleats of the same width for about two-thirds of the length.

Fold the napkin in half lengthways so the pleats are on the outside. Take up the bottom left-hand corner so that it overlaps the fold. Tuck the overlap underneath.

Gently lift up the top layer of pleats so that the napkin opens out into a fan, held up by the triangular spine.

Napkin folding

Enhancing a table with napkins

Use square napkins measuring at least 380mm (15in) across, preferably of lightly starched linen. Paper napkins can also be used, but are less elegant. The designs on the left can be accomplished quite quickly after a little practice. Make the folds as accurately and neatly as possible for good results.

Nappy changing

What to do if you have to cope

Washable terry-towel nappies are slightly less expensive than disposable nappies, they are more ecologically friendly, and you use them time and time again. Some babies get nappy rash more easily from terry-towels, while others are more prone to it from disposables. So choose whichever suits your purse and your baby better, or use both – terry-towels in normal circumstances, disposables when travelling.

Change nappies as soon as they become wet or soiled – certainly after every feed with young babies. Have ready a clean nappy, nappy pins and a nappy liner if you need them, slightly warm water, cotton wool, a soft towel and baby powder or cream (do not use both powder and cream together, as they can cause chafing in combination).

Lay the baby on his back on a waist-high table protected with waterproof padding. Never leave the baby alone in this position even for a moment in case he should roll off. Make the change a time of play and conversation; hang MOBILES above the table for young babies; give older ones a toy to hold.

Undo the wet nappy. Raise the baby's feet and slide the nappy from under him. Fold the outside edges over the centre and put the old nappy to one side, well out of the baby's reach or in a bucket, to deal with later.

Clean the baby's bottom with cotton wool soaked in water; wipe solids downwards from the anus and not towards the genitals, to prevent the risk of genital infection – particularly in girls. Rinse with a clean cotton-wool pad.

Once the baby's bottom is clean, pat it gently dry and give a light dusting with powder or apply a little cream. Make sure that the folds of skin around the groin and below the cheeks of the buttocks are perfectly dry.

Towelling nappy Fold the clean towelling nappy on the table beside the baby, and put it on as shown in the sequence of drawings on the next page.

When using terry-towelling, put a nappy liner on the nappy beneath the baby's bottom. It will make cleaning

NAPPY CHANGING

The kite-fold method

The kite fold is a popular method of folding a nappy, and can be adapted as the baby grows.

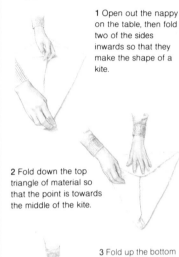

1 Open out the nappy on the table, then fold two of the sides inwards so that they make the shape of a kite.

2 Fold down the top triangle of material so that the point is towards the middle of the kite.

3 Fold up the bottom point towards the middle, bringing it up high for a small baby. As the baby grows, the point is raised less.

4 Raise the baby by the ankles, with a finger between them to prevent them rubbing. Slide the nappy under the baby's bottom, with the wide end level with the waist.

5 Bring the bottom flap between the baby's legs and adjust it so it comes to the waist. Bring the right back corner around and tuck it under the front. Pin it, with one hand between nappy and baby. Repeat on the other side.

much easier if the nappy becomes soiled. The liners can be bought in boxes and are easily flushed down the lavatory.

When inserting pins in the nappy, take great care not to injure the baby. Hold one hand between the nappy and the baby's skin so that you can feel the point of the pin as it comes through. Push the pin through all the layers of the nappy and back through to the front, fitting it in place in the head of the safety pin.

Lay the pin horizontally to the baby's body so that if it comes undone it will not prick him.

Disposable nappy These do not need to be folded, as they are shaped. There are two types: nappy pads are held in place with plastic pants (bought separately) which are held at the sides with fastenings; the all-in-one type is a combined nappy and plastic covering.

Dealing with a dirty nappy Once the clean nappy is on, remove the baby from the table and put him in a safe place while you see to the dirty nappy. If it is terry-towel, flush solid matter from it down the lavatory before putting it to soak in a nappy bucket containing water and a proprietary nappy sanitiser. Disposable nappies can usually be flushed down the lavatory.

QUICK TIP If you use terry-towel nappies, try to buy three or four dozen, so that you always have plenty clean. Do a nappy wash two or three times a week.

Nasal congestion

Relieve a stuffed-up nose

A blocked nose is usually associated with ALLERGIES or a common cold (see COLDS), and will clear of its own accord when the cold goes.

Consult a DOCTOR if the blockage persists for more than two to four weeks, or if there is a persistent blood-stained or yellow-green discharge.

Chemists sell decongestant medicines – drops and inhalers – to clear noses blocked by mucus. Many are available without prescription, but never use them to treat young children without seeking a doctor's advice.

Adults should be cautious, too; decongestants can make the blockage worse in the long run, damage the delicate tissues of the nose, and produce side effects such as dizziness in some people. They are dangerous when taken with certain other medicines. If in doubt, ask your pharmacist or doctor. As a general rule, do not use decongestants for more than three days, or anti-catarrh drops for more than ten days.

Blowing the nose is the most obvious source of relief: press one nostril closed and blow gently but firmly through the other one. Do not blow too hard, or you may damage an eardrum or provoke a NOSEBLEED.

Steam inhalations can help. Buy friar's balsam or a proprietary inhalant from the chemist – many contain eucalyptus oil or menthol, or both. Following the maker's directions, pour boiling water over the inhalant in a basin, bowl or jug, and allow the preparation to cool slightly.

Drape a towel over your head to retain the vapours, put your face over the bowl and breathe in the vapours. Never inhale the steam from water that is actually boiling – it can damage the tissues of the respiratory tract. Take precautions against scalding if you let a child use an inhalant.

The blockage may also be relieved if you can breathe slightly moist air. Spray your room occasionally with water from a vaporiser (the kind used to mist plants); attach humidifiers to central-heating radiators, or stand a wide, shallow bowl of cold water near them.

National insurance

What you can claim for what you have paid

Most employees and self-employed people must pay national insurance contributions while working, from the age of 16 to 60 (women) or 65 (men). The payments help to meet the cost of welfare benefits.

Some welfare services – health care and income support, for example – are available to all people who need them. Others – unemployment and sickness benefits, for example – are available only to people who have made national insurance contributions and fulfil certain conditions.

Local offices of the Department of Social Security (DSS) will advise you. A Citizens Advice Bureau can also give guidance.

What you pay
There are four classes of contributions:

Class 1 A percentage of earnings paid by employees who earn above a certain amount is deducted by the employer before the wage or salary is paid.

Class 2 A flat-rate contribution is made by the self-employed by direct debit payment from a bank or giro account to the DSS.

Class 3 Voluntary contributions are paid to maintain a right to benefits by people who are not obliged to pay anything – for example, if they have chosen temporarily not to work.

Class 4 These are paid in addition to Class 2 by self-employed people whose profits are more than a certain amount; they do not count directly towards any benefits.

Someone unable to work through force of circumstances – for example, illness or unemployment – may be credited with some contributions by the DSS to preserve the right to benefits. But you must have paid contributions at some time in order to get benefit.

A similar scheme of credits, called home responsibilities protection, maintains pension rights for someone obliged to give up work to look after children or a sick or elderly person.

What you can claim

Retirement pension Women over 60 and men over 65 who have paid the required number of Class 1, Class 2 or Class 3 contributions can claim retirement PENSIONS, often called old age pensions.

Unemployment benefit Only Class 1 contributions entitle you to claim unemployment benefit. It is payable for up to one year in any period of unemployment; after that, you must claim income support (see below). To qualify for unemployment benefit again, you must work as an employee for 13 weeks and a minimum of 16 hours in each week. The weeks need not be consecutive.

To qualify for any unemployment benefit, you must have contributed an amount equal to 50 Class 1 contributions in the relevant tax year.

You must register with your local employment office on the first weekday you are out of work.

Income support An unemployed person who does not have enough money to live on may be paid income support.

The benefit may be paid in addition to unemployment benefit, or if unemployment benefit is delayed, or if the person is not entitled to unemployment benefit.

In addition, the person may get free milk and vitamins and free dental treatment, glasses and prescriptions. Children may get free school meals.

To claim, get form B1 from the unemployment benefit office.

Sick pay and sickness benefit Employees paying Class 1 contributions are entitled to Statutory Sick Pay for illnesses lasting from four consecutive days up to 28 weeks. The amount is linked to earnings and is paid through the employer, who can recover part of it from the DSS.

Report the illness to your employer, who will tell you what to do.

Self-employed people paying Class 2 contributions are not entitled to Statutory Sick Pay. Instead, they can claim sickness benefit from the DSS for illnesses lasting from four consecutive working days up to 28 weeks. Sickness benefit is also paid to Class 1 contributors who are not entitled to Statutory Sick Pay – for example, because they are employed as temporary staff for less than three months.

To get sickness benefit, you must have paid contributions equal to 50 Class 1 contributions or Class 2 contributions in the relevant tax year.

People who are still not fit to work after 28 weeks of receiving Statutory Sick Pay or sickness benefit may be entitled to invalidity benefit, which includes a flat-rate invalidity allowance if they become chronically ill before they are 55 (women) or 60 (men).

Maternity pay A woman who has a job is likely to receive Statutory Maternity Pay (SMP) from her employer when she has a baby – see MATERNITY LEAVE.

Widow's benefits If she is under the age of 60, or her husband was not receiving retirement pension when he died, a newly-widowed woman can get a tax-free cash lump sum of £1000 from the DSS.

If the widow has a dependent child under 19 years of age, or is expecting a child by her late husband, she may get a widowed mother's allowance from the date of her widowhood.

Widows without dependent children and who are more than 45 years of age may be entitled to a widow's pension. The amount is related to the widow's age at the time she qualifies. The full widow's pension is paid only to women widowed at 55 or older, or whose widowed mother's allowance ends then.

For a widow to qualify for widowed mother's allowance or widow's pension, her husband must have paid a certain minimum number of national insurance contributions. The widow makes her claim through a DSS office.

Death grant The grant formerly paid to help with funeral expenses has been abolished. But anyone who gets income support, family credit or housing benefit may be able to get help with funeral costs if they enquire.

National savings

Taking advantage of their tax benefits

The government's Department for National Savings runs several no-risk investment schemes that offer tax benefits to both small and large savers. The schemes are operated mainly through the Post Office, and leaflets available in all post offices give full details.

Savings Certificates The rate of interest is roughly equivalent to the tax-paid rate you would get from BUILDING SOCIETIES. But, unlike a building society rate, it is guaranteed for a fixed period, commonly five years. It is paid when the certificates are cashed, is not liable for income tax, and does not even have to be declared on your income tax return. That makes the certificates a good investment for higher-rate taxpayers.

People over the age of seven can buy National Savings Certificates for themselves. Adults can buy the certificates in the names of children under seven.

There are two types of certificate. With the ordinary certificates, the full amount of interest payable over their life is specified when you buy them. With index-linked certificates, the guaranteed interest is lower, but it is topped up by the rate of inflation as measured by the retail prices index. Index-linked certificates ensure that the value of your savings is protected. When inflation is low, you may earn better interest from ordinary certificates.

Certificates are sold in units with a fixed price (£25 in 1994). They can be cashed at any time – a process that normally takes eight to ten working days. However, if you cash them within a year of purchase you will get only the purchase price back. After the first year, interest or index-linking is paid, but to get the best return, you should retain them for the full five years. You need not cash them after that; ordinary certificates will continue to earn interest at the General Extension Rate, which is varied from time to time.

Periodically, the government launches a new issue of savings certificates with different interest rates. Previous issues continue to earn as before, but they can no longer be bought.

For regular savers Yearly Plan certificates are similar to other savings certificates, offering interest that is tax-free, but they are sold in a different way. To buy one, you must make regular monthly payments by standing order of between £20 and £200, for 12 months. You can withdraw and get your money back during that time, but you will not receive any interest. At the end of the 12 months, you will get your certificate which you should then hold for a further four years to obtain the best interest rate.

At the end of a year, you can maintain or alter your standing order to buy a further Yearly Plan certificate every 12 months; or you can cancel the order and simply hold on to what you have already bought. Interest rates on Yearly Plans are similar to those on ordinary certificates over their full life, but they may be more attractive for people who prefer to set aside the amount required each month.

Income and Capital Bonds The drawback with Savings Certificates and Yearly Plan certificates is that you do not receive the interest from them until they are cashed. For people with a lump sum to invest, income bonds provide monthly interest payments, at a high but variable rate. The interest is reduced on sums withdrawn in the first year. The interest is liable for income tax, but the tax is not taken off before the interest comes to you. This is an advantage for non-taxpayers, and for people on low incomes (from PENSIONS perhaps) who can avoid paying tax on the interest by setting their personal tax allowance against it. The minimum investment is £2000.

Capital bonds offer an interest rate guaranteed for five years. The interest is not paid direct to you but is added to the capital after every 12 months. It is credited in full without tax being deducted, but is liable for tax. The minimum investment is £100.

For both income and capital bonds, three months' notice is needed to withdraw money.

Savings accounts National Savings Investment Accounts are particularly suitable for children (although those under the age of seven are not normally allowed to make withdrawals) and other non-taxpayers who want to put aside money and withdraw some occasionally. The minimum deposit is £5.

The interest is taxable, but tax is not deducted at source. One month's notice is needed for withdrawals.

National Savings Ordinary Accounts pay 5 per cent interest on amounts over £500 and 2½ per cent on less than £500. The first £70 of interest each year is taxfree, but tax must be paid on any interest above £70. The account is an alternative to a bank account. You can withdraw up to £100 at a post office.

Premium Bonds Prize draws held weekly and monthly distribute tax-free prizes to some holders of Premium Bonds. No interest is paid on the bonds, so they are a less certain investment than other National Savings schemes.

It is possible to win up to £250,000 from a single Premium Bond; on the other hand, your bonds may win no prizes at all, in which case you will receive no income and your investment will be reduced by inflation. The minimum purchase is £10; the maximum is £10,000.

Gilt-edged securities The Department for National Savings also keeps a register of government stocks through which small investors can buy gilt-edged securities more cheaply than through a stockbroker.

See also BANK ACCOUNTS; INCOME TAX RETURNS; INVESTING; SAVING.

Nature photography

Taking intimate pictures of plants and wildlife

You need a good 35mm single-lens reflex camera (see PHOTOGRAPHY) to photograph flowers and wildlife successfully. Each requires different techniques, lenses and accessories.

Small flowers and insects can be photographed in close-up, with the object appearing on the film at life size. 'Macrophotography' is where the object appears on the film larger than life size.

Close-up of flowers For this you can use a close-up lens or an extension tube which fits between the regular lens and the camera body. An extension tube increases the distance between film and lens, and can give even greater magnification than a close-up lens. A zoom lens with a 'macro mode' will also allow you to shoot close-ups.

A lens hood should be used when shooting outdoors into strong sunlight; a tripod will steady the camera and allow better composition, and a cable release will avoid shake when the shutter is released. Focus on the parts of the subject which you want to look sharp – there is only a very shallow depth of focus at close range.

To maximise depth of focus, use a small aperture (f11 to f22); if there is sufficient light, also use slow-speed film (ISO 25 to 125).

Close range exaggerates any movement of the plant – to avoid a blurred image, choose a still day. If there is a breeze, tie the flower to a stake or make a windbreak with stakes and fabric or sheets of cardboard.

Backlighting – when the sun is behind the subject – gives a translucent effect to leaves and petals; sidelighting makes for sharply defined textures. Place a white card to reflect light into shadowy areas; to soften harsh sunlight, hold a thin white cloth above the subject, stretched on a frame.

Remove unwanted or distracting objects – such as stones, loose twigs or tall grass – close to the subject.

If you want to pick flowers to photograph indoors, choose only the most common plants; avoid damaging wild flowers in general, or trampling the area.

Photographing animals Most wild creatures are easily startled. Move quietly and slowly to avoid frightening them away; wear muted colours, and camouflage the shiny surface of your equipment with dull tape or cloth.

Animals are most likely to stay still when feeding; seek out their regular haunts, or the nesting sites of birds – but do not disturb the nest or the surrounding 'cover'. You may be able to attract birds by putting out food.

Look for natural cover with a good view, or hide in your car or in a dull-coloured tent. You may need to remain silently in one place for hours, or return day after day until your 'target' becomes accustomed to your presence.

To 'pull in' subjects from a distance, you need either a zoom lens or a 200 to 400mm telephoto lens. Telephoto lenses exaggerate camera shake and have a limited depth of focus – so steady the camera on a tripod and take extra care with focusing.

Try to anticipate the animal's actions and focus on a spot it is likely to move to. Use high-speed film (ISO 400 to 1000) and fast shutter speeds (no slower than $1/250$ of a second).

Nausea

Relieving the symptoms

The queasy, sick feeling that may precede vomiting can be a symptom of many disorders, from digestive ailments to migraine; it is common in the early months of pregnancy. Consult a DOCTOR if nausea is accompanied by abdominal pain, difficulty in swallowing, VOMITING blood or persistent DIARRHOEA.

However, the most common cause is overindulgence in alcohol or food. Rest and eat little or nothing for 12 hours or so, taking occasional sips of water.

Antacids between meals may help, though you should avoid aspirin, which can irritate the stomach. A chemist can give you advice. For a further day or two, eat only simple, bland foods you know agree with you – for example, clear soups and dry toast.

If you feel an attack of nausea coming on, take several deep, regular breaths.

See also TRAVEL SICKNESS.

Needlepoint tapestry

How to form basic stitches

One of the oldest forms of embroidery, needlepoint is often used to make hard-wearing covers for cushions and chairs. The stitches are worked, usually with wool, on open-weave canvas. Consequently the craft is also known as canvas work.

For working needlepoint tapestry you need three basic items: a canvas, thread and a round-pointed tapestry needle. There are two main kinds of canvas – single and double. They are usually made of hemp or linen thread and have different-sized meshes, according to the number of threads to the inch. Single canvas consists of horizontal and vertical single threads. Double canvas has a mesh of double threads.

The most commonly used threads in

NEEDLEPOINT TAPESTRY

Tent stitch and cross-stitch

Many stitches have been devised for needlepoint, but the main ones are the tent stitch and cross-stitch.

Tent stitch To work stitches diagonally, begin at the upper left, bringing the needle out through a mesh. Put it in one mesh up to the right. Take it down under two threads, then out to repeat the stitch.

After the last stitch of the down row take the needle down under two horizontal threads and to the left under one vertical thread, to begin the up row.

Put the needle in one mesh up to the right then take it under two vertical threads and bring it out. Repeat, working upwards, fitting stitches between down row stitches.

Cross-stitch Start towards the upper left. For the first half of the stitch bring the needle out through a mesh and put it in one mesh up to the left. Take it down under one thread and out. For the other half put it in one mesh up to the right, and bring it out one mesh to the right and one mesh lower.

To begin the second row take the needle vertically under two horizontal threads and bring it out. Push it in one mesh up diagonally to the left and come up one mesh below. Then go over and under diagonally to the right.

needlepoint are crewel wool and tapestry wool. Crewel wool is very fine and can be worked in a single strand on very fine mesh canvas; or up to four strands can be threaded together for coarser work.

Tapestry wool – about three times thicker than crewel wool – is usually worked on medium-gauge single or double canvas.

To start, buy a ready-made design painted on canvas. Threads of the right colour usually come with the canvas.

Nervousness

Calming yourself in moments of stress

A mild state of worry or fear before facing a difficult task or an awkward situation is perfectly normal. Veteran actors can still suffer stage-fright at each performance. Many people feel sick, need frequent trips to the lavatory, sweat or tremble before an examination or important interview.

Such nervousness, though unpleasant, is not medically serious. However, seek medical advice if the bouts are so severe that they prevent you from doing something relatively straightforward, or if they come on without apparent cause.

People prone to nervousness should ensure that in the weeks leading up to a stressful event – perhaps making a speech, or sitting an exam – their way of life is healthy and well-balanced. Eat and drink at regular times and in moderation, avoiding too many stimulants, such as strong coffee. Take regular, gentle exercise and get plenty of sleep. Allow time for relaxation and pleasant hobbies.

Try to put the event into perspective. If you play poorly in a tennis match or stumble over a speech it does not greatly affect your value as a person; the worst that can be said is that you tried something and did not succeed – which happens to everyone at some time. Do not allow the coming event to assume unreasonable proportions.

If an event is genuinely significant – such as any entrance examination – it may help to calmly consider alternative choices should things go wrong. Perhaps you can sit the exam again, or pursue your studies in another way.

Relaxation Breathing and RELAXATION EXERCISES have, since ancient times, helped offset a bout of nervousness. They form an essential part of YOGA and various types of MEDITATION, and are taught in maternity classes and to patients suffering from heart ailments. Often, the techniques are simple and can be used anywhere, unnoticed by others.

Alcohol and drugs A small drink may help to relax you before making a speech, for example; but alcohol is not appropri-

ate in many circumstances, such as a job interview or a driving test. Even a little alcohol may impair your performance; and a reliance on 'something to steady the nerves' can lead to alcoholism.

Never take tranquillisers or other drugs unless prescribed by a doctor, and then only in recommended doses. If you are prescribed a short course of tranquillisers, do not give them up without your doctor's advice, and do not mix them with alcohol.

Hiding the signs Before approaching a situation that makes you nervous, have a light snack, and visit the lavatory. Time your arrival so that you are neither far too early (allowing you to sit around worrying), nor late and in a perspiring panic. Make sure you have any equipment or documents that you need, and that they are in order.

If the situation requires you to speak, try to do so clearly and slowly (breathing exercises may help here). Do not gabble or mumble – if you talk too fast, you may lose your train of thought.

Many people suffer from shaky hands when nervous: usually it stops as you get into your stride. Until then, try lightly gripping the arms of your chair, or the table edge if you are standing.

In some circumstances, where it is acceptable (not, for example, during an interview), chewing a sweet or gum may calm nerves and aid concentration.

See also SHYNESS; STRESS.

Noisy neighbours

Steps you can take to quieten them

Every householder is entitled to the peaceful enjoyment of his own home. A polite request to a noisy neighbour often solves the problem. If that fails, and if the noise is occasional – for example, a rowdy party – dial 999 and call the police when it is at its height. Police will ask the offenders to quieten down, although they will not usually be prosecuted.

If the neighbours are council tenants, the local council may help in warning them to be quieter.

If the noise is persistent – perhaps a dog barking or pop music played at full volume – you can consult the environmental health officer at your council offices.

The council can issue an abatement order, requiring the offender to stop or reduce the noise, or to confine it to certain times of the day. In serious cases, the council can obtain a court injunction forbidding the noise, or it can launch a prosecution.

Before approaching your environmental health officer, prepare as much evidence as you can about the noise, such as dates and times. The officer is more likely to take action if several neighbours complain together.

If the council declines to act, the police might do so, if it can be shown that the noise constitutes a NUISANCE. Ask at your local police station.

You can also apply to your local magistrates' court for a noise abatement notice, which has the same effect as a council abatement order; again, you need evidence and the support of other neighbours. If all else fails, you can apply to the magistrates' court for permission to bring a private prosecution: seek legal advice first – see LAWYERS.

Noisy pipes

How to cure water hammer in domestic plumbing

A hammering noise in domestic water pipes is both annoying and may damage the pipes. If the noise is allowed to continue, pipes can eventually fracture. Old lead pipe tends to dampen down the noise, but modern copper piping transmits it over considerable distances.

The noise is caused by water under pressure being cut off suddenly, then restored, resulting in a shock wave which travels along a pipe. And because it travels, it is often quite hard to decide where the problem originates. Here are the most likely sources:

Stopcock in rising main This is the tap used to cut off the water supply to a house – see TAPS. If the jumper inside the tap, which holds the washer, is free to move, it can vibrate, leading to the hammering noise. So all jumpers in stopcocks must be what is termed *captive*.

Cold taps off rising mains The same rule applies as for stopcocks: the jumper must be a captive type.

Worn washer A worn or damaged tap washer may lead to pipe noise; so you should check it.

Ball float bounce Water entering a storage tank may cause the ball float which controls the entry of water (see BALL COCKS) to bounce up and down on the surface of the water. This in turn leads to rapid opening and closing of the valve –again causing water hammer.

To stop this, either buy a proprietary paddle damper, which clips onto the ball arm, or make up a simple anchor. For example, you can use a plastic yoghurt carton fixed rigidly to the ball arm by galvanised wire, which holds the carton below water level. When the ball tries to bounce, the action is damped out by the submerged carton.

If all your efforts to kill the noise fail, your water pressure may be too high.

Consult your local water authority: they may fit a pressure-reducing valve near your control valve.

A different noise, more like hissing than hammering, may be caused by an old pattern ball cock. The noise is caused by water passing through it into the tank. This can often be eased by fitting a later pattern ball cock designed to cut down the noise. Your local plumbers' merchant can supply one either in plastic or in metal.

North Star

How to find your way at night

If you are lost at night without a COMPASS, find the North Star (Polaris) and use it as a guide. To locate it, look for the Plough – seven bright stars in the Northern Hemisphere grouped roughly in the shape of a plough. The Plough may be at any angle in the sky, as it rotates around the North Star. The two stars at the end of the Plough's blade – whatever its position in the sky – point to the North Star.

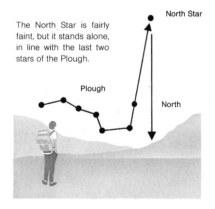

The North Star is fairly faint, but it stands alone, in line with the last two stars of the Plough.

North Star

Plough

North

Draw an imaginary line between the two end stars (the Pointers) and extend it by about five times. The line will lead directly to the North Star, which stands on its own about midway up the sky.

Face the North Star and you are facing north. Behind you is south; east is to your right, and west is to your left. See also STARGAZING.

Nosebleed

Stopping a minor attack

Sit the victim upright in a chair with his head tilted slightly forward. Firmly pinch the soft part of the nose, just below the bone, for at least 10 minutes, or get the victim to do it for himself.

Tell him not to swallow or spit out any blood running down the back of his nose into his mouth, and to breathe through the mouth. After 10 minutes, release the

nostrils; if bleeding restarts, squeeze them for a further 10 minutes.

Once bleeding has stopped, the victim should rest quietly for a while, and not blow his nose for at least three hours.

Consult a DOCTOR if the bleeding still goes on, if so much blood is lost that the victim becomes pale or dizzy, or if nosebleeds occur frequently.

Noughts and crosses

How to play – and how not to lose

Draw a grid with nine boxes, using two horizontal lines and two vertical lines. The first player marks an X in one of the boxes and the second player puts an O in another.

They continue alternately until one player gets three of his marks in a horizontal, vertical or diagonal line to win, or until all nine boxes are filled. As the player who starts the game has an advantage, take it in turns to begin.

There is no magic formula for always winning. However, the player who starts should aim to put his first three X's in such a way that, after his third move, he has a choice of two squares in which to mark an X to complete a line. His opponent can block one in his own third move, but not both, and is therefore trapped.

With practice (and a little advance information), the second player (O) can always force a draw: the secret is in O's first move (see panel below).

NOUGHTS AND CROSSES

How O can force a draw

The second player, O, can always avoid defeat, wherever the first player marks his X. Just follow these three ploys.

If the first player makes an X in a corner square, the second player puts his O in the centre square.

When the X is placed in the centre square, draw the first O in any one of the four corner squares.

If the first X is in the middle of a side column, put the O in the same column, or in the middle row.

Nuisance

Protecting your right to a peaceful life

Anyone who interferes substantially with someone else's reasonable enjoyment of his own property or of a public place – for example, by playing a tape recorder too loudly or by parking a car to obstruct access – is committing a nuisance. See also NOISY NEIGHBOURS.

The offender may be ordered under the law to stop it, and possibly fined. In addition, victims of the nuisance may be able to claim financial compensation.

If you believe you are the victim of a nuisance, and a polite request to end it does not bring results, consider seeking legal advice – see LAWYERS. The law offers many remedies, and your solicitor can help you find the one most suited in your case. There are, in law, four kinds of nuisance:

Private nuisances These affect someone in his own home, and may be caused by a neighbour who, for example, lights smoking bonfires on your washing day, or refuses to cut down a tree whose roots are undermining your house.

They can also be committed by outsiders – for example, drivers from a nearby factory park lorries outside your house and disturb you when they rev up early each morning.

Private nuisances are dealt with through the civil courts. Cases may be brought only by the owner or legal occupier of the place affected.

Public nuisances These involve misconduct in a public place or behaviour that annoys many people, such as a group of householders in a street. A public nuisance can be both a civil offence (in which case, any adult who is affected can bring a court action) and a crime entailing a prosecution either by the authorities or brought privately.

Obstructing the highway, urinating in public and atmospheric pollution by factory chimneys have all been held to be public nuisances.

Statutory nuisances Offences against the general public that have been singled out in specific laws passed by Parliament are statutory nuisances. Most of the statutes deal with matters of public health and safety: it is a criminal offence, for example, for a factory to cause blocked drains or release harmful or unpleasant fumes. Local council environmental health officers are, in the first instance, responsible for dealing with statutory nuisances – see below.

Bylaw nuisances Local authorities define these, using powers delegated to them by parliament. The bylaws vary from area to area, but most deal with such matters as noise, smells, rubbish dumping and keeping animals. Local councils are responsible for enforcing them – and they are criminal offences.

Ending a nuisance Before taking legal action, decide what you hope to achieve: do you want simply to end the nuisance, or do you expect compensation, too? If you are seeking compensation, you will have to prove in court that you suffered actual damage – for example, to your health or property.

Find out whether your local council or the police will act on your behalf to stop the nuisance. Local authority environmental health officers can initiate court proceedings against people committing bylaw nuisances and some forms of public nuisances – either as prosecutions or as applications for an injunction requiring the offence to cease.

In cases of statutory nuisance, the health officer can, without reference to a court, issue an abatement notice requiring the nuisance to end; if the offender disobeys, he can be summoned before a magistrates' court.

The police can act under common law against all types of public nuisance; ask for advice at your local police station.

If neither the police nor local council will act – for example, because they consider the nuisance is purely a private one – you have two choices: apply to the clerk of the local magistrates' court for a hearing to enable you to bring a private prosecution; ask your solicitor to apply for a court injunction ordering the offence to cease. Ignoring an injunction can be punished as contempt of court.

Nursing at home

Keeping the patient comfortable and happy

Looking after a sick person at home can put mental and physical strains on everyone in the household. Keep these strains to a minimum by encouraging the patient to do what he can for himself, and helping him to preserve his self-esteem.

See that his clothes and bedding are always fresh and clean (see STERILISING); take time to show love and affection; do nothing to make him more anxious than he is already. Follow the treatment prescribed by the DOCTOR. Call the doctor immediately if the illness worsens, or if recovery seems to be delayed.

Choosing the sickroom In all but minor illnesses, the patient needs a special room, large enough for a bed to be

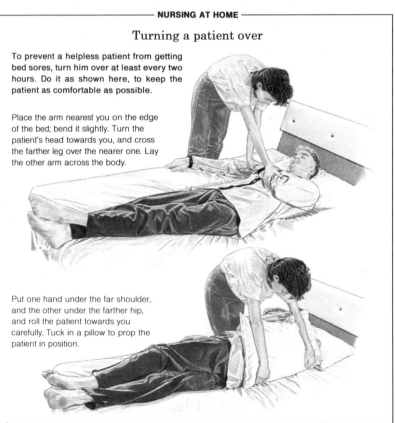

NURSING AT HOME

Turning a patient over

To prevent a helpless patient from getting bed sores, turn him over at least every two hours. Do it as shown here, to keep the patient as comfortable as possible.

Place the arm nearest you on the edge of the bed; bend it slightly. Turn the patient's head towards you, and cross the farther leg over the nearer one. Lay the other arm across the body.

Put one hand under the far shoulder, and the other under the farther hip, and roll the patient towards you carefully. Tuck in a pillow to prop the patient in position.

accessible from both sides, well-ventilated, well-lit and quiet. The temperature should be about 16°C (61°F), or 18°C (64°F) for babies, old people and those with chest complaints.

Ideally the room should contain an armchair for the patient, two chairs for visitors, a bedside table for books, radio, water jug, a reading lamp and, if necessary, an alarm intercom – see BABY ALARMS. Flowers or plants will help to brighten the room during the day, but remove them at night.

If the illness is likely to be brief, or the patient can move around freely when he is out of bed, his own bedroom will serve. In longer illnesses, try to convert a room closer to the centre of family activity, so that he does not feel cut off. A lavatory nearby will be useful; otherwise install a commode, if necessary.

Patients with mild illnesses can sleep at night in their bedrooms, but may appreciate a day bed – a sofa or stable sun lounger – in a family room. A young child, for example, will quickly become bored if left alone.

Storing medicines Do not keep medicines in the sickroom – a young child or elderly person in particular, may take a dose in error. Store them in the family medicine cupboard.

Beds and bedding The bed should be about 700mm (28in) high, so that the patient can get in and out easily and the bed is easy to make. The mattress should be firm; when dealing with back problems such as a SLIPPED DISC, it may be necessary to make the bed firmer by placing boards underneath the mattress.

Sheets and pillowcases should be made of easy-to-launder material; polyester/cotton blends are suitable. Use lightweight blankets or DUVETS.

If the patient is incontinent, put a waterproof cover or sheet of polythene over the mattress, with a normal sheet over it. Lay a smaller plastic sheet, about 900mm (3ft) wide, across the bed where the patient's buttocks go; then cover that with an incontinence pad or a drawsheet of the same width. The drawsheet should be as long as possible; tuck most of the surplus into one side of the bed, and gradually move it across as the exposed portion becomes wet, tucking the wet section into the other side.

Making the bed If you have to make a sick bed with a patient in it, do not allow him to be uncovered for longer than is necessary. Ensure that there is always at least one pillow under his head. Have the fresh top sheet ready to cover him as soon as you remove the dirty one. Cover him with a sheet or blanket while you change a duvet cover.

To change the bottom sheet, roll the patient gently to one side of the bed.

Tuck the other half of the old bottom sheet up against him. Spread the clean sheet on the vacant half of the bed, tucking it in, and leaving the surplus folded next to the patient. Then roll the patient the other way, onto the fresh sheet. Remove the dirty sheet, and spread the rest of the fresh one over the vacant half of the bed.

Clothing Pyjamas and nightdresses should not have thick seams that can press against the patient, causing discomfort or sores. A patient out of bed for short intervals should wear a dressing-gown and slippers: if he is up for longer periods, encourage him to get dressed.

Personal hygiene If a patient cannot go to the bathroom, give him soap, water and a face flannel and toothbrush to wash face and hands and clean his teeth twice a day.

To give a bed bath, prepare three flannels and towels (one each for the face, body and genitals), two large bath towels, talcum powder, soap and a good supply of warm water. Remove the top bedding, place one bath towel under the patient, and cover him with the other.

Wash and dry the face, neck and ears first. Then wash, rinse and dry each hand and arm. Take off the patient's nightclothes and wash and dry the chest, abdomen and sides, keeping as much of the body as possible covered with the bath towel. Wash and dry each leg. Then roll the patient onto his side to wash and dry the back and genital region. Dust the patient's whole body with talcum powder, remove the towels and put fresh nightclothes on the patient.

The patient's hair should be brushed and combed at least once daily, and washed once a week. If he cannot wash his own hair, protect him and the bedding with towels and a plastic sheet, and get him to lie on his back with his head over the side of the bed. Place a bowl on the floor to catch the water, then shampoo the hair and rinse with jugs of warm water. Dry at once, and comb.

Bed sores A patient bedridden for some time risks developing bed sores. The most vulnerable parts of the body are the buttocks, spine, hips, knees, ankles, heels, elbows, shoulders and back of the head.

Check regularly for bed sores: first signs are discoloured patches in the skin. If sores develop, get your doctor's advice.

When giving a wash, massage vulnerable areas with lanolin or soap. Keep his skin clean and dry. Change nightclothes promptly if they become damp. Keep the bed free of crumbs.

You can buy sheepskins on which the patient can lie or sit, to provide a soft, resilient surface; a bed cradle takes the weight of coverings off the body; buy one, or improvise with a stool or fireguard.

Nylon

Caring for fabrics; prolonging whiteness

Nylon is simple to care for and clean. Most spots can be washed off with warm water, and most oily stains removed with liquid detergent. For a complete clean, launder nylon articles by machine or by hand. See also LAUNDERING.

Always launder white nylon separately, as tints in coloured nylon tend to run. Washing white nylon at a fairly high temperature will help to prolong whiteness. If washed at too low a temperature, it will gradually become grey.

Machine-wash white nylon at 50°C (120°F) and coloured nylon at 40-50°C (105-120°F). Rinse in cold water and spin briefly.

Hand-wash white nylon in water as hot as the hand can bear, and coloured nylon in water that feels pleasantly warm. Rinse in cold water and drip dry.

To dry nylon CURTAINS, give them a very short spin, then hang them wet in the window and gently pull into shape.

Nylon ropes

Joining; sealing to prevent fraying

To splice or join together two lengths of nylon rope, unwind the strands at the meeting ends and weave the strands of one with the corresponding strands of the other. This way, the join will never part – because each pull on the rope will tighten the splice.

To get a good working length for splicing, unwind both sets of strands to about ten times the thickness of a strand. Push the stranded ends together and tie down the ends of one rope round the other with a piece of string. Then weave the free ends through the strands of the other rope at least four or five times. Untie the other ends and weave them into the splice. Cut off the surplus ends of the woven strands and pull the rope ends.

To seal a nylon rope, melt the cut end in the flame of a match, lighter or gas ring.

To prevent fraying, the rope should be sealed. Nylon or synthetic ropes can be sealed by softening their ends in a flame, then wetting your fingers and squeezing the melted ends together. See also SPLICING ROPE.

Obedience training

*Teaching your dog to obey
commands promptly*

Dogs can learn to associate certain commands, calls or whistles with actions and objects, if the same words and whistles are used repeatedly. Repetition and consistent use of these 'signals' will eventually trigger an automatic response from the dog, despite any distractions. The dog will learn quickly if every correct response is rewarded by praise. See also DOG CARE; HOUSE-TRAINING PETS.

Start or end each command with the dog's name. When it obeys, say 'Good dog!' and stroke or pat it. Praise quietly – exuberant petting will only make it want to play. Always use the same words of command; never vary them. Reward with an occasional biscuit or titbit.

Training sessions Begin with ten-minute sessions, extended later to 20 minutes. To start, you may need to repeat an exercise five or six times a day for several days – but not so often that the dog becomes bored.

Use a leather collar and about 2m (6ft) of lead for teaching your dog to sit, lie and heel. Use a longer lead for training it to come and fetch. Pet shops stock reels of retractable nylon lead that fastens to ordinary leather, nylon or chain lead.

Sit Position the dog on your left (if you are right-handed). Hold the lead close to the collar, then make the dog sit as illustrated. Praise the dog as soon as it sits. Repeat until it sits automatically.

Stay Make the dog sit and stay as illustrated. As soon as it stays for a minute or two, walk back and praise it.

Each time you take your dog out to a field or park, repeat the exercise (eventually, off the lead), gradually increasing the staying time and distance.

Lie Make the dog sit, then lie as illustrated. If the dog tries to get up, repeat the order to lie and say 'Stay'. Repeat the exercise until your dog obeys automatically, then give praise or a reward.

Kerb drill Each time you are going to cross a road, make your dog sit and give the order 'Stay'. When the road is clear, move off briskly, giving the lead a tug, at the same time saying 'Over'. Do not cross any road with your dog off the lead – it is illegal in a built-up area.

Heel Train the dog to walk next to your left leg with its nose just in front of your knee. While walking, use your left hand on the middle of the lead to pull it taut or slacken it, as illustrated.

If the dog lags behind or tries to press ahead, jerk the lead sharply and repeat the command. If it continues to strain at the leash, begin circling and turning or making figures-of-eight. This will keep the dog by your side.

Whenever you take the dog for a walk, judiciously mix praise with jerking until it learns to walk to heel.

OBEDIENCE TRAINING

Getting your dog to sit, stay, lie and walk to heel

Start training your dog to obey commands when it is about six months old – house-training starts earlier, but obedience training should wait until the dog is no longer too playful to concentrate. When training, never strike the dog for failing to obey – that will only make it dread training sessions. Just say 'No' in a firm, low voice – then repeat the exercise.

Sit With the dog on your left, hold its lead in your right hand. Press down its rump with your left hand and pull the lead gently back and up. Say 'Sit'.

Stay 1 Make the dog sit by your left leg. Say 'Stay' and hold your hand about 25mm (1in) from the tip of its nose.

Heel Train the dog to walk by your left leg on the command, 'Heel'. Hold the lead about 300mm (12in) from the collar and jerk it if the dog strains ahead.

Stay 2 Hold the lead loosely and take a pace or two back from the dog holding your palm towards it. If the dog follows you, return and start again.

Lie 1 Make the dog sit. With one hand slide its forepaws forward while pushing down its back or head. Give the command, 'Lie'.

Lie 2 Keep the dog lying by backing away, arm extended in front of you and hand raised. Tell it to stay.

Come Tell the dog to stay, then walk away, turn round and give the order 'Come!', at the same time tugging at a longish – say 3m (10ft) – lead. Praise the dog when it runs to you. Gradually increase the distance and finally, when the dog's response is prompt, practise without the lead.

Fetch Put a familiar object in the dog's mouth, to accustom it to picking things up and giving them back on the order 'Give'. Extend the exercise by moving away and saying 'Fetch'. Throw the object farther and then repeat the order. Praise and reward after successful retrieving.

Training classes These are held in many areas. Consult your vet, local police station, or the *Yellow Pages* under Dog training; or contact the Kennel Club (1 Clarges Street, London W1); it publishes a list of training clubs.

Obscene telephone calls

How to deal with them

If you receive an obscene or nuisance telephone call, hang up quickly and quietly. Any expression of anger, fear, or disgust – even slamming down the phone – may encourage a second call.

Most random callers are put off if they do not get the desired reaction – or gain information from you.

Do not answer the phone by giving your number, simply say 'Hello'. If someone asks 'What number is this?', ask what number they are calling. If it is not yours, do not give yours.

Tell your children to do the same – and never to say their parents are out.

If nuisance calls persist – and especially if the caller says nothing, or breathes heavily – he is possibly someone you know. So tell no one outside the household about such calls; if they *do* come from someone known to you, your annoyance, fear, or embarrassment may encourage more calls. A nuisance caller can be prosecuted under British law – report such a call to the police.

You should also contact the Customer Service Manager of your BT or Mercury Area Office, who will advise you on the best way of dealing with the problem. He may, for example, suggest:

Service interception The operator may be able for a limited period to intercept incoming calls and filter out the nuisance calls. This will discourage a persistent caller, but will not necessarily stop him.

Change of number You can be given a new phone number, provided there is a spare one available. It should be ex-directory, and you should give it only to

close friends, relatives and, if necessary, your employer. In 1994 the charge for this service was £30.50 plus VAT.

Incoming calls barred The exchange can adjust your telephone to make only outgoing calls. This may suit someone who normally does not receive many calls, but should be considered as a last resort. There may be a small charge for the service.

Other measures Take your own precautions – have friends use a prearranged code when calling. For example, they could ring three times – then ring off and dial again.

A woman should use just her surname and initials in the phone book, omitting 'Mrs', 'Miss' or 'Ms'.

Draining oil; replacing throwaway filters; removing replaceable ones

Before draining oil from a car, run the engine until warm, switch off and remove the oil filler cap – to help the oil flow out freely. Replace throwaway cartridge filters by unscrewing the old cartridge and screwing in a new one. Filters in many older cars consist of a filter element inside a metal bowl: replace the element.

Draining Put a container large enough to hold all the oil under the sump drain plug. Loosen the plug with a ring or socket spanner or drain-plug key. Remove carefully, making sure the hot oil does not scald your hand.

Cartridge filter Use a strap or chain wrench to loosen the filter, then unscrew it.

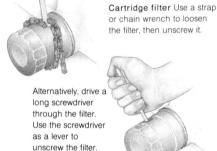

Alternatively, drive a long screwdriver through the filter. Use the screwdriver as a lever to unscrew the filter.

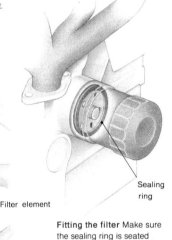

Sealing ring

Filter element

Fitting the filter Make sure the sealing ring is seated correctly on the new filter. Smear its outer face with clean engine oil. Screw on the filter until the sealing ring contacts the flange. Tighten it another three-quarters of a turn.

Removing filter element Unscrew the central bolt, then withdraw the bowl. Take out the old filter, also the plate and spring beneath. Remove the sealing ring from the flange on the engine's side.

Oil changing

Servicing your car; changing the filter

Change your car's engine oil and replace the oil filter as recommended in the owner's handbook. Use the grade of oil recommended by the manufacturer. Keep a record of oil and filter changes.

Draining the oil You can usually dispose of the old oil at a tank at one of the local council's refuse tips. It is illegal to put oil down a drain or to bury it. You may have to raise the front or rear of the car on axle stands to reach the sump drain plug – see JACKING A CAR.

Drain the oil as illustrated, with the

engine warm. Wait until oil stops dripping from the drain hole, then clean the drain hole threads with a clean rag; also clean the drain plug and check that its washer (if fitted) is in good condition. Replace the washer if it is damaged. Refit the plug and tighten it gently.

Changing the filter Place the draining bowl under the filter.

Remove a cartridge filter as shown on the previous page. Thoroughly clean the flange where the filter is screwed to the engine's side. Fit the new filter.

Remove a replaceable element filter as illustrated together with the sealing ring. Thoroughly clean the inside of the metal bowl with paraffin. Dry it, refit the spring and plate and insert the new filter. Clean the flange on the side of the engine and smear the new sealing ring – supplied with the filter – with clean engine oil. Fit the ring carefully into its groove. Hold the filter bowl against the mounting flange and locate the central bolt in its thread. Screw it in by hand until it is finger-tight, then tighten gently with a spanner.

Refilling with new oil Have the car on flat ground so you get a true oil-level reading. Remove the filler cap on the rocker box cover, and clean it with a paraffin rag. If the cap has a wire gauze filter in the body, rinse it in paraffin and blow dry with a foot-pump.

Use a plastic oil funnel in the oil filler hole to avoid spillage, and pour in only small amounts of oil at a time. Check the dipstick frequently, and cease filling when the level is at, or just below, the Full/Max mark.

Start the engine and allow it to idle for a few minutes. Stop the engine and wait about ten minutes. Check the level again on the dipstick and top up if required. Check also for OIL LEAKS at the filter and sump plug, tightening as necessary. Replace the filler cap.

Oil heaters

Maintaining and repairing them

Oil heaters are an economical form of home heating, but use and maintain them carefully, and never use them in a poorly ventilated room.

Never carry a lighted heater – even for a short distance. Do not stand it in a draught or near billowing curtains, and never allow anything to cover it. Never re-fuel a heater while it is alight, and always fill it in a safe place, preferably outside the house. Never use any fuel other than paraffin, and mark fuel clearly.

Convector heaters The heat is given out through a grille near the top. If there is a

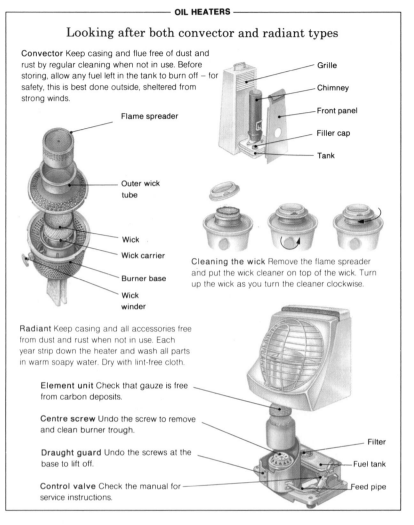

OIL HEATERS

Looking after both convector and radiant types

Convector Keep casing and flue free of dust and rust by regular cleaning when not in use. Before storing, allow any fuel left in the tank to burn off – for safety, this is best done outside, sheltered from strong winds.

Flame spreader

Grille
Chimney
Front panel
Filler cap
Tank

Outer wick tube

Wick
Wick carrier
Burner base
Wick winder

Cleaning the wick Remove the flame spreader and put the wick cleaner on top of the wick. Turn up the wick as you turn the cleaner clockwise.

Radiant Keep casing and all accessories free from dust and rust when not in use. Each year strip down the heater and wash all parts in warm soapy water. Dry with lint-free cloth.

Element unit Check that gauze is free from carbon deposits.

Centre screw Undo the screw to remove and clean burner trough.

Draught guard Undo the screws at the base to lift off.

Control valve Check the manual for service instructions.

Filter
Fuel tank
Feed pipe

smell, or if the flame is uneven and spiky, clean the wick as shown. If the wick is badly discoloured or too shallow for a maximum flame, replace it.

Methods vary for wick removal, but in most, when the wick has been exposed, it has to be wound off the winder cogs until it can be pulled free. If you have the handbook, order the correct size wick by using the reference number in the book. Or take the old wick to a hardware shop so that you can match size and thickness against a new one.

Take time getting the wick in place over the central tube, and ensure that the winder teeth engage properly, so the wick remains even as it is wound up and down. Before re-lighting, allow the wick plenty of time to soak up paraffin.

If the mica window has been damaged or is badly discoloured, get a replacement. Unscrew the cover plate holding the mica in place, then take the old mica with you to the shop to get the correct fitting.

Radiant heaters These have a gauze element that becomes red-hot and gives a direct heat. To dismantle the heater, first undo the retaining bolts or screws at the base to lift off the casing.

Remove the element unit which houses the wire gauze. Check that the gauze is clean and sits correctly in its groove. If the element is badly rusted, renew it.

Undo the screws holding the draught guard to the heater. Lift it off and wash it. Remove the centre screw in the top of the burner trough, remove the trough and clean with water and a brush.

Check in your manual how to service the control valve which monitors the fuel flow. There should be no signs of wear or rust. Also check washers on the control valve nut and fuel tank cap.

If the wick is contaminated or badly encrusted with carbon, check in the manual for size and type, and get a replacement. If you have no manual, take the old wick to a hardware store. Tell the retailer the make and model of heater.

Oil lamps

Servicing mantle and wick lamps

When any oil lamp is in use, make sure that it stands on a secure base or hangs from a soundly fixed hook. It should not be where it can be knocked over, or near draughts or billowing curtains. Never let anything get draped over a lamp.

A paraffin pressure lamp should be checked over at least once a year. When you reassemble a lamp, make all screw fittings finger-tight only.

Remove the head of the lamp, taking care not to knock the mantle, which is very delicate. If the mantle is broken, check in the manual and get another of the same type. If you have no manual, take the old mantle to a hardware shop, with details of the lamp make and model.

Remove the lamp glass and wash it in warm, soapy water. Dry with a soft cloth.

Feel if the needle tip in the vaporiser tube is broken; if so, fit a new needle following the maker's instructions. The vaporiser gradually becomes clogged by carbon deposits, so replace it after about 500 hours of burning. Wherever parts are screwed together – such as where the pump joins the fuel container – there are washers, often of leather. Each time you disturb one, lubricate the leather with thin oil. If washers show signs of deterioration, fit new ones.

If the pump fails to pressurise the container, unscrew the pump unit to expose the washer. Usually this has dried out and is no longer a tight fit in the pump tube. Lubricate the washer with thin oil and manipulate it with your fingers to swell it out. Shape it with your fingers so it will go back in its tube, then screw the unit back in place. Give one sharp pump to expand the washer against the walls of the tube.

Older lamps These simple wick-and-oil container types need very little in the way of maintenance. Keep the lamp glass

clean by washing in warm soapy water, and wipe the exterior of the lamp, particularly round the wick holder, to remove oil and grime.

As soon as the wick shows signs of turning black and brittle, turn it up and trim to expose new wick.

If the lamp starts to smell, unscrew the wick holder and empty the oil container. You may find debris, or even water, in the oil. Rinse out with fresh paraffin oil and refill the container. If the smell persists, suspect the wick. Remove it and fit a new one. If you are unsure of the width, take the old wick to your hardware store and buy one the same.

When a new wick is fitted, allow sufficient time for it to become saturated before re-lighting.

Oil leaks

Curing oil loss from your car's engine, rear axle and steering box

If you see oil under the car where it has been standing, trace the source of the leak immediately. First clean the area above the oil spill but remember that the leak may not be directly above the pool of oil. Use a wire brush to remove all caked oil and dirt and wash down with paraffin or a degreasing solvent (this can be a messy job; put down plastic sheeting and wear overalls).

Checking the engine Run the engine for a few minutes. Then switch off – unless you are looking only at the rocker or cam cover, when the movement will reveal a leak by spraying oil up against the cover. Most likely places for leaks are gaskets and seals.

Rocker box cover gasket Oil running down the cylinder head indicates a leak from this gasket. Tighten the cover screws or bolts evenly. Do not over-

tighten – this will distort both cover and gasket, making the leak worse.

Timing cover gasket Look for streaks of oil running from the bottom of the cover and along the sump cover. Tighten the timing cover bolts evenly. Look also for oil streaks radiating from behind the pulley wheel. This indicates a leaking oil seal – have it replaced by a qualified motor mechanic.

Side cover gaskets Some cars have a cover plate, or plates, over the tappet chamber on one side of the engine, usually below the inlet or exhaust manifold. Use a small mirror to look for leaks from the lower edge of a plate. A central bolt usually holds the plate; tighten it gently. Make sure the engine is cool if the plate is beneath the exhaust manifold.

Sump cover gasket Check for leaks around the sump cover flange. Tighten the sump bolts evenly. If there is a leak from the sump drain plug, tighten the plug. If the leak persists the plug washer must be changed, which involves draining the oil – see OIL CHANGING.

Oil filter The cartridge-type filter screws directly onto the crankcase. If there is a slight leak at the seal, try tightening the cartridge by hand. A heavy leak means that the rubber seal is damaged; fit a new rubber seal.

If the filter is of the replaceable element type, tighten the central bolt to stop a leak at the seal, or remove the filter housing and fit a new sealing ring. This filter is usually attached to the oil pump. Check for a leak at the pump flange and, if necessary, tighten the fixing bolts.

Rear axle leaks Curing serious leaks from the rear axle involves partial dismantling of the axle assembly, and should be left to a garage. However, it may be possible to stop a small leak round the differential casing by tightening the flange bolts. A leak from the axle filler or drain plug may be cured by fitting a new washer, if the plug is fitted with one (some plugs are tapered). Renewing the washer involves draining the oil and refilling.

Steering box leaks A leak from the top cover of the box may be stopped by tightening the bolts, or one from the filler plug by replacing the washer. All other leaks must be treated by a garage, as the steering must be readjusted after replacement of gaskets or seals. Tightening the top cover bolts may also disturb the adjustment, resulting in stiffness in the steering. If this happens have a garage readjust the box.

Not all oil gaskets on a car need to be changed by an experienced mechanic. On

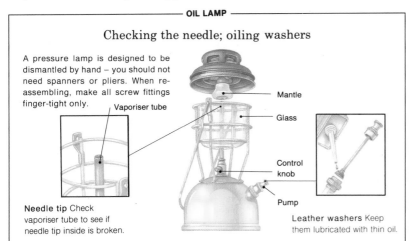

── OIL LAMP ──

Checking the needle; oiling washers

A pressure lamp is designed to be dismantled by hand – you should not need spanners or pliers. When re-assembling, make all screw fittings finger-tight only.

Vaporiser tube

Mantle

Glass

Control knob

Pump

Needle tip Check vaporiser tube to see if needle tip inside is broken.

Leather washers Keep them lubricated with thin oil.

most cars the rocker box or camshaft cover, for example, can be easily replaced by the owner. If you have a servicing manual for your car, check to see which gaskets can be changed with little dismantling and a basic tool kit.

Oil painting

Equipping yourself and learning basic techniques

Oil paint is usually mixed with pure linseed oil and turpentine, and brushed on; but it can also be applied thick with painting knives, poured or dripped on, or even squeezed on, straight from the tube.

To start, you need a small range of paints, brushes, paint and palette knives, palette, clip-on 'dipper' pots to hold linseed oil and turpentine – and something to paint on. This need not be canvas, which requires some preparation (see STRETCHING A CANVAS); art shops sell ready-primed canvas and oil painting boards which are cheaper and suitable for a beginner.

Paints Ready-made paints, sold in tubes, vary greatly in quality and durability. Check the manufacturer's grading for permanence, as some colours fade badly in sunlight. Buy the best you can afford, choosing a basic selection which should include Cadmium Yellow, Cobalt Blue, Cadmium Red, Viridian Green, Yellow Ochre, Ivory Black, Burnt Umber and Titanium White.

Mix and experiment to create a wide range of shades. You will need linseed oil to mix the paints and turpentine to thin them – buy pure turpentine, as substitutes could cause the paint to crack after it is on the canvas. You can use substitutes for cleaning brushes.

Brushes Oil painting brushes have bristles in four main shapes – square-edged 'flats'; shorter, square-edged 'brights'; 'longs' (longer flats); and 'rounds' which are rounded to a point. They are made of stiff hogs' bristle or a softer hair such as camel, squirrel or sable – again, buy the best you can afford.

In general, use broad, flat brushes to cover wide areas. Use bristle to emphasise the texture of brush strokes, and softer brushes for fine detail. You can also apply paint with knives, different shapes producing different effects. Use a palette knife to mix the paints.

Palettes The traditional artist's palette is made of mahogany, but you can also use glass, marble, melamine or buy disposable paper palettes. 'Dippers', which clip onto the palette, hold small quantities of linseed oil and turpentine, enabling you to dip into either pot quickly and

---

OIL PAINTING

How to paint a scene

Start by making a preliminary pencil drawing on a sketch pad of the scene you wish to paint. Lightly pencil in a grid over your drawing.

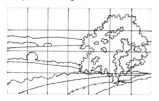

Using a grid Draw a scaled grid in charcoal on the canvas, then transfer your sketch to the canvas, using the grid as a guide and working square by square.

Sky and foreground Keep the blues light and blend in clouds while the paint is wet, to give a hazy effect. Paint the foreground and wait for it to part dry.

Finishing off Paint the dark areas of objects first, working towards the lightest shades which go on last.

---

conveniently as you work. A piece of clean rag is also essential for wiping the brushes as you paint.

Painting a scene Make a sketch of your proposed picture on paper. Use pencil and ruler to draw a light grid over the drawing. Then draw a grid of appropriate proportions on the canvas with charcoal. That way, as you transfer your sketch onto the canvas, you will know what should go into each square. See also PATTERN TRANSFER.

Sketch onto the canvas with charcoal or pencil, transferring the outlines square by square. When you have sketched in your outline, dust off excess charcoal. Mix the colours for the sky and apply them with a wide, flat brush.

Next, paint in the foreground, and wait at least a day until it is part dry. You could continue painting without a break, but this requires expertise to know how the colours will merge.

Paint the dark areas of your objects first, working towards the lightest shades, which go on last. When your picture is complete, wait a week before you start *glazing*.

Glaze is a layer of colour heavily thinned with linseed oil and turpentine, and is used to highlight certain areas – for example, you can use a translucent reddish-pink for a sunset. Try different colours for different effects, painting on lightly with a soft brush.

You can give the painting a final protective coat of matt or gloss varnish after about six months. Varnish in a dry place. See also WATERCOLOUR PAINTING.

Old people's homes

Choosing a suitable one; obtaining assistance

Finding the right old people's home for yourself or an aged relative entails shopping around to discover what is available in your area. There are three main kinds of residential-care homes: those run by local authorities; those run for profit; and those run by voluntary, non-profit-making organisations.

Local authority homes Approach your local social services department. They will assess your social circumstances and state of health (although a medical examination is *not* compulsory) and may consult your doctor. You will have to reveal your income and savings (if any).

If your application is accepted you will then probably have to join a long waiting list. Because of the shortage of accommodation, it is usually advisable to take the first place you are offered. There will be a charge, but help will be provided to people on low incomes.

Private homes To apply for admission, approach a home yourself – a selection is usually listed in *Yellow Pages* under 'Residential and Retirement Homes', or ask the social services department. Provided the home has at least four residents, it will be registered with the local authority under the Registered Homes Act 1984. This means it must fulfil certain standards of care and will be inspected by the social services department inspectorate at least once a year.

Fees can be expensive, and despite official scrutiny, homes can vary greatly in facilities and standards. If a resident is on a low income, the Department of Social Security (DSS) may provide financial help with the fees (but not with medical fees).

Voluntary homes To apply for admission, approach a home directly – again, you can consult *Yellow Pages* if necessary. Alternatively, your doctor or local social services department may put you in touch with a suitable home. Some homes accept only people of certain religions, or backgrounds. Although they are mainly non-profit-making, they charge fees to cover running costs.

Nursing homes As well as the three types of residential-care homes, there are nursing homes which provide nursing care. Most are run by private or charitable bodies. Lists can be obtained from *Yellow Pages*, social workers or the district health authority. People on low incomes may receive help with fees.

Before moving in Whichever home is chosen, first visit it in person beforehand (perhaps accompanied by a friend or social worker). If possible, stay there for a trial period. Prepare a checklist in advance.

Food Is it good, bad or indifferent? Are special diets catered for?

Rooms Will you have to share – and what happens if you cannot get on with your room mate?

Entertainment Is TV laid on, and who chooses the channel? Can you have a radio or TV in your room? Is there an area for reading and relaxing?

Books and papers Does the home have a library, or does the local public library run a special service for it? Are newspapers delivered?

Other considerations may include whether you can entertain visitors; take your own favourite armchair; keep your pet; consult your own doctor; have control over your finances.

Once someone has sold their home and belongings, and entered residential care, it is difficult to reverse the decision. Even so, any problems that may arise can be discussed with fellow residents, and with the staff. If this is not satisfactory, you can write to the registration officer of the district health authority, local councillors or, in extreme cases, your MP.

Age Concern publishes free fact sheets: *Local Authorities and Residential Care, Supplementary Benefit for Residential Care and Nursing Homes,* and *Finding Residential and Nursing Home Accommodation* (send a large stamped and addressed envelope).

Rights and safeguards No one can be forced into an old people's home just because they are old and infirm. But if the person concerned is severely mentally disturbed, or is a danger to himself or those around him, the local health authority can apply for a court order to put him in institutional care.

Most old people, however, enter homes of their own choosing – or on the well-meaning advice of relatives. They are seeking a cosy domestic environment, with an expert and caring staff of nurses and helpers. In most cases, that is what they get.

Ombudsmen

What they do and how to complain to them

An ombudsman helps members of the public to fight injustice or unfair treatment by the authorities. However, he cannot punish erring officials or reverse their decisions. His criticism of bad administration usually leads to it being changed – but his decisions cannot be legally enforced.

When a complaint is made, an ombudsman will hear both sides of the case in private. He has the same power as the courts in ordering people to give evidence.

Ombudsman is a Swedish word meaning 'agent' or 'representative'. In Britain, most ombudsmen are lawyers or senior civil servants, each with his own staff.

Parliamentary ombudsman Officially known as the Parliamentary Commissioner for Administration, he deals with complaints against central government departments and Crown bodies. All complaints to him must be made in collaboration with an MP – but not necessarily your own.

Alternatively, you can write to the ombudsman at Church House, Great Smith Street, London SW1P 3BW. He will then ask your MP (or another Member) if he would like to have the matter investigated. If the answer is no, then the ombudsman has no power to take your complaint any further.

Health ombudsman This is the Health Service Commissioner, who deals with complaints of maladministration in hospitals or other parts of the NHS. However, you must complain first to the health authority involved, and give it a few weeks to investigate.

If you are not satisfied with the investigation, you can write direct to the health ombudsman at Church House, Great Smith Street, London SW1P 3BW.

Local ombudsmen There are three for England (two in London, one in York) and one each for Scotland, Wales and Northern Ireland (where he is called the Commissioner for Complaints). They deal with complaints against county councils, borough and city councils, national park authorities, land authorities, regional water authorities, and police authorities.

They *cannot* investigate complaints

against individual police officers (complain in person to the duty officer at the police station, or write to the Chief Constable). Nor can they investigate complaints against parish or town councils (make any such complaints to the clerk or chairman of the council).

Complaints to the local ombudsman should first be made through a local councillor, but if he refuses to pass it on you can write directly to the ombudsman. The addresses are:

England 21 Queen Anne's Gate, London SW1H 9BU. Beverley House, 17 Shipton Road, York YO3 6FZ.

Scotland 23 Walker Street, Edinburgh EH3 7HY.

Wales Derwen House, Court Road, Bridgend, Mid Glamorgan CF31 1BN.

Northern Ireland Progressive House, 33 Wellington Place, Belfast BT1 6HN.

When to complain Complaints to all three categories of ombudsmen must be made within 12 months of the action being complained about. Their services are free, and there are no legal costs.

Ombudsmen's reports Copies of the reports made by parliamentary and health ombudsmen are sent to the department concerned and any individual named in the complaint. Copies also go to parliament.

Local ombudsmen send one copy of their reports to the complainants, one to the local authorities concerned, and one to any other persons named in the complaint. The local authority must then make the report available for public inspection for three weeks, and advertise the facts in the local press – unless the ombudsman rules otherwise.

Putting matters right If a parliamentary ombudsman upholds a complaint, the government department concerned will, usually, put the matter right. If it refuses to do so, the MP involved may raise the complaint again; or a Commons Select Committee may investigate.

Similarly, if a health authority refuses to act on a health ombudsman's recommendation, the matter can be taken up in parliament.

Omelettes

Cooking them plain and savoury

If possible, use an omelette pan or frying pan only about 150mm (6in) across to make your omelettes, so that the eggs do not spread out too thinly. Purists also use unsalted, clarified butter (see CLARIFYING BUTTER), so the fat will not burn easily or the omelette stick to the pan. Warm the pan before putting the butter in – it should make the butter sizzle.

Plain omelette Takes about 3 minutes to prepare and 2 minutes to cook:

Ingredients (for 1)
2 eggs
1 tablespoon milk or water
$\frac{1}{4}$ level teaspoon salt
Freshly ground pepper
Knob of butter

Break the eggs into a bowl, add the milk or water, salt and pepper. Beat lightly with a fork – just enough to blend. Heat the butter in the pan without letting it brown, then pour in the egg mixture.

Cook over a moderate heat and lift the edges of the omelette with a spatula, so that liquid egg runs underneath. When almost set, but still lightly runny on top, lift the edge with a spatula to make sure the underside is golden. When it is, tip the pan slightly backwards and use the spatula to fold the omelette in half. Finally, tip it quickly out upside down onto a warm plate. Serve immediately.

For a *ham omelette*, sprinkle 1 tablespoon of finely chopped ham over the omelette before folding. For a *cheese omelette*, add 25g (1oz) of finely grated cheese to the beaten egg mixture before cooking.

For *omelette fines herbes*, sprinkle the herbs, parsley, chervil, tarragon and chives, on top of the eggs before you beat them. See HERBS IN COOKING.

Orange trees
Growing fruit indoors

You can, even in Britain's cool climate, grow your own oranges in a greenhouse (see GREENHOUSES) or conservatory.

Buy an orange plant from a nursery. Alternatively, you can grow one from a pip or a cutting (see CITRUS HOUSEPLANTS), but the quality of the fruit will be unpredictable; also it will take two or three years to start fruiting.

An orange plant will grow to be 2.4m (8ft) tall or more. Grow it in a large pot or tub filled with a good potting mixture, such as John Innes No 2 – see JOHN INNES COMPOST. It needs to be kept under glass only in winter, at a constant temperature of 10-13°C (50-55°F). In summer, move it to a sheltered, sunny spot in the garden.

Caring for the plant Oranges are evergreen plants, and must be watered all year – plenty in summer, less in winter.

When the tree is carrying fruit, feed it once a week with diluted liquid manure. A constant temperature of 18-24°C (64-75°F) is needed for the fruits to ripen.

Under glass in winter, keep the atmosphere as dry as possible.

Calamondin oranges If space is limited, you can grow the dwarf calamondin orange. This seldom grows more than 1m (3ft) high. It produces clusters of three or four fragrant white flowers, followed by walnut-size fruit.

Orchids
Raising them as houseplants

Orchids are not nearly as difficult to grow as is commonly believed. There are several that thrive indoors if given the right amount of warmth, light and humidity. Different varieties flower at different times of the year.

Indoor varieties Orchids that can be grown indoors include the *cattleya* orchids; the *coelogyne* orchids, which include the white and yellow flowered *Coelogyne cristata* – one of the easiest orchids to grow indoors; the large, brightly coloured *epidendrum* orchids; *lycaste* orchids; *odontoglossum* orchids; and the *paphiopedilum* orchids – also known as slipper orchids.

Orchids grow either on the ground (terrestrial), or cling to trees, shrubs or rocky surfaces (epiphytic). Terrestrial orchids are usually grown in pots, using a special free-draining potting mixture, available from garden centres.

Creating the right conditions Orchids need plenty of light. Grow them in a draught-free window, so that they can get a few hours of sunlight in the morning or afternoon.

During winter, move epiphytic orchids to where they get as much direct sunlight as possible. Supplement this with artificial light for six to eight hours a day – so that they get at least ten hours light a day. Never expose *lycaste* or *paphiopedilum* orchids to direct sunlight.

Orchids also need humidity and warmth – a temperature during the day of around 20°C (68°F) in summer and 16°C (61°F) in winter. Night temperatures should be about 5°C (9°F) lower.

To provide humidity, stand the plants in trays of damp pebbles, gravel or moist peat. If the temperature is over 21°C (70°F), mist spray the leaves daily.

Watering and feeding Never overwater orchids. A moderate watering once a week is usually enough. To water epiphytic orchids grown in a hanging basket, or on a piece of wood or fern, soak the container or wood in a bucket for a few minutes.

During summer, spray orchids with a foliar feed every fourth watering.

Repotting orchids Do this once every two years. Repot when new roots begin to grow, usually in spring. Cut off dead

or damaged roots and carefully remove all traces of the old potting mixture.

With an epiphytic orchid soak the base of the plant in water for a few minutes, then let it drain for half an hour. Place some moss under the plant base and attach the roots to the wood or fern with copper wire or nylon string.

Do not water orchids for ten days after repotting, and then only sparingly for the next two weeks.

Organ donor
How to become one: authorising organ removal

Organs for transplant operations are obtained from live donors (kidneys only) and people who have just died (kidneys, heart, liver, lungs, pancreas and eyes). The laws and procedures governing each source are quite different.

Live donors Anyone over the age of 18 – being of sound body and mind – can be a kidney donor for a transplant operation involving a member of the family, but only if donor and recipient have the same blood group and tissue type. If a proposed donor is under 18, then the consent of parents or legal guardian is needed.

Consent will only be sought if the operation is in the donor's own interests – for example, to save the life of a brother or sister.

Future donors With certain exceptions, anyone can donate his organs for future medical use. After the donor's death, a transplant team will assess the medical suitability of the donated organs.

The best way for donors to ensure that their wishes are known and followed is to carry an official Donor Card, obtainable from hospitals and doctors' surgeries. This lists the organ or organs offered for transplantation, the donor's full name and home telephone number, and whom to contact in the event of sudden or accidental death.

Alternatively, potential donors can state their wishes in their will, or verbally in the presence of two witnesses. Provided one of these conditions has been met, relatives normally have no legal right to be consulted.

Liver organ donors must be aged under 50, and kidney donors can be anything between two years of age and 70.

Organ removal after death In order to save lives, organs must be removed shortly after death. A medical team *not* responsible for transplantation pronounces the person clinically dead.

When a potential donor dies in hospital or is dead on arrival there, the local health authority has legal possession of the body, and can authorise a surgeon to remove parts of the body – either for transplantation or for research. Otherwise, the executor of a dead person's estate has legal possession of the body and can also give authorisation.

But whoever provides the authority must ensure that, when alive, the dead person did not object to such a practice and that close relatives also have no objection. Under a separate law governing cornea grafts in eye surgery, however, relatives can overrule a dead person's wishes.

In the case of organ removal from a dead child, the law does not demand parental consent. Organs would not be removed unless the child had expressed a wish to be a donor – and in any case it is customary to obtain parental consent before any surgical action is taken.

Coming to a decision Before deciding to become an organ donor, make sure it is the right choice for you. Guidance can be provided by a family DOCTOR or religious adviser – and it may help to talk it over with relatives or close friends.

Orienteering

The thinking man's cross-country racing on foot

Armed with a map (see MAP READING) and a COMPASS, competitors have to navigate on foot routes between isolated controls, or checkpoints, set in rugged and unfamiliar terrain. Controls must be visited in correct order, and the winner is the person who completes the course in the fastest time.

Speed and stamina are important, but the real test is working out the quickest way over or around natural obstacles such as hills, woods, marshes and lakes.

Regular events are organised by local clubs of the British Orienteering Federation. You can write to them for a list – at Riversdale, Dale Road North, Darley Vale, Matlock, Derbyshire DE4 2HX. To stage a simple orienteering event yourself, choose an area preferably unknown to the participants – such as a wooded and hilly heath or common to which there is public access. Make sure it has enough natural or man-made features to serve as controls, has clear boundaries and is free of dangerous hazards.

At the starting point, give each participant a map of the full course, a description sheet and a control card. Control positions are shown on a master map, and competitors copy these onto their own maps.

For beginners, the course should be about 3km (2 miles) long, with about six controls.

After studying the course, competitors set out separately at one or two minute

intervals, making for the first control. They may be faced with two or more possible routes – and will have to decide which they can cover most quickly.

For example, it may be quicker to forge over a steep hill than take a longer but possibly easier route round it. Ideally, the routes should vary between short and arduous, and long and easy.

Each control is marked by a flag or sign carrying a number or symbol which the runners copy onto a card as proof of reaching the control. Sometimes the marker has a needle punch attached for marking the card.

Get friends to act as starter, timer and judge. You must hand in your card when you finish; if you do not, a search may be set up for you.

Origami

The decorative art of folding paper

All you need to make a start in origami is a piece of foldable paper about 150mm (6in) square, and directions to make a model. Books of origami are available.

Basic folds In the printed directions a line of dashes means fold the paper so that it faces you – a *valley fold*; a line of dots and dashes means fold the paper down behind or away from you – a *mountain fold*.

Animals' legs and necks are made with the *reverse fold*. Make a valley fold where indicated, open the paper slightly, push the creased section inside, and smooth down the folds. The illustrations show how to fold a popular origami model.

Outboard motors

Looking after your boat's engine

An outboard motor should be serviced at the intervals specified by the manufacturer, but between times, you can do routine maintenance yourself.

Even if the engine is running well, it is wise occasionally to remove and check the SPARK-PLUGS.

The fuel tank should need no attention unless the filler cap seal is cracked or split, in which case the seal must be replaced. On some two-stroke engines, the oil supply has a separate container which should be checked and topped-up as necessary. On four-stroke engines,

---

Folding a lucky crane

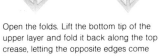

Fold a square of paper into a triangle, and again into a smaller triangle. Lift the top triangle and push its upper tip in to meet the lower tip. Smooth it out. Turn it over and repeat.

Lucky crane

Fold in the left and right corners to meet at the centre. Fold the top point down as indicated.

Open the folds. Lift the bottom tip of the upper layer and fold it back along the top crease, letting the opposite edges come together.

Smooth it out, turn the model over and repeat. Fold in the left and right corners to meet at the centre. Turn the paper over and repeat.

Reverse fold the bottom points up. Reverse fold the tip of one of the points down, to form the head. Pull out the 'wings' and blow into the hole underneath.

check the oil level with the dipstick. Change the engine oil at the intervals laid down by the manufacturer.

Periodically, clean the carburettor float chamber to remove any deposits or water droplets. Lubricate the throttle and choke linkages by applying a few drops of general purpose lubricating oil to the inner cable and linkage pivots on the carburettor.

On two-stroke engines the ignition timing is critical, for if it is wrong it can cause severe engine damage. Make sure that the setting accords with the handbook instructions. On engines with coil ignition, make sure that the electrical connections to the coils are clean and making good contact.

The gearbox at the base of the motor should not need topping-up, but check the contents from time to time by removing the filler plug. If the oil has become a greenish-brown sludge, it is contaminated with water that has got past a faulty seal. Check the gears and bearings for wear and corrosion, replace the seal, and refill with marine gear oil.

Before the motor is started, check the cooling water intake to make sure it is not blocked. It is fitted either low down near the propeller, or halfway up the driveshaft casing.

Hose down the outside of the motor thoroughly after each use, and dry it carefully.

Outside lighting

Fitting wall lights and power sockets outdoors

Make sure the wall light, or the socket you fit to plug a light into, is designed for outdoor use. A light fitting should be weatherproof (see LIGHT FIXTURES); a socket should be waterproof or protected by a tight-fitting cap attached by a chain and placed where it is not likely to be interfered with.

Installing the fittings First turn off the main switch (see FUSES AND FUSE BOXES) and withdraw the fuse for the circuit you are working on.

If the lighting circuit is wired on the loop-in system (see CEILING ROSE), you will have to transfer the connections of the most convenient ceiling rose to a JUNCTION BOX fitted above the ceiling and run cables from the junction box to the new light and its switch. If you use the existing mounting box, use a new two-gang switch over it.

If the lighting circuit is wired on the junction box system, connect the new cables to the most convenient box.

Decide and mark the exact position for the outside light. Now mark the corresponding position on the inside wall.

Make a route inside the house for the new light cable and switch cable. Lead it from the new or existing junction box to the indoor mark corresponding to the light position outside. Continue it from there to the position for the switch. If you are using an existing switch position, there will already be a cable running to it; take care not to damage this cable. Where the route is in plaster, chisel out a channel deep enough to take the cables and a filling of plaster at least 3mm ($\frac{1}{8}$in) thick.

Going back to your original mark for the light fitting, drill a hole from the channel in the inner wall through to the outside, drilling through both leaves if the wall is cavity construction – see MASONRY DRILLING. Use a masonry drill bit slightly larger than the diameter of the wiring cable – you may need to rent a long drill bit from a tool hire shop. If there is no existing switch at the switch position, fit a mounting box – see ELECTRIC SOCKETS AND SWITCHES.

Lay two 1.0mm² cables along the route (see ELECTRIC WIRING), taking the light cable through the hole in the wall, and the switch cable to its mounting box. Make good the damage and let any filler dry before you make the connections.

Prepare the cable ends for connection. Connect a new switch as shown in ELECTRIC SOCKETS AND SWITCHES. If replacing an existing switch with a two-gang switch, connect the cables as shown below. Connect both cables to the lighting circuit.

On the outside wall, hold the light mounting against the wall and mark the drilling spots. Drill holes and fit wall plugs – see WALL FASTENERS. Connect the

cable to the lampholder terminals as shown.

If the lampholder has a flex already attached, use a connector block to attach it to your new cable, putting red opposite brown, black opposite blue and sleeved green-and-yellow earth opposite green-and-yellow. The light mounting may have a rubber gasket to ensure a watertight seal when it is screwed to the wall – if it does not, coat the rim of the mounting with a waterproof sealant. Screw the light fitting in place, fit a bulb, put on the cover, and restore the power.

Fitting an outdoor socket The method is similar to wiring SPUR CONNECTIONS – the cable is taken from a convenient socket and run through a hole in the wall. Make sure the hole slopes down towards the outside and is above the damp-proof course in a cavity wall.

Seal the purpose-made, waterproof socket to the wall, either with a rubber gasket provided or with a waterproof sealant. An outdoor socket must be protected by an RCD – see CIRCUIT BREAKER.

Oven cleaning

Using cleaners; ovens that clean themselves

An oven is easiest to clean when it is still warm. Otherwise, leave an open container half filled with ammonia in a closed oven overnight. This will help to loosen grease and any food that has been burnt to the lining. Always follow the

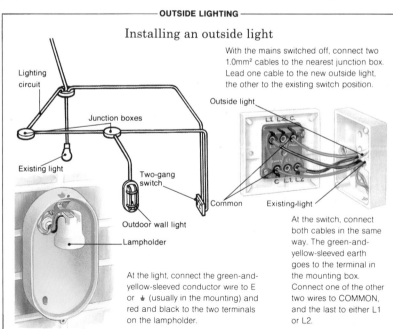

— OUTSIDE LIGHTING —

Installing an outside light

With the mains switched off, connect two 1.0mm² cables to the nearest junction box. Lead one cable to the new outside light, the other to the existing switch position.

Lighting circuit

Junction boxes

Existing light

Outside light

Two-gang switch

Common

Existing light

Outdoor wall light

Lampholder

At the light, connect the green-and-yellow-sleeved conductor wire to E or ⏚ (usually in the mounting) and red and black to the two terminals on the lampholder.

At the switch, connect both cables in the same way. The green-and-yellow-sleeved earth goes to the terminal in the mounting box. Connect one of the other two wires to COMMON, and the last to either L1 or L2.

manufacturer's instructions for the oven and the cleaner.

Remove the shelves and clean them with a soap-impregnated wire-wool pad. Clean the oven interior with detergent or washing soda in warm water, or a proprietary cleaner. If your oven has a vitreous-enamel lining, be sure to use a cleaner marked with a V symbol; this means that it is recommended by the Vitreous Enamel Development Council. Rub an inner glass door with a damp cloth dipped in bicarbonate of soda.

Badly stained ovens can be cleaned with a strong proprietary oven cleaner.

Self-cleaning ovens A special lining in self-cleaning ovens converts spattered grease into water and carbon dioxide when the oven is in use. Even so, heavier spills that drip onto the oven floor will have to be cleaned up: follow the manufacturer's instructions. Do not use abrasives or steel wool.

Cleaning a microwave Microwave ovens do not usually get as soiled as conventional ones – see MICROWAVE COOKING. Nonetheless, it is a good idea to wipe one regularly with mild detergent in water. Mop up spills at once.

If a microwave oven does get badly soiled, follow the manufacturer's instructions to clean it. Never use abrasives or steel wool to clean a microwave: scratches could distort the microwave pattern.

Oven mitts

A simple way to make them

To make oven mitts, you need 610mm (2ft) of 910mm (3ft) wide washable, thick fabric such as twill or some other very close weave; a piece of thick polyester wadding, measuring 360 × 400mm (14 × 16in); 2.5m (2¾ yds) of 25mm (1in) wide twill tape and thread to match the fabric.

Cutting out First make paper patterns, using tissue or greaseproof paper. Cut out two strips of paper measuring 840 × 150mm (33 × 6in) with rounded ends. These are the patterns for the insides of the mitts and the strip between.

Cut out two pieces measuring 180 × 150mm (7 × 6in), each with one rounded end to match the rounded ends of the long strips. These are the patterns for the insulated palms and the outside parts of the mitts.

Pin the two long patterns and the two smaller ones to the fabric and cut the patterns out in the fabric. Unpin the fabric, then use the smaller patterns to cut out four pieces of wadding.

Sewing together Place the long strips of fabric with the wrong sides together.

OVEN MITTS

How to make a pair

Insulating wadding · Glove palm piece · Glove fabric · Tape loop · Machine-stitch · Twill tape · Tacking

Place two layers of insulating wadding between two pieces of glove fabric, one at each end. Tack and then sew them in place. Sew tape to the straight edge of each glove piece. Tack the glove pieces in place at each end of the fabric, right side up. Sew tape all around.

Put two pieces of wadding between each end of the strips of fabric to make the insulated palms. Tack the fabric and wadding in place (see SEWING), then stitch through both layers of fabric and the sandwiched wadding across the straight edge of the palms.

Take the two smaller pieces of fabric. Fold the twill tape in half over the straight edge of each. Sew the tape to the fabric.

Lay the smaller pieces wrong side down in position at the ends of the long strips and tack in place. Fold some twill tape in half, then starting at the centre of one of the long edges of the long strips, stitch it in place all round the mitts. Make a loop in the middle with a piece of twill tape to hang them.

Overdraft

How to obtain and use one

An overdraft is a cheap and flexible way of borrowing money for short periods. It is an arrangement with your bank (see BANK ACCOUNTS), which gives you the option of drawing more money on your current account than you have in it – up to a limit agreed between you and your bank manager.

If you need money for a specific purpose (to buy furniture, for example) rather than for general expenses, it is usually cheaper to arrange a bank loan, or to use a credit card provided that you

can pay off the amount within a short period to minimise interest charges.

You will also have to pay a service charge for every cheque and cash withdrawal, and an arrangement fee, and interest is charged each day on the amount you are overdrawn. If you do not use the overdraft facility, you will not pay any interest or service charges.

Approaching the bank Anyone with a bank account can ask his bank manager for an overdraft. The manager will ask what the loan is for and how you plan to repay it. If it is for a large amount, he may ask for some kind of security – national savings or unit trust certificates, for example, or a deposit of share certificates.

If he agrees to give you an overdraft, he will set a date by which you must repay it.

Exceeding the limit Do not go beyond your overdraft limit. If you do, the bank has the right to return your cheques and withdraw the overdraft facility – though your manager will usually send a warning letter before doing so. If you need more money than you can get with your present overdraft limit, ask for a higher one or investigate alternative ways of borrowing money – see CREDIT AND CREDIT CARDS.

You are not entitled to any tax relief on interest you pay on an overdraft – unless it is for a business that you run – see also INCOME TAX RETURNS.

Overheating engine

Finding the cause, and getting moving again

The most common causes of engine overheating are a broken fan belt or a leaking water hose. Always carry a spare fan belt and a hose bandage in the car. Hose bandage – tape made of partially vulcanised rubber – is sold by car accessory shops. In an emergency, a temporary fan belt can be improvised with a length of rope, strong string or a nylon stocking, wound round the crankshaft pulley and fan pulley and secured with a slip knot – see KNOTS.

Changing or adjusting a fan belt If the belt is slipping – recognised by a squeal when the engine is revved - adjust the tension so that at the longest run of the belt it can be deflected by 6-13mm (¼-½in) under moderate thumb pressure. If the belt is still slack when the adjustment has been made to its limit, replace the belt with a new one.

To fit a new belt, slacken the pivot bolt and adjuster, push the generator towards the engine as far as it will go, and remove the old belt. Loop the belt

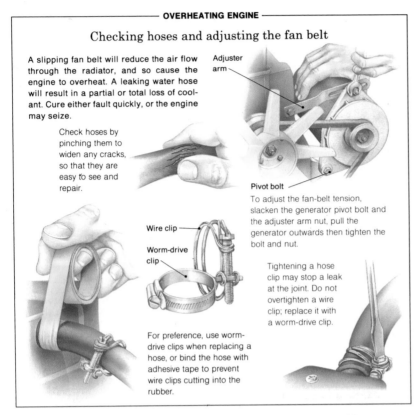

Checking hoses and adjusting the fan belt

A slipping fan belt will reduce the air flow through the radiator, and so cause the engine to overheat. A leaking water hose will result in a partial or total loss of coolant. Cure either fault quickly, or the engine may seize.

Check hoses by pinching them to widen any cracks, so that they are easy to see and repair.

Adjuster arm

Pivot bolt

To adjust the fan-belt tension, slacken the generator pivot bolt and the adjuster arm nut, pull the generator outwards then tighten the bolt and nut.

Wire clip

Worm-drive clip

Tightening a hose clip may stop a leak at the joint. Do not overtighten a wire clip; replace it with a worm-drive clip.

For preference, use worm-drive clips when replacing a hose, or bind the hose with adhesive tape to prevent wire clips cutting into the rubber.

into the bottom pulley, making sure it sits well into the groove, loop it over the waterpump pulley and feed it onto the generator pulley.

Turning the fan blades (if fitted) with one hand while pressing the belt into the pulley with the thumb of the other hand will help to ease the belt into place. Do not try to lever it on with a screwdriver – you may damage the belt or pulley. Adjust the tension as described above. Recheck the adjustment after 100 miles.

Hose leaks A leak at the end of a hose, where it connects to the engine or radiator, can usually be stopped by tightening the hose clip. Or the hose may be long enough to trim off the end with a sharp knife and make a fresh connection. Replace the hose as soon as possible.

To mend a split hose, clean the area around the split and wrap hose bandage tightly around it. Clear adhesive tape, insulating tape or adhesive vinyl tape will make an alternative, though less effective, temporary repair.

Radiator leak It may be possible to stem a small leak from the core with chewing gum, then drive slowly to the nearest garage. Or there are proprietary sealing compounds, available from garages and car`accessory shops, which you simply pour into the radiator when it has cooled enough to remove the cap. Never remove

the cap when the radiator is hot; scalding coolant will spurt out under pressure. Let the engine cool before opening the filler cap. Ease the cap off gently, holding it with rag or newspaper and stopping at the first position to ease the pressure. Drive with the filler cap off, as pressure in the system will damage the repair. Turn on the car heater, which will help to keep the water cool by dissipating heat into the car, and keep a close watch on the temperature gauge or warning light. Stop and let the engine cool off whenever it begins to overheat.

Other overheating causes If the top radiator hose is cold and the bottom one warm, the thermostat is stuck in the closed position. As an emergency measure the car can be driven a short distance with the thermostat removed – see THERMOSTATS IN CARS. Remove the bolts holding the thermostat housing (the top hose usually connects directly to it), take out the thermostat and refit the housing.

If the car has an electric fan, this may not be cutting in. Bridge the two wires at the radiator switch with a jump lead, or connect a wire from the battery positive terminal to the fan motor terminal, so that the fan runs continuously until you can get to a garage.

Getting on the move Any temporary repair must be made permanent as soon

as possible, so head for the nearest garage. If you have lost a lot of water, top up the radiator if you can – you may be able to get water from a nearby house, or even from a stream or pond. Alternatively, use water from the windscreen-washer reservoir.

Oysters

Opening, serving raw and cooking them

To open an oyster, grasp it firmly in a thick towel, with the flat shell up. Hold it over a bowl to catch any juice that may spill out. Insert the tip of an oyster knife – or a knife with a short, strong blade – into the point of the crack between the upper and lower shells.

Twist the knife hard to prise the shells open, then cut the muscle holding the oyster to the flat upper shell. Discard the flat shell, leaving the oyster lying in its juice in the rounded lower shell; add any spilt juice. Discard also any oyster that is already open, or not tightly closed – it will be dead or diseased.

Place oysters in their half-shells on a bed of cracked ice. Season them with salt and pepper, and serve with lemon wedges and thin slices of brown bread and butter. A little Tabasco sauce may be shaken on if desired. Traditionally, oysters are served with stout or a dry white wine such as Chablis or Muscadet.

One way to serve oysters cooked is to place them under a hot grill for 3 or 4 minutes (see GRILLING), then top them with a little cream and grated cheese. Oysters are usually eaten by the half-dozen or the dozen.

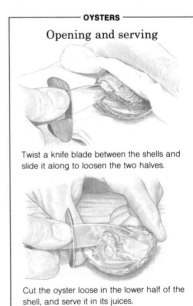

Opening and serving

Twist a knife blade between the shells and slide it along to loosen the two halves.

Cut the oyster loose in the lower half of the shell, and serve it in its juices.

Packing

*Keeping your clothes crease-free
and travelling light*

Unless you are going on a cruise, it is best to travel light. When flying, limit your cabin LUGGAGE to a shoulder bag or briefcase and a flight bag that will fit under the seat; the sum of its length, width and height must not exceed 1.15m (45in) and it must not weigh more than 5kg (11lb).

Keep with you essential toiletries and medicines, travel documents and valuables – plus, perhaps, a partial change of clothes, in case of delay.

Packing clothes in a garment bag, which you can hang up on arrival, helps to avoid creasing.

Packing a suitcase Choose a suitcase of suitable size; an overpacked case will result in creased clothes; in an underfilled case the clothes will shift about.

Place tissue paper in the shoulders and sleeves of dresses and jackets. Lay trousers flat, with the creases aligned; fold up the legs about 150mm (6in) below the knee, then again above the knee.

Fold the sides of a flared skirt inwards to form a rectangle; fold a skirt in half and a dress in thirds, with the first fold just above the waist and the second well below it.

A useful alternative for a skirt is to roll it into a sausage and pull it into an old stocking with the foot cut off – the skirt will not crease.

Layer clothes in the following sequence: shoes and other heavy items along the bottom; trousers; heavy dresses and skirts; jackets; shirts, ties, light dresses and sweaters; and lingerie on top. Tuck socks (if they are not in shoes), tights and underwear in crannies.

Pour shampoo and other liquids into leak-proof plastic bottles; fill them no more than three-quarters full, wrap them in small polythene bags and pack them in a vanity case. Use a plastic or rubber-lined toilet bag for your toiletries.

Remember that matches and lighters are prohibited in an aircraft baggage hold.

Labelling Replace all old destination tags and labels with new ones for your journey – typed, or written clearly in ink that will not smudge. As an extra precaution, tie or tape a label or card inside each case, giving your name, home address and phone number.

QUICK TIP If you mark your luggage with a distinctive label or tag, or with coloured tape, that will enable you to recognise and reclaim it quickly in the baggage claim area.

Padlocks

Choosing the right type for the job

A padlock is a detachable lock with a pivoted loop (shackle), usually fitted to a hasp-and-staple fastener. The strength of the hasp and staple is important: if the staple can be cut with a hacksaw or bolt cutters, the padlock is useless.

Padlocks vary tremendously in price and quality. Decide whether you want one mainly as a deterrent or whether you want a strong one to prevent entry into a garage or workshop.

Simple deterrent Choose either a lever-mechanism or combination-type padlock. A lever type is key-operated, and the more levers the better, because the lock is harder to pick without a key. The padlock may be automatic (snapped shut without the key) or non-automatic – needing the key to both lock and unlock it. For outdoor use choose a rustproofed model with sliding cover over the keyhole to keep out water.

A combination padlock has no key, but is opened and shut by using revolving tumblers, a dial, or a series of levers to set a particular combination of numbers.

High security Choose the padlock, hasp and staple together. The hasp should have no fixing screws visible when closed and should be held by bolts passing right through a door so that it cannot be levered off.

Make sure the padlock is close-shackled – fitting tightly in the staple so there is no room for inserting a jemmy; also that the shackle is hardened steel to resist the use of a hacksaw or bolt cutters. Look for a padlock with raised shoulders on a body machined from solid metal or one which has a case either welded and seamless or made up of laminated sheets. Choose a lock mechanism which has pins instead of levers, and with from four to six pairs of pins. This type of lock is harder to pick than the lever type.

Cycles and motorcycles Padlocks may have an extended, hardened shackle that fits through the spokes and round the fork, or be a cylinder lock incorporated in a very strong twisted steel cable with vinyl sheathing. Or you can buy a welded-link steel chain sheathed in plastic, with loops to take a high-security padlock. See also MOTORCYCLES.

If you are uncertain about which high-security padlocks and hasps to choose, consult a locksmith or your local Crime Prevention Officer.

Paintbrushes, pads and rollers

Choosing, using and cleaning

Brushes are suitable for painting a wide range of surfaces. Pads and rollers make covering large surfaces easier.

Paintbrushes The best types are still those made with Chinese hog bristle. Cheaper brushes may have bristle mixtures or synthetic bristles.

A fine finish depends on using a good brush. The better, more costly brushes are those with the densest bristles – the more bristles, the more paint the brush holds. Most new brushes will lose a few bristles, but if the brush is cheap and the bristles badly anchored, they are more likely to come out in clumps.

The most useful brushes are 13mm ($\frac{1}{2}$in), 25mm (1in), 50mm (2in) and 75mm (3in) wide for general painting work. Relate the width of the brush to the size of the surface. Other useful brushes are:

Wall brush This is 100mm (4in) or 125mm (5in) wide, for painting walls and ceilings – see PAINTING INTERIORS.

Cutting-in brush The bristles of this 19mm ($\frac{3}{4}$in) wide brush are cut at an angle for painting neatly against an edge such as glass in a window frame.

Paste brush It should be at least 100mm (4in) wide for pasting wallcoverings.

Paperhanging brush About 250mm (10in) or more wide, this is for smoothing on wallpaper – see WALLPAPERING.

Exterior wall brush It should be at least 125mm (5in) wide, for masonry paint and emulsion – see PAINTING EXTERIORS.

Creosote brush Keep this coarse-bristled brush, which should be at least 125mm (5in) wide, solely for applying WOOD PRESERVATIVES.

Using a paintbrush It is best to work from paint poured into a container with a handle. If the brush picks up something that contaminates the paint, the whole tin will not be affected. Dip only about one-third of the bristle length in the paint, and wipe off any surplus against the side of the container.

Brush paint down the length of the surface first, then across the width and finally down the length. Keep adjoining edges wet when covering a large area. Do not go back over paint that is drying.

When using normal gloss paint, spread it thinly to avoid drips and runs; apply two or three thin coats rather than one heavy one. If you are using one-coat non-drip paint (see PAINTS), load the brush heavily and spread a thick coat in horizontal bands, avoiding overbrushing.

Cleaning brushes There is no need to clean a brush if you have to stop work for only an hour or two – load it with paint and wrap it in kitchen foil.

A brush can be left loaded with paint overnight if the bristles are immersed in water to exclude air. Use a jam jar and suspend the brush on a piece of stiff wire pushed through a hole in the handle and laid across the jar top. The bristles should not touch the bottom or they will bend out of shape. Never leave a brush soaking in water for a long time. This rusts the ferrule and swells the bristles.

As soon as work is finished brush out excess paint on newspaper, then immerse the bristles in white spirit or proprietary brush cleaner. A brush used with cellulose or other special paints may need cellulose or other thinners to clean it; check the instructions on the paint tin.

Wash off the white spirit or brush cleaner in warm soapy water, then rinse in clean cold water. If you used emulsion paint, just wash the brush in warm soapy water, then rinse it.

After cleaning a brush, shake off as much water as possible, slip an elastic band loosely over the tip of the bristles to keep them in shape, and leave it somewhere clean and warm to dry.

Paint pads A pad consists of a fine layer of mohair stuck to a block of foam fixed to some form of handle. It is designed to apply a thin coat of paint quickly and without mess and is ideal for smooth surfaces. However, it can also be used on certain textured wallcoverings such as Anaglypta paper or foamed vinyl. It is not suitable for covering deep or rough surfaces such as textured compounds (see TEXTURED COATINGS), and is no good for exterior wall finishes.

Use a paint pad for water-based materials such as emulsion paint, which are easy to clean off. If you use an oil-based paint, the cleaner will tend to dissolve the adhesive holding the mohair to the foam.

Pads are available in a range of sizes from about 25mm (1in) up to 180mm (7in) wide.

Using and cleaning pads Work from a flat paint container. Dip the pad flat into the paint as deep as the mohair only. Do not overload it or it may drip. Apply the paint to the surface randomly but with strokes overlapping at some point.

Gently scrub the pad flat against the surface. Do not use too much pressure, or paint will be squeezed from the foam. Two or three coats may be necessary for a good covering.

As soon as work is finished, run the pad over newspaper to remove excess paint, and rinse it thoroughly. Leave to dry, then store it in a plastic bag to keep free from dust.

Paint rollers Most rollers are 180mm (7in) wide. Some have an integral handle and roller, others have a core to which a roller sleeve is fitted. Specially shaped rollers are available for getting into awkward places such as behind pipes and radiators.

The three main types of roller are: simulated mohair, foam and simulated sheepskin.

Simulated mohair This has a very fine, hard pile which is suited to smooth surfaces but not to textured surfaces. If used with gloss paint, cleaning may be difficult (see above). If necessary, try white spirit rather than proprietary paintbrush cleaner.

Foam rollers These give a reasonable finish on smooth and lightly textured surfaces, but they are more liable to spatter paint and they are not suitable for rough exterior work. Special textured foam sleeves are available for applying TEXTURED COATINGS (see also PAINTS) so that a pattern is produced as the surface is coated.

Foam rollers are best used with water-based paints, as some proprietary brush cleaners damage them. But if gloss paint is used, clean the roller thoroughly with white spirit.

Simulated sheepskin These very popular rollers are available with short pile for smooth surfaces, or medium or shaggy pile for exterior use. They are best used with water-based paint. Cleaning off gloss paint is difficult.

Using and cleaning a roller Work from a roller tray, filled about one-third full of paint. Dip the roller sleeve in the paint and run it along the tray to pick up the paint. Do not overload it or it will drip.

Apply the paint in two or three thin coats, rolling it steadily in all directions, but finish off in one main direction. Use a small paintbrush for cutting in.

Clean rollers as soon as work is finished. Run the roller over newspaper to remove excess paint (not twice over the same strip or you will pick paint up again). Then remove the sleeve, if possible, and wash it thoroughly.

Painting exteriors

Tackling outdoor walls, woodwork and metal

Because of the large areas involved, break the job down into manageable projects – such as one complete side at a time. Start with the side of the house that gets the most weathering, leaving a sheltered side to perhaps next year. The whole house need not be completed in one go.

Complete the preparation of the whole side first; piecemeal preparation spreads dirt onto newly decorated areas. The usual order for painting is high woodwork and metalwork, such as bargeboards and gutters, then walls, then downpipes, window frames and doors.

Protect any areas not being decorated such as tiled porches, windowsills and patios with dust sheets, preferably old, heavy cotton curtains, sheets or bedspreads.

Make sure you can safely reach the high areas. A ladder should extend at least three rungs above the work area, to give you a secure hold while painting, and should be firmly anchored – see LADDERS. If there is a lot of wall work, hire a SCAFFOLD TOWER kit from a local hire centre – see HIRING.

When working from a scaffold tower or ladder, paint only as much as you can reach without leaning forwards or sideways, then move it to a new position.

Tools and materials Apart from ladders, scaffolding and dust sheets, you will need a shave hook, a scraper, glasspaper, flexible sander or pumice stripping block, PAINT STRIPPING preparations, exterior-grade plaster and wood fillers, flexible sealant and cartridge gun, PUTTYING knife, paintbrushes (see PAINTBRUSHES, PADS AND ROLLERS), PAINTS, masking tape, perhaps a paint shield, a wire brush, safety spectacles, and an old paintbrush for dusting woodwork. You may also need wood hardener or a wood-repair system for rotten wood.

General preparation Where there are cracks and gaps between woodwork and masonry – such as between a window frame and a wall – rake out loose material and fill it with a flexible outdoor sealant applied with a cartridge gun – see SEALANTS. Sealant can be overpainted later – follow directions given on the container.

If there are small areas of wet rot, dig

out all soft wood with a chisel and apply a wood hardener to toughen up the remaining fibres, then fill with an epoxy-based wood filler. Or use a proprietary wood-repair system. If there are areas of DRY ROT, have the wood replaced.

New woodwork Examine new, unpainted woodwork for cracks and gaps, and fill them with an exterior-grade wood filler – see STOPPERS AND FILLERS. When dry, rub the whole of the wood with fine glasspaper, working only with the grain of the wood. Brush off dust with an old paintbrush.

Unless using microporous paint direct onto the bare wood, apply knotting fluid over any exposed knots, then coat with wood primer, undercoat, and two top coats. If you use a microporous paint, apply two coats.

With all types of paint, smooth over lightly with very fine glasspaper between coats to remove any small specks of dust embedded in the paint.

Painted woodwork For paintwork in good condition, wash with sugar soap, and rinse well. Smooth the surface lightly with a fine flexible sander or a pumice stripping block dipped in water, to provide a good key for the new paint.

Where there are only small areas of damaged paint, strip them down to bare wood and apply primer and undercoat before lightly rubbing down the whole surface.

Wipe the smooth surface clean with a lint-free cloth dampened with white spirit. When the surface is dry, apply new gloss paint over all the paintwork.

Metalwork Look for signs of RUST. On modern galvanised or alloy windows there should not be any, but on old iron or steel frames rust may be pushing the paint off.

Scrape back paint until all rusted areas are exposed, then use a wire brush and emery paper to remove all loose rust. Treat the exposed metal with a rust-inhibitor and metal primer or with cold galvanising paint before applying an undercoat and one or two coats of exterior gloss.

If the rust has made holes in the metal, clean off the rust and fill with an epoxy-resin filling compound before painting.

For other metal surfaces, remove loose rust and then paint with rust-inhibiting enamel paint.

Brick walls Never paint good-quality facing bricks – not only does paint spoil the appearance, but once applied it can never be removed. Clean bricks with a hard-bristled brush and water only – soap will stain them.

Examine rendered walls for cracks and gaps – see PEBBLEDASH; STUCCO WALLS. If the wall is discoloured with mould,

treat the affected area with a fungicidal wash – see EFFLORESCENCE. Leave for a week, then brush off any dead mould before applying a masonry primer or stabilising fluid.

If a rendered wall is being painted for the first time, coat it with stabilising fluid or masonry primer before applying exterior-grade masonry emulsion.

Paint the masonry in sections, starting from the top. Apply paint liberally. If it looks transparent after drying, give it a further coat.

Paint pebbledash and spar dash with a shaggy exterior-grade paint roller. However, a roller cannot reach corners so you need a paintbrush to get into them.

Painting interiors

Ceilings, walls, doors, windows and skirting boards

As far as possible, clear the room to be painted. Remove furniture, curtains and curtain rails and lift the carpet and underlay. Take down light fittings and shelves, and any other fitments that can be dismantled. If anything remains in the room, move it to the centre and cover it with dust sheets.

Cover the floor with old newspapers, but not near any part where you will be heat-stripping paint.

Apart from painting tools (see PAINTBRUSHES, PADS AND ROLLERS), you will need PAINT STRIPPING preparations, PAINTS, rag, masking tape, interior wood and plaster fillers (see STOPPERS AND FILLERS), a putty or flexible-bladed knife, a flexible SANDING block, safety spectacles, stepladders, and a simple scaffold (perhaps a box, a pair of steps and a scaffold board) to bring your head within 75mm (3in) of the ceiling.

Ceiling Tackle the ceiling before stripping paper from the walls.

If the ceiling is in good condition wash it thoroughly with sugar soap, then rinse well. Washing is particularly necessary in a kitchen, where there will be grease deposits from cooking (see also DISTEMPER REMOVAL). It is traditional to paint a coving as part of the ceiling, using the same paint, but if the ceiling is to be coloured you may prefer to paint the coving white.

When the ceiling is dry, repaint it. Work in strips parallel with the main source of light, starting near the light. Apply two thin coats of paint rather than one thick one – especially when painting a textured surface. See also TEXTURED COATINGS.

Alternatively strip and repaper the ceiling if necessary – see WALLPAPERING; WALLPAPER REMOVAL.

Walls Wash walls to be repainted with

sugar soap (see WASHING WALLS), then rinse with cold water. Do not use sugar soap on embossed paper such as Anaglypta (which is designed to be painted) – clean it with a soapy sponge or cloth before repainting.

Overpainting old patterned wallpaper is not advisable, but if you want to try, test a small hidden area first. The paper may expand and bubble, but if it dries smooth go ahead. However, any metallic colours in the pattern, may bleed through the paint; if so, strip the paper.

Paint walls before painting woodwork such as windows, doors and skirting boards. But if you are going to paper the walls, paint the woodwork first.

After stripping, you can paint straight onto plaster that is in good condition. Prime it with a coat made up of half emulsion paint and half water, then paint on two full coats of emulsion. Work down the wall in strips, starting from the top.

If the plaster has hairline cracks or other minor blemishes, either fill them with a suitable filler, or cover the wall with lining paper before painting.

Woodwork Remove fittings such as door handles, escutcheon plates and window stays and catches whenever possible before painting. They should not be painted, and it is hard to paint round them. If you have to paint round them, mask their edges with strips of masking tape, and remove it while the paint is still wet.

If the existing paintwork is in good condition, wash it with sugar soap dissolved in water, then rinse with cold water. Rub down the surface with a flexible sanding pad or stripping block dampened with water, then rinse again. This will remove both grime and glaze to give a good surface for repainting with a top coat. Use an undercoat first if the colour is being changed.

If the paintwork is in poor condition, strip all the old paint back to the bare wood. Fill any cracks with interior wood filler and rub smooth with abrasive paper. Wipe clean, then repaint with a primer, undercoat and top coat. Where only small areas of paint are damaged, strip the damaged area only then apply primer and top coat; smooth off the rim round the stripped area with fine glasspaper. Rub down all the paintwork and wipe it clean before applying the top coat. For new, bare wood apply knotting fluid to any visible knots. Smooth the wood with fine glasspaper. Apply primer, undercoat and top coat.

Wooden window frames Prepare the woodwork as described above. If the paintwork is in good condition but has become so thick from repainting that the windows will not close properly, strip the meeting edges back to bare wood for repainting.

Before painting, mask the glass with

How to paint doors

Flush door Paint the door in square sections as numbered, starting from the top and linking each section before the edges dry. Brush up and down, then across, and up and down again, finishing on an upward stroke. When the paint is dry, paint the door frame.

Panelled door Starting on the top hinge-side panel, proceed as numbered. Work on each panel in the same way as you would paint the squares on a flush door. Paint the crosspieces from top to bottom, then the hinge-side upright and then the lock-side upright. Again, paint the door frame last.

---

masking tape, positioning it about 2mm ($^1/_{16}$in) from the frame so that when you paint, a fine strip of paint left on the glass keeps moisture out of the frame and prevents it from rotting.

The best order for painting casement window frames is: crossbars and rebates, top and bottom cross-rails, hanging stile and hinge edge, meeting stiles and outer frame. The best order for painting sash window frames is: meeting rail, vertical bars (as far as possible for each with the window open each way), inner bottom sash cavity, lower runners, cross-rails, upper sash cavity and outer frame.

Metal window frames Check for signs of RUST. If you find some, scrape off the paint to expose every trace of it. Remove loose rust with emery paper or a wire brush, then treat any remaining rust and corrosion with either a rust inhibitor or cold-galvanising paint (see PAINTS), which neutralises rust and acts as a primer.

Paint bare metal with a metal primer before a top coat. No undercoat is needed unless the colour is being changed.

If the windows are hard to close, strip off the paint on the meeting edges, then prime and repaint them.

Doors Prepare the woodwork as described above; paint as illustrated. For a flush door, use a paintbrush about 75mm (3in) wide.

Skirting boards Prepare the woodwork as described above. Slide a piece of cardboard under the bottom of the skirting to avoid picking up dust.

Painting problems

The right way to deal with them

Problems arising are mostly faults in painting rather than in paint. Here are some causes and remedies:

Paint will not dry The usual cause is a greasy or dirty surface. Strip the paint back to a bare surface. If needed, use an aluminium primer-sealer (see PAINTS), then repaint – see PAINTING INTERIORS.

Flaking off The paint is on an unsuitable surface, such as emulsion over distemper, or gloss on a glazed surface. Or the wood is rotting. Strip paint and deal with the surface (see DISTEMPER REMOVAL; PAINT STRIPPING) before repainting.

Wrinkles or crazing An orange-peel effect can be caused when gloss is applied before the undercoat is dry – or because paints are incompatible. Strip and start again. For a small area, wait until paint has dried hard, then smooth with wet-and-dry abrasive paper dampened with water. Repaint with gloss.

Flies and gnats If small insects settle on the paint while it is drying, wait until the paint is hard – about a week – then brush them off.

Runs and sags Too much paint has been applied. Wait until hard – this may take some weeks – then rub smooth with fine dampened wet-and-dry abrasive paper. Wipe clean and apply a new top coat.

Cracks forming Usually caused by

wood opening up into cracks that are too wide for the elasticity of the paint to cope with. It often occurs on oak, which has an open-grained surface. Strip down the paint to bare wood and fill the cracks with an epoxy-based wood filler – see STOPPERS AND FILLERS. Smooth when set, then repaint.

Blisters Paint is pushed up into blisters when the sun's heat expands air or water trapped underneath. If the blister is dry, air has been trapped in a surface crack. If it is wet, the timber is damp.

If the damage is very local, rub off the paint and fill any cracks with an epoxy-based wood filler. If damp is present, dry with a hot-air blowtorch. Cover with primer and undercoat and rub smooth, then touch up with gloss.

One way to avoid blistering is to use a microporous paint, which allows the wood to breathe.

Dull glaze This is usually caused by applying gloss paint to unprimed wood. The gloss soaks into the wood, leaving a matt surface. Strip the paint back to bare wood and apply a primer and undercoat before repainting with gloss paint.

Stains These occur most often on emulsion paint and are caused by impurities in the plaster bleeding through the paint. A ceiling may show stains after a burst pipe in the loft, or if a loft has been coated with too much wood preservative, which seeps through the ceiling.

Strip off the emulsion paint and treat the stained area with an aluminium primer-sealer. When it dries, repaint.

Dark stains on painted wood The cause is probably resin from unsealed knots. Expose the knot using fine abrasive paper and seal with knotting fluid. When it is dry, repaint the area.

Mould See MILDEW AND MOULD.

Show-through When an under-colour can be seen just showing through a new top coat (sometimes described as grinning), the cause is failure to obliterate the old colour with an undercoat. More than one undercoat may be necessary – never rely on a gloss coat, which has little actual covering power.

Wait until the gloss is hard, then rub it down with wet-and-dry abrasive dampened with water. Wipe the area clean and apply an undercoat, then gloss paint once the colour is hidden.

Bitty surface A gloss surface may be spoilt by impurities such as bits of skin, paint, or fluff carried by the brush.

Wait until the surface is dry, then rub spoilt areas smooth with wet-and-dry abrasive paper used wet. Wipe the area clean with a lint-free rag moistened with white spirit, then repaint using a clean brush and uncontaminated gloss paint.

QUICK TIP If the paint you want to use is dirty, stretch a piece of clean nylon stocking over a paint kettle and strain the paint through it. Repaint using the paint from the kettle.

Paints

Choosing the right type for the job

There are many types of paint, each suitable for a particular job or range of jobs. A good result depends on choosing the right one for each job. Here are the commonest types:

Knotting A varnish high in shellac, used to coat bare knots in wood to seal in the resin. Otherwise knots can bleed (exude resin) and ruin a painted surface.

Primer A paint coating used to seal a porous surface or to grip on smooth metal. There are separate wood, metal and plaster primers, or you can buy an all-purpose primer to suit any surface. A primer-sealer contains fine scales of aluminium and forms a barrier over surfaces with coatings likely to seep through new paint – such as stains, preservatives or old bituminous coatings.

Cold galvanising paint This has a high zinc content and prevents further rusting when applied to rusted metal after loose and flaking rust has been removed.

Undercoat Use this paint to cover a primer before applying gloss paint. It has a high pigment content, so is good at hiding any colour showing through the priming coat. Use the undercoat recommended on the tin of gloss paint.

Top coat Top coats have a low pigment content but are high in varnish. They will not obliterate under-colours but give good surface protection, and are available in a gloss, satin or eggshell finish. For the best protection, apply at least two coats of gloss.

One-coat paint A jelly-like non-drip paint that is a combined undercoat and top coat. It is not stirred before use, and is laid on more thickly than separate coats. Even so, you may need two coats to obliterate another colour.

Enamel paint This gloss paint, which is usually expensive, has pigments finely ground to give a very high glaze. It can be used on bare wood or metal without primer or undercoat.
 Some enamels will inhibit rust and are useful for decorating metal garden furniture or wrought-iron work.

Microporous (acrylic) paint Designed to be painted directly onto bare wood, this water-based paint will allow timber to breathe but will keep out damp, and does not easily flake or blister with weathering. The paint is quick-drying and the finish gives a sheen rather than a high gloss. However, it will lose these advantages if put on top of existing paint.

Emulsion paint A quick-drying water-based paint, emulsion is used on walls and ceilings. Prime with a coat diluted with equal quantities of water. No undercoat is necessary, but more than one coat of emulsion may be needed.

Masonry paint Use masonry paint on rendered exterior walls. Most types have an additive such as mica flakes, nylon fibres, or sand – which improves weathering properties and fills minor cracks in a rendered surface.

Bituminous paint This is for waterproofing metal surfaces such as outside pipes and guttering. It is generally black. Other paints cannot be used on top. Clean brushes with paraffin.

Heat-resisting paint Surfaces such as stove pipes and radiators, which get hot enough to ruin other paints, can be painted with this.

Anti-condensation paint This emulsion paint absorbs moisture when air is heavy with water vapour, then breathes it out as the air becomes drier, so no water drops form on the surface. Useful in kitchens and bathrooms where CONDENSATION is a problem.

Textured (plastic) coating A very thick compound, generally applied with a shaggy or textured foam roller (see PAINTBRUSHES, PADS AND ROLLERS), for use on outside or inside walls and ceilings with uneven or cracked surfaces – see TEXTURED COATINGS.

QUICK TIP Get the primer, undercoat and top coat from the same maker to ensure that the paints will be compatible.

Paint stripping

Preparing for repainting or a new finish

If paintwork is in good condition, do not strip it unless a build-up of paint layers is making doors and windows difficult to open and close. Rub down the existing paintwork just enough to provide a key for new paint and wash it with warm water containing sugar soap. But if paint is in poor condition and needs stripping, there is a choice of methods:

Dry stripping Some surfaces – particularly rounded ones such as banisters – can be stripped dry, using a scraper with a very sharp blade to reveal bare wood or metal. Wear safety spectacles to protect your eyes from flying paint. If the paint is very old wear a gauze mask to keep the dust out of your lungs. The particles may contain harmful lead.
 Angle the scraper blade until you feel it bite into the surface, then draw the scraper towards you applying steady pressure. Take care not to damage wood, and sharpen or replace the blade as it becomes blunt.

Chemical stripping There are two types of chemical stripper – liquid and paste.
 Certain timbers are affected by chemical strippers, so test to see if the wood discolours. If different woods have been used in the construction, bleaching and recolouring may be necessary after stripping – see BLEACHING WOOD; STAINING WOOD.

PAINT STRIPPING

Two techniques to soften up

Heat stripping Keep a hot-air blowtorch moving to avoid scorching wood or cracking plaster; move it ahead of the scraper.

Chemical stripping Brush the stripper on thickly, then wait until paint has crinkled and broken up. Do not scrape too soon.

More than one coat of stripper may be necessary to get rid of several paint layers. Protect your eyes with goggles and hands with rubber gloves. Wash any stripper off your skin immediately.

Paste stripper resembles cold porridge, and is useful on carved or moulded surfaces. Trowel on a layer about 3mm ($\frac{1}{8}$in) thick, and leave it to dry. Then lift off the stripper, and old paint, with a scraper. If the paint is stubborn and the stripper seems to dry out too quickly, lay polythene sheeting over the wet stripper to hold in the solvents. This will increase the effectiveness of the chemicals.

All chemical strippers need neutralising before new paint is applied. Check on the pack or can for details.

Heat stripping An electric-powered hot-air stripper can be used to soften paint. Nozzle attachments are available – such as deflectors to shield glass, because the heat can crack windows, especially in cold weather. Hold the stripper as near as 50mm (2in) from the surface. When the paint starts to bubble, remove it with a scraper or shave hook.

QUICK TIPS When using a hot-air stripper, do not spread newspaper to protect the floor, in case any paint shavings catch fire and fall. Keep a bucket of water handy in which to drop burning or smouldering paint. Use a scraper at an angle, so hot paint cannot drop onto your hand, and wear old gloves. See also BLOWTORCHES.

Watch for nests in eaves, or for rotten timber, which could be set alight.

Paint touch ups

Dealing with chips and scratches on your car

Exposed metal rusts very quickly. Repair chips or scratches in car bodywork – often caused by small stones thrown up from the road – with touch-in paint of the correct colour as soon as possible. Use touch-in paint straight onto newly damaged paint, but if bare metal is exposed, a priming coat and RUST treatment is necessary.

Scrape off loose flakes of paint and any rust with a knife, and clean the area with white spirit on a soft cloth or tissue to remove grease or wax polish.

Treat surface rust with either a proprietary rust remover or a rust-neutralising primer that combines with the rust to form an undercoat. Make sure the rust-neutralising primer is suitable for use with cellulose paint, and follow the maker's instructions carefully. If you use a rust remover, coat the damaged area with cellulose metal primer before applying touch-in paint.

Stir touch-in paint with a piece of clean wire before you use it, to blend the colour evenly. A brush is supplied with the can, but it is better to use an artist's watercolour brush. Brush the paint on evenly, not too thickly, with as few strokes as possible, and overlap the existing paint by about 6mm ($\frac{1}{4}$in) all round. Leave it to dry, then apply a second coat.

Wait at least 24 hours before polishing the area gently with a mild cutting compound to blend in the new paintwork.

See also DENTS IN CARS; SPRAY PAINTING.

Pancakes

Making them and tossing them

Pancakes form the basis of many sweet and savoury dishes, from the traditional lemon pancakes of Shrove Tuesday to exotic CRÊPES SUZETTE. The secret of success lies in the batter, which should be like thin cream.

Ingredients (for 8-10 pancakes)
115g (4oz) of flour, plain or self-raising
Pinch of salt
1 egg
285ml ($\frac{1}{2}$ pint) milk

Making the batter Sift the flour and salt into a large bowl. Using a wooden spoon, make a hollow in the centre of the flour. Beat the egg lightly and drop it into the hollow. Slowly pour half the milk into the hollow, using the spoon to work the liquid into the flour. Then beat the mixture with the spoon, a whisk or a rotary beater until it is smooth and free of lumps. Let it stand for a few minutes. Add the rest of the milk, beating all the time until the mixture is bubbly and the consistency of single cream.

Cooking and tossing Use a heavy-based frying pan that measures about 180mm (7in) across the base; it should be shallow, with sloping sides. Cover a large plate with cooking foil, set it over a saucepan of boiling water, and stack each pancake on it as it is cooked. Keep the pancakes covered with a clean teacloth.

Grease the frying pan very lightly with butter or lard, and put it onto the ring at maximum heat. The pan must be really hot. Pour in just enough batter to form a thin film over the base of the pan, and tilt the pan to spread the mixture evenly. Use the first pancake or two to adjust the heat; it is right if the underside of the pancake becomes golden in 1 minute. Lift up a corner of the pancake with a spatula to check.

When the underside is golden, flip the pancake over with a palette knife or spatula, or toss it. To toss a pancake, lift the pan away from the stove; then flick your wrist so that the pan is thrust upwards and away from your body, starting the movement at about waist-level.

Cook for another minute then flip over again and slide out onto the plate.

Serving Lemon pancakes for desserts can be lightly sugared before stacking. Sprinkle caster sugar onto a sheet of greaseproof paper. As each pancake is cooked, put it on the sugared paper, dust the upperside with caster sugar and sprinkle with lemon juice. Fold it in half and then in half again, and stack until all the pancakes are ready. If you are adding a sweet or savoury filling, or storing the pancakes, do not fold them for stacking.

Pans burnt

Soaking off the black deposits

Burnt food stuck to the bottom of a saucepan or frying pan is best left to soak. Cover the blackened area with hot water and add salt, washing soda or biological washing powder. The amount to use depends on the extent of the burning. Try with about a dessertspoonful.

If the black deposits will not come off easily after soaking all night, put in fresh solution and bring it to the boil, then leave it to soak again. See also CLEANING AND POLISHING MATERIALS.

Paper aircraft

Folding your own aeroplane

Practise making simple darts before developing designs of your own. Use rectangular sheets of fairly stiff paper that can be folded easily – typing paper is suitable.

┌─ PAPER AIRCRAFT ─

Making your own model Concorde

Make a central crease along a rectangular sheet of paper. Fold the corners at one end to make two triangular flaps.

Fold each side over again, to the centre, so that two larger triangular flaps overlay the first.

Fold the sides to the centre a third time. Turn the paper over and fold in half. Open out the wings.

To make the dart fly straight, bend the back corners of the wings up slightly. To help it climb and loop, make two 13mm (½in) cuts at the back of each wing, and turn up the flaps they produce.

See also ORIGAMI.

Paper hats

A clown's hat and an Indian headdress

To brighten a children's party make colourful paper hats. You can make them before the party, or give guests the fun of making their own from cut-outs prepared in advance. As basic material, use large sheets of coloured semi-stiff card; large stationers sell them in sizes of about 510 × 610mm (20 × 24in). For sticking, use rolls of single-sided tape

Party hats Stick a feather in a circlet of corrugated cardboard to make an Indian headdress. For a clown's hat, cut a segment from a circular sheet of stiff paper to make a cone. Decorate with cut-out stars.

and double-sided tape. Have crayons and felt-tips and a supply of homemade baubles (ribbon curls, cut-out flowers or shapes, for example) for decorating the hats. Thin elastic or string cut to length can be used for chin-straps.

Paper logs

Making fuel from old newspapers

Paper logs cut down fuel costs, get rid of old newspapers, and are a good way of lighting a fire with the minimum of kindling. See also FIRELIGHTING. Use only newsprint, not glossy magazines, and make sure it is dry.

Use a large-format paper closed, but open out a small paper. Roll the whole paper tightly round a central rod such as a broomstick and bind it with strong string or adhesive tape. Then remove the rod to leave an airspace down the centre.

Experiment to find the right mix of paper and wood logs for your stove (see STOVES) or fireplace. Try laying a fire of two wood logs and one paper log. Not all wood-burning stoves will burn paper logs – check the maker's instructions.

Papier-mâché

Making things with paper and paste

Modelling with papier-mâché – mashed paper – is a simple craft requiring only old newspaper, glue and wallpaper paste. There are two methods – one uses paper strips, the other a mash of paper. They are applied over an *armature* – the base or skeleton for the model – which can be anything near to the shape of the model, such as a cardboard tube, a ball of kitchen foil or bent chicken wire.

For the strip method, tear newspaper into strips and soak them in wallpaper paste made of 1 part powder to 10 parts water. Do not use a powder containing fungicide. Allow several minutes for the paper to soak, then dip the strips in a mix of equal parts of PVA glue and water.

Apply the strips to the armature, overlapping each strip by about one-quarter of its width. Allow 12 hours for the layer to dry, then apply the next layer. Three layers is the minimum. Strips of paper towels make a good final layer if the model is to be painted.

The strip and mash methods can be combined to make a simple face mask.

PAPIER-MÂCHÉ

Making mash; using an armature

Make a mash by soaking pieces of paper in water overnight. Boil in a saucepan, stirring to make a pulp. Cool, strain off excess liquid, then stir in 2 tablespoons each of PVA glue and wallpaper paste.

Use galvanised wire of 1.6mm (¹⁄₁₆in) diameter to make the armature for this giraffe. The paper-strip method is used for the body (see text), with a last layer of paper towels.

Inflate a balloon for the armature, and half cover it with papier-mâché layers. Then add the features – eyebrows, nose, ears, mouth and chin – moulded from a mash (see illustration). Allow the mask to dry and deflate the balloon. Paint with a water-based paint.

See also MODELLING IN CLAY.

Parcel tying

Wrapping it securely

A parcel to go by post must be robust enough to withstand the journey. If the item is not conveniently rectangular, put it in a suitably sized box with crumpled paper to prevent it from moving, or wrap it in corrugated cardboard, with the corrugations inside.

Wrap the box or cardboard-covered item in brown paper, shiny side out, as for GIFT WRAPPING a rectangular parcel. Use extra-strong waterproof parcel tape to seal down the entire length of all flaps.

If you wish, use string instead of tape to secure the brown paper. Use good quality string, such as hemp or jute, and bind the parcel lengthways and across the width. Pull tight and finish off with a reef knot – see KNOTS.

Parquet flooring

Using wood mosaic panels to create a parquet effect

The thick blocks of a parquet floor should be laid by an expert, but a similar effect can be had by using wood mosaic panels. The panels range in size from 305mm (12in) square to 610mm (2ft) and are made up of strips of 10mm (⅜in) thick hardwood glued to a paper, felt or net backing. The panels are flexible, allowing for slight unevenness of the floor. If the floor is very uneven cover it with sheets of hardboard or, on a concrete floor, use a levelling compound – see UNEVEN FLOORS.

Laying the panels Two days before laying the panels, unwrap them and leave them in the room where they are to be laid. This will prevent expansion or contraction of the wood after laying.

To lay the panels, first set them out on the floor, leaving a wide border around the room for which tiles must be cut. Avoid leaving a narrow border as this will be difficult to cut. Where possible, arrange the layout so that the panels to be cut can be sliced between the wood strips. Allow a 13mm (½in) gap between the border and the wall or skirting board. This gap will allow for expansion and contraction; without it the new flooring could buckle.

Use the floor adhesive recommended

PARQUET FLOORING

Cutting wood mosaic panels to size

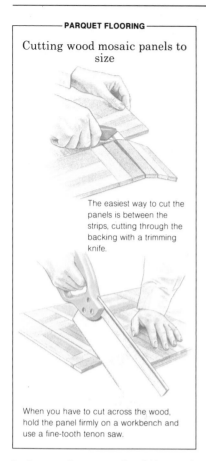

The easiest way to cut the panels is between the strips, cutting through the backing with a trimming knife.

When you have to cut across the wood, hold the panel firmly on a workbench and use a fine-tooth tenon saw.

by the manufacturer, and apply it according to the instructions. Lay the panels working outwards from the centre of the room, as for VINYL FLOOR COVERING.

When you have laid the floor, cover the gap round the edge with wood moulding (see MOULDINGS), or fill it with strips of cork tile.

Partitions

Building a timber-framed dividing wall

Use 75 × 50mm (3 × 2in) timber for the frame, which will consist of: a head plate which is attached to the ceiling; a sole plate, attached to the floor; the uprights, called studs; and horizontal bracing timbers, called noggins.

The head plate must be attached to ceiling JOISTS. If the partition is to run parallel to the joists, position it so that the head plate is directly under a joist. You can find the positions of joists by noting where the floorboards are nailed in the room above, or looking for them in the roof space above an upper room or using a metal detector to locate the lines of nails holding the ceiling plasterboard to the joists. If the head plate is to

be attached at right angles to the joists, measure between them, centre to centre, to determine the fixing points.

Saw the head and sole plates to length, and mark on them the positions of the studs, at 400mm (16in) centres. Mark the position of the head plate on the ceiling, and use a PLUMB LINE to find the positions for the end studs and the sole plate. Cut recesses in the skirtings (or, if more convenient, recess the end studs to accommodate the skirtings).

Fix the sole plate to the floor with woodscrews, making sure that the screws enter the floorboards, not pass between them. Use expanding BOLTS if the floor is concrete. Place the head plate in position, fixing it to the ceiling joists with woodscrews. Attach the end studs to the walls with expanding bolts or 100mm (4in) frame fixings, and use a spirit level to ensure they are vertical. If a wall is not true, pack gaps with pieces of hardboard.

Measure and cut each stud individually. Make them a tight fit between head and sole plate, position them as marked and use a plumb line or spirit level to ensure they are upright. Then skew-nail them (see NAILING) to the plates. Decide where you want the doorway to be, and leave out one stud at this point – to leave a gap of 810mm (32in). Measure the height of the doorway – the standard height of house doors is 1980mm (6ft 6in) – and cut a length of timber and nail it in to span the gap across the top of the doorway. Cut a short stud to fit centrally between the door head and the head plate and nail it in. Measure the width of the door (see DOORS) and nail softwood casings to the inside of the doorway to

obtain the required width. Attach 13mm × 25mm (½ × 1in) BATTENS on the sides and across the top of the doorway to provide a doorstop. Saw through and remove the sole plate at the base of the doorway.

Brace the studs with noggins, nailed midway between the sole plate and head plate, with extra ones to support wall-cupboards or pictures; use a spirit level to ensure they are horizontal. Cover both sides of the frame with 2.4 × 1.2m (8 × 4ft) sheets of PLASTERBOARD, using plasterboard nails at 150mm (6in) intervals and setting them in 13mm (½in) from the edge of the plasterboard.

Passport

Documents for travelling abroad

A passport establishes your identity and nationality when you are travelling abroad, and when you are seeking readmission to Britain after a spell overseas. British citizens are not legally obliged to have passports to leave this country. However, without one you may find yourself refused admission to other countries, and unable to buy airline or shipping company tickets.

There are two types of British passport:

Standard passports These are valid for ten years when issued to someone over the age of 16; for people under 16 at the time of issue, they are valid for five years, renewable for a further five years. Under an EC agreement, an EC passport is being introduced in all member-states.

PARTITIONS

Constructing a partition wall

This shows how a timber frame, lined with plasterboard, is used to partition a large room – see text. To improve sound insulation, lay 75mm (3in) sheets of glassfibre wool between the lining boards.

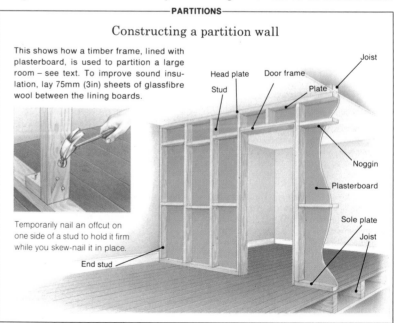

Temporarily nail an offcut on one side of a stud to hold it firm while you skew-nail it in place.

End stud

Head plate
Door frame
Joist
Stud
Plate
Noggin
Plasterboard
Sole plate
Joist

The EC passport for British subjects is gradually replacing British standard passports as those expire, and is similar to them in most respects.

British visitors' passports Valid for one year, they are intended only for holidaymakers going on trips of up to three months to certain countries that recognise them – the nations of western Europe, Bermuda, Turkey and Tunisia. They cost about half the price of standard passports, and can be obtained from post offices.

British excursion documents Valid or France only and for stays of up to 60 hours at a time.

Families On standard and British visitor's passports, the holder's wife or husband and children under 16 can be included at the time of issue, for an extra charge. The children of relatives may be entered, too. However, someone included on another's passport can travel only in the company of the passport holder.

How to apply Main post offices have application forms for both types of passport, and leaflets explaining how to fill in the forms. For a standard passport, you need a witness of professional standing who has known you for at least two years and is not a relative, for example, a JP, clergyman, lawyer, doctor, school teacher, to countersign the application, certifying the information you have given is correct.

With the standard passport application form, you must supply:
● Proof of British birth or citizenship (normally a birth certificate or naturalisation papers).
● If the name you are now using is different from the one you were born with, proof of the change – usually a marriage certificate.
● Two identical recent photographs (and two of your husband or wife, if included), taken full-face without a hat and measuring no more than 64 × 50mm (2½ × 2in) and no less than 50 × 38mm (2 × 1½in). One photograph must be signed on the back, stating that it is a true likeness, by the same person who countersigns your application.
● The fee.

For a visitor's passport, you must produce a birth certificate or other proof of nationality, proof of identity (such as a driving licence or bank card) and two identical photographs of each adult to be included; the photographs must measure 45 × 35mm (1¾ × 1⅜in) and be taken full face without a hat. You do not need a witness.

For a British excursion document, you need to show a birth or adoption certificate, a National Health Service medical card, or a pension book or pension card;

you must also provide a photograph of yourself. The application form and the photograph must be countersigned by a witness, in the same way as for a standard passport. Husbands and wives must have separate excursion documents; children who are under the age of 16 can be entered on the excursion document of a parent or guardian.

For British visitor's passports and excursion documents, hand in the completed form at a main post office. The passport or excursion document is issued on the spot.

For a standard passport, send or take the application and other documents to the regional passport office, as shown on the form. Applications normally take about two to four weeks to process. In an emergency, telephone the regional passport office; you may be able to obtain the passport in a few hours. See also VISA.

Pasta
Making it yourself and cooking it

This recipe will make enough flat pasta, such as fettucini or tagliatelle, to serve four to six people.

Ingredients
300g (11oz) strong bread-making flour
1 level teaspoon salt
3 large eggs
1 tablespoon olive oil

Sieve the flour and salt into a bowl, then make a well in the centre. Beat the eggs and oil together and pour into the well. Slowly draw the flour into the mixture with a knife, stirring well.

Mix until the egg and oil mixture is absorbed completely by the flour. If the dough is too sticky, add a little flour. If it is too dry, add a little water.

Knead the dough (see BREAD-MAKING) for about 15 minutes. Cover with a cloth and leave for an hour.

Using a heavy wooden rolling pin, roll out the dough on a well-floured surface to a paper-thin rectangle. Work quickly or the dough will become dry and unmanageable. When the dough is rolled out, drape it over a clean coathanger, until you are ready to cut it out.

Flour the dough lightly, then roll it up. To make fettucini, slice across the roll at 3mm (⅛in) intervals, so that it unrolls into thin strips; for tagliatelle, cut it into strips 6-13mm (¼-½in) wide. Shake out the strips and dry for an hour on a teacloth sprinkled with flour.

Cooking pasta Allow 75-115g (3-4oz) of pasta for each person. Bring to the boil plenty of water – at least 2.8 litres (5 pints) for every 450g (1lb) of pasta. Add 1 level teaspoon of salt and 1 teaspoon of oil for every 2.8 litres (5 pints) of water.

When the water is boiling rapidly, drop in the pasta. Stir the pasta well and then bring the water back to a rapid boil.

When it is firm to the bite (*al dente*) but cooked through, remove from the heat. Fresh pasta may take only 3 minutes or so to cook; dried pasta may take up to 12 minutes.

Pour the pasta into a colander and shake thoroughly. Transfer it to a hot serving dish and mix with a sauce – see SPAGHETTI. Eat as soon as possible.

Pastry
Getting it perfect every time

Keep everything as cool as possible when making pastry – or the fat will melt and the pastry become tough. If your hands are hot, hold them under cold water.

Shortcrust pastry This recipe makes 225g (8oz) of pastry (it is measured by its weight of flour), suitable for PIECRUSTS, TARTS and QUICHES.

Ingredients
225g (8oz) plain flour
½ teaspoon salt
50g (2oz) butter
50g (2oz) lard
2-3 tablespoons cold water

Sieve the flour and salt into a mixing bowl. Cut the butter and lard into small pieces and scatter over the flour.

Using just the tips of your fingers, rub the fat into the flour, lifting them up to keep them cool. Continue until the mixture looks like breadcrumbs.

Sprinkle the water over the mixture, a little at a time, then stir into the mixture with a round-bladed knife. Carry on stirring until the mixture forms a smooth dough that is not sticky.

Turn onto a floured surface. Knead lightly (see BREAD-MAKING) then cover for 20-30 minutes with the bowl.

Roll out the dough on a floured work surface, using a lightly floured rolling pin. Roll with light strokes in a forward direction. Lift the pin after each stroke. Turn the pastry regularly to roll it in a different direction. Do not roll the edges or you will roll out air pockets.

Puff pastry Recipes asking for 225g (8oz) of pastry are indicating the amount of flour in the pastry – unless they suggest using a pack of frozen puff pastry, which is marked with the total weight of flour and fat. Use the pastry for VOL-AU-VENTS, sausage rolls and jam puffs.

Ingredients
225g (8oz) strong white flour
150ml (¼ pint) iced water
1 teaspoon lemon juice
225g (8oz) unsalted butter in a block

Sieve the flour into a mixing bowl. Add the iced water and lemon juice, then mix using a knife with a round-ended blade, until the mixture forms a firm dough that is not hard.

Turn onto a lightly floured surface and knead for 5-10 minutes until smooth and silky. Wrap in a polythene bag and leave in the refrigerator for 15-20 minutes.

Place the butter between two layers of greaseproof paper or polythene. Beat with a rolling pin to make a rectangle about 19mm (¾in) thick. Smooth the top of the butter with the rolling pin. Roll out the dough (as shortcrust) to a rectangle about 25mm (1in) wider than the flattened block of butter is long, and about three times as long as the butter is wide.

Place the dough with a short side towards you and lay the butter across the centre. Fold the bottom third of dough over the butter, then fold the top third down over this. Press the open edges with the rolling pin to seal them.

Turn the dough so that a short side is facing you, then roll it out to its original size. Make sure the butter does not break through the surface. Fold up the bottom third, then fold down the top third of dough and seal the edges as before. Wrap and chill for 30 minutes.

Repeat the rolling, folding, sealing and chilling process five more times. After chilling the last time, roll out the pastry to the thickness you want, then leave it in a cool place for 10 minutes before cooking. Uncooked pastry can be kept in a fridge for 3 days, or in a freezer for 3 months.

Patching

Repairing large holes in fabrics

If a hole is too big to be darned, or is in a fabric that cannot be darned, it will need to be patched. Cut the patch as a rectangle from matching fabric, or an unseen part of the item being patched if possible; it should overlap the hole by 50mm (2in). Make sure any pattern on the patch matches the torn area.

Trim the edges of the hole to make it rectangular, and cut a diagonal snip about 6mm (¼in) long at each corner.

Lay the patch evenly over the hole, with its right side to the wrong side of the fabric. Pin and then tack the patch in position (see SEWING), turn the edges under about 6mm and slipstitch them to the fabric – see SLIPSTITCHING. Then remove the tacking.

Working from the right side of the fabric, turn under the edges of the hole about 6mm all round and slipstitch them to the patch.

QUICK TIP If the patch looks newer than the torn fabric, age it by soaking it in biological washing powder.

Patchwork

Making cushions or covers from scraps of material

Patchwork is made from small pieces of different-coloured fabric sewn together in a pattern. This forms the material for making items such as CUSHIONS or bedspreads. The pieces can be cut from scraps of fabric – see SEWING.

Commonly used shapes are squares, diamonds, triangles and hexagons. Plan the pattern on paper before you start, taking into account how much suitable fabric of each colour is available. Patches must be joined with the grain matched, or the patchwork will pucker.

To find the grain direction, run your finger along the cut edge of the fabric. If the direction is with the grain, the edge will be left smooth; if it is against the grain, the threads will pull apart and begin to fray.

Making fabric shapes Patches are formed round stiff paper cut to the required shape, and the paper is removed before the patchwork is lined. Metal templates can be bought for cutting out various shapes, or you can make your own from stiff cardboard. Make a solid template the same size as the finished patch, and a window template about 13mm (½in) bigger all round, with its centre cut-out the same size as the finished patch.

Use the solid template for cutting out the paper shapes for patch backings. Use the window template on the fabric to get the right part of the pattern within the frame and then cut round the outside. This allows for the turnover round the backing.

Place the paper shape centrally on the back of the cut out fabric patch, then fold the fabric over and tack-stitch it to the paper. Fold corners neatly.

Joining the patches Put two patches face to face and oversew them together along one edge, taking care not to stitch the paper backing. Use cotton to match the darkest colour.

When a number of patches are completely surrounded, remove the tacking threads and paper backing.

Once the patchwork is complete, press it and stitch a suitable lining material to the wrong side before making it into the required article.

Pâté

Making a savoury spread

Pâtés combine a meat or fish base with herbs and SPICES to make a savoury spread. Although some recipes require lengthy preparation, chicken liver pâté and kipper pâté are both simple and quick to make. Here are the recipes:

Ingredients (for 6)
450g (1lb) chicken livers
50g (2oz) butter
1 small onion, freshly chopped
2 bay leaves
Pinch of dried thyme
Salt and black pepper
2 tablespoons brandy

Clean, trim and chop the chicken livers. Melt the butter in a saucepan and fry the onion, bay leaves and thyme for 2-3 minutes. Add the chicken livers and cook over a low heat for 5 minutes. Take out the bay leaves and blend the mixture in a liquidiser. Season with salt and pepper and stir in the brandy.

Store the pâté in a jar in the refrigerator.

Ingredients (for 4)
2 boned kippers
1 tablespoon double cream
75-115g (3-4oz) softened butter
1 tablespoon lemon juice
Cayenne pepper
¼ teaspoon ground mace

Place the KIPPERS head down in a jug of boiling water for 5 minutes. Drain and skin the kippers and remove any small bones. Set aside to cool.

Use a wooden spoon to pound the kipper meat in a bowl until smooth. Add the cream, butter and lemon juice. Alternatively, give these four ingredients two ten-second bursts in a food processor. Season with cayenne and mace. Store in a jar in the refrigerator.

Patents

Protecting your invention

If you invent a new device or process, a patent will prevent other people from copying it for 20 years. During that time you alone will have the right to manufacture, use or exploit your invention commercially.

A patent can be obtained for almost anything, provided that it is new and not obviously developed from an existing invention. There are exceptions, however. You cannot patent an invention which has application to the Defence of the Realm, nor can you patent the discovery of a law of the universe that did not demand the intervention of men to bring it into creation. Similarly you cannot patent scientific theories, mathematical methods or new business methods. You can patent a new game, for example a board game such as Trivial Pursuit, but not new rules for a card game.

Applying for a patent To get a patent, you must file an application with the Patent Office, State House, 66-71 High

Holborn, London WC1R 4TP. Study their free information leaflets first; patents and patent agents are expensive. Applications must be made on special forms available from the Patent Office.

The most important part of the patent is the part known as *the claims*, where you state precisely what you are claiming as your own invention. Get a patent agent to help draw up the claims. If they are badly drawn up, someone may be able to copy the invention without infringing your patent.

To find a patent agent, contact the Chartered Institute of Patent Agents, Staple Inn Buildings, London WC1V 7PZ.

Keeping an invention under wraps Be careful not to publicise an invention before applying for a patent. To be granted a patent, an invention must be new according to patent law. If an invention has been shown in public or a description of it has been published before the application, it is deemed to be no longer new.

You can, however, show your invention to a potential manufacturer – so long as it is done in confidence.

When an invention is protected Exactly 18 months after an application is filed and before a patent is granted, an invention is published by the Patent Office. Provided the patent is subsequently granted, the invention is protected from the date of publication.

If, however, the invention is copied in the period between publication and the granting of the patent, the inventor will have to wait until the patent is granted before taking legal action. If, after all, the patent is not granted, the inventor will not be able to take legal action.

Amending claims The Patent Office may make you amend your patent application in the light of existing patents. In this case, you will have to revise the application so that it is acceptable. An acceptable reapplication must be made within four and a half years of the date the original application was filed – or the application lapses.

Patience

A card game for one player

The many different versions of patience include some for two players. Here is a game popular with lone players:

Shuffle the pack and deal the *tableau* (as shown above).

Place the remainder of the pack face down in front of you to form the *stock*, and look at the tableau. If an ace is exposed, move it above the tableau to start a *foundation* on which cards of the same suit will be built up in ascending order. Turn up the face-down card that

Dealing a tableau and starting foundations

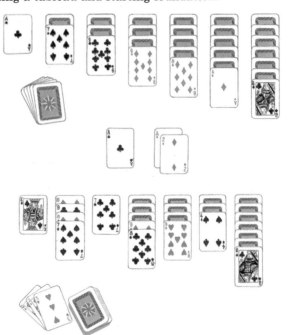

The tableau Deal seven cards from left to right, the first face up, the rest face down. Deal the next row on the last six cards, one face up, the rest face down. Continue to the seventh row – of one face-up card.

The foundation Here the ace of clubs and ace of diamonds have been moved from the tableau to start foundations. Sequences are made from turned-up cards or stock. The three stock cards will go – red three on the black four, red jack on black queen and red queen on black king.

was under the ace. If any cards exposed in the tableau can be moved from one row to another to fit into a sequence of descending order and different colour move them and turn up the face-down card at the bottom of the column.

When no more exposed cards can be moved on the tableau, turn up the top card on the stock and fit it into a row or foundation if possible, then make any movements it allows on the tableau. If you cannot use it, put it face up in front of the stock and turn up the next stock card. As the game progresses, columns of face-up cards build up on the rows, blocking the face-down cards. Only the top and bottom face-up cards in a column can be moved, the bottom card on its own, the top card with the rest of the column below it.

Replace a tableau row that falls empty using a king. Work a new sequence down from it. Once an exposed ace has been laid down as a foundation, put the two, three, and so on of the same suit on it as they become exposed.

When you have gone right through the stock, turn over the waste pile and start again. The aim is to build up all the suits on the foundations. Whether you succeed depends on key cards becoming exposed during the course of play.

Clock patience In this game the cards are laid in a circle face down in 12 piles of four cards, corresponding to the numbers on a clock face. The four cards left over

are dealt face down at random singly in the middle of the clock.

The player starts by turning up the top card on the one o'clock pile. He transfers it face up to its appropriate time pile (for example, a seven goes to the position of seven on a clock), then picks up the top unexposed card from that pile and moves it in the same way. Jacks count as 11, queens as 12. Kings are exchanged for a card in the middle.

The aim of the game is to complete the clock with all the numbers face up in their right places before all four kings are face up in the middle.

Patio building

Making an attractive garden terrace

Paving slabs provide an attractive surface for a patio or terrace. They are available in various finishes and colours, including natural stone, grey, buff, red and pastel colours. Sizes vary; common ones are 460×690mm (18×27in), 610×610mm (24×24in), and 610×460mm (24×18in). The thickness may be 38mm ($1\frac{1}{2}$in) or 50mm (2in). Paving slabs laid against the house should be at least 150mm (6in) below the damp-proof course (dpc). The patio should also have a slight fall (slope) away from the house for drainage. A fall of 25mm (1in) in 1.5m (5ft) will be sufficient.

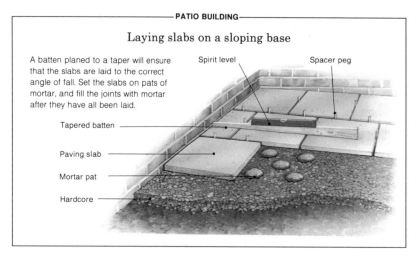

PATIO BUILDING

Laying slabs on a sloping base

A batten planed to a taper will ensure that the slabs are laid to the correct angle of fall. Set the slabs on pats of mortar, and fill the joints with mortar after they have all been laid.

Spirit level

Spacer peg

Tapered batten

Paving slab

Mortar pat

Hardcore

Preparations If the site slopes sharply away from the house, build a low retaining wall to contain the built-up soil and hardcore needed to raise the outer edge of the patio. If the site slopes towards the house, you can level the ground and build a retaining wall at the outer edge to hold back the soil. You may want to build a low wall as decoration round a patio on a virtually level site – see BRICKLAYING. In any case, leave a gap of 150mm (6in) between wall and patio. Fill with gravel to act as a soakaway.

Laying the slabs Remove at least 100mm (4in) of topsoil from the area to be paved, and consolidate the base by rolling or treading. Lay a 100mm base of compacted hardcore, firming it by rolling or with an earth rammer. Fill any gaps with ballast and cover with a layer of sand sufficient to level the surface.

Bed each slab on five generous dabs of MORTAR (at the corners and the centre).

Pattern transfer

Tracing and enlarging patterns and pictures

To transfer a pattern or picture from, say, a magazine onto another surface, such as a piece of fabric or wood, first trace it in pencil onto tracing paper. Then position the tracing, with a sheet of carbon paper underneath, on the surface to which you want to transfer the pattern.

Retrace over the lines of the tracing using a hard pencil (1H or 2H), a ballpoint pen or (on wood or other rough surfaces) a dressmaker's wheel.

Enlarging To enlarge a pattern when transferring it, draw a grid of uniform squares over the tracing. Then draw a larger grid, but with the same number of squares, on the new surface.

Use the grids to help you to transfer the pattern by hand from the tracing to the new surface. Re-draw it, square by square, on the larger grid. For very precise work, add diagonal lines to the grid to subdivide it further.

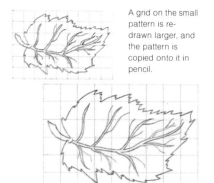

A grid on the small pattern is redrawn larger, and the pattern is copied onto it in pencil.

Three-dimensional patterns The easiest way to copy three-dimensional patterns is to use a PROFILE GAUGE. Alternatively, to trace the contours of a skirting board onto a board that will be fitted against it, use a compass.

Hold the board against the section of the skirting against which it will stand. Hold the compass with its point on the skirting and its pencil on the wood. Draw the point down the skirting so that the pencil traces its contours onto the wood.

Pawnbroker

Pledging valuables to secure a loan

A pawnbroker's shop is recognisable by a 'three balls' sign outside. Money can be borrowed from him, up to a maximum of £15,000, by leaving goods as a 'pledge' – security for the loan – on agreed interest terms. Almost any goods

can be pawned, but a pawnbroker is unlikely to accept any perishable goods, or something that could go out of fashion. Many pawnbrokers will only lend on jewellery or precious metals.

The person who pawns an article must be given a receipt at the time. If he loses it, he can recover his goods by making a formal declaration (for example, through a solicitor) that they are his, then repaying the loan plus interest. The loan is less than the full value of the goods – sometimes considerably so.

Usually the goods must be redeemed within six months. If they are not, the pawnbroker is legally entitled to make a charge for their safekeeping, or sell them. If he decides to sell them, he must serve written notice on the borrower, preferably by recorded-delivery letter. For loans of £25 or less, the pledge becomes the pawnbroker's property.

If a pawnbroker makes more money by selling the goods for more than he is owed, he is legally bound to hand over the balance to the borrower. If he makes less, he is not entitled to recover the loss from the borrower unless he can prove in court that he genuinely tried to get the true market value.

A pawnbroker must be licensed by the Office of Fair Trading, and his credit arrangements are subject to the rules of the Consumer Credit Act 1974 – which cover the total cost of a loan, including interest. If a borrower encounters problems about this, he should consult a solicitor (see LAWYERS) or his local Citizens Advice Bureau.

A pawnbroker who does not comply with the Act can be fined. In extreme cases, following a sequence of complaints, his licence could be withdrawn.

If you are unlikely to be able to redeem your pledge with a pawnbroker it is better to raise the money by selling the goods – you will get more for them and will not have to worry about interest.

Pay rise application

How to put it to your boss

Asking for a salary increase can be a delicate matter, and such requests to an employer should be couched in firm but respectful terms. For example:

Dear Mr Smithfield,

I have now been in your employ for 18 months, and I should be grateful if you would consider the question of increasing my salary. I believe I have given you every satisfaction in my work and general conduct, and have recently undertaken new responsibilities. (Give brief details.)

When I joined the company it was understood that my salary should gradually increase until it reached a maximum

of £..... a month. I am now receiving £.....,
and therefore take the liberty of asking
for at least part of the deficit to be made
up to me.

I am very happy with my work and the
conditions here, but find it increasingly
difficult, with a home and family to provide for, to meet my financial commitments on my present income. In view of
the circumstances, I trust you will give
my request your urgent and sympathetic
attention.

You can vary this basic theme according to circumstances. Never write a fawn-
ing application, and always make a point
of justifying your request.

Pebbledash

*Repairing rendering that is flaking
from a wall*

Apart from being unsightly, damaged pebbledash rendering will allow rainwater
to creep behind it and penetrate the brickwork. You should repair any damage as
soon as you notice it. You need about
5kg (11lb) of pebbles to cover a square
metre. Wash and drain them just before
use.

Where the rendering is flaking away,
remove all the loose material by hand
and then cut back the edges of the damaged area with a bolster chisel and club
hammer, to where the rendering is firmly
bonded to the wall. Clean out any crumbling mortar joints in the brickwork or
masonry to a depth of 13mm (½in), using
a plugging chisel or narrow cold chisel
and club hammer. Brush out all the
debris and moisten the area for repair
thoroughly.

Mix a filling of 6 parts plastering sand,
1 part cement and 1 part hydrated lime
mixed with enough water to make it easy
to use – spreadable but not too sloppy.

Apply a coat of the mix with a steel
trowel, spreading it evenly until it is
about 6mm (¼in) below the level of the
sound rendering on the wall. After about
20 minutes, scratch a crisscross of lines
in the rendering with the tip of an old
trowel. Let the coat dry for at least 14
hours.

For the top coat mix 5 parts sand, 1
part cement and 1 part lime, using
enough water to make a slightly softer
mix that will receive the pebbles. Lay
on the top coat, then spread a sheet of
polythene below the repair while you
throw small scoops of pebbles onto the
rendering. Press them in lightly with a
wooden float. Collect the pebbles that
fall onto the polythene sheet and use
them again.

If the area for repair is large, work
on it in sections that you can complete
within 20 minutes. The rendering starts
to harden after that time and will not
take the pebbles.

Peephole viewer

*Look to see who's knocking
at your door*

A peephole viewer contains a lens with
a wide field of vision (160-200 degrees,
depending on the model), making it
impossible for anyone standing outside
your front door to be out of view. The
lens acts like a one-way mirror, so that
while you can look out through the
peephole, the caller cannot see in. You
can inspect each visitor and see if it is
someone who appears suspicious.

A standard peephole viewer is about
13mm (½in) in diameter and can be
bought at most hardware shops. To
install one, drill a hole in the centre of
your front door at a height convenient
for the shortest adult – see DRILLING.

The adjustable halves of the viewer
can then be hand-screwed together
through the hole.

After dark, a peephole viewer is best
used in conjunction with a porch light –
see OUTSIDE LIGHTING. See also BURGLAR
ALARMS; BURGLAR-PROOFING.

Pelmet

*Making a decorative topping
for curtains*

A box pelmet can be made from planed
softwood TIMBER and PLYWOOD or hardboard, then painted or covered in fabric
to match the CURTAINS.

Use 150 × 13mm (6 × ½in) softwood
for the top and sides. Cut the top board
at least 100mm (4in) longer than the window width so the curtains can overlap
onto the wall – and even longer if possible or the curtains will not draw back
far enough to let in maximum daylight.
For a window up to 760mm (30in) wide,
use 3mm (⅛in) plywood or hardboard for
the front panel, but for a larger window a
thickness of 10mm (⅜in) will make a
stiffer panel.

Make the two side pieces 150mm (6in)
wide; the depth should be about an
eighth of the curtain length. Drill two
holes down into the ends of the top board
and through into the edges of the side
pieces, and assemble the top to the sides
with No 6 countersunk wood SCREWS.

Make the front panel to match the
depth of the side pieces and the length
of the top board. Attach it to the top and
sides with glue (see GLUING) and hardboard or panel pins – see NAILING.

If desired, you can fit curtain track
(see CURTAIN RAILS) to the underside of
the top board and near its back edge, so
the curtain fabric does not rub against
the bottom edge of the pelmet. Mount
the pelmet about 50mm (2in) above the
window with angle BRACKETS screwed
and plugged to the wall – see MASONRY
DRILLING; WALL FASTENERS.

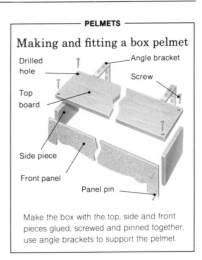

PELMETS

Making and fitting a box pelmet

Drilled hole

Angle bracket

Screw

Top board

Side piece

Front panel

Panel pin

Make the box with the top, side and front
pieces glued, screwed and pinned together,
use angle brackets to support the pelmet.

To cover the pelmet with fabric, stick
the material in place with latex-based
adhesive, taking it round the edges of
the board. Instead of making the pelmet
front with wood, you can use purpose-
made thick, sticky-backed stiffening
material to back fabric that matches or
tones with the curtains. The peel-off backing is squared to help you cut out accurately; there may be pelmet designs
already printed on the backing.

Pensions

*Getting your entitlement; private
schemes available*

State retirement pensions are paid to
people who have reached retirement age
(65 for men, 60 for women) and who have
paid the requisite number of NATIONAL
INSURANCE contributions. The pension
can be paid regardless of whether you
retire from work or not. If you do not take
your pension at retirement age, the eventual amount may be bigger.

Basic state retirement pension To
qualify for the flat-rate, basic state pension you must have paid the following
annual national insurance contributions, or have been credited with contributions by the Department of Social
Security (DSS).

● For tax years since April 6, 1975, class
1 contributions on 52 times the weekly
lower earnings limit – the amount below
which national insurance contributions
do not have to be paid (£57 in 1994-95) –
or 52 class 2 or 3 contributions.

● For tax years before April 6, 1975,
50 flat-rate contributions.

If you have paid or been credited with
the necessary contributions for nine-
tenths of your working life (generally
reckoned as the years between the age
of 16 and retirement age), you should
qualify for a full basic pension.

If you have contributed for less, the pension is reduced proportionately. If you have contributed for less than about 22 per cent of your working life, you are not generally entitled to a pension.

Married women, widows and widowers can receive the basic pension on their spouses' contributions if they are not entitled to them on their own. But people in these categories will not be able to get the pension until their spouses start receiving theirs.

Home responsibilities protection If you cannot work regularly because you' have to stay at home to look after some-one, you may be able to claim home responsibilities protection.

To claim you must, for a full tax year:
● Have received child benefit for a child under 16.
● Have looked after a' disabled person receiving a disability living allowance or a constant attendance allowance.
● Have received income support to look after an elderly or sick person at home.

The number of tax years for which you claim protection reduces the number of years for which you must have paid the necessary national insurance contri-butions to qualify for a basic pension.

Additional state pensions If during your working life you paid class 1 national insurance contributions on earnings above the lower earnings limit (see above), you are entitled to additional state retirement pension. The size relates to the amount you have earned above the limit.

You do not qualify for an additional state pension during any time you are self-employed or belong to an occu-pational pension scheme (see below) that is contracted out of the additional part of the state scheme.

Occupational pensions Many compan-ies run private pension schemes which are additional to the state pension.

Most pay a pension that is a pro-portion of either your final year's salary before retirement or your average salary over a number of years. By law, the lar-gest pension you can get from a private occupational scheme is two-thirds of your final salary.

These schemes are generally contrac-ted out of the state additional earnings-related pension scheme – but guarantee a pension at least equal to that paid by the state. Contributions are paid either by both the employer and employee or by the employer alone.

Employers can now offer schemes where the employee can make additional voluntary contributions to improve the retirement pension. Tax relief is given on the extra contributions. No employee can pay more than 15 per cent of earnings as contributions.

Personal pension schemes If you are self-employed or work for a company that does not run an occupational pension scheme, you can contribute to a personal pension scheme to provide an additional, earnings-related pension when you retire. These schemes are generally run by life insurance companies.

In 1988 the Government introduced a new pension system under which you can opt out of either your employer's scheme or the state earnings-related scheme and arrange your own personal pension scheme.

Pergolas

Building an attractive archway to shade a patio or path

A pergola is a framework of columns and beams, designed to carry climbing plants and provide a pleasant walkway, or shade for a patio – see PATIO BUILDING. It can be freestanding or built against a wall. Any building material can be used for the columns, such as wood, bricks or stone blocks; or TIMBER self-assembly kits available from garden centres.

You can design and build your own timber pergola quite cheaply and easily.

For the uprights use timber posts at least 75mm (3in) square and about 3m (10ft) long; for the side beams and cross beams use 150 × 50mm (6 × 2in) timbers. Use any softwood, provided it is well treated with a wood preservative. When buying, check each piece carefully to see that it is not warped or bowed; avoid wood that is excessively knotty.

Use pegs and a string line to mark out the ground area. Sink each upright 610mm (2ft) into the ground, in a bed of hardcore and CONCRETE – see FENCES.

After fixing the first upright, get a helper to hold the next one in its hole while you lay a batten across from its top to the first upright – check with a spirit level to see that the tops are level, and adjust the height if necessary by making the hole deeper, or by packing under the upright with hardcore. Repeat this check for each upright. Saw a length

A free-standing pergola. You can train plants such as honeysuckle or climbing roses along the timbers, or supported on TRELLISES between uprights.

of 150 × 50mm timber for each side beam, allowing about 150mm overhang at each end, shape by rounding or bevelling – see CHISELLING; SAWS AND SAWING.

Mark the side beams where they will fit onto the uprights, then cut recesses to half their thickness at these points for the ends of the uprights. Secure them by skew-nailing – see NAILING.

Cut the cross beams in the same way as the side beams, with overhangs that can be shaped. The number and spacing of the cross beams is a matter of choice – the closer together they are, the more shade they will provide below. Saw and chisel 50mm (2in) notches 75mm (3in) deep at each end, leaving the required width of beam in between, then slot the cross beams over the side beams and secure them with skew nails.

If the pergola is to stand against a wall, cross beams can be supported in metal joist hangers (see JOISTS), or not-ched and nailed to a 100 × 50mm (4 × 2in) batten attached to the wall with expansion BOLTS.

Period pains

Obtaining relief

Pains that come when a period starts – not before as with PREMENSTRUAL TEN-SION – have the medical name dys-menorrhoea. There is pain in the lower abdomen, perhaps a continuous dragging feeling or sharp, cramp-like spasms. There may also be aching in the lower back, nausea and a feeling of faintness. The worst of the discomfort ends during the first or second day of the period.

The condition is common in girls and young women, but ‾causes no lasting harm and usually disappears during the mid-twenties or after a pregnancy.

The pains are often caused by the womb contracting (as during childbirth) to expel menstrual blood. Sometimes pains are caused by a contraceptive i.u.d. They may be aggravated by tension, so can be eased by relaxing.

Once the pain starts, several remedies may be effective in bringing relief; relax-ing with a hot-water bottle against the back or abdomen; having a long warm bath; taking exercise; taking a safe pain-killer such as a paracetamol, aspirin or ibuprofen.

Pesticides

Using them safely; which to use

There are chemicals to control almost all garden pests – but do not use them indiscriminately, because they can all do harm as well as good.

Examine crops and decorative pot plants thoroughly and regularly for pest damage. Treat them only when you see they are affected – and even then, treat only the individual plants that are infested, and perhaps their nearest neighbours, not whole beds.

When treatment with a chemical is necessary, use one that will do as little general harm as possible – and use it strictly according to the directions on the label. Carry HOUSEPLANTS outside to treat them; if this is not possible, stand them in the bath, which can be rinsed thoroughly afterwards.

Keep rubber gloves and utensils to use solely when applying chemicals – a plastic watering can, mixing stick, spray, for example – and hose them thoroughly after use, or rinse them with clean water from another watering can.

Read the label carefully to check what the active ingredient is, and whether any particular plants are harmed by it. Do not use sprays or dust-on powders unless there is absolutely no wind. Even a slight breeze will carry the chemical onto plants that do not need treating, or into a neighbour's garden where it may harm children, pets or plants.

Dusts are best applied in the early morning so that they stick to the dew and coat the plant. You should make sure that stems and both sides of leaves are treated.

Greenflies and blackflies are the most widespread pests and multiply rapidly. They suck a plant's sap and carry diseases from one plant to another, so swift control is essential. Use a preparation containing pirimicarb, the most specific chemical control. It kills APHIDS but not bees (see BEEKEEPING), ladybirds or other insects. It is sprayed or watered on; the effects are of short duration.

A more general pesticide is one containing pyrethrum, derived from pyrethrum flowers. This is harmless to warm-blooded animals, and is quick-acting against aphids, WHITEFLIES, THRIPS, small CATERPILLARS, leafhoppers and beetles. It should be sprayed on frequently – and in the evening, because sunlight makes it ineffective. Synthetic compounds with similar effects are resmethrin, which lasts a little longer, and permethrin which is active for up to three weeks.

Derris (also called rotenone) is another more general pesticide. It kills aphids, small caterpillars, cuckoo spit larvae, thrips, raspberry beetles, flea beetles and red spider MITES.

Crawling pests can be controlled by spraying or dusting with a pesticide containing gamma HCH (formerly called lindane), fenitrothion, dimethoate, pirimicarb or pirimiphor methyl. They get rid of ANTS, cabbage root fly larvae, capsid bugs, caterpillars, EARWIGS, leafhoppers, leaf-miners, leatherjackets, millipedes, springtails, WEEVILS, wireworms and woodlice, as well as aphids, beetles and thrips.

On FRUIT TREES and bushes, overwintering insects and the eggs they have laid to hatch the next year, or hibernating caterpillars can be killed by tar oil solution sprayed on in late winter. This is poisonous to humans, animals and fish. Do not get any on your skin. It will discolour paint and damage plants under the sprayed bush or tree.

Do not spray when there is any wind, nor when the tree bark is wet or rain is likely, or the solution will simply run off. A spray is not effective when there is a frost. Tar oil rids the trees and bushes of aphids, suckers, scale insects, winter moths and mealy bugs.

See also SLUGS AND SNAILS; WASPS.

Pet injuries

Dealing with cat and dog emergencies

The most common animal injuries are: bites, bleeding, broken leg, choking, foreign objects in a paw, heat stroke, limping, poisoning, and stings. In all cases, get the animal to a vet as soon as possible. But before taking it, there is much you can do to relieve distress or pain.

Bites Use your fingers to find the site of the injury. Use small scissors to cut away the fur around the wound, and clean it with warm water containing a little antiseptic lotion. If possible, cover the wound with a pad of clean cloth – such as a folded handkerchief – or gauze, then bandage it. Have the wound checked by a vet, as bites and scratches suffered in

a fight may turn septic without proper treatment.

With CATS, the first sign of a bite may be an abscess or swelling – and the cat may become listless and off its food. Bathe the swelling with warm water and a mild disinfectant, and take the cat to a vet for treatment as quickly as possible. It may need antibiotics.

Bleeding If a cut is bleeding badly, cover it with a clean pad and bandage it firmly in place. Get the wounded animal to a vet without delay – especially if the bleeding does not stop.

Broken leg If an animal's leg is lying at an awkward angle, it may mean that a bone is broken. Ease the leg into as comfortable a position as possible, and stop any bleeding. Gently straighten the leg into a more normal position. Then bandage it gently but firmly to a piece of wood or hardboard of roughly the same shape as the leg. In some cases, a stick would make a perfect splint. Then take the animal to a vet – in a car, if possible, so as not to disturb the leg.

Choking Quickly remove the collar of a choking animal. If something is lodged in its throat – such as a piece of bone or stick – hold its mouth open and pull the obstruction out. To stop the animal's jaws closing, push a bar such as a spoon handle across the corners of its mouth.

If a ball gets stuck in a dog's throat, try to get a finger behind the ball and hook it out. Or put the fingers of both hands on the outside of its cheeks as far back as you can – and press forward from behind the ball. See also DOG CARE.

PET INJURIES

Removing a hook; applying a tourniquet

Barbed hook First bandage a dog's muzzle, so that it will not bite; try to get someone to hold the animal's head. Cut the hook free from any attached fishing line. Push the hook through to expose the barb. Cut off the barb with cutters or pliers. Pull the shank back and out. Dress the wound and consult a vet. See also FISH HOOK REMOVAL.

Tourniquet To stop excessive bleeding, apply a tourniquet. Tie a bandage around the limb, insert a stick and twist it. Release the pressure for at least one minute every 10-15 minutes.

Keep the dog warm, do not let it eat or drink, and get it to a vet without delay. Its throat could be cut or bruised and in need of expert attention.

Foreign objects in a paw Barbed objects such as fish hooks can become embedded in an animal's skin. Cut a hook free from any fishing line it is attached to – but if the wound is covered by hair, leave enough line to show where the hook is. If the hook will not pull out easily, gently ease it through until the barb is exposed – try to get a helper to hold the animal while you work. Cut off the barb with wire cutters or pliers, then ease the shank back and out through the original incision. Clean and dress the wound, then take the animal to a vet.

Do *not* try to remove a hook that has pierced a particularly sensitive part of an animal's body – such as the lips or eyes. The treatment may require an anaesthetic and should be left to a vet. Do not try to remove glass from an animal yourself, as slivers of it may be left behind. Again, this is a job for a vet.

Heat stroke Never leave a dog in a closed car on a hot day. The animal can rapidly become seriously overheated, and possibly collapse. If you must leave a dog in a car, make sure that two side windows are open about 50-75mm (2-3in), so that there is a cross-current of air.

If the dog is overheated, get it immediately to a cool, shaded place and soak it in cold water, using sponges or towels. Wrap cold, wet towels around its head and body as well. If possible, give it cubes of ice to suck, wrap it in more wet towels and take it to a vet.

Limping If a cat or dog develops a limp, examine the affected leg gently. Feel the limb from the paw upwards, looking for swelling, heat and pain. Look for cuts also – particularly in the pads – and for grit, thorns and splinters. Remove any foreign bodies that will come out easily, and clean any cuts in cold water. If something is firmly embedded get the animal to a vet.

If the leg is strained or swollen, bathe it in hot water containing some mild disinfectant. Then take the animal straight to a vet. If limping is caused by a septic wound, apply a hot poultice to reduce inflammation – especially if there is any delay in reaching a vet. Make the poultice from hot kaolin paste – available from chemists – spread on a bandage.

Poisoning Persistent vomiting and diarrhoea – often combined with shivering, tremors or convulsions – are usually signs that an animal has been poisoned. The symptoms can lead to a state of coma. If your pet is already in a coma, take it to the vet at once. If it is still

conscious, and you think it has swallowed a corrosive poison, such as acid or caustic soda, wash its mouth out with milk or water.

If necessary, use a disposable plastic syringe to squirt in the liquid. Hold a cat's head up and push the nozzle of the syringe between its teeth; with a dog, slide the nozzle alongside its teeth. Alternatively, hold the animal's mouth open and pour in the liquid from a jug or cup.

After washing its mouth out, give the animal plenty of milk or water to drink. This will dilute the poison without causing vomiting – which would burn the throat and mouth for a second time. Follow this with a heavy meal of porridge or bread and milk (if the animal can eat), then take it to a vet.

If you are sure the animal has swallowed a non-corrosive poison, such as household detergent, make it vomit as quickly as possible. Feed it a solid crystal of washing soda as you would give it a pill – see PET MEDICATION. The soda should make it sick in about five minutes. If washing soda is not available, use a solution of 1 part mustard powder to 20 parts of water. Feed it with a syringe.

If you are not sure what type of poison your pet has swallowed, treat it for corrosive poisoning. With either kind of poisoning, get the animal to a vet as quickly as possible, taking along labels or samples of the poison.

Stings Cats and dogs sometimes chase wasps and bees, so when they are stung it is usually on or around the face. If the sting is on the skin, rub in a proprietary antihistamine (see ALLERGIES), keeping the cream away from the eyes and mouth. If the sting is inside the mouth, get the animal to a vet immediately.

Before giving treatment As soon as an animal is injured, get it under control. Put a dog on its lead and take it to a quiet spot for examination. If there is no lead, use rope, string or a belt.

If the dog cannot stand, slide it onto an improvised stretcher – such as a blanket or a large towel.

Grasp a cat by the scruff of the neck with one hand, and support its bottom with the other. Take it to a quiet place – you can wrap it in a blanket if it is nervous or struggling.

Pet medication

Giving them pills and medicines

Medicine for pets falls into three main categories: pills, powders and liquids. These are best administered directly, and – if possible – not mixed in food.

When giving medicine, be firm but gentle; speak reassuringly to your pet. Cats are more nervous than dogs, and more

likely to resist. If one does, get a helper to hold it gently but securely around the neck from behind; alternatively, wrap the cat in a towel with just its head showing.

Pills Grasp a dog's muzzle or a cat's head with one hand so that your thumb and forefinger are on opposite sides of its mouth. Press its jaws apart by squeezing the animal's lips against its teeth just forward of the jaw hinge. Keep a dog's lips curled over its teeth to protect your fingers from being bitten.

Hold the pill between the thumb and forefinger of your free hand, and place the pill as far back on the animal's tongue as possible. With a cat, make sure the pill goes behind the hump of its tongue. Quickly close the mouth and hold it shut while stroking the throat. With a cat, it helps to blow briskly once or twice in its face.

If an animal still refuses to swallow, put the pill in a small lump of butter or meat and give it to the pet that way.

Powders The easiest way to administer these is in a bowl of water or milk. If

Dosing a dog and a cat

Giving a dog a pill Hold the muzzle, with your thumb inside the mouth. Push up with your thumb, keeping the dog's lips curled over the teeth. Put the pill on the back of the tongue, then close the mouth.

Giving a cat medicine Fill a plastic disposable syringe with the medicine. Push the nozzle into the side of the mouth, behind the large canine teeth, and trickle the liquid in slowly. Hold the mouth up while you inject the medicine, so that it does not dribble out.

an animal will not drink, mix another powder in its usual meal.

Liquids Gently pull out a dog's lower lip just in front of the corner of its mouth, making a small pocket. Using an eye-drop-type syringe, squeeze the medicine into the pocket a drop at a time. After each drop, close the pocket, lift the muzzle slightly, and wait for the dog to swallow. With a cat, hold its lips open at one side of its mouth and administer the liquid drop by drop with the syringe.

If an animal refuses to swallow the liquid, mix it with its food or drink. See also CATS; DOG CARE; PET INJURIES.

Pewter cleaning

Restoring and polishing old and new pewterware

Old pewter is an alloy of tin and lead which darkens with age. Dust it regularly, then burnish it with a soft cloth.

If old pewter is badly spotted, the only way of cleaning it without scratching is to rub it vigorously with a chamois leather. Do not use steel wool. If it is badly discoloured all over, get the advice of an antique dealer or jeweller.

WARNING Do not eat or drink from old pewter utensils. The lead content could lead to poisoning.

Britannia metal Modern pewter, or Britannia metal, is normally an alloy of tin, antimony and copper. Use a metal polish, following the manufacturer's instructions. Modern pewter is slow to discolour, and is safe to drink from.

Philodendrons

Growing a durable houseplant

Decorative foliage and easy care make philodendrons excellent HOUSEPLANTS. Their leaves vary considerably in shape and size from species to species. They may be heart-shaped, lance-shaped or rounded. Some have smooth edges; others are deeply indented. The leaves of some species may be up to 610mm (2ft) long. Most philodendrons are climbing plants.

Where to grow them Grow philodendrons in bright but filtered light – direct sunlight softened by a net curtain or thin blind, or by a leafy tree outside the window. They will not survive for long in temperatures below 13°C (55°F), but normal room temperatures are fine.

Watering and feeding Water so that the potting mixture is moistened throughout – but stop when drops start to appear

in the hole in the bottom of the pot. Let the top 13mm ($\frac{1}{2}$in) of potting mixture dry between waterings. Philodendrons slow down or stop growing briefly in winter. During this period, water the plant just enough to stop the potting mixture from drying out completely.

To feed philodendrons, give them a standard liquid fertiliser (see FERTILISERS) every two to three weeks. Do not feed during the winter rest period.

Repotting Once or twice a year lift a philodendron's rootball out of the pot. If the roots have completely filled the pot, repot the plant (see POTTING HOUSEPLANTS). Use an equal mixture of leaf mould or peat substitute and soil-based potting COMPOST. Do not repot during the winter rest period.

Propagation Take tip cuttings (see PROPAGATING PLANTS) in late spring or early summer. The cuttings should be 75-150mm (3-6in) long, ending just below a node. Remove the lower leaves and put three or four cuttings in a 75mm (3in) pot in a half-and-half mixture of moistened peat and perlite or coarse sand.

Enclose the pot in a plastic bag – kept away from the plants by small stakes – and stand it in bright filtered light indoors. After three to six weeks new growth should start to appear. Take the bag off and water the cuttings very

lightly. Feed them once a month. After about three months, pot individually and treat as mature plants.

Staking As they grow, tie climbing philodendrons loosely to a stake inserted into the potting mixture. Use garden twine, raffia or wire-and-paper twists.

To encourage the plant to cling to the stake with its own aerial roots (so that you will only have to tie it in at the beginning), tie a 50-75mm (2-3in) layer of sphagnum moss to the stake or nail some cork bark to it. Spray the moss or bark with water once a day. Make sure the stake is tall enough to support the plant when fully grown.

Photographing action

Getting split-second pictures

How can you photograph people, animals or vehicles in motion without blurring? The key to action photography is anticipation.

If need be, move closer to the action or, if you have a camera with interchangeable lenses, use a telephoto or zoom lens to 'pull' the action closer to where you are positioned.

Try to visualise in advance how to compose the picture, and exactly where and when the action will be at its

---

PHILODENDRONS

Recognising climbers and non-climbers

Most philodendrons are climbers – their name comes from the Greek for 'tree lover'. There are two varieties of the fast-climbing *P. scandens*; *P.* 'Burgundy' is a slow climber and *P. bipinnatifidum* is non-climbing.

Philodendron scandens (large-leaved variety)

Philodendron bipinnatifidum

Philodendron 'Burgundy'

Philodendron scandens (heartleaf)

PHOTOGRAPHING ACTION

Freezing the action with a panning shot

When you take a panning shot, the subject will appear clear and sharp, and the blurred background will heighten the impression of speed.

To 'stop' the action immediately in front of you, focus on the subject as it approaches you and keep it in the centre of the viewfinder all the time, moving the camera in an arc. Shoot when the subject is dead ahead, without slowing or stopping the panning movement.

---

height – as a runner breasts the tape, for example. Follow the action with your camera, adjusting the focus until just before you press the button.

To minimise blur in these 'frozen motion' shots, use a fast shutter speed – see PHOTOGRAPHY.

If your camera has adjustable settings, first select and set the aperture. If your camera does not have a built-in light meter, the instructions accompanying the film will tell you which 'f' number is best for different light conditions.

The closer the subject is to the camera, the faster the shutter speed needed to catch the subject in one position without time for movement to be recorded; similarly the faster the subject is travelling, the faster the shutter speed needed.

Outdoor action shots Suppose, as an example, you want a shot of a man walking briskly across your line of vision, parallel to the camera or diagonally across the picture. If he is at a medium distance, so that his height occupies about half the height of the viewfinder, a shutter speed of $^1/_{125}$ of a second will freeze his movement. But if he is walking towards or away from the camera, a speed of only $^1/_{60}$ of a second is needed.

For someone running or cycling across the picture or close to the camera when you press the button, a speed of $^1/_{250}$ of a second or faster is necessary to freeze the action; for photographing a moving car or boat – perhaps $^1/_{500}$ or $^1/_{1000}$ of a second.

Film Using a medium-speed film (ISO 100-200), the 'magic eye' of most point-and-shoot cameras will capture a person walking at a moderate pace or an animal moving slowly, without blurring. For faster action or frozen motion shots in dull light, buy a fast film (ISO

400-1000) – which will enable you to use a fast shutter speed with a moderately high 'f' number. Best results are obtained with a single-lens reflex (SLR) camera, but a point-and-shoot camera can also be quite effective.

Using a simple fixed focus or fixed setting camera, there will probably be some blurring, even in bright sunlight or with a fast film.

Freezing action with flash Indoors, electronic flash, which generally gives a burst of light lasting $^1/_{500}$ of a second, will freeze movement because of its short duration. But an average electronic flash will only light a subject up to about 4.6m (15ft) away.

Sometimes you can 'control' the action. For example, at a birthday party set your camera to flash, then say '1-2-3, blow', and press the button as the candles begin to flicker.

Accentuating speed To create an impression of speed in a photo of a racing car, say, or a skier, try a panning shot. Set the shutter speed at no faster than $^1/_{125}$ of a second and focus on a spot where the action will be at its most spectacular – for example, on a fast bend. Then follow the subject with your camera, keeping it in the centre of the viewfinder. This is easier if you use a tripod. Press the button as the car or skier reaches the chosen spot, without interrupting the smooth panning movement, and follow the subject for a moment as it continues on its way.

Since there is an element of chance in such split-second action shots, you may have to take several pictures and try different shutter speeds in order to obtain an ideal photo with the subject sharply defined against a background of streaked speed lines.

Photographing landscapes

Capturing natural vistas

Light, colour, cloud, weather and time of day all affect a landscape shot – but perhaps the most basic influence is how you compose the picture. Here are some pointers towards achieving good results:
● Compose the shot in the viewfinder; a camera with a standard lens cannot see as much as your eye can.
● Avoid shots of distant scenery, with a flat and featureless foreground and a backdrop of empty sky.
● To create a sense of depth, use fences, low walls, paths or hedgerows in the foreground.
● Choose a visually exciting object, say a ruined farmhouse, or a bare winter tree, as a focus of interest.
● Centred landscape shots tend to look boring. Try composing the picture with the main feature off-centre or to one side. Climb a rock or kneel for a more interesting angle.
● The 'rule of thirds', often used by painters, will help in achieving a satisfying visual balance.

In your mind's eye, draw lines dividing the picture into thirds, vertically and horizontally, like a noughts and crosses grid. Try to position the main subject and interesting lesser features along the lines, or at the points where the lines cross. The four points of intersection are the strongest focal points in the picture.

Try to compose the photo so that the horizon, or the edge of a field, lies along one of the horizontal lines.
● Avoid taking landscape shots around midday. The best time is early morning or late afternoon, when shadows are longer. Dawn and dusk provide particularly intriguing light effects. If you must shoot with the sun high, use a lens hood to shade the lens from glare.

For sharp results, use a small aperture (high 'f' number) and a slow film; ISO 64-100 should give a good result, but even slower film – ISO 25 and 50 – is available. For long exposure shots, a tripod will reduce camera shake.

If you have a 35mm camera with variable settings, you can modify colour or tonal contrast by fitting a filter in front of the lens.

Contrast filters Used only with black and white film. They make details stand out more boldly.

Ultraviolet filter Use this to eliminate the murky blue haze which often disfigures seascapes, photographs of lakes and landscape shots taken at high altitudes. You can keep it on the camera all the time to protect the lens.

Polarising filter The harsh glare reflected by water or shiny surfaces is reduced by a polarising filter, which can also be used to make the sky look darker.

When buying filters, make sure they are suitable for your camera. Contrast and polarising filters require you to increase the length of exposure by one or two stops.

Photographing pets

Persuading them to pose for you

Photographing pets takes patience, quick reactions and, often, a degree of cunning. The animal may suddenly turn away from the camera, refuse to budge from an inaccessible position – or settle in an ideal pose, then move the moment before you press the button.

Helpful hints Try to distract the animal's attention and/or get it to look towards the camera a split second before you take the picture. It is more likely to be relaxed and cooperative in familiar surroundings; a favourite spot or activity will also help you to gain its cooperation and to anticipate movements.

Cats, kittens and small animals – such as hamsters, guinea pigs, gerbils, rabbits and pet mice – often freeze for a moment when placed on a glass table. Ask a member of the family or a friend to help you; it is virtually impossible to handle an animal and use a camera at the same time.

You can take pleasing pictures of pets with people; for example, a child holding or playing with a pet or the two of them gazing at each other – or a cat or dog watching its owner absorbed in some activity.

Outdoors, a fast film (ISO 400-1000) allows you to work in poor light and with a faster shutter speed, reducing blur if the animal moves as you shoot – see PHOTOGRAPHING ACTION. Using flash indoors, avoid reflection in the animal's eyes, which makes them look red, by bouncing the flash off a wall or ceiling, or shoot a side view. Or, if possible, use a flash bracket to mount the flash unit slightly to one side of the lens.

If your camera has adjustable settings, select and set the aperture and shutter speed well in advance, so that all you need to do is focus and compose the picture in the viewfinder before pressing the button. Take several shots, then choose the best.

Close-ups If you creep up close, cats and dogs may simply think you want to play. A telephoto or zoom lens lets you take close-ups from a distance. If you do not have a special lens, enlarge the most interesting part of the picture, leaving out any unwanted background or foreground.

For normal close-ups, kneel, crouch or lie down, so you are at the pet's level.

Talk to it, or whistle, to grab its attention. Shoot when it adopts an interesting pose or lively expression.

To photograph a bird or small animal in a cage or behind glass, keep the camera as close as possible to the bars, mesh or glass. To make the mesh, or bars of a large hutch or cage unobtrusive, hold the camera almost parallel to the bars or wire and use a large aperture (low 'f' number).

Photography

Choosing and using a camera

The commonly used types of camera are:

Fixed focus compact Cheap and easy to use, these are adequate for family snapshots. Some can be set for dull skies, a weak sun and bright sunlight.

Automatic compact These generally give better results than fixed-focus cameras, and are equally easy to use – but cost more. The best have a 'magic eye' which focuses automatically; you simply point the camera at the subject and press a button. Some have a limited choice of positions to set manually for focus. Most use 35mm film and have built-in flash. There are also compacts with auto-zoom lenses.

Single-lens reflex (SLR) The camera lens serves also as a viewfinder in SLRs. You and the camera 'see' the same image, so focusing and composition are easy and accurate. The camera has variable settings for aperture and shutter speed. The film used is 35mm film and a variety of lenses and attachments can be fitted. Some SLR cameras now use a sophisticated automatic focusing system, requiring a special body and lenses.

Instant cameras These print and develop a colour snapshot within minutes. Film for them is expensive and you cannot obtain extra prints. However, there are no developing or printing costs.

Choosing a camera Tell your camera dealer how much you want to spend and the kind of photos you plan to take; he will advise you which cameras are best for which purposes. Price generally reflects quality.

If you find the complexities of apertures and shutter speeds daunting, buy a simple fixed-focus camera – or, for more money, a fully automatic compact.

Lenses A huge range of interchangeable lenses is now available, mostly for SLR cameras. The standard SLR lens has a focal length (the distance between lens and film) of 50mm with a 47 degree angle of view – like a human eye.

Telephoto lenses bring distant objects closer. Focal length ranges from 80mm to 500mm or more.

Using wide-angle lenses, trees and tall buildings can be photographed at close range. Focal length of the lens is usually 28mm or 35mm.

Zoom lenses allow you to switch rapidly from long-distance to close-up without changing lenses.

Apertures and shutter speeds A camera with variable settings has a series of 'f' numbers (sometimes called *stop numbers*). On a standard 50mm lens the numbers are 1.8, 2, 2.8, 4, 5.6, 8, 11, 16.

Just as the iris of your eye opens wider in darkness and narrows against bright light, so (unless the camera is automatic) you must adjust the iris-like diaphragm in front of a camera lens to suit the light available. The 'f' number indicates the size of the opening, or *aperture*.

The *shutter speed* is marked in fractions of a second. The shutter opens for a moment when you press the button, thus letting light into the camera through the aperture.

Films On film packets you will see the letters ISO (International Standards Organisation) or ASA (American Standards Association) and a number. The higher the number, the faster the film. Most films are also marked DX, which means the film speed will be set automatically on DX-rated cameras. Otherwise set your camera to the ISO/ASA setting.

A film speed of ISO 100 or 200 is suitable for fair-weather outdoor photography or family snapshots. Working indoors, or in dim or wintry light, use a faster film, such as ASA 400.

Using flash Electronic flash units come in two main forms.

Built-in units are provided with many types of cameras, including inexpensive ones. Some operate automatically when the light is poor; others have a warning light indicating that flash is needed.

Separate units are fixed to the camera with a 'hot shoe', and must be compatible with the camera.

Common problems

Blurred images To eliminate accidental blurring caused by camera shake, use a shutter speed of $^1/_{60}$ of a second or faster; squeeze the button gently.

Picture too pale/dark If you are not sure how much exposure to use, take three shots at three different exposures.

Too much contrast In strong sunlight, the brightly lit parts of a picture may come out bleached, the shaded parts almost black. To avoid this effect position your subject in light shade. Alternatively, use flash to illuminate parts of the subject in deep shadow.

Piano

Cleaning the instrument and making minor repairs

Most repairs to a piano should be done only by an expert, but there are some common faults that you can tackle yourself. To get into the piano, open the top and undo the end fastenings, pull the upper panel forward at the top and lift it out. Grasp the hinged lid over the keys in the middle at the front and rear and lift it straight up. If there is a rail on top of the keys, undo the screws to free it.

Replacing ivory If, on an older piano, an ivory key covering comes off, depress the keys on each side and lift up the key until you can slide a piece of hardboard under it to rest across the neighbouring black keys. Scrape off the old glue from the key and ivory with a sharp blade.

Carefully stick the ivory back in place using the thinnest possible clear contact glue – see GLUING. Press the ivory towards the joint with your thumb. Wipe off excess glue with your fingers and put the key back in place. It is ready for normal playing immediately.

Freeing stuck keys One cause of a stuck key may be damp and swollen bushings – small, cloth-lined holes that receive the balance and guide pins.

Lift the sticking key up to clear the balance pin and forward to clear the action lever. The guide pin hole is under the front of the key, the balance pin hole halfway along on the top.

Compress a swollen bushing gently with a warm screwdriver. To refit the key, lift the lever, fit the key under and on its balance pin, and push it down.

Cleaning keys Lift up five or six white keys at a time and hold them with the fingers of one hand while using the other to wipe them with a damp cloth. Use a little mild soap if necessary, but never detergent or methylated spirit. Dry and polish with a soft, clean cloth.

Repairing a split hammer shank A broken shank – the stick holding the hammer head – must be replaced by a professional piano repairer, but if it is split you can mend it yourself.

Apply some PVA woodworking glue to the inside of the split and press it together. Slip a loose loop of thread or thin twine over the hammer and onto the shank and pull it tight. Then bind the shank as illustrated.

Pickling

Preserving with vinegar, salt and spices

Most pickles are preserved in spiced vinegar, whose ingredients and flavours vary greatly according to the recipe and to individual taste – see SPICES. The most suitable vinegars are good-quality bottled malts, either brown or white.

Ideally, spiced vinegars should mature for four to eight weeks before being added to the pickle. Use spices such as cinnamon, cloves, dry root ginger, mace and peppercorns, and adjust amounts for a hot or mild spice. Use them whole – ground spices make the vinegar cloudy. Tie the whole spices in a muslin bag and let them steep in a closed, airtight, vinegar-filled jar, shaking occasionally. A suitable mixture and amount for each

litre (1¾ pints) of vinegar is a piece of dry root ginger, a few peppercorns and 7g (¼oz) each of cloves, mace, allspice and cinnamon. Ready-mixed pickling spices are also available.

To make spiced vinegar for immediate use, put the vinegar and the spices (whole but loose) in a bowl and cover with a lid. Place the bowl in a saucepan with cold water halfway up the bowl. Bring the water to the boil and take the pan from the heat. Leave the bowl in the water until the vinegar is cold, then strain the vinegar through a fine sieve.

When making pickles, do *not* use any copper or brass utensils – the vinegar will react with them and spoil the preserve. Use aluminium, enamel, heat-proof glass or stainless-steel pans, stainless-steel forks, nylon sieves and wooden spoons. Seal the glass storage jars with clip-on or screw-on plastic or plastic-lined tops.

Preparing for pickling Use only firm, young vegetables and sound fruits that have just ripened. Peel, wash and drain the vegetables. Then, according to the recipe, shred, chop or leave them whole. Among the many fruits suitable for pickling are apples, apricots, currants, damsons, gooseberries, grapes, peaches, pears and plums. Prick whole fruits with a fork to prevent shrinkage.

Salting vegetables Vegetables keep better by being salted before pickling. Do not use table salt, as this contains chemicals that may cloud the pickle. Immerse the prepared vegetables in a brine solution of 115g (4oz) of coarse salt to 1 litre (1¾ pints) of water.

Put an upturned plate over the vegetables to keep them immersed. Leave the vegetables in salt for 24 hours. Then drain off the brine, wash thoroughly in cold water and drain.

Bottling pickles Pack raw salted vegetables – such as beans, cabbages, cauliflowers, cucumbers and onions – into large coffee or fruit-juice jars. Leave a headspace of 25mm (1in). Fill with cold spiced vinegar, covering the vegetables by at least 13mm (½in) to allow for evaporation. Seal the jars.

For fruit pickles, dissolve about 1kg (2lb) of sugar in 1.1 litres (2 pints) of vinegar for each 2kg (4lb) of fruit. Use a saucepan. Then add the spices, tied in a muslin bag, cover the pan and bring to the boil. Simmer the fruit until tender, but not mushy. Carefully strain off the vinegar into a bowl or jug, remove the muslin bag, and pack the fruit into heated glass jars. Leave a headspace of about 25mm (1in). Boil the vinegar quickly in an uncovered saucepan until it is thick and syrupy. Then pour it over the fruits, covering them by at least 13mm (½in). Seal the jars.

PIANO

Keeping an upright in trim

A sticking key can be freed by easing the guide pin and balance pin bushings. To level a low key, put a thin paper washer under the cloth bushing on the balance pin.

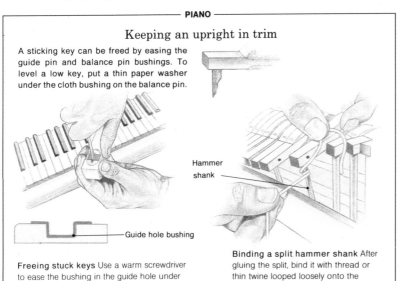

Hammer shank

Guide hole bushing

Freeing stuck keys Use a warm screwdriver to ease the bushing in the guide hole under the front of the key, shown here, and in the balance pin hole halfway along the key at the top.

Binding a split hammer shank After gluing the split, bind it with thread or thin twine looped loosely onto the shank. Pull the loop tight, bind the split spirally, tie a knot and trim loose ends.

Storing pickles Keep in a dry, dark, cool place. Uncooked pickles should mature for about eight weeks, except for pickled cabbage, which is ready within a week. Cooked pickles are ready to eat after about a week. Fruit pickles are ready in six to eight weeks, and can be served with cheese or as the basis of a winter salad. See also PRESERVING.

Picnic

Planning and preparing an outdoor meal

For a successful picnic, take simple food that will survive a possibly warm journey better than anything fancy. Dishes that can stand the hot weather – such as SANDWICHES and SALADS – can be made well in advance. And non-fizzy drinks – such as plain water or white wine – do not need time to settle.

Sandwiches can also be made fresh on the spot if you take bread, butter and fillings. Salads should be made from raw, crisp vegetables – such as carrots, courgettes, celery and cauliflower – rather than soft lettuces, which go limp in heat.

To preserve crispness, pack the salad ingredients in sealed plastic boxes and keep the dressing separate in a screw-top jar or bottle. Toss the salad and dressing (see SALAD DRESSINGS) together shortly before you are ready to eat.

Ready-made sandwiches are best wrapped in protective aluminium foil or greaseproof paper – as are PASTRY, PATÉ and cold meats.

Keep wine, beer and fruit juice chilled in insulated coolboxes fitted with ice packs. Make your own coolbox, if necessary, by packing a large cardboard box with crumpled newspapers as insulation, keeping the lid tightly closed.

Keep food intended for coolboxes in the refrigerator until the last minute before packing. Tea and coffee are best carried in vacuum flasks. To stop milk from going sour or curdling, boil it in advance, cool it again and carry it in a separate flask. Wide-necked flasks can be used for carrying foods such as thick soups and stews, for winter picnics.

Put food and drink in the coolest part of the car – usually the boot – and stack it firmly so that it does not slide about at every corner. Food that does not need to be kept cool can be packed in cardboard boxes or shopping bags and stood upright in the back of a car.

The luggage shelf in a hatchback car makes a useful sunshield; cover food and drink in an estate car with a rug. On a hot day, try to park the car in shade.

Traditional wickerwork hampers are fine for carrying plates and cutlery, but rarely have enough room for much food. Unbreakable plastic plates, cups and mugs weigh less than chinaware and are also more serviceable than paper ones.

Plastic knives and forks tend to break; try to take steel cutlery – plus a bread-knife, bottle opener and corkscrew. Wrap napkins round cutlery and put it between plates to stop it from rattling. Take plenty of paper napkins, a damp dish-cloth or sponge in a small plastic bag, and a large plastic dustbin liner for putting all the rubbish into afterwards.

When you have packed all the food in the car, put a tablecloth over it – and stack rugs and fold-up chairs around it so they can be taken out first. It is also advisable to take a basic FIRST AID KIT.

Ideally, a picnic should be held on level ground with some shade. If picnicking on the beach, try to shelter from the wind – which could blow sand into the food. The same applies to more elaborate and sophisticated picnics – involving china plates and silverware, sparkling wine and ice buckets, linen napkins and PLACE MATS. For more humble picnics, undertaken on foot, take food that can be eaten with your hands – and pack it in lightweight, leakproof, squash-resistant containers for carrying in a rucksack.

Picture frame repairs

Refixing corners, restoring mouldings

Opened corner joints or broken mouldings are the commonest damage on old picture frames. Corners normally have MITRE JOINTS held together with glue and veneer (or moulding) pins, which are finer than panel pins – see NAILING.

It may be possible to glue a loose corner as long as the pins are not bent, but if the frame is very loose it needs dismantling and rebuilding. Or you can strengthen the corners with plates or dowels. Get a valuable frame repaired by an expert.

Gluing a corner Brush out dirt and scrape off any old glue. Use a PVA woodworking adhesive – see GLUING. Then hold the joint together with a frame clamp until the glue has set, after about 24 hours. If you do not have a frame clamp, use string and wood blocks – put two blocks on the centre of each side of the frame, tie the string firmly round, then move the wood blocks towards the corners to tighten the string.

Strengthening a corner Use a corner plate screwed to the back, as illustrated. L-shaped or angle (triangular) metal corner plates can be bought from hardware shops, but may be suitable for larger frames only. Alternatively, cut triangular plates from PLYWOOD.

Restoring a moulding Small chips in mouldings can be filled with plastic wood or a cellulose filler – see STOPPERS AND FILLERS. For larger damaged areas of ornate moulding, take an impression from a piece of undamaged moulding and use it to make a mould for casting a replacement piece from glass-fibre paste. Make the impression as shown, using model-casting rubber or dental-impression compound (sold by dental suppliers). Use glasspaper to smooth and shape the back of the newly cast piece

---

PICTURE FRAME REPAIRS

Mending split corners and making a new moulding

If a picture frame starts to come apart at the corners, screw diagonal or triangular plates to the back of the frame to hold them in place. If the moulding on an otherwise sound frame is damaged, make a replacement section of moulding from glass-fibre paste.

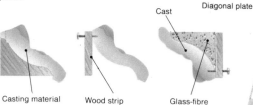

Cast

Diagonal plate

Triangular plate

Casting material on frame

Wood strip tacked to cast

Glass-fibre paste

Making a mould for casting Press the casting mould material onto the frame and let it set hard. Remove the mould from the frame and file a flat on the top edge, then tack a wood strip to the filed edge. Invert the mould and fill it with a proprietary glass-fibre paste. When set (after about an hour) remove the casting.

Frame clamp This simple but effective clamp can be bought at most tool stores. The corner pieces are tightened by pulling the cord through a non-slip toggle.

of moulding to fit the space, and glue it into position.

Finishing Touch up the repaired area with paint or gilt (see GILDING) to match the rest of the moulding.

Picture framing

Making frames, glazing and backing

To make a wooden picture frame you need picture moulding (see MOULDINGS), glass – unless the frame is for an oil painting – and a backing board. Also glazier's sprigs or swivelling clips, gummed tape to secure and seal the backing board, hanging eyes for fixing a picture cord or wire, veneer pins (small panel pins), glue and sticky tape.

Choosing the materials Buy ready-rebated picture moulding in a length of plain wood from a DIY centre or picture-frame suppliers. It is best to buy one length for the whole frame, as it is difficult to match mitred corners (see MITRE JOINTS) cut from separate pieces. The length should equal the total length of the outer edges of the frame plus about 50mm (2in) for wastage.

If you want to make a frame to fit a ready-cut piece of glass, the moulding should be the total length of the glass sides plus eight times the width of the moulding (less the rebate). Add on an extra 1-2mm (about $^1/_{16}$in) for each side to allow for clearance between glass and frame. Make sure the rebate is deep enough for the combined thickness of glass, mount, backing board and sprigs.

Use picture glass 2mm ($^1/_{16}$in) thick for pictures up to 500mm (about 20in) long, and 3mm ($^1/_8$in) thick for larger pictures. For a backing board use 3mm thick hardboard – or 6mm ($^1/_4$in) thick PLYWOOD for frames about 1m (roughly 3ft) long or longer. Cut the hardboard to the same size as the glass.

Making the frame Accurately measure the outer side length plus 1-2mm (about $^1/_{16}$in) for glass clearance on each side and mark it on the back of the moulding. Use a try square to ensure right angles. Cut each length, making a mitre joint at each end.

Join the mitred corners with glue (see GLUING), holding them together in a clamp until the glue sets. Use either a frame clamp or the cord-and-block method described in PICTURE FRAME REPAIRS to join one corner at a time; or use a belt clamp to hold all the glued joints at once. When clamping the whole frame, check that it is square by measuring the diagonals. They should be equal in length. Adjust any misalignments before the glue sets. Wipe away any excess glue.

If you decide to use pins as well, for extra strength, use veneer (or moulding) pins for small frames. Use two for each joint, driven in from one side and positioned in the thickest part of the frame.

When the glue has set, smooth the joints with glasspaper if necessary and paint or apply a suitable finish – see also GILDING; VARNISHING.

Assembling the frame Clean the glass with methylated spirit and lint-free cloth, and make sure it is quite clean and dry before framing. Lay the frame face down and fit the glass into the rebate. Lay the mounted picture (see PICTURE MOUNTING) onto the glass and fit the backing board over it.

Hold the frame against a clamped block of wood while you drive in sprigs along each side with a pin hammer. Drive them in to the thickness of the frame near the surface of the rebate, flat against the backing board, as illustrated. After fixing one or two sprigs each side, turn the picture over and check that it is straight, before you complete fixing. If using swivelling clips, fix them at each corner and the centre of each side.

Seal over the edge of the frame and the backing board with gummed tape set slightly in from the edge of the frame. Fix hanging eyes in the centre of the frame moulding on each side. Position them about one-third of the side-length from the top. Drill small starter holes before you screw them in, to avoid splitting the wood.

Picture hanging

Where and how to fix pictures on the wall

Hang a picture where there is enough light for good viewing, but not where the sun will be on it for a long time, causing the colour to fade. Avoid a position where lighting reflects from the glass.

Pictures can be hung with either picture cord or picture wire through the hanging eyes. Wire is strongest and will not stretch, but the ends must be securely twisted and taped over to prevent them coming undone.

Supporting the weight With the hanging eyes positioned about one-third down the picture sides, the cord just out of sight below the top, and the picture hung on a central hook, the load is about three times the weight of the picture. It increases if the cord is tauter and straighter. Use cord 3mm thick for loads up to 4.5kg (10lb), or 4mm for loads 4.5-7kg (10-15lb). If the load is too heavy, double the cord.

For wide pictures, hang the cord over two wall hooks, one positioned near each side. Otherwise, the load on an almost-straight cord from a central hook is about six times the weight of the picture.

Hang a really heavy picture on mirror chain – preferably one short chain at each side fixed to a wall hook. Or support it on interlocking BATTENS – one batten with a down-pointing outer edge fixed to the picture, the other with an up-pointing outer edge fixed to the wall.

PICTURE FRAMING

Assembling the frame and securing the backing

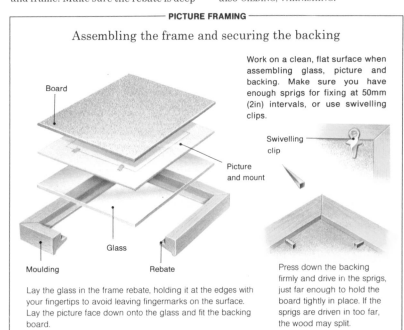

Work on a clean, flat surface when assembling glass, picture and backing. Make sure you have enough sprigs for fixing at 50mm (2in) intervals, or use swivelling clips.

Board

Swivelling clip

Picture and mount

Moulding

Glass

Rebate

Lay the glass in the frame rebate, holding it at the edges with your fingertips to avoid leaving fingermarks on the surface. Lay the picture face down onto the glass and fit the backing board.

Press down the backing firmly and drive in the sprigs, just far enough to hold the board tightly in place. If the sprigs are driven in too far, the wood may split.

Picture hooks Pin-type plastic or metal hooks that can be hammered into masonry are suitable for light or medium-weight pictures. Use the larger sizes for medium-weight pictures, or use a round-headed screw fitted into a wall plug – see MASONRY DRILLING; WALL FASTENERS.

To position a pin hook or screw, hold the picture against the wall in the place you want it, and lightly pencil mark the top corners on the wall. Then lay the picture on its face, use the hook to pull the cord tight, and measure the distance between the top of the hook and the frame. The cord should be tensioned to be as steeply angled as possible, with the hook still within the frame area. Tighten it, if necessary, by tying a loop at the centre.

On the wall, mark the centre point between the two corner marks, then measure down and mark the distance between the top of the hook and the frame. Hammer in the hook with the top against the mark.

Picture mounting

Providing a border for a framed picture

A mount can enhance a framed picture, particularly a watercolour or print, by giving it a border that separates it from the frame. The picture can be mounted directly onto the mount board, but a cut mount, which has a 'window' in it

--- PICTURE MOUNTING ---

Marking out and fitting a cut mount

Use a set square to mark out the 'window' in the mount. To fix the picture to the mount, use strips of adhesive tape.

Cutting Align the set square with the edges of the mount, to get a true right angle when marking the position of the 'window'.

Fixing Use short strips of tape to hold the picture centred on the mount. Now tape along the top edge of the picture.

through which the picture is seen, gives a better and more professional-looking finish. A cut mount also protects delicate pastels and watercolours, by separating the picture from the glass.

Mount boards can be bought from art-supply shops, in various thicknesses, sizes and colours. Colour is a matter of personal taste, but should either contrast or blend with the colour of the frame, the colour of the wall on which the picture is to be hung and the general tone of the picture itself. A thickness of 2mm ($^1/_{16}$in) is suitable for most purposes.

Making a cut mount You will need: a straightedge; heavy-duty trimming knife; set square; rule and a cutting board. The board can be a piece of 25mm (1in) thick wood which is longer and wider than the length of the straightedge.

Position the straightedge along the centre of the cutting board, and partly drive in two small screws for the straightedge to butt against. Measure and mark on the face of the mount the rebate size of the frame (see PICTURE FRAMING) and the size of the picture. Allow for the edges of the window to overlap the picture by about 6mm ($^1/_4$in).

Make the bottom margin 13mm ($^1/_2$in) wider than the rest; this is to compensate for an optical illusion, which causes the margin around a centrally mounted picture to look narrower at the bottom. The side and top margins should be not less than twice the thickness of the frame moulding.

Use the set square to mark the position of the window on the mount, and check that the corners of the window and the mount are at right angles, and that the sides of both are parallel.

Lay the mount on a piece of spare card, and slide them under the straightedge. With the straightedge held firmly against the screws, cut out the window, using firm pressure on the trimming knife. If you wish, you can hold the knife about 45 degrees from the vertical, to give the window a bevelled edge. Remove the cut-out centre and carefully clean out the window corners with the knife and a piece of fine-grade glasspaper. Use the straightedge and knife to cut the mount to the frame size.

Mounting the picture Lay the picture, with the mount on top of it, on a table, with both picture and mount projecting over the table edge. Position the picture so that it is central in the window. Use one hand to hold the mount and picture together, and with the other hand apply two strips of adhesive tape to the underside of the picture and mount. Turn over the mount and picture, and fix a strip of tape along the top edge of the picture. Remove the tapes from the bottom edge.

Pie crust

Making a crispy topping

A covering of shortcrust PASTRY makes an attractive and tempting crust for a pie. The crust is held to the pie-dish rim by a rim of pastry, which also prevents juices from leaking during cooking.

To make the rim, roll out the pastry to form an oval not more than 6mm ($^1/_4$in) thick and 50-75mm (2-3in) larger than the top of the dish all round. Turn the dish over onto the pastry and trim the pastry so that it is about 19mm ($^3/_4$in) larger than the dish all round. Set aside both the pastry and the strip you have cut off.

Wet the top edge of the dish and lay the strip of pastry firmly in place on it. Now put the filling – meat, fish, vegetables or fruit – into the dish. If there is not enough filling to make a pile in the centre of the dish, put an egg cup or pie funnel in the centre of the dish to support the pastry.

Brush the pastry rim with water. Then lift up the crust on the rolling pin and carefully lay it over the dish. Gently press the two edges of pastry together. If the filling has been partially cooked beforehand, make sure it has cooled before covering it or the pastry will become soggy.

Trim off any excess pastry with a sharp knife. Hold the knife at a slight angle so that the trimmed edge slopes outwards from the rim. This allows for a little shrinkage during cooking.

With the back of your forefinger, press down lightly just behind the edge of the pastry. At the same time make a series of shallow horizontal cuts in the edge beneath with the back of the knife. If desired, decorate the edge by fluting. Pinch the top edge of the pastry between a finger and thumb. Then take a sharp knife in the other hand and make a vertical cut in the pinched edge. Continue in this way all round the pie. Cut two vents in the top of the crust to let steam escape.

For a glazed, golden-brown finish, brush the lid with an egg beaten in an equal amount of milk or water.

Pigeons

Keeping and racing them

About a quarter of a million Britons are pigeon fanciers. The best way to start is to join a club, seek advice and buy young birds for breeding from reputable fanciers. If you have difficulty finding a club, write to the Royal Pigeon Racing Association, Reddings House, The Reddings, near Cheltenham, Gloucester GL51 6RN.

A housing pen, known as a loft, can be bought ready made – lofts are advertised in pigeon-fancy publications. Check first whether you need permission from the local authority to have one.

Size depends on the number of birds you want to keep, but each bird must have about 0.6m³ (20cu ft) of space.

The loft must be dry and well ventilated. Ideally, it should face south or south-east in a site where it will have plenty of sun and be protected from east winds.

You feed the birds chiefly on corn and seed, plus some green food. Balanced mixtures of corn and seed can be bought from pet shops or special suppliers. On average, a pigeon eats 25-40g (1-1½oz) daily. A supply of grit is also needed, to aid digestion.

Breeding is usually at the beginning of the year, but birds earmarked for long-distance races are often mated in March, so they will be in peak condition at the right time. Young birds hatch about 30 days after mating, and are feeding themselves at three weeks to a month old. When six to eight days old, they are permanently ringed with an identification number allocated by the Royal Pigeon Racing Association, perhaps through your local club. An RPRA ring will consist of the initials GB, a year date, and a letter and five numbers.

Pigeon racing This is a sport that can involve the whole family. Some 36 countries are affiliated to the Fédération Colombophile Internationale in Belgium, where the sport originated.

Birds entered in a race are taken to a designated liberation point, then released to fly home to their lofts. The winner is the bird which covers the distance at the highest average speed. Racing is highly organised. Every bird in a race is fitted with a coded rubber leg ring, and groups of clubs usually have their own vehicles for driving birds to liberation points in sealed baskets. They are accompanied by officials known as convoyers, who feed and water them on long journeys, and also decide if weather conditions are suitable for release.

Every racing loft must have a timing clock, and when the pigeon returns the rubber ring is removed and placed in the clock to record the time to the second. Club officials know the liberation time and the precise location of each loft, and use an approved formula to calculate the average speed in yards per minute from the time recorded. The highest average speed recorded in a race is 110.07mph from East Croydon to East Anglia in 1965, with a following wind.

However, before a bird can be raced it must be trained to travel and to fly home to the loft – seek advice at a club.

Races for first-season birds are in July, August and September. For yearlings and old birds (third season and older), racing begins in late April and finishes in autumn. Long-distance races are in late June and July.

Young birds are generally raced up to 320km (200 miles), yearlings up to 480km (300 miles). Long-distance races can cover 1290 (800 miles) or more, from points in southern France or Spain.

Older birds are often raced by what is called the 'natural system' – both hen and cock are raced separately while breeding and rearing. An alternative is the 'widowhood system' – the cock only is raced, and the hen remains in the loft as an incentive for his return.

Although substantial sums can be won in prize money, the cost of housing, feeding and club and racing fees is not cheap. Most fanciers get satisfaction from breeding and training birds and keeping them in good condition for racing.

Apart from the Royal Pigeon Racing Association, which has 13 regional groups, there are five Homing Unions – the Irish, North of England, North West, Scottish and Welsh.

High fliers and show birds Pigeons kept for high-flying competitions fly for long hours within sight of their loft to test their endurance and stamina.

Show birds include Fantail, Pouter and Modena breeds. Fantails are named for their habit of fanning out their tails and Pouters for the way they puff out their chests by inflating the air sacs round their large crops. Modenas are noted for the colours of their wing bars.

Showing is controlled by the National Pigeon Association, high flying mostly by the National Federation of West Tumblers and Exhibition Flying Tipplers.

Pilot lights

What to do if you smell gas and the light goes out

A smell of gas may indicate that the pilot light has gone out in a water heater (see GAS WATER HEATERS), gas CENTRAL HEATING boiler, or gas cooker with automatic ignition – see COOKERS. If the pilot light will not relight using the normal method, the jet may be blocked, or a water heater jet may need adjusting.

Do not attempt to clean the pilot jet in any gas appliance; turn off the gas supply at the meter and telephone the gas emergency number listed under GAS in the telephone directory.

Pineapple cutting

Preparing fresh fruit for serving

To slice a fresh pineapple, lay it on its side. Slice off the bottom and leafy top, then cut it into rings 13mm (½in) thick. Use a sharp knife to cut off the skin, and the knife tip to poke out the 'eyes' – or remove them with an apple corer or small pastry cutter.

Pineapple quarters Alternatively, you can serve a pineapple quartered – rather like a melon. Slice off the bottom only, then cut the entire pineapple, leaves and all, lengthways into quarters. If you wish, cut out the core from each quarter.

Pineapple quarters Slice off the bottom and cut the pineapple lengthways into four. Serve each quarter with the flesh cut into slices.

Lay each quarter skin side down. Use a sharp knife to separate the flesh from the skin, then cut the flesh vertically into slices. Serve the slices on the skin, each quarter making a serving.

Kirsch or a fruit-flavoured liqueur can be poured over fresh pineapple, for a more interesting flavour.

Pineapple plant

Growing one from the top of a fresh fruit

A pineapple plant can be grown from the sprouting top of a fresh pineapple. Slice it off, along with about 25mm (1in) of the fruit. Cut away the fleshy part to the hard, stringy core attached to the leaves. Leave this to dry for two or three days, to prevent it rotting.

Trim off the lower leaves, set the pine-

Setting the top Put the pineapple crown on a shallow layer of sand sprinkled over compost in a 100mm (4in) pot.

apple top on sand, as shown, and keep the pot in a light, warm place, with a temperature around 23°C (73°F).

After a month or so, repot in a mixture of 2 parts fibrous soil, 1 part leaf mould or peat, and 1 part sand – all by volume. Use a 125mm (5in) pot and support the plant with sticks, if necessary. The room temperature should not drop below 18°C (64°F). Spray regularly, but do not let the potting mixture become too wet. As the plant grows, water and feed it regularly. It may eventually fruit – but the fruit is unlikely to be edible.

Pipe bending

*How to do it without kinking
the bend*

To prevent a copper pipe kinking or flattening when being bent, use a bending spring, which you can buy from a tool shop, or a bending machine which you can rent from a tool hire shop – see HIRING. Springs are suitable only for 15mm and 22mm diameter pipe. Use one that is the same size as the pipe to be bent. A bending machine can bend larger pipes, will make tight bends and can make bends close to the end of a pipe.

Insert the tapered end of the spring into the pipe, and twist it in clockwise until it covers the area to be bent. You can make a slight bend over your knee.

To remove the spring, slightly overbend the pipe, then ease it back to its correct bend. Insert a screwdriver through the loop in the spring and remove it – turn it clockwise as you pull.

Using a bending machine Hire one with the correct size former, or formers, and guide blocks for the pipes to be bent. Fit the semicircular former into the machine, lay the section of pipe against it and place the correct size guide block between the pipe and the movable handle. Squeeze the handles together until the pipe is curved to the required angle round the former.

Bending plastic piping Polythene can be bent without the use of a spring, to an inside radius of not less than eight times the outside diameter of the pipe. For sharper bends, insert a bending spring and immerse the pipe in hot water. Bend the pipe when it becomes supple. Let it cool before removing the spring. Metal formers are available to hold polythene pipe in a right-angle bend.

Pipe lagging

*Saving heat and preventing
freeze-ups*

Hot water and CENTRAL HEATING pipes waste heat if they are not insulated; cold water pipes, especially in the roof space, may freeze up in cold weather if they are not protected. See also INSULATION. The insulating of pipes, called lagging, can be done using plastic foam, or glass fibre or mineral fibre strip; or using foam or felt tubing. Tubing is easier to fit, especially to pipes near a wall.

Lagging strips Plastic foam strip is self-adhesive when the backing paper is peeled off. It is 50mm (2in) wide and comes in rolls up to 10m (32ft) long. Glass fibre and mineral fibre strip is not always stocked, but you can cut insulating blanket into strips about 75mm (3in) wide. Wear gloves when you handle it.

Wrap the strip round the pipe so that the edges overlap by about half the width of the strip. Strip that is not self-adhesive needs tying on with string at every three turns. When you come to the end of a strip, overlap the next one with a complete turn and bind the string.

Wrap the lagging round the neck of valves and stopcocks, with a generous overlap. At the end of the pipe, make one full turn and tie non-adhesive tape with string. When lagging cold water pipes, do not forget to lag the overflow on the outside of the house.

Lagging tubes Flexible plastic lagging is available to fit pipes from 6mm ($\frac{1}{4}$in) to 75mm in diameter. Get the right size – lagging that does not fit will not insulate the pipe properly.

Tubular foam lagging is sold in 900mm (about 3ft) or 1.8m (6ft) lengths and comes split along its length so that it can be sprung over the pipe.

Open the lagging at one end and spring it over the pipe. Make sure the edges are closed and bind with plastic adhesive tape. Spring the rest of the lagging over the pipe, and at bends hold the edges together and seal with tape lengthways along the join. To seal joins between sections, wrap tape round to overlap both pieces. At valves and stopcocks, wrap tape round the lagging as close as possible to the neck of the valve.

Felt sleeving is for slipping over new pipes before installing, but by running scissors along the seam, can be opened to fit on existing pipes. It is sold in packs of about 22m (72ft) and fits 15mm ($\frac{5}{8}$in) and 22mm ($\frac{7}{8}$in) diameter pipes. Wrap the opened sleeve round the pipes and tie at frequent intervals with string.

Using a spring to shape copper piping

Pipe-bending springs are available in sizes to suit 15 and 22mm diameter pipes – standard in domestic water supplies.

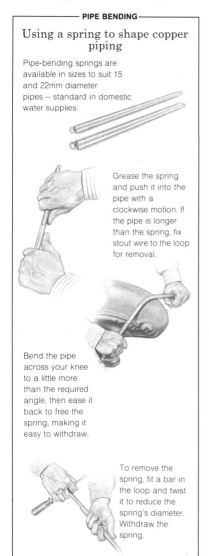

Grease the spring and push it into the pipe with a clockwise motion. If the pipe is longer than the spring, fix stout wire to the loop for removal.

Bend the pipe across your knee to a little more than the required angle, then ease it back to free the spring, making it easy to withdraw.

To remove the spring, fit a bar in the loop and twist it to reduce the spring's diameter. Withdraw the spring.

Insulating pipes with tubing or strips

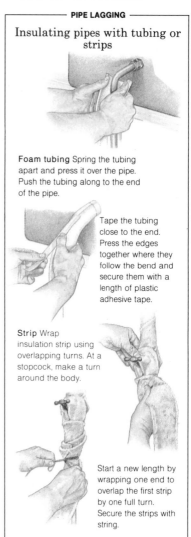

Foam tubing Spring the tubing apart and press it over the pipe. Push the tubing along to the end of the pipe.

Tape the tubing close to the end. Press the edges together where they follow the bend and secure them with a length of plastic adhesive tape.

Strip Wrap insulation strip using overlapping turns. At a stopcock, make a turn around the body.

Start a new length by wrapping one end to overlap the first strip by one full turn. Secure the strips with string.

Piping

Sewing in a decorative seam

Use piping as a rounded trimming to emphasise a shape or add a decorative touch. You can buy ready-made piping in different thicknesses and a selection of colours from the haberdashery departments of stores; or you can make your own to match the fabric you are using, or to pick up and enhance one colour in a patterned fabric.

To make piping, you need shrink-resistant cord and bias binding. If you cannot buy shrink-resistant cord, boil

---

PIPING

Making piping

To make piping, prepare a strip of bias binding, sew it round a length of cord and attach it along the seams of cushions or loose covers.

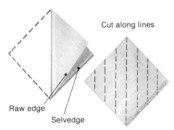

Cut along lines

Raw edge

Selvedge

Fold a square of fabric diagonally in half so that the raw edge meets the selvedge, and pin along the fold. Open out the fabric and cut strips parallel to the pin line.

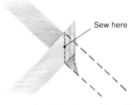

Sew here

Place the strips right sides together with their ends meeting in a V shape, and sew them together. Trim off the points, fold back the top strip to make a straight length and iron the seam.

Sew along the cord

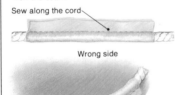

Wrong side

Right side

Lay the cord along the binding, fold the binding over, and sew along it as close to the cord as you can. Tack the seam edge of the piping to the edge of the fabric.

---

ordinary cord in water for three or four minutes and dry it thoroughly.

To make the bias binding, fold the straight raw edge of your chosen fabric back diagonally until it lies exactly along the selvedge. Put pins along the fold to mark it, then open out the fabric and cut along the line of pins. Cut strips of fabric parallel to the diagonal cut; they need to be 38mm (1½in) wide.

Join strips together by placing them in a V shape, right sides together and short ends aligned. Machine stitch (see SEWING) across the bottom of the V about 6mm (¼in) from the edge and snip off the projecting points of fabric.

Lay out the binding reverse side up and put the cord along the centre. Draw the edges of the fabric up to meet each other. Pin the two layers together, then tack and machine them – made easier if you fit the zipper foot in the machine. Remove the tacking.

To fit piping in place, align the raw edge of the piping with the edge of the fabric. Then tack in place the second piece of fabric, putting the right sides together and again aligning the edges. Machine along the seam as close to the cord as possible – using the zipper foot again. Remove the tacking.

If you have to join the two ends of the piping – when it is fitted round a cushion, for example – let them overlap by 13mm (½in), undo 13mm of the stitching at one end and cut off that amount of cord. Fold in the raw end of fabric, lap it over the other end of the piping and secure the join with tiny hemstitches.

Pizza

Preparing the dough and the topping; cooking

Making pizza at home is economical and gives scope for creating imaginative toppings.

Here is a traditional pizza recipe to serve four to six people or make 24 party portions. The yeast used must be left to rise, so allow about 2½ hours preparation time.

Ingredients
1 level teaspoon sugar
4 tablespoons tepid milk
15g (½oz) dried yeast
400g (14oz) plain flour
2 level teaspoons salt
3 tablespoons olive oil
About 9 tablespoons tepid water

For the topping
2 tablespoons olive oil
2 cloves of garlic, finely chopped
400g (14oz) tin of tomatoes, drained and chopped
½ teaspoon dried basil
Salt and black pepper to taste

350g (12oz) Mozzarella cheese
175g (6oz) Gorgonzola cheese
175g (6oz) Italian salami
10 black olives, stoned
1 heaped teaspoon dried oregano

Mix the sugar and milk together and whisk in the dried yeast. Leave in a warm place for 10 minutes until frothy.

Sieve the flour and salt into a bowl. Add the yeast mixture and stir in with a fork. Add the oil and enough water to make a dough. Knead the dough well until smooth and elastic. Place it in a floured bowl, cover with a cloth and leave in a warm place for about an hour.

Fry the GARLIC gently in the oil until lightly coloured. Add tomatoes, basil, salt and pepper, and simmer for 15-20 minutes.

Grease a baking sheet at least 380 × 330mm (15 × 13in). Roll out the dough to the same size on a floured surface. Lay it on the baking sheet, pulling up the edges to create a shallow lip all round.

Spread the tomato mixture over it and top with the remaining ingredients.

Leave to rise for 30 minutes, then bake in an oven preheated to 220°C (425°F), gas mark 7, for 25 minutes or until the dough has risen and the topping is bubbling.

Place mats

Making your own

Place mats must be sturdy enough to form a stable, heat-resistant base for plates. Reversible quilted cotton material is especially suitable.

Alternatively, use two layers of thick, firmly woven, washable fabric back to back. Avoid slippery or thin fabrics.

Each mat should measure at least 250 × 380mm (10 × 15in). For an oval or round table you could make oval mats.

Double-layered mats For a rectangular mat, cut out two pieces of fabric 13mm (½in) larger all round than you want the mat to be. Stitch the pieces together 13mm from the edge with the right sides facing each other. Instead of making a sharp right-angle turn at a corner, stitch diagonally for 6mm (¼in). At one end, leave a 100mm (4in) opening.

Trim the raw edges to 6mm (¼in) from the stitching.

Turn the mat inside out, push out the corners and seams, then slipstitch across the opening – see SLIPSTITCHING.

Single-layered mats Cut out the fabric to the size you want the mats to be. To finish each mat use 13mm (½in) fold-over braid. Simply tack the fold-over braid in place, overlapping the ends where they meet by about 25mm (1in) and turning under the raw edge of the top layer.

For a four-course meal Working towards the centre, lay the butter knife, soup spoon, fish and meat knives and pudding spoon on the right; lay the fish, meat and pudding forks on the left.

Place setting

The correct way to lay a table

The main rules for laying cutlery are:
1 Knives and spoons go on the right of each place setting and forks on the left.
2 Cutlery is always arranged in the order in which it will be used, starting from the outside.

Forks are placed with the prongs facing upwards and knife blades should face inwards. If there is a dessert or fruit course at the end of the meal to be eaten with special knives and forks, these are generally brought on with the fruit.

These rules apply for any sit-down meal, no matter how formal or informal or how many courses it has. The only common variation is to put the pudding spoon and fork above the place setting – very often to save space on the table. Put the spoon above the fork with its handle to the right. The fork should be pointing in the other direction.

China and glasses Lay side plates on the left of the setting. In Britain, other plates are generally brought in with each course. If you are going to serve a dish that has to be eaten with the fingers, provide finger bowls of warm water containing a slice of lemon.

If you are serving a single wine, put the wine glass just above the tip of the meat knife. For more than one wine, provide a different glass for each wine – see WINE WITH FOOD. Those for red wine are usually larger than those for white wine – see GLASSES.

A simply folded napkin is laid on the side plate or to one side of the glasses. If it is arranged in a complicated fold, it goes in the centre of the setting or on the side plate – see NAPKIN FOLDING.

Buffet parties Wrap each knife and fork in a napkin. Put them near the plates so that they can be picked up by the guests before moving on to the food. In the same way, put the pudding spoons and forks near the pudding plates.

Planes

Types of woodworking planes; keeping them sharp and correctly adjusted

There is a wide range of woodworking planes, to cope with all kinds of work, but for most basic jobs two patterns will suffice – a bench plane and a block plane.

Bench planes are 360mm (14in) or 380mm (15in) long, with a blade 60mm

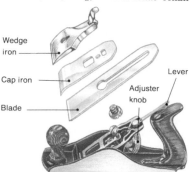

Wedge iron

Cap iron

Blade

Lever

Adjuster knob

Assembling a bench plane Screw the blade and cap iron together; hold them in place with the wedge iron. Adjust the depth of cut by turning the knurled knob.

(2⅜in) wide. They are used for levelling long lengths of timber – see PLANING.

A block plane is useful for small work and for end-grain trimming. It measures 90mm (3½in) to 200m (8in) long and has a blade 25mm (1in) or 40mm (1⅝in) wide.

Adjusting a plane On both bench and block planes, the depth of cut is adjusted by turning a knurled adjuster knob behind the blade.

A lever in front of the blade adjusts the lateral alignment with the face of the plane. Hold the plane upside down, look along the face and align the blade edge by moving the adjustment lever, then adjust the depth.

The blade is bolted to a steel plate called the cap iron, which has a rounded nose set fractionally above the cutting edge of the blade to break and turn the trimmed shavings. Its position is adjustable by a slot in the blade, and it should be set so that as the blade cuts the shaving is curled forward. To adjust the cap iron, use a screwdriver to loosen or tighten the cap screw.

Blade sharpening Plane blades are sharpened in the same way as chisels (see CHISELLING and SHARPENING HAND TOOLS), but some modern planes have replaceable blades that are thrown away when they become blunt.

Power planes For big jobs, a power plane will take the hard work out of planing. A rotating cutter block shears away wood fibres at speeds up to 25,000 revolutions per minute, and can be used to cut across and even against the grain of the wood.

WARNING Care must be taken when using a power plane:
● Make sure the work is fastened securely in a vice or portable workbench.
● Keep hands on the plane at all times, and never curl your fingers under the face to guide it.
● Never set the plane down after planing until the motor has stopped completely.
● Always set the depth adjustment (by a knob at the front of the plane) before switching on, and let the plane reach its maximum speed before beginning to cut.

Planing

Smoothing a board; squaring the edge; trimming end grain

Using a plane accurately calls for a degree of skill: practise the techniques outlined below on scrap wood, until you feel confident enough to tackle real jobs – TIMBER is expensive.

Use a bench plane (see PLANES) to level and smooth a length of sawn timber. Secure the board between two end stops on a workbench, and plane it in two stages.

First set the plane to make deep cuts, about the thickness of a postcard, then plane across the board at an angle of 45 degrees to the grain, overlapping each stroke. Check that the board is level by

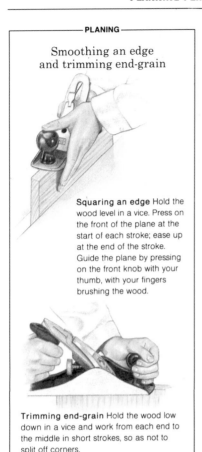

Smoothing an edge and trimming end-grain

Squaring an edge Hold the wood level in a vice. Press on the front of the plane at the start of each stroke; ease up at the end of the stroke. Guide the plane by pressing on the front knob with your thumb, with your fingers brushing the wood.

Trimming end-grain Hold the wood low down in a vice and work from each end to the middle in short strokes, so as not to split off corners.

looking along it frequently. When all high spots and the rough sawn finish have been removed, reset the plane to make tissue-thin shavings and plane the face with straight strokes along the grain.

Squaring the edge Secure the wood in a carpenter's vice, or an engineering vice with two pieces of scrap wood between the jaws. Check that the board is parallel to the vice jaws.

Set the front of the plane squarely on the edge, and guide it with the thumb pressing downwards and the fingers brushing against the wood. Make each stroke the length of the board. Use a try square frequently to see that the edge is square with the planed face.

Trimming end-grain Fix the piece of wood in a vice, as low down as possible, and plane from each end, working towards the centre. Use short strokes that do not go the full length. Make sure that the blade of your plane is sharp.

QUICK TIP Beeswax or candle grease applied to the face of a plane will make planing easier when the entire face of the plane is in contact with the wood.

Planning permission

How to apply; who to apply to

Any substantial addition or alteration to a property, from adding an extension to building a new wall or fence, is likely to require planning permission from your local council.

If in any doubt whether you need planning permission for an alteration, check with your local planning department. If the work requires permission and you go ahead without it, you can be ordered to stop – and pull down at your own expense any building that has been done.

If your property is 'listed' – classified as being of special historic or architectural interest – any alteration that may affect its character, such as a new roof, will need Listed Building consent from the local council.

Getting permission Fill in the planning application form available from your local planning department. You will probably have to submit plans showing the position of the site; the relationship of the proposed building to other buildings and the highway; plus drawings showing what the building will look like. If your plans are at all complicated, get your builder or architect (see ARCHITECTS; CONTRACTORS) to help you to make the application. You will also have to pay a fee on making an application.

The council may take up to two months to decide whether to grant permission. If it needs more time to make its decision, it will contact you. If the permission is granted, it is valid for five years. Permission lapses, though, if work is not started within that time.

Plant care during holidays

Keeping houseplants healthy while you are away from home

If you are going away for more than a few days, give your HOUSEPLANTS a thorough watering just before leaving. Put them in a cool room where they will be away from direct sunlight. As an added precaution, place them on trays or saucers of moist pebbles, or plunge them into large containers of moist sand.

For longer absences – say, two or three weeks in summer – you can install self-watering devices. Buy some moisture-conducting plant wicks from your local garden centre. Put one end of a wick in a water-filled jar, and let the other hang over the top of a plant pot standing at a lower level than the jar.

Another method is to cover your plants with plastic bags as soon as the potting mixture has been well watered and allowed to drain. Support each bag on three or four thin sticks pushed into the edges of the mixture. Make sure the plas-

tic does not touch the foliage and tie the bag around the rim of the pot.

The bags will retain moisture for two or three weeks. If you plan to be away for less than ten days, simply let the bags hang loosely. Store the bagged pots out of direct sunlight in the summer, or at a temperature of 13-16°C (55-61°F) in the winter.

If you are going away for more than three weeks, you can grow your plants in self-watering pots or troughs, which are available from garden centres. They have a water reservoir that needs filling up from time to time.

Plant galls

How to deal with abnormal growths on plants

Plant galls are abnormal growths on leaves, branches or roots, ranging from tiny blisters to sizable irregular swellings. Some have larvae of insects such as wasps inside. Others are caused by bacterial diseases.

Crown gall This is a bacterial disease that chiefly attacks woody plants such as apples, pears, plums, peaches, and raspberries. See also FRUIT TREES.

Chains of galls appear on trunks and stems at ground level. They also form on roots and can cause pale foliage and slightly stunted growth.

There is no cure for crown gall. If a plant is severely diseased, destroy it. Plants that are only mildly affected will generally survive.

To prevent crown gall, make sure the soil is well drained and avoid injuries to the roots of plants.

Gall midges The larvae of these tiny flies – bright red, yellow or white maggots – feed on the tissues of many cultivated plants. They cause galls on the leaves, stems and flowers and can check growth.

To control, spray with a persistent insecticide, such as gamma-HCH (see PESTICIDES), in late spring or early summer. This will kill the adult flies before they can lay their eggs.

Gall mites These are tiny mites that feed on or in plant tissues and cause galls on leaves and buds. For measures to control them, see MITES.

Gall wasps The galls found on oaks, willows and ROSES can be caused by any of several species of gall wasp larva.

The galls grow out of the leaves of affected trees or plants in many different shapes. Some resemble peas; others look like cherries, silk buttons or spangles. They are sometimes alone, sometimes numerous. They usually do no harm.

Planting

*Basic guidelines for putting plants
into the ground*

Whether you are planting an oak tree or a cabbage, the same rules apply: do not plant when soil is frozen or waterlogged; dig a hole that is comfortably larger than the plant's root mass; disturb the roots as little as possible; surround them with rich moist soil.

Make sure you set the plants at the correct depth, so that their roots are neither too near the surface nor too deeply buried. The correct depth is often indicated by a soil mark left on the plant when it was lifted. Plant herbaceous stock so that the soil is level with the point where stems and roots join. If you are unlikely to be able to plant for some time, set the plant at an angle against the side of a V-shaped trench and cover the roots with soil.

Planting trees and shrubs Trees (including FRUIT TREES) and SHRUBS may come with bare roots or in a container. If the roots are bare, soak them in water for a few hours before planting; cut off any damaged roots just before you plant. With container plants, keep the soil moist.

As you dig a hole to plant a tree or shrub keep the topsoil separate from subsoil. Mix plenty of peat substitute, manure or garden COMPOST into the topsoil and add a handful of bone meal – see FERTILISERS. You will not need the subsoil.

If a stake is needed, drive it into the hole before planting. Put enough topsoil back into the hole to support the tree or shrub at the right depth when packed down. For bare rootstock, make a cone of the enriched topsoil at the bottom of the hole and spread the roots over it. Add more topsoil, carefully working it in around the roots, until the hole is about two-thirds full.

When a plant is in a light plastic container, put it in the planting hole still in its container then cut away and remove the plastic. If the container is too strong to cut, carefully lift out the plant and all the soil and put in the planting hole.

Pack the soil down firmly and fill the hole with water. Let it drain, then fill the hole with more topsoil. Do not tread this soil down, but, as it settles, add more to top it up.

Make a shallow saucer-shaped dip around the stem of the plant and pour on a watering can of water. Make sure the plant gets at least a watering can of water a week during its first summer.

Planting seedlings Do not enrich the soil a hole at a time. Instead, prepare the whole bed – see SOIL PREPARATION. If planting in rows, mark each row with a string stretched between stakes.

Dig holes at regular intervals. Base the

spacing on the nature of the plants – tall, slender plants can be fairly close; spreading ones need more space.

Take each seedling from its container, unless the container is peat or fibre. Tap the container's bottom and sides, then tip it just enough to let the rootball slide out into your hand. Put the rootball in its hole and surround with soil as for larger plants. Seedlings in peat or fibre pots are planted still in the pots. The roots will grow through them.

See also PROPAGATING PLANTS; PRUNING SHRUBS; SEED SOWING; STAKING PLANTS.

Plasterboard

Using it to line walls and ceilings

Plasterboard consists of a layer of gypsum plaster faced on both sides with tough paper. It can be used for lining walls and PARTITIONS or for constructing a ceiling. Two thicknesses are available, 9.5mm (about $\frac{3}{8}$in) and 12.5mm (about $\frac{1}{2}$in), in sheets measuring from 1800mm (6ft) to 3600mm (12ft) long and in widths of 600, 900 and 1200mm (2, 3 and 4ft). Store sheets of plasterboard flat, in piles no more than 1m (3ft) high.

One face of plasterboard consists of an ivory-coloured paper that needs no other finish and can be painted or papered. The other side is grey and must have a skim coat of board-finish plaster before decorating. There are boards with expanded polystyrene backing or moisture-resisting metallised polyester backing. Both give greater insulation than standard ones. For the smoothest finish, use boards with tapered edges on the ivory side.

Lining a wall Nail the sheets, with the ivory side facing you, as described in BATTENS. Allow 3mm ($\frac{1}{8}$in) gaps – but no larger – between the boards. Use a broad-bladed filling knife or a plasterer's trowel to press joint compound into each joint and in a 25mm (1in) band along each side of it. While the compound is wet, press jointing tape on the compound with the knife, making sure there are no bubbles under it. After five minutes apply another layer of joint compound over the tape. Smooth it flush with the board, then use a damp sponge to remove the excess and feather out the edges. Rinse the sponge frequently.

When the compound is dry, apply a final thin layer 230-305mm (9-12in) wide and feather the edges with a sponge.

Before decorating, apply one or two coats of plasterboard primer/sealer over the whole board.

Making a new ceiling If a lath-and-plaster ceiling bulges to the extent that it cannot be repaired, it can be replaced with plasterboard. Removing the old ceil-

ing is a dirty job – it will create much dust, dirt and rubble. Clear the room of all furniture and furnishings, open all windows and wear old clothing, safety goggles and a mask. Make sure you have a safe footing on a soundly supported scaffold board.

Use a blunt chisel or an old screwdriver to cut through the old plaster and to prise the laths away from the JOISTS. When all the ceiling is down, pull out any nails remaining in the joists and chip away any remnants of plaster.

Measure the distance between the centres of the joists. For joists 400mm (16in) apart, fit 9.5mm (about $\frac{3}{8}$in) plasterboard with 30mm (1$\frac{1}{4}$in) galvanised plasterboard nails; for joists farther apart – up to 610mm (24in) – use 12.5mm ($\frac{1}{2}$in) board with 40mm (1$\frac{1}{2}$in) nails. Each end of each board must be nailed to the middle of a joist, so choose lengths that will suit the joist spacing. If the ceiling is in a top room it may be worth fitting insulated plasterboard, foil side up.

Plasterboard is heavy, so you will need a helper to lift the boards into place. To support the board at your end while you nail it, use a T-shaped floor-to-ceiling prop. Start in one corner of the room, drive in a few nails to hold the board in place, then secure it to each joist with nails spaced 150mm (6in) apart and at least 13mm from the edge. Drive the nails in until they dimple but do not break the board surface. Leave a 3mm ($\frac{1}{8}$in) gap between this board and the next, and between all subsequent boards.

When you come to the end of the row, you may have to cut a board to fit. Cut it, ivory side up, with a trimming knife or panel saw. Use the offcut to start the next row, so that the ends of the boards are staggered. If the boards fit exactly, start the second row with a board cut in half, then fit a full-length board and so on – again, to stagger the joins.

When all the boards have been fixed, fill the joints as for a wall.

See also PLASTER PATCHING.

Plaster patching

*Repairing cracks and holes in
walls and ceilings*

When repairing large cracks or holes in plasterwork, it is generally best to use special DIY plaster. This is available either ready-mixed in a bucket, or as a powder to which you add water. Some brands are sold with a plastic applicator; for others use a plasterer's trowel or, for smaller areas, a filling knife.

If the cracks are small, use cellulose filler – see STOPPERS AND FILLERS.

Preparing the surface Rake out all loose and crumbling material from the area to be patched. Test the surrounding

PLASTER PATCHING

Replastering a large hole

Chisel away all loose plaster surrounding the hole. Cut back the edges about 25mm (1in) to form a chamfer to provide a good key for the new plaster.

Load plaster onto a plasterer's trowel and press it into place to ensure that it keys firmly to the brickwork. Allow it to harden, then apply the next layer.

Level the final layer with a batten, working quickly while the plaster is still pliant and keeping both ends of the batten in contact with the surrounding plaster.

plaster with the tip of a trowel to check that it is adhering firmly to the wall. If it is not, chip it away with a cold chisel and hammer until you reach firm plaster. Brush the area clean with an old paintbrush.

If the surface to which the new plaster is to be applied is smooth (for example, laths in a lath-and-plaster ceiling or wall), coat with a layer of PVA adhesive. This will improve the bond between the new and old materials.

Applying the plaster Mix powdered plaster according to the manufacturer's instructions, or stir ready-mixed plaster. Load some onto a carrying board (hawk) and apply it to the wall, pressing it firmly in place with the special applicator, or with a plasterer's trowel or filling knife held at a slight angle. Build up in thick layers, allowing each layer to stiffen before applying the next, until the new plaster is a little higher than the old.

When the final layer begins to dry, level the surface with a straightedged wooden batten (see BATTENS) or ruler, moving it across the plaster with a slight zigzag motion. Finish off by smoothing with a trowel, then, for a fine finish, rub lightly with a damp sponge.

A one-coat plaster may be applied as a single coat up to 50mm (2in) thick, without risk of sagging.

Repairing external corners Prepare the wall as described above. Take a batten about 50mm (2in) wide and longer than the length of the area to be repaired. Drive a masonry nail through the batten near each end and with both the nails closer to one edge of the batten.

Hold the batten vertically across one face of the damaged corner with the nails nearer the inner side. With a straightedge, align the batten with the plastered surface of the adjacent wall above and below the hole. Nail the batten gently to the wall, heads protruding.

Fill the hole on the adjacent wall as described above so that it aligns with the edge of the batten. When the plaster has dried, remove the nails, then carefully pull the batten straight back, away from the wall. Nail the batten to the other face of the corner and repeat the process. To finish, before the plaster hardens fully, put on a rubber glove, then wet it and run your finger gently down the edge to round it off slightly.

Filling holes in partitions To fill a hole in hollow PARTITIONS made with PLASTER-BOARD, cut the edges of the damaged area so that it forms a square.

Cut a square from hardboard or a plasterboard offcut, small enough to go through the hole diagonally, but large enough to overlap it all around. Bore a hole in the middle of the square, and thread a length of string through it. Tie a nail to one end of the string to anchor it behind the board.

Put a few blobs of plaster round the edges – on the front of the hardboard or on the grey side of plasterboard, then feed the board through the hole in the plasterboard and pull it up tight against the back of the plasterboard.

Hold the string taut while you fill the hole with plaster as described above. When the plaster has set and is holding the hardboard securely to the plasterboard, cut the string.

Plastic laminates

Cutting and using them to decorate surfaces

Plastic laminates are made by building up layers of resin-impregnated paper, the top one being coloured and patterned. A tough coating of melamine is added to provide a practical surface – and this may be smooth or textured.

Normal sheet size is 2400 × 1220mm (8 × 4ft), and 1.5mm ($\frac{1}{16}$in) thick, but most stores offer a cutting service – at a cost. However, specialist stores sell offcuts as part of their service, which can reduce costs.

Before choosing, ask to see pattern swatches. A very large range of patterns and textures is now available, including a number of wood grains and copies of materials such as slate, woven bamboo – even copper.

Gluing You can stick laminate to any flat, dry surface which will provide an adequate key for the adhesive: PLY-WOOD, blockboard or CHIPBOARD are ideal. However, it is important to remove or break down painted or varnished surfaces, so that the adhesive can grip. If, for example, you stick a laminate onto a painted surface, all that holds it in place is the strength of the paint film.

Use a rubber-based contact adhesive for fixing laminate in place – see GLUING.

Cutting Cut laminate with a saw or strong craft knife. For sawing, use a sharp, fine-toothed tenon saw – see SAWS AND SAWING. Support the main part of the laminate, decorative side up, on a flat surface such as a table, and anchor it with clamps. If there has to be a considerable overhang of laminate, support this too (perhaps with a kitchen chair) to avoid the risk of snapping as cutting proceeds. Smooth the cut edge with fine glasspaper wrapped around a sanding block.

If you use a craft knife, it should have a special laminate scoring blade. Lay the laminate, decorative side up, on a flat surface, then lay a straight-edge or steel rule along the line of cut. Make a number of passes with the knife until the laminate surface is scored. Now lay a piece of wood along the scored line and bend the free side of the laminate *up* until it snaps. Clean up the edge with fine glasspaper.

Check that the laminate fits the surface you intend it for, then use a notched spreader to apply contact adhesive to both surfaces. Ask for a free spreader when you buy the adhesive, if it is not already provided – some water-based adhesives come with a sponge spreading pad.

Leave the coated surfaces until the

adhesive is touch-dry – usually about 15-20 minutes. This is vital, because otherwise solvent which has not evaporated will be trapped between surfaces, causing a permanent bulge.

A major problem is lining up the two surfaces so that they do not touch each other – because this type of adhesive bonds to itself instantly. The answer is to slide a sheet of brown paper between the two, line up the laminate, then slide out the paper and press the two coated surfaces into contact.

Once the laminate is down, thump it with your fist to get good contact, or tap it with a soft-face hammer. Allow 30 minutes for the glue to set fast before trimming the edges with a flat, fine-cut file or a small block plane – see PLANES; PLANING. File downwards: if you file upwards you could chip the surface.

Edging strips are usually available in stores selling laminates. One type is stuck in place with contact adhesive.

Alternatively, you can buy edging strip with a self-adhesive backing. Cut a strip to fit, place it on the edge and cover it with brown paper. Use a hot iron and moderate pressure to fix it in place, moving the iron backwards and forwards as you advance inch by inch along the edge. As you work, check frequently that the strip is in line and thoroughly bonded. Leave the strip to cool, then use a flat file or abrasive paper to trim the edges and ends.

Where an edge is too deep for a proprietary edging strip, cut strips of matching laminate and stick these in place with contact adhesive, using a block plane to trim back when the adhesive has set.

Scratches Special scratch cover in a tube is available for many of the Formica range of laminates.

See also WALL CLADDING.

Plastic pipes

The correct pipe for the job

Plastic pipe has several advantages over copper: it is less prone to furring up (see DESCALING); it will not burst if water freezes in it (see FROZEN PIPES); and it offers good INSULATION – though it should still be lagged to increase insulation – see PIPE LAGGING.

Its disadvantage is that it cannot withstand very high temperatures. You must not use it within 380mm (15in) of a boiler; you will have to link it to copper piping at that point.

You can buy flexible, semi-rigid or rigid plastic piping. It is available in two sizes – 15 and 22mm. You can connect one plastic pipe to another or to a copper pipe.

Use a standard compression fitting to make the joint – see PLUMBING. If the

Making joints and fitting a waste trap

Join lengths of plastic piping with stainless-steel inserts. These make the pipe ends rigid so that standard compression joints can be used.

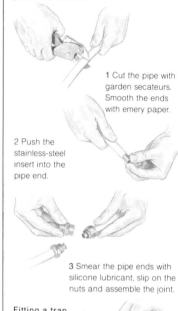

1 Cut the pipe with garden secateurs. Smooth the ends with emery paper.

2 Push the stainless-steel insert into the pipe end.

3 Smear the pipe ends with silicone lubricant, slip on the nuts and assemble the joint.

Fitting a trap
Unscrew the locking nut on the trap inlet and place the rubber washer in position.

Push the trap inlet into the waste outlet and screw the nut onto the outlet thread.

Slacken the nut on the trap outlet and slide the waste pipe into it, as far as it will go. Hand tighten the outlet nut.

olive (the sealing ring) supplied with the compression fitting is too tight a fit to position correctly, put the olive in place before you push home the copper insert. If correctly assembled, no sealing compound or tape is necessary.

The pipe will need some support, so use pipe clips at intervals of 510mm (20in) horizontally, and 1000mm (40in) vertically when using 15mm pipe. For 22mm pipe, support at 610mm (24in) and 1200mm (47in) centres. The pipes can be decorated with normal domestic gloss or emulsion paint.

Other uses Plastic pipe is also used for waste pipes and overflow systems. It is usually 38-42mm (1½in) for sinks, 32-36mm (1¼in) for washbasins and 21-23mm (¾in) for cistern overflow pipes. There are two ways of assembling the pipes:

● By a locking ring-seal connector, which engages a screw thread on one section with a plastic nut on the other; the seal is made by a tapered washer, usually ready-fitted.

● By a push-fit system – one pipe is simply pushed into a mating piece, where a seal is made by a rubber O-ring.

Using either system, always ensure that pipe ends are cut square, and that all swarf is rubbed away with fine emery paper. Fitting can be made easier by putting a little liquid detergent or petroleum jelly on the meeting surfaces, as a lubricant.

When measuring a pipe, add enough to fit fully into joints – usually about 25mm (1in). Make screw thread joints finger-tight only. Never use a spanner: overtightening will cause stripped or jumped threads.

Plastic wall cladding

Fitting 'weatherboard' that is maintenance free

Check with your local council whether you need permission to alter the appearance of your house with WALL CLADDING.

Plastic cladding not only makes a decorative finish to exterior walls, but will also, if properly fitted, stop rain from penetrating walls in exposed positions. There are two main types, both made of UPVC. One is a thin moulding with little structural strength; the other has a cellular core of PVC and is stronger.

All plastic expands and contracts with changes in weather conditions, and the hollow moulding is held by plastic channelling – never nailed to the wall. Expansion is less with the cored type, which can be nailed.

Thin-moulding cladding Frame the area to be clad with 38 × 19mm (1½ × ¾in) softwood BATTENS using two battens butted side by side for the uprights, single battens for the horizontal. The timber should be pre-treated to withstand rot. Within the frame, use single pieces of batten upright at about 400-460mm (16-18in) intervals. Secure them with masonry nails or hammer-in fixings. If the area to be clad exceeds 3m (10ft) in width, use a plastic panel joint, supported on two adjoining battens, as for the outside vertical frame.

Use a spirit level to check that the framework gives a flat surface. Plane any parts that stand out, and use small bits of timber to pack out any that are recessed.

Use a fine-toothed saw to cut the vertical plastic side channels to length, and fix them to the outer uprights with aluminium nails. Cut a starter strip and nail this to the bottom horizontal batten.

Cut the first shiplap plank to length, allowing a 10mm (⅜in) expansion gap at each end. Put the plank within the side channels and engage it with the starter strip. Fix it to vertical battens with the aluminium cleats supplied, held in place by aluminium nails.

Cut and interlock succeeding planks, checking regularly with a spirit level that they are horizontal.

To fit the final plank, cut from the top edge to give the required depth of plank. Nail the finishing strip in place, then insert the last plank, feeding it under the lip on the finishing strip.

To weatherproof around windows and doors, use a silicone sealant. Solvent cement may be used during construction of the cladding, to bond boards together. Follow the cladding manufacturer's instructions.

Cellular core cladding This tougher material has all the properties of timber without the risks of rot and the need to paint. The fixing method is similar to that for thin sections, except that planks are nailed to battens.

Make a frame as before, then fix vertical 50 × 25mm (2 × 1in) pre-treated battens to the wall at 400mm (16in) centres. Fix a starter channel at the base of the area to be clad. Fix the side channels. Nail the first plank in place using 32 or 38mm (1¼ or 1½in) steel nails, securing the plank to each wall batten.

Use the universal channel supplied to house the edges at internal corners and against windows; use batten cover strip at exposed external corners. If a corner has to be turned, use the special trim for the ends of meeting planks.

Other accessories available include joint trim; drip trim to fix above windows; and butt joint cover strip, to hide joins in horizontal runs.

Cleaning To clean cladding, wipe it with washing-up liquid in warm water, then hose it down with water. Avoid rubbing it dry, as this builds up static in the plastic, which in turn attracts dust.

Plucking birds

How to deal with a bird in its feathers

Ideally, POULTRY should be plucked immediately after killing, while still warm. GAME birds, however, should not be plucked until after hanging. They should be hung by the neck in a cool, dry, airy place for seven to ten days. When buying a game bird in feather, enquire how long it has already been hanging.

Start with the legs and wings, drawing out two or three feathers at a time with a slight, backward pull against the way they lie. Be careful not to tear the skin. Pluck the breast last, beginning at the top and pulling down towards the head. After plucking, singe the remaining down and hairs from the bird with a lighted taper. Wipe the bird with a clean cloth and pluck out any remaining long hairs or quills with a pair of tweezers.

Plugs

Fitting and replacing electric connectors

Most electrical appliances are supplied with a plug and flex moulded together. The plug should contain the correct cartridge fuse – 3amp for appliances up to 720 watts and 13amp for those over 720 watts – see FUSES AND FUSE BOXES. The wattage is given on the appliance or the packaging.

Modern insulation colours in flex are brown for live, blue for neutral and green-and-yellow for earth – see ELECTRIC WIRING.

To remove a plug, undo the large screw securing the cover and remove it. Loosen the screws at the terminals and pull out the wires (in a no-screw plug, lift the clamps to release the wires). Release any screws clamping the flex in place and withdraw the flex. The wire ends may need baring afresh if they are blackened or have broken strands. A new flex will also need to have the ends bared.

New plugs usually have a diagram attached showing how much insulation to strip off. Lay the flex on a firm surface and use a sharp knife to make a cut lengthways through the outer sheath – about 38mm (1½in) usually needs stripping off. Bend the sheathing back and trim it off, taking care not to nick the insulation on the wires inside.

Use adjustable wire strippers to take off about 16mm (⅝in), or the recommended amount, of sheathing from each wire. Set the strippers carefully, so that they do not cut into the fine strands of wire. If the plug cover has a sleeve or hole at the base, feed the flex through it. Press the flex between the clamping flanges or secure it under the screw-down

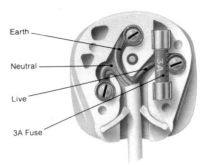

Wiring a plug Connect the brown wire to the live terminal, green/yellow to earth and blue to neutral. Wrap wires round terminal posts clockwise, or they will loosen when the screw is tightened. Make sure you have the right fuse; a 3amp fuse takes up to 720 watts.

clamp. The clamp must grip the outer sheath, not just the conductor wires.

Gently prise out the cartridge fuse if it is obscuring one of the terminals. Make the connections as shown.

Press the correct fuse gently in place. Fit the cover and screw it in place. On a no-screw plug the cover is secured by a quarter turn of the lock; on some models the lock turns automatically as you slide on the cover.

Plumbing

How the system works, and basic repairs

Get to know how your plumbing system works, so that you can deal with any trouble quickly and efficiently.

Locate your stopcock, which enables you to cut off the mains water supply if necessary – for example, when renewing a tap washer – see TAPS. The stopcock is normally inside – usually in the kitchen. Check that the stopcock turns easily, and show everyone in the household how to turn it off, to reduce damage should you get a burst pipe indoors.

Copper pipe joints There are three common types: compression, soldered capillary and push-fit. They are available from DIY stores in several configurations – such as T-joints, straight ones and elbows. All joints need the pipes to be cut absolutely square at their ends, using a fine hacksaw. Remove any burrs or roughness with a fine file, and smooth with emery cloth.

Compression joints The joint is made using a connector body, cap nuts which screw onto it, and 'olives' – soft copper compression rings – which fit between cap nut and connector.

Soldered capillary joint Integral-ring types have rings of solder set inside the

Understanding a domestic water system; making repairs

In most systems a mains pipe feeds the kitchen cold tap and then a storage tank in the loft, from which cold water is piped to other cold taps, the lavatory cistern and hot-water storage tank. In the system shown, the storage tank also supplies a feed and expansion tank, which feeds a boiler, from where hot water passes through a coil in the hot-water tank to heat it.

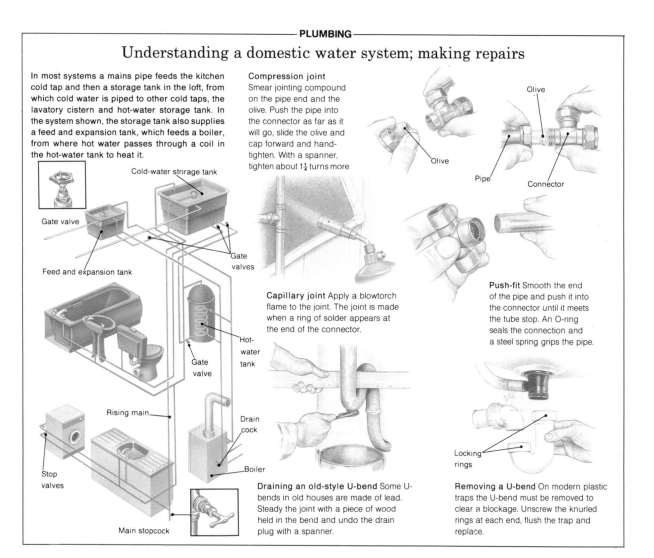

Compression joint Smear jointing compound on the pipe end and the olive. Push the pipe into the connector as far as it will go, slide the olive and cap forward and hand-tighten. With a spanner, tighten about 1¼ turns more.

Olive

Olive

Pipe

Connector

Cold-water storage tank

Gate valve

Feed and expansion tank

Gate valves

Gate valve

Hot-water tank

Rising main

Drain cock

Stop valves

Boiler

Main stopcock

Capillary joint Apply a blowtorch flame to the joint. The joint is made when a ring of solder appears at the end of the connector.

Push-fit Smooth the end of the pipe and push it into the connector until it meets the tube stop. An O-ring seals the connection and a steel spring grips the pipe.

Locking rings

Draining an old-style U-bend Some U-bends in old houses are made of lead. Steady the joint with a piece of wood held in the bend and undo the drain plug with a spanner.

Removing a U-bend On modern plastic traps the U-bend must be removed to clear a blockage. Unscrew the knurled rings at each end, flush the trap and replace.

---

connector by the manufacturer. Use steel wool to clean the cut end of the tube inside and out. Apply flux to the cleaned surfaces. Push the pipe well into the connector. Place some fireproof material such as glass fibre between the repair area and any woodwork, then apply a blowtorch (see BLOWTORCHES), until a silver ring of solder appears all round the mouth of the joint. Solder all openings on the joint in the same operation. Let the joint cool before any more work is done.

When making a soldered joint close to an existing joint, apply a damp rag to the existing joint to prevent heat from the soldering affecting it.

Push-fit joint This is made using a fitting which incorporates a circular coiled spring. Prepare the pipe as for a compression joint, then simply push it firmly into the fitting. The spring will allow the

pipe in, but will not let it be withdrawn. To break the joint it would be necessary to break the ring and later replace it with a new one.

Common problems
Dripping tap Probably means the washer needs changing – see TAPS.

Blocked sink Try clearing the blockage with a length of flexible curtain wire. If this fails, put a bucket under the sink and undo the nut on the waste trap. This may mean unscrewing a plug at the bottom of the U-bend, or unscrewing and removing a section of plastic pipe. Clean out any obstruction, re-connect and flush with boiling water and detergent.

If the blockage is further down than the trap, block the overflow outlet with a wet rag, then use a rubber suction cup on the waste outlet, pumping it up and down to build up pressure in the pipe,

forcing the obstruction out.

Leaking lavatory-pan joint Bail out most of the water from the lavatory bowl, then examine the waste outlet behind the pan. In older systems there is a caulked gap between the pan outlet pipe and the waste pipe; the caulking material may have failed.

Dig this out with an old knife, clean the interior surfaces and dry them off. Then reseal the joint with non-setting mastic filler and a waterproof building tape or cord.

More modern systems have a plastic pipe connected to the pan by a special rubber sleeve which is a push-fit on pan and pipe. You may find it has perished and split; if so, replace it with an identical sleeve, available from plumbers' merchants. No sealant should be needed, as long as the sleeve is pushed well home, but it is a wise precaution to use some.

Blocked lavatory Do not flush a blocked toilet until an attempt has been made to unblock it. Buy a large suction cup from a hardware shop or plumbers' merchant, and pump the cup up and down in the base of the pan. The water pressure built up in this way will often clear the blockage. If not, the outside drain may be blocked – see DRAINS.

Once the blockage is cleared, flush with water and brush until clean.

Running overflow pipe Overflow pipes protruding from the wall give warning of a fault. Check what the pipe is connected to: a lower one may be from a lavatory cistern; a high one from the cold-water storage tank. The fault will almost certainly be linked to a faulty ball valve – see BALL COCKS.

Leaking waste pipe On a basin or sink, water dripping from underneath may be caused by lack of sealant under the waste grid in the sink. Disconnect the waste pipe under the sink and lift out the waste grid. Clean off any old sealant, apply a thin ring of mastic sanitaryware sealant and bed the waste grid onto this. Refit the waste assembly. You may need to borrow a large spanner or adjustable wrench for the back nut – see SPANNERS AND WRENCHES.

If there are leaks at joints in plastic waste pipes, screw locking nuts only finger-tight to get a good seal. Tightening with a spanner can cause a stripped or crossed thread.

Leaking storage tank Older tanks are usually made of galvanised steel. At any signs of rusting and weeping at pinholes in the metal, have the tank replaced by a modern polythene one.

Plumb line

Finding a true vertical

Sometimes known as a plumb bob, this little device is used to establish a true vertical when erecting FENCES; GUTTERS AND DOWNPIPES; BRACKETS and GATES. It is also useful when decorating, to find the vertical line to which you can match the first length when WALLPAPERING. You can buy one from a DIY store, or use a small weighty object, such as a bolt, tied to a length of builder's line.

To use a plumb line, extend the line and hold it near the top of the wall, allowing the bob to settle three-quarters of the way down. Once swinging stops, get a helper to press the line to the wall and mark where it lies; then mark the top of the line before removing it.

If you are putting up wallcovering, make sure the edge of the first length touches both pencil marks.

To find a vertical over a short distance, it is possible to get 1m (3ft) long spirit levels with vertical and horizontal vials. See also LEVELLING.

Plywood

Choosing and using the correct grades

Grades of plywood vary from interior – which must not be exposed to damp – to marine ply, used for boatbuilding and impervious to water. The durability of the adhesive determines the grade.

The main classifications are recognised by these letters: WBP, weather and boil-proof, suitable for exterior use; BR, boil-resistant; MR, moisture resistant; and INT, interior use only. Thickness ranges from 1.5mm ($^1/_{16}$in) to 32mm ($1\frac{1}{4}$in). The commonest sizes are 4mm ($^5/_{32}$in), 6mm ($\frac{1}{4}$in) and 9mm ($\frac{3}{8}$in).

If you are planning to make furniture, and need a decorative plywood, ask a good timber merchant for details of the range. Plywood is available faced with a decorative VENEER such as beech, birch, redwood, sapele, mahogany, gaboon, walnut, teak and oak. However, these decorative boards are dearer than standard plywood.

Cutting Plywood tends to fray at the edges when sawn. To avoid this, use a craft knife and straightedge to score a line on both surfaces along the proposed cut. use a dovetail or small tenon saw for plywood up to about 6mm, a tenon saw for 6-12mm ($\frac{1}{4}$-$\frac{1}{2}$in) thick plywood, and for thicker boards use a panel saw, a circular saw or a power jigsaw – see SAWS AND SAWING.

Always cut through the decorative veneer first, to avoid damaging it.

Bending Use only thin plywoods – three ply – for bending. Plywood bends best at right angles to the direction of grain of the surface veneers.

To make bending easier, damp the plywood with water. Applying a hot iron to the damp veneer makes it even more pliable. But let it dry thoroughly before GLUING.

Smoothing Use fine glasspaper, working with the grain to avoid scratch marks. Use a SANDING block for edges, but rub with a downward action, never upward, or you may lift off and split the top layer.

Poaching

Cooking gently in a simmering liquid

To poach food, simply cook it for a few minutes in a gently simmering liquid, kept just below boiling point. The two most popular poached dishes are EGGS

and fish – see also FISH CLEANING. Some fruits can also be poached.

Poached eggs Fill a heavy-based frying pan with cold water to a depth of 25mm (1in). (Or use a ready-made egg poacher, available from hardware shops.)

Add a pinch of salt and bring to the boil. Reduce the heat and keep the water just simmering. Break the eggs, one by one, onto a saucer and slide them carefully into the water. Take a spoon in each hand and quickly gather the whites over and round the yolks. Cover the pan with a lid and cook the eggs for 4-5 minutes, or until the yolks are still soft and the whites just set.

Poaching fish All types of fish – whole, filleted, or steaks – can be poached. Use a large saucepan or fish kettle on the cooker hob, or a shallow covered dish in the oven at 180°C (350°F), gas mark 4. To remove the cooked fish easily, tie it loosely in muslin.

Cover the fish completely with lightly salted water – $1\frac{1}{2}$ level teaspoons to 1.1 litres (2 pints) of water. Add to the pan a few parsley or mushroom stalks, a generous squeeze of lemon, a slice of onion and carrot, together with a bay leaf and half-a-dozen peppercorns.

Bring the liquid to a boil over a moderate heat. Then cover the pan and lower the heat. Simmer the fish until it flakes when tested with a fork (allow 8-10 minutes per pound).

Pocket mending

Repairing holes and tears

To repair a large hole in a pocket, cut off the section with the hole or tear in it. Obtain some new pocket material; you can buy it at a sewing shop or a department store haberdashery counter, or use fabric similar to the original pocket.

Fold the new material in two and cut it to size. Machine-stitch the edges together – see SEWING. Sew two separate seams about 1mm ($^1/_{32}$in) apart to give extra strength to the join.

Pin the new piece to the cut-off pocket, then tack and machine it in place. Remove the tacking.

If a hole or tear is near the outside edge or corner of a pocket, machine-stitch a seam above the fault in a slight curve. Cut away the material below the new stitching. If the hole or worn area is within the body of the pocket, either darn or patch it – see DARNING; PATCHING.

Patch pockets sometimes come loose at the top corners. To secure them, sew up to the corners with straight machine-stitches; then sew down for about 13mm ($\frac{1}{2}$in) for a firm finish. To sew the corner by hand, whipstitch for about 6mm ($\frac{1}{4}$in) on either side of it.

Poinsettias

Looking after them all year round

The poinsettia's chief beauty is its flower-like bracts (modified leaves) – normally a brilliant red, though sometimes pink or white. The plant's flowers, by contrast, are small and a dull yellow-green colour.

The bracts can be made to form at any time of the year, if the plant is kept in a dark place for 14 hours a day for eight weeks. Most commercial growers make the bracts on their poinsettias 'flower' in time for Christmas, when their colour makes them especially popular.

Looking after a flowering plant Water a poinsettia with flowering bracts only when the foliage begins to droop. When watering, saturate the potting mixture thoroughly. Do not feed.

Keep the plant at normal room temperature, out of draughts and in bright filtered light – such as sunlight through a blind or net curtain.

Encouraging new growth The bracts flower for at least two months. When they fade and fall, cut the plant down to 25-50mm (1-2in) from the base. Allow the potting mixture to get almost, but not quite, dry, so that the plant stops growing.

Leave the dormant plant for about a month (until April if it was flowering at Christmas) at normal room temperature in bright filtered light. Then flood with water. When new shoots start to appear, repot (see POTTING HOUSEPLANTS) in fresh soil-based potting mixture. Do not repot into a larger pot or the plant will not produce good bracts.

Alternatively, instead of repotting the old plant, grow new plants from 75mm (3in) tip cuttings taken from the new shoots – see PROPAGATING PLANTS. After a month the cuttings should develop roots and start growing actively. Repot in fresh soil-based mixture.

Pointing

Restoring mortar joints in brickwork

Pointing on brickwork (see BRICKLAYING) not only gives a neat finish but helps keep rainwater out of the joints. Repoint any cracked or crumbly areas quickly.

Chip out the old mortar to a depth of about 13mm ($\frac{1}{2}$in), using a cold or plugging chisel and club hammer, and protecting your eyes with goggles. Work back to soundly pointed joints. Dust out the cavities with an old paintbrush, then damp them with clean water about five minutes before pointing.

Trowel a small heap of freshly made MORTAR onto a hawk, then use the trowel to press mortar firmly into the joints,

over-filling them slightly. The way you finish off the joints is governed by how the rest of the wall is pointed. The commonest finishes are flush pointing and weathered pointing.

Filling joints Press mortar liberally into the joints, prodding it firmly with the trowel edge to make sure there is no gap behind it. Trim off the excess with a flush or weathered finish.

Flush pointing When the mortar is almost dry, trim off excess flush with the bricks using a pointing trowel. Rub the joints smooth with sacking.

Weathered pointing This is finished sloping inwards from the bottom of the joint, so that water runs off the mortar.

Hold the pointing trowel down a vertical joint and use the trowel edge to push one side of the joint in. Draw the trowel across to the other side to cut off surplus mortar. Shape all the same way.

On a horizontal joint, use the trowel edge to push in the mortar at the top of the joint by about 3mm ($\frac{1}{8}$in). Hold a straight timber batten below the joint and trim off surplus mortar with the trowel leaving the lower edge projecting slightly. When almost dry, rub the surface with a dusting brush.

Poisoning

Emergency – the action and treatment

Ordinary domestic chemicals such as bleach, cleaning fluids, white spirit and weedkillers often cause poisoning – especially if left within reach of children or stored in drink bottles.

Someone who has taken poison will probably show one or more of the following symptoms – retching or VOMITING; pains in the stomach; UNCONSCIOUSNESS; DIARRHOEA; delirium and convulsions; or difficulty in breathing.

If the poison was corrosive, there will be BURNS round the mouth and severe pain in the mouth, gullet and stomach. Take immediate action:
- Call an ambulance.
- If the victim is unconscious, gently put him in the correct RECOVERY POSITION.

- If breathing ceases, start ARTIFICIAL RESPIRATION, first cleaning the victim's mouth to make sure that none of the poison gets into your own mouth.
- Try to identify the poison. If the victim is still conscious, ask what it was. Otherwise look around for any container or, say, the remains of a poisonous plant that might give a clue.
- When the ambulancemen arrive, give them the container or any other clue, such as a sample of vomit.
- If the victim is still conscious and has swallowed something that burns – bleach for example – persuade him to sip water or milk slowly, to dilute the poison.
- Do *not* try to induce vomiting. It may be harmful and simply wastes time.

Poker

Playing a favourite card game

There are numerous variations of the game. In all, however, the basic object is to assemble the highest ranking hand of five cards – no matter how many cards are dealt, or in what manner – and thus win the 'pot', the total of all the bets wagered.

Before any cards are dealt, each player puts an 'ante' (a set amount of money, or an equivalent plastic 'chip') in the pot.

One player is named banker and takes charge of holding and distributing the chips. Traditionally, blue chips are worth most, red come second and white third. Other wagers are made during the course of the play (the amounts are usually limited by prior agreement).

The players usually cut cards for dealer, and the player with the highest card deals the first hand. Cards are dealt clockwise, and the betting proceeds in the same order. The next hand is dealt by the person on the previous dealer's left, and so on.

Stud poker This is perhaps the most popular form of the game. The dealer gives each player one card face down (the *hole* card), then a second face up; players may look at their hole cards.

Betting is started by the player with the highest face up card. If there is a tie for the highest card, the player who received his card first bets. The other players must bet the same amount, or they may drop out by turning over their face-up card. A player can drop out during any betting round.

After the first round, the competing players are dealt another card face up. Dealing and betting continue until all the competing players have four cards face up. At the final betting (called the 'showdown'), the remaining players turn over their hole card. The highest hand wins the pot.

Stud poker is sometimes played with up to four 'wild' cards (say the four deuces), which can assume any value the player or players who hold them choose. For example, with a wild card and four aces, it is possible to have five of a kind – five aces, for example – the highest-ranking combination of all.

Among the many other variations of poker are Draw Poker, which often involves an element of bluffing (hence the expression 'a poker face'); One-Eyed Jacks, in which the two one-eyed jacks (the Jack of Hearts and the Jack of Spades) are wild; and High-Low, in which a player plays his hand for either high or low, but does not state which way he is playing until the last card is dealt. The pot is split between the two players with the highest and lowest hands.

Winning hands
In order of value, the highest hands are:

Royal flush – ace, king, queen, jack and ten of the same suit.

Straight flush – five numerically consecutive cards of the same suit, the highest being that led by a king and so on down the rank.

Four of a kind – any four cards of the same value, the highest being four aces. The fifth card in the hand does not count.

Full house – three cards of one value, together with two of another, the highest being three aces and two kings.

Flush – any five cards of the same suit, the value of the flush depending on the value of the highest card.

Straight – five numerically consecutive cards of any mixture of suits, the value depending on the highest card.

Three of a kind – any three cards of the same value, ranking from three aces downwards. The other two cards in the hand do not count.

Two pairs – two cards of the same value and of any suit, and two of another. The higher fifth card in the hands decides the winner between two pairs of equal value.

One pair – two cards of the same value and of any suit. The highest ranking pair is the winner. If the two competing pairs are of equal value, then the player holding the highest of the remaining cards wins the hand.

If no one has a better hand, the player with the highest single card (starting with an ace, and working down) wins the pot. If the winning card is an ace, then it is a case of *Ace high*, and so on through the ranking.

Pomander

Making an aromatic room freshener

A thin-skinned orange studded with cloves makes a simple, fragrant pomander. First, stick a line of cloves round the circumference of the orange starting at the stalk, then stick another line round the middle of the orange.

Now work outwards from these lines, pressing the cloves in firmly with one clove width of space between the heads. Cover the entire orange like this.

Mix 1 teaspoon each of orris root powder and cinnamon and roll the clove-covered orange in the mixture.

Wrap the orange in greaseproof or waxed paper and store in a dark place for several weeks to dry. As it dries out and shrinks, the cloves will be more closely packed.

Pony trekking

Where to go and what you need

Pony trekking is an enjoyable way of exploring attractive countryside – generally in mountains or moorland, such as Dartmoor, Wales or the Scottish Highlands.

You do not need to be an experienced rider. A reputable trekking centre will provide riding instructors (see HORSE RIDING), and guides to lead the treks. The normal pace on a pony trek is a gentle walk, with an occasional trot.

Trekking centres Choose one of the trekking centres that are approved by the following equestrian organisations.

They produce lists of centres that are available on written application.

Ponies UK, Chesham House, 56 Green End Road, Sawtrey, Huntingdon PE17 5UY.

The British Horse Society, British Equestrian Centre, Stoneleigh, Kenilworth, Warks CV8 2LR.

Scottish Trekking and Riding Association, Tomnagairn Farm, Trochrie, by Dunkeld, Tayside.

The Welsh Trekking and Riding Association, Standby House, 9 Neville Street, Abergavenny, Gwent HP7 5AA.

What to take You must wear a hard riding hat – many centres have hats which you can borrow. For legwear, take strong corduroy or cavalry-twill riding trousers, or knee breeches with woollen stockings. Do not ride in shorts; they provide no protection for your legs.

Strong walking shoes with a well-defined heel are acceptable in place of riding boots. Wellington boots can be useful in wet weather. Remember to take a light, waterproof mackintosh or anorak and waterproof overtrousers.

Pool

How to play a popular game

Pool is played with 15 coloured object balls, 50mm (2in) in diameter, and a white cue ball slightly smaller. Originally, the object balls were all numbered and half of them had striped colouring. Modern contests, however, increasingly use unnumbered balls – seven red, seven yellow and one black.

Two players compete, and the first to

POOL

The playing table and arrangement of the balls

Cue-ball 'D'

String line

Pocket

Black-ball spot

Cushion

Cue-ball spot

A pool table is marked with a spot for the black ball and a line, the 'string line', behind which is the 'D' from where play starts.

Place the object balls in a triangle, with the leading ball nearest to the 'D'. Place the black on its spot in the centre of the third row. Place the remaining balls as shown.

pocket his own seven balls, plus the black, wins. The players do not know which set of balls is theirs until one ball has been pocketed.

The players decide – usually by tossing a coin – who is to *break* (make the first shot).

The break The opening player places the cue ball anywhere within the 'D' marked at the bottom end of the table.

Using his cue, he drives the cue ball at the triangle of balls, aiming to pocket an object ball or drive at least two balls (one of which can be the cue ball) against a cushion. If he does neither, it is a *foul break* and the game restarts, with the opponent having two shots.

The first time a player pockets a ball, the colour of the ball determines his set. If he pockets a red and a yellow ball then he can choose his set. If a player pockets the black from the break, the game will be restarted by the same player. When a player legally pockets a ball or balls, he continues by playing another shot. This carries on until he either fails to pocket one of his set of object balls or commits a foul. Then his opponent takes a turn.

Fouls When a foul is committed, the offending player not only ends his turn but also loses his next turn at the table. Fouls occur when:
● The cue ball is pocketed (*in-off*). The ball is then replaced anywhere within the 'D'.
● The cue ball strikes an opponent's ball before a player's own ball or balls.
● A player fails to hit any ball with the cue ball.
● The cue ball jumps over any part of any ball (*jump shot*).
● The cue ball hits the black on the first impact before a player's own balls have been pocketed (except at the break).
● A player pockets an opponent's ball or balls. If he pockets the black before all his own balls are down he loses the game.
● A ball goes off the table. Any object ball or the black is returned to the black spot, or as near to it as possible, in a direct line between there and the centre of the 'D', without touching another ball. If the cue ball goes off the table, it is replaced anywhere inside the 'D'.
● A player's body or clothing touches any of the balls, whether they are stationary or moving.
● A player fails to have at least one foot on the ground when playing a shot.
● A player strikes with his cue any ball other than the cue ball.
● A player plays out of turn.
● A player plays before the balls have come to rest.
● A player plays before the ball or balls have been respotted.
● A player strikes the cue ball with his cue more than once.

See also BILLIARDS; SNOOKER.

Porcelain

Restoring chipped and broken pieces

Broken porcelain is repaired in the same way as CHINA, and missing chips can be replaced with a filler. But always have valuable pieces restored by a professional, as poor restoration reduces value considerably.

Repairing chips or small pieces Fill chips with a mixture of slow-setting epoxy resin adhesive (see GLUING) and finely powdered chalk, called whiting. Whiting is stocked by specialist paint shops; you can use talcum powder as a substitute. To rebuild a small piece that is missing, put gummed tape across the back of the area – or if it is curved use model-casting rubber or dental impression compound. Fill the gap with a stiff mixture of the epoxy resin and chalk until it is just above the surface. When the filler has set, rub it smooth with very fine glasspaper. Take care not to scratch the adjoining glazed surface.

Remodelling a patterned piece If the missing piece is a shaped part of a repeated pattern, make a mould from a similar unbroken part, using model-casting rubber or dental impression compound. When the mould has set, fill it with ready-mixed, fine-surface cellulose filler paste – see STOPPERS AND FILLERS. When the filler is hard, remove it from the mould and trim and file it to shape. Stick it in place with epoxy resin adhesive.

Pork pie

Making a great English treat

The best-known English pie is the pork pie, served hot or cold and excellent for picnics or buffets. It is made with hot-water crust or 'raised' pastry.

This recipe makes a pie for four to six people:

Ingredients
For the stock:
2 veal knuckles chopped into pieces
1 bouquet garni (or 1 sage leaf, 1 bay leaf, 1 sprig marjoram, 1 sprig thyme)
$\frac{1}{2}$ level teaspoon salt
6 peppercorns

For the pastry:
350g (12oz) plain flour
$\frac{1}{4}$ level teaspoon salt
115g (4oz) lard
4 tablespoons milk
1 egg, beaten for glazing

For the filling:
700g (1$\frac{1}{2}$lb) lean pork
Salt and freshly ground black pepper

First make the stock – see also SOUPS AND STOCKS. Rinse the veal bones in cold water, then put them in a large pan with the bouquet garni, salt and peppercorns. Cover with cold water. Bring to the boil and skim off the surface scum with a large spoon.

Cover the pan with the lid at a slight angle and simmer gently for 2 hours, skimming off the scum from time to time. Then boil rapidly to reduce to 285ml ($\frac{1}{2}$ pint). Strain through muslin or a fine sieve into a small jug. Leave to cool, then remove the fat from the surface.

Meanwhile, make the pastry. Sieve the flour and salt into a bowl. Put the lard, milk and 4 tablespoons of cold water into a large pan and bring slowly to the boil. When boiling rapidly, pour into the centre of the flour. Beat with a wooden spoon until the mixture clings together, coming away cleanly from the sides of the bowl.

Turn onto a lightly floured surface and knead well (see BREAD MAKING) to a smooth dough. Add a few drops of boiling water if it is too stiff, or a little flour if it is too sticky.

Thoroughly grease a 180mm (7in) loose-based cake tin with a single-layered base. Set aside one-third of the dough for the lid of the pie. Keep it warm on a plate over boiling water.

Roll out the rest of the dough to about 6mm ($\frac{1}{4}$in) thick while still warm and carefully line the inside of the tin. Make sure that the dough is even and that there are no holes through which meat juices could escape. Keep back a little dough to plug any holes that may appear. Leave for 10 minutes to set.

With a sharp knife, cut all excess fat from the pork. Cut the meat into 13mm ($\frac{1}{2}$in) cubes. Season with salt and pepper to taste and pack into the pastry-lined tin to within 19mm ($\frac{3}{4}$in) of the top. Moisten with 2 tablespoons of cold water.

Roll the remaining pastry to a circle for the lid. Moisten the pie edge with cold water, then place the lid on top. Pinch the edges together to seal them, trimming off any excess. Cut a hole in the top to let steam escape.

Place the tin on a baking tray and bake in an oven preheated to 190°C (375°F), gas mark 5, for 1 hour. Remove the pie from the oven and let it cool for 5 minutes, then push the pie up out of the tin, but leave it on the base. Brush the top and sides with beaten egg.

Reduce the oven heat to 180°C (350°F), gas mark 4, and cook on a baking tray for a further 1-1$\frac{1}{2}$ hours. Remove from the oven and leave until nearly cold.

Pour the stock into the pie, through a small funnel placed in the hole in the top. If the stock has set, heat it until it becomes liquid again before you pour it into the pie. Set the pie aside for a few hours while the stock sets and becomes a jelly.

Portrait photography

*Taking lively photos of family
and friends*

A snapshot taken when someone is absorbed in some activity and unaware of the camera can bring the subject vividly to life. To take a 'candid camera' shot, set aperture, shutter speed and focus in advance (see PHOTOGRAPHY) then watch and wait for the ideal moment.

Such a natural effect is much more difficult to obtain when someone is 'sitting' for a portrait. Faced formally with a camera, many people become stiff and ungainly, with strained expressions. Here are some tips for achieving a lively, natural result.
● Relax the 'sitter' – if possible, photograph him at home or in his own garden – perhaps in a comfortable chair, or leaning against a tree or wall. Otherwise try to put him in familiar surroundings.
● A three-quarter view or half-profile is best for most faces. A full profile accentuates forehead, nose and jaw line. A front view makes sharp features less prominent.
● Avoid full-length portraits with the subject standing stiffly to attention; most people feel and look awkward standing upright. It is better to let them lean against something.
● Take full-length portraits with your camera level with the subject's midriff, and close-ups or head-and-shoulder shots

with the camera at eye level. Focus on the subject's eyes or the bridge of the nose; if they are in focus, with a small aperture (high 'f' number) the whole face will be sharp.
● When taking a formal seated portrait, if the subject adopts an awkward posture or posed expression ask him to look away from the camera, then press the button as his head turns back towards you.
● The best results are usually obtained at a distance of 2-3m (6-8ft). Fixed focus and automatic cameras usually give blurred results at a distance of less than 1.2m (4ft).

Outdoor shots In bright sunlight, position your subject in light shade – under a large, leafy tree, for example, or on the shady side of a building.

For soft contrast and even lighting, choose slightly dull, overcast days. Or work in the early morning or late afternoon on sunnier days.

Indoor lighting Work either with all natural light *or* with all artificial lighting. Do not use fluorescent lights, which are too harsh, or mix different kinds of lighting.

For a dramatic effect, try side lighting which accentuates skin texture and facial contours. Place a light at one side of the subject – and possibly a sheet of white cardboard at the other side to bounce light back and soften shadows.

PORTRAIT PHOTOGRAPHY

Choosing the best way to photograph people

Crouch down with one leg tucked under you to photograph subjects that are at a low level. Brace elbows against knee and leg to minimise camera shake.

When photographing subjects indoors and in natural lighting, place them beside a window which receives indirect sunlight.

Photograph a child when he is absorbed with something, to avoid a formal pose. Record his changing expressions with several shots.

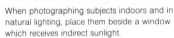

For a very low viewpoint, lie along the ground with your feet apart, and elbows resting on the ground. When you do not want to disturb a subject use a telephoto lens.

Posture

*Testing and correcting the way
you stand*

Correct posture is a comfortably erect stance in which head, trunk and legs are balanced one on top of the other in a relaxed but straight line. Rigidly erect military bearing is no longer considered a healthy posture – see BACKACHE.

How to test your posture Stand against a wall with your upper back, buttocks and heels pressed to the wall. Slip a hand between the small of your back and the wall. It should just be able to move in and out without touching your back or the wall.

If there is much extra space between your back and the wall, your back is probably arching forward more than it should – a condition known as *lordosis*, or hollow back.

Correcting mild lordosis Lordosis is generally caused by a heavy abdomen or weak abdominal muscles. It can often be corrected by losing weight and exercising the abdominal muscles to strengthen them.

Corrective exercises include sit-ups – see EXERCISES. Another is to stand against the wall with your feet a few inches from the wall. Tilt your pelvis forward so that you can touch the wall with your lower back.

When standing or sitting, straighten your lower back slightly. Women should keep to a minimum the wearing of high-heeled shoes.

Slumping This is a common problem with adolescents. It usually corrects itself as they grow older – and more confident. Encourage, but do not nag about, good posture.

Consult your DOCTOR about increasing or painful problems with posture.

Potatoes

Growing new potatoes successfully

Potatoes require a lot of room, so unless you have a large garden, grow a small crop of new potatoes which you can eat while shop prices are still high. To raise a sack of potatoes (25kg, 56lb) you need to plant 3kg (7lb) of seed potatoes in rows totalling 13.5m (45ft). Yield depends partly on variety and weather.

Digging a bed Dig over the bed in late autumn or early winter. For light soil, fork in two buckets of well-rotted manure per square metre; for heavy soil, dig in a generous dressing of strawy manure, well-rotted garden COMPOST, leaf mould or peat, plus some grit or sharp sand – see SOIL PREPARATION.

Leave the ground rough, to let the frosts break it up for spring planting. Just before planting, top-dress the bed with a general fertiliser at the rate of 175g (6oz) per square metre – see FERTILISERS.

Preparing seed potatoes for planting Seed potatoes are available from garden centres and seed firms. Buy 'first earlies' from the end of January, choosing only those which are certified 'disease-free'. Place them immediately in tomato trays (which have posts at each corner for stacking) laid out in rows with the rose ends – those having most 'eyes' – uppermost.

Keep the trays in a bright, cold, dry, airy room or greenhouse, where they will begin sprouting after four or five weeks when they are ready to be planted. Discard any that look diseased. The sprouts should be ideally about 6-13mm ($\frac{1}{4}$-$\frac{1}{2}$in) long. Always dust them with a non-toxic fungicide recommended for potatoes – see PESTICIDES.

In sheltered regions, the best time to plant is mid-March; in frosty or exposed areas, delay planting until as late as the end of April.

Planting Use a draw hoe to scoop out a straight 'drill' (furrow) for each row of potatoes, about 100mm (4in) deep in light soil or about 150mm (6in) deep in heavy soil. Space the drills about 600mm (2ft) apart.

Place the seed potatoes, sprouts uppermost, at the bottom of each drill every 300mm (12in). Cover them lightly with a ridge of soil and do not press them down with your feet.

Hoe a little extra soil over young shoots as they appear. As they turn into tufts of leaves, and if there is still a danger of frost, cover with dry straw.

Earthing up When the plants are about 230mm (9in) tall, begin earthing up. Break up the soil between rows and scatter a general-purpose fertiliser over it at the maker's recommended rate. Then hoe the loose soil and fertiliser to form a steep ridge over each row. The ridge should be about 150mm (6in) high with its top about 125mm (5in) wide and its base about 200mm (8in).

A week later, hoe more soil onto the ridge to raise it by about 25mm (1in). Three weeks later, when the plants are at least 300mm (12in) tall, raise the ridge by another 25mm.

Harvesting New potatoes should not be lifted until you want to eat them – they grow rapidly and can double their weight in a fortnight. In June, scoop away some soil from the side of the ridge with your fingers and see if the potatoes are large enough to cook. Pick a first 'boiling' and leave the rest to increase in size. Eat potatoes as soon as possible after lifting; dry off any that are not wanted immediately.

Before the final harvest, cut off the foliage; then use a garden fork for lifting, inserting it well clear of the plants and pushing it in fairly deep, so that it does not pierce the potatoes.

Forcing an early crop If you have a greenhouse, with space to spare, try forcing a small high-quality crop of new potatoes – see GREENHOUSES; GREENHOUSE GARDENING.

Buy first earlies as soon as available. Lay pieces of broken clay pots at the bottom of 250-300mm (10-12in) plastic pots and cover them with about 50mm (2in) of JOHN INNES COMPOST No 3. Place one or two seed potatoes in each pot, eyes or sprouts uppermost. Cover them with a 25mm (1in) layer of compost.

Start them into growth at 4-7°C (39-45°F); water sparingly at first. Then as foliage develops, add more compost round its base weekly until the level is 25mm below the rim of the pot. Increase watering, raise the temperature to 10-13°C (50-55°F) and feed every 10-14 days with dilute liquid manure.

About 12-14 weeks after planting, pick off the largest potatoes, repot in larger pots and continue growing.

Pests Common problems include wireworms and eelworms. To counter them, see PESTICIDES.

Potpourri
Giving your rooms a fragrant atmosphere

A potpourri is a mixture of flower petals and leaves, preserved in a bowl or pot and used to scent the air. Favourite ingredients include ROSES, lavender, fragrant polyanthus, verbena, geraniums, rosemary and bergamot – but any flowers or leaves that keep their scent when dried can be used – see FLOWER DRYING.

Start organising your potpourri in the spring and add to it throughout the flowering season. You need clean storage jars that can be tightly sealed, and a fixative to help preserve the scents. Traditionally, musk, civet or ambergris were used as fixatives, but they are expensive. You can make your own from spices:

Ingredients
25g (1oz) allspice
25g (1oz) cloves
25g (1oz) ground nutmeg
115g (4oz) ground orris root
The juice and grated rind of 3 lemons

Mix the ingredients together and allow them to stand for a few hours. If you wish, add dashes of oil of geranium, essence of lemon, oil of bergamot or spirit of lavender to enhance the scent.

Preparing the flowers The flowers should be picked early in the morning of a dry day, after the dew has evaporated, but before the sun is at full strength. Strip the petals from the flower heads and lay them to dry in the sun, spreading them out so that they are not touching each other. If you use rose petals, trim away the white area from the base of each petal.

Allow the petals to dry for two or three hours. Then mix them in an open bowl, adding a pinch or two of salt and the same amount of saltpetre to each handful. Let that mixture stand for two or three hours.

Put the petals into a storage jar and add the fixative in the proportion of 25g (1oz) to each eight handfuls. When you have used up all the petals, seal the jar.

Add more petals as they become available, resealing the jars afterwards. The petals after the first batch do not need to be dried, and the mixture should remain slightly moist. If it dries out, sprinkle on a few more pinches of salt. When the jars are full, stir the contents again and empty them into bowls to put on display.

Pottery
Making plates and dishes in clay; firing and glazing

Pottery clays are mixed in several types:

Earthenware These clays have a range of colours but are porous when fired.

Stoneware This fires to a hard, non-porous texture.

Porcelain Difficult to use because of their poor plasticity and the high temperatures needed to fire them, porcelain clays fire to a translucent white.

Self-hardening Beginners can start with this natural clay because it needs no firing; a glaze or varnish will make it non-porous, but it is not suitable for vessels intended to hold liquids.

Preparing and modelling the clay Pottery clay can be bought wet or dry from a crafts shop. The less bulky dry clay must be mixed and sprinkled with water to make it workable, then allowed to sit, in a sealed container or wrapped in plastic, for a few days.

Add plenty of water to wet clay to break it down and then mix it well to remove any lumps. Let the clay sit for several days before draining off excess water. The remaining clay must dry out until it is firm enough to use.

Clay must always be stored in an air-

POTTERY

Hand-building pottery without a wheel

There are two methods of hand-building pottery where the only tools you will need are fingers and thumbs. If you use self-hardening clay you will not need a firing kiln either. In the pinch method, the pot is formed by squeezing the clay into shape. The coil method uses clay rolled into strips and built up in coils on a flat base.

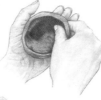

Pinch pottery Start with a ball of clay and sink your thumbs into the centre. Shape the pot by squeezing the clay from the outside.

Coil pottery First make a circular base of flat clay. Roll out a strip and use a piece of wood to press it onto the base.

Build up coils, applying slip (a thick mixture of clay and water) to each coil. Smooth the exterior with your thumbs.

Narrow the top of a large pot by tightening the coil. Let it dry for a few minutes periodically to stop it sagging.

tight container. Put a damp towel in with it to stop it drying out completely.

You will need a few modelling tools (see MODELLING IN CLAY), a large sponge or cloth for mopping up, and a board to work on. Have a plant spray or bowl of water ready to damp the clay as you work. Make your own wedging wire for cutting the clay, by attaching metal wire or strong nylon to two wooden handles.

Work on a very strong flat surface and place a board beneath the clay. 'Wedge' it by cutting the block in half, putting one half on top of the other and banging the two together hard. Do this until the clay is of even texture, cutting in different directions. Then knead the clay for at least ten minutes – until it is easy to handle and not at all sticky.

Simple pots or dishes can be fashioned by hand. Two simple methods – pinching and coiling – are illustrated. The items made can be textured in various ways. Use everyday objects such as nuts, bolts or shells, or roll twigs or leaves onto the clay to create patterns.

If the clay has to be fired allow the pots to dry out thoroughly for at least a week beforehand. Self-hardening clay will harden fully after two days. Learn to make or 'throw' pots on a wheel at evening class before buying equipment.

Firing Clay is fired at temperatures usually exceeding 1090°C (about 2000°F) to make it rigid and non-porous. This requires either an electric or fuel-burning kiln: new ones are expensive but secondhand kilns are advertised in specialist pottery magazines.

If you consider buying a kiln, make sure the manufacturer is reliable and accessible for servicing and parts. Check an electric kiln's capacity, to avoid overloading your domestic power system.

Most fuel-burning kilns use natural gas, but some burn oil, coke and wood.

Clay is fired in two stages: *biscuit* firing, then *glaze* firing.

Biscuit This is done at relatively low temperatures, usually 890-900°C (1634-1652°F), and stiffens the clay, making it safer to handle and ready to absorb glaze. The temperature has to be brought up slowly to allow any moisture that remains in the clay to evaporate gradually, rather than as an explosive steam which could crack the pot. Cooling must also be gradual.

Pots can be stacked on top of each other for biscuit firing, but should stand at least 6mm (¼in) apart for glaze firing.

Glaze A variety of 'glazing' materials is available from craft shops – follow the makers' instructions. Low-firing glazes come in a greater range of colours than those for high-firing temperatures, but are softer and more liable to scratch.

Before glazing wipe any dust off the biscuit-fired pots with a damp sponge or cloth. Apply the glaze, either by pouring it into the pot and rotating it until all areas are covered, or by dipping the pot in glaze and shaking off the excess. Use a brush to touch up the patches where you were holding the pot. Do not glaze the underside of a piece, or it will stick to the kiln shelf.

Do not touch a piece after glazing. Let the glaze dry completely, then fire it again, at the temperature specified for the glaze you are using.

Potting houseplants

How and when to repot

Houseplants need to be repotted as soon as they become 'pot-bound' – telltale signs are little or no growth, unusually small, pale or yellowish foliage, roots poking through the base of the pot.

Remove the plant from the pot and examine the roots. If they are densely matted or twisted in a thick spiral, have reached the outer edge of the soil or compost, or are beginning to push out new tips all over the surface, it is time to repot.

The best time is in spring or early summer. Young plants usually need larger pots once a year; older ones, every two or three years. Once a plant has reached the maximum convenient pot size or has reached full size, every year or two scoop out the top 50mm (2in) of soil, without exposing the main roots, and refill to the original level with fresh potting mixture – see HOUSEPLANTS.

Potting mixtures The mixture must contain nitrogen, potash and phosphates in correct proportions. Buy only sterilised mixtures.

Of the JOHN INNES COMPOSTS, use No 1 for young or slow-growing plants; No 2 for larger or established plants; and No 3 for well established, vigorous, fast-growing plants, such as chrysanthemums.

Soilless (peat substitute-based) potting mixtures, with fertilisers and added sand for drainage, are also suitable for pot plants, but feeding is essential within two months. Using a soil-based mixture, feeding is not necessary until after three months.

Pots You can use either plastic or clay pots. Plants in unglazed clay pots are less likely to become waterlogged, but need more frequent watering.

Repotting Place drainage material at the bottom of the new pot. If the pot is clay, with a large drainage hole, place a crock -- a fragment of broken clay pot – over the hole, curved side up.

A large plastic pot with three or four drainage holes requires a piece of crock over each hole. A pot with a single drainage hole needs a shallow layer of gravel on top of the crock. This will prevent waterlogging, if a pool forms in the container.

Place a layer of slightly moist, fresh potting mixture over the drainage material in the new pot, seat the plant on it and fill and firm well. When repotting is complete, the compost surface should be from 13mm (½in) below the rim of a 125mm (5in) pot to 50mm (2in) of a 380mm (15in) one.

If need be, take out the plant and increase or reduce the depth of the bottom layer of potting mixture, then

Removing a plant and repotting

Support the plant stem between two fingers, turn the pot upside down and tap the rim with a piece of wood.

To prepare a firm mould for the rootball, place the old pot inside a larger one and fill the space between them with fresh mixture, firm, then remove the small pot.

replace the plant. Make sure the plant is centred and hold it steady with one hand so that the stem is vertical. Use the other hand to pour fresh mixture around the rootball until you have filled the pot up to the correct level.

Tamp the mixture down gently with your fingers or a small piece of wood. Pack soil-based mixtures more firmly than peat substitute-based ones – but not too firmly, or water will not soak in.

Fill air pockets and settle the mixture evenly round the rootball by knocking the bottom of the pot gently on the table while filling. Water thoroughly, wetting the perimeter of the compost rather than the centre. If need be, top up the mixture after watering.

Poultry

Preparing and cooking birds

Most poultry is sold ready for cooking. If not, it should be plucked immediately after killing (see PLUCKING BIRDS), then hung head down in a cool, airy place. Hang chickens for about 24 hours; allow one or two days for geese and ducks, three to five days for turkeys. See also GAME BIRDS.

Once the bird is hung, draw it. Pull the skin away from the neck, cut off the head neatly, and sever the neck close to the body, leaving a loose flap of skin. Remove the crop and windpipe and loosen the entrails with your fingers through the neck cavity. Then enlarge the vent under the tail with a sharp knife, and draw out the entrails and any excess fat through it. Wash the bird,

inside and out, with cold water. Finally, slit the skin around the knee joints, draw out the tendons, twist and dislocate the shanks and cut off the legs at the knees.

The prepared bird Once plucked and drawn, poultry should have smooth skin, no hairs or discolorations, a clean cavity and no apparent odour. Fresh birds can be cooked immediately. Frozen ones should be allowed to thaw, still bagged, for 24-48 hours in a refrigerator.

Almost any cooking method is suitable for young birds. An older one should be roasted or braised (see BRAISING), while very old ones (more than a year) must be stewed. Whatever the method remember that breast meat cooks faster than thighs and drumsticks (see below).

Stuffing and trussing Remove the bag of giblets from oven-ready birds. Season the cavity with salt and pepper. If you are roasting the bird whole, stuff it just before cooking – see STUFFING. Do the neck cavity of turkeys (not necessary for other poultry), setting the bird on its tail in a bowl. Fill the neck loosely (stuffing expands during cooking) and pull the neck skin over the stuffing. Stuff the tail end of all poultry, placing the bird neck down in the bowl. Sew the openings shut, or close them with small skewers.

Secure the wings and legs by trussing with a piece of string or twine about 1m (3ft) long. Lay the bird on its back with the feet pushed upwards towards the neck. Put the middle of the twine under the tail, and cross it over the top of the tail tightly. Bring the string around the drumsticks and cross it on top, pulling the drumsticks as close together as possible. Pass the string under the tip of the breastbone and pull it back towards the wings. Turn the bird over and bring the string over the wings, pulling them against the body. Knot the string.

Roasting Rub the skin of chickens and turkeys generously with butter or oil; pierce the skins of ducks or geese with a fork or skewer to allow the fat to run out. Cover the breast of all poultry with bacon rashers to prevent drying while cooking – a process called *barding*.

Place the barded bird in a roasting tin in the centre of an oven preheated to 220°C (425°F), gas mark 7. Reduce the temperature to 180°C (350°F), gas mark 4 after 30 minutes. Baste the bird with the juices from the pan every 10-20 minutes. Remove the bacon 10-15 minutes before the end of cooking to brown the breast.

A large turkey, which is difficult to turn, should be placed breast up and covered with foil for half to two-thirds of the cooking time.

Cooking times Stuffed poultry takes 20-30 minutes longer to roast than an unstuffed bird, and smaller birds need

proportionately more cooking than larger ones. Here is a rough guide to cooking times:

Minutes per 450g/lb

Chicken	12-15
Turkey	10-11
Duck	20-24
Goose	11-12

Chickens and turkeys can also be roasted at 160°C (325°F), just under gas mark 4; allow 16-22 minutes per 450g (1lb).

Insert a skewer in the thigh near the end of the cooking time. The bird is done if the juice runs clear.

Power cuts

What to do if the electricity fails

Check first to see if all the circuits in the house are affected. If not, check whether a fuse has blown see FUSES AND FUSE BOXES. If all the power is off, check with neighbours to see if the cut is general. If the fault is in your supply only, ring the electricity board on their emergency number. Do not tamper with the board's sealed unit.

In the case of a general power cut, switch off all electrical appliances except those that are normally on all the time, such as clocks, refrigerator and freezer. When the power is restored the initial surge could blow a fuse if several appliances are left on particularly high wattage rated ones such as electric fires. Leave one or two lights switched on, to let you know when power is restored.

Avoid opening a freezer during a power cut. Keeping it closed should allow food inside to keep for at least 12 hours, and up to 48 hours if it is full.

Be prepared Sometimes the electricity board give warning of an impending power cut, which gives you time to prepare. Keep a small torch by your bed, and a large hand lamp in the kitchen. Stock up with candles and holders.

In an all-electric house, try to arrange alternative heating, such as a paraffin heater. Set freezer and fridge controls to maximum 24 hours before the power goes off the colder they are the longer the food will keep.

When power is restored Reset electric clocks and time switches. Check the freezer contents, and if the food has not thawed keep it closed for six hours, to lower the temperature to a safe level.

QUICK TIP If raw food has started to thaw, cook it and refreeze. Do not refreeze raw food. Precooked food that has begun to thaw should be reheated and eaten at once, or thrown away.

Power of attorney

*When one person acts on behalf
of another*

Anyone can engage an agent to act for
him or her in business matters, such as
negotiating contracts or buying a house.
The agent needs authorisation of his
right to act – especially for signing a
deed (a document under seal, such as a
covenant). This authority is given by a
deed called a Power of Attorney.

There are two kinds of power of attorney. One authorises someone to act on
your behalf for a specific reason or
period; it should be in the form laid down
in the Powers of Attorney Act, 1971.
Power under this deed lasts only as long
as the giver can act – death, bankruptcy
or mental disability end it.

You can also make an enduring power
of attorney, which does not end if the
giver becomes unable to look after
himself. It must be drawn up in a special
way and filed with the court, but it is a
wise precaution against relatives being
unable to use, for example, the bank
account of someone too senile to sign
cheques.

Ask a solicitor (see LAWYERS) to draw
up a power of attorney; you might
appoint the solicitor as your attorney.

An agent using a power of attorney
when it is no longer valid can be sued
for breach of warranty of authority.
While the power is valid, only the person
giving it can be sued.

Power steering

*Checking the oil; tensioning or
replacing the belt*

Check the oil level and belt tension on
power-assisted steering at least every six
months, or at the period recommended
in the car handbook, or if the steering
becomes heavy and jerky.

A pump at the front of the engine
provides the power; its oil is in a reservoir on or near the pump. There may be
a dipstick on the filler cap, or lines on the
reservoir, marking the levels required
when the oil is hot or cold.

Check the level when the car is standing on flat ground, and replenish as necessary with hydraulic-transmission oil. If
the level is very low, or constant topping
up is needed, look for leaks in the pipework; if you find a leaking joint, tighten
it. Have an untraceable or persistent
leak fixed by a garage.

After topping up, run the engine in
neutral ('park' for an automatic), with
handbrake on, until it is at running temperature. Then, let it idle and turn the
steering from lock to lock several times.
Switch off the engine. Look into the reservoir; if there are bubbles, there is air in
the system and it must be bled.

Bleeding the system Raise the front of
the car on axle stands (see JACKING A
CAR) so that both wheels are just off the
ground. Turn the steering from lock to
lock three times. Check the fluid level
and top up if necessary. Start the engine.
Slowly turn the wheels from lock to lock
three times, then check the fluid level
again. Note the exact level, replace the
filler cap and switch off the engine.

Lower the car to the ground and
restart the engine. Turn the steering lock
to lock five times, then centre it. Switch
off the engine and check the fluid level;
it should not have risen by more than a
small amount. If the fluid is bubbling or
has risen considerably, repeat the bleeding process. Finally, recheck for leaks. If
there is still a problem, have the system
checked by a garage.

Checking the drive belt The belt that
drives the pump is turned by a pulley on
the crankshaft. You should check the
belt for wear and tension whenever you
check the oil.

Slacken the pivot and adjuster bolts
on the pump and push it inwards, until
the belt is slack enough to ease off the
pulley. Inspect it for splits, fraying and
cracks. If you find any, fit a new belt.

To check belt tension, and to adjust
it after replacement, lay a straightedge
across the two pulleys and push the belt
down at the centre of the run. Measure
from the deflection to the straightedge.
The correct deflection should be in the
car handbook; if not, 10mm (⅜in) is about
right. Slacken the adjuster and pivot
bolts and move the pump inwards or
outwards as necessary. Tighten both
bolts and recheck the deflection.

Some cars have an adjuster arm, with
a pulley that rides on the outside of the
belt. Slacken the bolt on which the arm
pivots, and the locking bolt through the
slot in the arm. Slacken the locknut on
the adjuster bolt above the arm, and turn
the bolt to adjust the tension. Tighten
pivot and locking bolts, checking the
tension at each stage. Finally, tighten
the adjuster bolt locknut.

Power-tool safety

*Avoiding injury when using power
tools*

All electric drills, saws and other such
power tools can be dangerous if they are
not properly maintained and not handled
carefully. Always make sure a power tool
is earthed, with the green-yellow-
insulated conductor wire in the flex
connected to the earth pin of the plug.
The majority of tools are double-
insulated, with only two insulated
conductor wires in the flex – a brown and
a blue. Check the flex regularly, and
replace it if it becomes worn or damaged.
Change the plug if it is damaged – see

PLUGS. Fit an RCD in the socket before
plugging in the tool – see CIRCUIT
BREAKERS.

Always unplug the tool when changing parts, such as a bit in a power drill,
the blade in a circular saw or the disc on
a sander. Always unplug a power tool as
soon as you finish using it. Wear safety
goggles; do not wear loose clothing, a
tie or jewellery. Keep children and pets
away from the area where you are
working.

Take a firm grip on the tool, using
both hands where possible; use the side-
handle attachment on a power drill
rather than hold the body (see DRILL-
ING). When using a vice or adjustable
workstand, make sure the workpiece is
securely clamped.

Stand to one side of a circular saw as
you use it, not behind – if the blade
binds, the saw may kick back. If the
blade starts to bind, switch off and wait
for the blade to stop moving. Then
withdraw it from the cut and start again.
Whenever you have finished making a
cut, check that the saw's blade guard
drops into the closed position.

See also EXTENSION LEADS; HEDGE TRIM-
MERS; ROUTERS; SAWS AND SAWING.

Prams and pushchairs

*Care and maintenance; using
them safely*

The brakes, the safety locks and the harness attachments are the points to check
on prams and pushchairs.

The brakes should prevent all but the
slightest movement of the wheels when
applied on a slope with the child aboard.
Make sure the brakes press securely on
both back wheels. Replace the rubber
pads if they do not grip.

Check that the locks on a folding pram
frame or a pushchair are secure – not
only the lock that moves as the chair is
being unfolded but also the main lock
that holds it in the unfolded position.

When the child becomes very active,
keep an eye on the harness rings and
straps. Get replacements from the pram
shop if any parts wear or loosen.

Do not pile shopping onto the pram.
Many prams and pushchairs can accommodate a rack under the body.

Premenstrual tension

Simple ways of obtaining relief

Many women suffer the unpleasant but
generally harmless symptoms of premenstrual tension (PMT) during their fertile
years. Commonly, the symptoms appear
between two and seven days before the
monthly period is due, and clear up soon
after it starts. They may include moodi-

ness and fatigue, as well as discomfort in the breasts, back and abdomen. Often, there is also a slight weight gain.

Sufferers should avoid stress during the week before a period. Cut down on salt, which makes the body retain fluid, and on caffeine and alcohol, which can make you more irritable. Extra Vitamin B6 (see VITAMINS) taken on the days when PMT occurs may reduce symptoms.

If the physical or mental symptoms are severe, consult your doctor, who may prescribe hormone treatment.

See also PERIOD PAINS.

Presentations

How to make or receive them

If you are asked to present someone with a gift or an award, remember that the occasion is intended to honour the receiver, and your presentation speech should reflect this. Do not use the opportunity for your own purposes, and keep your choice of words moderate, direct and sincere.

Speak of the person's achievements, but do not exaggerate them wildly (do not diminish them, either) or indulge in false emotion. Otherwise, you will turn the event into an embarrassment for all.

In planning a presentation, use the same techniques as you would for other forms of speech-making – see PUBLIC SPEAKING. Ask yourself who your audience is, and what it expects from you. Aim for a tone appropriate to the occasion – respectful but informal in a gathering of family or friends, more formal for a business awards ceremony or prizegiving.

Remember that, at the end of the speech, you must make the presentation itself, and then fade into the background while the recipient takes the spotlight.

Gifts At many presentations, the choice of prize or gift is automatic – a trophy, perhaps, or a gold watch. For others, the gift has to be chosen. Try to ensure that it is both appropriate and something the receiver wants; if the gift is to be wrapped, make it look as attractive as possible – see GIFT WRAPPING.

When you hand over the present, say what it is. If it is an award, repeat what it is for. If it is a gift, say who it is from.

Receiving awards If you receive an award or gift and have to make a speech of thanks, be modest – but not to the point of falsity. You cannot say 'I thoroughly deserve this', but 'I do not deserve this at all' grates just as much. Pay tribute to the person who made the presentation, and to the organisation or group of people on whose behalf it was made. Thank everyone concerned during your speech, and again at the end.

Preserving

Bottling fruit in jars

All types of fruit are suitable for bottling, which preserves the flavour and colour almost intact. The fruit should be carefully chosen and carefully prepared. Make sure it is fresh, ripe and without the slightest blemish or sign of disease or decay.

Use purpose-made bottling jars, checking that they are unchipped, that the screw-bands are not distorted and that the rubber seals are not perished. You can buy new seals and tops from specialist kitchen shops or some hardware shops.

Before starting, remove stalks, stems and leaves from soft fruits such as blackberries, loganberries, raspberries and strawberries. Top and tail gooseberries, and cut rhubarb into even lengths.

Apples, pears and QUINCES should be peeled, cored, and quartered or sliced. Apricots and peaches can be bottled whole or halved and stoned. Peel peaches – and apricots if you wish. Plums and damsons are usually bottled whole, although very large ones can be halved and stoned if preferred. Cherries can be bottled with or without stones.

Wash the prepared fruit scrupulously, again inspecting it for disease and blemishes.

Making the syrup Although water can be used for bottling, homemade syrup gives a better flavour and colour. On average, the strength of the syrup is 225g (½lb) of sugar to every 570ml (1 pint) of water. Add the sugar, preferably granulated, to half the water. Bring to the boil, stirring until the sugar dissolves, and boil for 1 minute. Then add the rest of the water and bring it to the boil. The syrup can be poured over the fruit hot or cold. Golden syrup can be used instead of sugar, but it brings its own strong flavour to the fruit.

As sweet cherries are low in acid, add ¼ teaspoon of citric acid to every 570ml (1 pint) of syrup.

Packing the fruit Wet the insides of glass bottling jars with cold water and slip the fruit carefully into them. Choose fruits of uniform size, and use a bottling spoon to pack them closely, but without squashing them. Allow about 275-350g (10-12oz) of fruit to a 450g (1lb) jar.

Pour in the syrup and release any air bubbles by inserting a sterilised knife blade down one side of the bottle. Top up with syrup and loosely screw on the lids, so that steam can escape during sterilising and the jars will not burst.

Sterilising The two best ways of sterilising bottled fruit are by water bath or PRESSURE COOKER. The *water bath* method is more reliable, but it calls for a cooking thermometer. Take a large, deep pan and fit it with a false bottom – such as a grill rack, double cake-tin base or a thick wad of folded newspaper.

Place the jars on the false bottom, making sure they do not touch each other; a cloth tucked between them will ensure this. Fill the pan with cold water until the bottles are completely submerged. Put the thermometer in the water and heat the pan slowly, gradually raising the temperature until it reaches 54°C (about 130°F) in 1 hour – and the required temperature within 1½ hours.

Soft berry fruits and apple slices should be held at 74°C (165°F) for 10 minutes; all other fruit should be held at 82°C (180°F) for 15 minutes, with the exception of pears, which should be held at 88°C (190°F) for 30 minutes.

When the fruit has been sterilised, remove the jars from the pan (wearing thick kitchen gloves to protect your hands) or bail out the hot water before lifting the bottles with tongs. Put the jars on a dry, warm surface. Tighten the screw-bands immediately and leave the jars to cool overnight.

The *pressure-cooker* method is quick – but take care not to overcook the fruit. Put the cooker's rack or a false bottom (as above) in the cooker, and cover it with water to a depth of 25mm (1in). Set the prepared jars in the cooker and fasten the lid, leaving the vent open. Heat gently until steam comes out in a steady jet. This should take between 5 and 10 minutes. Put on the pressure weight and bring up to 2.25kg (5lb) pressure.

Hold the pressure for 1 minute for apples, rhubarb, all soft fruits, damsons and plums. Extend this to 3-4 minutes for tightly packed apples, and also for halved apricots, peaches and plums. Pears need 5 minutes.

Remove the cooker from the heat and leave it to cool for 10 minutes. Then take off the weight to release the pressure. Finally, open the cooker, remove the jars and tighten their lids. Put the jars on a dry, warm surface and leave them to cool overnight.

Testing the seal Whichever sterilising method is used, allow the bottles to cool completely. Remove the screw-bands and test each bottle by picking it up with your fingertips, holding only the lid. If the seal works, the vacuum inside the bottle will hold the lid securely. If the seal is faulty, the lid will come away.

Storing Coat the inner sides of the screw-bands with cooking oil and replace them. Wipe any stickiness from the outsides of the jars, label them, and store in a cool, dry, dark, well-ventilated place. Open the fruit as and when needed by removing the screw-band, standing a jar in hot water for a few minutes, and gently prising off the lid with the tip of a knife.

Pressing

Keeping clothes in good shape

When pressing fabrics, always press down with no movement of the iron (see IRONS) over the surface of the cloth. Simply press lightly, lift the iron, press the next section, lift, press, lift, and so on. Unlike IRONING, pressing flattens and shapes fabrics rather than simply smoothing out wrinkles. It takes out bagginess caused by wear and restores body to the fabric.

Before starting, smooth and straighten the fabric carefully. As a general rule, press on the reverse side of the material. Place a damp, colour-fast cotton or linen cloth over the fabric and press with a hot dry iron. If pressing on the right side, do not overpress as this can damage the fabric and make it shine.

Afterwards, iron the fabric through a sheet of brown paper or another cloth.

On completion, turn the materials back the right way and then press in any pleats or necessary creases.

See also SUIT PRESSING; SHINE REMOVING.

Press-studs

How to sew them on

Press-studs are fitted as illustrated. Sew on the ball side first on the lap of the opening. Sew by hand, making at least four stitches into each of the four holes. To sew on the socket, align the two parts of the stud by putting a pin or needle through their centres. Then stitch as before.

Press-stud
Position the ball half on the underside of the overlap and the socket half on the underlap. Whipstitch over the holes in each half.

Press-studs are best used where there is not much strain on the opening. For more holding power – needed on waistbands and at necklines – use HOOKS AND EYES.

See also VELCRO FASTENERS; ZIPPERS.

Pressure cookers

Caring for, cleaning and repairing them

Wash a pressure cooker in hot soapy water. Store with the lid off so that air can circulate inside the pan. Make sure the rubber safety valve is free of dirt.

To remove stains inside the pan follow the maker's instructions; otherwise, boil up a weak solution of cream of tartar and water in the cooker. Leave for three hours, then empty out, wash and dry.

Replacing the safety valve If the pin in the rubber safety plug blows frequently, it is time to replace the plug.

Remove the pin by pressing it down and pulling it out from the underside, then pull out the plug, if necessary, using a screwdriver to lever it out carefully.

Push in place the new plug (available from kitchen or hardware shops) from below. Make sure the side marked TOP is uppermost.

Replacing the sealing gasket If steam escapes around the cooker lid, the rubber gasket needs replacing – again, kitchen and hardware shops stock gaskets.

Follow the maker's instructions for replacing; otherwise, turn the lid upside down and use a screwdriver to lever out the gasket. Wash the inside of the rim with lukewarm soapy water. If any rubber adheres to the rim, you can use a wire wool soap pad to clean it off. Dry the lid thoroughly, then fit the new gasket, making sure to press it into place all around the rim. This may be easier if you soften the new gasket first in hot water.

Pressure cooking

Getting the best from your pressure cooker

By putting a sealed container of water under pressure the temperature at which the water boils can be considerably increased. PRESSURE COOKERS – large pans with closely fitting lids – use this principle to cook some food in less than half the usual time.

When to use a pressure cooker Pressure cookers can be used to cook any food that would normally be stewed, boiled or steamed, such as SOUPS AND STOCKS, pulses, steamed puddings, and POULTRY and large meat joints.

They are not good, though, for cooking such delicate foods as fish. You can cook more than one food at a time in the separate baskets in the cooker.

How to use a pressure cooker Put the food in the pan with the recommended amount of liquid – never less than 285ml ($\frac{1}{2}$ pint) – then close the lid. Put over a high heat until steam flows steadily through the vent.

Put the pressure weight on the vent. When the cooker starts to hiss loudly, set the heat to low until the cooking time is completed. For cooking times, see the manufacturer's recipe book.

You must reduce the pressure before taking off the pressure weight and opening the cooker. Stand the cooker in cold water or run cold water over its lid.

The safety valve If the pin in the rubber safety valve blows during cooking, remove the cooker from the heat and wait for steam to stop escaping.

Check the steam vent, unblocking it if necessary. Then reset the plug by pressing the pin back into place.

Prickly heat

Clearing up a hot-weather rash

Children and overweight people are particularly susceptible to prickly heat (known medically as *miliaria rubra*). It is caused by excessive sweating in hot, humid weather. A rash of small pimples and blisters appears in the skin creases and wherever clothing has been tight; in infants, the skin around the neck, chest, armpits and groin is affected.

There is no quick remedy, but frequent bathing in cool water, using little soap, may relieve irritation. Apply calamine lotion or spirit with 0.4 per cent phenol to the affected areas. Consult a doctor if the irritation is intense, or if the victim becomes weak and lethargic. See also HEAT EXHAUSTION; HEAT STROKE.

Loose-fitting clothing can reduce the risk of prickly heat, or ease discomfort. Susceptible people should try to stay in cool places, or take a rest-break in a cool room around midday.

Profile gauge

Using it to mark awkward corners

When laying VINYL FLOOR COVERING, it is often difficult to make a snug fit round awkward shapes, for example pipework or door-frame mouldings. A profile gauge, sometimes called a shape tracer, makes the task easy.

The gauge consists of a row of closely set steel needles in a centre bar – looking rather like a double-sided steel comb. The needles are a sliding fit in the centre bar, so that when one side is pressed against an object its profile is reproduced on the other side.

Before using the gauge, press it against a flat surface to align all the needles. Then press it against the shape you want to copy. Make sure the gauge completely

Profiling a door frame The needles on one side of the gauge are pressed against the frame, reproducing the profile on the other side.

fills any recesses or grooves. Transfer the gauge to the material you wish to cut and use a pencil to mark the profile outlined by the needles.

Cut the floor covering to shape with a craft knife.

Propagating plants

Growing new plants from old

Most techniques of propagation do not need much expert knowledge. But a few, such as *grafting* and *budding* – both used for ROSES and FRUIT TREES, in particular – require special skills.

Some plants regularly produce smaller versions of themselves. *Plantlets* grow at the end of runners on spider plants; *suckers* or *offsets* appear around the bases of shrubby plants such as lilacs, and bulbous ones such as tulips and gladioli; some lilies produce small *bulbils* at their stems. You can separate any of these from the parent plant and grow it.

Dividing Use *division* to propagate such clump-forming plants as michaelmas daisies, chrysanthemums, delphiniums, peonies and primroses. Dig up the root mass or take it from its pot, and pull or cut it into sections; replant or repot each section separately. Divide late-flowering plants in spring; those that flower early, in autumn. Divide the bulb masses of spring-flowering tulips and daffodils as soon as their foliage has died down.

Divide plants that grow from rhizomes, such as some irises, hostas and lily of the valley, just as growth begins in early spring. Dig up the mass of rhizomes and clean the soil from it. Use a sharp knife to cut off vigorous young sections from the edge for replanting; each should be 50-100mm (2-4in) long, with roots and at least one growth bud. Discard the centre of the mass.

Taking cuttings A cutting is simply a piece of plant. A *tip cutting* is taken from the top growth of a non-flowering shoot when the stem is either soft or semi-hard (in summer). A *stem cutting* is taken when the wood is hard (in autumn). Cut straight across the stem with a sharp knife, just below a leaf, and strip the lower leaves from the cutting. You may be able to tear away a 'heel' or sliver of the old wood with it. Dip the cutting into rooting powder and plant it in moist JOHN INNES COMPOST (seed) with a thin top layer of coarse sand. Enclose the pot in a clear plastic bag and keep it in a warm, shady place for a month or longer. Hardwood cuttings are slow to root, and can be set in an outdoor bed for a whole growing season. Remove the pot (see page 361) so that you can check that roots have formed. If they have, place the pot in

Dividing bulbs and taking cuttings to grow new plants

Plants can reproduce themselves from parts of their roots, stems, shoots, leaves or buds, depending on the species. Using the methods shown here you can stock your garden with new plants, which in time can also be propagated.

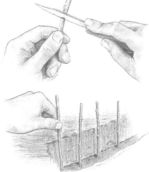

Dividing To propagate bulb-growing plants, separate the bulbs and replant each one. Cut the rhizomes of irises (right) from the edge of the clump, each with one or two leaf fans. Trim the leaves and re-plant.

Stem cuttings Trim the hardwood stem of a shrub to 300mm (12in) long in autumn. Cut just below a bud or joint at the base, and just above a bud at the top. Stand the cuttings in a trench, replace the soil and firm it with your foot.

Leaf-bud cuttings Take cuttings from a shrub or climber in August or September. Cut off a shoot with several leaves and trim by cutting just above a leaf axil and about 19mm ($\frac{3}{4}$in) below it. Pot the cutting in equal parts of peat and sand.

Tip cuttings Shrubby perennials, such as sedums and saxifrages, are best propagated by tip cuttings. Snip off non-flowering side shoots, 75-100mm (3-4in) long, in September. Plant in compost and cover the pot with a plastic bag. Make a wire frame to support the plastic.

Layering Flexible shrubs such as honeysuckle can be layered. Bend a shoot to the ground, make a cut underneath and at that point peg it into a 50mm (2in) hole. Fill the hole with seed compost. After a year, cut it from the shoot.

the light, without its plastic bag, and keep it moist; or transplant a hardwood cutting to its permanent site.

Young soft tips of many plants, such as mints and ivies, will also grow roots in a small jar or rooting flask of tap water. Pot them in seed compost when the roots begin to sprout.

AFRICAN VIOLETS and gloxinias are among the plants with thick leaves that

can be grown from *leaf cuttings*. Detach a healthy young leaf with its stem, dip the end in rooting powder and pot it as you would a tip cutting. You should make sure the leaf itself is not touching the compost.

To propagate rex and iron cross BEGONIAS, remove a large leaf and make several cuts on the underside across the points where main veins meet. Put the leaf, cut side down, on the surface of some moist peat substitute in a pot and weight it with a few pebbles. Cover the pot with clear plastic and keep in a warm place. When tiny plants appear, remove the plastic and put the pot in a warm, shady spot for about four weeks.

Layering The stems of such plants as strawberries, border carnations, clematis and other climbers, magnolias and rhododendrons will root where they touch the soil. To *layer* a plant with flexible stems, bend the stem to the ground, make a small cut in the lowest point of the stem just below a bud, and remove any surrounding leaves.

Apply hormone rooting powder to the cut and bury it 25-50mm (1-2in) deep. Pin or weight it down and water it well. After six weeks or so, roots will form. The new plant can then be severed from the parent and transplanted.

Chinese layering can be used on branches that are too stiff or too high to be layered at soil level – for example, rubber plants *(Ficus)* can be propagated in this way in spring or summer.

Make a slanting cut just below a node or leaf stalk and 150-380mm (6-15in) below the growing tip. Wedge it open with a matchstick. Apply hormone rooting powder to the cut, and wrap a clear plastic sleeve around the area, tying the bottom. Pack the sleeve with a damp mix of compost and moss and tie the top. When roots appear, after about ten weeks, cut the shoot just below the roots. Pot the new plant in suitable compost.

See also BULBS, CORMS AND TUBERS; PLANTING; POTTING HOUSEPLANTS.

Pruning shrubs

How to guide their growth

Pruning keeps SHRUBS to the required shape and size, prevents them from being weakened by disease or damaged growth and often improves the quality of their flowers or fruit. Many shrubs, including most evergreens, need little pruning once they are established, other than to combat disease or overcrowded growth. Others, such as deciduous flowering species, benefit from annual attention.

Check your shrubs each spring, to see what pruning is needed.

Deciduous shrubs that flower on the current season's growth – such as *Buddleia davidii* and fuchsia – should be pruned early in spring, cutting off about three-quarters of the previous year's growth, back to about three buds from the base. Remove dead or diseased wood, cutting back to the healthy growth, and weak or awkwardly growing stems.

Shrubs that flower on last season's shoots – such as forsythia, deutzia and philadelphus – should not be pruned until flowering has finished; cut the branches back by about one-third. And remove any that are old, dead, diseased, weak, or growing awkwardly – rubbing another branch, for example.

Tools you need Secateurs are suitable for cutting shoots and small branches; long-handled lopping shears or hedge shears with a pruning notch in the blade can be used for thicker stems. For the thickest branches, you need a pruning saw; long-arm or pole pruners are useful for high branches. Keep all pruning tools clean and sharp.

Pruning techniques Make all pruning cuts cleanly and just above an outward-facing bud. Start the cut level with the base of the bud but on the opposite side of the stem and angle it upwards to finish just above the tip of the bud. If you are removing whole branches, cut them flush with the trunk or main branch. Make a small cut on the underside first to prevent tearing of the bark as you finish the cut. If you wish, treat the bare wood where a thick branch has been cut with pruning compound (sold at garden centres and some hardware shops).

Shaping Create the basic shape of the shrub by careful but hard pruning when planting. After that, it will need less attention. Work with the natural shape. To encourage compact, bushy growth, prune each main branch or side-growth back to a suitable outward-facing bud. To create a tall plant, remove entire stems or branches. Trim dense-leaved hedging shrubs with shears.

Reviving old shrubs Overgrown, straggly or neglected shrubs can often be rejuvenated by hard pruning in spring. Cut off the oldest branches at the base, and saw the younger branches or stems to 300-610mm (1-2ft) from the ground. Remove suckers from around the base. Fork one of the general FERTILISERS lightly into the soil around the roots and spread well-rotted manure over it.

See also FRUIT TREES; HEDGES; TREE PRUNING.

Public speaking

Preparing and delivering a speech

In planning a speech, think first about the occasion and your audience. Will it be formal or informal? Who will be listening? Why is your subject of interest to them? Jot the answers down and keep them in mind as you proceed.

To organise your speech, write down the main points you want to make, as they occur to you (unless you are giving a lecture or a technical exposition, three or four main points are enough). Summarise each in one clear sentence, and group any relevant information around each.

Facts and statistics may be important to your topic, but dramatic stories involving real people will have greater impact. So will an occasional well-told and appropriate joke. Consider whether you will need visual aids, such as charts, drawings or slides, to make some points more effectively.

When you have assembled your main points, organise them in a logical order so that one idea flows from another. Pay particular attention to the opening few sentences. They should set out your theme, attract your listeners' attention and show the line of your thoughts.

Use the main body of the speech to develop your theme. Then, in the last two or three sentences, summarise the main points again. Depending on the occasion, you may need to bring in a toast, proposal or message of thanks. In any case, try to make the ending as strong as the beginning.

Rehearsing Once your thoughts are in order, and the beginning and ending prepared, the speech is ready for final polishing. You can, if you wish, write it out in full to learn it. But unless you intend to read it to your audience (inadvisable in most circumstances, because it looks unnatural and puts listeners off), writing a speech word for word has drawbacks – interruptions can easily fluster you, causing you to lose your thread.

A better plan is to write out the opening and closing paragraphs in full, keeping the material between in summarised form, to fill out as you speak. Set out each main point, and the beginning and ending, on postcards or small file cards, numbered in order. Those are easy to handle while you are speaking, and slip into a pocket or handbag.

Rehearse your speech, timing your delivery to match the time allotted. Use words and sentences that are short and clear, without unnecessary jargon. Avoid words you have difficulty in pronouncing, and any whose meaning you are not certain of. Practise in front of your family or friends, and ask for their honest opinions. Record the speech and listen to it to see where you could improve the delivery or clarify a point. If you can, rehearse with any visual aids you will be using.

Try to visit the place in which you will be speaking beforehand. Familiarise yourself with the space, the acoustics and any technical equipment.

Delivery Use your cards to aid your memory, but glance at them as little as possible. As you cover the points on each card, slip it to the bottom of the pack.

Speak loudly and a little more slowly

Finding the pulse on wrist or neck

The wrist pulse is about 25mm (1in) below the thumb and 13mm (½in) from the edge of the arm. Time it with a digital watch.

Feel for the carotid pulse by pressing in the hollow of the neck, to one side of the Adam's apple.

---

faster in children – as many as 90 beats for a ten-year-old, and up to 140 a minute for babies. At any age the rate rises during and immediately after exercise.

To time a pulse, you need a digital watch, or one with a second hand. The pulse can be felt at the wrist or carotid artery, as illustrated. Feel for it with your first three fingers (not your thumb), and press lightly. Count the beats for a minute; or for just 30 seconds, multiplying by two.

In all but minor injuries, take the casualty's pulse rate while you are giving first aid, and every 10 minutes while you are waiting for medical assistance. Keep a note of the rates for the doctor.

Punting

Poling along the river

Flat-bottomed, shallow punts are tricky craft to handle, best suited to sheltered waterways where the depth is an even 1.2-1.5m (4-5ft), and where the bed is firm gravel. There are, for example, appropriate conditions on stretches of the River Thames between Oxford and Kingston, and on the River Cam at Cambridge.

Punts are propelled with a pole about 4m (13ft) long, made of wood or metal and usually forked or slightly bulbous at the lower end. In the simplest method of poling (quanting) the punter stands in the bow of the boat and puts the pole upright into the water so that the end rests on the bottom. Gripping the pole and pressing it down hard, the punter then walks towards the stern, levering the boat forward as he walks. When he has reached the stern, he lifts the pole clear, carries it to the bow again and repeats the process.

There are, however, more stylish ways of punting. In the most traditional, you stand about 1m (3ft) from the stern of the boat facing forward with one foot hard against the side of the punt. (Racing punts, which are much narrower than ordinary punts, are propelled from the centre.) Insert the pole into the water vertically, or tilted slightly forwards, until it hits the river bottom. Then press down on the pole to push the boat along. Move your hands up the pole as the punt moves forward, and when they reach the top of the pole give the pole a sharp twist to extract it from the riverbed. Bring the pole upright and repeat the process.

You should always have the punt facing the desired direction before you push on the pole, and always push parallel to the long axis of the boat to keep it moving in a straight line.

Steer the boat by using the pole as a rudder, letting it trail behind the boat and sweeping it through the water to the left or right depending on which way you want the boat to turn. You cannot steer

successfully when you are pushing on the pole to move the boat forward.

These manoeuvres need practice if you are not to lose the pole, drench yourself with the dripping pole, be left clinging to it while the punt drifts on, or precipitate some other disaster.

As you become more proficient you will feel confident enough to let the pole slide or drop between your hands into the water vertically and return it to its vertical position with a flick of the wrist – so preventing water from running down your wrists to your elbows.

River 'rules of the road' decree that punts travelling downstream give way to those travelling up. Punts being poled have precedence over all other craft.

See also ROWING; SAILING; SCULLING.

Puppet making

Creating hand and finger puppets

Attractive finger puppets can be made very simply from an old glove. Cut off the fingers of the glove. Stuff a small piece of cotton wool into each fingertip to make the head of the puppet, then tie some string round the glove finger just below the cotton wool to make the neck.

Sew on sequins for eyes, and red embroidery thread for a mouth. For the hair, unravel the strands of some knitting wool and sew on. Use odd scraps of fabric to make the clothes.

Repeat the process with the other fingers to create a cast of characters.

Paper finger puppets These can be made looking rather like the glove finger puppets described above. Cut a 75mm (3in) square of thick paper or thin card for each puppet. Roll the piece into a tube around your finger and tape it together. Pinch in the top and glue on string or wool for hair. Use felt-tip pens to draw in the eyes, nose and mouth.

Costumes can be made, as before, from scraps of fabric, or you can use coloured paper, glued onto the body shapes. To fit the puppet to the finger, wrap the lower flaps around the finger and tape them to make a close fit. The puppets will last for some time if you do not make them too tight, and take them off carefully.

Hand puppets Place your hand on a sheet of paper with the thumb and little finger spread. Trace round it with a pencil about 25mm (1in) away.

Using the paper as a template, cut out two thicknesses of a heavy fabric, such as felt or wool suiting. Pin the pieces of fabric together, wrong sides out. Stitch them together (see SEWING) 13mm (½in) from the edge. Leave the wrist end open. Trim the raw edges with pinking shears.

Hem the wrist opening, then turn the

---

than in normal speech, but not so slowly that you sound pompous. Stand in a relaxed manner, with your feet slightly apart and your hands by your sides or resting on the table or lectern in front of you. Convey interest and enthusiasm with your voice, avoiding a monotone. Look at your audience as much as you can. When you have finished, pause for a moment before sitting down.

Do not let last-minute nerves worry you. They are common. Try a few breathing or RELAXATION EXERCISES shortly beforehand. See also NERVOUSNESS; PRESENTATIONS; YOGA.

Pulse-taking

Checking the beat; what it tells you

The pulse rate corresponds to the beat of the heart. A rapid or weak pulse may be associated with FEVER, BLEEDING, SHOCK, fear or exertion. A rapid or irregular pulse occurring when someone is at rest may occasionally be a symptom of a serious heart disorder.

The normal adult pulse rate, at rest, is 60-80 beats a minute for men, 70-90 for women. It is slower in old people, and

---

PUPPET MAKING

Using gloves to make figures of fun

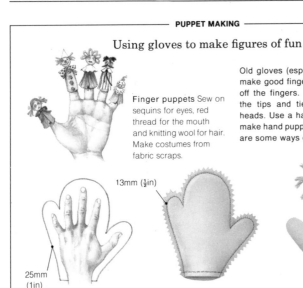

Finger puppets Sew on sequins for eyes, red thread for the mouth and knitting wool for hair. Make costumes from fabric scraps.

Old gloves (especially knitted ones) make good finger puppets if you cut off the fingers. Stuff cotton wool in the tips and tie them off, to form heads. Use a hand as a template to make hand puppets – illustrated here are some ways of decorating them.

13mm (½in)

25mm (1in)

Hand puppet Trace around your hand on paper as shown. Cut out the shape as a template.

Cut two thicknesses of felt in the same shape. Sew together, leaving the wrists open.

Turn inside out and sew on buttons for eyes, wool for hair and felt for features.

---

puppet right side out. Sew on two buttons for the eyes and strands of wool for the hair and eyebrows. Cut out a round or triangular piece of felt to make the nose, and a curved piece for the mouth, and stick or sew them on.

Puréeing

Making fruit or vegetable pulps

Fruit or vegetable purées are appetising and ideal for children and invalids. They are also the basis for many SAUCES and soups – see SOUPS AND STOCKS.

Ripe soft fruits such as strawberries, raspberries and skinned peaches may be puréed without cooking. Harder ingredients, such as apples or parsnips, should be cut up and stewed first.

Rub or press the ingredients (cut up, peeled, or stoned as necessary) into a bowl through a fine nylon sieve; metal sieves may give an unpleasant flavour. Alternatively, you can put the ingredients into FOOD MILLS, FOOD PROCESSORS or BLENDERS and reduce them to the texture you want. As a rough guide, 450g (1lb) of prepared fruit or vegetables give 285ml (½ pint) of purée.

Season vegetable purées with salt, pepper, herbs and butter to taste – see HERBS IN COOKING. If the purée needs thinning, add a little of the cooking liquid, or water or cream. To thin fruit purées, use orange or lemon juice. To thicken a purée, cook it briefly in a saucepan with a little cornflour or cream, or add an egg yolk (see SEPARATING EGGS) – do not let the mixture overheat, or it will go lumpy.

Push-starting

Getting your car going – with a little help

When your car battery is too low to start the engine you may be able to get going with a push-start – see also BATTERIES; JUMP-STARTING A CAR. You cannot push-start a car with automatic transmission.

Get helpers to push from the back – they must not push at the sides, on the door pillars or handles, because they will not get a firm enough grip and could fall under the rear wheels.

Move the car onto a *flat* surface, or one with a slight downward slope, and straighten the front wheels. Depress the clutch pedal, engage second gear and switch on the ignition.

When your helpers get the car rolling well, take your foot off the clutch. As the engine fires, quickly depress the clutch, disengage gear and press the accelerator. Charge the battery up at the earliest opportunity.

Puttying

Sealing the glass in a window; renewing old putty

When you fit glass in a window frame (see WINDOW PANES), you must seal it in with putty. For a wooden window frame, use linseed-oil putty; for a metal frame use metal-casement putty; or you can use universal or acrylic putty for either. You will also need a filling knife and a putty knife. Use an old chisel to chip away any old putty, and pincers to pull out any pins or clips that held panes before. Brush away any dust and paint the rebate with primer paint.

You will need about 1kg (2¼lb) of putty for 3.7m (12ft) of frame. First knead a handful of the putty until it is soft and pliable. Press in the putty as illustrated. Fit the glass, pushing it gently at the edges. Knock in glazing sprigs with the side of a chisel (or fit metal strips on a metal frame) to hold the glass. Fit them 250mm (10in) apart and let sprigs stand up 5mm (³⁄₁₆in) from the frame.

Press more putty round the front of the glass and shape it with the putty knife, as shown. Now use the knife to trim off any excess putty inside the window. Run a moistened paintbrush over the putty when it has been trimmed and shaped, this will help to ensure that it sticks to the glass. Allow the putty to harden for about two weeks, then paint it – otherwise it soon crumbles.

Renewing old putty Prise off the putty all round with an old screwdriver or a chisel. Replace any sprigs or clips that have corroded. Brush away all dust, prime the rebate and apply putty over the glass as described above.

QUICK TIP If putty sticks to the putty knife when shaping, dip the knife in clean water. Similarly, wetting your hands stops it sticking to your fingers.

PUTTYING

Securing a window pane with putty

Holding the putty in your palm, squeeze it out between thumb and forefinger into the window rebate, forming a layer 3-6mm (⅛-¼in) thick. Press pane in and secure with sprigs.

Press more putty round the front of the pane. Use a putty knife to smooth it into a neat bevel which covers the sprigs. Make neat mitres in the corners.

Quarantine

Bringing an animal into Britain

To prevent the introduction of RABIES, cats and dogs have to spend six months in approved quarantine (isolation) kennels when they are brought into Britain – even if they are returning from a brief stay abroad or have been immunised against rabies.

Similar rules apply to most pets and domestic animals, including hamsters, guinea-pigs and monkeys. There are special rules for importing horses, farm livestock, wild animals, captive birds, reptiles and endangered species, including tortoises and terrapins. Details can be obtained from the Animal Health Division (see 1 below).

The penalties for evading or failing to comply with quarantine regulations are an unlimited fine and/or imprisonment, plus seizure of the animal. Because of the presence of rabies in Europe and other parts of the world, offenders are usually dealt with severely.

If you want to bring an animal into the United Kingdom, you should:
1 Ask the Animal Health Division of the Ministry of Agriculture to send you application form ID1 for an animal import licence, together with a list of approved quarantine kennels, catteries and carrying agents. Their address is: Animal Health Division 1B, MAFF, Hook Rise South, Tolworth, Surbiton, Surrey KT6 7NF.
2 Choose a convenient quarantine kennel from the list and book a place.
3 Decide on a convenient port or airport of entry, which has facilities for keeping the animal in isolation for 48 hours before delivery to the quarantine kennel. Such facilities are available at Dover, Harwich, Hull, Liverpool and Southampton seaports; Heathrow, Gatwick, Edinburgh, Glasgow, Birmingham, Leeds, Manchester and Prestwick airports; and Ramsgate hoverport.
4 Arrange for an approved carrying agent to collect the animal from the port or airport of entry and deliver it to the quarantine kennel selected; you are not allowed to take it yourself.
5 Apply for the import licence, using form ID1 and submitting it at least eight weeks before the animal is due to travel. A licence will not normally be granted until the transport arrangements have been made.
6 Ask the airline or shipping company how you can arrange for the animal to be transported in a crate, and what documents are required.

What does quarantine involve? To obtain approval from the Animal Health Division, quarantine kennels must provide veterinary care and supervision, adequate sleeping accommodation and exercise space. Rules vary, but most quarantine kennels prefer the owner not to visit during the first 14 days.

On arrival at the kennels, the animal is given an anti-rabies vaccination. If there is any suspicion of rabies, it may be destroyed.

Quarry tiles

Choosing and cutting heavy-duty tiles; replacing a broken tile

Quarry tiles are unglazed and provide a hard-wearing floor in a kitchen, laundry room, hallway or lavatory. They are best laid on a concrete floor which is perfectly smooth and level – see UNEVEN FLOORS. A timber floor usually needs strengthening to bear the weight of the tiles. Lay quarry tiles on floors in the same way as CERAMIC TILES.

Tiles range in size from 75 × 75mm (3 × 3in) to 230 × 230mm (9 × 9in), and in thickness from 13 to 25mm ($\frac{1}{2}$ to 1in). They can be either machine or hand made. For a level floor with a smooth finish and regular joints, use machine-made 150 × 150mm (6 × 6in) tiles with a thickness of 13mm ($\frac{1}{2}$in) or 16mm ($\frac{5}{8}$in). Handmade tiles may vary in size.

Because they are dense and hard, use a platform tile cutter to cut quarry tiles, or hire a heavy-duty tile cutter (available from tool hire shops – see HIRING). No matter how careful you are, some tiles are likely to crack during cutting, so it is best to buy a few more than you need.

Measure the gap to be filled and mark the line on the face of the tile with a pencil. Then mark another line, the cutting line, slightly inside it to allow for the grouting on both sides. Place the tile on the cutter, aligning the cutting line with the pointer. Push the lever to score the tile, then press it firmly on the bar to snap it cleanly.

— QUARRY TILES —

Cutting with a chisel and replacing a cracked tile

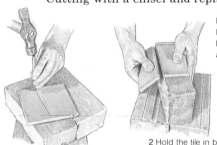

If you do not have a tile cutter, and have only a few tiles to lay, they can be cut with a small cold chisel. Mark and cut a tile on its underside.

1 Lay the tile on a brick and tap a row of indents along the line with a hammer and cold chisel.

2 Hold the tile in both hands and strike it against the brick corner.

3 After cutting the tile, smooth the cut edge with a rough carborundum stone.

Cracked tile 1 To remove it, chip out the broken pieces and any old cement with a hammer and cold chisel.

2 Spread on a thin layer of adhesive with a pointing trowel and fit the new tile.

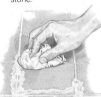

3 After 24 hours, grout the joints with a 4:1 sand and cement mix.

Alternatively, you can have the tiles cut for you in the tile shop.

Replacing a tile Use a hammer and cold chisel to break up a broken tile that needs replacing. Start at the centre. Remove the pieces and brush away dust.

Place the new tile in position and check that it will be level when fitted. Check also that it is just below the surface of the surrounding tiles, to allow for the thickness of the new adhesive. Spread a thin layer of adhesive and press the tile into place. Remove any surplus adhesive with the edge of a trowel. Leave for 24 hours before grouting the joints – see TILE REGROUTING.

Quicksands

What to do if you are trapped

Getting trapped in quicksands – or in a bog or marsh – can easily prove fatal. To survive, stay calm and obey these rules:
● The moment you realise you are stuck, fall gently backwards onto the sand or mud. As you drop, spread your arms as wide as possible, so that your body weight is evenly distributed. You will stay 'afloat' in this position.
● If you are wearing a haversack or cape, leave it on – it may increase your buoyancy. If you have a walking stick, slide it underneath you.
● If you are with someone, lie still and get your companion to throw you a line, or hold out a stick to you. Grasp the stick or line and pull yourself out, hand over hand, using long, firm and deliberate movements.
● If you are alone, stay on your back and deliberately, and *very slowly*, try to pull your feet out of the mire. Allow plenty of time for the sand or mud to flow around your limbs as you move. Abrupt, jerky movements will only create vacuum pockets under the surface, which will suck you in deeper.
● When your feet are more free, use your arms and legs as paddles and propel yourself – *extremely slowly* – towards firm ground. Use roots or large clumps of grass to pull yourself along.
● Do not rush. With rests, it may take an hour or so to cover only a few feet.

Danger spots A quicksand is often difficult to spot. When walking in the country, beware of black stretches of ground without vegetation and bright green expanses covered with moss.

If you have to cross boggy ground, keep to the highest parts where there are bushes and trees. Wherever possible, tread on clumps of grass or heather – they usually grow on drier ground.

When exploring beaches, spongy areas, or moorland, always carry a stick or pole as a probe.

Making a simple, hand-stitched quilt

Spread out the backing reverse side up, and lay the wadding on it, smoothing out each layer. Unfold the quilt top carefully, smoothing it over the wadding. Tack, then stitch the layers together, finishing with a self-edge or using the backing as a border.

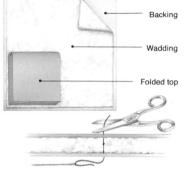

Backing

Wadding

Folded top

Tacking layers together Working from the centre of the quilt outwards, tack the three layers together in a sunburst pattern.

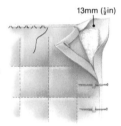

Quilting Knot the thread, then push the needle from the top through the layers. Pull the thread so that the knot slips into the wadding. Snip the extra thread.

13mm (½in)

Self-edging Trim the top and bottom layers 13mm (½in) wider all round than the wadding. Fold their edges in and whipstitch them together.

Hand-stitching Take a few small stitches at a time, then draw the needle through.

Turn under 13mm (½in)

Tacking

Bordering Tack the quilt top to the wadding. Fold in the backing edges 13mm (½in).

Slipstitch the backing to the top. Fold the corner of the backing.

Turn over the adjacent backing edge; slipstitch it to the top.

Quilting

Making a warm bedcover

A quilt consists of a soft layer of filling sandwiched between two layers of fabric and held in place by rows of stitching.

Top layer For the top layer of the quilt, use smooth medium-weight material such as cotton, poplin or polyester/cotton. It can be a printed material, or you can use a sheet of PATCHWORK. You can decorate a plain fabric with APPLIQUÉS or EMBROIDERY, but the stitching itself can make a pleasing geometric pattern.

Bottom layer Avoid slippery material, so the quilt does not tend to slide off the bed. A medium-weight fabric that is easy to sew through – such as fine cotton, muslin or flannelette – is ideal. You can use a bed sheet or buy sheeting – perhaps in a colour that complements the top.

Filling Use polyester wadding, which is warm, washable, easy to sew and sold in a range of widths and thicknesses.

Equipment No 8 or 9 needles are suitable for quilting most fabrics; No 7 is best for heavier material, No 10 for material that is fine or delicate. Buy 'betweens' 32mm (1¼in) long, or 38mm (1½in) 'sharps'. Try both and see which you like best.

The thread you use must be strong; No

40 cotton thread, silk or buttonhole twist, or polyester sewing thread, are all suitable. If using cotton thread, rub it on a cake of beeswax to reduce tangling and fraying.

For small items you can buy a quilting frame or hoop to hold the layers taut as you sew; major stores or haberdashery shops sell them. Alternatively, you can use a tapestry frame, though a full-size bed quilt is best done on a purpose-made frame. You will also need a thimble, a rubber finger pad (sold by stationers), scissors for cutting templates, and dressmaker's scissors.

Measuring and cutting Plan the design and measurements on graph paper. Make templates of thin card for the different shapes of your pattern. The rows of quilting can be as much as 150mm (6in) apart when you are using polyester wadding, because it does not easily disintegrate. To compensate for take-up when stitching, the wadding should be about 25mm (1in) larger all round than the size of the finished quilt.

For the same reason, when cutting fabric for the top and bottom layers, allow 20-50 millimetres (an inch or two) extra all round.

If the backing is to be used as a border the bottom layer should be larger than the top layer by twice the width of the proposed border, plus 13mm (½in) for turning under.

Assembling, tacking and quilting the layers Spread out the backing and lay over it the wadding and the quilt top.

Measure the four sides and mark the centre of each with a pin. Tack (see SEWING) one horizontal and one vertical line connecting the midpoints of the opposing sides and intersecting at the centre of the quilt, so that it is divided into quarters. Tack all round the quilt from the middle to the edges in a sunburst pattern.

Work slowly and carefully – good tacking is essential for an even, unpuckered finish, and must be particularly secure if you plan to quilt without using a hoop or frame. Do not kneel or lean on the fabric – this can create hidden wrinkles in the wadding and backing. The tacking can be snipped out during actual quilting.

Mark any patterns for quilting on the top layer, using your templates and dressmaker's chalk.

If you are using a hoop or frame, secure the part for stitching in it. Start at arm's length and work towards yourself, using short, even, running stitches. Make sure each stitch penetrates all three layers.

Self-edging Fold the edges of the backing over the wadding; then turn the edges of the top layer under. Whipstitch the folded edges together all round, making the stitches as small and neat as possible.

Backing as border After quilting, turn under the edges of the backing. Then fold the part of the backing that is to become the border, SLIP-STITCHING the turned-in edge of the border to the edge of the top layer of the quilt. Mitre and slip-stitch the corners neatly.

Quinces

*Growing a tree; making
quince jelly*

Quince trees (*Cydonia oblonga*) are easy to grow – but not many garden centres offer quince trees for sale, so you may have to buy one from a specialist nursery. They are self-fertile, so can be grown singly and produce fruit.

The most commonly grown varieties are 'Vranja' and 'Portugal'. Another variety, 'Meach's Prolific', grows more slowly than these two but bears fruit earlier, often after only three years. The others may take five to seven years before fruiting.

Quinces fruit best in the south of England. They should be grown as bush trees and planted in late October or November, in a sunny, open position or the shelter of a wall. Quince trees can be grown in ordinary garden soil, but do best in moist loam without too much chalk or lime – see SOIL PREPARATION. They sometimes top 5.5m (18ft), though 3-4.6m (10-15ft) is more usual, with a spread of 3m (10ft).

In northern areas, the fruit seldom ripens outdoors, except when the tree is trained against a sheltered, sunny wall – see FRUIT TREES. They do not like heavy pruning.

Pale pink or white flowers – rather like apple blossom – appear in May, followed by hard, golden, pear-shaped fruit, up to 100mm (4in) long, in autumn. Pick the fruit in October, before the frosts, and store in a cool, dry room. Quinces continue to ripen indoors, and can be stored for six or seven weeks. Keep them apart from other fruit – which may be affected by their pungent aroma. The fruit can be made into a delicious jelly or jam. See also JAM MAKING; JELLIES; PRESERVING.

Quince jelly This has a rich amber colour and a sweet, slightly lemony scent. It is delicious on hot buttered toast, on bread and butter, scones or muffins, and with highly flavoured meat, especially pork, venison or game. Make it with preserving rather than granulated sugar, since it produces less scum.

Ingredients (for 1.8-2.3kg [4-5lb])
1.8kg (4lb) quinces
Water
Preserving or granulated sugar
Juice of 2 lemons

Wash the quinces, chop them roughly and place the pieces in a large heavy-bottomed saucepan, with just enough water to cover them. Bring to the boil, cover and simmer for 1-1½ hours, until very soft. Ladle the fruit and liquid into a scalded jelly bag, slung from the legs of an upturned stool, with a plastic or earthenware bowl beneath the bag to catch the juice. Leave it to strain for about four hours. Do *not* squeeze the jelly bag, or the jelly will look cloudy.

Heat the oven to 110°C (225°F), gas mark ¼. Measure the strained juice, and weigh out 450g (1lb) of sugar for each 570ml (1 pint) of juice. Warm the sugar in an ovenproof dish in the middle of the oven for 10-15 minutes.

Next, warm the quince juice in a preserving pan or large, heavy-bottomed saucepan. Add the lemon juice and stir in the warm sugar until it dissolves. Bring to the boil and cook rapidly. The jelly should set after boiling for about 10-15 minutes. Test for set as in JAM MAKING.

Skim off any remaining froth or scum, then pour immediately into clean, warmed jam jars. Seal as jam and leave to cool before storing.

Quoits

Playing a ring-pitching game

Quoits is similar to HORSESHOES; but instead of open-ended horseshoes, circular metal rings, or *quoits*, are used.

The players try to throw the quoits so that they land over a stake in the ground – or at least nearer to it than the opponent's. A standard quoit weighs about 1.4kg (3lb); it has a hole in the centre 100mm (4in) in diameter and a rim 50mm (2in) wide. The stakes are anything up to 150mm (6in) high. The court consists of two stakes, or *hobs*, driven into the ground 16.7m (54ft) apart. Children, using quoits made of rope or rubber, can place the stakes 6-9m (20-30ft) apart.

The players stand just behind one of the stakes, and take turns pitching their quoits (two each) at the second stake. The players then move to the second stake, add up their scores, and pitch back at the first stake.

A quoit that encircles a stake (a *ringer*) scores 3 points; a quoit that leans against a stake (a *leaner*, or *hobber*) scores 2 points; and one that lands closer to the stake than an opponent's scores 1 point. A ringer topping an opponent's ringer scores 6 points; a ringer topping two others scores 9 points. If there are four ringers, the top one scores 12 points. Two leaners against an opponent's ringer count 7 points each.

The winner is the first player to reach 21 points; and the winner of two out of three games takes the match.

Rabbits

How to house, feed and care for them

Do not keep adult rabbits together – particularly adults of the same sex who will almost certainly fight. Put a doe with a buck only for mating.

It is generally best to keep a rabbit in a hutch outside in a sheltered spot, or in a well-ventilated shed or outbuilding. Do not keep rabbits in a garage – car fumes could kill them – or in a greenhouse, conservatory or in the home, the heat will be too much for them.

Ideally the rabbits should have a movable pen, in addition to a hutch, where they can be put out for exercise on the grass every day in good weather. Unless the pen is very secure, you will need to keep an eye on them to prevent them from escaping or being molested by dogs or cats.

The hutch This must be roomy enough for the rabbit to stretch and sit up – no less than 900mm (3ft) long, 600mm (2ft) wide and 450mm (18in) high – and well off the ground to protect the rabbit from damp and frost. The roof should be sloped, with a fall of about 50mm (2in) from front to back, and covered with roofing felt. It should overhang all round the hutch – at least 75mm (3in) at the front.

About one-third of the hutch should be closed in with a solid door for a sleeping and nesting area. The rest of the hutch should have a separate door covered with 13mm ($\frac{1}{2}$in) wire mesh. Both doors should be securely bolted. Make sure nothing inside the hutch could injure the rabbit – the mesh should be sandwiched between laths and the door frame.

A good construction is a hutch made from 13mm plywood panels inside a frame of 50 × 25mm (2 × 1in) softwood BATTENS so that the rabbit cannot easily gnaw the woodwork. All the woodwork should have been treated with one of the WOOD PRESERVATIVES not toxic to animals. If the floor is slightly sloped to the rear, with a drainage slot of about 6mm ($\frac{1}{4}$in) at the base of the back panel, it saves a lot of cleaning out.

Feeding Feed rabbits twice a day at the same times each day. See how much they eat within half an hour of feeding and offer this amount at future feeds. Put the food in a heavy earthenware dish.

Give plenty of fresh hay each day, as well as grass, cabbage, sprouts, lettuce (sparingly), carrot, turnip, or radish tops. Do not feed potato tops, rhubarb or broad-bean haulm. You can also give parsnips or swedes. Suitable weeds include dandelions (sparingly), clover, chickweed, shepherd's purse, groundsel, and coltsfoot – but do not give daisies or buttercups. Make sure that any weeds – from a garden or hedgerow – are not likely to have been sprayed with a pesticide in the previous week or so.

Never feed a rabbit with lawn mowings unless they are very fresh or have been properly dried – not if they have been left in a heap and have started to ferment.

Many rabbits also like leftovers, such as toast, cold porridge or apple or potato peelings.

Special, nutrient-rich rabbit pellets are available in pet shops, but rabbits generally prefer other foods as well. They also need fresh water – put it in a heavy bowl or a water dispenser.

Do not be disturbed if you see the rabbit eating some of its own droppings – this is a normal part of digestion.

Keeping a hutch clean Line the floor of a hutch with layers of newspaper covered with straw, sawdust or wood shavings, leaving only the area with the feeding pots uncovered. Change the covering once or twice a week – more often if there is a litter of young.

Handling a pet Put a hand under the rabbit's abdomen to lift it up, and quickly put the other hand under its rump to support its weight. Hold it against your chest, supporting its head and ears. Handle the rabbit frequently to win its confidence. Make slow, quiet and gentle movements. Unexpected or abrupt movements or noises will frighten the rabbit – and it can be difficult to regain its confidence. Never lift a rabbit by its ears – it is both cruel and unnecessary.

Young rabbits A doe produces young about 31 days after mating. Make sure she has plenty of hay and straw for nesting for about a week beforehand. She will make the nest herself, lining it with fur from her chest. The young are born blind and without fur, and do not leave the nest for two to three weeks. Do not disturb the nest – the litter is usually covered with fur, which can be seen rising and falling as the youngsters breathe. Make sure the doe has plenty of food and water while she is nursing.

Do not take young rabbits away from their mother before they are at least six weeks old. Do not let young rabbits eat too much wet grass or green stuff – this causes bloating or diarrhoea. Bramble leaves help stem diarrhoea.

Rabies

What to do if you are bitten

Rabies is a highly dangerous and infectious viral disease, carried by animals – particularly dogs and foxes. It is transmitted through the bite of an infected animal. The disease occurs in most parts of the world except Britain, Scandinavia, Australia, Japan and Antarctica.

Anyone bitten by a rabid animal must be treated *before* symptoms develop, otherwise there is no effective treatment, and death occurs usually within days.

Symptoms can take from ten days to a year after the bite to develop – but usually take 20-90 days. Initially they include fever, headache, sore throat and muscle pains, followed by pain or numbness in the area of the bite. A day or two later the patient becomes restless, agitated and confused, and may have hallucinations, muscle spasms, stiffness of the neck and back and areas of paralysis. Sufferers also foam at the mouth, have painful throat spasms and a fear of liquids.

If you intend to travel to an area where the risk of being bitten by a rabid animal is high, see your doctor about immunisation before you go.

If you are bitten In any country where rabies may be present, go to a local DOCTOR straight away if any animal bites you. Unless it can be proved beyond doubt that the animal is free of rabies, you must be given an immediate course of injections. If possible see that the animal that bit you is isolated. If it escapes, notify the local police. See also DOG BITES.

Radiator flushing

Clearing your car's cooling system

If your car engine is overheating and you have eliminated other possible causes (such as a broken fan belt or water leaks), the cooling system is probably blocked. The most likely place for the blockage is in the narrow passages of the radiator.

RADIATOR FLUSHING
Cleaning it out

Bottom connector stub
Top connector stub
Hose

Push a hose into the top connector stub; jam it with rags. Flush water through the radiator until it runs clear from the bottom hose connector stub.

Before flushing the radiator, drain the coolant from the system and discard it. (Use fresh ANTIFREEZE when refilling the system.) Disconnect the top and bottom hoses from the radiator and push a garden hose into the top radiator connector. Seal it with rags packed round the hose. Make sure the radiator pressure cap is on and fitting correctly, then turn on the hose. Flush until the water runs clear from the bottom hose connector.

If the water does not start to run clear within a few minutes, reverse flush the radiator. Put the garden hose in the bottom connector and seal it. Cover any electrical components near the radiator with plastic sheeting; or fit another hose – or a long plastic bag with a hole in the bottom – onto the top connector, to take away flushed water. Reverse flush until the water runs clear.

If the radiator remains blocked, try removing it – it is usually held by only a few small bolts. Stand it upside down near a convenient drain. Reverse flush again. If the radiator cannot be easily removed, consult a garage.

While the radiator is out of the car, check and clean the radiator fins. Use a stiff nylon brush to loosen dirt, then hose water through from the back.

Radio aerials
Getting better radio reception

Most modern radios have an aerial that is adequate for receiving medium wave (MW) and long wave (LW) transmissions. For very high frequency (VHF) and frequency modulation (FM) reception, most battery and battery/mains portable radios have a telescopic aerial which can be angled to the best position for distor-

tion-free reception. Radio tuners used as part of a hi-fi stereo system generally have only a socket for an FM aerial.

Switch off your radio or hi-fi and unplug it from the mains before working on an aerial.

If MW/LW reception is poor you may be able to improve it with a length of plastic-insulated wire. Bare about 19mm (¾in) at one end and push it into the radio's AM (amplitude modulation) socket. Bare the other end and lead it to a picture rail or over a curtain rail, experimenting to find a spot that improves reception. If the radio has an earth terminal, you can also reduce interference by pushing one end of a separate wire into the earth terminal and connecting the other to an earthed metal pipe.

Making an FM aerial In all but the very worst reception areas, a simple dipole aerial mounted in the loft will suffice. A dipole aerial (two rods with a small gap between them) can be made from two lengths of 10mm (⅜in) diameter alloy tubing, fixed over a piece of hardwood dowelling – see DOWELS. Saw each length of tubing to exactly 760mm (30in) (see SAWS AND SAWING) and push them over the dowelling, leaving a gap of not more than 25mm (1in). Drill a 3mm (⅛in) hole through the tube ends and the dowelling (see DRILLING), and fit a solder tag to each with a nut and bolt.

To make the aerial lead, use 75 ohm coaxial cable and a coaxial plug, obtainable from electrical stores. Using a sharp knife, bare the inner conductor wire and

solder it to one solder tag, soldering some of the twisted copper braid to the other solder tag.

Attach the other end of the cable to the coaxial plug, making sure that the copper braid is gripped firmly and the conductor is central in the plug body.

Suspend the aerial in the loft by cords attached to rafters, keeping it well clear of metallic objects such as water cisterns. Run the aerial lead from the radio by the shortest possible route.

The aerial should hang broadside-on to the direction of the local FM transmitter – if you are not sure of the direction, position the aerial until you get the best reception. At the radio end of the lead, connect the plug to the aerial socket in your radio.

Raffles
Running one according to the rules

If you want to run a lottery or raffle, you must normally obtain a licence. However, you do not need a licence to run a small lottery or raffle as part of an event such as a fête, sale of work, dinner, dance or sports event, provided it is not run for personal gain, and the rules laid down in the Lotteries and Amusements Act 1976 (as amended) are observed (see SWEEPSTAKE).

All other lotteries must be registered with either the local council or the Gaming Board for Great Britain,

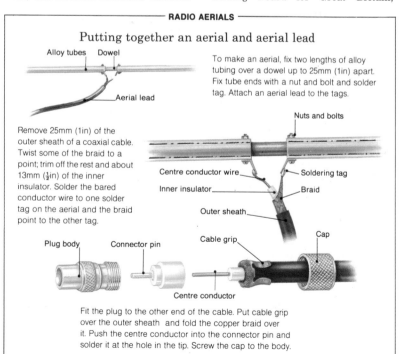

RADIO AERIALS
Putting together an aerial and aerial lead

Alloy tubes Dowel
Aerial lead

To make an aerial, fix two lengths of alloy tubing over a dowel up to 25mm (1in) apart. Fix tube ends with a nut and bolt and solder tag. Attach an aerial lead to the tags.

Remove 25mm (1in) of the outer sheath of a coaxial cable. Twist some of the braid to a point; trim off the rest and about 13mm (½in) of the inner insulator. Solder the bared conductor wire to one solder tag on the aerial and the braid point to the other tag.

Nuts and bolts
Centre conductor wire
Inner insulator
Outer sheath
Soldering tag
Braid

Plug body Connector pin
Cable grip Cap
Centre conductor

Fit the plug to the other end of the cable. Put cable grip over the outer sheath and fold the copper braid over it. Push the centre conductor into the connector pin and solder it at the hole in the tip. Screw the cap to the body.

Berkshire House, 168-173 High Holborn, London WC1V 7AA. Lotteries must be registered with the Gaming Board if the value of tickets to be put on sale is more than £20,000 for any one lottery, or £250,000 in total in any year. In these cases, the society running the lottery must register with the Board, and it must make a return to the Board in respect of each lottery it has held. The registration fee is £510. A separate fee is payable in respect of each lottery held, when the return is made.

Once a society is registered with the Gaming Board, it must make a return of all lotteries made within three months of the date of the lottery concerned. The society must renew its registration every three years. A society which does not have to register with the Gaming Board must register with the local council.

The turnover limit for a society lottery is £1,000,000 for an individual lottery, or £5,000,000 in a year. No prize may be greater than £25,000 or 10 per cent of the total value of tickets sold, whichever is the greater.

By law, the organiser of a registered lottery must also be a member of the registered club or society and must make a detailed return to the local authority or the Gaming Board after the lottery. The return must state the date of the lottery, how much money was raised, how much went on expenses and prizes and for what the profits were used.

Tickets, notices and advertisements must specify the lottery date, the name and address of the promoter, and the name of the promoting society. All tickets must carry the same price and give the name of the registration authority. They may not be sold in licensed gaming premises, from vending machines, on the street, and by or to anyone aged under 16. No more than half the proceeds can be spent on prizes and no more than 30 per cent (15 per cent for bigger lotteries) on expenses.

Rag dolls

Making your own soft toy

Use the pattern shown here and enlarge it – see PATTERN TRANSFER.

Trace the pattern twice onto pale pink, brown or beige fabric. On the outer side of one head, pencil in the mouth, nose and eyes. Embroider the mouth with a backstitch, the eyebrows with a stem stitch (see EMBROIDERY) and fill in the nose and eyes with satin stitch. Alternatively, draw on the face with felt-tip markers or sew or glue on felt shapes.

Cut out the bodies and, with the right sides facing, sew them together 6mm (¼in) from the raw edge with a machine, or backstitch by hand – see SEWING. Leave

a small opening on one side. Snip the seam allowance round curves and turn the doll right side out.

Stuff the body with soft, washable material, such as pieces of old nylon tights, or foam. Use a pencil to push the stuffing tightly into the arms and legs. Close the opening with SLIPSTITCHING.

Make some hair from wool and sew it on. Sew some clothes, using the doll outline enlarged as a guide.

RAG DOLLS

Cutting out and putting one together

Grid

Trace the pattern onto paper and enlarge it to 325mm (12¾in) on a grid of 25mm (1in) squares.

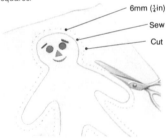

6mm (¼in)
Sew
Cut

Cut out the enlarged pattern, place it on two pieces of fabric, and draw round it, adding a 6mm (¼in) seam allowance all round. Embroider, draw or stick on the features. Cut out and sew the shapes together and stuff the body.

Stitch through lengths of wool and sew them to the head.

Plait girl doll's hair or gather it into bunches with ribbons. Enlarge the original pattern on a 25mm (1in) grid, for clothing. Cut out and sew the clothes.

Raincoats

Choosing, caring for, and reproofing them

Most raincoats, or mackintoshes, are treated (proofed) with a water-repellent chemical compound. This should keep out showery rain, as should lightweight plastic macs, often made of treated nylon. Nylon with an inner lining of plastic such as polyurethane should have greater water resistance.

Fully waterproof raincoats or oilskins are fabrics coated with PVC, oil or rubber compounds, but they restrict air circulation and can cause sweating, as do lightweight plastic macs. Jackets made of tightly woven waxed cotton allow air circulation and have fairly good water resistance.

How well a raincoat keeps out the rain depends also on the tightness of the fabric weave, the design and the workmanship of the manufacturer in places where water can penetrate (such as seams, button stitching and buttonholes), and also the styling.

Look for a raincoat with a close weave, good lining, bonded or well-sewn seams and buttonholes, and well-protected button stitching. Some makers use water-resistant thread for exposed stitching. Choose a style that is protective, with close-fitting sleeves and collar. Make sure the label gives information on LAUNDERING or cleaning.

Before putting away a wet raincoat, hang it on a coathanger to dry – but not too near high heat. Oilskins or PVC fabrics can be sponged clean with warm water, and lightweight plastic macs should normally be washed according to the instructions on the cleaning label, never dry-cleaned.

Raincoats with water-repellent proofing normally have to be dry-cleaned. If they are washable, follow the instructions on the cleaning label, but there is a risk of shrinkage. The water-repellent proofing diminishes with wear and cleaning, so it is best to have a raincoat re-proofed each time it is dry-cleaned.

Waxed cotton rainwear should be re-waxed at intervals of about 18 months to two years.

Raised flowerbeds

Giving your garden a lift

A raised flowerbed can be simply an attractive garden feature or a means of making gardening easier for those who find bending difficult or are confined to wheelchairs. Choose an open site, away from trees.

A raised bed should be no more than 1.2m (4ft) wide if it can be reached only from one side, or 2.4m (8ft) if it can be reached from two sides. A height of 460-

Making a small raised bed

Build tiers of dry stones or bricks laid closely together, sloping them towards the top. Fill the bed and any crevices with soil.

610mm (1½-2ft) is suitable for most purposes.

Clear and level the site, ensure that drainage is adequate, and destroy perennial weeds – see WEED CONTROL.

Making the walls For the walls, you can use stones or bricks – or peat blocks for acid-loving plants. Set the base layer at least 150mm (6in) firmly into the ground. The stones in one layer should bridge the gaps between those in the tier below, as shown. Each layer should be set slightly in from the previous one.

Alternatively, bind the stones or bricks together with MORTAR (see BRICK-LAYING) when there is no need to slope the walls. But first dig a base trench and lay a strong foundation. Leave some gaps without mortar, so that you can fill them with earth and plants.

Smaller raised beds can also be made with wooden surrounds, using rot-resistant planks or beams. The bottom layer of timbers should be set in a trench 50mm (2in) deep. If you use planks, place them on edge and fasten the corners with angle brackets. If you build layers of beams, peg the bottom layer to the ground with 1m (39in) reinforcing bars, and fasten each succeeding course to the one below with large nails – see NAILING.

Filling the bed The soil should retain moisture while draining well. Add 1 part of peat and 1 part of coarse sand to every 2 parts of soil, with several handfuls of base fertiliser (see FERTILISERS) to each barrowload. Fill the bed to about 25mm (1in) from the top. Soak the soil well and leave it to settle for a few weeks before planting. See also SOIL PREPARATION.

Rape

What to do if a rapist attacks

Weigh up the circumstances quickly. If you can run away, do so. Try to head for a well-lit place where there are other people. Yell for help.

Fight only if you have to – and then only if you have a chance of getting away. Be brutal, and if you have time, get a hard object into your hand – a metal comb or a bunch of keys, perhaps. Keep it concealed until the attacker is at close quarters. Then use it suddenly; without warning and with all your strength, jab it into the attacker's face. Keep fighting and yelling until the attacker lets go, then run for help.

If you have no weapon, scream at the attacker to leave you alone. Use forceful language; it may upset the rapist's fantasy about his victim and make him abandon his attack.

Calling the police If you escape from a would-be rapist, dial 999 as soon as you are safe and ask for the police. Give full details of the incident, and a detailed description of the attacker.

If you are sexually assaulted, report it to the police as soon as you can. This gives them a chance to arrest your assailant, and could save someone else from attack.

The police will do their best to help and reassure you. You can have a relation, friend or anyone you like for company during the interview.

Do not wash or tidy yourself up, as that may destroy evidence and lessen the chance of a conviction if the rapist is caught.

The police will also want to make an examination. Most police forces have specially trained rape incident teams, but you have the right to ask to be examined by your own doctor or a woman doctor. The examination will be made in a special suite, or else in a doctor's surgery.

The police will need a detailed statement of what occurred to help their enquiries, and for later use in court. If an arrest is made you may be asked to identify your attacker from among a group, or from a video film. If possible the police will provide a specially trained officer to help you in court, or else a Victim Support volunteer will keep you company.

If you feel you cannot face the trauma of questioning by the police, get help from the nearest Rape Crisis Centre. If there is no centre in your area, telephone either London (0171) 837 1600 or Birmingham (0121) 766 5366 at any time of day or night.

Reducing the risks Many rapes are perpetrated by someone the victim knows, but some are by an attacker who forces his way into the home. So be very cautious in opening the door to anyone if you are alone; friends will understand.

Fit a stout chain and a PEEPHOLE VIEWER to the outer door (see also BURGLARPROOFING) and ask callers such as meter readers or charity collectors for identification before undoing the chain. Pretend to have company by calling something like 'OK, I'll go, Fred' as you approach the door.

If you live alone in a flat use only your initials, not your full first name, on the nameplate. You could consider adding a fictitious name under yours on the plate, so that it appears you are sharing.

Self-defence In many areas, there are self-defence classes for women, run by the local council or other groups, often supported by the police. You can get details from your local library or newspaper. See also JUDO.

You may also consider buying a gas screech alarm. Carry it in your hand at night if alone in a place such as a car park or an almost empty train. Aim it into an attacker's face. An aerosol spray, such as hair lacquer, squirted at the face can also deter an attacker. See also MUGGERS.

Rashes

Finding what causes them and treating them

There are three main kinds of rash: those which affect the whole body and are accompanied by other symptoms, such as COUGHS or FEVER; those which affect the whole body but are not accompanied by other symptoms; and those which affect one part of the body only.

Rashes on the whole body If the rash is accompanied by other symptoms, it is probably a symptom of an infection, such as GERMAN MEASLES, MEASLES or chicken pox – more common in children.

Consult a doctor. He may simply advise you to treat the infection with rest, fluids and painkillers.

Allergic rashes Rashes that are not accompanied by other symptoms are usually due to ALLERGIES. They can also be caused by SUNBURN or ECZEMA.

Find out (by a process of elimination, if necessary) what is causing the rash and avoid it. If it is a prescribed drug, consult a DOCTOR. Consult the doctor if the rash is severe or persistent or caused by a substance used at work.

Partial rashes The part of the body affected will usually indicate the cause – commonly IMPETIGO and COLD SORES for face rashes, ATHLETE'S FOOT and eczema.

Rats

How to get rid of dangerous disease carriers

Rats carry diseases and are a danger to health. They also breed rapidly – one female rat may produce 50 young a year.

Rats rarely infest the average home, but may get into sheds and outhouses. If you find signs of them, get in touch with the Environmental Health Department at your local council offices. The signs that they are around, apart from damage to food stores, are oval droppings about 13mm ($\frac{1}{2}$in) long, gnawed woodwork, pipes or electric plugs or cables, and grease-stained edges round holes in woodwork or masonry.

Rats soon become wary of traps or poisoned bait – baits based on difenacoum or bromadiolone, that you can lay down yourself, are sometimes effective. However, the Environmental Health Department should get rid of them free, or for a small charge.

Preventing infestation Rats are more likely to be found in cellars, outhouses and warehouses near water or livestock, but will thrive in any environment that provides food and shelter. They will eat all sorts of stored or waste food, particularly cereals or root crops, and can easily climb into lofts or roof spaces.

Do not leave waste food lying about, and make sure that dustbins are secure. In cellars or outhouses store any food, bulbs, seed potatoes, even soap and candles in tins or bins.

Block holes under sheds or in masonry or woodwork with cement (see CONCRETE)

or strong metal mesh. Do not leave piles of rubbish in a yard or garden corners. Rats will often burrow under a protective heap of rubbish to find food.

Reading music

Understanding basic musical notes and terms

Most people can sing the basic scale – doh, ray, me, fah, soh, lah, te, doh. When you read music, you relate this and many other sound patterns to a system of written notes.

Notes are written on or between the lines of the treble and bass staves (see opposite), each pitch having its own position on the keyboard. Each has a letter-name from A to G. Starting on any letter, repeated patterns of eight (octaves) run alphabetically.

Bottom A is in the first space of the bass stave; B is on the first line and so forth to A on the top bass line. Middle C is suspended on a short line below the treble stave or just above the bass stave.

We tend to sing notes in a sweet 'major' sequence or key. But they can also be sung in 'minor' keys which give a mournful evocative sound, often used for sadder passages of music.

Sharps and flats The interval between two successive notes is either a tone or a semitone.

A sharp sign in front of a note (as shown) raises the pitch a semitone. A flat sign lowers it by a semitone; a natural restores it to its original pitch.

All scales except C major include at least one note that has to be flattened or sharpened to preserve the correct sound pattern. Because the key of a piece is always related to a scale, it will include the scale's sharps and flats. Instead of these being shown each time they occur, they are indicated in the key signature, at the start of the passage, as shown. Flats and sharps that occur outside the key are called accidentals.

Note values Notes are sung or played at different lengths or time values and this is shown by the way they are written.

The longest normally used is an open note called a semibreve. The minim (shown opposite) is half its length. The crotchet, a filled note with a tail, is half the minim's length. A quaver, a filled note with a tail and a tick or beamed to other notes, as shown, is half the length of the crotchet. Subsequently shorter notes are indicated by the number of ticks or parallel beams.

Each note has its corresponding 'rest' sign which is written to mark a break in the music for that exact space of time.

A note or rest can be lengthened by one half of its time value by adding a dot. A note can also be 'tied' – coupled to a following note which is not sounded but which extends the length of the first note by its own time value.

Time The rhythm of a piece of music depends on which notes are accented. This usually falls into a pattern, marked by a regular number of beats in a bar. To show where these divisions come, a vertical bar-line is placed across the

---

READING MUSIC

How to interpret the language of sounds

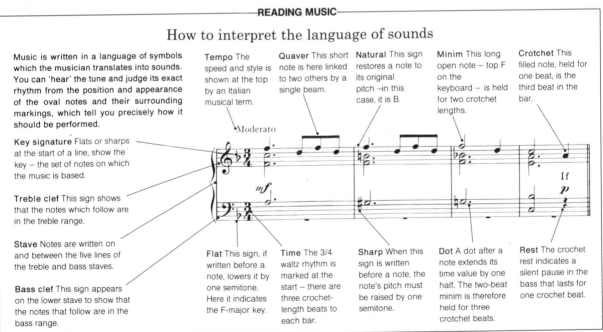

Music is written in a language of symbols which the musician translates into sounds. You can 'hear' the tune and judge its exact rhythm from the position and appearance of the oval notes and their surrounding markings, which tell you precisely how it should be performed.

Key signature Flats or sharps at the start of a line, show the key – the set of notes on which the music is based.

Treble clef This sign shows that the notes which follow are in the treble range.

Stave Notes are written on and between the five lines of the treble and bass staves.

Bass clef This sign appears on the lower stave to show that the notes that follow are in the bass range.

Tempo The speed and style is shown at the top by an Italian musical term.

Quaver This short note is here linked to two others by a single beam.

Natural This sign restores a note to its original pitch –in this case, it is B.

Minim This long open note – top F on the keyboard – is held for two crotchet lengths.

Crotchet This filled note, held for one beat, is the third beat in the bar.

Flat This sign, if written before a note, lowers it by one semitone. Here it indicates the F-major key.

Time The 3/4 waltz rhythm is marked by the start – there are three crotchet-length beats to each bar.

Sharp When this sign is written before a note, the note's pitch must be raised by one semitone.

Dot A dot after a note extends its time value by one half. The two-beat minim is therefore held for three crotchet beats.

Rest The crotchet rest indicates a silent pause in the bass that lasts for one crotchet beat.

stave. A double-bar (two bar lines) indicates the end of a passage.

The number of beats in a bar is shown numerically by the time signature, as illustrated. The bottom figure shows what length of note is the basic unit – a figure 2 denotes a minim, a 4 a crotchet, an 8 a quaver and so on. The top figure tells you how many units are in a bar.

A more general description of the speed and style of a passage is shown by a musical term, often in Italian, written above the stave – as shown.

Passages may also be marked specifically with, for instance, 'p' (*piano*) meaning soft or 'f' (*forte*) meaning loud or marked for a crescendo (increasing sound) or diminuendo (dying away).

Chords, one base note combined with related notes, played or sung together, add to the strength and richness of music. In a choir, different voices will take different notes of the chord.

Further study You can learn the rudiments of music at home, but to become proficient, seek expert tuition. Music teachers often advertise in *Yellow Pages* (Music teachers; Music schools) and in local newspapers. The Incorporated Society of Musicians produces a national list of qualified teachers, *Professional Register of Private Teachers of Music*. It is available in large reference libraries, or from the society. Many evening schools offer music classes. If you like singing, join a local choral or operatic society. See also PIANO; RECORDERS.

Receipts

Making one and getting one

A receipt is a written acknowledgment that someone has received money, goods or services under an agreement, or it is evidence that a transaction between two parties has been undertaken.

Giving a receipt The law does not specify the form a receipt should take; nor, in general, does it oblige you to issue one, but refusal to do so may suggest dishonesty. The receipt should include your name, the date of issue and what it is for – or the price paid.

If you occasionally sell goods privately – for example, furniture you no longer have use for – you should give a receipt to the buyer in case of any later dispute. You can write or type it (keep a copy), or buy a book of receipts from a stationer.

If you are in business for yourself, and you are registered for VALUE ADDED TAX, you must issue an invoice with any sale to anyone else who is registered for the tax. This must identify you, and set out all the details of the sale, including the amount of tax charged.

Getting a receipt Always ask for a receipt – and keep it carefully – if you believe that there could be any dispute afterwards. It is evidence of purchase if goods later turn out to be faulty (see also COMPLAINTS; SALE OF GOODS), or if you hope to recover part of the money – for example, on an expense account, or as a tax allowance – see INCOME TAX RETURNS.

Check the receipt when you are given it, to make sure the amounts and date are correct. Examine any small print – delivery receipts for goods often include conditions stating, for example, that acceptance of the receipt indicates that the recipient has checked the quality and quantity of items supplied.

Insist on a receipt, too, if you are registered for value added tax. You should be given a tax invoice as receipt, so that you may claim a deduction for the VAT you pay out.

Sometimes, you may want a receipt to prove that someone has received an important document – for example, notice to quit served on TENANTS, or dismissal notice for an employee. If you are delivering it by hand, prepare a receipt and a copy and get the recipient to sign both, or use recorded or registered post.

Recorders

Playing, cleaning and maintaining them

The recorder, like other woodwind instruments, is played by breathing into the mouthpiece while your fingers cover various combinations of holes to produce notes. See also READING MUSIC.

The small descant recorder is the most suitable type for a child to begin on, but an adult is more likely to prefer the slightly larger treble, which is not as shrill. There are other sizes, both smaller and larger – the bass recorder, for example – but they are more difficult for beginners to play.

Most recorders are sold with an accompanying fingering chart, but a tutor or detailed instruction book is also needed.

How to play Hold the recorder with both hands, the left at the top and the right at the bottom, and support the instrument on your right thumb. Hold your left hand with the thumb covering the hole on the underside of the recorder, and the pads of the first three fingers covering the three upper holes – the fourth finger is unused. Hold the fingers of the right hand over the four lower holes.

Uncover all the holes except those held by the left thumb and first finger, keeping the other fingers about 10mm (⅜in) above their respective holes, ready to lower again when needed.

Feel the two holes that you are cover-

ing, and make sure you are sealing them completely. Then add the other fingers again, one at a time, to get the feel of the whole instrument.

Place the mouthpiece between your lips, not so far in that it touches the teeth. Use just the left thumb and first finger to cover their two holes, and breathe a gentle 'doo' to make the sound.

The fingering you are using will give the note B on a descant recorder, or E on a treble recorder. Play several long Bs (or Es) until you are making a steady pleasant note. Add the second finger of your left hand and the note is A (or D). Adding the third gives G (or C).

Master these notes before you try to play any that involve the right hand. Your tutor or instruction book will tell you how to finger them, as well as how to read the music, breathe and phrase correctly, and play musically.

After practising steadily for a few weeks, you may want to play in company with other people. The Society of Recorder Players can put you in touch with a group or class if there is one in your neighbourhood. Contact the membership secretary at 469 Merton Road, London SW18 5LD.

Looking after your recorder Keep the instrument in its case when not in use. Before playing, warm the head joint in your hand or pocket to reduce condensation from your breath.

Clean the recorder to remove dust and moisture after use. Allow a wooden instrument to dry naturally first, do not dry it in direct heat. Separate the recorder into three sections for cleaning by gently untwisting the joints.

When cleaning, never touch the sharp lip of the instrument, as this controls the tone quality and is easily damaged. Clean the windway with a feather or a strip of folded paper. Clean the bore with a soft cloth held in the cleaning rod slot.

Records

Cleaning and taking care of them

Careless handling is the usual cause of dirt on records and compact discs. Once they become smeared or dusty, their sound reproduction is impaired.

Do not pull a record straight out of its sleeves. The friction will charge it with static electricity, which attracts dust. Hold apart the sides of the sleeves and pull out the record carefully by the rim. **Do not** touch the grooves with your fingers.

Do not leave records lying about uncovered; they will collect dust.

To prevent damage during playing, clean records regularly, but never while they are revolving on the turntable. The simplest and most effective cleaner is a carbon-fibre brush. The fibres bring out dust from the grooves, while a felt pad collects it.

An alternative cleaner is a fluid, but this removes only the surface dust.

An antistatic gun is another alternative. It shoots a stream of electrically charged atoms onto the record surface. Antistatic cloths are rarely effective.

Compact discs need little cleaning as long as they are handled properly and are put away in their cases after use.

Recovery position

Helping an unconscious person to lie in a safe position

Do not leave an unconscious person lying face up. Vomit, saliva or blood could block the windpipe, or the tongue could slide back over the windpipe's opening. Turn the person over carefully (see below). Get someone to dial 999 for an ambulance. If there is no one, do it yourself, but get back to the casualty as soon as possible.

If the casualty is heavy, try to find a helper. Grip the clothing at the hip with one hand while pulling at the knee with the other, as your helper supports the head.

If the casualty is not breathing, administer ARTIFICIAL RESPIRATION.

Redundancy

Your rights when your job disappears

When an employer goes out of business, or his business changes or declines, he often has to declare some or all of his employees redundant. Employees made redundant are entitled to proper notice and may claim redundancy pay. But if the employer is not really making an employee redundant, but is in fact getting rid of him for some other reason, the employee may be able to claim UNFAIR DISMISSAL and higher compensation.

When redundancy arises An employer can declare someone redundant if his job is no longer needed because:
● The employer is ceasing that business.
● Work is ending at the employee's workplace, or
● There is no work, or not enough work of the kind the employee does.

Unless an employer shows that one of these reasons applies, and the employer is not dismissing the employee because of misconduct, the worker can usually claim unfair dismissal even though the reason given is redundancy.

Giving notice An employer thinking of making staff redundant must give advance notice to any trade unions involved. If ten or more staff are to be declared redundant, 30 days' notice is needed. If the number is over 100, there must be 90 days' notice. Notice is not needed for fewer than ten job losses. Employees can claim compensation if notice is not given.

In addition, employees must be given proper notice, up to 12 weeks, that the job is coming to an end.

Claiming redundancy pay Someone who has worked for his employer for more than two years when made redundant can claim redundancy pay, but the following people cannot claim:
● Men over 65 and women over 60.
● Civil and public servants.
● Part-time workers, unless thay have worked for at least 16 hours a week for five years.
● Those on fixed-term contracts.

If the employer offers a replacement job on the same terms as the job lost, the employee cannot claim redundancy pay if he unreasonably refuses the new job.

Redundancy pay is usually made automatically. If not, it must be claimed

---

RECOVERY POSITION

Turning over an unconscious person

Check that the casualty is breathing. Put your ear to her nose or mouth and listen. Watch her chest to see if it rises and falls, or rest your hand lightly on it to feel for movement.

Straighten casualty's legs and put nearer arm at right-angles to body, elbow bent, palm up. Fold other arm across her chest and hold that hand under cheek, palm down.

Tilt casualty's chin up to keep her airway open. Ensure that her hand is still supporting her head.

If casualty is breathing, use your finger to clear her mouth of any foreign matter, Tilt her head back and lift her chin to open airway.

With your other hand, pull up knee and roll casualty towards you, stopping roll with your knees and supporting her head.

Adjust upper leg to keep knee and thigh at right angles and casualty propped securely. Never put pillow or coats under head.

Call emergency services, or get someone else to do so. Never leave casualty unattended for more than a minute or two. Check her breathing and pulse regularly.

within six months, or an action started in an Industrial Tribunal.

The amount of pay The amount of redundancy pay depends on the employee's age, and how long he has been at his job. The employer must make a payment for each full year's service up to 20. When the employee has worked more than 20 years, the last 20 count.

Disputes Disagreements about redundancy are decided by an Industrial Tribunal. If you are being made redundant, get advice from your trade union, a Citizens Advice Bureau or solicitor (see LAWYERS) to check that you get your entitlement.

References

How to write them; your legal responsibilities

Letters of reference deserve proper thought and care. They can affect not only an applicant's future, but your own credibility – and pocket.

Always be aware of the legal implications involved. For example, someone who has been given a bad reference can sue successfully for libel – but only if he can prove that the referee knew that what he wrote was untrue, and deliberately wanted to harm the applicant. On the other hand, do not give a good reference to someone whom you have dismissed for, say, dishonesty. The new employer can sue you for any loss that he has suffered if the person steals from him.

Again, if you said mistakenly that the subject of a reference was trustworthy – without bothering to check that this was true – you could be sued for negligence by the person's new employer. But you can avoid this by stating that the reference is given in good faith but is not a guarantee of perfect character.

Begin a letter of reference by stating how long you have known the person in question and in what capacity. Follow this with your opinion as to how well he may suit the position for which he is applying.

If you feel he is the right person for the job, be as enthusiastic as you like. A reserved recommendation could be interpreted as half-hearted.

If you do not think highly of the applicant, you can show your true feelings by writing a lukewarm recommendation – implying your reservations rather than stating them outright.

If for some reason you do not want to tell the truth in a reference, it is better not to give one. No one can demand that you do so. If you feel that someone is totally unsuited to the position being sought – then tell him, firmly but tact-

fully, that you are not the best person to approach.

Refrigerators

Maintaining and repairing them

Wipe the inside of the refrigerator regularly with a cloth wrung out in a solution of bicarbonate of soda and warm water. Or use a fridge/freezer cleaning liquid. Take particular care with the door compartments and the salad drawer, which get dirtiest.

Do not use detergent, as the smell could be transferred to the food. Do not use abrasive cleaners either, they could damage the cabinet lining. Occasionally unplug the refrigerator and gently dust the radiator-like condenser at the back. See also FREEZERS.

Defrosting Unless the refrigerator defrosts automatically, defrost it when the ice in the frozen-food compartment is about 6mm ($\frac{1}{4}$in) thick. Remove the food from the compartment, wrap it in newspaper and put it in a cool place.

If defrosting is manual, turn the temperature control off. If it is semi-automatic, push the button that starts the defrosting. Put a tray of warm water in the frozen-food compartment to speed up the process. If there is a drain hole to the outside, put a tray to catch the water.

Leave the refrigerator door open and wait for the ice to melt into the drip tray. Do not try to scrape ice off, as you may damage the lining of the compartment.

A semi-automatic refrigerator turns itself on again when defrosting is complete. Before returning food to the compartment, wipe the packages and the interior of the compartment; moisture will cause ice to form again faster.

Replacing a bulb If the interior light fails, turn the bulb in its socket to make sure it is connecting properly. Make sure the switch is not stuck. If the light still does not work, replace the bulb.

Faulty switch If the switch does not work properly – it either fails to light the bulb or to turn it off as the door is closing – get it checked by a qualified engineer. If the light stays on, the heat it gives out will affect the cooling.

Excessive noise This is often caused by vibration because the refrigerator is not level. Adjust the feet as necessary.

Door sagging Tighten the hinge screws. If necessary, get replacement hinges from the supplier. Unplug the refrigerator while fitting them. Never slam the door or overload door storage compartments.

Poor cooling The cause may be a

deteriorating door seal. Check it and find out from the maker's handbook whether it is removable. Seals held by screws (often concealed under a flap) can usually be replaced. Unplug the refrigerator before attempting any maintenance. Do not attempt to remove a seal clipped into a recess, have it replaced by a qualified repair man.

Gas refrigerators Some have a flue which should be removed and cleaned every six months. Check in the maker's handbook, or ask the local gas board.

Refunds

Compensation or your money back

Unless a product is defective, you cannot legally force the seller to take it back. But if you return the item promptly and in good condition, together with the receipt, you may be able to exchange it, receive a credit note, or even get your money back.

If you unwittingly buy faulty goods from a retailer, you are legally entitled to your money back or compensation under the SALE OF GOODS Act 1979.

If you are refused a refund for the defective goods, you can take legal action against the shopkeeper through a County Court. You can bring the action yourself under the Supply of Goods (Implied Terms) Act, or employ a solicitor to act for you – see LAWYERS; SMALL CLAIMS.

However, the supplier is not obliged to make a refund on faulty goods if he pointed out at the time of sale that they were in some way defective, or disclaimed any knowledge of whether the goods were fit for a particular purpose – or if you examined them and failed to notice an obvious flaw.

But a manufacturer may be legally responsible if defective goods cause the buyer or user any injury or damage. For example, if you buy a faulty hot-water bottle which bursts and scalds you or your family or guest without any fault on your part, the injured person can sue the manufacturer for personal injury compensation.

Relaxation exercises

Ways to reduce tension

Relaxation exercises form an integral part of such disciplines as YOGA and MEDITATION; they are also increasingly taught as an adjunct to orthodox medicine for conditions such as INSOMNIA, heart disease, STRESS and drug dependency (including SMOKING and over-use of tranquillisers), and to help women in CHILDBIRTH.

There are some simple relaxation exercises you can learn for yourself. At most, they need one or two 15 minute sessions a day. However, if you suffer from a breathing disorder such as asthma or hyperventilation (over-breathing), seek medical advice before attempting them.

Consider obtaining medical advice before taking up relaxation programmes – some are linked to posture control.

Deep breathing Take a very deep breath through your nose. Hold it for a moment and then breathe out through your mouth until your lungs are completely empty, ending with a sigh. Hold the left hand just above the waist, to check diaphragm movement, and the right on the chest. As you breathe in, expand your rib cage and diaphragm so the left hand is pushed out; the right hand should not move. As you breathe out relax your neck and shoulders.

Try to take at least 40 deep breaths a day, after rising in the morning or before going to bed at night, or for a minute or two at particularly stressful times.

Slow breathing Breathe in and out to a rhythm, counting slowly backwards from 10 to 1 to mark each complete breathing cycle. Start at 10 as you begin to breathe in and count 9, 8, 7; pause on 6 and 5; then breathe out to the count of 4, 3, 2, 1. As you breathe, become aware of which of your muscles are tense and let them sag.

Relaxing muscles Sit comfortably in a chair, or lie down on your back, with your shoes off and your clothing loosened at collar and waist.

Close your eyes and breathe deeply several times. Beginning with your feet, concentrate on one part of the body at a time, and relax it. Move your concentration to the legs, the knees and so on, relaxing each part.

As your body begins to feel warm and heavy, imagine that you are floating in warm water or in a peaceful place, such as a deserted sunny clearing in the woods. Stay in this floating, relaxed state for 10-15 minutes. See also NERVOUSNESS.

Repossession of property

*How to avoid losing your home
in hard times*

Most mortgagees – BUILDING SOCIETIES, banks and local authorities – are generally sympathetic to borrowers who may, through financial circumstances, be unable to keep up mortgage payments. It is important, however, to inform the lender as soon as you realise that you may not be able to make regular payments.

The worst thing a borrower can do is let arrears mount up without explanation, because by that time the lender

may not be able to offer any help at all.

If the borrower's plight is likely to be only temporary, the lender may agree to accepting interest-only payments for a time. However, this is of little help in the case of relatively new mortgages since in the early years the repayments of a capital-repayment mortgage consist largely of the interest anyway.

In the case of an endowment mortgage, the insurance company may agree to suspend the insurance premiums, leaving the home-buyer to pay only the interest to the lender.

It may also be possible to extend the period of the mortgage, which will reduce the cost of monthly repayments.

A home-buyer who falls on hard times through unemployment may be able to obtain income support (see NATIONAL INSURANCE) and should contact the Department of Social Security.

If repayment problems look like being permanent, it may be best for the home-buyer to sell the property outright or buy something requiring a much smaller mortgage. Otherwise the lender can apply for a court order to repossess the property, evict the borrower and sell the property to recover the loan, although any surplus money would go to the borrower.

Reptile pets

Keeping snakes and lizards

Snakes Those most commonly kept as pets in Britain, are from southern Europe – the green European tessellated or dice snake (often sold in pet shops as a grass snake), the brown four-lined snake, and the drabber Aesculapian snake.

Keep a snake in a vivarium that has a lid of gauze or fine wire mesh. For snakes up to 1m (3ft), the vivarium should measure at least 610 × 300 × 300mm (24 × 12 × 12in). For snakes up to 1.5m (5ft) long, it should measure 910 × 460 × 460mm (36 × 18 × 18in).

Hang a high wattage or infra-red bulb low over the vivarium to provide a temperature of 18-20°C (64-68°F) for temperate snakes and 24-30°C (75-86°F) for tropical snakes.

A snake will also need a shaded spot in very hot weather, and to avoid the heat rays from the lamp, such as a piece of curved bark or some stones piled together. Provide a bowl of water in which the snake can immerse itself.

Snakes frequently slough their entire skin. Difficulty in doing this can be related to undernourishment or dehydration. The simplest solution is to place the snake in a cotton bag containing moist sphagnum moss. The skin is usually discarded within 12 hours. Make sure the eye-shields have come away. If

these have been retained, remove them gently by hand.

A pet shop specialising in snakes will supply suitable food. Smaller snakes will eat small frogs, minnows, goldfish, whitebait or chunks of raw white fish. Always place the food in water.

Larger snakes generally require a mouse, young rat or chick once or twice a week. Many species prefer live food but will usually accept freshly killed or prey that has been dead longer.

Lizards Among those easy to keep are the small European green and wall lizards, the larger European eyed lizard, and tropical geckos.

Keep lizards in a covered vivarium at a constant temperature of 24°C (75°F). Cover the floor with sand and gravel and bury a bowl of water in it up to its rim. Provide a lamp for heat, rocks for the lizards to bask on and sheltered crannies for shade.

Feed lizards live flies, blowflies and other insects, maggots, mealworms, and egg and mince mixed together.

Resigning

Giving your boss formal notice

Anyone can resign from his job when he wishes. However, there are some rules he must obey, or he may be sued by his employer for breach of contract. That is unlikely – but an aggrieved employer might refuse to supply a reference and withhold money owed to the employee, challenging the employee in turn to sue. An employee who resigns without having another job to go to, may find himself unable to claim unemployment benefit for up to six weeks – see NATIONAL INSURANCE.

Most employees are required to give advance notice if they are leaving. The only exceptions are people who have worked for their employer for fewer than four weeks, or for fewer than 16 hours a week, those who work their duties outside Britain and if the employer changes the terms of the job without agreement, to the extent that it constitutes breach of contract.

In all other cases, the basic notice period required is one week for someone who has been with his employer for from four weeks to two years. After that, it becomes one more week for each additional year of service, up to a maximum notice period of 12 weeks. These basic arrangements may be altered by a collective agreement between the employer and a trade union, or in the employee's employment contract – see CONTRACTS.

The law does not require notice of resignation to be put in writing, as long as it is clear to the employer that notice has been given. However, a written resignation may be required by collective agreement or in an individual employment contract, and it is sensible as well as courteous to write and to keep a copy of the letter, to avoid any argument.

How to resign Find out, by checking your written details of employment or contract or by asking around in your company, how much notice you are supposed to give. Unless your employer has broken his contract with you, you must continue to work for him during the notice period if he wishes. He may not want you to, but he must still pay your wages for that period if you have kept to the rules, and unless you agree otherwise.

Write to your employer, putting his name and work address, and your own at the head of the letter. Make sure it is properly dated. State clearly and courteously that you are resigning, with a sentence such as: 'Would you kindly accept this letter as formal notice of my resignation.'

Make it clear when you expect to leave: 'I am happy to serve my required notice if you wish, to expire on December 31.' If you want to leave before your notice is officially completed – for example, to start a new job – say something like: 'I realise that my terms of notice require me to remain with you until November 30; however, I would be extremely grateful if you could release me earlier to take up my new post – say, on November 15.'

If your employer agrees, he need not pay you for the time by which the notice is reduced.

In most cases, it is appropriate to give your reason for leaving, and to thank your employer – though you are not obliged to do either. Remember, though, that you will probably be seeking a reference from him, so politeness is worth while.

On the other hand, if your reason for leaving is your belief that your employer has broken his contract with you, say what you think and why, and that you feel unable, on those grounds, to observe a notice period. You will need a copy of the letter as evidence if you decide to sue your employer, or to take him to an industrial tribunal for unfairly forcing you to leave. See also UNFAIR DISMISSAL.

Retiring

Planning for life after work

For someone who has spent most of his adult life working full-time, the sudden switch to retirement can be a deeply unsettling experience. Many employers now recognise that, and some companies have introduced programmes to make the transition easier for their older employees – for example, by allowing them to reduce their working time gradually as retirement approaches, by granting longer holidays, or by running in-company pre-retirement courses.

Try to plan your retirement several years in advance. It is particularly important to think ahead if you are in a job where early retirement may be used as one way of reducing the size of the staff or the job is contractual.

Guarding your income Employees and self-employed people who have made NATIONAL INSURANCE contributions are entitled to state PENSIONS when they retire at or after retirement age – 65 for men, 60 for women. In addition, employees may be entitled to an extra pension that is earnings-related – partly linked to the wages they received while working – either directly from the state, or through occupational pension schemes run by their companies. Self-employed people are not entitled to this benefit, so they need to make their own arrangements privately with an insurance company – see SELF-EMPLOYMENT.

A good time for many people to review their retirement pension prospects is at about the age of 50. Find out what you can expect from the state and any company schemes, or any private pension arrangements you may already have. Try to work out what it will be worth when you reach retirement age, bearing in mind that, while prices inexorably go up, the adjustments made, for example in the state pension payments, to counteract them do not really keep pace. INSURANCE policies that pay a lump sum at a certain age, or after you have contributed for a certain number of years, may seem much less attractive when you come to collect the money, because of the effects of inflation.

If you have some spare cash, get advice from an insurance broker or your bank manager on how best to invest it to increase your retirement income – see INVESTING. Decide whether you would prefer to take part of your pension as a lump sum on retirement and have the remainder paid to you at fixed intervals in your retirement years, or have the full amount paid at intervals.

If your earnings from work leave little to spare, consider cashing in on your home, if you own it. Now may be an appropriate time to sell, for example, a family house and move into a smaller and cheaper place – see HOUSES AND FLATS. The profit you make can be used towards your retirement.

Moving house Many people cherish the dream of moving to the seaside or a favourite spot in the country when they retire. This needs careful planning if it is to be realised. Again, start studying the idea seriously several years before you expect to leave work; if you can make the move while you are still working, and can combine it with reinvesting some of the capital tied up in your present home, so much the better.

Moving is considered by psychologists to be one of the biggest traumas faced by people in the course of normal life – see also MOVING HOUSE. To combine it with the loss of a job can be a recipe for disaster.

If you are set on moving, pick your location carefully. Do you already have friends or relatives in the area? If not, could they visit it easily? Are there shops and places of entertainment within easy reach? Could you still get to them if, in a few years, you become infirm? Would the property you choose itself be suitable if you became an invalid?

If you choose a place where you do not already have connections, make some before deciding to move there. Pay several visits – one holiday trip is not enough. If you are a churchgoer, make yourself known to the minister and attend services.

If you have other interests – for example, golf or another sport – see if you can enrol as a visiting member in the local club. Have the local newspaper mailed to your present home; it will help you keep an eye on properties for sale, as well as telling you what is going on.

Above all, talk over your plans with your wife or husband. Both of you must be convinced that the move will be a success, and be prepared to work to make it one. However unpleasant the idea, recognise that one partner could die fairly soon after the move; could the other cope in new surroundings alone?

Using your time Someone with a full-time job spends about three-fifths of his waking hours at work or travelling to it each week. That leaves a large gap to be filled when he retires.

Even if you have a wide range of interests already, they may not be enough. The golfer welcomed enthusiastically at his club on a Saturday may be shunned as a bore if he is there all day every day; the wife of a keen reader may become exasperated if that is all he does all day.

Perhaps the skills you used previously at work can be deployed in your local community – for money, or simply for your own fulfilment. Churches, charities, clubs and hospitals all welcome voluntary workers with a talent they can use, from accountancy to the simple knack of getting on with people.

Try a mixture of active and more relaxing pursuits, that use both your brain and your body. Gardening and walking are two of the best forms of exercise, and can be as strenuous or as gentle as you choose. A dog may give purpose to your walking – and the care of any pet is considered beneficial to health by doctors.

Take up at least one new pursuit. It can be anything from studying a language at evening classes to hill-walking.

Clubs for old people Most local authorities run activities intended for older people, through Darby and Joan clubs or similar organisations. They range from bingo sessions to amateur theatricals. Details are available at local libraries.

Reupholstering

Renewing sprung and drop-in seats on upright chairs

You can repair upholstered chairs and refurbish secondhand bargains with modern materials and a few special tools – a tack lifter, an upholsterer's hammer and a webbing stretcher. For a sprung seat, you will also need a strong curved upholstery needle and No 1 twine. All materials are available from upholsterer's suppliers.

For valuable ANTIQUES, put the work in the hands of a craftsman who will use traditional methods.

Drop-in seat Take the chair seat and lay it upside down on a table. Use the tack lifter to remove the tacks, and remove the hessian and other coverings.

Plane off a little wood from the seat frame for about 50mm (2in) at each side of the corners (see PLANING) to ease the fit of the padding when the new upholstery is fitted. Fill all the old tack holes with wood filler (see STOPPERS AND FILLERS) and sand the frame smooth with abrasive paper – see SANDING.

Cut three lengths of woven upholstery webbing to fit from back to front of the seat plus 200mm (8in). Fold under 25mm (1in) of the first strip and fix it to the centre back on the top face of the frame, using five upholstery tacks arranged in the shape of a W.

Stretch it with a webbing stretcher and then hammer in three tacks to hold the webbing, then trim the webbing 25mm from the tacks. Fold the surplus over the tacks and drive in two more tacks. Fit two more strips from back to front, spacing them equally on either side of the first.

Fit webbing in the same way from side to side of the frame. Weave the centre strip under, over and under the first set of strips; weave the other two over, under and then over the first set of strips.

Cut a piece of hessian 25mm larger than the frame all round. Centre it over the webbing and drive a temporary tack halfway in at the middle of each side. Fold over the surplus hessian along the back, take out the temporary tack, and drive a tack in fully at the centre.

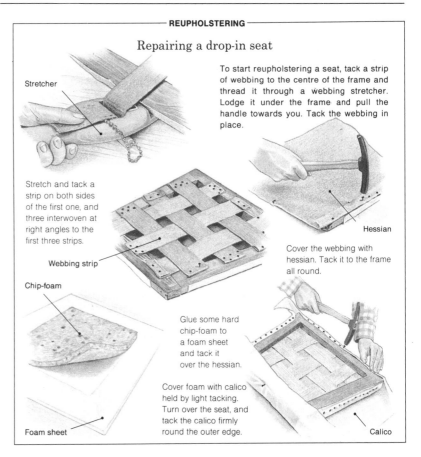

REUPHOLSTERING

Repairing a drop-in seat

To start reupholstering a seat, tack a strip of webbing to the centre of the frame and thread it through a webbing stretcher. Lodge it under the frame and pull the handle towards you. Tack the webbing in place.

Stretcher

Stretch and tack a strip on both sides of the first one, and three interwoven at right angles to the first three strips.

Webbing strip

Chip-foam

Hessian

Cover the webbing with hessian. Tack it to the frame all round.

Glue some hard chip-foam to a foam sheet and tack it over the hessian.

Cover foam with calico held by light tacking. Turn over the seat, and tack the calico firmly round the outer edge.

Foam sheet

Calico

Stretch out the fold towards each corner in turn and secure it with tacks. Drive in tacks at 25mm intervals along the rest of the fold. Secure the hessian in the same way along the front of the frame and then along the two sides.

Cut a sheet of 25mm thick foam the size of the seat plus 13mm ($\frac{1}{2}$in) all round. Use a hacksaw (or an electric carving knife) to trim all round the upper edge to chamfer it to an angle of 45 degrees, but leave the bottom 6mm ($\frac{1}{4}$in) of the sides untouched to form a lip. On the underside of the foam sheet, centre and glue a 13mm thick piece of hard-grade chip-foam 50mm smaller all round than the seat, using a water-based adhesive – see GLUING.

Arrange the foams, chip-foam down, over the hessian. Tack the 6mm lip to the top of the outer face of the frame. Work outwards from the centre of each side; space the tacks 13mm apart, and stop 50mm from the corners. Cut a V-shaped notch out of the foam at each corner, overlap the sides of the V and use one tack to secure the overlap to the frame. Finish the tacking at the corners.

Cut a piece of calico the size of the seat plus 100mm (4in) all round. Centre it over the foam and hold it to the outer face of the frame at the centre of each

side with a temporary tack. Turn the frame base-up and tack the calico in place near the outer edge of the frame's underside, turning under the surplus and working out from the middle of each side. Tack the calico at 25mm intervals and draw it taut as you work. At the corners, smooth the point of the calico over the angle and tack it. Fold the surplus fabric into a neat pleat at each side, overlap the pleats at the bottom and secure them with single tacks.

Lay a piece of upholstery wadding over the calico cut to the size of the seat. Fit the main cover fabric over it. Use the same method as used for the calico, but drive in the tacks at the inner edge of the frame's underside.

Fixed sprung seat Remove the old upholstery and chamfer the outer edge of the frame. Cut the hessian 75mm (3in) larger than the seat all round. Centre it over the seat.

Lay a 13mm ($\frac{1}{2}$in) wide strip of cardboard on it all round the seat and 6mm ($\frac{1}{4}$in) from the outer edge of the frame. Tack through cardboard and hessian at 25mm (1in) intervals, drawing the hessian taut and working from the middle out on each side.

Lay handfuls of fibre stuffing over the

cardboard all round the seat. Pull the stuffing out to give an even layer all round. Use enough to make a 19mm (¾in) roll when it is squeezed tight. Fold the hessian tightly over the stuffing roll and secure it with tacks 25mm apart driven into the frame close to the inner edge of the cardboard. Fold the hessian into neat pleats at the corners.

Cut the hard chip-foam to fit just inside the roll, and the sheet of foam to reach comfortably over the foam onto the wood. To make the seat more domed, put a layer of fibre stuffing over the hessian before you fit the foam.

Fit the calico, wadding and top cover as for a drop-in seat, but tack the calico halfway down the outer face of the frame and the top cover just below it. Glue on a decorative braid to hide the tacks. At the back corners, where the legs are inset in the frame, make a diagonal cut from the corner of the calico (and later of the main cover), but do not make it too long. Fold under the two points and pull the fabric down very tight before tacking it, or the foam will show when the seat is sat on.

Springs If the padding and covering of the seat are in good condition but the springs are worn or broken, you can fit new springs without tampering with the top coverings. Put the chair seat upside down on a table so that the chair back hangs down. Prise out the tacks holding on the bottom hessian and remove it. Prise out the tacks holding the bottom webbing, and snip the twine holding the top of each spring to the top layer of webbing. Lift out the springs with the bottom webbing attached.

Check on the condition of the top layer of webbing. Replace any worn webbing strips, tacking them to the inner face of the frame as near its top as possible – you will not be able to use the webbing stretcher. Weave new strands in and out of the old strands. Fit new springs about 75-100mm (3-4in) high – too tall and they will wear the cover. Put one spring at the centre of the seat and arrange the others in a square around it. Attach them where webbing strands cross.

Use the curved needle and one long piece of twine to sew in the springs. Secure the centre spring to the webbing with a slip knot (see KNOTS), then make a half hitch over the slip knot. Sew that spring to the webbing at two other points with half hitches. Carry the twine to each of the four outer springs in turn, sewing each with half hitches at three points. Finish the last stitch by making it a double hitch.

Fit webbing strands to the base of the frame as for a drop-in seat (but working on the base not the top face). Sew the bottom of the springs in place in the same way as the top. Fit the hessian cover (or a replacement) to the base.

If the springs and outer upholstery need replacing, fit webbing and springs first and then the hessian with edge roll, padding and covers; you will have access to both top and base of the frame so there is no need to fix webbing to the inner face of the frame.

Rhythm method

Controlling birth by natural means

In the natural rhythm of the monthly menstrual cycle, there is a spell of approximately eight to ten days during which the egg produced by the ovaries can be fertilised. If sexual intercourse takes place only during the remaining 18 or so days, and is avoided during the 'unsafe' time, the woman cannot, in theory, become pregnant. That is the basis of the rhythm, or natural, method of birth control.

Unfortunately, because the menstrual cycle varies in both length and regularity in many women, the rhythm method is not as safe a form of contraception as, for example, the birth-control pill, condom, or intrauterine devices.

The risks can, however, be reduced by using a combination of three methods to estimate when, during the month, it should be safe to have sexual intercourse: the calendar method; the temperature method; and the ovulation, or Billings, method.

The calendar method This should never be relied upon by women whose menstrual cycles are short or irregular. Using this method, the first day of menstruation is counted as Day 1. A woman with an absolutely regular 28 day cycle will have her unsafe time – when intercourse should be avoided – between Day 9 and Day 18.

For greater security, note the precise length of each menstrual cycle over 12 months. The first unsafe day can then be worked out by deducting 19 from the shortest of the last 12 cycles. If the shortest cycle was 25 days, conception is possible from Day 6 (25 –19). The last unsafe day is calculated by deducting 8 from the longest of the cycles. If the longest was 31 days, the last unsafe day is Day 23 (31-8).

In this example, conception is therefore possible from Day 6 until Day 23 inclusive. Intercourse would be safe from Day 1 to Day 5 inclusive (there is no medical reason for avoiding intercourse during menstruation, although many have aesthetic or religious objections) and from Day 24 to the end of the cycle.

Temperature method A woman's temperature rises fractionally – by 0.2-0.5°C (0.5-1°F) – during the time when her body produces an egg capable of fertilisation. To detect the change, the TEMPERATURE should be taken by mouth and recorded every morning, before getting out of bed or consuming food or drink.

Leave the thermometer in place for at least three minutes: if the temperature has not risen, ovulation (egg production) has not occurred. However, a temperature rise may be for reasons other than ovulation – such as a cold.

Chemists and family planning clinics sell ovulation thermometers and charts for recording daily temperature.

Ovulation method Biological changes take place at ovulation. They include an increase in the production of mucus, the jelly-like substance usually found at the entrance to the vagina; the mucus also becomes more watery. The wettest day is normally the fourth after ovulation. Women can learn to watch for changes in vaginal mucus and, with the temperature chart, to predict ovulation.

Rice

Cooking white and brown rice successfully

Two ways of cooking rice are boiling and frying. Always put the rice in a strainer before cooking and rinse it under cold running water. Allow 50g (2oz) of uncooked rice per person – during cooking, it almost trebles in bulk.

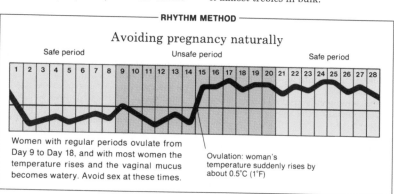

RHYTHM METHOD

Avoiding pregnancy naturally

Safe period · Unsafe period · Safe period

| 1 | 2 | 3 | 4 | 5 | 6 | 7 | 8 | 9 | 10 | 11 | 12 | 13 | 14 | 15 | 16 | 17 | 18 | 19 | 20 | 21 | 22 | 23 | 24 | 25 | 26 | 27 | 28 |

Women with regular periods ovulate from Day 9 to Day 18, and with most women the temperature rises and the vaginal mucus becomes watery. Avoid sex at these times.

Ovulation: woman's temperature suddenly rises by about 0.5°C (1°F)

If possible, measure the rice. For each 150ml (¼ pint) of rice, allow 285ml (½ pint) of water, chicken or vegetable stock and half a teaspoon of salt. Alternatively, two average-sized cups of liquid for every cup of rice. Either way, boil the rice in a large pan.

Brown rice – which is coarse and contains more fibre – must always be cooked *twice as long* as white rice. Brown rice is stronger-flavoured than white rice, and has a nutty taste.

Boiled rice Bring the water or stock to the boil. Add the rice and salt, bring back to the boil and stir once. Cover the pan with a tightly fitting lid.

Turn the heat down very low and cook very gently, without lifting the lid, for 15 minutes for white rice, or for 30 minutes for brown rice, or until all the liquid has been absorbed.

Then stir with a fork and separate the grains. Season the rice with salt and pepper to taste.

Rice can also be cooked in the oven. Put the rice in a casserole, cover with boiling salted water, stir thoroughly and cover the dish with foil and a lid. Cook in the centre of a preheated oven at 180°F (350°C), gas mark 4, for 30-45 minutes, or until all the liquid has been absorbed and the grains are soft.

Fried rice This is a good way of turning leftover boiled rice into a tasty dish. There are several varieties of fried rice – which can, for example, be served with Chinese food.

The following basic fried rice dish takes 5 minutes to prepare, 30 minutes to cook and serves four people:

Ingredients
115g (4oz) long grain rice
2 rashers streaky bacon
1 onion
25g (1oz) butter or oil
285ml (½ pint) chicken stock
Salt and black pepper

Remove the rind and gristle from the bacon and chop the rashers roughly. Peel and finely chop the onion. Fry the bacon in a deep frying pan over a low heat until the fat runs. Then add the butter, rice and onion, and continue frying – and stirring until the onion is transparent and the rice faintly coloured. Pour half the stock over the rice and cook over a moderate heat until all the liquid has been absorbed.

Stir occasionally, and add more stock as required until the rice is just tender. Season to taste.

Grain sizes White and brown rice come in three grain sizes: long, medium and short. Long-grain rice (fluffy when cooked) is suitable for savoury dishes such as curries (see CURRY POWDER),

paellas, pilaus, risottos and SALADS. Medium-grain rice (slightly sticky when cooked) is most suitable for CROQUETTES, fritters and STUFFINGS. Short-grain rice (creamy when cooked) is the traditional rice for sweet milk puddings.

Ringing in the ears

Coping with an annoying complaint

A condition in which the sufferer is conscious of continuous ringing, buzzing or tinkling noises in the ears is called tinnitus. There are several causes, including ear wax, deafness and hypertension (high blood pressure).

Brief tinnitus may also be the forerunner of an attack of epilepsy or fainting. In old people, deafness due to ageing is often the cause.

Unless there is a simple cause, such as wax in the ears, there may be no cure for tinnitus, but sufferers should consult their DOCTOR to make sure that it is not caused by a serious disease. Sometimes tinnitus is aggravated by anxiety or depression, which can lead to a vicious circle. That is, the sufferer becomes anxious or depressed because of the complaint, which in turn makes the condition worse – see also STRESS.

In Britain, tinnitus sufferers can keep in touch with the most recent research into the problem through the British Tinnitus Association, 14–18 West Bar Green, Sheffield S1 2DA.

Rivets

Setting them by hand and using a pop riveter

Riveting is a way of joining metals or some other materials – see also SOLDERING AND BRAZING; WELDING. Rivets are made from malleable metals such as iron, steel, copper, brass, aluminium or aluminium alloys.

There are three main types of rivet:
● Snags, or roundheads, are used for general metalwork where countersinking would weaken the plates and where a flush finish is not required.
● Flat heads are used for thin plate work, often for repairing gardening equipment such as grass boxes and metal WHEELBARROWS.
● Countersunk 90 degree rivets are the most common form of countersunk rivet, and they are used when a flush finish is required – provided the metals used are thick enough to accommodate the countersink.

When choosing a rivet, its diameter should be not less than the thickness of one of the plates to be riveted, and not more than three times its thickness. To

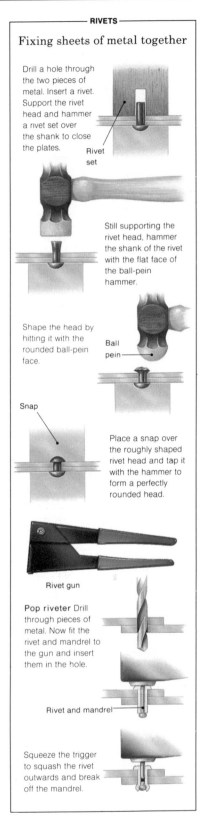

Fixing sheets of metal together

Drill a hole through the two pieces of metal. Insert a rivet. Support the rivet head and hammer a rivet set over the shank to close the plates. Rivet set

Still supporting the rivet head, hammer the shank of the rivet with the flat face of the ball-pein hammer.

Shape the head by hitting it with the rounded ball-pein face. Ball pein

Snap

Place a snap over the roughly shaped rivet head and tap it with the hammer to form a perfectly rounded head.

Rivet gun

Pop riveter Drill through pieces of metal. Now fit the rivet and mandrel to the gun and insert them in the hole.

Rivet and mandrel

Squeeze the trigger to squash the rivet outwards and break off the mandrel.

form a round head, the shank of the rivet must project $1\frac{1}{4}$ times the diameter of the shank, and for a countersunk head an amount equal to the diameter. In every case, the rivet must fit exactly the hole in which it is to be used.

When calculating the number of rivets required, spacing between rivets should be three times the diameter of the rivet across the width of the metal and twice the diameter down the length.

Rivets should be set $1\frac{1}{2}$ times their diameter from the edge of the metal they are to hold. Tools needed for riveting are:

Set and snap A rivet set is a piece of metal which has a hole the same diameter as the rivet shank. It is placed over the shank of a rivet after it has been pushed through the materials it is to fix. The set is then struck with a hammer to drive the plates tightly together.

The rivet snap, or dolly, is a solid piece of metal with a concave hole in one end, the same shape as a rivet head. It is used to form a neat, rounded head to the rivet after it has been roughly shaped.

The set and snap are available separately, or they may be combined. If combined you will need an additional snap or a piece of hardwood to support the rivet head while the shank of the rivet is being formed.

Ball-pein hammer This has a rounded head, opposite the flat face, which is used to rough-shape a rivet – see HAMMERS.

Riveting Firmly clamp the two pieces of metal together in a vice. Mark the position of the holes, then use a high-speed twist drill the same diameter as the rivet and drill through both sheets – see DRILLING.

Check there is no swarf. If there is, use a file to remove it, then pass the rivet through the holes. Take the metal out of the vice and hold the rivet head on a piece of hardwood. Place the set over the shank and strike it with a hammer to bring the two sheets in close contact. Use the flat face of the hammer to swell the shank of the rivet, then use the ball-pein end to rough-shape the rivet.

If countersunk rivets are to be used, use a countersink bit to form the countersinks in the metal sheets. Check with a rivet to ensure the countersinks are deep enough to take the head. Support countersunk heads on a flat metal block while the rivet is formed. Then use a file to smooth the rivet flush with the sheets.

Pop riveter As an alternative to hand-riveting, you can use a small tool resembling a pair of pliers. It has the advantage of fixing rivets from one side of the work only. The only disadvantage is that, being hollow, the rivets are not as strong as solid rivets of the same diameter. They are best suited to thin metals, such as

car bodywork. The hollow rivet contains a pin, called a mandrel, which is inserted into the riveting tool.

Drill through both materials to be riveted, then select a pop rivet of suitable length and insert it in the riveting tool. Press the rivet through the hole; hold firmly in place and squeeze the trigger of the tool. This draws the mandrel towards the tool, expanding the rivet on the far side of the hole. Keep squeezing, and the mandrel will break away from the head, and can be withdrawn from the tool.

Riveting kits, containing the tool and a selection of pop rivets, are available from tool stores and car accessory shops.

Roasting meats

Cooking different joints of meat in an oven

Prime cuts are best for a good roast. Buy the best joint you can afford from a good butcher. The meat should be at room temperature before cooking. Pat it dry with absorbent kitchen paper; wet meat will not brown properly.

If frozen, all meats must be thoroughly thawed before cooking.

Beef A joint of beef should be marbled – having little lines of fat running through it. The best cuts are sirloin, ribs and topside. A joint weighing 1.4kg (3lb) or more roasts better than a smaller one.

To prepare the joint rub it all over with freshly ground pepper or mustard. For a joint containing the bone, lay it on a wire rack in a roasting tin with the fat side up.

Then put in the centre of an oven preheated to 220°C (425°F), gas mark 7.

After 20 minutes, lower the heat to 190°C (375°F), gas mark 5, then leave for 15 minutes for every 450g (1lb) of joint if you want it rare, or 20 minutes for every 450g (1lb) if you want it medium rare. Leave joints which have had the bone removed to cook for 25 minutes for every 450g (1lb).

During cooking, baste the joint occasionally by spooning up juices from the bottom of the tin and pouring them over the meat.

Towards the end of the roasting time, stick a skewer into the centre of the joint near the bone. If the juices that emerge are pink, it is still rare. If they are clear and golden, it is well done.

Alternatively, test with a meat thermometer. Push the thermometer into the meat, avoiding bone. If it reads 65°C (150°F) the meat is rare; at 70°C (160°F) it is medium rare; at 77°C (170°F) it is well done.

After cooking cover the joint with foil and leave it for 15-30 minutes in a warm place before carving – to allow the juices to settle.

Use the juices in the tin to make GRAVY. Serve with YORKSHIRE PUDDING and horseradish sauce.

Lamb This is always tender, so all cuts, apart from scrag end of neck and middle neck, make good roasts.

A good way to roast lamb is to lay the joint fat side up on a bed of vegetables – such as sliced carrots and onions – in the roasting tin. Put into an oven preheated to 180°C (350°F), gas mark 4. With a joint on the bone, roast it for 20 minutes for every 450g (1lb), then for 20 minutes extra. With a boned joint, roast for 25 minutes for every 450g (1lb), then for 25 minutes extra.

Baste during cooking as for beef. Towards the end of the roasting time, test with a skewer as for beef or with a meat thermometer. When the thermometer reads 70°C (160°F) the meat is medium rare; at 80°C (176°F) it is well cooked.

Leave the joint to rest as for beef. Serve the joint with redcurrant jelly or mint sauce.

Pork If frozen, a pork joint must always be thoroughly thawed before cooking. All cuts are good for roasting, but leg, hand and spring have particularly large areas of rind which makes tasty crackling.

Use the tip of a sharp knife to score the rind with deep, even cuts. Rub some olive or vegetable oil into the rind, then sprinkle with plenty of coarse salt.

Lay the pork rind side up on a wire rack in a roasting tin. For a joint on the bone, roast in an oven preheated to 220°C (425°F), gas mark 7, for 25 minutes for every 450g (1lb), plus 25 minutes extra. For a joint off the bone roast in an oven preheated to 190°C (375°F), gas mark 5, for 35 minutes for every 450g (1lb), plus 35 minutes extra.

Test with a skewer as for beef, but the juices must be clear and golden. If you use a meat thermometer, the temperature should be 90°C (194°F).

Leave the joint to rest as for beef. Serve with apple sauce.

Venison A joint of venison (deer flesh) is dark, closely grained and very dry.

At least two hours before cooking the venison, rub plenty of oil into the surface of the joint and sprinkle with salt and freshly ground pepper.

Alternatively, sprinkle with salt and pepper and spread a generous layer of lard over the surface, or wrap the joint in streaky bacon rashers. Venison can also be marinated – see MARINATING.

Wrap the joint loosely in kitchen foil, sealing the edges of the foil, then roast in an oven preheated to 200°C (400°F), gas mark 6, for 20 minutes for every 450g (1lb), plus 20 minutes extra.

About 20 minutes before the joint is

cooked, pull back the foil. Dust the meat with flour and baste well.

Carve and serve venison immediately with redcurrant jelly.

See also CARVING MEAT AND POULTRY; POULTRY.

Rock garden

Planning and building one

Choose an open site, with uninterrupted sunlight and good air flow. Avoid the shade of large trees. If there is a natural slope, take advantage of it. Remember, however, that a slope facing south or south-west gets most sun, while your rock garden will create most impact if it is facing up your garden, towards the house. If you cannot reconcile the two conditions, RAISED BEDS may be more suitable than a rockery, and can serve many of the same purposes.

Good drainage is vital. Dig the topsoil out to a depth of about 610mm (2ft) and partially fill it with hardcore or builder's rubble. Cover that with a layer of gravel, stones or small rocks, and put inverted turves on top. Finally, replace the topsoil.

Choosing the stones If you live in an area where building stone occurs naturally, use that. It will look appropriate, and is relatively cheap to transport. Otherwise, you must rely on your local garden centre or builders' merchant, who may be able to order what you want. Limestone resists frost and is attractive when weathered. Sandstone weighs less, so is cheaper than limestone by volume, but some kinds are subject to frost damage.

Light, porous tufa is good for rock gardens, but expensive. You can make your own imitation tufa, however, as described below.

If you are buying stones, try to choose a balance of large and small ones – the mixture will look more natural, and help to create crevices for the plants.

How to build Effective rock gardens are not just mounds of earth with stones sticking out. They should look as much as possible like a natural outcrop. On a flat site, you can achieve that appearance best by keeping your rockery relatively low, but broad.

Before placing the rocks, study them carefully. Note which way the strata – the natural layers in them – run, and which faces are weathered. The rocks should be positioned with the strata all running the same way (usually horizontally), and with weathered faces outwards.

Lay your base to form a small plateau, the edges of which will define the shape of the rock garden. Start with a large, triangular stone to sit point outwards at the centre front of the base. Dig a hole about half as deep as the stone itself, and sloping downwards slightly from front to back. All the large stones in the rock garden should be positioned with this backward tilt, to carry rainwater to the centre to drain away, rather than run down its face.

Firm the soil around the centre-front stone. Lay others from it to create the front line you require. Then work towards the back until you have formed the complete base. Butt each stone as close as possible to its neighbours. Make sure each is firmly set in the soil.

When the base has been laid, fill the gaps to overflowing with a well-firmed mixture of 2 parts small stones or coarse gravel to 1 part of gritty soil.

Lay a second tier of rocks on the base,

setting them well behind the lower layer to create the slope at the front and sides. Try to place them so that they bridge the crevices in the base rather as you would with bricks – see BRICKLAYING. This helps to stop soil being washed away. Again, work from the centre front and then backwards down the sides. Fill the crevices with your stone-soil mixture. Add further layers of stones and filling until the rock garden is the height you require.

Planting Leave the rock garden to settle for a few weeks before you begin PLANTING. Pot-grown alpines can be planted at any time of year, except when the ground is frozen or covered with snow. Bare-rooted heathers and shrubs such as dwarf conifers should go in during November. Use campanula and dwarf phlox for the shaded back of the rock garden, and groups of alyssum, primula and saxifrage at the front.

When you plant, ensure that each crevice is firmly packed with soil mixture, to lessen the effects of erosion. Sprinkle a top layer of fine grit to help to keep down weeds. Check all rockery plants in spring, to ensure that they have not become loosened during the winter. Do not allow fallen leaves to lie on the rock garden in autumn.

Making your own rocks Lightweight imitation rock, known as hypertufa, can be made from ordinary Portland cement, sharp sand and peat substitute. Mould the mixture to any shape you want round an existing rock or an old tin or box, which can be removed when the material has set, leaving a hollow centre.

Thoroughly mix 1 part cement, 2 parts sand and 2 parts peat substitute together dry on a smooth surface. Make a crater in the top of the pile and add water a

---

Arranging the rocks, and planting for pleasing effects

Arrange a rock garden to look as natural as possible. Group the rocks together with the weathered sides facing out, and build them up in terraces. Create pleasing effects using alpines, which take up little room. Plant conifers at the back, to add height, and plants with colourful flowers in front.

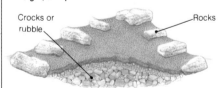

Crocks or rubble · · · Rocks

To build a rock garden, dig out a hollow and fill it with crocks or rubble for drainage. Cover it with gravel and soil. Build up the stones and soil in tiers, with the stones tilted inwards.

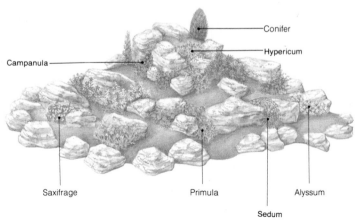

Conifer

Hypericum

Campanula

Saxifrage

Primula

Alyssum

Sedum

little at a time, shovelling the dry material to the centre, until the mixture is round the base in a thick layer. Once it has set you can chip it with a hammer and cold chisel to give it a natural, rough-hewn appearance.

The same mixture can be used to make an outer cover for an old sink or trough. First score the glazed surface with an old chisel to provide a good gripping surface, then coat it with PVA adhesive (see GLUING) as a binding agent before applying the hypertufa in a thick layer.

Roller skating

Choosing and maintaining skates; learning to skate

Skates with attached boots are generally more comfortable than clip or strap-on ones. Try on the boots wearing the socks or tights you would normally wear when skating. The boots should fit snugly yet let your toes wiggle.

For a beginner, cheaper skates are perfectly adequate. But if you are taking up the sport seriously, buy hand-made skates from a specialist shop, or a shop attached to a roller-skating rink.

First steps It is best to learn on a rink or other large level surface, such as a playground. Wear gloves and sturdy, loose-fitting clothes. Hold onto a fence or a friend until you gain your balance.

Start with the skates forming a T, as illustrated. Push off from the rear one, and skate by alternately pushing off with one skate and gliding on the other. As your momentum slows, lower your back leg, setting the skate down pointing forwards to form another T. Shift your weight onto this skate, then push off with the other.

Gliding and stopping When you are gliding forwards, hold yourself comfortably erect. To turn in a large arc, lean slightly in the direction you want to go.

To stop, bring your raised back skate down behind the other in the T-position. Set the skate down gradually so that the wheels' edges slow you.

Do not drag the toe stop at the front of the skate to slow yourself down. This will wear out the stop and may unbalance you on a rough surface.

Looking after your skates Each time you wear your skates, check that the toe stops are tight. Spin the wheels. If they do not spin freely, slacken the axle nut slightly. If they wobble, tighten the nut.

At regular intervals, put a drop of oil on each side of each wheel. If the wheels' spin begins to slow, take the skates to a shop that deals in them to have them cleaned. See also ICE SKATING.

── ROLLER SKATING ──

Learning to skate

Toe stop

Axle nut

The boots They should hold the heel and fit snugly. Toe stops should be tight and the wheels should spin easily.

Start by placing the skates in the T-position, with one skate pointing forwards and the other at right angles behind it.

Push off by pressing gently against the inside wheels of the back skate. Shift your weight to the front skate, then lift your back leg behind you.

Balance over the centre of the front skate and relax, but do not bend at the waist or look down at your skates.

Roman blinds

How to make them

When lowered, Roman BLINDS are like roller blinds. But as they are raised, they fold into horizontal pleats, instead of coiling round a cylinder as a roller blind does.

You can fit Roman blinds inside or outside a window recess, to overlap the wall a little. They are mounted on 38 × 38mm ($1\frac{1}{2}$ × $1\frac{1}{2}$in) BATTENS fixed in or just above the top of the recess.

The fabric should measure the length required for the finished blind plus 75mm (3in) at the top and the same at the bottom, for turnings. In width, it should

be the width required for the finished blind plus 38mm ($1\frac{1}{2}$in). If you have to join panels of fabric to make up the width, put a full-width panel at the centre and equal part-width panels at the edges. Make sure any pattern matches are exact if you join panels; the joins show much more than in CURTAINS, where the gathers hide them.

The blind needs a lining to give it more weight. Cut lining fabric to the width and length required for the finished blind, but 6mm ($\frac{1}{4}$in) bigger all round.

With the main fabric reverse side up, fold in and press a 19mm ($\frac{3}{4}$in) turning down each side and a double 38mm turning across both top and bottom. Turn the lining fabric reverse side up, fold in and press a 13mm ($\frac{1}{2}$in) turning all round.

Attach the lining right side up to the wrong side of the main fabric, using SLIPSTITCHING.

Pin lengths of heading tape up the back of the blind, putting one at each edge and spacing others equally about 150mm (6in) apart between them. Start the tapes about 150mm from the top of the blind and finish them about 60mm ($2\frac{1}{2}$in) from the bottom. Turn in the tape ends for a neat finish and make sure that each row has a pocket at the top and bottom. Tack the tapes in place then machine sew them down each edge – machining from top to bottom to avoid wrinkling – see SEWING. Attach curtain rings, one at the top of each tape, another at the bottom and others at 200mm (8in) intervals between.

Drill a clearance hole through the batten about 50mm (2in) from each end. Hold the batten in place in or just above the recess, then push a bradawl through each hole (from the bottom if inside the recess, from the front if outside the recess) to mark a drilling spot. Take down the batten, drill the marked spots and insert wall plugs – see MASONRY DRILLING; WALL FASTENERS.

Fix the blind to the face of the batten with decorative dome-headed upholstery nails driven in 50mm apart. If the batten is to be screwed from the front, leave the last 75mm of blind at each side without nails until later, so that you can get at the screw holes. Fit screw eyes to the batten as illustrated overleaf.

Cut a length of non-stretch cord for each row of rings, making it the width of the blind, plus twice its length.

Starting at the right-hand side, tie a cord to the bottom ring of the row. Thread it up through the other rings of the row, then from right to left through the screw eye above the row of tape and through all the screw eyes to the left.

Fit the other cords in the same way; do not pull them tight enough to pucker the fabric, nor leave them loose enough to sag. When all the rows are corded, knot all the cords together 38mm from the left-hand end of the batten. Plait the

ROMAN BLINDS

How to make a pleated blind

This shows the arrangement of the cords. Each cord runs through curtain rings fitted to curtain tapes and screw eyes in the top batten, to a cleat on the wall. Below are three stages in making the blind.

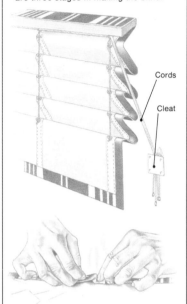

Cords

Cleat

Attach the lining right side up to the reverse side of the fabric, aligned at the top and 6mm (¼in) in on each side.

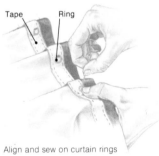

Tape   Ring

Align and sew on curtain rings at the top and bottom of each tape and at intervals of about 200mm (8in).

Batten

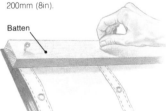

Spread out the blind (with batten attached), reverse side up. Fix a screw eye into the batten opposite each row of tape. The screw eye should end up at right angles to the window pane.

loose cords together, or knot them at intervals and trim the ends to an even length.

Screw the batten into the prepared holes. Finish nailing or tacking the edges of the blind to it if it is screwed from the front. Screw a brass cleat into drilled and plugged holes in the wall near the bottom of the plaited or knotted cord.

To raise the blind, pull on the cord. Wind the slack round the cleat to hold the blind at the required height.

Roman numerals

Making numbers with letters

Although the Roman system appears to be based on letters of the alphabet, it did not start that way. The I (1 in Arabic) was originally just a single stroke corresponding to one finger, as the earliest counting was done on fingers. The V (5) was a rough drawing of a hand, while the X was originally two Vs, or two hands, signifying 10. Later, letters were introduced to represent bigger numbers, such as C for 100 (*centum* in Latin).

The basic principle of Roman numerals is that when a smaller number comes before a larger number, the smaller number is subtracted. When a smaller number follows a larger one, the two are added together. You can see the idea at work in the first ten numbers, which are I, II, III, IV, V, VI, VII, VIII, IX and X. Thus, 4 is IV (V less I) and 6 is VI (V plus I).

A letter repeated repeats its value – so XX is 20 (10 + 10) and XXX is 30 (10 + 10 + 10). Other numerals are L for 50, D for 500 and M for 1000. So 40 is XL; 60, 70, 80 are LX, LXX and LXXX, and 90 is XC. The year 1988 is MCMLXXXVIII. The letters V, L and D are never repeated, as X, C and M

ROMAN NUMERALS

Counting the Latin way

Most people are familiar with the clock-face symbols corresponding 1 to 12, but many are baffled by large numbers. The table below shows how they are formed.

1	I	17	XVII
2	II	18	XVIII
3	III	19	XIX
4	IV	20	XX
5	V	30	XXX
6	VI	40	XL
7	VII	50	L
8	VIII	60	LX
9	IX	70	LXX
10	X	80	LXXX
11	XI	90	XC
12	XII	100	C
13	XIII	500	D
14	XIV	1000	M
15	XV	5000	$\overline{\text{V}}$
16	XVI	10,000	$\overline{\text{X}}$

serve that purpose. For example, X, not VV, C not LL and M, not DD.

A dash line over a numeral increases its value by 1000; X is 10,000 and CMXLIV is 944,000.

Roof repairs

Replacing slates and tiles; repairs to flat roofs

Do not venture onto the roof unless you have the right equipment and a head for heights. You need a ladder (see LADDERS) which extends at least three rungs above gutter level, for a good handhold.

Place a sandbag on the ground against the front of the ladder feet. Screw a ring bolt into the fascia board and lash the ladder to it. Hire a roof ladder (see HIRING) or buy an attachment which can be bolted to a standard ladder. The roof ladder has wheels which make it easier to run the ladder up the roof. When the top reaches the ridge, turn it over, so that the hooked top rests over the ridge.

When you reach the work spot, lash a rope to the ladder and through your belt. Put your tools and materials in a pouch strapped to you or in a bucket which you can tie or hook onto the ladder.

A ridge or hip tile that is dislodged will have to be mortared in place again. A common problem is cracking and crumbling of the MORTAR between these tiles. Such cracks also need repairing with mortar to prevent water from getting into the roof space. Use a cold chisel and hammer to chip away the remaining mortar from the tile, from each side of the ridge where the tile sits, and from the sides of adjacent tiles.

Prepare a firm mortar, adding PVA adhesive (see GLUING) to the mixing water. Brush plenty of PVA adhesive round the repair area. Spread mortar on both sides of the ridge or hip. If the roof tiles have a curved profile, fill the hollows with slips of tile.

Dip the tile in water and bed it on the mortar. Do not let the mortar squeeze up into the gap between the two roof slopes; air must circulate there. Point the gaps at the sides of the tile, giving a smooth finish to the mortar so that water will run off – see POINTING.

If the tile is at the end of the ridge, fill the end with mortar and slips of tile. If it is at the bottom of the hip, seal the end with mortar and make sure that the hip iron is firmly bedded in it.

Cracks in the mortar at the verge of a roof – where the roof meets the gable end – can be repaired with mortar. Brush out any loose mortar and coat the gap with PVA before filling with the new mortar and smoothing off.

If a tile has to be replaced, make two wooden wedges to raise the neighbouring tiles. Use 19mm (¾in) thick wood and

---

ROOF REPAIRS

Making repairs to a slate or tiled roof

Most roof tiles are hooked to battens and can be removed by raising neighbouring tiles. All slates, and some tiles, are held by nails and a slate ripper is needed to free them.

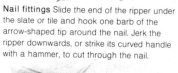

Nail fittings Slide the end of the ripper under the slate or tile and hook one barb of the arrow-shaped tip around the nail. Jerk the ripper downwards, or strike its curved handle with a hammer, to cut through the nail.

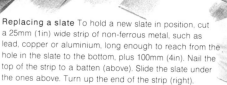

Replacing a slate To hold a new slate in position, cut a 25mm (1in) wide strip of non-ferrous metal, such as lead, copper or aluminium, long enough to reach from the hole in the slate to the bottom, plus 100mm (4in). Nail the top of the strip to a batten (above). Slide the slate under the ones above. Turn up the end of the strip (right).

Interlocking tile To remove, wedge under the tile to the left in the same course and the one to the right in the course above. Tilt the tile to disengage it from its neighbours.

Plain tiles These may be hung on a batten by projections, called nibs. Wedge the two tiles above and slide a large builder's trowel under the tile. Lift the tile clear of the batten and withdraw it.

make the wedges about 200mm (8in) long, tapering them from 32mm (1¼in) at one end to a point at the other. If the tile courses are staggered, push the wedges under the two tiles overlapping onto the damaged one from the course above. If the tiles are single lap, push one wedge under the tile to the left of the damaged one and the other under that to the right but in the course above.

Wiggle the damaged tile sideways until it is freed from the batten or interlocking grooves. Some tiles are nailed in place; you will have to hire a slate ripper to remove these. Slide the ripper under the tile, then cut through the nails by jerking the ripper with a sharp blow on its handle. There is no need to nail the replacement tile. Simply slide it up into place until it aligns with the rest of the

course. Remove the wedges. If the tile is in a prominent place, remove another tile from a spot not seen and use this to fill the gap. Then put your new tile in the unobtrusive spot where its brighter colour will not show.

Slates are always held by nails and have no nibs, so if the nails rust away, slates will slip. You cannot nail them back because the fixing points are overlapped by higher courses.

If the problem seems widespread you may be able to repair from inside the roof space – if the roof is unfelted. Push slipped slates back into place from the outside. Then use an aerosol can of foam filler to coat the slates from the inside. This will bond the slates together – and to the roof timbers.

Fill cracks in slates with epoxy repair

paste. Or for extra strength, use a strip of glass fibre bandage coated in paste.

Chimney-stack repairs are not DIY jobs, apart from repairing or replacing FLASHINGS that are within easy reach.

Flat roofs Problems occur on a flat roof, especially if rainwater gathers on it rather than draining off and if the roofing felt begins to blister. Rain and melting snow will find a way through any small cracks that develop.

Usually a flat roof is built up of layers of bitumen felt, often covered with small stones or chippings to dissipate summer heat. If you find blistering or cracking, scrape off the stones, sweep the roof and check the damage. Cut a cross in blisters with a knife and peel back the four points. Press a proprietary roof sealant under them, or paint on cold felt adhesive. Press the four points back in place, cover the cuts with self-adhesive flashing strip and replace any chippings. Fine cracks can be sealed with liquid rubber, but serious cracks are best reinforced with glass fibre bandage or hessian scrim bandage, sandwiched between layers of liquid bitumen waterproofing compound.

If a roof is more than ten years old but still sound, coat it all over with one of the bitumen-rubber waterproofing compounds. These are laid on thickly, usually after priming the surface with a special primer. A tough skin forms, which will add 20 years' extra life to the roof if properly applied.

Where a roof surface is in poor condition, strip off all the old felting and re-cover with two layers of medium-grade felt followed by a top sheet of heavy grade. Nail the first layer at 150mm (6in) intervals each way. Glue down the other two layers at the edges with felt adhesive, overlapping each strip 50mm (2in) onto the previous one. Fit new flashings at the house end of the roof.

A felted pitched roof can be refitted with new strips. Work from eaves to ridge overlapping the higher strip onto the lower by 75mm (3in). Nail the upper edge of each strip but glue overlapping lower edges, so that no nails show on the slope. Overlap the felt onto the eaves and fascia boards and secure it with galvanised clout nails at 50mm (2in) intervals.

Roses

Choosing, growing and caring for a garden favourite

Almost any part of the garden can be brightened with roses, blooming from early summer until late autumn. They need a well-drained soil so they do not get waterlogged, but the soil should be organically rich so that it retains moisture in summer – see SOIL PREPARATION.

ROSES

Pruning roses correctly

Prune large-flowered bush (hybrid tea), cluster-flowered bush (floribunda), climbing and standard roses quite severely, but trim shrub roses, miniatures and hedge roses lightly. Prune repeat-flowering varieties in March and climbers, weeping standards and single-flowering shrubs in September.

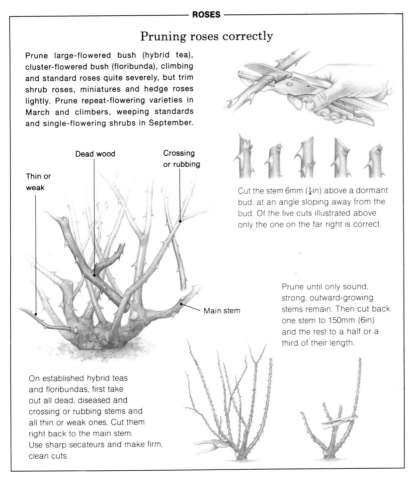

Cut the stem 6mm (¼in) above a dormant bud, at an angle sloping away from the bud. Of the five cuts illustrated above only the one on the far right is correct.

Prune until only sound, strong, outward-growing stems remain. Then cut back one stem to 150mm (6in) and the rest to a half or a third of their length.

On established hybrid teas and floribundas, first take out all dead, diseased and crossing or rubbing stems and all thin or weak ones. Cut them right back to the main stem. Use sharp secateurs and make firm, clean cuts.

Roses do best in slightly acid soils with a fairly high proportion of clay, and most roses like a sunny spot, but one that is sheltered from strong winds.

Hybrid tea These bush roses, known also as large-flowered bushes, have large, shapely flowers and, sometimes, a sweet scent. They are repeat-flowering and vary in height from 760mm-1.2m (2½-4ft). Plant about 600mm-1m (2-3ft) apart.

Floribunda Known also as polyantha or cluster-flowering bushes, they bear trusses of flowers from June until autumn, and grow from 600mm-2m (2-7ft) high. Plant the bushes about 600mm-1m (2-3ft) apart.

Both hybrid teas and floribundas can be grafted onto single, straight, brier stems to grow as standards about 1.5m (5ft) tall. Plant about 1.2m (4ft) apart.

Climbers These are suitable for walls and fences; many are repeat-flowering.

Ramblers Grow them against screens and pillars; they flower only in early summer, and have small blooms. Weeping

standards are ramblers grafted onto upright briar stems. Plant climbers and ramblers 2.4m (8ft) apart and weeping standards 1.8m (6ft) apart.

Modern shrub roses Their showy blooms are often sweet-scented. Most grow about 2m (7ft) high and many are repeat-flowering. Old garden roses (formerly called old-fashioned roses) are SHRUBS with large, heavily scented blooms and a short flowering season. Species roses are also grown as shrubs, sometimes reaching heights of 3.7m (12ft). Their flowering season is brief but some have attractive foliage and hips.

Miniature roses These rarely grow more than 250-300mm (10-12in) high, and look attractive in tubs, WINDOW-BOXES and a ROCK GARDEN. Those in tubs can be brought indoors when in bloom, but should be returned outside once they have flowered.

Choosing plants Pot-grown roses, available from nurseries and garden centres, can be planted at any time if the soil is not waterlogged or frozen. They tend to

be expensive and may be limited in variety. Order bare-rooted plants in August from catalogues, or buy them from nurseries and shops. Choose those with well-developed, bushy roots and strong green stems. Plant bare-rooted roses in dry, frost-free weather – see PLANTING.

Alternatively, buy container-grown roses; get them between spring and autumn, when you can judge their vigour from the leaves and flowers.

Planting At least a month before planting, work plenty of manure or COMPOST into the soil. Just before planting, fertilise the topsoil – see FERTILISERS. Cut back dead or damaged stems and trim very long or damaged roots on bare-rooted plants; soak the roots in water for up to 24 hours before planting.

Dig planting holes wide enough for the roots and deep enough for the crown to lie just below the soil surface.

Sprinkle peat substitute, leaf mould or COMPOST, and bone meal into the hole. For standards, which need staking, drive the stake in the hole – see STAKING PLANTS. Replace the soil, firm it down and water it well. In cold weather cover the soil round the plant with a layer of straw or newspaper.

Care of roses All roses need to be pruned once a year. Remove the blooms on repeat-flowering roses as soon as they fade, to encourage new ones.

Feed roses with rose fertiliser, hoed into the soil in April and July. Apply an additional feed of wood ash or sulphate of potash in September.

Mulch rose beds with a layer of compost or grass cuttings in April, to help conserve water and keep down weeds (see MULCHING). Water the plants thoroughly in dry spells, particularly new ones and those close to walls. Apply paraquat to kill weeds in April, and hoe rose beds regularly throughout the summer – see WEED CONTROL.

Fighting disease Use a systemic insecticide, spraying regularly from April to mid-October (see PESTICIDES). In May, begin regular spraying against fungus diseases, such as black spot and rust, with a systemic fungicide. Remove any rolled-up leaves that contain caterpillar grubs, or any with black spot or rust.

Roulette

Gambling on the turn of a wheel

Roulette is played using a shallow, lipped bowl enclosing a revolving wheel, which has numbered slots alternately coloured red and black. A steel, nylon, or ivory ball is thrown into the revolving wheel and lodges in a slot when the wheel slows.

There is also a baize betting board (or

ROULETTE

How to play the game

Here is a roulette wheel and betting layout. You bet on which slot or colour the ball will finally come to rest.

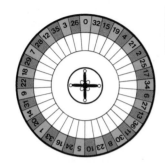

To bet, place chips on a chosen number, colour or combination. On the layout, *Manque* means low (numbers), *Passe* high, *Pair* even and *Impair* odd. Boxes marked ¹²P, ¹²M and ¹²D indicate first (*première*), middle (*milieu*) and last (*dernière*) 12 numbers.

layout) and coloured chips of nominal values used for placing bets on the board. Bets can be made on single or combinations of numbers, or on red or black.

Players bet against the *bank* (or *house*), which offers odds that vary according to the type of bet – for example, long odds (35-1) on single numbers; short odds (even money) on red.

Players place their bets and the banker then spins the wheel. Once the ball has dropped no further bets may be placed and no bet can be altered. The slot in which the ball lodges marks the winning number and colour.

Odds paid by the bank The wheel's 37 slots are numbered 1 to 36 (alternately red and black), plus a 0 (zero) slot which is green. Odds paid by the bank are:

● On any single number including the zero – 35-1.

● On the line between two numbers, when either number comes up – 17-1.

● At the end of a row of three numbers (for example, 31, 32 and 33) when any of the three numbers comes up – 11-1.

● On the intersection of four numbers, when any of them comes up – 8-1.

● At the end of the line horizontally separating the 0 and the numbers 1, 2 and 3 (a four-number combination) – 8-1.

● At the end of the line horizontally separating two rows of three numbers (a six-number combination) – 5-1.

● At the bottom of a vertical column of 12 numbers or on the 'dozens' (1-12, 13-24 or 25-36) – 2-1.

● Evens are paid on high numbers (19-36), low numbers (1-18), odd numbers, even numbers, black or red.

When the 0 (zero) comes up, the bank pays off for bets placed on it and on combination bets between it and any adjacent number or numbers. The bank takes all other chips, except those placed at evens. On these it returns half the stake.

On the Continent, rules differ slightly and American roulette has a double zero in addition to the zero.

Roulette sets for home recreation and parties are available at good sports shops.

Route-planning

Pre-journey map work to make the going easier

Do not journey into an area with which you are not familiar without good maps. You need them not only to plan and follow the route to your destination, but also if you have to make any unforeseen detours – because a road is temporarily closed, for example.

Choosing maps and guides You will need a fairly small-scale through-route map to get you to the area you are heading for and larger-scale maps to give more detail of the area where you are going to stay.

For through-routes in Britain, use a map on a scale of 1:625,000 or 1:950,000 (about 10 or 15 miles to 1in), showing motorways and major roads and with road numbers and place names clearly marked. For Western Europe or other places overseas, a scale of 1:1,250,000 or 1:3,000,000 (roughly 20 or 50 miles to 1in) is more practicable – see MAP READING.

For touring in a particular area, use a more detailed map on a scale of about 1:250,000 (roughly 4 miles to 1in) – or for abroad; about 1:500,000 (8 miles to 1in). If you are WALKING or BICYCLE TOURING in an area, you will need even more detailed maps on a scale of about 1:50,000 or 1:25,000 (1 mile or 2½ miles to 1in).

Although most large towns have sign-posted through-routes, it is easier to pilot yourself through them if you have a town plan. The motoring organisations can

supply guidebooks giving lists of accommodation and garages, as well as through-route maps, caravan and CAMP-ING sites or places to visit and how to get there.

Buy maps that are as up to date as possible, because roads are often renumbered or altered.

Finding distances Many maps and guides supply mileage charts that give distances between large towns and cities by the most direct route. These are not necessarily exact, because of new roads or road alterations. On all good road maps, distances between certain towns and intersections are printed on the map itself alongside roads.

Choosing a route in Britain Mark your starting and finishing points on the through-route map and decide what sort of route you want between them – fast, quiet, scenic, or one that will take in some interesting places on the way.

The shortest route is not always the fastest; motorways are not always shorter than other routes, but are usually much faster – see MOTORWAY DRIVING; MOTORWAY SIGNS. A quiet route with light traffic depends on the time of day you travel – peak traffic hours are around 9am and 5pm, or on Saturday mornings in towns. A road running near a motorway usually has less traffic, but is slower.

Take note of the towns to be negotiated on the route, and whether there are bypasses. Check also on car-ferry crossings, which may delay you.

Your journey time and route may be affected by roadworks or bad weather. Find out about these before you set out by telephoning the Traveline numbers for the areas you will be going through. They are listed in Telephone Directory information sections, or in motoring organisation handbooks.

Choosing a route overseas Plan a route to take you to Europe with your car in three stages – choose the most convenient Channel crossing for your destination, your route in Britain to reach the port, and your route from the port to your destination.

A motoring organisation will be able to give you all the details. They also have travel schemes that offer INSURANCE and lists of accommodation.

Planning overnight stops Decide roughly how much time you want to spend driving each day and how far.

Your average speed on a motorway is likely to be about 60mph, on a main road 40-50mph, and on a minor road 30mph.

Allow time for rest stops – never drive for more than three hours without a break. When driving abroad you will probably need to stop more often, because unfamiliar driving conditions

may tire you more easily. See also INTER-
NATIONAL ROAD SIGNS.

Plan to arrive at an overnight stopping
area in good time to find accommodation.
Booking ahead may be advisable in popular tourist venues at peak periods.

Navigating on the route Make a written summary of the route and keep it in
a place where you or your navigator can
glance at it quickly and safely at stops.
In Britain, list the main road numbers
and place names, and whether a road-
change is to the right or left. In Europe,
go by major place names – often more
prominent on signposts than road numbers, which may change at borders.

Routers

*Using and maintaining a handy
woodworking tool*

A router is a special type of plane (see
PLANING) used for making accurate
grooves of uniform depth in wood. The
standard size router is usually supplied
with three cutting blades – two with
chisel-shaped tips, for general cutting –
and a vee-shaped cutter for smooth
finishing, undercutting and getting into
corners. There are also attachments for
working across narrow sections of wood
or close to an edge.

To cut a groove, insert the chisel cutter
in the cutter clamp from below. Set the
depth gauge and adjust the cutter to it
with the adjustment nut, starting with a
fine cut. Mark the required width and
depth of the groove on the work. Make
a saw cut with a fine-tooth tenon saw
(see SAWS AND SAWING) to the waste side
of each edge of the proposed groove.
Make the first routing cut, gripping the
two hand knobs and using a series of
short forward strokes. End with a final
long sweep. Then reset the cutter in
stages, repeating the cuts until all the
waste is removed.

Sharpen the cutters like chisels (see
CHISELLING), but because of the 90 degree
set of the blade you will need to clamp
the oilstone near the edge of a bench so
that the cutter shaft can overhang.

Power router An electric router can
be fitted with a wide range of cutters,
making it a very versatile tool. Apart
from cutting grooves, it can be used for
making dovetails, rebates and a whole
range of decorative edgings.

To make a groove, fit the selected
cutter in its holder. Keep a firm grip
on the two handles to counteract the
tendency of the tool to twist. Let the
motor reach its maximum speed before
starting to cut, and then feed it in against
the clockwise rotation of the cutter, so
it pulls itself into the work. Move the
router slowly, steadily into the wood.

Rowing

Learning the basic strokes

Do not go rowing unless you are capable
of SWIMMING. Do not row in rough weather or when a storm threatens; if the
weather is uncertain, wear a life jacket.
Do not row in a strong current; on a
river, find out if any weirs are nearby.

The rowing cycle Step carefully into
the centre of the boat and sit erect, facing
the stern. Rest your feet securely against
the sides of the boat or the stretcher – a
raised board running across the boat.
Put the oars into the rowlocks.

Grip the oars so that the blades are
vertical and just out of the water. Push
the oar handles down slightly and away

Using your wrists

Change the angle of the blades by raising
or dropping your wrists. The blades must
be vertical while in the water.

Keep your wrists level with your
hands as you pull the blades
through the water.

Push your hands down at the end of the
stroke and drop your wrists to 'feather' the
blades.

Push the oar handles
forwards, keeping your
wrists bent and the
blades feathered, until
your arms are straight.

Turn your wrists to
square the blades
again. Raise your
arms to drop the
blades into the
water.

from you until your arms are straight.
Raise the handles until about two-thirds
of the blades are submerged.

Now pull steadily straight back, keeping your hands parallel. At the end of
the pull, lower the handles and drop your
wrists so that the blades are out of the
water and horizontal. Push the handles
down and away from you, then turn the
blades to the vertical and repeat.

Rowing stern first and turning To
advance stern first, reverse the rowing
stroke so that you push, rather than pull,
the oar through the water.

To turn a boat, exert greater force on
the oar opposite the direction in which
you want to turn.

Approach a quay or landing raft
against the wind or the current, whichever is stronger. Row to shore bow first.

If your boat capsizes, stay with it and
try to right it by pulling on the keel.

RSVP

*Correct ways to request or
respond*

If you are sending out formal or informal
invitations and want to know in advance
who will be coming and who will not,
put the letters RSVP – from the French
Répondez, s'il vous plaît, meaning 'please
reply'. Write them at the bottom of the
invitation, above the address to which
you want the answer to go.

It is always assumed that the address
below RSVP is the one at which the
event will be held, unless the invitation
states otherwise. For invitations issued
by organisations, you may add, above the
address, the name or title of the person
to whom the reply should be sent – for
example, the Secretary.

As a matter of courtesy, an RSVP invitation should be answered in writing several days before the event.

If you issue an informal invitation to
someone in conversation, and he accepts,
but you then send an invitation card,
cross out RSVP if it appears, and write
above it 'To remind'. A card altered in
this way does not need to be
acknowledged.

See also INVITATIONS.

Rug making

*Using canvas and wool, needles
and hooks*

Two common methods of making rugs
are hooking (by hand, or with a punch
needle) and knotting with a latchet hook.
See also RUG PLAITING.

Hooking by hand This is done by pushing a hook through hessian (or jute

Hooking and knotting

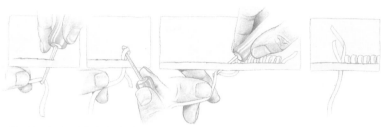

Hooking by hand Push the hook down through the rug base and catch one end of the fabric strip. Pull the hook back up, together with the end of the strip. The cut ends should later be trimmed level with the pile.

Working from right to left, push the hook down through the base again. Catch the strip and bring it up to form a loop. Continue along the row, making the loops the same height as the fabric strips are wide.

To end a strip, bring the cut end up through the hole. Begin the next strip in the hole where the last strip ended.

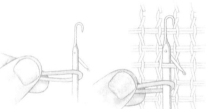

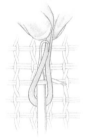

Knotting with a latchet hook Loop a strand of yarn round the shank of the hook.

Push the hook under a set of horizontal threads and through until the bar falls open.

Bring the ends of the yarn up and round, lodging them in the open latchet.

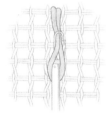

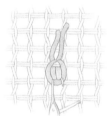

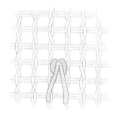

Carefully start to pull the hook down. When the bar closes, release the yarn.

Pull the hook down and under the horizontal threads. Pull the ends through.

Pull on the cut ends to tighten the knot and make the yarn ends even.

embroidery cloth) to catch a strip of fabric below and pull a loop of it through to the surface (see illustrations).

The size of hook used depends on the width of the fabric strip. A straight-weave, fine woollen fabric such as flannel is best for the strips. Wash the fabric first to pre-shrink it. You will need an area of fabric four times the area of the finished rug. Cut the fabric into strips about 6 or 10mm ($\frac{1}{4}$ or $\frac{3}{8}$in) wide, cutting along the line of a thread.

Knotting with a latchet hook A latchet hook has a bar which makes it easier to knot loops. Buy ready-cut rug wool, or wrap wool from a skein around a cardboard gauge and then cut along one edge. The length of each strand should be twice the desired pile depth plus 16mm ($\frac{5}{8}$in).

Work the knots (see illustrations) by row across the canvas and from the bottom edge up so that the hook can slip easily through the canvas. Work a knot in every hole across the canvas. For a very dense pile, work knots on every row of horizontal threads; for a less thick pile work across alternate sets of threads.

Preparing the base For all rug making, the backing must be held taut while you

work. Buy a frame, or improvise one by screwing two large hooks into a wooden batten longer than the rug width. Tack the backing to the wood, then loop rope round the hooks and tie it round the two legs on the far side of the work table. As you work down the backing, adjust the rope to move the wooden strip farther away from you. Hold the free end of the backing taut.

The base should be the size of the finished rug plus about 75mm (3in) all round. If you have to join hessian or jute embroidery cloth, trim the selvedges from the edges to be joined. Overlap one 19mm ($\frac{3}{4}$in) onto the other, then machine sew down both edges of the overlap 3mm ($\frac{1}{8}$in) from the raw edge – see SEWING. Pierce both thicknesses when you are hooking the rug. Machine a 10mm ($\frac{3}{8}$in) turning round each side.

To join canvas, trim the selvedges off the edges to be joined. Overlap one over the other by four threads and oversew the four rows together by hand. Bind the edges with masking tape.

Mark the centre of the backing fabric and the mid-point of each edge.

Marking the pattern You can buy rug bases already marked with a pattern. To design your own, trace or draw the pattern on paper. For working on hessian or jute embroidery cloth, stab a thick darning needle through the paper at frequent intervals along the lines of the design. Centre and pin the pattern on the base – right side up.

Sprinkle pounce (a powder sold in craft shops) or powdered French chalk over the pattern and rub it over the rows of holes with a wad of fabric. Lift off the paper carefully. Join up the dots with a dressmaker's pencil and shake off the loose pounce.

For canvas, centre the canvas over the paper pattern and hold the two together with small clothespegs or bulldog clips. The pattern is visible through the canvas: use a waterproof marking pen to trace the design on the canvas.

Finishing off Paint latex adhesive on the back of hooked rugs to secure the pile. Trim the base 32mm ($1\frac{1}{4}$in) from the outer loops. Sew 50mm (2in) wide binding tape on the right side of the rug. Butt its edge up to the outer loops and make a running stitch with carpet twine 3mm ($\frac{1}{8}$in) from the tape edge. Fold the tape onto the back of the rug and hemstitch it to the rug base.

At corners, fold the excess tape into neat mitres.

Caring for the rug Shake the rug outdoors regularly to get rid of grit; vacuum it frequently – see VACUUMING. Knotted rugs can be dry-cleaned, but latex-backed hooked rugs cannot because the cleaning solvent dissolves the latex.

Rug plaiting

*Making mats from scraps
of material*

Heavy or medium-weight woollen fabrics with a close weave make the hardest-wearing plaited rugs. You can use other fabrics, but it is best not to mix different materials; they wear and attract dirt at different rates. Many man-made materials attract static. Avoid fabrics that are stiff – they are not pliable enough to plait and shape easily.

Old coats, suits and skirts are suitable – with zips, seams and worn areas cut out. Usually old clothes in a range of colours can be bought extremely cheaply at jumble sales. Remnants bought in fabric shops will be much more expensive. You need about 450g (1lb) of fabric for about 900sq cm (1sq ft) of rug. Wash the pieces of fabric before you use them – wash by hand to avoid felting.

You can plait colours together at random or sew together one-colour plaits at random. If you want to plan a pattern, it is best to put lighter shades in the centre and the darkest shade at the edge.

Preparing the strips Follow the straight lines of the weave when you cut the strips. Make the strips 38-65mm (1½-2½in) wide, depending on how slender you want the plaits to be. It is not easy to do the necessary fold on heavy fabric if the strip is too narrow. With a thin fabric you can overlap the folds (see below) for added body. Make some test plaits with different strip widths before cutting up much fabric. Once you choose

the width, cut all strips the same width.

To join strips, put two together with right sides facing. Sew across the join as illustrated below. Cut off excess fabric and open out the joined strip. Continue joining on strips in the same way. Start the folding as soon as the strip is a metre or two long.

To fold a strip, lay it out wrong side up, turn the two raw edges to the centre, then fold the strip in half lengthways. Iron or steam press lightly to fix the folds. Wind the folded strip round a length of stiff card; secure the end of the strip in a slit at the end of the card.

You can join and fold strips, and wind them round the card until it is full. When you have three cards of folded strips, start plaiting.

Making a plait Join two of the strips (as illustrated below). Fold the joined piece and lay it out with the open edge towards you. Insert the third strip between the two layers at the open edge to make a T shape; its open edge must be to the right. Secure the third strip in place with a few stitches.

Fold the right half of the T cross bar over the stem of the T; its open edge should then be on its right. Over this strip, which is now at the centre of the three, fold the left-hand strip – again folding it so that the open edge ends up on its right. Now fold the right-hand strip over the centre strip.

Continue like this, folding left and right in turn over the centre strip. Each time, fold a strip so that its open edge ends up at the right. Plait the strips

tightly, so that the rug will be firm and strong.

To make the plait easy to coil, and to keep the finished rug flat, you have to build in turns. To make a turn, take the left-hand strip over the centre strip twice in succession before taking right over centre.

For a round rug, make 6 to 12 turns in succession at the beginning of the plait. After that, the circle will be large enough for a normal plait to curve round.

For an oval rug, subtract the planned width of the finished rug from its planned length; the remainder is the length to make the plait before introducing a turn. For example, if the rug is to be 910 × 1110mm (36 × 44in), make a 200mm (8in) plait before building in a turn. Make three turns in succession, then plait straight until you get back to the starting end. Make another three turns in succession there, and from then on plait normally.

Start a rectangular rug in the same way as an oval, but after the first turn build in an angle at each of the four corners in each row of plaiting. To make the angle, take the left strip over the centre three times in succession, before taking right over centre.

Joining up and finishing off Use a tapestry or tape-threading needle and carpet twine to lace together the coils of plait, but for a firm centre, sew one round with a sharp needle and strong thread.

To lace the remainder, take the needle through the inside loop of a plait and then through the adjacent loop of the

---

Making a rug with three-strand plaits

When making a three-strand plait, always keep the open edges of the strips to the right. To make a tight plait, pull each strip to the side, not down. When you break off, secure the plaited end with a clothespeg.

Fold in the strip edges – to overlap on thin fabrics, to meet on thick. Fold again and press.

To sew strips together, place them at right angles with the right sides facing. Sew together, trim the seam and press it open.

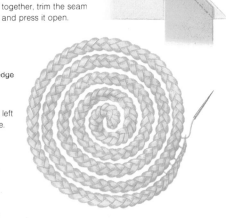

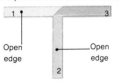

Sew strip 3 into the fold where strips 1 and 2 join.

Bring strip 3 over strip 2, then strip 1 over strip 3.

Plait by alternately folding left and right strips over centre.

For a round turn, take each strip over the centre once.

After this, bring the left strip (3) over the centre strip.

Bring the new left strip (2) over the new centre strip (3).

Bring the right strip over the centre. The plait now curves right.

Make 6 to 12 round turns for the centre, then plait as normal. Sew the centre and lace the coils together.

next row. Do not pierce the fabric as with sewing, but pass the needle under the entire strip. Pull the thread tight so that it does not show. At turns, miss out some of the loops on the coil that is being joined on, or else the rug will buckle.

To finish off, cut the three strips to different lengths and taper them to long points – about 150mm (6in) long. Fold in the raw edges and hand sew them. Fold the strips in the usual way as far as you can. Continue plaiting as long as possible, then tuck the tip of each strip under a loop of a matching colour in the previous coil. Sew the tips in place with small, unobtrusive stitches.

Shake the rug outside regularly to remove grit, which would damage the fabric. Vacuum it frequently. The rug can be dry-cleaned, but will lose its shape if washed. See also RUG MAKING.

Rummy

*Playing a popular family
card game*

Seven-card rummy is played with two packs and any number can play – provided that a reasonable number of cards remains in the undealt stack in the middle of the table. This is unlike GIN RUMMY, which is played with only one pack and is best suited to two people.

The object of each player is to compile sets of three or more cards of the same value (for example, three sevens) or three or more cards making a sequence in the same suit (for example, the five, six, seven and eight of hearts).

Aces can count high or low in sequences; twos are 'wild' and may be used to represent any card. The dealer shuffles the two packs (see SHUFFLING CARDS) and deals cards face down and one by one round the players, until each has seven. The rest of the pack is placed face down in the middle of the table, and the top card is turned face up beside it.

Starting with the player on the dealer's left, each player in turn has the choice of taking the top card from the unexposed pack or the exposed card beside it, to try to improve his hand.

After he has taken his card, he must discard one onto the exposed pile. The next player then has the choice of that card or the top one from the unexposed pack as play moves round the table.

Once a player has at least six of the cards in his hand organised into sets or sequences, and if any remaining card is a seven or lower, he may 'go down', declaring his hand and ending that round of play. A player may not go down in a turn when he has already changed a card. He must wait for his next turn.

When one player goes down, he and all the other players must lay their hands face up on the table, so that scoring can

begin. If the player going down has one unplaced card – say, a six – other players with spare sixes not included in a set or sequence can add them to his; they do not then count in the scores.

The cards in each player's hand not forming part of a set or sequence are added up and count against him. Picture cards count as ten, aces as one, and twos as nothing. Each player's score is recorded, and the next round of play begins. If a player should achieve a seven-card sequence, this is 'Rummy' – and removes any points so far counted against the player.

Each player is eliminated when his score reaches a previously agreed figure, usually 100 points, until a winner emerges. When seven-card rummy is played for money, each player must put an agreed stake into a central kitty, or pot, at the start of each round he plays in (sometimes the person going down is exempt from the stake for the next round). The winner then takes the pot.

In some variations of seven-card rummy, the pot is divided between the two last players remaining, in proportions agreed in advance.

Rust

How to prevent and cure it

Iron and steel rust when they get damp, and the metal is gradually eaten away. Rust is formed by chemical action between the metal, oxygen in the air, and water made into a weak acid by dirt and dust. Iron and steel will not rust if you keep them protected from the combined effects of air and water, so most preventive measures involve doing just that.

Preventing rust Paint iron or steel in need of decoration as soon as possible. First remove grease with white spirit and allow the metal to dry. Then paint with metal primer, followed by gloss paint – see PAINTS. This will exclude air and water.

Repaint even small scratches in paintwork before rust can form – see PAINT TOUCH-UPS.

During winter, when roads are being salted, wash the underside of your car as often as possible – particularly the sills and wings – because chemicals such as salt accelerate rusting.

Protect metal that cannot be painted, such as hand tools, with a thin film of oil or grease. Or use one of the moisture-displacing oils available as aerosol sprays. Thin coatings soon evaporate, so renew them regularly.

Use silica gel crystals to keep small cupboards dry (they have little or no effect in large spaces). The crystals absorb moisture from the air and need drying off in an oven from time to time to keep them effective.

Many tools and appliances are now made from materials that will not rust – such as stainless steel or aluminium alloy – or have chrome or other coatings that discourage rust. When you buy tools, check the labels about the materials used; it can save problems in the future.

Curing rust Deal with any rust formation, however slight, as soon as possible. Minor attacks may need only a rub with fine emery cloth.

For serious rusting, use a wire brush (either a hand-held brush or one fitted in a power drill) to remove all loose scale from the rusted area. Protect your eyes with safety goggles while you do it.

Once loose scale has been removed, treat the area with a proprietary rust-neutralising fluid that converts any remaining rust into a harmless black coating which can be overpainted with an undercoat if necessary and finished with gloss paint.

Alternatively, use cold-galvanising paint or zinc-rich paint. These not only neutralise any remaining rust, and provide a silvery priming coat, but also inhibit further rusting. Once dry, the coating can be overpainted with any good exterior gloss paint.

Another alternative is to use a rust-inhibiting enamel paint. Remove all loose rust, then paint the enamel straight onto the bare metal. No primer or undercoat is necessary. Work fairly fast, as the paint dries faster than standard paint, especially in warm weather.

When treating rusted areas on painted metalwork, be sure to strip off the paint until you come to bright metal – see PAINT STRIPPING. If you leave any hidden rust untreated, it will quickly spread and push up the paint in blisters.

Where rust has caused staining of a surface such as ceiling plaster (after water damage, for example) paint the stained area with aluminium primer-sealer – see PAINTS. This isolates the stain from any new paint or paper.

Repairing hollows and holes Where rust has eaten into the metal, first remove all loose and flaking rust. Fill up a hollow with an epoxy-based repair filler paste – see STOPPERS AND FILLERS. The paste inhibits any further rusting, so no priming paint is needed.

Back a small hole with glass-fibre matting, if necessary, or for a larger hole use expanded zinc-alloy mesh.

Stick it in place with a little repair paste, then build up the surface with the filler keyed to the mesh.

Build the filler a little higher than the surrounding metal. When it has hardened, smooth it level with wet-and-dry abrasive paper, used wet, before cleaning and painting the area. See also DENTS IN CARS; SPRAY PAINTING.

S

Safes

Installing a small home safe

As a last line of defence against a burglar (see BURGLARPROOFING), a small home safe will give better security for valuable items, such as jewellery and cash, than locked drawers or cupboards. Various models are available from security equipment stockists, and most are easily fitted. There are designs for floor, wall or cupboard installation. Some are key operated, others have combination locks.

Although safes are strongly made and tamper-proof, secrecy gives additional security. Models designed for underfloor installation are screwed between the JOISTS of a wooden floor (see FLOOR REPAIRS) and can be covered by a carpet or item of furniture. The size is governed by the joist spacing, but a larger model can be fixed on top of a wooden floor and concealed in a cupboard.

Other ingenious devices are the 'not what they seem' safes. One such looks like a double power socket. It fits into a wall (see ELECTRIC SOCKETS AND SWITCHES) but is not wired.

Safety seats

Choosing and fitting a child's seat

The safest way for a child to travel in a car is by using a restraint system that suits the child's weight and size, and is properly used and correctly fitted. All approved child restraints must carry either the BS Kitemark or the United Nations 'E' mark.

Up to nine months The safest type of restraint for small babies is a rear-facing infant carrier (BS AU202a or ECE44). It can be used in the front or rear of the car, wherever there is a lap-and-diagonal seat belt. Never use it facing forwards.

A carrycot with restraining straps (BS AU186a) provides much less protection than a rear-facing infant carrier. The carrycot is not designed to withstand the forces involved in an accident, and can only be used in the rear seat. However, it is better to use this system than to travel with your baby unrestrained.

Nine months to five years A forward-facing child seat with integral harness (BS 3254 or ECE44) should be fitted. The child is carried in a sitting position facing the front of the car. It is restrained

SAFETY SEATS

Providing your child with safe car travel

Rear-facing infant carrier Can be used in front or rear of car; never facing forwards.

Forward-facing child seat Provides safe ride when a child outgrows its carrycot.

Booster cushion The raised seat enables a small child to use an adult seat belt.

Carrycot restraint Use a harness with a quick-release buckle to secure a carrycot.

Booster seat The raised seat allows a small child to use an adult seat belt. It has a back, and usually sides.

in a harness which may have four or five straps. Two pass over the child's shoulders, two come around either side of the waist, and the fifth, if fitted, comes up between the child's legs.

Some rear-facing seats are 'two-way', and can be used as forward-facing seats when the child is ready for them.

The seat is fitted into the car either by its own tether straps, or by lap seat belts or lap-and-diagonal seat belts. Each type of seat should only be attached according to the manufacturer's instructions.

Over five The booster seat (ECE44) is designed to improve the positioning of the adult belt for a small child. It consists of a base cushion on which the child sits, a back, and usually sides. The restraint is provided by the adult lap-and-diagonal seat belt going around the front of the child, or a lap belt with some seats. A

booster cushion (BS AU185 or ECE44) does a similar job, and consists of a firm cushion. It can be used whenever a lap-and-diagonal seat belt is fitted.

Fitting a safety seat There are three main ways of fitting restraints into a car:
• A lap-and-diagonal seat belt.
• A lap seat belt.
• A special fixing kit consisting of two or four tether straps.

Some restraints can be fitted by more than one method.

Remember that not all restraints fit every model of car. It is important to check that the restraint can be fitted correctly before buying it. Always check that it has been fitted correctly.

If a child restraint is not fitted correctly, it may not perform as it should in an accident, and may cause injury or worse.

Who can fit a restraint? You can, so long as you follow the manufacturer's instructions. You may need to drill new anchorage points. If you do not have any fitting instructions, or are in any doubt, contact the manufacturer, or ask your local road safety officer for a list of local garages or other agencies which specialise in in-car safety.

Make sure that other people, such as grandparents, who are likely to move the restraint, also know how to fit it.

What the law says

	Front seat	Rear seat
Child under 3	Appropriate child restraint must be used	Appropriate child restraint must be used if available
Child aged 3-11 and under 1.5 metres tall	Appropriate child restraint must be worn if available. If not, adult seat belt must be worn	Appropriate child restraint must be worn if available. If not, adult seat belt must be worn if available
Child aged 12-13 or younger child 1.5 metres tall or more	Adult seat belt must be worn if available	Adult seat belt must be worn if available

Sailing

The basic techniques

Before attempting to sail your own boat, seek the advice and help of an experienced sailor. Better still, join a sailing club or sailing school. Consult the *Yellow Pages*, or write for information to the Royal Yachting Association, Romsey Road, Eastleigh, Hants SO50 9YA.

Start by learning how to sail a dinghy, under the guidance of an instructor. Always keep an anchor, bucket and paddles on board and make sure you know the rules regarding rights of way, especially when sailing on a river.

Sailing a dinghy For an absolute beginner, one with a mainsail only is the best choice. Select a day with a steady, but not strong, onshore wind.

Start by reaching, sailing across the wind – the easiest way to sail. Sit on the windward side, with one hand on the tiller and the other holding the main-

Handling a boat to make the best use of the wind

Sailing any kind of craft requires a basic knowledge of seamanship – how to use the wind to drive a boat. Try to learn the basic techniques on a sailing dinghy, which will provide you with experience enough to transfer with confidence if offshore voyaging is your aim.

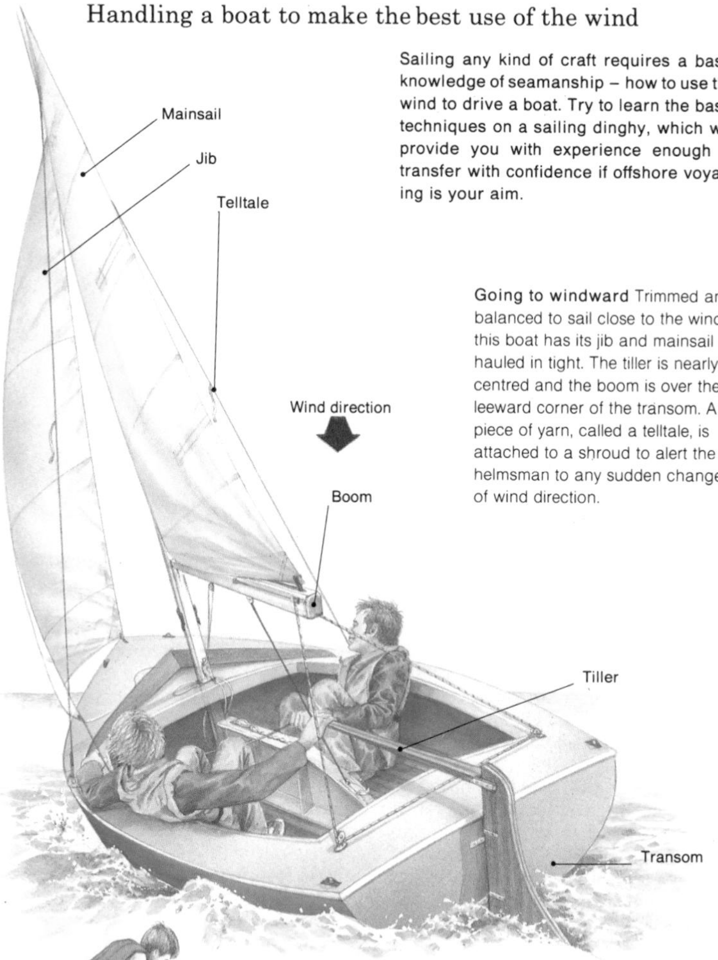

Going to windward Trimmed and balanced to sail close to the wind, this boat has its jib and mainsail hauled in tight. The tiller is nearly centred and the boom is over the leeward corner of the transom. A piece of yarn, called a telltale, is attached to a shroud to alert the helmsman to any sudden change of wind direction.

Mainsail
Jib
Telltale
Wind direction
Boom
Tiller
Transom

Righting a capsized dinghy Step onto the centreboard and grip the side of the boat with both hands. Lean back so that your weight pulls the boat upright. As the boat comes up, drop back into the water and climb in from the stern.

sheet (the rope controlling the boom).

To control speed, slacken the mainsheet until the sail begins to flap free, then slowly haul in the mainsheet until the sail fills. Control your course by moving the tiller and adjusting the angle of the sail in relation to the wind. If the boat heels (leans over) too much, slacken the mainsheet.

To tack, or change course, build up speed then push the tiller away from you to steer the bow through the wind. Duck under the boom as it swings across the

boat and move to the other side, changing hands on the tiller and mainsheet. Repeat the procedure to go onto the opposite tack.

Take care when moving the tiller – do not push it further than is necessary to bring the boat round smoothly from one tack to another, or you may not have time to cross to the windward side, and may capsize.

Come into a dock or mooring with the wind as nearly ahead as possible; stop by slackening the mainsheet to let the sail flap. If you must dock with the wind behind, lower the sail about 10-15m (30-50ft) away and coast in.

Sailing safely Always wear a buoyancy aid approved by the Ship and Boat Builders National Federation, even if you swim well. If you cannot swim, wear a life jacket approved by the British Standards Institution, marked BS3595.

A capsized boat is easy to right, but the techniques need some practice – try them out by deliberately capsizing the boat in calm, shallow water. If the boat is on its side, free the sheets so that the sails swing free, otherwise the wind will fill them as the boat is righted and capsize it again. Climb onto the centreboard – the stabilising keel under the hull – keeping your feet close to the hull. Hold onto the gunwale and lean back. Your weight should pull the boat upright. Drop back into the water, without letting go of the boat, then move round to the stern and climb in.

If the boat is upside down, and you are trapped underneath, take a deep breath in the air space left under the boat and swim out under water. The air trapped beneath the boat may create a partial vacuum, sucking the boat against the water and making it difficult to right – pull down or climb onto one corner of the stern to break the vacuum, then roll the boat onto its side and right it as described above.

Do not leave the boat, even if you cannot right it. If you let go it may drift or be blown away faster than you can swim. You also stand a better chance of being rescued, as a capsized boat is easier to spot than a swimmer. Climb onto the hull if you cannot right the boat.

See also DISTRESS SIGNALS.

Salad dressings

Mixing them for different dishes

A good dressing is essential to SALADS, but it should vary according to the salad ingredients. The first recipe below is for a sharp vinaigrette dressing, good for a green salad; vegetable, egg, fish and meat salads are enhanced by a smooth French dressing – the second recipe. See also MAYONNAISE.

Ingredients – 150ml ($\frac{1}{4}$ pint)
6 tablespoons oil
2 tablespoons wine vinegar
1 dessertspoon finely chopped herbs
Salt and black pepper

Put the oil and vinegar in a bowl or in a screw-top jar. Whisk with a fork or shake vigorously before seasoning the dressing to taste with herbs (see HERBS IN COOKING), salt and freshly ground black pepper.

Ingredients – 200ml ($\frac{1}{3}$ pint)
8 tablespoons oil
4 tablespoons wine vinegar
2 level teaspoons French mustard
$\frac{1}{2}$ level teaspoon each salt, black pepper
$\frac{1}{2}$ level teaspoon caster sugar (optional)

Whisk or shake all the ingredients together. Any of the following ingredients can also be added: 1-2 crushed garlic cloves; 2 tablespoons chopped tarragon or chives; 1 tablespoon tomato paste and a pinch of paprika.

Salads

Making meals of fresh fruits and vegetables

The two most common types – mixed salad and fruit salad – are easy-to-make, light dishes.

Mixed salad Any edible greens can go into a mixed salad – but use only those that are crisp and free of yellowing, spotting or bruising. Wash them carefully, swirling those with loose leaves at least twice in a bowl, discarding the water each time. Dry thoroughly by blotting them gently and rolling them in a clean towel or paper towels. Or you can shake them dry using a salad spinner, salad basket or colander.

In general, tear loose-leaved vegetables such as lettuce – and cut compact types such as celery and chicory. To crisp the greens you can put them in the refrigerator in plastic bags or a covered bowl for anything from 2 to 12 hours. If you are adding juicy vegetables such as tomatoes or beetroot, wash and keep them separate from the greens until ready for the salad bowl.

Pour the dressing (see SALAD DRESSINGS) over the salad. Then toss the

Waldorf salad A mixture of apple, celery and walnuts goes well with duck or pork.

ingredients thoroughly by lifting them from the bottom of the bowl with a salad fork and spoon half-a-dozen times. Serve as soon as possible.

Salad ingredients are very much a matter of personal choice. Generally, mild-flavoured greens, such as lettuce, benefit from being mixed with more pungent vegetables, such as watercress. Other flavourful and colourful additions include avocados, artichoke hearts, asparagus, carrots, green peppers, olives, onions, radishes and red cabbage.

Fruit salad This recipe for a fresh fruit salad takes about 30 minutes to make, and should be chilled for 2-3 hours.

Ingredients (for 6 people)
2 oranges
225g ($\frac{1}{2}$lb) black grapes
$\frac{1}{2}$ ripe honeydew melon
2-3 ripe pears
2 bananas
115g (4oz) caster sugar
150ml ($\frac{1}{4}$ pint) dry white wine
2 tablespoons kirsch

Use a sharp knife to cut a slice from the top and base of each orange; then cut down each orange in strips to cut away the peel and white pith. Ease out each segment and peel off the thin skin.

Peel and halve the grapes and remove the seeds. Place them in a bowl on top of the oranges and sprinkle with a little sugar. Remove the seeds from the melon, and dice the flesh. Add the melon to the bowl with another sprinkling of sugar.

Quarter, peel and core the pears, then slice thinly. Peel the bananas, cut them in half lengthways then dice them. Put them in the bowl with the remaining sugar.

Mix the fruit carefully, then pour over the white wine and kirsch. As the fruit soaks in the liquid, press it down so that it is covered with juice and is less likely to discolour.

Chill, and serve with cream.

Sale of goods

What to do if you have bought goods that are unsatisfactory

However small the purchase, when you buy goods you have rights against the seller, under the Sale of Goods Act, if they are faulty. See also TRADE DESCRIPTIONS ACT.

You cannot return goods simply because you do not like them. To obtain compensation, your complaint must satisfy one of three main conditions: the goods are not what you asked for, or do not match the seller's description; the goods are not fit for their common, everyday usage; the goods do not do the job for which they were sold.

Your claim will not succeed, however, if the fault was pointed out to you by the seller before you bought the article, or if you examined the article closely enough to have been able to spot the defect yourself. The seller can also refuse to compensate you if you bought something for a specific purpose after he had advised against it.

Even when goods are sold under a manufacturer's guarantee, the responsibility for compensation may be with the seller, *not* the manufacturer, though the seller has the right to claim in turn against the manufacturer. The seller is obliged to refund the full purchase price only if the goods are totally unsuitable or have a major defect. He can offer to have the defect put right and pay the costs or, if the defect is small, can refund part of the purchase price.

Act quickly if you want to return defective goods – do not keep them longer than is reasonably necessary to find the defect. If you ask for a refund, either full or partial, you are entitled to cash – you cannot be made to accept a credit note. If a trader refuses to meet his obligations you can sue him (see SUING), but that could be a costly business.

See also GUARANTEES; REFUNDS; WARRANTIES.

Salt on roads

Protecting your car from corrosion by salt deposits

A mixture of salt and sand or gravel is used by local authorities to prevent icing of roads, and the salt, combined with dirt and moisture, will accelerate the corrosion of bare metal.

Most cars are undersealed by the manufacturer, but stones thrown up by the wheels may chip away the sealant in time. Before winter, raise the car onto axle stands (see JACKING A CAR) and examine the underseal for damage.

The main type of body sealant used by manufacturers on exposed surfaces is a hard-setting bitumastic compound. When repairing damaged sealant, make sure to use the same type on the car.

Remove loose sealant and clean the exposed area with a wire brush. Treat the area with a proprietary anti-rust preparation (see RUST), available from car accessory shops, following the maker's instructions. On bare metal, a coat of zinc-based primer will give additional protection. Allow the treatment to dry, then brush on the sealant thickly, working it into any crevices.

If your car has not been undersealed, it is best to have it done professionally. The treatment, to be effective, involves steam cleaning before applying the sealant with a high-pressure spray gun.

Whether undersealed or not, clean under the wings of your car as soon as possible after you have been driving on salted roads. Place the car on axle stands and remove the wheels. Cover the brake drums or discs with plastic sheeting, taped in place. Loosen and remove as much accumulated mud and dirt as possible with a length of wood.

Connect a garden hose to a mains tap and turn it fully on, with the nozzle adjusted to give a concentrated jet.

Hose each wheel arch in turn, moving the hose round in an arc to direct the jet into every corner. Continue hosing until clear water runs down from under the wheel arch. After hosing, finish off with a stiff brush dipped in hot water. Replace the wheels and lower the car. See also CAR WASHING.

Sanding

Smoothing by hand and power tool

A surface is sanded to get it really smooth before decorating. A power sanding tool may also be used to shape and round timber. The material used for sanding is paper or cloth coated with grains of an abrasive such as silicon carbide. The coarseness of the abrasive is graded from fine to coarse, by words or by a series of numbers ranging from 60 to 400 (the higher, the finer).

When sanding wood, work only with the wood grain – never across it. Scratches across the grain are very hard to get rid of, and finishes such as varnish (see VARNISHING) show them up.

Do not use abrasives to remove paint and varnish. The heat generated by friction melts the paint, which clogs the abrasive and soon makes it useless. Strip a surface before sanding – see PAINT STRIPPING.

Types of abrasive available include:

Glasspaper (or sandpaper). Use it dry for woodwork that does not need to be very smooth, such as when rubbing down before painting. This is the cheapest abrasive.

Garnet paper A harder, better-quality abrasive, garnet is used for the fine finishing of furniture that is to be sealed, varnished or polished. Use it dry.

Emery paper or cloth Use them wet or dry according to the maker's instructions, for cleaning and finishing metal. Emery is tough but tends to clog easily. Use cloth on curved surfaces – tear off a strip and hold an end in each hand, working it back and forth.

Silicon-carbide paper Often called wet-and-dry, this paper can be used either way. Use it wet for removing the glaze

from paint before repainting – the water acts as a lubricant and also keeps down paint dust, which may contain lead.

Tungsten-carbide disc, block or file A casting of very tough material is brazed onto a metal backing to make these abrasive tools, which are available in coarse and fine grades. Use for coarse sanding or for removing paint.

Sanding pads These are foam blocks coated with an abrasive on the two large surfaces. Use wet for rubbing down paintwork before repainting (but not for paint removal). Use dry for smoothing curved and shaped surfaces.

Steel wool Graded by Os – the more Os, the finer the wool. Use fine grades, with white spirit as a lubricant, for taking the gloss off sealers and varnishes before re-coating. Very fine grades are also useful for removing scuff marks from vinyl floorcoverings. Never use coarse grades on woodwork.

Sanding by hand For smoothing curved and shaped areas use an abrasive sheet folded and shaped in the hand. For smoothing flat surfaces use an abrasive with self-adhesive backing and mount it on a rubber-faced hand-sanding block.

When rubbing down old paint and varnish for repainting, use a flexible-pad sander lubricated with clean water. For breaking up the surface of painted-over wall coverings, use a coarse-grade tungsten-carbide sanding block or file.

Power sanding Be extra careful when power sanding – it is easy to take off too much material. Use coarse abrasives for shaping and rounding, and fine ones for smooth finishing.

Power sanding is done either with an attachment to a power drill or with a tool made specially for sanding. Popular power-drill attachments are a disc sander, a drum sander, and a flapwheel. A disc sander is a flexible backing pad that holds a removable abrasive disc by either a screw and washer or self-adhesion. Keep it for rough work, as the disc always cuts across the grain of the wood, leaving marks which are hard to remove. A drum sander is a foam drum with a band of renewable abrasive fixed round it. Various grades of abrasive band are available.

A flapwheel consists of a spindle and core with numerous flaps of abrasive fitted round it. As the abrasive wears, it disintegrates, exposing new material, until the flaps are completely worn away. Various grades are available. Use it for cleaning and smoothing wood such as windowsills or furniture, or metal.

An orbital sander is available as either a drill attachment or (preferably) a separate tool. It has a very fine orbital movement that removes only a little material. Use it for fine finishing work on flat surfaces such as a table top.

A belt sander is a semi-professional tool that has a belt of abrasive rotated at fairly high speed. Use it for final smoothing after planing, for levelling floorboards, or for getting into corners where a floor sander cannot reach.

A floor sander is an industrial sanding machine that can be hired – see HIRING. Abrasive belts of various grades are supplied. Start with coarse for levelling and progress to fine for finishing. Use it for cleaning or stripping timber floors and levelling large areas of uneven floorboards. See also FLOOR REFINISHING; UNEVEN FLOORS.

Sandwiches

Making them tasty; keeping them fresh

Sandwich fillings can be very simple – such as sliced cucumber or hard-boiled EGGS. Or they can be rich and fancy – such as cream cheese and pineapple, or smoked salmon and lemon juice on thinly sliced brown bread.

For afternoon tea, sandwiches should be small and elegant, made of fresh or ready-sliced bread, with crusts removed. For other occasions, they can be as thin or as thick as you like – crusts and all.

Among the most popular types of sandwiches are:

Open sandwiches A Scandinavian speciality, they make an excellent breakfast. This Danish version has a preparation and cooking time of 20 minutes.

Ingredients (for 4 people)
4 slices black rye bread
Unsalted butter
4 eggs
1 tablespoon single cream and 1 tablespoon double cream *or*
2 tablespoons single cream or top of the milk
Salt and freshly ground black pepper
4 pickled herring fillets, flat or rolled
8 thin onion rings
4 small wedges of lemon
4 sprigs fennel or dillweed

Generously butter each slice of bread, up to the edges. Beat the eggs with half the cream (or top of the milk), and season with salt and pepper to taste. Heat 25g (1oz) of butter in a pan, add the egg mixture, and cook over a low heat. Stir constantly until the eggs form creamy flakes. Remove from the heat and stir in the remaining cream (or milk). Spoon onto the slices of thickly buttered bread. Top each one with a herring fillet, two onion rings, a wedge of lemon, and a sprig of fennel or dillweed.

Club sandwiches These hefty, tripledecker sandwiches originated in America. They have a preparation time of 15 minutes, and a cooking time of 5 minutes.

Ingredients (for 4 people)
12 slices white bread
50g (2oz) unsalted butter
4 small sliced tomatoes
8 rashers streaky bacon
8 small lettuce leaves
8 thin slices cooked chicken or turkey
4 level dessertspoons MAYONNAISE
4 stuffed olives (optional)

Toast the bread and remove the crusts; butter eight slices on one side, and the remaining four slices on both sides. Cover four of the partly buttered slices with tomato and top with the bacon, fried crisp and golden. Put the slices buttered on both sides on top of this, and cover with lettuce and cooked meat.

Spoon mayonnaise over the meat and cover with the last four slices of toast. Press the piled-up sandwiches firmly together and quarter them; spear each with a cocktail stick (with a stuffed olive on top if desired) and serve.

Fried sandwiches One of the most popular hot, fried sandwiches is the French croque-monsieur – consisting of grated cheese and ham. It has a preparation and cooking time of 20 minutes.

Ingredients (for 4 people)
8 pieces sliced bread
75g (3oz) butter
4 slices lean ham
115g (4oz) grated Cheddar cheese
Fat or oil for frying

Butter the bread and cover four separate slices with ham and cheese. Top with the remaining bread, and press the sandwiches firmly together. Remove the crusts and cut each sandwich into three fingers. Fry the bread fingers in hot fat until golden-brown on both sides. Drain onto absorbent paper before serving as a snack, hors d'oeuvre, or savoury.

Children's sandwiches For children's parties, make small sandwiches of thinly sliced white bread. Use biscuit-cutters to cut them into round, oval, or other fancy shapes. Butter the sandwiches lightly and spread them with a variety of fillings – such as sardine, cream cheese, egg and cress, meat and fish paste, honey, and Marmite.

Keeping sandwiches fresh Sandwiches taste best when eaten soon after they are made. But they can be kept fresh on plates by covering them with non-PVC clingfilm and storing in the refrigerator. This is effective for 6-8 hours. Alternatively, they can be kept fresh for a few hours in airtight sandwich tins.

Sand yachting

Sailing on land

This exhilarating sport is popular wherever there are wide, flat beaches, such as in North Devon, Cornwall, Lancashire, Wales, Scotland, east Yorkshire and Lincolnshire.

In its basic form, a sand yacht is an open seat on a three-wheeled tubular chassis with a mast and 5m² (54sq ft) of sail. A single sail is used, controlled in the same way as when SAILING on water, but instead of a rudder, the front wheel is steered.

More advanced designs have a slender body – often of fibreglass – and a sail area of up to 7.35m² (79sq ft).

These boats are capable of high speeds and delicate manoeuvres – a speed of 142.26km/h (88.4mph) was attained in America in 1976. The speeds attained by even simple sand yachts call for skill in handling and quick reaction. Even experienced dinghy sailors should seek advice or join a club to learn the art.

The British Federation of Sand and Land Yacht Clubs, 23 Piper Drive, Long Whatton, Loughborough, Leicestershire LE12 5DJ, can supply a list of clubs in Britain, together with other useful information about the sport.

Sashcords

Removing broken ones and fitting new

Sashcords usually fail with age, so if one breaks renew the other three as well. New sashcord is sold at most hardware shops; Terylene cord is best. You also need 25mm (1in) galvanised clout nails for securing the cord – see NAILING.

Removing the windows Remove the inside beading – see illustration. Use an old, broad chisel and work up and down from the centre – try not to damage the beading, as you will want to refit it.

Lift out the bottom sash, cutting an unbroken cord. Tie a length of string to the cut end so that you can feed it over the pulley to gently lower its weight. The string will also help when threading the new cord. If the cord is broken and the end lost, weight the string with a nail and feed it over the pulley. Next prise out the centre beading and lift out the upper sash. Use pincers to pull out the nails securing the cord to the window.

Fitting new cords Prise off or unscrew the pocket covers. Lift out the weights. Remove the old cord from them and cut new cords – see illustrations. Thread the new cords through the pulleys, using the string, then attach them to the weights. Lift the weights back into the boxes through the pockets. Refit the covers.

SASHCORDS

How to replace a broken cord in a sash window

First remove the sashes. Prise off the inside beading, then lift out the bottom sash. Cut cords. Tie string to cut or broken ends to lower a weight over its pulley. Remove the centre beading and upper sash. Remove pocket covers and lift out weights. Cut off old cords. Measure from the top of the window to the sill; add two-thirds again. Cut new cords to this length. Use string over pulleys to thread cords down to boxes and out through pockets.

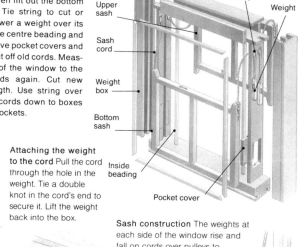

Upper sash

Pulley

Weight

Sash cord

Weight box

Bottom sash

Inside beading

Pocket cover

Attaching the weight to the cord Pull the cord through the hole in the weight. Tie a double knot in the cord's end to secure it. Lift the weight back into the box.

Sash construction The weights at each side of the window rise and fall on cords over pulleys to counterbalance the weight of the sashes.

Marking the sash Hold the sash against the top of the window. Mark on each side of the sash the mid-point of the pulley. Lower the sash to the sill.

Fixing cord to sash Nail the cord into the groove at the sash's side, below the mark indicating the position of the pulley.

Hold the upper (outer) sash against the top of the frame and mark on each side the mid-point position of the pulley. Lower the sash then pull down a cord until its weight is just touching the pulley. Wedge something – a pencil will do – into the pulley to hold the weight. Nail the cord to the sash as illustrated. Repeat on the other side.

Place the sash in position and check that it will rise smoothly to the top of the frame. Then tap in the centre beading.

Fix the bottom (inner) sash window to its cords in the same way, then refit the inside beading using 25mm (1in) oval nails. Before you drive the nails home, check the operation of the window. If it rattles, move the beading closer to the window.

Satellite television

Receiving it; getting the equipment

A variety of world sports, films, entertainment, news, foreign and children's programmes is now broadcast to Britain by various companies via the Astra television satellite.

To receive programmes from it, you need an outside dish aerial to intercept the satellite signals, an indoor receiver tuned to the different channels, and a television set.

The dish, typically 60 or 90 cm (2 or 3ft) in diameter, should be securely fixed and directed, clear of any obstructions, towards the satellite in the southern sky. Trees, hedges and buildings may all cause interference by blocking the satellite signals. Various systems are available and may be bought from high street electrical chain stores or specialist traders. Although you can install your own satellite system, by following the maker's instructions, you may prefer to have it installed professionally, bearing in mind the importance of correct positioning and the need to avoid any obstructions. The shop where you bought the system will put you in touch with installers, or arrange to have the dish installed themselves.

A cable links the outside dish to the receiver (located close to the television set), and a cable from the satellite receiver plugs into the aerial socket on the television set. Some satellite receivers have video and audio outputs and/or a SCART socket, which connect to similar inputs on the television set, providing superior picture and audio quality. More expensive systems incorporate a remote satellite controller, allowing the satellite dish to be moved over a wide angle to allow reception from other satellites.

Costs Basic systems start from around £200 plus installation charges, with multi-satellite systems costing around £750 plus installation.

Some satellite broadcasters charge for viewing their programmes by 'scrambling' the signal, so that only those who have paid for the service can watch the broadcast. Some satellite companies offer to add a channel temporarily, for perhaps one sports event. The subscriber can telephone the broadcaster and, by using a credit card for payment, request an additional channel or channels.

Sauces

Making basic sauces for meat and fish dishes

The three basic sauces are: white, used mainly for fish and poultry dishes; brown, mostly for red meat; and emulsion sauces, which are usually served with fish, chicken and vegetables.

White and brown sauces are thickened with a mixture of flour and fat known as a *roux*.

White sauces Easiest to make of the white sauces is *Béchamel*. It takes 20 minutes or so to prepare and 5-10 minutes to cook.

Ingredients – to make 285ml ($\frac{1}{2}$ pint)
285ml ($\frac{1}{2}$ pint) milk
$\frac{1}{2}$ small bay leaf
Sprig of thyme
$\frac{1}{2}$ small onion
$\frac{1}{4}$ level teaspoon grated nutmeg
25g (1oz) butter
25g (1oz) plain flour
Salt and black pepper
2-3 tablespoons single or double cream (optional)

Put the milk – together with the bay leaf, thyme, onion and nutmeg – in a saucepan and bring slowly to the boil. Remove from the heat, cover with a lid and leave the milk to steep for 15 minutes. Melt the butter in a heavy-based pan and stir in the flour to make the roux. Cook for 2-3 minutes, then remove the pan from the heat.

Strain the milk through a fine sieve and gradually blend it into the roux. Return the pan to the heat and bring to the boil, stirring continuously, then simmer for 2-3 minutes. Season with salt and pepper to taste – and, if wanted, stir in the cream.

Brown sauce One of the classic brown sauces is *Espagnole*. It takes 10 minutes to prepare and 1¼ hours to cook.

Ingredients – to make 285ml (½ pint)
1 carrot
1 onion
50g (2oz) green streaky bacon
25g (1oz) butter
25g (1oz) plain flour
450ml (¾ pint) brown stock – see STOCKS AND SAUCES
Bouquet garni
2 level tablespoons tomato paste
Salt and black pepper

Peel and dice the carrot and onion. Remove the rind and gristle from the bacon and chop the rashers. Melt the butter in a heavy-based pan, put in the vegetables and bacon and cook over a low heat for 10 minutes – or until light brown.

Blend in the flour, stirring the roux until brown. Gradually blend in 285ml (½ pint) stock, stirring constantly until the mixture has cooked through and thickened. Add the bouquet garni, cover with a lid and set a fireproof mat under the pan. Simmer for 30 minutes, then add the remaining stock and the tomato paste.

Cover the pan again and continue cooking for 30 minutes, stirring frequently. Strain the sauce through a sieve, skim off the fat, and season with salt and pepper to taste.

Emulsion sauces One of the simplest of these rich sauces is *Hollandaise*, which has a preparation and cooking time of 20 minutes. See also MAYONNAISE.

Ingredients – to make 285ml (½ pint)
3 tablespoons white wine vinegar
1 tablespoon water
6 black peppercorns
1 bay leaf
3 egg yolks
175g (6oz) soft butter
Salt and black pepper

Boil the vinegar and water with the peppercorns and bay leaf in a small pan, until reduced to about 1 tablespoon. Leave to cool.

Cream the egg yolks with 15g (½oz) softened butter and a pinch of salt. Strain the vinegar into the egg mixture and set the bowl over a pan of boiling water. Turn off the heat. Then whisk in the remaining butter, 7g (¼oz) at a time, until the sauce is shiny and has the consistency of thick cream. Season with salt and pepper to taste.

If the sauce thickens too quickly during cooking, remove it from the heat and add 1 tablespoon of warm water. If it is too thin, put 1 teaspoon of the sauce into a warm bowl and beat until thick. Then beat in the rest of the sauce, ½ a tablespoon at a time. If the Hollandaise

curdles during cooking, remove it from the heat and beat in 1 tablespoon of cold water, a little at a time, until the sauce becomes smooth. If this fails, beat an egg yolk in a clean pan until it thickens. Then gradually beat in the curdled sauce until smooth.

Sauerkraut

Making pickled cabbage at home

Sauerkraut is shredded cabbage which has been salted and left to ferment. The name means 'pickled cabbage' in German. To make it yourself, quarter, core and finely shred 2.7kg (6lb) of firm, white cabbage. Wash and scald a 4.5 litre (1 gallon) earthenware pot. Pack the cabbage and 2oz (50g) of sea salt into the pot in layers, finishing with a layer of salt. Press it down with a wooden spoon or potato masher. The brine that forms should cover the cabbage.

Cover with a clean cloth, its edges tucked into the pot. Then place a hot, snugly fitting plate in the pot over the cloth. Weight it down so that the brine comes up to, but not over, the plate. Let the cabbage ferment in a cool place – under 15°C (59°F) – for 5-6 weeks. It will ferment faster at a higher temperature, but will not be as good. When bubbles stop rising to the surface, the fermentation is over.

Remove scum from the top of the brine daily and wash or replace the cloth. At the end of the period, store the sauerkraut, still weighted down in its pot, in a cool cellar or larder until wanted.

Before use, rinse the sauerkraut and then soak it for 10-20 minutes to remove the harsh flavour. Drain it well. It can then be eaten raw, but is more usually cooked. One way to cook it is to put it in a pan with just enough water, or wine, to cover and then simmer it for 15-30 minutes. It is often flavoured with caraway seeds, juniper berries or apple. Sauerkraut goes well with veal escalopes, pot roasts, stews and German sausages.

Saunas

Getting maximum benefit; taking precautions

A Finnish tradition, the sauna is a steambath taken in a room lined with untreated, moisture-absorbing timber. The temperature should not rise higher than 79°C (174°F).

The heat raises the skin temperature above the normal body temperature of 37°C (98.6°F), increasing the flow of blood to the skin's surface. The sweat glands open, cleansing pores in areas that do not normally perspire. The process is designed to relax the bather, easing

aches and pains and cleansing the skin.

Before taking a sauna, remove clothes, spectacles or contact lenses and jewellery. Wear a loosely draped towel and sit on another thick towel. Stay in for 5-15 minutes – or less if you feel uncomfortably hot or breathless. Then leave, take a short swim or a shower in tepid water, and return for 5-10 minutes. Leave again and take another swim or shower – then have a 20 minute rest so that you cool down thoroughly. Do not go straight from the sauna into cold air – this can cause a dangerously rapid rise in blood pressure. Drink at least 1 litre (2 pints) of water to replace body fluids lost through perspiration.

You can have a sauna installed at home, or build one yourself from prefabricated parts – look under 'Sauna and solarium equipment' in *Yellow Pages*.

WARNING Saunas should not be used by people with high or low blood pressure, with heart conditions, diabetes – or with any kind of illness. They should also be avoided by the elderly and by pregnant women.

Sausage making

Giving them extra flavours

You can make your own sausages to your taste – either plain or with added herbs and spices. Sausage skins can often be bought from butchers, but if not you can always make the sausages without skins. Use a kitchen mincer or food processor (see FOOD PROCESSORS) to mince the meat yourself.

This recipe for herb sausages takes up to an hour to prepare, depending on your skill in filling the skins. Following it is a recipe for adding a spicy flavour to ready-made sausages.

Ingredients (for 20 large herb sausages)
900g (2lb) lean beef or pork, finely minced
350g (12oz) shredded suet
225g (8oz) fresh white breadcrumbs
1 level teaspoon dried sage
½ teaspoon dried marjoram
½ teaspoon dried thyme
¼ teaspoon grated nutmeg
1½ level teaspoons salt
½ teaspoon freshly ground black pepper
Sausage skins (synthetic or real)

Mix the ingredients together thoroughly in a bowl. To put the mixture into the skins, use a forcing bag with a long, wide nozzle. Knot one end of a length of skin 1m (3ft) long. Place the other end over the nozzle and push it on until the knot is as near the nozzle as possible.

Force the meat in, drawing the filled skin back from the nozzle. Do not overstuff. Knot the open end and twist the filled skin every 75-100mm (3-4in). Stuff the other skins. Leave in a cool place for up to an hour to set. They can be stored in a refrigerator for 2-3 days.

To cook, pierce with a fork to prevent them from bursting during cooking, then fry or grill for 12-15 minutes, turning once. To cook the mixture without skins, shape it into sausages, roll them lightly in flour, and then fry them.

Ingredients (spicy sausages for 4)
450g (1lb) plain beef or pork sausages
2 tablespoons olive oil
2 level tablespoons tomato ketchup
2 level teaspoons English mustard
½ teaspoon Worcestershire sauce
Salt and black pepper

Use ready-made sausages, or make your own as described above – but without the herbs. Prick the sausages all over with a fork. Lay them in a single layer in a roasting tin or ovenproof dish. Mix together the oil, ketchup, mustard and Worcestershire sauce in a bowl. Season with salt and pepper and pour the mixture over the sausages. Leave them to marinate for at least an hour, turning occasionally.

Bake in the centre of a hot oven, preheated to 200°C (400°F, gas mark 6) for 20 minutes. Baste them frequently until they are well browned. Serve hot with mashed potatoes and grilled tomatoes, or cold in buttered rolls with a leafy salad as accompaniment.

Saving

Putting your spare cash away for the future

If you wish to save up for a particular purpose – perhaps a car, furniture, holiday or wedding reception – you can open a special deposit account with your bank (see BANK ACCOUNTS) or an account with a building society (see BUILDING SOCIETIES) expressly for that purpose, and pay in a sum every month or week. The accumulated money will be there in full whenever you want to withdraw it – and it will have earned some interest in the meantime.

Other ways of putting money aside safely, with longer-term interest gains, include NATIONAL SAVINGS and Save As You Earn (SAYE) schemes.

SAYE Most building societies offer schemes for regular savers. You pay in a regular amount each month and at the end of the fifth and seventh years are entitled to bonuses, which are free of tax and are not affected by fluctuations in interest rates. Alternatively, you can pay a lump sum to the building society initially and they will transfer the appropriate amount into the SAYE account every month.

Unit-linked savings plans These are available from life INSURANCE companies or via insurance brokers. You pay in a monthly sum and the company invests it in UNIT TRUSTS – see INVESTING.

School fees plans These are available from specialist agencies and from some insurance companies and most brokers. If you wish to save up enough money to educate your child or grandchild privately, pay monthly instalments (or a lump sum) in advance into a scheme which will meet the full fees, or part of the fees, when the child is of school age. You do not have to specify which school at the outset and, as with life insurance policies and pension plans, the earlier you initiate a scheme, the greater the saving.

It is no longer possible to gain tax advantages by making a COVENANT in favour of another person such as a grandchild, or child over the age of 18.

Fixed-term savings plans These are offered by a number of insurance companies. You make monthly payments over a period of ten years or more and a guaranteed sum, usually plus bonuses, is paid to you at the end of the period or when you reach a specified age. The younger you are when you start such a scheme, the larger the guaranteed sum and bonuses will be.

Take advice However you decide to save, remember that interest rates and the value of stocks can fall, as well as rise. Also, tax regulations may alter, new savings schemes are constantly being offered, and a form of saving advantageous for one individual may be less so for another. It is therefore wise to obtain advice – from an accountant or bank manager. See also ANNUITIES; PENSIONS.

Saws and sawing

Choosing and using hand and power saws

The secret of successful sawing is to hold the work securely and to use the right saw for the job. A vice or clamps can be used to hold small pieces of wood, and saw horses to hold longer pieces, but the most versatile support is the folding portable workbench. This has a vice running the full length of the workbench top which will grip anything from a small piece of wood to a whole door.

Sheet materials need firm clamping at a number of points while being sawed. The cut section should also be supported, so that it does not break off and leave a splintered edge.

Hand saws There are two main types of

hand saw – those with flexible blades for cutting wood to size, and those with braced blades – usually having smaller teeth – for more accurate cutting.

Hardpoint saws have hardened teeth, and in normal DIY use will never need sharpening. Saws are also available with coated blades that reduce friction considerably, so making sawing easier.

Using a hand saw Grip a hand saw with your index finger extended along the side of the handle, and push from the shoulder – see illustration overleaf.

If the teeth do not bite into the wood, they need sharpening – see SHARPENING HAND TOOLS. If the saw wanders to one side, the teeth need repositioning with a purpose-made tool called a saw set.

Always mark a cutting line on the wood. Saw just on the waste wood side of the line; if you saw along the line itself, the workpiece will be fractionally too small. If sawing a coated board – such as veneered or melamine CHIPBOARD – score a deep cutting line on all four edges with a sharp knife held against a straightedge. Saw from the top, as the underside of the board may chip slightly.

Flexible hand saws The most common flexible saws are the crosscut, panel saw and ripsaw. A crosscut saw has its teeth sharpened at an angle of about 70 degrees on each edge, so they cut in both directions. Use the saw to cut across the grain of timber. It is about 640mm (25in) long and has six to eight teeth per 25mm (1in). Use it at an angle of about 45 degrees to the wood. A panel saw is a smaller version – about 510mm (20in) long and with ten teeth per 25mm. Use it for sheet materials such as PLYWOOD.

Ripsaw This has its teeth sharpened at right angles to the blade. It is about 650mm (25½in) long with five teeth per 25mm (1in). Use it to cut along the grain of the wood, working at a steep angle – about 60 degrees.

General-purpose saw A plastic handle which can be angled to suit the work in hand is common on this type. Its blade is designed to cut either wood or metal – or both together. Use this saw for cutting secondhand or scrap timber which could have hidden nails in it. Take great care if you use it to cut floorboards – it will cut through pipes and cables very easily.

Padsaw Also called a keyhole or compass saw, this is used for awkward interior cuts such as KEYHOLES or making a square cut-out in PLASTERBOARD. Fit the blade with its teeth sloping forward; some padsaws take a range of blades, including broken hacksaw blades. Drill a start hole in the waste part of the wood, then saw using short, gentle strokes.

Rigid hand saws The tenon saw is the most widely used type. It has a steel or brass strip folded along the top edge to keep the blade rigid, and is usually 250mm (10in) long with 14 or more teeth per 25mm (1in). A dovetail saw is a smaller version. These are the saws to use for cutting WOODWORKING JOINTS.

Coping saw A bow-shaped metal frame and handle is used to hold a thin, fine-toothed blade which is secured by clamping. Keep the tension on the blade tight. The blade holders can be swivelled so the saw can cut in any direction. For normal work, have the cutting teeth facing forwards so that you cut on the push stroke. For very thin materials, set the teeth backwards and cut on the pull stroke. To make an internal cut, first drill a hole through the wood. Thread the blade through, then connect it to the saw frame.

Fretsaw The frame holding the fine-toothed blade is deeply bowed, so that you can cut well into a thin piece of wood. The blade is secured at each end by a thumb screw. Clamp the wood flat, so that the area to be cut overhangs the bench. Cut with the handle below the work and with the teeth facing the handle. Use short, steady strokes.

Hacksaw This cuts most metals and also plastic pipes. It has a bow frame and handle, into which blades are inserted with teeth pointing forwards. Some frames are adjustable to take different blade lengths. There is a range of tooth sizes and spacing; as a general rule use fine teeth for sawing thin sheet materials, and coarse teeth for soft materials like aluminium. There are Junior and Mini hacksaws for fine cutting, and for working in confined spaces.

Sheet saw This is used to cut large sheets of metal, where a hacksaw cannot be used because the frame limits the length of cut. It resembles a rigid saw, but has a hacksaw blade attached to its cutting edge.

Log saw This garden saw has a tough tubular-steel frame to hold a steel blade. Sizes range from 610mm (2ft) to 910mm (3ft). The teeth are designed to cut the wood and clear the sawdust. The blade cuts equally well on both push and pull strokes.

Pruning saw A simple handle holds a curved blade which has teeth facing backwards, so you only cut on the pull or downward stroke.

Power saws For safety, always plug a power saw into a plug-in CIRCUIT BREAKER. Unplug the saw whenever you are not actually using it. Always use a sharp, unbent blade and fit it the correct way round. Keep the cable well away from the blade.

Wear safety goggles to protect your

SAWS AND SAWING

Using each kind of hand or power saw efficiently and safely

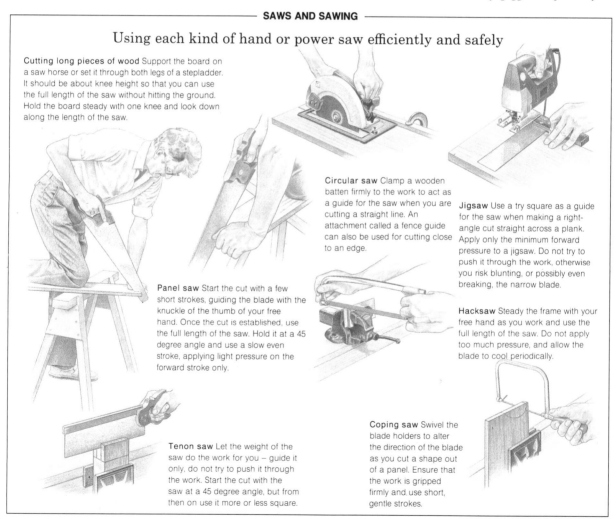

Cutting long pieces of wood Support the board on a saw horse or set it through both legs of a stepladder. It should be about knee height so that you can use the full length of the saw without hitting the ground. Hold the board steady with one knee and look down along the length of the saw.

Circular saw Clamp a wooden batten firmly to the work to act as a guide for the saw when you are cutting a straight line. An attachment called a fence guide can also be used for cutting close to an edge.

Jigsaw Use a try square as a guide for the saw when making a right-angle cut straight across a plank. Apply only the minimum forward pressure to a jigsaw. Do not try to push it through the work, otherwise you risk blunting, or possibly even breaking, the narrow blade.

Panel saw Start the cut with a few short strokes, guiding the blade with the knuckle of the thumb of your free hand. Once the cut is established, use the full length of the saw. Hold it at a 45 degree angle and use a slow even stroke, applying light pressure on the forward stroke only.

Hacksaw Steady the frame with your free hand as you work and use the full length of the saw. Do not apply too much pressure, and allow the blade to cool periodically.

Tenon saw Let the weight of the saw do the work for you – guide it only, do not try to push it through the work. Start the cut with the saw at a 45 degree angle, but from then on use it more or less square.

Coping saw Swivel the blade holders to alter the direction of the blade as you cut a shape out of a panel. Ensure that the work is gripped firmly and use short, gentle strokes.

eyes from fragments and sawdust. Make sure that the blade cannot damage anything underneath it. See also POWER TOOL SAFETY.

Using power saws Hold the saw back from the wood, press the trigger, and when the saw reaches full speed, start the cut. For a clean cut, set the cutting depth 3mm ($\frac{1}{8}$in) deeper than the wood.

Do not force the saw along – you will only slow down the blade, which needs to be at full speed to work best. When the cut is finished, allow the blade to stop before removing it from the wood.

Power saws cut from underneath or on the upstroke. Because of this, you should put coated boards face down for cutting; score the face with a sharp knife and draw a guide line on the reverse for following with the saw.

Circular saw Although these are available as attachments to an electric drill, it is better to use a purpose-made one, which is more powerful.

Use the saw for straight cuts in TIMBER and board. However, it is limited by the maximum depth of cut – normally 48mm ($1\frac{7}{8}$in) on a 150mm (6in) blade. Blades may be set to cut to full or partial depth, or to cut at a given angle.

A selection of blades is available – for general sawing of timber and boards; for finer cutting across the grain of hardwood and softwood; for coarse cutting with the grain of the wood; for very fine cuts on all timber and board; for cutting abrasive materials like CHIPBOARD where the bonding material would quickly blunt an ordinary blade; for cutting copper, lead and brass or other alloys; and for cutting masonry and ceramics.

Jigsaw More versatile than a circular saw, a jigsaw will take a range of blades for cutting wood, plaster, metal, leather and rubber. The saw can have variable speed, a dust extractor, a swivelling head to cut curves, and a pivoting and retractable sole plate.

Reciprocating saw Also known as the power sabre saw, this relatively new tool is really a powered hand saw. It will cut a variety of materials, from thick tree branches to metal tubing. You need both hands to hold it. See also CHAIN SAWS; SHARPENING HAND TOOLS.

Scaffold tower

Working safely at heights

The scaffold tower has a number of advantages over a ladder, particularly when you are working on the outside of your house. It offers a platform where you can stand comfortably and move freely; it gives you somewhere to put your tools

---

Working on a safe base

Check that any wheels on the scaffold tower can be firmly locked; also that the platform has movable planks, a guard rail, and a toe board to prevent you from accidentally knocking tools over the side.

and materials while working; and perhaps most important of all, it lets you work in perfect safety at height while using both hands.

You may not use a tower often, so decide whether it is economic to buy one outright; whether you have neighbours or relatives who would share the cost and therefore the use, or whether it would be better to rent one from a hire centre – see HIRING.

The scaffold comes in easily handled H sections, made either of steel or alloy tubing, which slot into each other. Half-section frames are available as extras. Use them to make a narrower tower if a passage is not wide enough for a full one; they can also be used for indoors to work on a staircase.

Two people should be able to set up a 4m (13ft) scaffold tower in about ten minutes. Make sure the tower is stable and level: base plates at the feet are

---

adjustable and you can put paving slabs or stout boards under the feet on soft ground. Outriggers give extra stability.

Always anchor the tower to the house. Place a plank across the inside of an open window and rope the scaffold securely to the plank. A rainwater downpipe is *not* a safe anchor point. A tower that has wheels is easy to move on level ground, but the wheels must lock to fix them securely when the scaffold is in use.

Always climb up the inside of the tower; do not have your weight outside it. Do not lean forwards or sideways from the tower to reach the work. Set up the tower against one area of the work spot; when you have completed work on that area, climb down and move the scaffold along to the next window or section of gutter, for example, making sure that you anchor it to the house again.

Scalds

Treating and preventing injuries

Soothe minor scalds by immediately running cold water over them until the pain begins to subside. Then cover them gently with a sterile gauze dressing or a piece of clean linen, taking care not to break any BLISTERS. Do not apply lotions, creams, butter or other fats.

For severe scalds, remove any saturated clothing that has not become stuck to the skin, cutting it if necessary. Cool the injury with cold water and cover it with a sterile dressing or clean cloth, and get immediate medical help.

Guard against scalds to young children by ensuring that your cooker has a protective rail round the hob, by turning the handles of saucepans away from the edges of the cooker, and by placing an electric kettle well above the child's reach, with the spout facing a wall. Do not allow a kettle flex to trail where a child can grab it. See also CHILD SAFETY; BURNS.

Scars and blemishes

Getting cosmetic surgery; what it can and cannot do

Cosmetic surgery can be obtained under the National Health Service, which employs consultant plastic surgeons. They mainly correct embarrassing deformities and disfigurements such as scars and blemishes, misshapen noses, bags under the eyes, sagging jowls and tattoo marks.

Cosmetic surgery can rarely be performed without leaving a scar but the scar may be slight, or hidden near the hairline, for example.

To obtain treatment, consult your DOCTOR. If he feels that cosmetic surgery would be beneficial – physically or psychologically – he will recommend an operation and arrange for you to see a consultant. However, the wait may be a year or more.

To avoid this delay, you can be operated on in a private clinic specialising in such work. Ask your doctor to recommend a reputable clinic, where the consultant surgeon is fully trained and qualified. He should be a Fellow of the Royal College of Surgeons, with the initials FRCS after his name. If in any doubt, look up his qualifications in *The Medical Directory* in any public library.

What cosmetic surgery can do There are five main ways in which you can benefit:
● Surgery can often improve – but not remove – an ugly scar. Most deep scars are permanent; but they can be cut out and the surrounding skin sewn neatly together. This leaves the area flatter and less unsightly.
● Moles and some birthmarks and pockmarks can be removed.
● Excess skin can be removed from the face, eyelids, breasts, stomach, thighs, buttocks and hips.
● Small breasts can be made bigger by inserting a silicone implant behind the breasts.
● The breasts, chin, nose and stomach can be made smaller or more symmetrical.

What cosmetic surgery cannot do It cannot – despite popular belief – make anyone look younger than they are. But it *can* prevent them from looking older than they are. For example, it can turn an ageing 60-year-old into a well-preserved 60-year-old.

Surgery cannot, simply by changing someone's appearance, make them any more successful – personally or professionally – than they are. For example, a 'new' nose will not necessarily ensure promotion, or save an unhappy marriage.

Nor can surgery turn a patient into someone he is not, or into someone he admires. For example, surgery cannot reproduce an 'ideal' chin from a photograph of a film star or a fashion model.

Birthmarks, such as 'port-wine stains', cannot be removed, but can be well disguised by ordinary COSMETICS.

The risks and the cost In skilled hands, only about 2 per cent of cosmetic surgery operations in Britain end in failure. Even so, there is always the risk of infection and excessive bleeding. There is also a slight risk of wound breakdown, delayed healing, and the build-up of blood beneath the skin – which may spoil the result of face-lifts and so on.

In 1994, the average cost in a private clinic of a nose operation was £2500, and a full face-lift about £4000.

Scavenger hunts

Organising search-and-find games for children or adults

A scavenger hunt is a good way to break the ice at a children's party, or occupy a group during a school or club outing.

Hide items of 'buried treasure' or select a number of objects within a defined area, then hand each team a list of objects (either the same or different) to bring back within a limited time.

The objects may be commonplace or out-of-the-ordinary; the area, can be a room, house, garden or the countryside; and the time may be measured in minutes, hours or days. To make the hunt more of a challenge, instead of listing the objects by name, provide mysterious or amusing clues for the competitors to puzzle out.

The winning team is the first to return with all the objects – or, if they fail to find everything on the list, the one that has brought back the largest number of objects when time is up.

A variation – designed to keep children amused on a long car journey – is a roadside scavenger hunt. The objects are things that can be spotted through the car window – the children jot them down with a pen or pencil and note pad. See also HALLOWEEN GAMES; TRAVEL WITH CHILDREN.

Scents

Infusing your own toilet waters

Infusions of fragrant herbs or flowers can be made and bottled easily and cheaply, using white wine vinegar as the infusing agent.

Lavender has always been popular for its refreshing scent; fill a bottle or jar with lavender flowers and cover them with white wine vinegar. Leave the bottle in a warm, sunny place for two weeks, shaking it daily.

Strain the vinegar and set it aside. Refill the bottle with fresh flowers, and cover them with the strained vinegar. Repeat the infusion procedure, and then a third time, making three infusions in all. Strain and bottle.

Sweet violets Fill a jar with violet blossoms and cover them with white wine vinegar. Seal the jar and leave in a warm place for four or five weeks, then strain the scented vinegar and bottle.

A fragrant refresher Infuse 115g (4oz) of rose petals and 25g (1oz) each of violet, jasmine and lavender flowers in white wine vinegar, with 285ml ($\frac{1}{2}$ pint) rose-water added. Tightly seal the bottle and leave it in a warm place for two or three weeks, then strain the scent and put it into smaller bottles.

Schools

Getting the best for your children

State schools are maintained and managed by their governors either on local authority funds or with direct grants from the government. All schools now control their own admissions policies. Voluntary schools, which are partly church-run, can take children's religions into account.

Discovering what is available Get a list of schools in your area from the local education authority. Draw up a short list, ask each for a prospectus, and arrange to visit them.

Assessing the school atmosphere You will start forming an impression of the school from the first moment of your enquiry – how it is dealt with, for example. Does the school head seem enthusiastic when talking to you about the school? Does the head's attitude to staff, and that of the staff to the pupils, seem friendly or formal? Is class control good when you visit? Is there an active School Association?

Assessing the curriculum Find out the range of subjects taught, and what options there are for specialising in various subjects. Does there appear to be an emphasis on arts subjects rather than science? How many modern languages are taught? Are there music, drama and craft classes? What kind of religious education is provided?

Ask or check in the prospectus if there is a library, a laboratory and provision for computer training. The choice of games may be important to the child – also the outside activities available.

Find out the average number of children taking and passing GCSE exams, and how many go on to take A or AS levels. This information should be in the prospectus, or available from the school head. Check on the careers advice available, and see what you think of it.

Choosing a school You may be refused the school you want because it is full, or because another school is nearer your home. You can appeal to the local education authority.

Your appeal will be heard by a local appeal committee. The school should have published an admissions policy showing how it decides to let children in. Usually, preference is given to brothers and sisters, and to children living nearby. Ask to see the policy, and prepare to argue before the appeal committee why your child should be admitted on the basis of that policy. Get medical or other evidence to support your appeal if you think this will help.

If you choose to pay to send your child to an independent school, ask at your local library for a book listing them.

SCISSORS

Correcting and tightening the blades

Restoring the curve Hold the blade in a vice between three equally spaced wood blocks. Tighten the vice slightly so that the centre of the blade is forced outwards.

Tightening loose joints Gently tighten the pivot screw with a screwdriver. Place the screw head on a solid metal surface. Hit the other end with the pein of a ball-pein hammer (see HAMMERS) until flattened.

Scissors

Keeping them in good repair

Do not allow scissors to be misused. Use them only for the cutting jobs for which they were designed – manicuring, food preparation, paper-hanging, needlework.

Blunt cutting edges Grip a steel knitting needle or the neck of a glass bottle with the cutting edges, and run them backwards and forwards a few times to renew the edges. Sharpen totally blunt scissor blades with a fine slipstone, held at right angles to the face of the blade. See also SHARPENING HAND TOOLS.

Damaged edges Run your nail along each blade, if it snags on damage to the edges use the slipstone to remove the snag. Apply a little oil to the stone, then rub it over the inner face of the blade until it is quite smooth.

Flattened blade Scissors are designed with a blade set so that it rubs for its full length against the other blade. This is what makes the scissors cut. Gently bend the blade in a vice, as illustrated.

Loose pivot joint The smaller the scissors, the more common this problem. Tighten the pivot joint as illustrated, then check and tighten it further if necessary until the scissors operate tightly but easily.

Scones

Making a teatime treat

Freshly baked scones, served hot and buttery or sandwiched with cream and strawberry jam, are quick and easy to prepare.

Ingredients (for 12 scones)
225g (8oz) plain flour
Pinch of salt
$\frac{1}{2}$ level teaspoon bicarbonate of soda
1 level teaspoon cream of tartar
40g ($1\frac{1}{2}$oz) firm margarine
About 4 tablespoons each milk and water, mixed
Milk for glazing

Preheat the oven to 220°C (450°F), gas mark 7. Sieve the flour, salt, bicarbonate of soda and cream of tartar into a wide bowl. Cut up the margarine and rub it into the flour. Using a round-bladed knife, mix in enough milk and water to give a soft dough.

Knead the dough lightly on a floured surface. Roll it out to a thickness of 13mm ($\frac{1}{2}$in). Cut out the scones with a 50mm (2in) pastry cutter and place on a warmed, ungreased baking tray.

Brush the scones with milk and bake on the top shelf of the oven for 10 minutes, or until they are well risen and light golden brown.

For fruit scones, mix in 25g (1oz) sugar and 50g (2oz) sultanas before the milk and water.

Scratch marks

Removing them from furniture

A light scratch in wax-polished wood can often be rubbed gently away with fine sandpaper or garnet paper dipped in linseed oil, then blended into its surroundings with wax furniture polish.

If the scratch is deep, it can be removed only by stripping the whole surface and applying a new finish (see FRENCH POLISHING; VARNISHING) or VENEER. Alternatively, you may be able to disguise it by rubbing in beeswax coloured with a wood stain (see STAINING WOOD) slightly darker than the damaged surface. Let the wax set, then rub it into the scratch. After a few hours, polish with wax polish.

If the surface is varnished, apply varnish mixed with methylated spirit as illustrated. Level it with fine glasspaper, or wet-and-dry abrasive paper used dry.

SCRATCH MARKS

Disguising scratches; raising small dents

Scratches On varnished wood, use a soft watercolour brush to apply diluted varnish along the scratch in the grain's direction. Let it dry, then apply more. Repeat until the surface is slightly raised.

Dents Cover the area of the dent with a damp cloth. Iron over it, keeping the iron moving. Leave for a few hours to let the wood swell. Iron again if necessary.

Wipe away the dust, then restore the gloss by rubbing gently with wax polish. Methylated spirit has no effect on polyurethane varnish or cellulose lacquer, but these are not easily scratched.

Filling dents Use a wood filler of a matching colour – see STOPPERS AND FILLERS. Or melt coloured beeswax in a spoon and drip it into the dent; when it cools, shave off any excess with a razor blade and smooth the area with fine glasspaper before repolishing.

Alternatively, try filling the dent by swelling the wood with a damp cloth and iron (see illustration), but make sure the wood is not a veneer. When the wood has swelled, level and repolish.

Screws

Choosing the right screw for the job; fitting and removing

There is a myth that the harder it is to drive in a screw, the tighter the screw will hold. It is quite untrue – in fact too tight a fit can split the wood.

Screws are made of a variety of materials including mild steel, brass, cop-

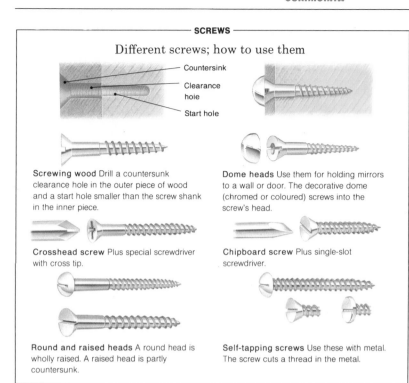

SCREWS

Different screws; how to use them

Countersink
Clearance hole
Start hole

Screwing wood Drill a countersunk clearance hole in the outer piece of wood and a start hole smaller than the screw shank in the inner piece.

Crosshead screw Plus special screwdriver with cross tip.

Round and raised heads A round head is wholly raised. A raised head is partly countersunk.

Dome heads Use them for holding mirrors to a wall or door. The decorative dome (chromed or coloured) screws into the screw's head.

Chipboard screw Plus single-slot screwdriver.

Self-tapping screws Use these with metal. The screw cuts a thread in the metal.

---

per, gunmetal and aluminium. They may be black japanned, galvanised or plated with nickel, tin, zinc or chromium. Standard screws have a single start thread, but some have a twin-start thread, which almost halves the number of turns needed to drive the screw in. These screws are also hardened, so can be safely driven with a power tool.

Apart from the length, a screw size is determined by the diameter of its shank – and this is referred to as the gauge. You can find the gauge by measuring across the screw head in sixteenths of an inch. Double this measurement and subtract two, to find the gauge. For example, a No 8 gauge screw measures $^5/_{16}$in across. Five by two gives 10; minus two is 8. The smaller the gauge number, the finer the screw. The screws most used for general purpose work are No 8s, and No 10s for heavier fixing jobs. The type of screw head required depends upon the nature of the work. There are five main types:

Countersunk The screw head is bevelled to the shank, and recesses into a countersunk hole so that it lies flush with, or just below, the surface.

Raised head Part of the head is countersunk, but a raised section is visible.

Round head. Mainly used for metal fittings which have no countersinks in screw holes. The heads remain above the work and can look decorative.

Dome head This has a threaded hole in the centre of the head into which a decorative dome can be screwed.

Clutch head This is a special security screw that can be tightened, but offers no grip for unscrewing it. Use with any fitting, like a hasp and staple, where you want it to be impossible to remove.

These designs (apart from the clutch head and dome head) are available as single-slot screws, or as cross-slot.

Screws called self-tapping screws are also used for metalwork. When fitted into a hole of recommended size, they are tough enough to cut their own thread, giving a secure fixing. They are often supplied with security devices for fixing to metal window frames.

Where heavy sections of timber are to be joined use coach screws – heavy-duty screws with nut heads screwed into a start hole with a spanner.

Fitting a screw Make a clearance hole in the piece to be fixed, slightly larger than the shank of the screw. Then bore a countersink with a countersink bit if the screw is to be recessed. Drill a start hole – just smaller than the shank of the screw – in the second piece of wood.

Removing a screw To remove a stubborn screw, try clamping a self-grip wrench to the shaft of a standard screwdriver, or use a carpenter's brace fitted with a suitable screwdriver bit. If this fails, use an impact driver. This is a tool with a selection of screwdriver blades. Hitting the handle with a hammer not only jolts the blade, but also turns it anticlockwise. The tool can also be adjusted to turn clockwise to tighten screws hard.

If a screw is rusted in, apply penetrating oil and leave for at least six hours. There are also proprietary chemical releasing agents that will dissolve RUST in a matter of minutes. If this fails, apply a hot soldering iron (see SOLDERING AND BRAZING) to the head. The heat will cause it to expand, breaking the rust bond and allowing the screw to be turned. As a last resort, drill off the screw head, remove the fitting, then unscrew the rest with a self-grip wrench.

QUICK TIP Smear woodscrews with petroleum jelly to make them easier to drive in and unscrew.

Scrimshaw

Engraving bones the sailors' way

Whalers used to carve or engrave designs on whale bones or teeth, or on walrus or narwhal tusks, and pick out the inscribed lines in black ink, soot or tobacco juice. This scrimshaw work, as it is called, is quite easy to do yourself.

SCRIMSHAW

Engraving and painting horn and bone

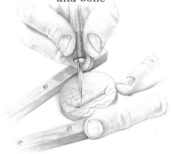

Wedge the piece between two strips of wood screwed down in a V shape. Engrave the design with a craft knife, penknife or bradawl.

Apply colour with a fine watercolour brush. Wipe off excess colour from the surface with a soft cloth. When dry, polish the surface with grade 0 steel wool.

Materials and tools Whalebone is no longer available, but animal bones, cow horns, deer antlers or even SHELLS can be used; or you may have old ivory knife handles or piano keys which can be used. Alternatively, some plastic surfaces, such as imitation ivory, are suitable.

Boil bones or antlers for several hours to remove all traces of flesh and dirt. Buff them with grade 0 steel wool and seal with clear polyurethane varnish – see VARNISHING. Cut the piece to size with a hacksaw, and position it on the work surface as illustrated.

Engraving a design Plan the design on paper and trace it onto the surface to be carved (see PATTERN TRANSFER) or lay the design on the surface and prick through to mark the lines at essential points. Then sketch the design in with a soft pencil.

Cut the heaviest lines of the design first, using firm, even pressure. Then add detail. For shading, scratch light parallel lines or crosshatching, making the lines close together for deeper shading.

Paint the design using any medium that will not run if it gets wet.

Scuba diving

Underwater swimming with your own air supply

The term scuba comes from the initial letters of Self-Contained Underwater Breathing Apparatus, and the sport has boomed in recent years.

The apparatus consists of one or more compressed air cylinders (usually referred to as 'air bottles' or 'air tanks'), and a mouthpiece connected to an automatic air supply regulator ('demand valve').

The regulator supplies air to the lungs at a pressure equivalent to that of the surrounding water. Exhaled air floats straight up to the surface as bubbles. The length of time you can stay underwater is governed by the depth at which you are diving and the capacity of your tank.

An air supply that will last an hour at the surface is enough only for a half-hour dive at 6m (20ft), or 20 minutes at 18m (60ft). Except in warm, shallow water, you will need to wear a neoprene (synthetic rubber) wet suit to protect you from cold. Most watersport shops hire out the necessary breathing equipment – commonly called an aqualung – and wet suits. Most divers use an aqualung with two air tanks and wear a lifejacket (see SAILING) inflatable by means of a small cylinder of compressed air for emergency surfacing.

Before making your first dive, you must complete a training course with a qualified instructor. Many watersport shops will refuse to hire out aqualungs

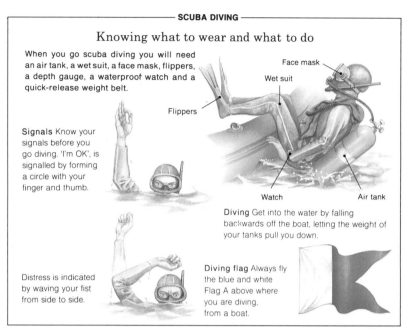

Knowing what to wear and what to do

When you go scuba diving you will need an air tank, a wet suit, a face mask, flippers, a depth gauge, a waterproof watch and a quick-release weight belt.

Face mask

Wet suit

Flippers

Signals Know your signals before you go diving. 'I'm OK', is signalled by forming a circle with your finger and thumb.

Watch

Air tank

Diving Get into the water by falling backwards off the boat, letting the weight of your tanks pull you down.

Distress is indicated by waving your fist from side to side.

Diving flag Always fly the blue and white Flag A above where you are diving, from a boat.

or fill air bottles if they suspect you are inexperienced or untrained. A list of diving schools and sub-aqua clubs that run courses can be obtained from the British Sub-Aqua Club, Telford's Quay, Ellesmere Port, Cheshire L65 4FY. Clubs and diving schools either lend equipment or hire it to you for each session.

If you have never used scuba equipment, go on a BSAC Novice Diver Course, which offers ten hours' theory and a total of ten hours' practice in a pool. You will then need to attend a BSAC Sports Diver Course – consisting of ten hours' theory and ten practice dives, totalling not less than three hours.

To enroll on a course, you must be a competent swimmer and reasonably fit. You will also have to have a medical examination and chest X-ray, to check that you do not suffer from respiratory or heart trouble, and that your middle ear and sinuses are able to stand changes of pressure.

Safety underwater Never dive alone; you and at least one other diver should be responsible for each other's safety and be trained in LIFESAVING techniques. Never go into the water until you have checked *all* your equipment thoroughly. Panic underwater can be fatal, so Stay Calm Underwater, Breathe Always (SCUBA).

Precautions to take before diving:
● Enquire at the harbour master's office, or the place where you hire your tanks, about tides, current, hazards and local regulations.
● Avoid shipping lanes, fishermen's markers and nets, and areas where there

are likely to be powerboats and WATER-SKIING. Listen and look around you when surfacing.
● If you are diving from, or are escorted by, a boat, fly the blue and white Flag A of the International Code of Signals.
● Make sure your escort boat has a radio transmitter/receiver or a portable telephone with adequate range.
● Stick to an agreed dive plan. If a diver fails to surface promptly, summon help without delay.
● Keep clear of sharp rocks and seaweed. Carry a knife with a floating handle in a sheath attached to your belt, in case you need to free yourself from weed or netting.
● If you go underwater fishing, never point or fire a spear gun directly below you or in the direction of other divers. On land, never leave or store a spear gun loaded.

For further safety measures, see SKIN-DIVING.

Sculling

Rowing with one oar; handling a solo racing boat

Sculling has two quite different meanings – either to propel a boat with a single oar or paddle, or to row a racing boat with a pair of oars. See also ROWING.

One-oar sculling In sculling, a single oar, held by an oar-lock or ring, is moved back and forth to propel the boat. It can be performed sitting, kneeling or standing. The key to the stroke is the angle of the blade, determined by the angle of the

---

SCULLING

Propelling a boat with one oar

Begin with the oar pushed over to one side of the boat. Hold it so the blade is at an angle between flat and upright.

Push the oar across your body, keeping the blade at the same angle as it pushes through the water.

At the end of a stroke, turn the blade with a flip of the wrist so the same side of the blade pushes the water.

Continue the movement from side to side, always with the blade angle between flat and vertical.

The boat goes forward in a series of zigzag movements as the oar is sculled to the left and right.

---

wrist. If the blade is too vertical, the stern will swing wildly from side to side, too flat, and the oar will slice through the water and the boat will not move.

Two-oar sculling A sculler has a pair of lightweight oars (or sculls), whereas in rowing races, each oarsman mans a single heavy oar which he pulls with both hands. The hull of a solo racing boat is a lightweight 'skin' or shell of wood or a plastic and carbon-fibre composite. As it is less than 3mm ($\frac{1}{8}$in) thick, balancing and steering it requires first-rate timing and coordination.

The sculler sits on a sliding seat so that he can power his stroke by driving his body backwards with his legs while pulling the oars. He slides forward again ready for the next stroke as the oars are feathered (lifted from the water and held flat) between strokes and the boat glides forward. At the start of the next stroke, the sculler should be at the front of the slide with arms stretched forward and the oar blades squared (vertical) when they enter the water.

Fast sculling demands a strong, smooth stroke with a regular rhythm and a powerful, well-timed leg drive, as well as skilled slide control. 'Catching a crab' – putting the blade into the water before it is vertical – can put the boat wildly out of control.

At rowing regattas there are generally events for single sculls, double sculls (two scullers in one boat) and sometimes quadruple sculls.

Scything

Using the traditional grass cutter

A scythe blade is curved and generally about 860mm (34in) long. It is set at an angle to the long shaft (or snaith), which is also curved and has two handgrips (called nibs, or doles) fixed at right angles to it.

Cutting with a scythe The art of scything lies in keeping the blade sharp and working with a steady swing. Stand comfortably straight with legs about 460mm (18in) apart and your right foot a little in front. Hold the handgrips from behind the shaft so that your right hand is on the lower grip and you are sideways on to the blade, which is pointing forwards in front of you.

Start the swing with your right hand in front of your right leg, and the blade held at the base of the grass, just above the ground surface. Swing the scythe smoothly, keeping the blade level, until your right hand is in front of your left leg. Then swing the scythe back and repeat, moving slowly forward as you work. Sharpen (whet) the cutting edge of the blade frequently with a scythe stone.

Whetting the blade Lubricate the scythe stone with light oil or water. Hold the scythe upside down with the shaft dug into the ground and one hand gripping the back of the blade. Starting from the shaft end, rub the stone along the cutting edge, keeping it flat against the blade so that the edge is honed to a fine point, not rounded off (given a shoulder). Sharpen both sides of the blade the same way.

Seafood cocktails

Making a popular meal starter

Whatever their basis – whether it is lobster, prawns, white crabmeat, or mixed shellfish – seafood cocktails have the same recipe. They take about 15 minutes to prepare.

Here is a recipe for prawn cocktail, a popular first course.

Ingredients (for 4 people)
225g (8oz) shelled prawns
8 level tablespoons tomato sauce or smooth chutney, such as apricot
150ml ($\frac{1}{4}$ pint) double cream or
MAYONNAISE
Worcestershire sauce or Tabasco
1 level dessertspoon grated horseradish
Lemon juice
4 tablespoons shredded lettuce heart
4 thin lemon slices, slit to the centre

Remove any grey veins from the prawns and set aside four of the largest for trimmings.

Blend the tomato sauce (or chutney) and cream (or mayonnaise) with the grated horseradish. Flavour to taste with a few drops of Worcestershire sauce (or Tabasco) and lemon juice.

Divide the shredded lettuce into four equal portions and place in the bottom of serving glasses. Arrange the prawns over the lettuce and cover with the creamy, tangy sauce. Chill in a refrigerator for 1 hour. Just before serving the dish, hang a prawn and a lemon slice over each glass as a garnish.

Sealants

Using flexible gap-fillers

Modern sealants, unlike putties (see PUTTYING) and MORTAR, set on the surface but remain flexible underneath. So if there is a slight movement between the two sealed surfaces – a timber frame shrinking away from masonry, for example – the sealant will not crack or pull away but stretch to maintain the seal.

Sealants are available in various forms, such as in cartridges for use in a dispenser gun, tubes with a screw end, and aerosol sprays.

There are also different types of sealant made for different jobs, although most are based on either acrylics or silicone rubber. Check the type you want when buying. Tube and cartridge-packed sealants are forced out through a tapered nozzle, and you can vary the thickness of the seal according to where you cut off the end of the nozzle to make an exit hole. Err on the small side, and cut the nozzle at an angle. You can always cut away a bit more if necessary, but you cannot make a hole smaller once it has been cut.

Sealing frames in masonry Gaps round window and door frames can let in DAMP. Clean out old putty or mortar, dust the gap, and if it is damp direct a hot-air gun (or a hair dryer) into it to dry it. Force sealant deep into the gap, allowing it to build up to just above the surface. Use a wet rag or your finger to smooth the surface of the sealant while it is still wet.

Gutter repairs Clean all debris from the gutter, then seal gaps and cracks with gutter sealant, preferably working on the outside of the gutter to avoid building up an obstruction within the gutter itself, which would impede the flow of water. See also GUTTERS AND DOWNPIPES.

Fitting a vanity basin Ceramic vanity (or countertop) basins have no clamps to hold them in place – use a sanitary-ware sealant, which contains a fungicide to prevent mould growth. Lay a bed of sealant round the opening cut in the countertop, and press the basin firmly in place. Weight the basin until the sealant has set. See also PLASTIC PIPES.

Caulking WC joints On older sanitary-ware, joints between lavatory pans and soil pipes may be filled with putty. Carefully dig out the old material, and clean and dry off the joint with a hair dryer. Seal with sanitary-ware sealant pressed well into the joint. Smooth it with a damp cloth while still soft.

Sealing baths and basins Use a silicone-rubber sealant (made in sanitary-ware colours) to seal a gap between a bath or basin and the wall. Clean out the gap and make sure it is dry before applying the sealant according to the maker's instructions. Depending on which type of sealant you use, you may have to push the tube's nozzle along the gap as you squeeze; or, if the tube has a winged applicator, pull the tube along as you apply the sealant.

Before tackling a long stretch, such as the side of a bath, experiment to get used to handling the sealant. Then do as much as you can without stopping. While the sealant is still soft, smooth it with a wet lint-free rag or a wet finger. Before sealing a deep gap fill it to within 6mm ($\frac{1}{4}$in) of the top with pieces of expanded polystyrene ceiling tile, which is flexible enough to jam in and provides a good base for the sealant.

If the gap is wider than about 10mm ($\frac{3}{8}$in), cover it with plastic moulding and

use the sealant as an adhesive. Where there is considerable flexing – such as with a badly supported acrylic bath – fix the moulding to the wall only and let it overlap the bath.

Removing excess sealant If you drop sealant where you do not want it, wait for it to dry, then cut it away from the surface with a craft knife. Do not try to remove it while it is wet.

Seat belts

Checking the webbing and mountings

Both for personal safety and for getting your car through the MOT TEST, check the seat belts regularly.

Use a spanner to see that the belt mountings are tight. Note, however, that when the bolt on a swivelling anchor plate is tight, the plate must still pivot freely. Check that when a belt is fastened the webbing is not twisted, and that the belt can be released easily. Renew the belts if the webbing is frayed, torn or coming unstitched at the mountings.

Pull the webbing of an inertia-reel belt to check that it runs freely from the reel and retracts fully. To test an inertia-reel belt, take the car on the road with a front-seat passenger. Make sure the road is clear behind you, then apply the brakes sharply at about 20mph. Both seat belts should lock as you and your passenger are thrown forward – hold the wheel or dashboard firmly in case of malfunction. If a belt does not lock, it may be out of alignment.

To work correctly, the inertia-reel box must be horizontal when the car is level and unladen. Check each box with a spirit level and reposition them if necessary.

Static belts may become worn or dirty if not stowed when not in use. Always hook or clip the snap-in buckle on its stowage point on the door pillar when leaving the car. If the hook or clip breaks, make a hook with plastic-covered wire. See also SAFETY SEATS.

Seed sowing

Sowing seeds in your garden

In January, study the seed catalogues and plan your growing programme. Order immediately – popular varieties sometimes sell out quickly. Consider buying F1 hybrid seeds; they cost more, but produce more vigorous and uniform plants than other seeds.

Tomato seeds remain viable for about five years, but other vegetable and also flower seeds often keep for only a year or two.

Preparing a seedbed Take time to prepare the bed well; sowing in cold, heavy, clogged soil wastes time and seed – see SOIL PREPARATION; COMPOST.

Before sowing, firm the soil by treading on it lightly and rake it until the surface is as fine as breadcrumbs.

Sowing Sow seeds outdoors when the weather is dry and still. Stretch a length of string between two sticks as a guide for a row and draw a drill with a draw hoe. Sow thinly; that way you will make the seed go farther, and you will save yourself much of the work of thinning out the seedlings.

Generally, sow the seeds at such a depth that they will be covered by their own length of compost or soil. Close the drill with the back of a rake and firm the soil lightly. Some seeds are sown in boxes or a propagator in warmth (see GREENHOUSE GARDENING) and planted out as seedlings – see COLD FRAMES, PLANTING.

Precise sowing instructions are given on the seed packet.

Keep the seedbed moist but not soggy, to speed the seeds' germination.

Thinning out Thin out the seedlings to the spacing you require as soon as two or three 'true' leaves have developed. True leaves are the leaves that grow after the initial seed leaf or pair of seed leaves.

Keeping birds away To protect seeds and seedlings from birds, cover the rows with strands of cotton or with plastic netting.

SEED SOWING

Protecting seeds from birds

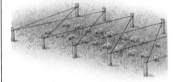

Covering with strands Stretch black cotton between rows of pegs on both sides of the seed patch, forming a crisscross pattern.

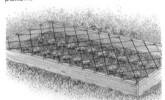

Covering with netting Build a wooden frame 100mm (4in) high to surround the patch. Fix black cotton or plastic netting to it with tacks or staples. Or support the netting over half hoops of wire, like a cloche.

Self-employment

Setting yourself up in business

Any paid work that you do, or service that you give, for someone other than an employer is, in law, classified as self-employment.

As soon as you start working for yourself, whether full or part-time, notify your tax inspector, and the local social security office. Register for VALUE ADDED TAX, if the income from your business is likely to exceed a specified amount – your VAT office can tell you how much.

If the name of your business is not your own you must display your name and address at your place of business, and put that name and address on all business documents. You can also consider forming a company – see COMPANIES.

If you intend to use your home for business, you may need to get PLANNING PERMISSION from your local authority. If the conversion involves structural alterations you also need Building Regulations approval – see BUILDING PERMITS.

Keep accounts from the start (see BOOK-KEEPING) and collect RECEIPTS, invoices, bank statements and so on, to show to your income tax collector. It is wise to engage an accountant to handle your accounts, and to discuss your plans with your bank manager – see BANK ACCOUNTS; HOME WORK.

You may need a bank loan; the bank may also offer special services for business firms. A separate bank account for your business will help you to avoid confusing your business income and expenditure with your personal ones.

You will have to pay NATIONAL INSURANCE contributions, but you are only entitled to sickness and pension benefit at the basic rate. You cannot claim unemployment benefit if your business ceases.

To provide for possible sickness, consider taking out sick pay INSURANCE.

You will also have to pay National Insurance contributions for anyone you employ, if you pay them above the lower earnings limit; arrange with the local tax office to deduct tax from their wages under PAYE.

Forming a partnership You can start a business with someone else, or with several others, by forming a partnership, which can be arranged informally or formally by a legal deed. Each partner shares the responsibility for the debts of the partnership, but some partners may limit their liability.

Limited liability As a sole trader you have unlimited liability for your debts, which means that if you owe money and cannot pay you face BANKRUPTCY. In a partnership, however, one or more partners can claim limited liability if they supply some of the cash but take no part in running the business. If the business fails, partners with limited liability lose only the money they invested. At least one partner in a partnership must have unlimited liability.

Septic tanks

How they work and how to maintain them

In many country areas, where mains drainage is not available, a septic tank provides a private sewage-treatment plant. The drain from the house feeds sewage into an enclosed chamber where, within one or two days, it is liquefied by anaerobic bacteria – microorganisms that are present in all sewage.

The action of the bacteria produces a surface scum that keeps in smells. Incoming waste enters low down the chamber so that it does not disturb the surface. At the base of the chamber a sludge forms, which must be pumped out from time to time.

You can arrange for emptying through the environmental health department of your local council or engage a private contractor from those listed under Waste Disposal in *Yellow Pages*.

The effluent between scum and sludge passes through a pipe into an adjoining second chamber where it filters through coke. The liquid is then safe enough to run into a ditch or stream, or to drain into the surrounding ground.

If you wish to have a septic tank installed, ask advice from a builder or contractor, and from the environmental health officer of your local council.

There are a few simple rules to keep a septic tank working efficiently:

● Do not use too many disinfectants or too much detergent. Too much disinfectant will kill the bacteria. Detergent can emulsify the contents of the chamber, causing clogging.

● Lift the cover off the main chamber to see if there is a scum on top. If there is, the sewage has not emulsified. If there is not, cut down on detergents or have the tank emptied.

● Keep rainwater well away from the septic tank. It must never be drained into it, as the whole balance of bacterial action would be upset.

Severed limbs

What to do in an emergency

If someone severs a finger, toe or limb, get medical help as quickly as possible. Call – or have someone call – 999 and ask for an ambulance or take the victim to the Accident and Emergency Department of the nearest hospital.

Do not try to restore the severed part yourself. You will only inflict a great deal of pain and may damage the tissues.

Immediate action Lay the casualty flat. Your first priority is to stem the BLEEDING. Without delay, raise the stump or injured part and prop it up with a pillow or folded coat, or rest it on your knee. Stop bleeding by pressing a large, thick wad of gauze or a clean handkerchief or piece of cloth onto the wound.

If you can, keep the wad in place by BANDAGING or with a scarf, necktie, shirt or strip of sheet. Otherwise, hold it firmly in place with your hands. If it becomes soaked with blood, do not remove it – add another layer of wadding.

Do not apply a tourniquet yourself; this should be done only by trained medical staff.

Reassure the patient and try to make him keep still.

Once you have dealt with the bleeding and are sure that the injured person is not in immediate danger, place the severed part in a clean polythene or plastic bag. Keep it cool by placing the bag inside a larger one, or in a suitable container, and pack ice (not too tightly) between the two bags.

Give the severed limb or digit to the ambulance crew or doctor, to go to the hospital with the injured person. It may be possible to stitch it back on.

Although limbs may be lost in road or rail accidents, the most common cause of severed fingers and toes is careless use of LAWN MOWERS and CHAIN SAWS, and disregarding POWER TOOL SAFETY.

Sewing

Stitching by hand or machine

The basic essentials for sewing are the right equipment, a knowledge of the basic stitches and seams for joining pieces of fabric together, and a well-lit working space with an electric socket for an iron and a sewing machine – see IRONS; SEWING MACHINES.

Basic equipment Needles are sized by number from 1 to 24, the higher numbers being the finest. *Sharps* in sizes 7 and 8 are of medium length and are commonly used for general sewing, but they have small eyes and many people prefer *crewels*, also called embroidery needles, because their larger eyes make them easier to thread. *Betweens* are short needles for fine fabric and *milliners* are longer needles for tacking.

Sewing machines have a supply of various needles. The machine's handbook lists fabrics suitable for each needle.

Thread is made of polyester or mercerised cotton, sized 40-60 (higher numbers are finer thread for finer fabric).

Other essentials include: tape measure; dressmaker's pins; small sharp scissors for cutting thread; quick-unpick or seam ripper for unpicking seams and cutting buttonholes; fabric shears for cutting cloth; pinking shears for finishing raw edges liable to fray; thimble; workbox for storing equipment.

Threading a needle Cut the thread at an angle with small, sharp scissors – do not break it, or it will fray. A good working length is about 600mm (2ft), with 150mm (6in) of it drawn through the eye. Use a longer length for tacking.

Basic stitches Use a sewing machine wherever possible. The basic machine stitch can be adjusted in length – and in width to make zigzag stitching – to suit different fabrics and seams. Below are the main hand stitches. See also SLIP-STITCHING.

Tacking A long temporary stitch, this can also be used for marking patterns on fine fabrics. Tacking can be done on a machine, but not if the needle holes will show once it is removed.

Running stitch A short, straight stitch used for fine seams, gathering or tucks.

Backstitch A small, strong stitch for making seams where machining is not possible, for securing stitching at both ends of a row, or for reinforcing stress points.

Hemstitch For fixing turned-up edges on light or medium-weight fabric – see HEMS. Blind hemming is stitched inside the hem so that no stitches are visible.

Herringbone stitch A strong hemming stitch for fixing heavy hems.

Oversewing Slanting stitches over the raw edge of a fabric to prevent fraying. On a machine a zigzag is used to make an overcast stitch.

Whipstitch Slanting stitches over the finished edges of two pieces of fabric joined together. It can also be used to fix a raw edge to a flat surface.

Basic seams A seam is a method of joining two pieces of fabric together. The method varies according to the strength required and how visible the join will be. In dressmaking the standard width for the fold-in (the seam allowance) is 16-19mm ($\frac{5}{8}$-$\frac{3}{4}$in) and it is usual to stitch from the wider to the narrower part – from a skirt hem to the waist, for example.

Plain seam A simple seam for joining where there is no heavy strain. Stitch with the right (outer) sides of the fabric together.

Tackling some basic stitches and seams

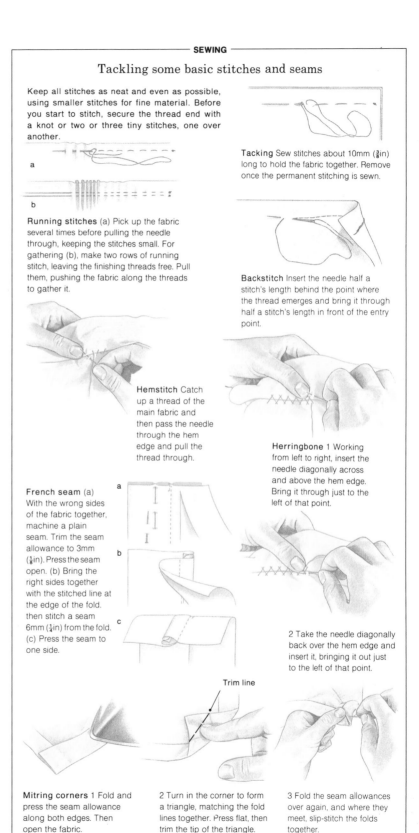

Keep all stitches as neat and even as possible, using smaller stitches for fine material. Before you start to stitch, secure the thread end with a knot or two or three tiny stitches, one over another.

a

b

Running stitches (a) Pick up the fabric several times before pulling the needle through, keeping the stitches small. For gathering (b), make two rows of running stitch, leaving the finishing threads free. Pull them, pushing the fabric along the threads to gather it.

Tacking Sew stitches about 10mm ($\frac{3}{8}$in) long to hold the fabric together. Remove once the permanent stitching is sewn.

Backstitch Insert the needle half a stitch's length behind the point where the thread emerges and bring it through half a stitch's length in front of the entry point.

Hemstitch Catch up a thread of the main fabric and then pass the needle through the hem edge and pull the thread through.

Herringbone 1 Working from left to right, insert the needle diagonally across and above the hem edge. Bring it through just to the left of that point.

French seam (a) With the wrong sides of the fabric together, machine a plain seam. Trim the seam allowance to 3mm ($\frac{1}{8}$in). Press the seam open. (b) Bring the right sides together with the stitched line at the edge of the fold, then stitch a seam 6mm ($\frac{1}{4}$in) from the fold. (c) Press the seam to one side.

a

b

c

2 Take the needle diagonally back over the hem edge and insert it, bringing it out just to the left of that point.

Trim line

Mitring corners 1 Fold and press the seam allowance along both edges. Then open the fabric.

2 Turn in the corner to form a triangle, matching the fold lines together. Press flat, then trim the tip of the triangle.

3 Fold the seam allowances over again, and where they meet, slip-stitch the folds together.

413

Flat fell seam (or run and fell) A strong enclosed seam with a flat finish on both sides. Stitch with the wrong (inner) sides of the fabric together, then open flat. Trim one flap to half width, fold the other one over it, turning in the edge, then stitch down along the folded edge.

French seam A narrow enclosed seam for fine fabrics that fray easily (see illustration on previous page).

Curves and corners Use a plain seam with short stitches for joining on a curve. After stitching, for an outward curve cut slits in the seam allowance so that the fabric can spread. For an inward curve cut out V-shaped notches so that the fabric can lie smooth.

Mitre hems at corners to reduce bulk.

Sewing machines
Using and maintaining them

A sewing machine uses two threads to sew a seam. One unwinds from a reel, lies on top of the fabric, and is pushed through the fabric by the needle. On the underside it loops through the second thread, which unwinds from a bobbin in the shuttle and runs under the fabric.

The tension draws the threads taut, so that the loop is centred between the layers of fabric, and the stitches on top and underneath are identical.

Choosing thread, needle and foot
Choose the thread and needle to suit the fabric. Use a cotton or silk thread for natural fibres, such as cotton and linen; use silk or synthetic threads with woollens; and a synthetic thread for man-made fibres. One thickness of polyester thread suits most synthetics.

Cotton thread is made in a range of thicknesses – the higher the number on it, the finer the thread; 60-100 is for light-weight cottons, 50-60 for medium-weight, 30-40 for heavy fabrics such as corduroy and towelling, and 20 for canvas. For upholstery fabric, use a strong thread such as flax, polyester, or heavy-duty cotton (size 20), or cotton-wrapped polyester.

Use a sharp-pointed needle on woven fabrics, a rounded tip on knitted fabrics, and a wedge tip for vinyl or leather. Your machine manual will tell you which size to select. Generally, the sizes are: 70 metric (11 old system) for fine fabrics such as silk; 80 (14) for normal use; 100 (16) for heavy fabrics; and 110 (18) for very thick fabrics. Round tips are 70 (lightweight), 80 (medium) and 100 (heavy); wedge tips are 70 (soft leather), 80 (medium) and 100 (very thick). Fit the needle as the manual indicates.

Fit the correct presser foot for the seam you are sewing. The foot fitted as standard is for straight seams – and sometimes zigzag seams. The range of alternative feet varies with the price of the machine; it may include feet for ZIPPERS, BUTTONHOLES, embroidery, oversewing, invisible hemming (see HEMS), DARNING, narrow hems, stretch stitches, and twin needles.

Threading and adjusting Fill the bobbin for the shuttle with thread – most machines now have an automatic winder which disengages the needle while the bobbin is filled. Fit the bobbin in the shuttle with a tail of thread coming off clockwise as you hold the shuttle bobbin-side up. Push the shuttle in place and pull the tail of thread up to the work surface of the machine.

The sequence for threading the machine is generally the same. Take the thread from the reel round the tension control device, through the take-up lever and then down to the needle; there are thread guides to ensure that the thread is not pulled off course.

Raise the needle by turning the fly-wheel. Make sure you thread the needle in the direction shown in the manual; some machines have a built-in needle threader. Raise the lower thread – see illustration.

Plug in an electric machine and place the pedal conveniently. Adjust the controls to produce the stitch you want. A dial controls the stitch length; usually the thinner the fabric the shorter the stitch. The machine manual will have a chart to show the setting for any fabric.

Set the stitch width control; this may be zero for a straight seam, or a swing to right or left for a buttonhole, or an even swing for zigzagging. Higher numbers give wider stitches. Some machines will set length and width automatically when you touch a panel to select the stitch pattern.

Adjust the thread tension control dial as the manual recommends for the fabric, then do a test seam on scrap fabric. If the two threads are engaging on top of the fabric, release the tension by turning the control to a lower number; if they are engaging below the fabric, increase the tension.

The dial alters the tension of the top thread; there is a screw on the shuttle to alter the tension of the lower thread – but this is rarely necessary.

Sewing With the presser foot, take-up lever and needle raised, put the fabric under the foot with the seam edge to the right and the main volume of fabric to the left. Turn the flywheel to insert the needle tip into the fabric at exactly the right point. Lower the presser foot to grip the fabric. Press the pedal to start the machine.

Most electric machines have a button which you can press to reverse the direction of sewing. This is useful for securing the seam ends. When you are starting a seam, insert the needle a short way in from the beginning of the seam, and sew in reverse to the edge before releasing the button and sewing forwards.

At the end of the seam, sew in reverse for a short way. Raise the foot and needle and pull the work backwards to draw out a length of thread before cutting off both threads. Pull the top thread to the underside, and cut off both threads with the built-in blade or with scissors. If your machine does not sew in reverse, pull the top thread to the underside and tie the threads together to secure them before cutting them off.

Do not push or pull the fabric through the machine. Simply prevent it from wandering to left or right. Use the edge of the presser foot as your visual guide as you sew.

At a corner, stop with the needle in the fabric but on its way up. Raise the presser foot and swivel the fabric round

---

— **SEWING MACHINES** —

Raising the lower thread

1 Lightly hold the tail of the upper thread. Turn the flywheel so that the needle goes right down through the feed-plate.

2 Continue turning the flywheel until the needle reaches its highest point again. The upper thread will pull up a loop of the lower thread with it.

3 Release the upper thread. Pull the lower thread loop until the tail comes up through the feed-plate.

4 Draw the ends of both threads to the back and one side. The thread ends should be at least 100mm (4in) long.

to the required position. Lower the presser foot and start sewing again. To sew a curve, go along slowly, turning the fabric gradually as you sew. If the curve is sharp or the edge begins to buckle, stop with the needle in the fabric, raise the foot, reposition the fabric and then lower the foot and continue sewing; you may need to do this several times round the curve.

Maintenance After using the machine, clean and oil it with the fine brush and oil dispenser supplied. Have the machine serviced by the dealer regularly.

When the machine is out but not in use, put on its carrying case to keep out dust, and unplug it.

Sharpening hand tools
Giving them a fine edge

The cutting edges of hand tools need to be kept sharp and honed. Apart from being more efficient, a sharp tool is far safer: it is the blunt tool that slips rather than biting into the wood.

Saw teeth are sharpened with files; knives, planes and chisels with an oilstone; scissors with a slipstone.

Planes and gouges. Sharpen plane blades and WOODCARVING gouges on an oilstone as for chisels – see CHISELLING. Check the angles of the cutting edge of a plane blade (see PLANES) with a protractor or use a honing guide. Sharpen the outer bevel of a gouge with a side-to-side movement on the oilstone. Rub the inside with a tapered slipstone.

Saws Clamp the saw blade in a vice, teeth up, between two pieces of scrap wood positioned with their edges no more than 6mm (¼in) below the teeth. Make sure that a long saw is clamped at both ends as well, to stop it whipping.

If sharpening a well-worn saw, look along the level of the teeth, or place a straightedge on them, to check that they are all the same length. If they are uneven, run a flat file down the length of the saw blade to level them.

Reshape the points with a triangular saw file. For a ripsaw (see SAWS AND SAWING) first file the back of the teeth angled away from you. Start at the handle end of the saw, and with smooth, light strokes, keeping the file at right angles to the blade, work along the blade. When you reach the end, reverse the saw blade in the vice and sharpen the remaining teeth.

File a crosscut, panel or tenon saw in a similar way to a ripsaw, but angle the file across the blade at 60 to 70 degrees to sharpen the teeth leaning away from you first. Then reverse the saw blade to sharpen the other teeth.

To ensure the correct 'set' of the splay of the saw teeth, use a saw set. It is a small tool resembling pliers, with a head that adjusts to suit the size of the teeth.

A dovetail saw does not have to be set.

Knives Many craft knives are supplied with disposable blades, or with blades marked in sections that are snapped off in turn as they become blunt to expose a new cutting edge.

To sharpen a knife with a permanent blade, stroke both sides of the knife blade on an oilstone, using a circular motion. Keep sharpening until the blade will slice cleanly through a sheet of paper held by its top edge. Finally, strop the blade on a leather strap dusted with polishing compound.

Secure the strap at one end and pull it taut, then draw the knife down the strap, blunt edge towards you, with the cutting edge pressed against the strap. Turn the blade over and go back up the strap again, with the blunt edge away from you.

Drill bits The angles on a drill bit are critical. If you plan to sharpen your own, use a sharpener that fits your electric drill and buy a drill sharpening guide from a tool shop. Most good tool shops will sharpen bits for you.

Shells
Finding and collecting seashells; preparing them for display

Shells are the hard protective outer covering of a large group of soft-bodied animals known as molluscs – and more than 800 species live in the seas surrounding the British Isles. The beaches of the south-west are particularly fruitful hunting grounds.

Searching for shells The best places to go shell-hunting are rocky coves and sandy beaches; the best time is at low tide, especially during spring tides which coincide with the full moon and new

---

SHARPENING HAND TOOLS

The equipment you need and how to use it

Sharpen saw teeth with files: a medium flat file and a double-ended saw file for panel, rip and crosscut saws; a fine flat file and a needle file for a tenon saw. First file teeth to the same level with the flat file.

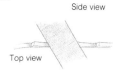

Side view

Top view

Reshape panel saw teeth with a triangular saw file. Hold it at 60° to the flat surface of the teeth angled away from you. Reverse the saw to file the others.

Locking screw

Scaled anvil

Use a saw set to readjust the angle of the saw teeth. Squeezing the handles presses the teeth to an angled anvil.

Window

Plunger

Count the number of teeth in 25mm (1in) and loosen the locking screw to set this number at the centre of the window number on the saw set. Working from the saw handle end, clench the saw set on all the teeth pointing away from you, then reverse the blade and repeat the process.

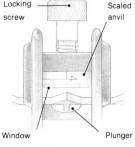

Planes To use a honing guide when sharpening a plane blade, clamp the blade into the guide, adjust it to the correct angle and rub across the oilstone.

Scissors Draw a fine slipstone along each blade at right angles to the blade's face – a slipstone is like an oilstone but is applied to a blade.

moon, or after a storm. Take with you a tool such as a long-handled gardening fork for combing through seaweed and debris, a knife and a plastic container for your finds. Wear gloves (some shells are rough or sharp to handle).

Record the place, date and time that you find each shell – it will make identification easier when you are preparing the shells for display.

Cleaning and polishing If the mollusc is still in its shell, boil it in water for five minutes and then remove the flesh with a bent pin or a knife.

Scrub the shells with a stiff brush and wash them thoroughly. You may prefer to leave interesting encrustations intact; otherwise, carefully scrape off encrusted material.

If encrustations are particularly persistent, soak the shells in equal parts of warm water and household bleach, wearing rubber gloves to protect your hands. Check the shells frequently during soaking and take them out if the bleach is beginning to dull or pit them.

After soaking, rinse the shells well. If remnants of flesh still remain inside the shell, soak it in methylated spirit for a few days to prevent the encrusted flesh from smelling. Dry and then plug the shell with tissue paper.

To enhance colour and lustre, rub your shells with a lint-free cloth moistened with baby oil, then buff with a clean, dry soft cloth.

Displaying your collection Label the shells, then mount them on cardboard and display them in glass-topped cases, similar to those used for exhibiting butterflies. Alternatively, arrange the shells on a layer of cotton wool in open trays or clear plastic boxes.

Shelves
Some simple ways to support them

Many different forms of shelving are available, so consider what you want the shelving for, and whether it needs to look attractive or just be functional.

The simplest form of shelf consists of a plank resting on BRACKETS. Before you start, decide on the width of shelf required. For example, most small books can be housed on a shelf 150mm (6in) wide; larger books may need a shelf 230mm (9in) wide. The easiest material to use is coated CHIPBOARD finished either in a wood VENEER or in white plastic.

Tracks fixed to the wall to support adjustable brackets form the basis of widely available shelving systems which are both simple and flexible.

Another type of flexible shelving system uses wooden or metal ladders, with shelves supported on metal rods hooked

between the rungs. The system is sold complete with shelves and rods. The ladders stand against the wall, at right angles to it. They can be cross-braced or anchored in place by SCREWS where necessary. Shelves can be varied in height by spacing different numbers of rungs between them.

Shelving can be fitted in an alcove by fixing BATTENS to the side walls. Use countersunk screws and wall plugs (see MASONRY DRILLING; WALL FASTENERS), and check with a spirit level to see that the supports are horizontal. The shelves can be rested on the supports, but for extra security drive lost-head nails through the shelves into the battens, and fill the holes with wood filler – see NAILING.

Alternatively, fix the shelves with mirror plates or shrinkage plates.

No other support is necessary unless the span is more than 1m (3ft). If it is, glue (see GLUING) and screw a batten to the front edge to strengthen it, and decorate the batten to match the shelf.

Angle-aluminium fittings for alcoves are also sold in DIY centres. They can be used with the shelf either fitted on top or slotted in.

If alcove shelving is only temporary, use piles of bricks, which can be painted with emulsion, as shelf supports.

Cupboard shelves Often, wall CUP-BOARDS have shelves too far apart, and valuable space is lost. Make up extra shelves using coated chipboard. Make two uprights from chipboard, each as wide as the shelf and to the height you want it less the thickness of the shelf. Glue and screw the shelf to the uprights and then stand the unit in the cupboard.

SHELVES

Shelving an alcove

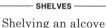

Timber or chipboard shelf

Batten angled at front

Fix 50 × 25mm (2 × 1in) battens to the side walls of an alcove to support the shelves. Angling the battens at the front ends makes them unobtrusive.

Shine removing
Taking the polish off your suit

Heavy, dark material, particularly wool or wool mixtures, can develop a shine as a result of direct IRONING or hard wear. The best remedy is to have the garments dry-cleaned, but you can remove the shine yourself almost as well.

Spread out the garment and dampen the shiny area evenly, using a cotton cloth such as a clean tea towel or pillowcase wrung out in cold water. Then spread the damp cloth over it and press lightly with a hot iron – lift the iron on and off, not backwards and forwards, as for smoothing. See also PRESSING.

Afterwards spread a sheet of brown paper on the garment and iron over the paper to dry the fabric.

Shine restoring
Bringing back a sparkle to car paintwork

Dull paintwork may be caused by chemical pollution in the atmosphere, which covers the car with a thin haze, or by fading with age or strong sunlight. The shine can be restored with a mild abrasive cleaner, available from car accessory shops. The cleaner lifts a thin surface film of paint, but may damage some metallic paint finishes – check with your handbook, or dealer, to see if it is safe to use on your car.

Wash the car (see CAR WASHING) and let it dry. Apply the cleaner with a damp cloth or piece of muslin and cover an area of about 460 × 460mm (18 × 18in) at a time.

Do not rub it in too hard, or you may cut through the top coats of paint to the undercoat, or bare metal. Let the cleaner dry to a white, powdery finish, then wipe off with a clean, dry cloth.

Once the shine has been restored, apply a wax or silicone polish with a soft cloth, and buff it with a cloth or lambswool mop in a power drill as soon as it is dry.

Renew the shine only when it begins to fade – do not use a paintwork restorer regularly as it will eventually cut through the finish and expose the undercoat. See also PAINT TOUCH-UPS.

Shingles
Relieving and treating a painful infection

Shingles is caused by the chickenpox virus which lies dormant in the nerve cells. The virus is known medically as *herpes zoster* and affects only those who have had chickenpox – usually when they were children.

Symptoms Severe pain, usually on one side of the body, followed two or three days later by a blistered, localised skin eruption over the painful area. There may be a mild FEVER and a general upset.

Duration The rash usually disappears after two or three weeks, but the pain can persist for weeks or months after – a condition known as post-herpetic neuralgia.

Treatment Consult a DOCTOR at the first sign of symptoms. Any eruptions near the eye can damage the sight if not treated early.
● Wear loose-fitting clothes to reduce pressure or rubbing on the affected area.
● Painkillers will give relief.
● Cool bathing and applications of calamine lotion can also help.
● Avoid contact with women in late pregnancy – the newborn baby could become ill with chickenpox.
● Keep away from children, who can catch chickenpox from a shingles sufferer.

The doctor may prescribe an antiviral drug to reduce the length of the attack and help prevent post-herpetic neuralgia.

Shin splints

Easing and avoiding pain in the lower leg

Joggers, sports players and athletes, especially marathon runners, are particularly prone to shin splints – pains at the front of the leg caused by inflammation of the lower leg muscles and tendons, or by a hairline fracture resulting from over-exertion or sudden, hard or repeated jolting.

If you have symptoms that could be caused by shin splints, do not try to diagnose what is wrong yourself. See your DOCTOR or go to a Hospital Accident and Emergency Department or a sports injuries clinic.

Prevention To guard against shin splints:
● Wear cushion-soled shoes for jogging, running and sports on a hard surface.
● Avoid running or jogging on hard or uneven ground – see also JOGGING INJURIES.
● Keep fit by regular exercise, without over-exertion or overtaxing your leg muscles. Occasional bouts of energetic exercise often lead to injuries of this kind or to other SPRAINS AND STRAINS.
● Always go through a stretching and warming up routine before activities that impose stress on muscles and tendons – see EXERCISES.

Recuperation Given a rest for a month or so, the damaged muscles and tendons

should repair themselves. Avoid vigorous exercise until they have completely recovered, otherwise the condition may become chronic. Once the pain has vanished *gentle* exercise such as SWIMMING will help you return to fitness. Remedial physiotherapy may also be beneficial.

Shirt collar turning

Giving an old shirt a new lease on life

The fold line of the collar usually wears thin long before any other part of a shirt. You can double the shirt's life if you turn the collar.

Fold the collar point to point, and put in a pin to mark the centre at the back. Sew a running stitch of bright thread up the centre of the neckband and another up the collar, making the stitches show

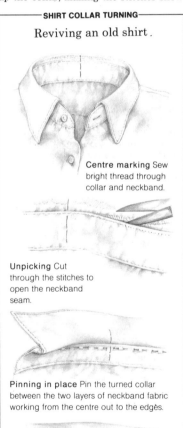

SHIRT COLLAR TURNING

Reviving an old shirt.

Centre marking Sew bright thread through collar and neckband.

Unpicking Cut through the stitches to open the neckband seam.

Pinning in place Pin the turned collar between the two layers of neckband fabric working from the centre out to the edges.

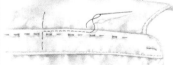

Tacking in place Tack along the line of pins, through all layers, as close to the edge of the neckband as you can.

on both sides – see SEWING.

Unpick the row of stitching at the top edge of the neckband; ease away the released layer of fabric. Inside, you will usually find another row of stitching holding the neckband fabric. Unpick this stitching and separate the collar from the neckband.

Lay down the collar, worn side up. Ease down the edge of the worn layer of fabric by about 3mm (⅛in) and tack right through the collar along the open edge. This will make the new face of the collar slightly deeper than the new underside so that it will fold easily.

Sandwich the collar between the two layers of neckband fabric. Align the running stitches in neckband and collar. Pin the collar in place, pinning through all the layers of fabric. Check that the pins are holding the bottom layer of fabric all the way along. Tack along the pinned line, then machine along the seam, just inside the line of tacking. Finish off the ends and remove the tacking.

If you are going to sew the collar in by hand, pin and tack it first to the inside layer only of the neckband. Sew it with backstitch. Then pin and tack in place the outer layer of the neckband. Sew it in place with a fine hemstitch, making sure that the stitches do not go right through all the layers and show on the other side.

Shock

Recognising the symptoms; emergency treatment

Clinical shock is a condition caused by the body channelling blood to the heart, brain, lungs and other vital organs as an emergency measure, temporarily neglecting less vital areas such as the muscles and the skin.

Shock often follows severe BURNS or profuse BLEEDING, fractures, crushing, violent VOMITING or DIARRHOEA or a bad fall. The effects may be immediate or be delayed by as much as 24 hours.

Obvious shock Shock can produce a variety of symptoms:
● Pallid or ashen skin that is clammy (cold and moist) to touch.
● In the earlier stages, agitation, anxiety and restlessness. Later, the victim may become unresponsive and, finally, unconscious – see UNCONSCIOUSNESS.
● A weak, rapid or irregular pulse.
● Shivering and sweating.
● Weakness, dizziness and faintness; blurred vision, nausea, a chilled feeling and thirst.

What to do Summon medical help or an ambulance the instant you are able to do so. Shock requires prompt treatment, and its severity is not always apparent.

Meanwhile, act as follows:

● Lay the victim on his back, with his head low and, if possible – unless you suspect a head injury or brain haemorrhage – legs raised about 200mm (8in). Prop them up on a cushion or folded coat so that the blood is directed to the brain.

● Give any necessary first aid – see BURNS; BLEEDING; BROKEN BONES; DISLOCATED JOINTS; HEAD INJURIES; HEART ATTACK; SEVERED LIMBS.

● Comfort and reassure the victim.

● Loosen any clothing at the neck, chest or waist likely to restrict breathing or circulation.

● Keep the victim warm with a coat or blanket.

● Do not apply hot-water bottles. Artificial heat will draw blood to the skin, starving the vital organs of blood.

● If the victim is thirsty, moisten his lips with water.

● Do not give anything to eat or drink, because it may cause delay in giving an anaesthetic in hospital.

● Do not move the victim unnecessarily.

● Do not let him smoke.

● If his breathing becomes difficult or he appears to be about to vomit or to lapse into unconsciousness, turn the victim over into the RECOVERY POSITION.

● If his breathing stops, administer ARTIFICIAL RESPIRATION immediately.

Anaphylactic shock Some people react very dramatically to wasp or bee stings – see INSECT BITES AND STINGS. Within minutes weals develop all over the body; the face and lips may swell enormously, and there is a massive drop in blood pressure so that the victim develops a rapid heartbeat and may faint. The victim may be short of breath, as in severe asthma. Get medical help at once.

Shock absorbers

Checking a car's shock absorbers for wear or damage; replacing them

The shock absorbers (or dampers) in a car's suspension system smooth out the recoil action of the springs as they absorb shocks transmitted by bumps in the road. One or more faulty shock absorbers will adversely affect a car's handling, and cause it to fail an MOT TEST.

Most modern cars have telescopic shock absorbers, in which a piston operated by the movement of the car displaces oil at a controlled rate from one end of a cylinder to the other.

A telescopic shock absorber forming the main suspension leg and with a coil spring at the top, is called a MacPherson strut, and is used on many cars. Rear suspensions usually have a leaf or coil spring, with separate shock absorbers fitted between the axle or suspension arms and the bodywork.

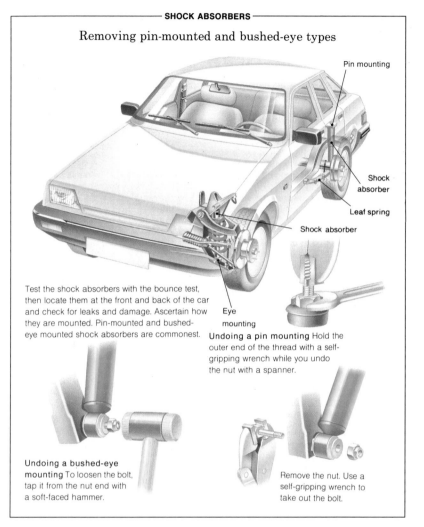

SHOCK ABSORBERS

Removing pin-mounted and bushed-eye types

Pin mounting

Shock absorber

Leaf spring

Shock absorber

Eye mounting

Test the shock absorbers with the bounce test, then locate them at the front and back of the car and check for leaks and damage. Ascertain how they are mounted. Pin-mounted and bushed-eye mounted shock absorbers are commonest.

Undoing a pin mounting Hold the outer end of the thread with a self-gripping wrench while you undo the nut with a spanner.

Undoing a bushed-eye mounting To loosen the bolt, tap it from the nut end with a soft-faced hammer.

Remove the nut. Use a self-gripping wrench to take out the bolt.

Checking shock absorbers Loosen the wheel nuts, jack up the car and support the chassis on axle stands so that the wheels hang free – never work under a car supported only by a jack. Remove the wheels.

Inspect each shock absorber for fluid leaks, which show as dark stains in the road grime that collects on its body and mounting points. Examine the body for deep dents, and the piston rod for signs of pitting or rusting. Any of these faults call for a replacement unit.

The ends of the shock absorber are bolted through rubber bushes. Grip the upper and lower part of the unit and try to move it backwards and forwards; then twist it about its mounting bolt. If there is any movement, replace the bushes.

The bounce test Grip the bodywork above a wheel and bounce it vigorously a few times, then let go. The body should continue to bounce about twice more and then stop in its normal position. If it

continues to bounce, the shock absorber at that point is weak, and will not pass an MOT test.

Removing a shock absorber With the car still on axle stands, place a jack under the suspension arm for a front shock absorber, or under the axle at the rear.

Locate the top mounting, which may be like the bottom one, or may be a threaded end of the piston called a pin mounting – it may protrude into the boot and you may have to remove some trim to get at it. For a pin mounting, count the number of threads above the nut: the same number must show when the shock absorber is replaced.

Note the positions of any washers and spacers while removing a shock absorber, and if you are fitting a new one use the new fixings supplied.

Replacing units for a MacPherson strut is better left to a garage, as special tools are needed.

Replacing bushes An eye-type rubber bush may be in two halves, with a steel sleeve through the middle. Pull out the old bush and lubricate the eye with a soap solution. Fit one half of the new bush with the sleeve inserted and push in the other half as far as possible. Place the eye in a vice and tighten it to squeeze the bush into place.

To replace a one-piece bush, take a socket (see SPANNERS AND WRENCHES) large enough to take the bush and place it in a vice on one side of the eye. Place the new bush on the other side and squeeze with the vice to push the old bush into the socket as the new one is forced into the eye.

Shoe care

Cleaning, storing and repairing

Polish new leather shoes or boots before you wear them for the first time, to give them a protective coating. You can treat suede with a water-repellent spray. Rub new leather soles with abrasive paper before walking on them; they are very slippery.

Cleaning leather shoes Wipe or brush off dirt once the shoes are dry – very dirty shoes can first be washed with leather soap. Remove salt, grease or tar stains with a proprietary remover.

Use polish or cream of a suitable colour for the shoe. Rub polish well in with a soft cloth, then rub it over with a clean duster or soft brush. Polish the surface to a shine with a fresh soft cloth. After polishing, rub or spray on a leather protector to repel water.

Cleaning suede shoes When the shoes are dry, scrape off heavy mud with the back of a knife blade, then brush the shoes with a suede brush made of wire, bristle or rubber, using it with a circular motion. Sponge away small kick and scuff marks gently with a mild soap and water solution. Remove any ingrained dirt with a suede shampoo, carefully following the maker's instructions to avoid flattening the nap (short surface fibres). Use a proprietary remover for stubborn stains.

Cleaning fabric shoes Brush off dust and mud when the shoes are dry. Dirt stains can be washed off. Shoes can be placed in a pillowcase and machine washed according to the type of fabric. Apply a fabric cleaner of suitable colour when the shoes are dry.

Storing shoes Use shoe or boot trees to keep the shoes in shape, and store them in bags or boxes to avoid scuffing and to keep out dust. Do not wear the same shoes continually – they will last longer

and keep in shape better if you rest them occasionally. Put them on using a shoe horn to avoid damaging the backs.

Shoe repairs Get heels repaired before they wear right down. For mending old or inexpensive shoes, you can buy ready-made rubber soles and heels complete with instructions for fixing them to leather or rubber soles or heels. Do not attempt to put them on PVC soles or heels. To identify PVC, heat a piece of copper wire in a flame, touch the hot wire against the sole, then put the wire back in the flame – if it burns green, the shoe material is PVC.

Rubber heels are fixed with cement and nailed through ready-made holes. Remove the old heels first – if they are leather, you may have to remove two layers to accommodate the depth of the new rubber heel. Use a hammer and punch to drive the nails below the surface. Use a sharp knife to trim the heel all round to bring its edge level with the rest of the heel.

Shortbread

Making a popular biscuit

Rich shortbread, a Hogmanay tradition in Scotland, has only three ingredients – butter, sugar and flour.

Ingredients (for 20 finger-biscuits)
225g (8oz) butter
130g (4½oz) caster sugar
350g (12oz) plain flour
Caster sugar for sprinkling

Preheat the oven to 180°C (350°F), gas mark 4.

Rub together the butter and sugar. Work the flour in lightly with your fingertips.

Pat the dough into an oblong shape about 6mm (¼in) thick and 75mm (3in) wide and cut into fingers. Space them out on a greased baking sheet, and prick rows of shallow holes in each finger with a fork. Bake for 20-25 minutes until a pale golden-brown. Dust with caster sugar and serve warm or cold. Shortbread keeps well in an airtight tin.

Short circuits

Tracing the causes and restoring power

When electric current takes the wrong route, it is called a short circuit. It happens because of a fault in the circuit between the consumer unit (see FUSES AND FUSE BOXES) and the appliance. For example, two wires may touch because they have come loose from their terminals, or their insulation has crumbled.

Extra heavy current flows through the wiring and takes the route which offers least resistance until it comes to a deliberate weak point – a fuse or MCB (miniature circuit breaker – see CIRCUIT BREAKERS), which blows or trips so that the circuit is broken and current ceases to flow. If there were no weak points, the short circuit could cause a fire by overheating the wiring or the connections.

You may hear a fuse blow – in a plug as you push it into a socket, for example. In this case you can check the connections in the plug and fit a new fuse – see PLUGS.

Locating the fault Switch off the power supply at the consumer unit or main fuse box first. Never check with the power still on. Each fuse carrier or box should be marked to show which circuit it protects.

If the fuse carriers are not marked, examine each one in turn. In the older type of carrier with a rewirable fuse, you will be able to see if the wire is broken, or see blobs on the wire, or detect a break when you gently press the wire.

If you have a consumer unit with MCBs you can see which button or switch has tripped.

If you have carriers with cartridge fuses, you will have to test each fuse in turn; remove the end of a metal-cased torch and hold the cartridge with one end touching the battery and the other end touching the torch case. When the torch is switched on, it will light only if the fuse is sound. See also TORCHES.

Fault in a lighting circuit Turn off the lights – as well as the main switch at the consumer unit. Examine the flexes of pendant lights. Flex perishes eventually and any movement – such as the draught from an open window – can then make the bare wires touch. Examine also the connections in the CEILING ROSE, the lampholder and the light switch to see if a wire has come loose from its terminal – see ELECTRIC SOCKETS AND SWITCHES.

Another possibility is that a cable has been damaged during work on walls or floors. Use a circuit tester to check for damage – see CIRCUIT TESTING. If the circuit cable is damaged it will have to be replaced – see ELECTRIC WIRING.

When you have remedied any faults, replace the blown fuse or reset the MCB in the consumer unit and turn on the main switch again. If the fuse blows again or the MCB trips, call in a qualified electrician.

Fault in a power circuit Disconnect all plugged-in appliances so that all socket outlets are clear. If there are any triple sockets or a FUSED CONNECTION UNIT on the circuit, test the fuses in them to make sure they are sound. Use a circuit tester to check that the cable is sound – if it is not, it will have to be replaced.

Fit the repaired fuse back in the consumer unit or reset the MCB and turn the main switch back on. If the fuse blows again or the MCB trips, call in a qualified electrician. If the fuse or MCB remains sound, the trouble must be with an appliance.

Fault in an appliance Disconnect all the appliances and examine each for signs of a faulty flex, or a blown fuse or loose wires in the plug. Never examine an appliance while it is connected to the power supply.

If you find nothing, connect appliances one at a time to the circuit and switch on. When you turn on the faulty appliance, the fuse will blow again. If the fault in the appliance is more than a single flex or wiring fault, have it serviced or repaired.

Shrubs

Growing and caring for them

Shrubs are among the garden's most versatile plants. Evergreens provide patches of green all year round; scented shrubs such as lavender or honeysuckle planted round a window can fill a room with their fragrance, and bushy shrubs will hide ugly corners.

Most common shrubs can be bought from a garden centre. They can be planted at any time of the year, but if planted in summer the soil must be kept moist until autumn. Evergreen shrubs not bought in containers should be planted in October or April.

Planting First remove weeds (see WEED CONTROL), then dig over the soil to a spade depth. If you intend to plant the shrubs immediately, tread down the soil. If not, let it settle for two weeks.

Space the plants apart by at least half of their total spread. For example, the space between a shrub with a spread of 1.8m (6ft) and one with a spread of 1.2m (4ft) should be 1.5m (5ft). Mark out the planting positions with bamboo canes.

Dig a hole to the depth of the shrub's container, and slightly wider. Mix the excavated soil with peat substitute or COMPOST plus bone meal – about 1 part to 2 parts of soil. If you use manure, it must be at least a year old or it may burn the roots and check growth.

Hold the plant by the base of its stem and remove the container. Place the root still in its ball of soil in the hole and fill in with the prepared soil. Tread the soil firmly, then top up with more soil and tread again. Soak thoroughly round the base of the plant with water.

Watering and feeding Soon after planting, and each spring, spread a 50mm (2in) deep mulch of leaf mould, garden compost, manure or spent hops over the soil – see MULCHING. Do not water if the shrub was planted in autumn, winter or early spring, but water liberally during prolonged dry weather. If the soil is poor, apply a general purpose fertiliser each February – see FERTILISERS.

If pests or diseases appear, deal with them as promptly as possible – see PESTICIDES. Spray during a dry period, but not in bright sunshine, and cover the undersides and the tops of the leaves.

See also PLANTING; PRUNING SHRUBS; SOIL PREPARATION.

A large deciduous shrub, *Cornus alba* 'Variegata', creates a bright splash with its creamy-white edged leaves. It grows up to 3m (10ft) tall, and in this case has been underplanted with pinks.

SHUFFLE BOARD

Playing the game

Drive a disc along the deck with the driver to land in a numbered area, or to improve the position of one of your earlier discs – or to remove an opponent's disc.

Shuffle board

Playing a popular shipboard game

The game is usually played on deck aboard cruise ships and ocean liners, and is a variation of the old pub game shove ha'penny, greatly enlarged. It is played as singles or doubles.

Each player has four wooden discs, about 150mm (6in) in diameter, and a long-handled driver with a semicircular shoe used to push the disc.

The scoring area consists of nine 305mm (12in) squares numbered 1 to 9, so that any row of three totals 15. At each end of the group of squares is a semicircle, one marked +10 the other marked −10. There are two scoring areas placed 10m (32ft) apart, and there are two start lines for each, one for ladies and one for gentlemen.

Opponents play alternately, delivering their four discs. If a disc fails to reach the ladies' line it is removed so as not to be an obstruction. A disc is often moved, deliberately or accidentally, by those played later. The score is counted when all eight discs have been played. Each disc must be fully inside a square to score (or lose) the number of points indicated. Play continues by playing in the opposite direction to the other group of squares. The game ends when one player has scored 50 or 100, as agreed before the start of the game.

Shuffling playing cards

Ensuring a fair deal

Ensure that the bottom card is not exposed to the other players by shuffling the pack without lifting it from the table. Stack the pack squarely, with the long edge facing you. Split the pack in half and place each half on the table. Riffle the inner corners with your thumbs pushing the two halves together. Repeat and prepare to deal. See also BLACKJACK; CANASTA; CRIBBAGE; GIN RUMMY; PATIENCE; POKER; RUMMY; SNAP; WAR; WHIST.

Shyness

Learning to overcome it

Unrealistic expectations of oneself and excessive fear of failure lie behind much shyness. Some people, for example, believe they should be able to handle any social situation with perfect ease and confidence. When they fall short of the unrealistic standard they set themselves, they feel themselves failures and become afraid of trying again.

Other people feel a need to be approved and accepted by everyone – a practical impossibility – and the slightest rejection, real or imagined, upsets them.

Pinpointing your shyness Most people are a mixture of shyness and confidence. Certain situations or people make them feel shy – in other situations, or with different types of people, they are perfectly confident.

The first step in overcoming shyness is to find out who or what causes it. For a week or so, keep a record of every occasion when you feel shy. Note the people involved and your reactions – your thoughts and feelings as well as the way you behave.

After a while study your notes. Does a pattern emerge? Are there, for example, particular people, situations or subjects of conversation that make you shy? What are your thoughts, fears and feelings in these circumstances? Why are you reacting as you do?

Many people, for example, are embarrassed when approaching people in authority, such as doctors, teachers or local authority officials when they need help or information – they are afraid of seeming foolish.

Others become reticent and tongue-tied with people they would really like to be friendly with, thinking irrationally that the other person would probably not like them. Or if they do talk to that person they avoid eye contact and soon run out of conversation.

Changing your reactions Try to change the thoughts or feelings that lie behind your shyness. If you have to ask for information, for example, tell yourself firmly that you are no more a fool than anyone else, that your question is perfectly worth asking and that you have every right to the information.

Do not allow yourself to assume, for no reason, that somebody does not like you. Remind yourself that you honestly do not know whether the person likes you or not – and that it is pointless to assume that he or she does not.

Try to change your behaviour too. Speak confidently; make yourself look people in the eye more often.

Try to develop new ways of coping with certain situations. Imagine how you would like to behave in these situations, then try to behave like that – but do not despair if you do not quite manage it at first. Observe how people you respect behave in these situations, and get ideas from them.

Basic conversational skills Learning certain basic conversational skills also helps. For example, volunteer your opinions and feelings more when talking to people – they help to carry forward the conversation.

Offer free information about yourself. When asking questions of someone, make them open-ended so that the other person has to answer with more than one or two words.

Try sincere compliments to initiate conversations – 'What a beautiful garden you have!' Or ask for help – 'I believe you've lived here for a long time. Do you know where I can get my lawn mower mended?'

Alternatively, offer assistance, if assistance is needed – 'Can I help you carry your bag?'

Do not be afraid either to use the most obvious method of opening a conversation – 'I'm Fred Burns. What's your name? Have you lived here long? What's your job?' It usually works.

Sign language

Talking with your hands

People who are totally deaf communicate with a mixture of sign language, finger-spelling and lip reading. The techniques can be learned fairly easily by other people who wish to converse with someone who is deaf.

British Sign Language consists of 6000 signs, from a total of about 100,000 words in the English language. Consequently, when deaf people use a word that has no sign they spell it out with their fingers. To reinforce the signs and finger-spelling they often mouth the words as well.

British Sign Language Hand and arm movements express whole words. Most signs are like mime and are easily memorised: rocking cradled arms means 'baby'; beckoning is 'come'; a balancing movement of the upturned palms is 'compare'; the first two fingers touching the ear is 'deaf'.

A horizontal hand moving up to the chin is 'enough'; an upturned thumb is 'good'; pushing away with both hands is 'hate'; fingers crossed is 'hope'; two fingers upright on the back of the other hand is 'stand'; the index finger touching the forehead is 'think'; the index finger touching the arm where a wristwatch should be is 'time'.

Facial expressions reinforce the signs. A look of sadness accompanies the signs for 'I am sorry to hear that . . .' Raised eyebrows go with a question.

For those wishing to communicate with deaf people, the greatest difficulty is not in learning the signs, but in watching and 'reading' them – especially when they are done at speed. Deaf people, however, will usually reduce their speed if you are trying to learn.

Someone deaf from birth cannot usually understand as many words as someone who has become deaf later. To ease communication it is best to keep sentences short and direct, to avoid figurative language, and to arrange ideas chronologically.

Signs differ in different countries, and even in parts of the same country. For example, the sign for 'old' in Britain is usually to indicate the lines on each side of the nose, while in some other countries it indicates a beard.

Inexpensive booklets on sign language can be bought from the Royal National Institute for the Deaf, 105 Gower Street, London WC1E 6AH.

Finger spelling In this system, the letters of the alphabet are indicated by placing the fingers of the two hands in 26 different positions. The consonants are formed by roughly imitating the shape of the letters, and the vowels are represented by touching the tips of one of the five fingers of the left hand (see illustrations overleaf).

Skilled finger-spellers make no pause at the end of each word, unless the person they are conversing with is a beginner.

Lip reading Deaf children learn to lip-read at school, but the skill is difficult to master, as many sounds are made with the same lip movements. Consequently many deaf people like to use sign language in conjunction with lip-reading.

Spelling with your fingers

In finger spelling, the sign for each consonant imitates the shape of the written letter. The five vowels are indicated by using the right index finger to touch the five digits of the left hand.

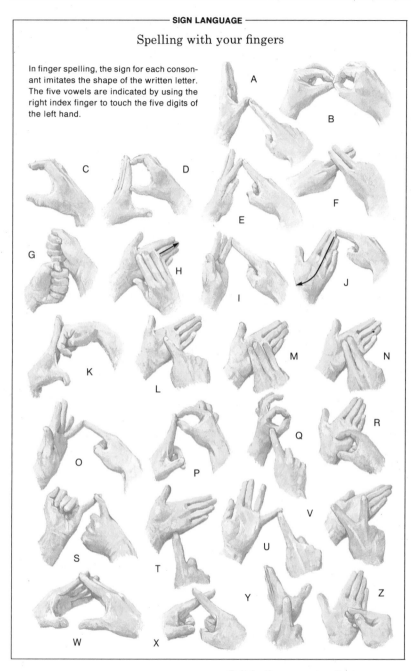

Silver

Caring for it; removing tarnish

Wash silver tableware immediately after use, using hot suds and a soft cloth, then rinse in hot water and dry. Keep each item in a lined cutlery box; and in a large service rotate the use of the pieces, so that their finish will mellow uniformly. To keep ornamental silver bright, dust or wash it regularly.

Polish silver occasionally to preserve its deep lustre. Wash the silver first in hot soap suds, then apply a proprietary polish. Use a soft grit-free cloth or CHAMOIS LEATHER and rub in straight, even strokes until the silver is clean and bright, then wash again to remove all traces of polish. Do not rub too heavily, as minute amounts of silver may be removed. Clean heavily embossed objects with a foam cleaner which washes off. On smaller items, use silver dip applied with a cotton-wool bud.

Removing tarnish Light tarnish is best removed by polishing, as described, but heavy tarnish can be treated by dipping in a 'silver dip', or by cleaning by the electrolytic method.

When using proprietary dip-shine fluids – make sure any fluid does not come into contact with other material such as stainless-steel knife blades or any other non-silver attachments.

To clean by the electrolytic method, line a porcelain bowl with aluminium foil, place the pieces in it and pour in a solution of a cup of washing soda and 4 pints of hot water. As with dip-shine fluids, do not immerse non-silver attachments, or knives that have handles fastened by cement.

As soon as the tarnish disappears from the items, remove then wash in running warm water. You can improve the finish by buffing after cleaning.

QUICK TIP To keep stored silver bright and clean, wrap it in acid-free tissue paper (available from some chemists) and store it in a bag specially designed for the purpose, available from jewellers.

Silverfish

Getting rid of a household pest

These silvery insects, about 13mm ($\frac{1}{2}$in) long, thrive in damp, warm places such as kitchens and bathrooms. They hide in floor cracks and under skirtings and are active at night.

To prevent an invasion of silverfish, minimise CONDENSATION and check for leaking PLUMBING or rising DAMP. Fill in cracks in floorboards (see FLOOR REPAIRS) and SKIRTING BOARDS.

If silverfish appear, use a spray or powder labelled 'for use against crawling insects' – see PESTICIDES. Do not use sprays where they may ignite, such as near an open fire or gas PILOT LIGHTS.

Siphoning

Transferring a liquid from one place to another

All you need to start a siphon is a length of flexible tube. Fill it with the liquid, immerse one end in the liquid, and hold the other end lower than the liquid level.

To empty a water butt or a raised pond, for example, immerse a length of hose pipe in the water. Squeeze along it and move it about to make all the air bubble out. Place your thumb firmly over one end and lift it out of the water, making sure that the other end stays submerged. Position the outlet end of the hose lower than the level of the water, and remove your thumb. Water will flow out and continue to flow as long as the end of the hose is lower than the level of the water – or until all the water is emptied out. The lower you hold the end of the hose the faster the water will flow out.

For smaller amounts of harmless liquid, you can use transparent tubing (so you can see what is happening) and suck liquid up it to fill it. When the tube is full, pinch its end tightly and move it until it is lower than the liquid level. Release the tube and liquid will flow.

With dangerous liquids, you may be able to fill the tube by using a garden spray. Wear strong rubber gloves and use a transparent tube. Attach the spray tube to the end of the plastic tube with insulating tape. Immerse the free end of the tube in the liquid, then draw on the spray handle until liquid is drawn up almost the entire tube. Pinch the tube firmly near the spray tube while you peel off the sticky tape. Move the tube end lower than the liquid level and release – liquid will flow.

Remember that if you lift the immersed end of the tube out of the liquid, air will enter it and the siphon will be broken. Just re-immersing it will not start the siphon again. You must refill the tube and expel all the air.

Where siphoning is not possible you can use a small pump attachment which will fit on most power drills; you can hire a pump from tool hire shops – see HIRING.

Skids
Avoiding and correcting them

Driving carefully will always minimise the risk of skidding, which occurs when the wheels fail to grip the road surface and slide over it rather than rolling along it. Ice, mud, wet leaves, oil and grease, shingle and sand are all potential causes of skidding. See also DRIVING IN BAD WEATHER.

There are three types of skid, calling for different driving techniques:

Rear-wheel skid If you feel the rear end start to break away, take your foot off the accelerator and steer *into* the skid. That is, if the back swings to the right, steer to the right, and vice versa.

Do not brake or declutch. Hold the steering on until you feel the tyres gripping again, then immediately centre it so that all four wheels are back in line. Resume steering normally.

Front-wheel skid The front wheels lose grip when cornering and the car slides forward, without responding to the steering wheel. Do not brake or declutch.

In a rear-wheel-drive car, take your foot off the accelerator and centre the steering wheel, so that the front wheels are in line with the direction of travel. When grip is restored, accelerate gently.

In a front-wheel-drive car, ease the accelerator, but retain just enough power to keep the car moving. Keep steering into the corner, straighten the wheels and accelerate gently.

Four-wheel skid Sudden, violent braking may cause all four wheels to lock; the car slides forward and cannot be steered. As soon as the wheels start to lock – the screech of rubber should warn you – reduce braking enough to allow the wheels to roll, then brake again (without declutching) in a series of quick on-off movements.

Skiing
Choosing the equipment; basic techniques

In Britain, skiing on snow is mostly confined to Scotland. There, and at ski resorts abroad and on artificial slopes at leisure centres, you can try out the sport on hired skis. If you become enthusiastic, you can buy your own.

Choosing equipment Skis for downhill skiing vary little in width, and for a beginner should be no longer than the skier's height – longer skis are harder to control. Skis for cross-country touring are longer and narrower, because they glide over the snow more efficiently.

Modern skis are made of fibreglass. Skis are arched so that when there is no weight on them they touch the ground only at the front and rear. Under your weight they will make full contact with the snow.

Buy the best ski boots you can afford. Modern boots are plastic, and the most expensive ones generally have the most adaptable inner linings to give the snug fit essential for you to be able to feel contact with the skis and the snow. Remember to wear socks when trying on boots. A perfect fit means that you cannot lift your heel inside the boot but your toes are not cramped and can be wiggled.

The clamp holding the boot to the ski is called the binding. For downhill skiing, the binding holds both toe and heel rigidly to the ski. But for cross-country skiing, the binding allows the heel to rise – cross-country bindings can often be adjusted for downhill as well. When you buy skis, bindings can be fitted to suit your boots.

The poles, or ski sticks, with which you propel yourself forward, need to be the right length. With the pole upturned and held under the basket (the hoop near the tip), your arm should be bent at a right angle at the elbow.

Ski clothing is a matter of personal choice and pocket. The essentials are a woollen hat to prevent body heat from escaping through the head, mittens or gloves which fit snugly round your wrists and hands, a warm jacket, and sun glasses – or wide-angle goggles if it is snowing.

Skiing technique One way to learn is to attend a ski school. You can find the nearest one to you by writing to the Ski Club of Great Britain, 118 Eaton Square,

---

SKIING

Learning how to start and stop

Good balance and control are needed in skiing. To ensure them it is important to perfect the basic techniques. Two of the first techniques taught are how to stand on your skis, and the snow plough, which enables you to stop.

Starting position Bend your knees slightly over your toes and get your weight slightly forward. Keep your body upright – do not bend too far forward from the waist.

Knees flexed

Weight slightly forward

Arms relaxed

Heels pushed apart

Snow-plough position As you are skiing, keep your knees bent and force your heels apart to bring the tips of your skis together.

London SW1W 9AF. Alternatively, you can have lessons on the nursery slopes at the ski resort.

Before skiing on snow, learn to walk wearing your skis. Push with your poles and walk round in circles. Try walking up a slight incline, using side steps if you begin to slide backwards. Then glide down.

When you fall – and you will – relax and fall on your side. Before you get up, turn your skis across the slope, draw your legs up under your hips and crouch. Then plant your poles firmly to give you support, and stand up.

To start skiing down a gentle slope, propel yourself forwards with the poles, then hold them so that they point backwards and are clear of the ground. Once started, you can glide down the slope with no further assistance from the poles.

To turn and stop, learn the snow plough position, as illustrated. To make a right turn, for example, exert more pressure on the left leg. Then ski down the slope in wide S turns, always exerting pressure on the downhill leg to make a curve. Turn uphill to stop.

Having mastered gliding, stopping and turning, you can start to ski faster by leaning forwards a little more and making fewer S turns, pointing your skis more downhill.

Skin-diving

Snorkelling safely with mask and flippers

Snorkelling enables you to see fish, shells and rocks on the seabed. The only items of equipment you need are a face mask to protect your eyes, a snorkel (breathing tube) and a pair of flippers.

Face masks The best masks have toughened safety glass (not plastic which scratches and mists up easily) firmly encased in a flexible rubber or silicone surround with soft edges, so that the mask fits snugly.

Buy a mask that covers your eyes and nose only; masks that enclose the mouth or have a built-in snorkel are dangerous. A shaped nosepiece will allow you to hold and blow your nose while underwater to clear blocked ear tubes.

To check if a mask is the right shape and size, hold it against your face without putting on the straps and breathe in through your nose; if the masks fits properly, the suction will keep it in place.

Snorkels Do not buy a breathing tube with an air valve or ping-pong ball attachment. Balls and valves jam easily, cutting off the air supply. Buy a simple J-shaped tube 300-360mm (12-14in) long, with a mouthpiece that fits comfortably between your teeth without bruising

SKIN-DIVING

Safe equipment underwater

Snorkels

Clearing your mask underwater Look up. Press the top of the mask. Breathe out through your nose until the mask is clear.

Face mask

Flippers

Foot gear Some flippers surround the heel like a shoe, others have open heel straps. They should be a close fit, but should not cut into your feet.

your gums. The best snorkels conform to British Standard BS4532.

To prevent misting up, before you enter the sea spit into your mask, smear the glass with saliva and wash it out, or rinse the glass with demisting solution.

Flippers Large, stiff fins give the most thrust, but if they are too unwieldy they may cause aching calf muscles. You can buy buoyant flippers which are less likely to get lost – see illustration.

Swimming with flippers Make strong, rhythmical movements, using slow crawl leg-strokes – see SWIMMING. Kick from the hips, keeping your knees slightly bent and your toes pointed. Do not let your fins break the surface.

In order to plunge to the bottom, do a 'duck dive': take a deep breath, filling your lungs with air, then bend from the waist and glide smoothly down towards the bottom. The snorkel will fill with water, which you must expel when you resurface.

Water in tube or mask After surfacing from a dive, or if water enters your breathing tube while you are at the sur-

face, bring your head up out of the water then thrust your chin upwards to tilt the tube – making sure the end of the tube is clear of the surface – and blow forcefully into the mouthpiece to expel the water.

To clear water from your mask when you are at the surface, tread water while you lift the lower edge of your mask so the water drains away.

To empty water from your mask while underwater, tilt your head back, keep the top of the mask pressed firmly against your forehead and breathe out slowly through your nose so that air fills the mask and forces the water out from the bottom. Stop exhaling as soon as the mask is clear, so you retain enough air in your lungs to return to the surface – see illustration.

Safety measures

● Do not go snorkelling unless you can swim well.

● Get used to using a mask, snorkel and fins in a swimming pool or in calm water well within your depth close to the shore.

● Wearing flippers, practise treading water, using your legs alone, with your hands above the surface, until you can keep it up for at least a minute.

● Never go skin-diving unaccompanied, or if the sea is rough or cold. Stay within easy reach of land or a boat, raft or jetty. Take lifesaving lessons.

● Avoid areas where there are power-boats or water-skiers. Listen for power-boats when you are surfacing.

● Do not stay in the water too long; come out immediately if you start to suffer cramp.

Signals

The following signals are used by skin divers and scuba divers, and may be understood by coastguards and some boat owners too:

Help needed To signal that you need assistance, raise one arm and wave it from side to side with fist clenched.

Help not needed To indicate that you are OK, raise your hand with thumb and forefinger joined to make an 'O' and the other fingers pointing upwards.

For safety precautions when spearfishing underwater or swimming near submerged seaweed – see SCUBA DIVING.

Skipping games

Jumping over a whirling rope

In one of the simplest group skipping games, two players hold the ends of a rope about 3m (4yds) long and swing it in a steady rhythm. The others stand in line between them and jump over the rope as many times as they can.

Sometimes the game starts with the

rope already turning, the jumpers stepping in one by one.

An onlooker, or a rope turner, keeps a count of the score by chanting a counting rhyme, such as 'one, two, buckle my shoe'. When a player misses a jump, he or she takes over one end of the rope so that eventually everyone has a turn.

The game can be varied so that players hop on one foot, or pick up and set down a stone or ball. Or the rope is whirled so fast that it passes under the jumpers twice between jumps. Another variation is for each player in turn to step in, hop once, then step out without breaking the rhythm. Next time, each player hops twice, then three times, then four, and so on, until one player misses and drops out. The game continues until only one player remains – the winner.

For 'follow the leader', each player copies the leader's actions – hopping on one foot, for example – as well as jumping in and out of the rope. And in 'salt and pepper', the rope alternates between fast and slow.

Skirting boards

Repairing and renewing them

The purpose of skirting boards is to protect the wall from damage by knocks from feet and furniture. But they may also be attacked from behind, for if a wall gets DAMP they may be affected by wet or DRY ROT.

If you have a damaged section to replace, measure the length and thickness of the skirting board, allowing 50-75mm (2-3in) for mitring – see MITRE JOINTS. The timber merchant may be able to match it exactly, or you can buy a board of the correct dimensions and shape it yourself at home. For one simple curve, use a drum sander with a fairly coarse sanding belt – see SANDING.

How skirting boards are fixed depends upon the nature of the wall. If the wall is masonry, they may be nailed to pieces of BATTENS set in the wall below plaster level, as shown. Or they may be nailed into wooden plugs knocked into the joints between the bricks, or nailed direct into the MORTAR joints.

The easiest boards to remove are those attached to stud PARTITIONS or hollow PLASTERBOARD walls, where quite small nails are set into the floor plate or timber blocks set in the partition.

To remove a skirting board, if possible start at an external corner where mitres meet. Scrape away the surface paint and clear the patches of filler covering nail heads. Try to remove the nail with pincers, but if no grip can be obtained, use a nail punch and hammer to sink the nail below the wood so that you can prise the board off and pull the nail out later. Lever the board off with a wrecking bar

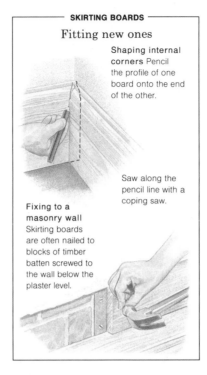

Fitting new ones

Shaping internal corners Pencil the profile of one board onto the end of the other.

Saw along the pencil line with a coping saw.

Fixing to a masonry wall Skirting boards are often nailed to blocks of timber batten screwed to the wall below the plaster level.

or a claw hammer, protecting the plaster surface with scrap wood.

If you encounter cut nails (see NAILING) which will not move – in or out – and the skirting board is to be scrapped, use a tenon saw (see SAWS AND SAWING) to make cuts close to the nails, at right angles to the run of the board, then lever away the board until it breaks. Or simply split the board free using an old wood chisel and mallet – see CHISELLING.

If the skirtings are nailed to vertical mouldings, such as door frames, locate the nail heads and punch them in with a nail punch to release the board.

If the same boards are to be used, make a note of where they fitted. Or if one piece is to be replaced, keep it as a template for the new piece of board – and as a guide for cutting the corners.

Treat the rear surface of the new skirting board liberally with one of the WOOD PRESERVATIVES. Make sure the wall is dry and that any fault has been dealt with before fitting new wood.

Mark any fixing points on the floor so you know where to position nails when the skirting board is held in place – you may need to renew timber fixings on masonry walls. Also mark the position of pipes and cables so you do not damage them with nails.

External corners will need to be mitred. On internal corners, mark the profile of one board against the other, as illustrated, and cut away the end along the mark – or use a PROFILE GAUGE. Fix the boards with the cut boards overlapping the uncut board.

Take care when hammering not to bruise the wood surface. Leave nail heads slightly above the surface, and use a nail punch and hammer to drive them below the surface. Fill the holes with wood filler – see STOPPERS AND FILLERS.

Skittles

Playing an ancient pub game

Skittles is mostly played in special narrow alleys attached to country pubs in England and Wales. The object is to knock down a group of nine wooden pins by bowling a heavy wooden or rubber ball at them. Rules vary but the basic game is played as follows:

Two teams of six to ten players assemble at one end of the wood or asphalt alley (see illustration), which is usually about 15-24m (50-80ft) long. They take turns to bowl the ball underarm at the wooden pins, which are usually numbered 1-9, with the nine, or 'landlord', sometimes the tallest pin at the centre of the diamond.

Some alleys have a long, narrow, wooden 'pitchboard' running parallel to the side walls, along which the players must pitch the ball before it heads towards the pins. The players can rest their heels for purchase on a raised wooden ledge called the 'oche', which runs across their end of the alley. But, when bowling, they must not overstep the oche (throwing line), and the ball must not bounce after the 'foul line'.

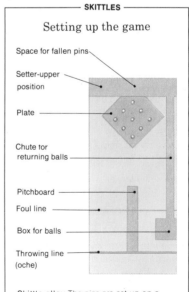

Setting up the game

Space for fallen pins

Setter-upper position

Plate

Chute for returning balls

Pitchboard

Foul line

Box for balls

Throwing line (oche)

Skittle alley The pins are set up on a diamond-shaped plate. The player throws from behind the throwing line and the setter-upper replaces fallen pins and returns the balls down the side chute.

In some versions of the game, a ball which rebounds off a side wall and knocks down the skittles is valid; in others it is not.

Each player has three consecutive throws, his score depending on the number of pins he knocks down. For example, if he knocks down all nine pins with his first ball – called a 'floorer' or 'flopper' – he scores nine points. The pins are set up again by someone appointed 'setter upper', or 'sticker-upper', and the player can go on to score a maximum of 27 points (three nines). The pins are only set up again if and when all nine have been 'floored'. Otherwise, the setter-upper clears away the fallen pins. So, if the player knocks down only one with his first throw and one with his second, the maximum he could score with his final throw would be seven.

At the end of an agreed number of throws – usually 18 or 21 – the players add up their scores to see which team has knocked down most pins. See also TABLE SKITTLES.

Sleep

Fighting insomnia; do's and don'ts for poor sleepers

Millions experience some form of insomnia – they have trouble falling asleep; they waken very early and cannot get back to sleep; or having slept for a few hours, they waken periodically until morning.

Insomnia can have a number of causes, such as pain, anxiety, depression or over excitement. But in most cases the cause is far simpler: too little exercise (see EXERCISES); too much to eat or drink; too much heat or cold; too much noise or light; or too many daytime naps.

Some basic do's and don'ts can relieve short-term insomnia.

Don't take stimulants – coffee, tea, tobacco – in the evening.
Don't eat rich, heavy foods shortly before going to bed.
Don't get into an excited state – watching a horror film, or tackling work problems – in the evening.
Don't put too many, or too few, blankets on the bed. Use bedding that is appropriate to the room temperature.
Don't worry about not sleeping – this only makes matters worse.
Do try to take exercise in the afternoon or evening.
Do develop a night-time routine, such as taking a stroll or walking the dog, locking up the house, reading in bed.
Do try to relax after turning out the light. For example, recite poetry to yourself, make up a story, or just let your mind wander down memory lane.

Do try RELAXATION EXERCISES or take up YOGA.
Do make sure the mattress is both firm and comfortable.
Do take a hot bath shortly before retiring, and have a drink of warm milk.

If you still have trouble sleeping, and particularly if you get off to sleep easily but wake in the early hours, consult your DOCTOR. If you are suffering from depression the doctor may prescribe anti-depressant tablets. Alternatively, you may be prescribed sleeping pills as a temporary solution; these do not remove the cause of the insomnia and are best avoided if possible.

Sleeping bags

Choosing and caring for them

Buy the best-quality sleeping bag you can afford. A good sleeping bag is made like a quilt – its filling compresses when rolled up, expands when unrolled – see QUILTING.

Choosing a bag Bag quality varies with the filling. The best are those filled with soft, fluffy feathers – finest goose or duck down. Not only will a down bag keep you snug and warm in temperatures as low as $-20°C$ ($-4°F$), but it is light to carry (a bonus when BACKPACKING or BICYCLE TOURING). They range in price from around £80 to £140 or more.

A drawback with the down bag, however, is that it soon loses insulation efficiency when wet. It needs two or three days in the air to dry out – unlike a polyester-filled bag, which dries out quickly. But down bags will last 12 years or more, whereas the synthetic-fibre bag may need replacing after five years.

Synthetic-fibre bags (around £12 to £30) are suitable for use under canvas in summer – see CAMPING. A third type of bag (£40 to £50) has a thicker polyester hollow fibre filling and is suitable for all seasons. Like down bags, it is barrel shaped to give snugness and warmth.

Try a sleeping bag before you buy it by climbing inside. It should be more than 1.8m (6ft) long, have good zips and allow freedom of movement; children's bags should be 1.2m × 610mm (4 × 2ft) for 7-8 year olds. Rectangular bags with all-round zip fasteners can often be zipped together as double bags.

Some bags come with a cotton liner, but you can buy liners separately. Only the liner need be washed regularly. Liners tend to twist when you turn over.

Caring for your bag Air thoroughly after each trip, and store loosely in a large laundry bag; or hang the bag on a coat hanger. Clean or wash in accordance with the maker's instructions.

Always carry a needle and thread, nylon tape patches and safety pins, to repair rips or holes promptly – see MENDING. Use a safety pin to replace a broken zip-pull – see ZIPPERS.

WARNING A sleeping bag can become a trap if a tent or caravan catches fire. Do not waste time trying to unzip it: kneel up, push the bag down, then kick it off.

Slides and slide shows

Storing and projecting your pictures

Always handle a slide by the mount, and put a label on the mount to show the date and subject. Put a self-adhesive spot on the lower left corner of each mount to make sure you feed it into a projector the correct way.

Storing slides Keep the slides in boxes or in plastic display sheets that can be held in files or binders and store in a dry, dark, cool place. In humid conditions store them with packets of moisture-absorbing silica gel.

Showing slides To get the best image, use the slide projector in a completely blacked-out room. Projectors vary from simple hand-operated models that carry only two slides at a time to remote-control machines with rotary magazines taking 80 or more slides.

Project the image onto any flat white surface, such as a wall or a screen. Screens may be matt or beaded. Beaded screens give a more brilliant image, but reflect in a relatively narrow angle so that the audience has to sit almost directly in front of the screen.

Editing slides Before giving a slide show, weed out slides with bad exposure and uninteresting shots. Avoid frequent jumps between bright and dark scenes or between horizontal and vertical images. Put the slides in a logical, storytelling sequence. See also PHOTOGRAPHY.

Sliding doors

Choosing and fitting them

A sliding cupboard or wardrobe door occupies no space when open, but hides a part of the contents.

Types vary according to weight; light, small sliding doors are usually fitted in runners, whereas heavy doors are hung on a roller track.

Light doors The simplest system, for CABINETS or CUPBOARDS, involves two wood or plastic runner tracks in which a hardboard or PLYWOOD door can be housed. When you buy the track, make sure you have a shallow one for the base, and one with channels about twice as deep for the top. Screw the tracks to the cupboard base and top (see SCREWS), flush with the front edge. Make sure that the screws do not stick up in the grooves.

Chamfer and smooth the bottoms of the doors, then dust with a dry lubricant. Keep the channels clear of debris.

Heavy doors When heavier and larger doors are involved, such as those used on wardrobes, hang the doors on rollers running in a steel channel as shown. Guides on the floor may either fit in a groove in the underside of the doors, or pass either side of the doors.

If the upper track is at ceiling height, you must screw it through the plaster into secure timber above – or into an upper frame that is screwed to the JOISTS. If the frame or track runs at right angles to the ceiling joists, locate the joists and screw into them. If the frame or track runs parallel to the joists, it is unlikely that a joist is in just the right place; fix sturdy struts between joists and screw into the struts. Never rely on ceiling plaster alone to take the weight of heavy doors.

Some channels are designed to take a single door on rollers, while others are shaped so that one set of rollers runs on the back edge of the channel and another on the front so the doors can pass freely. Whichever system is used you need the doors to overlap at the centre when both doors are closed.

Apart from straight sliding doors, gear is available which allows door sections to fold. This has the space-saving benefits of a sliding door but enables the whole of a wardrobe to be exposed. Hang the door sections as for normal sliding doors, then for each pair of folding doors fit a door pivot to run in the track. You will also need HINGES to hinge each door section to its neighbour.

Sliding door gear needs very little maintenance. Just make sure that channels are kept free from dust and debris, and oil wheel pivots occasionally.

Slings

Supporting a broken arm – or an injured hand

Slings give added protection and support to someone who has already been treated for an injury to the ribs, chest, hand or arm – see BROKEN BONES. If an arm is bandaged, check that the fingernails are not blue; if they are, loosen the bandage before fitting the sling.

Slings are normally made from a triangular bandage – obtainable from any chemist. But you can use any material

---

SLIDING DOORS

Fixing a roller track and runners

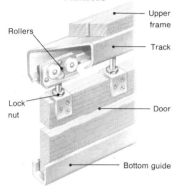

Rollers — Upper frame — Track — Lock nut — Door — Bottom guide

The adjustment nuts on the roller brackets alter the height of the door, so that it will run freely in the guide. Tighten the adjustment lock nuts when the height has been set.

In a simple cabinet system, lift the top of the door into the upper, wider track, and drop it into the shallow bottom track.

---

about 1m (3ft) square, either folded or cut diagonally.

Arm sling Use a conventional arm sling for a wounded arm and for some rib injuries. It works only if the casualty can stand or sit.

Get the casualty to support the injured arm with the other hand. Place the bandage between the chest and forearm – its point stretching well beyond the elbow. Take the upper end over the shoulder on the uninjured side, and round the neck to the injured side.

Take the lower end of the bandage up over the hand and forearm and tie the ends with a reef knot – see KNOTS.

Pin the point near the elbow, or twist and tuck it in.

Elevation sling Use this type if a hand must be raised to control bleeding, if a collarbone has been broken or if there are complicated chest injuries. It will also support the arm of a casualty who cannot stand or sit, and provides extra support if a rough journey has to be undertaken.

Raise the injured arm – or the arm on the injured side in the case of a chest injury – so that the hand rests on the opposite shoulder.

Put one end of the bandage over the casualty's shoulder on the uninjured side, letting the rest hang over the injured arm with the point extending beyond the elbow.

Gently push the base of the triangle under the arm and take the other end of the bandage round the casualty's back on the injured side. Tie the ends together at the shoulder on the uninjured side.

Fold the point of the sling at the elbow and fasten it with a pin, or instead twist and tuck it in.

Improvised slings Improvise a sling if you do not have a triangular bandage and you cannot make one. A sling can be made from a belt, tie, scarf or roller bandage – see BANDAGING.

Wrap or loop the improvised sling

SLINGS

Making three types of sling

Arm sling Take the top end of the bandage round the neck. Take the lower end under the injured arm. Then bring it up over the arm and tie the ends together just above the collarbone.

Improvised sling Loop the sling round the wrist of the injured arm. Take the ends round the neck and tie them together.

Elevation sling Stretch the sling diagonally across the chest to support and bind the injured arm to the opposite shoulder. Bring the lower end round the back. Tie above the collarbone.

round the casualty's wrist on the injured side of the body.

Put one end of the sling over the shoulder on the uninjured side. Then take the other end round the neck.

Tie the ends in the hollow above the collarbone on the uninjured side. The casualty's hand should usually be just above elbow level – but at shoulder level for forearm or hand wounds.

Alternatively, if you have a large pin, turn up the bottom edge of the casualty's jacket and pin it firmly to the jacket at chest level. The arm will then be well supported inside the fold.

Or, his hand can be pushed inside the fastened jacket at chest level, supported by a button or zip.

Slipped disc

Treating and avoiding one; warning signs

Symptoms of a slipped disc include severe pain in the lower back after lifting something heavy, or when straightening up after bending.

The pain may strike suddenly, or develop gradually. It may become more severe when you bend, sit on or rise from a chair, cough or strain. It may spread to the buttocks and hips, and one or both legs. You may be numb in the lower leg and outer foot. The pain is often eased when you lie flat, stand up or walk.

The spinal discs that cause the problem are made of jelly-like substances, contained in a tough fibrous casing. After the age of 25 these discs gradually degenerate – and the five in the lower back are the most likely to 'slip'.

When this happens, the soft core bulges from its fibrous casing and presses on a spinal nerve, causing acute pain.

Sometimes a mild attack clears up in a few days and never recurs. Some 75 per cent of the more severe attacks recur but are usually eased by resting.

Treatment at home Rest on a flat, firm bed – a soft bed should be 'hardened' with a wide board under the mattress. Do not attempt to move heavy weights.
● Take painkillers (aspirin, paracetamol) in recommended doses.
● Apply a heat-lamp or hot-water bottle to the affected area.
● Call your DOCTOR if the pain does not lessen, or gets worse, after two or three days' rest. The doctor may prescribe stronger painkillers and further rest, and arrange for physiotherapy or manipulation. In an extreme case, you may need surgery or a plaster jacket or corset.

Avoiding the slipped disc Remind yourself to keep your back straight and to bend at the knees when lifting or lowering something heavy; and to hold the weight close to your body. Never twist at the waist when lifting – lift first and then turn – see LIFTING AND CARRYING.

General back pain Most people suffer back pain at some time of their lives, but in very few cases is it a symptom of a serious disease. However agonising, it is usually the result of a minor injury, such as a slipped disc or muscle strain. Nearly 75 per cent of sufferers recover in a week, and 90 per cent of the remainder in a month – see also BACKACHE.

Slipstitching

Joining two folded edges with 'invisible' stitches

This is an almost invisible hand-made stitch used for joining two folded edges or for joining one folded edge to a flat surface. You can sew an even or an uneven slipstitch.

Even slipstitch Use this for joining two folded edges – for example, a seam that has come undone where you cannot reach the underside; the opening of a cushion cover or any other stuffed item (see TEDDY BEAR REPAIRS); a mitred corner – see SEWING.

Uneven slipstitch Use this for joining a folded edge to a flat piece of fabric – for example, for sewing linings in CURTAINS and garments; for PATCHING; or as an alternative to hemstitch for sewing HEMS.

SLIPSTITCHING

Even and uneven stitching

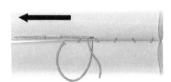

Even slipstitch Push the needle into one folded edge, slide it inside 6mm (¼in) and pull it out on the fold edge. Exactly opposite that point, push it into the other fold. Repeat.

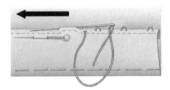

Uneven slipstitch Catch up two or three threads of the flat fabric and slide the needle inside the fold for about 6mm (¼in). Pull it out on the fold edge and repeat.

Sloes

Making sloe gin and sloe-and-apple jelly

Sloes are the blue-black fruit of the blackthorn, a large shrub or small tree that grows throughout Britain. The bushes occur in thorny thickets, and make dense and unapproachable hedges. They may be a parent of damsons and other types of plum.

Pick sloes – taking great care to avoid the thorns – in late October, when they are a ripe, deep blue, with a 'bloom' on them. See also BERRIES.

To make sloe gin, gather about 450g (1lb) of sloes and jab them with a sharp kitchen fork. Mix them with an equal weight of sugar, then divide the mixture between two bottles. Top them up with gin. Seal the bottles.

Leave for at least three months when the beverage will have matured to a warm, red colour. After this, strain several times through double muslin or filter paper until the gin is clear, then leave for another six months in a cool, dark place.

Here, too, is a recipe for sloe-and-apple jelly:

Ingredients
900g (2lb) sloes
1.8kg (4lb) cooking apples
Juice and peel of a lemon
Sugar

Wash and drain the sloes and prick them. Put them in a pan with the lemon juice, peel and just enough water to cover. Simmer until pulpy.

Wash and chop the apples, then simmer in a separate pan, with water to cover – again until soft and pulpy.

Strain the two pulps through scalded jelly-bags or fine muslin hung overnight over bowls – do *not* squeeze the bags, which will result in cloudy jelly.

Mix and measure the juices, bring to the boil, add sugar at the rate of 450g to 570ml (1lb to 1 pint) and stir until dissolved. Boil until the setting point is reached – see JELLIES.

Slugs and snails

Protecting your seedlings and leafy vegetables

Slugs and snails feed mostly at night and are particularly active in damp weather. They eat most types of leafy vegetables, but are particularly damaging to seedlings and young plants, as well as low-growing fruits such as strawberries. Keeled slugs live and feed underground and may damage potatoes, bulbs and root vegetables.

The surest way to protect plants is to surround them with proprietary slug pellets or slug-killer gel, which are based on metaldehyde or methiocarb – see PESTICIDES. These also poison other small creatures that eat them or eat slugs – particularly birds.

Protect birds – and also any hedgehogs that may come into your garden – by hiding pellets under propped-up slates, or preferably cover plant rows and pellets with domed wire-netting.

If you do not want to use poison, milk or beer traps can be effective. Sink small dishes about 25mm (1in) or more deep into the ground and fill them with watered-down beer or milk. The slugs are attracted to the beer or milk, then fall in and drown.

Another method is to surround plants with material such as soot, wood ash or lime, which slugs and snails cannot easily slide over. Keep it well away from plant stems. It needs renewing when it gets wet.

Slugs like to hide by day in damp, moist places under stones, bricks, flowerpots or garden litter. Either remove these to discourage them, or use them as a lure, regularly collecting the slugs from underneath and dropping them in a bucket of soapy water in order to kill them.

Another bait is half a potato or halves of grapefruit or orange skins set upturned on the ground. Slugs and snails can be regularly collected from these, and drowned.

A vulnerable young plant can be shielded until it is well established with a collar made from a tin with ends removed, or a cylinder of roofing felt, sunk into the ground round the stem. Shield clusters of strawberries with flat collars, or lift them off the ground with galvanised wire supports.

Potatoes can sometimes be protected from keeled slugs by planting them in plenty of garden compost, which offers an alternative food source as a distraction.

Small claims

Using a county court to recover a debt

Suing someone who owes you money, or who has refused to compensate you for faulty goods or services, can be done through the county court without having any legal knowledge or the assistance of LAWYERS.

Claims not exceeding £1000 are heard before an arbitrator, usually the court registrar, and the proceedings are informal – see ARBITRATION.

By agreement of both parties, claims above £1000 can go to arbitration on request to the registrar, but the request may be refused if the registrar considers the case should go to court. In that case

it will be heard by a judge in court, and all the usual court formalities will be observed.

How to sue Before suing someone for payment of a debt, be sure that your opponent will be able to pay if you win the action. See also SUING.

You should also make every effort to settle your dispute by agreement. A court may refuse to award costs to you if you sue someone without first giving him the chance to meet his obligations.

If you are owed money, write to the person concerned reminding him of the debt and asking him to settle as soon as possible. In the case of a claim for faulty goods or services, write to the supplier detailing the nature of your complaint and requesting recompense – see COMPLAINTS; SALE OF GOODS.

Allow no more than two weeks for a reply, and if your letter is ignored or your request refused, write again and state that unless you receive satisfaction within seven days you will issue proceedings in the county court. Keep a copy of the letters, and keep all invoices and receipts.

If you have difficulty in writing suitable letters, or there are complications in the claim, ask your local Citizens Advice Bureau. They may draft a letter for you, or write on your behalf.

To start an action you must fill in a form called 'a 'request', and enter the details of your claim on a form called 'particulars of claim'; you should fill in three copies of this, keep one and send the others to the court, one for their records and the other for sending to the defendant. The forms are available free from any county court office. The court in which you seek action must be the court for the district in which the defendant resides or carries on his business. A court fee, based on the size of the debt or recompense, must be paid with the request form.

When giving the particulars of your claim, make sure that you have the correct name and address of the defendant. This applies particularly if your claim is against a shop or company.

Set out a brief statement of your claim and the sum of money or other recompense you are claiming. The person suing is known to the court as the plaintiff, and it is usual to write in the third person – for example: 'The plaintiff claims £300 which he lent to the defendant in January 1994.'

The court will issue a summons, which will be served on the defendant by post. The summons can, at your request, be delivered by a court bailiff, but you will be charged a small fee for this.

Whether a dispute is to be settled by arbitration or in court, the registrar will usually first call both parties together to discuss, in his presence, ways of resolv-

ing it. You will be asked to bring receipts, bills and other relevant papers and may have to provide photocopies of them for the defendant. He will have to do the same. Quite often an amicable agreement is reached at this meeting, and the case goes no further. If not, a date for the hearing will be set.

Both plaintiff and defendant may take a relative, friend or social worker to the arbitration, to help them conduct their case, and the arbitrator can allow another person to address him on behalf of either party.

The arbitrator will ask you to state the details of your claim. Do so clearly and dispassionately, and speak slowly, as he will be making notes of what you say. The arbitrator may ask you questions – it is important that you give the right answers, so if you do not understand a question, say so.

The arbitrator will also question the defendant and any witnesses and will then give his judgment, called, in a case of arbitration, the award.

If the case is heard in court you will have to give evidence on oath, in the witness box. You can be cross-examined by the defendant, or his lawyer, and similarly you have the right to cross-examine him.

Where neither you nor the defendant is represented, the judge will usually listen to each of you in turn and then ask questions to clarify any particular points, or give the opportunity for you or the defendant to qualify or explain anything that has already been said during the hearing.

If judgment is given in your favour you can ask that the defendant pay all your court costs, but only if you have been awarded the full amount that you have claimed.

Seeking further advice Consult your local Citizens Advice Bureau or your local council's Consumer Advice Centre. From either of these, or from a county court office, you can also obtain the booklet *Small Claims in the County Court*, free of charge.

Smells

Ridding your home of unpleasant odours

The best way to keep a home smelling fresh is to keep it clean and well-aired. Open doors and windows regularly to let draughts of air circulate round the house. Install a ventilator (see VENTILATION) or an EXTRACTOR FAN in the kitchen to clear cooking smells.

Kitchen smells Wipe up spills promptly and open the window or ventilator or switch on the extractor fan during or after cooking. Get rid of fish, garlic and onion smells by rubbing a cut of lemon over utensils, pans, chopping boards and even your hands.

To get rid of persistent smells, simmer a small pan of white vinegar on the cooker.

Use a solution of bicarbonate of soda and water to clean the inside of a refrigerator and rid it of stale smells, or to freshen a vacuum flask.

Clean bins with domestic bleach. To clear a WASTE DISPOSAL UNIT of unpleasant smells, grind lemon or orange peel in it.

At least once a year, clean food cupboards and leave them empty with the doors open for a few hours.

Lavatory smells Light a match, candle or piece of string, then put it out and leave it in a dish in the lavatory for five minutes. Air fresheners are also useful.

Paint smells Slice an onion in half and leave it, sliced sides uppermost, in the room. It will absorb much of the smell. Throw the onion away afterwards.

See also CIGARETTE SMELLS; ANIMAL SMELLS; DRAINS; MILDEW AND MOULD.

Smoke detectors

Giving your home an early fire warning system

A fire in a house at night is particularly dangerous because it may take hold before it is noticed.

One type of smoke detector can detect light changes in the particle structure of the air as it passes through an ionisation chamber. The change sparks off an alarm. Another type, a photoelectric detector, has an alarm which is triggered when smoke scatters a light beam.

Detectors are powered by a long-life battery; choose a detector that gives visible or audible warning that the battery needs replacing. There should also be a test switch so that you can try out the alarm at regular intervals.

Try to install a smoke detector in each room where there is a possible source of fire – except the kitchen, where cooking could spark it off. If this is not possible, put one in the main hall and another on the landing. Screw each unit to the ceiling, taking care to screw into the JOISTS – not just the plaster or PLASTERBOARD.

It is important that the alarm is loud enough to wake sleeping occupants – at least 85 decibels – and it may be necessary for upstairs rooms to have the doors ajar if the alarm is to be heard. Downstairs doors and especially those leading onto a staircase, should always be kept shut at night to slow the spread of a fire. See also FIRE; FIRE EXTINGUISHERS.

Smoking

Helping yourself to kick the habit

First you must make your own decision to stop smoking. If you do it just to please others, you will probably fail.

Make a list of the reasons to give up. Bear in mind its effects on your health and think of other people affected – your family and perhaps future children.

Be realistic and make a list too of the reasons for continuing to smoke.

Preparing to stop When you decide to stop, pick a date in the near future. If possible, choose a time when you are faced with an agreeable change in routine, such as a holiday or trip. Do not try to give up smoking in times of anxiety.

Tell your family and friends; they will reinforce your resolve. Try to team up with someone else who is stopping – sharing the experience helps.

Make a note, too, of the moments when you most want to smoke so that when you stop you can prepare for them.

Stopping When the day to quit comes, stop carrying cigarettes, matches or lighter. Hide all ashtrays. It can be helpful to smoke all your remaining cigarettes the evening before – to give you a temporary aversion to smoking.

For the first few weeks you will have moments of great anxiety. Endure them; they will pass. To help, keep busy and take more exercise – see EXERCISES.

When you feel the urge to smoke, take some deep breaths. Carry nuts or other nutritious snacks to nibble on – but stay away from sweets. Drink lots of water and fruit juice.

Do not worry about never smoking again. Simply conquer the habit one day at a time.

Many have found help from 'stop-smoking' groups. Ask your DOCTOR for the address of a local group or contact Action on Smoking and Health (ASH), 109 Gloucester Place, London W1H 3PH. Some people have also found hypnosis treatment, YOGA, acupuncture and nicotine chewing gum or patches helpful.

Snakebites

Emergency action if you are bitten

A bite from an adder, Britain's only venomous snake, will require medical aid as soon as possible. However, adder bites are seldom fatal, and fear provoked by the bite can sometimes cause more harm than the bite itself. In hot countries, it is important to tell the doctor or emergency services the size, colouring and skin pattern of the snake to help them decide if anti-venom serum is needed. Even in the tropics, however, deaths from snake bite are rare.

If the bite is from a pet snake, ask the owner exactly which species it is.

Warning signs Signs that you have been bitten are a sharp pain, swelling round the affected area and one or two puncture marks. There may also be a feeling of NAUSEA, VOMITING, disturbed vision and breathing difficulty.

What to do Remain calm and still. If you move unnecessarily this will increase the heartbeat and hasten the rate at which the venom is absorbed into the bloodstream. Ask someone to call 999 for an ambulance.

While waiting for help, rest in a comfortable position and try to keep the bite area below the level of the heart. Any venom round the bite should be removed by wiping outwards, away from the wound.

Do not try to suck the venom out, or cut round the wound, as both actions will simply increase the flow of blood.

Snap

A fast and noisy card game

A pack of playing cards and up to six players are all that are needed to play this game, and the rules could not be simpler.

The cards are dealt among the players, who stack them face down in front of them. Starting from the left of the dealer, each player turns over the top card of his stack and places it face up in front of him. Whenever a player turns up a card of the same value as a card already showing – for example, two fours – the first player to call 'snap' picks up all the face-up cards of the player who has laid the matching card, and adds them to the bottom of his face-down stack. If the player who laid the matching card calls 'snap' first, he takes the face-up pile of the matched card. The object of the game is to win all the cards.

There may be arguments as to who called 'snap' first – arguments that do not arise in a quieter but more vigorous version of Snap in which a matchbox is grabbed by a player instead of calling 'snap'. The game is called, not surprisingly, Grab. See also SHUFFLING CARDS.

Snooker

Learning a popular table-top game

Snooker is played with 22 balls of different colours on a level table covered with green baize cloth. Round the table there is a cushioned rim interrupted by a pocket at each corner and at the centres of the two long sides. A full-size championship table is 3.7m (12ft) long and 1.8m (6ft) wide. Half-size and quarter-size tables are also made.

The object of the game is to score points by striking balls into the pockets – but not directly. Players use one hand to slide a cue (usually of ash or maple) over a bridge made by the other hand to strike the white cue ball; this in turn hits a coloured ball into any of the six pockets. The cue tip is rubbed with chalk so that it does not slip on the ball.

The game starts with the 15 red balls arranged in a triangle, other coloured balls on their starting spots (see illustration) and the cue ball anywhere in the marked 'D'. One player 'breaks' – strikes the cue ball to touch one of the reds, which makes the triangle break open. He tries to make the cue ball return to the baulk area – behind the marked line – so that the opponent has to make a long shot to strike one of the reds.

When a player pots one of the reds, he scores one point, and can attempt to pot any one of the other colours; another red must be potted before another colour, and so on. Once potted, red balls remain in the pockets but other colours are returned to their spots, until all 15 reds have been potted. Then the colours are potted in sequence: yellow (two points), green (three), brown (four), blue (five), pink (six) and black (seven).

A player continues until he fails to pot a ball – or strikes the wrong colour (a foul), or pots the cue ball (a foul). A foul gives four points to the opponent (or more if the ball wrongly struck counts for more than four points). A sequence of successful shots is called a break. The highest possible score – for potting all the balls in one break – is 147.

The skill lies in controlling the cue ball with spin, speed and rebounds off the cushions so that it comes to rest in the right position for potting the next ball. The balls run more easily from the baulk end to the black ball end; when they run the other way, or across the table, there is more resistance from the nap of the baize cloth.

When a player cannot hope to pot the right ball, he tries to make the cue ball touch it and then run to a position where the opponent will have a difficult shot; if the opponent is left with no direct path for the cue ball to reach the correct coloured ball, he is said to be snookered, and must take another course of action.

The 'frame' or game ends when all the balls have been potted or one of the players concedes. There is no set number of games. In a tournament, the number of frames usually increases round by round. See also BILLIARDS; POOL.

Snoring

What you can do to try to reduce or stop it

People are most likely to snore while in deep SLEEP or while dreaming. The cause is a loss of basic muscle tension in the tongue and jaw. This is why people tend to snore when lying on their backs – a position in which the jaw tends to drop down and the tongue slides back.

Some of the habits and conditions that have been blamed for snoring are SMOKING, drinking, heavy meals, COLDS and enlarged adenoids or tonsils. After middle age, when muscles and tissues in the respiratory area loosen, there is often an increase in snoring.

Often a snorer is woken by the volume of his own noise; at other times he may wake from lack of oxygen or shortness of breath. However, snoring is not harmful and is more likely to be a nuisance to the snorer's partner, particularly if the partner is a light sleeper. Usually, it is a simple matter to induce a snorer to turn onto his side, which often stops the snoring.

The snorer may alleviate the problem by lying on his side before going to sleep and by repeatedly telling himself: 'I am lying on my side and will go on lying on my side.' With time and practice, this 'command' will be carried over into sleep and begin to work like a well-learned resolution.

Another remedy is to sew a small rubber ball, or something uncomfortable, into the back of the snorer's pyjamas to prevent the snorer from lying on his back.

Other remedies worth a try are:
- Increasing the humidity in the bedroom.
- Avoiding alcoholic drinks for several hours before going to bed.
- Pressing against your jaw, forcing it to press back; and pressing your tongue against the lower teeth. Do both for about two minutes.
- Saying 'Aahhh' silently for three or four minutes.

If none of these works, the snorer's partner may have to wear ear-plugs or move into another room.

Snow blindness

Protecting your eyes against dangerous dazzle

Snow blindness is a painful but temporary condition caused by the glare of the sun's ultraviolet rays reflected by snow. It can occur even on overcast days, causing painful inflammation and gradual loss of vision during the three to five hours following exposure.

Protect your eyes with dark glasses or a mask or helmet with narrow eye-slits.

If snow blindness occurs, cover the eyes with patches or a blindfold – for example, a clean scarf or handkerchief. Rest in a dark room and get medical help as quickly as possible. With prompt treatment, the pain will go and normal vision will return within three days.

Snowbound

Surviving at home or in a car; taking precautions

If you live in an area where heavy snow is likely, you may find yourself housebound for several days or more. In remote areas, electricity and telephone lines could be out of action.

In a car, driving becomes impossible in a snowstorm, or if snow reaches more than about 300mm (12in) deep. See also DRIVING IN BAD WEATHER; SURVIVAL.

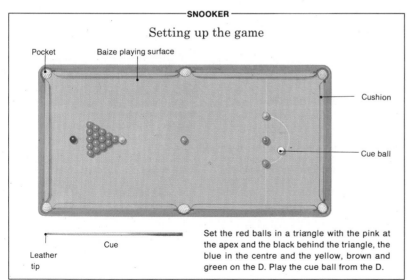

SNOOKER

Setting up the game

Pocket

Baize playing surface

Cushion

Cue ball

Cue

Leather tip

Set the red balls in a triangle with the pink at the apex and the black behind the triangle, the blue in the centre and the yellow, brown and green on the D. Play the cue ball from the D.

Whether trapped in a house with little or no heat, or in a snowbound car, you must keep warm to survive.

Keeping warm Wrap up in as many layers of clothing as possible, and keep your head well covered – a lot of body heat is lost through the head. Pad newspaper under your clothing if necessary, and wrap it round your legs. In a car, wrap it round your head if you have nothing else to use.

Eat as well as you can – food generates heat. Avoid drinking alcohol. It dilates the blood vessels and encourages loss of body heat. It also induces drowsiness, and if you fall asleep when very cold, you could succumb to HYPOTHERMIA or FROSTBITE.

Gentle EXERCISES will keep your blood circulating, but avoid violent exercise, which uses up body heat and makes you tired.

Surviving in a house If the electricity supply has failed and you have no other heating, find something you can burn, such as old wooden, non-upholstered furniture, and light a fire for warmth and cooking – see FIRELIGHTING.

If there is no open fireplace, improvise a brazier – knock holes in an old metal bucket or bath, for example. Use it on a stone floor, or take precautions against falling cinders. Melt ice if the water supply is frozen – it requires half as much fuel as snow does to give the same amount of water.

If you cannot reach a neighbour and are desperate for help, hang out a large written sign from an upper window or where it can be seen by a helicopter or local rescue services.

To avoid such extremes, at the beginning of winter make sure you have some form of alternative heating such as OIL HEATERS or gas-canister STOVES or COOKERS and plenty of fuel. In remote areas, a wood-burning stove and perhaps a small generator are an advantage.

Stock up with tinned food and dried food, matches, candles and spare torch batteries. Make sure that shovels and salt or grit are kept *inside* the house, so that you can dig paths to outhouses or to a neighbour if necessary.

Surviving in a car Stay in the car and keep as warm as possible. Do not walk along the road looking for shelter – people have died in drifts only yards from help. Before the snow piles too high, clear the area round the exhaust tailpipe and get anything you want from the boot – particularly rugs, newspapers, any warm clothing – and something such as a jack handle for poking through the snow later, if needed.

Run the car heater for about ten minutes every hour to raise the temperature.

Do not keep the car lights on or play the car radio or tape deck to help you to stay awake; you will drain the battery. Open the window for air occasionally, and do gentle exercises such as stretching your neck, shoulders, arms, legs, fingers and toes.

If the snow piles above the roof, poke an air channel up through the snow, and check regularly that it is still open. It may also help rescue services to spot you. Where several cars are stranded close together, collect everyone in one car, if possible. It will help you to keep warmer and stay awake.

Be prepared when driving in areas where heavy snow is likely. Keep a shovel, sacking and grit in the boot, as well as rugs, wellingtons, and snow chains or traction clamps for the tyres. Carry a torch, see TORCHES, spare batteries, and emergency rations such as chocolate, boiled sweets, biscuits and a hot drink in a vacuum flask.

Soap bubbles

Simple amusement for children of all ages

You can blow soap bubbles with a bubble pipe – most toy shops sell them – or you can make your own pipe from a drinking straw, by cutting four 13mm ($\frac{1}{2}$in) slits in one end and folding them back. Alternatively, make a bubble loop, about 19mm ($\frac{3}{4}$in) across, out of a length of stiff wire.

Mix half a cup of washing-up liquid with 1$\frac{1}{2}$ cups of warm water. Dip the pipe or straw into the solution, then blow gently until a bubble forms. Jerk the bubble-maker to free the bubble, so that it floats in the air.

If you are using a loop, dip it into the solution so that a thin film stretches across it. Blow the film gently to form a bubble, or wave the loop through the air.

Take care not to let the mixture drip or splash into your eyes. It will sting sharply.

Social security

Who can claim benefits; how to claim; appealing against a rejected claim

Social security benefits fall into two categories: contributory and non-contributory. Contributory benefits are made to people who have paid NATIONAL INSURANCE contributions, and include retirement pension, unemployment benefit and sickness benefit. Non-contributory benefits may be paid to anyone who has resided in the United Kingdom for a specified time, whether such a person has paid national insurance contributions or not.

The Department of Social Security booklet *Which benefit?* lists many of the benefits, and tells you which other leaflets will give further information. The booklet and leaflets are available from your local social security office or Citizens Advice Bureau – both of which can also advise you on what benefits you may be eligible for.

Income Support This is the benefit generally available to those in need.

The conditions for obtaining Income Support are fairly straightforward: you must be over 18, not working full time, and unable to live on your income. You can claim even if you have some savings, and you automatically get health benefits, help with housing costs and COUNCIL TAX, MORTGAGES and INSURANCE premiums.

Those eligible for Income Support include single parents, people unfit for work, people needed at home to look after a disabled relative, and unemployed people who do not get sufficient, or any, unemployment benefit. Payments are made weekly, the amount being decided by a means test that takes into account your income after stoppages, and your requirements. Income Support may be taxed if you are signing on as unemployed.

In addition to rent or mortgage relief, called Housing Benefit, there is a living allowance to cover daily expenses. The amount depends on such factors as the amount of your personal allowance, the size of your family, the ages of your children, whether you are a single parent, or sick, disabled, or over the age of 60.

Family Credit This is available to people in full-time employment who are unable to bring up children on a low wage. Full-time employment means at least 24 hours a week for one of a couple, or for a single parent. Self-employed people can claim – see SELF-EMPLOYMENT.

The benefit also includes free prescriptions, dental treatment, glasses, and travelling to hospital for treatment. You may also be able to get these benefits even if you are not entitled to Family Credit.

The amount of Family Credit you receive depends on your income, your partner's income, how many children you have, and their ages.

Child Benefit A set amount of cash a week is payable for each child under 16 (or under 19 if still in full-time, non-advanced education). It is paid tax-free and regardless of national insurance contributions to anyone responsible for the child. Payments are made in arrears, usually monthly.

How to claim Call at your local social security office or Citizens Advice Bureau and ask for the appropriate claim form. If necessary, the staff will assist you in making the claim. Some forms and information leaflets are available at post offices. General advice on benefits and national insurance is available on a free telephone service: 0800-666555. If your claim is turned down, you may have the right of appeal; you will be told when the decision is given. Appeal forms are available at social security offices.

Soft drinks

Making a ginger-beer plant and real lemonade

Homemade lemonade and ginger beer are two refreshing soft drinks. You can brew endless quantities of ginger beer with a 'ginger beer plant' – a fermenting mixture fed with sugar and dry ginger every day. To start it, you need:

285ml (½ pint) warm water
Juice of 1 large lemon
10 sultanas
1 level tablespoon sugar
2 level teaspoons ground ginger
Screw-top jar

Mix all the ingredients in the screw-top jar. Cover tightly and leave in a warm place (such as an airing cupboard) for three days or until the mixture is foaming gently. Every day for seven days add 1 level tablespoon of sugar and 2 level teaspoons of ground ginger. Then, to make it into 6 litres (10 pints) of ginger beer, you will need:

570ml (1 pint) boiling water
450g (1lb) sugar
3.4 litres (6 pints) cold water
Juice of 2 lemons
6 sealable 1 litre bottles

Pour the boiling water and sugar into a large bowl and stir until the sugar dissolves. Add the cold water and lemon juice. Strain the ginger beer plant into the bowl through a double layer of clean muslin or a fine sieve lined with absorbent kitchen paper. Squeeze out all the liquid and keep the residue. Stir the liquid in the bowl to blend the flavours. Pour into clean bottles and seal. Keep in a cool place for at least three days before drinking.

To continue the plant, divide the residue in two. Place half in the cleaned screw-top jar, add 285ml (½ pint) cold water, feed for a week and repeat the process described. Discard the other half.

Lemonade To make 3.7 litres (6½ pints), you need:
6 lemons, scrubbed
285ml (½ pint) water
450g (1lb) caster sugar

Use a potato peeler to remove the rind in thin sections from the lemons. Discard any white pith, as this would make the drink bitter. Simmer the rind in the water in a large, covered pan for 5 minutes; do not let the water boil. Remove from the heat. Squeeze the lemons and pour the juice into a large bowl. Add the sugar.

Strain the liquid from the pan over the juice and stir until the sugar has dissolved. This syrup is the basis of your drink, and will keep in the refrigerator for up to two weeks. When required, dilute it with still or sparkling mineral water. Add ice cubes and lemon slices just before serving.

Soil preparation

Laying the groundwork for successful growing

Good soil for growing plants is dark, moist and crumbly, and rich in decaying organic matter and earthworms. To get it into condition and maintain it, keep the soil well supplied with bulky organic manure (see COMPOST) and the right balance of plant nutrients – see FERTILISERS.

Digging The topsoil, the most fertile soil, may be 50-300mm (2-12in) deep, but in well-tended, old gardens it may be 610mm (2ft) deep. You can usually tell where the topsoil ends because the subsoil is a lighter colour. The topsoil must be kept open and well drained; rake it fine for seed sowing and planting.

Dig beds where plants or crops have been removed as they become vacant, remove any perennial weeds (see WEED CONTROL) and fork in compost. Do not dig round SHRUBS and fruit bushes or you will disturb the roots. Lay compost round them (not touching the stems).

Different soil types The best soil is loam, a blend of sand and clay. Sandy soil is light and open, needing little digging, but dries out fast. It needs plenty of compost to give it bulk and keep it moist.

Clay soil is heavy to work and slow to warm up. Its fine particles cling together as clods and make it sticky when wet and rock hard when dry. It is often rich but poorly drained, so needs compost, manure or leaf mould added. Digging in sharp sand or weathered ashes helps to break it up, as does liming.

SOIL PREPARATION

Digging cleared ground; rotating vegetable crops

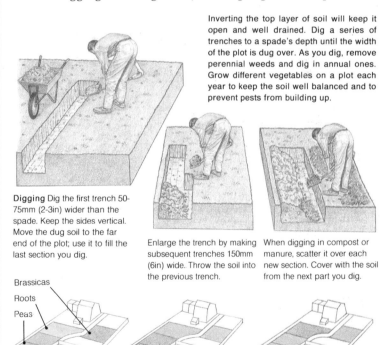

Inverting the top layer of soil will keep it open and well drained. Dig a series of trenches to a spade's depth until the width of the plot is dug over. As you dig, remove perennial weeds and dig in annual ones. Grow different vegetables on a plot each year to keep the soil well balanced and to prevent pests from building up.

Digging Dig the first trench 50-75mm (2-3in) wider than the spade. Keep the sides vertical. Move the dug soil to the far end of the plot; use it to fill the last section you dig.

Enlarge the trench by making subsequent trenches 150mm (6in) wide. Throw the soil into the previous trench.

When digging in compost or manure, scatter it over each new section. Cover with the soil from the next part you dig.

Brassicas
Roots
Peas

Crop rotation Divide a vegetable garden into three plots. Manure Plot One for peas, beans, and salad vegetables. Dress Plot Two with fertiliser for roots and potatoes.

Dress Plot Three with fertiliser and lime for cabbages and other brassicas. Cycle plots yearly so that each is prepared for and grows peas, then brassicas, then roots.

Do not dig wet clay. Wait until it does not stick to your boots. Clay is best dug in late autumn so that winter frosts break it up ready for spring.

Chalky soil is usually shallow. It drains quickly, but gets sticky when wet. It needs plenty of compost added to supply bulk and nutrients.

Peaty soil tends to get waterlogged and is usually acid and deficient in phosphates and potash. Deep trenches can fairly easily be dug at intervals and half filled with rubble or ashes before the soil is replaced. Raising the soil level overall will help to improve drainage.

Liming All soils except chalky soil need liming occasionally, or they become acid. Most plants grow best in neutral soil – a balance between alkalinity and acidity. Soil acidity or alkalinity is measured on a scale known as the pH scale. Neutral soil is pH 7. If the number is higher, it is alkaline and needs no liming; if it is lower, the soil is acid. You can buy soil test kits, but the balance can vary in different places at different seasons.

Apply hydrated lime as a top-dressing at the rate of about 225g per m² (8oz per square yard) on a neutral loam; halve the amount on sandy soil and double it on clay. Repeat the dressing once every three years or so in late February or early March. Lime washes into the soil quickly, but does not take effect immediately. On acid soil use double the amounts for neutral soil, but do not overlime, as this can cause iron and magnesium deficiency. Do not mix lime with farmyard manure or other fertilisers because the lime will destroy valuable nutrients in it. Apply lime at least a month before or at least two months after manure or fertiliser.

If soil is too alkaline, increase its acidity by digging in peat substitute.

Applying manure and fertiliser Garden compost and farmyard manure not only improve soil structure but also supply nutrients. Chemical fertilisers supply nutrients but do not improve structure. The structure deteriorates if they are applied continually without manuring.

Do not put fresh farmyard manure straight on the soil unless you bury it well down and leave the ground fallow over winter. It is too rich, and inhibits plant growth. Compost small amounts or stack it in a tight heap and leave it until it rots. Collect the drainage water and put it back on the heap, as it is rich in nutrients. Fork in compost or well-rotted farmyard manure when you dig – about a bucket per square metre (square yard).

Rotation of vegetables Crops vary in the amounts of different nutrients they take from the soil. A common rotation is to have three plots with a cycle of peas, brassicas and roots, as illustrated.

SOLDERING AND BRAZING

Soft and hard solder techniques

Use soft soldering for small jobs, such as joining electrical terminals. Use hard soldering to make stronger joints.

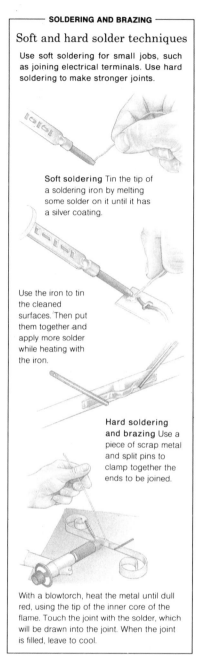

Soft soldering Tin the tip of a soldering iron by melting some solder on it until it has a silver coating.

Use the iron to tin the cleaned surfaces. Then put them together and apply more solder while heating with the iron.

Hard soldering and brazing Use a piece of scrap metal and split pins to clamp together the ends to be joined.

With a blowtorch, heat the metal until dull red, using the tip of the inner core of the flame. Touch the joint with the solder, which will be drawn into the joint. When the joint is filled, leave to cool.

Soldering and brazing

Bonding metal to metal

Soldering joins pieces of metal by running a molten alloy between them, then allowing it to cool. There are two basic types, soft soldering and hard soldering – which is akin to brazing.

Soft soldering You need a soldering iron, soft solder and a flux, which keeps

---

the metal clean and helps the solder to flow. Soft solder is a mixture of tin and lead, sometimes with traces of bismuth and antimony, sold as wire or sticks. Resin-cored wire solders are useful for small jobs, as they contain resin flux. Otherwise you need a separate flux in liquid or paste form. There are several types. Ask at a DIY shop for the best type for the job you are doing.

To make a joint, clean the parts to be joined back to bright metal with a file, emery cloth or wire wool. Coat both metal surfaces with flux – if not using cored solder. Clean the tip of the iron with emery cloth, allow the iron to heat, then tin the tip and assemble the joint, as illustrated. Remove the iron and allow the metal to cool. For soft soldering using a flame, see BLOWTORCHES.

Hard soldering and brazing More heat is needed for hard soldering and brazing, and different alloys are used. A gas blowtorch will give sufficient heat.

Hard solder alloys are made of copper, silver and zinc (known as silver solder); those for brazing are made from copper and zinc (called spelter). Both are supplied in strip or wire form, which is dipped into flux before applying it to the preheated work. Borax is the main flux, used either as a powder or mixed with water to form a paste.

To join two strips of metal, clean the mating areas to bright metal. Lay them on a glass-fibre cloth, or on a piece of fire-resistant insulation board. Brush flux onto the ends to be joined and bring them into contact. Make a simple clamp from scrap metal and two split pins, as illustrated. Bend the metal strip to a bridge shape so it is well away from the area to be joined, then secure it with the two split pins. Assemble the joint as shown. Wash off the flux with hot water and file off surplus solder.

WARNING With any kind of soldering, heat is easily transmitted along metal. Protect areas not to be soldered with a damp rag. For small electrical and electronic work, buy heat sinks – small devices designed to dissipate heat.

Sorbet

Preparing a delicate summer sweet

Sorbet – a light water ice – is a refreshing sweet to serve alone or following a rich main course.

The main ingredients are usually fruit juice, water, egg whites and sugar; the amount of sugar used is varied, according to the sweetness of the juice.

This recipe for orange sorbet also includes gelatine, for a smoother consistency.

Ingredients (to serve six)
175g (6oz) caster sugar
285ml (½ pint) water
1 level teaspoon powdered gelatine
175g (6oz) can frozen concentrated orange juice
2 egg whites

Add the sugar to the water in a pan. Sprinkle in the gelatine and leave to soak for 10 minutes. Heat the mixture gently until the sugar and gelatine have dissolved. Set aside to cool.

Break up the frozen block of orange juice and add it to the mixture. Stir until the juice has melted enough to give a smooth consistency.

Pour the mixture into freezing trays or a plastic container. Freeze for 1½ hours, or until ice forms around the edges and the centre is beginning to freeze.

Whisk the egg whites until stiff but not dry. Add the orange mixture to the whites and whisk until light and smooth. Refreeze the mixture for one hour. Remove and whisk again. Then refreeze for 4 hours until quite firm, then cover and leave in the freezer until required.

Sore throats

Identifying causes; getting relief

Rawness at the back of the throat may result from nothing more than an evening of drinking, smoking and loud conversation. It can also be a symptom of common illnesses such as COLDS, FLU glandular fever or tonsillitis.

Treat a sore throat by resting, sucking throat lozenges and drinking warm drinks. Painkillers in recommended doses and gargling every few hours with warm water and salt can also help.

When to see a doctor If a sore throat persists longer than a week, consult a DOCTOR. Consult a doctor too if the tonsils are swollen and inflamed and there are white spots on them. These may be symptoms of tonsillitis – others are a high fever and tender neck glands.

A sore throat accompanied by fever, swollen neck glands, fatigue and weakness may also be a symptom of glandular fever. If you have these symptoms, see a doctor.

Soufflés

Baking them so they do not collapse

Soufflés can be sweet or savoury, but either way, it is beaten egg whites that give them their attractive puffiness.

Always cook them in straight-sided buttered soufflé dishes. Do not let the soufflé mixture come more than three-quarters of the way up the side of the dish. Never open the oven door while a soufflé is cooking.

Serve as soon as the dish comes from the oven – before it has a chance to fall.

Savoury soufflés Here is a recipe for a basic savoury cheese soufflé – enough to serve four people. Serve with SALADS.

To make a ham soufflé, simply substitute 75g (3oz) cooked chopped ham for the cheese in this recipe.

Ingredients
3 eggs
40g (1½oz) butter
40g (1½oz) plain flour
225ml (8fl oz) milk
115g (4oz) finely grated mature Cheddar cheese
Salt and black pepper

Lightly butter the inside of a 140mm (5½in) or 1 litre (1¾ pint) soufflé dish. Separate the eggs into yolks and whites – see EGG SEPARATING.

Melt the butter in a saucepan, then add the flour and cook over a low heat, stirring all the time, for 1 or 2 minutes. Remove from the heat and gradually stir in the milk. Return to the heat and bring to the boil, stirring constantly. Simmer gently for 2 or 3 minutes until the mixture is very thick.

Stir in the cheese and season with salt and pepper. Stir over gentle heat until the cheese has just melted, then remove from the heat and leave to cool slightly.

Lightly beat the egg yolks, then fold a little at a time into the cooled cheese mixture. Whisk the egg whites in a clean, dry bowl until stiff and standing in peaks. With a large metal spoon, fold carefully into the cheese mixture.

Spoon the mixture into the soufflé dish. Bake in the centre of an oven preheated to 200°C (400°F), gas mark 6, for 35 minutes until well risen with a golden-brown crust.

Sweet soufflés A sweet hot soufflé makes a festive pudding. A simple chocolate soufflé can be made by omitting the salt and pepper from the cheese soufflé recipe and substituting 50g (2oz) plain melted chocolate for the cheese. Add a little rum as well.

Alternatively, here is a recipe for an orange soufflé – enough to serve four people.

Ingredients
2 large oranges
50g (2oz) lump sugar
285ml (½ pint) milk
50g (2oz) butter
25g (1oz) cornflour
3 egg yolks
4 egg whites
1 tablespoon orange liqueur or orange juice

Butter a 1.1 litre (2 pint) soufflé dish. Wash and dry the oranges, then rub the sugar lumps all over their skins – this will extract the oil from the skins.

Over a low heat, dissolve the orange-flavoured sugar lumps in all but 4 tablespoons of the milk. Bring to the boil and remove from the heat.

Melt the butter in a saucepan over low heat. Mix the remaining milk with the cornflour, then add to the butter and stir until thick. Slowly add the milk and sugar mixture, the egg yolks, then the liqueur or orange juice, stirring all the time. Remove from the heat.

Whisk the egg whites as for cheese soufflé, then with a large metal spoon fold into the mixture in the pan. Turn into the soufflé dish and bake, set in a pan of hot water, in an oven preheated to 180°C (350°F), gas mark 4, for 35-40 minutes.

Serve the soufflé with the oranges, cut into segments and free of peel and pith.

Soundproofing

Reducing noise indoors

Unfortunately there are few practical ways of keeping noise out of your home.

The most effective cure is good neighbourliness: re-siting a TV or sound system away from a shared wall, or laying thick carpet and underlay on a hard floor does more to solve the problem in adjoining properties than any amount of insulation.

Walls To reduce the noise through a shared wall, consider fitting built-in wardrobes in bedrooms. Filled with clothes, they act as noise absorbers.

A more expensive way is to build a new wall spaced away from the existing one using timber BATTENS and PLASTER BOARD, filling the cavity between with glass-fibre blanket. See also PARTITIONS.

Ideally the timber should be cushioned with foam or expanded polystyrene at floor and ceiling to reduce sound transmission. But do not expect more than a 20 per cent improvement in noise level.

If conversion work is undertaken to give extra living space, arrange for passages and storage areas or spare rooms to be on shared walls – not living rooms, bathrooms or toilets.

Floors Soft materials such as thick underlays will damp down noise. However, dense materials, such as 25mm (1in) of dry sand between a floor and a ceiling below it, are the best sound absorbers.

Doors Most noise entering through an outer door comes through small gaps between door and frame – even through a loose letterbox. Efficient DRAUGHT-PROOFING will reduce the level.

Windows Again, efficient draught-proofing will help; standard DOUBLE-GLAZING helps a little. To improve matters, you can add a third pane of glass spaced at least 75mm (3in) from the double glazing. Using glass of different weight for this third pane will avoid generating sympathetic vibrations which can carry the noise from one sheet to the next.

However, opening just one window lets noise in again: air conditioning might be the answer if the expense is thought worth while.

Outside noise At best this can be reduced by high closeboarded FENCES, brick walls, and tall HEDGES, all of which can absorb sound. If you live near an airport ask the local authority about GRANTS towards insulation.

As a last resort you can seek the help of the law to restrain NOISY NEIGHBOURS. See also NUISANCE.

Soups and stocks

Making your own using fresh ingredients

Stock is the basis of well-flavoured soup, SAUCES or a CASSEROLE. Although stock cubes are useful spur-of-the-moment aids, they lack the subtlety of a homemade stock.

Use a large, thick-based pan with a lid for meat and vegetable stocks. PRESSURE COOKERS or ELECTRIC SLOW COOKERS can be used instead of saucepans.

Ingredients About 450g (1lb) of solid ingredients to 2 litres (3½ pints) of liquid will make about 1.1 litres (2 pints) of stock. Solid ingredients are usually bones, meat and vegetables.

Use beef (or lamb) bones with scraps of cooked or uncooked meat for brown stock. For a white stock, use fowl or game carcasses (with their giblets), rabbit or veal.

Add a mixture of onion, celery and carrot, leaving them in large pieces. Cooked vegetables and peelings can also be used – but avoid too many greens and starchy ingredients such as potatoes, which give an unpleasant flavour.

For a brown stock, fry the meat and vegetables in a little butter or dripping to brown them – but not for a white stock.

Be sparing with spices and herbs – see HERBS IN COOKING. Use only 1 teaspoon of salt. The stock is a background ingredient and must not have a dominant flavour.

Fish stock is made with heads, skin, trimmings and cheap fish pieces, but avoid oily fish such as MACKEREL or herring. Add a little lemon zest, mace or fennel, but no vegetables.

To make vegetable stock (for VEGETARIAN MEALS) use uncooked or leftover vegetables – see LEFTOVERS. Use the water RICE and PASTA has been cooked in to increase the nutritional value.

Preparing Before you use bones, break them up with a hammer – or ask the butcher to saw them for you. For the best flavour, roast the bones in a low oven for 30-35 minutes before putting them to simmer. Simmer the meat and bones for about 3 hours before adding the vegetables, then simmer for about 2 hours more. The bones should be pitted with small holes by the end of the simmering.

For vegetable stock, about 2 hours simmering is needed. Fish stock differs in needing a maximum of 30 minutes.

For all stock, bring the ingredients in the pan to the boil, skim off the white scum that rises, then cover with a tilted lid and reduce the heat to maintain a simmer. Do *not* skim off brown scum that forms later; this is part of the protein content.

When the stock is cooked, strain immediately through muslin or a fine sieve into a clean bowl (not a metal bowl, which would spoil the flavour). Let it cool until the fat has risen, then draw several sheets of kitchen paper over the surface to absorb the fat. Alternatively, refrigerate the stock until it has set, then lift off every bit of fat.

Cover the stock and store it in the refrigerator. Use fish stock within 24 hours and vegetable stock within 48 hours. Meat and vegetable stock can be kept for 4-5 days, but must be boiled up every second day. Deep-frozen stock will keep for 3 months – see FREEZING FOOD.

Always bring stock to the boil before you use it.

Soups To make consommé, the thinnest of soups, simmer shin of beef for 2 hours in brown or white stock with an onion, carrot and bouquet garni. Or use 225g (8oz) of fresh uncooked beef to 1.7 litres (3 pints) of stock. Make it a day in advance – so that you can chill it and lift off the fat.

To clarify before serving, heat, stir in a beaten egg white (see EGG SEPARATING) mixed with crushed ice and stir until the consommé boils. Solid particles will be trapped by the coagulating egg whites. Strain, taste and correct the seasoning. Serve hot in winter, chilled and jellied in summer.

To make other thin soups, cook diced meat, vegetables or both in stock until tender. Serve piping hot with no further preparation.

Thick soups To make thick soups, pass solid ingredients, such as vegetables, through a sieve or mill – see FOOD MILLS. Or use a liquidiser (see BLENDERS) – but this will give the soup an emulsified, rather than a more palatable, grainy texture.

To stop the solid ingredients settling to the bottom – add thickening such as flour, cornflour, semolina or arrowroot worked to a smooth paste with milk and stirred into the soup. Or cook starchy items such as potato, sago, oatmeal, pearl barley, lentils and other pulses, with the rest of the soup ingredients.

Spaghetti

Cooking it 'al dente'; making spaghetti bolognese

The fresh pastas now widely on sale in delicatessens and supermarkets do not usually include spaghetti, but you may find it in specialist Italian provision shops. Usually, however, the spaghetti you cook will be dried.

Cook spaghetti as other pastas (see PASTA). Fresh spaghetti needs 3-4 minutes cooking, dried spaghetti 8-10 minutes, depending on the thickness of the strands. It is ready when it is firm to bite but without a gritty core – *al dente* (to the tooth). Do not mix different brands of spaghetti, unless they are of the same thickness – thin strands will be sticky before thick ones are cooked.

When cooked, strain the spaghetti immediately through a large sieve or fine colander and put it in a heated dish. You can stir in butter and freshly chopped herbs, or stir in a sauce, or simply pour the sauce on top; in any case, serve it very hot. Hand around finely grated Parmesan cheese to sprinkle on top.

A traditional sauce recipe for spaghetti is bolognese – see also SAUCES. Fry 75g (3oz) of finely chopped unsmoked bacon in a little butter. Add an onion, a carrot and a stick of celery, all chopped. Let them brown before adding the mince. Stir in 225g (8oz) of lean minced beef over a high heat until it separates into grains and changes from red to pale brown.

Authentic recipes also stir in 115g (4oz) of chopped chicken livers, but some recipes omit these. Add 3 teaspoons of concentrated tomato purée, 150ml (¼ pint) of white wine and 285ml (½ pint) of beef stock. Sprinkle in a pinch of nutmeg or oregano, bring to the boil and cover the pan. Simmer gently for about 30-40 minutes. Taste to see if salt is needed – the bacon may have provided enough.

Spanners and wrenches

Using the right ones to make the job easy

For a spanner to do its job efficiently, it must fit the nut or bolt perfectly, or it will damage the nut and make it more difficult to turn. Also, an ill-fitting spanner will slip and may cause injury.

BOLTS and the nuts that fit on them

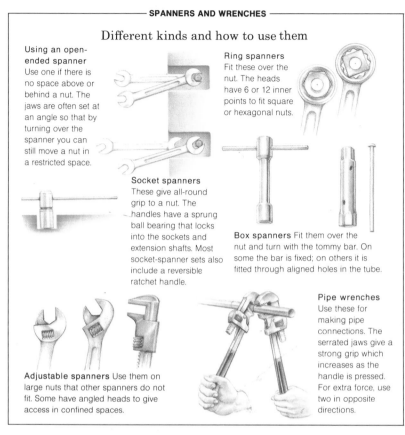

SPANNERS AND WRENCHES

Different kinds and how to use them

Using an open-ended spanner
Use one if there is no space above or behind a nut. The jaws are often set at an angle so that by turning over the spanner you can still move a nut in a restricted space.

Ring spanners
Fit these over the nut. The heads have 6 or 12 inner points to fit square or hexagonal nuts.

Socket spanners
These give all-round grip to a nut. The handles have a sprung ball bearing that locks into the sockets and extension shafts. Most socket-spanner sets also include a reversible ratchet handle.

Box spanners Fit them over the nut and turn with the tommy bar. On some the bar is fixed; on others it is fitted through aligned holes in the tube.

Pipe wrenches
Use these for making pipe connections. The serrated jaws give a strong grip which increases as the handle is pressed. For extra force, use two in opposite directions.

Adjustable spanners Use them on large nuts that other spanners do not fit. Some have angled heads to give access in confined spaces.

Self-grip wrench The jaws of this adjustable tool can be set to grip a given size of object and lock onto it – leaving the hands free. It is also useful for releasing tight nuts, but the jaws may well damage the nut while doing so. In the same way, it will hold a bolt still while you loosen its nut with a spanner.

Spark-plugs

Cleaning, gapping and fitting them

Check and clean your car's spark-plugs every 5000-6000 miles, and replace them after 10,000 miles. Always use the type of plug recommended by the manufacturer.

For most cars the plug size is 14mm (though it may be 10, 12 or 18mm) and

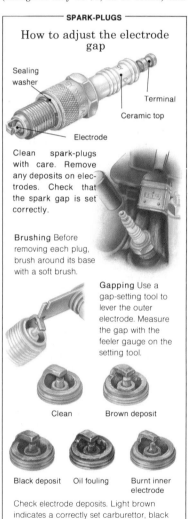

SPARK-PLUGS

How to adjust the electrode gap

Sealing washer

Terminal

Ceramic top

Electrode

Clean spark-plugs with care. Remove any deposits on electrodes. Check that the spark gap is set correctly.

Brushing Before removing each plug, brush around its base with a soft brush.

Gapping Use a gap-setting tool to lever the outer electrode. Measure the gap with the feeler gauge on the setting tool.

Clean

Brown deposit

Black deposit

Oil fouling

Burnt inner electrode

Check electrode deposits. Light brown indicates a correctly set carburettor, black too much choke or a too-rich mixture, oil fouling worn piston rings or valves, a burnt inner electrode pre-ignition.

---

may be imperial or metric. Both types are measured across opposing flats; imperial are termed AF (Across-Flats) sizes and measured in fractions of an inch, metric nuts are measured in millimetres.

Imperial and metric spanners are not interchangeable, so you need a set of each. If you work on older machinery – such as prewar cars or MOTORCYCLES – you will also encounter Whitworth and BSF (British Standard Fine) nuts and bolts. These are measured in fractions of an inch, but this is the bolt shank diameter, not the nut size. Both types need matching spanners.

Smaller bolts called BA (British Association) bolts were used mainly for electrical work (these are now metricated). For many jobs, a small adjustable spanner may save you carrying too many fixed spanners. Apart from different sizes of spanner, there are also different types:

Open-ended spanner These approach a nut from the side. They are often double-ended with different-sized jaws at each end, reducing the number of individual spanners you need.

Ring spanner This has a circular end with inner points to engage the nut or bolt. It is fitted from above, so must have enough clearance to do so. A ring span-

ner is stronger and grips better than an open-ended one, but is slower to use.

Box spanner This is a tube with a different size of hexagon shaped at each end. It needs room both to fit it and to turn it with a tommy bar. It can be strained by using too much leverage from an overlong bar and may split at the corners.

Socket spanner Socket spanners consist of a number of different types of handle which can be attached to several different types of socket. The sockets vary in size to fit different nut sizes.

The handles include a sliding bar and a reversible ratchet type for confined spaces – one or two 'clicks' of the ratchet will keep the nut moving.

Adjustable spanner The jaws of this open spanner can be adjusted to fit any size of nut up to the limit of the jaw opening. It is not as strong as a fixed spanner and easily strained, but is invaluable for light work.

Pipe wrench Similar in appearance to a large adjustable spanner, this has serrated jaws designed to grip circular objects such as pipes. The more pressure applied, the tighter the jaws bite – but they will mark the pipe.

you will need a plug spanner of the correct size for plug removal and replacement. Do not try to use any other type of spanner.

The inside of the plug spanner has a rubber sleeve that supports the spanner on the plug which lessens the chance of the socket tilting and breaking the ceramic insulator. A plug spanner with a universal-jointed bar will also help if the plugs are difficult to reach.

Removing the plugs First label the plug leads, if necessary using pieces of masking tape with the number of the cylinder each lead serves. Pull each lead from the plug, holding it by the cap, not the lead itself. Clean round the base of each plug with a soft brush.

Fit the spanner over the plug, pushing it down as far as it will go and keeping it straight. Use even force to unscrew the plug; jerking the plug spanner may damage it.

Cleaning Plugs that have a build-up of powdery deposits can be cleaned by grit-blasting. Many garages have grit-blasting equipment and will clean plugs for a small charge, or you can buy a home grit-blaster from a car accessory shop.

If the plugs are not too dirty, clean the electrodes with a fine, flat file or a carborundum board from a manicure set. If the threads are dirty, clean them with a soft wire brush. Wipe over each plug with a soft cloth dipped in paraffin. Make sure the ceramic top is clean – a build-up of dirt can cause tracking of the current between the terminal and the plug body.

Setting the gap The gap between the spark-plug electrodes should always be maintained at the distance specified by the manufacturer. If the gap is too large, misfiring may occur; if it is too small, poor engine performance will result.

It is best to set the gap with a gap-setting tool – see illustration. Alternatively, use pliers or a small screwdriver to lever the electrode open.

Use a feeler gauge (there is one on the gap-setting tool) to measure the gap – it should slide easily through the gap with a small amount of resistance. Measure the gap with the plug at eye level to check that you are holding the feeler at right angles to the centre electrode.

Refitting the plugs If the plugs have screw-on terminals, check that they are tight. Screw in the plugs by hand, taking care not to cross-thread them.

Tighten each plug with the plug spanner, a quarter of a turn beyond hand-tight. Do not overtighten them as this will make it very difficult to remove them again.

Refit the leads to the correct plugs, pushing the caps well onto the plug terminals.

Spatter prints

Making silhouette designs using an old toothbrush

You can make prints by spattering paint round simple shapes to create silhouettes. They can be used as party decorations using, for example, hearts for a Valentine's party or stars for CHRISTMAS DECORATIONS.

Cut out the shapes from stiff paper and lay them or pin them on a large sheet of white paper. Cover the work surface with newspaper and wear an overall to protect your clothes.

Prepare a water-soluble paint, such as poster paint, by diluting it slightly. Dip an old toothbrush into the paint and then spray paint dots onto the paper using an old table knife – as illustrated. Make the dots thickest at the edges of the shape.

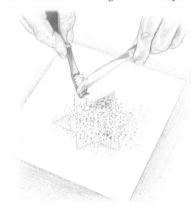

Paint spray Scrape the blade of a table knife towards you over the paint-filled bristles of a toothbrush, so spraying paint onto the paper.

Lift the shape from the background. When the paint is dry, position the shape on another part of the paper and make another silhouette, with paint of a different colour if you wish.

You can make a frame for making spatter prints. Nail four pieces of 25 × 75mm (1 × 3in) BATTENS together – the length and width can be whatever you choose – and cover the frame with fine mesh. Place the shape on its background and place the frame on top. Dip the toothbrush in the paint and brush across the mesh. Rinse the frame with water from time to time to prevent clogging.

Spectacles

Spectacles care; making small repairs

Always use a very soft clean cloth to clean lenses, especially plastic lenses, which scratch easily. When you are not wearing your spectacles, keep them in a spectacles case. Never lay them down with the lenses touching a hard surface.

Making running repairs

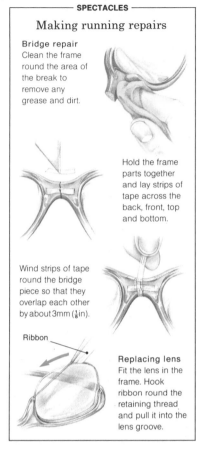

Bridge repair
Clean the frame round the area of the break to remove any grease and dirt.

Hold the frame parts together and lay strips of tape across the back, front, top and bottom.

Wind strips of tape round the bridge piece so that they overlap each other by about 3mm ($\frac{1}{8}$in).

Ribbon

Replacing lens
Fit the lens in the frame. Hook ribbon round the retaining thread and pull it into the lens groove.

If you wear reading glasses, hang them about your neck with a cord or chain (lanyard) that attaches to the arms – they are available from opticians. Remove your glasses by holding the arms between the fingers and thumb of each hand and moving them forward. Holding one arm and pulling them sideways may bend the other arm, and break the hinge.

Frame repairs If plastic frames break across the bridge, you can make a temporary repair using clear adhesive tape. Clean round the area of the break. Cut six 25mm (1in) strips of adhesive tape, 6mm ($\frac{1}{4}$in) wide and use to join the broken bridge, as illustrated.

A broken arm, if it is wire reinforced and the wire has not snapped, can be mended with epoxy adhesive – see GLUING – although this is a temporary measure only. Check regularly to see that the hinge screws are tight, using a watchmaker's screwdriver or the point of a kitchen knife. If a screw comes out and is lost, use a piece of a paperclip or safety pin to make a temporary hinge.

Refitting a lens Only frames which are partly rimless or a wire frame can be refitted with a lens by someone without professional experience. In half-frame spectacles, the lenses are usually held in place by a taut nylon thread, which is attached to the frame and runs in a groove in the lens. This can be fed back into the groove using a piece of ribbon.

Wire frames have tiny screws that hold the two halves of the lens holder together. If a screw becomes loose tighten with a watchmaker's screwdriver. Place a few drops of nail varnish on the thread before tightening.

Spices
How to use and store them

Keep spices in small screw-top jars in a cool, dry cupboard or larder away from heat and light. Stored whole, most spices keep well for up to a year; ground spices, on the other hand, lose their pungency within two or three months.

For maximum flavour, grind, crush or grate spices (as appropriate) immediately before use. Many spices can be ground finely, either in a spice mill or coffee grinder, or crushed lightly using a mortar and pestle. Some, such as nutmeg, can be ground or grated.

Before adding whole spices to casseroles and other dishes, tie them in muslin or cheesecloth for easy removal. Use spices cautiously – a pinch is enough.

Keep a selection of the following in your kitchen. They offer a range of flavours and are useful for many dishes.

Allspice The flavour resembles a blend of cinnamon, nutmeg and cloves. Use whole in pickles, soups, marinades and stews; and ground in cakes, puddings, fruit pies and root vegetable purées.

Caraway seed Use the tiny pungent seeds to flavour cakes and bread, SAUERKRAUT, and lamb or veal stews. Sprinkle over pork before roasting.

Cardamom The pods are used crushed in curries and other Indian dishes (see CURRY POWDER). The seeds flavour custards, baked fruits and Danish pastries.

Cayenne A very hot powdered pepper. Use sparingly. Sprinkle on egg, cheese and fish dishes. Adds extra flavour to prawn cocktails and smoked salmon.

Chilli powder Chillies are small red peppers, even hotter than cayenne. Use chilli powder sparingly in meat loaves, hamburgers and spicy meat dishes, such as chilli con carne.

Cinnamon Use ground to flavour cakes, biscuits and milk or fruit puddings. Sprinkle on hot drinking chocolate. Cinnamon sticks add spice to stewed or preserved fruit and to mulled wine.

Cloves Very pungent, so use sparingly. Use them whole to flavour stewed apple, fruit pies and cooked gammon; use them ground in bean dishes and milk puddings. Stick cloves into a whole orange to flavour hot wine cups.

Coriander The mild, aromatic seeds are much used in Mediterranean and Indian cooking. Use ground in stews and vegetable dishes and to season roast lamb; also, in MARMALADE and in syrup for fruit salads.

Cumin One of the basic ingredients of curry powder. Use whole in cabbage and pork dishes; use ground in curries and in cheese and egg dishes.

Dill seed Similar to caraway, but milder. Use whole in potato salads, lamb stews and to flavour pickled cucumbers and gherkins; use ground in SALAD DRESSINGS and cheese dips.

Ginger Use ground for gingerbread, cakes, biscuits, puddings and in apple sauce. Lightly crush or bruise a piece of root ginger to add a tang to poached or stewed fruit, especially rhubarb, and to chutneys, preserves and mulled wine. It is much used in Chinese cooking.

Fennel seed The delicate aniseed flavour goes well with fish, especially MACKEREL, and roast pork. Also used in coffee cakes.

Juniper Use the berries whole when cooking vegetables; add lightly crushed berries to game and pork dishes.

Mace The husk of the nutmeg, with a stronger taste. Use whole when stewing meat or cooking fruit; use ground in biscuits, milk puddings, soups, fish dishes, sweet pastries and with vegetables.

Nutmeg Grate a little of the kernel, into custards, cakes, biscuits, SAUCES and vegetables, particularly spinach.

Paprika A mild, red, powdered pepper. Use in goulash, in spicy chicken and veal stews, and to garnish fish, meat and egg dishes, and cream soups.

Pepper Both black and white pepper have most flavour when freshly ground. Use whole peppercorns in PICKLING, PRESERVING, marinades and when boiling whole pieces of meat. Ground pepper is used for general seasoning.

Saffron This bright yellow spice is used to flavour or colour RICE, cakes, fish sauces and some chicken and seafood dishes. Buy saffron in strands and, instead of grinding, steep a few strands in a little hot water for 30 minutes, then strain the liquid into the dish.

Turmeric Aromatic bright yellow powder used in curries and pickles and to colour rice. Use sparingly with EGGS and fish. See also HERBS IN COOKING; MARINATING; MULLING ALE AND WINE; SOUPS AND STOCKS.

Spider plants
Growing and caring for them

These popular houseplants (botanical name *Chlorophytum comosum* or *capense*) require little effort to grow. All have grasslike leaves arching from one centre and long straw-coloured stems which carry small white flowers at the tip, followed by plantlets. The most common variety, 'Vittatum', has leaves 150-300mm (6-12in) long with a broad white or pale cream stripe down the centre.

Spider plants need bright light and some direct sunlight, especially in the

Baby spiders Propagate by rooting the long-stemmed plantlets.

winter, to maintain the colouring – but keep them out of hot midday sun. They grow most happily in a moderately warm room – maximum summer temperature 24°C (75°F) – but do not thrive in temperatures below 7°C (45°F). In summer they can be moved out into the garden.

Care Water plentifully in summer, but in winter, water more moderately, letting the compost dry out between waterings to a depth of 13mm (½in). If the mixture dries out too far, the leaf tips turn brown. Feed with liquid fertiliser once a fortnight all year – see FERTILISERS.

Grow spider plants in a soil-based mixture such as JOHN INNES COMPOST No 1 or No 2. When the roots have forced the compost up to the rim, it is time to repot – see POTTING HOUSEPLANTS.

Propagating Peg down the plantlets – still on their stems – in small pots of compost. Separate them from the parent when they are well rooted. Or cut off the plantlets and keep them with their bases in water until they have roots at least 25mm (1in) long – see PROPAGATING PLANTS.

Spinal injuries

What to do – and not to do – in an emergency

Moving a person who has a broken neck or back can lead to their death, or permanent paralysis. Do not touch an injured person – not even to put them in the RECOVERY POSITION – until you have assessed whether a spinal injury is likely. If the person is in danger – in a burning building, for example – drag him to safety by grasping his clothing at the shoulders, and using it as a head support.

What to look for First look for signs of what has happened. Spinal injury is likely if a person is lying at the foot of a ladder or a flight of stairs, for example, or if he has been hit by a vehicle or something heavy has fallen across his back. The spine may have been jarred if someone has jumped from a height, or slipped and fallen on their buttocks or head. Someone in a car collision may injure his neck by a violent backward jerk of the head (whiplash).

Symptoms of spinal injury
- Loss of feeling and movement below the injured area – sometimes a sensation of having been cut in half.
- Pain at the site of the injury.
- Tingling or pins and needles in hands and feet (suggesting a neck injury).
- Inability to move fingers, wrists, toes, or ankles when asked to, but with no signs of a broken arm or leg.
- No feeling of pain when the skin is gently nipped.
- Difficulty in breathing.

What you should do Do not move the injured person, not even to slip something under his head. Reassure him and tell him to lie still while you call an ambulance. While waiting, place rolled clothing or blankets alongside head and trunk, and cover him with a blanket.

If he is unconscious and lying face up, clear his mouth of any obstructions to breathing with your fingers and hold his jaw forwards. Carefully watch his breathing, and if it stops gently administer ARTIFICIAL RESPIRATION, even though tilting his head risks further spinal injury.

Spin dryers

Maintaining them; fault-finding and simple repairs

All spin dryers have a rotating drum driven by an electric motor. The motor switches off automatically if the dryer lid is lifted, and a brake slows and stops the drum. Some dryers empty through a spout at the base (gravity types); other, more expensive types, pump out water through a hose hooked over the sink.

Dealing with a leak A leak is usually from the pump or one of its hoses which may be split or perished. The pump may need a new gasket on the flange. To remove the pump, undo the hoses, stretch the drive belt and ease it off over the pulley edges, and undo the nuts and bolts holding it to the frame.

The pump normally has two halves joined by small bolts through the flange. Unscrew and prise the parts open, taking care not to scratch the faces. Gently scrape off any gasket pieces from the faces. Before renewing the gasket, check the impeller shaft for signs of wear – to remove it, punch out the pin through the pulley collar, using a hammer and centre punch. If the impeller is worn, a new pump is needed.

If you cannot buy a new gasket, make one. Measure the internal diameter of the pump before refitting the impeller, then cut out a circle of the same size in a piece of gasket cork 2mm ($\frac{1}{16}$in) thick. Place the gasket face down on it and mark the shape of the joining faces. Cut out the shape, making sure the screw-hole positions are accurate. Coat both faces with gasket cement; fit the gasket and reassemble the pump. If leaking continues, the pump may have a worn gland and need replacing.

Pump not working The reason may be that the pump is blocked or the hoses kinked, or if it is driven by a belt from the motor, the belt may be broken or slack. Check for a blockage by removing the pump as for fitting a gasket. Adjust the belt by tightening the pulley wheel. You may have to remove and refit the wheel to fit a new belt.

Problems with the drum If the drum revolves unevenly and noisily, clothing may be caught between the drum and the casing. Or the brake may be binding on it. If the drum fails to stop spinning, the brake lining may be worn or the brake cable slack. The brake can be adjusted if it is accessible – it is usually at the base of the drum. The brake cable usually has two nuts, a locknut and an adjuster nut. Loosen the locknut with one spanner while you turn the adjuster nut to slacken the cable if the brake is binding, or to tighten it if the drum will not stop spinning.

If the drum fails to turn at all, check whether there is a broken drive belt between the drum and motor (not all drums are belt-driven). If the dryer vibrates excessively, the clothes are not evenly loaded, or the bearings may be worn. If the motor does not work, or

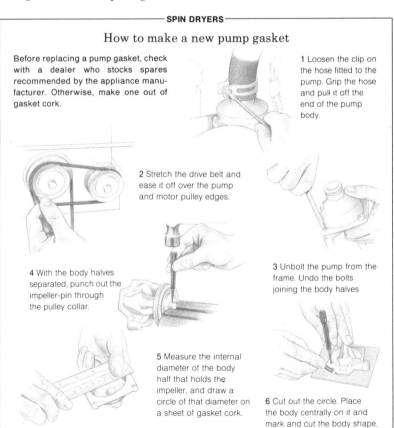

SPIN DRYERS

How to make a new pump gasket

Before replacing a pump gasket, check with a dealer who stocks spares recommended by the appliance manufacturer. Otherwise, make one out of gasket cork.

1 Loosen the clip on the hose fitted to the pump. Grip the hose and pull it off the end of the pump body.

2 Stretch the drive belt and ease it off over the pump and motor pulley edges.

3 Unbolt the pump from the frame. Undo the bolts joining the body halves

4 With the body halves separated, punch out the impeller-pin through the pulley collar.

5 Measure the internal diameter of the body half that holds the impeller, and draw a circle of that diameter on a sheet of gasket cork.

6 Cut out the circle. Place the body centrally on it and mark and cut the body shape.

works intermittently, either it is broken or faulty or there is an electrical fault such as a loose connection (see PLUGS) or a blown fuse – see FUSES AND FUSE BOXES. If the motor is faulty or there are signs of rust or corrosion, it is safer not to attempt any repairs. Ask an electrical shop if spares are available.

Spinning yarn

*Hand-spinning wool using
a simple spindle*

The basic techniques of hand-spinning have remained largely unchanged for thousands of years. All you need is a spindle and some fleece – both available from craft shops. Fleece is sold unscoured (in its natural state) or washed and carded. If the wool is unscoured you must *tease* and *card* it before spinning. For this you need two cards – wooden bats set with short wires – also available from craft shops.

Teasing Take a small handful of fleece and gently pull it apart with your fingers. Work through the whole fleece in this way until it is fluffy with no coarse lumps. Pull out any grass or seeds.

Carding Take one card in your left hand and lay a thin layer of fleece evenly across it, catching the fleece in the wires. Rest the card on your left knee. Draw the other card lightly across it with an upward motion at the end of the stroke. Repeat the brushing motion until all the wool is transferred to the second card.

Now repeat the process again to transfer the wool back to the first card. Transfer the wool from one card to the other until all the fibres are spread evenly over one card.

Hold the cards at right angles and draw the empty one up across the other to make a light, fluffy roll of wool – known as a *roving* or *rolag*. Gently roll the roving between your hands until even. Make about 24 rovings.

Spinning Take a piece of finished wool yarn and tie it to the spindle above the whorl, as illustrated. Wind it around the spindle shaft below the whorl, then bring it up and loop it around the notch at the top of the shaft.

Cut the yarn 250mm (10in) from the notch, then fray the end. Hold the frayed end and an end of roving together between the fingers and thumb of your left hand. Let the spindle dangle, then twirl it with your right hand so that the fibres and yarn are twisted evenly together as far as your left hand.

With your right hand, gently draw out some more fibres from the roving, then twirl the spindle again so that the fibres are evenly twisted. Repeat the rhythmic process of drawing out more fibres and spinning until the spun wool is so long that the spindle is near the floor.

Unfasten the spun yarn from the notch and beneath the whorl. Wind the yarn in a cone shape around the spindle shaft. Loop the yarn around the notch once more and resume spinning. Once spun in this way, the yarn becomes what is known as *a single*.

Plying yarn To make yarn suitable for weaving, ply together two singles. Place two cones of single in a bowl on the floor – to keep them contained and to allow them to unwind easily.

Attach them both to the spindle and twist together as for spinning – but twirl the spindle in the direction opposite to that used for making the singles.

As the yarn is plied, wind it into a *skein* around pegs set 460mm (18in) apart – or around a chair back. Tie the ends together, then tie several figure-of-eight knots through the skein to keep it from tangling.

Washing Soak the skein in mildly soapy, tepid water. Squeeze gently. Rinse in cold water several times. Hang up to dry on a rod outdoors in the shade. Move it around the rod so that it dries completely. Wind into a ball ready for WEAVING.

Splicing rope

*Joining two ropes; sealing
the ends*

The ends of all the ropes used on a boat need to be sealed to prevent fraying and unravelling. To seal a rope made of synthetic fibre, see NYLON ROPES.

A common method used to seal ropes made of natural fibre, such as hemp, jute or sisal, is to bind the strands with strong twine (preferably, sailmaker's yarn). This is called 'whipping'.

Whipping To whip the end of a three-strand rope:
1 Untwist – the technical term is 'unlay' – the end of the rope about 50-75mm (2-3in) and separate the strands. Loop the twine over one of the strands. Hold the loop, so that it is left dangling

Whipping a rope end and making a splice

Whipping Open the strands of the rope and loop a length of twine over one of them. With the loop and its short end protruding, rewind the strands and wind the twine around them.

Lift the loop over one strand and pull the short end to tighten it. Take the short end up outside the binding and tie it to the long end.

Splicing Interweave the strands and tie down the ends of one rope (left). Weave the free ends through the rope. Untie the other ends and weave them into the rope (right).

Making carded fleece into spun yarn

Tie yarn above the spindle whorl. Loop once below the whorl, then around the spindle top.

Twist the end of the yarn on the spindle to a piece of yarn on the roll.

Twirl the spindle, and the twist will run up the yarn to your fingers. Pull out the roll to even thickness. Keep rotating the spindle until the spun wool is so long that the spindle reaches the floor.

and does not run tight. With the other hand, bring the ends of the twine out between the other two strands.

2 Twist the strands back together – and wind the long end of the twine tightly round the rope, with the short end of the twine protruding from the bottom of the whipping. The whipping should be at least as deep as the rope diameter.

3 Hold the short end of the twine, slip the loop over one of the strands and pull the short end hard to tighten it, like a slip knot – see KNOTS.

4 Bring the short end of the twine up over the whipping. Cut the long end, so that it is approximately the same length as the short end, and tie the two ends together between the strands of rope with a tight reef knot. Trim the ends and cut off the end of the rope neatly, about 6mm ($\frac{1}{4}$in) above the top of the whipping.

Splicing To join two ropes together:

1 Untwist the strands at one end of each rope to a depth equivalent to ten times the thickness of one of the strands. Work the strands of the two ropes together so they are interwoven, then tie a short length of twine around the loose strands of one rope as illustrated.

2 Weave the free strands of one rope through the strands of the other three or four times. Untie the remaining strands and weave them into the splice. Trim any loose ends then tug both ropes to tighten.

Splicing is also used to create an 'eye' (permanent loop) at the end of a rope:

1 Twist open some strands in the body of the rope at the point where the splice is to be made. Untwist the rope end that is to make the eye, about 100mm (4in).

2 Bend over the rope end and weave the strands between the loosened strands in the rope body.

3 Twist the rope body to open strands more and weave in the end strands, passing each over and under the open strands at least three or four times until all the loose strands are woven in. Pull the two 'arms' of the eye to tighten.

If an eye splice or a splice joining two ropes together has been done properly, the eye or join will remain secure, and will tighten as the rope is tugged.

Splinters

Removing them safely

Removing a splinter safely means avoiding infection and pulling it out neatly in one piece. If the splinter – a thorn, or small sliver of wood or metal – is protruding from the skin, remove it as soon as possible. But for large or deeply embedded splinters – get medical help.

Use a pair of tweezers with spade ends. Wash your hands thoroughly then sterilise the tweezers either by passing them through a flame (do not wipe away the soot) or boiling them in water for ten minutes – see STERILISING.

Clean the skin round the splinter carefully with warm, soapy water, wiping away from the wound. Dry the skin gently then grasp the end of the splinter with the tweezers and pull it out – use a magnifying glass if you cannot see it easily. Wash the wound with antiseptic and cover it with a plaster dressing.

If the splinter will not come out, or breaks, or if the area round it swells or becomes painful, get medical advice.

Split ends

What to do about them; how to avoid them

Exposure to sun and wind can cause hair to split at the ends. More avoidable causes are too much colouring, bleaching or perming, using sharp combs or brushes that tear the hair, too frequent use of heated rollers, or blow-drying at too high a heat. These all rob the hair of the natural oils that keep it lubricated and prevent brittleness.

Once the damage is done, it cannot be repaired. The only remedy is to have a cut that will remove all the split ends, then use a conditioner formulated for damaged hair. Use it at least once a week until your hair is back to normal.

Alternatively, instead of applying a special conditioner, warm two or three tablespoons of olive oil, rub it into the scalp and comb it through your hair. Then wrap a towel round your head and leave the oil to soak in for 15 minutes. Follow with a mild shampoo and rinse.

If you wash your hair more than once a week, use an ordinary conditioner between the weekly conditioner treatments – see HAIR CARE.

To prevent split ends, treat your hair kindly. Use a mild shampoo, use conditioner from time to time and dry your hair gently – since hair is most easily damaged when wet. Avoid BACKCOMBING and use heated rollers no more than twice a week; also, avoid overbleaching and colouring and do not have your hair permed more than twice a year. See also HAIR COLOURING; HOME PERMS.

Sprains and strains

Getting relief from joint and muscle injuries

Sprains occur when the ligaments connected with a joint are wrenched or torn. The ankle is the joint most commonly affected by sprains, though the wrist, elbow, knee, hip and shoulder are also vulnerable joints. Symptoms of a sprain are: pain when the joint is moved; swelling of the joint, perhaps with some dis-coloration, and tenderness over the area of the torn ligament.

Strains occur when a muscle is overstretched by sudden or unaccustomed physical exertion, or by an accident such as a fall. The symptoms are: pain over the muscle, which becomes rigid, with possible bruising, swelling or cramp.

Treating a sprain Remove the shoe, if it is an ankle sprain, and raise the foot above the level of the head. Apply a cold compress and bandage it in place for 20-30 minutes. Remove the compress and bandage the joint firmly. For an ankle sprain, take the bandage in a figure-of-eight round the ankle and the instep several times – see BANDAGING.

Treating a strain Lie in a comfortable position with the injured limb above the level of the head. Apply a cold compress to the strained muscle, and bandage it in place for 20-30 minutes. Remove the compress and bandage the muscle firmly, but not too tightly because the muscle may swell. Support a strained arm with an arm sling – see SLINGS.

Spray painting

Covering large objects the quick way

The simplest form of spray paint for domestic use is the aerosol can – ideal for painting textured surfaces such as wickerwork or wrought iron work.

Make up a spray booth from sheets of cardboard to contain the spray, and lay newspaper on the ground. Work outside if you do not have a workshop separate from the house, and work on a dry, windless day. Mask areas you do not wish to paint with masking tape and newspaper.

Shake the can well until the paint is thoroughly mixed, then hold the can about 300mm (12in) away from the object to be painted. Press the button and move the can horizontally, keeping it an even distance from the object and moving all the time. Apply only a thin coat; do not try to cover the object with one coat.

Allow the paint to start to dry, then make another pass. Shake the can occasionally to keep the paint mixed. Keep applying coats until the object is fully covered with an even coat. When you stop work, upend the can and press the nozzle until only clear propellant comes out. This ensures that the nozzle is kept clean.

If you prefer to use a spray gun, there are two types from which to choose, the compressor and the airless – both electrically powered. The *compressor type* is the bulkiest form of spray, but gives fine control of paint so that thin, even coats are easy to apply. Most hire shops stock this equipment.

With the *airless spray gun* considerable pressure is needed to force the paint out, so fine control of the spray is not so easy, and you can get uneven spattering when paint is low in the container. One advantage of the airless gun is that there will be far less over-spray drifting around. This is the most suitable DIY spray, because of its compactness.

Spray guns are best used with cellulose paints – say for car body repair work – see DENTS IN CARS. But they can be used with oil-based gloss paint if it is thinned down as recommended by the instruction leaflet with the gun. Do not use with emulsion paint; it tends to clog the nozzle very easily and can block it if cleaning is not thorough.

The technique is similar to that already described for aerosol. Hold the gun about 300mm (12in) from the item to be painted, press the trigger and move the gun back and forth, keeping it parallel to the work so that an even coating is applied. Keep the coat thin, and do not expect to cover in one coat.

The most common fault is 'curtaining' caused by a flow of excess paint, or 'runs' trickling down from areas overloaded with paint. Build coat on coat until the required coverage is reached.

With items like wickerwork, approach from different directions for each coat so that all crevices are reached. But try to keep the gun the same distance from the item all the time so the coats are even.

As soon as work is complete, empty the container of remaining paint, and spray the appropriate thinner for the paint in use through the gun until every trace of paint has been removed.

Spur connections

Adding an extra power socket to a ring circuit

You can add a single or double socket to a ring circuit (see ELECTRIC WIRING) by leading a spur from an existing socket – see ELECTRIC SOCKETS AND SWITCHES.

You cannot, however, take a spur from a socket that is already on a spur, or has a spur running from it. You can have only one single or double outlet on a spur. The spur must not increase the likely load on the circuit to more than 7.2kW.

Directions given here apply only to a ring circuit – to add a spur on a radial circuit, consult a qualified electrician.

First turn off the main switch at the consumer unit and remove the fuse for the circuit you want to work on – see FUSES AND FUSE BOXES. Then check whether the socket from which you plan to run the spur is suitable.

Unscrew the socket and draw it forward carefully until you can see the wiring on the back of the socket. If there

are only three conductor wires coming from one cable, the socket is already on a spur and cannot be used; if there are three cables, one of them is a spur so the socket cannot be used.

If there are two cables, the socket should be safe to use – unless it is the first of a two-socket spur. These are no longer allowed, but one could have been fitted earlier.

To make sure, check with a circuit tester – see CIRCUIT TESTING. Disconnect the two red wires at the socket and fasten the clips of the tester to them, one to each red wire. If the bulb on the tester lights, the circuit has been completed, and so the socket is on the ring circuit and is safe to use. If the bulb does not light, the socket is on a spur and cannot be used.

To wire a spur socket you will need: 2.5mm^2 twin-core-and-earth cable; cable clips; green/yellow sleeving; a mounting box with grommets; and a single or double switched socket.

When you have found a safe supply socket, unscrew the conductor wires from the terminals and remove the socket and mounting box.

Cut a cavity to receive the mounting box for the new socket. Plan a route for the spur cable then check with a metal detector or probe carefully with a fine bradawl to see if any wires or pipes in the wall obstruct the route. If any do, plan a different route.

Prepare the route and lay the cable along it, secured with clips at 250mm

(10in) intervals, leaving enough spare to make the socket connections. Knock out an entry hole in each mounting box and fit grommets if the boxes are metal. Feed the cable ends through the holes and screw the boxes into drilled and plugged holes in their cavities – see MASONRY DRILLING.

Make good damaged plaster and wait for it to dry before you make the connections – see PLASTER PATCHING.

At both ends of the cable, cut back about 38mm (1½in) of the outer sheath with a sharp knife, and bare about 16mm (⅝in) of each wire. Slip green/yellow sleeving over the bare earth wires, leaving 16mm exposed at the tip. Connect the new spur cable and existing cable to the terminals at the supply socket and the other end of the spur cable at the spur socket – see illustrations.

Gently press each socket onto its mounting box, making sure that no wires are kinked or dislodged. Screw in place until there is no gap between socket and box.

Squash rackets

Playing a fast indoor ball game

Although easy to learn, squash rackets – usually called squash, for short – requires agility, concentration, fast reactions and the ability to outwit one's opponent. It is usually a singles game.

A squash court is an enclosed area

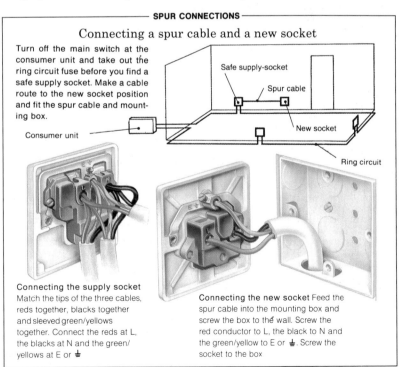

— SPUR CONNECTIONS —

Connecting a spur cable and a new socket

Turn off the main switch at the consumer unit and take out the ring circuit fuse before you find a safe supply socket. Make a cable route to the new socket position and fit the spur cable and mounting box.

Consumer unit

Safe supply-socket

Spur cable

New socket

Ring circuit

Connecting the supply socket Match the tips of the three cables, reds together, blacks together and sleeved green/yellows together. Connect the reds at L, the blacks at N and the green/yellows at E or ⊕

Connecting the new socket Feed the spur cable into the mounting box and screw the box to the wall. Screw the red conductor to L, the black to N and the green/yellow to E or ⊕. Screw the socket to the box

9.75m (32ft) long and 6.4m (21ft) wide with a wooden floor. At the bottom of the front wall is an area reaching 480mm (19in) up from the floor, topped by a strip of wood painted red, and called the 'tin'. If the ball strikes the tin, it is out; it is also out if it strikes any of the four walls above the out-of-court line – which is 4.6m (15ft) high at the front of the court and 2.1m (7ft) high at the back. The front wall and back wall lines are joined by a red line on each side wall. The rear half of the floor is divided into two service courts. Each court has a service box, 1.6m (5ft 3in) square.

A squash racket is similar to a BADMIN-TON racket but is slightly longer, much sturdier and has a smaller head; it is strung with natural or synthetic gut and may have a wooden, composite or metal frame. The small black or green ball is soft rubber and hollow. A coloured dot indicates the speed of the ball, which can be varied to suit the court temperature and players' ability. Players must wear white-soled squash or tennis shoes.

Play A spin of the racket decides who serves.

When serving, the server must have at least one foot inside the service box marked on the floor. For a serve to be 'in', it must strike the front wall direct, above the red service line (officially called 'the cut line'), and rebound into the opposite service court. If it is not served correctly, the server is allowed a second attempt. The receiver can either volley the ball or return it after it has bounced off the back wall, one of the side walls or the floor.

Both forehand and backhand shots are hit with a short swing.

During play, after a player has hit the ball, each shot must strike the front wall above the tin, either direct or after bouncing off one of the other walls, before the ball touches the floor. After it has struck the front wall, the ball may either bounce off one of the other walls or drop onto the floor. If it goes out or bounces on the floor more than once before being returned, that is the end of the rally.

Scoring In the international version of the game, only the server can score. If he wins the service or a rally he scores a point; if he serves a double fault or loses a rally, his opponent takes over the service and is then in a position to score. The first player to reach 9 points wins the game – unless the score is eight-all, in which case the first player to reach 8 points has the option of extending the game to 10, if he so prefers. A match is normally the best of five games.

If a player accidentally hinders his opponent or obstructs his view of the ball, the other player can claim a 'let'. The point is then replayed.

Squatters

What to do if they move into your property

If squatters move into your usual home or into a property that you intend to make your home they can be evicted quite simply. Show them proof that you live there or intend to (a sworn state-ment, for example, or a local council's letting agreement to you).

If they do not leave, they are commit-ting the criminal offence of 'adverse occu-pancy'. Call the police. They will either evict the squatters on the spot or pros-ecute them.

Evicting squatters yourself You can force your way in and evict the squatters yourself, provided you use only 'reason-able force'. How reasonable force is defined, though, depends on the circum-stances – it is usually better to leave the eviction to the police. If you use excess-ive force you could be charged with assault.

Until the squatters leave you may have to stay with friends or in a hotel. Check your home INSURANCE policy – you may be able to reclaim the cost of temporary accommodation, and even the cost of damage done by the squatters.

An unoccupied property If squatters move into a property you do not live in permanently (a holiday home, for exam-ple), they are not committing a criminal offence. You cannot therefore get the police to evict them, or force your way into the house.

If the squatters refuse to leave, get a solicitor (see LAWYERS) to apply to the county court for a possession order. When the order is issued, a court official will evict the squatters so that you can regain possession of your property.

Alternatively, wait until the squatters go out shopping, for example, then move in and take possession.

Do not destroy any property squatters leave behind. You have a legal responsi-bility to look after it until it can be collected. See also EVICTION NOTICE.

Squeaky shoes

Making them tread quietly

When the sole is not sewn tightly enough to the upper part of a shoe, the material of the upper and sole may rub together, making the shoe squeak. The squeak gen-erally stops when the shoe softens.

If the squeak persists, take off the shoe and twist it in your hands until you locate the source of the squeak. Rub a proprietary shoe cream or saddle soap around the stitches in that area. The cream may soften the leather and stop the squeak.

If your shoe still squeaks, the part that is rubbing may be in the interior of the shoe, and you will have to take the shoe to a shoe repair shop. The shoemaker may be able to put a few tacks in the area of the squeak to hold the sole and upper together more tightly – or possibly resole the shoe using masking tape as interfacing between upper and sole.

Stained glass

Making ornaments or panels

In the Middle Ages, stained-glass win-dows were made by fitting pieces of colou-red glass into lead channels – a method still used for some windows. But many ornaments and lampshades are now made by the copper-foil technique.

The edges of the glass pieces are wrap-ped with copper foil and fitted together. All exposed surfaces of foil are then coated with solder for strength.

Rolls of paper-backed copper foil, sheets of coloured glass, Chinagraph pen-cils and a selection of patterns can be bought at arts and crafts shops. Begin by tracing two copies of the original design. Cut one into patterns – templates for the individual pieces of glass in the work. Using the patterns as guides, as illus-trated, cut all the glass (see GLASS CUT-TING), laying each piece in place on the second copy of the design.

Wrap the edges of each piece with copper foil, paper-side out and starting at a corner, as illustrated. Centre the edge of the glass on the foil and, peeling off the paper backing as you go, work round each piece, ending at a corner that will not be on the rim of the finished piece, where it might be knocked and loosened, and allowing a 6mm ($\frac{1}{4}$in) over-lap. Use your thumb and forefinger to crimp the foil tightly over the glass on both sides, and replace it on the pattern. Tape each piece to the adjoining pieces with short strips of masking tape.

Next, join the foil-covered edges of the glass pieces with spots of solder at inter-vals, using a heavyweight SOLDERING IRON and soft solder – see SOLDERING AND BRAZING.

When all the pieces are joined apply a thin coat of solder to all the visible foil, front and back. As solder solidifies quickly but cools slowly, do not touch a newly soldered surface.

Unless the iron has a thermostat, it will overheat as you work, so keep swit-ching it on and off to maintain the correct soldering temperature.

Wearing rubber gloves to protect your hands, rub down the solder on the fin-ished piece with copper sulphate or pot-assium permanganate and a soft cloth to give it the appearance of antique copper. Wash the finished piece with detergent and water, then rinse dry.

Making a panel of stained glass

To make a stained-glass panel you will need one traced design and one with the shapes cut out; coloured glass and a Chinagraph pencil; a straightedge, a glass cutter and pliers to cut the glass with; and copper foil, masking tape, solder and a soldering iron.

Trace each shape onto the glass with a Chinagraph pencil. Cut the pieces out and arrange them on the traced design.

Wrap the edges of each piece of glass with copper foil, crimping it down, and replace the pieces on the tracing paper.

Hold the pieces in place with strips of masking tape and drop spots of solder along the joining edges. Remove the tape as you solder. Apply a thin coat of solder to all the foil on both sides of the panel. Rub the solder on the finished piece with a cloth dipped in copper sulphate so it resembles antique copper.

Staining wood

Improving its natural look

Many TIMBER hardwoods are expensive and difficult to obtain, but they can be imitated by colouring cheaper softwoods. Stains are available in a wide range of wood colours, from light oak to ebony and, with careful preparation, they are easy to apply.

The colours are mainly solvent (spirit) based or water-based. If you use a solvent-based stain, work in a well-ventilated room and do not smoke.

Water-based stains are easy to apply and can be diluted and mixed to produce the exact colour you want. The only disadvantage is that the water raises the grain of the wood slightly, so use fine glasspaper to smooth down after the wood has dried – see SANDING.

Colours may change slightly as they dry, so experiment on a scrap piece of wood, or an area which is not seen.

Prepare the wood by stripping off all old finish back to clean wood – see PAINT STRIPPING. Any paint or varnish left in the wood grain will resist the stain and cause patchiness. Remove also any traces of glue, perhaps from repaired joints. This too will resist stain.

Fill all cracks and gaps with a proprietary wood filler – see STOPPERS AND FILLERS. These are designed to accept stains, so that filled areas will blend in with the wood. When set, sand the whole of the wood smooth – working only with the grain of the wood. Scratches across

the grain will be highlighted by the colour. Make sure the surface is clean and dry and free of dust or grease.

Shake the stain well, pour some into a non-plastic dish then apply quickly and evenly with a lint-free rag made into a pad. For large areas use a paint pad – see PAINTBRUSHES, PADS AND ROLLERS.

Once the stain starts to dry, do not go over areas already done. You will darken the colour. Once dry, an extra coat can be added if you wish to darken the wood further. See the manufacturer's instructions for drying time.

When the stain is dry, rub lightly with fine glasspaper. Go over the piece again lightly with stain to coat any high points that have been bared by sanding. Leave overnight before VARNISHING or sealing.

Where an item of furniture is made up of woods of different colours, bring the whole piece to a neutral tone by using wood bleach. This is available from most hardware departments. Protect your eyes and hands while applying.

Stainless steel

Keeping it gleaming

Stainless steel can be generally maintained by washing it in detergent and drying with a soft cloth (to avoid water spots) after use. To keep stainless-steel tableware shining, use a proprietary stainless-steel cleaner, available from hardware stores.

Wash stainless-steel sinks, draining boards or oven tops with a non-abrasive

cleaner, preferably a cream or liquid. Glass cleaner or a paste of baking soda and water will keep a polished stainless steel finish shiny.

Avoid abrasives as much as possible, but if baked-on food is difficult to remove from pans, use a non-abrasive cream cleaner or soap-impregnated steel wool. See also PANS BURNT.

Stain removal

Treating soiled fabrics with water and cleaners

There are many proprietary dry-cleaning products available (see CLEANING SOLVENTS), and often stains can be removed using common household materials – see CLEANING AND POLISHING MATERIALS.

Rinse washable materials immediately with cold or lukewarm water. Stains in materials other than wool, silk, non-colourfast and flameproof fabrics may then be removed by soaking in the appropriate cleaner.

Fresh stains on white or colourfast linen can sometimes be removed by drenching the stained area with boiling water. Stretch the fabric over a basin and sprinkle a little dry borax or detergent on the stain, pour boiling water through, then rinse. If the stain remains after rinsing, gently rub some cleaner into it, rinse then wash – see LAUNDERING.

Treat non-washable materials by first sponging gently with cold water or, if possible, stretch the fabric over a jug and pour cold water through the stain. If the stain remains, place an absorbent pad under it and work in the cleaning solution with another pad. Sponge with clean water and blot dry.

Stair carpets

Choosing and laying

Stair carpeting can be bought in a standard width of 690mm (27in), and laid centrally on the stairway with the exposed wood on either side protected with PAINTS or VARNISHING. Fitted carpeting, laid the full width of the stairs, is more difficult to fit and should be left to an experienced carpet layer.

Stair carpet is subject to heavy wear, so choose a good quality pile carpet, such as Axminster or Wilton. Avoid cord, needlefelt and sisal which, although hard-wearing, do not grip the feet and could be slippery.

Estimating length First measure from the front to the back of one tread, and multiply by the number of treads. On a curving staircase, or a spiral staircase, take the widest measurement. If the stairs turn a corner on a half landing, measure its length and add it to the total, also the length of the upstairs landing if you want the carpet to run to the far end.

Now measure the height of a riser, the vertical part of a stair, and multiply that figure by the number of risers. Add this total to the one you already have to find the length you need to carpet the stairs. It is advisable to move the carpet from time to time to even out wear – to allow for this, add the depth of the bottom tread and the height of the bottom riser.

In addition to the carpet and underlay pads, you will also need carpet adhesive and metal stair grippers – angled strips with projecting teeth that grip the carpet backing. The length of the grippers should be the same as the width of the carpet, and you will need one for each tread.

Preparing the stairs If you have removed an old carpet, check the condition of the woodwork – see STAIRCASES. Remove old nails, tacks, old grippers and any patches of adhesive. Brush the stairs thoroughly.

Put a pad centrally on the first tread down from the top landing, with one edge against the riser and the other overhanging the front of the tread. Place a gripper in the angle between the tread and the riser and nail it through the pad to the tread, then nail it to the riser. To avoid hitting the teeth of the gripper, use a small hammer to drive the nails partly home, then finish off using a nail punch – see NAILING. Fit grippers and pads to all

the stairs except the bottom one, and do not fit a gripper where the bottom riser meets the floor.

Laying the carpet Unroll the carpet and run your hand over it; it will wear better if the direction which feels smooth runs from the top of the stairs to the bottom. Reroll it so that the decorative side is inwards.

Start at the bottom of the stairs. Unroll a little of the carpet, and if the end is starting to fray spread a little adhesive on it, taking care not to get any on the decorative side. Lay the carpet working from the bottom tread up, doubling back on the first tread, as illustrated.

Carpeting a curved staircase Use wooden gripper strips, nailing one to the tread and one to the riser. Cut the underlay pads to the shape of each tread and tack them in place, butted against the gripper on the tread. Lay the carpet from the bottom as described, folding it on the inside curve as illustrated.

Using stair rods For a more decorative effect, stair rods can be used instead of grippers. The method of laying is the same, except that the pads must be held in place with tacks. Make sure that the clips for the rods are close against the carpet edges, to prevent sideways movement.

Carpet landings On a half-landing, where the stairs make a 90 degree turn, treat each set of stairs as a separate

flight, using two lengths of carpet. Lay the first length on the lower flight and continue it across the landing to the wall. Turn the end under and tack it down. Butt the next length to it at right angles, with its end folded under and tacked.

If the staircase makes a dog-leg (180 degree) turn, there may be a wide landing to be covered with a separate strip of carpet laid at right angles to the two flights of stairs. Carry both stair carpets to what will be the far edge of the landing carpet, cut them off and tack them in place without underlay.

See also CARPET LAYING.

Staircases
Getting rid of squeaks and creaks

Timber expands and contracts according to its moisture content, and in a house which is well heated, squeaks and creaks may be heard, especially in staircases. But they will also creak if any of the fixings have worked loose, and the treads and risers are rubbing against each other or other adjoining wood.

When the stair carpet is next replaced, or lifted to move it to spread wear (see STAIRCARPETS), walk up the stairs, pressing on each tread to try to force a squeak. Also look for gaps in the long strips of TIMBER at each side, called the strings, to which the ends of the stair treads are fixed.

There are two types of strings – cut and closed. Cut strings have their upper edge cut in steps and have the treads fixed to the top edge of each step. Closed strings are not stepped; instead the treads are set in grooves in the strings.

Securing loose fixings If you locate squeaks, try to get at the affected steps from underneath.

If the stairs have closed strings, you will see the undersides of the treads and risers housed in grooves in the strings and held by wooden wedges glued and tapped in place. Pull out loose wedges; replace with new ones if necessary. Glue the wedges (see GLUING) and tap them back in place. Check also any blocks securing treads and risers.

If you cannot get at the underside of the stairs, drill holes through the tread into the riser at 250mm (10in) intervals – see DRILLING. Countersink the holes, then use long SCREWS to pull the tread and riser tightly together. Cover the screw heads with filler and sand them smooth.

Sealing gaps Use an epoxy resin filler to seal all cracks and gaps between stairs and strings. Do not use ordinary cellulose fillers because they are not strong enough – see STOPPERS AND FILLERS.

Seal gaps between walls and strings

STAIR CARPETS

Carpeting a straight and a curved staircase

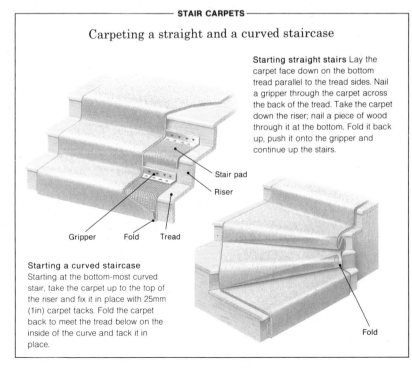

Starting straight stairs Lay the carpet face down on the bottom tread parallel to the tread sides. Nail a gripper through the carpet across the back of the tread. Take the carpet down the riser; nail a piece of wood through it at the bottom. Fold it back up, push it onto the gripper and continue up the stairs.

Stair pad
Riser
Gripper   Fold   Tread

Starting a curved staircase
Starting at the bottom-most curved stair, take the carpet up to the top of the riser and fix it in place with 25mm (1in) carpet tacks. Fold the carpet back to meet the tread below on the inside of the curve and tack it in place.

Fold

Fixing squeaky stairs

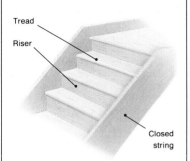

Tread

Riser

Closed string

Check for gaps between strings, treads and risers and fill them with an epoxy resin filler; fill gaps between strings and wall with a flexible sealant.

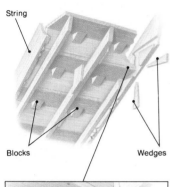

String

Blocks

Wedges

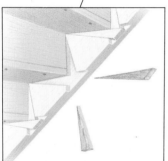

Look underneath the stairs and check if any triangular blocks holding treads and risers together, or wedges securing them in the strings, are loose. Remove loose wedges or blocks, clean off old glue, and apply PVA wood glue. Tap in wedges and screw blocks back in place.

with an acrylic flexible sealant. This comes in a cartridge for use with an applicator gun. It is better than normal fillers because it retains a degree of flexibility – see SEALANTS.

While working on the stairs, fill all cracks and tack holes with plastic wood, then smooth when set – see SANDING.

See also BALUSTERS.

Staking plants

Lending support to your garden

Many tall-growing, or top-heavy plants – for example, delphiniums, tomatoes and beans – cannot stand upright without support from posts or canes. Some trees and shrubs also need supporting for the first few years.

To prevent damage to roots or bulbs, stake plants early.

Stake trees and SHRUBS when PLANTING them, allowing up to 760mm (30in) of the stake for driving into the ground. With most perennials, put the stakes in position in April. Make sure the stakes are tall enough to reach just below the flower head or uppermost fruits of the plant when fully grown and to push as much as 300mm (1-2in) into the ground.

Supporting single stems For most plants a thick bamboo cane will give sufficient support – but for heavier plants such as dahlias use a wooden pole with a 25mm (1in) square cross section.

Secure the stem firmly but not tightly to the stake with raffia, twine or wire rings. Add more ties at 300mm (12in) intervals as the stem grows.

Supporting groups of plants To support a group of plants – or a plant with several stems – drive three stakes or canes into the ground in a triangle round the plants. Tilt them slightly outwards and join them with twine tied 150-230mm (6-9in) above ground. As the plants grow, tie in more twine at 230mm intervals.

To support clumps of herbaceous plants that grow more than 1.5m (5ft) tall – filipendulas, for example – make a cylindrical cage around the plants with 200mm (8in) square galvanised mesh. Hold the cage in place with bamboo

canes threaded through it and pushed into the ground.

Pea sticks Small floppy plants, such as dwarf sweet peas, are best supported by pea sticks – trimmings from small trees or HEDGES, available from garden centres or nurseries.

Staking a young tree or shrub Support a young tree or large shrub at planting time with a stout wooden pole treated with one of the WOOD PRESERVATIVES. The pole should reach just below the lowest branch and be driven in until very firm.

Secure the tree to the stake with tree ties – available from garden centres or nurseries. Loosen the ties periodically as the tree grows.

Stammering

Fighting a common speech problem

Children may stammer as a reaction to a severe trauma, such as a serious illness or bereavement, while learning to talk. This is normal and the most effective treatment is to relax and listen patiently as the child gains confidence with words. Do not appear anxious – it could make the child even more prone to stammer.

If stammering persists, it could be due to a delayed mental reaction as the brain checks what it has heard, or to impaired coordination between the palate, tongue and lips.

Consult your health visitor or doctor, who should be able to refer you to a speech therapist. The therapist will be able to tell you which of the many aids and techniques might help to improve fluency.

Some sufferers find that they do not

Supporting single and grouped plants

Staking single stems Drive a stake into the ground near the plant. Tie the stem to the stake at mid-stem and near the crown.

Staking grouped plants Drive three stakes into the ground in a triangle round the plants and join them with twine.

Staking with pea sticks Push two or three pea sticks into the ground near the centre of the plants. Interlace and tie the tops together.

Staking a sapling or shrub Drive a treated wooden pole firmly into the hole before planting. Secure the plant to it with tree ties.

stammer while singing or acting in a play. Taking up these activities can help boost confidence and give relief from the strain of stammering.

For further information write to the Association of Stammerers, 15 Old Ford Road, Bethnal Green, London E2 9PJ. This organisation is run by people who stammer, and can tell you about local groups, a library service and access to self-help tapes.

Stamp collecting

Making a start in philately

The easiest way to start is to buy a packet of 1000 different stamps. This will give you an immediate representative collection and help you decide what theme – bird or animal, for instance, you want to collect. They can be bought by weight quite cheaply from stamp dealers, who can be located in *Yellow Pages*.

Equipping yourself There are several types of stamp album: buy the kind you find easiest to handle – ring-fitting, loose leaf and multi-ring are among those available from a good stationer or stamp dealer.

You also need stamp mounts or 'hinges' – small, near-transparent slips of paper, gummed on one side, which when folded hold the stamp to a page. Or, to avoid hinge marks, you can use 'strip mounts' – slipping the stamps between a black backing which sticks to the page and a clear plastic front.

Handle your stamps with blunt-nosed tweezers (made of nickel or another non-rusting material) that are perfectly smooth on the inner sides.

You also need a small, strong, magnifying glass, to examine the stamps in detail.

Finding stamps Apart from stationers and dealers, you can buy them at stamp fairs, often held during weekends and advertised in local papers and collectors' magazines. You may also wish to contact the British Philatelic Centre, 107 Charterhouse Street, London EC1M 6PT, for details of stamp clubs in your area.

Consult catalogues such as those published by Stanley Gibbons (British), Yvert and Tellier (French), Michel (German) and Scott (USA). You can buy them, or study them at good local reference libraries. They will tell you what stamps are available and list prices.

Buy stamps which still have strong paper and are fresh-looking, with good colour and even perforations. Avoid any that are blemished by brown fungoid spots.

Sorting and handling Sort your packet of stamps initially by country, discarding any damaged or dirty ones.

Examine the stamps under the magnifying glass to pick out differences in colour, perforations and water marks. These differences will become more easily recognisable as your collection grows.

Weed out duplicates and any other stamps you do not want, and store them in a stock book, which has pockets to hold loose stamps that you may later want to trade.

Keep your collection at room temperature – if they get too dry, the paper cracks; if too damp, they become mildewed.

Soak used stamps, face upwards in a bowl of clear water, to remove all traces of the paper they were stuck to. Most will float free within a few minutes. Alternatively, lay them, face upwards on damp blotting paper or newspaper. After a short time, you should be able to peel the stamps from their backing.

Handle them always with tweezers, and let them dry face downwards on clean paper, lifting them from time to time to stop them sticking.

Stamp duty

Cutting the tax on home buying

Stamp duty is a tax that the buyer of a home above a certain value has to pay – see also HOUSES AND FLATS. The duty is a percentage of the price paid – at present, 1 per cent on properties over £60,000.

Both the amount of duty and the thresholds change from time to time so if you are considering house purchase you should find out how much, if any, stamp duty you will have to pay, so that you can include that amount in your total costs. An estate agent or your solicitor can advise you.

Avoiding stamp duty You do not have to pay stamp duty on fixtures and fittings, such as carpets, curtains and gas or electrical appliances, and if these are included in the purchase price you may be able to come to an agreement with the seller to pay for these items separately, and thus lower the price on which stamp duty is payable. Such an agreement must be made *before* the contract for the house purchase is made.

Staple gun

Using and maintaining a fast tacking tool

The staple gun has replaced the use of tacks for many household jobs, including upholstery (see REUPHOLSTERING), fixing carpet underlay (see CARPET LAYING), and holding garden mesh and netting.

In most instances you can use a gun

one-handed, which leaves the other hand free to hold the work. The only exception is when a heavy-duty gun is used with long staples, in which case you have to apply pressure to the gun to hold it in contact with the work to ensure that the staple goes right home.

Instructions for loading the staples in the chamber are supplied with each gun. Never try to overload, and always use the staples recommended by the manufacturer. As guns come in a number of sizes, check when buying what size of staple you can use. They can be safely driven into most wood-based materials including CHIPBOARD, blockboard, PLYWOOD and hardboard, and the longer the staple, the more secure the fastening. Some power staplers will also take nails – ideal for fixing down hardboard over UNEVEN FLOORS.

You have a choice of hand or power operation. A power tool is less tiring to use for repetition work, and most can be regulated to set the amount of impact applied to the staple. This is important if thin materials, like paper and card, are being fixed, as too much pressure would push the head of the staple straight through the material.

For wires and cables, it is advisable to use a special U-shaped staple, plus pressure control so that the staples do not damage or cut into the cable.

Observe the safety rules for your chosen staple gun at all times – especially when closing the gun to put it in its case. With some guns, compressing the handle will fire a staple.

Keep the gun clean by storing it in its case when not in use. Give an occasional wipe over with a rag dipped in machine oil to ensure staples run freely in the chamber. Stop immediately a staple fires incorrectly, and clear the blockage.

Stargazing

Locating the planets and constellations

You do not need an expensive astronomer's telescope to enjoy gazing at the stars and planets in the night sky. On clear nights you can see the constellations and many of the brighter planets and star clusters with the naked eye.

But for more detailed observations, you need a pair of good binoculars. A pair with 50mm (2in) lenses will gather 40 times as much light as the eye, enabling you to see the Moon's mountains and craters, star clusters and clouds of cosmic gases. As a beginner, you will also need a book on general astronomy, with maps and charts, to help you find your way about the sky.

As the sky becomes dark, the stars appear one by one – the brightest first, until you can see thousands.

The stars in the west 'set' soon after they appear, but the stars rising in the east appear to move across the sky towards the west. These movements of the stars across the sky are merely apparent motions caused by the Earth turning.

If you watch long enough you will see that the entire sky appears to move like a huge wheel round a fixed point. Near that point you will find the NORTH STAR.

Groups of stars form patterns, called constellations, which the ancients named after living creatures, common objects, or mythological gods or heroes – Sagitta (the Arrow), Hercules, and Ursa Major (the Great Bear) are three examples. The Plough, also known as the Big Dipper, forms part of the constellation of the Great Bear.

The Plough This forms part of the Great Bear and is easily identified by its seven stars. 1, 2, 3 and 4 form the handle; 4, 5, 6 and 7 form the blade.

Constellations are the observer's signposts by which the brighter stars and planets can be located. If you view the southern part of the sky every night at a certain time, a constellation will be seen slightly farther to the west than on the night before. In a year this nightly difference adds up to one complete turn round the North Star, due to Earth's yearly journey around the Sun. Sometimes a constellation is not visible, because it rises and sets during daylight.

Some of the ZODIAC constellations are hard to find, but it pays to recognise them. They are a great help in locating planets, because the planets pass through each zodiac constellation as they circle the Sun.

WARNING Never look at the Sun through binoculars unless they are fitted with protective filters or prisms.

Steaming

Cooking over boiling water

Fish, vegetables and puddings are the foods best suited to steaming. Fish keeps all its nutrients and flavour when steamed; so do vegetables, and they do not lose their fresh colour or firm texture. Sponge or suet puddings are lighter and more digestible than when cooked by other methods. See also POACHING.

Place fish or vegetables directly into a steamer (a container with a perforated

---

Using a steamer

Make sure the water is rapidly boiling, then place the food in the perforated container and see that the lid is tight. Fit the food pan into the water pan so its base rests above the water level.

base) or wire colander and fit it over the top of a pan containing 50mm (2in) of steadily boiling water. A pudding is placed in the steamer in its basin – or the basin can be put directly into water coming halfway up the side of the basin.

Vegetables Sprinkle the prepared vegetables with salt, allowing 1 teaspoon to each 450g (1lb) of vegetables. Steaming will take about 5 minutes longer than boiling the vegetables. Artichokes, asparagus and broccoli can be steamed without a steamer, by placing them in the pan with their stems resting in the boiling water.

Fish Use fillets or thin cuts of fish. Roll them or lay them in the perforated container. Sprinkle them with salt and freshly ground pepper, and cover tightly. Steam for 10-15 minutes.

Puddings Puddings take at least 2 hours to steam and are not harmed by slightly longer cooking. Christmas puddings take longer – 6 hours or more depending on the recipe. Grease the pudding basin well and cover the pudding with greaseproof paper or kitchen foil, greased on the underside, folded into a 25mm (1in) pleat across the middle and tied round the basin. From time to time add boiling water to the pan to keep the water halfway up the basin. You can add a few drops of vinegar or lemon juice to prevent the pan from discolouring.

Stencilling

Making and using your stencils

Stencilling is a technique for using cutouts to transfer patterns onto almost any surface, including wood, plaster, metal, glass, paper, fabric, walls and furnishings.

Stencils of lettering, numbers and design motifs can be bought in artists' materials shops. They are suitable for making signs, or decorating walls, furniture or fabrics.

You can use any type of colouring agent to paint your design, but you should always ask the shop's advice on what agent is best suited to the type of surface you are stencilling.

When using paint, blend it to a creamy consistency. A thin colouring agent must be applied in several thin coats, to prevent it from seeping under the edges of the stencil.

Before starting, test the colour on scrap paper or on a part of the surface which is normally not seen.

Position the stencil and brush the colour over it, stroking away from the edges towards the centre; and clean the back of the stencil before re-using it to avoid smudging a new surface.

Creating a rose design

Cut the design, showing inner detail by expanding contours to make bridges linking cut-out areas to stencil edges.

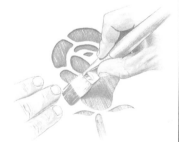

Paint the stencil by brushing gently from the edges towards the centre of the design. Press firmly on a bridge to hold it in place.

Making your own Draw a design on stiff paper or cardboard and use a craft knife to make the cut-outs. Be sure to include 'bridges' – strips that separate the shapes and link the cut-out areas to the edges of the stencil. Bridges should be at least 3mm (⅛in) wide, so that they will not break easily.

When making a cut-out rotate the stencil as you cut so that the knife is always moving towards you. Trim the corners and straighten the edges with scissors. You can mend a broken bridge with masking tape, trimming any excess tape to conform with the outlines of the stencil. See also LETTERING A SIGN.

Step repairs

Mending damaged brick and concrete steps

Damaged steps can be dangerous, so make their repair a priority.

Damaged brickwork Where a brick has been damaged, use a club hammer and cold chisel to remove the surrounding MORTAR until the damaged brick can be freed. Clean off all old mortar from both brick and cavity; make up some fresh mortar mix and dampen the damaged brick in water.

Turn the brick round so you have an undamaged face at the front, and re-fix the brick in the cavity on a bed of new mortar. Re-point when set – see POINTING. If the removed brick is too badly damaged to use again, try to find a matching brick to replace it.

Damaged paving slab Where part of a slab has been broken off, use a club hammer and cold chisel to loosen the slab away from any holding mortar. Ease the slab out and clean the underside, chipping off any old mortar. Make up a new mortar mix, adding just enough water to keep the mix fairly dry but workable.

Damp the underside of the paving slab, then turn it so that a new edge aligns with the step edge, and lay it on a bed of new mortar. Make the bed high enough so that when the slab is laid it will be the same height as surrounding slabs.

Tap the slab down with the handle of the club hammer, and check with a spirit level that it is true in both directions see LEVELLING. If any gap is left at the rear of the step by the missing piece of slab, fill it flush with mortar.

Cracked slab This usually caused by poor support under the slab. Ease the section of slab out, and clean off any old mortar from the underside. Mix new mortar and lay a bed which will give good support along the line of the crack. Damp the underside of the slab pieces.

then lay them on the mortar, tapping them in place with the handle of the club hammer. Bring the cracked edges close together and run a little mortar over the line of the joint. Check with a spirit level. Alternatively, discard the pieces and fit a new, matching slab.

Damaged concrete Where damage is slight, use an epoxy-based concrete repair material. This is usually supplied as a powder to be mixed with water to form a dryish mix.

STEP REPAIRS

Restoring crumbling concrete steps

To make up a concrete mix, use 3 parts shingle, 2 parts sand and 1 part cement. Just before you are ready to start using it, add 1 part water and 1 part PVA adhesive.

1 Using a club hammer and cold chisel, cut away 50-75mm (2-3in) of concrete round the damaged part of the step. Brush it clean.

2 Cut a board the height of the step and wider than the damage. Hold in place with bricks. Coat the exposed surface of the concrete with neat PVA adhesive.

3 Fill the hole with the new concrete. Tamp it down firmly with a trowel. Leave the board in place for at least 24 hours.

Where there is considerable damage, repair with new CONCRETE as illustrated. Make the concrete fairly dry.

An offcut of laminate is useful for the board formwork which forms the face of the new step. Or use oil-tempered hardboard. If ordinary timber or plywood is used, rub oil on the face in contact with the new concrete to avoid sticking.

Slippery steps Mould or moss growing on steps can become very slippery. Remove it with a proprietary mould or moss killer. Leave until the mould or moss dies off and blackens, then sweep the steps clean.

Stereo systems

Choosing and using hi-fi

There is a wide range of stereo hi-fi systems on the market, at prices ranging from around £100 up to many hundreds. When choosing a system, decide first how much you want to spend, then what kind of system you want.

Most systems consist of a packaged unit consisting of a record turntable, CD player, amplifier, FM radio tuner, one or two cassette recorders and a pair of speakers. However, some systems do not now include a turntable, so if you have a collection of records and LPs, look for a system that has an input into which one can be plugged.

Many systems also offer graphic equalisers, allowing you to adjust the high (treble), mid and low (bass) frequencies, and a remote control permitting you to operate the tuner, CD and cassette player and adjust the volume from your seat.

There are three main systems – the rack system, the midi system, and the mini (or micro) system.

Rack system This is a floor-standing unit, usually in a cabinet with a hinged glass door, and is designed to hold all the components, stacked one above another.

Midi system Similar to a rack system, the midi is much smaller and can be mounted on a shelf or console.

Whatever system you choose, make sound quality the top priority. Ask a reputable dealer for a full demonstration of models within your price range. Listen for a clean, crisp sound with no background noise, and a good bass response. Check that there is plenty of scope for adjusting the tone.

Listen for distortion at high volume. All but the most expensive systems have a small amount of distortion at full volume, so choose a model with at least 10 watts output, so that you do not have to turn the volume high for normal listening.

Mini (micro) system Similar to a midi system but even smaller, most units measuring about 305mm by 305mm (12in by 12in) or less. They have all the features found in the larger systems but do not offer a turntable. Because of their very compact size, these systems may be placed in confined spaces.

Speakers They should be at least 2.4m (8ft) apart. Floor-standing speakers should be at least 460mm (18in) from a wall; shelf or bracket-mounted ones at about ear level. In a rectangular room try to site the speakers at one end – experiment until you get the best stereo effect at the point where you will usually sit when listening.

The sound will also be affected by materials such as curtains and carpets absorbing sound from one speaker more than from the other. Overcome this effect by adjusting the balance control.

Headphones If you live alone, or are the only one in the household interested in listening to hi-fi stereo, good headphones are a worthwhile investment. They provide the best stereo effect, without interruption from extraneous noises and without disturbing neighbours.

See also CASSETTES AND RECORDERS; CAR CASSETTES AND RADIOS.

Sterilising

Making sure things are germ-free

Sterilisation ensures that objects are free from bacteria, viruses and other micro-organisms that can cause infection.

In the home, a baby's bottle and the teats can be sterilised by boiling in a pan of water for 15 minutes. Alternatively, they can be immersed, after washing, in a sterilising solution made up following the manufacturer's instructions.

Use sterilising solution also for DENTURES. A preparation is made specifically for sterilising CONTACT LENSES; take care to dilute it to the recommended strength.

A powder to be added to the water is sold for sterilising babies' nappies and soiled linen. If an illness is likely to cause infected clothing or bed linen, make sure the items are made of fabrics that can be boiled or disinfected in a solution of domestic bleach or a sterilising powder.

Keep a sick room well ventilated (see NURSING AT HOME) and vacuum the floor, furnishings and mattress (see VACUUM-ING). Certain organisms can remain alive in dust for several days.

Hands should always be thoroughly cleansed after contact with someone suffering from an infectious disease, or before dressing a wound. Wash hands in warm water, using plenty of soap and a clean nailbrush, and then rinse them with an antiseptic solution.

Skin around cuts and WOUNDS should be thoroughly washed with soap and water, then treated with a proprietary antiseptic solution or iodine before a sterile dressing is applied.

Sticking windows

How to get them working again

Never use force when trying to open a sticking window. You could damage the frame, or even crack the glass – see WIN-DOW PANES. Find the cause and cure it.

Slight sticking On a casement window, insert a piece of carbon paper between the meeting frames and close the window. The carbon will leave a mark at the tight spot. Try rubbing a candle on the tight part; or sand it (see SANDING) and then re-paint.

Damp Timber expands and contracts with changes in moisture content, so some windows may stick in winter but move freely in summer. Cure the problem by PLANING during damp weather. Take off at least 3mm ($\frac{1}{8}$in), then re-paint.

Paint problems Too many coats of paint often lead to sticking. Before re-painting a sticking frame, always strip it back to bare wood on meeting surfaces.

Make sure frames are not closed before the paint is absolutely dry. See also PAINT-ING EXTERIORS; PAINTING INTERIORS; PAINT STRIPPING.

Loose hinge If a casement window sticks along the closing edge, check that the hinge screws are tight.

Draught strip Sometimes a tight-fitting sprung draught strip will make a window hard to open. Prise off the strip, sand or plane down the wood and re-paint; then re-fit the strip – see DRAUGHTPROOFING.

Metal frames These may stick through too much paint or because of RUST. Use an old chisel or a wire brush to scrape or scratch away all loose rust down to sound metal. Rub clean with emery paper, apply a rust inhibitor and re-paint.

Sticky tapes

Choosing the right ones for household jobs

Sticky tape can simplify a wide range of household tasks, repairs and DIY jobs.

Double-sided tape ensures neat GIFT WRAPPING, and extra-strength tape replaces string in PARCEL TYING. These tapes, and decorative tapes for gift packages, can be found at most stationer's.

When decorating, protect areas that should not be painted, such as glass, with masking tape.

Cover small holes and cracks in plaster walls (see also PLASTER PATCHING) with glass-fibre wall repair tape – a self-adhesive mesh that is put on the repair area and then has filler pressed into it.

Use self-adhesive carpet tape to stick a patch on a carpet (see CARPET REPAIRS), use double-sided tape to secure the patch to the underlay or floor.

For repairs to leaking GUTTERS AND DOWNPIPES and roof FLASHINGS, use self-adhesive metal-backed flashing tape coated in mastic. Clean the area to be repaired, apply flashing strip primer to the repair area then press on the tape and roll an old wallpaper seam roller over it to ensure firm contact.

A transparent glazing tape is made for sealing glass into GREENHOUSES and sealing the overlapped edges of corrugated plastic panels. An alternative is self-adhesive aluminium tape. The transparent tape can be used to make temporary repairs to cracked glass and to leaking pipes.

A tape made for PLUMBING work is PTFE tape, used as an alternative to jointing compound to make threaded connections watertight.

Tape may sometimes be used instead of SEWING, to secure the HEMS of garments or CURTAINS. This bonding web is placed between the layers of fabric and sealed in place by PRESSING with a hot iron over a damp cloth.

Stiff necks

Relieving a neck that is stiff or sore

Stiff or sore necks can have a number of possible causes – nervous tension, for example, or sitting or sleeping in a draught or in an awkward position.

To treat a stiff neck, rest for a day or two. Take painkillers and lie with a hot-water bottle or other heat source against your neck to reduce pain.

Wearing a soft surgical collar, available from your DOCTOR or chemists, can also bring relief. Wear it 24 hours a day for two days. Alternatively, roll up a towel and fasten it around your neck with a safety pin.

When to see a doctor Consult a doctor if you have prolonged or repeated attacks. Consult a doctor immediately if a stiff neck is severe and accompanied by FEVER, HEADACHES and NAUSEA. In children in particular, these could be the symptoms of meningitis.

You should also see a doctor if the stiffness is caused by an injury such as whiplash, when the head is jerked forwards then backwards violently and unexpectedly – as may happen if you are in a car which is hit from behind.

Stir-frying

Fast frying over a high heat

Stir-frying is a Chinese method of cooking in which small pieces of food are fried in very hot oil. Because cooking is fast, all foods keep their nutrients and vegetables remain crisp.

Food is usually stir-fried in a wok – a bowl-shaped pan – but you can use a round, thick-based metal casserole or a deep frying pan.

Woks work best on gas hobs – on an electric hob you will need a wok stand. You will also need a metal wok spatula or long-handled spoon.

Frying Cut all the ingredients into uniform bite-sized strips, slices or cubes. Prepare seasonings such as finely chopped garlic, root ginger and spring onions. Heat the wok rapidly until very hot.

Add some groundnut or corn oil and swirl it round inside the wok. Leave for a little under a minute until the oil is very hot. Add the chopped seasonings and toss them for a few seconds.

Add the main ingredients one at a time, stirring and tossing all the time around the wok. Start with any meat and cook until pink, then add vegetables – those that have to be cooked longest first. Continue stir-frying until the food is cooked through but still crisp and with a bright colour.

Add liquid seasonings such as soya sauce or stock, and stir and toss for another minute. See also FRYING.

Stomach aches

Finding the cause and getting relief

Stomach pain has many causes, some serious, but more commonly a result of an overindulgence in food or drink.

Treat stomach ache by resting and taking small amounts of liquid, but not food, for 24 hours. During the next 24 hours, eat bland, easily digested foods (such as roast chicken, steamed fish or scrambled eggs) in small helpings.

Antacid tablets, available from chemists, may give some relief. The pain should go within 48 hours.

When to see a doctor Stomach pains generally go without medical treatment. If, though, the pain is unchanged or getting worse after four hours, contact your DOCTOR immediately. Tell the doctor if there are signs of bleeding – blood in vomit, for example, or black stools.

Consult your doctor if a stomach pain persists for more than two days or if you have stomach aches often. You may together be able to identify a cause such as ULCERS, gallstones, STRESS and anxiety, hurried meals, SMOKING or drinking too much alcohol or coffee.

A severe stomach ache can sometimes produce symptoms similar to those of a HEART ATTACK, including pains in shoulders and arms. Do not ignore such symptoms. Get to a doctor.

For other forms of stomach or abdominal pains, see CONSTIPATION; HEARTBURN; INDIGESTION; FOOD POISONING; NAUSEA; PERIOD PAINS; VOMITING.

Stonework

Cleaning and repairing

Many of the stones used for building are quite soft and porous, and in time become dirty from general weathering.

To clean grubby stonework, use a stiff scrubbing brush and plenty of warm water. Do not use soap or detergent, as these leave stains and can also cause crumbling. To remove the surface completely, use a wire cup brush in a power drill. Wear safety goggles and a simple face mask to protect eyes and lungs.

When the stone is clean and has dried off, treat exposed stone with a silicone water repellent. This dries perfectly clear, and it will protect the stone from rain and frost.

Repairing damaged stonework Where the stonework is badly damaged, use a club hammer and a brick bolster to cut out all the damaged material, making a rectangular hole.

Take a piece of the removed stone to a garden centre that supplies stone, and match it for colour. Dress the new piece with bolster and club hammer until the stone fits the cavity in the wall.

Make up a MORTAR of 4 parts soft sand to 1 part cement (measured by volume) and add PVA adhesive (see GLUING) to the mixing water in the proportions one to ten. Keep the mix on the stiff side. Damp the stone so that it does not absorb moisture from the mortar. Apply mortar inside the hole, insert the stone, then point the mortar when it has set to match the surrounding stonework – see POINTING.

If you find it impossible to match the stone, make up mortar and tint it with dry colour to match the wall. A good mix would be 12 parts crushed stone to 3 parts cement and 3 parts lime (measured by volume), plus colorant. Use a minimum of water to make a dryish mix, adding PVA adhesive to the water in the proportions one to ten.

If the hole to be filled is large, stuff it with pieces of old roofing tile set in mortar, to within 19mm ($\frac{3}{4}$in) of the surface. Then fill the remaining space with the mortar mix. Smooth it to the surrounding wall surface while still soft, then mark it to imitate the surrounding mortar joints. See also STUCCO WALLS.

Small areas of damage can be filled

in with an epoxy-based CONCRETE repair material. Take out all loose material beforehand.

Stoppers and fillers

Using the correct type for the job

When filling cracks and holes, it is important to use the correct filler or stopper for the job. Here are the main types:

Cellulose fillers These come in powder form, for mixing with water, or readymixed in a tub or tube. Use them for filling holes in walls and ceilings where the repair will be covered with some form of decoration. Most are suitable only for interior use.

Wood stopping A traditional filler which has very good adhesion. You can smooth and shape it when hard. It is available in interior and exterior grades.

Plastic wood This is a material specially formulated to resemble wood when dry. It is sold in several wood shades. Use plastic wood for repairing damaged furniture. It is solvent-based and has a strong smell, so work in a well-ventilated area. Once set, it can be shaped and smoothed like wood, and stains take to it readily.

Epoxy-resin based filler Available in a wood colour, this material has very strong adhesion, and it sets very hard. To get the best bond, treat the wood to be repaired with a hardening liquid first, to toughen up any soft wood fibres. Mix only as much filler as you can use in a few minutes. It sets quickly by chemical action which cannot be stopped. Quantities of filler and hardening agent are mixed according to the instructions.

Similar fillers are available in a grey colour, suitable for repairs to any hard materials, including metals. They are available to set hard or be semi-flexible. Where there may be slight movement of surface, such as on car bodywork, use the flexible type. See also SEALANTS.

Expanding foam filler This material, supplied in aerosol form, is ideal for sealing awkward holes; for instance, where waste pipes come through an external wall. The foam expands to many times its original volume.

Stoves

Choosing and maintaining them

There are two basic types of solid-fuel stove – the Aga variety (which give heat, incorporate COOKERS and supply domestic hot water) and the wood-burning or multi-fuel type which give heat and can sometimes be adapted to provide domestic hot water and CENTRAL HEATING also.

Before considering either type, make sure you have a sound chimney or flue; if your house was built before 1965, you will probably need to install a flue liner. Take expert advice if you have any doubts – the Solid Fuel Advisory Service (listed in the telephone directory) will give free advice.

A wood-burning or multi-fuel stove is an attractive option, particularly if you have access to well-seasoned wood.

Install the stove forward of the chimney breast to gain most benefit from its radiated heat. It should stand on a level stone, brick or tile hearth, which must project the required safety minimum of 300mm (12in) in front of the stove and 230mm (9in) on each side of it. Usually a flue pipe passes either upwards through a horizontal plate across the chimney base, or back through a vertical plate which seals off the fireplace opening.

The type you choose depends on the existing fireplace and size of the hearth. Make sure the flue pipe extends at least 100-150mm (4-6in) above a horizontal closure plate; with a vertical closure plate, allow at least 150mm between the pipe end and the back of the chimney.

In all solid-fuel systems, the air that goes up the flue has to be replaced by incoming cold air. While this may enter naturally through draughts from doors and windows, it is better to improve the DRAUGHTPROOFING and increase the air supply by installing an air brick (see AIR BRICKS) in the wall, or a grille in the floor, near the fire. This may also solve any smoking problems.

Wood ash from a stove should be removed regularly, as wood burns best on a layer of ash at least 25mm (1in) deep. Clear the grate every day if you use coal or coke. Chimneys and flues must be swept at least once a year.

Stranded on holiday

How to cope in an emergency

If you lose travel tickets, cash or credit cards while on holiday in Britain, report the loss immediately to the police, the travel company that issued the tickets and the bank and credit card companies – see CREDIT AND CREDIT CARDS.

Travelling abroad, keep a note of your credit card and travellers' cheque numbers, but separate from your other money and documents. Record every cheque cashed. Report loss or theft to the local police and, if possible, to an agent of the bank or company that issued them. Immediate refunds up to a certain limit will be given by some travellers' cheque companies, provided you can supply full details of your loss.

Consider also leaving card and cheque numbers with a friend at home, whom you could contact (by reverse-charge call, if necessary) in an emergency.

Should you run out of funds but still retain a major credit card, you can normally obtain money from a foreign bank displaying the particular credit card symbol. Although the British Consulate will often advise and assist with the transfer of funds, they will not normally lend money or cash a cheque. If you lose your passport (see PASSPORTS), the Consulate can issue a travel document.

Travel agents If the collapse of a holiday firm leaves you temporarily stranded, a rescue scheme should be mounted within a day or so by the Association of British Travel Agents (ABTA), the Civil Aviation Authority (CAA) or the Association of Independent Tour Operators (AITO), provided the company has an Air Travel Organiser's licence (ATOL). Check this before leaving, as it is required by law – the ATOL number should be quoted on the firm's publicity.

If air travel is not involved, make sure your company is a member of ABTA or AITO. Even when you are protected by a rescue scheme, it is advisable to take extra money to cover bills that might be incurred. Keep all receipts, booking documents and ticket stubs – you will need them to obtain a refund or compensation.

Airlines Should your airline go out of business, the holiday firm you bought your ticket from must find a replacement airline, or pay you compensation. If you bought your ticket direct from the airline, you may be able to use it with another airline on the same route, particularly if both are members of the International Air Transport Association (IATA).

If you miss your plane, your entitlement to another flight depends on the kind of ticket you hold. With a charter, special excursion or cheap ticket, you will not usually be able to get a free flight home, but the charter company may offer to find an alternative flight.

A normal unrestricted air ticket is valid for a year, and the airline is obliged to accommodate you on the first flight with seats available – possibly with another carrier.

Travelling by car If you are driving to your holiday destination, it is advisable to belong to a motoring organisation that operates a roadside-repair and breakdown-recovery service. If you are taking your car abroad, you should have a Green Card, which extends your normal insurance for the duration of the trip, and insurance to cover breakdown – such as the AA's Five Star Insurance. See also CAR ACCIDENTS and CAR INSURANCE. Your driving licence must be valid for the country you are visiting.

Stress

Alleviating life's strains and upheavals

Everyone at some time in their life experiences stress – the feeling of being 'wound up' and unable to cope with everyday worries and problems. A warning signal that you are allowing things to 'get on top of you' is when a minor irritation, such as being caught up in a traffic jam, causes an angry outburst.

This kind of everyday stress is relatively simple to alleviate. Regular EXERCISES, MEDITATION, YOGA, deep breathing (see RELAXATION EXERCISES), country walks, listening to music or caring for a pet (see CATS, DOG CARE, RABBITS) are particularly effective in reducing tension.

But stress caused by a major upheaval in your life – a bereavement, for example, or a new baby in the family – is usually more difficult to remove. The degree of stress is often severe and unremitting. If allowed to continue, it can lead to HEADACHES, INSOMNIA and depression.

Self help Talking your problems or worries out with family, friends, a trusted confidant or your DOCTOR can help to reduce stress. Your local clergyman may be helpful, too; many are skilled counsellors.

In self-help groups you will be meeting people who are learning to cope with similar problems. A Citizens Advice Bureau or local health authority should have a list of contacts. Discussing your situation or problems should not, however, become a substitute for facing up to them. Sooner or later you must decide which of your problems are real and which are imagined, then deal with them one by one.

Take comfort in regular routines: proper mealtimes, good food, customary standards of dress and hygiene, hobbies, and friendly relationships.

Those who cope best with stress usually have a flexible, positive attitude and do not become depressed or annoyed if events do not turn out as they expected. Those who blame 'life' or other people for their predicament cope least well with stress. Being positive and taking charge of your life will help to create a feeling of being 'in control' of events.

Stretching a canvas

Preparing it for painting a picture

You can buy canvas ready stretched and primed for painting, but you may prefer to buy untreated canvas, which is cheaper, and to stretch, size and prime it yourself. You can buy a stretcher frame, size and primer at an art supply shop.

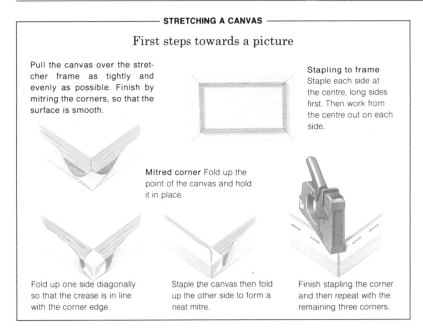

--- STRETCHING A CANVAS ---

First steps towards a picture

Pull the canvas over the stretcher frame as tightly and evenly as possible. Finish by mitring the corners, so that the surface is smooth.

Stapling to frame Staple each side at the centre, long sides first. Then work from the centre out on each side.

Mitred corner Fold up the point of the canvas and hold it in place.

Fold up one side diagonally so that the crease is in line with the corner edge.

Staple the canvas then fold up the other side to form a neat mitre.

Finish stapling the corner and then repeat with the remaining three corners.

The stretcher frame consists of four wooden bars with tongued-and-grooved ends which fit into each other tightly. When assembling, make sure that all the corners are square by checking with a try square, tapping home with a hammer if necessary.

Lay the stretcher frame, bevelled side down, on a sheet of canvas and use scissors to cut round the canvas 32mm (1¼in) outside the frame edge. Fold the overlap over one of the long sides of the stretcher frame and staple (see STAPLE GUN) or tack it to the edge in the middle of the bar.

Pull the canvas tightly over the opposite side and staple or tack it at the middle, then staple the two shorter sides in the same way, making sure that the canvas is taut. Working outwards from the middle of each bar, staple the overlap at intervals of 75mm (3in), pulling the canvas taut as you go along, but leaving about 75mm unstapled at each corner. At one corner, fold one of the two canvas ends under the other so that the tucked-in part is snug and neat against the frame. Then staple this corner fold into the widest part of the corner. Do the same with the other corners. Finish the corners with neat mitres, as illustrated. Finally, staple the surplus canvas over the back of the frame.

The canvas is now ready for sizing and priming. Size and primer can be bought at an art supply shop.

Sizing Traditionally, rabbit-skin size is used to ensure that the paint sticks to the canvas properly; it comes in concentrated form and must be mixed with water and heated before being applied. It is not necessary to size if you intend to use an acrylic primer.

Priming The traditional primer for OIL PAINTING is white lead in linseed oil, but you can buy cheaper primers, such as titanium in oil, or use acrylic-paint primer. Give the canvas several coats, using a flat varnish brush, and allow to dry between coats.

String art

Using string and nails to create an art form

Swirling patterns, abstract or pictorial designs and even complex geometrical structures can be created by string art.

This is a simple technique in which string is stretched between nails hammered into a wood board, to form a variety of shapes and patterns. You can also use thread, yarn or fine wire (copper, brass or galvanised wire should be 28 or 30 gauge).

To design a string art picture, you will need a pencil, coloured crayons, paper, masking tape, and a compass and protractor to draw circles and mark equal divisions on them.

Any TIMBER into which you can hammer the nails easily is suitable for the board; a piece of 13mm (½in) PLYWOOD is ideal. Paint, varnish or cover the board with fabric. If using fabric, overlap the edges of the wood base and staple the fabric to the back – see STAPLE GUN.

Use a pin hammer (see HAMMERS) – it will give you more control when NAILING. You can use any kind of nail, but 16-gauge panel pins are recommended. Gilt or nickel-plated nails are the most attractive, but are more expensive.

Begin by drawing your design on paper. Tape the drawing to the front of your prepared board. Hammer a nail into each dot on your drawing, keeping the nails upright and at a uniform height (a piece of cardboard cut to size will serve as a gauge). Once the nails are in position, pull off the drawing and begin stringing, following the design you worked out.

When tying string to the first nail use a simple overhand knot – see KNOTS. Following the lines of the design, wind the string round successive nails. To finish off, tie a double knot, cut the string and tuck the end out of sight or fix it with a dab of glue.

You can add a second layer of string, using a different colour and omitting some of the nails.

--- STRING ART ---

Creating delicate curves

A curve made by joining equally spaced points is the most versatile pattern. Complex forms can be created by combining curves. Fix a nail at each point.

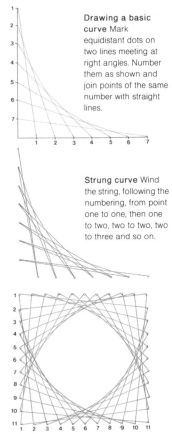

Drawing a basic curve Mark equidistant dots on two lines meeting at right angles. Number them as shown and join points of the same number with straight lines.

Strung curve Wind the string, following the numbering, from point one to one, then one to two, two to two, two to three and so on.

Complex pattern Four basic curves, sharing nails where they overlap, form this shape.

Stucco walls

Patching cracks and holes

Stucco consists of a cement/sand or cement/lime/sand mix, and has lines scored on its surface to simulate blocks of stonework. If it is correctly applied to exterior walls it will give years of trouble-free protection, but any cracks and gaps must be treated as soon as you find them.

Hairline cracks These are quite common and are not a serious problem. Decorate the wall with a masonry paint which has an additive such as sand, nylon fibre or silica, and all the tiny cracks will be filled – see PAINTING EXTERIORS; PAINTS.

Deeper cracks Dig out all loose and crumbling material and, if possible, undercut the crack (making it wider at

Repairing large holes

Removing loose stucco Clear back to the brickwork with a bolster and club hammer. Rake out the brick joints.

Applying mortar Press the mortar well into the wall, spreading it with an upwards motion. Leave it just above the surrounding surface.

Levelling Slide a piece of planking up or along the wall, in a zigzag motion.

the wall than at the surface) to afford a better grip to the repair material. Coat inside the crack with undiluted PVA adhesive (see GLUING) to improve bonding, then fill with a fairly stiff, dry MORTAR mix. Press it well in with the point of a trowel, then level off.

Persistent cracks If a crack opens after careful filling, it may be caused by slight movement of the building, or by subsidence. Get a small square of glass and bond it across the crack with epoxy resin adhesive. If the glass breaks over the next few months, seek expert advice from an ARCHITECT or building surveyor.

Mould This usually looks worse than it is, discolouring masonry paint. Treat it with a fungicide; wait until the mould goes brown or black, then brush it off with a stiff broom. Protect your eyes with safety goggles and wear a simple dust mask while tackling the brushing.

If you are going to repaint the wall, use a stabilising solution available from builders' merchants – before applying the masonry paint.

Blistering and dropping off If patches of stucco fall off, tap the remaining stucco lightly and wherever there is a hollow sound, chisel it off. Rake out the joints between the bricks with a narrow cold chisel or plugging chisel, brush out all dust, then brush PVA adhesive over all the repair area.

Use a mortar mix of 1 part Portland cement, 1 part lime and 6 parts sand, all measured by volume. Keep the mix to a dryish consistency so that it does not sag or slump.

Place some mortar on a hawk, hold it close to the wall, and lift the mortar off onto the wall with the upper front edge of a steel float. Press the mortar firmly onto the wall. Then use a length of wood to skim off the surplus by sliding it back and forth across the wall.

Leave the mortar for an hour to dry, then damp it with clean water. Smooth it over with the steel float and score it to match the simulated masonry joints on the surrounding wall.

Where the rendering is to be thicker than 13mm ($\frac{1}{2}$in), build it up in two layers. Score the first coat deeply to provide a good key, then leave it to dry for 24 hours. Apply fresh mortar over the first coat, following the procedure as for the single coat repair.

Where stucco is in generally poor condition, remove it down to the brickwork and re-render. The easiest way to do this, if you have little experience, is to use a Tyrolean projector. This throws a soft mortar mix onto the wall, giving a fine textured surface. The tool can be obtained from most hire shops, who will advise you of the mix required: See also PEBBLEDASH.

Stuffings

Making savoury fillings for meat and poultry

Stuffings add flavour when ROASTING JOINTS of meat and POULTRY. They also keep the flesh moist and help to make the meat go further.

Chickens can be stuffed at the neck or in the body cavity. Ducks and geese are stuffed in the body cavity. Turkeys are stuffed at both ends. Do not pack the stuffing in too tightly – it needs room to expand. Allow about 115g (4oz) of stuffing for every 450g (1lb) of bird.

Chicken stuffing To make a basic bread and herb stuffing, mix 115g (4oz) of fresh breadcrumbs with 25g (1oz) of melted butter.

Mix in 1 or 2 tablespoons of chopped fresh herbs, such as parsley, marjoram or tarragon (see HERBS IN COOKING), and a small onion finely chopped. Add a lightly beaten egg and enough stock or water to give the mixture a firm yet moist consistency. Season to taste with salt and pepper.

Turkey stuffing Stuff a turkey at the neck end with a bread and herb stuffing as for chicken. The body cavity is traditionally filled with a sausagemeat stuffing to keep the flesh moist.

Lightly fry a finely chopped onion and 450g (1lb) sausagemeat in 25-50g (1-2oz) butter. Turn into a bowl and add 25g fresh breadcrumbs, a lightly beaten egg and enough stock or water to bind. Season with salt and pepper.

Duck and goose stuffing Duck and goose are best given a sharp fruit stuffing to cut the richness. To make an apple stuffing, replace the herbs in the bread and herb stuffing with two medium-sized cooking apples, peeled and chopped. Substitute 25g (1oz) of finely chopped streaky bacon or bacon fat for the butter.

Pork stuffing Blade or loin of pork joints are often cooked with a fruit-based stuffing. Get the butcher to bone the joint. Stuff the resulting pouch. Roll the joint up and tie it with string.

To make an apple and nut stuffing for pork, peel and finely chop a small onion and roughly chop 50g (2oz) of cashew nuts or peanuts. Dice 50g of white crustless bread. Peel, core and dice a cooking apple. Wash and finely chop a stick of celery.

Melt 25g (1oz) butter in a small pan over a moderate heat and fry the nuts with the onion until they are just turning brown. Add the bread, apple, celery and a dessertspoon of chopped parsley and continue cooking until the apple softens. Add half a teaspoon of chopped sage and season to taste with salt, pepper and lemon juice.

Stumps

*Removing the boles and roots
of felled trees*

Tree roots can reach deep down into the soil, or extend outwards under the soil for a long way. A stump can usually be pulled out with a tractor and chains if there is room, or with a small hand-operated tree winch. Or you can grind it up with an engine-driven stump chipper. Winches and chippers can usually be hired from plant hire firms – see HIRING.

The tree winch is slung on a wire rope hitched to the stump at one end and a nearby tree trunk at the other. Before pulling, check the course of any large roots going under a lawn or building, for example, and saw them off – in case the soil disturbance causes damage.

A stump chipper has strong, sharp blades that cut from side to side to grind a bole into fine chips to about 150mm (6in) below ground.

Another way to get rid of a stump is to accelerate rotting, then burn it. Drill holes in the top of the stump and fill with sodium chlorate – available as a weed-killer. After about a month, burn the stump. Set light to it carefully, as the sodium chlorate may still be volatile if the weather has been dry.

Styes

*Treating painful small infections
on the eyelid*

The stye is a common bacterial infection of the glands at the eyelash roots. It begins as a painful swelling of the area and later fills with pus, develops a 'point' and discharges. Untreated, a stye will often last for a week or ten days.

To expedite matters, dip a small pad of cotton wool into boiling water and when it has cooled off a little, gently apply this to the eye, keeping it in place for 10-15 minutes. Repeat every two or three hours. Wash your hands thoroughly before and after each treatment.

Bathing will encourage the stye to discharge, after which wash the area well. If the eyeball is inflamed or vision affected, consult your DOCTOR.

See also EYES.

Subletting

*Acting as landlord for your
leased property*

Short-term tenancy agreements (see also TENANTS) generally have an absolute ban on subletting. Longer-term agreements may forbid subletting 'without the consent of the landlord'. In this case, though, the landlord cannot refuse permission unreasonably.

If the landlord unreasonably refuses consent to sublet to responsible people, you can still sublet to them – and expect to be supported by the court.

If you lease a property without a tenancy agreement and your landlord did not forbid subletting when the tenancy began, you can sublet without permission.

Evicting subtenants If the tenancy agreement allows you to sublet and you are ordered to give up a property, the subtenant will not be evicted. If you have sublet without authority, though, the subtenant would face eviction – see EVICTION NOTICE.

Before subletting, ask the subtenant for financial and character REFERENCES and obtain a deposit to cover breakages and redecoration.

A prospective subtenant should always ask for a written undertaking from the original, or head, landlord that subletting is allowed.

Succulents

Caring for and propagating them

Succulents are plants that have adapted to a naturally arid habitat by developing thick fleshy leaves or stems to store moisture. There are many types of succulent (including CACTI) that make suitable HOUSEPLANTS and need relatively little attention.

Moonstones Among popular succulents is the *Pachyphytum oviferum*. Its pink-tinged grey leaves give it a strangely lunar look – hence its common name 'moonstones'.

Some, such as agaves, can be left outside in sunny spring and summer weather, but those with more delicate leaves should be under a covering of glass or transparent plastic to protect them from heavy rain.

Species of sedum, such as stonecrop, occur in the wild, nestling in cliffs and outcrops, and their attractive colours and shapes make them ideal rockery plants. See also ROCK GARDEN.

Indoor succulents usually need as much direct sunlight as possible and should be turned daily during the brightest seasons to achieve even growth. They tend to thrive in a warm dry atmosphere, although a few need a period of cool winter rest.

Some watering is essential; over-watering, however, will cause the plants to rot. Rainwater is best, but ordinary tap water is acceptable. Water reasonably freely when the plants show signs of active growth, but during the rest period allow only enough moisture to prevent them from drying out.

Splashes of water can permanently deface succulents with delicate leaves and stems; to avoid this, stand the pots in water 50mm (2in) deep until enough has been absorbed to moisten the soil to its surface.

Rewatering is not advised, even during the active growth period, until the top 13mm (½in) of the potting mixture has dried out completely.

Fast-growing succulents can be fed monthly with one of the standard liquid FERTILISERS during the active growth period.

Succulents are usually quite easy to propagate (see PROPAGATING PLANTS), either from leaf cuttings or from seed, according to species. When leaf or stem cutting is feasible, allow the cut leaves to dry for several days. Then lay short leaves on the surface of the potting mixture; push the base of longer leaves just into the mixture. A stem of any branching succulent can be cut and planted like an offset; succulents that grow in clumps can be divided and immediately repotted. See also POTTING HOUSEPLANTS.

There is one basic method for growing succulents from seed. The best time to sow is in late spring or summer – see SEED SOWING. To provide effective drainage, cover the base of the seed pot or tray with 13mm (½in) gravel or perlite.

Fill the pot to within 13mm of the rim with a mixture of 1 part medium or coarse sand to 3 parts standard rooting mixture such as John Innes seed compost (see JOHN INNES COMPOST), measuring by volume.

Moisten the mixture evenly and sprinkle a fine covering of sand over it. Scatter the seeds on the sand, taking care not to bury them. Cover the container with plastic or glass and stand it in a temperature of at least 18°C (65°F) away from direct light until germination begins.

This usually takes two or three weeks, but may take longer according to species. Place the seedlings in direct light and open the glass or plastic slightly to allow them to breathe.

Suing

Seeking satisfaction through law

To sue a person or organisation is to institute legal proceedings against them. The object is generally to get financial compensation for an injury or damage caused by someone else's negligence, or to reclaim a debt.

Suing for negligence If you are injured or your property is damaged through the carelessness or negligence of another person, you may be able to claim compensation, or damages, if you can prove that the other person had a duty to take care, that he failed in that duty, and that his failure caused the injury or damage.

For example, somebody who makes or repairs goods has a duty to take care that they do not harm anyone who uses them. If you can prove that you or your property were harmed by goods because they had not been made or repaired with sufficient care, you should normally be able to claim compensation from the maker or repairer. See also REFUNDS; SALE OF GOODS.

Making a claim First get your solicitor (see LAWYERS) to write to the person whose negligence you believe caused injury or damage, claiming compensation from him. You may get LEGAL AID to help with the costs.

If you do not get a satisfactory reply, consider suing him in the courts. But do not sue unless you believe he has the means to pay compensation. Otherwise you are likely to end up with substantial legal costs and no compensation.

Make sure, too, that you have a reasonable chance of winning your case.

Suing for debt If someone has failed to repay a debt, write to him setting out clearly what you think he owes you. Try to find out why he has failed to pay. If you do not get a satisfactory reply, consult your solicitor and consider suing. Sue only if you believe he can repay.

Issuing a plaint note or writ If you decide to sue, get your solicitor to start an action in the county court (by issuing a plaint note) or in the High Court (by issuing a writ). Alternatively, you can start a county court action yourself. The High Court deals with large claims, the county court with lesser claims – see SMALL CLAIMS.

The court requires the debtor to admit or deny your claim within 14 days. If he ignores the request, the court will make an order against him on your terms. But if he disputes the entire claim, the case proceeds to trial.

If he admits the claim, he must propose terms for repaying. If you reject them, the court will decide how much the debtor can afford to pay, and when.

If the case goes to trial, you may be given judgment – official confirmation that the debtor owes you money. If the debtor ignores the judgment, you must apply to the court to have the judgment enforced – either by having a bailiff seize the debtor's goods which can be sold to meet the debt, or by intercepting wages or debts due to him. See also DEBT COLLECTORS.

Suit pressing

Avoiding shine and scorch marks

Taking care over PRESSING your suit will keep it looking new and extend its life.

The best method is to give the suit a first pressing with a damp cloth, then iron it through a sheet of brown paper – see IRONING. The moisture from the cloth is absorbed by the paper and the creases will be held in better. A damp cloth used on wool and other heavy fabrics also removes the risk of scorching and unwanted shines – see SHINE REMOVING.

Even when using a steam iron (see IRONS) it is advisable to press from the underside and through a damp cloth to obtain the best finish.

To remove bagginess at the knees of trousers, lay the inside of the front of each leg uppermost. Place a damp cloth over it and press with a hot iron until the cloth is flat. Iron again with brown paper. Then using the same procedure, lay the legs flat in the normal way and iron in the creases.

To ensure a knife-edge crease, put a block of natural pine wood on each pressed area immediately after ironing. The pine wood will absorb the steam as the fabric cools, leaving a flat crease. The wood should be about 2 × 4in (50 × 100mm) and 6-12in (150-300mm) long.

On men's and women's suits, the lapels should be gently folded over, rather than ironed flat. So when pressing, pad the crease with a folded cloth; the lapel will lie flat, but without a knife-edge crease.

Summons

What to do if you receive one

A summons is a document issued by a magistrate or justice's clerk, ordering a person to appear in court to answer a charge that an offence has been committed. The order gives the name and address of the defendant, the charge against him, brief details of the case and the time and place of the hearing. It may be delivered by a police officer, or court official or through the post by registered or recorded delivery.

If you receive a summons do not ignore it. If you do not appear in court at the stated time the magistrate can issue a warrant for your arrest. If you cannot attend through illness, ask your doctor to write a note which you can send to the court, and ask for an adjournment.

You can also request an adjournment if the summons gives you less than a week's notice of the hearing and you want time to prepare your defence.

If the offence is a minor one, such as failing to observe a traffic signal or illegal parking, you may be able to plead guilty by post – the summons will tell you if you can do so.

Alternatively, you can appear in court to plead guilty and ask for leniency, explaining any extenuating circumstances. Since you have pleaded guilty, this will not affect the verdict, but may lessen the punishment.

You cannot plead not guilty by post, and if the charge is a serious one you should consult a solicitor before deciding on your plea – see LAWYERS.

Time limit A summons is based on information laid before a magistrate, usually by the police, though it can be by a private individual. The information must be given within six months of the alleged offence. If the summons shows that the information was not laid within that time, the case must be dismissed.

You may also receive a summons to appear as a witness or for JURY SERVICE. Do not ignore either of these or you may be fined.

Sunburn

How to treat it

A SUNTAN is the skin's natural defence against the power of the sun, and is produced by melanin, a pigment that is activated by ultraviolet rays. We all have different amounts of melanin, and the less you have the more likely you are to suffer from sunburn instead of acquiring a deep suntan. Fair-skinned people generally have little melanin and burn very easily.

Minor sunburn produces a red skin; if you immediately avoid further exposure to the sun, the redness will disappear in a few days and a tan will often follow. More severe sunburn starts with painful, tender, swollen skin which may blister, and usually is at its worst 48 hours after exposure – see BLISTERS.

Treat severe sunburn with calamine lotion or cold compresses. Leave blistered areas exposed to the air, but do not allow further exposure to the sun. Avoid clothing that rubs the sore areas. Take painkillers if necessary.

If you have HEADACHES, NAUSEA or FEVER, or if the sunburn is very distressing, consult a DOCTOR – see also HEAT EXHAUSTION; HEAT STROKE.

Sunlamps

Getting a home tan safely

A sunlamp provides ultraviolet rays – the same rays that radiate from the sun. If not treated with respect, a sunlamp can be just as harmful as the sun – see SUNBURN; SUNTAN. Follow the manufacturer's instructions carefully. Wear goggles, not sunglasses, to protect your EYES and begin with short exposures and build up to longer ones gradually. Some lamp kits include a timer/buzzer – alternatively use a kitchen timer to avoid falling asleep under the lamp. Always use a body lotion or oil after tanning to prevent dryness of the skin. Do not wear perfume, cosmetics or moisturising creams while tanning.

WARNING Do not look directly at an ultraviolet bulb, even when wearing goggles, because it could permanently damage your eyes.

Suntan

Staying in the sun without burning

Never over-expose yourself to the sun or SUNLAMPS. If you do, you will simply end up with a lobster-pink SUNBURN, which can be both painful and dangerous, rather than a smooth brown tan.

An unprotected fair skin may take 15 minutes or less to begin to burn on a clear day in hot sun. An average skin may take 20 minutes and a darker one 25 minutes.

Sunbathing do's and don'ts

Do avoid exposing yourself to the sun as much as possible if you have a very fair or freckled skin.
Do keep small children covered or in the shade.
Do limit your exposure to the sun to no more than 30 minutes on the first day, gradually increasing it as the days go by to build up a protective tan.
Do use a good suntan preparation (see below) and reapply it every two hours at least. Protect particularly your nose, lips, forehead, ankles, shins and shoulders – where the skin is thin – and the skin round the edges of a swimsuit.
Do remember that artificial tanning lotions may not necessarily protect you from sunburn.
Do remember that you can be burnt both in and on the water.
Do use a suntan preparation when skiing.
Don't sunbathe at midday, or when the sun is hottest.
Don't assume that because it is cloudy you will not get burnt; 80 per cent of ultraviolet rays (that cause burning) penetrate cloud.
Don't use aftershave lotion or perfumes. Many contain light-sensitive substances that can cause unpleasant burns in hot sun.

Suntan preparations Most preparations now have a sun protection factor (SPF) number, indicating how much protection the lotion or cream gives. One with SPF 8, for example, should allow you to stay in the sun about eight times as long as you could without it.

Try to use a high SPF preparation at the beginning of a holiday; change to one with a lower SPF as you build up a protective tan.

Water-resistant preparations are available, and also ski preparations.

Superfluous hair

Removing unwanted hair

There are a number of ways in which hair can be removed from the face, body, arms and legs. Only one method, electrolysis, will remove hair permanently. It should be done only by a qualified electrologist. This is expensive and takes time. Home treatment for hair removal needs to be repeated regularly.

Shaving This is probably the most popular way to remove leg and underarm hair, but the hair grows again quickly, forming a stubble in two or three days. Razor manufacturers produce ladies' razors, both safety and electric. Men's razors of both types are more efficient but the risk of skin abrasion and subsequent infection is greater. A safety razor gives a closer shave, and the disposable types are cheap.

There is no need to use a shaving cream – ordinary soap will do. Lather the area and shave against the direction of hair growth.

Depilatories These products dissolve hair so that it can be washed away. The treated area stays hair free for two or three days.

Depilatories can be bought in cream, lotion or aerosol form, but all are expensive and messy and time-consuming to apply. Use a depilatory on the face only if the label tells you it is safe to do so. Follow the manufacturer's instructions for application, carrying out a patch test first. Clean a small area behind one ear with surgical spirit and apply a little cream. Leave it for 48 hours, and if no irritation or inflammation occurs it is safe for you to use.

Abrasion Hair-removing mitts, which are coated with very fine sandpaper, can be used to rub away stubble on the legs when it begins to appear after shaving. The mitts can also be used to thin downy hair on arms. Do not use on any other part of the body.

After shaving the legs, use the mitts every day or so, with gentle circular movements to remove the stubble. Do not try to rub away long hairs, as this will make the skin sore.

Waxing Large areas of hair can be pulled out by the roots by waxing, and therefore the treatment lasts longer than other methods, apart from electrolysis.

A warm, melted mixture of beeswax and resin is spread on the area with a spatula. When the wax hardens it is pulled quickly away, taking the hairs with it. The hairs must be at least 6mm ($\frac{1}{4}$in) long for this treatment to be effective. Cold waxes are also available.

Beauty salons use the waxing method for hair removal, but home kits are available from chemist shops. Follow the manufacturer's instructions exactly.

Bleaching This is a method of disguising hair, rather than removing it. It is most effective on growths of soft, dark hair on the upper lip, or on the legs where the growth is meagre. Bleaches for facial and body hair are sold by chemists. Follow the instructions carefully, and carry out a patch test (see above) first.

Surety

Acting as security for someone's debt or court appearance

If you stand as a surety for someone's cash loan, or for goods he is buying on credit, you must pay the debt if that person does not.

Similarly, by being a surety for a person released on BAIL pending a court hearing on a criminal charge, you guarantee a sum of money to the court to ensure that he answers the charge. If he does not turn up at the court when required, you may forfeit your money.

Before entering into such agreements, be sure that if the worst happens you can afford to lose the sum involved. After all, the creditor would not ask for a surety if he had no doubts about the borrower's ability to pay. And when magistrates grant bail only on condition of sureties, the implication is that the accused may not turn up for trial.

Under the terms of the Consumer Credit Act, there are three ways in which you can be a surety for a debt:
1 You can be a guarantor – you agree to pay the debt if the borrower defaults.
2 You can give an indemnity, in which you agree that the supplier can approach you directly for payment without any recourse to the borrower.
3 You can deposit an agreed sum against non-payment of the debt.

Under the Act, you are entitled to two copies of the credit agreement, the one signed by you and the one signed by the lender. If you are not supplied with the proper copy documents, the lender cannot recover any money from you without permission from a court.

If the borrower pulls out of the agreement legally – under the terms of the Act – the surety cannot be made to pay anything. Nor can a surety be made to pay more than the borrower could have been forced to pay.

SURFING

Using the bodysurfing technique

Waiting for a wave
Start swimming hard towards the shore when the crest of a wave approaches, watching the wave over your shoulder as you go. Stiffen your body as the force of the wave catches you and let it push you ahead of it.

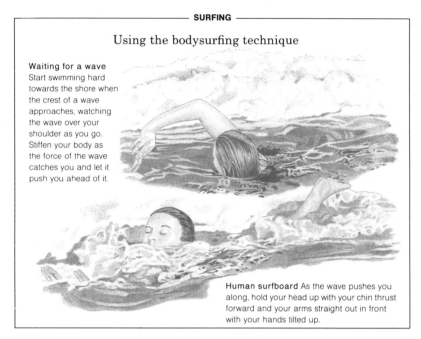

Human surfboard As the wave pushes you along, hold your head up with your chin thrust forward and your arms straight out in front with your hands tilted up.

Also, if you stand surety for someone who defaults on his debt and have to pay his creditor, you can sue (see SUING) the borrower for your loss – making him bankrupt if necessary.

If you have stood as a surety for someone on bail, and have reason to fear that the accused will abscond, you can cancel your surety by informing the court of your suspicions.

Surfing

Riding the crest of a wave

The Atlantic coasts of the Channel Islands, Cornwall, Devon and Wales are the best places in Britain for surfing; but riding the big waves as they roar in from the open sea is only for competent swimmers (see SWIMMING) and should never be attempted by anyone not fully aware of their abilities and limitations.

There are two types of surfboard: the short or belly board, traditionally made of plywood but now also made of polystyrene, and the 'Malibu' board, made of glass fibre – the most modern and most popular 'short Malibu' is about 1.8m (6ft) in length and the 'long Malibu' over 2.4m (8ft) in length. Boards can usually be hired at popular surfing beaches.

As its name implies, the belly board is ridden by the surfer grasping the sides with his hands and pressing the board close to his body. In this position his legs are clear of the board. A belly board can be used by beginners in gentle surf.

Malibu riders begin by lying full length on the board, but spring directly up to a standing position once they have joined an incoming wave. The direction and speed of the board is controlled by body movement which creates weight shift. Tuition is usually available at surfing centres and when hiring or buying a Malibu board, ask an expert for advice on the right board for your experience and body weight – a board that is too long will be difficult to manoeuvre; one that is too short will not support you properly. A Malibu board should have an ankle leash so that when you fall off, you will not lose the board and be stranded.

Before you go surfing, find out what local regulations apply and insure yourself against public liability in case you accidentally injure someone. Some beaches have areas for surfing, indicated by black-and-white quartered flags. You must surf between these markers, and avoid swimming areas which may be marked by red-and-yellow flags.

Watch out for undertow and rip currents – fast-running water that may pull you out to sea. If you get caught in a rip current on a Malibu board, do not leave your board but paddle across the current until you are in an area of breaking water that will propel you to the shore.

Belly-board surfing Walk out through the surf to a point where the waves are breaking, carrying your board well clear of the waves. Do not walk out of your depth. Stand side on so you can watch the incoming waves, holding the board at an angle to your body with both hands. When you see a promising wave – one that is long and about to break – get into position so that you throw yourself onto the board in front of the wave just as it breaks. The surf will catch you and carry you forward. Steer with your feet or by tilting the board. Take care to avoid anybody who might be bathing in the shallower surf.

Bodysurfing This is a technique used by many swimmers, and consists of stiffening the body to provide a human surfboard, as illustrated.

The British Surfing Association, Champion's Yard, Penzance, Cornwall TR18 2SS, will supply more information, including locations of controlled surfing beaches.

Survival

Staying alive in emergencies on land and water

Survival on land or water in an emergency will depend on cool, clear thinking and making good use of any equipment that is available.

Make sure you are properly equipped – whether mountaineering (see CLIMBING SAFELY), CAMPING, BACKPACKING, SAILING or SCUBA DIVING. But circumstances may sometimes demand ingenuity.

Immediate priorities for survival are:
● Signalling for help.
● Shelter from the elements.
● A supply of food and water.

For signalling, use, as appropriate, bright clothing, flares or smoke – see CAMPFIRES. If you have a whistle, six blasts a minute followed by a minute's pause is one of the internationally recognised DISTRESS SIGNALS. Use a mirror or shiny tin lid to reflect the sun during the day and a torch at night.

On land

Shelter A vehicle may provide temporary cover from a snowstorm (see SNOWBOUND), or its shadow can shield you from the desert sun. On foot you may be forced to seek shelter in caves or under overhangs when possible – they may also contain some water or moisture. Avoid them during storms, when lightning may strike them. Also stay clear of potential landslide or avalanche areas.

In snow, protect yourself from wind chill by tunnelling into the side of a snowdrift for about 600mm (2ft), then scoop out a cavity. Cover the opening with evergreen branches and packed snow, then pierce an airshaft for ventilation. If possible, lie or sit on a foam pad to protect from damp cold. Keep as warm as possible; wiggle toes and fingers, and stay awake.

Food and water In a desert, DEHYDRATION is the major hazard, so protection from the sun is essential, particularly in the heat of the day. If you are on foot, cover your head and the back of your neck. Whether on foot or in a vehicle, travel in the early morning or evening to avoid HEATSTROKE.

You need, if possible, to drink a minimum of 2.3 litres (4 pints) of water a day, but avoid drinking during the heat of the day as this may prompt excessive sweating and consequent loss of body salts. If you are short of water, ration yourself as necessary. You can survive only a few days without water, even in a temperate climate; in average conditions, a fit person can survive for four weeks or so without food.

You should be able to obtain some water from your environment – even in a desert. If you are carrying a large sheet of plastic or a foil space blanket – both of which pack up small – make a dew trap at night and a solar still by day to collect any available moisture.

Dew trap Spread the sheet or blanket over a large, shallow depression in the ground and pile clean, smooth stones in the centre of the cover. At night, dew will condense on the stones and must be collected from the sheet before dawn, as the sun will quickly evaporate it.

Solar still Transparent plastic sheet is best for this, as the aim is to use the sun's heat to draw the moisture from the ground; foil tends to reflect heat rather than letting it reach the ground.

Dig a hole at least 1m (3ft) across, and place a clean can or other wide-rimmed container at the centre. Surround it with any leaves or shrubs you can find, as they also exude moisture in the heat.

Spread the plastic over the hole and use stones or other heavy objects to keep the edges in place. Put one stone on the sheet – directly over, but not touching, the tin. As the ground heats up, moisture from it will condense on the underside of the sheet, and trickle into the tin. A well-made still may collect up to 2 litres (3½ pints) of water a day.

Only if starvation threatens should you experiment with unfamiliar plants as food. Try one plant at a time, letting a small piece lie on your tongue. Wait for four or five minutes. If you detect a stinging, burning or putrid sensation, which may signal poison, discard it.

If the plant seems harmless, chew and swallow a 50mm (2in) portion and wait two hours for possible ill effects. Repeat with a larger 150mm (6in) portion and again wait two hours. Do not eat a plant that brings on VOMITING or DIARRHOEA. If possible, boil a safe plant well to improvise a meal; discard the juices.

On water

When SAILING or pursuing any other aquatic activity, observe all the recommended safety precautions – such as wearing a buoyancy suit to keep afloat

Staying alive in the water

Always wear a life jacket on the water – to keep you afloat in an emergency. In cold water, curl up in the HELP position (Heat Escape Lessening Position) to conserve heat and energy until rescuers arrive. Do not swim for shore unless it is very close.

Life jacket Choose a life jacket with the British Standards Institution's kite mark. Use one with a whistle to attract attention. Put the jacket on over your clothes. Fasten securely.

Help position Bring your knees up and hug them to your chest. Trust your life jacket to keep you afloat. In this position you will survive for longer in cold water.

in an emergency. If you are sailing, WIND-SURFING or SURFING, never abandon your craft or surfboard unless it is about to sink or unless staying aboard it becomes dangerous.

Even then, try to make a distress signal. If possible, put on warm clothing to combat the effect of the cold water. If you take to a life raft, do not discard your wet clothing – it will help to protect you against heat loss. Try to stay as near to the wreck as possible, to help rescuers locate you; use a sea anchor if the raft has one. Seasickness quickly weakens the body, so take anti-seasickness pills if you have them.

If abandoning ship for open water, leap in from the side facing the wind, so that the boat does not drift into you. Swim well clear of a large sinking vessel, which could suck you down with it.

Never swim for the shore unless it is near; stay on a life raft or cling to wreckage, keeping as much of your body as possible out of the water to reduce heat loss. If there is nothing to cling to, hug your knees to your chest, which further conserves body heat, and rely on your life jacket to keep you afloat. If you are among other survivors, huddle together for warmth, for mutual support and to increase the chances of being spotted by rescue teams.

If adrift in a small boat, send out regular DISTRESS SIGNALS protect yourself as much as you can from exposure, and conserve water supplies. Avoid drinking sea water, as the salt content (three times greater than the body can tolerate) is potentially lethal.

Collect any rainwater in a waterproof sheet or container; any water that condenses at night on the cold parts of the craft should be wiped off with a clean, dry cloth before the sun can evaporate

it; squeeze out the water immediately into a container.

If the craft is not being buffeted by salt spray, which would contaminate any fresh moisture, you may be able to construct a dew trap (see left) on a clean metallic surface.

Survival kits Survival aids and kits are available but you can make up your own to suit your individual needs. Make sure you carry FIRST AID KITS and specific medicines for the area in which you are travelling, such as SUNBURN prevention ointment, insect repellent, laxatives, anti-diarrhoea pills and seasickness pills if you will be on water. Also include scissors and a good cutting blade plus a booklet or illustrations of first aid skills.

The following items can form a basic survival kit:
- Empty tin with a lid – to contain the survival kit and to use as a cooking vessel. You can use the shiny inside of the lid for signalling.
- Foil space blanket – for warmth, shelter and making a dew trap.
- Large plastic sheet – for shelter (see BIVOUAC TENT), to lie on and for making a solar still.
- Whistle, flares, torch – for signals.
- Clasp or sheath knife – for cutting, opening tins, cooking.
- Potassium permanganate – for purifying water, disinfecting and firelighting.
- Waterproof matches.
- Thin nylon line – for repairs and for tying down your shelter.
- COMPASS.

In addition, on land or water, you should try to carry a small two-way radio, fishing gear, a water bag and basic food supplies such as concentrated fruit or meat and glucose sweets.

Swarms

*Dealing with unwanted bee
swarms and wasp colonies*

Should you find yourself in the path of swarming bees, move out of their way, or lie flat and cover your face and other exposed skin areas with clothing. Do not flail your arms at them in the hope that it will drive them away; such action is more likely to make them sting you.

In the garden, move indoors quickly but calmly, closing doors and windows. Remain indoors until the insects have moved on. See also BEEKEEPING.

If WASPS should invade the house, close all doors and windows and ring for expert advice from the environmental health department of your local council, or from a pest-control firm listed in *Yellow Pages* under 'Pest and vermin control services'.

If bees are the problem, ring the police or the environmental health department of your local council, who will put you in touch with a local beekeeper. He will either remove the swarm himself, if it is accessible, or advise you what to do.

A wasp colony in a wall or bank, or in the ground in your garden, can be destroyed, if necessary, with a proprietary wasp-nest killer based on carbaryl and applied with a puffer – see PESTICIDES. But wasps help to keep down insect pests and are only troublesome in late summer and autumn.

Apply the killer at dusk when the insects are inside their nest. Direct a few puffs into the nest entrance where the wasps will come into contact with the killer as they emerge and return. They will die within two days.

WARNING Do not attempt to destroy a wasp colony unless you are wearing the proper protective clothing. Never try to destroy an active colony in an enclosed place. See also INSECT BITES AND STINGS.

Sweepstake

Keeping a local lottery legal

To comply with the Lotteries and Amusements Act 1976 there are certain rules that you should follow when arranging a sweepstake.

It must not be run for personal gain, but proceeds can go to a club, group or charity. Organiser's expenses must be limited to printing and stationery costs.

All the sweepstake tickets must cost the same price and be stamped with the organiser's name and address.

No tickets can be mailed and the sweepstake must not be advertised.

When sweepstakes are run at fêtes, bazaars or dances, they are generally classified as 'small lotteries'. Provided they are not the main attraction and the motive is not personal gain, they are usually legal. But money prizes at such events are not legal and the prizes awarded must not cost more than £50. All tickets must be sold and the draw must take place during the event.

Prosecutions for illegal sweepstakes are rare, but serious contraventions can incur a heavy fine or even imprisonment.

For anything more than a small lottery, you need a local authority or gaming licence – see RAFFLES.

Sweets

Making little treats

A variety of sweets, including peppermint creams, coconut creams and fruit fondants, can be made using a simple recipe that requires only two basic ingredients – icing sugar and egg white.

Sieve 275g (10oz) of icing sugar into a bowl. Put the white of one egg in another bowl (see EGG SEPARATING) and beat with a whisk or fork until it is frothy.

Now beat in about one-third of the icing sugar, using a wooden spoon, then add the flavouring for the sweet required as described below:

Peppermint creams Add a few drops of peppermint essence to the basic mixture and knead it in well.

Coconut creams Mix in 1 tablespoon of sweetened condensed milk, then work in 75g (3oz) of desiccated coconut.

Raspberry fondant Mix in a few drops of raspberry essence and a few drops of cochineal.

Cherry fondants Add chopped glacé cherries to the mixture and top each finished sweet with a glacé cherry.

When you have added the flavouring, turn the mixture onto a chopping board sprinkled with icing sugar, and knead in the rest of the icing sugar.

Divide the mixture in two and roll it out with your hands into two sausage shapes about 25mm (1in) thick. Cut the rolls into 6mm (¼in) slices. The recipe makes about 30 sweets.

Put them on a sheet of greaseproof paper, sprinkled with icing sugar, and leave for several hours to set.

You can divide the basic mixture into several batches, and flavour each batch individually for a variety of sweets. You can also dip some in melted chocolate when they are set. To melt the chocolate, fill a saucepan about half full with water and heat it. Then find a mixing bowl which will fit over the saucepan rim without its bottom touching the water, and sit it on top. Simmer the water and break a bar of chocolate into the bowl. Stir occasionally as the chocolate melts.

Swimming

*Basic techniques; breast stroke,
crawl and backstroke*

Learning to swim can be not only an introduction to a healthy and enjoyable pastime, but also a valuable aid to lifesaving – both yours and others. If possible, learn from an instructor qualified by the Amateur Swimming Association, especially if you want to take up the sport competitively, as there are strict rules governing how each stroke must be executed. Most municipal swimming baths arrange courses, or you can get details from the ASA, Harold Fern House, Derby Square, Loughborough, Leicestershire LE11 0AL.

Learn to swim in shallow water, either in a pool or on a calm, sandy beach. Start by practising breathing out under water, floating and treading water, then move onto the three basic strokes – breast stroke, crawl and backstroke.

Breathing out under water Stand chest-deep in the water and practise submerging your face while holding your breath. Then practise exhaling under water – exhale through your nose and mouth, blowing bubbles, then bob up to the surface and inhale. Also practise seeing under water by looking for and picking up objects on the bottom.

Practise breathing rhythmically. Standing chest-deep in the water, lean forward with your face to one side and one ear submerged. Breathe in, turn your face down into the water and exhale through your mouth and nose. Rotate your head sideways clear of the water again to inhale. Repeat the sequence turning your head to the right and left to find out the more comfortable side. Stay with that side and continue to practise until you can do it smoothly.

Floating Crouch in chest-deep water with your shoulders submerged. Stretch your arms in front of you. Breathe in deeply, submerge your face and push off gently with your feet to float horizontally, as illustrated overleaf.

Turn the float into a glide by pushing off from the poolside. Learn to glide on your back. Crouch in chest-deep water. Tilt your head back until your ears are submerged. Push off from the bottom, lifting your hips to the surface.

Treading water In water deep enough to allow it (but not out of your depth), keep your body upright and your head just clear of the water; kick your legs as if you were cycling and paddle with your arms, as illustrated overleaf. Treading water allows you to conserve energy and stay afloat for a long time.

Breast stroke Breathe in and start by lying straight in a face-down position, arms and legs fully extended. Drop your palms down and pull your arms outwards and down towards your feet, inhaling as you do so. Terminate the pull about 150mm (6in) in front of the shoulders, then draw your feet up by bending and parting knees and thighs until they are slightly wider apart than hip width. The feet should now be sole uppermost with toes pointing backwards.

Bring your hands together in front of your face. Then kick the feet backwards and slightly outwards, bringing the legs together and straight. As you kick, push forward with your hands until fully extended in a forward glide, and exhale.

Crawl Floating face down, with your face submerged and arms fully extended in front of you, begin to exhale slowly through your mouth and nose. With your hands flat and your fingers together, pull your right arm downwards, bending your elbow slightly so that your hand passes beneath your body.

Start turning your head to the left. Complete the pull at your hip and bend your elbow upwards. At the same time, begin the pulling action with your other arm and complete the head turn so that your mouth clears the surface. Inhale deeply, then roll your face back into the water, exhaling slowly. If it is more comfortable, you can breathe in while the left arm is pulling and your head is turned to the right.

Your arm should leave the water elbow high, wrist low, with your fingers together and slightly above the surface. Bring your arm forward and extend it fully, then spear your fingers into the water to start the next pull.

While pulling with your arms, kick up and down with your legs, using a scissor movement from your hip joints. Flex your knees slightly and point your toes downwards, keeping your feet just below the surface. Kick in a relaxed way but quickly – six kicks to each stroke cycle of both arms. The kick is primarily to balance your body in the water.

Backstroke There are two forms of back-stroke. One is an upside-down version of the crawl and is properly termed the back-crawl stroke.

The other backstroke, sometimes cal-led English backstroke, is a more relaxed method and the basis of the lifesaving stroke. Float on your back with palms facing down and toes pointed.

Bring both arms up to armpit level and extended straight out, with your hands slightly above shoulder level. Rotate your palms perpendicular to the water surface, and at the same time bend your legs with heels together and knees spread. Pull your arms in to your thighs, and thrust outwards with your legs, pro-pelling yourself backwards in a glide. As the glide slows, repeat the action.

Learning the basic skills

The first essential for learning to swim successfully is to gain suf-ficient confidence to support your-self and feel at ease in the water. Learn to control your breathing so that you can submerge comfortably and breathe out underwater. Learn also to open your eyes and look about you underwater. Practise keeping afloat in shallow water where there are swimmers nearby, and do not go out of your depth until you are competent to do so.

Breathing Bob in and out of the water. Hold your breath to submerge. Exhale through your nose underwater.

Floating Crouch in the water with your shoulders submerged and your arms stretched out in front of you. Take a deep breath, submerge your face, and push up gently with your feet so that you lie prone at the surface of the water (left, top). Relax your body. To recover from the float, lower your arms and bring your knees up in a crouch, and at the same time raise your head above the water (left, bottom). Straighten up and stand on the bottom.

Treading water In deep enough water, keep your head above the surface by cycling with your legs and paddling with your arms, holding your body upright. Alternatively, raise your knees, holding them slightly apart, then kick your legs down straight together. A third way is to kick your legs alternately below the knee.

Breath control Practise kicking and breathing sequences while holding onto the side. Raise your body and legs, keeping your face submerged. Kick with a scissors action. Turn your face up on alternate sides to breathe.

Water safety Never swim alone, even in a pool. Swim in supervised pools or at beaches with a friend. Watch children at all times. Avoid vigorous swimming for at least an hour after you have eaten. Leave the water when you get tired.

Stay out of the water during storms.

At a beach, swim parallel and close to the shore. If caught in a current, swim with it or across it – not against it. If you feel tired, rest by floating, not by treading water.

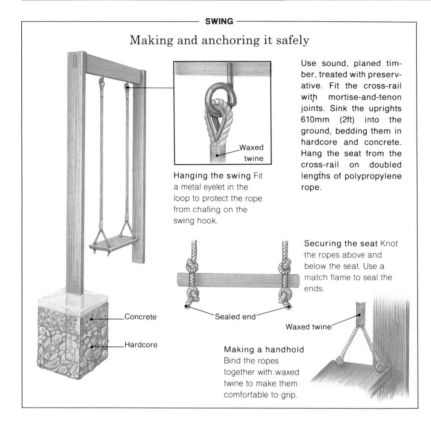

SWING

Making and anchoring it safely

Use sound, planed timber, treated with preservative. Fit the cross-rail with mortise-and-tenon joints. Sink the uprights 610mm (2ft) into the ground, bedding them in hardcore and concrete. Hang the seat from the cross-rail on doubled lengths of polypropylene rope.

Hanging the swing Fit a metal eyelet in the loop to protect the rope from chafing on the swing hook.

Waxed twine

Concrete

Hardcore

Sealed end

Securing the seat Knot the ropes above and below the seat. Use a match flame to seal the ends.

Waxed twine

Making a handhold Bind the ropes together with waxed twine to make them comfortable to grip.

Swing

Building one in your garden

A garden swing must be strong enough to be used by older children – and even adults. To make one, use 150 × 50mm (6 × 2in) softwood TIMBER planed all round for the uprights and cross-rail. You will need two uprights 2.7m (9ft) long to allow you to sink 610mm (2ft) into the ground for a solid foundation. Use pressure-treated timber or soak the bottom 610mm in wood preservative. Allow 1170mm (46in) for the cross-rail.

For the seat, use 230 × 38mm (9 × 1½in) planed softwood. You will need to cut a piece 560mm (22in) long – see SAWS AND SAWING.

You will also need: waterproof glue; abrasive paper; wood preservative or an exterior-grade varnish or seal (see VARNISHING; WOOD PRESERVATIVES); CONCRETE; 8m (26ft) of 10mm (⅜in) polypropylene rope, with two metal eyelets (sold as 'thimbles' in sailing equipment shops) to fit the rope; two strong-swing hooks with screw threads; waxed twine.

Method Join the cross-rail to the uprights using mortise-and-tenon joints (see WOODWORKING JOINTS) and GLUING them. Allow the glue to set. Plane off the protruding ends of the tenons – see

PLANING. Carefully smooth all wood with abrasive paper (see SANDING) to remove snags or splinters. Coat liberally with preservative, varnish or seal.

Using the frame as a guide, mark out two holes and dig to a depth of 760mm (2ft 6in). Pack a 150mm (6in) layer of rubble into each hole, to ensure good drainage. Now fit the frame uprights into the holes, keeping the frame square. Compact more rubble round each upright, to 150-250mm (6-10in) from the surface. Fill with stiff concrete; smooth the surface and slope it away from the wood.

Cut the rope in half. Fold one length in half again, fit a metal eyelet (or thimble) in the loop and bind it in place with waxed twine. Repeat for the other rope.

Drill four holes in the seat (see DRILLING) – two on each side, set in about 38mm (1½in) from the corners. Measure the length between the holes and mark it up on the cross-rail, so that the hooks will hold the ropes straight.

Screw the hooks into the cross-rail and slip the rope eyelets over them. Thread the rope ends through the seat and adjust its height, taking care to allow plenty of leg clearance between ground and seat. Finally, knot the ropes securely above and below the seat and fuse the strands of the frayed ends together, using the flame of a match – see also NYLON ROPES. Bind each pair together with waxed twine about 200mm (8in) above the seat.

Ready-made swings Many garden centres and larger toy shops offer garden swings in kit form. Most are made of tubular or angled metal sections and come with assembly instructions. Make sure the sections fit tightly – if necessary tap them home with a rubber mallet.

This kind of frame is quite light, so it is essential to anchor the swing firmly to the ground – especially if older children are going to use it. Long metal hooks may be included for this purpose, but in soft ground they could pull loose. To ensure a good foundation for the swing, sink a narrow, deep hole for each hook, then fill in round each hook with concrete.

Check the swing regularly for chipped paint and RUST. Rub away any rust or loose paint with emery cloth, then treat bare metal with rust-inhibiting enamel.

Swollen glands

What they might mean and what to do about them

A glandular swelling in the body is usually a symptom of an illness or infection, but occasionally it can be a side effect of a vaccination or be caused by an insect bite or a cut. In most cases swollen glands are not painful, but are usually accompanied by a feeling of being unwell or below par.

The swelling will disappear once the cause subsides, but see a DOCTOR if the glands remain swollen for more than a few days, or harden or enlarge with an attendant fever.

The glands of the throat may swell during upper respiratory illnesses such as colds, coughs and flu, particularly if the throat is sore or the tonsils are involved. Swollen glands can also be a sign of MUMPS or GERMAN MEASLES.

If the condition lasts for a week or more, with swelling in the neck, armpits and groin, the cause may be glandular fever (infectious mononucleosis) or a sign of something more serious.

Occasionally swelling may be caused by a salivary stone, a chalklike stone, in a salivary gland, which blocks the duct through which saliva normally flows into the mouth. The gland may swell painfully as saliva is produced but cannot drain into the mouth: avoid sharp, acid food and drinks, such as vinegar and lemon, as these will stimulate saliva production. Your doctor may be able to manipulate the stone with his fingers and 'milk' it out of the duct. Failing that, a simple operation will remove it.

In the case of glandular fever, which is common in children and young adults, the doctor may advise rest during the acute phase and taking painkillers and extra drinks, but avoiding alcohol as the liver is often affected.

T

Table decorating

*Making an attractive setting
for a meal*

Whether you are planning a simple family lunch or an elaborate dinner party, decorating the table attractively and imaginatively will set the scene to make the meal a special occasion.

Choose a colour scheme and decorations that will complement the room, and reflect the occasion and the season. Take care not to clutter the table with too many decorations, which may make it difficult for guests to eat or converse. Good glass, china or silver rarely need anything but the simplest decoration. See also PLACE SETTING.

If the table has a fine surface, it should be protected from spillage and heat by mats or a cloth. Choose a cloth to complement your china.

Mats for plates should be heatproof and non-slip. Use small mats, called coasters, for the wine GLASSES. Fine mats, especially those that are lacy or embroidered, will not protect the table from heat and must have extra protection underneath them.

Flowers and leaves Use low arrangements or a single bloom at each place, so that guests' views of one another are not obscured – see FLOWER ARRANGING. Avoid flowers with a strong perfume,

which may conflict with the aroma of food or wine. A long table can be decorated with garlands of flowers or leaves trailed across it, but a central arrangement is best for a round or square table.

When there are not many flowers to be picked in the garden, leaves, small branches and fir cones make an attractive alternative.

Candles The only guideline when choosing candles is that the taller the candlestick, the shorter the candle you put in it. The light should be cast on the food and people's faces – not on the tops of their heads.

Candles now come in many colours and shapes – see also CANDLEMAKING. You need not use all the same colour; you could, for example, mix a white one with pink or pale green. You can decorate them with flowers or ribbons tied to the base.

Use non-drip, unscented candles and make sure they are long enough to last through the meal and are positioned where they will not be knocked over.

Fruit bowls A bowl of fruit with shiny polished skins makes an ideal centrepiece. The arrangement of fruit can be decorated with camellia or bay leaves, or studded with silver or gold dragees – sweets with hard sugar or chocolate centres, used for cake decoration.

Napkins Linen napkins are the most stylish, but paper ones are increasingly popular, especially for large buffet parties, as they are discarded after use. Choose the large multi-ply type.

Napkins can be folded into simple triangles or rectangles or into elaborate designs – see NAPKIN FOLDING.

Table repairs

*Bracing corners; mending legs
and frames*

Normal wear and tear and the drying effects of central heating can damage a table. You can carry out many repairs yourself, but take fine ANTIQUES to an expert.

Uneven legs Make sure the unevenness is in the table, not the floor. You can test this by standing the table on several different areas of floor. When you are sure the table is at fault, place it on a truly flat surface – perhaps a sheet of thick plywood laid on a floor.

Pack thin scrap pieces of wood under the leg or legs where the table rocks until the table stands firm and level. You may find one leg shorter or longer than the other three.

With the table standing correctly, set a pair of compasses so that the pencil touches the table leg just above the thickest amount of packing. Mark all four legs with the compass pencil, keeping the compass point on the floor each time.

Carefully saw off the excess from each leg, using a fine-toothed tenon saw – see SAWS AND SAWING. Rub the cut edges with fine glasspaper. The table will now stand firm on all four legs.

Loose legs Have a look under the table to see how the legs are fixed. Tighten any loose screws or wing nuts.

Where there are simple WOODWORKING JOINTS, tap apart any loose ones with a wood mallet or rubber-faced hammer; clean off all old glue with a chisel, then re-glue, clamping the joints together while the glue sets – see GLUING.

To strengthen the joints, use metal corner braces, available from most hardware stores. Fit a brace across a corner, setting its ends into slightly recessed slots chiselled (see CHISELLING) or sawn into each piece of wood. Remove the brace once you have established its posi-

Table for two Shells, fruit and flowers glow in soft candlelight.

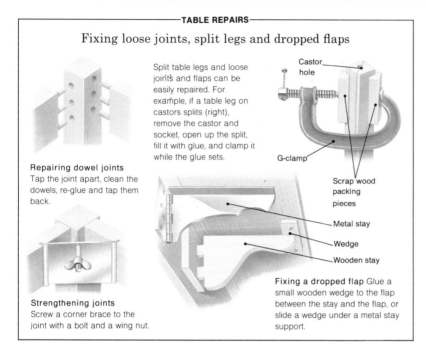

Fixing loose joints, split legs and dropped flaps

Split table legs and loose joints and flaps can be easily repaired. For example, if a table leg on castors splits (right), remove the castor and socket, open up the split, fill it with glue, and clamp it while the glue sets.

Castor hole

G-clamp

Repairing dowel joints
Tap the joint apart, clean the dowels, re-glue and tap them back.

Scrap wood packing pieces

Metal stay

Wedge

Wooden stay

Strengthening joints
Screw a corner brace to the joint with a bolt and a wing nut.

Fixing a dropped flap Glue a small wooden wedge to the flap between the stay and the flap, or slide a wedge under a metal stay support.

---

tion and screw the special bolt provided with the brace into the corner, so that its threaded length will protrude through the hole in the brace. Screw the brace in place with the bolt protruding. Screw a wing nut onto the protruding bolt.

Loose dowel joints Use a mallet or rubber-faced hammer to knock apart any loose joints made with DOWELS. Use a chisel and abrasive paper to clean off all old glue from the dowels and from the holes in which they fit. If stubs of broken dowel are stuck in the holes, drill and clean them out.

Prepare new dowels, making sure they are grooved, then apply new wood glue. Tap the joints together, putting a piece of hardboard between the hammer and the wood to avoid bruising the wood, then clamp the joints until the glue has set. Wipe away any surplus glue while it is still wet.

Split leg Splits can occur on coffee-table legs that have been fitted with CASTORS or glide-feet. Remove the castor and socket or the glide, and open up the split as far as possible with a chisel blade so that you can inject wood glue into the crack. Use plenty of glue, then clamp the parts together and wipe away surplus glue while it is wet. When the glue has set, clear out the hole and refit the castor and socket or the glide.

If the glide is held by small SCREWS, some of which have split the leg, repair as above, then fill the screw holes with plastic wood. Drill new start holes for the screws before screwing the glide back in place on the leg.

Drop-leaf hinges Wood can split along the screw line of HINGES, perhaps through too much pressure on the flap. Remove the flap and hinges; open up the crack with a chisel and insert wood glue in the split. Clamp the wood until the glue sets.

Fill the screw holes with small tapered plugs of wood, glued and tapped into place. When the glue has set, cut or saw off the surplus plugging.

Re-position the hinge or hinges over the repair, and use a bradawl to mark the positions of new start holes for the screws. Drill start holes then screw the hinges back in place.

Dropped flap Where a flap is not level with the table, up-end the table and check that the flap supports are firmly screwed in place. They should just be touching the flap. If they are not, shape small slivers of wood and glue them either under the flap or on top of the stays, so there is no gap between stay and flap.

If the table has metal stays, an alternative cure is to loosen off the screws holding the stays, then slide in a slim wedge under the bottom of the stay support before tightening the screws.

Table skittles

Playing skittles in miniature

Also known as Devil Among the Tailors, this pub game is played on a baize-bottomed table about 760mm (2½ft) square, surrounded by a wall 75mm (3in) high. Nine hardwood skittles about 75mm high are arranged in a diamond shape on a platform 230mm (9in) square in the middle of the table.

They are knocked down by a wooden ball which hangs from a post, about a third of the way along one side. This post, or mast, is about 1 metre (3ft) high and has a swivel top so that the ball can swing freely. Some boards have a CRIBBAGE-style scoreboard at the top.

Variations of the game include 31-up and fives-and-threes. In the first, each player has three turns and scores for each pin knocked down. The aim is to score 31 exactly. In fives-and-threes multiples of these two numbers must be knocked down to score: 3 or 5 wins 1 point; 6 or 10, 2 points; 9, 3 points, etc, 15 wins 8 points as it is a multiple of 3 and 5.

Knocking down the pins

Swivel

Post

Arc of ball

230mm (9in)

760mm (2½ft)

Skittles

The game can be played by two opponents or by teams. Stand behind the line of the post and take it in turns to swing the ball round behind the skittles to knock them down. Each pin knocked over scores a point. The aim is to reach the targeted score exactly.

Platform

Table tennis

Playing a fast, skilful indoor game

The object of table tennis is to score points by hitting the ball across a low net so that it bounces where your opponent cannot hit it back.

The dark green wooden table is 2.7m (9ft) long, 1.5m (5ft) across, and 760mm (2ft 6in) high; you need at least 1.5m clearance at each end and about 1m (3ft) each side. The net across the middle – 150mm (6in) high – divides the table into two courts, outlined in white around the table border. A white line divides each court into a right and left half for doubles. In doubles, partners must take it in turns to hit the ball during play.

Each player strikes the hollow celluloid ball with a rounded wooden bat, about 125-165mm (5-6½in) across and usually covered with pimpled rubber. There are two ways of holding the bat – with your palm round the handle (the lawn tennis or shake-hands style), which allows a wide range of strokes, or by gripping the blade with the handle projecting upwards between your thumb and forefinger (the penholder style).

To serve, hold the ball on your palm at table level and toss it upwards, then strike it as it descends. It must bounce once on each side of the net – if it brushes the net, serve again.

A continuous exchange is a rally. Your opponent scores if you miss the returned ball, hit it before it bounces, or hit it after it has bounced twice on the table or struck the floor, wall or ceiling. A player loses a point if he touches the table with his free hand, or jars the table.

Each player delivers five services in turn, but serving alternates after each point if the score becomes 20 all. The winner is the first to score 21, but if he is not then leading by two points, play must continue until one player leads by two points. The winner of a match is the winner of two out of three games – three out of five in a championship.

The sport is controlled by the International Table Tennis Federation, 53 London Road, St Leonards on Sea, E. Sussex TN37 6AY.

Taps

Repairing a spindle or leaking spout

There are two main types of tap, the bib tap and the pillar tap. The bib tap has a horizontal water inlet and is mostly used for garage or garden water supplies. The pillar tap has a vertical inlet and is used in kitchens and bathrooms.

Two main methods are used to control the flow of water. The first is a washer and valve pressed into a seating by turning the tap handle clockwise. Undoing it lifts the washer so water flows.

The second method uses two ceramic discs held in close contact, with holes through them. When the tap is turned on the holes are aligned and water flows through; turn the handle 90 degrees, and the holes move out of alignment.

Taps with washers may leak after a lot of use. In those with ceramic discs, the seal between discs improves with age.

There are also two common types of tap handle which have to be dismantled differently – the traditional capstan or cross-top handle, above a bell-shaped cover; and the modern shrouded-head handle, usually a fluted knob.

Repairing a drip from the spindle If the drip is coming from above a bell cover adjust or repack the gland without turning the water off. Remove the handle from its spindle by undoing a small grub screw at one side of the handle and then tapping gently upwards. If there is no grub screw it may pull straight off, or pull off after being given a half turn. Then unscrew the bell-shaped cover.

The hexagonal nut nearest the handle is the gland nut. Give it a half-turn with a spanner, turning clockwise. Often this will stop the drip, as the gland packing material is pressed more tightly to the spindle. Check by temporarily slipping the handle back to turn the tap on.

If there is still a leak, undo the nut and remove it to reveal the gland packing. If this has deteriorated, replace it with similar packing. In a more modern tap this seal may be graphite or a rubber O-ring; in an older tap it may be string or hemp, which can be poked out with a fine knitting needle. String packing can be replaced with a length of knitting wool coated liberally with petroleum jelly and pressed into the recess. Replace the gland nut and tighten it until the tap spindle turns with just slight resistance. Do not over-tighten the nut or the tap will be hard to turn on and off.

O-ring seals in shrouded-head taps rarely need replacing. If one should, cut off the water supply, remove the tap handle, and take out the headgear as for repairing a dripping spout (see below). Turn the spindle clockwise to release the washer unit. Prise out the O-ring at the top of the washer unit. Grease the new ring with petroleum jelly; fit it and reassemble the tap.

Repairing a drip from the spout If water drips from the tap spout, the washer usually needs renewing. Renew both washers on mixer taps. Cut off the water supply before you dismantle the tap – at the mains stopcock for a mains tap or, for stored water, at a gate valve on the supply pipe. If there is no gate valve, tie up the ball valve in the cold-water storage tank (see BALL COCKS) and drain the tank by running taps and flushing toilets. When the water stops running, put the plug in the sink or basin where you are working to avoid losing parts down the waste pipe. Put a cloth in the basin to protect it against knocks.

For a shrouded-head tap, lift off the handle, usually held by a screw under the top plate. This reveals the tap headgear. On a traditional tap, unscrew the bell cover and lift it to reveal the hexagonal headgear nut.

Unscrew the hexagonal nut holding the headgear in place. You can use an adjustable spanner after removing a shrouded head, but on a traditional tap the gap made by the lifted bell cover is wide enough for an open-ended spanner only. Hold the tap nozzle firmly in your other hand as you unscrew, and apply

---

TABLE TENNIS

The serve and the two basic grips

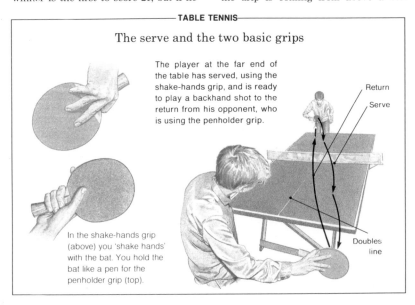

The player at the far end of the table has served, using the shake-hands grip, and is ready to play a backhand shot to the return from his opponent, who is using the penholder grip.

Return
Serve
Doubles line

In the shake-hands grip (above) you 'shake hands' with the bat. You hold the bat like a pen for the penholder grip (top).

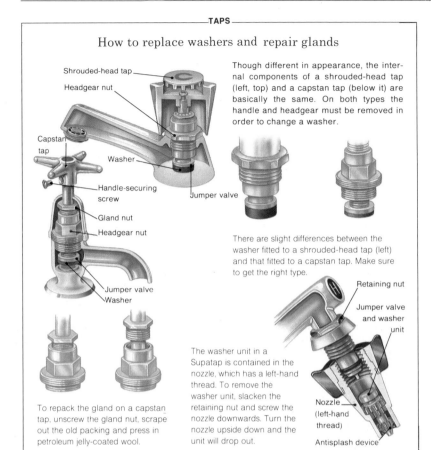

How to replace washers and repair glands

Shrouded-head tap

Headgear nut

Capstan tap

Washer

Handle-securing screw

Gland nut

Headgear nut

Jumper valve
Washer

Jumper valve

Though different in appearance, the internal components of a shrouded-head tap (left, top) and a capstan tap (below it) are basically the same. On both types the handle and headgear must be removed in order to change a washer.

There are slight differences between the washer fitted to a shrouded-head tap (left) and that fitted to a capstan tap. Make sure to get the right type.

Retaining nut

Jumper valve and washer unit

Nozzle (left-hand thread)

Antisplash device

The washer unit in a Supatap is contained in the nozzle, which has a left-hand thread. To remove the washer unit, slacken the retaining nut and screw the nozzle downwards. Turn the nozzle upside down and the unit will drop out.

To repack the gland on a capstan tap, unscrew the gland nut, scrape out the old packing and press in petroleum jelly-coated wool.

counter-pressure to avoid twisting the base of the tap. Otherwise, if the headgear is tight, the force exerted could crack the basin.

Lift out the headgear. At the bottom you will see a small rod and plate called a jumper valve with a washer attached. In tank-fed taps the jumper may be fixed in the base of the headgear, but in mains-fed taps the whole unit may be loose. If there is a small washer-retaining nut, remove it to release the washer; otherwise prise the washer off.

Replace the washer with a new one of similar size and material. Sometimes a bell-shaped washer will work when a conventional washer will not. If you cannot remove the washer, replace the whole jumper valve unit. To remove a fixed unit, you may have to undo a small grub screw. If you cannot undo it, prise out the unit by force. If replacing it with a metal valve, roughen the jumper rod to help it grip.

Reassemble the tap and make sure it is turned off before you restore the water supply. If the tap continues to drip, the tap seating may be damaged.

Repairing the tap seating Cut off the water supply and dismantle as described

above. Feel the metal seating in the tap body with your finger. If it is rough, or a piece is missing, allowing water to bypass the washer, buy a reseating tool from a hardware shop to re-grind the surface smooth. Alternatively, you can buy a reseating set (usually supplied with a washer). It has a nylon seat that can be pressed over the existing seating to provide a new smooth surface. Be sure the set is designed for the size of tap being repaired.

Repairing a Supatap There is no need to turn off the water supply. To fit a new washer, hold the nozzle in one hand while you loosen the retaining nut at the top of the nozzle with a spanner. Then hold the loosened nut with one hand while you unscrew the nozzle anticlockwise. As the nozzle comes away in your hand, a check valve drops into place to prevent the flow of water.

Tap the base of the nozzle against a firm surface to loosen the antisplash device (which contains the jumper valve and washer unit). Then turn it upside down, so the unit falls out. Fit a new washer and jumper unit, then reassemble the tap by screwing the nozzle clockwise.

See also PLUMBING.

Tarts

Making jam and fruit-filled pastries

Tarts are usually made with shortcrust PASTRY. They can be made in a shallow tin or a flan ring, or as individual tartlets in patty tins. The fillings can be any flavour of jam, or fresh or cooked fruit.

Roll out the pastry to line the tin; for patty tins cut out tartlets with a pastry cutter. Allow an extra 6mm ($\frac{1}{4}$in) of pastry for shrinkage during cooking. Make sure the pastry is firm against the sides and bottom, with no air bubbles beneath it.

If you are filling with jam, keep it well below the rim or it will boil over.

Apples are a popular fruit filling; use Bramleys peeled and sliced and scattered with 115g (4oz) of sugar to 450g (1lb) of fruit. Hard fruits such as gooseberries should first be simmered with a tablespoon of water in a closed pan for 5 or 6 minutes and then allowed to cool.

Bake for 10 minutes in an oven preheated to 200°C (400°F), gas mark 6, then reduce the heat to 190°C (375°F), gas mark 5, and cook until the pastry is golden and the fruit tender – about 20 minutes more.

Tea

Choosing blends and brewing a perfect cup

All teas come from the same species of evergreen shrub, *Camellia sinensis*. The differences in flavour depend on the type of soil, the altitude and climate of the growing area, and the production methods. Various types of tea are produced by blending teas from different areas or by adding flowers and natural fruit oils to the leaves during processing.

Black tea The leaves are fermented after picking, and produce flavours typical of each growing area – rich and malty Assam tea, delicate and grapey Darjeeling, light but strong Ceylon. Most brands are blends from different regions, chiefly in India, Sri Lanka (Ceylon) and East Africa.

The terms Orange Pekoe, Pekoe and Pekoe Souchong denote leaf grades in descending size. As they get smaller they are prefaced with the words Broken, Fannings and Dusts. Pekoe tips are leaves from the shoots of tips, which make the finest tea.

English Breakfast Tea is a blend of Ceylon and Assam teas which give flavour and strength. Earl Grey is a blend of China tea scented with oil of bergamot.

Indian and Ceylon teas are usually served with milk; China teas – more delicate in flavour – are served on their own or with lemon. China teas include Keemun, Ching Wo and Lapsang Souchong.

Green tea The leaves are not fermented and produce pale-coloured tea of mild flavour. Most green teas are from China or Japan. They include Hoo Chow and Gunpowder.

Oolong tea The leaves are partly fermented, and have a flavour between that of black and green teas. Oolong tea comes from China and Taiwan. Formosa (Taiwan) Oolong is said to be one of the world's finest – as well as one of the most expensive – teas.

How to make tea Warm the pot with hot water, then empty it. For medium-strength tea, use one rounded teaspoon (or one tea bag) for each person and an extra one for the pot. Take the pot to the kettle when the water boils, and pour the boiling water onto the tea. Do not add too much water – judge by the amount of tea used and the size of the teapot.

Stir the tea, and let it stand for five minutes – or two or three minutes for green tea, which infuses more quickly. Do not leave tea standing for more than a few minutes, or it will be 'stewed' and taste bitter. Strain the tea into the cups. Refill the pot with boiling water for serving second cups – but the flavour will not be quite as good.

Store tea in a dry place away from direct light, and use an airtight container (tea caddy) so that it keeps its flavour.

Teddy bear repairs

Taking care of a child's favourite toy

Many teddy bears are extremely long-lived, being cherished well beyond childhood. They need occasional washing, but should not be dry-cleaned because poisonous fumes can be retained in the stuffing. If you use a machine wash, set a warm wash programme for fine fabrics and make sure the teddy bear's fabric is sound first, or the stuffing could escape into the machine.

Mending loose limbs Sewn-on limbs that are loose or have come off can be restitched, but on some toys the limbs are jointed with a split pin or piece of wire through wooden discs, in the end of the limb and inside the body.

Sometimes a weak split pin will snap. To get at the body disc to refix or tighten the limbs, unpick the back body seam and remove the stuffing.

The eye of the split pin is usually inside the limb. Put in a new wire or pin if necessary to replace a limb, or tighten the existing pin using long-nosed pliers to pull and twist the curled end.

Renew the seam with SLIPSTITCHING, using strong double thread.

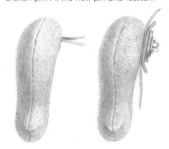

--- TEDDY BEAR REPAIRS ---

Giving an old friend a new lease of life

Metal washer — Fur fabric of arm
Twisted tail of pin
Wooden disc — Fur fabric of body
Fabric shield
Wooden disc — Metal washer
Eye of pin

Fitting a new limb joint The joint consists of two wooden discs held by a split pin (above) and two retaining washers. Straighten the legs of the split pin inside the body and remove the limb. Unstitch the fabric around the joint and remove the broken pin. Fit the new pin and restitch.

Push the tail of the split pin into the body and slip the outer disc and washer over it. Pull the split pin tight with a pair of long-nosed pliers and bend back the pin's legs against the disc. Restitch the body seam.

Repairing a split seam If the material is sound, the seam can be resewn with slipstitching. If the material is worn, remove a little of the stuffing so that you can turn in the material edges slightly and resew through sound fabric.

If a large area around the seam is thin, it needs PATCHING with suitable material. You will probably have to undo an opposite seam and remove the stuffing to fit the patch from behind. Or reinforce the area by sewing on some new material

in the form of a garment, such as a vest.

You can buy kapok or plastic foam chips to replace stuffing where necessary.

Repairing the eyes Modern teddy bears usually have either felt eyes or plastic safety-lock eyes that are unlikely to come out. If an eye is lost or damaged, it is best to replace both, to make a matching pair. It is easier to use felt for eyes, as plastic safety-lock eyes have to be inserted with a special tool.

Glass eyes are dangerous to young children because, if they come off, the wire retaining loop is exposed and can cause scratches; also the child may swallow and choke on the eye. But to refix an existing glass eye in an old and cherished teddy, first undo a seam at the back of the head, and if necessary patch or mend the eye area, leaving a small hole for the wire loop at the back of the glass eye.

Check that the wire loop is securely wound so that the thread will not slip out, then put a double length of thread (or string) through it and tie the eye at the centre of the threads with a slip knot – see KNOTS. Pass the threads through the eye hole and the head, and out through the opposite ear. Restuff the head and sew up the seam, then pull the threads comfortably tight, knot them together and sew the ends into the fabric.

Teeth

Fighting tooth decay and gum disease

Thanks to recent research, effective action against the teeth's major adversaries – decay and the gum disease called gingivitis – can now be taken by everyone. To achieve the best protection, make personal dental care a daily habit. Start a dental regime for a baby as soon as it begins TEETHING.

A baby's first teeth may be cleaned with a cotton-wool bud or piece of gauze; you can introduce a toothbrush as soon as the child will accept it. Avoid toothpaste until the child can rinse out his mouth; brush his teeth for him until he can do so himself.

Sugar combines with the sticky bacterial plaque which coats teeth and gums, increasing the level of acid which attacks tooth enamel and starts decay. Avoid it, if possible. Treats should be fresh or dried fruit rather than sugary sweets – a 'sweet tooth' is a habit that need never develop.

A build-up of plaque between tooth and gum, when not removed by regular brushing, can cause gingivitis, characterised by bright pink gums which bleed.

The plaque hardens to form tartar, which collects more plaque and causes gum inflammation. If neglected, this condition loosens teeth by destroying the fibres which attach them to the jaw, and the teeth fall out or have to be removed.

Brush your teeth immediately after eating for about three minutes, using a fluoride toothpaste – fluoride has been shown to reduce decay by about 25 per cent. Do not wet the brush before use as this produces too much froth, which may impede cleaning.

Use gentle upward and downward strokes on the outer and inner surfaces, tilting the brush to gain proper access to all teeth. Then, with a horizontal action, brush the biting surfaces of the upper and lower teeth. For best coverage, start the brushing process in a different part of the mouth each day.

Use nylon dental floss or wooden dental sticks to clean between your teeth, following the instructions on the pack.

See also DENTURES; TOOTHACHE.

Teething

Easing babies' discomfort

A few lucky babies grow TEETH without a single tear, but many fret and drool because of the pain when they first appear. But contrary to popular belief, teething does not cause fever or illness in babies. Nor is late or early teething of any medical significance.

A baby eventually has 20 teeth. The first to appear are usually the two front teeth of the lower jaw, when the baby is between five and ten months old. The back molars appear last – between 24 and 30 months.

However, different babies develop at different rates – and teeth may emerge before or after these times.

Teething discomfort When teething, a baby is often irritable and flushed. Discomfort may make the baby wake up a lot at night.

Chewing can give relief and it helps the teeth to come through. Offer the baby a chilled teething ring to bite on; or a clean flannel soaked in cold water then wrung out; or a soft washable toy.

Be sure to keep out of a baby's reach all sharp objects, or small ones that could be swallowed.

If the baby wakes up at night and cannot go back to sleep easily, a drink of water may help. Do not offer food; night-time feeds could quickly become a habit.

Teething cream or gel (available from chemists) can be rubbed into the gums to relieve the discomfort. Such treatment may cause allergic reactions in some babies. A mild painkiller, such as paracetamol, will relieve pain.

Consult your doctor if you suspect that symptoms such as FEVER and excessive crying could be caused by something more serious than teething.

Telephone answering machines

How to choose and use one

A telephone answering machine automatically answers the telephone while you are out. It gives an opening message in your own voice (or you can buy a recorded message); then it records the caller's message.

Some answering machines are easy to install, requiring only two connections, one to a power socket and one to the telephone socket – see also TELEPHONE EXTENSIONS; TELEPHONES. You can also get telephone systems with integrated answering machines.

When buying an answering machine, make sure it is approved by the British Approval Board Telecommunications (BABT). Look for a white label with a green spot bearing the words: 'APPROVED for use with telecommunications systems run by BT in accordance with the conditions in the instructions for use.' A machine should be BABT approved even if your telephone service is supplied by Mercury Communications Ltd.

For many answering machines you can get a remote controller. With this you can phone your number from anywhere and listen to any messages on the machine. Some machines also have a monitor feature so that when you are at home you can leave the machine on and listen to a message as it is recorded – then decide whether or not you want to answer the call.

Recording a message Write out the message, read it aloud, and time it before you record it. On many machines the message should last no more than 30 seconds.

A suitable message might be: 'Hello, this is 123-4567, Tony Warren speaking. I'm afraid I'm not able to answer your call at the moment, but if you leave your name, number and any message, I'll return your call as soon as possible. Thank you for calling.'

Some people, though, prefer to omit their name – or even the number. The manufacturer's instructions usually give several sample messages.

Telephone extensions

Buying and installing your own

A wide range of TELEPHONES is available from many electrical shops, DIY centres and department stores. If you already have a telephone line to your home you can install extensions easily, provided your line is connected in the house to a master socket – a square white box with a shuttered socket aperture – which

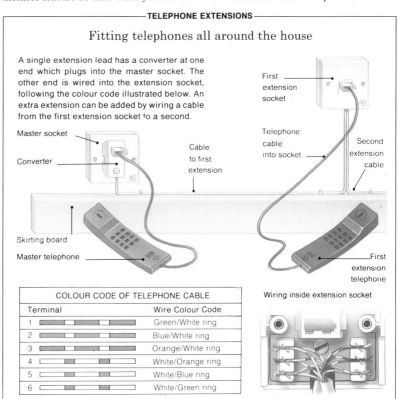

— TELEPHONE EXTENSIONS —

Fitting telephones all around the house

A single extension lead has a converter at one end which plugs into the master socket. The other end is wired into the extension socket, following the colour code illustrated below. An extra extension can be added by wiring a cable from the first extension socket to a second.

Master socket

Converter

Cable to first extension

Telephone cable into socket

First extension socket

Second extension cable

Skirting board

Master telephone

First extension telephone

Wiring inside extension socket

COLOUR CODE OF TELEPHONE CABLE	
Terminal	Wire Colour Code
1	Green/White ring
2	Blue/White ring
3	Orange/White ring
4	White/Orange ring
5	White/Blue ring
6	White/Green ring

must be fitted by the telephone company (BT, Mercury Communications or Kingston-upon-Hull Telephone Department).

Once you have a master socket you can fit extensions throughout the house, but there must not be more than 50m (54yds) of cable between the master socket and the farthest extension socket.

You can use up to four telephones at the sockets. If you have more than four sockets, you can move the telephones as required and simply plug them into the sockets; or you can have just one telephone and plug it into different sockets as you move, say, from the living room to your bedroom.

When you buy your new plug-in telephone or telephones (which come with plugs already fitted), buy also a socket converter, which plugs into the master socket and has a length of cable attached, as many extension sockets as you need, enough cable cleats to fix the cable at 300mm (12in) intervals, extra cable if needed and an insertion tool.

Decide where you want to fit the extensions and plan a route for the cable, using the shortest route possible. It can be fitted along walls or skirting boards, above ceilings and below floors, but for safety reasons it must be kept at least 50mm (2in) away from mains electric cables.

Starting from the master socket, fit cable in place with cleats; allow for the socket converter to reach the socket easily, but do not plug it into the master socket until all the extension sockets have been fitted and connected. When the cable reaches the point of the first extension, cut it, leaving about 75mm (3in) to spare.

Unscrew the front plate from the extension socket and use a sharp knife to cut away the cable entrance hole, marked at the bottom of the plate.

An insertion tool is supplied with the extension kit; use it to connect the cable's six wires to the socket. First strip off about 32mm (1¼in) of the outer sheath with a trimming knife; there is no need to bare the ends of the six wires.

Use the insertion tool to push the green wire with white rings into the connection marked 1; the blue wire with white rings into 2; and the orange wire with white rings into 3. On the other side of the socket, fit the white wire with orange rings to connection 4; the white with blue rings to 5; and the white with green rings to 6.

Screw the socket into a drilled and plugged hole in the wall (See MASONRY DRILLING; WALL FASTENERS), or screw it to a skirting board. Fit the front plate using the two screws provided. To add more extensions, wire them from the first extension, connecting the wires in the order as before and pushing them into the connections on top of the existing wires.

Telephones

Choosing one for your home

Telephone and electrical shops and many large department stores offer phones in a variety of styles and colours. Many models can 'remember' selected telephone numbers, to redial them if necessary, and have other useful functions. Most are press-button operated, though old-style dialling models are available.

When buying a new phone, always look for the 'green spot' label, which shows that the instrument is approved by the British Approval Board Telecommunications (BABT); in practice this means that it can be used with the equipment owned by BT, which is still responsible for the telephone network. See also TELEPHONE EXTENSIONS; TELEPHONE ANSWERING MACHINES.

Although modern telephones can perform many functions, and the language used to describe them can be confusing, the following definitions will help you to choose the instrument most suited to your needs:

Call progress monitor With this function you can dial a number without lifting the handset until the moment that you hear you are connected.

Call timer A device that times your calls. In a large household it is useful for working out who owes what towards paying the telephone bill.

Cordless telephone A useful alternative to extension phones, the base station is plugged into a telephone socket in the normal way, and the handset will receive and transmit calls by a radio frequency at a distance of up to 100m (109yds), enabling you to use it anywhere in the house, or garden.

Follow-on call facility By pressing a 'cancel' button you can clear the line to make consecutive calls instead of having to put the phone down or depress the receiver rest.

One-piece phone The press buttons or dial in the handset are between the earpiece and the mouthpiece. The phone is disconnected when you put it down on a firm surface. A wall-fixed holder is available for it.

Hands-free operation A speaker and microphone in the telephone base enable you to make and receive calls without holding the phone, leaving your hands free to take notes.

Last number redial At the touch of a button or two the phone will automatically redial the last number you called, taking the effort out of redialling a number that is engaged for a long time.

Memory store With this facility you can store electronically the numbers you use most – as many as 24 numbers on some models. When you want to call one of the numbers, the phone will dial it automatically at the press of a button or buttons.

Secrecy button By pressing a button, you can talk to someone near you without the person on the other end of the phone hearing you.

Some instruments have aids for the hard of hearing, such as an adjustable volume control on the earpiece, adjustable volume control for the bell and a light that flashes when the phone is ringing.

Telephone solicitations

How to discourage callers

People trying to sell you things over the telephone can cause irritation and annoyance if they interfere with your leisure time – and you are not interested in what they turn out to be selling.

When dealing with an unwanted telephone solicitation, ask immediately who is calling, what they are selling and how they obtained your number. The caller should tell you, enabling you to write or telephone your protest to the company involved.

However, direct answers to these questions are not mandatory. Guidelines on selling by telephone, prepared by the Office of Fair Trading, are printed in the back of every phone book. They recognise that unsolicited calls can be of benefit to the subscriber if made in a responsible manner, and if guidelines are adhered to should not cause inconvenience or annoyance.

But if you agree to buy something over the telephone, you have entered into a CONTRACT, even though there is nothing in writing. Remember that the call may have been recorded.

If subscribers are desperate, they can change to an ex-directory number; BT charges £30.50 plus VAT for making the change.

Television aerials

Choosing and positioning them

Television broadcasts are made on a certain waveband or group of channels and it is essential for your receiving aerial to be matched to the appropriate band or group.

There are five aerial groups: A receives channels 21-34; B receives 39-53; C/D receives 48-68; E receives 39-68; and W receives 21-68 (that is, all channels). A television dealer or rental firm can

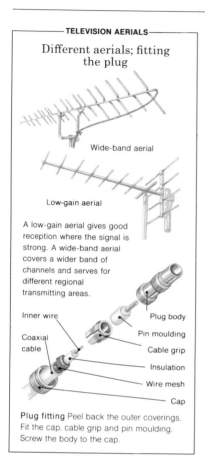

Different aerials; fitting the plug

Wide-band aerial

Low-gain aerial

A low-gain aerial gives good reception where the signal is strong. A wide-band aerial covers a wider band of channels and serves for different regional transmitting areas.

Inner wire

Coaxial cable

Plug body

Pin moulding

Cable grip

Insulation

Wire mesh

Cap

Plug fitting Peel back the outer coverings. Fit the cap, cable grip and pin moulding. Screw the body to the cap.

usually advise you on which group will serve you best.

The size and type of aerial will also affect the quality of signal you receive. If you live near a main transmitter or very near a relay station, an aerial with six to eight elements will suffice. If you live towards the edge of the transmission coverage area, you may need 18 elements.

If you live well within the coverage area in a spot where the signal is strong, a typical nine element *low-gain* aerial (of the right group) will give good reception. If you live far from the transmitter and the signal is weak, perhaps because of nearby hills, a multi-element *high-gain* aerial will strengthen the signal.

A *wide-band* (*log-periodic*) aerial will not strengthen the signal, but will pick up a moderate signal if it can be directed at the transmitter with no obstacles between; it covers a wide band of channels – useful if you are likely to move often and take the aerial with you.

Positioning the aerial is crucial: it must be as high as possible and with a clear view to the horizon, because television signals travel principally by line of sight. The rod elements should be horizontal or vertical depending on the transmitter.

The direction in which the aerial

should point will have to be worked out by trial and error to find the best position for all channels; the direction of your neighbours' aerials can be the starting point.

If you live in an area where reception is poor – tucked under a hill, for example, or among large trees – the aerial may have to be put on a tall mast or fitted with a booster to improve the signal strength. You can get advice on what aerial to use from BBC Engineering Information, White City, 201 Wood Lane, London W12 7TS or your local ITV station.

If you live near to a high-power transmitter, you may be able to get a good picture with an indoor aerial. However, passing cars, trees waving in the garden or even people moving in the room are likely to cause interference. You can improve the picture by putting the aerial as high as possible – in the loft, for example.

A 'ghosting' effect is sometimes seen on a set with an indoor aerial; it can also occur in hilly and built-up areas – the set is receiving two or more signals, a direct one and others reflected from hills or buildings. A good directional low-gain aerial may reduce the ghosting.

Ghosting and interference can also happen during unusual weather conditions. Announcements are usually made between programmes when this is happening. No adjustment to the set or aerial can correct it.

Aerial lead The lead connecting the aerial to your set should be a low-loss 75 ohm coaxial cable. There is some loss of signal strength between aerial and set. Keep the loss to a minimum by making the cable run as short as possible, by avoiding sharp bends in it and by avoiding use of a thinner coaxial cable.

Signal loss is greater with the higher channel number – those covered by a C/D group aerial, for example – because the frequency is higher.

Make sure that the connection of the plug at the end of the aerial is sound. Sometimes the cable from the aerial ends at a socket on the wall and a short length of aerial is plugged in there and leads to the set. Make sure that all these connections are sound.

If any connections are damaged, prepare the cable end afresh and reconnect it to the plug. Plugs vary in detail but have the same basic design; they may be male or female to suit the outlet.

Use a sharp knife to make a 32mm (1¼in) slit lengthways at the end of the PVC outer sheath. Peel back the sheath and cut it off. Fold or push back the mesh of copper wire to clear 19mm (¾in) of the hard plastic inner insulation. Use wire strippers to remove 13mm (½in) of this inner insulation and reveal the single copper wire at the core.

Slide the cap down the cable. Open the

jaws of the cable grip and fit it over the exposed mesh and the outer sheath. Make sure no whiskers of the mesh are sticking out; the mesh must not touch the inner wire. Squeeze the cable grip with pliers to close the jaws tightly on the sheath. Feed the inner wire into the pin moulding and insert the moulding in the plug body. Slide the cap up the cable sheath and screw it to the plug body.

Television sets

Choosing them; maintaining them

Buy or hire a television set of an established make from a reputable dealer. Screen sizes vary from around 50mm (2in), found on hand portables, to 660mm (28in) on larger sets. The small 2in personal sets use LCD (liquid crystal display) screens. Many models are available with various facilities and extras including FST (flatter squarer tube), Nicam stereo, Dolby Surround, Fastext, sound controls for bass and treble, and on-screen 'menus' for controlling various options. Nicam stereo allows you to hear the programme in stereo if the broadcast is in stereo, while Dolby Surround adds depth to the broadcast with the addition of two 'rear' speakers. To hear this surround sound, the broadcast must be in Dolby Surround as well.

Fastext is 'fast' teletext, giving you access to news, weather, sports results, traffic and travel information, and subtitles for the hard of hearing.

Most TV sets have an 'audio out' facility allowing you to feed the sound into your hi-fi system, which improves the sound quality. Some TV sets are fitted with a SCART socket (also known as a Euro Connector), which permits direct connection to a video recorder without the need to use an aerial socket. Using the aerial socket is only possible if the video, too, is fitted with one of these connectors.

Before buying, visit a specialist TV retailer to investigate what is available, and ask for a demonstration of the various models that fit your budget.

Maintenance A television set from any reputable manufacturer should last seven to ten years without major repairs. A poor-quality picture more often reflects poor reception than a fault in the set itself.

Most models can be easily adjusted on the set or by remote control. Always study the manufacturer's instructions to make sure you understand the set's controls and functions and can make the best use of them. But, if something goes wrong, do not tamper with the components inside the set. Have the set repaired by a qualified television repairer.

Temperature

*Using a thermometer to check
body heat*

A rise in temperature above the norm of 37°C (98.6°F) is a symptom of many illnesses – often they are common and need no medical treatment, but some are more serious. Take the temperature of someone who is unwell to see if it is so high that you should call your DOCTOR. See also FEVER.

Using a mercury thermometer Rinse the thermometer under cold water and dry it with a tissue. Holding the thermometer at the end opposite the bulb, shake it sharply a few times to get the mercury back into the bulb. Make sure the reading on the thermometer is below 35°C (95°F).

Put it under the tongue for two minutes. Then hold it over the back of your hand to read the line of mercury.

Under-arm temperature If there is any chance that the patient may break the thermometer in his mouth – if he has difficulty breathing, for example, or is very young – it is better to take the temperature under the arm; this avoids the risk of swallowing broken glass or mercury.

TEMPERATURE

Using a mercury thermometer

Put the bulb under the patient's tongue for two minutes, making sure that it is held by the lips, not the teeth.

Alternatively, slip the bulb into the patient's armpit. Fold the arm across the chest to ensure that the bulb is touched all round.

Rinse, dry and check the thermometer, then put the bulb in the armpit for three minutes. Remove it and read the temperature.

Forehead thermometers These consist of narrow plastic strips divided into bands corresponding to different temperatures. When applied to the forehead, liquid crystals inside each band change colour to indicate skin temperature.

These thermometers have the advantages that they read a patient's temperature more quickly than a traditional mercury thermometer and are unbreakable.

To use a forehead thermometer, first make sure the patient's forehead is dry. Press the thermometer firmly to the forehead, holding it at both ends, then wait 15 seconds.

During this time different bands will change colour. The band that turns green is the one that indicates the patient's temperature.

Read the temperature while the thermometer is still on the forehead – if you are taking your own temperature, use a mirror.

See also HYPOTHERMIA.

Tempura

Frying Japanese style

This Japanese dish of seafood and vegetables fried in batter then dipped in a piquant sauce is ideal for serving informally to friends or family. It is a filling dish and needs only fruit to follow.

Prepare the sauce in advance.

Sauce
175ml (6fl oz) chicken stock
6 tablespoons soya sauce
6 tablespoons sweet sherry or Japanese rice wine
1 tablespoon grated radish or horseradish
1 teaspoon grated fresh ginger root

Mix the ingredients well and serve in small bowls with the tempura. You can vary the fish and vegetables, making use of what is readily available. You can give added authenticity by including slices of lotus root; tinned roots are sold.

Use a wok or a deep-fryer and lift out the cooked items with metal tongs or a slotted spoon.

Ingredients (for 6)
8 giant prawns
350g (12oz) monkfish (filleted)
1 large aubergine, cubed
2 small green peppers, cut into wide strips
1 large onion, sliced
6 courgettes, thickly sliced
175g (6oz) of small mushrooms
6 sprigs of broccoli or cauliflower
1 or 2 eggs

175g (6oz) white bread (strong) flour
340ml (12fl oz) iced water
Cooking oil

Shell the prawns, discarding the veins that run down their backs but leaving the tails intact. Cut the monkfish into strips or pieces.

To make the batter, beat the egg or eggs in a bowl with the iced water. When mixed add the flour and beat for a short time, but do not over-mix. The batter should be slightly lumpy and used immediately.

Heat the oil in the wok or deep-fryer to 180-195°C (360-380°F). Test the temperature with a cooking thermometer or drop in a cube of bread – it should start to colour immediately.

Dip a few prawns and monkfish strips in the batter and drop them into the hot oil.

When the prawns and fish are cooked – in about 2 minutes – the batter should be pale but crisp. Lift them from the oil onto absorbent kitchen paper to drain, then keep hot. When all the prawns and fish strips are cooked, fry the other vegetables in batches and serve in hot dishes.

Ideally, you should eat tempura using CHOPSTICKS, but a fork or fingers will do just as well.

WARNING Do not leave the kitchen when the oil is heating or when you are FRYING: the oil may overheat and catch fire while you are out – see CHIP PAN FIRE, FIRE EXTINGUISHERS.

Tenants

*Knowing your rights in
a rented home*

Before you agree to rent any domestic property, make sure you know exactly what is being offered; a shorthold tenancy or lodgings, for example, do not give you the security of tenure afforded to tenancies which come under the Rent Acts and Housing Act.

Council and housing association tenants now normally enjoy some security of tenure under the Housing Acts. Rent and rates payments, repairs, and whether you can keep pets or sublet, should be discussed before you move in.

Council tenants Council tenancy agreements are legal and binding, and, under the Housing Acts, must be made public. They may either take the form of a written contract, or be contained in the housing director's offer of accommodation, according to the particular council's practice. If the rent is payable weekly, the council must give you a rent book. Council rents are payable in advance.

Unless the home is let under special

conditions – for example, to a council employee or homeless person – the possibility of eviction is unlikely, unless you fail to pay rent, severely damage the property, cause a NUISANCE or use your home for unauthorised, illegal or immoral purposes. An EVICTION NOTICE must be in writing and you cannot be evicted unless the council obtains a court order for possession of the premises. The council is responsible only for major repairs and outside maintenance; tenants are expected to look after minor household repairs and inside decoration. The council must inform the tenant in writing about who is responsible for repairs. If the council fails to carry out essential repairs you can:

● Complain to your local councillor.
● Tell the council you will do the repairs. Keep the receipted accounts (as proof of work done), then deduct the cost from your rent payments.
● Contact the local magistrates' court which can order an environmental health officer to inspect the premises. The council may be fined if the premises are found to be unfit.
● Consult a solicitor (see LAWYERS), local law centre or Citizens Advice Bureau, who may help you to start a county court action to enforce essential works.
● Complain to the local government ombudsman – see OMBUDSMEN.

If you want to make improvements at your own expense, the council cannot reasonably refuse and cannot increase your rent because of them – but you must inform the council before you start.

A council tenant can also, on reasonable grounds, exchange his home for a larger or smaller property, or move to a property in another area. This depends on the councils involved and the availability of the properties.

Private tenants Never rent without viewing the premises. Always make sure you know the exact terms of the lease, which may be outlined in a written agreement. Key points to observe are:
● The nature and length of lease. For example, shorthold tenancies, college or university accommodation or premises where the landlord is resident offer less protection from eviction than those fully covered by the Rent Acts.
● Rent and Council Tax payments. If the rent is due weekly, the landlord must provide a rent book specifying the amounts due, and also bearing his name and address, that of his agent, and details of local rent allowances. The Council Tax is usually included in the total rent payment.

If payments are due at longer intervals, ask for receipts if paying in cash; these or the bank's records of cheques made payable to the landlord are the only way you can prove you are the legal tenant if there is no written agreement.

Rent If, after taking the property, you feel you are being overcharged, check with the local Rent Office to see whether a fair rent has already been fixed; if not, you can ask the Rent Office to decide whether you are paying too much. However, you then risk them deciding that the rent is too low. They will advise you on this.

Repairs Make sure everything is in working order before you move in. The lease may require you to 'put in repair' – which means undertaking *all* repairs from the time you become the legal tenant. It may also oblige you to 'yield up in good repair' which means the property must be well maintained at the time that you leave it.

However, unless the tenancy is for longer than seven years, the landlord is responsible by law for the exterior and structure of the building; also for gas and electric fittings, heating and plumbing. You should report any defects to him.

Subletting Short-term agreements usually ban subletting and this is legal and enforceable. Other agreements may forbid it 'without the consent of the landlord' – in which case permission cannot be refused unreasonably, provided the subtenants are responsible people.

Complaints If, for any reason, your landlord fails to satisfy a justified complaint, consult a solicitor or Citizens Advice Bureau.

Tennis elbow
Painful swelling round a joint

Although sometimes caused by sports such as tennis and BADMINTON, tennis elbow is just as likely to result from building work, joinery, KNITTING, or any unaccustomed or repetitive activity of the hand and forearm.

All the forearm muscles are attached to the lower end of the arm bone at the elbow. Repeated or excessive use of the muscles can produce inflammation at the points where they join – over the bone at the outside of the elbow – causing tenderness there and a pain in the forearm that is aggravated by exercise. Even movements such as turning stiff door handles, shaking hands or pouring tea may be painful. The pain often develops gradually and may spread up and down the arm. A similar condition, known as golfer's elbow, causes pain in the forearm and tenderness on the inside of the elbow, which is worse when gripping with the hand.

Without treatment tennis elbow and golfer's elbow can take up to two years to go away. If you think you have either, strap the elbow with an elastic bandage,

rest it, and take an anti-inflammatory painkiller (such as ibuprofen), available from a chemist. If there is no improvement, consult your DOCTOR. He will check that the pain is coming from the elbow, not from another cause such as a trapped nerve in the neck, elbow or wrist. He may prescribe stronger anti-inflammatory painkillers, inject the tender spot with hydrocortisone and a local anaesthetic, or arrange a course of physiotherapy. In severe cases, the arm may be put in plaster for up to six weeks.

No matter how painful tennis or golfer's elbow may be, it almost always clears up without lasting effects. See also SPRAINS AND STRAINS.

Tennis rackets
Choosing and repairing them

The most important factors in choosing a racket are grip size and weight, then head size and composition. Make your choice on the basis of 'feel'. If possible, find a specialist tennis shop or a sports shop that has demonstration rackets you can try out on a court; you normally have to pay a deposit on the rackets. Buy the one that feels most comfortable.

The grip circumference of adults' rackets ranges from 108mm (4¼in) to 120mm (4¾in); for juniors, a 100mm (4in) grip is usually the most suitable.

The weight of a racket is indicated by the letters L (light), LM (light-medium), M (medium) or T(top). A light racket is easier on the arm and more manoeuvrable for the beginner.

The head size varies from 477cm² (74sq in) for very young children to 710cm² (110sq in) for adults. The larger area makes it easier to hit the ball on the strings, but the medium size 548-580cm² (85-90sq in) has greater power.

Rackets made of wood are scarce now, and frames of aluminium or compression-moulded graphite composites, or injection-moulded graphite are used. Their advantage is that they do not warp, and as they are hollow they are even better than wood for absorbing vibrations.

Rackets are pre-strung to the manufacturer's recommendation – from 18 to 20kg (40 to 45lb) for juniors and 24-27kg (53-60lb) for adults – but there is no hard-and-fast rule.

Stringing The stringing and tensioning of non-wood rackets is best done by a shop, as specialist equipment is needed. But you can repair broken strings in a wooden racket at home, provided the repair does not involve more than six strings and an exact tension figure is not vital for your particular racket.

The new strings, either gut or synthetic fibre, are fitted in one continuous piece. The racket must be held in a vice

TENNIS RACKETS

Restringing a racket

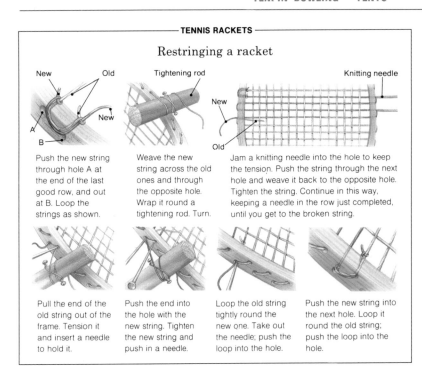

Push the new string through hole A at the end of the last good row, and out at B. Loop the strings as shown.

Weave the new string across the old ones and through the opposite hole. Wrap it round a tightening rod. Turn.

Jam a knitting needle into the hole to keep the tension. Push the string through the next hole and weave it back to the opposite hole. Tighten the string. Continue in this way, keeping a needle in the row just completed, until you get to the broken string.

Pull the end of the old string out of the frame. Tension it and insert a needle to hold it.

Push the end into the hole with the new string. Tighten the new string and push in a needle.

Loop the old string tightly round the new one. Take out the needle; push the loop into the hole.

Push the new string into the next hole. Loop it round the old string; push the loop into the hole.

ies to knock down all tenpins, he scores a 'spare'.

For a strike he scores ten points and a bonus equal to the number of pins he knocks down in his next two deliveries; for a spare, he gets ten points and a bonus equal to the number of pins he knocks down in his next delivery. A player who scores a strike in the tenth frame bowls two extra balls; when a spare is scored in the tenth frame a third ball is bowled.

In a ten-frame game a player who bowls 12 strikes in succession makes the maximum score of 300 points. A score of 120, however, is very good for a beginner; and a player who regularly achieves 170 is good enough for serious competitive play.

The ball should fit your fingers comfortably. Check with one of the bowling-centre staff to get a correct fit.

To find out about competitions or bowling alleys nearest you, contact the British Tenpin Bowling Association, 114 Balfour Road, Ilford, Essex IG1 4JD.

See also SKITTLES; TABLE SKITTLES.

by the shaft (remember to protect the shaft with a thick cloth).

To tension a new string, make a tightening rod by fixing two screws (slightly staggered) into opposite sides of a piece of broom handle. Trap the end of the string under the 'loop' between two adjacent holes.

Handle Most sports shops stock adhesive tape for repairing a worn handle-grip. On some rackets the end of the grip tape is held by a strip of narrow adhesive wound round the shaft. If a tack is used, take care not to damage the shaft when removing and replacing the tack.

Remove the old tape. Overlap the spirals of the new tape slightly.

Tenpin bowling

Playing a popular indoor game

Tenpin bowling – rolling a heavy ball to knock down pins – can be played by individuals or teams. The smooth wooden lane on which it is played is 1.06m (42in) wide and 19.16m (just under 63ft) long, with an additional approach area of at least 4.5m (15ft). The pins are bottle-shaped and 380mm (15in) tall. The balls have a thumb and two finger holes; they should not weigh more than 7.26kg (16lb) or have a circumference of more than 690mm (27in).

The pins are set in a triangle at one end of the lane, with the apex towards the player, who is positioned at the other end. Markers on the lane floor help the

bowler to aim. If a player's foot crosses the foul line when rolling the ball, he commits a foul, and any pins he knocks down are discounted. For fallen pins to count, the ball must go direct from hand to pins without bouncing off pins lying in the gutter.

The game is played in ten 'frames', or turns, and each player has two deliveries per frame. A point is awarded for every pin knocked down. If a player knocks all ten pins down in one delivery he scores a 'strike'; but if it takes him two deliver-

Tents

Choosing, looking after and repairing them

Tents are available in a variety of shapes and sizes, from simple BIVOUAC TENTS for a quick shelter to expensive types that fold out from a purpose-built car trailer. Many types have clear polythene or PVC windows, with overflaps that zip or roll up, and a porch or side awning. Larger models often have several compartments.

The main types are ridge tents, dome and tunnel tents and frame tents (see

TENPIN BOWLING

Knocking down the pins to win

In tenpin bowling, each player in turn rolls two balls down a lane of polished wood in an attempt to knock down the pins. If a bowler puts a foot over the foul line, the electronic eye detects it and the score from that ball is discounted.

Indicator board It shows which pins are still up. Flashing X means a strike (all pins down).

Foul line

Ball return

Ridge, dome and frame tents; how they can be used

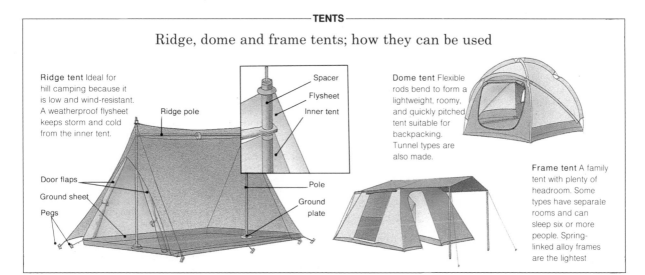

Ridge tent Ideal for hill camping because it is low and wind-resistant. A weatherproof flysheet keeps storm and cold from the inner tent.

Ridge pole

Spacer

Flysheet

Inner tent

Dome tent Flexible rods bend to form a lightweight, roomy, and quickly pitched tent suitable for backpacking. Tunnel types are also made.

Frame tent A family tent with plenty of headroom. Some types have separate rooms and can sleep six or more people. Spring-linked alloy frames are the lightest

Door flaps

Ground sheet

Pegs

Pole

Ground plate

illustration). Also available are trailer tents which stow away inside a trailer for travelling and storage. They usually have fold-out flooring and a cabin section that can be erected quickly for overnight stops. The more expensive ones are equipped with beds, mattresses, curtains, seats, storage lockers and kitchens.

Buying a tent Choose a tent with strong fabric that breathes, such as proofed cotton, PU (polyurethane-coated) nylon or ripstop nylon (which is corded to prevent tearing). Look for an integral ground sheet, mosquito netting, waterproof flysheet, mudwalls (washable panels sewn or bonded to the lower part of the walls), nylon rather than metal zips, and lightweight poles or rods.

Do not buy a tent that is too small. Clothes and cooking equipment can take up a lot of space. For comfortable CAMP-ING, buy a three-person tent for two people, or a six-person tent for four.

For a BACKPACKING or BICYCLE TOURING holiday, choose a tent that will pack up small and will be light to carry, for example, a bivouac, small ridge, dome or tunnel tent.

Looking after a tent Before you go camping with a new tent, practise erecting and dismantling it. Try to arrive at camp sites before nightfall – you are less likely to damage your tent if you put it up in daylight.

Before each camping trip, set up your tent and inspect it for holes and tears and mildew – see MILDEW AND MOULD. Many tent manufacturers produce repair and spare-part kits – see also EYELETS AND GROMMETS. Apply waterproof sealant to both sides of seams, allowing plenty of time for it to dry out and the smell to clear – see SEALANTS.

Take ripstop nylon repair tape, a tube of seam sealant and some ready-proofed

patches (all available from camping shops) with you on a camping trip. Pack beeswax or a stick of lip salve for sealing small leaks where no hole is visible.

● When pitching your tent, first clear the site of sharp sticks and stones that could puncture the ground sheet. Put pieces of cardboard or other packing under the feet of chair legs and camp beds, to avoid tearing or otherwise damaging the ground sheet.

● Do not park your car with the exhaust pointing towards the tent – exhaust fumes can scorch the fabric, as well as pollute the air.

● Never place STOVES or gas lamps near a tent wall or on a ground sheet. Do not cook inside a tent unless it has a VENTILATION flap in the roof and the stove is set on bare ground.

● If possible, pack up your tent only when it is dry. The best way to dry a tent is to erect it with the fabric stretched tight. If you hang it to dry with the fabric unstretched, it may shrink. If you do have to pack a tent when it is wet, be sure to erect it and allow it to dry out within the next two days.

● CONDENSATION often forms inside tents at night, unless there is adequate ventilation. Air the tent during the day to dry it and prevent mildew.

● Store your tent in a dry, light, airy place. Bring it out and air it occasionally during the winter.

Repairing a hole Mend small holes and tears temporarily by sticking ripstop nylon tape over them. Cover larger holes and tears with a temporary patch, sticking down the edges with ripstop nylon tape. Always patch on the inside, except near or over seams, and never use pins to hold patches in place.

To make a permanent repair, sew on a ready-proofed patch, using polyester thread and a fine, long sewing needle.

Cut the patch about 50mm (2in) larger than the hole all round, then hemstitch it over the hole (see HEMS) on the inside of the tent fabric, making small stitches close together. Do not pin the patch in place first; this punctures the fabric unnecessarily. From the outside, make a short diagonal cut from each of the four corners of the hole then turn the fabric under to give a hem about 13mm ($\frac{1}{2}$in) deep all round. Hemstitch the folded edges to the patch, wax the stitching, and treat the edges of the patch with seam sealant.

For a tear beside a seam, cut the patch to cover the adjacent seam as well as the torn area. Sew the patch on the outside (with edges folded under) to outer seam edges. Cut, turn in and hemstitch the tear on the inside.

Fitting new springs Spring-linked metal poles have a clip at one end of the spring and a connecting chain and clip at the other. Replacement springs are sold in packs with a spring-inserting tool. Make sure you buy the right size.

Pull out the damaged spring with pliers. Compress the clip at the chain end of the new spring and push it into the narrower of the two tubes. Then use the inserter to push it down until the spring touches the tube end.

Compress the other clip and push it into the larger tube. Push it down with the inserter until it is completely hidden.

Reproofing If small areas leak, you can spray them with an aerosol reproofer. At least once every three years it is advisable to reproof the whole tent. To do so, lay the tent flat, outside up. Dip a broad brush, such as a whitewash brush, into water then into a can of reproofer and brush on firmly. Allow the solution to dry, then apply wax sealant to the outside of all seams, working it in well.

Textured coatings

*Applying a raised-pattern finish to
a wall or ceiling*

A textured finish on a wall or ceiling not
only hides a poor surface but also fills
any fine cracks. If you decide to apply
one, look on it as a permanent decoration
because it is very hard and messy to
remove.

Make sure the surface to be coated is
dry, clean and grease-free. Remove all
loose and flaking paint or old distemper – see DISTEMPER REMOVAL; PAINT
STRIPPING.

Apply texturing compound thickly
with a paint roller – either a shaggy pile
type or a textured foam sleeve – see
PAINTBRUSHES, PADS AND ROLLERS.

If you use a shaggy pile roller, you will
also need something to stipple or pattern
the surface after applying the coating,
such as a sponge, a stippling brush or a
plasterer's comb.

Whichever method you use, before
tackling a large area, experiment on a
sheet of hardboard until you get the
effect you want.

If you find the coating is pulled up
into points as you apply it, dab over the
surface with a damp sponge to smooth it
down a little before the compound sets.

Once the coating has dried, decorate
with emulsion paint, applied by brush or
by shaggy pile roller – see PAINTS.

Removing textured finishes Empty
the room before you start, and cover
the floor with a layer of old newspapers.
Many old textured finishes contain
asbestos fibres, so never sand them down.

Hold a steam wallpaper stripper
against the surface – see WALLPAPER
REMOVAL. When the coating has softened,
remove it with a scraper.

The alternative is to use a textured
paint remover – a chemical stripper
made especially for textured coatings.
Wear protective gloves and goggles and
apply it thickly with a brush, spatula or
plasterer's float. Leave it for about half
an hour before stripping with a broad-
bladed scraper.

Thatching

*Care and repair of a straw or reed
roof*

If you are considering buying your dream
cottage with a thatched roof, have it
checked by a qualified thatcher recommended by the Thatching Advisory
Services Ltd., 29 Nine Mile Ride,
Finchampstead, Berks RG11 4QD. Replacement of a thatched roof could cost
thousands of pounds.

You can make minor repairs – not
extensive ones – to areas within reach
from a ladder, but do not go on the roof –

thatch is easily destroyed. Be sure to use
the correct materials – the NSMT can
advise you.

Fitting new rods and spars Thatch is
held in place by horizontal rods made of
hazel branches split into strips about
13mm (½in) in diameter and between
610mm (2ft) and 1.8m (6ft) long. The rods
are anchored by spars positioned about
every 150mm (6in) along the rods.

Where you find damaged rods, pull
out the spars far enough to release the
damaged pieces. Cut new rods from hazel
branches, position them where the old
rods were, and refasten with new spars.

A spar is a piece of hazel 610mm long

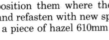

Repairing a thatched roof

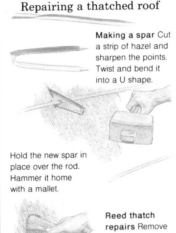

Making a spar Cut
a strip of hazel and
sharpen the points.
Twist and bend it
into a U shape.

Hold the new spar in
place over the rod.
Hammer it home
with a mallet.

**Reed thatch
repairs** Remove
loose reed and
insert a bundle of
cut reed as far as
possible.

Pack the hole with
new reed. Trim the
ragged edges flush
with the old, using
secateurs.

**Straw thatch
repairs** Remove
loose straw. Hook
up some straw
bent into a U shape
round a spar.

Push the spar and
straw into the hole,
hold a batten on
the spar and
mallet it home.
Trim the ends.

and about 13mm wide, with the ends
sharpened to points, then twisted and
bent into a U shape.

Small holes If the thatch is of straw,
pull out any loose material, then plug
the hole with straw bent into a U shape.
If the roof has reed thatch, clean out the
loose reed and pack it with lengths of
cut reed.

Emergency patching Where damage is
extensive, make an emergency patch by
inserting heavy gauge polythene sheet
over the damaged area to keep out the
weather until a thatcher can be
employed. Bear in mind that thatchers
are usually very busy, and you may have
to wait months.

Netting Wire-netting – used to prevent
birds and mice nesting in the thatch –
usually lasts from 10 to 15 years, but
check it annually for signs of rusting
away. You can replace any which is
within reach from a ladder, but if damage
is extensive, call in a thatcher.

Cut out the damaged wire with wire
cutters, then cut a patch of new wire of
the same gauge and mesh size to overlap
by at least 100mm (4in) all round. Tie the
new netting to the old with lengths of
galvanised wire every 150mm (6in), pressing the wire ends down into the thatch.
Hook the loose ends around the edges of
the new wire into the old with long-nosed
pliers, and at the eaves bend the new
netting over the old and shape it by hand
to match the angle of the eaves. To finish
the shape, lay a length of batten (see
BATTENS) on the wire along the top edge
of the eaves then hammer lightly along
the netting below with a mallet before
fastening the old and new wire together.

Thawing food

Defrosting it safely

The best way to thaw frozen food is on
one of the open shelves in a refrigerator
(see REFRIGERATORS), and in its original
wrapper. Allow eight to nine hours per
450g (1lb) for meat and three to four
hours per 450g for poultry. A 450g package of fruit takes six to eight hours.

To thaw meat, fish or poultry more
quickly, immerse it in cold water (in its
plastic bag). This method takes about
one-eighth of the refrigerator time. Some
foods can be thawed safely at room temperature; fruit thaws in two to four
hours, bread in three to four hours, and
cakes and sandwiches in two to four
hours. An even faster method of defrosting is to unwrap it and put it in a microwave oven, set on *Low* or *Defrost* – see
MICROWAVE COOKING.

Once thawed, use the food immediately. Do not refreeze thawed food.

Thermometers

Using different types

The commonest type of thermometer is a sealed, thin glass tube with a bulb at one end containing mercury. As the mercury expands or contracts with heat or cold, it moves along the calibrated tube. This type of thermometer is used for measuring body heat – see TEMPERATURE.

Glass thermometers used for measuring ambient temperatures – the temperature of the surrounding air – may also be filled with mercury, or with coloured alcohol.

Another type, the bimetallic thermometer, has a dial scale with a pointer. The pointer is connected to the end of a coil. As the outer metal expands or contracts, it alters the curvature of the coil and thus deflects the pointer along a calibrated scale. Such thermometers are often used in conjunction with aneroid BAROMETERS.

To get accurate readings from an outdoor thermometer, locate it out of direct sunlight and away from heat generated by the house.

Fix an indoor thermometer to an inside wall, away from draughts or heat.

In GREENHOUSES you can use a thermometer for measuring the ambient temperature. A soil thermometer can be used in a cable-heated propagator, garden frame or greenhouse bed.

A cooking thermometer accurately tells when a joint or jam is ready – see ROASTING MEATS; JAM MAKING.

Thermostats in cars

Checking and changing a faulty thermostat

If your car engine takes a long time to warm up, or if it overheats quickly, the cause could be a faulty thermostat.

In most cars the thermostat is under a domed housing at the front end of the cylinder head. The housing is connected directly to the top radiator hose. Sometimes the thermostat is in the hose.

For a quick and easy test of the thermostat, start the engine from cold and then put your hand on the top hose to check its temperature.

If the hose begins to get warm almost immediately, the thermostat is stuck open; if the hose stays cool when the engine is at normal operating temperature, the thermostat is stuck in the closed position.

Ideally the hose should start to warm up after about three minutes; if it takes longer than that, the thermostat may be working sluggishly.

To remove a thermostat, first partly drain off the coolant (see ANTIFREEZE; RADIATOR FLUSHING) so the level is lower than the thermostat housing.

Remove the hose and then the nuts or bolts securing the thermostat housing. If it does not lift off easily, tap it gently with a piece of wood – do not try to prise it off with a screwdriver.

Lift out the thermostat – again it may need a gentle tap. It should be in the closed position, with the coil spring under the bellows fully extended. If it is closed, and you want to check that it opens correctly, suspend it in a pan of water with a cook's thermometer (see THERMOMETERS) and heat the pan. The thermostat should open within three or four degrees of the temperature marked on its rim.

You can buy a new thermostat from a garage or car accessory shop. Before fitting it, block the hole in the cylinder head with a piece of rag to prevent debris falling in, then scrape away all traces of the old gasket from both the housing and cylinder head.

Remove the rag from the hole. Insert the new thermostat. Smear non-setting gasket sealing compound on both sides of the new gasket and fit it to the cylinder head with the thermostat housing.

Tighten the housing bolts or nuts alternately, a little at a time, to avoid distorting the housing. Do not overtighten. Refit the top hose.

Top up the cooling system and run the engine. Check for leaks round the housing and the hose. Let the engine cool, then repeat the hose-touching test.

Top hose thermostat Some cars, particularly Renaults, have the thermostat fitted inside the top hose, where it connects to the water pump. To remove

it, disconnect the hose and slacken the hose clip which holds the thermostat in place, then pull out the thermostat. Insert the new one (making sure it is the correct way round), tighten the hose clip and reconnect the hose.

Threading needles

Doing it the easy way

By far the easiest way to thread a needle is to use a needle-threader – a loop of fine wire with a foil grip – which you can buy from a sewing shop for a few pence. Or use a diamond-shaped loop of thin fuse wire.

Push the wire loop through the eye of the needle, slip the end of the thread through the loop, pull it back through the eye, and the needle is threaded.

Push the loop of a needle-threader through the eye of a needle, pass the thread through the loop and pull it through the eye.

Wool Before attemping to thread wool – through a darning needle, for example – fold the end of the yarn round the pointed end of the needle, stretch the folded wool by pulling it and pinch it flat. Slip it off the needle, then pass the flattened fold through the needle's eye.

Threadworms

Countering an irritating infection

The two most frequent causes of anal ITCHING are HAEMORRHOIDS and threadworm infection (enterobiasis). Also called seat worm and pinworm, this type of infection is extremely common and has been recorded since ancient times.

The worms look like threads of white cotton, less than 13mm ($\frac{1}{2}$in) long, and can be seen in the faeces. They live in the lower bowel or other parts of the intestine.

The females prefer to lay their eggs outside the intestine. During the night they emerge from the rectum and lay thousands of minute eggs round the anus and on nightclothes and bed linen, secreting a sticky substance that causes intense itching.

In women, the worms can take up residence in the vagina, causing irritation and slight blood-stained discharge.

Children suffering from threadworms keep scratching their bottoms and often wake up complaining of a painful or

---

THERMOSTATS IN CARS

Removing and testing a thermostat

Thermostat housing

Hose clip

Drain the cooling system partially. Undo the hose clip; ease off the hose.

Thermostat

Remove the housing and lift out the thermostat.

Hang the thermostat in hot water. Note the reading on a cook's thermometer (not touching the pan) when the thermostat opens.

---

itching bottom. Sometimes they also get stomach ache.

Although tiresome and uncomfortable, the infection can be easily and quickly cleared up. See your DOCTOR or chemist, who can recommend anti-infestive drugs for the whole household to prevent the infection going round the family.

To guard further against reinfestation, keep fingernails short and scrub them frequently. If necessary, wear shorts and gloves in bed.

Thrips

Fighting a tenacious garden pest

These minute, sap-sucking insects, popularly called 'thunderflies', are about 1.6mm ($^1/_{16}$in) long and look like elongated black, yellow or green specks.

Thrips puncture leaves and flowers, leaving a tracery of mottling or streaking and black specks on the foliage – so the leaves have a silvery or flecked appearance – and disfiguring white spots or blotches on the petals. Eventually, the leaves and petals turn brown and shrivel up.

As soon as symptoms appear, remove and burn infested blooms and leaves. Treat the rest of the plant with a pesticide – see PESTICIDES.

There are numerous species of thrips, which attack different plants. Here are the most common ones – and ways to tackle them:

Gladiolus thrips These infest the corms, leaves and flowers of gladioli – and sometimes irises, lilies and freesias, too. To prevent thrips overwintering on the corms, dust them with HCH after lifting and again before replanting – see BULBS, CORMS AND TUBERS.

Dust or spray the growing plants thoroughly (the danger period is June to September) with HCH or another suitable pesticide as symptoms appear.

Rose thrips ROSES are particularly prone to thrips in warm, sheltered areas. The flowers may be malformed and the petals covered with insects. Spray them with derris, malathion or dimethoate as symptoms appear.

Pea thrips Broad beans, as well as peas, are attacked – especially during hot, dry weather from June to late summer. Severe attacks stunt plants and inhibit flowering and pod production.

Spray or dust with fenitrothion or malathion as soon as you see symptoms. If need be, repeat after ten days. After applying chemicals, allow two weeks before harvesting.

Other outdoor plants that attract thrips include pinks and carnations, privet and chrysanthemums. Dust or spray with malathion, HCH, derris or nicotine as soon as symptoms appear. Repeat until symptoms vanish.

Greenhouse thrips Cyclamens, carnations, FUCHSIAS, roses and TOMATOES are the chief hosts in GREENHOUSES. Fumigate with nicotine or use derris, dimethoate, malathion or HCH smokes or sprays. Repeat as necessary.

Houseplants Remove spoiled flowers and badly damaged leaves of HOUSEPLANTS. Spray with an appropriate pesticide, such as malathion, and maintain a cooler and more humid atmosphere to discourage rapid breeding.

In each case, continue dusting or spraying until symptoms vanish.

Ticks

Removing safely; taking precautions against

Ticks are blood-sucking creatures, about 6mm ($^1/_4$in) long, that frequent shrubs, ferns and long grass in woods and fields. They attach themselves to animals or humans when they brush against them. Ticks can transmit certain diseases, such as typhus.

Do not try to pull a tick out – you may leave the head embedded and increase the risk of infection. Insecticide spray such as fly-spray or the glowing end of a cigarette or a lighted match held close to the tick's body will make it fall off; alternatively, cover it with cooking oil or light machine oil to close its breathing pores. Wash with soap and apply antihistamine cream.

When walking in country where you know there may be ticks, wear garments that cover legs and arms. If, after being bitten by ticks, a rash appears, accompanied by a fever or nausea, see a DOCTOR immediately.

Tiddlywinks

A game of skill for children and dedicated squidgers

For many people, tiddlywinks comes in the same category as blow football and snakes and ladders, but it also has its serious followers and there are strict rules drawn up by the English Tiddlywinks Association. As a children's game, however, the rules can be simplified to provide lively competition between two or four players.

The game is played on a rectangular mat of convenient size placed on a flat, level surface. In the centre of the mat is the pot, which should have concave sides 38mm ($1\frac{1}{2}$in) high.

The object of the game is to propel plastic discs (winks), into the pot by pressing on their edges (called squidging), with a larger plastic disc (squidger). Each player has six winks of the same colour – blue, green, red or yellow – and a squidger.

The players squidge from the corners of the mat. If there are four players, those sitting diagonally opposite each other play as partners, red partnering blue and green partnering yellow.

To determine who plays first, each player has one squidge at one wink. The wink that lands nearest the pot, or goes into it, wins. If two or more winks are the same distance from the pot, or in it, the players concerned squidge again until a winner emerges.

The winner plays first and the others follow in turn, clockwise round the mat. Each player shoots once at his turn, but gets another shot for potting a wink. The first to pot all his winks (potting out) scores four points.

If a wink lands on top of, or partly covers, another wink, the lower wink is 'squopped' and cannot be played until one player has potted out, when all winks

Squidging winks Press on the edge of the wink with the larger squidger to shoot it into the pot.

are desquopped by moving (manually) the winks that cover them to new positions which are the same distance from the pot. Play continues until all winks are potted; any squopping winks are moved at once during the play after the first player has potted out.

The second player to pot out scores two points, the third one. Partners' points are added together, and one point is transferred from the losing pair to the winning pair.

Tie-backs

Adding an elegant touch to your curtains

Straight or shaped tie-backs are easy to make. They can match the CURTAINS or be in a contrasting colour and material. For an informal appearance there is no need to stiffen the tie-backs, but for a more elegant arrangement – perhaps

Keeping curtains in place

Tie-backs can be simply rectangular, with the corners left square or rounded, or the ends tapered. It is just as easy, though, to shape them into a crescent. Whatever shape the pattern, the method for making is the same.

Size Measure the distance from the hook, around the curtain and back to the hook.

Curved pattern Draw half a crescent on folded paper with the centre at the fold.

Fabric Pin the pattern on the fabric and cut round it leaving a 19mm (¾in) turning allowance.

Interlining Fold the turning allowance over the interlining. Clip the curves and tack.

Lining Pin the lining in place, with allowance turned in, then slipstitch it.

Taking the basic steps

Wash and tie the fabric to be dyed, then dip it into cold water.

Immerse the fabric in dye. Stir for five minutes then leave for the recommended time.

Rinse the fabric until the water runs clear, then untie the bindings.

Unfold the fabric, then iron out the creases while it is still damp.

Marbled effect Crumple the fabric into a ball then tie it crisscross with string.

Stripes Fold and iron the fabric evenly, then tie it at regular intervals with thin string.

---

with full-length velvet curtains in a large window – stiffen them with buckram.

First decide the position of the tie-backs, and screw a decorative hook into the wall (see MASONRY DRILLING; WALL FASTENERS) or window frame each side of the window. Make sure the hooks are at the same level by measuring up from the floor.

Open the curtains fully, slip a tape measure round one curtain, adjust it to the amount you wish the curtain to be gathered in and measure the length of the tie-back. The width can be whatever you prefer, but at least 100mm (4in).

Draw a pattern on stiff paper, making it the length and width of the finished tie-back.

If you want the tie-back to be shaped, draw the pattern on a piece of paper folded in half. Cut through both thicknesses of the paper, following the drawn lines then unfold the paper.

Pin the pattern on the fabric, making sure that it is straight on any design. Cut out the fabric, making it 19mm (¾in) larger than the pattern all round. Cut lining material to the same size.

Cut a piece of interlining fabric to exactly the size of the pattern. You can stiffen it with buckram, cut to the same size and oversewn to it all round the edge.

Tack the interlining to the wrong side of the main fabric (see SEWING), fold the 19mm turning allowance over the interlining and pin it in place, or hold it in place with clothes pegs. Cut V-shaped notches in the allowance along any curved edges and snip off any corners. Tack

and press the turning and sew it in place with herringbone stitching. Remove the tacking.

Place the lining over the interlining right side up, and centre it carefully. Notch the edges where necessary to avoid bulky overlaps. Turn in the edges to finish 6mm (¼in) from the edge of the tie-back. Press and pin the lining in position, or secure it with clothespegs, and sew the lining in place with SLIPSTITCHING.

Sew a small curtain ring at each end of the tie-back, for securing to the hook.

Make the second tie-back in the same way. If the material has a design, make sure the details that will show are the same as those on the first tie-back.

Tie-dyeing

Creating colourful patterns on fabrics

Tie-dyeing is a simple and effective way of creating colourful patterns on fabric. The material is folded, pleated, rolled or twisted, then tied in position and immersed in dye. The folded or tied areas are not touched by the dye, so retain their original colour, but the remainder of the fabric absorbs the dye and is coloured by it. It is also possible to combine tie-dyeing with BATIK.

Lightweight fabrics such as cotton, linen and unbleached silk are best. Non-iron and crease-resistant fabrics are unsuitable. String, sewing thread, raffia, elastic bands and pipecleaners can all be used for tying, or you can knot the material itself. Pleasing patterns can be made by tying or sewing in small objects such as pebbles, buttons, milk-bottle tops or dried peas.

Natural, synthetic, hot-water and cold-water dyes are all suitable (see DYEING) but use only cold-water dyes if tying in dried peas. The immersion time varies, depending on the dye used, but often no more than 30-60 minutes is needed.

Basic technique Wash the fabric, whether old or new, to remove grease and size (stiffening agent) then iron flat.

Tie the fabric then dye it – see previous page. Soak it for the time recommended by the dye manufacturer. The longer you leave it, the deeper the colour. If a second colour is wanted, unfold, re-tie and repeat the process after rinsing out excess first dye.

How to tie-dye small pieces Use a pencil to mark the place where the material is to be tied. Gather it into a point, push a needle through the pencil mark and leave it inserted.

Hold the material firmly while you tie a 100-125mm (4-5in) length of thread round it in a tight slipknot just below the needle – see KNOTS. Wind the thread round the fabric several times, binding it tightly. Slip the end of the thread through the last loop, pull it tight, then remove the needle and snip off any excess thread. Check that all threads are tight before dyeing.

Ties

How to tie four-in-hand and Windsor knots

The traditional tie knot, sometimes called a four-in-hand, is small and tubular shaped. To tie it:
1 Put the tie round your neck with the wider end on the right and about 250mm (10in) longer than the narrower end.
2 Bring the wide end over and round the narrow end one and a half times, so that it is pointing to the left.
3 Take the wide end up behind the knot and forwards out over it.
4 Tuck the wide end through the crossways loop at the front of the knot, and pull to tighten. The wide end should cover, and be a bit longer than, the narrow end.

Windsor knot This is wide and triangular, and sits more evenly at the throat than the four-in-hand. It is suitable only for a narrow tie made of thin material. To make it, start the tie in the same way as for a four-in-hand but with the wide end even longer:
1 Pass the wider end across the narrower one, half under it, through the loop at

your throat and again out to the front.
2 Pass the wider end to the right then left under the narrow end to enter the loop at your throat from the front.
3 Pass the reversed wide end to the right, and then left across the front of the knot.
4 Bring the wide end upwards through the loop at your throat from behind, tuck it through the crossways loop, and tighten.

See also BOW TIES.

Tight lids and stoppers

Ways and means of removing them

To undo a stuck screw-top lid, try doubling a wide elastic band around the lid to improve your grip (special strap spanners can be bought), or wrap coarse sandpaper round it, abrasive side in, and grip that.

If the lid still refuses to come undone, hold the lid under hot running water.

Small screw-top lids can often be opened using hinge-type nutcrackers or the ridged grip built into kitchen scissors between the finger holes and the blades.

Several inexpensive models of screw-top lid openers are sold in hardware stores.

Glass stoppers To unjam a glass stopper, run hot water over the neck until the stopper is released.

Alternatively, mix 2 parts white spirit, 1 part glycerine and 1 part salt. Apply the mixture between the neck and stopper and leave for a day. Tap the stopper gently with your hand, or a piece of wood wrapped in cloth, to loosen it.

Tile regrouting

Renewing the filling between tiles

Once the grouting between CERAMIC TILES becomes crazed or discoloured, it is best to remove it and apply fresh grouting.

Use a pencil-point tile-cutting tool for scraping out hard grout, but if the grout is fairly soft, use a piece of bent wire or the tip of a small trowel or scraper. Take care not to chip the edges of the tiles.

Once the grout is out, brush away all loose dust with an old toothbrush, then treat the cracks with a proprietary fungicide to prevent mould growth.

The grout may be supplied as a white powder to be mixed with water, or ready-mixed in a tub. Apply it with the squeegee supplied or a piece of sponge. Press it into the cracks and wipe away the surplus with a clean damp sponge. For a neat finish, run a thin piece of dowelling (see DOWELS) along each grout line. Leave until dry, then rub with a soft cloth. Grout is available in a range of colours as well as white.

Timber

Buying softwood in the sizes and grades you need

The term softwood refers to timber cut from conifers such as spruce or pine. Generally speaking, all other timbers are hardwood. Much of the softwood stocked by timber merchants or DIY stores is European redwood and European whitewood.

Redwood – often known as deal or pine – is recognised by its reddish inner heartwood and whitish outer sapwood. Whitewood – called spruce, white pine or white deal – looks lighter than redwood and is all one colour.

Softwood is sold in grades according to its freedom from knots and other blemishes. For making furniture, you may want knot-free timber, whereas wall panelling may be enhanced by well-anchored knots. Consider this when buying.

Timber for load-bearing must be of the stress grade required by the Building Regulations. Ask your timber merchant to advise you on the grade you will need for structural work.

Timber adjusts its moisture content according to the humidity of its surroundings, so timber stored outside for any length of time is not suitable for indoor work, such as furniture making. As the wood dries out it may shrink or warp. Make sure the timber you buy has been kiln-dried to no more than 18 per cent moisture content – just about the content likely in an unheated room. With CENTRAL HEATING, the percentage drops to as little as 10 per cent. It is advisable to buy timber for indoor use two or three weeks in advance, and store it in the conditions in which it will be used, to allow for adjustment of the moisture content.

Timber is usually sold in metric sizes, and for domestic use ranges in thickness from 12mm ($\frac{1}{2}$in) to 75mm (3in) and in width from 25mm (1in) to 225mm (8$\frac{7}{8}$in). It is usually sold in lengths cut to 300mm (about 12in) increments. Keep this in mind when deciding sizes and ordering. For example, if you order 8ft lengths, the nearest metric equivalent is 2.4m (7ft 10in). You would have to buy 2.7m (9ft) lengths.

Timber sizes may be rough sawn or ready-planed – referred to as 'planed all round' (p.a.r.). Planed timber is 3-5mm ($\frac{1}{8}$-$\frac{5}{32}$in) smaller in width and thickness, even though it may be referred to by the rough-sawn size. When making framework, measure the pieces of timber as you use them to get the dimensions correct.

Softwoods are prone to attack by insects and fungus, so for constructional work, especially where DAMP or CONDENSATION may be encountered, always choose pretreated timbers. See also WOOD PRESERVATIVES.

Timesharing

Owning your holiday home part-time; avoiding pitfalls

Timesharing means buying the use of holiday accommodation in Britain or abroad for a specific time of the year, usually for a contracted number of years. Some timesharing schemes are in perpetuity and can be bequeathed. Most timesharers agree to buy one, two or three weeks of the year.

Rules to follow when buying Timesharing has received adverse publicity because of the high-pressure sales tactics employed by some companies.

If you go to a timeshare presentation, do not sign anything without considering carefully what is being offered: exactly what the accommodation is, its running costs, its local amenities and the probable climate during the vacation period you would choose. Legal safeguards should be evident.

It is not unusual to discover that the property on offer is not yet completed. You must, if you decide to buy, know the schedule for completion. You must also be satisfied that your money will be held by a responsible trust fund until the final purchase is made. There are organisations, whose members include developers, consultants and trust funds, that offer such guarantees. They include The Timeshare Council, 23 Buckingham Gate, London SW1E 6LB.

If you have any doubts, get legal advice (see LAWYERS) before signing any documents or paying any money – even a small deposit. Make sure there is a 'cooling off' period that allows you to change your mind and withdraw if you wish. An agreement signed in Britain must contain a cooling-off period; but act quickly if you change your mind. Outside Britain the local law applies. Get all details in writing; talk to existing timeshare owners; shop around and compare the quality and prices of other locations and schemes.

Costs Prices can range from a few thousand pounds up to £15,000 or more, according to the resort and time of year you choose. You also pay a variable maintenance charge during the weeks you spend there – the current average is about £120 per week – which covers local management and operating expenses, refurbishments, and a sinking fund for major repairs.

A further feature of many timeshare deals is membership of an exchange scheme. This allows you to swap weeks or homes with other members, and frequently offers benefits on travel, car hire (see HIRING) and INSURANCE. Membership itself may be free for the first few years, but members have to pay an additional fee each time they use the exchange.

Timesharers are frequently offered attractively priced air travel to their holiday homes; always check that the carriers have proper coverage to offer you appropriate assistance in an emergency – see STRANDED ON HOLIDAY.

A final consideration: your holiday home time may be difficult to resell.

Tipping

Guidelines for being a fair tipper

Tipping is essentially a gesture of thanks for good services rendered, not usually an obligation. But it is widely accepted that gratuities are paid for certain services – to a waiter, hairdresser or taxi driver, for example.

The practice differs somewhat from country to country, but as a rough guide anyone who gives you a personal service can be tipped at your discretion. Conversely, a tip can be withheld as a sign of disapproval – but you should be prepared to explain why.

Restaurants Check your bill to see whether a service charge has been added before giving a tip. If it has not, 10 per cent of the total is acceptable, 12½ per cent is very adequate and 15 per cent denotes exceptional service.

There is no need to tip if the service charge has been included, but a small amount can be left to express appreciation. Your tip may or may not go direct to whoever served you; some restaurants insist that all tips are pooled.

Hotels Porters, waiters, chambermaids and shoe-shiners can be tipped a few pounds for their services at the end of a stay of a week or two, even if the hotel has a fixed service charge. If the hotel does not make a service charge and you are uncertain how much to give, add 10 per cent to the bill when you leave and ask the manager or receptionist to distribute it equitably among the staff. You do not tip a chef or manager.

Hairdressers A tip of 10 per cent is perfectly acceptable. As well as tipping the stylist, a woman usually gives a smaller tip to the person who has washed her hair.

Taxis Wherever you are, taxi drivers tend to expect a tip – 10 to 15 per cent is acceptable, and more can be given for courteous service such as helping you to lift luggage in and out of the taxi.

Cloakrooms and powder rooms Where there is an attendant, he or she will often have the sort of tip expected displayed in coins in a saucer. Tip the same amount or slightly less than what is shown.

Toasters

Some simple repairs when a toaster goes wrong

A few home repairs are possible on a toaster, but if the pop-up mechanism is faulty or the element breaks, get the toaster repaired by a qualified repairer. Unplug a toaster from the mains socket before carrying out any repairs.

No power Check the plug for loose connections – see PLUGS. If they are all right, fit a new 13amp cartridge fuse. If this does not restore the power, unplug the toaster and check the connections inside the toaster. Remove the screws holding the casing, lift off the casing and ensure that the connections are not loose. If the connections are all right, test the flex for continuity – see CIRCUIT TESTING. If the flex is faulty, replace it with one of the correct rating – see ELECTRIC WIRING.

Intermittent power Check for loose connections or damaged flex as described above.

Safety check After repairing and reassembling a toaster, check with a circuit tester to see that the casing is earthed and that there are no SHORT CIRCUITS between the casing and either of the flex wires – the brown and blue leads. Carry out the checks with the bread carriage down and in the locked position.

WARNING If toast gets stuck in the toaster, never attempt to free it with a knife or other metal utensil. First unplug the toaster, then use a wooden spoon or spatula to dislodge the toast.

Toasts

Making short speeches while raising a glass

Informal or formal toasting can take place during any celebration. Those gathered raise their glasses and drink to the health, happiness or success of a person or project. If the person is present, everyone else will usually stand, raise their glasses and take a sip; the recipient should remain seated and not drink until the toast is completed.

During a formal dinner, toasts are made at the end of the meal, or towards the end, and may be announced by a toastmaster.

The first toast – before which smoking is not usually permitted – is the loyal toast to the Queen. Subsequent toasts may be preceded by a short speech which can be humorous, serious or sentimental, according to the occasion – see PUBLIC SPEAKING.

If you have to propose a toast, make sure everyone has a drink to toast with, and begin by addressing the company as appropriate.

At general celebrations, a toast can be proposed by anyone in a fairly informal way. But there is a traditional procedure for WEDDINGS.

Toboggan
Building a sturdy sledge

The toboggan illustrated below is sturdily designed and big enough for two children to ride on together.

Runners Cut two runners from 22mm ($\frac{7}{8}$in) TIMBER softwood, each 1250mm (49$\frac{1}{4}$in) long and 170mm (6$\frac{3}{4}$in) wide. On the bottom of each runner, cut the back end to a 70 degree angle. Curve the front end as if part of a circle with a radius of 175mm (6$\frac{7}{8}$in). Curve the other three corners as if part of a circle with a radius of 25mm (1in).

Cut a 16 × 2mm ($\frac{5}{8}$in × $\frac{1}{16}$in) metal strip into two 1430mm (56$\frac{1}{4}$in) lengths. Drill countersunk screw holes as shown (see also DRILLING) and round off the ends of the strips.

Rails and footrest Cut four lengths of 22mm thick softwood 530mm (20$\frac{7}{8}$in) long and 70mm (2$\frac{3}{4}$in) wide, for the rails and footrest. Cut double tenons and twin mortises in the rails and runners as illustrated. Round off the edges of the footrest – see SAWS AND SAWING; WOODWORKING JOINTS.

Glue the runners, rails and footrest together (see GLUING) and clamp them, using adjustable clamps or simple tourniquet clamps – see CHAIR REPAIRS. When the glue is set, screw steel angle BRACKETS to the rails and runners for added strength. Plane the tenons flush with the runners (see PLANING), then use a coarse SANDING block to smooth the ends. Drill two holes in the footrest 75mm (3in) from the runners to take a towrope. Bend the metal strips to fit the runners, then, starting on top at the front, screw the strip in place.

Platform Cut this from 16mm ($\frac{5}{8}$in) exterior grade PLYWOOD; it should measure 780 × 480mm (30$\frac{3}{4}$ × 18$\frac{7}{8}$in). Position the platform centrally on the rails. Fix it to the rails with 32mm (1$\frac{1}{4}$in) countersunk SCREWS; screw through the rails into the platform.

Paint the woodwork (see PAINTING EXTERIORS) or give it a natural finish – see VARNISHING. Thread in the towrope and knot it under the footrest.

Toddy
A traditional recipe for a warming winter drink

Scotsmen swear by toddy as a remedy for a bad head cold – it may not cure the cold but it alleviates the misery.

First warm a tumbler, then put in three or four lumps of sugar, or 2 teaspoons of granulated sugar. Stand a metal spoon in the tumbler before you half-fill with boiling water. When the sugar has dis-solved, fill up the tumbler with whisky and stir (with a silver spoon according to tradition). If necessary, repeat the dose.

A slice of lemon can also be added and a spoonful of honey is sometimes used instead of sugar. Rum can be used instead of whisky.

Toffee apples
A children's treat on a stick

To make eight toffee apples you will need eight small, crisp eating apples, eight wooden skewers and a saucepan of home-made toffee.

Thoroughly wash and dry the apples, remove the stalks and push a wooden skewer into the centre of each apple.

Ingredients (for toffee)
225g (8oz) soft brown sugar
25g (1oz) unsalted butter
1 tablespoon golden syrup
5 tablespoons water
1 tablespoon vinegar

Put all the ingredients in a heavy-based saucepan and heat the mixture gently, until the sugar has dissolved. Bring to the boil and cook fairly briskly, until a drop of the mixture put in a bowl of cold water separates into threads cleanly.

Dip each apple first into the toffee, twisting it round to coat it evenly, then into cold water to set the toffee. Stand the apples on a greased or non-stick tray and leave until the toffee has set fully. Then wrap each apple in Cellophane or plastic film.

Toilet training
When and how to start it

Patience, perseverance and a measure of child psychology are needed in training a young child to use the toilet. The best time to introduce a child to the pot is when he or she is old enough to under-stand its purpose – there is no point in attempting training before the child is capable of learning, and sitting a baby on the pot immediately after a feed merely takes advantage of a natural reflex.

At about 2 to 2$\frac{1}{2}$ years, a child begins to develop an interest in learning, and also to have control of bodily functions. The best method of teaching is praise each time the child uses the pot success-fully, and no comment for failure.

Days and weeks may pass before training succeeds; do not get over anxious, and persevere with the method described. Failure to learn bowel control is almost always confined to children subjected to excessive training.

If after a time the child shows no sign of learning, abandon training for a

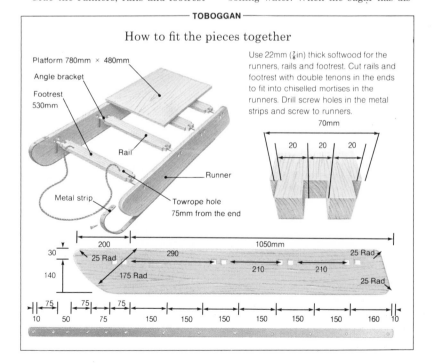

─ **TOBOGGAN** ─

How to fit the pieces together

Platform 780mm × 480mm
Angle bracket
Footrest 530mm
Rail
Metal strip
Runner
Towrope hole 75mm from the end

Use 22mm ($\frac{7}{8}$in) thick softwood for the runners, rails and footrest. Cut rails and footrest with double tenons in the ends to fit into chiselled mortises in the runners. Drill screw holes in the metal strips and screw to runners.

70mm
20 20 20

200   1050mm
30   25 Rad   290   25 Rad
140   175 Rad   210   210   25 Rad
75   75   75
10   50   75   150   150   150   150   150   150   160   10

month, then try again. Avoid scolding, mocking or bribery with treats – they are more likely to make things worse than better. Most children will be clean by the age of three and dry at night by three and a half.

Tomatoes

*Growing your own crop
from seed*

You can grow tomatoes indoors or outside, but only certain varieties are suitable for outdoors – check on the seed packet when you buy. Seeds sown in early spring should provide ripe fruit in late July (indoors), August or September.

Raising seedlings Start seeds in the warmth in a propagator or in seed boxes on a warm windowsill in late March or early April – see PROPAGATING PLANTS. Prick out the strongest, straightest seedlings into individual 75mm (3in) pots filled with JOHN INNES COMPOST (No 2 potting) once they have formed the first pair of leaves – probably about ten days after sowing. Hold a seedling by its leaves when potting. Keep them moist.

Growing outdoors Prepare a bed in a sunny, sheltered spot, digging in plenty of well-rotted manure or COMPOST – see SOIL PREPARATION. Add one of the general FERTILISERS a fortnight before planting out. In mid or late May transfer to a covered COLD FRAME on a warm day. Gradually open the frame a little more each day, closing it at night. Eventually it can be left open 24 hours.

Plant the tomatoes in the prepared bed once there is no danger of frost. Remove the plants from their pots by inverting and tapping the rim (see page 361). Plant and water in. Insert a 1.5m (5ft) cane firmly in the ground beside the plant. Space plants 460mm (18in) apart and rows 760mm (2ft 6in) apart.

Protect the plants from slugs (see SLUGS AND SNAILS) until they are well established. If a prevailing wind strikes the plot, rig up a shelter on the windy side – using canes and transparent plastic sheeting, for example – to protect the plants for a week or two.

Growing in a greenhouse Prepare a bed in a greenhouse border, digging in plenty of peat or straw – see GREENHOUSE GARDENING.

Plant out the seedlings in a cold greenhouse about mid-April, either in the prepared bed, in bags (see below) or in rings – open-ended pots on a 150mm (6in) deep bed of aggregate such as washed gravel or coarse vermiculite. Buy the rings from a garden supplier or staple roofing felt into cylinders about 230mm (9in) high and 230mm across.

Stand the rings on the aggregate bed about 460mm (18in) apart and fill them with No 3 compost, setting out the young plants into the compost. Water thoroughly after planting, but after that water into the aggregate only, keeping it moist.

Growing in bags Garden suppliers sell plastic growing bags for tomatoes. The bags are filled with peat and all necessary nutrients. Plant the seedlings in holes cut in the bag.

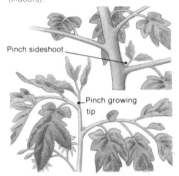

── TOMATOES ──

Where to pinch off

Pinch off all sideshoots before they are 25mm (1in) long. Pinch off the growing tip two leaves above the fourth truss (outside) or the sixth (indoors).

Pinch sideshoot

Pinch growing tip

Tending and harvesting plants Tie each plant to its support with raffia or garden twine as it grows. Nip out sideshoots from leaf axils as they appear. Water regularly to keep the soil moist.

After fruit has formed on the first truss of flowers, feed the plants with liquid fertiliser once a week. In August pinch off the growing point two leaves above the top truss – see illustration.

Pick the tomatoes as they ripen. If any outdoors are still green when autumn frosts become likely, pick them and ripen them in a drawer.

Tomato sauce

*Making your own sauce using
fresh fruit*

Fresh, homemade tomato sauce makes an excellent accompaniment to PASTA, RICE, meat or vegetables. The flavouring suggested here can be varied by adding red wine and lemon juice, or by using fresh parsley and basil or basil and marjoram instead of oregano. This recipe is for four to six people:

Ingredients
900g (2lb) ripe tomatoes

2 cloves garlic, peeled and chopped
2 tablespoons vegetable cooking oil
1 level teaspoon sugar
1 level teaspoon dried oregano
Salt and freshly ground black pepper

Nick the skins of the tomatoes with a sharp knife. Plunge them in boiling water, and as soon as the skins begin to crack quickly remove the tomatoes, cool them and peel them. Chop the flesh coarsely.

Fry the onion and garlic gently in the oil for five minutes until soft, then add the tomatoes. Stir in the sugar, oregano and seasonings to taste. Cover the pan and cook the mixture over a gentle heat for 30 minutes.

Allow the sauce to cool slightly and then sieve or liquidise it. Reheat the sauce and serve quickly.

Toothache

*Getting relief from the pain until
you see a dentist*

Pain in the TEETH, jaws or gums is usually a symptom of tooth decay, gingivitis or other dental disorder. The pain may be constant, throbbing or intermittent and is often made worse by food or drink.

Sometimes, however, it may result from a disorder such as sinusitis or neuralgia – if the pain persists after the disorder clears up, you should consult your dentist.

If chewing causes the pain, the tooth may be fractured, but with prompt attention it may be saved. If there is swelling as well as pain, the cause may be an abscessed tooth. This needs urgent treatment, especially if the swelling has spread to your face and neck.

It may not be possible to see a dentist right away, but there are measures you can take to ease the pain in the meantime.

● Paint the tooth with oil of cloves, a surface anaesthetic available from most chemists; or pack the cavity area with cotton wool soaked in oil of cloves.

● Rinse the mouth from time to time with a solution of antiseptic mouthwash and warm water. This will encourage an abscess to burst and will also wash away the pus.

● Take aspirin or other painkillers in the doses recommended by the manufacturer.

● Hold a covered hot-water bottle or heated pad against the affected side of the face.

After dental work you may get a painful reaction when eating or drinking. This usually passes within a few hours, but it can help to rinse your mouth with warm, salted water after eating or drinking.

Torches

Choosing and looking after them

There are three kinds of torch – small, flat, pocket or pen-size types, cylindrical, hand-held ones; and large reflector hand lamps with carrying handles. The light from small torches is generally low, and they are for occasional, emergency use; a robust cylindrical torch is best for household uses.

Many torches are available with knock-proof and waterproof rubber casings and durable bulbs, reflectors and switches. The large reflector-style torches can make effective area or hazard lights and are particularly useful for motoring, CAMPING or caravanning.

Rechargeable torches are also available: they avoid the inconvenience and expense of buying new batteries, but should never be allowed to run down completely, which could damage them beyond repair.

Maintenance If you do not use a torch regularly, test-light it occasionally; contact points may become dirty or corroded, and batteries discharge slowly even when the torch is unused.

Torches usually have a reflector. Do not try to clean it, even with a soft cloth, as the metal surface is easily damaged.

Leaking batteries corrode any metal parts; always remove batteries if the torch is out of use for some time. Corrosion on the battery terminals or at the contact between bulb and spring can usually be removed with fine glasspaper. If the light is not working well, check that these points are in proper contact and that the battery is correctly inserted.

A fading beam usually indicates that the battery needs replacing. If the torch fails to light, suspect a 'blown' bulb. Remove the bulb and hold it up to the light – if there is a break in the filament or the glass is blackened, fit a new bulb.

If it is difficult to determine where the fault lies, remove both battery and bulb, hold the centre connection of the bulb against one terminal and connect the bulb base to the other.

If the bulb fails to light, test the battery with a second bulb; if that also fails to light, buy a replacement battery of the same size and voltage.

If you use bulbs which have a slightly lower rating than that indicated, the beam will remain strong even if the batteries are running low. The higher the bulb rating, the sooner the battery will be exhausted.

Batteries are rated as high-power (HP) and super-power (SP). HP batteries are used with bulbs of more than 0.5amp rating, SP batteries are used with bulbs up to 0.5amp.

The head of some torches is a sealed unit. If the bulb fails you have to fit a complete unit.

Touch-typing

Teaching yourself at home

Typing by touch is using all the fingers of both hands without looking at the keys. It allows you to read what you are typing (and copying) as you do it. Most typewriter keyboards have the letters and figures in the same positions, although some symbols and controls may vary, so once you can touch-type on one machine, you can do it on another.

Sit comfortably in front of the typewriter with your wrists relaxed and your arms bent at a little less than right angles. Place the fingers of your left hand on the home keys (the second row from the bottom) on the letters asdf, and the fingers of your right hand on the keys ;lkj. Use your index fingers to control the keys ghf and j.

Start by using the appropriate fingers to type all the letters in this row, first with the left hand (little finger first) and then with the right. To begin with, type slowly and rhythmically, aiming at accuracy. Speed comes with practice.

Use your thumbs to operate the space bar (used to space between words) after each word, and your little finger to operate the shift key on each side to type the same letters as capitals – see TYPEWRITERS.

When you can confidently and accurately type asdfg ;lkjh without looking at the keys, practise on the third row (qwert poiuy) and the bottom and top rows in the same way – possibly zxcvb $\frac{1}{2}$.,mn and 12345 09876, depending on the machine.

Get a typing manual and practise the exercises in proper sequence. The exercises are designed to introduce use of all the letters of each row. Finally, practise the sentence that includes all the letters of the alphabet – the quick brown fox jumps over the lazy dog.

Tourniquet

Using one in an emergency when treating a bleeding animal

A tourniquet may be used on animals such as CATS or dogs (see also DOG CARE; DOG FIGHTS; PET INJURIES) which are bleeding profusely from a gash or bite. But a tourniquet should be only a temporary measure, used while the animal is being taken to a vet.

Treating the wound Before applying the tourniquet, cover the wound with a clean pad – a piece of cloth or gauze – and bind it on with bandage, or hold it firmly in place.

If the wound is on a limb and a pad will not stop the flow of blood, apply a tourniquet above the wound. Tie a bandage or clean handkerchief round the limb and slide a stick under it. Twist the stick to tighten the bandage, cutting off the flow of blood to the wound below. Loosen the tourniquet for at least a minute every 10-15 minutes, to avoid the risk of gangrene.

Calming the animal Before applying a tourniquet, try to calm and reassure the animal. Even the most placid pet is likely to bite or scratch if it is frightened and suffering pain.

Approach slowly and talk soothingly. Grip the animal firmly and, if possible, get a helper to assist you. With a dog, tie a handkerchief firmly round its muzzle so that it cannot bite.

Try to get the animal onto a smooth surface, such as a kitchen table or linoleum floor, where it will be difficult for it to get a foothold and escape.

Towel rails

Installing and repairing them

Most towel rails are supplied complete with fixing SCREWS which are adequate for attaching the rail to wood, such as the back of a door, but they may not be long enough for wall fixing. If not, change them for longer screws of the same gauge.

With one type of towel rail, the rail and brackets are in one piece. To fix it to a wall, hold the rail in place and mark through one hole. Drill and plug the wall (see MASONRY DRILLING; WALL FASTENERS), then fit a screw. Now use a spirit level and adjust the position of the rail so that it is horizontal, before marking through a hole in the other bracket. Drill and plug; screw in place. Mark the two remaining holes, remove the rail, drill and plug; now screw the rail in place.

With a rail with separate brackets, fix one bracket to the wall using only one screw. Insert the metal tube and check for length. If the rail is too long, remove the tube and cut it to the correct length using a hacksaw – see SAWS AND SAWING. Smooth the end with a file so that it enters the bracket easily.

Re-insert the tube in the fixed bracket, slip the remaining bracket in place, then use the spirit level to make sure that the rail is horizontal. Mark through one of the holes in the unfixed bracket; drill, plug, and secure in place, then remove the rail, mark, drill and plug the remaining holes and screw on the rail.

With another type of rail a metal anchor piece is first fixed to the wall, then the rail bracket is located over it. To simplify locating the holes, most rails of this type include a template which can be held on the wall to mark the hole positions. Again check with a spirit level to ensure that the rail is horizontal.

Drill and plug one hole for each

anchor, and secure both in place. Insert the rail in the brackets, then locate the brackets over the anchors. Remove the brackets and drill and plug the remaining holes. With the brackets and rail in place, tighten the small grub screws located under the brackets. These lock the brackets onto the anchors.

Repair work The most common problem with rails is that the anchorage fails, usually due to the use of screws which are too short. Remove the rail and pull or drill out any remaining wall plugs. Select new screws of the same gauge but at least 19mm (¾in) longer.

Drill the wall deeper at each screw point; insert new, longer wall plugs, then screw the rail back in place.

If plaster has been pulled away, this should be repaired before re-drilling – see PLASTER PATCHING.

Where the original holes were made too large, try to re-locate the rail so that new holes can be drilled and the old ones will be masked by the brackets. If this is not possible, plug the holes with a fibrous plugging compound. Allow it to set, then re-insert the screws.

Towing

Pulling a vehicle out of trouble

Towing may be necessary to move a stranded vehicle, but it can be dangerous unless done properly. If possible, use a purpose-made tow rope, which has loops and attachments for both vehicles (carry one in your car). The towing vehicle should be at least the same weight, size and power as the one to be towed.

A vehicle with automatic transmission can be damaged by towing – the gearbox may overheat because the lubrication pump works only when the engine is running. Check in the car handbook whether towing is advisable.

Fitting a tow rope The maximum distance between the two vehicles should not exceed 4.1m (13ft 6in). Fit the rope to the towing eye brackets on each vehicle, if there are any. If not, use a substantial part of the chassis sub-frame or, if fitted, a tow bar bracket on the towing car.

Do *not* secure the rope to a bumper or to any part of the steering or suspension.

Make sure the rope will not chafe against the car body or damage a number plate or exhaust pipe.

Tie a piece of coloured rag to the rope halfway between the cars, so that it can be seen. You are not obliged to display an 'On Tow' sign on the rear vehicle, but it is safer to do so.

Driving the towing car Before starting, arrange signals with the towed-car driver, in case it is necessary to stop or pull off the road. Switch on your headlights in daylight as a warning to other road users that you are in tow.

Move off very slowly, so that the rope tautens without jerking. Change gear smoothly. More clutch slip than usual is necessary. Because of the extra weight and slow speed, you may find you have to remain in third gear. Although the maximum permitted towing speed is 96km/h (60mph), it is wiser not to exceed about 48km/h (30mph).

Signal well in advance, and take corners as widely as possible, to keep down chafing and strain on the rope. Be particularly careful on downhill stretches – especially if the towed car has servo-assisted brakes, because the engine-operated servo will not be working.

Driving the towed car Turn on the ignition to ensure that the steering lock remains disengaged and the signals can be used. Switch on the lights (if they are working and the battery is not too low). If you have a long way to go, disconnect the ignition coil to prevent it from overheating.

Use the brake as necessary to keep the rope reasonably taut. You will need to brake much more than usual – use the handbrake as well if necessary. If the brakes are servo-assisted, keep the engine running in neutral if possible. If you cannot run the engine, you will need to exert more pressure than usual when braking. The same applies when steering, if the car has power-assisted steering. Without power, the steering will feel heavy, and the wheel difficult to turn.

Toy tank

Making a cotton-reel motor

To make this creeping, turning, climbing toy, you need an empty cotton reel, a used matchstick, a strong rubber band, a short piece of household candle, a sharp knife and a stick or pencil about 100mm (4in) long.

Use the knife to cut notches equally spaced round each end of the cotton reel, to provide grip as the 'tank' moves. Thread the rubber band through the central hole, so that a loop hangs out at each end. Slip a short piece of matchstick (smaller than the reel's diameter) through one loop. Pull the other loop to hold the matchstick tightly against the reel, then fix the match in place with sticky tape.

Cut a 13mm (½in) slice cleanly off the bottom end of the candle. Bore out the centre with a scissor blade to remove the wick and provide a hole through the piece. Thread the free loop of the rubber band through the hole and tie a knot in the band to secure the candle to the reel.

Pull the knot outwards and slip the stick through the rubber band, between the knot and the piece of candle. Rotate the piece of candle firmly against the end of the reel, to coat it with a thin layer of wax, which will help the toy to move more easily.

Finally, twist the band about 20 times by rotating the stick. Set the toy on the ground and it will creep along and also climb over surfaces that it can grip – just like a tank!

Tracking

Recognising some common animal tracks

Mud and snow are good places to find animal tracks, although in snow they soon get enlarged and distorted. Apart from the shape of the footprint itself, look for other clues that help to identify the animal – for example, droppings, the location, and the way it walks, indicated by the position of a series of footprints.

Large tracks Dogs, cats and foxes make similar marks, which show pads and four toes on each foot, but the shape and gait help to distinguish the tracks. Sizes vary widely, dog marks especially, but the paw marks of an adult badger or otter can be 50-60mm (2-2½in) across.

TOY TANK

How to assemble the parts

Cut equally spaced notches round each end of the cotton reel. Use a rubber band to provide the 'power'. Rotate the pencil 20 times to tension the 'motor'.

Pencil
Knot
Rubber band
Notches
Looped end
Matchstick
Candle
Cotton reel

Dogs Their marks often have the toes spread out. The two left paw marks and the two right paw marks are staggered in separate lines.

Cats The paw marks are distinguished by their rounded toes, with no claw marks showing. Sizes are commonly 32-38mm (1¼-1½in) across.

Foxes The two middle toes are close together; the paw marks are in a single line, with hind feet on top of fore feet.

Badgers The marks are broader than they are long, with a wide pad visible. The five toes are almost in a straight row and show claw marks. The feet point inwards, and hind foot marks cover the back of the larger fore foot marks.

TRACKING

Identifying animal tracks

Cat   Dog   Fox

Compare dog tracks with those of a cat and fox – cat's toes are rounder and leave no claw marks; the middle toes of a fox lie closer together.

Dog trail

Fox trail

Study the gait of different animals – dog prints are staggered on both sides of the body line; a fox places one foot in front of another, leaving a single line of prints.

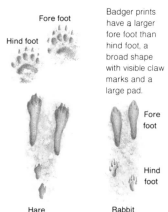

Fore foot

Hind foot

Badger prints have a larger fore foot than hind foot, a broad shape with visible claw marks and a large pad.

Fore foot

Hind foot

Hare   Rabbit

Hare and rabbit tracks are similar but differ in size. The hind feet are in front of the fore feet when the animal is bounding.

Otters The five toes are curved round a pad. Marks of the webbing between the toes may be visible, and also drag marks from the tail. The tracks are usually beside water, but are found only in certain areas (mink tracks, also usually by water, are very similar and now much more common).

Small tracks It is difficult to distinguish the tracks of small rodents such as rats and squirrels. Look for other clues – a rat's tracks, for example, are more likely to be near water, a squirrel's in a wood leading from a tree.

Brown rats The paw marks are long and narrow, with four toes on the fore foot and five on the hind foot, where the two outer toes are virtually at right angles to the centre toes. An adult's hind foot may be about 35mm (1⅜in) long. Water vole tracks are similar but smaller.

Grey squirrels The paw marks have four toes on the fore foot and five on the hind; and are usually in groups spaced about 500mm (20in) apart because of the animal's bounding gait.

Rabbits The tracks have long hind feet – often about 90mm (3½in) – and short, round fore feet. When the rabbit is bounding the hind feet are in front of the fore feet. When it is hopping, the fore feet are in front. This is often clearly visible in snow near woodland and hedges.

Hares The tracks are similar to rabbits' tracks but larger – hind feet can be 150mm (6in) long. They are more likely to be seen in open country, not in woodland.

Moles There are five long-clawed toes on each foot; the fore feet curve inwards as moles tend to walk on the inner side, and only the claw tips show. Often there is a body drag mark between the paw marks.

Stoats and weasels The paw marks have five toes curving round a pad – similar to an otter's, but much smaller. A stoat's may be 22-25mm (⅞-1in) across, a weasel's 10-13mm (⅜-½in).

Trade Descriptions Act

What to do if goods are not as described

The Trade Descriptions Act lays down that goods must be correctly described in all signs, advertising material and labelling that is used.

The Act also strictly controls sale prices. A shopkeeper cannot state that an item has been reduced from, say, £10 to £8 unless the item had been charged at

the higher price for at least 28 consecutive working days in the six preceding months. The shopkeeper is not committing an offence, however, if it is clearly stated on the sale card that the higher price was charged for a shorter period.

Similarly, when a special range of goods is bought for a sale, the shopkeeper must make it clear that these are special purchases, not reduced prices on stock which has been selling in the preceding six months.

The Act demands that goods that have slight defects must be clearly marked as such. If the faults are serious, the item must be described as 'imperfect' or 'substandard'. Seconds must be of merchantable quality and fit for their purpose.

Services The Trade Descriptions Act also covers services, for example, the accommodation offered by a hotel or the facilities advertised by a holiday firm. A hotel advertising that 'all rooms have a sea view' when in fact some overlook the local gasworks is committing an offence under the Act, as is a holiday firm that offers holidays close to a sandy beach when the beach is shingle.

If you think you have been misled, take your complaint to your local council's trading standards department. The Act applies to commercial transactions only, not to goods sold privately. See also SALE OF GOODS.

Travel emergencies

Delayed journey; medical help abroad; lost luggage; if someone dies abroad

If your journey is delayed by bad weather, technical faults or industrial disputes, the airline, ferry company or coach firm you have booked with often provide refreshments and even overnight accommodation during the delay. However, they are not obliged to do so and you cannot claim compensation for the delay. You can claim compensation only under an INSURANCE policy that covers such risks.

You can get travel insurance from travel agents, motoring organisations and insurance companies, and a typical policy will cover medical emergencies (see also STRANDED ON HOLIDAY), loss of luggage or money, and cancellation, as well as delays.

Before travelling abroad, read the DoH leaflet *Health Advice for Travellers*, which tells you which countries offer free or cheap medical treatment. When holidaying in EC countries, you are entitled to basic medical care if you hold an E111 form. This can be obtained by filling out an SA30 leaflet, available from your local social security office. Do it as soon as you know your departure date.

Even if you are visiting a country where most treatment is free – make sure you are insured.

If you are taken ill while abroad (or another member of your party is), go to the nearest hospital. If you are staying in a hotel, contact the reception clerk – most hotels in foreign major cities or resorts have an English-speaking DOCTOR on call.

If you show your insurance policy to the doctor or hospital, you may be able to delay any payment until you get home. If you have to pay on the spot, get a receipt and send it to your insurance company with a claim form. Check with your policy how soon you have to notify them if you need to make a claim – you may have to make a phone call as soon as possible.

Lost luggage If your luggage fails to appear at an airport baggage collection point, first report it to an airport official in the collection area. If it cannot be traced, go to the airline desk immediately and fill in a claims form.

If you are travelling with a holiday firm, their representative at the airport will assist you.

Death abroad If someone you are travelling with dies while abroad, get in touch with the local British consulate or the embassy. The staff will advise you and help you to make arrangements for the funeral, or for bringing the body back to Britain.

Travel sickness

Avoiding that queasy feeling

Many travellers suffer from the effects of travel sickness at some time, whether they go by air, sea, road or rail. The symptoms may include a feeling of NAUSEA, VOMITING, sweating and DIARRHOEA.

They are caused by the movement of a vehicle disturbing the relationship between what the eye sees and what the balance mechanism in the inner ear feels. The eye adjusts to the movement but the ear does not; the resulting 'signals' from eye and ear do not tally.

There is no cure for travel sickness when it strikes, but there are measures you can take to prevent or alleviate the condition.

Take a travel-sickness pill, available from chemists, at least half an hour before you start your journey. Take care, however – they may cause drowsiness and impair driving performance. Never drive or operate machinery until the effects have worn off, usually within four to six hours.

The pills usually contain hyoscine or an antihistamine, both of which can have side-effects. If you are already taking

medication for another condition, check with your DOCTOR or pharmacist before taking travel-sickness pills.

Do not travel on an empty stomach and do not drink alcohol. Eat bland, easily digestible food before and during the journey.

If you feel at all queasy, do not try to read or write on a bus or in a car – again the movement of the page may affect your eyes. But try to keep your mind occupied: games, toys, puzzles and audio tapes are useful distractions, particularly for a child sufferer – see TRAVEL WITH CHILDREN.

Look out of the front of the car. Watching objects flashing past side windows can make nausea worse. Look at the horizon, not at things close by. This helps to keep the head still and lessens queasiness. Here are some other do's and don'ts for sufferers:

Don't allow SMOKING in a car – it could trigger an attack.
Don't talk about the possibility of being sick in front of a sufferer; this may cause an attack.
Do take plastic bags in case all else fails.
Do keep a car well ventilated: open a window or the air vents.
Do Sit in the most stable area of a vehicle: near the driver in a bus, or in the front seat of a car. Stay on deck in a ship or boat, rather than in the cabin.

Travel sickness is rarely a problem on large jet aircraft. They rapidly penetrate bad weather and cruise high above it, so that the effects of motion are minimal. If you are prone to sickness, however, try to get a seat away from windows, beside one of the central aisles.

Travel with a disabled person

Organising a trouble-free trip

Book your trip as early as possible. If booking through a travel agent, give details of your companion's disability – so that the agent can arrange for appropriate facilities.

If your companion is in a wheelchair, for example, find out the width of a hotel room's entrance and bathroom doors. Make sure there are grab bars in the bathroom, and access ramps where they are needed. If your companion has a guide dog, make sure arrangements will be made for it. Get the hotel to confirm in writing that it can meet your needs.

When going abroad, make sure your companion has proper INSURANCE cover.

Check that your disabled companion is taking any necessary equipment and all the drugs he or she will need – and knows the exact medical names of the drugs if more are needed; brand names often differ from country to country.

Travelling in Britain If you are going by rail or coach, contact the local British Rail area manager or coach company at least two days before travelling. Give full details of your companion's disability, when you plan to travel and where to. A ramp can be provided to help the wheelchair passenger to board and leave.

Arrive at a railway station in plenty of time. If the platform is difficult to reach, you can be taken in a goods lift but may have to wait for a while.

Many Inter-City trains have special seats with extra leg room for disabled travellers – but they must be reserved in advance. On other trains, travellers in wheelchairs can transfer to ordinary seats. Or they can sit in their wheelchairs in the guard's van, provided that you ask British Rail in advance for a permit.

Disabled people in wheelchairs are entitled to reduced fares on British Rail; one companion is entitled to the same fare. There is also a disabled person's railcard giving fare concessions to the disabled who are not in wheelchairs. Details are given on a leaflet available at British Rail stations, travel centres, Citizens Advice Bureaus and post offices.

Coach company staff will help disabled travellers on and off coaches – folding wheelchairs are generally carried free, as are guide dogs.

Local transport systems – buses and underground railways – are generally difficult for disabled people to use. If possible, use taxis or minicabs. There are some cabs with entry ramps and wheel clamps for wheelchairs.

Travelling abroad Most airlines and airports provide wheelchairs to carry disabled passengers through the terminal and onto or off the aircraft. Airlines will provide special food for those with dietary problems if they know in advance.

When making a reservation, tell the airline or travel agent exactly how your companion is disabled, and what kind of help will be needed at the terminal and during the journey. Then telephone the airline a few days before travelling, to check that the correct information has been fed into its computer.

Cross-Channel ferries also provide facilities for disabled people, including special cabins.

Facilities on public transport abroad vary greatly from country to country. Consult *Holidays and travel abroad* – published by RADAR (the Royal Association for Disability and Rehabilitation), 12 City Forum, 250 City Road, London EC1V 8AV.

Holidays for the handicapped RADAR publishes annual guides to holidays for the handicapped. A holiday information service is also run by Holiday Care Service, 2 Old Bank Chambers, Station Road, Horley, Surrey RH6 9HW.

Travel with children

*Keeping them safe and occupied
on the road*

Most children are apt to get bored, restless or irritable on a long car journey. Much of the tedium can be removed by making the ride into a pleasure trip.

Make sure that the children can see out of the car. Insist that older children wear seat belts. If your car does not have rear seat belts, it is advisable to have them fitted. Younger children should have properly installed SAFETY SEATS.

The day before you set out, get older children involved in looking at maps to help plan the route. Select interesting places to look for or visit on the way.

When calculating your arrival time at your destination, or an overnight stop, allow extra for holdups; and do not try to clip an hour or two off your time to prove how fast you can do the trip.

Be sure you have plenty of drinks and nutritious snacks, baby foods and disposable nappies, and plastic bags in case of TRAVEL SICKNESS or other mishaps.

Keep the car well ventilated, make frequent stops and provide light, nongreasy snacks. Make use of motorway service areas where the children can run around and let off steam under your supervision. Keeping toddlers amused can be a challenge. In addition to familiar toys, try packing some surprises and bring them out at intervals.

Driving through large towns can involve lots of stops and starts. Alleviate the children's boredom by playing a guessing game at traffic lights. When the car stops at a red light, each occupant makes a guess at how long it will be before the light turns to amber. When a player thinks the light is about to change, he cries 'Now!' The winner of the round is the *last* person to call before amber shows.

Travel with pets

*Making your journey safe
and pleasant*

Before taking a pet on holiday in Great Britain, make sure it is in good health and that it will be welcome wherever you are staying. A publication entitled 'Pets Welcome' is available from newsagents, and lists holiday accommodation where pets are accepted.

Consult your vet if you think your pet may suffer from travel sickness. Do not give human remedies or tranquillisers. See also PET MEDICATION.

Going by car If your dog or cat is not accustomed to car travel try taking some short rides before embarking on a longer journey. Consider fitting a grille behind the driver's seat if you have an estate car. Car accessory shops stock suitable grilles and also window grilles which allow you to open a window for ventilation. In a smaller car keep a dog on the rear seat or on the floor. Safety belts to fit all dogs are available in pet shops.

A cat or small dog is best kept in a travelling kennel or basket. Line it well with newspaper and put it where it will get the least amount of jolting. Keep the car well ventilated throughout the journey and do not leave it unattended for more than a few minutes at a time. Make frequent stops so that dogs may exercise and relieve themselves and keep drinking water available. For their sake, park in the shade, particularly in hot weather.

Going by train Small pets in the charge of a passenger travel free on British Rail, up to a maximum of two animals. No passenger may take more than two animals. Dogs may travel in the passenger compartments as long as no other passenger objects. If there is a complaint, the guard may require the dog to be muzzled and travel in the guard's van. Uncaged cats and dogs are charged at half the adult fare up to £3.50 single and £7 return. Guide dogs for the blind travel free.

Going by coach Restrictions vary with different companies, but in general pets are taken at the discretion of the driver and should not occupy a seat. Pets may be banned on coaches where food is served. Guide dogs travel free.

At your destination Make sure your pet has an identity disc with your holiday address. Note the telephone number of a local vet in case of need.

Travel abroad A holiday abroad with a pet is not practicable, owing to our stringent QUARANTINE regulations.

If you wish to take an animal out of the country permanently consult the Animal Health Division of the Ministry of Agriculture for a list of regulations, and also notify the embassy of the country concerned. The animal may require certain inoculations, which should be done at least three months before departure. See also MOVING HOUSE.

Treasure

How finders can be keepers

Anything valuable found in the ground – whether ancient or modern – should be reported to the police. The police will report the find to the coroner, who must decide if the treasure was hidden deliberately or merely lost.

Hidden gold or silver plate, coins, bullion or other valuables are termed 'treasure trove' and belong to the Crown unless their original owner can be found.

If the owner is not found, Crown officials may allow the finder to keep his treasure. When the Crown does keep it, it is usual to pay the finder what it is worth as a reward. But if the coroner decides that the treasure has been lost or abandoned – if coins are scattered over a wide area, for example – and the original owner cannot be traced, they belong to the owner of the land they were found in or, if not in the ground, they become the property of the finder.

Lost property If you find lost property, you must take reasonable steps to trace the owner. If you keep it, you are guilty of theft. If you hand the property to the police they will keep it for a month if it is worth less than £50, or six months if it is worth more. If the owner is not traced, the article will be handed back to you. Report even beachcombing finds to the police if they seem valuable. Keeping them could amount to theft. See also METAL DETECTING.

Tree house

Making a lofty den for youngsters

A tree house must be made to measure for the tree, and construction must be safe and solid. Build it on the guidelines given here, with a TIMBER frame bolted together, a wooden LADDER, safety rails and floorboards slightly spaced to allow for drainage. An awning can be rigged as a roof to give shade and shelter.

Choose a tree with sturdy, spreading branches 1.5-1.8m (5-6ft) above the ground, such as an old apple tree. Make sure the tree limbs are not rotten and that the ground below is not too hard.

Timber Lengths needed depend on the dimensions of the structure. Buy pre-treated timber, or treat it with one of the WOOD PRESERVATIVES.

For the two or more supporting beams use 150 × 50mm (6 × 2in) timber. For the base frame you need four lengths of 100 × 50mm (4 × 2in) timber to form the sides – allow also for a centre support if the frame width is more than 600mm (2ft). Five lengths of 50 × 50mm (2 × 2in) timber will make corner and door posts.

For floorboards and side rails use 100 × 25mm (4 × 1in). The ladder is made with 60 × 38mm (2½ × 1½in) timber for uprights and 50 × 25mm (2 × 1in) for the 300mm (12in) long rungs.

Fixings For each corner joint, use three 10mm (⅜in) diameter 115mm (4½in) long coach BOLTS (with nuts, washers and timber connectors). Use two more coach bolts for the door post and two for fixing the ladder. For fastening the frame to the supporting beams, use four or more

A guide to the basic support and construction

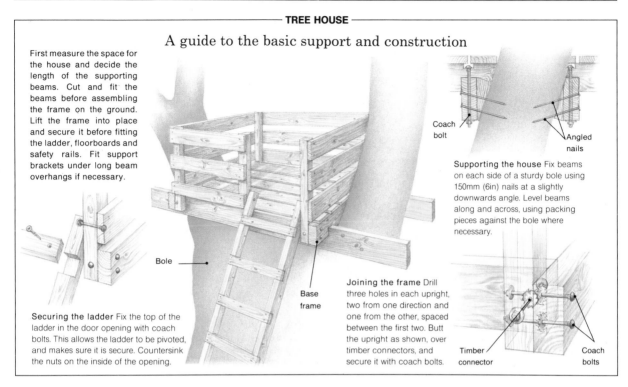

First measure the space for the house and decide the length of the supporting beams. Cut and fit the beams before assembling the frame on the ground. Lift the frame into place and secure it before fitting the ladder, floorboards and safety rails. Fit support brackets under long beam overhangs if necessary.

Coach bolt

Angled nails

Supporting the house Fix beams on each side of a sturdy bole using 150mm (6in) nails at a slightly downwards angle. Level beams along and across, using packing pieces against the bole where necessary.

Bole

Base frame

Joining the frame Drill three holes in each upright, two from one direction and one from the other, spaced between the first two. Butt the upright as shown, over timber connectors, and secure it with coach bolts.

Securing the ladder Fix the top of the ladder in the door opening with coach bolts. This allows the ladder to be pivoted, and makes sure it is secure. Countersink the nuts on the inside of the opening.

Timber connector

Coach bolts

200mm (8in) coach bolts. You also need 50mm (2in) galvanised countersunk SCREWS, for ladder rungs, side rails and floorboards, and 150mm round wire nails to fix the beams to the tree – see NAILING.

Making the ladder Clamp the uprights together with 38mm (1½in) edges upwards. Use a tenon saw and chisel to cut out matching housings for each rung, spaced 250mm (10in) apart top to top – possibly less for small children – see CHISELLING; SAWS AND SAWING; WOOD-WORKING JOINTS. Cut the housings 25mm (1in) deep so that the rungs and uprights lie flush. Screw the top and bottom rungs in place first, to give a 300mm (12in) total width. Round off the top front edge of each rung with a file.

Constructing the house Cut the supporting beams to length and fix them to the tree – see illustration. Cut the base frame and uprights to length – see SAWS AND SAWING. Make two base side pieces to the full length of the frame, the other two to butt between them. The uprights are fixed to the base frame with three bolts – two from one direction and one from the other, as illustrated.

Carefully mark the bolt-hole positions on the bottom of each upright and the 100mm (4in) face of each base piece, then drill the holes using a 13mm (½in) bit – see DRILLING. Also drill two bolt holes for the door post in a side piece – make the doorway 315mm (12½in) wide so the ladder can fit inside it. Mark the undersides

of the base pieces where they will fit over the supporting beams, and cut out housings 50mm (2in) deep.

Put the frame together on the ground, with the base pieces standing on their edges. Butt the pieces together, insetting two of the pieces 50mm at each end to accommodate the uprights. Bolt each joint together, fitting the timber connectors over the bolts between the two pieces of wood. Secure the bolts with washers and nuts and tighten them firmly with a spanner. Get a helper to lift the frame onto the beams and slot it in place. Secure it with coach bolts as illustrated, counterboring the holes 13-19mm (½-¾in) as necessary.

Drill holes in the door uprights and fix the ladder as shown. Screw the floorboards to the frame, leaving a gap of about 25mm between each board. Screw side rails to the uprights to a height of at least 760mm (30in).

Tree pruning

When and how to cut back branches

In general, trees rarely need pruning, but it may be necessary to cut off or shorten branches to preserve the shape. Dead or damaged branches should always be removed, as they are dangerous if they fall. Sound branches may have to be removed if they overhang a road or a neighbour's garden. Leave the top prun-

ing of a tall tree, or the felling of a diseased tree, to a professional tree surgeon. If you have to use a ladder (see LADDERS) to reach the branch for cutting, make sure it is secured and that you have a helper to support the weight of the branch; otherwise you could lose your balance.

FRUIT TREES are pruned regularly to train them into convenient shapes and encourage fruiting. Prune other deciduous trees in winter – from the beginning of November to the end of February – after the leaves have fallen. Exceptions are the Japanese cherry, which should be pruned in late summer, and birches, maples and walnuts, which tend to bleed sap if pruned later than November.

Do not prune conifers unless it is absolutely necessary. If it is unavoidable, do it in March or April.

Preserving tree shape Use secateurs to cut off unwanted sideshoots low down on the trunk of a young tree, and to cut off feathering – sideshoots that grow out on an older tree where a large branch has been sawn off. Also use secateurs or lopping shears to cut off as necessary some of the sideshoots growing in towards the centre of the tree, to keep the branches well spaced.

If a young tree starts to fork at the tip, it can spoil the shape – especially on a single-stemmed pyramidal conifer. Cut off such a secondary leader entirely on a conifer. On a deciduous tree prune it back to half its length, cutting diagon-

─ TREE PRUNING ─

Removing a single branch

Use a pruning saw or a log saw to cut the branch into lengths. To stop the branch from tearing or swaying as you saw, tie a rope round it and then tie the rope to a higher branch – or loop it over the higher branch and give it to a helper to hold taut.

Manageable length Cut back the branch in several stages if necessary, until there is only 300-460mm (12-18in) of stump remaining.

Cutting off the stump Saw through close to the trunk, cutting first from below, then from above.

Sealing the wound Paint over the cut wood with tree-pruning compound if you do not like the look of the raw wound on the trunk.

Neatening the cut Trim the ragged edges of the wound with a sharp knife to leave a smooth surface.

ally just above an outward-facing bud. This will induce the shoot to put out horizontal sideshoots.

If an over-vigorous branch begins to destroy the tree's overall outline, cut it back by about two-thirds of its length. Use lopping shears, a pruning saw or a log saw, depending on the branch size – see SAWS AND SAWING. Make the cut just in front of a sideshoot growing in the same direction. Saw off completely any diseased, dead, or damaged branches, or any that cross or rub each other.

Cutting off an unwanted branch Use a log (bow) or pruning saw. Do not try to cut off a long branch in one go, it may well rip away from the trunk and damage the bark. Cut it off in convenient lengths to about 460mm (18in) from the trunk. See illustration.

To make the final cut at the base of the branch, saw from the underside as close to the trunk as possible for about one-third of the thickness. Then saw down from the top to meet the cut. Trim off ragged edges with a sharp knife.

Sealing the wound After sawing off a branch more than about 25mm (1in) across, you can cover the raw wood with pruning compound. Tree experts disagree about sealing the wound in this way – some say it keeps out disease spores, some think it unnecessary and perhaps harmful. But many people prefer the painted appearance.

Trellises

Making a support for climbing plants

A trellis support for climbing plants can be fitted against a fence or wall, on top of a fence, or be used between fence posts as a fence. Sections of ready-made trellis are available from garden and DIY centres and TIMBER merchants, but you may want trellis of non-standard size to fit a particular space.

A trellis panel has thin strips of wood – generally 19mm ($\frac{4}{4}$in) wide and 10mm

Backyard beauty In a backyard with no flowerbeds, a trellis attached to a wall can be used to display pot plants.

($\frac{3}{8}$in) thick – spaced 100-150mm (4-6in) apart to form squares or diamonds, the whole fixed to a rectangular frame of 38 × 19mm (1$\frac{1}{2}$ × $\frac{3}{4}$in) wood. For fencing, add a wider capping strip to the top of the frame.

Decide whether you want a square or diamond pattern and sketch out your plans on squared paper to calculate how much timber you will need.

Western red cedar is recommended but the cheaper and more readily available yellow deal is quite suitable, and can be treated with WOOD PRESERVATIVES more effectively than white deal. Do not use creosote, which will harm plants.

Assembling Make the frame using suitable WOODWORKING JOINTS. Lay the thin strips on the ground in the required pattern, and use galvanised nails to join them at the crossings. Use a second hammer behind each joint to support it while nailing. Nail the assembled trellis to the frame.

Secure the frame to timber fence posts (see FENCES) using coach BOLTS or fence panel clips, or to concrete posts using wall plugs and zinc-plated woodscrews.

If you are fitting the trellis against a wall, plug the wall (see MASONRY DRILLING) and use anchor BOLTS or hammer-in fixings. Leave at least 25mm (1in) space between the trellis and the wall – use wooden blocks as spacers – see SCREWS; NAILING; WALL FASTENERS.

Trusts

Organising your assets for the benefit of others

Money or assets put in a trust belong legally to the trustees, who manage it on behalf of the beneficiaries – usually quite different people, often children too young to own property.

In this way, those who provide the assets for the trust – the settlors – ensure that the beneficiaries get the benefits of the assets (perhaps income from money, or use of property) but the assets are looked after and administered by the trustees. Trusts are also used to set up charities, and can save the settlors significant amounts of tax.

Setting up a trust Get a solicitor (see LAWYERS) to help draw up a signed, legal document, naming trustees, beneficiaries and assets to be administered. It should also lay down how the trust is to be run – how, for example, the income should be used to benefit children; or how a charity should help people.

The settlor appoints the trustees, usually two or more, who must be over 18. They should be reliable people with business experience, who also know the beneficiaries. They are usually unpaid.

However, if the trust is complicated or long running, appoint and pay a professional trustee – a bank trustee company, solicitor or accountant.

The trustees must fulfil the terms of the trust and, under the Trustee Investment Act, may be liable for losses through improper investments.

Charitable trusts must be registered with the Charity Commissioners, but for other trusts, it is necessary only for the trustees to be registered as the owners of any land or stocks and shares that are held in the trust.

Tug of war

Testing the combined strength of two teams

Tug of war is a long-established rural sport, in which two teams pull at opposite ends of a thick rope in a contest of strength. Playing it strictly to the rules, the rope should be 100-125mm (4-5in) in circumference and at least 32m (35yds) long if the maximum eight-man teams are competing. Such ropes are expensive; try to borrow one from a tug-of-war club for a one-off event. Thinner ropes can cause rope burns on hands.

Mark the rope with red tape at its exact halfway point, and with white tape at points 4m (13ft) on either side of it. Mark the ground with a line to show the halfway point.

When the contest starts, the centre of the rope must be directly over the centre line on the ground. The hands of the first team member on each side must be behind a blue tape mark placed 5m (16½ft) from the centre of the rope.

The rope is gripped with both hands, palms uppermost, and passes under the right arm of each team member, down to the last or anchor man (usually the heaviest member of the team), who may hold the rope under one arm and over the other shoulder, but must let the end hang free.

The contest starts on a signal from the judge, and is over when one team pulls the opposing team's white marker over the line on its side. The best of three pulls usually decides the contest.

Tumble dryers

Hints on using and maintaining them

The basic components of a tumble dryer are: a revolving drum; a fan; an electric motor and a heating element. Some models have a vent to carry the moist air outside. This can be a flexible tube and stored when not in use, or permanently fixed. More expensive types of dryer have a condenser that collects the moisture.

Do not overload the machine – this results in poor drying and causes the clothes to crease. Spin or wring clothes before putting them in. Remove loose items such as safety pins, close zips and tie belts. Turn jeans and other metal-studded garments inside out so that the studs will not damage the drum.

Because of the high temperature generated within the dryer, do not tumble dry flammable materials such as rubber, plastic foam, polythene, paper, nappy liners or waterproof pants. Similarly do not dry articles on which flammable substances have been spilt – for example petrol, cleaning solvents, hair lacquer and cooking oil – unless they have been well washed in detergent.

Do not tumble dry woollen items unless their label includes the 'may be tumble dried' symbol (a circle inside a square). Articles not to be used in a tumble dryer carry the same symbol with a cross through it.

After tumble drying, switch off the dryer at the socket or a FUSED CONNECTION UNIT. Empty the storage reservoir of a condenser dryer, unless it is fitted with a drain hose. Wipe inside the drum with a damp cloth. Clean the filter using a nailbrush or an old toothbrush. Build-up of lint can cause breakdown. Occasionally wash the filter in tepid water and dry it before replacing it.

Turfing

Preparing, laying down and repairing a lawn

Turfing is the quickest way of creating a lawn. It provides instant colour and cuts out the time and effort required for sowing and nurturing grass seed.

Turf should be laid between October and February (see LAWN CARE) to give it a chance to take proper root before the growing season. Start site preparation three to six months earlier, depending on how much work there is to do.

Preparing the soil Clear the ground and dig over the area, removing perennial weeds such as dock and couch grass – make sure all the roots are taken away. Ideally, the ground should be left grass-free for three months, during which time level it, if required, and dig in a well-rotted manure or COMPOST to improve fertility and drainage. On clay soil, add coarse sand to assist drainage (1 bucket of manure and 2 buckets of sand per square metre). Treat the soil with weed-killer – see WEED CONTROL.

Choose a day when the soil is dry to rake it smooth and even, free of lumps and hollows, then roll or tread it to a firm surface. Rake in Growmore fertiliser about a week before turfing – about 2-4 tablespoons per square metre. Just before you lay the turf, rake the surface smooth.

Choosing a turf Buy the best quality turf you can afford. Meadow turf is the cheapest, but may be full of weed grasses; cultivated turf is preferable.

The turf should be recently mown, with a good uniform colour and no evidence of pests, diseases, weeds or bare patches. The soil underside should be an even mix of clay and sand, free from stones, with plenty of white roots present. Examine a turf sample before you buy; check the turf again before laying.

Turves are normally sold in imperial sizes, sometimes by the square yard, sometimes by the number of turves, which may be of various sizes. A popular size is 4ft 6in × 16in.

TURFING

Laying an instant lawn

Mark out the area to be turfed with pegs and string. Start laying along the side nearest your stock of turves. Make a tamper by nailing two or three thick boards to the end of a pole.

Tamp the turves down gently. Add or remove soil from below to level any bumps or dips.

Work forwards, staggering the turves. Stand on a plank, not on the turves. End each row with a half or whole turf. Avoid small pieces at the edges.

Laying the turf Do not leave turf in stacks or rolls; spread them out flat and water if necessary, if the lawn is to be laid more than three days after delivery.

Choose a fine day, when the soil is reasonably dry. Lay the turf forwards in rows and tamp it down – see illustration. Stand or kneel on a plank while laying to avoid damaging the new grass.

After laying, fill the cracks with a top dressing of sieved, good quality soil mixed with sand and peat (4 parts sand, 2 parts soil, 1 part peat). Work this in between the turves; it will help knot them together. If you want a curved edge, trim the turves with a half-moon edging tool after filling the cracks. Roll the turves lightly – you can use the back roller of a lawn mower – and brush with a stiff broom to raise the flattened grass. Water with a sprinkler.

The new lawn will benefit from a quick-acting fertiliser in late spring – see FERTILISERS. It should be well watered during summer dry spells, as it will be more vulnerable to drought than established grass.

Turfing repairs Cut a square round a bare patch, rake the soil and fit in a new turf square. If the lawn edge is broken, cut round the square containing the broken edge and ease it outwards so that the damage is clear of the border. Trim off the damaged edge in line with the rest of the lawn and repair the inner gap with a rectangle of new turf. Use sifted soil to seal the cracks.

Twenty questions

Playing a guessing game

Twenty Questions (also known as Animal, Vegetable or Mineral) is an ideal game for long family car journeys – see also TRAVEL WITH CHILDREN. One player chooses a subject in one of the three categories, but does not tell the other players who or what it is. Animal can be anything that is a living being, human, animal or insect; vegetable, anything that is organic, such as a tree or plant; mineral, anything that is inorganic – a rock, metal or an object such as a table.

The other players must guess who or what the first player has chosen, by asking in turn questions that can be answered 'Yes' or 'No'. 'I don't know' and 'Partly' are also allowable answers. There is a limit of 20 questions.

The first question is usually 'Is it an animal (or vegetable or mineral)?' The remaining questions should gradually narrow down the possibilities.

If, after 20 questions, no one has guessed correctly, the next game is started by the same player. But if the subject is guessed, the player who guesses correctly can pick a new subject.

Twenty Questions can also be played as a competition between two players or two teams. Record the number of questions each player or team asks before guessing correctly. The player or team with the lowest score wins.

Two-way switches

Testing and replacing them

A two-way switch system allows you to switch a light on and off from two different switches. If the switches stop working, check first whether there is a power cut. Do other switches and power points work? Are your neighbours without power?

If there is no power cut, but other light switches on the same floor are not working, the circuit fuse may have blown – see FUSES AND FUSE BOXES. A blown fuse could indicate that the circuit is overloaded: the maximum the circuit can supply is 1200 watts, so, for example, 150 watt bulbs at ten lighting points would overload the circuit.

If only the two-way switches do not work check the light bulb – if it is sound, the cause is probably a faulty connection in one of the switches.

Turn off the electricity at the main switch and take out the circuit fuse. Remove the screws from the switchplates of each two-way switch in turn, and gently pull the switchplate forward until you can reach the terminals on the back.

One of the switches will have two conductor wires at two of the terminals – one from the twin-core-and-earth switch cable that comes from the CEILING ROSE or JUNCTION BOX (where it connects with the lighting circuit cable); the other from the cable leading to the second switch. This cable is three-core-and-earth, with conductor wires insulated in red, blue and yellow; the earth wire is bare (or sleeved at the switch). There will be one conductor at the other terminal.

The earth conductor wires are connected to a terminal in each switch mounting box – do not dislodge them. They will be covered in green-and-yellow sleeving, or left bare; if they are bare, sleeve them.

Pull gently at each wire to see if it is loose at its terminal. If so, undo the terminal screw, insert the wire tip afresh and tighten the screw firmly on it. If there are two wires at the terminal, insert both tips into it together – do *not* twist them together or the copper wire may crack. If a wire has cracked or broken, strip about 16mm ($\frac{5}{8}$in) of insulation from the end and reconnect it. Screw the switchplates back in place.

Check that the ceiling rose connections are secure. Replace the circuit fuse and turn on the main switch.

If the switches still do not work, the mechanism of one may be faulty. Use a circuit continuity tester to check them – see CIRCUIT TESTING. Turn off the main switch again and remove the circuit fuse. Grip the terminal marked Common with the tester's crocodile clip. Attach the other clip to one of the other two terminals and turn the switch up and down several times; the tester should light with the switch in one of the positions.

Test the other switch in the same way. If a switch is faulty, replace it. Different switches may have different patterns of connection, visible when they are removed. Reconnect them as you find them. One method is shown below.

TWO-WAY SWITCHES

Replacing and reconnecting: one method

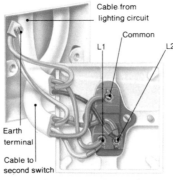

Cable from lighting circuit

Common

L1   L2

Earth terminal

Cable to second switch

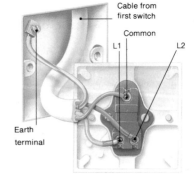

Cable from first switch

Common

L1   L2

Earth terminal

First switch Connect to the COMMON terminal the red wire from the cable to the second switch. Connect to terminal L1 the yellow wire from the second switch cable, also the red wire from the lighting circuit cable. Connect to terminal L2 the blue switch cable wire and black lighting circuit cable.

Second switch Only one cable leads to this switch – from the first switch. Connect the red wire to the COMMON terminal and the yellow wire to terminal L1. Connect the blue wire to terminal L2. Do not disconnect the earth wires on either switch – other than to put green-and-yellow sleeves on them.

Replacing switches Turn off the main switch and remove the circuit fuse. Undo the screws holding the old switch, pull it forward and note which terminal each wire goes to. Loosen the terminal screws and withdraw the wires.

All the conductor wires – not just the red ones – become live at some stage depending on the positions of the two switches; to indicate this, slip short pieces of red plastic sleeving over the yellow, blue and black wires.

Connect the wires to the new switches as illustrated. Screw the switchplates back on without pinching any wires. Replace the circuit fuse and switch on. See also ELECTRIC SOCKETS AND SWITCHES.

Typewriters

Servicing a manual machine;
cleaning electric and
electronic ones

Keep any typewriter covered when not in use. Manual and some electric typewriters can be given routine services at home – but they should have a professional service every two years if they are used more than four hours a day.

Servicing a manual typewriter Pull off the top plate covering the type bars, then stand the machine on its back edge and remove the base plate. Remove the side plates, if fitted.

Lift the ribbon free from the type guide, then release the spring retaining arms and lift off the spools. Remove the left-hand platen (roller) knob, then pull out the platen shaft. Lift out the platen and feed roller.

Using a stiff toothbrush, clean the character heads of the type bars. You can lift dirt from letter cavities by pressing on some plastic reusable adhesive, then removing it.

If any bars are bent, straighten them gently with pliers until they move easily when you press the key. Press down as many keys as possible and clean below the type bars with a soft, dry paintbrush. Use a thin knife blade to clean any grime out of the segment slots at the base of the type bars. Brush away any remaining dirt from the slots.

Brush the carriage clean, then move it from side to side to brush its track. Brush clean the parts accessible from underneath. Clean the platen with a cloth dampened with methylated spirit.

Apply a little light machine oil (3 in 1) to each end of the carriage track and to the pivot screw at each side of the shift key. Lubricate each ribbon shaft.

Electric typewriters Machines with type bars rather than golf balls can be cleaned in the same way as manual typewriters.

Golf ball and electronic machines Clean the golf ball or daisy wheel regularly, using a cloth dampened with methylated spirit. Also clean the guides for the ribbon and corrector ribbon.

If your machine does not work, check the power cord and the 3amp fuse in the plug – see PLUGS. If there is nothing wrong with either, do not attempt repairs – return the machine to the dealer. See also TOUCH-TYPING.

Tyres

Checking condition, pressure and
tread depth

Check the condition of your tyres at least once a fortnight and before any long or high-speed journey. Damaged or badly worn tyres are illegal (see also MOT TEST) and could cost you your life. Periodically take off each wheel and check the inside walls of the tyres for any obvious signs of damage – see JACKING A CAR.

Inspecting treads and walls Check for flaws in the pattern of the tread and for abnormal wear. Any abnormal widening of the grooves between the tread blocks is a sign of ageing.

Remove any sharp flints, nails or tacks. Then check that the tyre does not lose pressure without them – if it does, have it repaired. If the tyre has a series of cracks, replace it.

Look for any flattening or unevenness of the treads. Flat areas can be caused by fierce acceleration or braking; excessive wear on the centre of the tread is caused by over-inflation; on the edge of the tread it is caused by under-inflation. If there is excessive wear on one side of the tread only, have the tracking and suspension checked.

Do not drive fast on tyres that have bulges in the side walls. Renew them as soon as possible – though they may be used for a short time for local journeys, as long as you drive slowly.

Checking tread depth Check this regularly as illustrated, especially when tyres are beginning to show signs of wear.

In Britain the tread on tyres must be at least 1.6mm deep over 90 per cent of the tread width all round the tyre, but it is safer to have at least 2mm of tread. The remaining 10 per cent of the tread must have a clearly visible tread pattern.

Check all round each tyre, moving the car slightly so that you can measure the depths of the sections on which the car was standing.

Checking tyre pressure Do this fortnightly and always before long journeys. If tyre pressures are wrong – especially if they are too low – the covers will soon wear; also the car's handling will be affected.

Make your checks when the tyres are cold – the pressure inside increases when they are hot. Inflate them to the pressures recommended by the tyre manufacturer. Tyres on the same axle must be inflated to the same pressure.

Before carrying a heavy load, towing or driving at high speed, increase the pressure of the tyres as recommended by the manufacturer. Generally the pressure in rear tyres is increased by 4-6psi for carrying a load or towing, and the pressure in all tyres is increased by 3-6psi for sustained high-speed driving.

TYRES

Looking for wear or damage to treads and side walls

Cracks caused by ageing

Buckled rim and damaged side wall

Shoulder wear (under-inflation)

Centre wear (over-inflation)

Side-wall scuffing

Feathering of tread (misaligned wheels)

Inspect the tread for signs of abnormal wear and cuts. Prise out any nails or stones with a screwdriver. Check the side walls for cuts, cracks, scuffing or bulges.

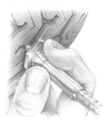

Tread depth Check this with a tread-depth gauge. Or hold a screwdriver blade in the groove and mark the depth with your thumbnail.

Ulcers

Relieving stomach problems

Stomach ulcers cause burning pain in the upper abdomen or below the ribs – often in the early morning and after meals. Men are more susceptible than women – young men are more likely to suffer from duodenal ulcers (in the first part of the small intestine), whereas gastric ulcers (in the stomach lining) tend to afflict middle-aged or older men.

The causes of both types of ulcer are similar – excess stomach acid, STRESS, anxiety, overwork and SMOKING, which can all prompt and aggravate the condition. Bouts of pain may persist for four to eight weeks and recur periodically. In severe cases, there may be bleeding and VOMITING of blood.

Treatment Stop smoking, avoid stressful situations and eat frequent small meals of non-fried, bland, milky foods to neutralise the acid. Proprietary antacids, available from chemists, may also be taken.

If home treatment fails to bring relief after a few weeks, or if you develop symptoms for the first time over the age of 40, visit your DOCTOR. He may prescribe medicine to block the release of acid. He may also refer you to hospital for a full examination.

Severe ulcers may ultimately require an operation; both duodenal and gastric ulcers can recur – particularly if a stressful life is resumed.

Umbrellas

Choosing and caring for them

There are two main types of umbrella – long types with fixed handles and short types with telescopic handles. Long umbrellas can be inconvenient to carry when not in use, but usually cover a wider area than telescopic types, which can be slipped into a bag or briefcase. Some long umbrellas have shoulder slings for carrying. Automatic umbrellas are opened by pressing a button near the handle.

Some umbrellas are 'windproof'; when they blow inside-out they can be restored to their normal shape without breaking.

Whatever type you buy, choose one with a strong, waterproofed nylon cover, firmly attached to its ribs. Always leave a wet umbrella open to dry.

Repairs A rib that has come away from the cover can often be repaired by sewing it back with button thread. Stitch through the hem and the 'eye' of the rib and secure with a slipknot.

A hole in the cover should be patched from inside, using a small piece of matching nylon stuck in with clear adhesive – see GLUING.

Replacement handles and tips are sometimes available for a favourite 'brolly' – consult *Yellow Pages* under 'Umbrella makers and repairs'. Remove a damaged wooden tip with pliers, and glue and twist on the replacement. Break off a damaged plastic handle and fix the new one with epoxy-resin glue.

Unconsciousness

On-the-spot emergency treatment

Unconsciousness is not always total insensibility. There are three basic stages, and a victim may go through all three or remain in one. The stages are:
● Drowsiness, in which the victim is easily roused but passes back into a sleep-like state.
● Stupor, in which the victim gives incoherent replies (or no replies) to questions.
● Coma, in which the victim cannot be roused and is motionless and silent.

An unconscious person is in danger of choking to death if left lying face up. Vomit, blood or saliva may block the top of the windpipe, and the base of the tongue may slide back over the windpipe. Normal reflexes do not function properly during total unconsciousness, so a victim with a blocked airway might not cough or turn over, as in sleep.

Do not move the victim more than is necessary; if he is breathing normally, put him in the RECOVERY POSITION at once, unless you suspect a back or neck injury. If there is such an injury, do not move him, but hold his jaw forward so that there is no obstruction to breathing. Stay with him in case he stops breathing, and get someone to dial 999 for the emergency services.

If he stops breathing, begin ARTIFICIAL RESPIRATION. If breathing does not begin, check the pulse for a heartbeat. If there is no pulse and you are trained in the technique of CHEST COMPRESSION, start it immediately.

Once breathing resumes, put the person in the recovery position with the head lower than the rest of the body.

Loosen any tight clothing at the neck, chest and waist, to assist breathing and blood circulation.

If nobody else is on hand to telephone for help, do so yourself at the first opportunity.

Underwater escape

Getting out of a sinking car

If your car plunges into deep water, you may manage to escape through a door or window before it sinks, but do not open the doors once it has started sinking.

If you cannot escape immediately, close all windows and doors before the car sinks, to retain air, and switch on headlights and interior lights, if possible, to help you to see better, and to help rescuers locate the car.

The engine end will sink first and an air pocket will form at the other end. Release your safety belt and those of any other occupants, and move everyone into the air-pocket area so that they can breathe.

Do not panic – water will enter the car, but will stop when the air pressure inside the vehicle equals the water pressure outside. At that point, you should be able to open a door or a window.

All occupants can then take a deep breath and get out through the opening. Form a chain by holding hands, to make sure no one is left behind. The air breathed inside the car will have been under pressure, so breathe out slowly as you rise to the surface, to avoid damaging your lungs. Swim to shore, with those who can swim helping any who cannot – see LIFESAVING.

Uneven floors

Levelling a timber or concrete floor

A level floor is essential for laying VINYL FLOOR COVERING and PARQUET FLOORING.

Levelling a timber floor Badly worn floorboards can be covered with sheets of 2.4 × 1.2m (8 × 4ft) tempered hardboard. First make sure that all the floorboards are firmly fixed, punching nail heads below the surface. Plane or sand down raised edges.

Two days before laying, wet the rough side of each sheet of hardboard with a pint of water and stack the sheets back

---UNEVEN FLOORS---

Laying hardboard and applying levelling compound

Concrete Start at the farthest point from the door and pour about a quarter of the levelling compound on the floor.

Hardboard Find the centre point of the room and lay the first sheet (1) exactly on it. Then lay the other sheets round it, in a clockwise direction.

Use a plasterer's trowel to spread the compound evenly to a thickness of 3mm ($\frac{1}{8}$in) over the floor, spreading and trowelling as you work your way towards the door.

to back on a flat surface in the room where they will be used.

Lay the hardboard smooth side down, and position sheets so that the joints between adjacent sheets are staggered, as shown. Hold them in position with spots of contact adhesive (see GLUING) at 300mm (12in) intervals, then secure them to the floorboards with hardboard pins – see NAILING. Start in the centre of one edge, then add second and third nails 150mm (6in) away on each side. Set the fourth nail 150mm towards the middle of the sheet. Nail the fifth and sixth nails beside the second and third, and the seventh towards the middle, and so on.

Levelling a concrete floor Sweep the floor and wash it with a strong sugar-soap solution. Fill any cracks or holes with MORTAR, adding PVA adhesive according to the instructions.

Mix up levelling compound following the manufacturer's instructions, and apply it to the floor. Allow an hour for it to set and wait 8-10 hours before laying any floor covering on top.

Unfair dismissal

Your protection against wrongful sacking

If you have worked full or part time for an employer for at least two years, you are entitled to apply to an Industrial Tribunal for compensation if you consider you have been unfairly dismissed.

This entitlement does not apply if you are over retirement age, a merchant seaman, or a registered dock worker.

Unfair dismissal is often difficult to define, though there are some clear-cut examples: a woman who is not allowed to resume her old job after having a baby has been unfairly dismissed; an employee who suffers REDUNDANCY, then finds someone else appointed to do the same job could claim unfair dismissal; dismissal for belonging to a trade union or taking part in trade union activities outside working hours is also unfair.

Reasons for dismissal that are considered 'fair' include lack of capability or qualifications for doing the job; misconduct; redundancy; when continued employment would lead to a breach of the law; and other 'substantial' reasons.

There are, however, areas within those reasons where unfair dismissal could still be successfully claimed. If, for example, an employee is sacked for lack of capability after working at a job for five years, a tribunal would ask why the employer took so long to discover the employee's shortcomings.

Serious misconduct, such as stealing from an employer, would warrant instant dismissal, but dismissal may not be justified if the misconduct was not of a serious nature – for example, occasional lateness – or if the employer acted without properly investigating the facts.

There is no legal definition of what constitutes other substantial reasons for dismissal, but one reason often upheld is incompatibility – when an employee causes disharmony among fellow-workers by offensive remarks or behaviour, especially if after warnings.

Dismissal for economic reasons – for example, replacing a highly paid employee by someone on a lower salary could be held to be unfair; but tribunal decisions vary, and some cases have ended in favour of the employer.

Claiming unfair dismissal First ask your employer to give you the reasons in writing for dismissing you – he or she is required by law to do so within 14 days. When you have the reply, get a Form IT1 from your local Citizens Advice Bureau, Job Centre or DSS office.

You can seek advice from the Bureau, a solicitor (see LAWYERS) or a trade union official on how to fill in the form. You will have to give your reasons why you feel your dismissal was unfair. If you decide you want a solicitor to represent you at the tribunal hearing, you cannot claim legal aid.

Within three months of your dismissal, send the completed form to the Secretary of the Tribunals, Central Office of the Industrial Tribunals, 93 Ebury Bridge Road, London SW1W 8RE.

Your former employer will be sent a copy of the form IT1 and invited to reply, giving the reasons for the dismissal. A copy of his reply will be sent to you.

Before the tribunal hearing both you and the employer may be approached by a conciliation officer of the Advisory, Conciliation and Arbitration Service (ACAS), to try to reach a settlement. Neither party is obliged to cooperate, but it is advisable to do so, as the officer may be able to negotiate a compromise.

However, if the claim proceeds, you will be notified of the date of the hearing. Write again to the employer, asking for 'further and better particulars' of the information given in the employer's reply to your form IT1, and ask for copies of any relevant documents, such as your personnel file and the company's disciplinary rules and procedures.

Again, the employer must supply the information within 14 days; if you do not receive it, write to the Secretary of the Tribunals and ask for an order to be made to the employer to supply it.

Prepare your case carefully, and read your employment contract and the company's rules thoroughly.

Ask any colleagues who can provide evidence that you were unfairly sacked to be witnesses. If a colleague is reluctant, write to the Secretary of the Tribunals and ask for a witness order to be made. However, it is up to you to serve the order on your colleague.

If you win your claim, you can ask for your job back; you can ask for a new job with your previous employer; or you can ask for financial compensation from the employer, up to a maximum of £13,420 in most cases.

Unit trusts

*Choosing one to suit your
investment needs*

When you buy unit trusts you join a pool
of investors whose investments together
make up a large enough fund to buy an
extensive portfolio of shares. Each trust
fund is divided into equal units and you
are allocated units in proportion to the
size of your investment – most trusts
require a minimum of £500 or £1000.

The risk is less than INVESTING directly
in shares because your money is usually
spread throughout a range of shares.
However, the trusts are affected by rises
and falls in the stock market. They
should be regarded as a medium to long-
term investment. Unless the timing is
right, withdrawal at short notice could
be costly.

Types of unit trust fund There are
three basic types of fund – 'income',
designed to produce a regular and
increasing income; 'growth', designed to
produce increased capital values; and
'general', designed to produce a combination of capital growth and income.
You can invest in unit trusts through
two types of unit: 'accumulation', which
automatically reinvests any income, and
'income', which distributes income twice
(or more) per annum.

It is important to select the type of
fund to suit your needs.

If you are in a high tax bracket, a fund
geared to growth would suit you best
because capital gains below £5800 are
exempt from capital gains tax. Dividends,
however, are taxed at the lower rate at
source and then may be liable for further,
higher-rate tax; non tax-payers can
reclaim the tax deducted.

Trusts vary in their type of investment:
some concentrate on the UK or international stock markets; some – gilts –
invest in British Government stocks;
others are highly specialist, and more
speculative.

How to make the investment A bank
manager, stockbroker, insurance broker
or building society can advise you and
invest your money; or you can get in
touch direct with a particular trust. The
Unit Trust Association publishes a useful booklet – *Everything you need to
know about unit trusts*. To obtain it send
a large stamped addressed envelope to
Unit Trust Association, 65 Kingsway,
London WC2B 6TD.

Charges The trust manager's initial
charge and any government duties payable are included in the cost of the units
when you buy them at the 'offer' price.
The offer price is usually 5-7 per cent
higher than the 'bid' price at which you
could cash in your units. The annual
management charge – between $\frac{3}{4}$ and 1

per cent of the fund's total value – is
usually deducted from income before it
is sent to you. It is wise to shop around
and compare charges before investing.

See also ANNUITIES; BANK ACCOUNTS;
BUILDING SOCIETIES; SAVING.

Unsolicited goods

*Dealing with goods you have not
ordered*

It is an offence under the Unsolicited
Goods and Services Act 1971 to demand
payment from people who have been sent
goods they have not ordered.

You do not have to pay for goods if you
have not agreed to buy them. Unpacking
the parcel to see what is inside is not an
agreement to buy. Nor are you obliged
to return the goods or write to say you
do not want them. It is up to the sender
to contact you to pursue the sale.

But do not use the goods – put them
away untouched. If they have not been
collected by the sender after six months,
you can dispose of them as you wish.
During the first five months you can, if
you wish, write to the sender giving him
30 days in which to remove the goods. If
he does not remove them in the 30 days,
they then become yours.

See also TELEPHONE SOLICITATIONS.

Used car

Making checks before buying

Few used cars are in tiptop condition,
so there is always a risk when buying.
Minimise the risk by making preliminary
checks, especially for a private sale,
which offers no redress for defective
goods. Compare the selling price for the
make, model and year with that given in
a used car price guide. Low mileage,
extra accessories, a 'long' road tax and
MoT (see MOT TEST) can add to a car's
sale price. Some dealers offer WARRANTIES
for a given period or mileage after purchase, to cover the cost of parts and
labour, or just parts. Check the terms of
the warranty carefully.

If there is no warranty, evaluate the
price against any repairs needed. Repairs
that affect the car's roadworthiness
should be carried out by the dealer
within the selling price.

If possible, take a knowledgeable person with you to help you inspect the
vehicle; or pay for an independent check
by an expert – the Automobile Association, for example – who will provide
you with a written report.

Inspect a car in daylight, preferably in
dry weather. Use a torch to look underneath for signs of wear and weakness:
rust on the chassis; bulges in inner tyre
walls; oil leaks; peeling or cracked under-

sealing; rust or small holes in the exhaust
system; rusted jacking points.

Other points to check are:
● Look at the engine for signs of recent
servicing – reasonably clean engine oil,
for example.
● Look at the front of the car from a
distance of about 6m (20ft). If the bumper
is not parallel with the ground, its mountings or the suspension need attention.
● Press hard on each corner of the car
in turn. When your weight is released,
the car should not bounce more than
twice. If it does, the SHOCK ABSORBERS
need renewing. Look under wheel arches
for fluid leaks from a suspect shock absorber. If it leaks it needs replacing.
● If body RUST is extensive the car will
not be a good buy, but small, isolated
rust spots can usually be treated. Check
inside for damp areas indicating water
entry and probably rusted floor panels.
● Check TYRES for tread wear.
● Turn the steering wheel back and forth,
up to about 150mm (6in), and get a helper
to tell you when the front wheels begin
to change direction. Up to 38mm (1½in)
free play at the steering wheel before the
front wheels turn is usually acceptable.
Clunks or rattles could mean worn steering joints. Excessive wear could entail a
replacement steering rack or box.

Test drive Drive the car for several miles·
if possible – to show up running faults
and to judge driving comfort. Note
whether the doors open and close easily
– misalignment could have been caused
by accident damage.

The car should start easily and idle
smoothly. Some blue smoke from the
exhaust on starting is acceptable, but if
it persists, the engine is probably burning
too much oil and needs overhauling.

If the clutch is jerky and gear engage-
ment sticky, the transmission may need
overhauling. On an automatic, a slight
lurch as drive is engaged is normal, but
a noticeable thump is suspect.

At 48km/h (30mph) the engine should
perform smoothly – any rumbling or
knocking noises indicate worn bearings.

Test the brakes. If they are well balanced, the car should stop smoothly in a
straight line, with no wheel-locking or
juddering. Check that lights, panel
lights, indicators, windscreen washers
and wipers all work. Finally, check the
spare wheel, jack and wheel brace.

WARNINGS A car more than three
years old should have an MoT certificate.
This shows that it met the required safety
standards when tested – *not* that it is
still roadworthy.

If you are buying privately, ask the
seller for written evidence of ownership –
preferably a bill of sale. If you buy a
stolen or leased car, the rightful owner
can claim it and you have no redress. If
you buy from a dealer, he is responsible.

Vacuum cleaners

*Choosing and caring for them;
simple repairs*

The two basic types of vacuum cleaner are upright and cylinder. Most have a range of attachments to clean different surfaces, and some will even suck up water and wet debris, as well as dust.

The cleaning power of any machine is determined by the suction power at the cleaning head, which depends on the design of the head and hose as well as the power (wattage rating) and design of the motor. Some models have a variable suction control. A reliable make should carry the British Electrotechnical Approvals Board (BEAB) safety label or similar recognised mark of approval.

Upright cleaners As well as using suction these use revolving brushes which make them efficient at picking up animal hairs and ingrained dirt from carpets. They are easy to push over large areas, but unless they also have a good length of flexible hose and cleaning heads, their use is limited to carpet and floors.

Cylinder cleaners This type may be cylindrical or spherical in shape and operates purely by suction. Various types of cleaning head, including brushes, can be fitted to the hose or its rigid extension tube, which is hand held. The cleaner is therefore suitable for dusting and cleaning upholstery, shelves, walls and ceilings as well as carpets and floors.

Its design also makes it easier to reach awkward corners and under furniture and to clean stairs than with an upright cleaner, but it takes more effort.

See also VACUUMING.

Maintenance and repairs If your cleaner fails to operate when switched on, check the plug fuse and connections – see FUSES AND FUSE BOXES; PLUGS. If the plug is all right, the fault is in either the flex or the motor. Have the cleaner repaired by an electrician.

If a cleaner fails to pick up dirt properly, the dust bag may be full.

If suction is weak on a cylinder cleaner, the hose may be blocked or split. On some cleaners you can clear a blocked hose by fitting it to the rear of the cleaner (you may have to remove a grille and filter). Direct the hose outdoors and switch on the cleaner – the blockage will be blown out. If the hose is split, make a temporary repair with adhesive tape. New hoses are usually available from shops selling your make of cleaner.

An upright cleaner may fail to pick up dust well because it needs new brushes or a replacement brush-drive belt. These can usually be fitted at home, except on some of the most modern models, but make sure you buy the correct brushes or belt for your particular model. Ask the dealer to advise you.

To examine the belt, first unplug the machine. On some makes a front cover plate must be removed in order to release the belt from the drive shaft. On other makes there is only a base plate. Remove the base plate to reveal the brush roller. The rubber drive belt should be intact and looped tightly to the motor drive shaft. If it has slipped off, the belt may be worn.

To replace a worn belt, release the roller as shown in the illustration and fit a new belt. You will need to twist the belt when looping it over the end of the drive shaft. It is usually twisted clockwise, but follow the maker's instructions. Switch on the machine to test whether the belt is turning the roller correctly. If it does not, you may have twisted it the wrong way.

If the belt is sound but the roller does not turn, check the roller for tangled hair or threads that may impede its action, and remove them. Replace the metal plate. Follow the manufacturer's instructions for replacing brushes; you may have to buy a whole new roller and brush fitting.

On a cylinder cleaner, the rear exhaust filter and, if there is one, the motor filter behind the dust bag, should be changed at least twice yearly, or as recommended by the manufacturer; buy replacements from your local dealer or hardware store and fit them according to the manufacturer's instructions. They usually push or slot into place.

VACUUM CLEANERS

Fitting a new drive belt

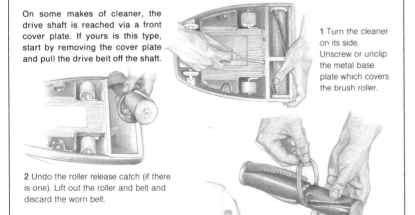

On some makes of cleaner, the drive shaft is reached via a front cover plate. If yours is this type, start by removing the cover plate and pull the drive belt off the shaft.

1 Turn the cleaner on its side. Unscrew or unclip the metal base plate which covers the brush roller.

2 Undo the roller release catch (if there is one). Lift out the roller and belt and discard the worn belt.

3 Fit a new belt round the groove in the roller. Refit the roller and base plate.

4 Twist the belt and stretch it over the drive shaft.

Vacuuming

Using your cleaner to the best effect

The range of jobs you can do with your vacuum cleaner will depend on the type – see VACUUM CLEANERS. Use the cleaner strictly according to the manufacturer's instructions, as forcing a machine to do something it was not designed for may damage it or the surface you are cleaning. Do not attempt to pick up hot cinders or lighted cigarette ends, or sharp objects such as needles.

VALANCES

Making a frilled edge for your bed

Sew the valance pieces together into one strip. Sew a double 16mm (⅝in) hem at each end and a double 20mm (¾in) hem along the bottom edge. Pin-mark the raw edge into eight sections. Run two parallel threads along the raw edge of each section.

Double hem 16mm (⅝in) Flat-fell seam Running threads

Double hem 20mm (¾in)

Bias binding

Base

Tacking

Draw the threads to gather the material, then pin and tack it to the base fabric.

Pin, tack and sew bias binding, wrong side up, along the tacked line.

Fold the binding back over the raw edges and sew it to the base material.

Guide the machine or cleaning head with firm regular movements; do not push it like a broom. Use the special head attachment for vacuuming along carpet edges. If you have an upright model with no such attachment, use a stiff brush to move dust away from the carpet edge to a position where the cleaner can deal with it.

If you are cleaning a staircase with an upright model, leave it at the bottom or top of the flight and use a hose attachment to clean each step. If the hose is too short, move the machine to the other end of the stair halfway through cleaning; do not overstretch the hose.

Empty the bag when it is full, and always fit a replacement bag of the type recommended by the manufacturer.

Carpets in regular use should be vacuumed at least once a week. If you have pets, you can buy a special cleaning-pad head that picks up animal hairs from upholstery and can be adapted to fit various models.

Valances

Putting the finishing touch to curtains and divans

Valances are like very short curtains that hang round a bed base to hide the legs, or hang across the top of a window to hide the curtain rail. See also CURTAINS; PELMET.

Making a gathered valance for a bed or divan Cut out (from inexpensive sheeting fabric) a piece of material for the base, the size of the mattress surface plus 13mm (½in) all round. Using pins as markers, divide the edge – apart from the bedhead edge – into eight equal sections.

You will need enough bias binding to go all round the base.

Measure from the base of the mattress to the floor and add on 50mm (2in) for seams and the hem. You need a strip of material this width for the gathered frill. Measure all round the bed from one top corner to the other; double this measurement to find the length of the strip.

Join together the pieces to make up the strip, using flat-fell seams – see SEWING. Hem each end and one long edge with a machine stitch or by hand – see HEMS.

Using pins as markers, divide the raw edge of the strip into eight equal sections. Run two gathering threads along near the raw edge of each section. Draw up the gathered sections until each one is the right length to match a section marked with pins on the edge of the base.

Pin the gathered strip to the base with wrong sides together, then tack the two together 13mm from the edge. Pin the top edge of bias binding along the tacked line with right side down. Then tack it in place and machine along the tacked line. Fold the binding over to lie flat on the base and cover the raw edges; fold the excess into neat pleats at the corners. Pin, tack and sew the free edge of the binding to the base.

Bind the bedhead edge of the base. Lay the valance on the bed under the mattress.

Making a curtain valance This is usually fitted onto the curtain rail using brackets and a valance rail. If your curtains are in the window recess, you can hang it at the front of the recess.

Allow 38mm (1½in) of valance to every 300mm (12in) of curtain drop plus 75mm (3in) each for the hem and top turning. To calculate the width, measure the curtain rail, multiply this measurement by

2-2½, and add on 60mm (2¼in) at each end.

Make up the valance as for curtains, fitting the heading tape so that the curtain hooks will be 50mm (2in) below the top of the finished valance. Draw up the tape cords and insert the curtain hooks.

Value Added Tax [VAT]

Calculating an extra cost on goods and services

Value Added Tax is levied at each stage of production and supply of certain goods and services, including the final stage of selling to the consumer. The 1994 rate was 17½ per cent. Knowing what is, and what is not, liable for VAT can often save you money. For example:

VAT is not payable on most foods in shops, but is payable on items such as potato crisps, salted nuts, ice cream, chocolate, sweets, alcohol and fruit juices. Take-away cold food carries no VAT, but hot take-away meals and food you eat inside a café, pub or restaurant are taxed. Feed for livestock is not taxed; pet food, however, is.

Prescription medicines and medical aids on prescription carry no VAT, but over-the-counter medicines and cosmetics are taxed.

You pay VAT on petrol and motor oil, and also on domestic heating oil, coke, gas and electricity.

You do not always have to pay VAT on constructing a building, but you do on repairs or maintenance work or on alterations unless they are to a listed building.

Public transport is exempt from VAT, provided the vehicle can carry 12 or more passengers – so taxis and hire cars are chargeable.

Dwellings, caravans as homes and houseboat homes are not subject to VAT if they are occupied for longer than three weeks. VAT is charged on hotel rooms, car parks, touring caravans and pleasure boats.

Non-profit-making education and courses are not taxed; profit-making private schools and private courses are.

Shops and restaurants have to show prices with VAT included, other traders do not.

If you are paying for goods or services liable for VAT, the supplier must give you an invoice indicating his name, address, VAT registration number, the date of supply, a description of the goods or services, the total payable including the tax, and the VAT rate in force.

Varnishing

Applying a clear finish to wood

Basically, varnish is a paint that contains no pigment, so the finish is transparent. It is used wherever you want a protective finish with the natural colour and grain of wood showing through.

Varnishes are available with a high gloss, slight gloss or matt finish, and there are interior and exterior grades. Exterior grades may contain fungicide, plus an ultraviolet filter to prevent the sun's rays from affecting the wood.

Varnishes may be virtually colourless, or may contain stains that colour the wood. They are available for brushing on, or in aerosol form for spraying.

Preparation If the wood is uneven in colour, perhaps through different woods being combined, use a wood bleach to produce an over-all neutral tone – see BLEACHING WOOD. Fill all gaps with matching wood filler, of a type that will take stains and varnish – see STOPPERS AND FILLERS. If in doubt, test a little first.

When the filler has set, rub the surface smooth with fine glasspaper – see SANDING. If you wish, apply a wood stain or dye by rag or brush to produce the colour you require before varnishing – see STAINING WOOD.

Whichever of the above treatments is used, give a final light smoothing with fine glasspaper, then dust off thoroughly.

The alternative to a wood stain is a varnish stain which combines colour and varnish. But keep in mind that every coat applied darkens the surface a little more. Experimenting is advisable if a number of coats are to be applied.

Application Ensure that there is ample ventilation when varnishing and work on a day when the air is still. Do not apply varnish in damp or very humid weather or the finish may be cloudy.

Look upon the first coat of varnish as a primer – it is best applied with a lint-free rag, such as a piece of old cotton sheet. Work the varnish well into the wood and leave to dry for the time recommended by the maker. Then rub over it with fine glasspaper, working only with the grain of the wood.

Dust off thoroughly, then apply the second coat of varnish with a clean, dust-free brush. Do not apply too thick a coat – apply several thin coats, allowing each to dry before applying the next.

Sometimes a high gloss looks artificial. To mellow its appearance, rub lightly with fine steel wool lubricated with white spirit. Wipe clean with a lint-free rag, then polish with furniture polish. A similar effect can be achieved by using matt varnish followed by wax polish.

An aerosol varnish is useful for coating textured or intricate surfaces, but it is not so good on large, flat surfaces. Preparation is the same as for applying by brush, but as varnish from an aerosol is very thin, plan to apply several very light coats. Too much varnish in one coat will almost certainly result in trickles, runs or sagging.

Hold the can the recommended distance from the surface to be coated, and move it parallel with the surface. Maintain the same distance all the time and keep the aerosol moving constantly. Allow each coat to dry before spraying on the next. See also SPRAY PAINTING.

Vegetarian meals

Planning meatless menus

If you are catering for a vegetarian, find out which diet is being followed.

The strictest of all vegetarian diets is the vegan, in which no animal products are eaten; this excludes not only meat, EGGS and dairy products but even such animal by-products as ASPIC. Other vegetarian diets exclude meat but include milk and other dairy products. Vegetarians may or may not eat fish or eggs.

Since the foods excluded from a vegetarian diet are rich in body-building proteins, you should serve other protein-rich foods in their place to provide a nutritionally balanced diet.

Four main food groups will supply all a vegetarian's dietary needs. These are: pulses (peas, beans, lentils) and nuts, cereals such as wheat and rice, fruit and vegetables, and dairy produce.

Include foods from each group daily to make up a balanced vegetarian diet. If dairy foods are not eaten, serve a wide range of green leafy vegetables such as broccoli, brussels sprouts and spinach, to provide the calcium usually supplied by milk. They also supply iron.

As many vegetarian foods are lower in both protein and calories than a regular diet, serve larger portions to make up

the deficiency – see CALORIE COUNTING.

Recipes combining vegetarian foods in delicious and nutritious ways can be found in the many vegetarian cookery books available. These may include dishes from the Far East and Middle East where there is a long tradition of vegetarian cooking, using a wide range of herbs and spices to add variety and flavour to meatless meals.

Velcro fasteners

Fixing on easy-to-use fastenings

Velcro fastenings consist of two tapes, patches or circles, which grip each other tightly when the one side, covered with tiny, nylon hooks, is pressed against the other side which has tiny nylon loops. Both tapes may have to be sewn on; both tapes may be self-adhesive; or one tape may be self-adhesive and the other for SEWING.

The sew-on type is generally most suitable for fixing to fabrics. It makes garments easier to manage for disabled people and small children because the fastening simply presses together and pulls apart. Use the tape instead of ZIPPERS, to fasten waistbands, in place of buttonholes, for detachable collars or hoods, or to close pockets. You can also use Velcro for the openings of loose covers and CUSHIONS.

Use the stick-on type on hard surfaces such as metal, wood, tiles and glass, and the combined sew-on and stick-on type for attaching fabrics to hard surfaces – for example a fabric pelmet to a wooden support – see PELMETS.

To sew the tapes to fabric, use a sewing machine (see SEWING MACHINES) with the zipper foot fitted and a small zigzag stitch. Thread the machine with a synthetic thread. Begin stitching along the sides of the tape rather than at the corners, which take the greatest strain when the fastener is opened. Stitch tapes wider than 25mm (1in) through the centre or diagonally from the corners as well as round the edge. Sew on small pieces by hand, using hemstitch.

Close a Velcro fastening before washing, and when IRONING, use nothing hotter than a 'warm' setting. If fluff gathers on the hook side clean it gently with a wire brush.

Velvet

Cleaning it and restoring the nap

Before cleaning velvet or velveteen (a velvet-like cotton fabric), check the label to see if it is washable. Non-washable velvet should be dry-cleaned professionally. If in doubt, treat as non-washable.

Do not press velvet unless you have a

needle board for pressing pile fabrics. Even then, it is difficult.

Cleaning washable velvet Remove any bad spots with a soft brush. Wash and rinse in lukewarm water – see LAUNDERING. Spin briefly, then hang out to dry. When completely dry, brush in one direction only with a soft brush.

Restoring the nap If velvet becomes crushed, restore the nap by steaming – if it is not too badly damaged. Tie muslin or cheesecloth over the spout of a kettle of water and heat the kettle. When the water is boiling rapidly, pass the velvet, with the reverse side towards the spout, to and fro through the steam – be careful, steam can cause SCALDS.

Veneer

Fixing an attractive new surface to wood

Veneer is widely used in furniture-making, both to give the appearance of expensive woods, and to provide decoration – see also MARQUETRY. It is produced by peeling very thin layers of wood from a revolving log. The usual thickness of a veneer is 0.6mm (less than $^1/_{32}$in).

If you plan to do veneering, contact one of the specialist timber companies which operates a mail order service. A catalogue will show that a wide range of timbers and grain patterns are available.

You will need a few special tools and materials. The most important is a veneer hammer, which you can get at a specialist tool or craft shop. You also need a steel straightedge and craft knife; abrasive paper and SANDING block; a roll of brown sticky paper tape; and hot, thin Scotch (traditional) glue. A PVA adhesive can be used for very small repair jobs, but traditional glue is best for larger areas – see GLUING.

To cover a sheet of PLYWOOD about 13mm ($\frac{1}{2}$in) thick, you need decorative veneer and a cheaper balancer veneer to go on the underside of the plywood to prevent bending. If the plywood is to be anchored firmly, say as a worktop, the under-surface can be painted instead.

Roughen the surface to be covered, using a coarse glasspaper. Work across the wood grain as well as with it, to give the glue a good key.

Cut the covering veneers roughly to size, matching the sheets for pattern. Overlap the sheets by about 19mm ($\frac{3}{4}$in) where they join and leave a similar allowance round the edges of the plywood. Sprinkle clean water on each side of the veneer sheets; stack them in a pile and hold them flat between two boards. After a few hours they will be pliable.

Make up some Scotch glue – follow any instructions on the packet. Otherwise break up the glue and soak it in water for several hours. Then cover it with more water and boil for 20 minutes in a double saucepan. Brush a thin layer on the plywood face. Leave it to dry.

Arrange your sheets of veneer in the order they are to be applied, then spread another layer of glue on the plywood, to the width of the first sheet. Lay the first sheet of veneer face down on the glued area and apply glue to the veneer.

Turn the veneer over and also glue the face side, then move the veneer into position, remembering the overlap. Now rapidly rub it with the veneer hammer, until it is firmly bonded to the plywood.

Gently tap the entire surface with the hammer. If there is a hollow sound, it indicates a bubble. Force the air out by pressing and scraping with the veneer hammer, working it towards the edges of the plywood.

Now treat the second sheet of veneer in a similar manner, overlapping the first by 19mm ($\frac{3}{4}$in). When the veneer is laid, use the craft knife and straightedge to cut through the centre of the overlap.

Remove the waste pieces, then close the joint by rubbing hard with the veneer hammer, working it in a herringbone pattern towards the joint, until the edges meet. To hold the joint in place, cover it with sticky brown paper tape. Remove it later, using a damp cloth.

Remove surplus glue from the laid veneer with a rag and hot water. Use a cabinet scraper to remove any residue, scraping only in line with the grain of the wood. Trim the edges with the craft knife.

Patching Veneer often gets chipped along the edge of a piece of furniture. To repair a small damaged area, first try to find a piece of veneer that matches the original. Cut and glue the patch as illustrated, using Scotch glue on old furniture and PVA adhesive on new pieces.

Cover the repair with non-sticky brown paper, then a piece of board, and put a weight on it or secure with clamps until the glue has set. Trim the edge. Finish as appropriate – see ANTIQUES; FRENCH POLISHING; VARNISHING.

If the damage is in the centre of an area of veneer, cut a diamond or boat-shaped patch and proceed as before.

Loose veneer Raise the loose area carefully with the craft knife blade. Remove all old glue, then stick the veneer back, using a resin-based adhesive on the veneer and the wood. Cover and weight or clamp, as for patching. Small loose areas can often be refixed by carefully heating the area, then pressing down the veneer into the melted glue.

Sand lightly with fine glasspaper, working as far as possible with the grain of the wood. Finish as appropriate.

Veneer tape

For neat edgings

Veneered CHIPBOARD is usually supplied with all edges veneered, but once a board is cut the chipboard is exposed. To cover it, VENEER in tape or strip form is available by the roll, ready-coated on one side with a heat-sensitive adhesive.

VENEER

Patching a damaged edge

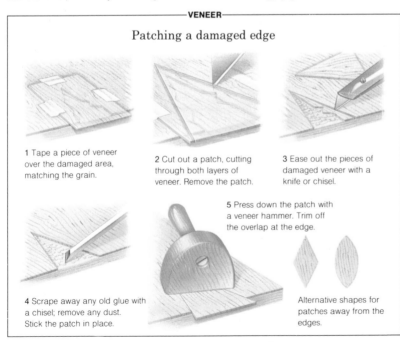

1 Tape a piece of veneer over the damaged area, matching the grain.

2 Cut out a patch, cutting through both layers of veneer. Remove the patch.

3 Ease out the pieces of damaged veneer with a knife or chisel.

4 Scrape away any old glue with a chisel; remove any dust. Stick the patch in place.

5 Press down the patch with a veneer hammer. Trim off the overlap at the edge.

Alternative shapes for patches away from the edges.

To veneer an edge or replace a missing edging, ensure that it has a clean, square face, free from loose material and smoothed with glasspaper wrapped around a SANDING block.

Clamp the board in a vice with the cut edge uppermost and level. Lay the strip in place at one end and cover it with brown paper. Press with the tip of a hot iron until the tape is anchored in place.

Brown paper

Veneer tape

Applying veneer tape Move the hot iron back and forth under moderate pressure to ensure that the tape is firmly stuck down.

Hold the strip in position with two fingers, moving them in advance of the iron while you press the rest of the tape in place, as illustrated. Finally remove the iron and press the tape down with your fingers, keeping the brown paper in place, to make sure that all the tape is in firm contact.

Use a craft knife to trim the tape at each end. If tape has to be joined, overlap it by 13mm (½in) where it meets, then cut through both pieces with the craft knife *after* sticking the tape in place. Remove the surplus pieces and press down to leave a perfect join.

If trimming is necessary along the length of the board, use the craft knife first, then smooth the meeting edges with fine glasspaper.

Dirty marks can be removed from plastic tape with a domestic cleaning paste on a piece of damp rag. Remove marks from wood veneer tape with abrasive paper.

Venetian blinds

Fitting them; three methods

Venetian BLINDS can be bought made to measure for the window; there are three or four slat widths to choose from.

There are three ways of fixing the head rail – in the window recess, screwed either to the side walls or the top; or to the wall above the window.

If you fit the blind within the window recess, measure the horizontal width both at the top of the recess and at the bottom in case there is any variation in width. Then measure the recess from top to bottom. Give these exact measurements to the store, and they will make

a clearance allowance when they calculate the size of the blind.

If the blind is to be fitted outside the window area, measure to allow at least 50mm (2in) extra on either side to stop the blind drifting into the window recess.

The made-up blind will be supplied with two holding brackets – marked 'left' and 'right' – for the head rail. They have a number of holes, allowing you to screw through the side, back or top.

Each bracket has a hinged flap, and this must be positioned to lift up at the front. Hold a bracket in place; mark the wall through the appropriate fixing holes, then drill and plug the wall – see MASONRY DRILLING. Screw the bracket in place, then repeat the process for the second bracket.

Open the hinged flap of each bracket and insert the blind, then close the flaps until they click shut.

With most domestic blinds, if the width exceeds 1.5m (5ft), a centre support bracket will be required. Check this with the supplier's leaflet when buying.

WARNING Make sure that the position you choose for your blind has no obstructions which would foul the blind when operated – such as window catches.

Ventilation

Making sure your home is well aired

In the draughty homes of the past, ventilation was never a problem. But with efficient DRAUGHTPROOFING and the blocking up of open flues, many homes have become like hermetically sealed boxes, allowing little stale air out and almost no fresh air in.

This allows germs to multiply, and the fug generated can lead to lethargy and HEADACHES. It may also create problems with gas and solid-fuel fires and boilers, which need a regular air supply to burn efficiently and safely.

In the winter when the heating is on, open small windows to allow in fresh air – particularly in bedrooms, where CONDENSATION can be a problem. Grilles and ventilators are of some value but they are affected by prevailing winds and air may blow in, but never out. If possible, install the type of ventilator that can be shut off.

Ensure that boilers have their own local air supply, and improve the burning of solid-fuel fires and stoves by siting small ventilators close by. Fit a small ventilator in the panel that blocks off any unused flue, so that air can circulate and keep the chill off the flue, otherwise there is the risk of condensation on the flue lining.

See also AIR BRICKS; EXTRACTOR FANS; FIREPLACES.

Verdigris

Removing green deposits from copper

Verdigris is the green deposit (a copper carbonate compound) that forms on copper that has been exposed for a long time to air or sea water.

To prevent it from forming, keep copper polished (see ANTIQUES), particularly copper cooking utensils – because, as with all copper compounds, verdigris is toxic.

If, however, verdigris does form, make a solution of lemon juice and salt or a paste of whiting and methylated spirit and rub it hard into the verdigris, using a soft cloth. If some stubborn patches remain, use very fine (gauge 0000) steel wool – but never harsh abrasives, which will scratch the metal.

Video recorders

Choosing one; setting up and handling it

A video recorder will record any programmes received in your area independently of your television. To play back, and view, the recorded programme the video must be plugged into a TV set. This can be accomplished via the TV's aerial socket, or else via a SCART socket (also known as a Euro Connector) if both the video and the TV are fitted with these connectors.

Buy or hire a recorder of an established make from a reputable dealer. The most common types are VHS and SVHS. Many models are now available with various facilities and extras, including Nicam stereo and Dolby Surround. Visit a specialist television and video retailer to investigate what is available before buying, and ask for demonstrations.

Nicam stereo allows you to hear the programme in stereo, if the broadcast is in stereo and you have a stereo television, while Dolby Surround adds depth to the broadcast with the addition of two 'rear' speakers. To hear 'surround sound', the broadcast must be in Dolby Surround.

Several video recorders have an 'audio out' facility, allowing you to feed the sound into your hi-fi system, so improving the sound quality. Long play is a common feature that doubles the length of your recording time – a three-hour tape becomes six hours and a four-hour tape, eight hours. Long play is useful when you want to record several programmes, but the quality is not as good as at normal speed.

Some video recorders can take two tapes allowing you to record a programme on one while viewing a tape on the other

Setting up and handling Before recording, study the instructions and make sure you understand the controls. Most timers are quite straightforward; some can be operated by remote control. To play back recorded programmes, the video and TV set must be set up, using a spare TV channel. Follow the step-by-step instructions carefully, or ask the dealer to set it up for you.

Keep the recorder on a shelf or in a video cabinet. Do not set it on the floor, where it can gather dust and possibly animal hairs from pets. Most machines are too complex for the user to clean or repair. Properly looked after, a good recorder should last at least five years.

Vines

Growing your own grapes

Grape vines are hardy and can withstand a temperature as low as –20°C (–4°F), but persistent lower temperatures will destroy them.

Best-quality dessert grapes do not generally do well outdoors in Britain's variable summers, and are best grown in GREENHOUSES. Some dessert varieties, however, yield good crops in the south of England. They include 'Royal Muscardine', 'Black Hamburgh', 'Siegerrebe' and 'Buckland Sweetwater'.

WINE-MAKING grapes are grown outdoors. Varieties successful in Britain include 'Triomphe d'Alsace', 'Müller Thurgau' and 'Seyve Villard 5276'.

An established vine against a wall or under glass may produce 7-10kg (15-22lb) or more grapes in a good season.

Outdoor vines If possible, plant vines against a sheltered, sunny, south or west-facing wall. Fix support wires to the wall 300mm (12in) apart and held 125mm (5in) from the wall with vine eyes – special galvanised eyebolts available from garden shops.

Buy year-old vines and plant between October and March. Vines will grow in any well-drained soil. Before planting, enrich the soil with garden COMPOST or rotted manure – a 10 litre (2 gallon) bucket to the square metre (about 1 square yard) – and 115g (4oz) general fertiliser (see FERTILISERS), to the square metre.

For each vine dig a hole slightly deeper and wider than its root system. Plant the vines 1.2m (4ft) apart and 230mm (9in) from the wall.

After planting, cut the vine above a bud about 150mm (6in) above the ground. During the first summer, allow only five strong shoots to grow; pinch out all the rest as soon as possible. In the first winter, cut the strongest shoot (the rod) back by half, and cut out the other four shoots completely.

During the second summer, tie all side-shoots (laterals) to the supporting wires. When they are 610-910mm (2-3ft) long, pinch out the tips. Let the rod grow.

In winter, trim the rod to the final height you want it to be; if it is still too short, leave it. Cut each lateral above the second bud.

In early spring, each bud will produce fruiting spurs. Cut off the weaker spur on each lateral, as well as any other unwanted shoots. Tie the remaining shoots to the supporting wires.

In early summer, a flower cluster will form on each spur; cut the spur two leaves beyond the cluster.

Soon after the grapes begin to form, use scissors to cut out any small, over-crowded fruits in the centre of bunches.

Repeat the winter, early spring and summer pruning each year.

Greenhouse vines A greenhouse vine can be planted in an outside border, then trained into the greenhouse through an aperture. This makes watering easier.

Plant greenhouse vines in early autumn. Before planting, fix support wires running the length of the greenhouse 300mm (12in) apart and 460mm (18in) from the glass. Attach them to the greenhouse framework with vine eyes.

Make up a bed with 3 parts loam and 1 part rotted manure. Plant the vines 1.5m (5ft) apart. After planting, cut back above a bud, leaving only 150mm (6in) above ground or inside the greenhouse if the roots are outside. Train as for vines grown against a wall (see above).

In late winter, start heating the greenhouse to around 7°C (45°F). In spring, raise the temperature to 16°C (61°F) at night and 18-21°C (64-70°F) during the daylight hours.

Keep the vines thoroughly watered in warm weather and spray the rods daily, to keep the atmosphere humid. Keep the greenhouse well ventilated.

Once the grapes begin to form, feed the vines with liquid fertiliser (following the manufacturer's instructions) and dried blood – 1 dessertspoon per square metre (square yard). During the winter, remove the top 25mm (1in) of soil and replace with compost or manure. See also MULCHING.

Vinyl floor covering

Laying and cutting tiles and sheet flooring

Ensure first that the floor is smooth and free from obstruction. Check timber floors for loose tacks or small nails; remove any with a tack lifter or pincers. Knock down any protruding flooring nails using a hammer and nail punch. If the floorboards are uneven, rent a floor sanding machine from a tool hire shop to level the boards; if there are gaps between, lay hardboard over the whole floor area. See also FLOOR REPAIRS; HIRING; UNEVEN FLOORS.

Check CONCRETE floors for rough spots. Chip these away with a club hammer and cold chisel, and fill any holes with sand-cement MORTAR to which some PVA adhesive has been added – see GLUING. Brush off all loose material. Level off any filling with a builder's trowel, and allow it to set and dry out before laying the covering.

VINYL FLOOR COVERING

Laying floor tiles and sheet vinyl

Laying floor tiles Bisect the floor each way using a length of string coated with chalk. Stretch the string and then release it to leave chalk lines on the floor. Start tiling from where the lines intersect.

90 degrees

Now position the sheet on the adjacent side so that it is 125mm (5in) from the wall, and scribe it in the same way as for the first wall.

Scriber

Laying sheet vinyl Place the first side 125mm (5in) away from the wall. Holding a scriber against the wall, draw it along the vinyl. Cut off the surplus along the scratched line and slide the sheet against the wall.

Laying the covering 'Stay-flat' types of cushioned vinyl are the easiest to lay, as they do not need to be glued and do not shrink.

The easiest way to lay vinyl is in tile form. Some tiles are self-adhesive, others are stuck down with flooring adhesive, which can be bought with the tiles.

If you are using adhesive, spread about a square metre (square yard) at a time, then lay tiles on the glued area at your central starting point (see illustration).

If adhesive oozes up between the joins, wipe it off at once with a cloth damped with white spirit or water, according to the maker's instructions.

WARNING Make sure there is adequate ventilation and turn off all pilot lights.

Once all full tiles have been laid, lay part tiles to fill in the gaps: lay a second tile over the top of the last full tile, then a third on top of the second and slide it into contact with the wall.

Mark on the second tile where the outside edge of the third tile comes. Cut the second tile along this line with a sharp knife, to leave a piece which will fit neatly into the gap. Continue until all gaps are filled.

Sheet materials Many floorcoverings are now available in rolls wide enough to cover the average room without joins. If a join has to be made, try to locate it in an area of least traffic, and where it will hardly show.

Cut the sheet with generous overlaps on all four sides – at least 50mm (2in) – and position the sheet on the floor. Make up a simple scriber with a fine-pointed nail sticking through a batten 150mm (6in) from the end – see BATTENS.

Now, holding the scriber to the wall, use it to make a scratch mark on the floorcovering for the full length of the sheet. It will follow accurately the contours of the wall. Cut off the surplus with a craft knife and slide the sheet in contact with the wall.

Repeat for an end wall, first making a mark at each end where the sheet needs to be cut, then pulling the sheet away from the wall until the scriber point just touches both marks. Scribe a line the full length of the sheet, cut off the surplus, then slide the sheet in contact with the end wall.

Repeat for the other two walls. Roll back the sheet over half the room, put adhesive on the floor, and reposition the sheet. Cushioned vinyls only need to be glued round the edges.

If two pieces are needed to cover a floor, deal with the outside walls first, allowing a generous overlap where the sheets meet. If the sheets are patterned, make sure the pattern will be maintained at the overlap. When fitting is complete, allow a week for settlement, then cut

through both sheets together with a sharp craft knife and straightedge.

Pull out the scrap piece from under the top sheet, and the two pieces should meet perfectly. Fix double-sided carpet tape under the join, to hold it firmly to the floor.

For marking around obstructions like door architraves, use a PROFILE GAUGE.

Violins

Making minor repairs and restringing

Valuable instruments are best repaired by a professional craftsman, but minor repairs to an inexpensive violin can be made at home.

Replacement parts are available from musical instrument shops. Rest the violin on paper or cloth while working.

Fixing a loose belly Scrape out the old glue from the gap between the belly and the rib with a flat-bladed knife. Then use the knife to insert fresh adhesive into the gap (use Scotch glue or PVA woodworking adhesive – see GLUING). Cramp the joint together with a G-clamp, padded with small pieces of hardboard to avoid marking the wood. Wipe off any excess glue and leave clamped for 24 hours.

Fitting a chin rest The rest is secured to the side of the belly with sleeve nuts tightened by a square-shaped key usually supplied with it, but stiff wire can be used instead. Make sure the chin rest does not touch the tail piece, as this will cause it to vibrate during playing.

Fitting new strings Do not remove all the strings at once, or the soundpost could be displaced. Replace one string at

a time, in the order E A D G. Fit each one at the tail-piece end first, then to the peg box at the scroll end (see illustration).

Fit the threaded end of the E-string adjuster through its hole in the tail piece and screw on the knurled nut and adjuster screw. Slip the looped end of the E string onto the adjuster and position the small plastic sleeve over the bridge to prevent the bridge being damaged.

Fit the other end of the string through the hole in its peg. The string should protrude about 25mm (1in) through the hole. Turn the peg clockwise until the string is taut, making sure that the wound string does not cross over itself.

The other strings are fitted the same way at the scroll end, but not at the tail-piece end. Knot the ends of the A and D strings and slip the knots through the holes in the tail piece; then pull the strings into the thin slots. Fit the G string by pushing its looped end through the hole in the tail piece and threading the string back through the loop.

Fitting a new peg When a peg becomes so worn that it cannot hold the string taut, replace it with a new one. This is usually slightly thicker than required. Shape it to fit, using a fine file, and finish off with glasspaper.

Put the peg through its holes and turn it a few times to form two shiny rings round it. These ensure correct fitting and smooth turning. Refit the peg and make a pencil mark at the protruding end 3mm ($\frac{1}{8}$in) from the edge of the peg-box. Remove the peg and saw off the surplus with a fine-toothed saw, and smooth the cut end with glasspaper. Replace the peg and mark its centre between the two sides of the peg-box. Take the peg out and drill a 2mm ($\frac{1}{16}$in) string hole through the marked centre.

VIOLIN

A guide to components, and restringing

Scroll

Fingerboard

Tail piece Fit a string to the tail piece first, then the peg-box. Work in the order E A D G.

Tail piece

Peg-box

Bridge

D   A

E

G

Plastic sleeve

Adjuster screw

Tail piece

Belly

Saddle

Peg-box Thread a string through its peg hole and turn the peg clockwise to tauten the string.

Purfling

'f' hole

Soundpost

Rib

End pin

Chin rest

Sleeve nut

Fitting a new bridge Bridges with self-adjusting feet are available but, depending on the instrument, it may be better to use fine glasspaper to shape the feet to the contours of the belly.

To do this, put a piece of glasspaper, rough side up, at the point where the bridge is to be fitted and rub the bridge back and forth over it. Then position the bridge on the belly between the f-shaped holes, in line with their centre cuts. Check that the feet fit against the surface exactly.

File the top of the bridge to roughly match the curve of the fingerboard. Viewed from the scroll end, the G-string side of the bridge should be 6mm ($\frac{1}{4}$in) higher than the fingerboard, and the E-string side 5mm ($\frac{3}{16}$in) higher. Finish with glasspaper.

Use a craft knife to cut four V-shaped nicks in the top of the bridge for the strings: make the two outer grooves 3mm ($\frac{1}{8}$in) from the edges, and space the inner ones equally between them. Rub a little pencil lead in the nicks, place the bridge in position (do *not* glue it) and restring.

The soundpost Do not attempt to reposition the soundpost – a thin stick of pine wedged upright inside the instrument immediately below the bridge. If it is dislodged by a hard knock or fall, get it repositioned.

Visa

Finding out if you need one and how to get it

A visa is an official authorisation which permits you to enter a foreign country and travel in it. The visa is usually stamped in or attached to your passport by a consular office of the foreign country. In most cases a visa states the purpose for which you are allowed to visit the country (tourism, for example) and for how long.

Before making a foreign trip, check with your travel agent, the airline you are using or the consulates or embassies of the countries you plan to visit, what the visa requirements are. Generally, British citizens do not need visas for EC countries or for Commonwealth countries, except Australia and India.

Applying for a visa Ask the country's consulate or the consular section of the embassy for an application form for a visa. Alternatively, get your travel agent to apply for you.

Make your application several weeks in advance – especially when visiting Asian or African countries whose consulates can take several days to process applications; and allow extra time if you are going to more than one country, as your passport will have to go to each consulate in turn.

Many consulates charge a fee for a visa and may require you to provide one or more passport-type photographs and supporting documents.

Changing plans The dates on your visa apply strictly. If you arrive early at a frontier, you may be refused entry. If you unexpectedly wish to prolong your trip, find out immediately from a British consul, the local police or a tourist bureau how to extend your visa.

Visiting hostile countries If you are visiting two countries that are hostile to each other (Israel and most Arab states, for example), ask the consulates of the countries concerned to stamp the visas on separate sheets of paper which can be clipped to your passport and removed after the visit. Or ask the Passport Office (see PASSPORT) for a second passport valid only for one or other of the opposing countries.

If you have previously visited a country hostile to the country you are now planning to visit and have its visa in your passport, it may be advisable to surrender the passport and buy a new one, or obtain a second one.

Vitamins

Getting those you need; good sources

Vitamins help your body to function efficiently – for example, they assist it to process other nutrients. They do not, however, provide tissue or energy.

Getting enough The best way to take vitamins is in food.

The chart shows foods that are rich in each particular vitamin. Make sure you eat some food from each category each week.

Buy food as fresh as possible, and process it as little as possible. Preferably, eat fruit and vegetables raw – if you do cook them, it is generally best to cook them in as little water as possible. Use meat cooking juices and vegetable cooking water for sauces, gravies and soups.

Vitamin tablets A healthy, balanced diet gives you more than enough vitamins of all kinds.

Vitamins in tablet form can be useful after an illness or if you are on a drastic weight-loss diet. In this case, take multivitamin tablets – the cheaper ones with synthetic vitamins are just as beneficial as ones with natural vitamins.

Contrary to popular belief, there is no conclusive evidence that large doses of vitamin C prevent colds. However, vitamin C does increase the amount of iron

Guide to vitamins	
Vitamin	Good sources
A	Liver, spinach, carrots, tomatoes, peaches, margarine, butter, yellow and orange fruit and vegetables, dark green vegetables, eggs, cheese, milk
B_1 (Thiamin)	Pork, liver, ham, bacon, potatoes, bread, breakfast cereals, pulses, nuts, vegetables, milk
B_2 (Riboflavin)	Liver, meat, milk, cheese, eggs
B (Niacin)	Liver, meat, bread, chicken, pulses, breakfast cereals
B (Folate)	Liver, green leafy vegetables, peas, oranges, breakfast cereals, wholemeal bread
B (Biotin)	Liver, pork, kidneys, nuts, lentils, breakfast cereals, cauliflower
B (Pantothenic acid)	Liver, kidneys, eggs, peanuts, mushrooms, spinach, cheese, pears
B_6 (Pyridoxine)	Liver, breakfast cereals, pulses, poultry
B_{12} (Cobalamin)	Meat, milk, cheese, eggs
C (Ascorbic acid)	Citrus fruit, fresh currants, green leafy vegetables, strawberries, blackcurrants, tomatoes, bananas, cauliflowers, potatoes
D	Skimmed milk, fatty fish, margarine, eggs, butter, sunlight
E	Vegetable oils, nuts, eggs, butter, wholegrain cereals, green leafy vegetables
K	Green leafy vegetables

you absorb from food and helps your body to break down cholesterol.

WARNING Keep vitamin tablets out of the reach of children. Overdoses of vitamins can be dangerous.

Vol-au-vents

Making light pastry cases with savoury fillings

You will need 450g (1lb) puff PASTRY for a dozen small cases, which are cooked and then filled with a thick, creamy chicken or fish-based mixture. Roll out the pastry to 13mm (½in) thick. Cut out rounds using a floured 75mm (3in) fluted biscuit cutter.

Transfer the rounds to a wetted baking tray using a palette knife. Brush the tops with beaten egg. Press a 50mm (2in) fluted biscuit cutter onto the rounds, cutting each halfway through.

Bake the cases in an oven preheated to 230°C (450°F), gas mark 8, for 20 minutes, or until risen and brown, then reduce the heat to 180°C (350°F), gas mark 4, for a further 20 minutes. Ease off the lids with the point of a knife. Scoop out and discard the soft pastry inside the cases to make hollows for the filling.

Ingredients

175-225g (6-8oz) diced, cooked chicken, ham, flaked salmon or shelled prawns
285ml (½ pint) milk
½ small bay leaf
Sprig of thyme
½ small onion
¼ level teaspoon grated nutmeg
25g (1oz) butter
25g (1oz) plain flour
Salt and black pepper to taste
2-3 tablespoons single or double cream

Heat the milk, bay leaf, thyme, onion and nutmeg in a pan and bring slowly to the boil. Remove from the heat, cover and leave for 15 minutes.

Heat the butter in a heavy-based saucepan. Stir in the flour, a little at a time, making sure that the mixture, or *roux*, remains smooth, then cook for 3 minutes. Strain the milk through a fine sieve and blend it gradually into the roux. Bring to the boil, stirring continuously so that it thickens evenly, and then simmer for 2-3 minutes. Remove from the heat and adjust the seasoning. Stir in the cream if you are using it, taking care not to thin the mixture too much.

Blend in the chicken or fish and spoon the mixture into the cases.

Volleyball

A game for playing on beach, lawn or court

As its name suggests, volleyball is played by returning a ball over a net before it touches the ground. It is a six-a-side game played on a court 18 × 9m (roughly 60 × 30ft). The net is stretched across the centre of the court at a height of 2.43m (8ft) for men, 2.24m (7ft 4in) for women, and 2.1m (7ft) for children.

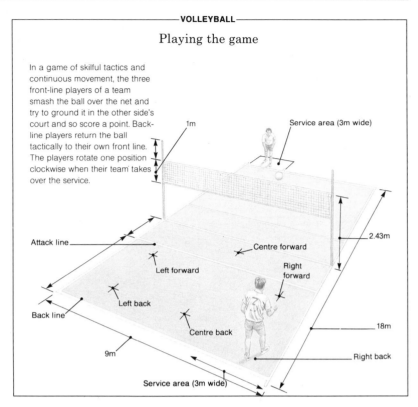

VOLLEYBALL

Playing the game

In a game of skilful tactics and continuous movement, the three front-line players of a team smash the ball over the net and try to ground it in the other side's court and so score a point. Back-line players return the ball tactically to their own front line. The players rotate one position clockwise when their team takes over the service.

1m

Service area (3m wide)

Attack line

Centre forward

Left forward

Right forward

Left back

Back line

2.43m

Centre back

18m

9m

Right back

Service area (3m wide)

The players try to volley a large ball 660mm (about 26in) in circumference into their opponents' court, and score if the other team allows the ball to touch the ground before returning it.

Only the three front-line players may smash the ball into their opponents' court. The opposing front-line players try to stop the ball with their hands near to and above the net.

Players are not allowed to catch, throw or carry the ball. Each team can hit the ball three times before sending it over the net, but it must still be kept off the ground and hit cleanly, and no player may hit the ball twice in succession.

The server stands behind the right-hand third of the back line and strikes the ball with one hand or arm. The served ball must clear the net; if it does not, or if it touches the net and goes over, the serve is lost – though a ball that touches the net and goes over during a rally (a succession of volleys) continues in play.

If the serving team succeeds in grounding the ball on their opponents' side, a point is scored. If, however, the ball is returned and drops on the serving team's side, their opponents do not score but take over the serve.

The first team to reach 15 points wins the set, but they must have a two-point lead or play on until one is established.

After each point, or rally, the players taking the service rotate clockwise, so that all take a turn in each position.

Vomiting

Coping with someone who is violently sick

Vomiting is a common but distressing symptom with many possible causes – see HANGOVER; INDIGESTION; MIGRAINE; NAUSEA; TRAVEL SICKNESS; ULCERS.

If there is blood in the vomit, if food eaten more than four hours previously is being vomited, if the vomiting continues for more than four hours, or if the patient also has DIARRHOEA or muscle CRAMPS, contact a DOCTOR.

Often small amounts of milk are vomited during BABY WINDING – this is normal, but frequent vomiting of moderate and large amounts may indicate a disorder. Again, contact a doctor.

Treatment at home Children – and often adults, particularly the elderly – may need support or reassurance when vomiting. Gently clean the face and clothes; supply clean clothes or linen, if you can. See also NURSING AT HOME.

Make sure the patient rests and has plenty to drink to prevent DEHYDRATION – initially provide water or glucose and electrolyte solution (available from a chemist). Give weak tea or broth later.

When the bout of attacks has ceased and the patient no longer feels nauseous, give light, non-greasy foods.

Waffles

Making crisp batter cakes

Waffles are crisp, dimpled squares of batter used as a base for savoury or sweet toppings. They are cooked in waffle irons, either electrically heated or used on a cooker hob. You can also cook them in sandwich-makers with waffle plates. This recipe will make enough waffles to serve six to eight people (to separate the eggs, see EGG SEPARATING).

Ingredients

225g (8oz) plain flour
1 level teaspoon baking powder
1 level teaspoon bicarbonate of soda
½ teaspoon salt
40g (1½oz) caster sugar (omit for savoury waffles)
3 eggs (separated)
1½ tablespoons lemon juice
340ml (12fl oz) milk
3 tablespoons oil

Sieve flour, baking powder, bicarbonate of soda and salt into a bowl and, for sweet waffles, mix in the sugar. Beat the egg yolks with the lemon juice, milk and oil and pour this into the dry mixture, beating well to make a smooth batter. Whisk the egg whites until stiff but not dry and fold them into the mixture.

Heat the waffle iron – check the instructions to see whether it should be greased first. Pour in enough batter to fill it, close the lid and cook for 3-4 minutes, or until the waffles are golden-brown in colour.

Top them with bacon, jam, honey or anything you like and serve immediately, as waffles go soft if allowed to stand.

Walking

Equipping yourself and getting started

When planning a walk spend some time choosing a suitable route; a leisurely 4-5 miles is a reasonable distance for beginners. This would take two or two and a half hours – for a route of average flatness.

The route Choose a circular route to avoid retracing your steps.

Buy a town guide or, if you plan to walk in the country, consult a detailed map – see MAP READING. For Britain, the Ordnance Survey Landranger Series shows public rights of way and also indicates viewpoints, local landmarks, monuments, information centres, public telephones, picnic sites and some pubs.

The larger-scale Pathfinder Series shows field boundaries and indicates footpaths and rights of way in more detail.

On the same scale, but covering larger areas, there are now some 30 Outdoor Leisure Ordnance Survey maps which cover areas of specific scenic interest, such as the Peak District, Aviemore and the Cairngorms and the Yorkshire Dales. These maps are ideal for people who want to explore on foot while holidaying in the region.

Over short distances a COMPASS is not essential, but it could prove useful in thickly wooded country, on moorland or in other areas without landmarks.

Clothing Walking boots are the best footwear for rough or wet ground, but you should wear them in at home and over short distances before undertaking a long walk. Rubbing dubbin or a softening agent into the leather will help to make them pliable. Strong, comfortable shoes with thick, non-slip soles are also suitable.

Trainer-type footwear is suitable for dry ground, but be sure to buy a type which provides proper heel support. Soft leather shoes or a pair of the hardier leather-look boots or shoes may be equally good, but avoid flimsy, thin-soled or stiff, new footwear which could cause BLISTERS.

Whatever shoes or boots you wear, make sure that they are roomy enough for you to wear two pairs of socks – a thin pair and a thicker pair over them. Wear your walking socks when you are buying new walking shoes or boots.

An anorak or the longer knee-length cagoule is another useful item – choose one with a front pocket large enough to hold your map and other small essentials. The lightweight, rainproof types will keep you dry and can be easily slipped off and carried if you get too hot.

Avoid jeans and tight clothing; try to wear clothing made of a natural fibre – loose-fitting cotton trousers are best.

You may also need a spare pullover and socks, depending on the weather.

Supplies Carry your supplies in a rucksack so that your arms are free. Put food and drink in lightweight plastic containers. Glucose or boiled sweets are handy refreshers along the way.

As a precaution, take a small first aid kit or sticking plasters in case of cuts or blisters – see FIRST AID KITS.

Always carry your map – even on short trips you can get lost.

Wall cladding

Timber boarding and panelling indoors and out

Timber cladding can be used indoors and out for decoration and to improve the insulation of the wall it covers; outdoors it is used also for weatherproofing an exposed wall.

Outdoors Fix weatherboarding horizontally, using shiplap boards, which have a curved groove along the top front edge and a square-cut groove behind the bottom edge. The square groove laps down over the curved one to shed water.

Make a framework of BATTENS as for PLASTIC WALL CLADDING.

Treat the timber with one of the WOOD PRESERVATIVES before applying the final stain, as soon as boarding is complete, then cap exposed ends with matching cover strips of treated wood. Nail these in place with small rustless nails – see NAILING. Finally apply an oil stain, exterior-grade varnish or microporous paint – see VARNISHING; PAINTING EXTERIORS.

Indoors There is a choice of materials for cladding internal walls – and some of them are also used on ceilings. Individual hardwood or softwood tongue-and-grooved boards nailed to battens look attractive, but add thickness to the wall, making a room slightly smaller. SKIRTING BOARDS, architraves and ELECTRIC SOCKETS AND SWITCHES may need some alteration.

If the added thickness is acceptable, fix battens to the walls with masonry nails. Secure boards either by pinning through the tongues, or by special metal clips which lock into each groove.

Switch off the electricity at the consumer unit (see FUSES AND FUSE BOXES) and remove the relevant circuit fuse before adjusting any switch or socket. Take out the screws holding the switch or socket to the mounting box behind it. Draw out the switch or socket and take out the screw or screws holding the mounting box to the wall behind it. Fit a piece of wood behind the box to bring it

Fixing boards to indoor and outdoor walls

Exterior cladding Fix vertical battens to the wall 460mm (18in) apart. Using a spirit level, nail the first board at the bottom. Use rustless nails, but secure every third or fourth board with countersunk screws. Space each board a little so that the wood can expand.

Interior vertical boarding Fix horizontal battens. Nail the first board in a corner – with a 3mm (⅛in) gap at the wall; butt the board on the other wall against it.

Quick tip If a tongue-and-grooved board proves difficult to slot in place, hammer it home with light blows from a mallet. Use an offcut of the board slotted into the board you are fitting to protect it from damage.

forward the required amount. Use longer screws to give a secure fixing into the same plugged holes in the wall. Cut the cladding board to fit snugly round the mounting box. Screw the switch or socket back in place. Replace the circuit fuse and switch on at the mains.

An alternative to using individual strips of board is to use wallboards designed to look like timber panelling. They measure 2.4 × 1.2m (8 × 4ft) and some are grooved to resemble strips, while others carry a photographic reproduction of real timber panelling. However, the photo-reproductions can look artificial, as the pattern repeats itself.

An advantage of some wallboards is that they are thinner and may not need battens; they can be fixed direct to a flat, dry, clean wall, using special panel adhesive. Cut the board to size, then apply contact adhesive in strips to the back and edges. Lift the board to the wall, press it in place, then pull it away and allow a few moments for the adhesive to dry. Now press it back on the wall, thumping all over the surface with the side of your fist to ensure good contact.

Again, holes must be cut for switches and sockets. Cut them to fit very snugly round the switch or socket, which will still stand out from the board.

If a wall is uneven, or you wish to improve INSULATION, fix the wallboards to battens. To improve insulation further, fill the gaps between battens with glass-fibre blanket, before pinning or gluing the boards in place.

Sheet materials may expand in a moist atmosphere, so cut wallboards 13mm (½in) short top and bottom, to allow for expansion. Hide the gaps by pinning on purpose-made matching cover strips.

Wall fasteners

Fixing things to solid and hollow walls

Wall plugs will ensure a secure fixing to most wall surfaces when fitting items such as wall CUPBOARDS and SHELVES.

Plug designs vary from simple fibre or plastic tubes to elaborate fluted ones with wings, but all work on the same basic principle. The plug expands inside a hole in the wall when a screw is driven into it. See also MASONRY DRILLING.

When using wall plugs, first select the size of SCREWS required – choose screws long enough to penetrate through the wall plaster or tiles and well into the masonry behind. Then choose plugs of a size to suit the screws.

Having chosen screws and wall plugs, select the correct masonry bit for the plugs. A wheelbrace should be sufficient for drilling soft material such as breeze block, but a power drill will be necessary for drilling brickwork.

Make sure the hole penetrates well into the masonry. CERAMIC TILES or plaster, or both, should not be relied upon to support any weight. Let the flutes on the bit bring out as much dust as possible, then push a plug into each hole, tapping each flush with the wall surface. The screws can now be passed through the item to be fixed, and screwed into the plug. Sometimes it pays to fit the screw first, remove it, then re-screw it through the item to be fixed.

Soft materials, such as breeze block (see BUILDING BLOCKS), tend to crumble as a normal plug expands. In such cases use a special wall plug designed for soft

materials, and use a wheelbrace or a power drill set for normal drilling rather than hammer-action drilling.

Where really strong fixing is required, use an expanding metal bolt. This has a special wedge section which is drawn up into the core of the bolt as the nut is tightened. Wings on the bolt are forced to spread, giving a very strong fixing. Such bolts usually require holes which are outside the range of normal masonry bit sizes, so you need a masonry drill bit large enough to make a hole for the chosen expanding bolt.

Apart from anchor bolts, hook and eye bolts are available. Anchorage is made by tightening a nut close to the hook or eye bolt.

Hollow walls There are special fasteners for hollow walls such as plasterboard PARTITIONS, which are not thick enough to take wall plugs. The fasteners have toggle arms, which either drop into place or expand within the cavity, and a fixing screw which is threaded through them.

──── WALL FASTENERS ────

Matching the wall fastening to your purpose

— Plastic wall plug

Strip plastic

Screws and wall plugs For fixing an item of medium weight to a wall use a wood screw and a fibre or plastic plug, or strip plastic plugging. Drill a hole in the masonry, push the plug into the hole, fit the screw through the item, then screw it into the plug.

Expansion bolt

Hook bolt

Expansion bolts For heavy fixtures use an expanding metal bolt; for hanging heavy objects use a hooked expansion bolt.

Gravity toggle

Spring toggle

Toggle fasteners For cavity walls use a gravity or spring toggle, which drops into place or spreads behind the wall.

When fixing something heavy, like a kitchen cabinet, do not rely on hollow fixings alone, because of the strain they will put on the plasterboard. Position a horizontal batten (see BATTENS), screwed to timber uprights within the wall, so that the cabinet base rests on it.

Find the uprights either by probing, or by using a simple metal-finding tool, which indicates where there are nails. If possible, drive the screws supporting the cabinet directly into the uprights.

Irregular holes Where it is difficult to make a neat hole in a solid wall, use a fibrous plugging compound, rather than a wall plug. Take a pinch of the dry compound, moisten it with water and work it until it is putty-like. Now roll it and ram it into the hole, pushing it firmly in place. Once firm, screw into it while the compound is still soft, but do not apply a load until it has set.

Wallpapering

Choosing and hanging wallcoverings

The term wallpaper covers a wide range of wallcoverings, made of materials that include fabrics, vinyls, woodchip and cork.

Wallpaper A roll of paper is printed with pattern and colour. Most British papers come in rolls 10.05m long by 520mm wide (11yds by 20½in). But check sizes carefully in Continental pattern books – roll widths vary from country to country.

Choose a fairly substantial paper for your first attempt. Cheap, thin papers tear and crease easily and are more difficult to hang.

Duplex wallpaper This is made from two papers bonded together during manufacture. The paper is strong and retains any relief pattern better than single-sheet paper.

Woodchip Two layers of paper bonded together with a sprinkling of wood chippings between them. Designed to be painted with emulsion paint after hanging.

Embossed paper A heavy paper embossed to form a raised pattern which is convex on the decorative side but concave on the underside. Embossed papers are mainly intended to be decorated with emulsion paint, though coloured and patterned ones are available.

Fabric wallcoverings Hessian, silk, Japanese grasscloth or velvet flock are bonded to a backing paper. In most types, paste is applied to the wall, not the covering.

Vinyl wallcovering A thin sheet of coloured and textured vinyl is bonded to a paper backing. The vinyl offers a tough, easy-to-clean surface and is suitable for kitchens and bathrooms.

Cork A thin veneer of cork is bonded to a backing paper, which is sometimes painted so that the colour shows through holes in the cork.

Blown vinyl A heat process produces a relief pattern on the vinyl surface – if the relief is compressed, it quickly recovers. It is available coloured and patterned, or plain for emulsion coating.

Foamed polyethylene The surface has the feel of fabric, and springs back into place if pressed gently. It is hung straight from the roll, and paste is applied to the wall, not the covering.

Easy-strip wallcoverings These are available in both paper and vinyl to make removal easier – see WALLPAPER REMOVAL.

Pre-pasted wallcoverings Both papers and vinyls are available with paste coated on the back. This is activated by dipping the cut piece of paper in a trough of water.

Lining paper Available for covering walls which have hairline cracks or uneven colouring. Preferably hang lining paper horizontally so that it is at right angles to the paper put over it – but it can be hung vertically, in which case make sure the seams of the lining paper and the paper put over it are not in the same place.

Paste A wide range of pastes is available, some are supplied dry in packets to be mixed with water, and others supplied in tubs ready for use. Make sure you select a paste recommended by the wallpaper manufacturer. Heavy papers need full-bodied pastes, and those for vinyls should incorporate a fungicide to discourage mould growth.

Tools You will need large decorators' scissors; small scissors for fine trimming; a craft knife and steel straightedge for trimming vinyls; pasting brush and bucket for water-mixed pastes; smoothing brush or clean paint roller; seam roller; steel tape; PLUMB LINE; sharp pencil; and a pasting table for all but pre-pasted papers.

Preparation Walls to be papered must be clean, dry and smooth. It is not wise to paper over old paper as the new wet material may loosen the paper beneath. Fill cracks with cellulose filler and smooth – see STOPPERS AND FILLERS. Decorate paintwork before papering.

Measuring and buying Divide the distance round the room, including doors and windows, by the width of your chosen paper. This gives the number of strips you need. Divide the roll length by the height of the wall plus one pattern repeat – this gives the number of strips you can get per roll.

Divide the strips needed by the strips per roll for the number of rolls to buy. Make sure all the rolls have the same printing batch number.

Cutting and pasting Measure the distance between ceiling or picture rail and skirting board and add 50mm (2in) for trimming, either at the top or bottom – or both. Cut the paper to length and lay it face down on the pasting table so that the top edge and all surplus paper hangs off the table to the right. Paste the paper from the centre out, herringbone fashion, making sure the edges are well coated. Fold it (see illustration). Leave the paper to soak for as long as the manufacturer recommends. One or two more pieces could be pasted while waiting.

Applying Start on a wall adjoining a window wall. Measure out from the corner the width of your paper less about 25mm (1in) so that the paper will turn onto the window wall.

Take your first length of paper; unfold the top end and align against the plumb line as illustrated. When you are sure the paper is in the correct place, release the lower folds and use the smoothing brush or roller to press the centre of the length to the wall. Then brush out from the centre, finally pressing down the edges. Pull the paper away top and bottom after pressing it into ceiling or picture rail and skirting board with the edge of the scissors, and trim off the surplus paper. Press the paper back in place, then use the seam roller to press the edges are stuck down. Do not use a seam roller on embossed patterns, except foamed polyethylene, as the pattern will flatten – instead, gently dab the edges with a dry sponge or a clean shaggy-pile roller.

Check the length for bubbles, and press out any trapped air, working to the edges. Small bubbles should disappear as the paper dries. If not, cut them with a razor blade and use a fine artist's brush to put new paste behind the flaps. Press back the paper and wipe off any excess paste with a damp cloth.

Match the next length against the hung piece, and trim to length. Unless you are very experienced it is not wise to cut too many pieces at a time. The exception is a paper where no pattern matching is involved.

Continue hanging until you come to a corner – either internal or external. As a general rule, cut paper so that no more than 25mm (1in) turns an internal corner, to allow for any irregularities in the plas-

---

WALLPAPERING

Pasting, folding, hanging the first length; papering the ceiling

Fold pasted paper and draw it to the left to pull unpasted paper onto the table. Fold long strips concertina fashion every 460mm (18in), without creasing the folds.

With shorter strips, fold the left-hand edge to about the centre of the length.

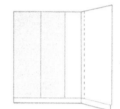

Papering a ceiling If possible get a helper to hold the folded paper close to the ceiling while you position the first folds.

Hanging Using a plumb line, make pencil marks to show a true vertical on the wall. Lay the paper's right-hand edge against the top pencil mark, leaving about 50mm (2in) excess for trimming. Keeping the left edge off the wall, align the rest of the paper on the wall with the other pencil marks. Use your hand to smooth the top to the wall.

Internal corners Cut the paper so that no more than 25mm (1in) turns the corner. This allows for plastering irregularities.

tering. On an external corner, never try to turn more than 25mm – the paper is likely to slant and look crooked.

If the turn is a good one, the cut-off piece can be matched and papering continued. If the corner is out of true, it will be necessary to overlap the join slightly to bring the paper back to a true vertical – again using the plumb line as a guide.

Obstructions When ELECTRIC SOCKETS AND SWITCHES are encountered, turn off the current at the mains and unscrew the fitting just far enough so that paper can be cut and a slight surplus tucked under the fitting. But where a fitting cannot be moved, mark its outer edges on the paper, then cut either a cross for square fittings or a star pattern for round fittings so that the paper fits around the obstruction. Press the paper in place, then trim off the surplus paper with small sharp scissors.

At door and window frames, allow just 3mm (⅛in) to turn onto the frame to hide any slight gap or irregularity where wall and frame join.

Normally, you can work round a room from the window wall, but where there is a focal point, such as a chimney breast, it looks more effective to paper the chimney breast from the centre, working into each internal corner. Slight mismatching of the pattern at this point will not show.

Wallpaper removal

Stripping walls to paint or paper

Some modern wallcoverings, including most vinyls, are termed 'easy-strip' – which means that the surface of the covering can be pulled away, leaving a backing paper – see WALLPAPERING.

If you have to strip wallpaper, try lifting one corner of a length to see if it will pull away. If it will, and the underpaper remains in good condition, leave the underpaper on the wall as a lining paper. But if the underpaper is damaged or creased, soak it with water and remove with a scraper.

If the wallcovering will not pull away, give it a good soaking. Put newspaper on the floor to absorb spilt water, then fill a bucket with warm water, add a little liquid detergent and a handful of cellulose paste, and mix well. The detergent acts as a wetting agent, and the paste holds the warm moisture in place while it softens the adhesive.

Apply it to the wall with a wide brush or paint roller – or you could use a garden spray. Allow plenty of soaking time – until the paper comes away easily with a scraper.

If the paper has a wipe-clean finish that the water cannot penetrate, use a coarse sanding block to break up the

surface before wetting. Do not use a wire brush, as small pieces of metal tend to embed themselves in the wall plaster, then rust, leading to rust spots on the surface of new wallcoverings.

Where there are many layers of paper on the wall, simplify stripping by renting a steam wallpaper stripper from a tool hire shop – see HIRING.

Hold the plate close to the wall, and the combination of heat and steam will quickly soften the paste, allowing many layers of wallcovering to be pulled off in sheets.

Where there are ELECTRIC SOCKETS AND SWITCHES turn off the current at the main switch and remove the circuit fuse (see FUSES AND FUSE BOXES), then unscrew and ease the fittings away from the wall to remove any paper tucked behind them.

Wandering Jew

Making it thrive and multiply

Tradescantias (also known as Wandering Jews) grow well in JOHN INNES COMPOST (No 2 potting), in 100-150mm (4-6in) pots or in hanging baskets. Keep them in a well-lit position but out of direct sunlight. They thrive in humid warmth with an even round-the-year temperature of 21-24°C (70-75°F). Do not let the temperature drop below 10°C (50°F).

Between May and September, keep the potting mixture thoroughly moist – and feed fortnightly with one of the houseplant FERTILISERS. In winter, water sparingly.

To encourage a rich growth of foliage, nip out the growing tips regularly during spring and summer. The plants deteriorate quickly and are best discarded after two growing seasons.

Tradescantia albiflora Wandering Jew's trailing cream-and-green foliage makes it a popular houseplant. A variety called 'Tricolor' has white and rose-purple striped foliage.

Propagation Take 75mm (3in) tip cuttings from the leaves at any time between April and September. Set them – four to six to a 75mm (3in) pot – in a barely moist mixture of John Innes potting compost No 1, at a temperature of 16°C (61°F). Water just enough to keep the compost barely moist. See also PROPAGATING PLANTS.

Roots should develop in about two weeks. Prick out the young plants which can then be potted separately – see POT-TING HOUSEPLANTS.

War

Playing a fast two-handed card game for children

Shuffle the pack (see SHUFFLING CARDS) and deal it all face down between the two players. The players then turn over their top card. The player with the higher card wins (aces are high), takes both cards and puts them face down under his or her pack.

The game continues in this way until both players turn up cards of the same value – this is 'war'.

Both cards are put in the middle of the table, then both players play three 'war' cards face down. They then turn up their first war card, and the one with the highest takes all eight cards. If the turn up reveals a second pair of equal value, however, each player adds another card face down to the array of war cards and the next pair of war cards is turned up, with the higher value card winning all ten cards.

The game ends when one player has captured the whole pack.

Ward of court

Seeking a court's protection for a minor

If a child under 18 is felt to need the law's protection, a juvenile court can place the child in the care of the local authority. Any interested party – a parent, guardian, relative or the local authority itself, for example – can make an application for a child to be placed in care.

When the special powers of the High Court are required to protect the child, a wardship application may be made. If it is granted, the High Court becomes the child's legal guardian until the child is 18, and during the wardship a judge makes any decisions concerning the ward's care or education.

An application to make a child a ward of court might be made, for example, if a girl under 18 ran away with a man against her parents' wishes. The judge could order her to return to her parents, and anyone who helped her to stay away would risk imprisonment for contempt of court. The man concerned could be charged with abduction.

If a wife who has custody of a child believes that her husband is about to try to take the child abroad, the child could be made a ward of court. The judge could then grant an injunction forbidding the child to be taken out of the country and empowering port and airport authorities to prevent it.

A local authority might apply for a wardship order if a juvenile court refused a request for a child to be taken into its care.

Any boy or girl under 18 in England and Wales can be made a ward of court, even if he or she is a foreign citizen. So can young British subjects living abroad, if the judge considers a young person's case should be investigated in Britain rather than in a court of the country of residence.

Applications are made in the Family Division of the High Court through a solicitor, and can be complicated and costly – see LAWYERS; LEGAL AID.

Under Scottish law there is no provision for a minor to be made a ward of court, but in a dispute the court decides who will take custody of a child. Anyone who then defies the custody order can be prosecuted for contempt of court.

Warranties

Making sure of your rights as a consumer

A warranty is another name for a GUARANTEE, and is often used in connection with mechanical or electrical goods, such as cars, record players, television sets, video recorders and washing machines.

The period of a warranty may be anything from six months to five years or more, and you can sometimes ask for an extended warranty, for which there is a charge.

A warranty can promise any protection or benefit that a manufacturer or trader sees fit – but you still retain your rights under the SALE OF GOODS Act or Unfair Contract Act. A warranty document must state that the buyer's statutory rights are not affected by the terms of the warranty.

Warts

Treating, removing and avoiding them

There are five types of wart – small, solid growths on the skin that are caused by viruses and are slightly contagious.

Types of wart Common warts, which have a rough, horny surface and may be brownish, are the biggest type. They can be up to 25mm (1in) across, and may be joined together. They are commonest on children, especially on the hands.

Another type common on children are plantar warts (which are also known as verrucas). They are embedded in the soles of the feet or toes, and are often painful. Plane warts are small, smooth clusters that often grow along the line of a scratch. Filiform warts – thin strips of skin up to 3mm ($\frac{1}{8}$in) long and with a hard tip – usually grow on the face or neck. Anogenital warts are multiple growths round the genitals or anus.

Treatment Warts sometimes disappear without treatment, but they usually persist or spread. Chemists sell proprietary paints and pastes for removing warts, but do not use them on facial or anogenital warts – for these, get a prescription from your DOCTOR.

The paint or paste should be applied to the warts daily (not on normal skin) and allowed to dry. When using paste, protect the surrounding skin with a corn pad and cover the wart with a dressing. Never scratch warts, as it could encourage them to spread.

Consult a doctor if you have anogenital warts, or if a wart becomes painful, or if paints and pastes have no effect. The doctor can often remove warts by freezing or burning them off, or by digging them out with a curette.

Prevention Avoid touching contagious warts, and if you have one, wear waterproof plasters in public showers, swimming pools, washrooms, gymnasiums or similar places.

Washing machines

Choosing an automatic; getting the best results; faultfinding and repairs

The choice of a machine depends on the space available, as they work best when permanently plumbed in. This means being near a water supply and a convenient outlet to a drain. Although most machines will work from a cold supply, it is usually more economical to connect to the hot water supply as well.

If there are no plumbing facilities for the machine, get professional help from the manufacturer or a local plumber.

Make sure the machine has all the programme options you want. Some useful options are: pre-wash; half load; and spin alone. Some machines have an integral tumble dryer.

Using the machine Sort garments for their correct wash programme – see LAUNDERING. Do not either overload or underload the machine. If you have to put in a small load, use the half-load option.

Check drain or lint filters regularly and rinse under a tap to get rid of accumulated fibres.

Faultfinding and repairs Home maintenance of a washing machine is restricted to minor repairs. Some common symptoms are:

No power or intermittent power Check the plug fuse and connections, or the main fuse box – see PLUGS; FUSES AND FUSE BOXES. If these are intact, the motor has failed or there is a fault in the electrical system.

Water leak Tighten the hose connector if it is loose. Fit a new washer if necessary.

Damaged hose Cut out the damaged area with a hacksaw. Use a short piece of brass or copper tubing, matching the internal diameter of the hose, to link the hose. Secure the hose to the tube at each end with hose clips. But always take into account any manufacturer's recommendations.

For all other faults, consult the dealer or service engineer.

QUICK TIP In areas where the water pressure is high, a washing machine may flood during the rinsing cycle. Reduce pressure by partly closing the cold-water supply tap.

Washing walls

Cleaning them and removing common stains

Painted or tiled walls, or walls with washable wallpaper, need regular cleaning – see DUSTING AND CLEANING; CLEANING AND POLISHING MATERIALS. Wallpapers such as over-painted Anaglypta need different treatment from other painted walls.

If you are not sure whether wallpaper is washable (see WALLPAPERING), test the cleaning agent on a small patch where it will not show. If the paper absorbs water or the pattern is affected, the wall is not washable.

Before washing walls, take up a movable floor covering and put down old newspapers to soak up splashes. Cover fitted carpets with waterproof sheeting.

Some stains on walls will not wash off easily. Crayon or scuff marks can be a problem. You can usually remove them from paintwork by applying a paste of baking soda and rubbing it lightly with fine steel wool. Rub with stale white bread to remove grease marks.

On washable wallpaper, use a light dab of washing-up liquid on a moistened cloth or paper towel – or if the stain is persistent, try a sparse sprinkling of abrasive powder.

To get rid of ink spots, use a solution of 1 tablespoon of chlorine bleach in a cup of cold water. Ball-point marks can usually be removed with a dab of methyl-

ated spirit on a cotton-wool bud. On washable wallpaper, test the stain remover on an inconspicuous part first.

To clean cement stains from a bare brick wall, use a proprietary masonry cleaner, available from DIY shops. Apply it with a brush, and after a few minutes scrub the area with a stiff brush. Rinse with clean water after ten minutes.

Wasps

Getting rid of them

There are seven species of wasp in Britain, but it is the Common wasp or the German wasp, living in large colonies, that can become a nuisance in late summer. Before that, their presence is beneficial because they kill APHIDS and CATERPILLARS to feed to their own larvae.

The colony breaks up about the end of August, when the wasps start looking for new sources of sugary food, and will eat fruit and jam.

The workers (sterile females) sting repeatedly if disturbed and angered. The stings are painful, but rarely serious – see INSECT BITES AND STINGS.

Dealing with wasps They can be killed with aerosol fly sprays, or lured and trapped by jars half-filled with jam and beer, in which they drown.

Nests can be found in cavities such as abandoned mouseholes, or in walls, sheds or lofts, or in a corner where you store plant pots. You may first suspect its presence by seeing a succession of wasps hovering near it; or by a stain developing on a ceiling.

If you have a nest in your house that is a nuisance, consult the Environmental Health Officer at your local council

offices, or one of the specialist firms listed in *Yellow Pages* under Pest and Vermin Control Services.

You can pay to have the nest destroyed if necessary, but the colony will disappear anyway by the end of the season and you can then block holes that allowed entry to the loft or other nest site so that it is not accessible for the following season. A nest outside can be destroyed with a proprietary chemical for wasp nests – see PESTICIDES.

Waste disposal unit

Fitting one in your sink and maintaining it

Powerful steel teeth inside a sink waste disposal unit grind up food wastes such as vegetable peelings so that they can be mixed with cold water into a slurry and washed down the drain.

There are two types of unit: continuous-feed units can have waste food and water added while in operation; batch-feed units have to be loaded and covered before they are switched on.

A unit is driven by an electric motor and plumbed in permanently just below the plughole. It needs a sink outlet with a diameter of 90mm (3½in). If your sink does not have an outlet of this size, you may need a new sink. Alternatively, if you have a stainless-steel sink, the existing outlet can be enlarged with a tool you can hire from the unit's supplier.

Most units have a seal which fits over the tail of the plughole outlet under the sink. A clamp fits beneath the seal, and the unit is bolted, screwed or clipped to the clamp. Fit a sink trap between the unit outlet and the waste pipe.

The unit must be permanently wired

WASTE DISPOSAL UNIT

Unblocking a waste disposal unit

Release tool

Sink fitting

Blade spindle nut

Grinder teeth

Grinder body

Switch off the electricity at the consumer unit. To free the blade of the waste unit, fit the release tool over the nut on the blade spindle, then jiggle the tool. To dismantle the unit, undo the screws, clips or bolts clamping the grinder to the sink fitting. The blockage can then be cleared by hand.

511

to the electricity supply through a FUSED CONNECTION UNIT fitted with a 13amp fuse.

How to free a jammed unit To unjam a blocked waste disposal unit, try switching to reverse, if the machine can be run in both directions. If this does not work, or if the unit has no reversing control, switch off at the consumer unit – see FUSES AND FUSE BOXES. Then use the release tool supplied with the unit to free the blockage.

Poke the tool through the plughole and fit it onto the nut on the blade spindle. Move the tool gently backwards and forwards to release the blade.

Remove the tool and switch on the power. If the motor still will not turn, switch off again at the consumer unit and disconnect the unit from the plughole tail. Take out the motor and grinder unit – it may drop out or it may be held by a bayonet fitting like a light bulb. Remove the obstruction and reassemble the unit.

How to clean it To clear out grime that has accumulated over a period of time, simply run a handful of ice cubes through the unit.

Watercolour painting

Learning techniques and composition

Watercolour paints are made in cakes or tubes. It is usually enough, especially for a beginner, to have about a dozen basic colours: reds (cadmium and alizarin crimson), yellows (ochre and cadmium), blues (prussian, ultramarine and cerulean), browns (raw sienna, burnt sienna, raw umber, burnt umber) and Payne's grey.

You also need brushes, paper, a drawing board, and a palette for mixing colours. Buy four brushes: a flat for applying washes and three rounds (small, medium and large). The best brushes are made of red-sable hair – expensive but long-lasting. If a brush starts to shed its hair, hammer the metal ferrule lightly to tighten its grip.

Different sizes of watercolour paper are available in three finishes – rough, hot-pressed (smooth), and not (short for not hot-pressed); not is for general use. The weight, indicated by the number of grams per square metre or pounds per ream (500 sheets), ranges from 85gsm (90lb) per ream (the flimsiest) to 850gsm (400lb) per ream (the thickest). All the materials and equipment listed above can be bought from an artists' supply shop.

Preparing the paper Paper weighing less than 300gsm (140lb) per ream needs to be stretched before being painted to

avoid cockling. Soak the sheet in cold, clean water for about 15 minutes, or until it is saturated. Lift it out by two corners, let water run off, then lay it on a drawing board. Lightly sponge off any excess water with a clean sponge, smoothing out wrinkles as you go.

Wet a wide strip of gummed paper and stick one of the watercolour paper's long sides to the board. Use more gummed paper to tape the opposite side, then tape the short sides. Press the tape firmly outwards so that the watercolour paper is flat, and leave it to dry before you start your picture.

Composing a picture Start by sketching your subject lightly, using a soft pencil. Try to position the major features – the face, say, in a portrait, or the horizon in a landscape – roughly a third of the way down or up the paper, not in the middle. In the same way, set vertical features – a foreground tree, for example – about a third of the way across the paper, not right on the edge or in the middle.

Artists call this composition tip the 'rule of thirds'; it gives a more pleasing result than a picture which is split in half horizontally or vertically.

Painting a landscape Use a wet brush to transfer paint to the palette. Thin it with water in varying amounts for different shades of a colour, or mix colours together with water for different hues. Rinse the brush in clean water before you transfer each new colour.

Begin to paint working from the background towards the foreground, applying the lightest shades first. Allow each colour to dry before applying another, or the colours will mingle. It is always possible to paint darker colours over lighter ones.

So, for example, you can paint a dark tree on top of a pale sky. But you cannot paint a light colour over a darker one, because the darker colour will show through. So if you want to paint a light-coloured house, say, in front of dark and distant hills, leave the area of the house white when you paint the hills.

Use your flat brush to paint the sky as a blue wash (a large area of one colour, evenly spread). Moisten the area with water first to ensure that the paint spreads evenly (this is a wet-on-wet wash). Dab patches of colour off with a rag before the paint dries, to indicate areas of cloud. Block in the distant landscape with a wash, leaving gaps for foreground features.

Paint in the lighter parts of the foreground, then gradually add darker details. You can use a half-dry brush and ragged strokes to achieve textures such as bark. To add highlights to painted areas – where the sun catches the edge of a branch, for example – carefully scratch off small areas of paint using a razor blade.

When your picture is finished, let it dry completely before removing it from the board and mounting it – see PICTURE MOUNTING. See also OIL PAINTING; PICTURE FRAMING.

WATERCOLOUR PAINTING

Painting a picture in watercolours

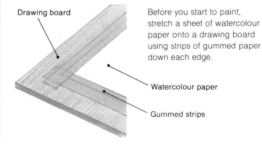

Drawing board

Watercolour paper

Gummed strips

Before you start to paint, stretch a sheet of watercolour paper onto a drawing board using strips of gummed paper down each edge.

Sketch in pencil the shapes you will be painting, making sure that the main elements are not grouped in the centre of the picture.

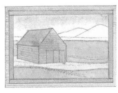

Moisten the paper and paint the broad areas, such as the sky and ground, with washes of light colour, using the flat brush.

Paint in the remaining areas. Use light greys and blues for the hills to make them recede and darker colours in the foreground.

Finally, add the darkest shadows and the details. Use an almost dry brush on the wet paint to add texture to the grass and building.

Water divining

Using dowsing rods to find water

If you want to try your hand at water divining – finding a hidden source of water through the reaction of a simple instrument – contact the British Society of Dowsers, Sycamore Barn, Tamley Lane, Hastingleigh, Ashford, Kent TN25 5HW, enclosing a stamped addressed envelope. The society can provide information on the theory and methods of dowsing, as it is called.

Do not expect immediate results from your attempts. You must be relaxed and in a receptive state of mind for divining to work. The most commonly used dowsing, or divining, instruments are angle and spring rods.

Using angle rods You can easily make a pair of angle rods from two wire coat hangers. On each hanger, use pliers to cut the bottom wire at one end, then the arm at the opposite end, 125mm (5in) up from the bend. Open up the bend so that the two arms are at right angles. Cover the short arm of each rod to make a handle, using thin tubing or cotton reels so that the wire rods can swing freely – hook the top of the wire to anchor it.

Hold each handle as near as possible to the horizontal bar with loosely closed fists. Relax completely with your arms hanging by your sides. Then bring the rods up to a horizontal position, keeping your arms and wrists body-width apart. The rods should be pointing away from you, roughly parallel to each other (the neutral position).

When they react the rods will swing inwards and cross over, or swing out, or swing roughly parallel in the same direction.

Practise walking about with them, trying to keep them in a neutral position but not holding them rigidly. Make a mental note of where and when any reactions occur.

With practice you will learn to recognise whether the rods are swinging because you are moving or are reacting to the presence of water. In England it is not difficult to find water; the problem is to ignore sub-surface trickles and concentrate on a main water line.

Using a spring rod The Y-shaped rod is made from a single twig, or of two strips of springy wood or metal fixed together. The best woods are hazel, hawthorn and cherry – remove any leaves. The arms of the spring rod should be 460mm (18in) long and from 6-13mm ($\frac{1}{4}$-$\frac{1}{2}$in) thick.

Hold the spring rod with the tip pointing away from or towards you and the arms of the Y clasped firmly in your hands with your palms face up. The rod will react by moving up and down, and where the reaction is strongest water is below its tip.

Practising on the water pipe As your first project, try to find the water service pipe that leads into your house and trace its course. Walk back and forth slowly over the likely area, concentrating your thoughts on the pipe, and note where your instrument reacts.

Go over the course two or three times and at different times of the day to make sure that the reactions occur at the same points.

Judging the depth There are several ways of establishing the depth of a water line, one of the simplest being the Bishop's Rule. Stand directly over a reaction point on the line. Relax and put your arms down by your sides. Then lift the instrument slowly into its neutral position and walk away from the line. At some point the instrument will react (this should not be one of the location points). Mark this point.

Go back to the line and walk away from it in a different direction until you notice another reaction. Repeat this until the signal points form a rough circle. Their distance from the centre is equal to the depth of the water from the surface. A water service pipe is normally 760mm (30in) below ground.

Water heating

How to heat your domestic hot water

A common and convenient modern water heating method is a side effect of CENTRAL HEATING. Water to supply the hot taps is stored in a cylinder and heated indirectly by a coiled pipe that passes through it carrying hot water from the central heating boiler. Fit a jacket – 75mm (3in) or more thick – round the cylinder to keep the water hot.

Most central heating boilers can be programmed to supply hot water even when the central heating is off, but this can make the boiler area too hot and an alternative method is needed.

Homes without a central heating boiler may have a kitchen boiler or a back boiler behind a solid fuel open fireplace or openable stove. Hot water rises from these boilers directly to the hot water storage cylinder. As with a central heating boiler, an alternative method is needed for the summer.

An IMMERSION HEATER installed in the hot water storage cylinder will heat the water directly. It does not need a boiler connected to it and can be your only method of water heating.

Dual element immersion heaters are made to provide either a full cylinder or a half cylinder of hot water. To make the most economical use of the heater, fit a jacket on the cylinder, have a timer fitted in the circuit to switch it on and off automatically, and, if possible, make sure it operates at off-peak times.

If your hot water temperature is controllable by a thermostat, set it at 60°C (140°F). This is adequate for domestic use and, in hard water areas, it avoids excessive scaling of the pipes.

In some cases it may not be practical to run stored water to a tap and a local supply of hot water may be more efficient. This may be provided by a GAS WATER HEATER or an electric one designed to deliver an almost instantaneous supply of hot water.

Water polo

Playing a tough game for experienced swimmers

A ball game for two teams of seven swimmers, water polo is played in a pool 20-30m (about 65-100ft) long and 8-20m (about 26-65ft) wide, with water at least 1m (3ft 3in) deep.

Goals 3m (10ft) wide, backed by a net, are set at each end, and the players use a round, inflated ball weighing about 450g (1lb). Each team has four reserves, who may serve as substitutes. The game is played in four quarters of five minutes each, with two minutes' interval in between. The teams change ends at the start of each quarter.

Play starts with the teams lined up along their goal lines. The referee blows a whistle and throws the ball into the centre of the pool. At least two players, from either team, must handle the ball before a goal can be scored. Any part of the body except a clenched fist can be used. As in football, the goalkeeper has greater licence in handling the ball, but must not go or touch the ball beyond the centre line. He can shoot at the opposite goal from within his half of the pool.

After a goal, the players can take up positions anywhere within their own halves. A player from the team that did not score restarts play, passing the ball to another teammate who must be behind the centre line when he receives it.

Ordinary fouls include moving over the goal line before the referee's starting signal; holding the goalposts, pushing off from the pool side, or standing or walking along the pool floor during play; touching the ball with both hands (goalkeepers excepted); and taking or holding the ball underwater when tackled. For ordinary fouls, the opposing side gets a free throw.

Major fouls include holding or sinking an opponent who is not holding the ball, kicking or striking an opponent or disobeying the referee. The offending player may be sent from the water, or, in certain circumstances, the other team may be awarded a penalty throw (a direct shot at goal).

Water-skiing

Getting started; practising on shore and in water; repairing skis

A water-skier is towed at speed behind a motorboat, so before you start water-skiing, make sure you know the safety signals between the tow-boat look-out and skier. Ask the British Water Ski Federation, 390 City Road, London EC1V 2QA, for the full safety code. You should be a good swimmer.

You will need a wet suit for early summer and winter water-skiing, and an approved water-ski safety jacket. Your tow boat should be able to maintain at least 48km/h (30mph). Use an approved tow rope, 23m (75ft) long. Except in authorised competitions, water-skiing is not allowed at night – between one hour after sunset and one hour before sunrise.

Water-skis These are made of laminated wood or fibreglass, in varying lengths for children and adults. The average adult length is 1700mm (67in). There are several types of ski for different skiing techniques, but for beginners general-purpose skis are best.

All skis have shoe-like rubber fastenings, called bindings, into which you slip your feet. The binding may be adjustable – with separate toe and heel rubbers, the heel part being mounted on a sliding runner for varying the foot size of the binding. Or the binding may be a plate binding, a single unit made to your shoe size.

Practising on shore Wet your feet and the foot bindings. Holding down the heel rubbers, slip your feet into the toe rubbers. Pull up the heel rubbers (adjusting the heel slide if your bindings are adjustable).

With your feet flat and set shoulder-width apart, crouch on your skis with your knees drawn up to your chest. Extend your arms forward outside your knees.

Hold the tow bar while someone draws the tow rope gradually taut. Keeping your feet flat, knees bent, arms and back straight and head up, let the rope pull you upright. Practise until you have mastered this movement.

Practising in water Start in waist-deep water, letting your safety jacket support you. Grasp the tow bar, crouch as you did when practising on shore, and keep your ski tips slightly above water, in line with the stern of the boat.

As the boat idles forward and the rope draws tight, you will begin to move. When the rope is taut, signal to the driver of the tow boat that you are ready and he or she will accelerate gradually. Hold your crouch position until the skis rise to the surface of the water and begin to plane, then straighten up slowly.

Learning how to start off in the water

Grasp the tow bar and crouch on your skis, arms held straight on either side of your knees, ski tips slightly out of the water. As the boat moves forward, hold the crouch position until the skis rise to the surface. Stand up slowly as the boat accelerates.

To stop, signal to the driver, then release the tow rope and allow yourself to sink into the water, supported by your safety jacket.

Repairing your skis Clean your skis every time you use them, rinsing them thoroughly in fresh water. Treat them gently – careless handling will crack the varnish. For minor cracks in the varnish, or scuff marks, rub in silicone wax polish with a soft cloth.

Do not leave your skis outdoors for more than a few days, and store them upright in a dry place at room temperature. Smear silicone grease onto any metal parts.

Skis need to be re-varnished every winter. Place them on a flat surface and remove the foot bindings. Rub the top surfaces with wet-and-dry paper, used wet. Wipe clean and let them dry. Then varnish both top surfaces with clear polyurethane varnish – see VARNISHING. When they are dry, varnish the undersides and edges.

With constant use the foot bindings perish and need to be replaced. Unscrew the aluminium strips that hold the binding to the ski, and place them on the new binding. Mark the screw holes with a pencil and then make holes through the rubber using a centre punch and hammer. Position the aluminium strips over the holes and push screws through them. Place the binding on the ski, line up the screws with the existing holes, and screw them in tightly.

If the fin on the underside of your water-ski is warped or broken, you can buy a replacement or make your own. Cut it from beech or mahogany using the fin of the second ski as a pattern, if possible. Otherwise, taper it to about 38mm (1½in) deep at the back and 19mm (¾in) at the front. Sand the sawn edges and rub down the bottom edge of the fin – see SANDING. Remove any bits of fin left on the ski, and sand the underside.

Position the fin on the ski and mark the screw holes. Drill a hole through the front of the fin and countersink it – see DRILLING. Apply a water-resistant, latex-based contact adhesive to fin and ski, then glue them together – see GLUING. Screw the fin to the ski from the top side of the ski, then screw into the ski through the countersunk hole at the front of the fin. Finally, varnish the fin.

Water softeners

Making domestic water easier to do washing

Hard water contains a high calcium or magnesium content. Soap will not lather easily in it and forms scum that, if left in clothes, makes them feel stiff, even after rinsing. Hard water also causes scaling in some CENTRAL HEATING pipes, washing machines and kettles – see DESCALING.

If you are not sure about the hardness of your domestic water supply, ask the local water authority, listed in the telephone directory under Water. The hardness, calculated in degrees Clark, is likely to be between 18 and 32 degrees.

Water softeners vary in their effect on water hardness. Not all prevent scum – some claim only to inhibit scaling (these are often called conditioners). There are three main ways you can use them:

● Add washing soda or a proprietary softening powder to your washing. Washing soda is the less effective option here, as it dissolves only in warm or hot water and can damage woollens and coloured fabrics. A good proprietary softener can be used for all fabrics, and will dissolve

Fitting different types of simple softener units

Portable softener Connect this by a hose to the hot or cold water tap. Top up the softening agent (usually common salt) regularly, according to the instructions.

Suspended softener Hang a capsule containing water-softening crystals in your cold-water storage tank, suspended from a batten placed over the tank.

Plumbed-in fitting Plumb the unit into the pipes after the branch to the kitchen tap – see PLUMBING. Top up the unit often with salt tablets.

in hot or cold water. Add it to a washing machine with the soap powder.

● Buy a portable softener, which you can attach by a hose to any hot or cold water tap to soften water from that tap.

● Fit a permanent softener unit to the water supply. Ion-exchange water softeners costing several hundred pounds are the most effective. They are plumbed into the rising main and most are also wired to the electricity supply. They have to be regularly topped up with salt, which is fed into the unit through a clock or meter control. Cheaper, simpler plumbed-in units – such as the one illustrated – prevent scaling.

If you fit a permanent softener, draw all drinking water from the (unsoftened) kitchen cold tap. Babies and people on low-sodium diets should not take softened water, and medical researchers have found that generally people who drink hard water are less prone to heart disease than those drinking soft water.

Weaning

Getting a baby to eat solid foods

When your baby is about four or five months old, you will find it more and more difficult to satisfy his appetite with milk alone. The time has come to start feeding him solid food.

As a first taste, try a baby cereal or a purée (see PURÉEING) of fruit and vegetables. Manufactured fruit and vegetable foods are convenient, but you can save money by preparing the food yourself. The less bland taste and consistency of home-prepared food will also ease the changeover to an adult diet later.

Introduce new foods one at a time, a few days apart. That allows time for you to identify any food that causes a stomach upset or allergy.

Do not add salt or sugar: too much salt can cause dehydration and sugar can encourage a 'sweet tooth'.

If the baby refuses a solid food, try a different cereal or purée – or leave it and try again in a few days.

When the baby is six or seven months old, the diet can include meat, liver, fish and chicken, provided it is strained or finely minced. Soft pieces of well-cooked vegetables can be added, but avoid large, hard lumps which might cause the baby to choke. You can also offer food that the baby can hold – rusks, toast fingers or sticks of fruit.

Once the baby accepts solids you can begin to replace some of the milk intake, and you may find that he drops from four to three meals a day because solids will satisfy his hunger for longer than milk. By nine months the baby will probably be fully weaned, eating normal food in mashed-up form.

See also BABY FOODS; BREAST FEEDING.

Weather forecasting

Reading nature's signs

The changeable nature of Britain's island weather has given rise to a mass of weather lore. Many popular sayings often hold true. One example is 'Red sky at night, shepherd's delight; red sky in the morning, shepherd's warning'. Most of our weather comes from the west and if the air to the west is dry and cloudless, the setting sun is clearly visible, giving a red sky. We see a rosy glow at dawn through clear weather to the east, which means the dry spell has passed. Because the weather changes so fast, a depression is likely to follow.

Reading the clouds Clouds may be high, medium or low, and in three basic types – cirrus (wispy or feathery), cumulus (large and fluffy) and stratus (flat and layered). The words are combined to describe clouds that are a mixture of types. Clouds bringing rain often include the word 'nimbus' in their name – cumulonimbus, for example.

High-level wispy cirrus cloud can also mean that bad weather is coming. Cirrostratus cloud, like a high milky-white sheet, often thickens to herald rain within the day.

Fluffy cumulus cloud is associated with sunny spells; tall cumulonimbus cloud, with a flat top and dark underneath, indicates a thunderstorm in spring and summer.

Low-lying grey stratus cloud, which often blankets hills like fog, may bring drizzle. A solid mass of dark, low cloud – nimbostratus – means imminent rain.

Forecasting from flowers 'Ne'er cast a clout, Till May is out' may refer to the hawthorn's may flower rather than the month. Weather lore experts prefer the flower interpretation because they say cool weather delays the bloom. Common flowers such as tulips, daisies and dandelions, close their petals before rain.

Insects and birds 'Fish bite the least, When the wind is in the east' is widely believed by fishermen and is usually true. In a dry east wind, the insects that fish eat fly too far above the surface for the fish to catch them.

Bees stay close to the hive when it is going to rain because nectar-gathering will be more difficult in the rain.

Swallows fly high when it is dry because the insects they feed on rise higher in settled weather.

Rooks circle noisily and dive close to their nests before bad weather. Before a storm, the mistle thrush may sit on a tree top and sing a song which countryfolk interpret as 'More wet, more wet'.

Other signs of rain Smoke stays closer to the ground in a humid atmosphere – a common precursor to rain; distant objects look closer and sounds seem louder. Seaweed, hung outside, feels damp in humid weather because it is coated with sea salt which absorbs moisture. See also BAROMETERS.

Weather vane

A simple wind guide for a youngster to make

A revolving pointer to show which way the wind is blowing can be made from odds and ends about the house and a handyman's workshop.

Materials needed Broomstick or 35mm (1⅜in) dowel; sizable round wooden bead; two wire coathangers; piece of planed wood 50 × 25mm (2 × 1in) about 510mm (20in) long; piece of 3mm (⅛in) PLYWOOD about 400 × 300mm (16 × 12in); 125-

---

Making one from scrap wood and wire coathangers

A few pieces of wood, a broomstick, a round wooden bead about 25mm (1in) across, and two wire coathangers are the basic materials for a simple weather vane. You will also need a hammer, a drill and bits, a long galvanised nail, panel pins, a vice, a saw, pliers with sidecutters and a knife or rasp. Treat the wood thoroughly with preservative before assembly.

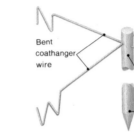

Long nail

Plywood

Plywood

Bead

Making the pointer Use plywood for the arrow head and tail. Pivot it on the bead and anchor it with a long nail.

N S

Setting up the weather vane Choose an open spot on soft ground. Drive the broomstick into the ground before carefully nailing the pointer in place.

Bent coathanger wire

N E

W S

Broomstick

Making the base Use a sharpened broomstick with coathanger wire pushed through holes drilled at right angles to each other through the broomstick. Place one about 230mm (9in) from the top end so that the pointer will not foul it, and the other about 13mm ($\frac{1}{2}$in) lower. Punch start holes with a nail before drilling each hole through the stick using a drill bit that gives a tight fit, so the wire will not move about. Coat the broomstick and the bead with wood preservative, especially the cut ends.

150mm (5-6in) galvanised round-wire nail; a few 19mm ($\frac{3}{4}$in) panel pins and one of the WOOD PRESERVATIVES. Do not use hardboard as it will curl up when damp.

Making the pointer Measure and mark two equal-sided triangles on the plywood for the head and tail of the arrow-shaped pointer. Make the tailpiece with sides about 300mm (12in) long, and the head with sides about 200mm (8in) long. Cut them out with a tenon saw – see SAWING.

Put the planed wood length in a vice edge up and drill a hole through the centre (or just to the rear of the centre) for the nail. You will probably need an 8mm ($\frac{5}{16}$in) bit. Smooth all rough edges with sandpaper, then soak the plywood and planed wood thoroughly in wood preservative before assembly.

Draw centre lines on each triangle and on the flat side of the planed wood. Position the head and tailpiece at each end of the wood, with the centres aligned, to form an arrow. Let the head protrude about 75mm (3in) from the front of the shaft, and the tail about 100mm (4in).

Making the holder Sharpen one end of the broomstick to a point with a sharp knife or rasp so that it can be driven into the ground. Cut the other end flat and drill a pilot hole at the

centre for the nail (see DRILLING); make it slightly smaller than the nail to give a tight fit. Check that the nail will pass through the centre of the bead – drill the hole wider if necessary.

Mark points for wire indicators to fit at right angles to each other through the broomstick. Place one about 230mm (9in) from the top end so that the pointer will not foul it, and the other about 13mm ($\frac{1}{2}$in) lower. Punch start holes with a nail before drilling each hole through the stick using a drill bit that gives a tight fit, so the wire will not move about. Coat the broomstick and the bead with wood preservative, especially the cut ends.

Straighten the coathanger wire with a pair of pliers to give two pieces about 860mm (34in) long. Thread the wires through the holes in the stick. Hold the end of the wire steady with one pair of pliers while you use a second pair to bend about the last 230mm (9in) into an N and S on one piece and a W and E on the other.

Fit the pointer to the broomstick with the long nail, threading it through the holes in the shaft and bead and into the pilot hole before carefully hammering it home to just above the top of the pointer shaft. You may need to weight the head end to balance it – using a lump of Plasticine, for example.

Weaving

First steps in learning a practical hobby

At its most basic, weaving involves threading one set of threads over and under another. It can be done on a loom or with your fingers – see FINGER WEAVING. Both forms rely on weaving horizontal threads (the weft) through vertical threads (the warp).

The most basic loom is a frame of wood with rows of nails hammered into the two ends. The warp is wound round the first nail at the top end, down to and round the first nail at the bottom end and up again and round the second nail at the top, and so on. Alternatively, you can use a roller frame in which the warp threads are attached to rollers at each end and are wound out further as the weaving develops.

The weft is usually wound onto a shuttle which is passed from side to side through the warp threads. A space, or shed, through which the shuttle is passed, is created between alternate warp threads with a shed stick. On a roller frame a rigid heddle separates alternate warp threads and is raised or lowered to make a shed.

There are different styles of weaving, but only plain weave or tapestry can be done on a frame loom. Plain weave is produced by taking the weft thread over and under alternate warp threads. In tapestry weave (a variation of plain weave) the weft is much thicker than the warp – so that in the woven fabric the weft shows and the warp is covered.

You can use almost any material for weaving. Experiment with the thickness and texture of different yarns in the weft, but it is important that the warp is strong and smooth.

Making a cushion cover on a frame loom To make a cushion cover 360mm (14in) square, construct a frame loom. Cut two pieces of 50 × 25mm (2 × 1in) softwood 380mm (15in) long, and two pieces 510mm (20in) long – make sure the ends are square.

Hammer 19mm ($\frac{3}{4}$in) panel pins into the two shorter pieces, spacing them 10mm ($\frac{3}{8}$in) apart and staggered as shown. Angle the pins slightly with about two-thirds of their length showing.

Lay the shorter pieces across the longer ones to make the frame, with the pins in the shorter pieces angled outwards. Fix together using overlap joints – see WOODWORKING JOINTS.

As well as the frame you will need a 400mm (16in) shed stick, a shuttle, about 58m (64yds) of yarn for the warp and 225g (8oz) of yarn for the weft (it is bought by weight, not length). The warp yarn can be knitted worsted, worsted warp yarn, rug warp or string. The weft yarn can be wool, mohair, chenille, rag strips, ribbon, metallic cord, or a mixture of all of them. For a balanced weave (with both warp and weft showing equally), choose a weft yarn the same size as the warp.

First, thread the warp (see above and illustration). Loop one end of the weft round the notch in the shuttle and then wind the yarn round the length of the shuttle leaving about 400mm (16in) at the loose ends. Insert the shed stick from the right over every other warp thread and stand it on its edge to lift the alternate threads, as shown.

WEAVING

Using a simple frame loom

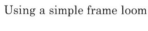

Shuttle

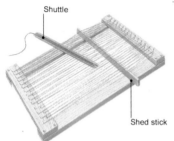

Shed stick

Turn the shed stick on its edge to lift up the alternate warp threads. Then slide the shuttle through the space between the threads, working from left to right.

Lay the shed stick flat and slide it towards you to push the weft thread firmly into place. Then slide the shed stick to the back of the frame ready for the next weft.

Keep the stick flat and weave in the next weft from right to left – pass the shuttle under the threads the first weft went over, and over those it went under.

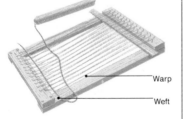

Warp

Weft

Do not pull the weft taut. Weave the weft tail into the warp and continue weaving, alternating sheds on each row.

Slide the shuttle from left to right through the space between the threads, and nearer to you than the shed stick. Leave a 50mm (2in) 'tail' of yarn on the beginning edge. Do not pull the weft taut; allow it to form slight curves across the warp. This prevents the warp from being pulled in at the sides.

When the shuttle reaches the other side, lay the shed stick flat and pull it against the weft thread to pack it straight and firmly into place. Slide the shed stick away from you again, keeping it flat. Now weave the shuttle from right to left under and over the alternate strands that lie behind the first weft; this is the second shed. At the end of this row, weave in the weft tail. Continue weaving, alternating the sheds on each row and packing the weft threads against each other with the shed stick.

After completing 13mm ($\frac{1}{2}$in), called a heading, introduce other colours and textures in the weft. To change yarns at the beginning of a row, leave a tail of each yarn; weave each tail into succeeding rows.

When you have woven 360mm (14in) of fabric, make another heading, and reintroduce the yarn used at the beginning. If the shed openings are tight, weave the last row or two with the weft threaded through a large darning needle. Push them into place with the shed stick. With the weft yarn, make an oversewing stitch (see SEWING) through each warp end and round the last two rows of wefts. Cut across the warp ends near the pins.

Weave a second square for the cushion back, or buy half a metre (half a yard) of fabric to use for the back.

See CUSHIONS for the way to make the cover.

Weddings

Making the arrangements; being best man

By tradition, the bride and her family make most of the arrangements for a wedding. Today, however, if couples are older or if either is remarrying, they may take that responsibility on themselves. See also MARRIAGE.

First, the couple must decide whether to marry in a church or a register office. For a church wedding, speak to the minister to discuss date, time and arrangements. For a civil wedding, contact a register office – look under 'Registration of Births, Deaths and Marriages' in the phone book. Make arrangements for the reception, booking the place, the caterers and a band or disco if you are having them.

Invitations Send out invitations between six and nine weeks before the wedding – they usually come from the bride's parents. The number of guests, from both the bride's and groom's sides, are agreed in advance. The invitations should be simple and formal, stating names and when and where the ceremony and reception are being held.

Wedding presents The couple may decide on a list of presents they would like to receive. The bride, her mother and the groom's mother usually keep a copy each – invited guests can ring them for ideas. It may also be convenient to leave a list with a local store.

Presents sent before the ceremony should be addressed to the bride – otherwise they are addressed to bride and groom. The bride should write thank-you letters from herself and the groom as soon as possible after receiving presents.

Dress Weddings are a chance for everyone to dress up, and the style of wedding will broadly dictate what guests should wear. The bride will often choose the traditional long white, cream or ivory dress and a veil, with complementary colours and designs for her attendants. The bride's mother usually chooses her outfit first, then tells the groom's mother the colour – so that they do not clash.

The bride's father, the groom, best man and ushers often wear morning dress which may be hired – look under 'Men's Wear Hire' in *Yellow Pages* (see also HIRING). If you want all male guests to wear morning dress, you should let them know well in advance.

Attendants The duties of the best man – usually the bridegroom's brother or closest friend – are mainly to take care of the bridegroom and to ensure that he arrives at the ceremony calm, on time, and correctly dressed. The best man looks after the wedding ring, orders buttonholes and supervises the hiring of any cars the groom requires.

The bride chooses her bridesmaids – unmarried girls or women. If the chief bridesmaid is married or a widow, she is called Matron-of-Honour. The bridesmaids' duties are to attend the bride, such as help her to dress, carry the bridal train and hold her bouquet during the ceremony. The bride may also choose pages to attend her.

Ushers show guests to their places in church – the bride's family and friends on the left, the groom's on the right. Ushers are usually men – friends of the groom and men from the bride's family.

Other arrangements Choose and order flowers for the church and reception, also bouquets for bride and bridesmaids.

Choose hymns, arrange for an organist, get service sheets printed and book a photographer well in advance. Order the cake at least three months beforehand – the flavour improves with age.

Arrange for cars to take the bride and her father to church, and the bride's mother with the bridesmaids. The groom should make bookings for the honeymoon well in advance and, if it is to be abroad, PASSPORT applications should be made at least six weeks ahead.

Receptions A wedding reception can be anything from a formal wedding breakfast to an informal buffet party. Receptions are generally held at a hotel, a hall or the bride's parents' home. For a large reception at home, a marquee may be put up in the garden – see 'Tent and Marquee Hire' in *Yellow Pages*.

At the reception the bride's parents, groom's parents and bride and groom form a receiving line to greet the guests.

Speeches usually follow the meal or refreshments. The first is made by the bride's father, who proposes a toast (see TOASTS) to the bride and groom. The groom replies, thanking the bride's parents for the wedding and guests for presents, then he toasts the bridesmaids.

The last speech is from the best man, who replies on behalf of the bridesmaids and may read any telegrams. The cake is then cut by the bride and groom together.

The bride and groom often leave shortly after the speeches. By tradition, the bride tosses her bouquet to an unmarried girl as she leaves.

Wedding expenses The bride's family traditionally bears most of the expense, but costs may be shared by agreement.

The bride's parents normally pay for the reception; flowers for the church and reception; and cars for the bride and her father, bridesmaids and mother.

The bridegroom pays for the wedding ring, and any fees such as those for the church, for publishing the banns, for the marriage certificate and licence, the minister or registrar and the organist. He also pays for his and his best man's car, the going-away car, and the various bouquets as well as buttonholes for himself, his best man, the ushers and close male relatives. He should give the bride's attendants a small gift and may give the best man a present. The groom also pays for the honeymoon.

The bride should pay for the groom's ring if he wants one and may contribute to the cost of her bridesmaids' dresses.

Weed control

Eliminating the competition from your garden

Weeds compete with cultivated plants for light, moisture and nutrients, and harbour pests and diseases. Regular hoeing and digging will keep most weeds at bay – use chemical weedkillers only as a last resort. Annual weeds such as groundsel and fat hen grow fast and produce many seeds. Pull them out by hand, cutting off their roots with a hoe, or turn them under before they go to seed. Perennials, such as dandelion and thistle, come back year after year. Dig up their roots with a border fork or keep the stems cut back to the ground for at least two seasons.

Alternatively, grow ground-cover plants, such as periwinkle or ivy, to smother weeds and prevent sunlight from reaching them.

If you are starting to cultivate a weed-infested area, remove as many roots or rhizomes of weeds as possible. Sow areas not immediately wanted for crops with grass; cutting the grass closely and regularly for two seasons should clear most perennial weeds.

Chemical weedkillers These may be selective – killing a limited range of plants; or non-selective – killing all plants. Use selective weedkillers on lawns to kill weeds, non-selective weedkillers to clear paths and uncultivated areas. Apply following the manufacturer's instructions exactly – some are poisons. Apply on a still day, to make sure the chemical does not blow onto cultivated plants. Use a watering can kept specially for weedkiller.

There are three types of weedkiller: contact types are applied to leaves; translocated types are applied to the leaves and absorbed into the roots; residual or pre-emergence types are applied to the soil – for example, around cultivated plants to prevent seeds germinating.

Weevils

Getting rid of a common garden pest

Small, night-feeding beetles with long, snout-like heads, weevils can cause damage in the garden by eating leaves, buds and plant growing tips, and their larvae burrow into seeds and fruit. There are more than 500 species in Britain, including carrot, nut, apple blossom, and pea and bean weevils. The most troublesome ones for gardeners are vine and clay-coloured weevils, which feed on VINES, soft fruit, and also rhododendrons, polyanthus, and the roots of pot plants such as cyclamens and BEGONIAS.

You can use HCH (see PESTICIDES) to combat weevils. But it may also kill the parasitic wasps that prey on the weevils. If you do not want to use a pesticide, you may be able to trap the weevils in folded sacking or corrugated paper laid near the plants – this is the kind of material they like to hide in by day. Shake the trapped beetles into soapy water or a disinfectant solution, or burn the material.

Basic drills

When weight training, learn to breathe in as you lift – or 'clean' – the weights, and out as you lower them.

Power clean Bend your knees, feet hip-width apart. Grasp the bar firmly with arms straight and back flat.

Straighten your legs keeping arms straight and back flat. As the barbell passes the mid-thighs, snap your elbows under the bar. Lift to shoulder level. For a heave press, bend your legs slightly, then lift the barbell above your head.

Forward raise standing Stand holding a dumbbell across each thigh. Raise your arms, keeping them straight, to just above shoulder level.

Weight training

Starting to exercise with weights

If you are over 30 or have not been exercising regularly, consult a DOCTOR before you start weight training. If possible, join a gym or health club where a qualified instructor can advise you.

Weightlifters train by lifting bars with

weights at each end. To train at home, buy a barbell and dumbbells. To start, choose types with adjustable weights in the 7-14kg (15-20lb) range.

Train three times a week on alternate days. Warm up before a session – see EXERCISES. Start with a weight you can lift comfortably for a set of eight repetitions of one exercise (see below).

Over a few weeks, progressively increase the repetitions to sets of 10 or 12; then add up to 10 per cent more weight to the barbell or dumbbells and go back to doing eight repetitions. To increase muscle size and strength, do fewer repetitions with heavier weights; for tone and endurance, do more repetitions with lighter weights.

Weight-training exercises Use one exercise, repeated, for each set. Here are three basic exercises.

Power clean Stand with your feet under the barbell. Bend your knees, curl your fingers over the bar and grasp it as illustrated. Breathe in and at the same time begin the lift by vigorously straightening your legs. Breathe out as you reverse the action to lower the weight.

Heave press Lift the barbell to shoulder level as for the power clean exercise. Keep the position as you breathe out and prepare for the second part of the lift as illustrated. Breathe in as you vigorously extend your arms. Breathe out as you lower the barbell by reversing the action.

Forward raise standing Take a dumbbell in each hand and stand with your feet hip-width apart. Breathe in as you raise your arms forward. Breathe out as you lower your arms.

Welding

Using an electric home welder

A portable electric welder will make a strong joint between two pieces of metal. Various types are available in DIY stores, or from tool hire centres. Follow the maker's instructions, and practise first on scrap metal. The thinner the metal, the more skill is required.

The pieces are joined by creating an arc – a discharge of electric current across a gap between the metal to be welded and a metal rod (a welding electrode). The current generates enough heat to melt the edges of the metal for welding and fuse them together. The metal rod also melts, adding more molten metal to the joint and filling any gaps.

The electric arc produces intense ultra-violet radiation, which can damage eyes and skin, so it is most important to protect your eyes with a special face mask. Wear heavy leather gloves and, if you

can, a leather apron to withstand sparks.

You should work at a sturdy workbench or table covered with a sheet of heatproof material or mild steel.

You also need a supply of suitable welding electrodes – follow maker's instructions regarding the size of rod.

Seam welding Lay the pieces to be joined on the bench top, and clamp them together in the exact position in which they are to be welded. Connect the earth cable clamp to the workpiece. Insert a welding rod in the electrode holder, then set the amperage on the transformer to suit the rod – consult your instruction book. Plug in the welder.

Hold the electrode about 15 degrees from the vertical and stroke it against the metal at the point to be joined – like striking a match – then immediately lift it about 3mm ($\frac{1}{8}$in) away from the metal surface. This will produce a spark. At the correct distance there will be a crackling sound and you will see the metal melting. Too close and the electrode may stick. Too far away and the arc will be lost. If the rod sticks, move it from side to side as you pull it away.

Move the electrode at a speed which allows the metal to melt and fill the space between the two sheets. At the end of the weld, lift the rod away to kill the arc.

When the weld is cold, chip away any crusty deposit with a steel chisel and hammer, wearing your face mask.

Spot welding In many repair jobs, you do not need to make a welded joint along the full length of the metal – spot or tack welds will suffice. This involves making welded beads, spaced about 6-13mm ($\frac{1}{4}$-$\frac{1}{2}$in) apart along the joint. The thinner the metal, the closer the beads should be.

To spot weld, prepare as for seam welding. Strike an arc and hold the electrode still, long enough for a bead of molten metal to form. Allow the molten metal to fill any hollows in the workpiece, then lift the electrode away sharply to kill the spark. Move along the required distance and repeat until the joint is complete.

You can make spot welds to hold pieces of metal together at strategic points before seam welding.

Wet suits

Choosing, looking after and repairing them

For some watersports, such as SAILING, SCUBA DIVING and WINDSURFING, you may need a wet suit for warmth and protection.

They are available in adult and children's sizes, and are made from a synthetic rubber called neoprene, frequently in bright fluorescent colours that are easily seen.

Scuba-diving suits are 3-10mm ($\frac{1}{8}$-$\frac{3}{8}$in) thick. For sailing or windsurfing, you need a 2-5mm ($\frac{1}{16}$-$\frac{3}{16}$in) suit, which is more supple. Many suits have a reinforced knee area.

One-piece suits have a nylon zip up the back, and may have detachable sleeves. Two-piece suits consist of a 'long john' – combined leggings and tunic top – and a jacket or bolero with a nylon zip up the front.

You may also need accessories such as a neoprene hood, gloves or mittens, and boots.

Make sure your wet suit is a good tight fit. It should let in only a minimal amount of water, which, warmed by the body, helps to insulate you from the cold. Suits seamed with 'blind' stitches, which do not penetrate the entire thickness of the material, are the most waterproof and generally warmer.

Caring for your suit Always wash and rinse a wet suit after use (but *not* in a machine) to remove all traces of salt, which can perish the rubber. Hang the suit to dry, but not in direct sunlight or heat, or the rubber may perish. Hang the suit to store it – do not fold it or leave heavy objects on it.

Repair of suits Small tears in wet suits may be repaired with a special liquid neoprene glue which hardens on contact with air, or with wet suit repair kits. These are available from good sailing or diving equipment shops. Follow the manufacturer's instructions for use carefully.

Pieces of neoprene material are sold for patching very small holes. Stick a patch in place with neoprene glue. Get large holes repaired professionally.

Wheelbarrows

Maintaining them; fitting new wheel bearings

A good wheelbarrow will last for years, if properly cared for, and should need few repairs. Whether it is metal, plastic or wooden, clean it after use and store it in a dry place. Do not leave it full of damp vegetation, which could either rust or rot the body.

Load it carefully to protect the body surface, particularly when transporting sharp or heavy materials. Lightweight garden wheelbarrows are not suitable for heavy building work, such as concreting. For this hire a heavy-duty wheelbarrow with a strong tubular-steel frame. Avoid bumping a barrow with pneumatic tyres up a kerb or step, as this could burst the tyre. If this occurs, you will have to refit a new wheel assembly, available from the supplier or builders' merchants.

Sand and dust can erode wheel bearings. To fit new ones, undo the wheel nuts, ease the wheel from the framework and pull out the spindle and hub centre. Use a screwdriver to force out the nylon bearings from the hub centre, and tap the new ones in with a soft-headed mallet.

Wheezing

Relieving noisy breathing

Wheezing – noisy and troubled breathing – when breathing in or out may be caused by CHOKING, laryngitis, respiratory infections or, in young children, croup. Wheeziness may also be a symptom of asthma, which requires medical care to control the condition.

Less frequently, in babies under 18 months, a wheeze when breathing out develops within a few hours of contracting bronchiolitis – an infection of the small air tubes called bronchioles.

General treatment Give cool drinks. Steam inhalations can also help, especially for croup. Fill a sink or bath with hot water and close the door to let the room fill with steam. Sit the child on your knee to breathe the steamy air for a few minutes.

Take great care to avoid SCALDS from the steam.

Consult a doctor:

● If the breathing stops or is difficult.
● If a baby under six months is affected.
● If a child is drooling and having difficulty in swallowing.
● If a young child's complexion turns greyish, or if the child's breathing becomes rapid, with the ribs being drawn in with each breath.
● If breathing does not become easier in the steam-filled room.
● If you suspect that the nose or throat is blocked by a foreign body.
● If there is a history of any heart disease.

Whist

A card game of trumps and tricks

Whist is a game for four players who play in pairs to win the highest number of *tricks*. The players cut a standard 52-card pack to choose partners. The two who cut the highest cards (ace is high) play the two who cut the lowest. Partners sit opposite each other at the table.

The players cut again and the one with the highest card has the first deal. The pack is cut again by the player on the right of the dealer. The dealer then deals each player 13, one at a time, face down, starting with the player on his left.

The last card the dealer deals to himself – he turns it face up. This card determines the *trump* suit – that is the suit

Dealing, scoring points and taking tricks

Every player takes his turn at dealing the cards – 13 to each one. The dealer deals the last card to himself, turning it face up on the table. This last card determines which suit is to be trumps.

Taking tricks The highest-ranking card in a suit wins the trick. But with diamonds trumps (right), the ace of clubs in the last trick, for example, could be beaten by any diamond.

Scoring points Teams show trump honours they are dealt before play begins. A team with three or four trump honours scores 2 or 4 points, respectively.

which can be used to override other cards when a player cannot follow the suit that has been led.

The players arrange their cards in suits, concealing them from other players. They expose their trump *honours* (ace, king, queen and jack) briefly on the table. If either team holds three trump honours, that team immediately scores 2 points; if a team holds all four, it wins 4 points. No points are scored if the honours are even.

The player on the dealer's left lays the first card of the game, placing it face up in the centre of the table. Play is then clockwise round the table. The other players must follow with cards from the same suit if they can.

If all players can follow the suit, the highest-ranking card wins the trick. If one player, having no card of the same suit, plays a trump, that card wins the trick. If two trumps are played, the higher-ranking trump wins. A player who cannot follow the suit may discard from a suit other than the trump suit.

The winner of each trick leads the next hand and the game continues until all 13 tricks are taken. Then the scores are counted.

No points are scored for the first six tricks or *book*, but each trick taken after that earns the winning team 1 point. The points scored for tricks are added to those scored for honours.

The cards are shuffled and cut and play begins again. The new dealer is always the player to the left of the previous dealer. The game continues until one of the pairs reaches an agreed number of points.

Whiteflies

Dealing with a garden and houseplant pest

Whiteflies – wedge-shaped white insects up to 2mm ($^1/_{16}$in) long – attack the leaves of green vegetables from May to September, and many HOUSEPLANTS and greenhouse plants (see GREENHOUSE GARDENING) all year round.

The winged adults can often be found in dense clusters on the undersides of the leaves, where they deposit eggs in vast numbers. The yellowish larvae remain attached to the plant and suck sap from the leaves, turning them mottled and yellow.

Whiteflies need persistent treatment with PESTICIDES such as resmethrin, permethrin and pyrethrum. Alternatively, in the greenhouse use biological control by introducing *Encardia formosa*, the efficient parasite now regularly available commercially.

Sprout enemy This is what whiteflies look like – clustered here on the underside of a brussels sprout leaf.

Wills

*Making and changing them; what
to do if there is no will*

A simple will can be made without a solicitor's help by any person of sound mind who is over the age of 18. It is, however, best to seek legal advice (see LAWYERS) particularly if the will is complex, or involves considerable property – which may entail setting up TRUSTS to minimise Inheritance Tax.

A will's purpose is to state who will get your possessions and who will wind up your affairs after your death. You can also name a guardian for your children and stipulate what kind of funeral you want.

Most stationers stock basic will forms or you can write your own. The will should begin: 'This is the last will and testament of me (your full name) of (your address). I hereby revoke all wills previously made by me.'

You must name the executor of the will – that is, the person who will see that your instructions are carried out. For practical reasons, this will often be the principal beneficiary or beneficiaries, or a solicitor or bank manager.

Make it clear that all outstanding debts and expenses must be paid from your estate first and then state clearly who is to get what. Identify beneficiaries by giving their relationship, if any, their full name, and if needs be, their address, so there is no doubt who they are.

When allocating sums of money, you can add 'tax free' to indicate that any tax must be paid from the rest of the estate. Describe possessions in detail so that they can be clearly identified.

Even if you think you have accounted for all you possess, to cover all eventualities, specify who should receive any residue.

The will must be clearly dated, and signed by you and two independent witnesses. They must not be beneficiaries or married to beneficiaries. The witnesses must see you sign together and must say so; for example 'signed by X in the presence of us who in X's presence and the presence of each other have hereto signed our names as witnesses'.

Changing a will You can always change or revoke your will with a later will or with a 'codicil' – an amending document, dated and signed by you and two independent witnesses, as in a will.

A codicil should state again your name and clearly outline the changes and what they are replacing.

If you marry or remarry, a previous will is generally revoked automatically.

If you get a divorce, your ex-wife or ex-husband should no longer be an executor. If she or he is to remain a beneficiary, you must amend the will to make the new relationship clear.

If there is no will If someone dies without leaving a will, a relative or friend can seek advice from the Probate Registry – usually listed in the local telephone book. A booklet entitled *How to obtain probate* can normally be obtained from the registrar of births and deaths when the death is registered.

The Probate Registry will supply a set of forms which must be completed if you wish to administer the estate. You must also attend an interview at the registry.

If your application is approved, you will receive from the registry a Grant of Representation. The estate must be distributed according to probate rules which determine who the beneficiaries will be – usually the nearest relative.

If someone dies without leaving a will and no claimants come forward, the estate passes to the Crown and is administered by the Treasury Solicitor's Department. In practice, the Treasury Solicitor takes the Grant of Representation and usually advertises for claimants to come forward. Claims are then examined by his office before anyone can benefit.

Window boxes

Making your own

A window box can stand on a windowsill, secured by a restraint, if the sill is wide enough. If not, it can be supported on metal BRACKETS on the wall below the windowsill.

The simplest window boxes to maintain are those designed to house pots or long containers. However, both the containers and window box must have drainage holes, otherwise the plants can become waterlogged – especially during heavy rain.

Use either 19mm ($\frac{3}{4}$in) softwood TIMBER or, for long life, use a similar thickness of exterior-quality PLYWOOD.

Windowsill Measure the length of the sill and deduct 25mm (1in). Measure the width then consider what size of pot or container the window box must house. For the height of the window box, 120mm ($4\frac{3}{4}$in) is reasonable, but make it high enough for the containers not to show above the front.

Cut the wood to size – a front and a back, two end pieces, and a base – see SAWS AND SAWING. Cut the base to fit within the front, back and end pieces, set level and slightly raised to leave a gap underneath for water to run away. Drill 13mm ($\frac{1}{2}$in) drainage holes along the base at 100mm (4in) intervals – see DRILLING.

Drill screw holes for all joints and treat all the pieces with one of the clear WOOD PRESERVATIVES before assembly. Apply waterproof wood glue (see GLUING) to each meeting surface and use fine brass or rustless SCREWS to fix the pieces together. Wipe away surplus glue before it sets.

Secure the back of the box to the window frame with angle brackets screwed firmly in place.

Wall-mounted box Make in the same way as for a sill-mounted one, but with the end pieces level at the bottom edges and the base fitted flush. The width is not so critical. Mark the positions for the brackets on the wall, allowing for the top of the box to be level with the sill when it is resting on the brackets. For a box up to 600mm (2ft) long, use two strong metal brackets, slightly shorter than the measurement from front to back of the box, and positioned 150mm (6in) from each end. For a longer box, fit extra brackets equally spaced between – one for each extra 300mm (1ft) of length.

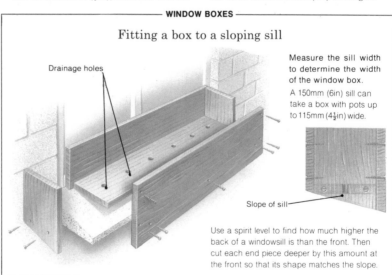

WINDOW BOXES

Fitting a box to a sloping sill

Drainage holes

Measure the sill width to determine the width of the window box.

A 150mm (6in) sill can take a box with pots up to 115mm (4$\frac{1}{2}$in) wide.

Slope of sill

Use a spirit level to find how much higher the back of a windowsill is than the front. Then cut each end piece deeper by this amount at the front so that its shape matches the slope.

Drill and plug the wall (see MASONRY DRILLING) and secure the brackets using strong screws inserted at least 25mm (1in) into the masonry – see WALL FASTENERS. Screw the box onto the brackets with rustless screws.

Window cleaning

Getting them crystal clear with minimum effort

Do not clean windows when the sun is shining on them, or they will dry too quickly and streaks will appear. Use lukewarm water, and if the windows are very dirty, add a little washing-up liquid or a tablespoon of methylated spirit.

Use two wash leathers – CHAMOIS LEATHER or chamois-substitute cloths are best – one to wash and the other to wipe. Dip the wash leather in the water and wring it out well. Clean from the edges of the pane towards the centre. Immediately wipe the glass from side to side with the second cloth, which should be slightly damp. Change the water often.

It may be quicker to use a window mop – a rubber blade on a stick – for large panes of glass. Use it on a long pole to reach high windows. Work from the top of the pane downwards, wiping the blade with a dry cloth after each stroke.

If you use washing-up liquid, rinse the windows with clear, cold water and a leather to avoid smears.

An alternative cleaning method is to use a proprietary window polish, but wash very dirty panes first. Apply the polish lightly with a soft cloth, and as it dries wipe the smears away with a clean soft cloth or paper towel.

Window panes

Replacing broken glass

There are several types of window glass ranging from patterned varieties to the crystal clear. If you plan something different for a window, ask to see samples or a pattern leaflet at your local glass shop. Glass varies in thickness too, and sizes (once graded by weights, such as 24oz) are now in millimetres. Glass 3mm thick is available for very small panes, such as for Georgian-style windows. For windows up to about 1sq m (11 sq ft), use 4mm glass. For larger windows use 6mm glass. For windows in very exposed positions, use thicker glass.

When you buy new glass, give the exact dimensions to your glazier, and explain the location of the window. He can then recommend a suitable glass.

If you need glass of an odd shape – perhaps for a front door – make a paper pattern of the shape for the glazier to use as a template. See also GLASS CUTTING.

You will also need linseed-oil putty and glazing sprigs for wooden frames, or metal-casement putty for steel frames.

Replacing a pane Use an old chisel or knife to knock out all the old putty, then wear leather gloves while you pull out the broken glass. If glass splinters are likely to fly, wear safety goggles as well.

Pull out old glazing pins – or any spring clips on a metal frame – with pliers, then clean out the rebate in the window frame. If the frame is metal, deal with any RUST. Apply wood or metal primer, then fit the new pane in place – see PUTTYING.

Windscreen washers

Maintaining and adjusting them, renewing motors

If a windscreen washer fails, the fluid reservoir may be empty, the spray jets clogged, or the connecting hose blocked or damaged. Top up the fluid reservoir before you start a long journey. Use a proprietary additive in the water to dissolve grease – do not use liquid detergent, which may clog the system. Clean clogged sprays with a pin or pricker, or

---

WINDSCREEN WASHERS

Replacing a motor

When fitting a new motor of a different type, it is often simplest to bypass the old motor. Disconnect the battery first.

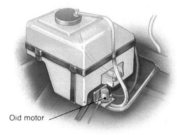

Old motor

Remove the old motor's wiring. Then disconnect its water outlet pipe and plug the stub with a brass woodscrew.

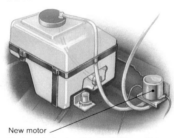

New motor

Fit the detached outlet pipe to the outlet stub on the new motor. Fit a new length of suction pipe from the motor's inlet stub to the reservoir.

---

replace them if they cannot be cleared.

If no fluid flows from the plastic connecting hose, it may be kinked or misshapen – you can usually straighten it by hand. If it is blocked, disconnect it from the pump and blow or pump air through it. Replace a damaged hose.

The washer system should have a filter and non-return valve at the bottom end of the pipe in the reservoir. Examine this for dirt and sediment. Clean or replace the filter if necessary.

Changing a motor If the motor does not work when switched on, check the switch and wiring by CIRCUIT TESTING. Make sure the motor is properly earthed and not too tight in its mountings. Replace the switch if necessary.

If current is reaching the motor but it still does not work, replace it. You may be able to buy a washer replacement unit for your make of car from a motor accessory shop. If not, disconnect and bypass the old motor and fit a new one of a different pattern nearby. You may need to lengthen the hoses or wiring to fit it on a new mounting. Disconnect the battery before disconnecting the old motor. Plug the outlet pipe.

Make sure you have a clear space behind the panel before DRILLING holes for the new motor. Fit it in place, following the maker's instructions.

The stubs for the inlet and outlet water pipes are usually marked with arrows showing the flow direction. Fit the disconnected outlet pipe to the outlet stub.

Fit a new length of suction pipe from the inlet stub to the plastic reservoir. Make sure you have a filter and non-return valve at the bottom end of the pipe in the reservoir.

Lastly, connect the wiring to the motor. If the car has a negative earth, fit the negative terminal to the car bodywork; if it has a positive earth, connect the positive terminal to the bodywork.

Reconnect the battery and test the system. Do not operate the washer when the fluid reservoir is empty – it could damage the pump impeller.

Windscreen wipers

Replacing and adjusting the blades and arms

There are several ways of attaching wiper blades and arms. When replacing either, get the correct type for your car. Fit a new arm with the blades on so you can check that it is at the correct angle to the screen and parks properly.

Bayonet-type blades The blade mounting pushes onto a small pin. Press the blade until the pin disengages, then withdraw it. Push on the new blade until the pin snaps into place.

Hooked-arm blades The blade has a U-shaped plastic insert that fits inside the hooked end of the arm. To remove the blade, squeeze the ends of the insert together and push the blade along the arm until it is clear of the hook. Remove the plastic insert. Thread the hooked arm through an aperture above the U-piece in the new blade and push the new insert into the hook until a locking piece of plastic engages with a notch in the hook.

Sidelock blades A waisted pin on one side of the blade engages in a hole in the end of the arm. Press the locking clip away from the pin and withdraw the pin. Push the pin of the new blade into the hole until the clip snaps into place.

Clip-on arm A spring-loaded clip behind the arm bears on the splined drive spindle. Prise the clip away from the spindle and pull off the arm. Push the new arm partway onto the splines, check that it is at the correct angle, then press it home until the clip snaps into place.

Nut or screw-held arm Prise up the hinged cover, remove the screw or nut and pull the arm from the spindle.

Maintenance and adjustment Every time you clean the car (see CAR WASHING) look for splits in the blade rubber or a thin, wavy edge. If the blade skates over water, fit a new arm. If it judders, the arm is loose or misaligned. Tighten the spindle boss nuts, and see if the blade hinge pins are worn – if they are fit a new arm. To adjust the arm alignment, switch the wipers on then turn off the ignition while they are vertical. Remove the blade and twist the arm gently with pliers so that, viewed end on, the flat part is parallel to the screen.

Windsurfing

Surfing with the wind

It is best to learn windsurfing – or board-sailing – from a Royal Yachting Association-qualified instructor. Details are available from their headquarters at Romsey Road, Eastleigh, Hants SO50 9YA.

Do not attempt windsurfing unless you are a good swimmer, and always wear a buoyancy aid. Wear suitable clothing, such as a WET SUIT and a light windproof jacket.

A sailboard consists simply of the board and rig, made up of a mast, boom and sail. Attached to the front of the boom is the uphaul (the line used to heave the mast upright). The boom is a chest-height elliptical rail which passes round the sail. The surfer grips the boom and uses it to change the angle of the sail to the wind.

Position the board at right angles to the wind, with the sail lying in the water downwind and at right angles to the board. Kneel in the middle of the board with your knees on either side of the mast foot. Check that the wind is at your back. Grasp the uphaul for stability. Move your feet on either side of the mast foot on the centreline, and stand up. Hold the end of the uphaul and lean back slightly. Bend your knees, keep your head up and use your body weight and leg muscles to pull the rig just clear of the water. Continue pulling hand over hand on the uphaul until the far end of the boom clears the water and the sail is at right angles to the board.

Hold the uphaul with the hand nearest the stern. Cross the other hand over the first and grasp the boom about 200mm (8in) from the mast. Release the uphaul and grasp the boom about 510mm (20in) from the other hand.

To steer a straight course at right angles to the wind, slowly pull in the sail until it fills and ceases fluttering; keep the boom parallel to the board. Lean back to counterbalance the pull of the sail in a strong wind.

To turn the front away from the wind, tilt the rig forward. To turn towards the wind, tilt the rig back. The board will stall if you sail directly into the wind. See also SAILING.

If you fall off the board, approach it from the opposite side to the rig. Place your hands on the centreline and hoist yourself back on in a kneeling position. Then stand and pull the rig up again.

Sailboard safety Never sail where there are no other people about. But keep clear of bathers, anglers and other craft.

Do not sail in an offshore wind until you are very experienced; if you find yourself far out and unable to sail back, remove the mast from its housing, roll up the sail and tie it to the mast. 'Scissor' the boom along the mast and tie the sail and boom securely. Lay them along the board. Lie face down on the board and paddle ashore.

To signal for help, kneel or sit on the board and raise and lower both arms, or shout.

Wine-making

Preparing a country vintage from the humble dandelion

A traditional country wine can be made from the petals of DANDELIONS. You can use some ordinary kitchen equipment – a large bowl, a large, heavy-based stainless-steel saucepan, a plastic funnel, and a muslin cloth or jelly bag for straining – and empty wine bottles and stoppers. You will also need two 4.5 litre (8 pint) glass fermentation jars, one with a bung and airlock (a U-shaped glass tube that

Using an airlock and siphon

You need an airlock and a siphon for the fermentation process – one to let gas escape, the other to get rid of sediment.

Airlock Push the stem of the airlock into the hole in the bung, so that the end of the tube just protrudes into the jar.

Siphoning Place the jars so that the top of the empty jar is lower. Suck the tube to start the flow. Keep the wine jar tilted.

stops air and bacteria getting in but lets gas out), polythene tubing – about 1.5m (5ft) – for siphoning, and a wine-maker's thermometer.

Sterilise all containers, stoppers and siphons in sulphite solution (available from a chemist) before use. If you pick the dandelions in April or May, the wine should be ready by Christmas.

Ingredients (for 3½-4 litres – 6-7 pints)
2.3 litres (4 pints) dandelion petals
3.4 litres (6 pints) boiling water
1.6kg (3½lb) granulated sugar
Juice and thinly peeled rind of 1 lemon
Juice and thinly peeled rind of 1 orange
15g (½oz) wine or baker's yeast

Pick the petals from the dandelion heads, discarding the green cup, put them in a large bowl and pour the water over them. Cover the bowl with a cloth, secured with elastic to prevent sagging. Leave the petals in the water for three or four days, stirring the mixture daily, to extract the full flavour.

Strain the liquid into the saucepan through muslin. Add the sugar, lemon and orange peel. Heat gently, stirring until the sugar has dissolved. Simmer for 30 minutes. Strain back into the cleaned bowl. Cool to about 21°C (70°F) before adding the lemon and orange juice.

Strain the liquid through the muslin and funnel into a fermentation jar, filling it about three-quarters full. Sprinkle the yeast onto the liquid.

Fit the jar with the bung and airlock, filling the curve of the airlock between the bulbs with sulphite solution (keep it topped up).

Leave the jar in a warm place – 21°C – for the first fermentation, which generally takes several days. Move it to a temperature of 16-18°C (61-64°F) as the bubbling slows down.

Sediment forms in the bottom of the jar as fermentation slows down. Rack – that is, siphon off the clear liquid from the sediment – several times as the wine ferments. Siphon it into the second fermentation jar. If there is not enough liquid to fill the second jar, top it up to the neck with a sugar solution of the same strength.

To check whether fermentation has ceased, move the wine back to a warmer temperature – 21°C. If it starts bubbling again, it is not completed. When the wine has stopped fermenting, bottle it, leaving a 25mm (1in) gap below the stopper. Store, in a cool, dark place for at least six months. See also BEER.

Wine storage

Keeping it in good condition

Most wines are now sold ready for drinking, and do not need to be left to mature. But all except very light-bodied wines or cheap red wines will improve in flavour if kept for a while before drinking, and stored in the right conditions.

Store wines in a cool, dark place where the temperature is fairly even – between 7°C and 18°C (45°F and 64°F) – to prevent premature ageing. A damp cellar is ideal. Your storage place could also be a ventilated cupboard near an outside wall or even a blocked-up fireplace.

Keep bottles on their sides in wine racks, so that the wine inside keeps the cork wet. If the cork dries out it will allow air through to the wine, which will oxidise and turn to vinegar.

Wine with food

Matching it to a meal; serving it correctly

There are some foods that do not combine well with any kind of wine; these include anything dressed in vinegar or large quantities of lemon juice, pickled foods, egg dishes, anything heavily spiced with chilli or curry, and chocolate.

When planning what wines to serve, choose according to the sauces to be used and method of cooking. A sauce of white wine, cream and mushrooms, for example, needs to be eaten with an assertive white wine such as an Entre-Deux-Mers or a white Burgundy.

Sauces made from horseradish or mint diminish the taste of fine wines – match them with a robust, everyday wine such as a Muscadet or a Dão. Fried dishes or fatty meats need robust wines to cut across the fat and freshen the palate; a white Spanish or Italian wine goes well with fried fish and a good red Burgundy with fatty POULTRY.

Basic dishes such as a CASSEROLE or a stew are best accompanied by straightforward red wines. Goulash, for example, is good with a strong red such as the Hungarian Bull's Blood; a white meat stew goes with a light red – a Merlot or Gamay, for example.

Serve dry wine before a sweet, because you are unlikely to enjoy a dry wine after eating or drinking something even slightly sweet. If you are serving the same type of wine throughout the meal, offer young wines before old. Go from the lightest to the heaviest wines, and always serve the finest last.

Shellfish are usually served with chilled dry white or pink (rosé) wines. Fish dishes also go well with pink wines, but it depends on the flavour of the fish: fish of subtle flavour such as trout, need a delicate wine such as an Anjou rosé or a Riesling: stronger-tasting fish need weightier wines such as a white Burgundy or Rioja.

Poultry can be accompanied by red or white wines: in France duck and goose are frequently served with a red Burgundy or Bordeaux (claret), although they also go well with a Gewürztraminer or a Riesling. As a general rule, choose the wine for meat according to the strength of the flavour and accompaniments – a light wine for lighter flavours and simple stuffings, a stronger wine for richer ones.

Serving the wine If your white wine has not been stored in a cool place such as a refrigerator, chill it for about 15 minutes in icy water or an ice bucket filled with crushed ice. Serve dry white wine and champagne at about 10°C (50°F), and dessert or sparkling wines at 4°C (39°F). The flavour of young reds usually benefits from decanting the wine at least an hour before the meal, but decant mature wines just before serving. Uncork the bottle to 'air' young wines for several hours, and mature wines for one or two hours. Old Burgundy, Chianti and Côtes du Rhône are best served at about 18°C (64°F), most other red wines and Bordeaux at 16°C (61°F), but young red Burgundy at 14°C (57°F) and Beaujolais at 11°C (51°F). See also GLASSES.

Winkles and whelks

Enjoying native shellfish

The whelk, a large marine snail, and the similar, but smaller, winkle are both plentiful on rocky coasts around Britain. They are generally sold ready-cooked and shelled, on stalls and in fishmongers. They should be eaten fresh, on the day of purchase.

To prepare Live winkles, gathered at the seaside, should be washed well in several changes of water to get rid of the sand. Then let them soak in fresh water for half an hour before washing them again. Traditionally, they are cooked in seawater but may also be boiled in fresh, salted water.

Strain them, shaking the sieve gently so that they withdraw into their shells before dropping them in the boiling water. Cook for 5-7 minutes.

When cooked, use a pin to remove the scale-like cap from the opening of the shell (which is discarded) and to extract the meat inside. Season the winkles with malt vinegar and pepper to taste.

Whelks are tougher than winkles and tastiest when small. Cover live whelks in fresh water and leave to soak for an hour so that they expel the dirt from their shells. Boil for 10-15 minutes in seawater or salt water. Pick them out of their shells and season to taste. Serve with brown bread.

WARNING Properly cooked, shellfish should pose no danger to health – any polluting viruses will be killed in boiling water. Nonetheless, in polluted estuaries in some parts of Britain, shellfish gathering is prohibited under public health regulations.

Woodcarving

Equipping yourself; choosing woods; basic cutting

For woodcarving you need a round mallet and a set of gouges (chisels with curved blades) of different widths – 25mm (1in), 13mm (½in) and 8mm (⁵⁄₁₆in) are best for beginners. You also need a parting tool, which is a narrow V-shaped gouge for channelling, and a flat chisel and corner chisel. Keep gouges and chisels sharp as you work – see CHISELLING. Blunt tools are likely to slip.

Other tools needed are a large rasp, and rifflers – variously shaped finishing tools with finer teeth – for preliminary smoothing; also a saw (see SAWS AND SAWING) to cut off excess wood, and a simple bench screw or clamp to hold the carving block in place. Alternatively, get a special vice which allows you to turn the piece as you work.

You will need a selection of glass-papers, from coarse to the finest grade, to smooth down the finished piece, and polyurethane varnish (see VARNISHING), beeswax and turpentine for polishing.

Choosing a wood Jelutong, from the Malaysian rubber tree, is a soft hard-wood suitable for beginners, and available from many timber yards. Mahogany, lime and fruit tree woods are also good; or you can use a shelf or leg from an old piece of furniture, after stripping off its varnish or polish. Softwoods (see TIMBER) are difficult to cut cleanly.

If you need to build up laminations of wood to form a block thick enough for carving, use PVA adhesive. Clamp the laminations while the glue is wet and leave to dry overnight.

Designing and carving Make rough sketches of your proposed carving from several angles. Plan the carving so that thin parts of the piece run with the grain of the wood to give it strength. Then make a clay model or 'maquette' to get a clearer idea of its three-dimensional shape – see MODELLING IN CLAY.

Make side and back outline sketches of the maquette, lay the two sketches against the wood and trace round them in pencil. Mark the areas to be cut away and remove the main unwanted areas with a saw.

Clamp the block to your work surface and begin cutting with a large gouge. Hold the gouge firmly in one hand and tap it gently with the mallet, working away from yourself. When cutting with the grain, remove small chips at a time to avoid splitting the wood, and work from the long grain towards the end grain. When cutting across the grain, remove long slivers and work from the edges to the centre.

Gouge out the basic shape at the front and back, removing roughly equal amounts of wood from each side. Keep the maquette close by as a guide.

To begin rounding the piece, mark unwanted areas with a pencil and start cutting them away with a flat chisel. Continue cutting with gouges, using the most appropriate size. Define detailed shaping by channelling with the parting tool. When you have finished shaping, smooth down the grooves with the rasp.

To sand the carving smooth, start with a coarse glasspaper, working through the grades to the finest grained paper – see SANDING.

Coat the model with polyurethane varnish and allow it to dry thoroughly. Rub down with fine glasspaper to take off the surface, leaving the varnish soaked into the wood.

Gently heat equal amounts of beeswax and turpentine. Place it in a tin standing in a pan of water; never heat it directly, as it could catch fire. Paint the mixture over the model. When dry, rub with a soft cloth to give a light sheen. Make further applications for a glossier finish.

Wood preservatives

Protecting timber indoors and out

To prevent DRY ROT and WOODWORM, buy only pre-treated timber, which has been pressure-impregnated with wood preservative at the mill, to use when doing un-painted construction or repair work in the house or garden.

If treated timbers are not available, treat the wood yourself with a wood preservative. Most preservatives available are either solvent-based or water-based, and are harmless to humans, pets and plants once dry, but avoid splashing. Solvent-based types are flammable – keep flames away until at least two days after application. Creosote, made from tar oil, is harmful to plants. If you apply it to outside woodwork, wear protective clothing and keep children and pets away until it is dry. A preservative may be clear or may contain pigments which colour the wood as it is applied.

The following methods can be used for applying preservatives:

Spray Mostly used for loft treatment, in which case it is best to hire spray equipment plus a protective industrial mask to filter out fumes. Follow the maker's instructions carefully. Preservatives may also be sprayed on fences – use water-based preservative in a pressure garden sprayer. Use a coarse spray nozzle to ensure a thorough coating.

Brush Use a brush about 75mm (3in) wide. Wear protective gloves and, if working above your head, headgear and safety goggles as well. Push preservative into cracks, and soak end grain by dabbing on preservative until it runs off. Keep the brush strictly for preservatives in future.

Soaking This is the most effective way of treating timber at home. Timbers for fence posts or rails are best treated in this way. Make up a simple trough, using a retaining wall of bricks, then line it with draped heavy-gauge polythene sheeting to form a 'pond'. Lay a length of timber in the trough and weight it down with bricks. Then fill the trough with enough preservative to cover the timber and leave it to soak overnight.

If it is not practicable to immerse the whole of the timber, fill a large can with preservative and stand posts in it. This will give maximum protection to that section of the post going below ground. The rest can be treated by brush.

Pellets Where decorated wood, such as a painted windowsill, may be at risk but applying preservative is not practical, use fungicidal pellets. Drill holes in the wood and insert a pellet in each hole. Then seal with waterproof filler or stopping. Should the timber become damp, fungicide will be released from the pellet, effectively preventing rot.

Wood splitting

Making logs into firewood

Use a felling axe (see AXES) to split logs up to 380mm (15in) in diameter. Alternatively, use a steel wedge and sledge-hammer. Tap the point of the wedge into the log along the grain line so that the wedge stands upright, then strike with the sledgehammer to split the wood.

With logs 610mm (2ft) or more in diameter, you may need a log grenade – a spiked, cone-shaped wedge, which is driven into the end of the log with a sledgehammer.

Place the log upright on a chopping block and drive the point of the grenade into the log's centre with a few taps of the sledgehammer. Then give the top of the grenade a few heavy blows with the hammer – the log will split into several pieces.

To split the log halves or pieces into kindling wood, use a billhook or a hatchet.

Woodworking joints

Marking, cutting and fitting some basic joints

Simple joints can be used for most general-purpose jobs, such as TIMBER framework, SHELVES and FENCES.

Construction can often be simplified by using modern adhesives which in many cases are stronger than the wood.

Tools you may need include: a fine-toothed tenon saw (see SAWS AND SAWING); a try square, for marking right angles; a scriber or knife and a pencil, for marking; a steel tape, for measuring; woodworking adhesive (see GLUING); nails (see NAILING) and SCREWS; a hammer and screwdriver; a drill and twist bits (see DRILLING); a chisel and mallet – see CHISELLING.

Butt joint The simplest of all joints, this is used to fix two pieces of wood at right angles to each other, to make a corner or a T. Mark the end of the piece to be butted using a square and scriber, then cut it dead square with the tenon saw, so that the surfaces to be butted together meet perfectly.

Drill a screw hole or holes through one piece of wood, then drill smaller start holes to take the screws in the end grain of the second piece of wood. Apply adhesive to the two meeting pieces, then screw them together until adhesive seeps from the joint. Wipe away surplus adhesive while wet.

End grain does not have much holding power, so if the joint needs to be strong, insert wall plugs (see WALL FASTENERS) into holes drilled in the end grain and drive the screws into these. Position the plugs so that they will expand where the wood is widest.

Overlap joint Simply lay one piece of wood on top of another at right angles to it, and secure with glue and nails or screws. Make sure both surfaces meet perfectly, then apply adhesive to them. Check with the square that the two pieces are at right angles before the glue sets. Secure with screws or nails driven through the thinner piece into the thicker. Drive in the nails at an angle (skew nailing).

Full lap T-joint The full thickness of a thinner piece of wood is set into a thicker piece – so that their surfaces are flush. Lay the thinner piece on the other piece. Mark its position with two small scribed scratches down each side of it on the thicker wood, then use the square to draw two parallel lines over the scratches across the wood.

Mark the depth of the piece to be inset, then use the tenon saw to cut down to this depth, cutting just on the inside of the two parallel lines. Use the chisel and mallet to remove waste wood until the piece to be housed is a good tight fit, with its surface flush. Apply adhesive to the meeting surfaces and nail or screw together.

Rebated joint One piece of wood is recessed to the thickness of the second piece, so it sits over the end grain of the second piece. Mark the first piece to the right depth and width with square and scriber, then cut out the waste with the tenon saw. Make the joint project just a fraction so you can square it up when the joint is finished. Do not make the depth of a rebate more than three-quarters the thickness of the wood into which it is cut.

Glue the meeting areas, then skew nail or screw them together.

Mortise-and-tenon This makes a very strong joint – but calls for a little practice to ensure a really good fit.

An extra tool is needed to make the joint – a mortise gauge, which has two points that can be set to mark the exact width of the tenon and the mortise into which it will go. The tenon can be up to a third the thickness of the wood it will slot into – but not thicker or strength will be lost. Mark the cutting lines for tenon and mortise first with the gauge,

---

┌─────────────────────────────┐
│ **WOODWORKING JOINTS** │

Making a mortise-and-tenon joint

Use a mortise gauge to measure the pieces to be cut out. Cut a tongue (tenon) in one piece to fit a slot (mortise) in the other.

Tenon Hold the wood in a vice and use a tenon saw to cut the tongue.

Mortise Drill holes through, within mortise marks; chisel out the remaining waste.

Fitting During final trimming, test the tenon in the mortise for a snug fit. Trim as necessary, then glue the joint.

└─────────────────────────────┘

then with a pencil and square to get them right-angled. Make the tenon a fraction too long so that it will protrude through the mortise slot.

Cut the waste from the tenon using the tenon saw.

Mark the mortise on both sides of the wood so you can cut away waste wood from both sides. Drill a series of holes through the marked area, then use a mortise chisel and mallet to cut out the remaining waste, keeping inside the scribed lines. When the tenon fits well, glue the tenon, then tap it into the mortise until it protrudes. Check with the square to see the two pieces of wood are at right angles, then leave the joint to set. When set, use coarse sandpaper wrapped around a block to smooth off the projecting tenon until it is flush with the surrounding wood – see SANDING.

A twin mortise and tenon is even stronger and withstands blows and twisting – to a TOBOGGAN, for example. Instead of a single tenon, cut two, side by side, to fit into twin mortise slots. Use a mortise gauge to mark cutting lines accurately and make the tenons and the gap dividing them the same width. Cut and glue as for a single mortise and tenon.

Single dovetail Use this strong joint to fix rails which have to bear a weight. A wedge-shaped dovetail, or 'pin', cut at the end of the rail is recessed into a similarly shaped slot in the piece to which it is being joined.

Mark out the shape of the pin on the rail, keeping the dovetail as wide as possible. Cut the pin accurately to shape with the tenon saw, keeping to the waste side of the lines.

Lay the dovetail on the second piece of wood, and mark its exact shape on the wood with the scriber or a knife point. Saw down at a number of points to the exact depth of the dovetail, then chisel out the waste, keeping all faces square. Test the dovetail in the recess until a tight fit is produced. Glue the two pieces and tap them together.

Woodworm

Getting rid of pests which can cause damage

The most likely beetle to attack the woodwork in your home is the common furniture beetle. It will attack rough timbers in a loft and any untreated wood, such as floorboards, the backs of furniture and similar surfaces.

It is worth making a search in late spring for signs of attack – small holes about 2mm (^{1}/$_{16}$in) in diameter, and little piles of wood dust. If left unchecked, the beetle can cause extensive damage.

The beetle lays as many as 60 eggs in cracks and crevices, and these hatch into grubs which bore down into the wood, forming small tunnels as they do so. The grubs will stay in the wood for up to three years, eventually coming close to the surface to turn into adult beetles. They then bite their way out to lay new eggs – and so the cycle continues.

For limited attacks, either brush or spray on woodworm killer fluid, allowing it to soak into the holes. Where large areas are involved (in a loft space, for example) hire a professional spray and industrial respirator and buy some fluid from your local hire centre (see HIRING). You will need 4.5 litres (1 gallon) of woodworm fluid for every 18.5m² (200sq ft) to be sprayed. For attacks in furniture, inject the fluid into every individual hole, using a can with an injector nozzle.

Beetles landing on the treated timbers will die, and emerging beetles also die, thus breaking the life cycle.

If you are unsure whether signs you find are made by woodworm, or how severe the attack is, call in one of the specialist companies which offer a free survey – look under 'Woodworm Control' in *Yellow Pages*. If they find trouble, they will quote for treating it –

some may give you the option of doing it yourself.

Protect furniture from attack by using an insecticidal furniture polish. Check any secondhand furniture you buy: a few holes do not necessarily mean there are living grubs inside, but as a precaution treat all holes with insecticide and use insecticidal polish.

A far more serious, though rarer enemy is the house longhorn beetle, which can burrow for up to six years. It makes an oval hole about 6 × 3mm ($\frac{1}{4}$ × $\frac{1}{8}$in) so close to the surface that you can usually see the tunnels.

If you are considering buying a house more than 20 years old, have a free survey done by one of the specialist companies to check the timbers. See also DEATH WATCH BEETLE.

When undertaking repair or constructional work, buy timber which has been pressure-impregnated with preservative. See also WOOD PRESERVATIVES.

Wormcasts

Ridding your lawn of unsightly blemishes

A morris dance (or any other vigorous dance) held on your lawn is a traditional, and effective, way to deal with worms. The worms are said to interpret the thumping feet as a heavy shower of rain – so they pop to the surface where they can be brushed up for dropping onto the compost heap.

Less energetic measures, however, are also available. If the problem is minor, it may be best to let the casts dry, then brush them over the lawn as a top-dressing; they contain valuable nutrients.

If, however, the worms are seriously disfiguring the lawn, irritants such as permanganate of potash or derris dust will drive them away. Dissolve the potash in water at the rate of 6g per litre (or 1oz per gallon) and sprinkle it on the grass. Scatter the derris dust on the grass dry – 25g per square metre (1oz per square yard) – and water it in.

For a more permanent treatment, use a wormkiller based on chlordane or carbaryl – but only as a last resort, for worms are beneficial to soils.

Wounds

First aid for cuts and abrasions

Slight cuts and grazes do not usually need professional attention – unless infected or caused by dirty or rusty objects. Nonetheless, treat even minor wounds with care to prevent infection from developing and to aid healing.

First control BLEEDING – in more serious cases this could save a life. To treat the wound, first wash your hands thoroughly, then fill a bowl with clean, lukewarm water containing soap or a mild antiseptic.

Expose the wound and use sterile gauze pads, cotton swabs or a clean cloth dipped in the water to clean the skin round the injury. Wipe outwards and away from the wound. Make sure the water does not run into the wound. When a pad or swab becomes soiled, change to a fresh one.

Now wash the wound itself. Rinse generously with plenty of soapy water from the bowl; do not rub the wound. Splash a cut hand or foot in the bowl; flush grit away by squeezing the water over it.

Dry round the wound gently with a clean swab. Apply a bandage – see BANDAGING.

Ingrained dirt Remove any visible grit or splinters with sterilised tweezers – see STERILISING. However, only remove the grit you can pick out easily – do not probe. Never squeeze a puncture wound to clean it; this can spread infection. If dirt is embedded in the injury, keep rinsing for at least 20 minutes. Dry and bandage as before.

Check the wound regularly over the following few days. Excessive pain or swelling, redness, or a red streak leading from the original injury may indicate infection or a foreign body. If so, see a doctor.

Always consult a doctor or hospital casualty department about a gaping wound that might need stitches. You may need an anti-tetanus booster injection every ten years (five years if you work with animals or the soil).

'Stab' wounds Wounds from nails, needles, glass and other sharp objects may look slight on the surface, but can result in serious internal injury. They can also carry dirt and germs deep into the flesh – and infection below can spread. Seek medical help as soon as the wound has been cleaned and bandaged.

If the object that created the wound remains embedded, do not try to remove it. Instead, use a ring-pad and bandage to cover the wound – so that the object is not forced in. Seek medical help.

Wreaths

Making them for Christmas and other seasons

To make a traditional Christmas wreath, collect evergreen branches or use the lower branches of your Christmas tree – see CHRISTMAS TREES. Stand them in a pail of water for a day or two in a cool place, such as a garage or garden shed.

For the frame, make a 300mm (12in) diameter hoop by bending a wire coathanger and twisting the ends together with pliers.

Cut two or three evergreen sprigs between 200mm (8in) and 300mm (12in) long and tie them in a bunch with thin wire. Attach a length of thin wire to the hoop, then wrap it round the base of the sprigs. Wire another bunch of sprigs behind the first one, then continue round the hoop until it is covered with an even mass of evergreen foliage. Brighten up the wreath with a ribbon bow and CHRISTMAS DECORATIONS.

For a wreath that will be attractive all year round, use dried flowers (see FLOWER DRYING) wired in the same way.

Wrinkles

Preventing premature facial creases and sagging skin

Facial wrinkles occur naturally with advancing years. People with fair skin tend to wrinkle sooner than those with darker complexions.

Typically, wrinkles appear first round the eyes, above the upper lip and on the neck. Cosmetic creams can soften and lubricate, but their effect is superficial and temporary – see FACIAL CARE. Surgeons and dermatologists can remove wrinkles for longer periods with cosmetic surgery, chemical peeling, or the injection of augmenting material, but all these techniques involve risks. See also SCARS AND BLEMISHES.

Delaying actions Many people believe that facial massage helps to stave off wrinkles. There is little or no evidence of this, but there are positive actions you can take:

● Stay out of the sun as much as possible.

● Avoid smoking, which has been linked to premature wrinkling, partly because it lessens circulation to surface blood vessels.

● Make sure that your vision is properly corrected, if necessary, and wear sunglasses when you are near water, on the beach or skiing, to prevent 'crow's feet' forming.

● Avoid losing weight too quickly, or constantly alternating weight gain with weight loss (see DIETING), which can cause skin to sag.

● Take care of your teeth, to preserve the jawline.

● Avoid STRESS; habitual contraction of facial muscles due to stress can cause premature wrinkling.

As part of your daily routine, pause for a moment now and then to relax your facial muscles. Avoid frowning; let your forehead remain smooth. Also avoid sitting with your chin on your hand (pushing your face out of its natural position) and rubbing your eyes (which can stretch delicate skin).

XYZ

Yoga

Exercising to relax body and mind

Experienced practitioners of yoga believe that yoga exercises (Hatha Yoga) can improve mental and physical health by helping you to relax, improve your posture, and tone up muscles, heart and nerves. They need take up no more than 10-15 minutes once or twice a day, and can usually be safely undertaken by people of all ages because they concentrate on breathing and stretching and should be done without straining. Check with your DOCTOR first, if you are suffering from any physical complaint such as ARTHRITIS or a bad back – see BACKACHE.

The best way to learn yoga correctly is to attend classes run by a reputable teacher. Enquire at your library to find a local evening class.

Practise in a quiet, moderately warm, airy room, with space to stretch out – coldness makes it difficult to relax, so lie on a carpeted floor or a rug or blanket. Wear loose clothing and no shoes. Hold a posture only as long as it is comfortable. Breathe normally through your nose and stretch slowly. Focus your thoughts on making a tense muscle relax.

Here are some beginner's yoga exercises which can be done in the home:

Resting posture Lie on your back, arms by your sides, palms up, legs outstretched and slightly apart. Close your eyes and imagine you are floating on water. Slowly roll your head from left to right and back ten times. Relax each part of your body, starting from the feet and working towards the head. Concentrate on each part until it feels free of tension.

Breathing exercise Lie on your back and relax. Slowly inhale to the count of four – bulging out your stomach and distending your lower ribs smoothly, without strain. Exhale slowly to the same count.

Hero posture Use a rolled-up blanket as a pad to support your feet, and another blanket placed on top of the first for sitting on.

Kneel on the floor. Support yourself with your hands on the floor and rest your feet across the rolled-up blanket. With knees together, spread your feet about 460mm (18in) apart. Lower your buttocks onto the top blanket and rest your hands on your knees. Do not place any body weight on your lower legs.

Lower your chin a little; lower your eyelids and look at the floor. Keep your shoulders down and spine straight. Try to maintain the posture for two to five minutes, breathing naturally.

Practising the Hero posture Breathe naturally, and keep your spine straight. Do not hold the posture for longer than is comfortable.

Salutation to the sun Try this next:
1 Stand with your feet together; inhale deeply, raise your arms over your head and stretch backwards.
2 As you exhale, bend slowly forward until your hands touch the floor.
3 Inhale deeply as you bend your left knee and extend your right leg behind you, stretching your neck forward. Then rest on your hands, arms straight, while you extend the left leg behind you, keeping your body in a straight line.
4 As you exhale, lower your knees, forehead and chest to the floor; then lower your hips and relax your feet.
5 Inhale again while you raise your upper torso on your extended arms, slowly stretching upwards with back arched and head back; do not hunch your shoulders.
6 Push up on your arms, putting your feet flat on the floor, and raise your hips until your legs are straight.
7 Bend your right knee and bring your right foot forward. Then bring the left foot forward and straighten your legs.
8 Slowly stand, resuming posture 1.
See also RELAXATION EXERCISES.

Yoghurt

Making your own

Yoghurt is made by adding bacteria called lactobacilli, in the form of live yoghurt or yoghurt ferment, to fresh milk at blood heat. The creamier the milk, the thicker the yoghurt.

While the yoghurt sets, it must be kept at a temperature of 35-43°C (95-109°F). To do this, use a large clean vacuum flask or a proprietary yoghurt maker with an electric heating element, or put the dish in a warm place such as an airing cupboard.

Preparing the yoghurt To make about 570ml (1 pint) of yoghurt, pour 570ml of milk into a saucepan, and bring it slowly to the boil. Cool to lukewarm – 37°C (98°F). If you have no thermometer, sprinkle a few drops of the milk on your wrist; it should feel neither hot nor cold. Stir in one tablespoon of live yoghurt.

Pour the mixture into the flask or yoghurt maker, screw on the top and leave for 6-8 hours. Alternatively, pour the mixture into a clean shallow dish, cover with a warm plate and wrap in a towel, blanket or thick cloth. Leave it for 6-8 hours in a warm place.

The yoghurt will keep in a refrigerator for up to six days. Use a tablespoon of it to start another batch.

Yorkshire pudding

Making the traditional companion for roast beef

Mix Yorkshire pudding batter before you put the joint of beef in the oven (see ROASTING MEATS). Cook the pudding in dripping from the roasting tin.

Ingredients (for 6-8 people)
115g (4oz) plain flour
½ teaspoon salt
1 large egg
285ml (½ pint) milk
2 tablespoons cold water

Sieve the flour and salt into a large basin and make a well in the centre of the flour. Break the egg into the well and add a little of the milk. Use a wooden spoon to draw in the flour gradually and mix the ingredients together, adding more milk a little at a time until you have a thick batter.

Beat with a wooden spoon until the batter is smooth, then stir in the remaining milk. Leave the mixture to stand for about an hour.

Remove the joint from the oven, put it to keep hot and increase the oven temperature to 230°C (450°F), gas mark 8. Cover the bottom of a baking tin with a thin layer of fat from the roast; put it in the oven until the fat is smoking hot.

Quickly stir the cold water into the batter, then pour it into the tin. Bake on the top shelf of the oven for 25 minutes, or until the pudding has risen and is crisp and golden-brown. While it cooks, prepare the GRAVY.

Youth hostelling

Seeing the countryside on a budget

Whether you are BACKPACKING, BICYCLE TOURING or CAMPING, youth hostels offer basic accommodation, washing facilities and food at reasonable prices. There are 350 youth hostels in the United Kingdom, in a variety of locations and in buildings ranging from castles to cottages.

The three United Kingdom Youth Hostels Associations offer members the use of 5000 hostels in 60 countries worldwide. There is no upper age limit on membership, but fees vary according to age. In 1994, membership fees were: England and Wales YHA £3 (under 18), £9 (18 and over), £18 (family); Scottish YHA £2.50 (under 18), £6 (18 and over); Northern Ireland YHA £4.95 (under 18), £5.95 to £8.50 (18 and over). You can join at any hostel (listed in the local phone book). Non-members can apply for two-night guest passes.

Facilities Hostels are normally closed between 10am and 5pm, although most offer some form of daytime shelter, and doors are shut from 11pm to 7am. They are graded in four categories according to their facilities. The simplest hostels may have no hot water, showers may be outside, and daily accommodation costs in 1994 ranged between £3.15 and £10.50, depending on the hosteller's age. Higher grades offer correspondingly more facilities such as heating, a resident warden, a shop, or a laundry, and cost a few pounds more. To keep down costs, hostellers are asked to carry out a duty allocated by the warden.

You can buy low-priced breakfasts, lunch packs or evening meals, or there may be a kitchen for self-catering. Many hostels (other than the simplest) offer both. Alcohol is not allowed.

There are separate dormitories for males and females; most have two-tier bunk beds with bedding (except sheets) provided. Hostellers must hire or bring their own sheet-type sleeping bag – approved size 2.1m × 0.8m (7ft × 2ft 7½in). Quilted bags are permitted only in simple hostels, during winter months.

Small dormitories can be booked for family use in some hostels or for use by a blind person accompanied by a guide dog. Hostellers may not otherwise bring animals into the hostel or grounds.

All hostels have a common room where board games, magazines, TABLE TENNIS or POOL may be provided. Some have a separate television room.

Certain hostels also offer a CAMPING site, charging campers half the senior overnight fee for use of all hostel facilities, excluding bedding.

Although the length of stay at a hostel is normally unrestricted, a warden can limit bookings to three consecutive nights if the hostel is busy.

The YHA also organises adventure holidays, which include activities such as parachuting and WINDSURFING. For further information write to the Youth Hostels Association (England and Wales), Trevelyan House, 8 St Stephen's Hill, St Albans, Herts AL1 2DY. The Scottish Youth Hostels Association, 7 Glebe Crescent, Stirling FK8 2JA; or the Youth Hostels Association of Northern Ireland, 22 Donegall Road, Belfast BT12 5JN.

Yo-yo

Fun on a string

A yo-yo consists of two rounded pieces of wood or plastic joined by a short axle, to which a length of string is attached. The string is wound round the axle and used to make the yo-yo rise and fall by its own momentum.

Make a loop in the free end of the string to slip over your middle finger between the tip and middle joint.

Wind the string round the axle and hold your hand palm down with the yo-yo in it. Raise your hand towards your shoulder with a brisk, rhythmic movement, letting the yo-yo fall. Do not let it touch the ground – when it reaches the end of the string, give a little tug and it should ride back into your hand.

Then try the 'sleeper' – send the yo-yo down the string, and let it spin, or 'sleep' in its loop. When it slows down, jerk your wrist upwards to make it climb back into your hand.

Alternatively, do the 'forward pass'. Rest your arm loosely by your side, holding the yo-yo in your palm. Bring your arm up sharply forwards and release the yo-yo horizontally to the end of the string. Turn your hand up to receive it as it returns.

Zabaglione

Making a frothy delight with eggs, sugar and wine

Zabaglione originated in Sicily, where the fortified Marsala wine is made. Throughout Italy it is served as a restorative tonic, but it has become popular in other countries as a dessert. This is how to make a classic zabaglione, which should be served hot:

Ingredients (for 4 people)
4 egg yolks
1 tablespoon caster sugar
6 tablespoons Marsala wine

Put the egg yolks and sugar into a mixing bowl or the top of a double saucepan and whisk them with a balloon whisk until the mixture thickens.

Warm the Marsala in a separate pan until it feels lukewarm. Place the bowl or pan of whisked egg and sugar over a saucepan half filled with simmering water, making sure that the water does not touch the bowl or top pan. Keep the heat moderate, so that the water never rises above a simmer. Pour the warmed Marsala into the egg and sugar and whisk the mixture constantly for five to seven minutes until it thickens and becomes foamy. Do not let the egg mixture overheat, or it will curdle. Take the bowl off the saucepan and spoon the mixture into warmed glasses. Serve immediately.

Zippers

Fitting and replacing a zip; renewing the slider

Zip fasteners in clothing are usually fitted into a seam, either lapped by one side of the seam only, or centred under both sides of the seam. Lapped zips are often used at the side of a skirt or ladies' trousers.

When making a garment, leave an opening long enough for the zip when sewing up the seam – see SEWING.

Fitting a lapped zip Turn the garment right side out. On the side that is to lap over the zip, fold under the seam allowance along the seam line and secure the fold with tacking.

Fold under the other seam allowance 3mm (⅛in) nearer the raw edge than the seam line, and tack it down. Fit the zip to this side first. Tack it under the fold with right side facing up. Then machine-stitch it close to the teeth, using the zipper foot (see SEWING MACHINES) and working from bottom to top. Remove the tacking stitches.

Place the lap over the zip to meet the seam line and tack the other side of the zip into place. Then machine-stitch it (through the garment fabric), first across the tape at the bottom of the zip and then from bottom to top.

Fitting a centre zip Work with the garment turned inside out. Fold back the seam allowances on each side, press flat, and oversew them together temporarily to hold them temporarily closed.

Put the zip in position face down, aligning the tapes with the top of the opening and the teeth with the butted seam edges.

Pin the zip in place and tack along both sides. Machine-stitch close to the teeth – work from the bottom to the top on each side, stitching across the bottom of the zip tape first. Remove the tacking and oversewing.

Replacing a zip on fly-fastened trousers Unpick the stitches holding the zip to the waistband and opening, and remove the zip. Tack the new zip in place between the folded edge and the facing fixed behind it and tuck the zip tape into the waistband. Machine-stitch that side of the zip in place from bottom to top and remove the tacking.

Turn the trousers inside out. Tuck the other tape of the zip under the waistband and tack that side of the zip in place 13mm (½in) from the edge of the flap. Hand-stitch across the ends of the two tapes at the bottom of the zip, then turn the trousers right side out and backstitch by hand along the tacked side, close to the teeth. Remove the tacking.

Overstitch the waistband on both sides of the zip, then overstitch across the bottom ends of the flaps inside the front of the trousers.

Replacing a zip on a skirt Unpick the waistband 25mm (1in) on either side of the old zip, and then along both sides of the zip. Take out the zip.

Pin the new zip carefully in position and tack it in place along the sides and bottom. Then oversew the seam edges lightly together to hold them in place temporarily. Remove the pins, and check that the edges of the seam still meet, before machine-stitching along the bottom and up each side of the zip with the skirt right side out. Remove the tacking and over-sewing.

Turn the skirt inside out. Slip the tops of the zip under the waistband, and hemstitch the waistband both inside and out. Overstitch the tapes at the bottom of the zip, then oversew the sides of the tape to the seam flaps. Press the seams flat with an iron.

Renewing the slider If the teeth of the zip on a bag or holdall come apart when the zip is fastened, but do not seem to be damaged, the slider is probably worn and unable to grip the teeth firmly.

Another possibility is that the top and bottom parts of the slider have pulled apart slightly. Take the zip to a leather or handicraft shop and see if you can get a slider and zip stop to match the old ones. If not, you may be able to take the slider and stop from an undamaged zip on a worn bag and fit them as a replacement.

Use a screwdriver to lever off the zip stop at the bottom of the old zip. Pull the old slider down and off the zip. Slip the new slider over the teeth at the bottom of the zip and partly close the zip. Fit the prongs of the new zip stop into the old

holes and use the blade of a small screwdriver to press them flat on the other side of the fabric.

QUICK TIP To free a jammed zip, use a cotton bud to coat the adjoining teeth carefully with a little soft soap or candle wax. Ease the slider backwards then forwards gently until the obstruction is cleared and it will slide freely.

Zodiac

How your birth sign influences your character

There are 12 signs in the Zodiac, each with similar names to the star constellations through which the Moon, Sun and principal planets pass.

Astrologers use the Zodiac to cast horoscopes. They claim to be able to analyse a person's character and prospects by linking the date, place and time of birth with the exact position of the Moon and planets at that time.

Each Zodiac sign has a ruling planet, which is said to influence the characteristics of persons born under that sign. For example, Aries is ruled by Mars, which represents drive and energy, and Taurus is ruled by Venus, representing harmony and partnership.

The signs are also grouped according to their ruling elements – the four elements of the ancient world: fire, earth, air and water. Each sign is said to be influenced by the nature of its element. Fire – Aries, Leo and Sagittarius: enthusiastic, energetic and positive. Earth – Taurus, Virgo and Capricorn: static, practical and negative. Air – Gemini, Libra and Aquarius: intellectual, communicative and positive. Water – Cancer, Scorpio and Pisces: emotional, impressionable and negative.

Astrologers claim that your birth sign – the sign through which the Sun was passing at your birth – is one of the many factors in your birth chart that can give you an insight into your own characteristics. The Moon's position also has a strong bearing on it.

ZODIAC

Typical character traits of the 12 birth signs

♑ Capricorn
Dec 23-Jan 19
Determined, reliable, patient, prudent, ambitious, inflexible.

♒ Aquarius
Jan 20-Feb 19
Independent, kind, friendly, original, dogmatic, obstinate.

♓ Pisces
Feb 20-Mar 21
Kind, sympathetic, adaptable, sensitive, vague, indecisive.

♈ Aries
Mar 22-Apr 20
Adventurous, brave, direct, energetic, selfish, impatient.

♉ Taurus
Apr 21-May 21
Practical, reliable, determined, loving, lazy, stubborn.

♊ Gemini
May 22-June 22
Versatile, lively, witty, adaptable, restless, two-faced.

♋ Cancer
June 23-July 23
Imaginative, kind, thrifty, protective, unstable, touchy.

♌ Leo
July 24-Aug 23
Generous, creative, cheerful, strong, pompous, dogmatic.

♍ Virgo
Aug 24-Sept 23
Modest, meticulous, logical, perceptive, critical, fussy.

♎ Libra
Sept 24-Oct 23
Romantic, idealistic, tactful, charming, gullible, frivolous.

♏ Scorpio
Oct 24-Nov 22
Imaginative, subtle, purposeful, intense, jealous, stubborn.

♐ Sagittarius
Nov 23-Dec 22
Open-minded, jovial, sincere, optimistic, extremist, restless.

Index

Page numbers in **bold** type indicate a main entry on the subject.

Abacus **8**
Abdominal thrusts 99–100
Abuse, drug 145–6
Accidents, bathroom 31
 car **76**
 chip pan fire **98**
 prevention **8–9**
 to children 96
Accounts, book-keeping 50–51
 building society 61
Acne **9**
Acrylic **9**
 insulation 141
Action on smoking and health 430
Adder bite 430
Addiction, drug 145–6
Aerials, car **76–77**
 radio **373**
 television **470–1**
Aerobics **9**
African violets **10**
Agreements
 contract **113–14**
 disputes 16
 guarantee **207**
 rental 225
Air, beds **10**
 bricks **10**
 filters **10–11**
 freshening 359
 layering 366
 locks in radiators 88–89
Aircraft, paper **326–7**
Airgun 208
Airline collapse 453
Alarms, baby 21
 burglar **62–63**
 car 82
 gas screech 375
Alcohol, for nervousness 306
 hangover from **218**
Alcove, shelves for 416
Ale, mulling **298**
Allergies **11**
 bee sting 38
 hayfever **218–19**
 hives **225**
 itchiness 242
 milk 107
 rashes 375
Allspice 439
Aluminium pans 115
Amber, cleaning 245
Ammonia 103
Anagrams **11**
Anal itching 242
Anaphylactic shock 418
Ancient lights **12**
Angina 94

Animals
 bats **33**
 photography 305
 quarantine **369**
 smells **12**
 tourniquets **484**
 tracks **485–6**
 See also Pets
Ankle sprain 28
Annuities **12**
Antibody production 11
Anticondensation paint 325
Antifreeze **12–13**
Antigen reaction 11
Antihistamines 11
 for bee stings 38
Antiques **13**
Ants **13**, 237
Aphids **14**, 335
Appendicitis **14**
Apples 188
 and sloe jelly 428
 ducking for 215
Appliqué **14–15**
Aquariums **15–16**
Arbitration **16**
Architect **16**
Arm, broken 59
 sling 427–8
Arrest, citizen's **102**
Arthritis **16–17**
Artichokes **17**
Artificial respiration **17–18**
Asparagus **18**
Asphalt driveways **18–19**
Aspic **19**
Aspidistra **19**
Assessor, local 376
Asthma 11
Astrology 530
Astronomy 448–9
Athlete's foot **19–20**
Attacks by muggers **297–8**
Auctions **20**
Avocado plants **20**
Awards, giving or receiving 363
Axes **20**
Axle, leaks 313
 stands 243

Baby, alarms **21**
 bathing **21**
 breast feeding **56–57**
 colic **107**
 emergency delivery 94–96
 external chest compression 159
 food **21**
 hypothermia **231**
 nappy changing **302–3**
 teething **469**
 weaning **515**
 winding **22**

Backache **22**
 lifting and carrying **268–9**
 lumbago **272**
 slipped disc **428**
Back-combing **22**
Backgammon **22–23**
Backpacking **23–24**
Back posture **358**
Backstitch 154, 413
Backstroke **462**
Bad breath **24**
Badger tracks **485–6**
Badminton **24–25**
Bail **25–26**
 surety for 458–9
Bailiffs 130–1
Baking powder as cleanser 103
Baldness 212
Ball cocks **26**
 noise from 307
Ball repairs **26**
Ballroom dancing **26–27**
Balm 223
Balusters **27–28**
Bamboo **74–75**
Bandaging **28**
 for head and face 219
Bank, accounts **28–29**
 loans 120
 overdraft 319
Bankruptcy **29**
Barbecues **30**
 kebabs **251**
Barking dogs **136**, 306
Barometers **30–31**
Basil 223
Basket repairs **31**
Bathing baby **21**
Bathroom safety **31**
Bathtub, sealing **31–32**, 411
 stains 32
Batik **32–33**
Bats **33**
Battens **33**
Batter, pancake 326
 waffles 506
 Yorkshire pudding **528–9**
Batteries **34**
Battleships **34–35**
Bay 223
Beadwork **35**
Beards **36**
Beauty creams **36**
 See also Health and beauty
Béchamel sauce 401
Bedding plants **36–37**
Beds, air **10**
 for nursing sick patient 309
 orthopaedic 22
 valances 498
Bedsores 309
Bedwetting **37**
Beef, carving 82–83
 roasting 385
Beekeeping **37–38**
Beer **38**
 glass 201
Bee sting 237, 418

Bee swarms **461**
Beetle, asparagus 18
 carpet **80**
 death-watch **130**
 furniture 526–7
Begonias **38–39**
Belts 264–5, 168–9
Benefits, social security **432–3**
Berries **39–40**
Bicycle, care **40–41**
 padlocks 321
 riding **41–42**
 touring 42
Bilberries 39
Billiards **42–43**
Bird, box **43**
 care 43
 table **43–44**
Birdwatching **44**
 weather forecasting from 515
Birth, certificate **44**
 control, rhythm method **383**
 marks 405–6
 signs 530
Biscuits **44**
Bites, dog **136**
 rabies from **372**
 in pets 335
 insect **236–7**
 snake 430
Bituminous paint 325, **389**
Bivouac tent **44–45**
Blackberries 39
 jelly 245
Blackcurrant, gall mite 288
 jelly 245
Black eye 161
Black-eyed susan, 103
Blackfly 14, 335
Blackjack **45**
Blankets, electric **150–1**
 Blanket stitch 154
Bleach 103
Bleaching, dishes 134
 superfluous hair 458
 wood 45
Bleeding **45**
 from severed limb 412
 in pets 335
Blemishes **405–6**
Blenders **45**
Blight 14
Blinds **46–47**
 Roman **387–8**
 Venetian **501**
 cleaning 147
Blisters **47**, 184
Bloaters **47**
Blocks, building **60**
Blood donors **47**
Blouses, ironing 241
Blowtorches **47–48**, 326
Board games
 backgammon **22–23**
 battleships **34–35**
 chess **93–94**
 Chinese checkers **97**
 draughts **143**

Boats, gas heating in 78
  sailing **397–8**
  survival on 460
  See also Rowing; Sculling
Body, massage **280–1**
  odour **48**
  temperature 166, 231
Boilers, maintenance 88–89
  water heater 513
Bolts **48**
  expansion 507
  security 63–64
Bonds for bricks 57
Bones, broken **58–59**
  broken in pets 335
  dislocated 134–5
  engraving **408–9**
Boning fish 171–2
Bonnet catches **48–49**
Bonsai **49**
Bookcase building **49–50**
Book-keeping **50–51**
Book repairs **51**
Boots 23, 104, 506
Borax 103
Border plants **51–52**
Borrowing see Credit; Loans
Bossout 277
Bottle-feeding 107
Bottle gardens **52**
Bottling fruit 363
Botulism 183
Boules **52**
Bouquet garni 224
Bowel problems, constipation **112–13**
Bowls **52–53**
Bow ties **53**
Brackets **54**
Braising **54**
Brakes, bicycle 40
  car 294 **54–55**
  pram 362
Brandy glass 201
Brass, cleaning 13
  rubbing **55**
Brazing 434
Bread, freezing 185
  -making **55–56**
  stale 266
Bread and butter pudding 266
Breast, examination **56**
  feeding **56–57**
  surgery 406
Breast stroke 461–2
Breath, bad **24**
Breathing exercises 380
Breeze blocks 60
Brewing beer 38
Bricklaying **57–58**
  mortar for **290–1**
Bricks, air 10
  cleaning 103
  cutting 58
  drilling 280
  painting 323
  pointing **355**
  repairing walls **194**
  steps 450
  types 57
Bring-and-buy sales **58**
Britannia metal cleaning 337
British Canoe Union 76
Broken bones **58–59**
  in pets 335
  slings for **427–8**
Bronchodilators 11
Bronze cleaning 13
Brushing, hair 210
  teeth 24, 468–9
Bryony 39

Budgerigars 43
Budgeting **59–60**
Buff-tip moth 86
Builders, contractors 113
Building, blocks 60
  design, architects for 16
  Inspector 60
  obstruction, preventing 12
  permits **60**, 227
  Societies **61**
Bulbs, corms and tubers **62**
  division 365
  forcing **61–62**
  scale mites 288
Bunions **62**, 184
Burglar, alarms **62–63**
  -proofing **63–64**
Burglary, car 79
  protection against 82
Burning bush 52
Burns **64–65**
  holes in carpets 81
  mark removal 13
  prevention 8
  to children 96
Burnt pans 326
Burping baby 22
Business, companies **107–8**
  letters **65**
  partnership 412
  self-employment 412
  See also Companies
Busy lizzie **65–66**
Butter, clarifying 102
  -making **66–67**
Butterflies **66**, 86
Buttonholes 67
Buttons 67

C

Cabbage, pickled **402**
Cabbage white butterfly 86
Cabinet **68**
  kitchen **253**
Cable, electric 153–4
Cacti **68–69**
Cake, baking **69–70**
  decorating 70
  freezing 185
  icing **233**
  marzipan for **279–80**
Calamondin orange tree 316
Calligraphy **70–71**
Calorie counting **71**
Cameras 305 339
Campfires **71–72**
Camping 24, **72**
  sleeping bags **426**
  tents **474–5**
Canapés **72–73**
Canaries 43
Canasta **73**
Cancer, breast examination for **56**
Candle, cooking with **114–15**
  for table setting 464
  lantern 243
  -making **74**
Cane, and bamboo **74–75**
  repair 31
Cannabis abuse 146
Cannelloni **74–75**
Canoes and kayaks **75–76**
Canvas stretching **453–4**
Cape jasmine 193
Capercaillie roasting 192

Car, accidents **76**
  aerials **76–77**
  breakdown abroad 453
  cassettes and radios **78–79**
  driving 145, **423**
  hire 225
  horns **79**
  insurance claims **79–80**
  jacking 243
  jump-starting 249
  keys locked in car **80**
  locks frozen **80**
  maintenance
    air filter **10–11**
    antifreeze **12–13**
    batteries 34
    bonnet catches **48–49**
    brakes **54–55**, 294
    dent repair **132–3**
    exhaust 78
    fan-belt adjustment 319–20
    fuel economy **190**
    lights 294
    oil changing **311–12**
    oil leaks **312–13**
    overheating engine **319–20**
    paintwork **326**, **416**
    power steering 362
    radiator flushing **372–3**
    shock absorbers **418–19**
    spark-plugs **437–8**
    thermostats **477**
    tyres 294, **493**
    undersealing against salt 399
    wheels 243, 294
    windscreen washers **522**
    windscreen wipers **522–3**
  MoT test **294–5**
  pets in 488
  push-starting **368**
  radio, aerials **373**
    interference **81–82**
  roof racks **82**
  safety seats **396–7**
  seat belts **411**
  security **82**
  skids 423
  snowbound in **431–2**
  towing **485**
  underwater escape from **494**
  used **496**
  washing and polishing **84**, 399
  See also Driving
Caravans and trailers **77**
  gas heating in 78
Caraway 439
Carbon monoxide poisoning **78**
Cardamom 439
Card games
  blackjack **45**
  canasta **73**
  casino **84**
  crazy eights **119**
  cribbage **120–1**
  gin rummy **199**
  grab 430
  patience **331**
  poker **355–6**
  rummy **395**
  shuffling for **421**
  snap **430**
  war **510**
  whist **520**
Card tricks 274
Carpet, beetles **80**
  cleaning **80**, 101, 146
  laying **80–81**
  mothproofing 292
  repairs **81**
  stair **445–6**

Carrycot restraint 396–7
Carrying **268–9**
Carving meat and poultry **82–83**, 192
Casino **84**
Casserole **84–85**
Cassettes and recorders **85**
  car 78–79
Cast-iron, pans 115
  plant 19
Castors **85**
Cataract 162
Catches **258–9**
Caterpillars 66, **86**
Cats **86–87**
  fleas **177**
  house-training **231**
  injuries 335–6
  lost **271**
  medication 336–7
  smells 12
  tracks 486
Cat's cradle **87**
Cauling 411
Cayenne 439
Ceiling, distemper removal 135
  painting 323
  plasterboard **349**
  rose **87**
    fixing light to 269–70
    junction box 249–50
Cellulose, fillers 452
  glue 201
Central heating **88–89**
  descaling 133
  frost protection **187**
  grants for 204
  pipe lagging **345**
Ceramic, mosaics **291–2**
  tiles **89–90**
Cereus peruvianus 68
Chafing dish cooking **90–91**
Chain saw **91**
Chain stitch 154
Chair, cane and bamboo 74–75
  garden **193**
  repairs **91–92**
  reupholstering **382–3**
Chamois leather **92**
Chamomile 207
Champagne glass 200–1
Charcoal 30
Cheese, sauce **92**
  soufflé **435**
Chemical, burns 65, 161
  poisoning **355**
  stripper 325–6
  toilets **92–93**
Cheques 29
Cherry fondant 461
Chess rules **93–94**
Chest, compression, external **158–9**
  pain **94**
Chewing gum removal **94**
Chicken, carving 83
  cooking and preparation **361**
  liver pâté 330
  stuffing 455
Chickenpox, shingles and 416–17
Chilblains **94**
Childbirth **94–96**
Children
  bedwetting **37**
  birth certificate **44**
  camping with **72**
  child benefit 432
  contracts with **113**
  diarrhoea **133**
  external chest compression **159**
  eyesight testing **162**
  fever fits 166

Children (continued)
flat feet **176**
naming **301–2**
safety **96**
schools **406**
stammering **447–8**
tantrums **96**
toilet training **482–3**
travel with **488**
ward of court **510**
Chilli powder 439
Chimes, door **138**
Chimney fires **96**
China **97**
repair 13
washing 134
See also Porcelain
Chinese checkers **97**
Chipboard **97**
Chip pan fire **98**
Chiselling **98**
Chives 224
Chocolate truffles **99**
Choking **99–100**
in pets 335–6
Cholesterol **100**
Chopsticks **100**
Christmas, cake 69–70
decorations **100**, 527
trees **101**
Cigarette scorch marks **101**, 186
smells **101**
Cinnamon 439
Circuit, breaker **101**
short **419–20**
testing **101–2**
Citizens Advice Bureau 263
Citizen's arrest **102**
Citrus houseplants **102**, 316
Cladding, plastic 351–2
wall **506–7**
Claims, settlement 266
small 109, **429**
Clarifying butter **102**
Clay, modelling **289**
pottery 359–60
Cleaning, and dusting **146–7**
and polishing materials **103**
carpets 80
chewing gum stain 94
clocks **104**
cookers 114
copper 501
duvets **147**
eiderdowns **150**
glassware **201**
handbag 217
ivory **242**, 340
jewellery **245–6**
lace 256
lampshades **257**
marble **276–7**
mirrors **287**
oven **318–19**
paintbrushes 322
pans **326**
pewter 337
piano **340**
shells 416
shoes 419
silver 422
solvents **103**
spark-plugs 438
spectacles 438
stainless steel **445**
stonework **452**
teeth 24, **468–9**
velvet 499–500
walls 352, **511**
window **522**

Cleansing cream 36, 117, 163
Clematis 104
Climbing plants **103–4**
Climbing, safety **104**
Clock, cleaning **104**
patience 331
Clothes
alterations **105–6**
bow ties 53
freshening with lavender bag 260
ironing **241–2**
laundering **259–60**
leather 264
mending **283**
mothproofing 292
on fire 64
packing **321**
pressing **364**
raincoats 374
shine removing **416**
storage **104–5**
ties **480**
tumble drying 491
washing **510–11**
Clouds 515
Cloves 439
Coal see Solid fuel
Coats, leather 264
Cockroaches **106**
Cocktails 144–5
seafood **410**
Coconut creams 461
wafers 44
Colding moth 86
Coffee, Irish 241
Coin tricks 274
Cold, frames **106**
hypothermia 231
Colds **106–7**
Coldsores **106–7**
Colic **107**
Collar turning **417**
Collections **107**
Colour blindness **107**
Compact discs 378
Companies **107–8**
book-keeping **50–51**
stocks and shares 240–1
Compass **108–9**
Compensation for crime 121
Complaints **109**
about homelessness 226
ombudsmen **315**
Compost **109**
for houseplants 360
John Innes **246**
Computers **109–10**
Concrete **110–12**
drilling 280
flagstones 175
levelling 267, 495
slabs, for patio 331–2
steps 450
Condensation **112**
Conditioning hair 210
Condolence letters **112**
Confectionery 461
Conjunctivitis **112**
Consommé 436
Constipation **112–13**
Contact lenses 113
Contents insurance 238
Contractors **113**
Contracts **113–14**
disputes 16
Convector heaters, gas 196
Conversational skills 421
Cookers **115**, 452–3
cleaning **318–19**
electric slow 151

Cooking
biscuits **44**
blenders **45**
bloaters **47**
braising **54**
bread **55–56**
butter, clarifying 102
butter-making **66–67**
cake-baking **69–70**
cake decorating **70**, 233
cannelloni **74–75**
casseroles **84–85**
chafing dish **90–91**
crab **118–19**
curry **125**
eggs **150**
escargots **156**
fish cleaning **171–2**
flambé **175**
fondue **182–3**
food mills **183**
food processors **183**
frying **189**
game birds **192**
garlic **194–5**
grilling **206**
herbs **223–4**
jam-making **244–5**
jellies **245**
jugged hare **248–9**
kebabs **251**
kippers **252–3**
leftovers **265–6**
lobster **271**
mackerel **273**
marinating **277**
microwave **286–7**
moulding food **295**
mushrooms **299**
mussels **299**
omelettes **315–16**
oysters **320**
pickling **340–1**
pie crust **343**
poaching **354**
poultry **361**
preserving **363**
pressure **363**, **364**
puréeing **368**
rice **383–4**
roasting meats **385–6**
smells **429–30**
spaghetti **436**
steaming **449**
stir-frying **452**
stocks and soups **436**
wine-making **523–4**
winkles and whelks **524**
with a candle **114–15**
See also Recipes; Vegetables
Cookware **115**
Coolant removal from cars 12–13
Copper, cleaning 13, 115, **501**
stains, bathtub 32
Coriander 439
Corks and corkscrews **115**
Corms **62**
Corn dollies **116**
Cornices and covings **116–17**
Corns **117**, 184
Cornus alba **420**
Cosmetics **117**, 161–2, 163
Cosmetic surgery **405–6**
Cottage pie 266
Couch grass 118
Coughs 118
Council, grants **203–4**
homelessness **225–6**
planning permission **348**
tax **118**

tenants 472–3
County court arbitration 16
Covenants 118, 227
Covings **116–17**
Crab **118–19**
Crab apple jelly 245
Cradle cap **119**
Crafts
acrylic **9**
appliqué **14–15**
batik **32–33**
beadwork **35**
candle-making **74**
corn dollies **116**
crochet **121–2**
découpage **131**
egg decorating **149**
embroidery **154–5**
enamelling **155–6**
figure drawing **167**
finger painting **168**
finger weaving **168–9**
flower drying **179**
flower pressing **179–80**
gift wrapping **198**
gilding **198–9**
hairpin crochet lace **212–13**
kites **253–4**
knitting **254–5**
lapidary work **257–8**
lavender bag **260**
leather work **264–5**
lino cuts **270**
macramé **273–4**
marquetry **278–9**
mobiles **289**
modelling in clay **289–90**
mosaics **291–2**
needlepoint tapestry **305–6**
oil painting **314**
origami **317**
paper aircraft **326–7**
papier-mâché **327**
patchwork **330**
pomander **356**
pot-pourri **359**
pottery **359–60**
puppet-making **367–8**
quilting **370–1**
rag dolls **374**
rug-making **392–3**
rug plaiting **394–5**
scents **406**
scrimshaw **408–9**
spatter prints **438**
spinning yarn **441**
stained glass **444–5**
stencilling **449–50**
string art **454**
tie-dyeing **479–80**
watercolour painting **512**
weaving **516–17**
woodcarving **524–5**
See also Hobbies; Woodwork
Cramps **119**
Crawl 462
Crazy eights **119**
Crazy paving **119**
Creams for skin **36**, 117, 163
Credit, and credit cards **119–20**
hire purchase 225
See also Loans
Crêpes suzettes **120**
Cribbage **120–1**
Crime compensation **121**
Criminal Injuries Compensation
Board 121
Crochet **121–2**
lace, hairpin **212–13**
Crocuses, forced 61

Croquet **122–3**
Croquettes **123**
Cross stitch 154, 306
Crown Courts, compensation 121
Crutches **123**
Crystal see Glassware
Cuckoo pint 39
Cultivator **124**
Cumin 439
Cupboards and wardrobes **124–5**
  catches 258–9
  hinges 224–5
  shelves 416
Curriculum vitae **128**
Curry powder **125**
Curtains **126–7**
  pelmets 333
  rails **125–6**
  tie-backs **478–9**
  valances 498
Cushions **127–8**
Cutlery **128**, 347
Cuts, bandaging 28
  first aid 527
  prevention of 8
Cutting, glass **200**
  hair **211–12**
  plastic laminate 350
  plywood 354
  tiles 89, **369**
Cuttings 66, **365–6**
Cutworms **128**
CV **128**
Cyanoacrylate glue 202

D

Dahlias **129**
Damp **129**
  condensation **112**
Damson jelly 245
Dancing, ballroom **26–27**
Dandelions **129**
Dandelion wine 523–4
Dandruff **129–30**
Darning **130**
Darts **130**
Deadly nightshade 39
Deafness, aids for **220**
  sign language for **421–2**
Death, abroad 487
  compensation for 121
  condolence letters **112**
  funeral arrangements **190**
  grant 304
  wills **521**
Death-watch beetle **130**
Debentures 240–1
Debt 29, 457, 458–9
  collectors **130–1**
Deckchairs **131**
Decongestants 303
Decorating cakes **233**
  eggs **149**
Decorations, Christmas **100, 527**
  gourds 203
  Halloween 243
Découpage **131**
Deed of covenant 118
Defence against attack 297–8, 375
Defrosting, food 287, **476**
  refrigerators 379
Dehydration **131–2**, 218
Delivery of baby 94–96
Delphiniums 51
Dents in cars **132–3**

Dentures **133**
Deodorants 48
Depilatories 458
Descaling **133**
Designer stubble 36
Devil Among the Tailors 465
Dew trap 460
Diamonds, cleaning 246
Dianthus 51–52
Diarrhoea **133**
Dictamnus albus 52
Dieting **133–4**
  calorie counting **71**
  cholesterol levels 100
Dill 224, 439
Dimmer switch **134**
Dinghy sailing 397–8
Diphtheria vaccine 234–5
Disabled person, travel with **487**
Disc, slipped 428
Dishwashing by hand **134**
Dislocated joints **134–5**
Dismissal, unfair **495**
Distemper **135**
Distemper removal **135**
Distress signals **135**
Diving **135–6**
Divining, water **513**
Division for propagating 365
Doctor **136**
Dog, barking **136**, 306
  bites **136**
  care **137**
  distemper **135**
  fights **137**
  fleas 177
  house-training **231**
  injuries **335–6**
  kennel **251–2**
  lost 271
  medication **336–7**
  obedience training **310–11**
  smells 12
  tracks 486
Doll repairs **137–8**
Domestic accidents 8, 31
Dominoes **138**
Donors, blood 47
  organ **316–17**
Doors **140**
  bells and chimes **138**
  damp 129
  draughtproofing **142**
  frame sealant 411
  garage **192–3**
  hanging 224–5
  keyholes **252**
  knobs **139**
  latches 258–9
  locks **139–40**
  louvre 271
  painting 324
  peephole viewer **333**
  security 63–64
  sliding **426–7**
  soundproofing 435–6
Double glazing **140–1**
Dough 55–56
  as cleanser 103
Dovetail joint 526
Dowels **141**
Down pillows **141**
Downpipes **208–9**
Dowsing rods 513
Drains **141–2**
Draughtproofing **142**
Draughts **143**
Drawer, construction **143**
  keyholes **252**
  repairs **144**

Drawing, figure **167**
Drawstrings **144**
Dressing head wounds 219
Dressings for salads **398**
Dressing up 215, 327
Drill bit sharpening 415
Drilling **144**, 280
Drinks **144–5**
  glasses for **200–1**
  Irish coffee **241**
  soft **433**
  sloe gin 428
  toddy **482**
Driveways **18–19**, 111–12
Driving, fuel economy 190
  in bad weather **145**
  in snow 432
  on motorway **293–4**
  skids and **423**
Drug overdose **145**
  recognition **145–6**
Dry-cleaning fluids 94
Drying, flowers **179**
  hair 210, 212
  herbs **223**
Dry-mounting photographs **146**
Dry rot **146**
Duck 83, 361, 455
Dusting and cleaning **146–7**
Duvets **147**
Dyeing **147**
  batik 32–33
  eggs 149
  hair **210–11**
  handbags **218**
  leather **265**
  tie- **479–80**

E

Earache **148**
Ears **148**
  ringing in **384**
Earthenware **148**
Earthquakes **148–9**
Earwigs **149**
Eczema **149**, 242
Efflorescence **149**
Eggs 6, **150**
  curried 125
  decorating **149**
  leftover 266
  poached 354
  separating **150**
Eiderdowns **150**
Elderberries 39
Electric, blankets **150–1**
  burns 65
  cooker 114
  circuit breaker **101**
  circuit spur connections 443
  circuit testing **101–2**
  dimmer switch **134**
  door bells and chimes **138**
  element replacing 234, 252
  extension leads **158**
  extractor fan **159–60**
  fluorescent lights **180–1**
  fused connection unit **191**
  fuses and fuse boxes **190–1**
  heating, central 88–89
  junction box **249–50**
  lawn mowers 262
  lighting see Lights
  plugs **352**
  sanders **399–400**

saws 404–5
shock 96, **151**
short circuit **419–20**
slow cookers **151**
sockets and switches **152–3**
tools 362
two-way switches **492–3**
wiring **153–4**
Electricity
  meters 285
  moving house and 297
  power cuts **361**, 379
  safety precautions 8
Elements, in heaters 234
  in kettles 252
Embroidery **154–5**
Employment, contract 113–14
  resignation from **380–1**
  retirement from **381–2**
  rights, home worker and 227
  unfair dismissal **495**
Emulsion paint 325
Enamelled pans 115
Enamelling **155–6**
Enamel paint 325
Endowment, mortgage 291
  policies **156**
Engraving bones **408–9**
Environmental health officer 306
Epileptic fit **156**
Epoxy-based filler 452
Epoxy resin 202
Escargots **156**
Espagnole sauce 402
Estimates 113
Eviction notice **156–7**
Exercise **157–8**
  aerobics 9
  backache relief 22
  backpacking **23–24**
  ballroom dancing **26–27**
  bicycle riding **41–42**
  jogging **246**
  punting 367
  roller skating **387**
  shin splints from **417**
  walking **506**
  weight training **518–19**
  See also Relaxation exercises
Exhaust system maintenance 78
Expanding foam filler 202, 452
Expansion bolts 507
Expenses, budgeting 59
Extension leads **158**
External chest compression **158–9**
Extinguishers, fire **169**
Extractor fan **159–60**
Eyebrows 160
Eyelets and grommets **161**
Eyes **162**
  colour blindness **107**
  conjunctivitis **112**
  contact lenses **113**
  injuries **160–1**
  make-up 160, **161–2**
  styes **456**
Eyesight testing **162**

F

Fabric, cleaning 147
  curtains 126–7
  dyeing **147**, 479–80
  joining 227, 364
  laundering **259–60**
  leather **264–5**

Fabric (continued)
mending **283**
nylon **309**
patching **330**
pressing **364**
reinforcing 161
scorch marks 101
stain removal **445**
velvet **499–500**
Facial, care **163**
injuries **219–20**
lift 406
make-up 117
Fainting **163–4**
Falls, preventing 8
Family Income Supplement 432
Family trees **164**
Fan, extractor **159–60**
Fan-belt adjustment 319–20
Fasteners, hooks and eyes **227**
Velcro **499**
wall **507–8**
Fats in diet 283
Feet, bunions on 62
care of **184**
flat **176**
Fences **165**, 267
Fennel seed 439
Ferns **165–6**
Fertilisers **166**
from compost 109
lawn 260–1
soil 434
Fever **166**
Fibre in diet 283
Fibreboard 97
Ficus pumila 103
Fiddle sticks 244
Fig, creeping 103
Figure drawing **167**
Filing **167**
Fillers 452
Films for photography 338, 339
Filters, air **10–11**
car, changing 312
Finance
annuities **12**
bank accounts **28–29**
bankruptcy 29
book-keeping **50–51**
budgeting **59-60**
building societies **61**
company 107–8
covenants 118
credit and credit cards **119–20**
debt collectors **130–1**
endowment policies **156**
grants **203–4**
hire purchase **225**
income tax **235**
insurance **238**, 240
investing **240–1**
legal aid **266**
mortgages **291**
national insurance **303–4**
national savings **304–5**
overdraft **319**
pawnbroker **332**
pay rise application **332–3**
pensions **333–4**
rate reductions and rebates **376**
receipts **377**
refunds **379**
repossession of property **380**
savings **403**
self-employment **412**
surety **458–9**
trusts **490–1**
unit trusts **496**
VAT **498–9**

Finches, caged 43
Finger, bandage 28
painting **168**
puppets 367–8
severed 412
spelling 421–2
weaving **168–9**
Fingernails **167–8**
See also Nails
Fire **169**
camp- **71–72**
car, claims for 79
chimney **96**
chip pan **98**
extinguishers 98, **169**
lighting **169–70**
warning system 430
Fireplace **170**
bricking in 58
Fires see Heaters
Firewood, making 525
Firework safety **170–1**
First Aid
artificial respiration **17–18**
bandaging **28**
bleeding **45**
blisters **47**
broken bones **58–59**
burns **64–65**
carbon monoxide poisoning **78**
chest pains **94**
childbirth **94–96**
choking **99–100**
dehydration **131–2**
diarrhoea **133**
dislocated joints **134–5**
dog bites **136**
drug overdose **145**
electric shock **151**
epileptic fit **156**
external chest compression **158–9**
eye injury **160–1**
fainting **163–4**
fish hook removal **172**
frostbite **187**
head and face injuries **219–20**
heart attack **220**
heat exhaustion **220**
heat stroke **221**
hypothermia **231**
insect bites and stings **236–7**
kits **171**
lifesaving **267–8**
lightning, struck by 270
nosebleed **307**
poisoning **355**
recovery position **378**
scalds **405**
severed limbs **412**
shock **417–18**
snake bites **430**
spinal injury **440**
splinters **442**
sprains and strains **442**
sunburn **457**
unconsciousness **494**
wounds **527**
Fish, cleaning **171–2**
crab **118–19**
freezing 185
grilling 206
kippers **252–3**
leftovers 266
lobster **271**
mackerel **273**
poaching 354
steaming 449
storage 183
tanks **15–16**
winkles and whelks **524**

Fishing **172–4**
flies 181–2
rights **174**
tackle **174–5**
Fits, epileptic **156**
fever 166
Flagstones **175**
Flambé cooking **175–6**
Flashings **176**
Flat feet **176**
Flats **230–1**
in Scotland **231**
Fleas **177**
Flex 154
connection, to fused unit 191
to plug 352
replacement 242
Flippers 424
Floaters 162
Float fishing 173
Floating 461, 462
Flooding **177**
Floor, cleaning 146, 290
draughtproofing 142
insulation 238
joists 247
parquet **327–8**
profile gauge for **364–5**
refinishing **177**
repairs **177–8**
soundproofing 435
tiles, ceramic 89–90
uneven **494–5**
vinyl **502–3**
Flowerbeds, raised **374–5**
Flowers, arranging **178–9**, 464
bedding **36–37**
drying **179**
for butterflies 66
photographing 305
pressing **179–80**
weather forecasting from 515
See also specific
flowers, e.g. Dahlias and
Gardening; Houseplants
Flu **180**
Flues, blocking off 170
Flummery **180**
Fluorescent lights **180–1**
Fly, casting 173–4
repellent 237
tying **181–2**
Flying kites 253–4
Foam mattress **182**
Fog, driving in 145
Fondue **182–3**
Food, baby 21
barbecuing **30**
calorie content 71
dieting and 133–4
fat content 100, 283
fibre in 283
for survival 459–60
freezing 185–6
garnishing **195**
leftover **265–6**
menu planning 283
microwaving **286–7**
mills 183
moulding **295**
pickling **340–1**
picnic 341
poisoning 183
processors 183
storage **183–4**
thawing and reheating 287, **476**
vegetarian **499**
vitamins in 504
wine with **524**
See also Recipes

Foot care **184**
Footpath guides 24
Foreign body, in cuts 28
in ears 148
in eye 160–1
Formaldehyde glue 202
Forms of address 65, **184**
Foundations, levelling **267**
Fox tracks 486
Frames, pictures **342**
Freezers **184–5**, 297, 361
Freezing, food **185–6**
herbs 223
French polishing **186**
Fretsaw 404
Fringe trimming 212
Frisbees **187**
Frostbite **187**
Frost protection **187**
Frozen, locks 80
pipes **187**
Fruit, for table decorating 464
freezing 185–6
jams **244–5**
jellies 245
pickling **340–1**
pineapple cutting **344**
preservation 363
quinces 371
sloes 428
storage 183
trees **188–9**, 371
spraying 335
Frying **189**
Fuchsias **189**
Fuel economy **190**
Funeral arrangements **190**
Fungicides 287, 525
Furniture, beetle 526
castors for **85**
dusting and cleaning **146–7**
scratch marks 407
scorch marks 101
Fused connection unit **191**
Fuses, and fuse boxes **190–1**
for car horns 79
Fusing web 15
Fuzz sticks 72

Gall mites 288
Galls, plant 348
Game birds **192**, 352
Games
anagrams **11**
billiards **42–43**
cat's cradle **87**
chess **93–94**
croquet **122–3**
darts **130**
dominoes **138**
frisbees **187**
Halloween **215**, 243
hopscotch **228**
horseshoes 229
jacks **243–4**
jackstraws **244**
jigsaw shapes **246**
magic tricks **274**
marbles **277**
musical chairs **299**
noughts and crosses **307**
pool **356–7**
quoits **371**
roulette **390–1**

Games (continued)
scavenger hunt **406**
soap bubbles **432**
shuffle board **420–1**
skipping **424–5**
skittles **425–6**
snooker **430–1**
table skittles **465**
tenpin bowling **474**
tiddlywinks **478**
travel 488
twenty questions **492**
yo-yo **529**
See also Board games; Card
games
Gaming Board 374
Gammon, carving 83
Garage, doors **192–3**
sales **193**
Garden chairs and seats **193**
Gardenias **193–4**
Gardening
accidents 8
bedding plants **36–37**
begonias **38–39**
bonsai 49
bulbs, corms and tubers **62**
busy lizzie **65–66**
cold frames **106**
compost 109, 246
couch grass **118**
cultivators **124**
dahlias **129**
ferns **165–6**
fertilisers **166**
fruit trees **188–9**
fuchsias **189**
geraniums **197**
gourds **203**
greenhouse **204–6**
ground cover **206–7**
hanging plants **218**
hedges **221**
hedge trimmers **221–2**
herbs **223**
lawn mowers **261–2**
lawns **260–1**
moles **290**
mulching **298**
pergolas **334**
planting **349**
plants for butterflies 66
ponds **194**
potatoes **358–9**
propagating plants **365–6**
pruning shrubs **366**
quinces **371**
raised flowerbeds **374–5**
rock gardens **386–7**
roses **389–90**
seed sowing **411**
shrubs **420**
soil preparation **433–4**
staking plants **447**
stump removal **456**
succulents **456**
thermometers **477**
tomatoes **483**
tree pruning **489–90**
trellises **490**
turfing **491–2**
vines **502**
walls **194**
weed control **518**
wheelbarrows **519–20**
window boxes **521–2**
See also Houseplants; Pests
Garlic **194–5**, 224
Garnet paper 399
Garnishing **195**

Gas, blowtorch 47–48
bottled 196
carbon monoxide poisoning **78**
cooker 114
escape **195–6**
heating, central 88–89
room **196**
water **196**
meters 285
moving house and 297
pilot lights **344**
pokers 170
refrigerators 379
Gasket leaks 313
Gastroenteritis 119
Gates **196–7**
hanging 225
latches for **258–9**
Genealogy 164
General Register Office 164
Geraniums **197**
Gerbils **216–17**
German measles **197**, 235
Gift, covenants **118**
presentation 363
wedding 517
wrapping **198**
Gilding **198–9**
Gilt-edged securities 305
Ginger 439
Gingerbread men **198–9**
Ginger drops 44
Gin rummy **199**
Glacé icing 233
Gladiolus 62, 478
Glands, swollen 463
Glandular fever 463
Glass, broken windows 263–4
cutting **200**
insulation 141
puttying 368
replacing in greenhouses 205–6
windowpanes 522
Glasses **200–1**, 347
Glasspaper 399
Glassware **201**
cleaning and repairing 13
heat-resistant 115
washing 134
Glaucoma 162
Glazes for pottery 360
Gloves, leather 264
Glue sniffing 146
Gluing **201–2**
chairs 91–92
china 13, 97
earthenware 148
leather 265
photographs 146
plastic laminates 350
Glycerine 103
Gold hallmarks **214–15**
Golf **202–3**
Goose 361, 455
Gooseberry jelly 245
Gouges, sharpening 415
Gourds 203
Gout 203
Grab 430
Grants **203–4**
Grapefruit pot plant 102
Grape ivy 103
Grass cutting 410
turf **491–2**
Gravel paths 204
Gravy 204
Greenfly 14, 335
Greenhouse, gardening **204–5**
thrips 478
tomatoes 483

Greenhouses **205–6**
`sealing tape for 451
Grilling **206**
Grommets, eyelets and **161**
Ground cover **206–7**
Grouse roasting 192
Grouting 90
Guarantee **207**
Guelder rose 39
Guinea pigs **216–17**
Guitar, repairs **207–8**
tuning **208**
Gullies 141
Guns **208**
Gutters and downpipes **208–9**, 411

H

Hacksaw 404
Haemorrhoids **210**
Hair, back-combing **22**
care **210**
colouring **210–11**
cutting **211–12**
dandruff **129–30**
lice **267**
loss **212**
perming **226**
pieces **212**
plaiting **213–14**
setting **214**
split ends **442**
superfluous **458**
transplants 212
-weaving 212
Hairdryers **212**
Hairpin crochet lace **212–13**
Halitosis 24
Hallmarks **214–15**
Halloween games 215, 243
Hamburgers **215–16**
Hammers **216**
Ham soufflé 435
Hamsters **216–17**
Handbag repairs **217–18**
Handbrake failure **54–55**
Handgun 208
Handle, for axes and hatchets 20
for baskets 31
for hammers 216
for handbag 217
for knives 128
for luggage 272
Hands, manicuring **275**
Hand sling 427
Hanging plants **218**
Hang nails **218**
Hangover **218**
Hard water deposit removal 32
Hare, jugged **248–9**
tracks 486
Hatchets, maintenance of 20
Hay fever 11, **218–19**
Headaches 219, 287
Head and face injuries **219–20**
Headphones 451
Health and beauty
beauty creams **36**
calorie counting **71**
cosmetics **117**
dandruff **129–30**
dieting **133–4**
eyebrows **160**
eye make-up **161–2**
facial care **163**
fingernails **167–8**

foot care **184**
manicures **275**
massage **280–1**
nail-biting **300**
posture 358
scars and blemishes **405–6**
sunlamps **457–8**
suntan **458**
wrinkles **527**
See also Hair
Health ombudsman 315
Hearing aids **220**
Heart attack 94, **220**
Heartburn 94, **220**
Heaters, immersion **233–4**, 513
oil **312**
gas **196**
solid fuel **452–3**
Heat exhaustion **220**
Heat-resistant paint 325
Heatstroke **221**
in pets 336
Hedera 103
Hedges **221**
Hedge trimmers **221–2**
Hems **222**
Herbaceous plants 51–52
Herbs 195
gardening **223**
in cooking **223–4**
preserving **223**
Heroin abuse 146
Herpes simplex virus 107
zoster virus 416–17
Herrings 47, 172
Hiccups **224**
Hi-fi 450–1
Hinges **224–5**
for gates **196–7**
Hire purchase 120, **225**
Hiring **225**
Hives **225**, 242
Hives, bee- 37–38
Hobbies
aquariums **15–16**
beekeeping **37–38**
beer brewing **38**
birdwatching **44**
brass rubbing **55**
calligraphy **70–71**
family trees **164**
flower arranging **178–9**
kites **253–4**
metal detecting **284**
photography 305, 337–9, 358
shells **415–16**
slides and slide shows **426**
stamp collecting **448**
stargazing **448–9**
See also Crafts; Exercise; Sport
Hock glass 201
Holidays
backpacking **23–24**
bicycle touring **42**
camping 72
caravan 77
car accidents abroad 76, 80
diarrhoea 133
disabled people 487
doctors 136
map reading **275–6**
passports **328–9**
pets and 488
pony trekking **356**
route-planning **391–2**
stranded on **453**
timesharing **481**
travel emergencies **486–7**
visas **504**
youth hostelling **529**

Hollandaise sauce 402
Holly berries 39
Home
    accidents in 8, 31
    nursing **308–9**
    old people's **314–15**
    perm **226**
    worker **226–7**
Homelessness **225–6**
Honey production 37–38
Hooks, and eyes **227**
    picture 343
Hopscotch **228**
Horn engraving **408–9**
Horse riding **228–9**
Hoses **229**
    gas, checking for leaks in 196
    leaks, car 320
Houseplants **229–30**
    African violets **10**
    aspidistra **19**
    avocado **20**
    begonias **38–39**
    bottle gardens **52**
    bulb forcing **61–62**
    busy lizzie **65–66**
    cacti **68–69**
    care during holidays **348**
    citrus **102**
    climbing plants **103–4**
    ferns **165–6**
    fertilisers **166**
    fuchsias **189**
    gardenias **193–4**
    hanging **218**
    ivy **103**
    orange trees **316**
    orchids **316**
    pests 14
    philodendrons **337**
    pineapple plant **344**
    poinsettias **355**
    potting **360–1**
    spider plant **439**
    succulents **456**
    wandering Jew **509–10**
Houses **230–1**
    alterations **348**
    design, architects for 16
    improvement grants **203–4**
    in Scotland **231**
    insurance 238
    purchase, stamp duty on **448**
    repossession **380**
    squatters **444**
    subletting **456**
    tenants **472–3**
House-training pets **231**
Housing benefit 376
Hyacinths, forced 61
Hydrogen peroxide 103
Hypothermia **231**

Ice, driving on 145
    removal **232**
    skating **232–3**
Ice cream **232**
Icing cakes 70, **233**
Immersion heaters **233–4**, 513
Immunisation **234–5**
    measles 282
Impatiens sultanii **65–66**
Imperial conversion to metric 285
Impetigo **235**

Income, bonds 305
    budgeting 59
    retirement 381
    support 304, 376, 432
    tax 235
Indigestion **236**
Infection, ear 148
    itchy 242
Information **236**
Ingrowing toenails **236**
Injury, compensation 121
    crutches for **123**
Ink, indelible **236**
    invisible **241**
Insect, bites and stings **236–7**, 418
    repellent **237**
    weather forecasting from 515
Insecticides see Pesticides
Insomnia **237**, 426
Insulation 187, **237–8**
Insurance **238**
    calculation of sum 240
    claims, car **79–80**
    endowment policies **156**
    home working and 227
Interest, building society 61
    on credit 120
    mortgage 291
    tax on 235
International road signs **238–9**
Introductions **240**
Inventions, patents on **330–1**
Inventory **240**
Investing **240–1**
    on retirement 381
    unit trusts **496**
Invitations **241**
    wedding **517**
Invoices 377
Irish coffee **241**
Ironing **241–2**, **364**, **457**
Irons **242**
Itching **242**
Ivory **242**
    piano cleaning and repairs 340
Ivy **103–4**

Jacking a car **243**
Jack o'lanterns **243**
Jacks **243–4**
Jackstraws **244**
Jam-making **244–5**
Jaw, broken 219
Jellies **245**, 371, 428
    aspic 19
Jet lag **245**
Jeweller's rouge 103
Jewellery **245–6**
Jigsaw (tool) 405
Jigsaw shapes **246**
Jogging **246**
    injuries 246
John Innes compost 246
Joints, caulking 411
    mitred **288–9**
    pipe **352–3**
    woodworking **525–6**
Joists **247**
Judo **247–8**
Jugged hare **248–9**
Juggling **249**
Junction box **249–50**
Juniper 439
Jury service **250**

K

Kayaks 75–76
Kebabs **251**
Kedgeree **251**
Kennel **251–2**
Kettles, descaling 133
    repairs **252**
Keyholes **252**
Keys **252**
    locked in car 80
Kilns 360
Kippers **252–3**
    pâté 330
Kiss of life 17–18
Kitchen, accidents in 8
    cabinets **253**
    smells **429–30**
Kites **253–4**
Knitting **254–5**
Knives, craft, sharpening 415
    table 128
Knots **255**

L

Labour, emergency birth 94–96
Lace, cleaning **256**
    hairpin crochet **212–13**
Ladders **256–7**
Lagging pipes 345
Lamb, carving 83
    kebabs **251**
    roasting **385**
Laminate cladding **350–1**
Lamp, oil 313
Lampshades **257**
Land registration, Scotland 231
Landscape, painting 512
    photography **338–9**
Lapidary work **257–8**
Laryngitis **258**
Latches, and catches 139, **258–9**
    gate 197
Laundering **259–60**
Lavatory, blocked 353–4
    chemical **92–93**
    cistern ball cock 26
    joint caulking 411
    leaking 353
    smells 430
Lavender, bags **260**
    scent 406
    sticks 260
Law centres 263
Lawn, care **260**
    chamomile 207
    dandelions in 129
    moles in **290**
    mowers **261–2**
    turfing **491–2**
    wormcasts **527**
Lawyers **262–3**
Laxatives **112–13**
Layering **365–6**
Leaded lights **263–4**
Leaks, ball cock repair for 26
    car 313–14, 319–20
    flashings **176**
    gas, checking hoses for 196
    lavatory 353
    pipes 354
    radiator 88–89

tanks 354
taps **466–7**
windows 263
Leather, chamois **92**
    garments **264**
    reinforcing 161
    work **264–5**
Left-handedness **265**
Leftovers **265–6**
Leg, broken 59
    in pets 335
    pain 417
Legal affairs
    ancient lights **12**
    arbitration **16**
    bail **25–26**
    birth certificates **44**
    building permits **60**
    car accidents **76**
        insurance claims **79–80**
    citizen's arrest **102**
    companies **107–8**
    complaints **109**
    crime compensation **121**
    eviction notice **156–7**
    fishing rights **174**
    guarantee **207**
    guns 208
    hire purchase **225**
    jury service **250**
    lawyers **262–3**
    noisy neighbours **306–7**
    nuisance **308**
    ombudsmen **315**
    organ donors **316–17**
    patents **330–1**
    planning permission **348**
    power of attorney **362**
    raffles **373–4**
    refunds **379**
    repossession of property **380**
    sale of goods **398–9**
    small claims **429**
    squatters **444**
    suing **456–7**
    summons **457**
    sweepstake **461**
    telephone solicitations **470**
    tenants **472–3**
    timesharing **481**
    treasure **488**
    unfair dismissal **495**
    ward of court **510**
    warranties **510**
Legal aid **266**
Lemon, juice as cleanser 103
    pot plants 102
Letters, business 65
    condolence **112**
    forms of address **184**
    references **379**
    resignation 381
    RSVP **392**
Levelling **267**
Lice **267**
Lids, unscrewing 480
Life jackets 460
Lifesaving **267–8**
Lifting and carrying **268–9**
Lifts, being trapped in **269**
Light, right to **12**
Lightning **270**
Lights, car 294
    ceiling rose fitting **87**
    circuits 154
    fixtures **269–70**
    fluorescent **180–1**
    junction box **249–50**
    outside **318**
    switches 152–3

Limbs, severed **412**
Liming soil 434
Liners for ponds 194
Lino cuts **270**
Lip reading 421
Lipstick stains **270–1**
Lizards 380
Loans 119–20
  arrears 380
  mortgage **291**
  overdraft **319**
  pawnbroker **332**
Lobster **271**
Locks 63–64
  car 82
    frozen **80**
    unlocking without keys 80
  door **139–40**
  keys broken in **252**
  padlocks **321**
Loft insulation 204, 237–8
Logs, paper **327**
  wood 525
Lordosis 358
Lost, dogs and cats **271**
  property 488
Lotteries 58
  raffles **373–4**
  sweepstake **461**
Louvre doors **271**
LSD abuse 146
Luggage **272**
  lost 487
  packing **321**
Lumbago **272**
Lupin 51

Mace 439
Machine-sewing **414–15**
Machine washing 259
Mackerel **273**
Macramé **273–4**
Magic tricks **274**
Magistrate's court order 121, 307
Magnet **274**
Mail, redirecting 297
Make-up, facial 117, **160**
  for eyes **160**, 161–2
  for Halloween 215
  removal 163
Mallet 216
Manicures **274**
Manure 434
Maps 23–24
  reading **274–5**
    compass for 108–9
  route-planning **391–2**
  walking 506
Marble **276–7**
Marbles **277**
Marinating **277**
Marjoram 224
Marmalade **277–8**
Marquetry **278–9**
Marriage **279**
Marzipan **279–80**
Masks, facial 163
Masonry, drilling **280**
  nails 300
  paint 325
Massage **280–1**
Maternity, leave **281**
  pay 304
Mattress, foam **182**

Mayonnaise **281–2**
Mealy bug **282**
Measles **282**
  German **197**
  vaccine 234–5
Meat, braising 54
  carving **82–83**
  freezing 185
  grilling **206**
  leftovers 265–6
  loaf **282**
  marinating 277
  roasting **385–6**
  storage 183
  See also specific meats
Medical care abroad 486–7
Medical problems
  acne **9**
  allergies **11**
  appendicitis **14**
  arthritis **16–17**
  athlete's foot **19–20**
  backache **22**
  bad breath **24**
  body odour **48**
  breast examination **56**
  broken bones **58–59**
  bunions **62**
  burns **64–65**
  chilblains **94**
  colds **106–7**
  cold sores **107**
  colic **107**
  colour blindness **107**
  conjunctivitis **112**
  constipation **112–13**
  corns **117**
  coughs **118**
  cradle cap **119**
  cramps **119**
  deafness 220
  doctor **136**
  drug recognition **145–6**
  earache **148**
  ears **148**
  eczema **149**
  eyes **162**
  eyesight testing **162**
  feet **176**, **184**
  fever **166**
  flu **180**
  food poisoning **183**
  gout **203**
  gums **133**
  haemorrhoids **210**
  hair loss **212**
  hang nails **218**
  hangover **218**
  hayfever **218–19**
  headaches **219**
  head and face injuries **219–20**
  heart attack **220**
  heartburn **220**
  heat exhaustion **220**
  heat stroke **221**
  hiccups **224**
  hives **225**
  immunisation **234–5**
  impetigo **235**
  indigestion **236**
  ingrowing toenails **236**
  insect bites and stings **236–7**
  insomnia **237**, 426
  itchiness **242**
  jogging injuries **246**
  laryngitis **258**
  lumbago 272
  measles **282**
  migraine **287**
  mumps **298**

  muscle aches **298**
  nasal congestion **303**
  nausea **305**
  nosebleed **307**
  nursing at home **308–9**
  period pains **334**
  premenstrual tension **362–3**
  pulse-taking **367**
  rabies **372**
  rashes **375**
  ringing in the ears **384**
  shingles **416–17**
  shin splints **417**
  slings **427–8**
  slipped disc **428**
  snoring **431**
  snow blindness **431**
  sore throat **435**
  stammering **447–8**
  stiff necks **451**
  stomachaches **452**
  stress **453**
  styes **456**
  swollen glands **463**
  tennis elbow **473**
  threadworms **477–8**
  travel sickness **487**
  ulcers **494**
  vomiting **505**
  warts **510**
  wheezing **520**
  See also First aid
Medicines, for pets **336–7**
  storage of 309
Meditation **282**
Memory improvement **282–3**
Mending **283**
Menu planning **283**
Mercury **283**
Meringues **283–4**
Metal, detecting **284**
  doors, repair of 193
  gates **196–7**
  greenhouses 206
  polish 103
Metalwork, drilling **144**
  painting 323, 324, 326
  riveting **384–5**
  rust **395**
  sawing **403–5**
  soldering **434**
  welding **519**
Metalworking **284–5**
Meter reading **285**
Methylated spirit 103
Metric conversion **285**
Mice **286**
Microwave, cooking **286–7**
  oven, cleaning 319
  ovenware 115
Midge bites 237
Migraine **287**
Mildew and mould **287**
Milk, allergy to 107
Minors see Children
Mint 224
Mirrors **287–8**
Mites on plants **288**
Mitre joints **288–9**
Mobiles **289**
Modelling in clay **289–90**
Moisturiser 36, 117, 163
Moles **290**, 486
Money see Finance
Monstera 103
Mops and mopping **290**
Morse code **290**
Mortar **290–1**
  for stucco walls 455
  pointing **355**

Mortgages 230, **291**
  arrears 380
  increasing 120
Mortise, -and-tenon joint 526
  lock **139–40**
Mosaics **291–2**
Mosquito bite 237
Moss 194, 450
Mothproofing **292**
Moths as pests 86
Motorcycles **292–3**
  padlocks 321
Motorway, driving **293**
  signs **293–4**
MoT test **294–5**
Mould **287**
  on brickwork 194
  on greenhouse glass 206
  on steps 450
  on stucco walls 455
Moulding food **295**
Mouldings **295–6**
  picture frames 341–2
  repair 116
Mounts, picture **343**
Moustaches 36
Mouth-to-mouth resuscitation 17–18
Moving house **296–7**
Muggers **297–8**
Mulching **298**
Mulling ale and wine **298**
Mumps **298**
Murder in the dark 215
Muscle, aches **298**
  relaxation 380
  strain 246, 442
Mushrooms 195, **299**
Music, copyright 58
  reading **376–7**
  See also Guitar; Piano; Recorders; Records; Violins
Musical chairs **299**
Mussels **299**

Nailing **300**
Nails (finger/toe), biting **300**
  hang **218**
  ingrowing **236**
  manicure **275**
Names **301–2**
Napkins **302**, 464
Nappy changing **302–3**
Narcissus, forced 61
Nasal, congestion **303**
  surgery 406
National insurance **303–4**
National Savings 304–5
Nature photography **305**
Nausea **305**
Neck, stiff **451**
Necklace, bead 35
Needlepoint tapestry **305–6**
Needles 412, 414
  threading **477**
Negligence, suing for 457
Neighbours, noisy **306–7**
  nuisance 308
Nervousness 306
Neurodermatitis 242
Noise, dog barking **136**
  neighbours **306–7**
  pipes **307**
  protection against 148
Non-stick pans 115

North Star **307**
Nosebleed **307**
Noughts and crosses **307**
Nuisance **308**
Nursing, at home **308–9**
   homes 315
Nutmeg **439**
Nuts and bolts 48
Nylon **309**
   ropes **309**

O

Obedience training **310–11**
Obscene telephone callers **311**
Oil, changing **311–12**
   checking in power steering 362
   -fired central heating 88–89
   heaters **312**
   lamp 313
   leaks **313–14**
   painting **314**, 454
Oilstone 415
Old people's homes **314–15**
Ombudsman **315**
Omelettes **315–16**
Opticians 162
Opuntia microdasys 68
Orange, marmalade 277–8
   sorbet **434–5**
   soufflé 435
   trees 102, **316**
Orchids **316**
Ordnance Survey maps 275–6
Oregano 224
Organ donor **316–17**
Orienteering **317**
Origami **317**
Osteoarthritis 16–17
Otter tracks 486
Outboard motors **317–18**
Outside lighting 318
Oven, cleaning **318–19**
   mitts **319**
   See also Cooker
Overdose, drug 145
Overdraft **319**
Overheating engine **319–20**
Oysters **320**

P

Packing **321**
   for moving house 297
Padlocks **321**
Pain, appendicitis 14
   arthritis 16–17
   back 22
   chest **94**
   colic **107**
   cramps **119**
   headaches **219**
   period **334**
   shin splints **417**
   stomach **452**
   toothache **483**
Paintbrushes, pads and
   rollers **321–2**
Painting, canvas for **453–4**
   cars 132–3
   eggs 149
   exteriors **322–3**

finger **168**
interiors **323–4**
louvre doors 271
oil 314
   problems **324–5**
   spatter prints **438**
   spray **442–3**
   stencilling **449–50**
   touch-ups **326**
   watercolour **512**
Paints **325**
   smells 430
   stripping 47–48, **325–6**
   textured coatings **476**
Pancakes 120, **326**
Panel adhesive 202
Pans, burnt **326**
Paper, aircraft **326–7**
   folding **317**, 326–7
   hats **327**
   logs **327**
Papier-mâché **327**
Paraffin as cleanser 103
Parcel tying **327**
Parliamentary ombudsman 315
Parlour palm 19
Parquet flooring **327–8**
Parsley 224
Parthenocissus 104
Partitions **328**
Partnership 412
Partridge roasting 192
Passport **328–9**
Pasta 74–75, **329**
Paste, wallpaper 508
Pastry **329–30**
   freezing 185
   pie crust **343**
Patching 330
Patchwork 330
Pâté **330**
Patents **330–1**
Paths, concrete 111–12
   flagstones **175**
   gravel **204**
Patience **331**
Patio building **331–2**
Pattern transfer **332**
Paving, crazy **119**
   slabs repairs 450
Pawnbroker **332**
PAYE 235
Pay rise application **332–3**
Pea, moth 86
   thrips **478**
Pears 188–9
   in brandy 91
Pebbledash **333**
Peephole viewer **333**
Pelargoniums **197**
Pelmets **333**
Pensions **333–4**
   retirement **304**, 381
   widow's 304
Pepper **439**
Peppermint creams 461
Perennials 51–52
Pergolas **334**
Period pains **334**
Perm, home **226**
Pesticides **334–5**, 390
Pets
   cats **86**
   distemper 135
   dogs 136–7
   fleas **177**
   hamsters, guinea pigs and
      gerbils 216–17
   house-training **231**
   injuries **335–6**

lost **271**
medication **336–7**
mice **286**
moving house 297
obedience training **310–11**
photographing 339
pigeons **343–4**
rabbits **372**
reptiles **380**
travel with **488**
See also Animals
Pewter cleaning 13, **337**
Pheasant roasting 192
Philately **448**
Philodendrons **337**
Phlox 51
Photographs, dry-mounting **146**
Photography **339**
   action **337–8**
   landscape **338–9**
   nature **305**
   pet **339**
   portrait **358**
Piano **340**
Pickling **340–1**, 402
Picnic **341**
Picture, frame gilding **198–9**
   frame repairs **341**
   framing **342**
   hanging **342–3**
   mounting **343**
Pie crust **343**
Pigeons **343–4**
   roasting 192
Pigtails **213–14**
Piles 210
Pillows, down **141**
Pilot lights **344**
Pineapple, cutting **344**
   plant **344**
Pinks 51–52
Pinworm **477**
Pipes, bending **345**
   frost protection **187**
   frozen **187**
   lagging **345**
   noisy **307**
   overflow 354
   plastic 351
   plumbing **352–4**
Pipe wrench 437
Piping as trimming **346**
Pizza **346**
Place, mats **346**
   setting **347**
Plaint note 457
Plaiting, hair **213–14**
   rug **394–5**
Planes **347**, 415
Planing **347–8**
Planning permission 60, 227, **348**
Plant care during holidays **348**
   See also Gardening; Houseplants
   or specific plants
Planting **349**
   shrubs 420
Plasterboard **349**
   battening 33
   nails 300
Plaster patching **349–50**
Plastic, bed repair 10
   insulation for windows 140
   laminates **350–1**
   pipes 351
   wall cladding **351–2**
   wood 452
Platinum hallmarks 214–15
Plucking, birds **352**
   eyebrows **160**
Plugs, electric **352**

Plumbing **352–4**
   descaling 133
   plastic pipes 351
   taps **466–7**
   water heating **513**
   water softeners 514–15
Plumb line **354**
Plums 188–9
Plywood **354**
Poaching **354**
Pocket mending **354**
Poinsettias **355**
Pointing 194, **355**
Poisoning **355**
   carbon monoxide **78**
   food **183**
   in pets 336
Poisons, household 96
Poker **355–6**
Polio vaccine 234–5
Polishing, antiques 13
   cars 84
   French **186**
   marble **276–7**
   materials 103
   shells 416
   silver 422
   stones **257–8**
Polygonum 52
   baldschuanicum **104**
Polystyrene cement 202
Pomander **356**
Ponds, garden **194**
Pony trekking **356**
Pool **356–7**
Porcelain **357**
Pork, carving 82–83
   pie **357**
   roasting **385**
   stuffing 455
Port glass 201
Portrait photography **358**
Posture 22, **358**
Potatoes **358–9**
Potpourri **359**
Pottery **359–60**
Potting houseplants **360–1**
Poultry **361**
   carving 82–83
   freezing 185
   grilling **206**
   leftover 266
   plucking **352**
   storage 183
Power, cuts **361**
   of attorney **362**
   steering **362**
   -tool safety **362**
   See also Tools
Prams and pushchairs **362**
Prawn cocktail 410
Premenstrual tension **362–3**
Premium Bonds 305
Presentations **363**
Preservatives, wood **525**
Preserving **363**
   herbs **223**
   See also Jam-making
Pressing **364**
   flowers **179–80**
   suits **457**
Press-studs **364**
Pressure cookers **364**
   cooking **364**
   preserving 363
Pressure points to stop bleeding 45
Prickly heat 242, **364**
Primula vulgaris 52
Printing, lino cut 270
   spatter **438**

Privet berries 39
Profile gauge 332, **364**
Propagating plants 197, **365–6**
Pruning, fruit trees 189
  hedges 221
  houseplants 229–30
  roses 390
  shrubs **366**
  trees **489–90**
Ptarmigan roasting 192
Public Record Office 164
Public speaking **366–7**
Pudding, steamed 449
Puff pastry 329–30
Pulse rate, for fitness levels 9
Pulse-taking **367**
Pump, gasket 440
  replacing, central heating 88–89
Pumpkin lantern 243
Punch 144–5
Puncture mending, air beds 10
  bicycle 41
Punting **367**
Puppet-making **367–8**
Puréeing 183, **368**
Pushchairs **362**
Push-starting **368**
Puttying **368**
PVA glue 201

Quail roasting 192
Quarantine **369**
Quarry tiles **369–70**
Quicksands **370**
Quickstep 26–27
Quill pens 70–71
Quilting **370–1**
Quinces **371**
Quoits **371**

Rabbits **372**
  tracks 486
Rabies **372**
Rackets, tennis **473–4**
Radial circuits 154
Radiant heaters, gas 196
  oil 312
Radiators, car, flushing **372–3**
  leaks from 320
  central heating 88–89
Radio, aerials **373**
  car 76–77
  interference in car **81–82**
Raffles 58, **373–4**
Rag dolls **374**
Raincoats **374**
Raised flowerbeds **374–5**
Rape **375**
Rashes 197, **375**
Raspberries 39
  fondant 461
Rates, home workers and
  business 227
Rats **376**
  tracks 486
RCD 101
Reading music **376–7**
Receptions, wedding 518

Recipes
  barbecue sauce 30
  batter, coating 189
  biscuits 44
  bread and butter pudding 266
  bread-making 55–56
  canapés **72–73**
  cannelloni 74–75
  cheese, sauce **92**
    soufflé 435
  chicken liver pâté 330
  chocolate truffles **99**
  Christmas cake 69–70
  cottage pie 266
  crêpes suzettes 120
  croquettes **123**
  dandelion wine 523–4
  dry martini 145
  eggs **150**
    curried 125
    omelette 315–16
    poached 354
  fish, poached 354
  flummery **180**
  fondue **182–3**
  ginger beer 433
  gingerbread men **198–9**
  gravy **204**
  hamburgers **215–16**
  ham soufflé 435
  ice cream **232**
  icings 233
  Irish coffee **241**
  jams 244–5
  jellies **245**, 371
  kedgeree **251**
  kipper pâté 330
  lamb kebab 251
  lemonade 433
  mackerel in cider 273
  marinade 277
  marmalade 277–8
  marzipan **279–80**
  mayonnaise **281–2**
  meat loaf **282**
  meringues **282–3**
  mulled ale and wine 298
  orange, sorbet 434–5
    soufflé 435
  pancake **326**
  pasta **329**
  pastry **329–30**
  pizza **346**
  planter's punch 145
  poires flambées **91**
  pork pie **357**
  potato chips 189
  prawn cocktail 410
  rice 384
  salad, fruit 398
    mixed 398
  salad dressing 398
  sandwiches **400**
  sauces, brown 402
    cheese 92
    emulsion 402
    tomato 483
    white 401
  sauerkraut **402**
  sausages 402–3
  scones **407**
  shepherd's pie 266
  shortbread **419**
  sloe and apple jelly 428
  sloe gin 428
  snail butter 156
  spaghetti bolognese 436
  sponge cake 69
  stuffings **455**
  sweets **461**

  tarts **467**
  tempura **472**
  tequila sunrise 145
  toddy **482**
  toffee apples **482**
  tomato sauce **483**
  Tom Collins 145
  vol-au-vents **505**
  waffles **506**
  yoghurt **528**
  Yorkshire pudding **528–9**
  zabaglione **529**
  See also Cooking
Receipts **377**
Recorder **377–8**
Recorders 85,
  video **501–2**
Records **377**
Recovery position **378**
Redcurrant jelly 245
Red spider mite 288
Redundancy **378**
References **379**
Refrigerators **379**
Refunds **379**
Reheating food 287
Relaxation, exercises **379–80**
  for nervousness 306
  massage **280–1**
  meditation **282**
  yoga **528**
Removals 296
Renting goods 225
Repossession of property **380**
Reptile pets **380**
Resigning **380–1**
Resin glue 201–2
Resuscitation 17–18
Retiring **381–2**
  pension 304, 333–4
Reupholstering **382–3**
Rheumatoid arthritis 17
Rhipsalidopsis gaertneri 69
Rhizome division 365
Rhoicissus rhomboidea 103
Rhythm method **383**
Ribs, fractured 59
Rice **383–4**
Riding, bicycle **41–42**
  horse **228–9**
Rifle 208
Ring circuit 154
Ringers 277
Ringing in ears **384**
Rivets **384**
Road signs, international **238–9**
  motorway **293–4**
Roasting, game 192
  meats **385–6**
  poultry 361
Rock climbing safety 104
Rock garden **386–7**
Roller blinds 46–47
Rollers, hair 214
  paint **321–2**
Roller skating **387**
Roman blinds **387–8**
Roman numerals **388**
Roof, damp from 129
  insulation 237–8
  racks, car **82**
  repairs **388–9**
  thatching **476**
Ropes, nylon **309**
  skipping 424–5
  splicing **441–2**
  whipping 441–2
Rosemary 224
Roses **389–90**
  thrips 478

Rot, dry **146**
  violet root 18
Rotary mower 261–2
Roulette **390–1**
Route-planning **391–2**
Routers **392**
Rowing **392**
  sculling **409–10**
RSVP **392**
Rubber-based glue 202
Rubella **197**
Rucksacks 23
Rug, making **392–3**
  plaiting **394–5**
Rummy **395**
Russian vine 104
Rust **395**
  repair, on gates 196–7
  stains, bathtub 32

Safes **396**
Safety advice
  bicycle 41–42
  car 82
  child **96**
  climbing **104**
  electricity 8
  fire 169
  firework **170–1**
  flambé cooking 175
  flooding **177**
  gas escape **195–6**
    pilot light **344**
  hedge trimmers 222
  ice skating 233
  ladders **256–7**
  lightning 270
  motorcycles **292–3**
  motorway driving **293**
  padlocks **321**
  ponds 194
  power tool **362**
  pressure cooker 364
  quicksands **370**
  rape **375**
  sailing 398
  sauna 402
  scaffold tower **405**
  skin diving 424
  sunlamps 458
  swimming 462
  toasters 481
  underwater 409
  See also Accidents
Safety seats **396–7**
Saffron 439
Sage 224
Sailing **397–8**
  knots 255
Saintpaulia ionantha 10
Salad dressings 281–2, **398**
Salads **398**
Salary increase 332–3
Sale of goods **398–9**
Sales, bring-and-buy 58
  garage **193**
Salivary stone 463
Salmonella poisoning 183
Salmon fishing 174
Salt, as cleanser 103
  on roads **399**
Salvo 35
Sanding **399–400**
  floorboards 177

Sandwiches **400**
Sand yachting **400**
Sashcords **400–1**
Satellite television **401**
Sauce **401–2**
  barbecue 30
  cheese **92**
  tempura 472
  tomato 483
Sauerkraut **402**
Saunas **402**
Sausage-making **402–3**
Saving **403**
  accounts 305
  budgeting 59–60
  certificates 304
Saws, and sawing **403–5**
  chain 91
  sharpening 415
Scabies 242
Scaffold tower **405**
Scalds 64, **405**
  prevention 8
Scalp wounds 219
Scars and blemishes **405–6**
Scavenger hunts **406**
Scents **406**
Schlumbergera × *buckleyi* 69
Schools 403, **406**
Scissors **407**, 415
Scones **407**
Scorch mark removal 101
Scotland, houses and flats in **231**
  marriages in 279
Scratch marks **407**
  removal 13, 186
Screen blocks 60
Screws **407–8**, 507
Scrimshaw **408–9**
Scuba diving **409**
Sculling **409–10**
Sculptures 289–90
Scything **410**
Sea, distress signals at 135
Seafood cocktails **410**
Sealants **410–11**
  for baths 31–32
Sealing, gaps in staircases 446–7
  strips 142
Seams 413–14
Seat belts 294–5, **411**
Seats, garden **193**
Seat worm 477
Security, for bail 25
  for loans 120
Seed sowing **411**
Seizures 156
Self-employment **412**
  home worker **226–7**
  pension 381
Sensor alarms 62–63
Septic tank **412**
Sewing **412–14**
  buttonholes **67**
  buttons **67**
  clothing alterations **105–6**
  curtains **126–7**
  cushions **127–8**
  darning **130**
  duvet covers 147
  embroidery **154–5**
  hems **222**
  hooks and eyes **227**
  lampshades **257**
  leather 265
  mending **283**
    pockets **354**
  oven mitts **319**
  patching **330**
  piping **346**

place mats **346**
press-studs **364**
quilting **370–1**
rag dolls **374**
Roman blinds **387–8**
shirt collar turning **417**
slipstitching **428**
threading needles **477**
tie-backs **478–9**
valances **498**
zippers **529–30**
See also Crafts
Sewing machine **414–15**
Shampooing 210
  carpets 80
Shares, term 61
Sharpening hand tools 20, **415**
Shaving superfluous hair 458
Sheds 60
Shells **415–16**
Shelter for survival 459
Shelves **416**
  levelling **267**
Sherry glass 200–1
Shepherd's pie 266
Shine, removing **416**
  restoring **416**
Shingles 94, **416–17**
Shirts, collar turning **417**
  ironing 241
Shock **417–18**
  absorbers 295, **418–19**
  electric **151**
    in children 96
Shoes, care **419**
  comfortable 184
  squeaky **444**
  walking **506**
Shortbread **419**
Short circuits **419–20**
Shortcrust pastry 329
Shotguns 208
Shrubs **420**
  planting **349**
  staking 447
Shuffle board **420–1**
Shuffling cards **421**
Shyness **421**
Sickness benefit 304
Sick pay 304
Signals, Morse **290**
  skin-diving 424
Sign language **421–2**
Signwriting **266**
Silicon-carbide paper 399
Silver **422**
  cleaning 13
  hallmarks **214–15**
  washing and drying 134
Silverfish **422**
Sink waste disposal unit **511–12**
Siphoning **422–3**
Skating, ice 232–3
  roller **387**
Skids **423**
Skiing **423–4**
  water **514**
Skin care, facial **163**
  cosmetics 117
  creams 36
  problems, acne **9**
    eczema **149**
    hives **225**
    impetigo **235**
    sunburn **457**
    wrinkles **527**
Skin-diving 424
Skinning fish 171–2
Skip hire 225
Skipping **424–5**

Skirt, alterations 105
  hems 222
  ironing 241
  zippers 530
Skirting boards **425**
  painting 324
Skittles **425–6**
  table 465
Slate roof repairs 389
Sledgehammer 216
Sleep **426**
  difficulties 237
  posture 22
Sleeping bags **426**
Slides and slide shows **426**
Sliding doors **426–7**
Slings **427–8**
Slipped disc **428**
Slipstitching **428**
Slipstone 415
Sloes 39, **428**
Slugs and snails **428–9**
Small claims 109, **429**
Smells **429–30**
  animal 12
  body 48
  cigarette **101**
  drains 141–2
Smoke detectors **430**
Smoking **430**
Snails, edible 156
Snakes 380
  bites **430**
Snap **430**
Snipe roasting 192
Snooker **430–1**
Snoring **430**
Snorkelling 424
Snow, blindness **430**
  bound **431–2**
  clearing 232
  driving in 145
Soap bubbles **432**
Social Security **432–3**
Sockets, electric **152–3**
  outside 318
Soft drinks **433**
Softwood 480
Soil preparation **433–4**
Soldering 48, **434**
Solicitors **262–3**
  for complaints 109
  for house purchase 231
Solid-fuel, central heating 88–89
  cooker 114
  stoves **452–3**
Solvent, abuse 146
  cleaning 103
Sorbet **434–5**
Sore throat **435**
SOS signal 135
Soufflés **435**
Soundproofing **434–5**
Soups 183, **436**
  garnishes 195
Sowans 180
Sowing seeds **411**
Spaghetti **436**
Spanners and wrenches **436–7**
Spark-plugs **437–8**
Spatter prints **438**
Speakers, hi-fi 451
  in car 78–79
Spectacles **438–9**
Speech, in public **366–7**
  presentation 363
  stammering **447–8**
  toasts **481–2**
Spices **439**
Spider plant **439**

Spillikins 244
Spinal injuries **440**
Spindle tree 39
Spin dryers **440–1**
Spinning yarn 441
Splicing rope **441–2**
Splinters **442**
Splints 59
Split ends **442**
Sponge cake 69
Sport
  badminton **24–25**
  boules **52**
  bowls **52–53**
  canoes and kayaks **75–76**
  climbing **104**
  diving **135–6**
  fishing **172–4**
  golf **202–3**
  guns **208**
  horse riding **228–9**
  ice skating **232–3**
  judo **247–8**
  orienteering **317**
  pony trekking **356**
  rowing **392**
  sailing **397–8**
  sand yachting **400**
  scuba diving **409**
  sculling **409–10**
  skiing **423–4**
  squash rackets **443–4**
  surfing **459**
  swimming **461–2**
  table tennis **466**
  tug of war **491**
  volleyball **505**
  water polo **513**
  water-skiing **514**
  windsurfing **523**
  See also Exercise
Spotlights 269–70
Spots, acne 9
Sprains and strains 28, **442**
Spray painting **442–3**
Spur connections **443**
Squash rackets **443–4**
Squatters **444**
Squeaky, floors 178
  shoes **444**
  staircases **446–7**
Squirrel tracks 486
Stab wounds 527
Stained glass **444–5**
Staining, floorboards 177
  wood **445**, 499
Stainless steel 115, **445**
Stain removal 103, **445**
  bath 32
  china 97
  dishes 134
  glassware **201**
  indelible ink 236
  irons 242
  lipstick **270–1**
  marble 276
  mildew and mould **287**
  paintwork, new 324
  wood 13, 186
Stair, carpets **445–6**
  cases **446–7**
  rail maintenance 27
Staking plants **447**
Stall hire 58
Stammering **447–8**
Stamp collecting **448**
Stamp duty 448
Staple gun 448
Stargazing **448–9**
Steaming **449**

Steam inhalation therapy 520
Steel wool 103, 399
Steering box, car 295
    leaks 313–14
    power **362**
Stencilling **449–50**
Step repairs **450**
Stereo systems **450–1**
Sterilising **451**
    bottled fruit 363
Sticky tapes **451**
Stiff necks **451**
Stings, bee **38**
    insect **236–7**
    shock reaction to 418
    to pets 336
Stir-frying **452**
Stitches
    back- 154, 413
    blanket 154
    chain 154
    cross- 154, 306
    hem 413
    herringbone 413
    knitting **254–5**
    oversewing 413
    running 413
    slip- **428**
    stem 154
    tent 306
    whip 413
Stoat tracks 486
Stocks, cooking 436
Stocks and shares 240–1
Stomach, aches **452**
    ulcers 494
Stone polishing **257–8**
    marble **276–7**
Stonework **452**
Stoppers, unjamming 480
Stoppers and fillers **452**
Stoves **452–3**
Strains **442**
Stranded on holiday **453**
Strawberries 39
    jam **244–5**
Stress **453**
    itchiness and 242
String art **454**
Stubble, designer 36
Stucco walls **455**
Stud poker 355–6
Stuffings **455**
Stumps **456**
Styes **456**
Subletting **456**, 473
Succulents **456**
Suede
    clothes 264
    shoes 419
Suffocation in children 96
Suffolk latch 258–9
Suing **456–7**
    small claims **429**
Suitcase, packing 321
    repair 272
Suit pressing **457**
Summons **457**
Sunburn **457**
Sunlamps **457–8**
Suntan **458**
Superfluous hair **458**
Surety **458–9**
Surfing **459**
Surveyors for house purchase 230
Survival **459–60**
Swarms **461**
Sweepstake **461**
Sweets **461**
Swimmer's ear 148

Swimming **461–2**
    diving **135–6**
    for survival 460
    lifesaving **267–8**
    skin-diving **424**
    underwater **409**
Swing **463**
Swiss cheese plant 103
Switches, electric **134**, **152–3**,
    492–3
Swollen glands **463**

T

Table, decorating **464**
    laying 347
    repairs **464–5**
    skittles **465**
    tennis **466**
Tacking 413
Talc as cleanser 103
Tangerine tree pot plant 102
Tank, toy **485**
Tanks, frost protection of 187
    leaking 354
Tantrums, children's 96
Tape recorders 85
Tapes, sticky **451**
    veneer **500–1**
Tapestry, needlepoint **305–6**
Taps **466–7**
    dripping 353
    noisy 307
Tarragon 224
Tarsonemid mites 288
Tarts **467**
Tax, allowances 235
    covenants and 118
    income **235**
    investments 240
    relief, for home worker 226–7
    stamp duty 448
    See also Value added tax
Tea **467–8**
Teddy bear repairs **468**
Teeth **468–9**
    aching **483**
    cleaning 24
    dentures **133**
Teething **469**
Telephone, answering machines **469**
    callers, obscene **311**
    extensions **469–70**
    solicitations **470**
Telephones **470**
Television, aerials **470–1**
    hiring 225
    satellite **401**
    sets **471**
    video recorders **501–2**
Temperature, body 166, **472**
    lowered 231
    measurement 477
Temper tantrums 96
Tempura **472**
Tenants **472–3**
    eviction notice **156–7**
    subletting **456**
Tennis, elbow **473**
    rackets **473–4**
Tenpin bowling **474**
Tents **474–5**
    bivouac **44–45**
    camping 72
Terrace, garden 331–2
Tetanus vaccine 234–5

Textured coating 325, **476**
Thatching **476**
Thawing food 287, **476**
Theft see Burglary
Thermometer 472, **477**
Thermostats, in cars **477**
    in heaters 234
Threading needles **477**
Threadworm **477–8**
Thrips **478**
Throat, sore **435**
Thrush 242
Thunbergia alata 103
Thyme 224
Ticks **478**
Tiddlywinks **478**
Tie-backs **478–9**
Tie-dyeing **479–80**
Ties **480**
    bow **53**
Tight lids and stoppers **480**
Tiles, ceramic **89–90**
    cleaning 147
    fireplace 170
    quadrant 32
    quarry **369–70**
    regrouting **480**
    roof 388–9
    vinyl 502–3
Timber **480**
    See also Wood; Woodwork
Timesharing **481**
Tinnitus 384
Tipping **481**
Titles, introductions and 240
    letter-writing and 65, 184
Toasters **481**
Toasts **481–2**
Toboggan **482**
Toddy **482**
Toe, severed 412
Toffee apples **482**
Toggle wall fasteners 507
Toilets see Lavatory
Toilet training **482–3**
Toilet water 406
Tomatoes **483**
    sauce **483**
    Vandyke 195
Tombola 58
Tools and equipment
    axes and hatchets **20**
    belts **48**
    brackets **54**
    chain saw **91**
    chisels **98**
    gouges 415, 524
    hammers **216**
    hedge trimmers 221–2
    hiring 225
    mallet 216
    nails 300–1
    paintbrushes, pads and
        rollers **321–2**
    planes 347
    power **362**
    profile gauge **364–5**
    riveting 384–5
    routers **392**
    sanders 399–400
    saws **403–5**
    scissors **407**
    screws **407–8**
    sharpening 415
    spanners **436–7**
    spray gun **442–3**
    staple gun 448
    wall fasteners **507–8**
    wrenches 437
Toothache **483**

Torches **484**
Tortrix moth 86
Touch-typing **484**
Toupee 212
Tourniquet **484**
Towel rails **484–5**
Towing **485**
Toy tank **485**
Tracking **485–6**
Track lighting 269–70
Tracks, curtain 125–6
Tradescantias 509–10
Trade Descriptions Act **486**
Trading standards 109
Traffic signs, international **238–9**
    motorway **293–4**
Trailers 77
Tranquillisers for nervousness 306
Travel, emergencies **486–7**
    sickness **487**
    with children **488**
    with disabled person **487**
    with pets **488**
Travel agent collapse 453
Treasure **488**
Trees, bonsai **49**
    Christmas **101**
    fruit **188–9**, 371
    house **488–9**
    planting 349
    pruning **489–90**
    staking 447
    stumps **456**
Trekking, pony **356**
Trellises **490**
Tricks 274
Trousers, alterations 105
    ironing 241–2
    zippers 530
Trout fishing 174
Truffles, chocolate **99**
Trusts **490–1**
Tuberculosis vaccine 235
Tubers **62**
Tug of war **491**
Tulips, forced 61
Tumble dryers **491**
Turfing **491–2**
Turkey, preparation and cooking 361
    stuffing 455
Turmeric 439
Twenty questions **492**
Two-way switches **492–3**
Typewriters **493**
Typing, touch- **484**
Tyres, car 294, **493**
    punctures, bicycle **41**

U

Ulcers **494**
Umbrellas **494**
Unconsciousness **494**
    recovery position for **378**
    resuscitation of 100
Undercoats 325
Underwater escape **494**
Unemployment benefit 304
Uneven floors **494–5**
Unfair Contract Terms Act 114
Unfair dismissal **495**
Unit trusts 241, **496**
Unsolicited goods **496**
Urticaria 225
Used car **496**
U/V activated glue 202

V

Vaccines see Immunisation
Vacuum cleaners **497**
Vacuuming **497–8**
Valances **498**
Valuation officer 376
Value added tax **498–9**
invoices and 377
Vanity basin fitting 411
Varnishing **499**
découpage 131
finger and toenails 275
floorboards 177
Vegetables
artichokes **17**
asparagus **18**
braising **54**
crop rotation 433–4
freezing 185
growing in cold frames 106
leftovers 266
pickling 340–1
potatoes **358–9**
steaming 449
storage 183
Vegetarian meals **499**
Velcro fasteners **499**
Velvet **499–500**
Veneer **500**
repair 13, 500
Veneer tape **500**
Venetian blinds 46–47, 147, **501**
Venison roasting 385–6
Ventilation **501**
for condensation 112
Verdigris **501**
Victim compensation 121
Video hire 225
recorders **501–2**
Vinegar as cleanser 103
Vines **502**
Vinyl, ball repair **26**
floor coverings **502–3**
Viola 52
Violet root rot 18
Virginia creeper 104
Visa **504**
Vitamins 283, **504**
Vol-au-vents **505**
Volleyball **505**
Vomiting **505**

W

Waffles **506**
Walking **506**
aids 123
and backpacking **23–24**
compass for **108–9**
Wall, block 60
brick 57–58
cladding **506–7**
cleaning 147
coverings 508
damp 112, 129
efflorescence **149**
fasteners **507–8**
garden **194**, 375
painting 323
partitions **328**
pebbledash **333**
plasterboard **349**

plastic cladding **351–2**
plugs 507
soundproofing 435
stucco **455**
tiles, ceramic 89–90
washing **511**
Wallpaper, removal **509**
washing 511
Wallpapering **508–9**
Waltz 26–27
Wandering Jew **509–10**
War **510**
Ward of court **510**
Wardrobes 124–5
Warranties **510**
Warts **510**
Washers, for bolts 48
tap 466–7
Washing, car 84, 399
clothes **259–60**
dishes **134**
machine **510–11**
nylon 309
powders 260
walls **511**
Wasps **511**
sting 237, 418
Waste disposal unit **511–12**
Water, divining **513**
for survival 459–60
heaters 78, **196**, **233–4**
heating **513**
leaks from radiator 89
mark removal 13, 186
softeners **514–15**
tanks, ball cock repair in 26
Watercolour painting **512**
Water polo **513**
Water-skiing **514**
Wax, batik 32–33
candle 74
removal from ear 148
Weaning **515**
Weasel tracks 486
Weatherboarding 351–2
Weather forecasting **515**
Weather vane **515–16**
Weaving **516–17**
finger **168–9**
Weddings 279, **517–18**
invitations 241
Weeding, posture for 22
Weeds, control **518**
couch grass **118**
dandelions **129**
lawn 261
Weevils **518**
Weight training **518–19**
Welding **519**
Wet rot **322**
Wet suits **519**
Wheelbarrows **519–20**
Wheels, car 294
changing 243
Wheezing **520**
Whelks **524**
Whisky tumbler 200-1
Whist **520**
Whiteflies **520**
Whooping cough vaccine 234–5
Wickerwork painting 442–3
Widow's benefit 304
Wigs 212
Wild flowers 66
Wildlife photography 305
Wills 164, **521**
Window boxes 521–2
Windowpanes **522**
Windows, cleaning **522**
condensation 112

damp 129
draughtproofing **142**
frame sealants 411
insulation 140–1, 238
leaded lights **263–4**
painting 323–4
puttying 368
sashcords **400–1**
security 63–64, 82
soundproofing 435–6
sticking 451
Windscreen washers **522**
Windscreen wipers **522–3**
Windsurfing **523**
Wine, corking 115
-making **523–4**
berries for 39–40
mulling **298**
storage **524**
with food **524**
Winkles and whelks **524**
Wiring, electric **153–4**
plugs **352**
See also Flex
Wisteria 104
Wood, bleaching 45
-burning stove 452–3
chainsawing 91
chipboard **97**
chiselling **98**
dowels 141
drilling **144**
dry rot **146**
filling 452
floor levelling 494–5
French polishing **186**
garden seats, repair 193
gates **196–7**
greenhouse 205
hinges **224–5**
joints, mitre **288–9**
joists **247**
mouldings **295–6**
nails for 300–1
painting 323
parquet flooring **327–8**
partitions **328**
pelmets **333**
pests 130
planing **347–8**
plastic laminates for **350–1**
plywood **354**
preservatives **525**
restoring 13
sanding **399–400**
sawing **403–5**
scratch marks **407**
screwing **407–8**
splitting **525**
staining **445**
varnishing **499**
veneer **500**
veneer tape **500–1**
wall cladding **506–7**
See also Floors
Wood ash as cleanser 103
Wood-burning stoves 452–3
Woodcarving **524–5**
Woodcock roasting 192
Woodwork
bird box **43**
bird table **43–44**
bookcase **49–50**
cabinet-making **68**
kitchen **253**
cupboards and wardrobes **124–5**
drawers construction **143**, **144**
fences 165
joints **525–6**
kennel **251–2**

marquetry **278–9**
pergolas **334**
picture framing **342**
rabbit hutch 372
shelf brackets 54
shelves **416**
swing **463**
table repairs **464–5**
toboggan **482**
tree house **488–9**
trellises **490**
weather vane **515–16**
window boxes **521–2**
Woodworm **526–7**
Wool spinning **441**
Word game 11
Work, safety at 8–9
Worktops 253
Wormcasts **527**
Wounds **527**
staunching 45
Wrapping, gift **198**
parcels **327**
Wreaths **527**
Wrinkles **527**
Writ 457
Writing, calligraphy 70–71
invisible **241**
left-handed 265
signs **266**
See also Letters
Wrought iron, painting 442–3

X Y Z

Yachting, sand **400**
See also Sailing
Yearly plan certificates 304
Yew berries 39
Yoga **528**
Yoghurt **528**
Yorkshire pudding **528–9**
Youth hostelling **529**
Yo-yo **529**
Zabaglione **529**
Zippers **529–30**
Zodiac 530

ACKNOWLEDGMENTS

The publishers would like to thank the following people and organisations for their valuable assistance in the preparation of this book:

Aerobicentre; Age Concern; John Alexander, Royal Greenwich Observatory; Bryan Allen; Laye Andrew; Penny Annand; Tommy Armstrong; Association of British & International Hairdressers; Banbury Homes and Gardens Ltd; Bank of Scotland; David Barriskill, Guildhall Library; Peter Bateman; Jeff Bellingham; Keith Betton, Association of British Travel Agents; Chris Bostock, Tynewear Theatre Company; Mary Brennan; Britax; British Seagull Ltd; British Tenpin Bowling Association; Ian Brown; Stephen Bunce, Royal Lifesaving Association; Ceri Burgum, British Horse Society; Sally Buxton, Unit Trust Association; Antony Byers, The Electricity Council; Major Camilleri, Royal Pigeon Racing Association; A.J. Camp, Society of Genealogists; Dr Neville Carrington; Eugenie Castle; John Castle; Michael Cazalet, Camping & Caravanning Club of GB; Charrington Bowl; Child Accident Prevention Trust; HM Coastguard; Tessa Coker, Ski Club of GB; Adrian Coles, Building Societies Association; The College of Insurance; Jill Colmer; John Crabbe; Mike Cunningham, British Surfing Association; HM Customs & Excise; S.P. Dance; Ian Dawson, RSPB; Guy Dehn, National Consumer Council; Andrew Dodwell, The Brass Rubbing Centre; Dennis Donovan; Jake Downey, National Badminton Centre; Brian Doyle; Philip Dyson, General Leather Company; Stephanie Edwards, Sight & Sound College; Margaret Ferris; G.C. Good, British Canoe Union; David Gower, Freewheeler Leisure Products; Fiona Griffiths; Jenny Hall; Mike Hampton, British Federation of Sand & Land Yacht Clubs; Helena Harwood, Wine Development Board; Terry Haydon; Heating, Ventilation & Air Conditioning Association Ltd; Mrs E.A. Hogg; Honda UK Ltd; Ted Hooper; Hubble & Freeman, Ltd; Damien Hunt; Denise Hunter, Moss Bros; Institute of Metals; Ralph Jackson, National Federation of Self-Employed; Christopher Jaques; D.C. Jardine, Forestry Commission; Joyce Jarvis; Phil Jones, UK Windsurfing Assn; R.C. Justice, Britannia Sailing; Andrew Lang; Roy Launder; Lowdon Dog Centre; LPC Mortgage Services Ltd; Mansell Collection; Mrs D. Marsh, St Anne's College; Steve May; Gina McGonigal, Association of British & International Hairdressers; John McGowan; Dr David Milman; Colin Mitchell, *Angler's Mail*; Bob Morris, Squash Rackets Association; Mothercare; Ron Murphy; Music, page 377, *If You Were The Only Girl In The World*, words by Clifford Grey, music by Nat. D. Ayer, published by EMI Publishing Ltd, arranged by Dan Fox; National Pawnbrokers Association; National Society of Master Thatchers; J.H. Nicholson, British Pétanque Association; Charles Nodder, British Field Sports Society; Olive Odell; Orienteering Federation; David Orr, British Telecom; John Orr; Barry Parker, MET Office; Passport Office; Ronan Paterson; Pre-Retirement Association of Great Britain & Northern Ireland; J. Presland, Queen's Ice Skating Club; Bruce Preston; Tim Preston; Roger Preston-Smith; Tom Randall; Tony Ray, British Judo Association; D.A. Reeves, Amateur Swimming Association; Stuart Reuben; Philip Ripley; Tom Robinson; Royal Institute of British Architects; Royal School of Needlework; A. Sabin, Tug-of-War Association; St Thomas' Hospital, Physiotherapy Dept; Sandy Sanderson, Clydesdale Bank; A.W. Shipley, English Table Tennis Association; M. Simmonds, Royal Philatelic Society; Jo Smith, Good Housekeeping Institute; Joan Smith, Royal Society for the Prevention of Accidents; Southwark Borough Council; J.W. Speake; Ivor Spencer, Guild of After Dinner Speakers; Hugh Steele, British Gas; Group Captain R.D. Stephens, British Casino Association; Roy Stobbs, Billiards & Snooker Control Council; Michael Stockman; Tony Stuart-Jones; Marion Thompson, Pitman's Tutorial College; Peter Turner; Tim Turner; Mark Vaux; John Vigurs; Chris Webb, Elgin Music Ltd; Sharon Webster; Kevin White; Paul Whitfield; Dave Wilkinson; Dr David Williams; Jim Williams; D.G. Williamson, Debretts Ltd; Reg Wing, National Small-Bore Rifle Association; Bob Woolley.

The publishers also acknowledge their indebtedness to the following books:

Alternative Health Guide, Brian Inglis and Ruth West (Michael Joseph); *The Angler's Guide to Coarse Fishing*, Bill Howes (Salamander Books); *The Art of Mixing Drinks* (Bantam Books); *The Ashford Book of Spinning and Weaving*, Anne Field (Dryad Press); *Baby and Child*, Penelope Leach (Penguin); *Ballroom Dancing* (Teach Yourself Books); *The Bed and Bath Book*, Terence Conran (Mitchell Beazley); *Beekeeping*, H.R.C. Riches (Foyles Handbooks); *Beginner's Guide to Domestic Plumbing*, Ernest Hall (Butterworth); *Berries*, Alison Copland (Blandford Press); *Berries and Fruits*, George E. Hyde (Frederick Warne); *Better Roller Skating*, Richard Arnold (Kaye and Ward); *Boat Handling* (Time-Life Books); *Book of British Birds* (Drive Publications); *Book of Childcare*, Dr Hugh Jolly (Allen and Unwin); *The Book of Dogs*, G.N. Henderson (Albany Books); *The Book of Photography*, John Hedgecoe (Ebury Press); *The Brain: Mystery of Matter and Mind*, Jack Fincher (U.S. New Books); *Camping*, Nigel Hunt (Brockhampton Press); *The Caravan Book*, Christina Fagg (Exley Publications); *Cat's Cradle and Other String Games*, Camilla Gryski (Angus and Robertson); *Choosing a School*, Felicity Taylor (Advisory Centre for Education); *Collecting Stamps*, Stephen Holder (Macdonald); *The Complete Book of Etiquette*, Mary and John Bolton (W. Foulsham); *The Complete Book of Gardening*, Ed. Michael Wright (Michael Joseph); *The Complete Book of Spirits and Liqueurs*, Cyril Ray (Cassell); *Complete Book of Tools*, Albert Jackson and David Day (Michael Joseph); *The Complete Guide to the Art of Modern Cookery*, G.A. Escoffier (Heinemann); *The Complete Indoor Gardener*, Ed. Michael Wright (Pan Books); *The Complete Practical Book of Country Crafts*, Jack Hill (David and Charles); *Concrete in Garden Making*, Nicolette Frank (Cement and Concrete Association); *The Cooking of Germany* (Time-Life Books); *The Cooks Companion*, Susan Campbell (Macmillan); *The Cooks Encyclopaedia*, Tom Stobart (Papermac); *Creative Soft Toys*, Snook (Dryad Press); *Debrett's Correct Form*, Ed. Patrick Montague-Smith; *Dictionary of Economics*, Ed. David J. Thomas (Bell and Hyman); *The Diviner's Handbook*, Tom Graves (Aquarian Press); *Elderly People: Rights and Opportunities*, Manthorpe (Longman); *Encyclopaedia Britannica*; *Encyclopaedia of Fishing in the British Isles*, Ed. Michael Prichard (Collins); *Encyclopaedia of Sports* (Marshall Cavendish); *Enquire Within Upon Everything* (Barrie and Jenkins); *Face and Beauty Book*, Miriam Stoppard (Windward); *The Face and Body Book*, Miriam Stoppard (Windward); *Face Values*, Vernon Coleman with Margaret Coleman (Pan); *The Family Creative Workshop* (Plenary Publications International Inc.); *Figure Drawing*, Wendon Blake and Uldis Klavins (Watson-Guptill Publications); *Fish Cookery*, Jane Grigson (Penguin); *Float Fishing*, Colin Dyson (E.P. Publishing Ltd); *Fly Tying*, Tony Whieldon (Ward Lock); *Fund Raising and Grant Aid*, Darnbrough and Kinrade (Woodhead-Faulkner); *Gambling*, Alan Wykes (Aldus Books); *Game Fishing*, Stanley B. Woodrow (E.P. Publishing Ltd); *A Golden Dolly*, M. Lambeth (John Baker Ltd); *Good Housekeeping Book of Wine* (Ebury Press); *Good Housekeeping Cookery Book* (Ebury Press); *Good Housekeeping Freezer Recipes* (Ebury Press); *Good Things*, Jane Grigson (Penguin); *Guide to the Social Services*, Ed. B. Preston (Family Welfare Association); *Hair Cutting For Everyone*, Harold Leighton (Book Club Association); *Handicrafts For All Seasons*, Rosalie M. Brown (J. Goodchild); *The Health and Beauty Book* (Mitchell Beazley); *Home Maintenance Manual*, Simon James (Sphere Books); *Home Management*, Phyllis Davidson (Batsford); *The Hostess Cook Book*, Anne Ager and Pamela Westland (Octopus Books); *How To Clean Everything*, Alma Chesnut Moore (Tom Stacey Ltd); *Hoyle's Rules of Games*, Albert H. Morehead and Geoffrey Mott-Smith (Plume); *Hugh Johnson's Wine Companion* (Mitchell Beazley); *IBA Yearbook*; *Iceskating*, Dennis L. Bird (A. & C. Black); *Illustrated Encyclopaedia of Beekeeping*, Ed. Morse and Hooper (Blandford Press); *Introduction to Accountancy*, H.C. Edey (Hutchinson); *Introductory Photography Course*, John Hedgecoe (Ebury Press); *Italian Food*, Elizabeth David (Penguin Books); *Jewellery*, Thomas Gentille (Pan Gulf Books); *Judo*, Syd Hoare (Teach Yourself Books); *Katie Stewart Cook Book* (Gollancz); *Left Over For Tomorrow*, Hanbury Tenison (Penguin); *Lightweight Boating*, P.W. Blandford (John Grifford Ltd); *The Lore of the Land*, John Seymour (Whittet Books Ltd); *Making Decorations*, Elizabeth Gundry (Piccolo); *Mammals of Britain: Their Tracks, Trails & Signs*, M.J. Lawrence and R.W. Brown (Blandford Press); *The Manual of Horsemanship* (The British Horse Society); *Mechanics of the Mind*, Colin Blakemore (Camb. University Press); *Microwave Cookery Course*, Cecilia Norman (Panther Books); *Mountaineering For All*, Richard Gilbert (B.T. Batsford); *Nature Photography*, Heather Angel (Fountain Press); *Newnes Family Lawyer*, Ed. Dudley Perkins; *1,000 Things You Ought To Know*, Ginette Chevallier (Airtrans Establishment); *The Oxford Illustrated Dictionary*; *Painting and Decorating*, Elizabeth Gundry (Ward Lock); *The Pan Book of Card Games*, Hugh Phillips; *Patons Book of Knitting and Crochet* (Heinemann); *Pears Medical Encyclopaedia* (Pelham Books); *Pétanque, The French Game of Boules* (Carreau Press); *Picture Framing*, Rosamund Wright-Smith (Orbis); *Pigeon Fancying*, Ron Bissett (David and Charles); *Pigeon Racing*, James Martin (W. Foulsham); *Plumbing and Wiring* (Time-Life Books); *Pony Trekking*, Glenda Spooner (J.A. Allen); *Pony Trekking*, Edward Hart (David and Charles); *Pool – Know the Game* (The British Association of Pool Table Operators); *The Practical Astronomer*, Colin Ronan (Pan); *Practical Letter Writing*, Ian Gordon (Heinemann Educational Books); *The Practical Microwave Handbook*, Jill McWilliam (Octopus Books); *Pub Games of England*, Timothy Finn (The Oleander Press); *Rabbit Keeping*, Gay Nightingale (John Bartholomew & Son); *Repairing Furniture* (Time-Life Books); *Richard's Bicycle Book*, Richard Ballantine (Pan); *Rudiments and Theory of Music* (The Associated Board of the Royal School of Music); *The Scented Garden*, Rosemary Verey (Michael Joseph); *Sea Fishing*, Tony Whieldon (Ward Lock); *Skin and Hair Care*, Linda Allen Schoen (Penguin); *Spinning and Dyeing*, Gill Dalby and Liz Christmas (David and Charles); *The Spur Book of Caving*, Jim Ballard; *The Stars: A New Way To See Them*, H.A. Rey (Chatto and Windus); *Stay Younger Longer*, Bronwen Meredith (Michael Joseph); *The Story of Astronomy*, Patrick Moore (Macdonald); *Successful Sailing*, Lou D'Alpuget (Nelson); *Supertips To Make Life Easy*, Moyra Bremner (Coronet Books); *Supertips 2*, Moyra Bremner (Andre Deutsch); *Take Care of Yourself*, D.M. Vickery (Allen and Unwin); *The Taste of Wine*, Pamela Vandyke Price (Macdonald and Jane's); *Teas of the World*, Nancy Hyden Woodward (Collier Macmillan); *Textile Crafts*, Ed. Constance Howard (Pitman Publishing Ltd); *Tips and Wrinkles*, Mary Sansbury and Anne Fowler (Pan Books); *Treat Your Own Back*, Robin McKenzie (Spinal Publications Ltd); *VAT Explained*, Ed. Alex Chown; *Vegetarian Kitchen*, Sarah Brown (BBC); *Vogue Guide to Hair Care*, Felicity Clark (Penguin Books); *Walker's Handbook*, H.D. Westacott (Penguin Books); *Webster's Sports Dictionary*, G. & C. Merriam; *We Learn to Ski* (Sunday Times); *The Which? Book of DIY* (Consumers' Association); *The Which? Book of Money* (Consumers' Association); *Woman In Your Own Right*, Anne Dickson (Quartet Books); *The Young Angler: A Complete Guide to Coarse Fishing*, Dave King (Pisces Angling Publications); *You And Your Back*, Dr David Delvin (Pan Books); *Youth Hostels Association Guide*.

Photographs appearing in this book came from the sources listed below. Work commissioned by Reader's Digest is shown in *italics*.

10 Eric Crichton; **14** A.J. Deane/Bruce Coleman Ltd; **36** Eric Crichton; **39** Eric Crichton; **51** Eric Crichton; **66** Biofotos; **91** *Philip Dowell, Reader's Digest, The Cookery Year*; **104** Eric Crichton/Bruce Coleman Ltd; **107** All photographs: Institute of Ophthalmology; **146** Biofotos; **201** *Laurie Evans*; **206** Tania Midgley; **221** Tania Midgley; **295** Michael Boys; **338** Tim Woodcock; **347** *Jan Baldwin*; **358** *left* Tim Woodcock, *right* Fotobank International; **398** *Philip Dowell, Reader's Digest, The Cookery Year*; **420** Photos Horticultural; **464** Syndication International; **490** Hugh Palmer; **520** Holt Studios Ltd.

Typesetting: Sprint Productions Ltd, London *Separations:* Litra Ltd, Edenbridge *Paper:* Hale Paper Ltd, London
Cloth: bn international U.K., London · Red Bridge (Bolton) Ltd, Lancs *Printing and Binding:* BPC Hazell Books Ltd, Aylesbury

40–176–4